International Law:
A Contemporary Perspective

STUDIES ON A JUST WORLD ORDER

Also of Interest

†Available in hardcover and paperback.

ABOUT THE BOOK AND EDITORS

International Law: A Contemporary Perspective

edited by Richard Falk, Friedrich Kratochwil, and Saul H. Mendlovitz

In a time when the international system is under increasing pressures from the problems of the arms race, overpopulation, food shortages, and ecological decay, *International Law* critically assesses the established practices and institutions for maintaining minimum global order. This ideologically balanced reader provides students with an understanding of the contributions and limitations of international law in creating a dependable environment in which nations can interact. The editors, while recognizing that the image of international law in political life has never been more tarnished, are certain that an opportunity for rejuvenating the international legal system—a new "Grotian moment"—is at hand.

This book avoids the pitfalls of either legalistic uniformity, wishful thinking, or cynicism with respect to international law. It critically probes the possibilities, trends, and processes that indicate opportunities for peaceful transformational change. The work addresses the traditional concerns such as lawmaking, the sources of law, problems of compliance, the interaction between power and normative preferences, and the classical issues relating to the regulation of force. But it is also sensitive to considerations usually inadequately treated in standard textbooks: new forces in world politics, demands for distributive justice, resource sharing, ecological protection, and human rights. Extensive introductions, carefully drafted study questions, and suggestions for further reading should make this book an invaluable teaching tool and reference work both for teachers and for concerned students of international law and international affairs.

Richard Falk is Albert G. Milbank Professor of International Law and Practice at Princeton University and a Senior Fellow of the World Policy Institute. **Friedrich Kratochwil** is assistant professor of political science and teaches international law and international relations at Columbia University. **Saul H. Mendlovitz** is professor of international law at Rutgers University—Newark, Ira D. Wallach Professor of World Order Studies at Columbia University, and coeditor of *Alternatives: A Journal of World Policy.*

STUDIES ON A JUST WORLD ORDER
Richard Falk and Saul H. Mendlovitz, General Editors

STUDIES ON A JUST WORLD ORDER, NO. 2

International Law: A Contemporary Perspective

edited by Richard Falk,
Friedrich Kratochwil,
and Saul H. Mendlovitz

WESTVIEW PRESS / BOULDER AND LONDON

Studies on a Just World Order, No. 2

Copyright © 1985 by Westview Press, Inc.

Published in 1985 in the United States of America by Westview Press, Inc., Frederick A. Praeger, Publisher; 5500 Central Avenue, Boulder, Colorado 80301

Library of Congress Cataloging in Publication Data
Main entry under title:
International law.
    (Studies on a just world order; no. 2)
    Includes bibliographical references.
    1. International law—Addresses, essays, lectures.
I. Falk, Richard A.   II. Kratochwil, Friedrich V.
III. Mendlovitz, Saul H.   IV. Studies on a just world
order; v. 2.
JX3091.I657 1985   341   85-3318
ISBN 0-86531-241-9
ISBN 0-86531-252-4 (pbk.)

Printed and bound in the United States of America

10   9   8   7   6   5   4   3   2   1

Contents

Credits

Selection 1: Reprinted with permission from *The British Year Book of International Law* (London: Oxford University Press, 1946), pp. 1–53.

Selection 2: Reprinted with permission from Richard Falk, *The End of World Order: Essays on Normative International Relations* (New York: Holmes & Meier, 1983), pp. 25–32.

Selection 3: Reprinted with permission from *Foreign Affairs* 51 (1973), pp. 408–421.

Selection 4: Reprinted with permission from the *Hastings Constitutional Law Journal* 9 (Summer 1982).

Selection 5: Reprinted with permission from Grenville Clark and Louis B. Sohn, *World Peace Through World Law*, 3rd ed. (Cambridge, Mass.: Harvard University Press, 1966).

Selection 6: Reprinted with permission from Oran Young, *Compliance and Public Authority* (Baltimore: Johns Hopkins University Press, 1977).

Selection 7: Reprinted with permission from Richard Falk and Cyril E. Black, eds., *The Future of the International Legal Order* (Princeton, N.J.: Princeton University Press, 1969).

Selection 8: Reprinted with permission from Wolfgang Friedmann, *The Changing Structure of International Law* (New York: Columbia University Press, 1964), Ch. 6, pp. 60–71.

Selection 9: Reprinted with permission from Mohammed Bedjaoui, *Towards a New International Order* (Paris: UNESCO, and New York–London: Holmes & Meier, 1979).

Selection 10: Reprinted with permission from the *American Journal of International Law* 53 (1959), pp. 1–29.

Selection 11: Reprinted with permission from Cyril E. Black and Richard Falk, eds., *The Future of the International Legal Order* (Princeton, N.J.: Princeton University Press, 1972), Ch. 9, pp. 331–383.

Selection 12: Reprinted with permission from Nicholas G. Onuf, *Law-Making in the Global Community* (Durham, N.C.: Carolina Academic Press, 1982).

Selection 15: Reprinted with permission from *Harvard International Law Journal* 18 (The United Nations, 31st session, 1977), pp. 559–575.

Selection 16: Reprinted, with substantial deletions acknowledged, with permission, from Thomas Franck, *The Structure of Impartiality* (New York: Macmillan, 1968).

Selection 17: Reprinted with permission from the *American Journal of International Law* 68 (1978), pp. 591–627.

Selection 18: Reprinted with permission from the *American Society of International Law Proceedings* (1963), pp. 13–15.

Selection 19: Reprinted with permission from Abram Chayes, *The Cuban Missile Crisis* (New York: Oxford University Press, 1974).

Selection 20: Reprinted with permission from *Alternatives: A Journal of World Policy* 6, no. 2 (1980), pp. 307–337.

Selection 21: Reprinted with permission from the *American Journal of International Law* 64 (1970), pp. 809–907.

Selection 22: Reprinted with permission from the *American Journal of International Law* 65 (1971), pp. 544–548.

Selection 23: Reprinted with permission from the *American Journal of International Law* 66 (1972), pp. 1–36.

Selection 24: Reprinted with permission from the *Annals of International Studies* 3 (Geneva, 1972).

Selection 25: Reprinted with permission from the *British Journal of International Studies* 3 (1977), pp. 121–136.

Selection 26: Reprinted with permission from *McGill Law Journal* 28, no. 3 (July 1983), pp. 519–541.

Selection 27: Reprinted with permission from the *British Journal of International Studies* 4 (1978), pp. 1–19.

Selection 28: Reprinted with permission from Giuliano Amato et al., *Marxism, Democracy and the Rights of Peoples: Homage to Lelio Basso* (Milan, Italy: Franco Angeli Editore, 1979).

Selection 29: Reprinted with permission from *Rutger's Law Review* 33, no. 2 (Winter 1981), pp. 435–452.

Selection 30: Reprinted with permission from the *Reports of Judgments, Advisory Opinions, and Orders* (International Court of Justice, 1950), pp. 174–185.

Selection 31: Reprinted with permission from Oscar Schachter, *Sharing the World's Resources* (New York: Columbia University Press, 1977), pp. 3–34.

Selection 32: Reprinted with permission from the *New York Journal of International Law and Politics* 11, no. 2 (Fall 1978), pp. 179–195.

Selection 33: This essay appeared in slightly different form as "The New Law of the Sea," in the *Journal of the American Law Association* 69 (February 1983), p. 156. Copyright © 1983, American Bar Association. Used by permission.

Selection 34: Reprinted with permission from the *American Journal of International Law* 77 (1983).

Selection 35: Reprinted with permission from the *Journal of World Trade Law* 16.

Selection 36: Reprinted with permission from Jan Schneider, *World Public Order of Environment* (Buffalo, N.Y.: University of Toronto Press, 1979).

Selection 38: This article is a revision of material delivered as the Sherill Lectures at Yale University, March 1974.

General Introduction

Perhaps not since the birth of the modern state system, usually associated roughly with the Peace of Westphalia in 1648, has the image of international law in the political life of the world seemed so tarnished. This is not, we believe, because there is "less" law or "more" sovereignty, but because the inability of law to satisfy steadily increasing minimal expectations about the requirements of global order and justice create an impression of "failure," deterioration, and disillusionment. Indeed, given the inability of international law to evolve at a pace comparable to that of increasing interdependence, *doing more* can still seem like *achieving less*.

Moreover, in recent years there has been an *absolute decline* in the perceived role of law with respect to the most basic ordering challenge of all—the prevention of war. Throughout this century, and especially since the end of World War I, there had been a sustained legal effort to prohibit all nondefensive uses of force in international affairs. The Kellogg-Briand Pact of 1928, which committed the major states of the world to a rule of law renouncing aggressive uses of force, was intended as a turning point, overcoming the earlier consensus that recourse to force was a matter of sovereign discretion, provided only that war was initiated by an appropriate declaration. After World War II, leaders of Germany and Japan were tried and punished as "criminals" before specially established international tribunals because they were found to have planned and waged aggressive war. The United Nations Charter proceeded from this central premise and required governments to submit all claims of self-defense for review by the Security Council. Work on an agreed definition of aggression went forward and culminated in a formulation accepted on all sides. Proposals for a standing international criminal court were seriously considered.

To be sure, there was a certain thinness or lack of credibility about this legal enterprise throughout the entire period. Realists dismissed the various steps taken by international law as window dressing or, in some cases, as victors' justice. The legal concepts were vague. The organized international community never possessed clear authority or relevant enforcement capabilities. The more ambitious undertakings, such as the security mechanisms to establish peacekeeping forces under United Nations auspices, were stillborn, apparent casualties of the cold war. The Security Council procedures were subject to a veto; the General Assembly was conceived of as only a recommending body. Major states, it seemed clear, had not given up their discretion to decide when force was appropriate for their pursuit of national interests. At most, they had committed themselves to justifying claims to use force by reference to defense against aggression. Since there was no way to resolve competing claims of defensive force, the new international law arguably did no more than prescribe new verbal forms for habitual political realities.

Yet there seemed to many careful observers to be some significant correlation between the verbal demands of international law and emerging practices of restrained statecraft. World War II could as readily be perceived to be a vindication of the legal claims as an instance of their irrelevance. After all, the international community successfully resisted and punished the aggressor states and established a postwar international organization designed to carry on the struggle against aggressors. As long as the United States dominated the voting processes in the United Nations, there seemed to be a coherent set of responses to "illegal" behavior, that is, to the nondefensive recourse to force by the main agents of communism—namely, the Soviet Union, China, and their allies. Notably, the United Nations condemned North Korea's attack on South Korea as "aggression" and treated China's entry into the war on North Korea's side as complicity in aggression. Later on, the United States stretched its "legalist" commitment beyond its alliance relationships when in 1956 it joined in opposing an attack launched by its main allies, Britain and France, on Nasser's Egypt, a state with whom it had strained relations at the time. Again, reality is never lacking in ambiguity; some interpreters have suggested that the United States, eager to displace Great Britain as the principal Western force in the Middle East, used the Suez attack to complete the process of weakening the British presence in the region.

The Vietnam War represented, as in so much else, a crossroads. The United States' decade-long effort to sell its role as a "defensive" one against communist "aggression" never took hold. Increasingly, even in the United States, the American role seemed interventionary in its essence. Such an impression was reinforced by the increasing capacity of Third World actors and groupings (e.g., the nonaligned movement) to get a hearing in international political arenas. The loss of American credibility in relation to the prohibition of aggressive force was, perhaps, the decisive turning point in perceptions. The Soviet Union, the other pace-setting state in international life, never made a secret of its suspicion about international attempts to regulate sovereign rights. Soviet diplomacy attacked, of course, the condemnation of its allies (North Korea, China) as aggressors in the Korea War and considered such an appraisal as reflecting nothing more than a confirmation of Western dominance of the United Nations. The United States, however, was seen by the Western world as championing a liberal international order, which, in the aftermath of appeasement associated with the response of the liberal democracies to Hitler in the 1930s, meant resistance to aggression plus renunciation of all nondefensive uses of force. Therefore, when the United States itself seemed to abandon the basic norm of restraint, not only in Vietnam but elsewhere in the Third World, the whole impression of a gradual growth of law in relation to international violence virtually disappeared.

This disappearance was reinforced by a loss of support, especially in the liberal United States, for the United Nations as a noble experiment that was pushing international politics in a more law-oriented direction. The rapid expansion of Third World influence, especially in the General Assembly, had engendered rapid disillusionment. More and more former supporters of the United Nations began to look upon the organization as an instrument for the expression of arbitrary and irresponsible views by a mere majority that neither had much weight in power politics nor contributed much to the overall budget (a 2/3 vote in the 1960s could be achieved in the General Assembly over the opposition of states that paid 95 percent of the annual dues). Particularly upsetting was the consistent UN espousal of the Palestinian cause, which, aside from its anti-Israeli features, was understood to be a virtual embrace of terrorism.

Almost unnoticed in the background, moreover, was the crucial and revealing failure of international law to address the use and development of nuclear weapons. Somehow, the basic legal enterprise described earlier survived the Hiroshima and Nagasaki explosions. Nevertheless, the continued development of nuclear weaponry, with all that it implied by way of rejecting restraint-in-war, further confirmed the limitations of international law, however optimistically assessed, to protect human society from catastrophe.

Now, in the decade of the 1980s, most of the earlier pretensions about legal restraint have been abandoned. Even such clear instances of aggression as the Iraqi attack on Iran in 1980, the South African "incursions" into Angola, and the Israeli invasion of Lebanon in 1982 have been ignored as "legal" events. Once more there is hardly even the necessity to provide a serious justification to the international community for recourse to force. The Soviet invasion of Afghanistan, although condemned and defended in East-West dialogue, represented further evidence of the deterioration of the modern regime of restraint, as have the indications by various U.S. leaders that the United States was quite prepared to protect oil resources with nondefensive force should a hostile revolution threaten to take power in a major producer country in addition to Iran.

This impression of deterioration has been further reinforced by the failure of the Law of the Sea negotiations. Year after year the negotiations had dragged on, only to result in the United States' suspension of its participation. In actuality, the process of disenchantment is even wider, as several of the most industrialized countries have moved steadily in unilateral directions, even with respect to deep sea mining. Germany and the United States, for instance, have already given out licenses for mining operations, thereby undercutting any prospect of preserving the deep sea as a "common heritage." Here again, the sense of futility about law is growing stronger as time passes. It was argued by some prominent international lawyers that the oceans were a much better test of international law than was war prevention. It was contended that international law could be expected to work only where regulatory regimes did not intrude on the fundamental self-help rights of states. Therefore, the war system could be mitigated only to a slight degree by legal approaches, but functional cooperation in an increasingly complicated world was an essential foundation for economic development and political stability, inasmuch as it serves as a major terrain for the growth of international law. However, the formulation of acceptable rules to govern the relations of diversely situated states has proved very difficult in a political order in which the poor, as well as the rich, are now genuine participants. It may still be the case that a consensus on the role of law will eventually develop, even if it fails to fulfill the hopes of those who had earlier expected a more comprehensive arrangement. The antilaw mood seems quite volatile. A major treaty on the status of the oceans or in the area of arms control might yet even generate a wave of enthusiasm for the role of international law in world affairs reoriented toward the track of mutual interests in regimes of order.

Our point of departure in this volume is that the evaluation of international law needs to proceed without regard for these shifts in mood. It is based on a conviction that the structure of human activity on a global scale necessarily has a normative element that is best studied in relation to the place of law. To deny law this role is to give way to the nihilism of the age, a posture sometimes struck behind the defenses of social-scientific canons of inquiry. In this fundamental regard, we believe that even the study of lawlessness in international life is one way to take seriously the normative potential of the human experience, a potential that embodies much of what hope remains for the future well-being of our species.

In addition to this article of faith, we focus in this volume on three central ideas about the place of law in the game of nations. First of all, there is a lot more ongoing law on a day-to-day basis than meets the eye of the casual newspaper reader. The relatively high stability of routine transactions (travel, commerce, communications) in international life is successfully sustained by an elaborate framework of law. A clear understanding of this framework is important, as international law enables an enormous volume of transnational life to proceed reliably, even if it does not altogether relieve our anxiety about the danger of war, the spread of repression, or the threat of chaos.

Furthermore, we place emphasis upon the *structural* limitations of international law, given the organization of international society into states of unequal power and varying traditions, ideological outlooks, and goals. In our judgment, international law by itself can never adequately secure peace, protect human rights, achieve economic well-being, or ensure ecological balance in such a political order, given current levels of vulnerability, complexity, and interdependence. The primacy of the state, perceiving and acting on the basis of its particular interests (rather than on the basis of shared interests or the public good), places very strong limits on what can be achieved by a "law" that transcends the particular. Indeed, the necessity for clarifying and understanding these limits is one important reason to study international law. Such study may help to disabuse those who may still harbor illusions that an enlightened development of law could overcome the main deficiencies of international society at this stage of international history.

Beyond this critical function of study is our view that the future of international political life stands on a threshold created by conflicting tendencies toward integration and disintegration. In many respects, this threshold resembles the situation that existed when the emergence of the state system gave rise to the felt need for an articulated legal framework. In the context of the late Middle Ages, the challenge was posed by the collapse of the integrative role of the Holy Roman Empire, and with it the partnership between the Catholic Church and the emperor. Hugo Grotius came along to validate the autonomy of the sovereign state while upholding a binding, overarching idea of law, derived from a shared Christian conscience, from the universal content of natural law, and from the agreed practices of states.

It is only accidental, perhaps, that we stress this world order quest around the time of the 400th anniversary of Grotius' birth, but it is certainly convenient to take note of the occasion. We suggest that a Grotius for our time might provide the vision binding past, present, and future into a credible whole. International law might thus provide one setting in which the dangers inherent in a system of autonomous states can be ameliorated to give rise to a more cooperative system based on global sentiments and on organizational capabilities to uphold the public or common good. The emphasis will be on global interests as well as national interests, planetary loyalties as well as national loyalties, nonstate actors as well as state actors; the objective is the construction of a vision of legal integration that does not jeopardize the diversity or autonomy of the parts but might even contribute to pluralism by defending the group rights of persons other than those in control of any given sovereign state.

Our overall aim in this book is to introduce to students the actual workings of law within the present arrangements of states, the inevitable limits of this type of legal order, and the possible role of international legal thought in transcending these limits.

SELECTED BIBLIOGRAPHY

This bibliography, and those at the end of each chapter, are limited to books in English that have not been utilized in the reader.

Michael Akehurst, *A Modern Introduction to International Law*, 3rd ed. (London: Allen & Unwin, 1980).

J. L. Brierly, *The Law of Nations,* 6th ed. (New York: Oxford University Press, 1963).

Ian Brownlie, *Principles of Public International Law* (Oxford: Clarendon Press, 1979).

Richard Falk and Cyril Black, eds., *The Future of the International Legal Order,* 4 vols. (Princeton, N.J.: Princeton University Press, 1969).

Wolfgang Friedmann, *The Changing Structure of International Law* (New York: Columbia University Press, 1963).

Hugo Grotius, *The Law of War and Peace,* Kelsey ed. (Oxford: Clarendon Press, 1925).

Morton Kaplan and Nicholas de Katzenbach, *The Political Foundations of International Law* (New York: John Wiley & Sons, 1961).

Hans Kelsen, Robert Tucker, eds., *Principles of International Law* (New York: Holt, Rinehart & Winston, 1966).

R. St. J. Macdonald and D. M. Johnston, eds., *The Structure and Process of International Law* (The Hague: Martinus Nijhoff, 1983).

Gary Maris, *International Law* (Lanham, Md.: University Press of America, 1984).

Myres S. McDougal and Associates, *Studies in World Public Order* (New Haven, Conn.: Yale University Press, 1960).

G. I. Tunkin, *Theory of International Law* (Cambridge, Mass.: Harvard University Press, 1974).

Charles de Visscher, *Theory and Reality in Public International Law* (Princeton, N.J.: Princeton University Press, 1957).

Burns H. Weston et al., eds., *International Law and World Order: A Problem-Oriented Coursebook* (St. Paul, Minn.: West, 1980).

CHAPTER 1

The Grotian Moment

As indicated in the General Introduction, the orientation of our perspective is shaped by the normative potential of international political life. To give concreteness to this perspective, we propose to examine the specific circumstances under which modern international law took shape. In particular, we wish to focus on the seventeenth-century Dutch jurist, Hugo Grotius, whose work has generally been regarded as seminal in these respects. Grotius is often called "the father of international law," although some dispute this attribution of paternity, emphasizing instead the earlier contributions of the Spanish School of international law.

Our emphasis on Grotius and the Grotian legacy reflects the judgment that Grotius fulfilled the normative potential of his historic epoch. The possibility of a similar relevance of law and legal thought to a comparable fulfillment in our time is the challenge we hope to pose for students.

We begin by drawing a distinction between international law and world order. International law consists of the rules, procedures, and practices that regulate the behavior of various actors within a world political system dominated by sovereign states of unequal power, wealth, and prestige. World order refers to the general framework of organization that prevails in human affairs, including the ways in which power and authority are distributed as well as the network of interacting institutions that administer whatever structure of governance exists at a particular time. International law has evolved within the specific world order system associated with the primacy of the state, but other systems are certainly imaginable. Indeed, some would argue that statist arrangements are gradually being superseded, and that a new system of world order will come into existence at some time in the course of the next century. In light of such impermanence, we seek to consider the possible role of law and legal thought in a time of transition between world order systems—a circumstance designated here, for reasons that should become evident, as the "Grotian moment."

The specific stimulus for Grotius's approach was the devastating impact on Europe of the pervasive religious warfare known to historians as the Thirty Years War. Grotius was especially eager to argue that the particular religious identity of a state was not a "just cause" of war. In this regard, the normative potential of that moment involved decentralism without anarchy. Accordingly, Grotius wanted to erode the normative authority of the Catholic Church and yet, simultaneously, raise the normative quality of international life.

The existence of other circumstances enabled his work to have the impact it did. Particular trends in economic, social, and political development favored both centralism within the state and loose ties in the relations among states. Favorable conditions of capital formation and economic growth, in particular, supported the emergence of the autonomous state.

One caveat is in order. The Grotian "world" was in reality a reflection of the regional circumstance of Europe. The European role in "discovering" and "colonizing" the rest of the globe has given the history of its international relations a prime importance. International law itself arose out of this largely regional experience, but it has been adopted over time as a basis for the exercise of sovereign rights by all states. In the process, this historical background of international law has left a Western cultural imprint and aroused hostility and suspicions. Some of the substantive rules of international law are challenged on these grounds: For instance, it is condemned for its tendency to vindicate colonialist claims.

Americans, especially, may remember when the Iranian revolutionary leader Ayatollah Khomeini insisted during the seizure of the U.S. Embassy and diplomats ("the hostage crisis" of 1979–1981) that international law was two-faced; that is, it condemned Iran for protecting itself against spies disguised as diplomats while ignoring the use of diplomatic facilities and personnel by the United States in 1953 (when the shah was restored to his throne, in part as a result of CIA intervention) to undermine the constitutional order of a sovereign state. Of course, Iran could have protected its "legitimate" concerns by declaring U.S. diplomats *personae non gratae* and ordering them to leave the country within 24 hours. But this procedure would not have resolved the earlier and fundamental Iranian complaint that embassy privileges had been abused to the extent that the United States found it necessary in 1953 to help organize an "illegal" takeover of power from the constitutional government. In addition to Third World objections, there are criticisms of international law from a Marxist/Leninist perspective. International law, or parts of it, has been alleged to be an expression of bourgeois society and interests, or of imperialism, and hence is no longer appropriate for a world of coexisting ideologies.

The first selection in Chapter One, by Hersch Lauterpacht, a famous international law scholar from England, emphasizes the Grotian tendencies of modern international law. In this respect, Lauterpacht regards the "Grotian tradition" as building up the normative expectations necessary to create a community of law that overcomes the limitations of a world order system based on the exclusive reliance upon state sovereignty. Indeed, Lauterpacht views innovations such as the Nuremberg trials of German war leaders after World War II and the willingness to protect the victims of aggression by commitments to collective security as rescuing international life from a barren positivism in which international society can do nothing more to protect itself against the prospect of destructive warfare and global aggression than rely upon the vagaries of balance-of-power arrangements (i.e., prenuclear "deterrence").

Lauterpacht's analysis was not generated beneath the nuclear shadow, yet its appeal can only be augmented by the realities of the nuclear arms race that have emerged in recent decades. Despite this objective situation, the evolution of international law since Lauterpacht's article in the late 1940s has turned in the disappointing direction discussed in the General Introduction. Put differently, the Grotian tradition has been eclipsed by a new geopolitics that is carrying the conflictual tendencies of the state system to the brink of catastrophic collapse.

In part, Lauterpacht's outlook may actually have been too optimistic, given that the world order structure is based overwhelmingly on territorially separate sovereign states. And, in part, forces of moderation have been superseded by the passions of nationalist and ideological politics, resulting in a long phase of subordination for the cooperative possibilities in international societies. If there is a swing back to moderation in the late 1980s or 1990s, Lauterpacht's hopes may seem far less "pie in the sky" than they do now.

The second selection, by Richard Falk, formulates the relevance of Grotius to the world order challenge we confront today. As in the seventeenth century, we need a jurist who is able to generalize the basis of normative authority so as to overcome the specific hazards of statism. At the same time, however, we cannot leap into a planetary order. It is important that we preserve the gains of autonomy and diversity associated with sovereign rights, as well as acknowledge various forms of societal identity, while working to overcome the dangers and injustices associated with the fragmentation of world society.

By linking the enterprise of international law with that of world order we hope, also, to introduce a skeptical note about what can be expected by way of legal reform considered apart from world order transformation. In this regard, we believe that the normative potential of international law is dependent on the overall political structure.

Our more optimistic perspective arises from the view that the inhibiting structure of the current world order system is not destined to last forever, but is in the process of eroding sufficiently to allow other types of world order to emerge. By remaining aware of these emergent possibilities, international legal thought can help orient beliefs and action in the direction of a more just world order.

QUESTIONS FOR DISCUSSION AND REFLECTION: CHAPTER ONE

1. How does the study of international law help us to understand international politics at various historical stages?

2. Is it reasonable to believe that the role of international law in guiding decisions can be increased in our present epoch?

3. Is the adoption of a world order perspective a heuristic means of thinking about the role of international law? In what respects?

4. What is the relationship between values, legal rules, and norms of behavior in international relations?

5. How would you summarize the Grotian perspective on international law? What is the justification for conceiving of the present epoch as creating a "new Grotian moment?"

SELECTED BIBLIOGRAPHY: CHAPTER 1

Charles Beitz, *Political Theory and International Relations* (Princeton, N.J.: Princeton University Press, 1979).

Hedley Bull, *The Anarchical Society: A Study of Order and World Politics* (New York: Columbia University Press, 1977).

Joseph A. Camilleri, *Civilization and Crisis: Human Prospects in a Changing World* (New York: Cambridge University Press, 1976).

Grenville Clark and Louis B. Sohn, *World Peace through World Law*, 2nd ed., rev. (Cambridge, Mass.: Harvard University Press, 1976).

Richard Falk, *A Study of Future Worlds* (New York: Free Press, 1980).

————, *The End of World Order* (New York: Holmes & Meier, 1983).

Johan Galtung, *The True Worlds: A Transnational Perspective* (New York: Free Press, 1981).

Stanley Hoffmann, *Duties Beyond Borders* (Syracuse, N.Y.: Syracuse University Press, 1981).

C. Wilfred Jenks, *A Common Law of Mankind* (London: Stevens & Sons, 1958).

Robert C. Johansen, *The National Interest and the Human Interest* (Princeton, N.J.: Princeton University Press, 1980).

Samuel S. Kim, *The Quest for a Just World Order* (Boulder, Colo.: Westview, 1983).

Rajni Kothari, *Footsteps into the Future* (New York: Free Press, 1975).

Ali Mazrui, *A World Federation of Cultures* (New York: Free Press, 1976).

Saul Mendlovitz, *On the Creation of a Just World Order* (New York: Free Press, 1975).

1. The Grotian Tradition in International Law

H. Lauterpacht

In a very real sense Grotius was one of the greatest international figures of his age—a prodigy, almost a miracle, of learning; an intimately familiar name to all interested in religious controversy at a time when questions of religious dogma and polemics were in the very centre of public attention; a brilliant literary scholar; the acknowledged greatest exponent of the law of nations. It would be necessary to go back to Erasmus to find a figure who was as much a household name wherever learning and culture reached. But we can well understand the doubts which beset Grotius as he lay on his death-bed in the town of Rostock, in Pomerania. He was then on his return journey from Stockholm, where he had gone to tender what was in fact an enforced resignation as Swedish Ambassador to the French Court and to attempt to obtain a diplomatic appointment of comparable dignity and usefulness. No such offer materialized. There he lay, shattered in body by a storm which made his ship a total wreck, and broken in spirit, his long and varied career unfolding itself before his mind's eye. According to a report, as to the authenticity of which there has been some controversy, among his closing words there was the exclamation of despair: 'By undertaking many things I have accomplished little.'[1]

Posterity has successfully challenged that self-deprecatory judgment. . . . But it is probable that he did not feel strongly about the set-backs in his diplomatic career, which for him was merely a source of livelihood. It is not even certain that international law had been or remained the centre of his interest. He was busy with the successive editions of *De Jure Belli ac Pacis*. But the mysteries of the doctrines of Atonement and of Transubstantiation were more real to him than the work on which his fame eventually rested. What affected him more deeply was the failure of his persistent efforts, through writings and otherwise, to promote the unity of the Church—a unity conceived as an aim praiseworthy in itself and as a pre-eminent instrument of peace.[2] He was not primarily a man of affairs, and his powers as negotiator were impaired rather than enhanced by the range and the conviction of his scholarship. His main literary activity— which was not in the sphere of international law but of poetry, literary criticism, religious dogma, and biblical exegesis—has proved of ephemeral value. There are very few, if any, who now draw their inspiration or knowledge from these writings.

What is perhaps more important is that the merits of that very work which has secured for him a permanent place in history are not by any means above controversy. The view is widely held that as an exposition of international law—or even as a presentation of a jurisprudential system— *De Jure Belli ac Pacis* is in many respects a somewhat superficial, hasty, and pretentious production. It is impossible to brush aside that view with astonished impatience. That monumental work is a dazzling exhibition of learning, but much of that learning creates the impression of being irrelevant. This is so not because he overwhelms the reader with a mass of ancient authorities while neglecting those nearer home. For this was the custom of the time. Witness, for instance, the way in which Machiavelli, the realist, relied almost exclusively upon the experience of antiquity. Hobbes, the atheist, devotes a substantial portion of the *Leviathan*—a secular work if ever there was one—to a discussion of the Scriptures. The principles and practice of the Greeks and Romans were used as the basis of the revival of the study of military science in the seventeenth century. This also was the case with political science and constitutional law. Neither is there more substance in the facile criticism pointing to Grotius's promiscuous reliance on what appears to the modern eye to be the exotic authority of poets, philosophers, schoolmen, scholastic writers, the Holy Scriptures and their innumerable commentators. For he is at pains to prove not only the law of nations—the evidence of which he sought in unbroken custom and the testimony of those skilled in it[3]—but also the law of nature in its diverse connotations. For the latter purpose it was legitimate for him to draw upon a manifold variety of opinions. The impression of irrelevancy is largely due to the ostentatiousness and prolixity in the piling up of authorities.

*   *   *

To that seemingly deficient and artificial construction of the treatise there must be added a defect of method which, apparently, has no redeeming feature. That defect does not consist in the fact that it is impossible to classify Grotius as belonging to any of the accepted schools of thought in the matter of sources of international law. He is not a pure positivist—a mere chronicler of events laboriously woven into a purely formal pattern of a legal system. Neither is he a naturalist pure and simple for whom an irresistible law of nature is the overriding—or the only—rule of conduct. We cannot even consider him as what is usually described as a 'Grotian' who has accomplished a workable synthesis of natural law and state practice. The fact seems to be that on most subjects which he discusses in his treatise it is impossible to say what is Grotius's view of the legal position. He will tell us, often with regard to the same question, what is the law of nature, the law of nations, divine law, Mosaic law, the law of the Gospel, Roman law, the law of charity, the obligations of honour, or considerations of utility. But we often look in vain for a statement as to what is *the* law governing the matter. Occasionally we obtain a glimpse of how useful the treatise would be if Grotius had adhered to these distinctions for the practical purpose of indicating the existing legal rule. Thus in discussing unjust causes of war he distinguishes between strictly legal obligations and those arising from generosity, gratitude, pity, or charity, which obligations must not be enforced by war any more than they can be enforced in a court of law. . . .[4]

Finally, while the treatise has appeared to some to fail in the achievement of its avowed object in respect of the law of war, it has drawn upon itself vehement condemnation as a servile and reactionary instrument of justification of established authority. The doctrine of the law of nature has been exposed to the reproach that it has served more often as a bulwark of the existing order of things than as a level of progress. Grotius seems to have given a semblance of support to that view. He justifies slavery by reference to the law of nature—a proceeding supported by a venerable array of authority from Aristotle to Locke. Although the social contract is an important component of his political theory, he attributes equal weight to the original acquisition of sovereignty by conquest on the part of the ruler. It is in this sphere that he has been denounced, in intemperate terms, as confusing law and fact.[5] He explicitly refuses to commit himself to any unqualified affirmation of the sovereignty of the people. He expressly rejects the view that 'everywhere and without exception sovereignty resides in the people so that it is permissible for the people to restrain and to punish kings whenever they make a bad use of their power.'[6] He supports his opinion by an elaborate and lengthy argument the gist of which is that any person may voluntarily enslave himself to anyone he pleases for private ownership.[7] For this reason he denies that the subjects are always entitled to regain their liberty—even if they lost it as the result of force. For, he says, subjection though due originally to force may receive subsequent confirmation by tacit acceptance: 'The will of the people, either at the very establishment of sovereignty or in connexion with a later act, may be such as to confer a right which for the future is not dependent on such will.'[8] In the same line of thought he denies the right of active resistance.[9] This view is qualified, as we shall see,[10] not only by the affirmation of the right and duty of passive resistance in face of orders contrary to the law of nature and the commandments of God,[11] but also by vast and significant categories of exceptions. Viewed in proper perspective, the denial of the right of resistance and the support for the sovereignty of the ruler appear less damaging to the character of the treatise than their intransigence suggests.[12] Yet they are not accidental; neither is the uncompromising expression with which they are affirmed. They are not, as we shall see, due to a perversity of thinking which makes us shrug our shoulders with incredulous astonishment. But they do not add to the greatness of De Jure Belli ac Pacis.

These faults of method and substance which we have traced in De Jure Belli ac Pacis are such that, indirectly, they suggest qualities so great and so permanent as to give the very fullest measure of compensation for these defects and to explain the enduring influence of that work in the realm of human thought in general and of international law in particular. We are concerned here only with the latter. The standing of De Jure Belli ac Pacis as an authority relied upon in judicial decisions, national and international, has been higher and more persistent than that of any other of the founders of international law. This can be seen, for instance, in the lengthy pleadings and arguments before and by the various Claims Commissions established by the Jay Treaty of 1794 between Great Britain and the United States, the first modern treaty of arbitration.[13] What is even more impressive is the reverent recourse to his treatise by the four greatest writers in the field of international law in the century which followed, namely, by Pufendorf, Bynkershoek, Wolff, and Vattel—even when, as often happens, they disagree with him. Undoubtedly, the general picture of international relations in the two centuries which followed the publication of De Jure Belli ac Pacis was not one pointing to any direct influence, in the sphere of practice, of the essential features of the Grotian teaching. But the view that, for that reason, Grotius's work was during that period consigned to oblivion[14] is unwarranted and pessimistic. If it were so there would have been no reason why Grotius should have been the first target of criticism in the opening chapters of Contrat Social.[15] Rousseau would have hardly thought it worth while to select for that purpose a writer who had become a dim memory. Voltaire, who, he said, was bored by Grotius's learned quotations masquerading as argument, would not have troubled to read him.[16] De Saint-Pierre's A Project for Settling an Everlasting Peace in Europe would not have its title-page adorned with a passage from *De Jure Belli ac Pacis* recommending the holding of international conferences for the purpose of settling disputes.[17] Between 1680 and 1780 there were thirty editions of the work in Latin; nine in French; four in German; three in English. . . .[18]

When in 1925 jurists of many nations united in celebrating the tercentenary of the publication of *De Jure Belli ac Pacis*, it was manifest that the inspiration which for three centuries emanated from that treatise had by no means become a thing of the past.

There are a number of factors which, in a sense, are external to the substance of Grotius's teaching and which had a share in securing its contemporaneous success and its place in the succeeding centuries. The first is its timeliness. At the time that *De Jure Belli ac Pacis* was published the historic process of the disintegration of European political society as hitherto known and the rise of the territorial sovereign state were being consummated. The Thirty Years War, which, to all appearances, was a war of religion, actually began and continued as a war of secular claims and ambitions of dynasties and nations. The rivalry between France and Spain had been a problem of European politics for three centuries. It had been kept in check by the overriding unity of religion. The Thirty Years War, when Catholic France allied herself with the Protestant cause in opposition to the dynastic ambitions of the Hapsburgs and when the Pope, for similar reasons, stood aloof at a time of deadly peril for the Catholic party, showed clearly the implications of the change. In a different sphere the demise of the feudal system gave a new and higher significance to the territorial state. The need for a system of law governing the relations of the independent states to replace the legal and spiritual unity of Christendom had thus become urgently obvious. If it is accurate to say that Grotius is the founder of modern international law, it is equally true that the necessity for an international law secured to the work of Grotius a place which otherwise it might not have acquired. Of that necessity the lessons of the Thirty Years War were a most compelling reminder. . . .

Secondly, however incomplete—when judged by reference to the present scope of international law—*De Jure Belli ac Pacis* may appear to be, it was the first comprehensive and systematic treatise on international law. Grotius was not the first writer on the law of nations. Belli in 1563,[19] Ayala in 1581,[20] and, above all, Gentilis in 1598[21] wrote learnedly on the laws of war; Vittoria about 1532[22] and Suarez in 1612[23] laid the foundations of the jurisprudential treatment of the problem of the international community as a whole. But no one before Grotius attempted the treatment of the subject in its entirety. There is in *De Jure Belli ac Pacis* a great deal of matter which is not and never has been within the proper sphere of international law, but there is in it all the international law that existed in 1625.

Thirdly, the very circumstance that a substantial portion of the treatise was devoted to matters which had little to do with what is generally regarded as belonging to international law proved a weighty contributory factor in the success which it achieved. For *De Jure Belli ac Pacis* is to a large extent a general treatise of law in its wider meaning (including constitutional law, the theory of the state, and the basis of legal and political obligation) and of jurisprudence. International law proper forms merely a part—though the most important part—of a wider system. The reason assigned by Grotius, and by others, for that prolixity is that that peripheral matter was necessary as an exposition of the rights which might be affected by unlawful action providing a legitimate reason for war.[24] But Grotius himself spoke of the treatise as one pertaining to philosophy of law.[25] There is no doubt that, on balance, what many critics regarded as pretentious irrelevancy proved to be an invaluable asset. For there was presented to the world an exposition of international law woven into the structure of a general system of law and jurisprudence—a significant affirmation of the unity of all law and of the final place of international law in the general scheme of legal science. The effect was to enhance the authority of the treatise and of its main theme, namely, the law of nations.

Finally, the probability ought not to be discounted that the contemporaneous success of the work was to some extent determined by the already great reputation of its author. In 1625 Grotius was a European figure in his own right. His name added lustre to and helped to launch a work which in the course of centuries became synonymous with his fame.

However, all these factors—the timeliness of the treatise, its comprehensiveness as an exposition of international law, its wide jurisprudential background, and the already considerable reputation of its author—are, in a sense, circumstances external to the work. While they may account for its success at the time of its publication and the period immediately following it, they do not explain the powerful and sustained influence of what may be called the Grotian tradition in international law. They do not explain why *De Jure Belli ac Pacis* has been in the history of modern international law more than a mere symbol. . . .

What are the aspects of the teaching of Grotius which, notwithstanding shortcomings of method and defects of substance, lift his work above the plane of a mere episode, however important, in the history of international law and of its development as part of jurisprudence? . . . The answer is that the principal and characteristic features of *De Jure Belli ac Pacis* are identical with the fundamental and persistent problems of international law and that in nearly all of them the teaching of Grotius has become identified with the progression of international law to a true system of law both in its legal and in its ethical content. These main features of the Grotian tradition will now be considered.

1. *The Subjection of the Totality of International Relations to the Rule of Law.* In the first instance, Grotius conceives of the totality of the relations between states as governed by law. This is the central theme of the treatise and its main characteristic. There are no lacunae in that subjection of states to the rule of law. Modern international law recognized for a long time the existence of gaps which obliterated altogether the border-line between

law and lawlessness in international relations. Of these gaps the admissibility of war as an absolute right of states, requiring no other legal justification, is the outstanding example. In laying down the distinction between just and unjust war Grotius rejected the claim to any such right. Neither did he concede to states the absolute faculty of action in self-preservation—a right which, till recently, writers coupled with the legal power of the state to determine, with finality and to the exclusion of any outside tribunal, the justification of action in self-defence.[26] The emphasis with which Grotius denies the absoluteness of the right to act in self-preservation is deeply impressive. That denial of an unqualified right of self-preservation was not a seed which fell on totally barren soil. For we find the same idea expressed in pregnant words two and a half centuries later by Westlake. Self-preservation, he says, does not constitute a principle. It is rather 'a primitive instinct, and an absolute instinct so far as it has not been tamed by reason and law, but one great function of the law is to tame it. . . . In principle we may not hurt another or infringe his rights, even for our self-preservation, when he has not failed in any duty towards us.'[27] In the same line of thought Grotius challenged the right of a state to go to war in order to ward off an anticipated attack. . . . It may also be noted in this connexion that he did not limit the orbit of international law to the states of Christian civilization. He recognized the binding force of treaties concluded with infidels. There was no room in his system for wars of religion—though he considered that there was a duty incumbent upon Christian states to defend one another against aggression by infidels.

2. *The Acceptance of the Law of Nature as an Independent Source of International Law.* With the affirmation of the rule of law as extending to the totality of the relations of states there is connected the second feature of the Grotian tradition, namely, the view that the law thus binding upon states is not solely the product of their express will. Grotius accepted as self-evident the proposition that the sovereign—the state—is bound by the law of nations and the law of nature.[28] The law of nations proper—*jus gentium voluntarium*—is, of course, the product of consent as manifested in the practice of states. Grotius's *jus gentium* thus conceived is not synonymous with public international law. It is distinguished from municipal law (*jus civile*), which emanates from the civil power of one state; it embraces all law—public and private, international and other—which has been sanctioned by the practice of all nations or of many nations.[29] It is one of the component parts of international law, but not the whole of it—a fact which seemingly escaped some of the early critics of Grotius such as Pufendorf and Barbeyrac, who reproached him with basing all international law on consent. Similarly, though a great deal of international law proper rests on consent, much, but not all,[30] of it follows from the precepts of the law of nature. In a wider sense, the binding force even of that part of it that originates in consent is based on the law of nature as expressive of the social nature of man.

It would be a mistake to judge the importance of the part played by the law of nature in *De Jure Belli ac Pacis* by reference to its use in relation to matters affecting international law proper such as treaties between states, the law of diplomatic immunities, and, above all, the law of war. For, as Grotius points out in the opening passages of the chapter on the Right of Legation,[31] in these matters he relies largely on the 'voluntary' law of nations as evidenced by international practice. The significance of the law of nature in the treatise is that it is the ever-present source for supplementing the voluntary law of nations, for judging its adequacy in the light of ethics and reason, and for making the reader aware of the fact that the will of states cannot be the exclusive or even, in the last resort, the decisive source of the law of nations.

This aspect of the system of Grotius has become an integral part of the doctrine and of the practice of the modern law of nations—a part more real than the accepted terminology in the matter of sources of international law has accustomed us to assume. For who are the positivists of whom it may be said, with any approach to accuracy, that they regard the will of sovereign states as the exclusive source of international law? Bynkershoek, generally regarded as the typical positivist of his period, not only repeatedly invokes custom and reason as a source of the law of nations.[32] When confronted with an apparently uniform chain of treaties and municipal enactments cited in support of a view which he considered unreasonable, he refused to accept them as an authority for an asserted legal rule on the ground that 'the law of nations cannot be deduced from these, for reason, the preceptress of the law of nations, will not permit a general and indiscriminate interpretation of these practices.'[33] Hall, the leading British positivist, who appears to limit the sources of international law to usage and treaties,[34] actually bases international law on the natural law foundation of postulates and assumptions. 'The ultimate foundation of international law is an assumption that States possess rights and are subject to duties corresponding to the facts of their postulated nature.'[35] What is that assumed nature? 'It is postulated of those independent states which are dealt with by international law that they have a moral nature identical with that of individuals, and that with respect to one another they are in the same relation as that in which individuals stand to each other who are subject to law.'[36] Kelsen, who denounces natural law as being both unscientific and, historically, an instrument of reaction, assumes as the basis of international law the same jurisprudential maxim on which, in substance, Grotius made it to rest, namely, the rule *pacta sunt servanda*—the difference being that for Grotius the rule *pacta sunt servanda* is a precept, perhaps the main precept, of natural law while for Kelsen it is a 'meta-legal' initial hypothesis. The methodological difference may be considerable, but we cannot be sure of its practical relevance.

The fact is that while within the state it is not essential to give to the ideas of a higher law—of natural law—a function superior to that of providing the inarticulate ethical premise underlying judicial decisions or, in the last resort, of the philosophical and political justification of the right of resistance, in the international society the position is radically different.

There—in a society deprived of normal legislative and judicial organs—the function of natural law, whatever may be its form, must approximate more closely to that of a direct source of law. In the absence of the overriding authority of the judicial and legislative organs of the state there must assert itself—unless anarchy or stagnation are to ensue—the persuasive but potent authority of reason and principle derived from the fact of the necessary coexistence of a plurality of states. This explains the pertinacity, in the international sphere, of the idea of natural law as a legal source. . . .

3. *The Affirmation of the Social Nature of Man as the Basis of the Law of Nature.* The place which the law of nature occupies as part of the Grotian tradition is distinguished not only by the fact of its recognition of a source of law different from and, in proper cases, superior to the will of sovereign states. What is equally significant is Grotius's conception of the quality of the law of nature which dominates his jurisprudential system. It is a law of nature largely based on and deduced from the nature of man as a being intrinsically moved by a desire for social life, endowed with an ample measure of goodness, altruism, and morality, and capable of acting on general principles and of learning from experience.[37] He admits that man is an animal, but one different in kind from other animals. That difference consists in his impelling desire for society—not for society of any sort, but for peaceful and organized life according to the measure of his intelligence. It is a difference the essence of which is the denial of the assertion that 'every animal is impelled by nature to seek only its own good.'[38] There is perhaps no political writer in whose system that conception of the nature of man is more prominent. The theme is, of course, one of the persistent problems—perhaps *the* problem—of political thought. For Machiavelli and Hobbes man is essentially selfish, anti-social, and unable to learn from experience; *homo homini lupus* is the fundamental truth; human nature does not change; pessimism as to the potentialities of its improvement is of the essence of sanity; the basis of political obligation is interest pure and simple; the idea of a sense of moral duty rising supreme over desire and passion is a figment of imagination fatal alike to action and to survival. This is the typical realistic approach of contempt towards the 'little breed' of man. On that line of reasoning there is no salvation for humanity but irrevocable subjection to an order of effective force which, while indifferent to the dignity of man, yet contrives to prevent his life from being 'solitary, poor, nasty, brutish, and short.' The approach of Grotius and—to mention a writer as distinguished and as influential—Locke is diametrically different.

One of the salient characteristics of *De Jure Belli ac Pacis* is not only the frequency of the reliance on and appeal to the law of love, the law of charity, of Christian duty, of honour, and of goodness, and to the injunctions of divine law and the Gospel: the element of morality and the appeal to morality are, without interfering decisively with the legal character of the exposition, a constant theme of the treatise. An equally persistent feature is Grotius's faith in the rational constitution of man and his capacity to see reason and to learn from experience. This aspect of *De Jure Belli ac*

Pacis goes a long way towards explaining the force of the Grotian tradition in the international sphere. . . .

4. *The Recognition of the Essential Identity of States and Individuals.* That all-pervading element of morality and rationality which is the result of Grotius's conception of law as based in the social nature and the intrinsic goodness of man is not limited to the conduct of individuals. It extends to the conduct of nations and of rulers acting on their behalf. In fact, one of the most decisive features of the teaching of Grotius is the close analogy of legal and moral rules governing the conduct of states and individuals alike. 'Populi respectu generis humani privatorum locum obtinent'[39]—this is a pregnant and persistent theme in the teaching of Grotius. This analogy of states and individuals has proved a beneficent weapon in the armoury of international progress. It is not the result of any anthropomorphic or organic conception of the state as being—biologically, as it were—assimilated to individuals, as being an individual person 'writ large.' The analogy is much more simple, more direct, and more convincing. The analogy—nay, the essential identity—of rules governing the conduct of states and of individuals is not asserted for the reason that states *are like* individuals; it is due to the fact that states *are composed of* individual human beings; it results from the fact that behind the mystical, impersonal, and therefore necessarily irresponsible personality of the metaphysical state there are the actual subjects of rights and duties, namely, individual human beings. This is the true meaning of the Grotian analogy of states and individuals. The individual is the ultimate unit of all law, international and municipal, in the double sense that the obligations of international law are ultimately addressed to him and that the development, the well-being, and the dignity of the individual human being are a matter of direct concern to international law. . . .

Undoubtedly, international law is primarily—though not exclusively—a body of rules governing the relations of states, i.e., of individuals organized as a state. But this circumstance cannot affect decisively the moral content of international law and of the dictates of reason and of the general principles of law which underlie it. It may be true to say that 'after all' states are not individuals; but it is even more true to say that 'after all' states are individuals. . . .

In stressing the practical analogy of states and individuals Grotius derived substantial assistance from the fact that in the century in which he wrote the emerging territorial state was a creature of personal rule. The history of Europe could still, to a large extent, be conceived as a history of dynasties and dynastic ambitions. . . . Thus the analogy of states and individuals, which is one of the crucial aspects of Grotius's teaching, was the twin result of two distinct causes. One, which was of a transient character, was the patrimonial character of a considerable number of European states. The other, more enduring, was the realization of the true nature of rules of international law as addressing themselves to individual human beings acting on behalf of the state. The cumulative effect of these two causes was to further the scientific development of international law and to emphasize the moral content of its rules. Largely on account of the recognition of that fundamental analogy, the door was wide open for the enrichment and advancement of international law with the help of rules of private law, Roman and other, as expressive of the general principles of law recognized by civilized states. Critics of the positivist complexion have frequently raised doubts as to the propriety of that process of borrowing from private law. Even if that criticism had been justified—and it is not believed that it was—it was a lament after the event. There have been few branches of international law which have remained unaffected by the influence of private law. We have only to think of Grotius's contribution, by reference to private law, to the development of the rules of law relating to acquisition of territorial sovereignty, the principle of the freedom of the sea, and the law of state responsibility. The very notion of sovereignty, which Grotius conceived, like property, as dominion held under law, helped to deprive it of the character of absoluteness and indivisibility. Neither was it a process confined to the exposition of international law by writers; governments and international arbitrators relied upon it frequently and effectively. If we were to ignore or to underestimate these 'illicit borrowings' we should be depriving ourselves of the possibility of understanding what is perhaps the major part of international law. To discard them as a matter of future practice is impossible. To do so would mean to jettison a substantial part of positive international law in which the rules derived by analogy have become crystallized. It would mean challenging the purpose of that significant provision of the Statute of the International Court of Justice which constitutes the general principles of international law as recognized by civilized states, one of the three principal sources of the law to be applied by the Court. To discard them as a matter of principle would mean to abandon the view, which is amply justified by experience, that upon the continued vitality of this aspect of the Grotian tradition depends the progressive approximation of international law to a system of legal rules worthy of that name.

5. *The Rejection of 'Reason of State.'* The recognition of the social and moral nature of man as the principal source and cause of law explains, when coupled with the persistent affirmation of the analogy of states and individuals, the fifth characteristic of the Grotian tradition, namely, his denial of the 'reason of State' as a basic and decisive factor of international relations. That denial of the principle of double morality is for Grotius so obvious and so fundamental that, it would seem, he regards it as below the dignity of his work to engage in the then customary argument *ad hominem* on the subject.

A startling feature of *De Jure Belli ac Pacis* is the absence not only of any polemics, but of all reference to Machiavelli. . . . But although he does not mention Machiavelli by name, he takes up the issue of 'reason of State' at the very beginning of the treatise. After remarking upon the usefulness of a knowledge of the law 'which is concerned with the mutual relations among states or rulers of states,'[40] he points to the special necessity of studying that branch of law. For, he says, there are 'in our day' persons who view it with contempt as having no reality; who consider that for a king or a state nothing is unjust which is expedient; and that the business of the state cannot be carried on without injustice.[41] He sees an intimate connexion between the rejection of the ideas of 'reason of State' and the affirmation of the legal and moral unity of mankind. He insists that if no association of men can be maintained without law, 'surely also that association which binds together the human race, or binds many nations together, has need of law.'[42] This means, he says, quoting Cicero with approval, that shameful acts ought not to be committed even for the sake of one's country.[43] It means also that the hall-mark of wisdom for a ruler is to take account not only of the good of the nation committed to his care, but of the whole human race.[44] 'The name of Minos became odious to future ages for no other reason than this, that he limited his fair dealing to the boundaries of his realm.'[45] While denying that law is based on expediency alone,[46] he was ready to meet the theorists of 'reason of State' on the ground of their own choosing, namely, that of advantage. He records the fact that according to many the standards of justice applicable in the relations of individuals within the state do not apply to a state or the ruler of a state. The reason usually given for that assertion of the double standard of justice is, he says, that law is indispensable to individuals who, taken singly, cannot protect themselves, while great states, which dispose of everything needed for adequate protection, are in no need of law. Grotius rejects this view. Such, in his opinion, is the impact of economic interdependence or of military security that there is no state so powerful that it can dispense with the help of others.[47]

Grotius's rejection of the ideas of *raison d'état* finds more direct expression in relation to concrete issues. It expresses itself in the denial of the right to resort to war unless in pursuance of a good legal cause;[48] in the rigid limitation of the right of self-defence (including the right of war in order to ward off an anticipated attack); in the concession of the right—indeed, in the injunction of the duty—of passive resistance against orders and laws contrary to the law of nature and the law of God;[49] in the concession to the subject of the right—and, again, in the injunction of the duty—to refrain from participation not only in unjust wars but also in wars the justice of which is doubtful;[50] in his stressing of the sacredness of the principle *pacta sunt servanda*. . . .[51]

The great issue of 'reason of State' is still with us and, while it will continue to be an absorbing dilemma of historical science, it is one of the main problems of international law—perhaps the central problem if by law we understand restraint and if by 'reason of State' we mean rejection of any substantial restriction upon the freedom of action of sovereign states in matters which matter. The '*raison d'état*' may no longer present itself in the international sphere in the cruder forms of treacherous violence, of brazen perfidy, and of outright deceit—although recent history has shown that species of *ratio status* to be not altogether obsolete. Modern formulae such as that international law is possible only as a 'law of co-ordination' effected by agreement of sovereign States express ideas of distinct affinity with those of 'reason of State.'

. . . It may be difficult to form an estimate of the influence of *De Jure Belli ac Pacis* in curbing the spirit of *The Prince*. But there ought to be no doubt as to the place which the rejection of the ideology of *raison d'état* occupies in the Grotian system—a repudiation significant both in the absence of direct reference to Machiavelli and, more particularly, in Grotius's attitude to the questions which 'reason of State' has pretended to solve in its crude and realistic fashion.

6. *The Distinction Between Just and Unjust Wars*. In the assertion of 'reason of State' and of the double standard of morality, the claim to an unrestricted right of war, though not the most conspicuous, is the most important. It is not the dagger or the poison of the hired assassin or the sharp practice of the realistic politician which expresses most truly, upon final analysis, the ideas of '*raison d'état*.' It is the infliction, without a shadow of a specific right and without a claim to any particular right, of the calamities and indignities of war and of the territorial mutilation and the very annihilation of statehood following upon defeat in war. Prior to the changes introduced by the Covenant of the League of Nations, the Pact of Paris of 1928, and the Charter of the United Nations, that central idea of 'reason of State' formed part of international law. States claimed—and had— the right to resort to war not only in order to defend their legal rights but in order to destroy the legal rights of other states. In the sphere of political theory Machiavelli put the position with his usual terseness: 'That war is just which is necessary.'

. . . But although this particular—and most important—manifestation of 'reason of State' became and for centuries continued to be part of international law, it was not an unchallenged doctrine. It was opposed by the parallel and powerful current of opinion that distinguished between wars which, in law, were just and those which were not. That current of opinion is represented by yet another aspect of the Grotian tradition, namely, his denial of the absolute right of war and his consistent differentiation between just and unjust wars. Grotius did not invent that distinction. It was part of the heritage of the Middle Ages. . . .

In the elaboration of the causes of just war Grotius made no obvious advance upon the already elaborate treatment of the subject by his pre-decessors. The merit of his own contribution lies in the clarity and in the emphasis with which he treated the subject. For a war to be just there must exist a legal cause for it—a reason which would be recognized by a court of law as a cause of action. As he points out, war begins where judicial settlement ends. It follows that a war undertaken to enforce a claim which 'is not an obligation from the point of view of strict justice'[52] is not a just war. He devotes an entire chapter to an enumeration, by way of example, of various kinds of unjust war.[53] On the other hand, the causes of just wars are limited to defence against an injury either actual or immediately threatening,[54] to recovery of what is legally due, and to inflicting punishment. He definitely excludes wars undertaken in order to weaken a neighbour who is a potential threat to the security of the state. He says, with regard to such a war, in a passage typical of the temper of the work in its challenging rejection of *raison d'état*: 'That the possibility of being attacked confers the right to attack is abhorrent to every principle of equity. Human life exists under such conditions that complete security is never guaranteed to us. For protection against uncertain fears we must rely on Divine Providence, and on a wariness free from reproach, not on force.'[55] He says in another part of the book: 'That defence may be just, it must be necessary; and it cannot be this, except there be clear evidence, not only of the power, but also of the *animus* of the party; and such evidence as amounts to moral certainty.'[56]

. . . The relevant section of Book II[57]—the shortest paragraph in the treatise—consists of one sentence, significant and impressive in its brevity, referring to the causes of war: 'Advantage does not confer the same right as necessity.' He also denies that there is any question of a justifiable war of defence in the case of those who deserved the war waged against them.[58]

But it was in the drawing of the practical consequences from the distinction between just and unjust wars that Grotius went beyond anything taught by his predecessors. This applies not only to the all-important question of neutrality,[59] or to such matters of detail as the rule that a state bound by treaties of alliance with states engaged in war ought to give preference to that engaged in a just war, for 'there is no obligation to undertake unjust wars';[60] that a treaty of alliance is not binding in relation to a state waging an unjust war;[61] or that a state engaged in a just war may, under certain strictly defined conditions, take possession of a place situated in a neutral country;[62] or, though apparently only as a matter of *interna justitia*, with regard to restoration of property taken in an unjust war;[63] or even to the assertion of the right of the belligerent fighting an adversary waging 'a very unjust war' to inflict capital punishment upon those carrying contraband.[64] It applies to the more fundamental question of the duty of the subject to serve in a war which is unjust or doubtful, an aspect of his teaching which is of particular significance in view of the respect—some thought servile respect—with which Grotius treated established authority and with which he discouraged any thought of rebellion. He is emphatic that the subject when ordered to take up arms in a clearly unjust war ought to refrain from doing so.[65] Moreover, after much careful deliberation and weighing of authorities, he considers that the obligation is the same when the justice of the war is doubtful. He admits the dangers of disobedience, but he is content to take the risk: 'For when either course is uncertain that which is the lesser of two evils is free from sin; for if a war is unjust there is no disobedience in avoiding it. Moreover, disobedience in things of this kind, by its very nature, is a lesser evil than manslaughter, especially than the slaughter of many innocent men.'[66] The only concession that he is prepared to make is that in the case of a doubtful war the ruler may impose an extraordinary tax upon those refusing to carry arms.[67] At the same time, in conformity with the view which has remained unchallenged and which is in accordance with the humanitarian character of his treatise, he lays down that the question of the justice or injustice of the war is irrelevant for the purpose of observing the rules of warfare as between the belligerents.[68] Any other rule would add to the inherent evils of war the horrors of unrestrained licence and cruelty accentuated by what must often be an unverified *ex parte* claim to wage a just war.

International law, in the three centuries which followed *De Jure Belli ac Pacis*, rejected the distinction between just and unjust wars. War became the supreme right of sovereign states and the very hall-mark of their sovereignty. To that extent international law was deprived of a reasonable claim to be regarded as law in the accepted sense of the word. The law on the subject has now undergone a fundamental change. War has ceased to be a supreme prerogative of states. . . . [A]mong the imponderables which have worked in that direction, the Grotian tradition occupies a high place.

7. *The Doctrine of Qualified Neutrality.* It followed from the emphasis of the distinction between just and unjust wars that no affirmation of absolute impartiality on the part of neutral states in relation to the state waging an unjust war was to be expected in a legal treatise in which the element of moral obligation was as prominent as in *De Jure Belli ac Pacis*. It is theoretically possible for international law to declare that some wars are illegal and criminal and yet to lay down that the neutral states not involved in the war must act with absolute detachment in relation both to the aggressor and to his victim. The legal consistency of such a system of international law would be questionable; its ethical impropriety would be obvious. In any case such a solution would not have been in keeping with the spirit of *De Jure Belli ac Pacis*. Grotius's view on the subject is expressed tersely in the brief chapter on neutrality entitled 'On those who are of neither side in war.'[69] He says: 'It is the duty of those who keep out of war to do nothing whereby he who supports a wicked cause may be rendered more powerful, or whereby the movements of him who wages an unjust war may be hampered.'[70] It will be noted that these duties do not include the positive obligation to assist actively the state waging a just war. But they clearly imply a right to do so. . . .

In general, the right of neutrals to form a judgment on the legal justice of the war waged by belligerents and to adopt discriminatory treatment in accordance with that judgment was generally recognized in the eighteenth century under the influence of Grotius.

The doctrine of qualified neutrality was rejected in the nineteenth century—with perfect logical consistency—by the overwhelming majority of writers. If every war is, in law, just, then neutrality must be an attitude of absolute impartiality. Occasionally writers of authority expressed their disapproval of neutrality thus conceived as being morally intolerable.[71] But that denunciation of neutrality was in fact a condemnation of a system of international law, fully in operation at that time, in which resort to war was an unlimited right of sovereign states.

With the drastic limitation of the right of war as adopted in the Covenant of the League of Nations and in the General Treaty for the Renunciation of War, the law restored the historic foundations of the doctrine of qualified neutrality as taught by Grotius. The Covenant of the League, in permitting neutrality and in obliging the Members to resort to sanctions and other measures of discrimination against the Covenant-breaking state, was, in this respect, based on the principle of qualified neutrality. When in 1940 and 1941 the United States committed itself to a determined departure from the customary and conventional rules of absolute neutrality as they obtained in the nineteenth century, it invoked, among others, the argument that with the general renunciation and condemnation of war as an instrument of national policy, the right, asserted by the founders of international law, to discriminate against the aggressor was fully restored. Grotius's teaching on the subject was adduced in support of the attitude thus adopted.[72]

Under the Charter of the United Nations neutrality is no longer an absolute right. Members of the United Nations are bound, if called upon to do so by a valid decision of the Security Council, to resort to war against a state waging an aggressive, an unjust, war. But it is possible that the call made upon them may fall short of a summons to resort to war. In that case, the principles of qualified neutrality would once more be applicable. . . .

8. *The Binding Force of Promises.* The denial of the right of war, unless for a cause recognized by law, and the principle of qualified neutrality constitute the main application, with regard to the law of war, of Grotius's rejection of the ideas of reason of State. In the sphere of the law of peace, that same tendency expressed itself most conspicuously in the emphasis which he placed upon the binding force of promises and the obligation of good faith in their fulfilment. The subject is treated at great length in the six chapters of Book II on Promises, on Contracts, on Oaths, on Promises of those holding Sovereign Power, on Public Treaties and Sponsions, and on Interpretation.[73] In addition, the five concluding chapters of the treatise are devoted to the subject of promises and good faith in war.[74] The last exhortation, in the final chapter of the treatise, is an appeal to the sacredness of good faith.[75] To Grotius the obligation to abide by pacts is not only the basis of municipal law and of civil society; it is of the essence of the social contract.[76] Without it the social contract is meaningless.[77] As such, the obligation to keep promises is the principal tenet of the law of nature. It is an obligation which binds the ruler in relation to the contract which he has entered into with his subjects; they derive a clear legal right under it. And this, he adds, 'holds even between God and man.'[78] It is not surprising that to him the binding force of treaties is the basis of international law. They must be kept even in relation to pirates and tyrants, in peace or in war;[79] they may be made, according to the Christian law and otherwise, with infidels,[80] and faith must be kept even with them.[81] He lays down the

modern and, in the circumstances, unexceptional rule that promises made during war or for the purpose of terminating a war are valid even if extorted by fear.[82] The reason for this seemingly repulsive qualification is that unless this rule were adopted most wars would be incapable of termination.

This categorical affirmation of the sanctity of promises—even in relation to God Himself—had a pointed meaning at a time when the Pope claimed the right to release rulers from the binding obligation of oaths and treaties, by way of interpretation or express dispensation,[83] and when the view was widely adopted and acted upon that there is no binding force in treaties concluded not only between Christians and infidels but also those between Catholics and Protestants. But its significance goes considerably beyond that. It supplies a scientific basis—that of the law of nature and of the social nature of man—for the 'volitional' law of nations, i.e., international law based on agreement whether expressed in a treaty or implied by custom. In modern terminology, the rule *pacta sunt servanda* is the initial hypothesis of the law of nations. . . .

9. *The Fundamental Rights and Freedoms of the Individual.* There is one perplexing aspect of the work of Grotius which appears to be alien to the spirit of his teaching as outlined so far and which calls for careful examination, namely, his attitude to the question of the freedom of the individual in his relation to constituted authority. The importance of this subject is not confined to the field of political theory. In many ways it is closely connected with international law. It has given rise to scornful and impatient reprobation of Grotius's work as a whole. What is the reason for this exception—if an exception it is—to the otherwise uniformly progressive trend of the treatise? On the face of it the record is disillusioning. Grotius justified slavery and claimed to have found support for it in the immutable canons of the law of nature. He rejected the idea of the sovereignty of the people.[84] He denied the right of resistance to oppression by the ruler.[85] He did not see why, if an individual can voluntarily sell himself into slavery, a whole people should not be able to do so collectively. He attributed an irrevocable legal effect not only to collective voluntary submission, but also to conquest. He completed this chain of reasoning by including in his examples of unjust wars a contest waged by an oppressed people in order to regain its liberty.[86] It is not easy to fit all this into the general pattern of the treatise. The matter becomes even more obscure when we consider the personal circumstances of its author. Here was a refugee who escaped from the sentence of a political court set up by an arbitrary decree. Yet he deprecated resistance to oppressive rule. Here was a Dutchman, the loyal son of a people which half a century before had by force thrown off the yoke of the Spanish oppressor who, at the very moment when *De Jure Belli ac Pacis* was being written, was preparing war against the United Provinces to reimpose upon them the tyranny of alien rule. Yet Grotius considered to be unjust a war waged by an oppressed people for the sake of its freedom.

What is the explanation of these views, so foreign to the spirit of his teaching and to his personal condition? It is true that, writing as he did in a country under an absolute monarch to whom he dedicated the treatise, who bestowed a pension upon him, and from whom he might have expected the favours of remunerative appointment, he could hardly write in the vein of *Vindiciae contra Tyrannos*. It is possible that, in view of the intransigence with which the right of resistance was advocated, both in the latter tract—which appeared in 1579 but which had not by any means fallen into oblivion—and in Hotman's *Franco-Gallia*, published in 1573, he felt it incumbent upon himself to give to the matter a special argumentative emphasis. But this in itself is an inadequate explanation. What is much more to the point is that this frowning upon rebellion and the favouring of authority were in accordance with what were considered to be the essential needs of the times. The horrors of civil war were foremost in the minds of political thinkers. There was not, in this respect, much difference between Hobbes and Bacon on the one side, and Hooker, Gentilis, and Bodin on the other. They discussed in detail the right of resistance; they all rejected it. So, perhaps with less justification, did Pufendorf.[87] At a time of general uncertainty and of loosening of traditional ties of society, national and international, order was looked upon as the paramount dictate of reason. In the period preceding the Thirty Years War the territorial sovereign state which emerged from the dissolution of the feudal system of society on the Continent of Europe had hardly taken over the functions of the feudal lord; the resulting vacuum accentuated the necessity for stability even at the expense of freedom.[88] Considerations of this order must have weighed heavily with one in whose work the desire for peace was the dominant motive and the ever-recurring theme. This particular feature of Grotius's outlook appears clearly from his unheroic advice given to defeated peoples to yield to fate rather than to engage in a suicidal fight for liberty, for, he says, reason prefers life to freedom.[89] Strange as it may sound, his attitude towards slavery was to a large extent determined by humanitarian considerations. Enslavement of those captured in war was an alternative preferable to the unlimited power, including the right to kill, which, in his view, the customary law of nations and, probably, the law of nature gave to the captor. His treatment of the institution of slavery is permeated throughout by a spirit of charity and mercy.[90]

What is more important than these explanations is the fact that behind the façade of the general disapproval of the right of resistance there lay qualifications so comprehensive as to render the major proposition almost theoretical. Thus, according to Grotius, there is a right of resistance in cases in which the ruler, by virtue of an original or subsequent contract, is responsible to a free people (as was the case in Sparta);[91] against a king who has renounced his authority or has manifestly abandoned it;[92] who attempts to alienate his kingdom (but only so far as is necessary to prevent the transfer);[93] who openly shows himself the enemy of the whole people—an elastic and formidable exception;[94] who attempts to usurp that part of the sovereign power which does not belong to him;[95] and, finally, where the people have reserved the right of resistance in certain cases.[96] These exceptions as laid down by Grotius were relied upon as an authority for the justification of the resistance to and deposition of James II. . . .[97]

Finally, in this connexion we must bear in mind other indications of Grotius's true attitude. Thus it is significant that, notwithstanding his reluctance to sanction recourse to war, he considers as just resort to war to prevent the maltreatment by a state of its own subjects. In such cases, he says, if a ruler 'should inflict upon his subjects such treatment as no one is warranted in inflicting, the exercise of the right vested in human society is not precluded.'[98] This is, on the face of it, a somewhat startling rule, for it may not be easy to see why he permits a foreign state to intervene, through war, on behalf of the oppressed while he denies to the persecuted themselves the right of resistance. Part of the answer is, perhaps, that he held such wars of intervention to be permitted only in extreme cases which coincide largely with those in which the king reveals himself as an enemy of his people and in which resistance is permitted.

However that may be, this is the first authoritative statement of the principle of humanitarian intervention—the principle that the exclusiveness of domestic jurisdiction stops where outrage upon humanity begins. The doctrine of humanitarian intervention has never become a fully acknowledged part of positive international law. But it has provided a signpost and a warning. It has been occasionally acted upon, and it was one of the factors which paved the way for the provisions of the Charter of the United Nations relating to fundamental human rights and freedoms. . . .

10. *The Idea of Peace.* The tenth—and not the least important—aspect of the Grotian tradition is his pacifism. He does not deny that war is a legal institution. On the contrary, he is at pains to show that war is not inconsistent with the law of nature and with many other kinds of law. There were good reasons—in addition to the recognition of a patent fact—for this initial legitimation of war. It would not be feasible to attempt to introduce a measure of legal regulation into a relation not recognized by law. A corresponding method suggested itself—and was adopted—with regard to the contents of the rules of warfare. Thus Grotius's treatment of the laws of war seems to be open to the charge that, after setting out to humanize rules of war, he gives the imprimatur of law to rules of pronounced inhumanity.[99] His answer to any such criticism would probably have been that the proper course was not to deny the character of law to practices which apparently had secured a wide degree of acceptance, but to urge a mitigation of their rigours. Ayala went as far as Grotius—and farther—in treating these practices as law, but he did not propose anything in the nature of *temperamenta*.

In general, there breathes from the pages of *De Jure Belli ac Pacis* a disapproval, amounting to hatred, of war.[100] There is nothing in that work reminiscent of the Baconian conception of war as a healthy exercise. Grotius is clear that where the question of legal right is doubtful, a state ought to refrain from war.[101] He proposes various methods of settling disputes, including negotiation[102] and arbitration.[103] He suggests that 'it would be advantageous, indeed in a degree necessary, to hold certain conferences of Christian powers, where those who have no interest at stake may settle the disputes of others, and where, in fact, steps may be taken to compel parties to accept peace on fair terms.'[104] He devotes a whole chapter to 'warnings not to undertake war rashly, even for just causes.'[105] Elsewhere, he distinguishes between justifiable wars, namely, those for which there is a true legal cause, and those in which the law is but a pretext. These latter he describes simply as wars of robbers.[106] He fully approved of the view of St. Augustine that aggressive wars of conquest are nothing but 'wholesale robbery.'[107] And he cited other distinguished authorities in support of the same opinion.[108] It is probable that his persistent striving towards the unity of the Christian Church and the appearance of leanings towards Catholicism[109] were the outcome of the realization that no other basis was as yet possible for the international organization and preservation of peace.

11. *The Tradition of Idealism and Progress.* The pacifist strain which runs through the entire work of Grotius is only one feature of the more general aspect—the last to be here considered—of the Grotian tradition, namely, what may not inappropriately be called the tradition of progress and idealism. He initiated or gave his support to progressive ideas in various fields in the sphere of international relations. He was one of the first to assist the cause of international co-operation in the suppression of crime by urging extradition of criminals as a matter of legal duty.[110] He did more than any of the other founders of international law in developing the theory and in elucidating the practice of diplomatic immunities. He supplied the basis of the modern law of state responsibility founded on fault as distinguished from absolute liability[111] and thus helped to displace the indiscriminating and anarchic practice of reprisals as a normal means of redressing grievances. He urged, and laid down as a rule of law, the principle of freedom of navigation on international rivers and canals.[112] His share in the evolution of the principle of the freedom of the sea needs no elaboration. In all these matters his teaching became part of international practice, wholly or in part. In others, although it has remained a mere postulate of reason, it is not without significance.

Thus in matters of economic freedom he spoke the language of uncompromising free trade expressed in terms of legal right. Men are entitled to obtain things without which life cannot comfortably be lived. And although this is an imperfect right inasmuch as the owner retains the power of disposition, no obstacles to the free acquisition of necessaries of life must be raised by 'law or by conspiracy.'[113] To do that, he says, quoting Ambrose, is 'to separate men from relation with their common parent, to refuse fruits freely produced for all, and to do away with the community of life.'[114] He reiterates that all men have the right to buy such things at a fair price unless, as in time of extreme scarcity of grain, they are needed by those from whom they are sought.' As if in anticipation of some modern monopolistic practices, he inquired, in this connexion, whether it is permissible for one people to make an agreement with another to sell to it exclusively products which do not grow elsewhere. He thought this permissible and not inconsistent with the law of nature provided the latter was prepared to re-sell at a fair price.[115]

It will be noted that these various claims are not postulates of mere ideal justice. They figure in the part of the treatise which is concerned with the causes of war—one of which is 'injury actually received,'[116] 'an injury to that which actually belongs to us.'[117] He was clearly in advance of his time when he urged that refugees driven from their homes have the right to acquire permanent residence in another country provided they submit to the government in authority;[118] that deserted and barren portions of national territory be given to immigrants who ask for it, and that they are entitled to take possession, subject to the sovereignty of the original people, of uncultivated land;[119] that a state is bound to grant freedom of passage through its territory to a people which has been forced to leave its country and is seeking unoccupied lands, or desires to carry on commerce with a distant nation;[120] that freedom of passage for the purpose of carrying on commerce extends, as a matter of right, not only to persons but also to merchandise;[121] and that such freedom of passage includes freedom from taxation unless in return for services rendered.[122] He urged with emphasis the right of the individual to expatriate himself from his country of origin,[123] and he acknowledged the right of self-determination to the extent of requiring the consent of the population to the transfer of national territory. . . .[124]

These then are the principal features of what has here been called the Grotian tradition in international law. They may be conveniently enumerated by way of conclusion. They are: the subjection of the totality of international relations to the rule of law; the acceptance of the law of nature as an independent source of international law; the affirmation of the social nature of man as the basis of the law of nature; the recognition of the essential identity of states and individuals; the rejection of 'reason of State'; the distinction between just and unjust war; the doctrine of qualified neutrality; the binding force of promises; the fundamental rights and freedoms of the individual; the idea of peace; and the tradition of idealism and progress. Some of these elements of the Grotian tradition have now become part of the positive law; others are still an aspiration. But they all explain why Grotius's work has remained an abiding force and not merely an episode, however important, in the literature of international law. They explain why writers and statesmen have turned to Grotius not only as a source of evidence of the law as it is, but also as a well-spring of faith in the law as it ought to be. Grotius did not create international law. Law is not made by writers. What Grotius did was to endow international law with unprecedented dignity and authority by making it part not only of a general system of jurisprudence but also of a universal moral code. To many, indeed, it may appear that *De Jure Belli ac Pacis* is more a system of ethics applied to states than a system of law. This would not inevitably imply a condemnation of the work. For it may be held that at that time—as, indeed, at any time—

it was important that the relations of states should be conceived and taught as part of ethics as well as part of law. Grotius's great merit is that he performed both tasks in one work. This combination of functions resulted in much methodological confusion offensive to the purist, who is in danger of forgetting that in the seventeenth century eclecticism was as important as systematic accuracy. *De Jure Belli ac Pacis* is pre-eminently a treatise which must be judged not by reference to its method, but by its influence on the doctrine and on the practice of the law of nations. It satisfied the craving, in the jurist and the layman alike, for a moral content in the law. In stressing and, on the whole, maintaining the distinction between law and morality it vindicated the place of the law of nations in legal science. Last—but not least—it became identified with the idea of progress in international law.

These considerations may help to answer, to a large extent, the question whether *De Jure Belli ac Pacis* is still a proper medium of study and instruction in international law. The reply is clearly in the negative if what we have in mind is assistance in the search for a legal rule which we may assume an international court would now apply in a case before it. From this point of view most text-books and treatises are obsolete. . . .

[However, by] gaining an understanding of the Grotian tradition as a whole—this has been the main object of the present article—we may not only fathom the secret of its influence upon generations of scholars and men of affairs. We may, and that is no less important, obtain an insight into the persistent problems of international law in the past, in the present, and, probably for some long time to come, in the future. It is a measure of the greatness of the work of Grotius that all these questions should have found a place in his teaching and that he should have answered them in a spirit upon the acceptance of which depends the ultimate reality of the law of nations as a 'law properly so called.'

NOTES

1. As quoted by Knight, *The Life and Work of Hugo Grotius* (1925), p. 289.
2. See section 10.
3. Book II, ch. i, § xiv. 2.
4. Book II, ch. xxii, § xvi.
5. See Book II, ch. xxii, § xvi, p. 1.
6. Book I, ch. iii, § viii. 1.
7. Book I, ch. iii, § viii.
8. Book II, ch. iv, § xiv. 1.
9. Book I, ch. iv, § ii. 1. He denies that the ruler who maltreats an innocent person by that fact necessarily ceases to be a ruler: Book II, ch. i, § ix. 2.
10. See section 9.
11. Book I, ch. iv, § i. 3.
12. See section 9.
13. See, e.g., *International Adjudications* (ed. by Moore), vol. iv (1931), Mixed Commission under Article VII of the Jay Treaty, pp. 357, 384–6, 390–2, 413–15 (on carriage of contraband), pp. 232–7, 269–79, 282–3 (on enemy character), pp. 246–

7, 251-2 (on reprisals and exhaustion of legal remedies), pp. 419-21 (on measure of damages).

14. See Van Vollenhoven, 'Grotius and Geneva,' in *Bibliotheca Visseriana*, vol. vi (1926), pp. 15, 16, 30-4.

15. Book I, ch. ii.

16. *Dialogues et entretiens philosophiques* (Œuvres complètes, 1824), vol. xxxvi, p. 232.

17. Book II, ch. xxiii, § vii. 4 (in the English translation of 1714).

18. For an exhaustive list see *De Jure Belli ac Pacis* (translation in 'Classics of International Law,' 1925), pp. 877-86.

19. *De re militari et bello tractatus.*

20. *De jure bellico; De officiis bellicis; De disciplina militari.*

21. *De jure belli libri tres.*

22. *De Indis; De jure belli* (published in 1557).

23. *Tractatus de legibus et Deo legislatore.*

24. *Proleg.* 33-5.

25. *Ibid.* 30.

26. Thus writers have interpreted the various declarations accompanying the General Treaty for the Renunciation of War and reserving to the Parties both the right of resorting to war in self-defence and of determining when such action is necessary as meaning that the Parties have the exclusive and ultimate right to pronounce upon the legitimacy of the action said to have been taken in self-defence. No such right is implied either in the Treaty or in the reservations thereto. The state which believes itself to be in danger is entitled to determine, in the first instance, whether action in self-preservation is necessary. The ultimate determination of the legitimacy of the action taken is a matter for decision by an impartial body. See the Judgment of 31 August 1946 of the International Military Tribunal at Nuremberg: 'It was further argued that Germany alone could decide, in accordance with the reservations made by the many Signatory Powers at the time of the conclusion of the Briand-Kellogg Pact, whether preventive action was a necessity, and that in making her decision her judgment was conclusive. But whether action taken under the claim of self-defence was in fact aggressive or defensive must ultimately be subject to investigation and adjudication if international law is ever to be enforced' (*Transcript of the Proceedings*, p. 16,853).

27. *Collected Papers* (ed. in 1914), p. 112. He says in the same chapter: '. . . although it is certainly indispensable for the welfare of men that they should be associated in some state tie, it does not follow that their welfare imperatively requires the maintenance in its actual limits, and with resources entirely unimpaired, of the actual state tie in which they happen to be engaged' (ibid., p. 113). And see T. H. Green, *Principles of Political Obligation* (1895), § 166, who says that a state that 'needs to defend its interest by action injurious to those outside it . . . by no means fulfils its purpose . . . it might perhaps be swept away and superseded by another with advantage to the ends for which the true State exists.'

28. Book I, ch. iii, § xvi. 1.

29. Book I, ch. i, § xiv.

30. There is probably no sufficient warrant for Sir Henry Maine's view (*Ancient Law* [1920 reprint], p. 103) that Grotius identified *jus gentium* and *jus naturae*.

31. Book II, ch. xviii.

32. *Quœstionum juris publici libri duo* (1737 edition), Book I, ch. vi, p. 46; ch. viii, p. 66; ch. x, p. 77.

33. Book I, ch. xii, p. 95 (Tenney Frank's translation in 'Classics of International Law,' 1930).

34. *A Treatise on International Law* (3rd ed. 1890), Introduction, p. 7.

35. *Op. cit.*, § 7 (p. 44).

36. *Op. cit.*, § 1 (p. 18).

37. *Proleg.* 5–9.

38. *Proleg.* 6. He says elsewhere: 'If other ties are wanting, the tie of a common human nature is sufficient. Nothing belonging to mankind is indifferent to man' (Book II, ch. v, § ii. 1 [Whewell's translation]).

39. *Mare liberum*, ch. v. See also *De Jure Belli ac Pacis*, Book II, ch. xv, § xii. 1. In the judgment given on 31 August 1946 by the International Military Tribunal at Nuremberg we find an illustration of the practical implications of the problem. The Tribunal said: 'It was submitted that international law is concerned with the actions of sovereign States, and provides no punishment for individuals . . . these contentions must be rejected. . . . Crimes against international law are committed by men, not by abstract entities, and only by punishing individuals who commit such crimes can the provisions of international law be enforced' (*Transcript of the Proceedings*, p. 16,878).

40. *Proleg.* 1.

41. *Ibid.* 3.

42. *Ibid.* 23.

43. *Ibid.*

44. *Ibid.* 24.

45. *Ibid.*

46. *Ibid.* 5, 22, 57.

47. *Ibid.* 21, 22. See also ibid. 18: 'For just as the national, who violates the law of his country in order to obtain an immediate advantage, breaks down that by which the advantages of himself and of his posterity are for all future time assured, so the state which transgresses the laws of nature and of nations casts away the bulwarks which safeguard its own future peace.' See also ibid., p. 24, n. 3, and p. 26, n. 2.

48. See section 6.

49. See section 9.

50. See section 6.

51. See section 7.

52. Book II, ch. xxii, § xvi.

53. Book II, ch. xxii.

54. Book II, ch. i, § ii. 1; § v; § xvi. In the latter paragraph he permits a state to forestall an act of violence not actually present but threatening from a distance. But even in this case he excludes direct action—which he considers unjust—and limits it to obtaining satisfaction for a delinquency begun but not yet consummated.

55. *Ibid.*, § xvii.

56. Book II, ch. xxii, § v. 1. (The translation is from Whewell's edition as it seems, on this point, more precise than that in the 'Classics of International Law.')

57. Ch. xxii, § vi.

58. *Ibid.*, ch. i, § xviii.

59. See Book II, ch. xv, § xiii, p. 40.

60. Book II, ch. xv, § xiii. 1.

61. Book II, ch. xxv, § iv. He regarded as not permissible military alliances concluded without regard to the cause of the war in which the ally may be involved. Book II, ch. xxv, § ix. 1.

62. Ibid., § x. 1.

63. Book III, ch. x, § iii. 1.

64. Ibid., ch. i, § v. 3.

65. Book II, ch. xxvi, § iii. 1.

66. Ibid., § iv. 5; ibid., § iv. 8. With this may be compared the view of Pufendorf, *De jure naturae et gentium libri octo* (1688), Book VIII, ch. i, *in fine*, who points to the dangers of destroying civil sovereignty and advises the citizen to 'leave the supreme sovereign accountable to God for the injustice of his war.'

67. Book II, ch. xxvi, § v.

68. Book III, ch. iv, § iv.

69. Book III, ch. xvii.

70. Ibid., § iii. 1. But he counsels impartiality in doubtful cases.

71. See, in particular, Westlake, *International Law*, vol. ii (2nd ed., 1913), p. 90.

72. See the speech of Attorney-General Jackson on 27 March 1941 (*American Journal of International Law*, 35 [1941], p. 351).

73. Chs. xi–xvi.

74. Book III, chs. xix–xxiii.

75. Book III, ch. xxv, § vii.

76. *Proleg.* 15.

77. This explains why he is prepared to base the right of punishment on implied contract (Book II, ch. xx, § ii. 3).

78. Book II, ch. xiv, § vi. 2.

79. Book III, ch. xix, § ii. 1, 2.

80. Book II, ch. xv, § x. 1.

81. Book III, ch. xix, § xiii. 1. Although he advises caution in concluding treaties of alliance with infidels, he regards such alliances as permissible and, above all, as binding (Book II, ch. xv, § ii).

82. Ibid., § xi—unless such duress is, in turn, contrary to the law of nations, as, for instance, in the case of a promise extorted from a captured ambassador (ibid., § xii).

83. For numerous examples of such releases see Laurent, *Histoire du droit des gens* (1865), vol. x, pp. 432–9.

84. Book I, ch. iii, § viii.

85. See in particular Book I, ch. iv, §§ i–vii.

86. Book II, ch. xxii, § xi.

87. *De jure naturae et gentium*, Book VII, ch. 8, §§ 5, 6.

88. He says, after stating that by nature all men have the right of resistance in order to ward off an injury: 'As civil society was instituted in order to maintain public tranquility, the state forthwith acquires over us and our possessions a greater right, to the extent necessary to accomplish this end. The state, therefore, in the interest of public peace and order, can limit that common right of resistance' (Book I, ch. iv, § ii. 1).

89. Book I, ch. ii, § xxiv. 6. See also ibid., § vi. 5, and ibid., ch. iii, § xxv. 4. Grotius, who in 1643 read *De Cive*, expressed agreement with Hobbes's view on political authority though he was unable to agree with the bases of the Hobbesian argument: 'Librum de Cive vidi, placent quae pro Regibus dixit. Fundamenta tamen quibus suas sententias superstruit, probare non possum. Putat inter homines omnes a natura esse bellum . . .' (*Epistolae quotquot*, 1687, Appendix No. 648).

90. Book III, chs. vii and xiv.

91. Book I, ch. iv, § viii.

92. Ibid., § ix.

93. Ibid., § x.

94. Ibid., § xi.

95. Book I, ch. iv, § xiii.

96. Ibid., § xiv.

97. An interesting illustration of this recourse to Grotius will be found, for instance, in an anonymous pamphlet published in 1689 in London by 'A Lover of the Peace of his Country' under the title *The Proceedings of the Present Parliament Justified by the Opinion of the most Judicious and Learned Hugo Grotius; With considerations thereupon. Written for the Satisfaction of some of the Reverend Clergy who yet seem to labour under some Scruples concerning the Original Rights of Kings, their Abdication of Empire, and the People's inseparable Right of Resistance, Deposing, and of Disposing and Settling of the Succession to the Crown.* The author invoked Grotius 'the famous Civilian . . . because of the great Credit and Authority he has obtained in the world, especially amongst the Clergy, and is above all other of his Faculty, most tender of the Rights and Prerogatives of Crowned Heads' (p. 6).

98. Book II, ch. xxv, § viii. 2. See also ibid., ch. xx, § xi. 1.

99. See Book II, ch. xxv, § viii, p. 12.

100. It is the same overriding desire for peace which explains the extraordinary passage in which, with some uneasiness, he elaborates the view that a state may surrender to an enemy an innocent subject in order to avoid a greater danger (Book II, ch. xxv, § iii).

101. Book II, ch. xxiii, § vi.

102. Ibid., § vii.

103. Book II, ch. xxiii, § viii.

104. Ibid., § viii. 4.

105. Book II, ch. xxiv.

106. Ibid., ch. xxii, § iii. 1.

107. Book II, ch. xxii, § iii. 2.

108. Book II, ch. i, § i. 3.

109. There seems to be no warrant for the suggestion that before his death, prior to leaving France on his journey to Sweden, he expressed the desire to become a Roman Catholic. That possibility is discounted by the most judicious of his biographers: see De Bourigny, *The Life of the Truly Eminent and Learned Hugo Grotius* (translation from the French, 1754), pp. 300 ff. See also Hanshagen in *Zeitschrift für Völkerrecht*, 23 (1939), pp. 13–48, and, in particular, the illuminating Preface of Schulte to Broere's *Hugo Grotius' Rückkehr zum kathclischen Glauben* (1871). However, the legend of Grotius's Catholicism dies hard. See, e.g., Pastor, *Geschichte der Päpste*, vol. xiii (1929), p. 783. The source of the belief, occasionally expressed, that Grotius was converted to Catholicism lies probably in the fact that much of his theological doctrine was in the nature of an approximation to or, at least, of a sympathetic understanding of the Catholic point of view. To what extent that tendency was, in turn, due to his desire to assist in bringing about the unity of the Christian Church must remain a matter of conjecture. In any case, it was that practical problem which constituted the main preoccupation of his life from the time that he entered the public service of his own country till his death. That cause he served with a sustained fervour and ability which reveal a stature more impressive than that of an essentially academic person who had never grown into full practical maturity—a picture presented by some biographers. See on this aspect of his life: Krogh-Tonning, *Hugo Grotius und die religiösen Bewegungen seiner Zeit* (1904); Schlüter, *Die Theologie des Hugo Grotius* (1919); Wernle, *Der schweizerische Protestantismus im XVIII, Jahrhundert* (1922), vol. i, pp. 471 ff. See also von Luden,

Hugo Grotius nach seinen Schicksalen und Schriften dargestellt (1806), and Knight, *The Life and Works of Hugo Grotius* (1925), pp. 245–90.

110. Unless the state of refuge itself chooses to mete out punishment (Book II, ch. xxi, §§ iii, iv. 3).

111. Book II, ch. xvii, § 20; ch. xxi, § 2.

112. Book II, ch. ii, § xiii.

113. Book II, ch. ii, § xviii.

114. Ibid.

115. Book II, ch. ii, § xxiv.

116. Ibid., § i.

117. Ibid.

118. Ibid., § xvi.

119. Ibid., § xvii.

120. Ibid., § xiii. 1.

121. Ibid., § xiii. 5.

122. Book II, ch. ii, § xiv.

123. Ibid., ch. v, § xxiv.

124. Ibid., ch. vi, § iv.

2. The Grotian Quest

Richard Falk

Especially in dark times like ours, decent men and women are often drawn toward the light, only to perish like so many moths. Rousseau perceived his utopian contemporary, Abbé Saint-Pierre, as such a victim: "This rare man, an ornament to his age and to his kind—the only man, perhaps, in all the history of the human race whose only passion was the passion for reason—nevertheless only advanced from error to error in all his systems, because he wished to make all men like himself instead of taking them as they are and as they will continue to be."[1]

While he opposed endowing illusions with solemn pretentions, Rousseau celebrated the enlivening effects of fantasy: "I created for myself societies of perfect creatures celestial in their virtue and their beauty, and of reliable, tender, and fruitful friends such I had never found here below."[2]

If, however, the purpose of our endeavors is to create a better world, then fantasy, whether self-deceived or self-aware, is of little help. We require instead a special sort of creativity that blends thought and imagination without neglecting obstacles to change. We require, in effect, an understanding of those elements of structure that resist change, as well as a feel for the possibilities of innovation that lie within the shadowland cast backward by emergent potential structures of power. Only within this shadowland, if at all, is it possible to discern "openings" that contain significant potential for reform, including the possibility of exerting an impact on the character of the emergent political realities.

This shadowland lies necessarily at the outer edge of the realm of politics, although its special emphasis is upon those political possibilities not yet evident to politicians. As such, it is dangerous intellectual work that often engenders rejection, and may even stimulate repression. Power-wielders tend to be scornful of the apparent challenge to their competence—while purists are likely to be alienated by the failure to extend the conception of reform to include structural changes. The more impressive the discernment of possibilities for change in the shadowland, the more likely it will be that those with vested interests will either co-opt the vision, or at least its rhetoric, to conform to their wishes and interests, or reject those who explore the shadowland of structural reform through some form of distortion. The relevance of the shadowland is especially great when an emergent new structure has not yet fully superseded an old structure, in times of transition when the need for bridges between the past and future is the greatest.

In many respects Hugo Grotius was an exemplary visionary of the shadowland, whose life in the late sixteenth, early seventeenth century, coincided with the culminating phase of the long transition from the old feudal order to the new order of sovereign states. It is probably not accidental, then, that he led such a difficult personal life, despite the triumphs of his precocious early years. Grotius became a political prisoner in his own country, escaped from jail with a daring plot, lived his remaining years in exile, became a diplomat on behalf of foreign royal leaders, produced his greatest work abroad, and was honored in death by burial close to the very Dutch princes who tormented him while alive. In essence, Grotius was a person of deep conscience who was neither radical nor acquiescent, and who yet was deeply committed to leaving the world a better place than he found it. It is also not accidental that Grotius' thought has been misconstrued over the years, by detracters and admirers alike, which is one of the fates of those who construe the shadowland.

Grotius came to maturity at a time of religious and political strife, of ripening claims of absolute state sovereignty by the leading monarchs of Europe, and of steadily declining prestige and capacity of the Church of Rome to assert even symbolic authority over the whole of Christendom. It was the time, also, when feudal traditions were being displaced by statist tendencies and administrative capabilities that emphasized territoriality and the domestic centralization of both legitimate authority and military power. Accompanying this process, as with any profound transition in the way collective life is organized, were bloody struggles between those who represented the new order and those who held fast to the old.

Grotius approved of this historical process, yet was appalled by its apparent tendency to generate brutality and unrestrained behavior, which resulted in an apparent relapse in the moral quality of relations among separate human collectivities. What Grotius attempted, whether wittingly or not, was to provide the foundation for a new normative order in international society that acknowledged the realities of an emergent state system and yet remained faithful to the shared heritage of spiritual, moral, and legal ideas that any Christian society could still be presumed to affirm as valid. Out of this heritage, Grotius fashioned a grand intellectual synthesis that culminated in the publication of *De Jure Belli ac Pacis* in 1625, over twenty years before the rulers of Europe assembled at the end of the Thirty Years War to produce the Peace of Westphalia, the occasion most often selected to mark the formal beginning of the modern state system.

The shadowland that Grotius explored rested on the idea that restraint and decency could be grounded in law despite the realities of the new age of statist diplomacy. Grotius' system of mutual legal restraint was premised on the reality of an overarching Christian conscience which it seemed reasonable to believe continued to matter for the rulers of the day, whose Christianity persisted despite the increase in their secular autonomy and sovereign stature. In effect, Grotius believed that by activating the Christian conscience of rulers, peaceful methods short of war could be promoted to resolve disputes between royal sovereigns, and that where, in those exceptional circumstances, war did occur, its character could be sufficiently regulated to moderate its cruel character and effects. In retrospect, what Grotius proposed seemed the only way to acknowledge sovereign prerogatives without endorsing their most nihilistic implications. By drawing on rationality and natural law, Grotius encouraged European rulers of his day to reconcile their practical pursuits as statesmen with their spiritual and intellectual heritage, and thereby fill, in an acceptable form, the moral vacuum created by the erosion, if not the total collapse, of the Roman Church as a source of international unity and authority. In what respects, if any, the Grotian approach did, in fact, moderate interstate diplomacy is a matter of controversial interpretation, although it has assuredly shaped subsequent efforts to introduce normative elements into the practice of statecraft. The sufficiency of the Grotian approach also needs to be considered in light of the evolving technology of war; whereas *moderation* might have been a sufficient seventeenth-century solution, *abolition*, or at least substantial abridgement, of the war system might alone suffice in the era of nuclear weaponry. That is, from our perspective in history, a shadowland approach only promises a sufficient result if we correctly discern emergent structures of a new globally oriented system of world order. It is a question of great current historical moment, whether those who discern emergent structures are wishful thinkers like Abbé Saint-Pierre or are shadowland explorers like Grotius. Given the dangers that confront us, it seems prudent to suspend critical judgment, and to remain as receptive as possible to approaches that depict and develop shadowland claims.

Perhaps, also, Grotius is vulnerable to the charge of accommodating statism to an excessive and unnecessary degree. Perhaps, the degree of his acknowledgment of statist legitimacy, as against the claims of popular sovereignty, did contribute to the neglect of human rights for so long in international legal theory and practice. Until recently, only states were subjects of international law, whereas individuals were objects, whose rights were derivative from the state and dependent upon its government for their protection. Even now, despite an upsurge of interest in human rights, practical and formal realities make individuals almost totally dependent upon the benevolence of their national government. And Grotius, so attentive to the shadowland, may also have been motivated, as Rousseau carps, by the logic of his personal situation to solicit royal patronage at the expense of individual or personal rights. In effect, Grotius' peculiar sensitivity to the implications of state sovereignty as the new ordering principle of world affairs seems to have been coupled with some insensitivity, from a normative standpoint, to the fate of individuals and groups confronted by repressive patterns of governance.

Charles Edwards has produced a magnificent new interpretation of Grotius' achievement that clarifies its peculiar relevance to our contemporary torments.[3] Edwards is scrupulous and precise in his appreciation of Grotius, neither exaggerating nor underestimating his contributions. We are gently guided by Edwards through complex thickets of academic controversy and thereby permitted a more accurate apprehension of Grotian thought. In particular, Edwards clarifies the extent to which Grotius combined religious with secular concerns, the degree to which he adapted the natural law tradition to new international circumstances, and the sense in which it seems appropriate to regard him as "the father of international law." Edwards provides a persuasive, well-documented account of these controversies. He also gives us an appreciation of the heroic scale of the Grotian question to blend disparate moral, legal, and political perspectives into a coherent conception of world order, that challenged the secular imagination without abandoning it for either backward-looking religious or forward-looking secularist utopian solutions.

What is more, Edwards speculates about what Grotius might do if confronted by the current international situation. This exercise sharpens the distinction between the temporality of the Grotian solution to the pre-Westphalian puzzle with its limited relevance for our situation and the timelessness of the Grotian quest for openings to the future through shadowland exploration. The particular applicability of the Grotian quest at this moment of history depends on whether the prevailing structure of world order can be sufficiently synthesized with that structure which is not yet apparent, to provide help in this period of transition—whether, in effect, the future order is sufficiently crystallized to cast its shadow backwards into the present.

Grotius makes clear that the sort of normative identity he attributed to human society did not then imply any belief in the necessity or desirability of institutionalization beyond the state, much less world government. On the contrary, any insistence on supranationalism would have run against the powerful current of territorial sovereignty that was so dominant in the seventeenth century. As such, it would have been a species of forward-looking utopianism, allowing wishes rather than the rigorous observation of possibilities to supply the identity of the emergent structure. In our period, in contrast, it is the state system that is being challenged by a variety of novel forms of supranationalism (regional, functional, global in scope and orientation), although in an ambiguous, and perhaps only preliminary, fashion.

Another important development in the 350 years that have elapsed since Grotius did his main work is the changed character of the sovereign state. The government of such a state can no longer be associated with the administration of power by a series of European Christian princes. In the contemporary world, the state is more typically dominated by a faceless bureaucracy that is governed by leaders who are selected and rejected at short intervals or are kept in power for longer periods by sheer brute force and whose religious and cultural background embraces the diversities of the main global traditions. The Grotian solution presupposed the personal character of royal rulership in Europe and is not fully transferable to the global bureaucratization and secularization of power that has evolved into the modern post-seventeenth century state and that has steadily diffused the responsibility and eroded the spirituality of political leadership. It is a mistake to suppose, as do such recent diverse commentators on Grotius as Hersch Lauterpacht and Hedley Bull, that the Grotian solution proposes substantive answers that are directly applicable to the transitional twentieth-century torments of the state system.[4] Such a mistake flows, it seems to me, from confusing the Grotian solution with the Grotian quest.

Given the peculiar burdens posed by nuclear weaponry, ecological decay, population pressures, and expectations of equity, the renewal of the Grotian quest in our time cannot credibly rely on a shared heritage of normative traditions as reinforced by the conscience of contemporary leaders. What makes our situation seem so desperate is the vagueness, and even dubiousness, of the normative heritage (especially for non-Western societies) and the uncertain contours of the emergent structure. We seem caught in a historical movement where the burdens on the old order are too great to bear, and yet the new alternative order that we hope lies out beyond the presently perceived horizon of attainability casts no shadow backwards from the future that can be reliably and persuasively discerned. As a consequence, the advocacy of global normative approaches are often understood to be neo-Machiavellian maneuvers by those governments of large states that harbor imperial ambitions, which, in recent decades, has meant mainly the United States and secondarily the Soviet Union. At the same time, within these imperial centers such globalist speculation is dismissed as the naive and sterile wanderings of alienated minds drawn like moths into the flames of utopian illusion.

Perhaps we should regard the faddish prominence temporarily accorded human rights diplomacy as a pathetic reenactment of the Grotian quest. The normative claim embodied in human rights is, quite simply, that leaders of governments can continue to pursue nationalistic economic, social, and political goals, if only they will abide by the most minimal decencies required by international law in governing peoples within their territory. No further accusation is mounted by most human rights advocates against the state system as such. Admittedly, the humanizing potential of adhering to human rights is considerable, and should not be belittled even in relation to globalist concerns about peace, justice, and ecological balance. Whether contemporary global and national structures of power actually allow this potential to be tapped is doubtful. Repression seems integral to the structure, rather than an aspect of the shadowland, although it may partake of both. And it is as revealing as it is disquieting to note that the international concern of governments for human rights, realized after it became a goal of American foreign policy at the outset of the Carter presidency, has receded as quickly as it was stimulated, here and elsewhere.

Compared to the ferment of the seventeenth century, with the new logic of the state system taking over from the feudal logic, our transitional challenge is more dangerous and bewildering. The statist logic has not yet been seriously challenged by an alternative logic that conceives the *whole* as necessarily prior to the *part* in matters of ecological stability and military security. The shadowland cast backward onto the present situation of world order does not yet seem to exist. Perhaps we await a Grotius who can teach us to "see" the shadowland, according sufficient status to international developments that depart from the premises of the state system without losing persuasiveness.

Grotius came from an independent state in the Protestant north of Europe that was the setting for revolt against holistic domination of all Europe by the Catholic south. One would similarly expect that our Grotius, if he or she emerges, will come from the Third World rather than from the advanced industrial countries. The shadowland is more accessible to those who are victims of the old order, apostles of the new order, but who yet see that the hopes for a benign transition depend on the success of an ideological synthesis.

Our prospects as a civilization, even as a species, continue to seem poor. We cannot manage the technology at our disposal and, at the same time, sustain present patterns of life. Our social and political relations are distorted by pervasive inequalities that make the powerful and weak alike seem dependent on violence, even terror. To submit to such a reality is tantamount to renouncing hope for the future. To project mere images of a viable future is to fiddle while Rome burns. To embark upon a revolutionary voyage, given all we now know about the tendency of revolutions to devour their children, is probably to opt for a violent course of terror that doesn't even contain much promise of genuine transformation.

Without indulging illusions, I believe that the Grotian quest remains our best hope. It offers no easy solace, or spectacular outcomes. Yet the Grotian quest remains constructive in our situation, because it is normatively grounded and future oriented, synthesizes old and new, and cherishes continuities while welcoming discontinuities. Our political life is now so bureaucratized that it is doubtful whether anyone who listens to the voice of conscience, or if he or she hears and heeds, could long remain influential. The Grotian quest should probably concentrate more on mobilizing the conscience of the people than on activating the conscience of their rulers.

Whatever else, no venture into the future will succeed without anchors in our past. At this time, we should not neglect this strong, tested, and reliable Grotian author.

NOTES

1. Jean-Jacques Rousseau, *The Confessions* (New York: Penguin, 1953), Book IX, p. 393.

2. Ibid., p. 398.

3. Charles S. Edwards, *Hugo Grotius: The Miracle of Holland* (Chicago: Nelson Hall, 1981).

4. See Hersch Lauterpacht, "The Grotian Tradition in International Law," *British Journal of International Law*, 23, 1946, pp. 1–53; and Hedley Bull, "The Grotian Conception of International Society," in Herbert Butterfield and Martin Wight, eds., *Diplomatic Investigations* (London: Allen & Unwin, 1966), pp. 51–73.

International Law and Problems of Compliance: Internal and External Aspects

In Chapter 2 the interaction of politics and law in the international arena is considered. International law provides a series of conceptual maps that are derived from and help guide the international political game. Law not only determines the participants by endowing them formally with actor status. It also informs them about the nature of the game they enter and puts forward a set of minimum conditions for social coexistence. In this regard, international law provides reasons for presuming that promises are kept (*pacta sunt servanda*) and that resort to violence is somewhat restricted even if states retain basic discretion; moreover, it clarifies "possessions" and boundaries so as to facilitate secure property relations.

By organizing the inquiry along these analytical lines, we have been able to chart the "development" of international law through a comparison of two polar types of legal order that Falk, in Chapter 3, calls the Westphalia System and the Charter Conception. The growth of international law conceived mainly in terms of a history of ideas (the teachings of international law) can also be approached in an analytical manner. The consequences for the structure and functioning of international politics brought about by changes in the rules designating actors, authorizing the use of force, and creating legal obligations can be assessed and important insights into the limits of law gained.

Understanding the functioning of the state system helps us understand the phenomenon of compliance or noncompliance with the prescriptions of law. One way to conceive of the problem is to compare "political" and "legal" decisionmaking. As might be expected, it is the specific interactions of politics and law that are most revealing. Patterns of compliance with legal prescriptions are not uniform for all existing norms and systems; rather, they are "system specific" such that following rules and/or deviating from them exhibits patterns that are connected with the systemic constraints imposed by the wider setting of world politics.

While it has been common to argue that the imperatives of bureaucratic decisionmaking in foreign affairs necessitate the utilization of standard operating procedures—which in turn explains the need for and the relevance of international prescriptions—such deference to international norms is usually granted only in the area of "low politics." Important issues, particularly the "high politics" of national security, have to be managed through "discretion and prerogatives" rather than by attentiveness to legal requirements. Although there is obviously some truth to the connection between discretion and high politics, the conventional wisdom needs substantial modification, as our first contribution in Chapter 2 demonstrates.

John Norton Moore's "Law and National Security" deals with the problem of compliance in a context of maximum insistence by state leaders on discretion to act. Noting the lack of concern with legal prescriptions on many levels, particularly within the national security bureaucracy, Moore argues that the national interest could better be realized by introducing legal advice at critical junctures of policymaking. Enhancing compliance with international legal norms to promote good international citizenship is not advocated by Moore, although that would be a desirable side effect, contributing to the prestige and diplomatic stature of the United States. Moore maintains that a more law-oriented foreign policy helps structure domestic debate and thereby build firmer support for a particular line of policy, as well as to induce leaders to put forward national goals with greater clarity. Thus, in principle, such legally dubious and adventurist foreign policy overreactions as the landing of U.S. Marines in the Dominican Republic (1965), as well as some of the more odious and counterproductive battlefield practices adopted by the United States during the Vietnam War, might have been avoided. In short, law can reinforce self-interest even in the context of national security considerations, just as it can provide leaders with a method of formulating the "national interest" that adds even to a realistic appraisal of short-run goals by stressing the significance of relevant norms, the observance of which is vital for a free society.

The other side of Moore's concern is highlighted by Jordan J. Paust's "Is the President Bound by the Supreme Law of the Land?—Foreign Affairs and National Security Reexamined." Paust is troubled by the judicial tendency to confirm presidential claims to be above the law when it comes to sensitive elements of national security (e.g., legal scrutiny of CIA activities), or even to foreign affairs generally. Paust questions the trend of decisionmaking that erodes this aspect of constitutional order, and he argues strongly for a more active role for domestic courts in upholding international law as against the executive branch. The argument is developed mainly as one of American constitutional law, but it is also relevant to the overall question of implementing international law *within* the governing processes of sovereign states. Given the weakness of international enforcement/compliance procedures, this domestic dimension of compliance is of critical relevance. Upholding international law in the domestic arena also has some positive effects with respect to civil liberties and the overall constitutional relationship between state and society.

The next selection, drawn from the introduction to Grenville Clark and Louis B. Sohn's seminal work, projects the case and imagery related to a much stronger set of external enforcement mechanisms. In the background of the Clark/Sohn emphasis on global reform is the authors' sense that a world of sovereign states cannot protect fundamental peace and security issues without a much stronger network of procedures and capabilities *beyond the state*, that is, at the international level. Surely self-enforcement offers little assurance that state behavior will be restrained by law in crisis situations, except possibly in the tactical sense advocated by Moore. Furthermore, it is the breakdown of law in crises that is responsible for shaping much of the overall climate of transition, anxiety, and realization that the old ways could easily generate catastrophe. At the same time, the path from the past to a safer future may not be primarily by way of strengthened international institutions. As yet, the requisite political will seems absent at both the governmental *and* the popular levels. The Clark/Sohn prescriptions raise questions about how compliance *could* be enhanced, but they do not necessarily suggest the most relevant possibilities.

Oran Young's theoretical essay on compliance in the international system enriches this inquiry into what makes international law as effective as it is and what might make it more effective. Young's analytic comparison of international relations with a group of subway riders that meet by chance for a short duration helps us grasp some of the salient features involved in securing compliance in decentralized social systems. First, a variety of situations are delineated to show that compliance with norms is the result of varying types of self-interest calculations. Naturally, situations of "pure coordination" are most likely to increase compliance to the highest levels, whereas situations resembling zero-sum games (in which one side's gains are another's losses) are unlikely to induce compliance, and even if compliance is obtained for some reason, by threats or external circumstance, such a pattern is unstable.

Some of the most interesting social situations are naturally those modeled after the classical prisoner's dilemma, insofar as they involve mixed motives on the part of the participants. In such a case the "rational" individual tends to be motivated by "free rider" incentives; that is, he or she wants everyone else to comply with relevant prescriptions while personally reaping the benefits of noncompliance. On the domestic level the solution to this dilemma is, of course, the introduction of a governmental agent to ensure uniformity of compliance. Yet even in an "anarchical system" in which no governmental force can be brought to bear, the compliance problem may be less hopeless than is usually assumed, provided certain conditions obtain: a limited number of participants, a more or less permanent relationship among these participants, and reasonably good chances of quickly detecting violations. Actors in anarchical circumstances are perhaps far more concerned about the dangers of the disintegration of what minimal social order exists than are participants in a system in which concerns about basic order are reliably delegated to the government. Although there are no theoretical reasons why this state of affairs should not lead to some tolerable "anarchical" ordering, historical experience suggests that the emergence of such spontaneous ordering does not consistently occur, especially in the context of national security concerns. Rather, what is more likely to occur is the emergence of a "hegemonic power" or at least a number of "Great Powers" that "police" the system, thereby mixing selfish motives with community needs. Such an analysis of how powerful states induce compliance can be associated with the discussion of international regimes in areas of complexity and interdependence in international life, and with writings of social scientists on the behavior of hegemonic powers in world politics. This latter point, in turn, is of particular interest to the world order approach given that the possibility of an "imperial peace" either by direct military imposition or by "structural" means (i.e., by determining and enforcing the rules of the game) seems historically and theoretically plausible. We are left with the world order question as to whether the realization of needed "central guidance" capabilities required for maintaining order can be achieved in a "contractarian" (voluntary agreement) rather than a "Hobbesian" fashion (involuntary agreement or coercion). Here again, the reality may well be mixed.

In sum, our concern in Chapter 2 is with the degree to which international law can operate effectively, given the way the world is currently constituted. The section also explores whether this effectiveness rests in reality on imposed solutions contrived by great powers policing the system. In the end we are left with doubts as to whether global security in the nuclear age can be managed over time with such a political order. The original Grotian quest of this historic epoch was to create reliable patterns of compliance based on institutional arrangements and voluntary acceptance on the part of the actors involved. Such a quest is distinct from the idea of recreating the world order framework—that is, doing for the late twentieth century what Grotius did for the seventeenth, but without effectuating Grotius's vision as such.

QUESTIONS FOR DISCUSSION AND REFLECTION: CHAPTER 2

1. Traditional conceptions of law stress the importance of centralized procedures and capabilities for enforcement. To what extent does this view of law need correction, or, if you are persuaded by it, does this lead one to adopt the Clark/Sohn proposals for limited world government?

2. What functions (other than "constraining" choices) are served by law in any society? In the specific setting of international relations?

3. What role do you believe is played by law in relation to the forming and execution of national security policy?

4. In what ways do law and politics interact in the context of domestic policymaking? In international arenas (e.g., the political organs of the United Nations)?

SELECTED BIBLIOGRAPHY: CHAPTER 2

Michael Barkum, *Law Without Sanction* (New Haven, Conn.: Yale University Press, 1968).

James Brierly, *The Nature of Obligation in International Law* (Oxford: Clarendon, 1958).

Richard Falk, *The Status of Law in International Society* (Princeton, N.J.: Princeton University Press, 1970).

Roger Fisher, *Improving Compliance with International Law* (Charlottesville: University of Virginia Press, 1981).

Louis Henkin, *How Nations Behave*, 2nd ed. (New York: Columbia University Press, 1979).

Stephen Krasner, ed., *International Regimes* (Cambridge, Mass.: MIT University Press, 1982).

Terry Nardin, *Law, Morality and the Relations of States* (Princeton, N.J.: Princeton University Press, 1983).

3. Law and National Security

John Norton Moore

The role of law in the management of national security has been debated throughout American history. Traces of the debate may be found as long ago as 1793 in the exchange between Hamilton and Jefferson about the relative importance of "interests" and "morality" in deciding whether the United States should support France in the war with England. Jefferson found an obligation to support France under the 1778 treaty of alliance and urged that the treaty obligation was binding on the nation. Hamilton countered that there was no obligation but even if there were it did not require the United States to jeopardize its "essential interests."

At the turn of the century the debate achieved clearer focus in the writings of Alfred Thayer Mahan, the great sea power strategist, and Elihu Root, Secretary of State and a distinguished American jurist. The core of this second round was the importance of arbitration and other third-party machinery for the settlement of international disputes. Root and other jurists urged greater resort to international arbitration. Mahan countered that law, while sometimes useful, was incapable of dealing with questions of national expediency such as the Monroe Doctrine.

In the aftermath of World War II the debate was resumed more sharply and with a broader focus. On one side were international relations theorists such as Hans J. Morgenthau and George F. Kennan, who saw only a small role for international law and who opposed their "realist" position to what they believed were dangers of a "legalistic-moralistic" approach in dealing with national security issues. On the other side were jurists such as Hardy C. Dillard and Myres S. McDougal, who warned that the realists had an incomplete understanding of the role of international law and that their view, if influential, could be costly for American foreign policy.

The realists have, throughout the debate, had an important message. Over-reliance on international law can be a prescription for disaster in a loosely organized and intensely competitive international system. If the disappointments with arbitration treaties and universal disarmament schemes during the interwar years did not drive this home, the advent of the cold war certainly did. All this, however, has led to an overly broad indictment of the legal tradition. For while we have been preoccupied with the dangers— some very real—of a "legalistic-moralistic" strain in American foreign policy, we have failed to see the cost resulting from the slender capacity of our national security process to take an international legal perspective into account.

*   *   *

II

National security decisions must consider a range of component issues. At a first stage these include: What are the national goals? Are they realizable in the context in which they must be pursued? If so, are they realizable at a cost-benefit ratio which makes their pursuit in the national interest? Are preferable alternatives available which will achieve the goals at a more favorable ratio? And how can policies, once chosen, be most effectively implemented and justified?

Legal considerations, like political, military and economic considerations, are relevant to each of these issues. Yet there are no international legal specialists on the increasingly important staff of the National Security Council even though that staff now comprises over 50 substantive officers. Similarly, there is virtually no reference in the Pentagon Papers to the legal dimensions of policy in the Vietnam War. These examples illustrate a structural weakness in the national security process which impedes the consideration of international—and sometimes constitutional—legal components of policy.

There are, of course, showcase examples of national security decisions in which legal considerations have played a constructive role. Chief among them are the Berlin crisis of 1948 and the Cuban missile crisis of 1962. The "Forrestal Diaries" indicate that Forrestal and President Truman discussed "the controlling legal rights and undertakings" as a starting point for policy in the Berlin crisis. The United Nations was also used extensively and helpfully during the crisis. Similarly, because of early involvement of the State Department's Legal Adviser's Office, international legal considerations played a significant role in shaping U.S. policy during the missile crisis.

Legal initiatives included designation of the action as a quarantine—since a blockade might have been construed as an act of war—and collective authorization by the Organization of American States (OAS).

Much more abundant examples can be found of insensitivity to international legal considerations. In order to justify the initiation of bombing of North Vietnam in February 1965, for instance, the raids were announced as reprisals for Vietcong attacks on the U.S. military advisers' compound at Pleiku. A case can be made that this bombing of the North, like U.S. participation in the War, was a lawful defensive response against a prior intervention by North Vietnam amounting to an armed attack under Article 51 of the U.N. Charter. But there is overwhelming authority that reprisal, which is a technical legal term for minor coercion in response to a breach of an international legal obligation not amounting to an armed attack, is barred by the Charter. By their unawareness of the relevant legal considerations or their unwillingness to take them into account, American policy-makers had chosen a public justification blatantly in violation of international law.

The April 1965 intervention in the Dominican Republic provides another example of insensitivity to legal considerations. The announced purpose of the first phase of the U.S. action in landing 400 marines was to protect U.S. nationals, a purpose which if carefully implemented would be lawful. But the action was neither implemented nor justified with the legal basis for such action in mind. And the second phase of the action, which committed more than 21,000 U.S. forces to an effort to end the Dominican civil strife, was undercut from the beginning by the failure to initiate the action under Article 6 of the Rio Treaty and by the overly broad rhetoric of President Johnson in proclaiming the inadmissibility of another Communist government anywhere in the hemisphere, a reason for the action which would make it in violation of Article 2(4) of the U.N. Charter. These failures subsequently obscured the real differences between the U.S. action in the Dominican Republic and the Soviet action in Czechoslovakia.

Still another, and poignant, example is the lack of vigorous effort in the Indochina War, at least during the early years, to implement the laws of war. The United States is party to a variety of treaties relating to the conduct of warfare, including the Fourth Hague Convention of 1907 Respecting the Laws and Customs of War on Land and the four Geneva Conventions of 1949. It also recognizes a substantial body of customary international law setting minimum humanitarian standards for the conduct of warfare.

As the Son My tragedy amply confirms, violation of these standards may undermine the national effort as well as offend moral sensibilities. But the Son My tragedy also raises broader problems concerning the present status and effectiveness of the laws of war, problems which have been insufficiently considered by U.S. policy-makers. First, officially defined restrictions on combat too frequently have not been understood or implemented in the field. For example, there seems to have been wide disparity in understanding among regional commands in Vietnam that the "body count" was to include prisoners of war as well as enemy casualties and that "specified strike zones" did not override the laws of war which hold that attacks on noncombatants are not permissible. Second, the manifest ambiguities and deficiencies of the law, in face of the complexities of a counterinterventionary setting and newer military technology, have largely gone unattended. For instance, the principal legal analysis for the massive use of chemical herbicides in Vietnam seems to have been a memorandum prepared in March 1945 by Major-General Myron C. Cramer, then Judge Advocate General, concerning the possible use of chemical anti-crop agents against pockets of Japanese on the Pacific islands. This example is symptomatic of a lack of adequate legal review of newer weapons and tactics.

Most important, adequate national and international machinery that can deal with the full sweep of these problems has been lacking. Though army regulations require compliance with the laws of war and many military and other government advisers made significant individual efforts to ensure compliance in the field, the chances for a more vigorous and imaginative implementation would have been improved if an international legal perspective sensitive to the issues had been systematically structured into higher levels of the national security process. This might have been supplied by an interdepartmental group charged with responsibility for oversight and development of the laws of war.

A fourth example of insensitivity to legal considerations is in the recurring failure to prepare an adequate constitutional basis for major military actions abroad. The failure of President Truman to secure explicit congressional authorization for the Korean War was followed by President Johnson's unnecessary reliance on an ambiguous series of attacks on American ships in the Gulf of Tonkin as the occasion for obtaining congressional authorization for the Indochina War. In both cases the failure to allow more adequately for the constitutional legal dimensions proved to be major weaknesses of policy.

The Cambodian incursion of April 30, 1970, provides a fifth example. There were at least three ways that more adequate consideration of international legal factors might have strengthened the U.S. response in the crisis.

First, North Vietnamese attacks on Cambodia might have been protested by the United States in the Security Council much as the Soviet actions in curtailing access to Berlin were taken to the Security Council to lay the groundwork for subsequent Allied action to reopen the city. The Cambodian complaint to the Security Council on April 22 would have seemed an opportune time to press such a complaint in the Council. And at a minimum, the incursion should have been immediately reported to the Security Council pursuant to the obligation under Article 51 of the U.N. Charter.

Second, the principal legal basis for the Cambodian incursion was that a belligerent state may take action to end serious violations of neutral territory by an opposing belligerent. Yet the important presidential address explaining the action to the nation did not mention the principle. This and other public pronouncements might have been more focused and carried greater weight had they emphasized the substantial international legal authority for the action.

Third, and most important, a prior understanding with Cambodia might have been obtained for public release at the time of the operation. In view of the requirement of Article IV, paragraph 3, of the SEATO Treaty, which provides that no action on the territory of a protocol state such as Cambodia "shall be taken except at the invitation or with the consent of the government concerned," such an advance agreement would have seemed particularly advisable.

Finally, and most recently, there is the example of the U.S. response to the Pakistan-Bangladesh-India war. Perhaps the lack of clarity in the U.S. position was attributable to the complexity of the situation. It is, after all, difficult to distinguish the damsel from the dragon when one side is engaged in mass murder of noncombatants and the other intervenes in a war of secession against a traditional rival. Nevertheless, America might have been more persuasive in focusing on the shortcomings of both sides if she had taken account of the legal aspects of the conflict.

Initially, the United States should have vigorously urged Pakistan to live up to the provisions of Article 3 of the Geneva Convention of 1949 Relative to the Protection of Civilian Persons in Time of War. Article 3 sets out a series of minimum standards for the protection of noncombatants "in the case of armed conflict not of an international character occurring in the territory" of a party to the Convention. In fact, the United States had an obligation under Article I of the Convention to undertake "to ensure respect for the . . . Convention in all circumstances."

With respect to the Indian action, the United States might have pointed out more specifically that the intervention violated a series of recent General Assembly Resolutions, including the 1960 Declaration on the Granting of Independence to Colonial Countries and Peoples and the 1965 Declaration on Inadmissibility of Intervention. The 1960 Declaration was particularly on point. Section 6 declares: "Any attempt aimed at the partial or total disruption of the national unity and the territorial integrity of a country is incompatible with the purposes and principles of the Charter of the United Nations."

The point is that the actions of both sides had their warts and that legal analysis could have helped to isolate the virus and prescribe the treatment.

The memoranda of the meetings of the Washington Special Action Group, made public by Jack Anderson, confirm that greater sensitivity to legal considerations was called for in the India-Pakistan crisis. These sources demonstrate that the National Security Council understood the advantages of utilizing the United Nations, a use which was helpful. But they evidence little awareness of international legal norms as a basis for appraisal of the Indian and Pakistani actions or for support of U.S. policy. For example, there was no mention of the General Assembly Resolutions condemning intervention in a war of secession—Resolutions which strongly supported U.S. opposition to the Indian intervention. Similarly, no mention was made of the 1949 Geneva Convention Relative to the Protection of Civilian Persons, despite a discussion of how best to ensure the safety of the Biharis in East Pakistan and the Bengalis in West Pakistan. More dramatically, although Henry Kissinger posed a question concerning the legal basis for the Indian naval blockade, there was no legal specialist present to answer it. The resulting discussion too easily suggested that there was no legal basis for an Indian blockade and failed to consider whether incidents involving American ships subsumed violations of international law even if the Indian blockade were legal.

The legal tradition is important in making policy as well as for its implementation and justification. The 1960 Bay of Pigs invasion illustrates the cost of failing to take an international legal perspective into account in planning for U.S. action. There is no evidence that the U.S. planners weighed the effects of supplying illegal assistance to the insurgents. It should have been evident that the effort—successful or unsuccessful—would establish a precedent for external assistance to exile insurgents which would work strongly against the national interest when transferred to Indochina or the Middle East. The effort was also likely to contribute to a loss of national influence as a result of the associated violations of the charters of the Organization of American States and of the United Nations. It would probably overstate the case to say that the abortive invasion would not have taken place if the legal tradition had been adequately considered, but it might have been less likely had there been full and candid presentation of the international legal costs of the action.

Quite apart from the utility of an international legal perspective in crisis management there is also a need for more systematic representation of the legal tradition in formulating a coherent and intellectually powerful foreign policy. Under the pressures of the cold war the nation has drifted away from a consistent vision of world order. Yet a foreign policy which focuses on the importance of the stability of the system and coöperative solution of global problems seems strongly in the national interest.

Internationally, such a foreign policy may be the best strategy for the United States to recoup its leadership; and nationally it may be a prerequisite to adequate domestic support of foreign policy. The present neo-isolationist tendencies within the United States are qualitatively different from the isolationism of the "America first" movement preceding World War II. Then the predominant strain was to avoid involvement in the affairs of Europe, whatever the moral cost. In contrast, the predominant strain in the present movement seems to be a pronounced—though sometimes misplaced—concern for the moral dimensions of American foreign policy. If such concern can be channeled into a coherent vision of world order, it may revive domestic support for the more active international policy which the nation must undertake in order to deal effectively with the myriad of problems in security, development and environment which lie ahead. The legal tradition has no monopoly of vision on world order; it does have a special contribution to make to the normative aspects of state conduct as well as global organization for solution of social problems.

III

The realist-jurist debate has done little to dispel widespread misperceptions about the value of the legal tradition in the management of national security. At least three such misperceptions continue to obscure its importance.

First, international law is thought of as saying what cannot be done, solely as a system for restraining and controlling national actions. No one proposes to exclude military or political considerations from planning simply because they do not always determine policy. Yet because of a misleading image of law as a system of negative restraint, we make such a judgment when it comes to law. In fact, the legal tradition can play a variety of important roles in planning and implementing national security decisions. These include, among others, focus on the long-run stability and quality of the international milieu; calculation of the costs and benefits resulting from violation of the law or compliance with it; focus on a range of international legal options for conflict management; concern with appraising and justifying national actions by reference to shared global interests; and supervision of the national interest in domestic operations that involve U.S. adherence to international agreements.

Law is also useful for solving social problems and communicating intentions. Examples include the 1967 Treaty for the Prohibition of Nuclear Weapons in Latin America, the recently signed Draft Convention on the Prohibition of the Development, Production, and Stockpiling of Bacteriological (Biological) and Toxin Weapons, and the ongoing efforts to reach agreement on an international régime for the resources of the deep seabeds. To focus exclusively on the difficulties of international law in constraining international behavior is to miss the creative opportunities which the law provides.

There are, of course, dangers in simplistic legal approaches to national security issues. These include, among others, equating general goals with specific policies without assessing the effectiveness of those policies, as, for example, to urge that since we wish a warless world we should unilaterally disarm; pursuit of policies which are unrealistic in the present international system, as, for example, to advocate submitting the Arab-Israeli or Indochina conflicts to the International Court of Justice; and over-reliance on the deterrent effect of international law or on formal legal arrangements divorced from power realities, as, for example, to rely solely on international law for the protection of the *Pueblo* despite the demonstrated willingness of North Korea to violate international law.

Though these dangers are real, none of them is inherent in a sophisticated legal approach. More important, the legal tradition complements the realist approach precisely where that approach is weakest, that is, in preoccupation with short-run goals at the expense of long-run interests in a healthy world order.

A second misperception is that a concern for international law is opposed to a concern for the national interest. But the "national interest" is not a self-defining concept. As it is understood by most theorists, it would include a strong interest in the stability and quality of the international system. Thus Raymond Aron says: ". . . the West must stand for an idea of an international order. The national interest of the United States, or even the collective interest of the Anglo-Saxon minority, will not win over any country nor will it cause any loyalties if it does not appear to be tied to an international order—the order of power as well as the order of law."[1]

International law may also help to elaborate the national interest in a variety of operational settings. For example, international law has distilled from centuries of experience a substantial body of norms for the conduct of hostilities. Not to comply with these is to risk breakdowns in military discipline, brutalization of participants with resultant social costs on return to civilian life, unnecessary escalation or continuation of conflict, reciprocal mistreatment of nationals, domestic loss of support and unnecessary destruction of human and material resources.

The real conflict between law and the national interest, when it arises, occurs in terms of the costs and benefits to the nation of pursuing a policy which is illegal. When the conflict arises, too often the legal costs are not adequately appreciated. In the case of the Bay of Pigs invasion, for example, the probable benefits to the nation deriving from a successful action should have been weighed against the short-run cost in loss of U.S. influence resulting from a blatantly illegal policy and the long-run cost of undermining legal constraints contributing to the stability of the international system.

A third misperception comes in judging the utility of the legal tradition on an oversimplified model of law. A common error in this regard is to underestimate the importance of community perceptions of legality as a base for increase or decrease in national power. International law, particularly on issues of war and peace, does not always manifestly control the behavior of states. But it is not as widely perceived that even when international law does not control behavior, there are international norms—community expectations about the authority of national action which may in a variety of ways translate into power realities. For example, an action such as the Korean War, in which perceptions as to lawfulness are high, is likely to produce more allies than actions which are controversial such as the Indochina War or widely regarded as unlawful such as the British and French invasion of Suez.

If beliefs about the illegality of a nation's actions are intense and widespread there may be a generalized loss of national influence. The Soviet Union seems to have paid such a cost in the invasion of Czechoslovakia, as indicated by the disaffection of Soviet-oriented Communist parties and front organizations throughout the world. Perceptions about legality may also influence votes within international organizations such as the United Nations, the OAS Council of Ministers or even the International Committee of the Red Cross.

Another error resulting from an oversimplified model of law is the tendency to overestimate the indeterminacy of international legal norms. The lack of centralized legislative and adjudicative competence in the international system is a real factor contributing to gaps and tears in the legal fabric. But it is wrong to conclude that all international law is amorphous. International law has areas of clarity as well as of uncertainty and in this respect is not as qualitatively different from national law as one who has never suffered through the confusion of first-year law school might suspect. It is virtually undisputed among international lawyers that the U.S. role in the Bay of Pigs invasion, the Soviet role in the invasion of Czechoslovakia, and the British and French Suez intervention violated Article 2(4) of the U.N. Charter, which proscribes "the threat or use of force against the territorial integrity or political independence of any state. . . ." It is also widely accepted that the allied intervention in the Korean conflict was a lawful exercise of collective defense under Article 51 of the Charter, that the Son My tragedy was in violation of Hague and Geneva rules and that the North Vietnamese mistreatment of allied prisoners is in violation of the Geneva Conventions. Many other examples of reasonably definite legal conclusions about war and peace issues could be given.

IV

One important reason for the failure to take legal perspectives into consideration in the management of national security is that the machinery, as presently structured, is inadequate to the task.

The principal international legal adviser to the government is the Legal Adviser of the Department of State. In addition, there are many other offices engaged to some extent in the process, including, among others, the Office of General Counsel of the Department of Defense, the General Counsel of the Arms Control and Disarmament Agency and the Office of Legal Counsel of the Department of Justice.

There are a number of structural problems which prevent full utilization of this plethora of legal offices. The most important is that there is little legal advice used by the important National Security Council and NSC staff portions of the security process. Since its creation in 1947, the NSC and its staff have played an increasing role in the management of national security. There are persuasive reasons for dividing the national security process between State and the NSC–White House. Unfortunately, a consequence of this division has been to minimize concern for international legal considerations since there are no international legal specialists on either the White House or NSC staffs.

A second structural problem is the lack of centralized responsibility for the general development and supervision of the international legal aspects of national security decisions. The press of day-to-day business within each legal office and the lack of clear lines of responsibility between offices have hindered vigorous efforts to strengthen and develop international law.

Although not to overemphasize the importance of structural change as such, certain changes might improve the present inadequate consideration of the legal component of policy:

First, make the Legal Adviser of the Department of State a regular member of the National Security Council. This would have the advantage of introducing international legal considerations into crisis management where they are most needed. It would also give the Legal Adviser, who is called upon to justify policy, a better opportunity to influence the making and implementation of policy. In his new capacity, the Legal Adviser would be available to advise the President as well as the Secretary of State. An obvious parallel to this dual advisory role is the dual role of the Chairman of the Joint Chiefs of Staff who advises both the President and the Secretary of Defense. As a corollary to this change the Legal Adviser might also be made a member of any NSC group dealing with security crises, such as the Washington Special Action Group.

Second, add a new position, which might be called Counselor on National Security Law, to the staff of the National Security Council. One of the important mechanisms for coördinated foreign policy planning is the National Security Study Memorandum supervised by the NSC staff. Of 138 such memoranda prepared from 1969 through October 2, 1971, some 20 to 30 have a significant legal component. These include memoranda on Indochina, Cyprus, the Middle East, southern Africa, the nonproliferation treaty, the Nuclear Test-Ban Treaty, tariff preferences, chemical-biological agents, toxins, the seabed treaty and U.N. China admission. Though legal considerations are undoubtedly present in many of these memoranda as a result of interdepartmental consideration, an in-house legal expert within the NSC staff could assist in recognizing and coördinating the legal components of such planning. The Counselor and his staff would also be available to the President to provide advice on the legal dimensions of national security issues when, for reasons of speed or secrecy, the President chose not to utilize the formal machinery of the National Security Council. Finally, the Counselor could serve as a liaison with other government legal advisers, particularly the Legal Adviser of the Department of State and the General Counsel of the Department of Defense. Indeed, the coördinating function might extend to many hitherto-domestic agencies. The U.N. Conference on the Human Environment and the upcoming conference on the law of the sea are illustrative of a new global consciousness that promises both a multiplication of national obligations and an increase in the impact of international law on national life. In this respect, the creation of a Counselor on National Security Law would parallel the recent addition of an Assistant to the President for International Economic Affairs.

Third, create a permanent Interdepartmental Group on International Legal Affairs chaired by the Legal Adviser of the Department of State. Its purpose would be to coördinate and initiate government programs for the implementation and development of international law. More specifically, the Group would coördinate the executive position on issues with a substantial international legal component, for example, the position on ratification of the 1925 Geneva Protocol on Gas and Bacteriological Warfare. It would also identify international legal problems in current U.S. foreign policy and prepare position papers for consideration by the National Security Council. An example would be the U.S. obligation under Article 25 of the Charter to accept and carry out the U.N. sanctions against Southern Rhodesia—sanctions which the United States supported and could have vetoed—by refusing to import Rhodesian chrome once such sanctions had been decided by the Security Council.

The Group would also have responsibility for assessing any government action against the legal obligations binding on the United States. This would include, for example, continuing appraisal of compliance with the laws of war during the course of hostilities. Another recent and practical example is the case of the Lithuanian defector, Simas Kudirka, who was hastily returned to Soviet custody on November 23, 1970, from the U.S. Coast Guard cutter *Vigilant* in violation of the U.N. Protocol Relating to the Status of Refugees. The incident might have been prevented if the Protocol had been previously incorporated in Coast Guard regulations (as it has been subsequently) by prohibiting the immediate return of defectors pending subsequent determination of status as required under the 1951 Convention Relating to the Status of Refugees.

Finally, the Group would have responsibility for promoting the progressive development of international law by the United States. In this capacity the Group might identify and promote areas in which U.S. leadership could strengthen international law. It might also encourage greater training in international law for government officials, for example, by enlarging the programs in international law offered by the Foreign Service Institute, the National War College and the Naval War College or by instituting such programs elsewhere. Similarly, it might identify and sponsor research in areas of international law which are unclear and which are of potential concern.

In its composition, the new Interdepartmental Group would be chaired by the Legal Adviser of the Department of State and would include the General Counsel of the Department of Defense and (if the position of Counselor on National Security Law were created) the newly created Counselor as well. In addition, the Group would include any government legal counsel deemed important for its effective functioning. In some respects, it might be modeled after the highly successful Interagency Task Force on the Law of the Sea which is chaired by the State Department Legal Adviser and responsible to the National Security Council. It would, however, be structured as a permanent interdepartmental group.

Finally, consultants on international law should be added to the Senate Foreign Relations and House Foreign Affairs Committees. The simplest and most effective way of doing so is to regularize the consideration of international legal factors in the day-to-day work of the principal congressional committees dealing with national security issues.

In the consideration of these proposals it should be remembered that the question is not whether international law will be controlling but the more modest one of whether it will be taken into account. As Stanley Hoffmann observes, "a comprehensive analysis of world politics and foreign policy cannot afford to neglect the law, both because of its *actual* importance and because of its *potential* importance for a better order. . . ."[2]

NOTES

1. Raymond Aron, "The Quest for a Philosophy of Foreign Affairs," in Stanley Hoffmann, ed., *Contemporary Theory in International Relations.* New York: Prentice-Hall, 1960.
2. Stanley Hoffmann, "Henkin and Falk: Mild Reformist and Mild Revolutionary," *Journal of International Affairs,* v. 24, 1970.

4. Is the President Bound by the Supreme Law of the Land?— Foreign Affairs and National Security Reexamined

Jordan J. Paust

INTRODUCTION

This article is concerned with whether or not the President and other members of the executive branch are bound by the United States Constitution and other laws comprising the supreme law of the land when "foreign affairs" or "national security" interests are involved. This general issue also involves more specific concerns about governmental attempts to control both access to and content of public information. For example, if the President could act without regard to the supreme law of the land, then, functionally at least, his control of access to and the content of information in a courtroom, a newspaper office, a television or radio station, a publishing house, a library, a classroom, or even the governmental "foggy-bottom" could be furthered by numerous strategies. New and dangerous meanings of "national security," "executive privilege," or "political question" might be conditioned by an unrestrained executive power. Indeed, if the precept that all are bound to comply with the law is not recognized as the preemptory norm conditioning the meaning of each of these phrases, then it is likely that the legal niceties and the nuances of judicial choice concerning public access to information will be trampled by an advancing, all-powerful executive immunity. . . . In the end, if amorphous phrases such as "national security" are used to justify various anticonstitutional and antidemocratic evils, then important freedoms of speech and press, including the public's right of access to and dissemination of information will become meaningless.[1]

In another article,[2] I sought to document related dangers posed to the human and constitutional rights of Americans by similar trends occurring in our society and, more alarmingly, in numerous other societies throughout the world. In that article, disturbing aspects of dicta in some United States cases and the unacceptable claims of Richard Nixon were discussed: (1) that "the President is like a 'sovereign' and can ignore constitutional prohibitions and federal law in order to protect national 'security,'"[3] and (2) that, when applying or interpreting law, so-called "governmental interests" can outweigh public interests and obviate democratic freedoms. What I did not predict, despite an awareness of the deprivations of human and constitutional rights suffered increasingly by most of our global neighbors, is that certain government attorneys, not long after the resignation of Richard Nixon, would vigorously reassert these and related claims with apparent sincerity. More importantly, I did not realize how easily certain federal judges would accept quite similar, if partially hidden, claims when "foreign affairs" or foreign persons were somehow involved. So quickly and so easily have democratic values and human rights been seriously threatened.

A recent four-four split among the members of the United States Supreme Court in *Kissinger v. Halperin*,[4] although generally reaffirming our constitutional values, creates additional concern as to whether or not a few justices might be dangerously close to considering a Nixonian view of both the presidency and the role of the judiciary in a democratic process.[5] In the following pages, an effort is made to identify and consider the general problem posed by recent claims of executive immunity from law, and a more specific question is raised with regard to a particular executive function: the operation of our intelligence system.

THE PROBLEM: RECENT EXECUTIVE CLAIMS TO IMMUNITY FROM LAW

Some of the trends during the past few years have been alarming. One hears more frequently of bills being drafted to allow the FBI and the CIA to violate civil liberties. These proposed bills even include attempts to shield government agents from prosecution for breaking the law if they "were following orders," a defense denied even to soldiers acting in the heat of battle during a time of grave national emergency.[6] More serious than such pernicious nonsense, however, are claims made openly by government attorneys that the Executive, in certain contexts, should not be bound by the Constitution or other elements of supreme federal law. Although it is difficult to believe that such claims could be made by attorneys working for a constitutional and democratic government, pledged as they are to uphold the United States Constitution, these claims clearly have been made in at least three cases.

The first such attempt occurred in 1979. *United States v. Tiede*[7] was a criminal proceeding, the result of the diversion of a Polish airliner by two East Germans from its scheduled landing in East Berlin to a landing in West Berlin. The United States prosecutors argued before Federal District Judge Herbert Stern, sitting in a specially convened United States court in Berlin, that both the proceedings and other governmental actions did not have to comply with the United States Constitution. The prosecution reasoned that because Berlin is a territory, governed as the result of military conquest, the court served only as an instrument of foreign policy, unable to protect rights that were not provided by the Secretary of State. The prosecution also argued that, in the court's words, "everything which concerns the conduct of [the government's occupation of a foreign territory] is a 'political question' not subject to court review."[8] Despite such claims, Judge Stern refused to deviate from legal and constitutional requirements, admonishing counsel for the government, "[E]verything American public officials do [at home or abroad] is governed by, measured against, and must be authorized by the United States Constitution."[9] As Judge Stern aptly noted:

[T]here has never been a time when United States authorities exercised governmental powers in any geographical area—whether at war or in times of peace—without regard for their own Constitution. *Ex parte Milligan*, 71 U.S. (4 Wall.) 2 (1866). Nor has there ever been a case in which constitutional officers, such as the Secretary of State, have exercised the powers of their office without constitutional limitations.[10]

Judge Stern further upheld the predominant trend and expectation that judicial attention to law must not be lessened merely because of the involvement of an executive power to conduct foreign relations. As far as the court was concerned, the existence of "foreign affairs" implications and separate executive powers, even in an international crisis, could never be raised to bar jurisdiction or to justify judicial inattention to the constitutionality, or permissibility under other federal law, of United States executive actions at home or abroad. Quite properly, the court noted that although laws might not directly regulate executive discretion concerning the conduct of otherwise permissible governmental operations, the Executive, in choosing among permissible options, must not violate the law. More specifically, the court recognized that "the talismanic incantation of the word 'occupation' cannot foreclose judicial inquiry into the nature and circumstances of the occupation, or the personal rights of two defendants which are at stake."[11]

Judge Stern's recognitions concerning the scope of executive and judicial powers have not always been shared by all federal judges. Indeed, the seemingly talismanic incantation of words like "crisis," "political," or "embarrassment," and phrases such as "national security," "governmental interests," "foreign affairs," "the conduct of our international relations," or "interacting interests of the United States and foreign nations" appears to have been reason enough for certain other federal judges to abdicate their judicial power and responsibility to identify, articulate, and apply constitutional or other supreme federal laws, even in the face of important allegations that such laws had been violated.

For example, quite recently, in *Rappenecker v. United States*, Federal District Court Judge Schwarzer, finding nonjusticiable the claims by former crewmen of the privately owned *S.S. Mayaguez* against the United States Government for personal injuries suffered as a result of United States military operations in response to the seizure of the vessel by Cambodian gunboats, wrote, "The textual commitment to the President as commander in chief of authority for military decisions entails that his decisions may be implemented without judicial scrutiny."[12] What seemed to impress the court was the indisputable but ever-present fact that "policy decisions" and a "basic policy judgment" were involved[13] and thus, perforce (we are led to believe), a nonjusticiable "political question" existed.[14] Curiously, the court concluded that claims arising out of the conduct of military operations "fall within the class of claims arising out of determinations entrusted to the executive branch and not subject to review by the courts, and are therefore nonjusticiable."[15]

What Judge Schwarzer seemed to ignore, however, is that although numerous "determinations" are "entrusted" to the Executive, a fundamental expectation has predominated elsewhere under our constitutional system that the Executive, in carrying out its own powers and responsibilities, is bound by the Constitution and other supreme federal law. Unlike Judge Stern in the *Tiede* decision, Judge Schwarzer appears to have been unaware of numerous cases that affirm that the Executive has, indeed, no power or authority to act except in accordance with the Constitution and the supreme law of the land. More specifically, it has long been held that during the conduct of "military operations," the President of the United States is not only bound by international law, which is part of the supreme law of the land under article VI, clause 2 of the Constitution, but is also subject to the court's jurisdiction and thus to judicial review in order to remedy any legal improprieties.[16]

As Professor Gordon recognized in a study of recent cases raising claims of "political" questions,[17] other cases have also contained similarly disturbing language. Among these is an absurd statement in a Fifth Circuit opinion, *Occidental of Umm al Qaywayn, Inc. v. A Certain Cargo*,[18] that "[i]n their external relations, sovereigns are bound by no law."[19] Later in the same opinion, the same judge made an equally egregious remark: "Should the president ever officially act on a political issue, we would be constitutionally bound to accept his act."[20] What this latter statement necessarily, but incorrectly, assumes is that when a president acts politically in a general sense, *i.e.*, "on a political issue," he may act in any way whatsoever and thus in violation of the Constitution or other supreme federal law. Richard Nixon undoubtedly would have welcomed such an excuse, but, as the Supreme Court emphatically has held, such a broad exclusion of judicial power and presidential duty remains constitutionally unacceptable. . . .[21]

In the case of *Narenji v. Civiletti*,[22] several judges for the Court of Appeals for the District of Columbia based their holding in the Iranian deportation case on similar matters of executive concern. Despite documented claims that constitutional and human rights were being violated by the executive branch during its attempt to deport Iranian students, and the acceptance of *amicus* briefs on the need for the judicial branch to enforce international law even against an unwilling executive, the majority opinions neglected these issues. They did, however, incorporate several of the touchstone phrases complained of by Judge Stern. The majority opinion, for example, speaks of "foreign affairs," a "crisis" and "foreign policy"[23] as if such matters obviate the need for inquiry into whether or not the President has violated the United States Constitution and international law. Judge Robb, writing for the majority in *Narenji*, declined jurisdiction, reasoning: "[I]t is not the business of courts to pass judgment on the decisions of the President in the field of foreign policy."[24] Elsewhere, he noted, "The present controversy involving Iranian students in the United States lies in the field of our country's foreign affairs and implicates matters over which the President has direct constitutional authority."[25] What Judge Robb seems incorrectly to have assumed, as did the Fifth Circuit opinion in *Occidental of Umm al Qaywayn, Inc.*,[26] is that whenever a president has general constitutional authority to act and "foreign affairs" are involved, the president may act in any way whatsoever and thus in violation of law. Numerous cases stand in opposition to such an assumption, most importantly in this instance, *The Paquete Habana*.

Judge Robb also seemed impressed by an affidavit from the Attorney General stating that his regulation was issued "as an element of the language of diplomacy . . . in response to actions by foreign countries. The action implemented by these regulations is therefore a fundamental element of the President's efforts to resolve the Iranian crisis."[27] As Judge MacKinnon added in concurrence, "in the situation with which we are here dealing, the President's power is at its zenith—right up to the brink of war."[28] What these judges did not address, however, is the fact that the Supreme Court and other federal courts have often stressed that, even in time of war, when executive powers are admittedly at their highest, the President is bound by international and United States constitutional law. A crisis circumstance, even war, does not obviate judicial power and responsibility.

In opposition to the denial of a rehearing *en banc*, Chief Judge Wright and Judges Spottswood, Robinson, Wald, and Mikva noted problems posed by "selective law enforcement"[29] involving, really, a form of unlawful collective punishment, discrimination, and retaliatory purpose.[30] At the conclusion of their opinion, they issued a trenchant warning that, unfortunately, still has gone unheeded by some. "These cases do . . . raise a grave constitutional issue. When the rule of law is being compromised by expediency in many places in the world, it is crucial for our courts to make certain that the United States does not retaliate in kind."[31]

Before the United States Supreme Court, during an attempted appeal, United States Attorneys McCree, Daniel, Kopp, Steinmeyer, and Singer openly argued against such a notion: "The Constitution does not forbid the President . . . to violate international law, and the courts will give effect to acts within the constitutional powers of the political branches without regard to international law."[32] Although case law belies the validity of such an argument, government attorneys openly argued once again that, in certain circumstances, the President of the United States should not be bound by the Constitution or other supreme federal law.

It is noteworthy that in the more disturbing "foreign affairs" and international law cases disclosed above, one professorial work is often used by those judges and attorneys who would support the claim that the President should not be bound by international law. That work, cited without question or attention to the actual trends in the case law as noted in Part II of this article, is the book, *Foreign Affairs and the Constitution*, prepared by Professor Louis Henkin. The language quoted in the government's brief before the Supreme Court in the Iranian deportation case and noted above is, in fact, Professor Henkin's.

Since Professor Henkin's work has been cited to support this misconception regarding presidential power, his statements are worthy of our attention, even though Professor Henkin would himself admit that "[t]here are no clear Supreme Court holdings, or even explicit dicta, upholding the power of the President to act contrary to international law."[33] Such a realization does not restrain him, however, from making remarks like those quoted above[34]—remarks that rest ultimately upon mere belief, and thus a personal preference,[35] and that are supported only by a misreading of dicta by Chief Justice Marshall in *Brown v. United States*. . . .[36] Professor Henkin also seems to fall into error by equating the President with "the sovereign."

Also worth mentioning in this section on disturbing claims to immunity from law are a series of developments occurring with regard to bilateral prisoner exchange agreements between the United States and several foreign countries. . . .[37]

Since the power and authority of the government "have no other source [and the government] can only act in accordance with all the limitations imposed by the Constitution, . . . [it having] no power except that granted by the Constitution,"[38] since "no agreement with a foreign nation can confer power on the Congress, or on any other branch of Government, which is free from the restraints of the Constitution,"[39] since no federal power exists to so incarcerate Americans;[40] and since the government is participating still in such an incarceration of American citizens; these developments amount to an impermissible claim by the executive branch, approved by Congress,[41] that it be allowed to act as if it were immune from the Constitution of the United States. As explained in other writings, federal courts should uphold the Constitution in the face of such a subversive threat to law and void attempted exercises of power not delegated by the Constitution. Similar threats occur and should be similarly voided where the government knowingly involves itself in foreign state illegalities by subsequently incarcerating the victims of such illegalities, especially if human rights deprivations have occurred.

Perhaps equally or even more disturbing in view of Richard Nixon's claim that "governmental interests" should be considered to outweigh public interests and democratic freedoms is the language from Chief Justice Burger's opinion in *Haig v. Agee*.[42] In providing the Secretary of State with broad discretion to deny travel abroad under an American passport to citizens whom the Secretary believes pose a threat to national security, the Chief Justice expressly recognized that even an "exclusive power of the President . . . in the field of international relations" is a power that "must be exercised in subordination to the applicable provisions of the Constitution."[43] Nevertheless, he declared that "freedom to travel abroad with a . . . passport . . . is subordinate to national security and foreign policy considerations . . . [or] to reasonable governmental regulation."[44] The Chief Justice added: "[N]o governmental interest is more compelling than the security of the Nation. . . . Protection of the foreign policy of the United States is a governmental interest of great importance . . . [and m]easures to protect the secrecy of our Government's foreign intelligence operations plainly serve these interests."[45]

Although his opinion is unclear on this point, presumably the existence of compelling or important "governmental interests" and measures needed to "serve these interests" were primary factors leading to his conclusion that the constitutional freedom being considered should be "subordinate to national security and foreign policy considerations." The Chief Justice may have reaffirmed the long-recognized expectation that the President cannot violate the Constitution in the name of "national security" or "foreign policy considerations," but that reaffirmance may make little difference if previously recognized constitutional freedoms are interpreted away or depleted in order to serve those same executive "considerations" or to assure that "governmental interests" in "national security and foreign policy" will always prevail. The point is all the more disturbing in view of the fact that the government will often have "interests" or "considerations" at stake when national security or foreign policy is somehow involved.

Moreover, in light of Richard Nixon's claims that the President can ignore the supreme law of the land in order to protect the national security and that "governmental interests" can outweigh public interests, the danger inherent in what appears to be an approach to constitutional choice that favors "national security and foreign policy considerations" seems potentially to be even more threatening to our constitutional process when these "considerations" are couched, not in terms of democratic values and the public interest, but in terms of a potentially antagonistic and more limited standard termed "governmental interest." If governmental interests are to outweigh public interests and democratic values (either through an open balance or through a failure to address effects upon public interests and democratic values at stake while "balancing" merely governmental interests as such), then the Chief Justice, at least, seems to have accepted one of Richard Nixon's earlier claims. In any event, an end run (e.g., an interpretive approach that makes the "rights" to be interpreted "subordinate to national security and foreign policy") would seem to be just as dangerous as a frontal assault (e.g., a claim that the Executive can disregard law when "national security and foreign policy" are to be served). In view of the general legal policies at stake and predominant trends in the case law, both attempts at derogation should be condemned.

REGULATING THE INTELLIGENCE COMMUNITY

In light of the above discussion and case law, it is clear that the FBI and the CIA, whether acting at home or abroad, are bound, like the President, by the Constitution, and other supreme federal law. For this reason, FBI or CIA charters adopted by Congress need no clause demonstrating that these entities are bound by all of the supreme federal law; that result is necessarily required as a matter of constitutional law. Nevertheless, a far more difficult problem was presented recently by Deputy Director of Central Intelligence Frank Carlucci. In a speech before an American Bar Association Conference on Intelligence Legislation, Director Carlucci explained that intelligence organizations like the CIA "must go forward with our task, often in disregard of foreign law."[46] As he explained, foreign law might simply forbid the collection of intelligence and the fact that a foreign agent has a contract with the CIA may itself "break the law of the agent's host country."[47] He added, "The problem . . . is . . . how we sanction this kind of activity within a carefully drawn legal framework. . . .[W]e must always bear in mind that we are legalizing an activity that is inherently antagonistic to the interests of other countries in which that activity is going to be conducted."[48] Surely, Director Carlucci did not have in mind assassination and torture directed by the United States, which would violate not only United States law and foreign law, but international law as well.[49] What he seemed concerned with is whether or not the CIA should be free to violate foreign law as long as our Constitution, federal laws, and international law are not violated.

Because neither article VI, clause 2 of the Constitution nor the case law mention foreign law as such, this question is interesting. One approach might be to distinguish the types of foreign law involved. For example, CIA violations of foreign laws that are similar to United States laws might be prohibited. Thus, otherwise unregulated CIA activities abroad could be prohibited if those activities would have been prohibited had they occurred, for example, in a United States territory or against United States citizens. Another approach might be simply to ignore violations of foreign law that do not also involve a violation of international law, United States federal law, or the Constitution.

In a case involving solely a violation of foreign law, the same types of legal policy might not be at stake. Although legitimate needs for effective intelligence and national security do not outweigh the supreme law of the land, they might still outweigh foreign law or certain types of foreign law. Certainly, the government cannot act abroad except in accordance with the supreme law of the land,[50] but if the government's public acts abroad violate only a foreign law, are the government and its agents acting within the scope of their public power entitled to immunity? Foreign government agents engaging in similar activities within the United States might add another variable to the inquiry. Does this latter concern depend upon whether or not foreign agent activities violate our own laws?

With regard to international law, if foreign law is violated on foreign territory (i.e., the territory of the "host" state) at the direction of our government, international law might not necessarily be violated, depending on the nature of the activity (e.g., the mere receipt of information within a country versus an active participation in its extraction from foreign government files). Does it matter that the activity is itself arguably protected by international law—for example, as part of a process of a relatively free exchange of information across national borders?

International law does prohibit many types of active and intentional interference with the essentially domestic or internal affairs of another nation,[51] especially the undermining of a foreign self-determination process through strategies of military or economic coercion. The extent of these prohibitions is complicated, however, by other competing interests that might internationalize a situation so that foreign "internal" affairs are no longer "essentially" domestic within the meaning of article 2(7) of the United Nations Charter. Examples include international concern about human rights deprivations engaged in by a foreign government against its own people and the relatively recent recognition of a right of self-determination assistance. It is certainly possible that intelligence agencies will participate in activities abroad that involve permissible efforts to further human rights and self-determination, whether or not such internationally permissible activities violate some foreign law. It must be assumed, therefore, that the mere fact of a violation of foreign law is not determinative since adequate inquiry must extend to consideration of all relevant legal policies, including international and United States domestic law.

In addition, commentators generally agree that the mere receipt of information from outside a nation's territorial jurisdiction, without more, is generally permissible. What about the gathering of intelligence from within, or the dissemination of information, not to coerce, but to inform a foreign populace so that they might themselves participate even more effectively in the shaping of their political process? Is there something like a global First Amendment freedom—one that even CIA agents can enjoy? In another article, I have documented the fundamental human right to freedom of opinion and expression, which international law affirms as including the freedom "to seek, receive and impart information and ideas through any media and regardless of frontiers."[52] Although such law has been challenged, United States and foreign intelligence agents who merely gather and disseminate public information "through any media and regardless of frontiers" would seem to be exercising an internationally protectable human right. They are engaged, to that extent, in an activity related to the public's "right to know" and are not thwarting another human right—the right to privacy.

Yet there are other complications. First, there is an exception to such a freedom: one conditioned by a strict test of necessity within democratic limits.[53] This exception, when properly implemented, allows the foreign government to limit the human rights of a foreign agent within its country. In the reverse situation, in which the human rights of foreign agents who gather public information in this country are involved, the test is also usable, as is any other part of human right, law, by our federal courts; it contains several limiting provisions that seek to accommodate important interests, including the "just requirements" and the "democratic society" phrase. Since the exception is strictly controlled and available only in a "democratic society," the human right to seek, receive and impart information and ideas should be available to United States agents in many countries under many circumstances, regardless of violations of foreign laws that seek to deny this human right and that do not comply with the test set forth in human rights instruments for a lawful exception to such a right. Again, the mere fact that a foreign law is violated should not determine legality under international law or under the supreme federal law of the United States. A second complication arises when intelligence agents seek and receive information that is not otherwise "public" in the "host" country. Then, at least, human rights norms might bend to a foreign country's interest in a right to privacy[54] and foreign espionage laws. The question arises, should the United States government authorize violations of foreign laws that are not themselves overridden by international law, so long as the activity to be engaged in by government agents would not itself constitute a violation of international law or other supreme federal law? Or, in such a circumstance, should we authorize nothing so precise, leaving the matter for executive decision and, realistically, leaving the agent who is caught to the foreign judicial system? The latter approach is the one presently operative, and for now there is no compelling need to change it where supreme federal law is not at stake.

Nonetheless, three important legal restraints on government intelligence agents operating here or abroad have been identified. American agents must not violate: (1) the Constitution, (2) international law, or (3) other supreme federal law. Also identified are three important rights or freedoms based on international law that government agents should be able to enjoy so long as they are not otherwise restricted by supreme federal law: (1) the general freedom to further human rights, (2) the general freedom to promote self-determination in accordance with international law, and (3) the general human right to seek, receive, and impart public information and ideas through any media and regardless of frontiers. These last three rights or freedoms should be available whether or not a foreign law is violated, unless international law recognizes the validity of a foreign law restraining a human right or freedom in accordance with the strict test of necessity within democratic limits. It has also been recognized that international law prohibits many forms of military or economic coercion, and that assassination, torture, or violations of basic human rights must not be allowed whether or not such conduct is compatible with foreign law. Yet, whether or not foreign laws can or should otherwise be violated is left for future consideration.

One final point involves judicial choice concerning limitations placed on the public's "right to know" sensitive and secret intelligence agency information. Although judicial tests are still being refined, greater attention should be paid to the "necessity within democratic limits" test developed as a part of human rights law. As noted above, the human rights test accommodates several important interests while seeking to assure democratic values, and it is usable by the federal judiciary with or without further attempts at guidance through congressional legislation. Nevertheless, no matter what test is finally adopted, there should always be an overriding constitutional exception to governmental secrecy when supreme federal law has been or is likely to be violated.

CONCLUSION

In conclusion, it might be useful to recall the observation of a sagacious Englishman who, when confronted with the notion that the King can do no wrong, reminded "that the King not only is capable of doing wrong, but is more likely to do wrong than other men if he is given a chance." Contrary to another old adage—that this is a government of laws and not of men—it seems wise to note that, realistically, we have a government of both. The trick is to make the second attentive to the first.

Choices will be made by real human beings, human beings who certainly can do wrong. Choices must be made about the content of law, and delegated authority does allow a measure of discretion, but one peremptory norm remains—all who exercise authority in the name of the people of the United States, all within the government, as all others living in our country, are bound by the supreme law of the land in their exercise of choice. For this reason, they may never lawfully violate such law.

If it were ever otherwise, then, functionally, as Judge Stern recognized implicitly in *United States v. Tiede*, there would be no Constitution, no First Amendment. Recently, there have been claims made that the President and others can violate the supreme law of the land. Clearly, this and other disturbing notions of executive immunity from law and judicial inquiry must be opposed. Whatever the boundaries of discretion as such, the President must not step outside the law. Furthermore, this line between permissible discretion and law is one that must be drawn by the judiciary—a line that must forever hold against every attempted break and any claimed exception.

NOTES

Jordan J. Paust is Professor of Law, University of Houston. A.B., 1965, J.D., 1968, University of California at Los Angeles; LL.M., 1972, University of Virginia; J.S.D. Candidate, Yale University. He is indebted to Margaret Harris, J.D., 1981, University of Houston, for her help in researching some of the cases noted in Part III of this article.

1. In a provocative article, Professor Arthur Miller has suggested that we have nearly arrived at such a level of governmental dictatorship with a far too frequent acceptance of a "doctrine" of *raison d'état* and a functional "Constitution of Control." Miller, *Reason of State and the Emergent Constitution of Control,* 64 MINN. L. REV. 585, 585 (1980) [hereinafter cited as Miller, *Reason of State*]. Elsewhere, he has warned that "crisis government" will soon be normal as "increasingly despotic governments" develop globally and the United States becomes more authoritarian in order to protect "interests of the state." Miller, *Constitutional Law: Crisis Government Becomes the Norm,* 39 OHIO ST. L.J. 736, 737, 739–41, 749–50 (1978). For evidence of global trends of emergency decrees often instituted in the name of "national security" and "interests of the state," see Paust, *International Law and Control of the Media: Terror, Repression and the Alternatives,* 53 IND. L.J. 621 (1978) [hereinafter cited as Paust, *International Law*], and note 7 *infra.*

2. Paust, *International Law.*

3. *Id.* at 622. *See also* A. MILLER, *supra* note 3, at 225–27; Dorsen & Shattuck. *Executive Privilege, the Congress and the Courts,* 35 OHIO ST. L.J. 1, 8–9 (1974) (presidential brief in *United States v. Nixon* arguing that Nixon was not subject to criminal law); note 110 *infra.*

4. 452 U.S. 713 (1981) (4-4 decision; Rehnquist, J., not participating; per curiam, mem.), *aff'g,* 606 F.2d 1192 (D.C. Cir. 1979), *reh'g denied,* 453 U.S. 938 (1981).

5. The effect of the four-four split is automatically to affirm the lower court ruling in Halperin v. Kissinger, 606 F.2d 1192 (D.C. Cir. 1979), but note that Nixon v. Fitzgerald, No. 79-1738 (D.C. Cir. June 24, 1982), *cert. granted,* 452 U.S. 959 (1981), may raise similar issues.

6. *See, e.g.,* U.S. DEP'T OF ARMY, FIELD MANUAL FM 27-10, THE LAW OF LAND WARFARE ₽509, at 182–83 (1956); Principle IV, Principles of the Nuremberg Charter and Judgment, U.N. GAOR Supp. (No. 12) at 12, U.N. Doc. A/1316 (1950); THE MILITARY IN AMERICAN SOCIETY 6-48, 6-66, 6-68 to 6-69; 6-74 to 6-96 (D. Zillman, A. Blaustein, E. Sherman *et al.,* eds. 1978).

7. Crim. Case No. 78-001A (U.S. Ct. for Berlin Mar. 14, 1979), *reprinted in* 19 I.L.M. [International Legal Materials] 179 (1980). This case is ably reviewed in Gordon, *American Courts, International Law and "Political Questions" Which Touch Foreign Relations,* 14 INT'L LAW. 297 (1980).

8. *Id.* at 188.

9. *Id.* at 192. During the trial, the judge also noted that it was not only unthinkable that conduct of government officials that thwarted due process standards would be permissible, but also that such conduct was ever contemplated. *See* Gordon, *supra* note 12, at 326.

10. 19 I.L.M. at 190.

11. *Id.* at 193.

12. Rappenecker v. United States, 509 F. Supp. 1024, 1030 (N.D. Cal. 1980) (citing Durand v. Holland, 8 F. Cas. 111 (C.C.S.D.N.Y. 1860) (No. 4,168)).

13. *Rappenecker,* 509 F. Supp. at 1027.

14. *Id.* at 1026, 1028. *Cf. id.* at 1028 ("[n]ot every question involving the exercise of these powers is necessarily nonjusticiable"). *See also id.* at 1029–30.

15. *Id.* at 1030. *See also id.* at 1028–29.

16. *See* The Paquete Habana, 175 U.S. 677 (1900) (voiding an executive seizure of an enemy vessel in time of war); Brown v. United States, 12 U.S. (8 Cranch)

110, 128–29, 145, 147, 149, 153 (1815); The Flying Fish, 6, U.S. (2 Cranch) 170, 178–79 (1804); Seery v. United States, 127 F. Supp. 601 (Ct. Cl. 1955). *See also* United States v. Robel, 389 U.S. 258, 263–64 (1967); Youngstown Sheet & Tube Co. v. Sawyer, 343 U.S. 579 (1952) (presidential order reversed because President is bound by the Constitution in time of war).

17. Gordon, *supra* note 7.

18. 577 F.2d 1196 (5th Cir. 1978), *cert. denied*, 442 U.S. 928 (1979).

19. 577 F.2d at 1204–05, *quoted in* Gordon, *supra* note 12, at 303. It is also possible that Judge Morgan, the author of the *Occidental* opinion, confused sovereignty, held by the people of the United States, with the executive branch.

20. 577 F.2d at 1205 n.16.

21. *See* United States v. Nixon, 418 U.S. 683 (1974). On Nixon's putative justifications, see also Paust, *International Law, supra* note 3, at 622; Paust, *Human Rights and the Ninth Amendment: A New Form of Guarantee*, 60 CORNELL L. REV. 231, 240–43 (1975) [hereinafter cited as Paust, *Human Rights*]. The Court also has recognized that the mere fact that important political issues are involved and important political consequences might follow from a decision of the Court, the case or controversy before the Court does not thereby involve a nonjusticiable political question. *See, e.g.,* Baker v. Carr, 369 U.S. 186, 217 (1962); J. NOWAK, R. ROTUNDA & J. YOUNG, *supra* note 19, at 100.

22. 617 F.2d 745 (D.C. Cir. 1979), *reh'g denied*, 446 U.S. 957 (1980). *Narenji* involved the constitutionality of a regulation requiring students who were natives or citizens of Iran to provide information as to their residences and maintenances of nonimmigration status in preparation for a major effort to deport Iranians.

23. 617 F.2d at 747–49.

24. *Id.* at 748. Judge Robb also declared that when the lower court found the executive action to be unconstitutionally discriminatory, "the District Court undertook to evaluate the policy reasons upon which the regulation is based. . . . In doing this the court went beyond an acceptable judicial role." *Id.* Since the circuit court also looked at several "policy reasons" in order to support its choice, it must not be impermissible *per se* to evaluate policy reasons. One must assume that what Judge Robb really meant was that if a court uses policy reasons to deny the validity of an executive decision, it is not engaged in an "acceptable" judicial role, but if it uses policy reasons to justify an executive decision, then the court is engaged in an "acceptable" role. Contrary to such an assumption, the Supreme Court has engaged in a second-guessing both of legal and nonlegal determinations made by the Executive, even in times of war or other national "crisis" or emergency, when law has been violated. *See* note 24 *supra*; notes 89 & 131–56 and accompanying text *infra*. When such an allegation has been made, the Court has proceeded to make a determination on the specific issue(s) raised. For this reason, Judge Robb's proffered formula for deference to the Executive (*i.e.*, if only the executive actions "are not wholly irrational they must be sustained." 617 F.2d at 747) must be opposed whenever law has been violated. Otherwise, courts would entertain the most ludicrous of arguments about the whole irrationality versus partial irrationality of any illegalities perpetrated by the President. For the jurisprudential point, see Cohen, *Transcendental Nonsense and the Functional Approach*, 35 COLUM. L. REV. 809, 819 (1935), generally condemning the so-called rational basis test as a mental institution test that also is far too myopic when compared with one that takes into account all aspects of law and all relevant legal policies at stake.

25. 617 F.2d at 748.

26. *See* text accompanying notes 30–32 *supra*. A similar notion was advanced by the United States Attorney in the *Tiede* case. *See* text accompanying note 15 *supra*.

27. Narenji v. Civiletti, 617 F.2d at 747 (quoting an affidavit from the Attorney General). Judge Robb continued, "Thus the present controversy . . . lies in the field of our country's foreign affairs. . . ." *Id.* at 748. An appropriate response is "So what?" *See also* note 39 *supra*; text accompanying note 42 *infra*.

28. 617 F.2d at 753 (MacKinnon, J., concurring).

29. 617 F.2d at 754 (joint statement of Wright, C.J., Spottswood, Robinson, Wald, and Mikva, JJ., in support of rehearing *en banc*).

30. Federal cases recognize that governmental actions taken against aliens that are "motivated by a retaliatory purpose" or that discriminate against nationals of a particular country are patently violative of international law and will not be enforced, upheld, or recognized in this country. *See, e.g.*, Banco Nacional de Cuba v. Farr, 383 F.2d 166, 170, 183–85 (2d Cir. 1967), *cert. denied*, 390 U.S. 956 (1968); Banco Nacional de Cuba v. Farr, 307 F.2d 845, 861, 864–68 (1962); Banco Nacional de Cuba v. First Nat'l City Bank, 270 F. Supp. 1004, 1010 (S.D.N.Y. 1967). *See also* Banco Nacional de Cuba v. Sabbatino, 376 U.S. 398, 402–03 (1964) (recognizing the State Department position on the violations of international law, as printed at 43 DEP'T ST. BULL. 171 (Aug. 1, 1960)).

31. Narenji v. Civiletti, 617 F.2d at 755.

32. Respondents Brief in Opposition at 18, Confederation of Iranian Students v. Civiletti, 617 F.2d 745 (1979), *cert. denied*, 446 U.S. 957 (1980) (quoting L. HENKIN, FOREIGN AFFAIRS AND THE CONSTITUTION 222 (1972)).

33. L. HENKIN, *supra* note 48, at 460 n.61.

34. *See, e.g.*, *id.* at 165 n,† (President can break or terminate treaties); *id.* at 170–71. (President can breach a treaty); *id.* at 188, 222, 460–61 (President can act regardless of treaty obligations). *But see id.* at 55 ("[the President] shall enforce the law of the United States (including international law and obligations . . .)"). As a member of a panel of the American Society of International Law on The Constitution and the Conduct of Foreign Policy, Professor Henkin apparently approved a recommendation that "we should do our utmost to have the two branches act together within a framework of *law*, especially on the vital issues of war and peace." Recommendation No. 5 concerning The Power to Wage War (emphasis added), *reprinted in* THE CONSTITUTION AND THE CONDUCT OF FOREIGN POLICY xiv, 4 (F. Wilcox & R. Frank, eds., 1976).

35. *See* L. HENKIN, *supra* note 48, at 460 n.61: "There are no clear Supreme Court holdings, or even explicit dicta, . . . but the principle is, I believe, the same."

36. 12 U.S. (8 Cranch) 110, 153 (1815). The only other possible footnoted "support" for such a dangerous allegation lies in an even more irrelevant quotation from another Supreme Court opinion: "'This court is not a censor of the morals of the other departments of the government.'" L. HENKIN, *supra* note 48, at 419 n.139 (quoting The Chinese Exclusion Case, 130 U.S. 581, 602–03 (1889)). The "morals" of another department are not directly relevant, and the quoted language is irrelevant to whether or not the President is bound by law. *See also* Paust, *The Seizure and Recovery of the Mayaguez*, 85 YALE L.J. 774, 803–04 n.131 (1976) (power to terminate does not imply power to breach law while it remains law); Paust, *Does Your Police Force Use Illegal Weapons? A Configurative Approach to Decision Integrating International and Domestic Law*, 18 HARV. INT'L L.J. 19, 43–4 (1977) (President bound by law while it is law, despite power to terminate treaties).

37. *See, e.g.*, Abramovsky, *A Critical Evaluation of the American Transfer of Penal Sanctions Policy*, 1980 WIS. L. REV. 25 (1980); Abramovsky & Eagle, *A Critical*

Evaluation of the Mexican-American Transfer of Penal Sanctions Treaty, 64 IOWA L. REV. 275 (1979); Bassiouni, *Perspectives on the Transfer of Prisoners Between the United States and Mexico and the United States and Canada,* 11 VAND. J. TRANSNAT'L L. 249 (1978); Paust, *The Unconstitutional Detention of Mexican and Canadian Prisoners by the United States Government,* 12 VAND. J. TRANSNAT'L L. 67 (1979) [hereinafter cited as Paust, *The Unconstitutional Detention*]; Robbins, *A Constitutional Analysis of the Prohibition Against Collateral Attack in the Mexican-American Prisoner Exchange Treaty,* 26 U.C.L.A. L. REV. I (1978); Vagts, *A Reply to "A Critical Evaluation of the Mexican-American Transfer of Penal Sanctions Treaty."* 64 IOWA L. REV. 325 (1979); Letter to the Editor from E. Freeman, N.Y. *Times,* May 20, 1980, at A18, col. 4. Most of these sources address questions of rights, waivers, and consent, but do not adequately address a more fundamental question of whether or not any federal power exists to incarcerate Americans who have violated neither United States' nor international laws.

38. Reid v. Covert, 354 U.S. 1, 6, 12 (1957). *See also* Balzac v. Porto Rico, 258 U.S. 298, 312–13 (1922); *Ex parte* Milligan, 71 U.S. (4 Wall) 2, 120–21 (1866); Bauer v. Acheson, 106 F. Supp. 445, 449, 451–52 (D.D.C. 1952).

39. Reid v. Covert, 354 U.S. at 16.

40. *See* articles cited in note 61 *supra. See also* 1 Op. Att'y Gen. 509, 521 (1821) (no presidential power to arrest anyone except for violation of our laws or possibly to extradite); 1 Op. Att'y Gen. 406, 408 (1820) (relevant British expectation that government can "inflict no punishment upon any [person] . . . unless warranted by the law of the land").

41. There has been congressional implementing legislation. *See* 18 U.S.C. § 3244 (Supp. II 1978). Nevertheless, Congress cannot obtain powers that do not exist through a treaty and its own acts any more than the President. *See* notes 62–63 and accompanying text *supra.*

42. 453 U.S. 280 (1981).

43. *Id.* at 289 n.17 (quoting United States v. Curtiss-Wright Export Co., 299 U.S. 304, 320 (1936)).

44. 453 U.S. at 306.

45. *Id.* at 307.

46. 2 A.B.A. STANDING COMM. ON L. & NAT'L SECURITY, INTELLIGENCE REP. no. 8. at 7 (Aug. 1980).

47. *Id.*

48. *Id.*

49. *See* Letelier v. Republic of Chile, 502 F. Supp. 259 (D.D.C. 1980) (prohibition of assassination recognized in both national and international law); Letelier v. Republic of Chile, 488 F. Supp. 665, 673 (D.D.C. 1980).

50. Note that the CIA is thereby restrained by international law, and relevant international law would apply regardless of the nationality of persons involved.

51. *See, e.g.,* U.N. CHARTER art. 2, paras. 4 & 7; Declaration on Principles of international Law Concerning Friendly Relations and Co-Operation Among States, G.A. Res. 2625, 13 U.N. GAOR Supp. (No. 18) at 337, U.N. Doc. A/8018 (1970).

52. Paust, *International Law, supra* note 3, at 625–31. *See also* Paust, *Transnational Freedom of Speech, supra* note 172.

53. *See id.* at 624, 626–29. Article 29, paragraph 2 of the 1948 Universal Declaration of Human Rights reads, "In the exercise of his rights and freedoms, everyone shall be subject to such limitations as are determined by law solely for the purpose of securing due recognition and respect for the rights and freedoms of others and of

meeting the just requirements of morality, public order and the general welfare in a democratic society." Universal Declaration of Human Rights art. 29, para. 2 (1948).

54. Since there is a human right to privacy, the foreign law violation may also involve a violation of international law. In such a case, our intelligence agents should be restrained. On the human right to privacy, see Universal Declaration of Human Rights art. 12 (1948); M. McDOUGAL, H. LASSWELL & L. CHEN, *supra* note 124, at 466, 548–49, 810, 816–17, 820–25, 840–56, and authorities cited therein. Concerning a related right to privacy in the United States, see Halperin v. Kissinger, 606 F.2d 1192, 1199–1200, 1210 (D.C. Cir. 1979), *aff'd in part*, 452 U.S. 713 (1981).

5. Introduction to World Peace Through World Law

Grenville Clark and Louis B. Sohn

The proposition "no peace without law" embodies the conception that peace cannot be ensured by a continued arms race, nor by an indefinite "balance of terror," nor by diplomatic maneuver, but only by universal and complete national disarmament together with the establishment of institutions corresponding in the world field to those which maintain law and order within local communities and nations.

A prime motive for this essay is that the world is far more likely to make progress toward genuine peace, as distinguished from a precarious armed truce, when a *detailed* plan adequate to the purpose is available, so that the structure and functions of the requisite world institutions may be fully discussed on a world-wide basis. Consequently, this essay comprises a set of definite and interrelated proposals to carry out complete and universal disarmament and to strengthen the United Nations through the establishment of such legislative, executive and judicial institutions as are necessary to maintain world order.

UNDERLYING PRINCIPLES

The following are the basic principles by which Professor Sohn and I have been governed.

First: It is futile to expect genuine peace until there is put into effect an effective system of *enforceable* world law in the limited field of war prevention. This implies: (a) the complete disarmament, under effective controls, of each and every nation, and (b) the simultaneous adoption on a world-wide basis of the measures and institutions which the experience of centuries has shown to be essential for the maintenance of law and order, namely, clearly stated law against violence, courts to interpret and apply that law and police to enforce it. All else, we conceive, depends upon the acceptance of this approach.

Second: The world law against international violence must be explicitly stated in constitutional and statutory form. It must, under appropriate penalties, forbid the use of force by any nation against any other for any cause whatever, save only in self-defense; and it must be applicable to all individuals as well as to all nations.

Third: World judicial tribunals to interpret and apply the world law against international violence must be established and maintained, and also organs of mediation and conciliation, so as to substitute peaceful means of adjudication and adjustment in place of violence, or the threat of it, as the means for dealing with all international disputes.

Fourth: A permanent world police force must be created and maintained which, while safeguarded with utmost care against misuse, would be fully adequate to forestall or suppress any violation of the world law against international violence.

Fifth: The complete disarmament of all the nations (rather than the mere "reduction" or "limitation" of armaments) is essential for any solid and lasting peace, this disarmament to be accomplished in a simultaneous and proportionate manner by carefully verified stages and subject to a well-organized system of inspection. It is now generally accepted that disarmament must be universal and enforceable. That it must also be complete is no less necessary, since: (a) in the nuclear age no mere reduction in the new means of mass destruction could be effective to remove fear and tension; and (b) if any substantial national armaments were to remain, even if only ten per cent of the armaments of 1960, it would be impracticable to maintain a sufficiently strong world police force to deal with any possible aggression or revolt against the authority of the world organization. We should face the fact that until there is *complete* disarmament of every nation without exception there can be no assurance of genuine peace.

Sixth: Effective world machinery must be created to mitigate the vast disparities in the economic condition of various regions of the world, the continuance of which tends to instability and conflict.

The following supplementary principles have also guided us:

Active participation in the world peace authority must be universal, or virtually so; and although a few nations may be permitted to decline active membership, any such nonmember nations must be equally bound by the obligation to abolish their armed forces and to abide by all the laws and regulations of the world organization with relation to the prevention of war. It follows that ratification of the constitutional document creating the world peace organization (whether in the form of a revised United Nations Charter or otherwise) must be by a preponderant majority of all the nations and people of the world.

The world law, in the limited field of war prevention to which it would be restricted, should apply to all individual persons in the world as well as to all the nations, to the end that in case of violations by individuals without the support of their governments, the world law could be invoked directly against them without the necessity of indicting a whole nation or group of nations.

The basic rights and duties of all nations in respect of the maintenance of peace should be clearly defined not in laws enacted by a world legislature but in the constitutional document itself. That document should also carefully set forth not only the structure but also the most important powers of the various world institutions established or authorized by it; and the constitutional document should also define the limits of those powers and provide specific safeguards to guarantee the observance of those limits and the protection of individual rights against abuse of power. By this method of "constitutional legislation" the nations and peoples would know in advance within close limits what obligations they would assume by acceptance of the new world system, and only a restricted field of discretion would be left to the legislative branch of the world authority.

The powers of the world organization should be restricted to matters directly related to the maintenance of peace. All other powers should be reserved to the nations and their peoples. This definition and reservation of powers is advisable not only to avoid opposition based upon fear of possible interference in the domestic affairs of the nations, but also because it is wise for this generation to limit itself to the single task of preventing international violence or the threat of it. If we can accomplish that, we should feel satisfied and could well leave to later generations any enlargement of the powers of the world organization that they might find desirable.

While any plan to prevent war through total disarmament and the substitution of world law for international violence must be fully adequate to the end in view, it must also be *acceptable* to this generation. To propose a plan lacking in the basic essentials for the prevention of war would be futile. On the other hand, a plan which, however ideal in conception, is so far ahead of the times as to raise insuperable opposition would be equally futile. Therefore, we have tried hard to strike a sound balance by setting forth a plan which, while really adequate to prevent war, would, at the same time, be so carefully safeguarded that it *ought* to be acceptable to all nations.

It is not out of the question to carry out universal and complete disarmament and to establish the necessary new world institutions through an entirely new world authority, but it seems more normal and sensible to make the necessary revisions of the present United Nations Charter.

MAIN FEATURES OF THE WHOLE PLAN

In harmony with these underlying principles, the most important specific features of the proposed Charter revision may be summarized as follows:

1. *Membership.* The plan contemplates that virtually the whole world shall accept permanent membership before the revised Charter comes into effect—the conception being that so drastic a change in the world's political structure should, in order to endure, be founded upon unanimous or nearly unanimous approval.

The assurance of assent by a great preponderance of the nations and peoples of the world would be accomplished by the revised Articles 3 and

110 providing: (a) that every independent state in the world shall be eligible for membership and may join at will; (b) that the revised Charter shall come into force only when ratified by five sixths of all the nations of the world, the ratifying nations to have a combined population of at least five sixths of the total world population and to include all the twelve nations which then have the largest populations. The assurance of permanent membership would be provided by the revised Article 6 whereby no nation, once having ratified the revised Charter, could either withdraw or be expelled.

The practical result would be that the plan would not even become operative until active and permanent support had been pledged by a great majority of all the nations, including as the twelve largest nations Brazil, France, the Federal Republic of Germany, India, Indonesia, Italy, Japan, Pakistan, the People's Republic of China, the United Kingdom, the U.S.A., and the U.S.S.R. . . .

The likelihood that there might not be a single nonmember nation is made the greater by the proposed requirement (under revised Articles 2 and 11) that every one of the necessarily small minority of nonmember nations shall, nevertheless, be required to comply with all the prohibitions and obligations of the disarmament plan. This provision that *every* nation in the world shall completely disarm and shall comply with the plan for the substitution of world law for international violence is deemed fundamental, since if even one small nation were permitted to possess the new weapons of mass destruction, such fears and suspicions might remain as to prevent the adherence of others, and the entire plan might be frustrated.

In view of the proposed requirement that every nation would, irrespective of membership, be bound to observe the world law in the field of war prevention, and the further fact that any minority of nonmember nations would necessarily be small, it may be argued that it would be simpler and legitimate to impose compulsory membership upon all the nations without exception. The plan set forth in a preliminary draft of the present proposals issued in 1953 did in fact provide that once the revised Charter had been ratified by a very large majority of the nations, all other nations should be deemed full and permanent members, even though they might have deliberately refused ratification. In deference, however, to the view that no nation should be *forced* to accept such affirmative obligations of membership as the duty to contribute financially, the present plan stops short of *compelling* membership by any nation, no matter how overwhelming the support for the revised Charter.

Nevertheless, the practical result would be little different from that of universal compulsory membership since, as already noted: (a) the maximum possible number of nonratifying nations could not exceed one sixth of all the nations and could have no more than a minor fraction of the world's population; and (b) even this small minority of nations, although exempt from certain positive duties of membership, would be bound equally with the member Nations to comply with the world law prohibiting international violence and requiring complete disarmament. This practical result would be accomplished, however, without the element of coercion involved in requiring active membership from the relatively few nations which might choose not to ratify.

2. *The General Assembly.* A radical revision is proposed as to the powers, composition and method of voting of the General Assembly.

Although the plan sets forth in the Charter itself all the *basic provisions* of the disarmament process and of other main features (such as the proposed world police force, the revenue system and the judicial system), it would still be true that in order to *implement* these basic provisions, the powers of the legislative and executive branches of the world organization must be considerable.

The plan calls for imposing the final responsibility for the enforcement of the disarmament process and the maintenance of peace upon the General Assembly itself, and gives the Assembly adequate powers to this end. These powers would, however, be strictly limited to matters directly related to the maintenance of peace. They would *not* include such matters as regulation of international trade, immigration and the like, or any right to interfere in the domestic affairs of the nations, save as expressly authorized by the revised Charter in order to enforce disarmament or to prevent international violence where a situation which ordinarily might be deemed "domestic" has actually developed into a serious threat to world peace.

To ensure the observance of these limitations, the delegated powers would be enumerated and defined in the revised Charter; while, as still further protection, there would be an explicit reservation to the member Nations and their peoples of all powers not thus delegated "by express language or clear implication." The delegated powers are defined in revised Article 11 and in various other provisions of the revised Charter, while the reservation of all nongranted powers is contained both in revised Article 2 and in the proposed Bill of Rights (Annex VII).

As above mentioned, the principle is followed that all the *main features* of the whole plan shall be included in the revised Charter itself as "constitutional legislation," having in mind that the nations will be more likely to accept the plan if all its principal provisions are clearly set forth in the constitutional document itself. The effect would be to bind the nations in advance not only to all the fundamentals but also to many important details, and thus to leave for the General Assembly a more limited legislative scope than might be supposed.

Since, however, the General Assembly, even with elaborate "constitutional legislation," would need to have some definite legislative powers, the plan calls for a revision of the system of representation in the Assembly. For it cannot be expected that the larger nations would consent to give the Assembly even very limited *legislative* powers under the present system whereby Albania, Costa Rica, Iceland, Liberia, etc., have an equal vote with the United States, the Soviet Union, India, the United Kingdom, etc.

The purpose is, by abolishing the present system of one vote for each member Nation, to substitute a more equitable system, and thus to make the nations more willing to confer upon the General Assembly the limited yet considerably increased powers that it would need.

The proposed plan of representation takes account of relative populations but is qualified by the important provisions that no nation, however large, shall have more than thirty Representatives and that even the smallest nation shall have one Representative. The upper limit of thirty would be imposed partly because weighted representation is not likely to be accepted by the smaller nations unless the differences in representation between the majority of the nations and the largest nations are kept within moderate limits, and also because without some such limitation, the General Assembly would be of so unwieldy a size as to be unable to transact business. At the other extreme the purpose is to ensure that even the very small nations shall have some voice.

The proposed formula divides the ninety-nine nations, generally recognized in early 1960 as independent states or likely to be so recognized by 1965, into six categories according to relative populations, with representation as follows:

The 4 largest nations.....30	Representatives each 120
The 8 next largest nations 15	Representatives each 120
The 20 next largest nations 6	Representatives each 120
The 30 next largest nations 4	Representatives each 120
The 34 next largest nations 2	Representatives each 68
The 3 smallest nations.... 1	Representative each 3
99 nations	551 Representatives

It is proposed that the populations of colonial and semi-colonial areas (i.e., the non-self-governing territories and dependencies, including territories under trusteeship administration) shall not be counted in determining the representation of the independent states but that, in order to afford equal treatment to the estimated approximately 95 million people (in 1965) of these areas, they shall be entitled to representation in proportion to population on the same average basis as the people of the member Nations. It is assumed that as of July 1965 this method would entitle these areas as a whole to seventeen Representatives. The General Assembly would allocate these Representatives among the various territories or groups of territories, taking into account their relative populations.

Of the assumed 568 Representatives, 551 would therefore represent the assumed ninety-nine independent states, while the non-self-governing and trust territories would have 17 Representatives.

The four most populous nations of the world—the People's Republic of China, India, the Soviet Union and the United States—would each have the maximum of thirty Representatives; and even the smallest nation (Iceland) would have one Representative. The 568 Representatives would represent a total estimated world population (as of July 1965) of 3,172,156,000, or an average of about 5,600,000 for each Representative.

The effect would be that, with relation to population, the smaller nations would still have a disproportionately large voice, but not nearly as much so as under the present system of one vote for each member Nation irrespective of population. . . .

As to the method of selection of the Representatives, it is proposed that a system of full popular election shall be gradually introduced. This would be done under a three-stage plan providing: (a) that in the first stage all the Representatives would be chosen by the respective national legislatures of the member Nations; (b) that in the second stage at least half the Representatives would be chosen by popular vote of those persons qualified to vote for the most numerous branch of the national legislature; and (c) that in the third stage all the Representatives would be chosen by the same sort of popular vote. The first two stages would normally be of twelve years each (three four-year terms of the General Assembly) but could each be extended by eight years by a special vote of the Assembly. The popular election of all the Representatives would, therefore, normally become mandatory twenty-four years after the ratification of the revised Charter and in any case not later than forty years after the revised Charter comes into force.

With regard to the terms of service of the Representatives, it is proposed that they shall serve for four years.

Concerning the procedure for voting in the General Assembly, it is proposed in place of the present method: (a) that a majority of all the Representatives then in office must be present in order to constitute a quorum; (b) that, except as to certain "important" and "special" questions, decisions shall be made by a majority of the Representatives present and voting; (c) that on these "important" questions which would be specifically defined, decisions shall be by a "special majority" consisting of a majority of all the Representatives then in office, whether or not present and voting; and (d) that in respect of several "special" questions, also specifically defined, there shall be even larger special majorities which in one instance would require the affirmative vote of three fourths of all the Representatives in office including two thirds of the Representatives from those nations entitled to fifteen or more Representatives, i.e., the twelve largest nations.

Two full-time Standing Committees of the General Assembly would be constitutionally provided for, namely, a Standing Committee on the Peace Enforcement Agencies and a Standing Committee on Budget and Finance. The former would be a "watchdog" committee to exercise legislative supervision over the process and maintenance of disarmament and over the United Nations Peace Force. The latter would have vital functions in submitting to the Assembly recommendations as to the amount and apportionment of each annual budget for all the activities of the strengthened United Nations.

With relation to the powers of the revised General Assembly, a clear distinction would be made between legislative powers and powers of recommendation. The *legislative* powers would be strictly limited to matters directly related to the maintenance of peace, whereas the extensive powers of mere recommendation now possessed by the Assembly would be retained and even broadened. To this end, the Assembly's legislative authority would, as above mentioned, exclude any regulation of international trade, immigration and the like and any right to interfere in the domestic affairs of the nations, save only as strictly necessary for the enforcement of disarmament or, in exceptional circumstances, for the prevention of international violence.

On the other hand, as distinguished from the power to legislate, the General Assembly would have the right to make nonbinding *recommendations* on any subject which it deemed relevant to the maintenance of peace and the welfare of the world's people.

3. *The Executive Council.* It is proposed to abolish the present Security Council and to substitute for it an Executive Council, composed of seventeen Representatives elected by the General Assembly itself. This new and highly important organ would not only be chosen by the Assembly, but would also be responsible to and removable by the Assembly; and the Council would serve for the same four-year terms as the Representatives in the Assembly.

Special provision would be made for representation of the larger nations, whereby the four largest nations (China, India, the U.S.A. and the U.S.S.R.) would each be entitled at all times to have one of its Representatives on the Council; and four of the eight next largest nations (Brazil, France, West Germany, Indonesia, Italy, Japan, Pakistan and the United Kingdom) would in rotation also be entitled to representation, with the proviso that two of these four shall always be from nations in Europe and the other two from nations outside Europe. The remaining nine members would be chosen by the Assembly from the Representatives of all the other member Nations and the non-self-governing and trust territories under a formula designed to provide fair representation for all the main regions of the world and to ensure that every member Nation, without exception, shall in due course have a Representative on this all-important Council.

In contrast to the voting procedure of the present Security Council, whereby any one of the five nations entitled to "permanent" membership has a veto power in all nonprocedural matters, the decisions of the new Executive Council on "important" matters (as defined in paragraph 2 of revised Article 27) would be by a vote of twelve of the seventeen Representatives composing it, with the proviso that this majority shall include a majority of the eight members of the Council from the twelve member Nations entitled to fifteen or more Representatives in the Assembly and a majority of the nine other members of the Council. All other decisions would be by a vote of any twelve members of the Council.

This Executive Council would constitute the *executive arm* of the strengthened United Nations, holding much the same relation to the General

Assembly as that of the British Cabinet to the House of Commons. Subject to its responsibility to the Assembly, the new Council would have broad powers to supervise and direct the disarmament process and other aspects of the whole system for the maintenance of peace provided for in the revised Charter.

The Executive Council would, for example, decide (subject to review by the General Assembly) as to whether each stage of the disarmament process has been satisfactorily completed and, once complete national disarmament has been achieved, would watch over its maintenance. Nevertheless, the Council would always remain subordinate to the Assembly, which would have final authority to make such crucial decisions as the possible postponement of any stage of the disarmament process, and the imposition of sanctions in case of any breach of the peace or serious violation by any nation of the authority of the United Nations.

4. *Economic and Social Council, Trusteeship Council.* These two Councils would be continued, but with a somewhat larger and different composition than under the present Charter designed to provide a wider and better-balanced representation on these Councils.

The Economic and Social Council, instead of its present membership of eighteen, would have a membership of twenty-four Representatives elected by the General Assembly from among its own number for four-year terms. They would be chosen pursuant to a formula whereby each of the twelve member Nations having the largest gross national products would be entitled to have one of its Representatives on the Council at all times, the other twelve members of the Council to be elected by the Assembly from among the Representatives of all the remaining member Nations and the non-self-governing or trust territories, with due regard to geographical distribution. . . .

5. *The Disarmament Process.* Annex I contains a carefully framed plan for the elimination—not the mere "reduction" or "limitation"—of *all* national armaments.

It calls for a "transition period" of one year following the coming into force of the revised Charter during which the first new General Assembly would be selected, the first Executive Council would be chosen by the Assembly, and the first Inspection Commission would be appointed by that Council, subject to confirmation by the Assembly. The plan then calls for a "preparatory stage" of two years, during which an arms census would be taken, an Inspection Service would be organized and other preparations would be made. Finally, it provides for an "actual disarmament stage" which would normally cover ten years during which there would be a step-by-step proportionate reduction in all categories of all national armed forces and all armaments at the rate of ten per cent per annum. As below mentioned, this normal ten-year period could be reduced to seven years by the General Assembly or could, on the other hand, be extended by the Assembly under certain circumstances.

The proposed Inspection Commission, the members of which would be appointed for five-year terms by the Executive Council subject to confirmation by the General Assembly, would consist of five persons, none of whom could be a national of any of the twelve nations having fifteen or more Representatives in the General Assembly and no two of whom could be nationals of the same nation. The administrative head of the Inspection Service would be an Inspector-General, who would be appointed by the Inspection Commission for a six-year term, subject to confirmation by the Executive Council, and would be removable by the Commission at will.

The Executive Council would have general supervision over the Inspection Commission with authority to issue instructions to the Commission and to remove at will any member of the Commission.

Very careful safeguards would be provided to ensure the competence and integrity of the personnel of the Inspection Service and their devotion to the purposes of the United Nations. These would include a provision limiting the number of nationals of any one nation among those performing duties of actual inspection to not more than four per cent of the total number of Inspectors; a requirement that all the personnel of the Service shall be recruited on as wide a geographical basis as possible; a prohibition against their seeking or receiving instructions from any government or authority except the United Nations; and the requirement of a solemn declaration that they will perform their functions impartially and conscientiously. On the other hand, all the personnel of the Service would be assured "fully adequate" pay and allowances and retirement pensions free from all taxation.

As a still further safeguard, the Standing Committee on the Peace Enforcement Agencies of the General Assembly would have the responsibility of watching over the proper performance by the Inspection Commission of its duties and also over the proper exercise by the Executive Council of its general authority over the Commission with full power to investigate and report to the Assembly itself.

The proposed powers of the Inspection Service are carefully defined in Annex I, and the General Assembly would be empowered to adopt further regulations, on the one hand, to ensure the efficacy of the inspection system and, on the other hand, to protect nations and individuals against possible abuses of power. While Inspectors would be given unlimited access to establishments with especially dangerous potentials, periodic inspections of less dangerous activities would be restricted to a reasonable number each year. Any additional inspection of activities subject only to periodic inspection and of places not ordinarily subject to inspection could be conducted only on the basis of a special authorization issued by one of the United Nations regional courts which would be established as explained below. Such an authorization could be granted only upon a showing to the court of reasonable cause to believe or suspect that a prohibited activity is being conducted in the place sought to be inspected. Regular aerial surveys would be provided for, subject to the limitation that no more than three regular surveys of any particular territory could be conducted in any year. Special aerial surveys could also be made, but only upon court authorization after a showing to the court of reasonable cause.

The reduction process during each year of the "actual disarmament stage" would be verified by the Inspection Commission, which would report fully to the Executive Council as to whether the required proportionate reductions had been duly carried out by all the nations. The General Assembly, advised by the Council, would have power to suspend the disarmament process for six months at a time if not fully satisfied that it was being faithfully fulfilled. On the other hand, after the first four years, the Assembly would have the power to cut in half the remaining six years, so as to achieve universal and complete disarmament in seven years from the beginning of the "actual disarmament stage."

This disarmament plan should, however, be thought of as a twelve-year plan if normally carried out without either delay or acceleration, i.e., [one consisting of] the two years of the "preparatory stage" and the normal ten years of the "actual disarmament stage." At the end of the latter period, no *national* military forces whatever would exist; and the only military force in the entire world (as distinguished from limited and lightly armed internal police forces) would be a world police force, to be called the "United Nations Peace Force," which would be built up parallel with and in proportion to the disarmament process.

No plan for universal and complete disarmament is practicable, unless *all* nations are bound by it. It is apparent to all that if any one of the larger and stronger nations were exempted from the disarmament process, no such disarmament would be feasible. But it is equally true in this world of novel weapons of tremendous destructive power that even a small nation might become a menace to the peace of the world. The disarmament system must, therefore, cover *every* nation, whether a member of the United Nations or not; and the plan includes appropriate provisions to this end. . . .

The proposed disarmament plan depends also on its *simultaneous* execution by all nations. It is obvious that no nation would be willing or could be expected to disarm ahead of the others; and therefore all necessary safeguards must be established to ensure that no nation would be put in a disadvantageous position because other nations have not simultaneously carried out their part of the plan. Accordingly the Inspection Commission would be empowered not only to approve annual disarmament plans for every nation but also to supervise and to ensure their simultaneous execution.

Still further, the disarmament plan must make sure that all nations will disarm *proportionately*. The year-by-year diminution of military strength must be equal for all nations, since no nation can be expected to disarm by a larger percentage than others and since no nation should be deprived of a main source of its military strength while other nations still retain their principal sources of strength. Thus a nation strong in nuclear weapons should not be entirely deprived of them while other nations retain a large proportion of their preponderant land armies. And similarly, a nation could not reasonably be asked to abandon its ballistic missiles while another was permitted to retain its bombing planes. For these reasons a *uniform percentage* reduction year by year is provided for as the fairest and most acceptable method to achieve total national disarmament.

It would not, however, be sufficient merely to provide for uniform percentage reductions in the *total* military forces and armaments of the various nations, since a particular nation might, for example, simply demobilize a large number of foot soldiers while leaving the strength of its air force and navy unimpaired. Similarly, some other nation might limit a required numerical cut in its air force to maintenance personnel while keeping all its pilots in the service. A requirement with respect to the reduction of weapons might also be easily evaded if a nation were permitted to divide the reduction unequally between its fighter planes and long-range bombers, or between its fissionable and fusionable weapons. A really fair and safe method of reduction requires, therefore, that each nation shall reduce in an equal manner the personnel not only of each major service (land, sea and air), but also of each major component thereof. Moreover, this principle of proportionate reductions would need to be applied uniformly to troops stationed in the home territory and abroad. For example, if in a given year the ground forces of a particular nation should consist of 500,000 men of whom 100,000 were stationed abroad, a ten per cent reduction of 50,000 in that year would have to be divided in such a way as to ensure that 40,000 be discharged from the forces stationed in the home territory and 10,000 from those stationed abroad.

Fairness and safety require similar equal and proportionate reductions in each major category of weapons and in all facilities for the production of armaments. Reductions of the same proportionate size should be made, for instance, in each nation's capacity to produce various categories of weapons; for example, with respect to guided and ballistic missiles, separate cuts would be necessary in the capacity for the production of short-, medium- and long-range missiles. . . .

The disarmament plan also includes provision for a United Nations Nuclear Energy Authority with dual functions: (a) to assist the Inspection Service in guarding against possible diversion of nuclear materials to any war-making purpose, and (b) to promote the world-wide use of nuclear materials and processes for peaceful purposes. To these ends, the Nuclear Energy Authority would have wide powers to acquire by purchase at a fair price all nuclear materials in the world, with the obligation to have them put to use at fair rentals for peaceful purposes in all parts of the world under arrangements that would apportion the materials fairly and safeguard them against seizure. It is contemplated that this new Authority, having wider scope and membership than the International Atomic Energy Agency established in 1956, would take over the personnel and functions of that Agency.

As in the case of the Inspection Service, the Nuclear Energy Authority would be under the direction and control of a five-member Commission. This body would be called the Nuclear Energy Commission. Within its field this Commission would correspond to the Inspection Commission and would be subject to the same careful provisions as the Inspection Commission in respect of the eligibility of its members and the authority of the Executive Council to supervise its policies and to remove any member at will.

The administrative head of the Nuclear Energy Authority would be a General Manager appointed for a six-year term by the Nuclear Energy Commission and removable by it at will. Safeguards corresponding to those provided in respect of the personnel of the Inspection Service would also be applicable to the personnel of the Nuclear Energy Authority, and the Standing Committee on the Peace Enforcement Agencies of the General Assembly would have responsibilities in respect of this Nuclear Energy Authority corresponding to its responsibilities in respect of the Inspection Service.

A new feature of the disarmament plan, made necessary by the recent penetration of outer space and its potentialities for the future, is a proposed United Nations Outer Space Agency. The broad objectives sought are: (a) to ensure that outer space is used only for peaceful purposes, and (b) to promote its exploration and use for the common benefit of all the people of this earth, rather than for the benefit of any nation or any part of mankind.

The Outer Space Agency would, subject to the over-all authority of the General Assembly and the Executive Council, be under the "direction and control" of a United Nations Outer Space Commission. This Commission, like the Inspection Commission and the Nuclear Energy Commission, would be composed of five members appointed for five-year terms by the Executive Council subject to confirmation by the General Assembly and would be removable at will by the Council.

Correspondingly also, the Outer Space Agency would have an administrative head who would be called the Managing Director.

Moreover, as to the personnel of the Outer Space Agency, there would be safeguarding provisions in all respects similar to the above-described provisions relative to the personnel of the Inspection Service and the Nuclear Energy Authority; and the Standing Committee on the Peace Enforcement Agencies would have "watchdog" responsibilities identical with those relative to the Inspection Service and the Nuclear Energy Authority.

Provision is made for reporting any violations of the disarmament plan; for correcting such violations; for the prosecution of serious individual violators in regional courts of the United Nations; and for sanctions against nations themselves in the possible event of defiance or evasion by any government. As a still further safeguard, there would be the above-mentioned committee of the General Assembly (the Standing Committee on the Peace Enforcement Agencies) with the function of keeping a sharp eye on all aspects of the disarmament process and of keeping the Assembly informed of any dereliction or defects.

It is a basic premise of this necessarily elaborate plan for universal and complete disarmament that, while the proposed system of inspection and control could not provide *absolute* assurance against the clandestine retention or manufacture of weapons, it could and would provide highly effective protection. It would be fallacious and a counsel of despair to reject the idea of the complete abolition of national armaments, including nuclear weapons, merely because no absolute or "foolproof" guarantee can be supplied that every ounce of dangerous war material has been accounted for and that no dangerous new weapon can ever be secretly made.

It is believed that the whole proposed system of inspection, including the inspection of all means of "delivery" of nuclear weapons, would, in practice, make it impossible for any group within a nation or any nation itself to assemble weapons that would constitute a serious danger. And it is also to be remembered that a powerful world police force would always be in the background for the very purpose of deterring or suppressing any rash attempt at international violence.

The guarantees of safety to be relied upon when all national armaments are abolished lie, therefore, in the *combination* of a comprehensive and highly organized inspection system with a coercive force of overwhelming power. Not exclusively on one or the other, but on the *combined* effect of both, the world could safely rely in the abandonment once and for all of all national military forces.

6. *A World Police Force.* The plan is framed upon the assumption that not even the most solemn agreement and not even the most thorough inspection system, or both together, can be *fully* relied upon to ensure that every nation will always carry out and maintain complete disarmament and refrain from violence under all circumstances. Moreover, it must be recognized that even with the complete elimination of all *military* forces there would necessarily remain substantial, although strictly limited and lightly armed, internal police forces and that these police forces, supplemented by civilians armed with sporting rifles and fowling pieces, might conceivably constitute a serious threat to a neighboring country in the absence of a well-disciplined and heavily armed world police.

In short, our conception is that if police forces are necessary to maintain law and order even within a mature community or nation, similar forces will be required to guarantee the carrying out and maintenance of complete disarmament by each and every nation and to deter or suppress *any* attempted international violence. In consequence, detailed constitutional provision is made for a world police, to be organized and maintained by the strengthened United Nations and to be called the "United Nations Peace Force." This world police force would be the only *military* force permitted anywhere in the world after the process of national disarmament has been completed. It would be built up during the above-described "actual disarmament stage," so that as the last national military unit is disbanded the organization of the Peace Force would simultaneously be completed. . . . This Peace Force would consist of two components—a standing component and a Peace Force Reserve—both of which would, save in the most extreme emergency, be composed solely of volunteers.

The standing component would be a full-time force of professionals with a strength of between 200,000 and 600,000, as determined from year to year by the General Assembly. The proposed term of service for its enlisted personnel would not be less than four or more than eight years, as determined by the General Assembly, with provision for the re-enlistment of a limited number of especially well-qualified personnel.

In respect of the composition of the standing component, assurance would be provided through various specific limitations in Annex II that it would be recruited mainly, although not exclusively, from the smaller nations. These limitations would include: (a) a provision whereby the number of nationals of any nation (including any non-self-governing or trust territory under its administration) serving at any one time in the standing component shall not exceed three per cent of its then existing total strength; (b) a provision that the number of nationals of any nation in any one of the three main branches (land, sea and air) of the standing component shall not exceed three per cent of the then existing strength of such main branch; (c) a provision that the number of nationals of any nation serving at any one time in the officer corps of either of the three main branches of the standing component shall not exceed three per cent of the then existing strength of the officer corps of such main branch; and (d) a provision that not less than two per cent or more than ten per cent of the total strength of the standing component shall be nationals of the nations or nation constituting any one of eleven to twenty regions into which the whole world would be divided by the General Assembly pursuant to paragraph 9 of Article 26 of Annex I.

The units of the standing component would be stationed throughout the world in such a way that there would be no undue concentration in any particular nation or region, and, on the other hand, so as to facilitate prompt action for the maintenance of peace if and when required. Proposed specific provisions in this respect include: a direction that the standing component shall be stationed at military bases of the United Nations so distributed around the world as to facilitate its availability in case prompt action to prevent or suppress international violence is directed by the General Assembly (or in certain circumstances by the Executive Council); a provision that no such base shall be situated within the territory of any nation entitled to fifteen or more Representatives in the General Assembly, thus ensuring that no United Nations military base would be located in any of the twelve largest nations; a provision that all the territory of the world outside that of the twelve largest nations shall be divided by the General Assembly into eleven to twenty regions for the special purpose of distributing elements of the standing component between such regions, with the proviso that not less than five per cent or more than ten per cent of the total strength of the standing component shall be stationed in bases in any one of those regions, save only when the Peace Force has been duly called upon to take action.

In order to ensure the greatest possible security for the standing component, provision would be made that its units be located to the greatest extent possible on islands or peninsulas, or in other easily defensible positions.

The mobility of the standing component would be of great importance, in order that its widely distributed units could be promptly brought together into a formidable force in the event of any serious threat of international violence or serious defiance of the authority of the world organization. The equipment of the standing component should, therefore, include an ample number of large and swift aircraft for the long-distance transport of men and supplies, and in voting the annual budgets for the Peace Force the General Assembly would have authority to provide for this need.

As distinguished from the active or standing component, the Peace Force Reserve would have no organized units whatever, but would consist only of individuals partially trained and subject to call for service with the standing component in case of need. It would have a strength of between 600,000 and 1,200,000, as determined by the General Assembly. Its members would be recruited subject to careful provisions as to geographical distribution identical with those applicable to the standing component. The proposed term of service of its enlisted personnel would be for not less than six or more than ten years, as determined by the General Assembly. They would receive a minimum amount of basic training during the first three years of their term of service and some further training during the remainder of their terms, but except for these training periods would remain in their home countries on a stand-by basis subject to call.

The officers of both components would be selected, trained and promoted with a view to "ensuring an officer corps of the highest possible quality" with adequate opportunity for the selection as officer candidates of highly qualified men from the rank and file. . . . It is contemplated that the United Nations Peace Force shall be regularly provided with the most modern weapons and equipment. . . .

With regard to the use of nuclear weapons by the Peace Force, the solution proposed is that neither component shall normally be equipped with any kind of nuclear weapons, but that some such weapons shall be held in reserve in the custody of a civilian agency for use only under the most careful precautions. This agency would be the Nuclear Energy Authority, which would be authorized to release any nuclear weapons for possible use by the Peace Force only by order of the General Assembly itself, and then only if the Assembly has declared that nuclear weapons (which might have been clandestinely hidden or clandestinely produced) have actually been used against some nation or against the United Nations, or that such use is imminently threatened. While it may be argued that nuclear weapons should be part of the regular equipment of a world police force so that it could immediately crush by ruthless action any defiance of the world law, this solution has been rejected as being no more consistent with the purpose of the Peace Force than the regular equipment of a city police force with weapons whereby thousands of citizens could be killed in suppressing a riot.

It is also realized that it can be persuasively argued that nuclear weapons should not be even potentially available to the Peace Force. On balance, however, it is believed wise to make it *possible* for the Peace Force to use nuclear weapons in extreme circumstances provided that, as called for by the above-described proposals, such possible use is safeguarded with the utmost care.

The immediate direction of the Peace Force would be entrusted to a committee of five persons—to be called the Military Staff Committee—all of whom would have to be nationals of the smaller nations, i.e., of those nations entitled to less than fifteen Representatives in the General Assembly. Beyond this safeguard, however, the Military Staff Committee would always be under the close control of civilian authority, i.e., of the Executive Council. Still further, the General Assembly, through its Standing Committee on the Peace Enforcement Agencies, would exercise a general supervision over the work of the Military Staff Committee and over the Executive Council itself in respect of the organization and all the activities of the Peace Force. In short, the plan includes the utmost precautions for the subordination of the military direction of the Peace Force under all circumstances to civilian authority as represented by the Executive Council and the General Assembly.

While a world police force, well equipped and strong enough to prevent or promptly to suppress *any* international violence is, we believe, indispensable, the danger that it might be perverted into a tool of world domination is fully recognized. It is with this danger clearly in mind that meticulous care has been taken to surround the proposed Peace Force with the above-mentioned careful limitations and safeguards, so as to make its subversion virtually impossible.

Even with these elaborate safeguards, it is realized that the danger of possible misuse of the Peace Force cannot be *wholly* eliminated any more than every *conceivable* danger of violation of the disarmament process can be eliminated. However, in order to achieve complete national disarmament and genuine peace, *some* risks must be taken. What we have attempted is to reduce these to the very minimum. On the one hand, we have sought to provide for a world police so strong as to be capable of preserving peace in any foreseeable contingency. On the other hand, we propose such careful checks and limitations that there would be every possible assurance that the power of this world police would not be misused.

It will be seen that despite all the proposed safeguards this plan calls for a world police that would be a strong and effective fighting force in case of need. The idea of some people that a world peace force somewhat similar as to arms and functions to the United Nations Emergency Force of 1957–1960 might suffice is, we believe, unsound and untenable. Even in a world in which all national military forces were abolished, there would, as above mentioned, necessarily remain internal police forces of substantial strength which would probably need to possess a considerable number of rifles and even a few machine guns. In addition, there would remain literally millions of sporting rifles and revolvers in the hands of private persons and thousands of nonmilitary airplanes, large and small. Accordingly, it is conceivable that, even with total disarmament, an aroused nation with a strong grievance could marshal quite a formidable armed force even if no one in it possessed any weapon stronger than a rifle. And while it is true that any such force, even of a million men, could not withstand a well-armed contingent of the world police of even one-twentieth its strength, that contingent in order to suppress the aggression promptly and with minimum injury would need to be a genuine fighting force, well equipped and highly disciplined.

Moreover, there would remain a lurking suspicion for some time at least that despite the most efficient world inspection system some nation or nations had contrived to hide or might produce secretly some forbidden weapons. In these circumstances it seems perfectly clear that in order to provide the necessary assurance to obtain general assent to universal and complete disarmament, it will be essential to provide a world police of such strength and armament as to be able *quickly* and *certainly* to prevent or suppress *any* international violence. We firmly believe that on no cheaper terms can universal and complete disarmament be achieved, while it is equally clear that without total disarmament, genuine peace is unattainable. We submit, in short, that a strong and well-armed police force is part of the indispensable price of peace and that the sooner the world faces up to this conclusion the better it will be for all peoples.

7. *The Judicial and Conciliation System.* In accordance with the conception that the *abolition* of national armaments is indispensable to genuine peace, and that if such armaments are abolished other means must be simultaneously provided for the adjudication or settlement of international disputes and for "peaceful change," provision is made for a world system of conciliation and adjudication.

In proposing such a system, recognition is given to the existence of two main categories of international disputes, namely: (1) those disputes which are capable of adjudication through the application of legal principles, and (2) the equally or more important category of disputes which cannot be satisfactorily settled on the basis of applicable legal principles.

With respect to those international disputes which are susceptible of settlement upon legal principles, it is proposed to empower the General Assembly to *direct* the submission of any such dispute to the International Court of Justice whenever the Assembly finds that its continuance is likely to endanger international peace. In case of such submission, the Court would have compulsory jurisdiction to decide the case, even if one of the parties should refuse to come before the Court.

The International Court of Justice would also be given authority to decide questions relating to the interpretation of the revised Charter, and to decide disputes involving the constitutionality of laws enacted thereunder. Compulsory jurisdiction would also be conferred upon the Court in certain other respects as, for example, any dispute relating to the interpretation of treaties or other international agreements, or as to the validity of any such treaty or agreement alleged to conflict with the revised Charter.

In order to strengthen the independence and authority of the International Court of Justice in view of these enlarged powers, it is proposed that the tenure of its fifteen judges shall be for life, instead of for nine-year terms as provided by the present statute of the Court, subject only to the possibility of dismissal if, in the unanimous opinion of his colleagues, a judge is no longer able properly to perform his functions or, as now provided, has in their unanimous opinion "ceased to fulfill the required conditions" of his tenure. The judges of the Court would be elected, not by concurrent action of the General Assembly and the Security Council, as at present, but by the General Assembly alone, from a list of candidates prepared by the Executive Council upon the basis of nominations received from the members of the highest courts of justice of member Nations, from national and international associations of international lawyers and from professors of international law. The Council would be required to present three candidates for each vacancy.

In respect of the enforcement of the judgments of the International Court of Justice, it is proposed that the General Assembly (or in certain special circumstances the Executive Council) could direct economic sanctions or, in the last resort, action by the United Nations Peace Force to ensure compliance. Any such action would, however, be limited, if at all possible, to air or naval demonstrations and would involve actual military operations against a noncomplying nation only if absolutely necessary.

With regard to the other main category of international disputes, i.e., those inevitable disputes which are not of an exclusively legal nature, it is proposed to establish a new tribunal of the highest possible prestige, to be known as the World Equity Tribunal. To this end it is proposed that the Tribunal shall be composed of fifteen persons elected by the General Assembly pursuant to safeguards and an elaborate procedure designed to ensure the choice of individuals whose reputation, experience and character would furnish the best assurance of impartiality and breadth of view. Thus no two of them could be nationals of the same nation, and it would be required that at least ten of the fifteen must have had more than twenty years of legal experience as judges, teachers of law or practicing lawyers. In addition, the General Assembly would be restricted in its choice to a list of persons nominated by the member Nations upon the recommendation of a committee in each member Nation which would have to include representatives of its principal judicial tribunals and legal associations, and of its leading academic, scientific, economic and religious organizations. Beyond this, the General Assembly would be required to pay due regard to the geographical distribution of the members of the Tribunal, so as to ensure fair representation of all the principal regions of the world.

To ensure the independence of the members of the World Equity Tribunal, they would be elected for life, subject only to the possibility of dismissal if, in the unanimous opinion of his colleagues, a member is no longer able properly to perform his functions or has ceased to fulfil the required conditions of his tenure.

In ordinary circumstances this World Equity Tribunal could not make binding decisions, as distinguished from recommendations, except with the consent of the parties. But provision is made that if the General Assembly votes by a large special majority, i.e., by a three-fourths majority of all the Representatives then in office (including two-thirds of all the Representatives from the twelve largest nations), that the carrying out of the Tribunal's recommendations is essential for the preservation of peace, the recommendations of the Tribunal shall become enforceable by the same means as a judgment of the International Court of Justice.

The purpose of this important departure is to supplement other methods for settling *nonlegal* international disputes (such as negotiation, conciliation and agreed arbitration) by providing an impartial world agency of so high a stature that, under exceptional conditions involving world peace, its recommendations may be given the force of law.

Through the adoption of these proposals in respect of both legal and nonlegal international disputes, world institutions would at last exist whereby *any* nation could be compelled to submit *any* dispute dangerous to peace for a final and peaceful settlement; and the world would no longer be helpless, for lack of adequate machinery, to deal by peaceful means with any and all dangerous disputes between nations.

In order to provide means for the trial of individuals accused of violating the disarmament provisions of the revised Charter or of other offenses against the Charter or laws enacted by the General Assembly, and to provide safeguards against possible abuse of power by any organ or official of the United Nations, provision is also made for regional United Nations courts, inferior to the International Court of Justice, and for the review by the International Court of decisions of these regional courts.

The proposal is for not less than twenty or more than forty such regional courts to have jurisdiction in regions to be delineated by the General Assembly, each regional court to be composed of not less than three or more than nine judges. The judges of these courts would be appointed by the Executive Council from a list of qualified persons prepared by the International Court of Justice, with the provisos that not more than one-third of the judges of any such court could be nationals of the nations included in the region of the court's jurisdiction, and that no two judges of any such court could be nationals of the same nation. Their appointments (which would be subject to confirmation by the General Assembly) would be for life, subject only to dismissal for cause by a vote of two thirds of all the judges of the International Court.

The regional United Nations courts, together with the International Court of Justice, would introduce a regime of genuine and enforceable world law in respect of all *legal* questions likely to endanger world peace, while the World Equity Tribunal would, as above mentioned, provide means for the authoritative and compulsory settlement of nonlegal situations seriously dangerous to peace.

In addition to these judicial agencies, it is proposed to establish a World Conciliation Board which could be voluntarily availed of by the nations, or to which the General Assembly could refer any international dispute or situation likely to threaten peace. The functions of this new Board would be strictly confined to mediation and conciliation; and, if it failed to bring the disputing nations to a voluntary settlement, resort could be had to the International Court of Justice or the World Equity Tribunal, as might be most suitable in view of the nature of the issues involved.

In order to achieve genuine peace we must have more than total and universal disarmament and more than an effective world police. We must also have world tribunals to which the nations can resort with confidence for the adjustment or decision of their disputes and which, subject to careful safeguards, will have clearly defined authority to deal with any dispute which is dangerous to peace even if a nation does not wish to submit to the jurisdiction of the appropriate tribunal.

8. *Enforcement and Penalties.* The plan envisages a variety of enforcement measures, including the prosecution in United Nations regional courts of individuals responsible for a violation of the disarmament provisions.

In order to aid the Inspection Service in the detection and prosecution of any such violators, it is proposed to have a civil police force of the United Nations with a strength not exceeding 10,000. This force would be under the general direction of an Attorney-General of the United Nations, to be appointed by the Executive Council subject to confirmation by the General Assembly. The Attorney-General, besides having supervision over the civil police force, would be responsible for making arrangements with national authorities for assistance in the apprehension of persons accused of offenses against the revised Charter and the laws and regulations enacted thereunder and for the detention of such persons pending trial. Provision would also be made for Assistant Attorneys-General of the United Nations who would be assigned to each regional court.

In case of a serious violation of the revised Charter or any law or regulation enacted thereunder for which a national government is found to be directly or indirectly responsible, the General Assembly could order economic sanctions against the nation concerned. In extreme cases the Assembly (or the Executive Council in an emergency and subject to immediate review by the Assembly) would also have authority to order the United Nations Peace Force into action. Any such enforcement action would correspond to the above-mentioned action, available for the enforcement of judgments of the International Court of Justice or of the recommendations of the World Equity Tribunal for the settlement of a dispute when the General Assembly has decided that a continuance of the dispute would be a "serious danger" to peace.

9. *World Development.* The plan further provides (revised Articles 7 and 59 and Annex IV) for the establishment of a World Development Authority, whose function would be to assist in the economic and social development of the underdeveloped areas of the world, primarily through grants-in-aid and interest-free loans. This Authority would be under the direction of a World Development Commission of five members to be chosen with due regard to geographical distribution by the Economic and Social Council, subject to confirmation by the General Assembly.

The World Development Commission would be under the general supervision of the Economic and Social Council, which would have power to define broad objectives and priorities. Since that Council would be composed of twenty-four Representatives of whom twelve would come from the member Nations having the highest gross national products and twelve from among the Representatives of the other member Nations selected with due regard to geographical distribution, there would thus be reasonable assurance that account would be taken both of the views of those nations contributing large shares of United Nations revenue, and also of the nations most in need of the Authority's assistance.

This proposed World Development Authority could, if the General Assembly so decided, have very large sums at its disposal, since the Authority's funds would be allocated to it by the Assembly out of the general revenues of the United Nations. With the large resources which the Assembly could and should provide, the World Development Authority would have the means to aid the underdeveloped areas of the world to the extent necessary to remove the danger to world stability and peace caused by the immense economic disparity between those areas and the industrialized regions of the world.

While universal, enforceable and complete disarmament, together with adequate institutions and methods for the peaceful settlement of disputes, are certainly indispensable, no solid and stable peace can be assured by these means alone. There is also required a more positive approach through the amelioration of the worst economic ills of mankind. To this end, the new World Development Authority, together with the Nuclear Energy Authority, would serve as important arms of the strengthened United Nations.

10. *A United Nations Revenue System.* It would obviously be futile to establish the proposed new world institutions called for by the plan (including the United Nations Peace Force, the Inspection Service, the World Development Authority, the Nuclear Energy Authority, the Outer Space Agency, the World Equity Tribunal and the World Conciliation Board) unless a well-planned system is provided for their sufficient and reliable financial support. Such a system should also, of course, provide for the adequate support of the already existing organs and agencies of the United Nations, which would be continued and, in some cases, would have enlarged functions and responsibilities. These include the revised General Assembly itself, the strengthened International Court of Justice, the Economic and Social Council, the Trusteeship Council, the Secretariat and the various specialized agencies already affiliated with the United Nations.

The United Nations Peace Force, with an assumed strength for its standing component of, say, 400,000 (midway between the proposed constitutional maximum of 600,000 and minimum of 200,000) and with an assumed strength for the Peace Force Reserve of, say, 900,000 (midway between the proposed constitutional maximum of 1,200,000 and minimum of 600,000) would alone require some $9 billion annually. The minimum annual amount required for the General Assembly and Executive Council, the judicial system, the Secretariat, the Inspection Service, the Nuclear Energy Authority, the Outer Space Agency and the other organs and agencies other than the World Development Authority may be estimated at $2 billion. To this should be added a large amount on the order of $25 billion, which should be annually appropriated by the General Assembly for the proposed World Development Authority in order to make a real impression on the vast problem of mitigating the worst economic disparities between nations and regions.

Upon first impression, this assumed $25 billion figure for world development may appear high, but is in fact moderate if the purpose is to accomplish a substantial change in the living conditions of the more economically underdeveloped areas of the world. This is so because before the machinery for supplying any such amount can become operative, there will probably be an increase in world population to nearly 4 billion, by which time the number of people living in poverty relative to the standards of the industrialized nations will certainly be not less than 2 billion. Accordingly, the annual expenditure of $25 billion to improve the condition of these people would represent only about $12 per capita, which is little enough to accomplish any substantial improvement in their living standards.

It is apparent, therefore, that the reasonable expenses of a world authority adequately equipped to deter or suppress any international violence, to administer a comprehensive system for the peaceful settlement of all disputes between nations and *also* to do something substantial for the economic betterment of the underdeveloped parts of the world could easily run to $36 billion per annum. And while this amount would be less than one half the 1960-61 budget of a single nation—the United States—it would, nevertheless, be so large a sum that reliance for supplying it should not be placed on a system of yearly contributions by the separate governments of nearly one hundred nations. Apart from a World Development Authority, the maintenance of a high level of efficiency and morale by the proposed Inspection Service, the Peace Force, the Nuclear Energy Authority and the Outer Space Agency would be of crucial importance; and it would indeed be folly to set up these and other vital organs without reliable machinery for supplying the necessary funds. To this end, a carefully devised *collaborative* revenue system is proposed.

A chief feature of this system would be that each member Nation would assign in advance to the United Nations all or part of certain taxes designated by it and assessed under its national laws. Each nation would undertake the entire administrative function of collecting the taxes thus assigned to the United Nations, these taxes to be paid directly to a fiscal office of the United Nations in each member Nation. In this way it would be unnecessary to create any considerable United Nations bureaucracy for this purpose.

Another important feature would be an *over-all limit* on the maximum amount of revenue to be raised in any year, namely, two per cent of the gross world product (total value of all goods produced and services rendered) as estimated from year to year by the above-mentioned Standing Committee on Budget and Finance of the General Assembly.

The General Assembly would adopt the annual United Nations budget covering all its activities, and would determine the amounts to be supplied by the taxpayers of each member Nation for that budget. These amounts would be allotted on the basis of each member Nation's estimated proportion of the estimated gross world product in that year subject to a uniform "per capita deduction" of not less than fifty or more than ninety per cent of the estimated average per capita product of the ten member Nations having the lowest per capita national products, as determined by the Assembly. A further provision would limit the amount to be supplied by the people of any member Nation in any one year to a sum not exceeding two and one-half per cent of that nation's estimated national product.

Taking 1980 as an example, and assuming that the gross world product for that year was estimated at $2600 billion, the maximum United Nations revenue which could be raised would be $52 billion. And if for the 1980 fiscal year a budget of $16 billion less than the maximum, or $36 billion, was voted, it being then estimated that the United States had thirty per cent of the gross world product, the amount which the taxpayers of the United States could be called upon to supply, allowing for the "per capita deduction" would be about $12.2 billion. This charge upon the taxpayers of the United States, while substantial, would still be less than one-third of the approximately $46 billion to be supplied by them in 1960-61 for military purposes alone. It follows that upon the completion of national disarmament, whereby this $46 billion item would be entirely eliminated, even the maximum possible charge for the budget of the strengthened United Nations would seem relatively small. The same would be true of any other nation with large military expenses.

In addition to the provisions for the raising of annual revenue, a United Nations borrowing power would also be provided for, with the limitation that the total United Nations debt outstanding in any year shall not (except in grave emergency declared by the General Assembly) exceed five per cent of the estimated gross world product in that year.

A more detailed explanation of this revenue plan is set forth in Annex V. It is believed that the plan would be effective to provide reliable and adequate revenues for the strengthened United Nations without involving the creation of a United Nations revenue-raising bureaucracy.

11. *Privileges and Immunities.* Annex VI relates to the privileges and immunities of the United Nations itself and of the greatly expanded personnel (including the United Nations Peace Force) which, under the revised Charter, would be in the service of the United Nations.

For the successful operation of an effective world organization to maintain peace, a body of genuinely international servants of high morale is clearly essential. To this end, it seems advisable to provide constitutionally and in some detail not only as to the privileges and immunities of the United Nations as an organization, but also as to the rights and privileges of all United Nations personnel and the limitations thereon.

12. *Bill of Rights.* Annex VII contains a proposed Bill of Rights having a two-fold purpose: (a) to emphasize the limited scope of the strengthened

United Nations by an explicit reservation to the member Nations and their peoples of all powers not delegated by express language or clear implication; and (b) to guarantee that the strengthened United Nations shall not in any manner violate certain basic rights of the individual, that is to say of any person in the world.

The reason for the former is to make doubly sure that the authority of the United Nations shall not be enlarged by indirection, but shall be confined within the limits set forth in the revised Charter.

The latter set of provisions would not extend to any attempted protection of the individual against the action of his own government. It may be argued that the time has come for a world organization to guarantee to every person in the world and against any authority whatever a few fundamental rights—such as exemption from slavery, freedom from torture and the right to be heard before criminal condemnation. We have not, however, thought it wise to attempt so vast a departure; and the proposed guarantees relate solely to possible infringements by the United Nations itself. Against such violations it does seem advisable and proper to have the explicit assurances which would be provided by Annex VII.

The assurances thus provided would include: guarantees, in considerable detail, of the right of fair trial for any person accused of a violation of the revised Charter or of any law or regulation enacted thereunder; a guarantee against double jeopardy, i.e., against being tried twice for the same alleged offense against the United Nations; and also a prohibition against any *ex post facto* law of the United Nations, i.e., against any law making criminal an act which was not criminal at the time the act occurred.

Provisions would also be included against excessive bail and any cruel or unusual punishment, including excessive fines; and the death penalty would be specifically prohibited. In addition, a remedy would be provided against unreasonable detention through a provision securing the right of any person detained for any alleged violation of the revised Charter or of any law or regulation enacted thereunder to be brought without undue delay before the appropriate United Nations tribunal to determine whether there is just cause for his detention.

Unreasonable searches and seizures would also be forbidden, subject to the proviso that this prohibition shall not prejudice searches and seizures clearly necessary or advisable for the enforcement of total disarmament.

Finally, it would be provided that the United Nations shall not restrict or interfere with freedom of conscience or religion; freedom of speech, press or expression in any other form; freedom of association and assembly; or freedom of petition.

The effort has been to provide protection for all the most fundamental individual rights which might conceivably be infringed upon by the United Nations without, however, going into undue detail. Necessarily, as in the case of any constitutional guarantees of the rights of the individual, there will be room for judicial interpretation and application of a United Nations Bill of Rights. This function would be performed by the International

Court of Justice which, in the exercise of its proposed jurisdiction to interpret the revised Charter and to declare void any law, regulation or decision conflicting with the revised Charter as so interpreted, would gradually build up a body of world constitutional law relative to the scope and application of the various provisions of the Bill of Rights.

13. *Ratification.* The proposed requirements for ratification of the revised Charter are: (a) that ratification shall be by five-sixths of the world's nations, including all the twelve largest nations, the aggregate of the populations of the ratifying nations to equal at least five-sixths of the total world population; and (b) that each nation's ratification shall be by its own constitutional processes.

At first glance, the requirement that so very large a preponderance of the nations and people of the world shall be necessary for ratification may appear excessively difficult. But it must be remembered that it would be impossible to accomplish the main purposes of the whole plan, namely, total disarmament and the establishment of an effective system of world law, unless there is a preponderant acceptance throughout the world of the constitutional document which would provide for the necessary world institutions. In practice, this means that the eight or ten principal Powers— especially the Soviet Union and the United States—would first need to agree. But once these Powers (containing together a large majority of the world's people) had reached agreement on the essentials of a revised Charter, there can be no doubt that virtually all the other nations would, as a practical matter, give their assent. Thus the obviously desirable object of obtaining the unanimous or nearly unanimous assent of all the nations appears also to be a practical one, once the indispensable assent of the leading Powers has been obtained.

14. *Amendment.* The proposed requirements concerning the procedure for amendments to the revised Charter are almost as strict as those provided for its ratification. Any future amendments would be submitted for ratification when adopted by a vote of two-thirds of all the Representatives in the General Assembly, whether or not present or voting, or by a two-thirds vote of a General Conference held for that purpose. In order for an amendment to come into effect, ratification by four-fifths of the member Nations would be required, including three-fourths of the twelve member Nations entitled to fifteen or more Representatives in the Assembly.

It will be noted that while the proposed provisions for ratification of the revised Charter would require that the ratifying nations shall include *all* the twelve nations having the largest populations, the provisions relating to the ratification of amendments would require the assent of only three-fourths of those twelve nations.

The reason for this difference is that in order to ensure the necessary overwhelming support for the revised Charter in its initial stage, it is considered essential to have the prior assent of literally all the world's largest nations—defined as the twelve nations with the largest populations. On the other hand, in the case of future amendments *after* the strengthened United

Nations is functioning under the revised Charter, it seems unduly severe to require absolutely unanimous approval by the twelve largest nations. Instead, it seems sufficient to require the assent of no more than a preponderant majority of those nations.

15. *Continued Organs and Agencies.* It should be emphasized that far from impairing the existing organs and agencies of the United Nations, which despite all obstacles have accomplished important results, the intention is not only to preserve but also to strengthen them. Thus the General Assembly would have much greater scope through having the final responsibility for the maintenance of peace, through the new system of representation and voting, and through the new, although limited, power to legislate.

The Security Council would, indeed, be abolished, but would be replaced by the veto-less Executive Council, chosen by and responsible to the General Assembly. The Economic and Social Council and the Trusteeship Council would be continued, with important changes as to their composition and functions, and with much stronger financial support under the new revenue system. The International Court of Justice would be continued with greatly enlarged jurisdiction and greater authority. And as to various other organs, and such agencies as the Food and Agricultural Organization (FAO), the United Nations Educational, Scientific and Cultural Organization (UNESCO), the International Labor Organization (ILO) and the World Health Organization (WHO), the revision would not only provide for their continuance but would also give opportunity for the enlargement of their activities and usefulness.

The intention is not to dispense with anything which has proved useful, but rather to revise, supplement and strengthen the existing structure so that the United Nations will be fully and unquestionably equipped to accomplish its basic purpose—the maintenance of international peace.

6. Compliance in the International System

Oran Young

COMPLIANCE IN DECENTRALIZED SOCIAL SYSTEMS

. . . I want to consider a number of attributes common to all decentralized social systems with respect to compliance. Any conclusions arising from this discussion will be fully applicable to the case of the international system.

Extreme Cases

It is widely assumed that the achievement of compliance in highly decentralized social systems is extremely difficult. Those who make this assumption generally regard some form of hierarchical organization as a necessary condition for compliance, and anarchy as a recipe for extreme disorder.[1] What is the basis of this point of view? I believe it rests on a tendency to single out certain extreme cases and to equate all problems of compliance in decentralized social systems with these extreme cases. To see this, let us consider a concrete example. Imagine a large group of individuals packed together in a crowded subway car. Assume also that there is no official present to detect violations of behavioral prescriptions and to apprehend violators. What are the chances that these individuals will comply with pertinent prescriptions concerning appropriate behavior while entering the car, riding in the car, and exiting from the car?

This situation exhibits a number of characteristics that combine to make the achievement of compliance difficult. First, the members of the group typically do not know each other and have no previous experiences with each other. Consequently, they will not possess stable expectations and viable rules at the outset. Second, interactions of this type are fleeting, and noniterative, so that the discipline of time cannot be expected to work effectively. Third, the membership of the group will fluctuate constantly as individuals enter the car and exit from the car. This makes it difficult for stable expectations to arise out of the situation itself. Fourth, mechanisms for the coordination of expectations are typically weak. It is extremely difficult for any single individual to exhibit effective leadership, and there are no built-in institutional arrangements to facilitate coordination. Fifth, the group will be sufficiently large so that it will be hard to develop effective rules through explicit processes of bargaining and negotiation. The shifting membership of the group will also act as a barrier to the emergence of such processes. Sixth, the members of the group are likely to have highly negative expectations about the behavior of the others because most of them will have had negative experiences in previous situations of a similar kind. Under the circumstances, members of the group are not likely to be willing to take significant chances in the hopes of encouraging compliant behavior on the part of others. . . .

Compliance Without Organization

It is relevant to inquire whether extreme cases of the type considered above constitute the exception or the rule. I see no reason to conclude that the extreme cases are predominant in most social systems. There are numerous situations in which subjects left to their own calculations in the absence of any organized sanctions nevertheless exhibit high levels of compliance. In Switzerland, for example, many public telephones and buses are operated on what amounts to an honor system in which compliance with prescriptions concerning payment is essentially voluntary. And it would not be difficult to compile a long list of other examples in which compliance typically occurs in the absence of any organized compliance mechanisms. How do we account for behavior of this type?

Above all, it seems clear that there are numerous situations in which simple self-interest dictates compliance. That is, when looked at in simple cost-benefit terms, the expected benefits of compliance often outweigh the costs without regard to any prospects of enforcement, inducement, or social pressure. In some cases, this flows from the fact that noncompliance carries its own penalty. This is true, for example, of rules requiring employees to undergo annual physical examinations or students to take introductory courses in a given subject before enrolling in advanced courses. In many other cases, the prospects of counter violations, retaliation, undermining the general viability of the prescriptions in question, or reducing the opportunities for profitable interactions in the future are sufficient to make the expected costs of violations outweigh the possible gains. . . .

There is, however, one major class of situations in which simple self-interest calculations are not sufficient to induce compliance. These are situations in which individuals experience free-rider incentives with respect to the relevant prescriptions. That is, they approve of the existence of the prescriptions and they want others to comply with them. But their preferred outcome would be compliance on the part of everyone else coupled with noncompliance for themselves. This would permit them to enjoy an orderly social system while reaping the benefits of noncompliance at the same time. . . .[2]

The classic response to this problem is the introduction of some arrangement whereby all members of the group agree to allow themselves to be coerced into complying with behavioral prescriptions. . . . I have some doubt, however, whether the introduction of some such enforcement mechanism constitutes a necessary condition for the achievement of compliance under these conditions.[3] Individuals operating in highly decentralized social systems will know that they cannot rely upon a government or some other centralized public authority to maintain order and to preserve the social fabric of the system. Therefore, they are likely to be far more concerned with the social consequences of their behavior than they would be in a centralized system, where such concerns can be allowed to atrophy without causing undue harm, at least in the short run (Taylor, 1976, especially pp. 134–140). . . .

In addition, there is no reason to assume that feelings of obligation will be inoperative as a basis of compliance in highly decentralized social systems, although such feelings may be linked more closely to explicit consent in such systems (Hart, 1958, and Fuller, 1958). Subjects are apt to regard themselves as highly autonomous in decentralized systems and to object to prescriptions that they themselves have not agreed to explicitly. But none of this suggests the irrelevance of obligation as a basis of their compliance. On the contrary, obligations may sometimes become even more binding in decentralized social systems than in centralized ones because there is no authoritative agency capable of exempting a subject from the force of an obligation under special or extenuating circumstances. . . .

Decentralized Institutions

Although decentralized social systems do not have centralized and formally organized governments, it would be a mistake to assume that they entirely lack institutions relating to compliance. A little reflection will make it clear that various institutional arrangements are perfectly compatible with the general condition of decentralization in social systems (Burke, Legatski, and Woodhead, 1975).

It is possible to distinguish at least three characteristics of compliance mechanisms in decentralized systems. First, activities relating to compliance are often performed by a wide range of actors rather than by a single actor specialized to the task of handling compliance problems. For example, some systems have authorized self-help arrangements in which it is entirely acceptable for individual actors to mete out sanctions under specified circumstances. Second, there are many systems in which compliance mechanisms are developed for individual functional areas, with the result that there is no centralized agency concerned with problems of compliance in general. In the international system, there are distinct arrangements for maritime transport, air transport, commodity trade, monetary transactions, specialized problems relating to the management of natural resources, and so forth (Tauber, 1969, and Fisher, 1971). Third, it is common in decentralized social systems for separate institutions to handle different aspects of the overall problem of compliance. Thus, there may be quite distinct arrangements for inspection and information gathering, the application of prescriptions, and the organization of sanctions (Oliver, 1971).

It is not uncommon for systems to develop institutionalized arrangements for inspection and surveillance even in the absence of clear-cut procedures relating to the other aspects of compliance (Falk and Barnet, 1965). The extent to which such arrangements become important will of course be a function of the chances for subjects to engage in clandestine violations. In some areas, it is exceedingly difficult to prevent violations from coming to the attention of others and explicit arrangements for inspection are relatively unimportant. In other cases, however, the knowledge that there is a high probability that violations will be detected may be a substantial incentive for individuals to comply, even if they do not expect sanctions to follow detection.[4]

DISTINCTIVE FEATURES OF THE INTERNATIONAL SYSTEM

. . . The international system is a member of the class of highly decentralized social systems. But it also exhibits a number of distinctive features that have important implications for the achievement of compliance. The purpose of this section is to identify the most critical of these features and to assess their consequences.

Nature of the Subjects

. . . No matter where we draw the line regarding membership in the international system, several points about international actors are worth noting with reference to the problem of compliance. First, the number of actors in the system is relatively small, no more than a few hundred by most criteria of membership in use at this time. While the system does not belong to the category of small groups as that concept is generally employed in social psychology, the number of actors involved is small compared with the massive numbers of autonomous actors we are used to thinking of in discussions of domestic societies. Above all, this means that it is possible to focus on the behavior of well-defined subjects rather than conceptualizing the problem of compliance largely in actuarial terms. Moreover, it suggests that the actors will typically consider the behavior of specific others rather than some undifferentiated environment in making computations regarding the costs and benefits of compliance. That is, they will make explicit calculations concerning the expected reactions of other individual members of the system in making choices between compliance and violation.[5] Because of this, the international equivalent of social pressure can be expected to be an important basis of compliance in this system, even in the absence of organized agencies dealing with enforcement and inducement (Kiesler and Kiesler, 1969).

Equally important is the fact that the actors in the international system are collective or corporate entities. Following the orientation of most theories of choice, I have been proceeding so far in my analysis of compliance on the assumption that the subjects of behavioral prescriptions are more or less integrated individuals (or at least that it is reasonable to think of them in this way). Thus, I have generally predicated my analysis on the premises that subjects are capable of formulating clear-cut preference orderings over sets of alternatives and that their behavior does not involve the coordination of a number of autonomous or semiautonomous component units. But such premises are clearly inappropriate when it comes to an examination of the external behavior of the members of the international system. In this case, external behavior is clearly a product of relatively complex internal processes (Allison, 1971 and Steinbruner, 1974). . . .

The basic implication of this first perspective for the problem of compliance is that collective entities are not likely to follow a consistent or undeviating path with respect to their external behavior. Unless one internal actor achieves an overwhelmingly dominant position, the entity is apt to shift back and forth between compliance and violation in response to the dynamics of its internal bargaining processes (Neustadt, 1970).

A second perspective on the external behavior of collective entities focuses on bureaucratic behavior and the operation of organizational routines (March and Simon, 1958). Large and complex collective entities invariably develop elaborate organizational arrangements and procedures that govern their external behavior. . . . Once a behavioral prescription becomes a standard operating procedure or norm of the bureaucracy, the tendency to follow rules on a routinized basis will take over as a determinant of external behavior (Chayes, 1972).

A third approach to the external behavior of collective entities is to view them as small groups or teams. Here the idea is to identify a small number of individual actors who constitute the crucial decision makers within the entity and to focus on the interactions among these actors. The external behavior of the entity then becomes a product of group dynamics, and it is possible to apply various insights from social psychology and the theory of teams to this problem (Thibaut and Kelley, 1959 and Buchanan, 1965). . . .

Thus, a special feature of the compliance problem for collective entities is the question of who is ultimately responsible for violations (Taylor, 1970a, and Taylor, 1970b). If the entity itself is held responsible, individuals are not likely to feel the force of sanctions or social pressure strongly. Yet, it is ultimately the actions of individuals which determine the external behavior of collective entities. Alternatively, if individuals are made responsible for the behavior of collectivities, other problems arise. One approach is to designate the sovereign as the responsible agent. But how is it possible to sanction a sovereign, and what is to be done when sovereignty resides with a group rather than with an individual? . . . While it would be wrong to overemphasize this factor, the prospect of escaping the immediate consequences of violations will undoubtedly serve to make individuals within collective entities less cautious about noncompliant behavior in some situations.

Character of the Prescriptions

The behavioral prescriptions that arise in the international system share numerous characteristics with similar prescriptions operative in other social systems. Nevertheless, there are several attributes of these prescriptions which are distinctive. International prescriptions commonly take the form of understandings, agreements, or treaties among specified sets of actors in contrast to more general or open-ended rules for the system as a whole. That is, the principal prescriptions of the international system are relatively closed agreements among well-defined groups of actors rather than broadly formulated rules applicable to any actor who finds himself in a given situation. In this sense, international prescriptions bear a distinct resemblance to contracts, in contrast to laws, in municipal systems. Moreover, these agreements typically deal with the problem of compliance in an *ad hoc* fashion; the arrangements they encompass are limited strictly to the agreements in question. The prevalence of such agreements, therefore, does not encourage the emergence of more centralized institutions pertaining to compliance.

Related to this is the fact that explicit consent is of central importance to the operation of behavioral prescriptions in the international system. Thus, the actors generally reject ideas of obligation emanating from mere membership in the system or various forms of tacit consent (Pitkin, 1965, and Pitkin, 1966). In many other social systems, when an individual actor becomes a member, he is assumed to accept the prevailing set of behavioral prescriptions in the system unless he makes a specific point of rejecting one or more of them. In the international system, however, new members can and often do reject existing prescriptions, and there is no automatic presumption that they have accepted them simply by accepting membership in the system.[6] The critical role of explicit consent is of course obvious with respect to agreements and treaties. However, the role of explicit consent is unusually important in this system even in the case of other types of prescriptions. For example, there has been some debate about the extent to which such things as United Nations resolutions can be regarded as binding on all members of the international system.[7] I do not mean to dismiss these devices as insignificant, but it seems to me that it would be a serious mistake to ignore the differences between the international system and most domestic social systems with respect to this question of explicit consent. Among other things, this implies that the set of widely accepted behavioral prescriptions will be smaller in the international system than it is in other social systems in which ideas of tacit consent are more viable.

Next, the behavioral prescriptions of the international system are more afflicted by ambiguity than those of many other social systems. In my judgment, the crucial source of this ambiguity does not lie in the often lamented fact that the international system lacks the centralized institutions of government we commonly associate with political communities (Mendlovitz, 1975). I would argue that this feature of the set of international prescriptions stems from two sources that are more fundamental than that. First, the system is both heterogeneous, in the sense that the interests of the actors diverge widely, and volatile, in the sense that patterns of relationships among the actors change rapidly. For these reasons, the status of individual prescriptions is responsive to changing relationships within the system itself, and it is often difficult to determine at any given time how specific prescriptions are regarded by various members of the system. Second, many important international prescriptions are intrinsically difficult to put into operation in real-world situations. It is simple enough to ban all nuclear tests in the atmosphere. But consider such prescriptions as the rules against aggression, the rules pertaining to nonintervention in the internal affairs of other actors, the rules concerning the recognition of new governments, the rules relating to the status of nonbelligerency, and the rules governing the conduct of overt hostilities (Kaplan and Katzenbach, 1961, especially part II). In all these cases, the nature of the behavior in question makes it difficult to eliminate substantial elements of ambiguity surrounding the relevant prescriptions.

In many social systems, violations of behavioral prescriptions remain largely private affairs; they do not become matters of widespread public attention. In some cases, such violations simply go undetected. In others, they are not of interest to many members of the system even if they are detected. In the international system, however, the violation of behavioral prescriptions is typically a much more public affair. Partly, this stems from the fact that the system is a relatively small one in which each actor is generally well aware of what the others are doing.[8] It is also attributable to the fact that many international violations automatically become matters of public record. This is true, for example, of most violations of the rules against aggression or the rules pertaining to the status of nonbelligerency.

But there are many cases at the international level in which the violating actor himself must sooner or later reveal his noncompliant behavior in order to reap the benefits associated with the violation. Thus, it is typically impossible to reap strategic advantages from violating an arms control agreement unless the violations are ultimately revealed in some dramatic fashion.[9] And the actor who violates an agreement to refrain from producing specified goods for an international market cannot benefit from his noncompliant behavior unless he reveals his violations openly.

Finally, I want to say something about the consequences of violating international prescriptions. The violation of any behavioral prescription is apt to be taken seriously by the actors immediately involved. But the distinctive feature of international violations is that they are far more likely to have extensive collateral or systemic consequences than violations in other social systems. For example, the consequences of a murder in a typical domestic society seldom extend beyond the families and friends of the individuals immediately involved, unless the victim is a figure of critical importance in the society. An act of aggression at the international level, however, may precipitate violent conflict involving many members of the system. And most members of the system are apt to feel the impact of such violations, at least indirectly. This feature of the international system can be expected to have important implications for the problem of compliance. Briefly, all those actors who are likely to experience collateral damage from the noncompliant behavior of others can ordinarily be counted upon to exert considerable pressure for compliance in specific situations. While the international system lacks a centralized public authority, therefore, it does possess a well-informed "public," which can be counted on to express concern about the occurrence of violations and which can be expected to exert pressures for compliance on potential violators.

International Institutions

It is undoubtedly true that the members of the international system are generally left to their own calculations in making choices concerning compliance. That is, behavior in this realm is not deeply affected by the activities of formal institutions organized at the systemic level. This is not to say that the subjects of international prescriptions will engage in noncompliant behavior lightly. It merely suggests that the activities of formal international institutions seldom play a crucial role in their decisions about compliance and violation. Nevertheless, it would be a mistake to conclude that international institutions are entirely irrelevant. The United Nations hardly conforms to our image of a centralized public authority. It was never intended to operate in this fashion, and its actual performance falls short of the relatively modest expectations incorporated in the Charter (Nicholas, 1962). Even so, actors in the international system cannot afford to ignore completely the actions of the Organization in making their own choices about compliance. Moreover, there is a considerable array of more specialized and decentralized institutions in the international system which have some relevance to the problem of compliance. The fact that these institutions are highly decentralized makes it easy to overlook their significance, but in fact they add up to a rather extensive network.

Inspection systems have been experimented with in a number of areas at the international level. For example, there are relatively well-developed inspection arrangements in some technical realms such as international air transport (Tauber, 1969), and substantial efforts have been made to introduce inspection systems relating to more highly politicized matters like the control of armaments (Falk and Barnet, 1965). Underlying many of these arrangements is the premise that inspection can play a significant role in eliciting compliance even in the absence of well-developed institutions for the organization of sanctions. Partly, this premise rests on the idea that other actors in the system are apt to react in such a way as to reduce the benefits of violations once they become aware of their occurrence. In some cases, however, it is also predicated on the idea of reducing the chances for an actor to gain major advantages through clandestine violations that can be revealed dramatically later on after extensive preparations have been made. It is worth noting here that considerable efforts have been made to develop international inspection procedures that are politically acceptable to the actors involved. Often this is essentially a matter of regulating certain externalities associated with international inspection. For example, attempts have been made in the realm of arms control to devise inspection systems capable of detecting violations of the relevant agreements without simultaneously obtaining too much information about the military preparations or other aspects of the societies in which the inspections are being carried out. Finally, it is important to note that international inspection is a function of the state of technology as well as the nature of the specific activities in question. Thus, there are cases in which technological advances have the effect of reducing the importance of international inspection systems by making it less and less feasible for actors to engage in otherwise undetected violations. Here too the area of arms control provides clear-cut examples.[10]

Traditionally, the application of international prescriptions was treated as a process that could not be subjected to institutionalization at the system level. The doctrine of state sovereignty led directly to the conclusion that each member of the system was to be its own judge concerning questions relating to compliance with international prescriptions. More recently, this tradition has weakened, and various steps have been taken to develop international institutions capable of providing authoritative judgments concerning alleged violations of such prescriptions. The International Court of Justice deals with issues of this type, and the United Nations itself has acquired some role in the application of the relevant prescriptions. It would be a serious error to overemphasize these developments; the Court is typically bypassed in important cases, and the decisions of the United Nations are frequently not accepted as authoritative. But the current situation certainly differs significantly from that obtaining in the nineteenth century (Rosenne, 1973). An important recent trend in this area concerns the authorization of individual members of the system to make applications of international prescriptions under well-defined conditions and according to agreed-upon standards. Such procedures are of course highly decentralized, but they differ fundamentally from the traditional arrangement based on unrestricted self-application. Arrangements of this type are most appropriate with respect to highly iterative activities that occur within the territorial jurisdiction of individual actors. Developments along these lines have already occurred in connection with some of the commodity agreements (Fisher, 1971). And there are trends in this direction in such areas as the management of marine fisheries and the regulation of various forms of pollution (Burke, Legatski, and Woodhead, 1975).

The organization of sanctions at the international level has followed much the same course as the application of prescriptions (Doxey, 1971). The traditional system was based almost exclusively on the idea of unrestricted self-help. Each actor was authorized to respond in its own way to the alleged violations of others, subject only to the most general rules pertaining to appropriate responses (for example, the criterion of proportionality). Here too, the twentieth century has witnessed some efforts to introduce more centralized institutional arrangements. But these have been even less successful than similar efforts relating to the application of prescriptions, and it seems highly unlikely that significant centralizing tendencies will emerge during the foreseeable future. As in the case of the application of prescriptions, perhaps the most important trend concerns the gradual emergence of decentralized sanctioning processes. This trend involves authorizing individual members of the system to organize sanctions against violators on the basis of standards that are relatively well-defined and explicitly accepted by the community. Such arrangements may be accompanied by the development of more centralized agencies (for example, within the United Nations) designed to oversee and to coordinate the employment of sanctions by individual actors. Significant developments along these lines have already occurred in some functional areas, such as international air transport (Tauber, 1969). In other areas (for example, the control of marine pollution), there are good reasons to believe that we will experience increased movement in this direction (*Yale Law Journal, 1973*). In my judgment, the impact of this trend is likely to grow rather than to decline during the foreseeable future.

International Externalities

What sorts of unintended side effects are generated by the highly decentralized systems of compliance mechanisms I have been describing in this section? At the level of the international system, it seems clear that it will not be necessary to worry about many of the types of negative externalities traditionally associated with the operation of compliance mechanisms. These externalities flow from the behavior of highly centralized public authorities, and there is nothing remotely resembling a set of institutions of this sort in the international system. But this does not mean that the problem of externalities can be ignored completely in thinking about compliance with international prescriptions.

The standard argument in this regard rests on the proposition that the international system is characterized by extensive ambiguity concerning the prevailing set of behavioral prescriptions and by generally low levels of compliance with those prescriptions. This, it is often argued, generates a variety of unintended by-products whose consequences are of far-reaching importance at the international level. These include such things as a generalized lack of predictability in the interactions among individual members of the system as well as a constant danger of escalating conflicts. In short, it is widely believed that many of the phenomena commonly associated with an uncooperative or even Hobbesian "state of nature" actually occur in the international system and that this situation is attributable to the absence of a more highly organized and centralized public authority.

I do not wish to assert that this line of reasoning is wholly without foundation. Nevertheless, I believe that it is seriously defective and that it overlooks some of the real virtues of highly decentralized social systems. To begin with, it is not at all clear that the level of compliance is strikingly low in the international system, although dramatic violations do occur with some frequency. On the contrary, it is a demonstrable fact that most acknowledged international prescriptions are complied with by the relevant actors most of the time. . . .

It is well worth noting that decentralization at the level of the international system has important compensating virtues, even if it is conducive to the occurrence of costly violations from time to time. Not only is it true that the negative externalities associated with the operation of highly centralized public authorities are notably absent in this system. It is also true that the members of the international system have far more freedom than the members of most other social systems to develop autonomously and to establish their own preferences and priorities. Efforts to compare these compensating virtues with the costs of decentralization raise a normative issue that I cannot of course hope to resolve here. But there is no doubt in my mind that it would be a mistake to condemn the decentralized compliance mechanisms of the international system without examining carefully the benefits as well as the costs of this response to the problem of compliance.

NOTES

1. To illustrate, compare the views of Hobbes (1962) on this question with those of leading anarchist thinkers like Kropotkin. For an account of anarchist thinking on such questions see Guerin (1970).

2. The issue here is analogous to the collective goods problem. See Olson (1965) and Frohlich, Oppenheimer, and Young (1971).

3. Note also that one might question whether the introduction of such an enforcement mechanism constitutes a *sufficient* condition.

4. I am reminded in this context of the traditional Harvard aphorism that it is acceptable for a gentleman to do as he pleases so long as he is not caught doing it.

5. For an extended discussion of this phenomenon in connection with the concept of strategic interaction see Young (1975).

6. This is so, in practice, despite the provision of Article 4 of the United Nations Charter, which specifies that a willingness to ". . . accept the obligations contained in the present Charter" is a condition for membership in the Organization.

7. For an expansive view of the significance of United Nations resolutions see Falk (1966).

8. The same phenomenon occurs in small communities composed of individual human beings. For a striking case study see Wylie (1974).

9. Note, however, that this is not always the case. Secret testing to maintain technological capabilities may help to set the minds of policymakers at rest even if it is never revealed. Similarly, cheating on the permissible number of strategic delivery vehicles might have the psychological effect of increasing confidence in the effectiveness of deterrence even (or perhaps especially) if the cheating is never detected. I owe this point to the comments of Robert L. Butterworth.

10. For example, recent improvements in seismology make it increasingly possible to detect nuclear explosions without on-site inspection. And orbital satellites have dramatically reduced the chances of concealing a variety of military activities.

REFERENCES

Allison, Graham. 1971. *The Essence of Decision* (Boston, Little, Brown).

Buchanan, James M. 1965. "An Economic Theory of Clubs," *Economica*, n.s. 32, pp. 1–14.

Burke, William T., Richard Legatski, and William Woodhead. 1975. *National and International Law Enforcement in the Ocean* (Seattle, University of Washington Press).

Chayes, Abram. 1972. "An Enquiry into the Workings of Arms Control Agreements," *Harvard Law Review*, vol. 85, pp. 905–969.

Doxey, Margaret P. 1971. *Economic Sanctions and International Enforcement* (London, Oxford University Press).

Falk, Richard. 1966. "On the Quasi-Legislative Competence of the General Assembly," *American Journal of International Law*, vol. 60, pp. 782–791.

Falk, Richard, and Richard Barnet, eds. 1965. *Security in Disarmament* (Princeton, Princeton University Press).

Fisher, Bart S. 1971. "Enforcing Export Quota Agreements: The Case of Coffee," *Harvard International Law Journal*, vol. 12, pp. 401–435.

Frohlich, Norman, Joe. A. Oppenheimer, and Oran Young. 1971. *Political Leadership and Collective Goods.* (Princeton, Princeton University Press).

Fuller, Lon L. 1958. "Positivism and Fidelity to Law: A Reply to Professor Hart," *Harvard Law Review*, vol. 71, pp. 630–671.

Guerin, Daniel. 1970. *Anarchism: From Theory to Practice* (New York, Monthly Review Press).

Hart, H.L.A. 1958. "Positivism and the Separation of Law and Morals," *Harvard Law Review*, vol. 71, pp. 593–629.

Hobbes, Thomas. 1962. *Leviathan*, original date 1651 (New York, Macmillan).

Kaplan, Morton and Nicholas deB. Katzenbach. 1961. *The Political Foundations of International Law* (New York, Wiley).

Kiesler, C.A. and Sara B. Kiesler. 1969. *Conformity* (Reading, Addison-Wesley).

March, James G. and Herbert A. Simon. 1958. *Organizations* (New York, Wiley).

Mendlovitz, Saul H., ed. 1975. *On the Creation of a Just World Order* (New York, Free Press).

Neustadt, Richard. 1970. *Alliance Politics* (New York, Columbia University Press).

Nicholas, H.G. 1962. *The United Nations as a Political Institution* 2nd ed. (London, Oxford University Press).

Oliver, Edward F. 1971. "Wet War—North Pacific," *San Diego Law Review*, vol. 8, pp. 621-638.

Olson, Mancur, Jr. 1965. *The Logic of Collective Action* (Cambridge, Harvard University Press).

Pitkin, Hanna. 1965. "Obligation and Consent—I," *American Political Science Review*, vol. LIX, pp. 990-999.

———. 1966. "Obligation and Consent—II," *American Political Science Review*, vol. LX, pp. 39-52.

Rosenne, Shabtai. 1973. *The World Court* 3rd rev. ed. (Dobbs Ferry, N.Y., Oceana).

Steinbruner, John. 1974. *The Cybernetic Theory of Decision* (Princeton, Princeton University Press).

Tauber, Ronald S. 1969. "Enforcement of IATA Agreements," *Harvard International Law Journal*, vol. 10, pp. 1-33.

Taylor, Michael. 1976. *Anarchy and Cooperation* (London, Wiley).

Thibaut, John W. and Harold W. Kelley. 1959. *The Social Psychology of Groups* (New York, Wiley).

Wylie, Laurence. 1974. *Village in the Vaucluse* 3rd ed. (Cambridge, Harvard University Press).

Yale Law Journal. 1973. "New Perspectives on International Environmental Law," vol. 82, pp. 1659-1680.

Young, Oran. 1975. *Bargaining: Formal Theories of Negotiation* (Urbana, University of Illinois Press).

Varying Perspectives, Emerging Structure

In Chapter 3 we consider how international law evolved in the centuries since Grotius's time. Throughout the history of international law, its legal nature has repeatedly been drawn into question. This partly reflects the alleged "ineffectiveness" of international law, including the absence of an enforcement capability, which has led some critics to contend that international law is not genuine law but rather a species of morality or a framework of prudence and convenience. Such allegations concern both problems of order in international life and problems of theory concerning the nature of law. Both sets of issues are important to consider throughout the book, although we focus upon them as the particular concerns of this chapter.

The first selection in Chapter 3, by Richard Falk, depicts a basic normative tension in the international legal order: state-centered law premised on sovereign consent (Westphalia) versus community-centered law premised on the existence of a general will and global public interests (UN Charter). This tension has always been present in some form, but since the creation of the League of Nations after World War I, the community-centered pole of legal order has been associated with the existence and constitutional framework of a general international organizational structure. The interplay of these two types of law also involves the transitional challenge in which no single explanation of law is entirely satisfactory. In this regard, we await a new synthesis, one we have labeled "the Grotian moment."

Wolfgang Friedmann's contribution clearly identifies the expanded scope and puts forth the case for the "relevance" of modern international law. Drawing a fundamental distinction between the law of the political framework (law of coexistence), the law of cooperation, and the law of community comprising the increasing functional interdependencies created by modern life, Friedmann offers a needed corrective to the "cops and robbers" model of law that often underlies the popular conviction that international law is not really a proper form of law. Friedmann's framework of three types of law is an elaboration of Falk's argument in the previous selection.

The next selection is taken from the writings of Mohammed Bedjaoui, an Algerian jurist and diplomat, who is currently a judge at the International Court of Justice (at The Hague) and is well-known as an articulate champion of Third World viewpoints concerning international legal issues. Bedjaoui is prominent among those calling for a revitalization of international law through a much more serious effort to accommodate the needs and expectations of the non-Western peoples of Asia, Africa, and Latin America. Whether the Westphalian orientation, or that associated with what Friedmann calls the law of coexistence, can make the kind of adjustments implicit in Bedjaoui's analysis is an important issue to bear in mind. There is also the further issue as to whether the international legal system can be "functional" and "legitimate" for the Third World without such adjustments.

A problem appears when "law" and "policy" are not analytically distinguished despite their obvious interdependencies. Rejecting traditional legal categories, Myres S. McDougal and Harold D. Lasswell in the final selection treat "law" as a matter of degree and bestow legal significance on "policy" to the extent that policies set forth by officials and leaders are interpreted as contributing to a postulated overarching goal of human dignity. Even if complete information about the value effects of a decision were available, such an appraisal based on the consequences of public choice upon human dignity can be performed only if problems of assessing value effects and of weighting competing values can be solved. To suppose a solution involves a heroic assumption that is not made much less heroic by the reliance placed by McDougal and Lasswell upon the findings of social science. These findings, even if otherwise conclusive, (and they generally are not) would certainly be incapable of assessing value tradeoffs in an objective manner. For instance, no economist can tell us convincingly how much inflation should be traded off against various quantities of reduced unemployment (despite the existence of the Phillips Curve). The problem of unintended consequences, especially in an arena in which even Great Powers have often little control over outcomes, makes the assessment of law according to a sliding scale of value effects a nearly hopeless enterprise. Thus, as important as McDougal and Lasswell's liberation of legal thinking from the fetters of formalism might be, some of the analyses inspired by their framework fail to persuade us about the content of law. Instead of firm guidance provided by legal rules in specific contexts, this alternative policy orientation encourages the insinuation of personal preferences in the garb of legal analysis. This tendency is unavoidable to some extent for any legal theory. And, indeed, one of the main points of criticism made by legal realism against other varieties of natural law centers on the inability to overcome subjective applications of law. Yet legal realism itself seems questionable as a jurisprudential theory on these same grounds, given its failure to conceive adequately of the nature of discretion in decisionmaking settings, overstating, as it does, the absence of boundaries and understating the role of rule guidance in stabilizing expectations about the proper outcome of legal disputes.

McDougal and Lasswell also help us grasp the extent to which ideological perspectives shape (and distort) ideas about international law, especially the central ideological encounter between East and West, between communism (Marxism-Leninism) and liberalism (or capitalism). It seems evident that the emphasis by McDougal and Lasswell on "human dignity" as the appropriate overall value focus involves taking ideological sides, choosing West over East. It is not clear whether this *ideological* level of discussion corresponds to the *geopolitical* patterns of conflict in which opposing power-centers compete for maximum control and influence in relation to foreign societies and markets as well as ocean and space domains. Whether ideological orientation, as such, works for or against compliance with international law is difficult to establish, although a recent militant ideological viewpoint would be likely to emphasize its repudiation of portions of the normative status quo.

The selection by Gidon Gottlieb, "The Nature of International Law," explores in some detail the special quality of international law as law. Gottlieb explains clearly why voluntary patterns of compliance are so central to the effective operation of international law. He shares with McDougal and Lasswell a belief in the significance of decisionmaking—that is, with respect to how and why decisions relating to authority are made and upheld. Such an orientation frees the concept of law from the positivist preoccupation with "sanctions" and implementation mechanisms that for a long time denied international law the status of proper law. This reorientation of perspective is not merely a matter of definitional convenience but has deep repercussions for our understanding of law in general, particularly for law dealing with "horizontal" ordering in the domestic arena, as is amply demonstrated by Gottlieb's analysis. His taxonomy of two ideal types of law (the "authority model" and the "acceptance model") helps break down and overcome the increasingly misleading distinction between "internal" and "external" reality—a distinction that reflects deeply held views that domestic law is true law, whereas international law is, at best, primitive or inferior in some way. Gottlieb also effectively makes the point that even for many areas of domestic law, such as certain areas of labor law, the acceptance model characteristic of international law is more descriptive of the actual legal process than is the authority model associated with a discrete enforcement capability. Thus not only can international law be called "true" law, but new insights into the process of legal ordering in the domestic as well as international arena can be gained. This is particularly important in the context of decisionmaking, in which the problem of guidance by rules— legal as well as others—is investigated.

Gottlieb wrestles with two problems that are significant for an under-standing of international law, namely, the problem of the relationship between law and policy, and the nature of the authoritative and effective decisionmaking process that the latter identifies with law in the international arena. If international law is a process of claim and counterclaim by which relevant decisionmakers pursue conflicting goals through policies on behalf of their constituencies, then this process can be traced and thereby appraised as "law" only if the identity of the relevant decisionmakers entitled to make such claims is adequately clarified. But clarification itself presupposes legal standards of recognition for the identification of the decisionmakers, standards that are external to the claiming process. Since the identification of such structures underlying the decision process is often the most hotly contested problem of international law, the identification and appraisal of claims and counterclaims as law become problematic. This dilemma is analogous to the problem of defining law as "what courts do" while failing to define what institutions shall count as a court, by law.

In terms of legal theory, our hope is that world order advocates will eventually help bring into existence a more humane set of global arrangements responsive to the tensions and dangers of the present situation. Such an endeavor recalls Grotius's earlier achievement in hastening the emergence of a new international order from the shambles of the Holy Roman Empire and the savageries of religious wars.

QUESTIONS FOR DISCUSSION AND REFLECTION: CHAPTER 3

1. Is Wolfgang Friedmann's image of a three-tiered interacting structure of international law helpful for the analysis of the contemporary international legal order? Does Friedmann's failure to emphasize diverse cultural perspectives limit the usefulness of his analysis? How would Gottlieb's approach to international law be helpful in answering such questions?

2. Bedjaoui emphasizes the failure of the international legal order to be fair and equitable between rich and poor states. Does this emphasis interfere with our understanding of the functions of law, or does it facilitate a better conceptualization of the progressive development of international law?

3. Is it realistic to expect a coherent and unified view of international law and its functions given the scope and depth of the political changes that have occurred in the international system since the end of World War II? How would you assess, in this context, McDougal and Lasswell's argument that the ideological differences between the socialist bloc and the West can be clarified and narrowed by the application of social science methods to the analysis of legal questions?

4. What is your view of the strengths and weaknesses of McDougal and Lasswell's focus on the decisionmaking *process* as opposed to the substantive content of the rules guiding decisionmakers in the international arena?

SELECTED BIBLIOGRAPHY: CHAPTER 3

R. P. Anand, *The New States and International Law* (Delhi: Vikas Press, 1972).
Adda Bozeman, *The Future of Law in a Multicultural World* (Princeton, N.J.: Princeton University Press, 1971).

Isaak Ismail Dore, *International Law and the Superpowers* (New Brunswick, N.J.: Rutgers University Press, 1984).

Taslim O. Elias, *Africa and the Development of International Law* (Leiden, Neth.: Sijthoff and Dobbs Ferry, N.Y.: Oceana, 1972).

Samuel S. Kim, *China, the U.N. and World Order* (Princeton, N.J.: Princeton University Press, 1979), especially chapter 8.

Manfred Lachs, *Teachers and Teaching of International Law* (The Hague: Nijhoff, 1982).

Richard Lillich, *Economic Coercion and the New International Economic Order* (Charlesville, Va.: Michie, 1976).

7. The Interplay of Westphalia and Charter Conceptions of International Legal Order

Richard Falk

There are many useful ways to speculate about the future.[1] This chapter is concerned with identifying certain evolutionary trends that seem to be influencing the shape and substance of the international legal order.[2] Inquiry is organized around a comparison between the Westphalia and the Charter conceptions of international legal order. The Westphalia conception, taking its name from the peace treaties of 1648, constitutes the classical framework of legal constraint postulated to regulate a highly decentralized world of sovereign states; this conception yields a permissive, voluntaristic system of law stressing matters of the allocation of competence among sovereign states.

The Charter conception, taking its name from the United Nations Charter, constitutes a major modification of the Westphalia system in a number of critical respects bearing on the status of war, the role of national sovereignty, and the degree to which authority structures are centralized.[3]

In the contemporary international system the Charter conception is far from fully realized, the Westphalia conception is far from fully displaced.[4] The purpose of calling attention to these two conceptions is to specify the prospects for a fuller realization of the Charter conception of international legal order in the years ahead by pointing to some relevant trends in belief and attitude. To promote this purpose, however, it is essential to emphasize the extent to which Westphalia considerations continue to prevail as a consequence of the national control of military power and human loyalty. The focus upon the interplay between these two conceptions of normative orientation is intended to contribute a basis for speculation about the future of international legal order. . . .

THE COORDINATES OF ANALYSIS

What Is the International Legal Order?

The international legal order is here conceived of as an aggregate conception embodying those structures and processes by which authority is created, applied, and transformed in international society. The distinctive focus, then, is upon the authority system as an attribute of the wider extralegal conception of an international system. Authority is understood to encompass established expectations and traditions about who is entitled to make and implement decisions; the authority perspective also is concerned with patterns of compliance that suggest a positive, if imprecise, correlation between the authoritative decision and the behavior undertaken in relation thereto.[5] In effect, the international legal order is a socio-historical product of convergent perspectives of formal authority and actual behavior.[6] The decentralized character of the present system of international legal order complicates the task of specifying the prevailing profile of authority. It is difficult, for instance, to deal realistically with "spheres of influence" that are tacitly and reciprocally acknowledged by principal sovereign states as creating special prerogatives about the exercise of national power.[7] For instance, the role of the United States in Latin America or the role of the Soviet Union in Eastern Europe are critical aspects of the constituted authority system that exists in international life even though these roles cannot be explained in terms of formal norms or even by reference to formal processes of decision.[8] To exclude these patterns of control from a conception of the international legal order tends to produce an artificially formalistic and legalistic conception, one that over-clarifies the distinction between the realm of law and the realm of politics in international affairs. To assimilate completely *de facto* regimes of control into a conception of the international legal order, however, would endanger a confusion of law and power such that it would no longer be meaningful to distinguish the standards of international law from the patterns of international politics.[9] We seek here an intermediate position, one that maintains the distinctiveness of legal order while managing to be responsive to the extralegal setting of politics, history, and morality.[10] In this spirit, the study of international law—as the specialized and disciplined inquiry into the structure and process of authority—gives the legal dimension in international relations the status of a quasi-dependent variable. By quasi-dependence is meant that law both tends to reflect and to be shaped by the international system as a whole and serves or may serve as a strategy by which to participate in or transform the international system.[11] As a consequence of such a conception of the international legal order it is essential to identify the wider systemic setting and to consider the strategic potentialities available in the various arenas of authority for system-reform and system-transformation.[12]

In this chapter attention will be given to the general characteristics of the present system of international legal order: its most characteristic and general level of existence.[13] The relatively permanent elements of structure are used as delimiting features: the number and kind of units, bases of international obligation, external aims and domestic public order systems, stakes and modalities of conflict, frameworks of constraint, and forms of conflict settlement.[14] Attention will also be given to dynamic elements of process: emerging units, converging and diverging external aims, alterations in the pattern of conflict, and shifts in loyalty and belief. . . .

It would seem most desirable to adopt a comparative method for the study of alternative systems of international legal order. Such a comparative method facilitates sharper delineation of the present system and a better appreciation of the relative desirability and attainability of alternatives to it.

The consideration of several models of the international legal order calls attention to the transition problem, i.e. to the problem of system-change on the macro-level of international society that is entailed in moving from an existing system to a preferred system. . . .[15]

To carry forward this method of inquiry we will postulate five highly abstract preferences that may on occasion interact nonharmoniously so as to make an explanation of priorities necessary in each setting of decision:

1. The minimization of violence;
2. The promotion of human rights of individuals and groups, especially national autonomy and racial equality;
3. The transfer of wealth and income from rich states to poor states;
4. The equitable participation of diverse cultures, regions, and ideologies in a composite system of global order;
5. The growth of supranational and international institutions.[16]

Priorities could be postulated in noncontextual or categorical form such that, for instance, recourse to violence is never justifiable. It seems preferable, however, to establish priorities within specific contexts of choice or to endorse authoritative procedures as competent to establish priorities. For instance, an international institution may be endowed with the competence to authorize violence to promote collective security, anti-colonialism, or racial equality. The Southern African issues of racism and colonialism illustrate a setting wherein it appears increasingly appropriate for community institutions to suspend prohibitions upon violence so as to secure other valued ends.[17] The failure of the Security Council of the United Nations in 1961 to oppose India's forcible seizure of Goa was a vivid instance in which a constituted international organ established a priority schedule on an *ad hoc* basis.[18]

In studying the future of the international legal order several prominent issues emerge: (1) alternative conceptions; (2) transition prospects and strategies; and (3) trends and countertrends within the existing system; (3) may prove to be the most rewarding focus as the prospects for (1) and (2) are not very favorable. No major structural modifications of international society appear likely to occur in the twentieth century unless a general nuclear war takes place. Over a longer term, an evolutionary erosion of the existing national locus of power and loyalty seem likely to take place, but such trends are indefinite and their eventual impact difficult to anticipate. The existing system of international legal order appears resistant to drastic change through conscious redirection, whether in the form of agreement by sovereign states or by a transnational political movement. The strategic variable in assessing prospects for change is the extent to which capabilities to wage war will remain under the control of national governments, and the further extent to which the leadership of a few of these governments have predominant capabilities as compared to the remainder. Of course, many sub-variables are associated with the future of the nation-state as the organizing power center of international life.[19] It is especially important to gauge regional integration, cosmopolitan belief systems, and the proliferation of nuclear weapons technology in relation to the role and function of the state. . . .

World order literature is often flawed by its sentimental naiveté, by its implicit faith that what appears desirable is automatically attainable.[20] Little attention is given in this aspirational literature to problems of transforming power relations and redirecting loyalty patterns in international society.[21] And yet these structures of power relations and loyalty patterns are typical ingredients of a social system capable of maintaining itself against pressures for change. Reasoned persuasion does not by itself provide any realistic prospect for altering the structure of international society.[22] World order analyses have in the past emphasized some sort of plan that is supposed to appeal to the rational intellect as preferable to the present system of world order.[23] The projection of a preferred future system of world order is not likely to be relevant to the historical future unless the awesome problem of attainability is confronted with great seriousness. Such a problem is, above all, one of studying the transfer of power and authority under various kinds of functional stress and depicting the nature of a new cosmopolitan ideology that would dissipate the hold of the state upon the loyalty of the individual and substitute new myths and symbols capable of arousing widespread support.[24]

The consequence of a more practical orientation, then, is to refocus a study of the future of world order on the specific problems of political engineering: What is desired? Under what conditions can it be attained? What can be done to bring these conditions about? In a world of hostile ideologies, of states at different levels of economic and political development, and of different patterns of belief and fear there is bound to be a very limited consensus on means, ends, and prospects. Without consensus the only strategy of directed change for a system as decentralized as international society would appear to entail coercion leading to wider systems of domination—imperial world order systems—lacking any genuine sense of community attachment by many caught within the imperial net. A dilemma is posed by the difficulties of consensus-formation and the dangers and deficiencies of domination that expresses the basic quality of the current international situation. Bipolarity on the fundamental level of stalemating any effort by a principal sovereign state to achieve overarching domination is a further aspect of the dilemma of world order. The diagnostic consequence is to predicate the persistence of the present international system, including its quasi-dependent authority pattern.

FIVE DIMENSIONS OF INTERNATIONAL LEGAL ORDER

Surprisingly little effort has been given to a specification of the attributes of the present system of international legal order. Until we have a clear image of the present system it is impossible either to interpret trends or assess proposals and prospects for change. In this section of the chapter a preliminary profile of the present system will be attempted. Heavy emphasis will be given to the role of authority perspectives—expectations about permissible standards and procedures of behavior.

There are problems of *characterization* created by my unwillingness to accept a conservative interpretation of the province of legal authority[25] as delimited by formal expression of consent by sovereign states. The authority system operative in international society is specified here to encompass *de facto* regimes that can come into effective being without any dependence upon the rhetoric or technique of lawyers—for instance, through the manipulation of the so-called rules of the game.[26] In opposite fashion, the authority system is also specified to include *de jure* regimes extant without much prospect of behavioral impact—for instance, the human rights provisions of the United Nations Charter or the General Assembly Resolution adopting the Principles of the Nuremberg Judgment. . . .[27]

On the basis of such an effort to grasp the international legal order as a distinctive legal system, it is possible to consider the principal components of authority and its implementation within the present framework of world affairs. Predominant emphasis will be placed upon the roles of the Westphalia and Charter conceptions, but other components will be briefly noted so as to present a reasonably comprehensive description of the current character of international order. The following components of the international legal order will be considered in sequence:

1. The Westphalia Conception;
2. The Charter Conception;
3. Geo-Political Conceptions (sphere of influence, deterrence);
4. Rules of the Game;
5. Decentralized Modes of Implementation.

1. THE WESTPHALIA CONCEPTION.[28] The basic formal ordering conception in international society since the seventeenth century has been the coordination of sovereign state units. It is convenient to identify this conception with the Peace of Westphalia of 1648, a dramatic event in the process of

transition from medieval society to the modern world. Medieval society was dominated by the image of a Christian commonwealth, a world order system hierarchically organized beneath the sway of the Pope and the Holy Roman Empire.[29] Westphalia evolved a new image of coordinated states, each sovereign within its territorial sphere. . . .

The Westphalia conception—giving legal status to a growing exercise of authority on a national level—has provided the main outline of structure and process in international society up to and including the present period. Sovereign states remain the dominant actors in international society and the contents of international law in its most formal sense is the result of voluntary action by states, exhibited either in the form of express agreement (treaties), tacit agreement (custom), or through the effective assertion of claims to control behavior in specified ways.

The state, as a spatial unit, results in the fundamental ordering of international relations through a central reliance on territorial conceptions. Respect for the boundary of states is crucial and results in derivative legal ideas of territorial jurisdiction, sovereign equality, and nonintervention. The confirmation of the exclusive internal governing authority of the national government followed from the triumph of nationalism over feudalism, another feature of the Westphalia system. Jurisdictional ideas about the reciprocal allocation of authority to govern territorially distinct units of space achieved great prominence through the logic of Westphalia. Mutual respect for territorial supremacy within well-defined boundaries provided a formal basis for international peace and a mutually beneficial endorsement of authority to govern the internal life of national societies. The oceans were an unregulated arena, originally a place of danger and chaos, but gradually, after a period of sporadic sovereign appropriation, subjected to the thinking of Westphalia. The horizontal structure of international society precluded the emergence of a supersovereign of the oceans or even some community regime of organized cooperation. Ships were given identity through national registration and regulated as a "floating territory" when on the high seas. Cooperative norms emerged through practice and agreement to promote common interests in safety, conservation, and convenience.[30] All states were made competent to pursue and capture "pirate" (nonflag) vessels, and otherwise to make unencumbered use of the oceans.[31]

The spirit of Westphalia did not prohibit recourse to war. In fact, the decision to wage war was vested in the sovereign, the highest source of legal authority in international society.[32] The role of international law as measured by the coordination of sovereign wills evolved the status of neutrality to enable the differentiation of participants from belligerent states according to legal standards and procedures that protected the two categories of interests.[33] In addition, rules governing the conduct of war evolved by custom and treaty, in a manner comparable to the law of the oceans, to serve common interests in safeguarding prisoners of war, caring for the sick and wounded, and exempting certain targets from attack and prohibiting some weapons from use. The idea of neutrality and the laws of war have suffered serious encroachment as a consequence of the progressive change in the character of war from a conflict between professional armies to a conflict between adversary societies. In modern warfare anything that weakens the enemy society tends to help the war effort, and there is little willingness on the part of belligerents to indulge neutral trade or to respect targets as "nonmilitary."[34] Neutrality rested on the presupposition that neutral states could engage in nonmilitary commerce with either side or even with both sides in a war without encroaching upon serious belligerent concerns. Neutrality also presupposes a balance-of-power mentality in which the stakes of conflict are limited and in which wars are not fought to transform the system.[35] In a bipolar world, or even in a highly heterogeneous international society,[36] principal states will tend to be drawn to one or the other side in a struggle and the stakes may involve the polar affiliation of a unit, and hence alter "the balance" prevailing in the system. Also the resurgence of a normative attitude toward warfare in the twentieth century, especially in the years since the Kellogg-Briand Pact of 1928, have produced some shift to a collective security consciousness. That is, the logic of neutrality is challenged by normative pressures to protect the victims of aggression.

Many attributes of the contemporary world render the state system less credible as a basis for organizing international society than in the past.[37] States are not nearly so autonomous in the present world with respect either to matters of security or welfare.[38] The territoriality of action does not provide as satisfactory a basis for allocating legal authority as it did at an earlier stage in international society. Communications, transportation, a world culture, and a world economy unify demands about internal social and political life. Interdependence makes all states vulnerable to the effects of decisions made outside their boundaries on matters as distinct as nuclear weapons testing and currency devaluation. Nuclear weaponry and electronic guidance systems make every state vulnerable to destruction at the will of a rival national power center. These factors appear to explain some loosening of the bonds between the individual and the state, especially in the principal societies possessing relatively democratic national traditions.[39] Transnational, regional, and even cosmopolitan trends are evident in behavioral and loyalty patterns. . . .[40]

At the same time the Westphalia conception remains very significantly central to the organization of international society. National governments retain predominant, if occasionally challenged, authority and control over events within territorial boundaries. Sovereign consent remains critical to the formation of serious new international obligations.[41] The retention of military capabilities at the national level ensures the continuing supremacy of state decisions in the area of war and peace. International institutions, with some notable exceptions, operate as instrumentalities for the realization of national purposes rather than as autonomous actors. The basic postulates of the Westphalia conception continue to hold true for the early decades of the nuclear age. Despite the political vitality of the Westphalia conception, its increasing inability to satisfy the needs of individuals and states is a social fact of prime importance for our time. At each stage of international history there has existed a peculiar tension between the logic of sovereign equality central to Westphalia thinking and the actualities of inequality in national wealth, power, and disposition.

The actuality of hierarchy has always influenced the shape of international society, especially the relations between the dominant states and the rest of the world. The Westphalia conception through its acceptance of force as a potential source of legitimation was able to accommodate in its authority system some of the consequences of inequality. This accommodation is most dramatically expressed by the legitimacy attached to peace treaties imposed by the victor in war.[42] The validity of imposed peace treaties contrasts sharply with the treatment of imposed contracts in domestic law wherein proof of duress or coercion relieves a party from the burden of performance. . . .

The colonial system—as with all *de jure* imperial relationships—rests upon the legitimation of a structure of domination; in addition, as has been already noted, quasi-legitimate spheres of influence accorded primary sovereign states also leads to structures of partial domination that are at odds with the ideology of sovereign equality. The contemporary reassertion of national autonomy throughout the world has been accompanied naturally enough by profound bitterness and skepticism on the part of Afro-Asian leaders about the validity of traditional international law.[43] The notion of oligarchy in international society has been perpetuated in our time on a political level by the distinction between nuclear and nonnuclear powers and on the authority level by vesting a veto in the five permanent members of the Security Council.[44]

To acknowledge hierarchy and oligarchy in the international system is not to imply that the Westphalia major premise of sovereign equality is something altogether nominal or epiphenomenal. In many areas of international life, including virtually all matters of international routine, the legal notions of sovereign equality enjoy political vitality. . . .

2. THE CHARTER CONCEPTION. A second main dimension of the international legal order centers upon the normative conceptions embodied in the United Nations Charter. The Charter conception overlaps in many respects the Westphalia conception, but it also complements this conception by centralizing some cooperative activities and contradicts this conception to the extent that community-oriented procedures come to displace sovereignty-oriented procedures.[45] On a formal level of norms these two dominant conceptions of international order are reconciled in Article 2, the provision of the Charter that sets out the Principles that are supposed to control the operation of the Organization; from the perspective of reconciliation Article 2(1) and 2(7) are particularly relevant, the former stating that "the Organization shall be based on the principle of sovereign equality of all its Members" and the latter asserting that "nothing contained in the present Charter shall authorize the United Nations to intervene in matters which

are essentially within the domestic jurisdiction of any state or shall require the Members to submit such matters to settlement under the present Charter." Thus the critical ideas of Westphalia involving sovereign equality and domestic jurisdiction are formally perpetuated in the Charter. The tension between the two conceptions of international legal order arises from certain other formal imperatives embodied in the Charter, modes of procedure by which "decisions" are reached and implemented, and patterns of practice that have evolved over the history of the Organization. A few of the more significant points of tension will now be taken up to illustrate the relationship between Westphalia and Charter approaches to world legal order.[46]

Status of War and Violence. The Charter purports to prohibit all recourse to force in the relations among states except individual or collective self-defense against an armed attack.[47] There is a sharp unresolved debate as to the scope of self-defense centering especially on whether allegations of covert infiltration or sporadic border infringement constitute "an armed attack" for Charter purposes. In General Assembly Resolution 2131 (XX), Declaration on Inadmissibility of Intervention, the ambiguity is maintained by condemning armed intervention and forms of interference with the sovereign character of a foreign state as "synonymous with aggression."[48] Article 51 makes self-defense available only "if an armed attack occurs" and makes no reference to aggression;[49] presumably "armed attack" is a narrower notion than aggression, and hence there is no real implication that action in self-defense is compatible with the Charter undertaken in response to aggressive acts that do not amount to an armed attack. In the absence of an authoritative definition of "armed attack," the formal scope of permissible force under the Charter will remain beclouded by controversy and subject to the vagaries of auto-interpretation.[50]

But the problem of clarification is vastly more complicated even than this. Article 51 asserts that "Nothing in the present Charter shall impair the inherent right of individual or collective self-defense . . . until the Security Council has taken the measures necessary to maintain international peace and security." Furthermore, "Measures taken by Members in the exercise of this right of self-defense shall be immediately reported to the Security Council and shall not in any way affect the authority and responsibility of the Security Council under the present Charter to take at any time such action as it deems necessary in order to maintain or restore international peace and security." But suppose the Security Council fails to reach any determination? Or suppose the member state fails to report immediately its exercise of self-defense?[51] These formal gaps are of particular importance because states have been reluctant to fulfill their procedural duty to submit claims to act in self-defense to the Security Council and the Security Council has often been unable to mobilize a relevant voting consensus whenever the issue touched closely upon the central Soviet-American international rivalry. In earlier years of the Organization, the United States sought to transfer competence to the General Assembly in the event that the Security Council was paralyzed by a veto or a division of sentiment.[52] The growth of more militant and anti-Western sentiment in the General Assembly, largely as a consequence of the expansion of Afro-Asian representation, and the outcome of the financing controversy disclosing the limits of Assembly effectiveness in peace and security matters involving superpower rivalry has fostered a gradual realization that it is either futile or self-defeating to circumvent the Security Council. . . .

The central consequence of these limits on the capacity of principal organs of the United Nations to interpret and apply its own Charter provisions is to revive the logic of Westphalia for many problems in the area of war and peace, especially those problems involving the direct participation of principal sovereign states. National governments self-interpret and self-apply the provisions of the Charter; the foreseeable consequence is to produce adversary rationalizations couched in the prevailing legal rhetoric.[53] In practical effect, however, principal states tend to reserve for national decision the determination of discretion as to the use of force. Shifts in beliefs about the utility of military power, concern about escalation, and some socialization of national elites in terms of Charter conceptions are among the factors that differentiate current patterns of decentralized decision-making on war/peace problems from earlier patterns.[54] The gradual reorientation of national elites toward the impartial acceptance of world community legal standards may be the most significant, if occasionally invisible, contemporary trend in support of world order. The Charter conception, by its authoritative formulation of governing norms, is a crucial factor encouraging this trend. The principal organs of the United Nations often provide communication facilities wherein international adversaries meet in periods of crisis and violence. Invoking norms to rationalize a national position may lead to a gradual assimilation of the normative directive as part of what is perceived to be reasonable behavior. In effect, the Charter conception through its application and invocation in the organization settings of the United Nations contributes to a vast global learning experience, the effects of which are difficult to calculate.[55]

A further element of the charter conception of authority, as it applies to governing the use of military power, entails a commitment to the logic of collective security.[56] The United Nations is entitled to use military power if its organs have acted in accordance with their own procedures. In any event, there is no higher decision-maker that can pass judgment upon a contested use of force by the political organs of the United Nations. There is no reason to suppose that the International Court of Justice would do more than render an Advisory Opinion on such a question.[57]

Members of the United Nations are obligated in Article 2(5) to give the United Nations "every assistance in any action it takes in accordance with the present Charter, and shall refrain from giving assistance to any state against which the United Nations is taking preventive or enforcement action." In a complementary fashion the Draft Declaration on Rights and Duties of States in Article 10 requires that "every State has the duty to refrain from giving assistance to any state which is acting in violation of

Article 9 [prohibition on illegal use or threat of force], or against which the United Nations is taking preventive or enforcement action."[58] In both documents the essence of the legal duty is to support the United Nations in its effort to establish peace and security. A state is obliged to defer to community judgment in a situation of conflict and violence. Such an obligation appears to take precedence over inconsistent duties arising from an alliance and over a policy preference for impartiality and neutrality.[59]

In practice, however, states have not been willing to support action by the United Nations with which they disagreed. The problem has been minimized to some extent because it has been difficult to organize support for action in situations of real confrontation between principal members. The U.N. Emergency Force organized after the Sinai Campaign of 1956 and the Congo Operation of 1960–1964 are two examples of action by the United Nations in the face of a split Organization. In both instances, however, an initial consensus was lost in the course of carrying out a mission deliberately couched in ambiguous directives so as to obscure the underlying conflict of objectives. The financing crisis arose from a backlash created by disappointment with the United Nations and expressing, perhaps, the concern of some members, especially France and the Soviet Union, that the Organization was infringing upon the prerogatives of state sovereignty.

The Charter conception of international order rests heavily upon the capacity of the international community to mount collective action based on a fair-minded interpretation of certain shared norms.[60] Such an approach can only hope to succeed if most states, especially principal states, are prepared to accord priority to Charter rules and procedures.[61] The effect of such priority is to subordinate alliance relations and balance-of-power considerations. In the nomenclature of this chapter, the Charter conception can only become embodied in international life to the extent that Westphalia approaches to national security lose their political vitality. . . .

At the same time the Charter conception is not without great significance. In the event a consensus on ends and means can be reached within the United Nations, then prospects for peace-keeping or peaceful settlement are considerable. On rare occasion, principal states have upheld Charter norms at the expense of alliance partners, as was done by the United States after Great Britain, France, and Israel invaded the Sinai Peninsula in 1956. More normally, however, the Organization can only hope to mobilize a consensus to oppose the use of violence when principal states agree on the identity of the wrongdoer and on the direction of policy response. Small conflicts at the margin of regional and sub-regional concern can be kept within tolerable limits by this means. For instance, in both Cyprus and the Yemen the United Nations has been able to play a peace-keeping role.

In general, then, governments continue to base national security planning upon Westphalia calculations. The Charter conception has greatly changed the rhetoric of diplomatic discourse, and this change in rhetoric may gradually produce shifts in attitude and behavior. As well, the institutional setting provided by the United Nations is an excellent forum for adversary communication and facilitates the identification and implementation of converging interests. The United Nations has changed the international environment more by facilitating international communications than by translating the norms of the Charter into operational rules of conduct. Finally, for states or groups of states with little military capability but with extensive political support from other governments, the United Nations provides a mobilization arena, within which to encourage the sharpening of sentiment. Such a process has been an essential part of African efforts to mobilize global support for their insistence on the elimination of racism and colonialism from the continent.

Basis for Obligation. The Westphalia conception of international order rests upon the essential role of consent in the process of forming international obligations.[62] The Charter conception superficially respects, or at least contains nothing to contradict, this traditional mode of law-creation.[63] Among the recent developments that have encouraged a growing role for consensus as a law-creating energy are the following: (1) The functional needs of unified regulation in an increasingly interdependent world; (2) the increase in the number of active national participants in international life; (3) the cosmopolitan sentiments generated by the existence of the United Nations; (4) the emergence of a global public opinion on many issues of international importance; (5) parallel developments on a domestic level in both socialistic and capitalistic societies that involve the displacement of individual choice and responsibility by community choice and responsibility.[64]

In several distinct subject-matter areas the General Assembly has come increasingly to formulate its "recommendations" and "declarations" in legal rhetoric. From a technical point of view, it would be possible to contend that the General Assembly is only giving formal expression to what the majority of its membership regards to be obligatory in any event. Given an expanded international society that needs and demands more rapid formulations of governing standards, the Assembly resolution can be understood as a modern adjunct to the traditional mode of law-creation by "international custom. . . ."

Among the sorts of issues that have been the subject of Assembly law-creation are the following:

1. The prohibition of nuclear weapons;
2. The withdrawal of legitimacy from colonial regimes;
3. The condemnation of racial discrimination as endangering international peace and as justifying coercive and interventionary undertakings;
4. The banning of nuclear weapons in outer space;
5. The acceptance of certain welfare responsibilities by developed countries in relation to poorer countries;
6. The enunciation of rules and procedures of operations internal to the United Nations and the interpretation of provisions of the Charter.

The importance of such law-creating acts varies greatly from context to context. The quality of the supporting majority is very important, especially whether the real targets of regulation join in the consensus. In certain contexts, a resolution may be almost a functional equivalent to an international treaty; such was the case, for instance, with respect to the resolution banning the introduction of orbital weapons into outer space.[65] In other contexts, the resolution may only posit aspirational standards as a technique of promoting an eventual legal standard; such was the case, for instance, with respect to the resolution prohibiting the use of nuclear weapons.[66] Other resolutions are designed to mobilize community action, put pressure on principal states, in contexts in which there is an adversary relationship between the organized international community and a particular state or group of states; such has been the case, for instance, with respect to the escalating confrontation between the General Assembly and South Africa over the issues of racial discrimination and over the status of South West Africa.

It is impossible to examine this development in any detail here. What has been described in the setting of the General Assembly is taking place in other international bodies of a more specialized nature. There is a noticeable drift toward consensus as a basis of legitimation; the will of the international community acquires a certain degree of legislative status when it manifests itself through formal actions of international institutions. These trends are indefinite and uneven, but their cumulative effect challenges the fundamental ordering principle of the Westphalia conception—that is, the centrality of the will or volitional behavior of individual sovereign states. . . .

There is no doubt that the Charter conception, with its increasing emphasis on the claims of the Afro-Asian majority, is challenging and eroding the consent-oriented basis of Westphalia thinking. At the same time, states have not shown any dramatic willingness to defer to community claims directed against their central interests or traditional prerogatives. Sovereign acquiescence continues to be an element in establishing "a sense of obligation" on the part of government elites. It is this sense of obligation, far more than any mechanism of enforcement, that makes for effective adherence to international standards of behavior. National governments have not shown much disposition to be responsive to community claims posited in the form of General Assembly resolutions. Westphalia conceptions about law-creation remain very much alive, although Charter developments are posing a formidable challenge. Most of the important considerations in evaluating these trends are sociological rather than juridical, depending for their basic interpretation upon the attitudes, beliefs, and actions of elites in national governments and in international institutions. If the officials formulating the claims *think* that the mode of formulation has a law-creating effect—imposes some sense of obligation in relation to some standard of behavior—then this expectation has a bearing on how officials on the national level perceive and react. At this point, the evidence of trend and countertrend is difficult to evaluate. The future shape of international society will reflect the progress of this ongoing struggle between a consensus-oriented and a consent-oriented international society. It represents one of the critical issue-areas of transition in the international political system.

Constitutional Authority. The Charter of the United Nations in Article 2(6) claims competence to ensure that states which are not members of the United Nations act in accordance with these principles [that is, the other provisions of Article 2] so far as may be necessary for the maintenance of "international peace and security."[67] The significant point here is that the United Nations Organization claims for itself whatever authority is necessary to establish global peace and security. The Charter embodies the claim and the Organization gives its continuing effect. Article 2(6) is a significant provision (one that carries forward the approach of Article 17 of the League Covenant) because it relies on a treaty instrument such as the Charter to establish the basis for communitywide authority that might be extended to nonparticipants in the treaty regime. . . .

The claim embodied in Article 2(6) is paralleled in the practice of regional organizations such as the Arab League, Organization of African Unity, and the Organization of American States. These institutions act on the assumption of regionwide competence that is not constricted by the nonparticipation of some national units within the region.

The development of constitutional authority for international institutions is complementary to the evolution of legislative authority discussed in the preceding section. In the latter case, the will of the relevant community is endowed with law-creating effect despite dissent, whether from members or not; in the latter case, the constitutional status of the organization allows its competence to extend beyond the activities of its members, and regardless of whether nonmembers assent or are given an opportunity to join. Since international institutions remain voluntary associations of states their stature depends upon a basic consensus as to ends and means and upon a level of participation that includes most, if not all, of the relevant states concerned. . . .

Erosion of Domestic Jurisdiction. We have mentioned the saving clause in Article 2(7) of the Charter that promises to uphold the domestic jurisdiction of states. The idea of domestic jurisdiction being invested exclusively in national governments is a prime element of the Westphalia conception. The abiding strength of this idea is suggested by the reluctance of states, even on the part of those states most committed to the growth of a stable system of world order, to entrust international institutions with the capacity to determine what falls within domestic jurisdiction. The famous debate occasioned by the Connally Reservation to the United States' acceptance of the compulsory jurisdiction of the International Court of Justice[68] is a familiar illustration of this reluctance to allow any risk of intrusion on matters thought to be within domestic jurisdiction. . . .

At the same time the practice of the Organization has increasingly removed from domestic jurisdiction various subject-matter in the area of human rights. The struggle to oppose apartheid in South Africa has created a whole range of precedents involving the claimed competence of the organized international community to determine for itself whether a particular national policy is within the reserved domain of domestic jurisdiction. Certainly in 1945 when the United Nations came into being it was widely assumed that policies used by a government to regulate internal race relations would have been thought to fall squarely within domestic jurisdiction. But the critical issue governing the shifting contents of domestic jurisdiction is the locus of authority to characterize subject-matter as domestic or inter- national. If, as has been increasingly the case, the international community is unified in its assertion of competence to make this judgment, then the appeals of a national government to some earlier understanding of the domestic jurisdiction principle are not likely to have much bearing on authority trends. The United Nations as an organization possesses an almost unquestioned competence to determine what constitutes a threat to inter- national peace and security, and by so determining, possesses the capacity to internationalize the status of a particular question. Over South Africa's vigorous objection, the policies of apartheid have been increasingly inter- nationalized in this manner. It makes little juridical difference that the threat to the peace comes from hostility toward apartheid by foreign countries rather than from the policies themselves. The essential juridical ingredients of this legal claim are a strong consensus within the United Nations and the expression of this consensus in a series of formal acts by the principal organs of the U.N. There has been parallel experience in other areas, especially arising from the Unilateral Declaration of Independence in 1965 by the Smith regime in Rhodesia and in connection with the various efforts of the United Nations to oppose Portuguese colonialism in Africa. . . .

There is a kind of common law energy that builds up expectations as to the character of permissible kinds of undertakings. A precedent established by overwhelming consensus (South Africa) or by overwhelming military superiority ("defensive quarantine" in the Cuban missile crisis), can be invoked in less compelling future circumstances. Thus the trend toward further erosion of the reserved domain of national governments may be expected to accelerate in the decades ahead. Such an expectation is reinforced by the fragmentation of national loyalty patterns in such a way that domestic pressures to conform national behavior to international standards are likely to grow stronger. As well, the functional necessities of unified regulation make the state a less autonomous unit for the conduct of practical affairs. . . .

Modern communications, transportation, highly specialized technologies of space and oceans, interdependencies in currencies, employment patterns, commodity pricing, and international trade are among the factors making for a world ever-less constituted by autonomous national states reciprocally deferring to exclusive patterns of territorial jurisdiction. Territorial space is declining as an indicator of formal authority. This decline is symbolized by the decreasing capacity of most governments to be able to provide for national security and national welfare. The ideology and practice of foreign aid expresses one dimension of this pressure upon the Westphalia conception at the unit level. In the present world, to put the point provocatively, the great majority of weak and poor states ultimately depend, for whatever marginal viability they may possess, upon the interventionary policies of the few strong and rich states.[69] The Charter conception of world legal order, as expressed in such recent developments as UNCTAD I and II and the Tehran Conference of 1968 on Human Rights, is evolving a primitive base for a welfare state on a world level.[70] Such an evolution, if it continues, will be of crucial importance in shaping the near future of the international legal order.[71]

Supranational Professionalism. There is a growing kind of cosmopolitanism arising from the proliferation of contact between various kinds of professional groups located in different national societies.[72] Science, for instance, is becoming an increasingly supranational enterprise. Cross-national loyalties evolve and there is a tendency to form opinions on a basis less expressive of place of national affiliation. The great growth of specialized international agencies, and the parallel development of nongovernmental and intergovernmental international organizations, is part of this continuing process. The ease and growth of travel, the emergence of "world companies" without any real national center of operations, and the beginnings of global television and telephone coverage are further expressions of this supranationalization of human experience. . . .[73]

Within domestic societies, especially those organized according to the principles of liberal democracy, there is evidence of increasing alienation of individuals from the nation-state as the central focus of their political loyalty.[74] More individuals appear socialized by Charter norms about violence than ever before in human history. The peace movement in the United States during the Vietnam War is probably the most dramatic example of the limits of national loyalty. The effort to organize draft resistance has rested heavily on normative considerations, especially drawing on legal standards of limitation applicable to recourse and conduct of war.[75] In several prominent domestic trials, defendants have attempted to introduce international law arguments to justify their refusal to cooperate with the Vietnam War effort. Courts in the United States have refused so far to examine the substance of these contentions, concluding that such issues are nonjusticiable because the subject matter of war and peace is entrusted to the discretion of the executive branch of government. The "Political Questions Doctrine" is also invoked to explain why domestic courts cannot examine the substance of arguments about the legality of war and warfare. It is an important event that such issues are being raised in a serious fashion. The reluctance of domestic courts to adjudicate seems to be a legacy of Westphalia thinking with respect to the discretionary nature of sovereign decisions to wage war. Charter norms provide guidelines; the head of state is obliged to conduct the affairs of government within a framework of legal restraint. The precedents of war crimes trials after World War II suggest an aggregate trend toward more cosmopolitan orientations of legal assessment than executive self-determination; the Judgment at Nuremberg surely established that the king can do wrong when it comes to war. Individuals are increasingly appealing above the heads of their elected national officials to global norms and procedures. These patterns of protest and appeal are currently at a rudimentary stage of assertion, but they represent important indications about what is going to happen in international society in the near future in the event that further cosmopolitan support develops.

The Charter is important in these settings because it provides individuals with a set of authoritative reference points that can be invoked against a national government that acts as though it was subject only to the minimal constraints of the Westphalia conception. On the level of individual loyalty, as on the level of elite predisposition, we live at a time of normative tension between the relatively permissive Westphalia restraints and the relatively restrictive Charter restraints. The two bodies of normative guidance coexist in uneasy irresolution, the clarity and proportionality of their eventual relationship depending on future events.

Supplemental Conceptions. As already suggested, the normative choices embodied in the Westphalia and Charter conceptions are qualified and complemented by certain additional ordering mechanisms at work in international society. These additional mechanisms are not "supplemental" in this sense of enjoying a secondary importance. On the contrary. The subordinate treatment is a consequence of the questionable normative status of these conceptions rather than their lesser impact on the shape of international behavior.

3. GEO-POLITICAL CONCEPTIONS. The stability of national boundaries is a consequence, to some indefinite extent, of the role of the predominant power wielded by principal sovereign states. Neither the Westphalia conception of sovereign units nor the Charter conception of a nascent world community can comprehend within its juridical logic the role of "spheres of influence," the special ordering prerogatives implicitly asserted by principal states and ambivalently acquiesced in by the rest of international society. The mapping of these "spheres of influence," a task beyond the scope of this chapter, is definitely a critical aspect of the quality of existing order, and the remapping prospect is an important element in the near future. It is also very relevant to assess whether Westphalia and Charter conceptions will erode the quasi-imperial claims and practices of principal sovereign states in the decades ahead.

The relationship between the Soviet Union and Eastern Europe or between the United States and Latin America is illustrative of clearly delimited spheres of influence wherein interventionary prerogatives exist. These spheres of influence are not symmetrical with one another, nor is the pattern of interventionary prerogative within any particular sphere stable through time. Each sphere can be conceived of as a sub-system possessing its own properties and its distinctive links to the global system. . . .[76]

Secondary spheres of influence also exist based upon unequal power relations of sovereign units within regional sub-systems. Militant actors such as Cuba under Castro, Ghana under Nkrumah, and the United Arab Republic under Nasser intervene, to some extent successfully, within their respective sub-systemic settings. Some efforts to establish spheres of influence generate intense geopolitical opposition. The United States' role in Southeast Asia since 1950 is partly a consequence of its determination to resist Chinese efforts to establish such a sphere of influence over the states contiguous to her borders. The Vietnam War is a culmination of an American exaggeration of the geopolitical dimension of post-colonial Asian conflict. It is an exaggeration because the forces of struggle in Vietnam are animated primarily by nationalistic considerations—the impulse toward national independence, modernization, and unity.

The relations between a dominant actor and its sphere undergo sharp shifts through time. Interventionary prerogatives may be moderated or intensified. The history of the role of the United States in Latin America illustrates clearly the various swings of the pendulum in response to factors taking place within the sphere and those directed at the sphere from outside.[77] The efforts of Latin American statesmen to secure a greater measure of autonomy in their relations with the United States was rewarded with the Good Neighbor Policy of the 1930's. . . .

Similarly, the Soviet experience of intervention in 1956 may have moderated its imperial prerogatives in East Europe throughout the subsequent period so as to avoid the need for a recurrence. The military pressure directed against the Dubcek regime in Czechoslovakia since 1968 contrasts at least in severity with the brutal coercion directed twelve years earlier at the Nagy regime. The Soviet claims against Czechoslovakia have been very extreme in the sense that they have concerned the domestic social and economic policies being pursued by a popular and stable government in Prague; there was no significant domestic unrest in Czechoslovakia *until* Soviet troops entered the country in August of 1968.

The normative point is that the existence of discernable spheres of influence is an important ingredient of the present system of international order. Expectations about the tolerable range of intervention are shaped by whether the locus of controversy is within or without a sphere of influence. . . .

The role of deterrence is closely linked to norms of international order, which incorporate some appreciation of spheres of influence. States are deterred by the added perception that a state is acting within certain prescribed limits. If such action is within a discerned sphere, then it may be tolerated in a manner that it would not be outside such a sphere. Threatened retaliation normally does not include "intra-sphere" aggression, but is limited to either "inter-sphere" aggression or to situations wherein contradictory or ambiguous geopolitical perceptions are experienced by rival governments. One major cause of war is the failure to delimit spheres of influence in a sufficiently clear way to establish shared expectations. The problem of delimitation is vastly complicated by the fact, already alluded to, that the very existence of spheres of influence contradicts the prevailing ordering ideals of Westphalia and the Charter. A geopolitical input, although very apparent in the structure of world affairs, is ideologically abhorrent to the subordinate units. Such abhorrence has been clearly manifest on many occasions in the ex-colonial sectors of the world, but never more vividly than during the Security Council debate which followed the Stanleyville Operation of 1964, justified as a humanitarian rescue of hostages in the West and attacked as a neocolonialist venture by militant statesmen of black Africa.[78]

4. RULES OF THE GAME. A further basis for order in international society arises from patterns of mutual adherence to "rules of the game." These are rules that do not qualify as legal rules, at least if the criteria of qualification are established by the traditional sources of international law. At the same time, these rules of the game moderate the scope and magnitude of conflict, and create an important secondary line of normative defense in the event that primary rules governing the conduct of states have failed to prevent violence.

Rules of the game are standards of behavior to which adherence corresponds with widely shared community expectations as to the character of reasonable behavior; a departure from a rule of the game, as with the departure from any rule of order, is likely to generate some escalatory response on the part of adversely affected actors, provided such actors possess the capability to make or threaten a credible response. Mutual adherence maintains some kind of framework of restraint even in situations of chaos, crisis, and warfare.

The nature and function of rules of the game can be illustrated in connection with the subject-matter of civil strife. Several rules of major significance appear to exist:

1. Nuclear weapons will not be introduced into battle by a belligerent;
2. Counterinterventionary targets will be limited to the territory wherein the civil strife is taking place;
3. States furnishing assistance short of combat troops to either interventionary or counterinterventionary actors will not be treated as belligerents.

The primary rules of intervention have not been very successful in prohibiting overt and covert forms of third-party participation in civil strife. These rules of the game are designed to moderate the destabilizing effects of third-party participation, assuming it takes place. The Vietnam War has been a major testing ground for the limitation of the scale and form of violent conflicts in this category. These limiting rules are highly dependent on the exercise of self-restraint by third-party states, especially those that are geographically distant and geo-politically powerful (and, hence, exempt from retaliatory responses, except possibly by third-party allies of the other side). In this regard, the U.S. decision during the Vietnam War to initiate large-scale bombing in North Vietnam[79] was a flagrant and prominent violation of rule (2), which undoubtedly has weakened the stability of such a regime of mutual, self-imposed and self-implemented restraints. Although a pattern of departure does not nullify a rule of the game, it does set a negative precedent of considerable weight for prospective violators in the future. Dominant states cannot induce compliance to these rules of restraint if their own behavior exhibits nonconformity. Atmospheric nuclear testing by the United States and the Soviet Union is a negative precedent of such strength that it virtually nullified any effort by these two states to object to subsequent testing claims of China and France. . . .

5. DECENTRALIZED MODES OF INTERNATIONAL ORDER. The Westphalia conception includes the idea that national governments are the basic sources of order in international society. National governments provide territorial order and share in authority to attach national law to activity on the oceans and in air space. Various allocational doctrines have evolved to identify which of several national governments can apply its regulatory authority in situations of overlapping concern. Doctrines of sovereign and diplomatic immunity, act of state, and various kinds of extraterritorial jurisdiction carry out the basic postulates of the Westphalia system: decentralized legal control by sovereign states.

In addition, however, to this jurisdictional kind of decentralization there exist a growing number of situations that allow national institutions to act as agents of the international system. Domestic courts can supply judicial institutions for the adjudication of international controversies, national legislative organs can posit and clarify standards of international behavior, and the executive branch can implement sanctioning procedures to promote international enforcement processes.[80] National institutions, without efforts at explicit coordination on an international basis, can reinforce the ordering potential of the international system. The contribution to an evolving legal order depends upon the extent to which decentralized processes operate as *agents* of the world community enjoying independence from directives of national policy. A tradition of independence and an explicit appreciation of the ordering contributions that could be made might increase the prospects for national institutions. As matters now stand, national institutions tend to apply international law in such a manner as to assure its conformity with national policy.

A special case of decentralized ordering concerns an activity such as piracy, which is universally condemned. Each state has the capacity to apprehend "pirates" on behalf of the overall international community. A somewhat comparable competence was claimed by Israel when it prosecuted Adolf Eichmann as a war criminal. Those individuals who have recourse to litigation in the United States to question the legality of the Vietnam War by invoking norms embodied in the Charter or in the Nuremberg Judgment are also trying to convert a domestic court into an agent of an emerging international system of order, an agent that accords precedence to the norms of international law when these norms come into conflict with the dictates of national policy. . . .

NOTES

1. A growing literature is concerned with speculation about the future. Several books are particularly useful as introductions—e.g., Erich Jantsch, *Technological Forecasting in Perspective* (Paris, Organization for Economic Cooperation and Development, 1967); Fred A. Polak, *The Image of the Future* (2 vols., Dobbs Ferry, N.Y. 1961); Bertrand de Jouvenel, *The Art of Conjecture* (New York 1967); Herman Kahn and Anthony J. Wiener, *The Year 2000—A Framework for Speculation on the Next Thirty-Three Years* (New York 1967).

2. As such, its emphasis is upon evolution within the existing system rather than with speculation about alternative international systems and the conditions of their emergence. For a discussion of this distinction see Falk, *Legal Order in a Violent World* (Princeton 1968), 8–38. A useful comparative analysis of alternative international systems is to be found in Oran R. Young, *The World System: Present Characteristics and Future Prospects* (Hudson Institute [HI-277-D], August 29, 1963).

3. The Charter conception is a continuation, in most essential respects, of the modifications of international society embodied in the ideas leading to the formation of the League of Nations. In some sense, it might be more accurate to compare the Westphalia conception with the Covenant conception. However, since the League is defunct, it seems more suitable merely to take note of the formation of the League as a critical date and to suggest sources for those interested in a comparison between the Charter and the Covenant. On this see Inis L. Claude, Jr., *Swords into Plowshares* (New York, 3rd rev. edn., 1964), Chapters I–II; Falk and Saul H. Mendlovitz, eds., *The Strategy of World Order: The United Nations* (New York 1966), Vol. III, 5–36.

4. These two conceptions of international legal order are ideal type characterizations that purport only to approximate the actual contours of behavior and order. Such intellectual constructs are useful in developing highly abstract images, but they must be adapted to the specific character of various sectors of international life.

5. There is a very suggestive discussion of authority, and its relationship to behavior, in Kenneth S. Carlston, *Law and Organization in World Society* (Urbana 1962), 64–123.

6. This viewpoint is well formulated in Oscar Schachter, "Towards a Theory of International Obligation," 8 *Virginia Journal of International Law*, 300–22 (1968).

7. For some discussion of the role of "spheres" or "zones" of de facto authority see pp. 41–69.

8. In certain instances, these extraterritorial prerogatives are given formal or quasi-formal legitimacy. The validation of colonial title is, of course, one kind of example. Another more subtle kind of legitimacy is that given the Monroe Doctrine by Article 21 of the Covenant of the League of Nations. Article 21 reads: "Nothing in this Covenant shall be deemed to affect the validity of international engagements, such as treaties of arbitration or regional understandings like the Monroe Doctrine, for securing the maintenance of peace." See comment on Article 21 in Ronald J. Yalem, *Regionalism and World Order* (Washington, D.C. 1965), 39–40. Professor Yalem reflects, perhaps, too narrow a view of international order when he concludes "the Monroe Doctrine was in no sense a regional understanding. It was a unilateral declaration of policy by the United States without any standing under international law" (39–40). Surely, this is true in formal terms of consensual authority, but claims to exercise authority that are acquiesced in by the community create expectations that are given de facto respect even if not accorded full de jure validity.

9. The intellectual risks of such a confusion are well identified in Stanley Hoffmann, *The State of War* (New York 1965), 123–33.

10. An attempt to specify this intermediate position is to be found in Falk, *The Status of Law in International Society* (Princeton 1969), Chapter III.

11. This is the major theme of a series of lectures: Falk, "The New States and International Legal Order," 118 Hague Academy Recueil des Cours 1–103 (1966).

12. Such an undertaking is the explicit orientation of Morton A. Kaplan and Nicholas deB. Katzenbach, *The Political Foundations of International Law* (New York 1961); see also Oran R. Young, "A Systemic Approach to International Politics," Research Monograph No. 33, June 30, 1968.

13. There are many recent efforts at characterization. See, e.g., Stanley Hoffmann, *Gulliver's Troubles, or the Setting of American Foreign Policy* (New York 1968), 10–51; George Liska, *Imperial America—The International Politics of Primacy* (Baltimore 1967).

14. Cf. the formulations of Ernst B. Haas in Chapter 6.

15. See Hoffmann, *Gulliver's Troubles*, 343–64; Young, *The World System*, 4:7–4:18, 5:7–5:13, 6:2–6:10.

16. A very tentative, initial acknowledgment of the following criticism directed at my past work: "One difficulty in the way of Professor Falk's efforts to formulate an international law that embraces both the noncommunist and communist worlds resides, thus, in his unwillingness to postulate a comprehensive set of inclusive policies, for which he as a scholar is willing to take responsibility in recommendation, relevant to appraising the detailed practices of both sets of participants." Myres S. McDougal, Harold D. Lasswell, and W. Michael Reisman, "Theories About International Law: Prologue to a Configurative Jurisprudence," 8 *Virginia Journal of International Law*, 188–299, at 288 (1968).

17. There is, of course, the correlative question about the extent to which priorities can be established by regional and national actors in circumstances where the organs of the global actor cannot or do not come to a decision. What are the residual capacities of subordinate actors to set priorities, especially in situations where the use of political violence is being authorized? Under what circumstances can the Arab League or the Organization of African Unity legitimize a contemplated use of violence to deal with an intra-regional adversary? Can even the United Arab Republic or Tanzania confer legitimacy on use of violence against a foreign state, at least to the extent of providing money, arms, and sanctuaries for insurgent and guerrilla groups? These questions probe the surface of a complex subject. There are different degrees of nonaction, authorization, and participation, as well as different normative expectations as to what it is permissible for various actors to do. There is a need for a systematic statement of these interrelations between different kinds of *actors* in different kinds of *conflict*.

18. That is, norms precluding recourse to international violence were subordinated to norms invalidating colonial title; other factors of preference and capability entered in. The fact that Goa was "an enclave," not "a state," meant that there was some ambiguity as to whether India was making an internal use of force protected from international scrutiny by the domestic jurisdiction principle or was making an external use of force subject to the prohibition that force is illegal except in self-defense.

19. In assessing this future, Stanley Hoffmann's differentiation of national consciousness, national situation, and nationalism is suggestive. See Stanley Hoffmann, "Obstinate or Obsolete? The Fate of the Nation-State and the Case of Western Europe," *Daedalus* (Summer 1966), 862–915, at 867–69.

20. For criticism of this defect in analysis see Falk, "The Revolution in Peace Education," *Saturday Review* (May 21, 1966), 59–61, 77.

21. For a very significant exception see W. Warren Wagar, *The City of Man* (Baltimore 1967).

22. The reasons why this is so have been ably stated by Walter C. Schiffer, *The Legal Community of Mankind* (New York 1954), esp. 273-301. See also F. H. Hinsley, *Power and the Pursuit of Peace* (Cambridge 1963).

23. The most widely known contemporary plan of this variety is Grenville Clark and Louis B. Sohn, *World Peace Through World Law* (Cambridge, 3rd rev. edn., 1966); for a very persuasive analysis of the reasons why such a reasonable objective is unattainable see the numerous writings of Reinhold Niebuhr. See especially *The Structure of Nations and Empires* (New York 1959); *The Children of Light and the Children of Darkness* (New York 1944).

24. A recent book is quite suggestive along these lines, despite its narrower focus. Robert Gilpin, *France in the Age of the Scientific State* (Princeton 1968).

25. An excellent presentation of these issues is to be found in Schachter, "A Theory of International Obligation," 306-22; also useful is Clive Parry, *Sources and Evidence of International Law* (Manchester 1965).

26. Suggestive writings include C.A.W. Manning, *The Nature of International Society* (London 1962), 64-181; Anatol Rapoport, *Fights, Games, and Debates* (Ann Arbor 1960); T. C. Schelling, *Arms and Influence* (New Haven 1966).

27. The General Assembly unanimously affirmed "the principles of international law recognized by the Charter of the Nuremberg Tribunal and the judgment of the Tribunal" on December 11, 1946, G. A. Res. 95 (I). The same Resolution also directed the International Law Commission to formulate these principles as part of an overall effort to evolve a codification of "offenses against the peace and security of mankind, or of an International Criminal Code." For a summary of United Nations activity in relation to the Nuremberg Principles see Louis B. Sohn, ed., *Cases on United Nations Law* (Brooklyn 1956), 969-70; for formulation of the Nuremberg Principles, and a summary of their discussion in the Sixth (Legal) Committee of the General Assembly see same, 970-83.

28. An analysis of the Westphalia conception as it applies to ocean fishery disputes is to be found in Falk, *The Status of Law*, Chapter XX.

29. Well-explicated in Leo Gross, "The Peace of Westphalia, 1648-1948," 42 *American Journal of International Law*, 20-41 (1948).

30. For a very ample documentation of these processes see Myres S. McDougal and William T. Burke, *The Public Order of the Oceans* (New Haven 1962), esp. 1-88, 730-1140.

31. Related claims to regulate extranational activity have resulted from the increasing interdependence of complex patterns of human behavior. One prominent and controversial area of such regulatory activity has involved the extension of the American antitrust laws to cover certain foreign operations alleged to have an anticompetitive impact on the United States economy. For a survey and analysis of the pattern of claim in the extraterritorial antitrust area see Falk, *The Status of Law*, Chapter IX.

32. The growth of rules of international law restricting the right to wage war is described in Quincy Wright, *The Role of Law in the Elimination of War* (Dobbs Ferry, N.Y. 1961); see further Ian Brownlie, *International Law and the Use of Force by States* (London 1963).

33. See Myres S. McDougal and Florentino P. Feliciano, *Law and Minimum World Public Order* (New Haven 1961), 384-519.

34. For a strong argument that the changing patterns of warfare require revision of the laws of war see Josef Kunz, *The Changing Law of Nations* (Columbus 1968),

831–68; in the context of the Vietnam War see John Gerassi, *North Vietnam: A Documentary* (New York 1968); Kuno Knoebel, *Victor Charlie—The Face of War in Vietnam* (New York 1967).

35. On the conception of a moderate (as distinct from a revolutionary) international system see Hoffmann, *Gulliver's Troubles*, 17–21, 356–64.

36. On heterogeneity, see Aron, *Peace and War*, 99–104, 373–403.

37. For useful specification of state system see William D. Coplin, "International Law and Assumptions about the State System," *World Politics*, 17 (1964), 615–35.

38. Such an argument is mainly related to security issues in John H. Herz, *International Politics in the Atomic Age* (New York 1959); to welfare issues in Gunnar Myrdal, *Beyond the Welfare State* (New Haven 1960); to circumvention via the growth of functional international organization in Ernst B. Haas, *Beyond the Nation-State— Functionalism and International Organization* (Stanford 1964).

39. Quite different trends are evident in nation-building settings and in the relatively more authoritarian and totalitarian societies.

40. See Galtung, "Future of the International System."

41. As has been explained by McDougal and Burke, *Public Order of the Oceans*, and Schachter, "A Theory of International Obligations," there has always been some compromise between "consent" and functional imperatives in the processes of formation of customary international law. See also Karol Wolfke, *Custom in Present International Law* (Warsaw 1964).

42. For an assessment of the juridical validation of coercion in the form of imposed treaties of peace see Julius Stone, "De Victoribus Victis: The International Law Commission and Imposed Treaties of Peace," 8 *Virginia Journal of International Law*, 356–73 (1968).

43. For some consideration of these matters see Falk, "The New States and International Legal Order," 118 *Hague Recueil des Cours*, 1–102 (1966); a more fundamental depiction of the alienation that follows from the colonial experience is to be found in the play "The Blacks" by Jean Genet. See also Frantz Fanon, *The Wretched of the Earth* (New York 1963).

44. The phenomenon of neocolonialism also needs to be examined. It would be desirable to assess the functional dimensions of colonial rulership and then use these dimensions to assess allegations of neocolonial equivalencies.

45. To derive the juridical basis of the Charter see R. B. Russell and J. E. Muther, *A History of the United Nations Charter* (Washington, D. C. 1958); for comparison of Covenant of the League of Nations and Charter of the United Nations see sources cited in note 3.

46. A parallel analysis of centralizing and atomizing tendencies of thought and action is examined in a very thoughtful, imaginative essay. See Hedley Bull, "The Grotian Conception of International Society," in Herbert Butterfield and Martin Wight, eds., *Diplomatic Investigations* (London, 1966), 51–73.

47. The relevant Charter provisions are Article 2(4) and 51; there has been a great deal of legal analysis devoted to the textual and contextual implications of the interrelations between the prohibition on the use of force and the authorization of self-defense; there are related issues concerned with the obligations to report a claim of self-defense to the Security Council, the procedural duty in Article 33 to exhaust pacific remedies, and the ambiguous status of various uses of forces made under mandate of a regional institution (Chapter VIII of the Charter) or in pursuance to a collective defense arrangement (Chapter VII of the Charter). Some of the basic interpretative issues are considered in McDougal and Feliciano, *World Public Order*, 121–260; see also D. W. Bowett, *Self-Defense in International Law* (Manchester 1958);

Julius Stone, *Aggression and World Order* (Berkeley 1958); Louis Henkin, "Force, Intervention and Neutrality in Contemporary International Law," *Proceedings American Society of International Law 1963*, 147–62.

48. For convenient text of G. A. Res. 2131 (XX), December 21, 1965, see Louis B. Sohn, ed., *Basic Documents of the United Nations* (Brooklyn, 2nd rev. edn., 1968).

49. As some commentators have noted, the French text of Article 51 uses the broader, more inclusive phrase "aggression armée" in place of "armed attack." As both texts are authoritative there is some ground for rejecting a strict construction of the English version. For a perceptive comment along these lines see Hardy C. Dillard, "Law and Conflict: Some Current Dilemmas," 24 *Washington and Lee Law Review*, 177–204, at 199–200 n. 28.

50. There are great difficulties of application in real-world situations arising from the occasional arbitrariness of identifying as "aggressor" the state that makes the initial recourse to force. Given alignments and the patterns of group voting in the political organs of the United Nations it is not possible to entrust the power of authoritative decision fully to the organized international community. Pariah states such as South Africa, Portugal, and Israel cannot expect to receive a norm-guided determination of a dispute involving a controversial use of force. The primacy of policy-implementation over norm-implementation is another way of expressing this attribute of the international system. Of course, if the community of states can engage in norm-creation, then some of the apparent contradiction between normative and policy imperatives can be eliminated. Efforts at norm-creation have taken place in relation to "apartheid" and "colonialism." For a favorable juridical assessment of these claims see Falk, *The Status of Law*, Chapter VI.

51. For some data see "Submission of the Vietnam Conflict to the United Nations," Hearings before U. S. Senate Foreign Relations Committee, 90th Cong., 1st Sess., October 26, 27, and November 2, 1967.

52. G. A. Res. 377 A (V), November 3, 1957; for convenient text see Sohn, *Basic Documents of the U.N.*, 99–102.

53. E.g., compare Legal Adviser of the Department of State, "The Legality of U. S. Participation in the Defense of Viet-Nam," in Falk, ed., *The Vietnam War and International Law* (Princeton 1968), 583–603; Consultative Council of the Lawyers Committee on American Policy Towards Vietnam, *Vietnam and International Law* (Flanders, N. J., 2nd edn., 1968); John Norton Moore, James L. Underwood, in collaboration with Myres S. McDougal, "The Lawfulness of United States Assistance to the Republic of Viet-Nam," 5 *Duquesne University Law Review*, 235–352 (1967).

54. Many of these factors are discussed in Klaus Knorr, *On the Uses of Military Power in the Nuclear Age* (Princeton 1966).

55. Such a suggestive viewpoint is developed in Kenneth E. Boulding, "The Learning and Reality-Testing Process in the International System," *Journal of International Affairs* 21 (1967), 1–15.

56. For skeptical assessments of the record and prospects for collective security see Roland N. Stromberg, *Collective Security and American Foreign Policy* (New York 1963); Bull, "Grotian Conception."

57. The experience of noncompliance by objecting members of the Organization with the Advisory Opinion of the Court in the financing context does not encourage present reliance on this mode of dispute settlement. For the various opinions of the International Court of Justice see Certain Expenses of the United Nations (Article 17, Paragraph 2, of the Charter), Advisory Opinion, ICJ Reports 1962, pp. 151–308. For the wider setting of the financing crisis see John C. Stoessinger and Associates, *Financing and the United Nations System* (Washington 1964); Falk and Mendlovitz, *Strategy of World Order*, Vol. 4, 693–789.

58. For convenient text see Sohn, *Basic Documents of the U.N.*, 26–27.

59. Article 103 of the United Nations Charter reads as follows: "In the event of a conflict between the obligations of the Members of the United Nations under the present Charter and their obligations under any other international agreement, their obligations under the present Charter shall prevail." Cf. also the consideration in other settings of the alleged existence of a *Jus Cogens.* See Egon Schwelb, "Some Aspects of International *Jus Cogens* as Formulated by the International Law Commission," 61 *American Journal of International Law*, 946–75 (1967).

60. Deep skepticism as to this possibility is the central theme of Stone, *Aggression and World Order* (Berkeley 1958).

61. For a discussion of the uncertain relationship between a treaty regime such as the Charter and its "amendment" through the practice of the Organization see Ervin P. Hexner, "Teleological Interpretation of Basic Instruments of Public International Organizations" in Salo Engel, ed., *Law, State, and International Legal Order—Essays in Honor of Hans Kelsen* (Knoxville 1964), 119–38.

62. For elaboration see references already cited in note 40 and James L. Brierly, *The Basis of Obligation in International Law and Other Papers* (Oxford 1958), 1–67, Percy Corbett, *Law and Society in the Relation of States* (New York 1951), 17–89.

63. Challenges directed at traditional modes of law-creation are considered in Falk, *The Status of Law*, Chapters V and VI; see also Falk and Mendlovitz, *Strategy of World Order*, Vol. III, 39–122.

64. Daniel Bell has written that "domestically the United States is becoming a *communal* society rather than a *contractual* one. Rights and claims against the community are becoming central." See Bell, "A Summary by the Chairman," in symposium, "Toward the Year 2000: Work in Progress," *Daedalus* (Summer 1967), 975–77, at 977. Such a statement of trend contrasts interestingly with the celebrated earlier distinction of Sir Henry Maine between *status* and *contract*, suggesting that modern society was a product of the transition from status to contract.

65. See in this connection Adrian S. Fisher, "Arms Control and Disarmament in International Law," 50 *Virginia Law Review*, 1200–19 (1964).

66. G.A. Res. 1653 (XVI), November 24, 1961.

67. For an extended discussion of the significance of Article 2(6) see Falk, *The Status of Law*, Chapter VII.

68. It will be recalled that the essential provision of the Connally Reservation precludes the World Court from adjudicating any controversy that the United States Government determines to be within its domestic jurisdiction: For convenient text of the United States Declaration of August 1946 accepting the compulsory jurisdiction of the Court subject to the Connally Reservation see Sohn, *Basic Documents of the U.N.* 272; for text of the optional clause permitting states to file declarations accepting compulsory jurisdiction, Article 26 of the Statute of the International Court of Justice, see Sohn, 227–28.

69. An interventionary capability often reflects relational factors of size, propinquity, access, modes, and geopolitical status. For example, a militant African state, although a feeble power if measured in European terms, might have a considerable sub-regional capability for military intervention. Another state may be able to make use of hostile propaganda to incite revolution in a neighboring state that is much more powerful than it is in terms of conventional military struggle.

70. For an assessment of recent developments pertaining to the economic dimension of the North-South split see Branislav Gosovic, "UNCTAD: North-South Encounter," *International Conciliation*, No. 568 (May 1968), 1–80. Raymond Aron is skeptical

about the capacity of the poor states to maintain a sufficiently cohesive position to influence the future character of international society. See *Progress and Disillusion— The Dialectics of Modern Society* (New York 1968), 176–79.

71. For creative speculation along these lines see Myrdal, *Beyond the Welfare State;* Myrdal, *The Asian Drama* (New York, 3 vols., 1968); Gustavo Lagos, *International Stratification and Underdeveloped Countries* (Chapel Hill, N.C. 1963).

72. See, in general, Vincent Rock, *The Strategy of Interdependence* (New York 1964); on the specific role of supranationalizing trends see Galtung, "The Future of the International System."

73. See, e.g., address by George W. Ball, "Some Implications of the World Company," Pace College, May 2, 1968 (mimeo).

74. Such evidence is analyzed in Falk, *The Status of Law*, Chapter XXIII.

75. My own analysis of this question is contained in a preface to *In the Name of America*, Clergy and Laymen Concerned About Vietnam (Annandale, Va. 1968), 22–27.

76. See useful analysis along these lines in Oran R. Young, "Political Discontinuities in the International System," *World Politics*, 20 (April 1968), 369–92.

77. See consideration of these issues in Falk, *Legal Order in a Violent World* (Princeton 1968), 156–223.

78. For discussion see ibid., 324–35.

79. For a description of the United States bombing patterns in North Vietnam see Gerassi, *North Vietnam: A Documentary* (New York 1968).

80. For extended consideration see Falk, *The Role of Domestic Courts in the International Legal Order* (Syracuse 1964).

8. The Changing Structure of International Law

Wolfgang Friedmann

THE THREE LEVELS OF CONTEMPORARY INTERNATIONAL LAW

The changing structure of contemporary international relations is reflected in more diversified patterns of modern international law. Just as modern international relations are no longer essentially a matter of diplomatic interstate relations, but affect groups and individuals and reach into many domains of social and economic life, so modern international law moves on different levels.

They can briefly be characterised as follows:

The International Law of Coexistence

First, there is the traditional sphere of diplomatic interstate relations, represented by the classical system of international law. These rules aim at the peaceful coexistence of all states regardless of their social and economic structure.

The principal object of these rules of coexistence is the regulation of the conditions of mutual diplomatic intercourse and, in particular, of the rules of mutual respect for national sovereignty. The substance of these rules is found in the classic texts on international law: the rules regulating membership of the family of nations, including the recognition of new states and governments; the rules governing the limits of national territories and of territorial jurisdiction; the jurisdictional and diplomatic immunities of foreign sovereigns; the principles of responsibility incurred by a state for injury done to the lives or properties of the subjects of another state; the adjustment of the rights of belligerent states and neutral states in the rules of war and neutrality, and the formal implementation of these principles by custom, treaty or adjudication.

In the original Marxist conception, which regarded the state as an instrument of capitalist domination to be replaced by international and world-wide class divisions, this system of international law would have lost all significance. In the actuality of the present world, where Communist régimes have adopted and indeed sanctified the traditional aspects of state sovereignty, it retains its universal validity. The conflicts that today confront states governed by entirely different political systems and ideologies, whether over the occupation status of Berlin or the legal status of the rival two Germanies, whether over the width of territorial waters, the rights to conduct nuclear bomb experiments in certain areas of the high seas, or sovereignty in outer space, these and scores of similar conflicts are not as such sensitive to the ideological or political differences between the parties, even though they may have been caused by cold war tensions. They are traditional interstate conflicts, matters of adjustment between national interests and sovereignties. To this extent, the traditional system of international law retains not only its validity but its universality. It is true that certain rules, notably those dealing with the immunity of foreign governments from jurisdiction, have been considerably affected by the assumption of governments of economic responsibilities not contemplated when these rules were evolved. But the need to qualify the rule of absolute immunity with respect to commercial enterprises conducted by governments or governmental institutions was first acknowledged by the Belgian Cour de Cassation in 1903.[1] State ownership and control of commercial enterprises, notably in shipping and other means of international transport, is spread throughout the world and a vast variety of states and political systems. It is in no way characteristic of the division between Communist and non-Communist nations.

What complicates the working of the rules of coexistence far more is the proliferation of sovereignties and the consequent multiplication of clashing national interests. This was clearly demonstrated by the two Geneva Conferences on the Law of the Seas of 1958 and 1960. The major agreement reached was on the Continental Shelf, i.e., an extension of exclusive national claims to resources hitherto included in the freedom of the seas. Neither in 1958 nor in 1960 was agreement achieved on the extent of territorial waters. But the fact that the U.S.S.R., Iceland or Indonesia, with support from some other states, claim a 12-mile limit; Norway, 4 miles measured by baselines, and Peru or Chile 200 miles, while the U.S. and Britain reluctantly concede 6 miles, is due not to ideological but to geographical, economic and military factors. This is not basically different from the opposing views on the freedom on the seas expressed by the Dutchman, Grotius, and the Englishman, Selden, on *mare liberum* and *mare clausum* in the early seventeenth century.

International Law of Co-operation: Universal Concerns

To this traditional sphere of diplomatic existence and the corresponding rules of international law, modern needs and developments have added many new areas expressing the need for positive co-operation, which has to be implemented by international treaties and in many cases permanent international organisations. This move of international society, from an essentially negative code of rules of abstention to positive rules of co-operation, however fragmentary in the present state of world politics, is an evolution of immense significance for the principles and structure of international law. As will be shown later this new dimension of international law deeply affects some of the most firmly established concepts concerning both the universality[2] and the reality of international law.[3] It affects both the meaning and the significance of sanction in international legal relations. The extension in the range of universal human concerns calling for international regulation is a response to the profound changes in the physical and social structure of international society. A preliminary survey of the legal organisation of these interests, as at present discernible, will be given below.[4]

International Law of Co-operation: Regional Groupings

To the extent, however, that international law expands from what is essentially a set of rules of abstention, to organised international co-operation, it becomes more sensitive to the divergencies of internal systems, as expressed in their political ideology, their legal structure and their economic organisation. The building of "co-operative" international law proceeds today on different levels of universality, depending on the extent of the common interests and values that bind the participants. Certain types of the new international law are developing today on the universal level, because they reflect universal interests of mankind. Others, depending on a more closely knit community of values and purposes, proceed on a more restrictive level of international organisation, mostly of a regional pattern (notably in the West European Communities). The borderline between the two groups is not an absolute one, and it will obviously shift in accordance with changing political configurations. It represents nevertheless a fairly definite and important division in the processes of international legal development.

The basic reason for the simultaneous development of international legal organisation and new substantive principles of international law derives from the fact that law must reflect and respond to such need and that at this time only some concerns of mankind are felt to be of sufficiently strong universal urgency to make some measure of universal legal organisation possible. But at the same time certain groupings of nations, more closely bound to each other by common values, common interests, common fears and stronger affinities in their social and legal structure, are proceeding to develop common legal organisations and a corresponding evolution of their substantive laws in fields where mankind as a whole is still too disunited or too disparate to attempt legal organisation and integration. It is possible though by no means certain that the intensity of international, transnational and supranational developments within these more closely knit groups, most clearly exemplified today, though in very different manner, by the European Communities on the one hand and the East European Soviet bloc on the other hand, will be pace setters that will furnish models of integration that mankind may later use on a universal level when it has reached a corresponding degree of community of values and purposes.[5]

In the present phase of international society, attempts at legal regulation on a universal level occur principally in three spheres: the international organisation of security from physical annihilation by war, the international organisation of certain aspects of communications, health and welfare, the tentative beginnings to control the conservation of resources by international co-operation and organisation.

While in theory such fields as the protection of human rights, as formulated in the United Nations Declaration of Human Rights of December 1948, is a universal concern of mankind, in fact, the disparity of standards, systems and values is too great to make an effective international organisation possible in this field. The more closely knit community of the nations joined in the Council of Europe, on the other hand, has been able to enact a Covenant of Human Rights and to establish a machinery, consisting of a quasi-judicial commission and a fully judicial court for their protection. In other fields, too, such as the assimilation of corporate laws, anti-trust laws, patent laws, the closer community of the six European nations joined in the European Economic Community has proceeded to a level of international legal co-operation not presently attainable in the world at large.

Subsequent chapters will deal with specific aspects of these different levels of international law. What is to be emphasised here is the necessity of studying them all as representing, in different ways, the legal organisation of mankind in our time.

THE NEW DIMENSIONS OF INTERNATIONAL LAW

The recognition that the structure of international society has undergone some basic changes, and that, correspondingly, international law is now developing on several levels, one continuing the traditional international law of diplomatic coexistence and the other two implementing the quest for both universal and regional international co-operation and organisation, must lead to a far-reaching reorientation in our conceptions of the science and study of contemporary international law.

Some of the new tasks and dimensions of international law were discernible in the inter-war period. This is true of the gradual extension, since the end of the First World War, of international law to new subject-matters,[6] or of the impact of new principles of state organisation and especially of the growing state control over economic activities, on the traditional system of international law.[7] But the horizontal expansion of international law, towards non-Western states and civilisations, with differing cultural backgrounds and differing stages of economic development, as well as the vertical extension of international law, from states to public and private groupings, as participants in the international legal process, are essentially, though not entirely, phenomena of the world as it emerged from the Second World War.

Shortly after the last World War, Maurice Bourquin[8] pointed out that the subject-matter of international law is not enclosed in "immovable boundaries." Taking as his principal illustration the transformation of labour and social welfare matters from the earlier nineteenth-century philosophy of *laissez faire* to active state intervention and from there to international legal concern and organisation, as expressed in 1919 by the International Labour Organisation (ILO), Bourquin described the development of the substance of international law as "a mounting flood which is far from having exhausted its momentum."[9] He pointed to the rapidly expanding number of fields affected by international legal regulation, such as labour, human rights, education, science, refugee assistance, civil aviation, communications, agriculture, international money and banking matters, and on the other hand, to the increasing participation of technical, scientific and other experts in the processes of international law and diplomacy. He characterised the entire development as one of both quantitative and qualitative renovation of international law.

More recently, the need to redefine the scope, impact and purposes of international law has been articulated by several other distinguished writers.

Philip Jessup, whose work, *A Modern Law of Nations*, had already foreshadowed the need to reassess the scope and purposes of post-war international law, has formulated the challenge in the following words:

> Obviously there is a delicate shading between the situations to which international law traditionally applies and those to which it does not. "Lawyers," writes Sigmund Timberg, ". . . have adhered to rigidly compartmentalized national legal systems, which are unable to cope with an economic order of international dimensions." The use of transnational law would supply a larger storehouse of rules on which to draw, and it would be unnecessary to worry whether public or private law applies in certain cases. We may find that some of the problems that we have considered essentially international, inevitably productive of stress and conflict between governments and peoples of two different countries, are after all merely human problems which might arise at any level of human society—individual, corporate, interregional or international.[10]

Myres McDougal, in his Hague lectures of 1953 and in other works, has spoken of the need for a contemporary study of international law that would include not only the nation state but also international government organisations, transnational political parties, pressure groups, private associations and the individual human being.[11] More recently, a Spanish jurist, in a survey of the structure of international society,[12] has emphasised that international society comprises inter-individual and inter-group relations, of which inter-state relations are only one specific aspect.[13]

The shift in the structure of international law has been vividly formulated by Wilfred Jenks:

[T]he emphasis of the law is increasingly shifting from the formal structure of the relationship between States and the delimitation of their jurisdiction to the development of substantive rules on matters of common concern vital to the growth of an international community and to the individual well-being of the citizens of its member States. We shall also find that as the result of this change of emphasis the subject-matter of the law increasingly includes cross-frontier relationships of individuals, organisations and corporate bodies which call for appropriate legal regulation on an international basis.[14]

The present writer,[15] and Dr. Röling,[16] have emphasised more strongly the shift, in the subject-matter of international law, from the more or less formal regulation of diplomatic relations between states to an international law of welfare.

In a brief but incisive survey[17] Frederick van Asbeck has stressed the extent of growth and movement in international law "in various forms and variegated shades of colour" in the last 100 years. He has singled out six factors as the most important new forces accounting for this change: first, the extension of inter-governmental consultation and co-operation from the foreign relations field to technical, economic and social affairs; second, the increasing substitution of a collective framework for bilateral dealings; third, the extension of the activities of international unions and other organisations to the non-European world; fourth, the entry of the technical expert on the international scene; fifth, the growth in the practice of regular political conferences and assemblies, of fixed composition and working according to a fixed procedure, based on a permanent secretariat of officials; and sixth, the quasi-parliamentary conference representing social groups as well as governments in the ILO.

Other basic challenges to the present structure and teaching of international law come, on the one hand, from the steady horizontal widening of its scope, the expansion of membership from a small group of Western nations to virtually all of mankind, including civilisations whose values differ profoundly from those of the Western-Christian world and, on the other, from the emergence of deep fissions in the social, economic and political structure of states, leading to the formation of groupings of states and of regional systems of international law in addition to, or possibly in derogation of, the traditional principles of universal international law.

Although the great majority of the treatises and case books on international law remain, to a surprising extent, dominated by the traditional scope and arrangement of international law, the awareness of new dimensions is increasingly reflected in the contemporary teaching of international law, at least in the United States. The study of international organisations, including the special UN agencies, international financial institutions and the regional groupings, notably the European Communities, now forms part of the curriculum of the teaching of international law in major law schools. In American law schools there has also been growing emphasis on the legal aspects of international investment, including both international economic transactions and consideration and characterisation of the relations between sovereigns and private investors, a field almost automatically excluded from the traditional study of international law, which recognises only states as subjects of international law.

The increasing preoccupation with the position of the individual and of the individual and the private corporation have further widened the horizons of international law from still another perspective.

A number of eminent authorities, such as the late Sir Hersch Lauterpacht, Judge Jessup and others, have stressed the need to include the individual as a subject of international law. The United Nations Declaration on Human Rights of 1948, the same Organisation's Draft Covenants on Human Rights and, perhaps more significantly, the European Convention on Human Rights, which for the first time enables an individual to bring an action against his own state before an impartial supranational forum,[18] give increasing substance to an international law of human rights.

In the post-war period, private corporations have become increasingly active participants in international transactions, mainly as investors concluding agreements on the exploitation of natural resources, or on industrial activities, with the governments of underdeveloped states, i.e., with sovereigns and, through their participation in certain international multilateral transactions, with governmental organisations or international public institutions such as the World Bank. The importance of the private corporation as a participant in the development of international law has been stressed among others by Berle, Jessup, McDougal, Schwarzenberger and Verdross.[19]

The widening scope of international law is reflected in the definition given at the beginning of the new semi-official digest of international law, prepared under the direction of an Assistant Legal Adviser to the U.S. Department of State: "International law is the standard of conduct, at a given time, for states and other entities subject thereto."[20]

THE EXPANDING SCOPE OF INTERNATIONAL LAW

Perhaps the most important of the revolutions in the dimension of modern international law lies in its steadily expanding scope, in the addition of new subjects to the field of international law. This expansion is due in large measure to the growing number of fields in which all or part of the family of nations co-operate for purposes of international welfare. In the present writer's earlier formulation, the term "co-operative international law" is tentatively chosen to describe the growing of international legal relationships and organisations which are . . . concerned with the regulation of experiments in positive international collaboration. The legal and institutional problems posed by this developing and increasingly important branch of international law are essentially of a different character from those posed by traditional international law. To speak in sociological terms, a developing co-operative international law represents community aspects, rather than society aspects, in the relations between states and nations.[21]

To some extent, this corresponds to the distinction between "the international law of reciprocity" and "the international law of coordination" as formulated by Dr. Schwarzenberger in various works.[22] Dr. Röling has spoken of an international law of welfare as the law concerned with the creation of conditions of well-being and the promotion of higher standards of living, full employment and economic and social progress and the development of all the members of the economic community.[23] Also, in this context, the efforts of Professor McDougal to reformulate international law in terms of policies and interests, rather than in terms of traditional analytical concepts, should be mentioned.[24]

Much of this new, and constantly expanding, body of international law is less than universal in dimension and character. Almost all of it is found in international conventions, i.e., in articulate law-making, rather than in the slow growth of custom or judicial interpretation. The extent of the universality of this new co-operative international law is of course closely related to the nature of the subject-matter. In certain fields there is a universal community of interest; in others, agreement on the formulation of common standards depends upon a community of interests, values, and institutions confined to a more closely knit and limited community. In the field of international communications and transportation, for example, there is generally a universal interest in common standards and a corresponding universality of international conventions. In matters of labour, differences of political organisation as well as of economic and social standards make universality far more difficult to attain. Effective international co-operation in cultural and educational matters or in the protection of human rights against arbitrary interference depends on a correspondence of values unattainable at this time in the world community but realisable within more limited groups of nations.[25] The acceptance of bilateral, multilateral, regional and other international conventions of less than universal scope as sources of modern international law is therefore no longer a matter of doubt.

The most serious challenge to the conception and in particular to the teaching of international law arises from the increasing diversity of the subject-matter regulated in hundreds of international conventions. These may affect company law, copyright law or patent law. They may regulate collective labour agreements, restrictive trade practices or the protection of foreign private investment. Many of the subjects thus regulated are the province of specialists in other fields of law who are not usually concerned with public international law. Yet it would clearly be inadequate and indeed disastrous to leave this field entirely to the experts in company law, commercial law, copyright law and the like, and to regard these matters as outside the province of the international lawyer. Collaboration of the experts in the particular field is of course indispensable since the international lawyer can hardly be expected to be an expert in the many fields that may become the concern of international law. But by virtue of becoming the subject of an international convention, of a public law agreement between states, these matters inevitably acquire significance from the public international law point of view as well as from that of the special field.

An international tax convention, for example, raises not only the highly complex questions of double taxation, remission of taxes and the respective competences of various jurisdictions, but also questions of national and international public policy of decisive importance for the control of national resources and the legal principles governing foreign investment. The international regulation of restrictive practices presents a great challenge to the comparative student of anti-trust law and also raises vital problems of international policy in regard to the respective functions of governments and private enterprise and indeed in regard to the whole economic and social organisation prevailing in the various countries involved. The constitution and the periodic re-negotiations of the General Agreement on Tariffs and Trade (GATT)[26] are not only a matter for the experts on tariffs and trade quotas; they also pose basic problems of international policy, such as the effect and significance of the "most favoured nation" clause in trade relations between states that have differing degrees of control over their economies. Given the close connection between trade and politics, the negotiation of a multilateral trade agreement also poses complex problems of a diplomatic nature. An international labour convention may have far-reaching effects on the relative competitive export capacity of the participants, or on their position with respect to non-participants. If it affects maritime wages, it may produce a significant shift in the registration of merchant shipping under the flag of a non-member country, as has indeed been amply demonstrated in recent years.

The changes in the dimensions of international law require a corresponding reorientation in its study; neither the international lawyer trained in the classical methods of international law and diplomacy nor the corporation, tax, or constitutional lawyer are equipped to handle this subject without co-operation with each other, and with economists and political scientists. International law is becoming a more and more complex and many-sided subject. Its scope is bound to expand as the organisation of mankind, on a universal or regional basis, increases. Private law may become public law and a comparative study of a particular subject may become the prelude for an international convention.

The time has come to attempt at least a tentative ordering of this bewildering mass of new developments, not only for the sake of classification or as a guide to a reorientation of the teaching of modern international law in contemporary universities, but principally as an aid to our understanding of modern legal problems that have arisen outside the traditional scope and methods of international law. To understand and interpret such modern phenomena as an investment and concession agreement between a group of private oil companies and the Indian government, or the legal relation of the anti-trust regulations of the European Economic Community to the public and private laws of its Member States, we must reorient our thinking. In particular, we must overcome the traditional distinction between public law and private law thinking, between diplomacy and political science thinking, on the one side, and "black-letter law" on the other.

The reordering of international law and an understanding of its new dimensions should proceed from five different perspectives:

1. the widening of the scope of public international law through inclusion of new subject-matters formerly outside its sphere;[27]
2. the inclusion, as participants and subjects of international law, of public international organisations and to a less definite extent, of private corporations and individuals;
3. the "horizontal" extension of international law, particularly through the accession of non-Western groups of states to the legal family of nations;
4. the impact of political, social and economic principles of organisation on the universality of public international law, particularly at a time when its scope and subject-matter are expanding;
5. the role and variety of international organisation in the implementation of the new tasks of international law.

NOTES

1. *S. A. De Chemins de Fer Liegeois-Luxembourgeois v. Etat Neerlandais, Belgium,* Cour de Cassation, 1903, Pasicrisie belge 1.294. See further below, p. 345 *et seq.*
2. See Chaps. 18–21 in Wolfgang Friedmann, *The Changing Structure of International Law* (New York: Columbia University Press, 1964). Subsequent references to "chapter" also pertain to Friedmann's book.
3. See Chap. 7, fn. 2, especially p. 88 *et seq.*
4. See Chap. 17, fn. 2.
5. This estimate is more cautious than that of a recent Dutch monograph (De Valk, *La Signification de l'Integration Européenne pour le Developpement du Droit International* (1962)), which asserts categorically that the community aspects of the new European organisations (from unanimity to majority rule) characterise the evolution of all modern international law, "La loi constitutionelle est la cristallisation européenne de la forme caractéristique du droit international moderne" (p. 97).
6. See Garner, "Le Développement et les Tendances Récentes du Droit International," 35 *Hague Recueil* (1931), 625, 641 *et seq.*
7. Friedmann, "The Growth of State Control over Economic Activities, etc.," 19 B.Y.I.L. (1938), p. 118 *et seq.*
8. "Pouvoir Scientifique et Droit International," 70 *Hague Recueil* (1947), 331, 359 *et seq.*
9. *Op. cit.,* at p. 361 (author's translation).
10. Jessup, *Transnational Law* (1956), pp. 15–16.

11. McDougal, "International Law, Power and Policy: A Contemporary Conception," 82 *Hague Recueil* (1953), 137.

12. Truyol y Serra "Genèse et Structure de la Société Internationale," 96 *Hague Recueil* (1959), 553.

13. In addition, see the distinction drawn by Reuter in *Institutions Internationales* (1956 ed.), pp. 10–11, between "groupes primaires" and "groupes secondaires."

14. Jenks, *The Common Law of Mankind* (1958), p. 17.

15. Friedmann, *Law in a Changing Society* (1959), pp. 417–419; "The Changing Dimensions in International Law," 62 Columbia L.Rev. (1962), 1147.

16. Röling, *International Law in an Expanded World* (1960).

17. "Growth and Movement of International Law," 11 I.C.L.Q. (1962), p. 1054 *et seq.*

18. This applies only to the nationals of those Member States that have accepted this part of the European Convention on Human Rights of 1954: 213 U.N.T.S. (1955), p. 221.

19. See Chap. 14, fn. 2.

20. Whiteman, *Digest of International Law*, Vol. 1 (1963), p. 1.

21. Friedmann, "Some Impacts of Social Organization on International Law," 50 Am.J. Int.L. (1956), 475; restated in *Law in a Changing Society* (1959), p. 460.

22. See, most recently, Schwarzenberger, *The Frontiers of International Law* (1962), pp. 29, 34.

23. Röling, *International Law in an Expanded World* (1960), pp. 83–86.

24. See McDougal and Associates, *Studies in World Public Order* (1960); McDougal and Feliciano, *Law and Minimum World Public Order* (1961); McDougal, "International Law, Power and Policy: A Contemporary Conception," 82 *Hague Recueil* (1953), 137.

25. A preliminary attempt to classify the various fields of international law from this point of view, i.e., with respect to their sensitivity to a community of standards, was made by the present writer in 1938. Friedmann, "The Disintegration of European Civilisation and the Future of International Law," 2 M.L.R. (1938), 194. See Chap. 20, fn. 2.

26. GATT, October 30, 1947, 6 T.I.A.S. No. 1700. The official text of the general agreement is issued as 3 *The Contracting Parties to the General Agreement on Tariffs and Trade, General Agreement on Tariffs and Trade, Basic Instruments and Selected Documents* (1958).

27. For a survey of the new emerging fields of international law, see Chap. 11, fn. 2.

9. Poverty of the International Order

Mohammed Bedjaoui

Traditional international law is derived from the laws of the capitalist economy and the liberal political system. From these two sources it derives the elements and factors of a certain consistency to be found in its theoretical construction and in the terms of its actual rules.

The judicial order set up by the former international society gave the impression of neutrality or indifference. But the laisser-faire and easy-going attitude which it thus sanctioned led in reality to legal non-intervention, which favoured the seizure of the wealth and possessions of weaker peoples. Classic international law in its apparent indifference was *ipso facto* permissive. It recognized and enforced a 'right of dominion' for the benefit of the 'civilized nations.' This was a colonial and imperial right, institutionalized at the 1885 Berlin Conference on the Congo.

In addition to ratifying the European countries' right to conquer and occupy the territories concerned, international law recognized the validity of 'unequal treaties,' essentially leonine, whereby the weaker peoples for a long time delivered up their natural wealth on terms imposed on them by the stronger States. Neutral or indifferent, international law was thus also a formalistic law, attached to the semblance of equality which barely hid the flagrant inequalities of the relationships expressed in these leonine treaties.

It was also a law eminently suited to the protection of the 'civilized countries'' privileges, through the interests of their nationals. By virtue of diplomatic protection and intervention, the law enabled the nationals of the countries concerned to obtain, in certain States, advantages which were not even awarded to the citizens of those States.

International law made use of a series of justifications and excuses to create legitimacy for the subjugation and pillaging of the Third World, which was pronounced uncivilized. As we shall see, these justifications were dropped as and when they had fulfilled their allotted function of mystification.

However, the consistency of the system required that the freedom of action allotted by international law to a 'civilized' State should be matched by the same freedom for any other civilized State. This accepted international law was thus obliged to assume the essential function of reconciling the freedom of every State belonging to the family of 'civilized nations' with the freedom of all the other States in the same family.

To keep in line with the predatory economic order, this international law was thus obliged simultaneously to assume the guise of: (a) an *oligarchic law* governing the relations between civilized States members of an exclusive club; (b) a *plutocratic law* allowing these States to exploit weaker peoples; (c) a *non-interventionist law* (to the greatest possible extent), carefully drafted to allow a wide margin of laisser-faire and indulgence to the leading States in the club, while at the same time making it possible to reconcile the total freedom allowed to each of them. However, this matter of controlling rival appetites was not taken very far.

Until the League of Nations came into being, this international law was simply a European law, arising from the combination of regional fact with material power, and transposed as a law dominating all international relations. The European States thus projected their power and their law on to the world as a whole. Here we come to the real nature of the so-called 'international' law, to its substance and even to the reality of its existence.

As it had been formed historically on the basis of regional acts of force, it could not be an international law established by common accord, but an international law given to the whole world by one or two dominant groups. This is how it was able to serve as a legal basis for the various political and economic aspects of imperialism.

This classic international law thus consisted of a set of rules with a geographical basis (it was a European law), a religious-ethical inspiration (it was a Christian law), an economic motivation (it was a mercantilist law) and political aims (it was an imperialist law).

Until the recent period of successive decolonizations, there was no perceptible change in this law as a backing for imperialism, apart from the fact that the emergence of the two super-great powers eclipsed the European influence and provoked a large-scale revision of the boundaries of spheres of influence in the world. . . .

A PLUTOCRATIC INTERNATIONAL LAW

After each of the two world wars, the great powers had lofty ideals and generous objectives to attain. The idea which inspired the creation of the League of Nations, and then, after the Second World War, the establishment of the United Nations, was completely in line with these ideals. Great hopes were thus entertained. The concept of 'peoples of the United Nations' embodied in the Charter was intended to embrace all countries and peoples in the international community. The proclaimed objectives of justice and social progress augured well for the institution of a new order breaking with the inequitable practices which international law had always covered.

But there were contradictions in the Charter and its environment. First, there was no political will to translate into practice what seemed to be the most advanced of the provisions of the Charter; and second, the conclusion of such parallel arrangements as the Yalta agreement on the political plane, and the Bretton Woods agreement on the monetary plane, was directly opposed to the principles and ideas proclaimed in the Charter. There had been no radical change in international law, which had merely come to terms with the new circumstances surrounding the emergence of the super-great. It had ceased to be a European law only to become a law of the great powers, thanks to the policy of the exclusive clubs both within and without the international organizations.[1] While it may in principle no longer have been serving political colonization, it did not cease for all that to be a means of economic domination and an excuse for it. In actual fact, it modified only the form, not the substance, of domination. The latter has been more subtly introduced into the legal rules governing the economic relations between developed and developing countries. . . .

Now, not only does this permissive international law serve the interests of a minority of States, but furthermore it shows a dangerous indifference to the common good of mankind as a whole, as it results in wastage, reckless over-exploitation of natural resources, destruction of the environment and the unfair distribution of wealth. 'The economic and social inequality of the contemporary world is not merely called in question on the moral plane, but also . . . as the driving force for an economic system which has consolidated the division of the world into two enormous spheres, the contrast between which is no less striking than during the colonial period. . . .'[2]

Thus, after having constituted a check on political decolonization, international law continues to be an obstacle to the development of the Third World countries on solid foundations. The baleful characteristics of this law have not changed: in the words of Professor Chaumont, this 'law, unjust because of what it justifies, is unrealistic because of what it ignores.'

We shall see later how international law has long concealed flagrant economic inequalities between States under cover of sovereign equality. The rules of free competition, reciprocity and non-discrimination are also among those which have made it possible to accentuate the unequal relationship which in fact directly affected the sovereignty of the developing countries.[3] The legal 'baubles' given to the developing countries, such as the most-favoured-nation clause or the system of generalized preferences, are only one variant of the legal formalism 'designed to float above things as they really are and thereby camouflage them, and finally enable the States to operate freely behind a façade of generalities.'[4]

. . . Just like the developing countries, international law is also a 'developing' law. The work done by Professor Wolfgang Friedmann on the 'changing structure of international law' has shown the profound changes that, with a certain quickening of tempo, this law is undergoing today:

Traditional international law is essentially a law of co-existence, composed for the most part of rules of mutual abstention. It is based on the political and legal sovereignty of States and it sanctions their, at least theoretical, equality. Its purpose is to regulate diplomatic relations between States in a juridical way on the basis of the mutual respect of national sovereignty. . . . This limited system of co-existence based on intergovernmental relations offers the advantage of taking no account of the States' internal legal and social conditions. At the very most, this law requires that States should satisfy three conditions: the existence of a territory, of a population, and of a government exercising the minimum of control and responsibility imposed by international relations.[5]

This limited system indeed offered the dominant powers the 'advantage' of ignoring the internal legal and social conditions of the Third World, meaning in the final analysis that they could ignore the conditions for the real exercise of sovereignty and independence by those States. However, the real equality of States depends on their development. The underdeveloped or non-aligned countries have, by their activities, compelled recognition of the existence of unequally developed countries. Traditional international law thus prospered on facticity, formalism, artifice and fiction and had no connection with a reality deeply marked by the underdevelopment and exploitation of the Third World. The merit of the underdeveloped and the non-aligned countries has been to show that, unless they wish to perpetuate the artifice, States cannot be equally sovereign if they are not equally developed. In that sense, the non-aligned countries have made an enormous contribution to exposing the deceit of traditional international law. . . .

International law must thus accept the challenge being made to it both by the structural disorder of the world economy and by the deeply felt desire of all peoples for a new international economic order. However, it is perfectly clear that to satisfy such hopes and to meet the needs of the international community seeking for this new order, international law cannot properly and effectively undertake its own transformation if it confines itself to its traditional sources alone, i.e., custom, treaties and general legal principles. The inadequacy of the traditional ways of forming the rules of international law is very sharply felt at the present time. What is to be done if not to make use of other sources? This is the new and fundamental problem raised by the establishment of the new international economic order. Another problem arises from the fact that the relationship between progress in standards on the one hand and institutional change on the other is fairly specific in international law as compared with domestic law. In the international field, the adoption of a new standard is not necessarily accompanied by the establishment of the executing body that should go with it. The shortcomings of 'institutional' international law in comparison with 'normative' international law, still to be seen today, are due to a variety of factors, most important of which is that the foremost component of the international community is still the sovereign State with its suspicions about international or supranational bodies of a legislative, executive or judicial nature. Nonetheless, the development of the body follows that of the standard and conversely, even if the process is somewhat tardy. Consequently, and this is the first conclusion of these preliminary observations, the surest way to meet, legally speaking, the challenges made by the inevitable establishment of the new economic order would be to concentrate on standard-setting activities. The international law of tomorrow will develop more through a consolidation of the normative fabric than through the more problematic proliferation of institutions. The second conclusion is that this approach is also the one which, by the reciprocal interplay of the standard and the executive body, will encourage the development of institutional international law.

If these remarks are accurate, the problem of the contribution of international law to the establishment of the hoped-for new economic order arises today more in terms of the elaboration of legal standards than in terms of the establishment of institutions. To achieve this objective, and as has been stated above, it is scarcely possible to hope for as substantial and rapid a development as possible of international law on the basis of its traditional sources, referred to in Article 38 of the Statutes of the International Court of Justice. If custom, treaties and general legal principles are in danger of contributing too little, all that is left is the resolution or, in more general terms, the legal standard elaborated in international organizations, in order to attain the sought-after goal. This leads on to a great number of problems, only some of which will be mentioned here, concerning the conditions under which the normative action of international organizations takes place, particularly the procedure for drawing up the international legal standard as well as its scope and its effects when effectively applied.

The word 'resolution' is, of course, to be taken here in its widest sense, whatever its content, form, designation or the procedure by which it is adopted. Whether it is called a wish, resolution, declaration, recommendation, decision, approbation, or anything else; whether it is economic, social, political, technical or cultural in content; whether it gives an order, makes a request, invites or asks for a particular action, recommends specific or general measures; whether it is addressed to a State, whether or not a member, or to a body of the same international institution or to a different international institution, a multinational or transnational firm or to an individual; whether it is adopted without a vote, by consensus or by a unanimous or majority vote—what is here called a 'resolution' or again a 'legal standard of an international organization,' covers any decision taken by a deliberative body belonging to an international institution of a world-wide nature.

THE ATTRACTION OF THE RESOLUTION

There is no doubt that the resolution holds a real attraction for the countries of the Third World because of its flexibility, its rapidity and the security it gives these countries through their control of the technique as a result of their numbers. It is equally certain, however, that by reaction, the development of resolutions as a means of formulating international law is linked with the very evolution of that law, which has become a law of transformation for a purpose. It is a system in motion, directed towards the requirements of development, and it was inevitable that the legal techniques for elaborating the rules should be affected by these successive waves of adaptation.

In the opinion of the developing countries, international organizations, and especially the United Nations, provide an ideal context for the drafting of a legal new deal with a view to the transformation of the international economic order and the development of all peoples. Through its egalitarian character, its majority basis and hence its democratic origins, the resolution seems to them to present sufficient guarantees as a method for the elaboration of international norms responding to today's needs.

The preference of Third World States for resolutions as instruments for the progressive development of international law can thus be explained: first, by the conception these States have of the role of international organizations and especially of the General Assembly of the United Nations; next by the speed of adoption of a resolution; and last, by the resolution's flexibility, since it can quite easily be changed to take account of developments in the world. In spite of the privileged position of the great powers within international organizations, in spite of the existence of limited-membership bodies and the practice of weighted voting, these organizations remain places favourable to contestation, to inspiration and to the creation of new guidelines furthering the interests of the international community.

But the question of how to draw up the 'rules of the international game' for the present and the future, with the participation of all States, new and old alike, leads us to one of the major problems of our time, which we can assume will have the most decisive impact on the fundamental rules of future international law. It concerns the 'reversal of the majority' on the international scene in favour of the new States, and hence the problem, formulated in new terms, of 'majority' and 'minority.'

NUMBER VERSUS FORCE

For thirty years, in addition to its veto in the Security Council, the club of the developed countries had an automatic majority in the General Assembly of the United Nations, owing as much to the number of Member States, at that time limited, as to the existence of certain clients.

Some fifty States were godparents to the United Nations at its baptism in San Francisco in 1945. Today, 150 States are members of the organization. This tripling of the number of Member States poses complex problems which lie at the heart of the new international economic order and the projected new legal order. The vast increase in the number of States which occurred in the post-war world cannot be considered merely in quantitative terms. For the elaboration of the new order, 'membership' must eclipse the 'leadership' of dominant oligarchies and must give pride of place to 'partnership.'

The problem, however, is that power and number have never been in such a paradoxical relationship as at present.

Formerly, Europe projected its law and power upon the world. It had written the history of the world with its soldiers, merchants, missionaries and lawyers. It dominated the globe in the name of its law, and until 1960 the Third World was virtually non-existent. Today, our world calls for conversions and metamorphoses, grafts and substitutions. We are living at a time of the necessary transfer of power and wealth within States as well as among them. We are likewise living at a time when nations are allergic to encroaching leadership.

The problem is not so much the 'transfer of the majority' in itself. This majority, held by the Western countries until the 1950's and 1960's, has passed to the States of the Third World. The problem is that for the first time in human history, international law is not on the side of force or power. The novelty of our time resides in this signal divorce between law and force. The Western world hitherto possessed material force and imposed on the world its own protective law, in the guise of universal international law. Might and right were therefore on the same side, without serious divisions or excessive tensions. . . .

If we venture to sketch out the future trend of this system of norms, we could say that international law will probably no longer be the expression of relations of domination which are inegalitarian or hegemonistic. Nor is it likely to be only a law of egalitarian relations, but rather a body of rules of which an increasingly large part will be reserved for relations of equity and solidarity. The principles of equity and solidarity will increasingly be the basis for the elaboration and observance of norms which allow room for corrective or compensatory inequality to enable the Third World States to grow. It can therefore only be a law which is elaborated and inspired by the final objectives of development.

The main question, and it is a complex one, is whether we can agree on a viable system and make it work through international co-operation. Some suggest what one might call 'separate development,' which would reserve a particular sphere of international law for each 'group' of countries, bearing in mind the nature and degree of its development.

An improvement in the international order cannot come about within the world-wide capitalist system, nor within the existing legal framework, still faithful to ancient principles. The transformation or even repudiation of the old framework does not in any way mean looking for a separate system designed solely for the Third World countries, and therefore the drafting of a 'non-law' or 'sub-law.' On the contrary, the aim must be to define a homogeneous international community. Hence the contradictory phenomena and tendencies which modern international law is required to eliminate, so as to allow the 'community' of States as a whole to take shape as such and to develop. . . .

It has been justly maintained that 'the history of international relations has been nothing but the simplified expression of the relationships of production that govern the various economic and social formations.' Indeed, the development of international law appears to result from a series of factors encompassed in what economists call the production mode. Socioeconomic phenomena are themselves the product of a series of interactions between them and the institutions of international law. Thus the idea of change is fundamental, and its driving force must be sought in the socioeconomic structure of the international system. It must be accepted then that this development may have a dual nature:

1. A *purely quantitative change* does not modify the fundamental nature of the international system. Thus the appearance of international European organizations constitutes a change which has taken place since the second World War, but the character of European society has not changed; it remains a society of sovereign States, even if their sovereignty has suffered some limitations.
2. However, these quantitative changes prepare the way for a *qualitative evolution in the international system*. Thus, for example, relations between the great powers on the basis of peaceful coexistence may introduce a qualitative change in international law. Similarly, a change in the present economic order must entail a qualitative evolution of the system.

International law is not homogeneous in character. Its various sectors, such as human rights, the law of nations, the law of the State and the law of international organizations, do not evolve at the same rate or in the same direction. And, more often than not, the law gets out of step with the relationships of all kinds which exist at the heart of the international community. The lack of homogeneity in the formation and composition of the international community and in the various branches of the law is matched by a particular type of relation, sometimes a relation of domination, sometimes a relation of transition. The latter is today tending to become more and more the rule. Thus the challenging and rejection of the classical legal principles governing nationalization were less a lasting phenomenon than a temporary effect. It was not a question of resolving in this way the *structural problems* which face the international community, but of overcoming difficulties arising from a particular set of circumstances and resulting from the hand-over of sovereignty at the end of the colonial period.

The procedures for drawing up this transitional law, the nature of the instruments used, as well as the institutional framework and the specific nature of what it covers do not imply that there is, on the legal plane, a tendency to erode international law, and still less that this happens to any real extent. The economic, social and political differences which exist between the various international orders give this law a differential character, without in any way splitting it up or dividing it into various legal rulings peculiar to each nation or group of nations.

Thus, the generalized adoption of the entity of the State implies a unity in the norms of international law. The industrialized States and the developing ones are certainly in different situations, but they exist within and belong to a unified system because there cannot be more than one world economy and therefore more than one sphere of international law. It would thus be a mistake to consider change and specific characteristics as being the opposite of unity. . . .

If we are to believe certain analyses,[6] there exists in this contemporary, transitional international law, or more exactly in international development law, an original, specific principle, that of the double standard. In other words, 'for a single body of rules uniformly governing all relations between States are henceforth substituted two bodies, parallel and of equal worth. On the one hand is the one which governs relations between developed countries and on the other, the one which governs, firstly, the relations between these and the developing countries and secondly, relations between developing countries.'[7]

. . . The supporters of the new international order, however, stress the coexistence, not of a double standard as such, but of the dual content of the same standard, which adds to the urgency of the development of the Third World countries. These writers take a more acceptable universalist view.[8] Development law is in fact to be seen at the present time as a wave of protest against the general norms drawn up and imposed by the Western countries, and whose application and effect the developing countries cannot tolerate. . . .

Indeed, international development law is first of all, and this is as much its *raison d'être* as its primary characteristic, the expressions of the social and economic life of the contemporary international community with its present needs. It is therefore the expression of an effort to think up concepts and to create norms which will provide a satisfactory solution to the problems of underdevelopment. It is a retrograde and fragmentary way of looking at things to see 'international development law' as a law on its own. Some lawyers, clinging to classical law as a harmonious whole, accept that it should grow a sort of pseudopod, but they limit the development of this limb by treating it as an appendage or excrescence whose existence they must, if need be, admit, but only so that it can govern relations within another world, that of the poor. *That is a law for the ghetto. . . .*

The characteristic of modern international law is not crisis but rapid change in a world which is itself in crisis. The main feature of international law is in fact its present multi-dimensional nature. It is to traditional international law what three-dimensional geometry is to plane geometry. To start with, it has for several years been undergoing an unprecedented horizontal expansion because of the 'explosion of States' which has brought a multitude of States on to the international scene. International law's horizontal field of action has not only been extended geographically but has also been diversified to the extent to which those actively concerned by international law have increased in number. The individual, non-governmental organizations, multinational or transnational companies, national liberation movements, peoples and mankind have made a notable entry into international relations as parties actively involved, either new or making a comeback. The 'vertical' dimension which international law possessed, to the extent to which it was already concerned with space, was extended to outer space and the cosmos and to the depths of the sea, which was known to traditional law only as regards its surface.

The 'frontiers' of international law have thus been considerably enlarged so as to make it a universal law. But what is even more spectacular is the new function assigned to international law, which has now been given the task of adjusting, not only inequalities due to human activity but even those due to nature. We all know the economic demands being made by the 'Group of 77,' made up of some 105 Third World States. But in this, they are attempting first to iron out inequalities resulting from human activity—in other words, to bring about the end of colonial, neo-colonial or imperialist exploitation. These are their aims in striving for effective implementation of the principle of compensatory inequality. If, however, we examine the problems of the new law of the sea, we come to the existence of 'States which are geographically disadvantaged' by nature, and whose interests or aspirations must be taken into account by the new norms of that law. Within this group, geographical origins or ideological divisions become blurred to the advantage of the interests of the whole.

Landlocked, geographically disadvantaged States want to have a ceiling fixed for the benefits derived in the economic zone and to have a share in these benefits. Similarly, and here it is a question of regulating competition between men in the exploitation of natural resources, the developing States want the exploitation of the deposits of the sea-bed in the international zone carried out according to rules which will provide protection for their mining production on land. And when there is a call for 'collective economic security' or for the extension of 'mankind's common heritage' to other areas, then an effort is being made at the same time to allot to the international law of the future the task of correcting the inequality due not only to men, but also to natural conditions.

It can nevertheless be seen that the considerable widening of the scope of international law makes it an even more complex and baffling task to evaluate the power relations between the industrialized and developing countries in the elaboration of the new international economic order. Beyond the common aspirations of the Third World States, communities of interest, born of circumstance, are continuously forming and dissolving, so that we may sometimes question the consistency of the Third World's influence in the elaboration of new international legal norms. In the new law of the sea, whereas the widely, differing interests of States were originally determined in accordance not with their ideologies, which divide the world, but with their degree of development, thus substituting a North-South confrontation to the opposition between East and West, the cohesiveness of the developing countries in their dealings with the industrialized countries has been gradually eroded over the sessions. The 'Group of 77' broke up as a result of the creation of the geographically disadvantaged group of States. Each country ended up taking its own stand according to its particular situation with relation to the sea, and according to the type of question being discussed. What common destiny is shared by Austria and Upper Volta, Switzerland and Uganda, Hungary and Nepal? And yet these States were on the same side in the demand for a share in the riches of the sea-bed and for as wide an extension as possible of the international zone. On the other hand, countries such as India and Chile, which belong to the Third World, and Canada and Australia, which are among the 'Western States,' are all to be found in the same camp, at least insofar as they refuse to share their continental shelf which stretches a long way. . . .

For all that, one cannot doubt the inevitable coming of the new international economic order. Like a river whose course is shaped by the obstacles it encounters but which will unfailingly flow into the sea, the concept of the new international economic order can prolong or delay its course in meanderings, or lose its way a thousand times in chasms which the speleologists of international law will explore, before finding concrete and complete expression in international relations.

NOTES

1. It is interesting to re-read after a lapse of time the statement by a member of the American Congress, James Hyde, who belonged to the United States delegation to the Interim Committee of the United Nations General Assembly: 'Our country

is a leader and a most powerful leader in the world community. Power confers leadership; power brings with it responsibility. . . . To a large extent the future of the United Nations depends upon us. It is fortunate that our own self-interest and our own idealism lead us along the same road. In my opinion, if the United Nations did not exist today, one of the first orders of business in American foreign policy would be to invent something that looks a lot like it.' *Annual Review of United Nations Affairs,* 1951, p. 255 and p. 260.

2. Message from Luis Echeverría Alvarez, President of Mexico, to the meeting of the Club of Rome, held in Algiers, 25–28 October 1976.

3. Éric David, 'Quelques Réflexions sur l'Égalité Économique des États,' *Revue Belge de Droit International,* 1974, p. 401.

4. Charles Chaumont, Cours de Droit International Public, *Collected Courses of The Hague Academy of International Law,* 1970, Vol. 130, p. 350.

5. Wolfgang Friedmann, *Revue Belge de Droit International,* 1970–71, p. 6.

6. See *Pays en Voie de Développement et Transformation du Droit International* (Aix-en-Provence symposium of the Société Française pour le Droit International, 1973), Paris, Pedone, 1974; Guy Feuer, 'Les Principes Fondamentaux dans le Droit International du Développement,' ibid., p. 225 (p. 191–234).

7. Ibid., p. 225.

8. Michel Virally, 'La Charte des Droits et des Devoirs Économiques des États,' *Annuaire Français de Droit International,* 1974, p. 74.

10. The Identification and Appraisal of Diverse Systems of Public Order

Myres S. McDougal and Harold D. Lasswell

. . . The problems connected with the identification of public order systems, and their appraisal in terms of impact upon the values of human dignity, have received so little systematic attention that scholars of many nations, in no sense exclusive of the United States, continue inadvertently to contribute to the confusions of everyday life manifest in the whole world community and all its component regions.[1]

. . . Among traditional legal scholars it has long been customary to give unquestioning verbal deference to the proposition that if there is any international law at all, it is a universal law, embracing the organized governments of the world community as a whole, or at least all those bodies politic admitted to the ever-enlarging European "family of nations."[2] The existence of regional diversities in the interpretation of allegedly universal prescriptions, and in the fundamental policies about the allocation of power and other values sought by such interpretation, has been cloaked in the shadows of "decent mystery" by hopeful insistence that such divergent interpretations are but occasional aberrations which will disappear when the real universality of the relevant concepts is appropriately understood. . . .

Professional lawyers and men of affairs the world over exhibit the most extreme oscillation between over-affirmation of the authoritativeness of what they term "international law" and over-denial of the validity of any significant claims put forward in the name of such a system. . . . Not the least obstructive result of this confusion is the failure to keep at the focus of responsible world attention both the *future-oriented* nature of the challenge contained in the idea of universal legal order and the crucial fact that a legal order of inclusive scope can only come into existence in a process of interaction in which every particular legal advance both strengthens a world public order and is in turn itself supported and strengthened by that order. The processes of law have as their proper office the synthesizing and stabilizing of creative efforts toward a new order by the procedures and structures of authority, thereby consolidating gains and providing guidance for the next steps along the path toward a universal system. By pretending in one mood that international law is a contemporary and presumably well-constructed edifice while insinuating in another that it is a pretentious and dubious fantasy, the true dimensions of the task are concealed. Effective, comprehensive universality, despite the faint shadows of worldwide organization, does not now exist. It is for the future and can be expected only as a reward of clarification and of relevant effort.

A pervasive present illusion is that lip service to the claim of universality for contemporary international law serves the cause of universality. On the contrary, the invocation of spurious universalism on all questions diverts creative concern from the vital issues on which the diverse systems of public order that now dominate the world scene are *not* united, and which, if they are to be resolved by peaceable persuasion rather than bellicose coercion, must be brought into the open and kept there as unremitting challenges to take appropriate action. . . .

Having full regard to the common interest in removing the cloud that overcasts the future, it must not, however, be supposed that all interests are identical, or that the existing decision-makers of all nation states are without what they regard as important stakes in continuing, rather than terminating, the present state of danger.

In view of the universal testimony in public and private about the suicidal peril of continuing the arms race, one may well exclaim: "How can such things be?" . . . We do not even need to make the assumption of malevolence, of individual depravity that prefers office to the sacrifices necessary to abate the nuclear danger. A much simpler explanation may very well account for the failure of leaders, notably of totalitarian leaders, to make whatever short-range sacrifices may appear necessary in order to install the operations essential to a truly universal system of international law.

We refer to the conditions that surround the political leaders of totalitarian systems. Such leaders have come to the top by surviving the chronic uncertainties and risks of a police state. . . . These top figures, despite all their braggadocio and bombast, have been effectively paralyzed as leaders of co-operative achievement by a polity of mutual and deadly intimidation;

they gyrate in endless convolution while the arms race gains breadth and malignance.

Yet the spokesmen of totalitarian Powers are the ones who, professing to be more orthodox keepers of the faith than their bourgeois opponents, pay most punctilious deference to the supposed universality of international law. And why? Strange as it may seem at first glance, the most convincing interpretation is that the existing imperfections of the system can be used by them to help prevent further advances toward a world order with genuine measures of security. For it is in the name of such allegedly universal doctrines of international law as sovereignty, domestic jurisdiction, non-intervention, independence and equality—all of which appear to fortify claims to freedom from external obligation—that the case is made to resist the institutional reconstructions which are indispensable to security.

In this grave posture of world affairs it can only make sense to put aside the veil that is provided by false conceptions of the universality of international law. An indispensable step toward a truly comprehensive system of world order is to disabuse all minds of the false myth that universal words imply universal deeds. The effective authority of any legal system depends in the long run upon the underlying common interests of the participants in the system and their recognition of such common interests, reflected in continuing predispositions to support the prescriptions and the procedures that comprise the system. The discrediting of claims to universality which are in fact false is thus a first necessary step toward clarifying the common goals, interpretations, and procedures essential to achieve an effective international order capable of drawing upon the continuous support essential to global security by consent. . . .

For the visible future at least the lead must of course be taken by scholars and public figures physically located in the non-Soviet world. It is obvious that scholars who reside in the non-Soviet world have much more freedom in the expression of unconventional ideas than their opposite numbers. . . . Scholars and public figures in the non-totalitarian world can use this relatively favorable environment to make critical appraisals—of the national self as well as the self of other nations. It is therefore feasible for them to dissolve the curtains of confusion created by the common practice of glorifying specific institutional practices instead of glorifying the goal values of human dignity and engaging in a *continuous reappraisal of the circumstances in which specific institutional combinations can make the greatest net contribution to the over-arching goal.*

Not the least of the institutionalized devices that call for reappraisal are the doctrines and operations having the name of international law. We suggest that major contributions to world order would be the divorce of many of these putative principles from the contexts that give them spurious significance and the vindication of authoritative prescriptions that have genuine relevance to the goal values of human dignity.

The task is a prime responsibility of the scholarly world, and especially of jurisprudence and the social sciences generally. Some of the work has been done by traditional scholars, though too often in scattered and incomplete form. We shall outline a map of the undertaking that we have in mind and in whose execution we invite all like-minded scholars to participate. It will be made evident that we are calling, not for a single research project to be done once and for all, but for a continuing process designed to become part of the intelligence and appraisal functions of the world community. In common with all institutional details this inquiry will be open to perpetual reappraisal.

The map we recommend begins with (a) orienting ourselves in world social process, (b) identifying within this, a process distinctively specialized to power, (c) characterizing as the legal process those decisions that are at once authoritative and controlling, and (d) defining as the public order those features of the whole social process which receive protection by the legal process. From this map we proceed to (e) outline our commitment to the realization of a universal system of public order consistent and compatible with human dignity, (f) analyze the intellectual tasks that confront the scholar who accepts this overriding goal, (g) indicate some of the specific questions that arise in the consideration of any system of public order, and (h) refer to the scholarly procedures by which the task of inquiry can be executed on a satisfactory scale of depth and coverage.[3]

WORLD SOCIAL PROCESS

Systems of public order are embedded in a larger context of world events which is the entire social process of the globe. We speak of "process" because there is interaction; of "social" because living beings are the active participants; of "world" because the expanding circles of interaction among men ultimately reach the remotest inhabitants of the globe. Interaction is a matter of going and coming, of buying and selling, of looking and listening, and more. The most far-reaching dimension is the taking of one another into account in the making of choices, whether these choices have to do with comprehensive affairs of state or private concerns of family safety. Such subjective events of mutual assessment tie people into the same process even when they retire behind the ramparts of castles and garrisons to prepare against an eventual day of reckoning.

The participants in the world social process are acting individually in their own behalf and in concert with others with whom they share symbols of common identity and ways of life of varying degrees of elaboration. Whether acting through one channel or the other the fundamental goal stays ever the same, the maximization of values within the limits of capability. A value is a preferred event; and if we were to begin to list all the specific items of food and drink, of dress, of housing and of other enjoyments, we should quickly recognize the unwieldiness of the task. Hence for the purpose of comparing individuals and peoples with one another we find it expedient to employ a brief list of categories where there is place for health, safety and comfort (well-being), for affection, respect, skill, enlightenment, rectitude, wealth and power. Human beings the world over devote their lives to the incessant shaping and sharing of values, activities which they accomplish by making use of patterns of varying degrees of distinctiveness.

Each identifiable "practice" is a pattern of subjectivities (perspectives) and of operations. The practices which are relatively specialized to the shaping and sharing of value we identify as an "institution." Hence we recognize institutions of government, specialized to the shaping and sharing of power; economic institutions, which focus upon the production, distribution and consumption of wealth; religious and ethical institutions, specialized to the grounding and specification of responsible conduct; mass media and other institutions of enlightenment; schools of arts, trades and professions, and associated institutions of skill; pervasive patterns of social class, which are basic institutions of respect; the institutions of family and friendship (affection); and of health, comfort and safety (well-being). These institutions, organized and unorganized, utilize the resources of nature in greater or less degree in the shaping and sharing of preferred outcomes of the social process. When we consider the globe as a whole we perceive that it is composed of communities of diverse size and degrees of institutional distinctiveness (culture). . . .

WORLD POWER PROCESS

Within the vast social process of man pursuing values through institutions utilizing resources, we are especially concerned with the characteristic features of the power process. A social situation relatively specialized to the shaping and sharing of power outcomes is an "arena"; and it is evident that the world at any given cross section in time is a series of arenas ranging in comprehensiveness from the globe as a whole, through great continental, hemispheric and oceanic clusters, to nation states, provinces and cities, on down to the humblest village and township. The identifying characteristic of an arena is a structure of expectations shared among the members of a community. The assumption is that a decision process occurs in the community; that is, choices affecting the community are made which, if opposed, will in all probability be enforced against opposition. Enforcement implies severe sanction.

When we scrutinize an arena in more detail, going beyond the minimum necessary for bare definitional purposes, it is possible to identify several categories of participants. Some are official organizations, or governments—national and international. Others are specialized to bringing influence to bear upon those who make the important decisions (political parties, political orders, pressure groups, gangs). Some are associations which, though active in the social process, do not concentrate upon power but primarily seek other values. The ultimate actor is always the individual human being who may act alone or through any organization.

Whatever the type of participants—group or individual—the actual conduct of participants in the power process depends in part upon their perspectives, which are value demands, group identifications and expectations. . . . Demands may be accompanied by structures of expectation that place great reliance upon strategies of persuasion (or coercion) as the most likely means of influencing results.

Each participant has at his disposal values that he employs as bases for the influencing of outcomes. An inventory discloses that all values—power, wealth, respect, and so on—may be used to affect a decision outcome.

Base values are made effective by the strategies used to affect outcomes. Strategies are often classified according to the degree to which they rely upon symbols or material resources. Diplomacy depends primarily upon symbols in the form of offers, counter-offers and agreements among elite figures. Ideological strategy also uses symbols as the principal means of action, the distinctive mode being communications which are directed to large audiences. Economic instruments are goods and services; military strategy employs weapons. Every strategy uses indulgences (such as economic aid to allies) or deprivations (such as boycott of unfriendly Powers), and proceeds in isolation or coalition. The coalitions within an arena at a given time reflect the number and strength of the participants interacting in the arena. . . .

The outcomes affect the value position of every participant in the world context in terms of every value and institutional practice. In addition, post-outcome effects may change the basic composition and modes of operation of the entire world community.

THE LEGAL PROCESS

Within the decision-making process our chief interest is in the legal process, by which we mean the making of authoritative and controlling decisions. Authority is the structure of expectation concerning who, with what qualifications and mode of selection, is competent to make which decisions by what criteria and what procedures. By control we refer to an effective voice in decision, whether authorized or not. The conjunction of common expectations concerning authority with a high degree of corroboration in actual operation is what we understand by law.

In order to identify and compare the role of law in the processes of power it is serviceable to distinguish seven functional phases of decision-making and execution. *Prescription* is the articulation of general requirements of conduct. Among the organs specialized to this function are constitutional conventions and legislatures. International law is articulated principally in the daily activities of foreign offices as they justify or attack, accept or reject, the claims put forward by themselves or others. Prior in time to prescription in a given sequence is *recommendation*, or the promoting of prescriptions. This function is actively performed by such official and semi-official bodies as international governmental organizations, national and trans-national political parties, and pressure groups. Also the *intelligence* function is typically prior in time to prescription or recommendation; it includes the gathering and processing of information about past events, and the making of estimates of the future, especially of the costs and gains of alternative policies.

Invocation consists in making a preliminary appeal to a prescription in the hope of influencing results. Hence invoking activities are conspicuous in negotiation; they also include the justifying of claims defended or attacked by counsel before tribunals of the world community. Invocation is the function of public officers or the community agents who are confronted by the responsibility for labeling specific patterns of conduct in reference to legal norms. *Application* is the final characterization of a situation in reference to relevant prescriptions. When a court speaks at the end of litigation, or an administrative organ decides a concrete case, each operation is an applying activity. The *appraisal* function formulates the relationship between official aims and subsequent levels of performance. Among special agencies of appraisal are auditors, inspectors and censors. . . . The function of *termination* is the putting to an end of authoritative prescriptions and of arrangements arising within them.

A PUBLIC ORDER SYSTEM

Within the distinctions thus developed, we are able to clarify what is meant by a system of public order. The reference is to the basic features of the social process in a community—including both the identity and preferred distribution pattern of basic goal values, and implementing institutions— that are accorded protection by the legal process. Since the legal process is among the basic patterns of a community, the public order includes the protection of the legal order itself, with authority being used as a base of power to protect authority.

In this perspective it is evident that our world is composed of a series of community contexts beginning with the globe as a whole and diminishing in territorial range and scope. To the extent that it can be demonstrated that the globe as a whole is a public order system, and only to that extent, do we speak of universal international law. To the degree that territories larger than national states comprise a public order system, we refer to regional international law. . . . Obviously today it is more accurate to speak of international *laws* or multi-national law than of international *law.*

Clearly, systems of public order differ not only in territorial comprehensiveness but also in the completeness of arrangements in terms of the different value processes regulated, and in the internal balance of competence for decision *inclusive* of the entire area in question and that for decision relating *exclusively* to component areas within it. To the extent that there is universal international law some prescriptions are inclusive of the globe; other prescriptions recognize self-direction by smaller units. Regional international law has a corresponding separation between region-wide prescriptions and sub-regional units. . . .

Among major distinctions between public order systems are the degree to which *specialized organs* have been developed to conduct the decision process in the inclusive territory, and the degree to which the organs employed by each component unit also carry on the decision process for the whole. It requires no demonstration that international law is largely the creation of organs of the latter type, since the bulk of the world legal system has grown up in the "custom" of communicating foreign offices, supplemented by special conferences, and more recently by intergovernmental bodies whose tasks, speaking formalistically, are not "legislative" (that is, are not regarded as performing "prescriptive" functions).

It is not possible at present to describe the public order structure of the world community, since for the most part existing knowledge is fragmentary and noncomparable. Nor can we proceed with confidence to set detailed limits upon the relative completeness of legal systems and hence of systems and near-systems of public order. It is sufficient to say that, whatever lines are drawn between a system that the scientific observer calls "complete" and systems that are "incomplete," the present absence of authoritative and controlling arrangements for minimal security will preclude the acceptance of the entire world community, as at present constituted, from being classified among complete legal systems, and hence among complete public orders.

TOWARD A UNIVERSAL ORDER OF HUMAN DIGNITY

Our overriding aim is to clarify and aid in the implementation of a universal order of human dignity. We postulate this goal, deliberately leaving everyone free to justify it in terms of his [or her] preferred theological or philosophical tradition.

The essential meaning of human dignity as we understand it can be succinctly stated: it refers to a social process in which values are widely and not narrowly shared, and in which private choice, rather than coercion, is emphasized as the predominant modality of power.

Given this overarching goal and the present posture of world affairs, what can scholars do individually and through the organization available to them to further the objective?

Manifestly, five intellectual tasks are pertinent to the solution of this as of any legal problem.

First, clarification of goal. Clarification can proceed in two directions, in justification of the commitment to the goal, or in detailed specification of what is meant in terms of social and power processes, and legal and public order systems. If we were to specify in detail the meaning of "widely shared participation" in social values, we would consider each of the value-institution processes of society in turn.

Second, description of trend. Having clarified the goal of human dignity, the next intellectual task is the discovery of the degree to which historical and contemporary events conform to or deviate from the goal.

Third, analysis of conditioning factors. Simple historical sequences are not enough to provide understanding of the factors which affect decision.

We need to ascertain the factors that condition the degree to which goals have been achieved or failed of achievement.

Fourth, projection of future developments. Assuming that our individual or group efforts will not significantly influence the future, what are the probable limits within which goal values will be achieved?

Fifth, invention and consideration of policy alternatives. Assuming that our efforts may have some impact upon the future, what policy alternatives will maximize our goals (at minimum cost in terms of all values)?

Each of these five intellectual tasks may be illustrated in further detail. We begin with the clarification of goals and indicate with a series of questions about each value what we mean by the sharing of values.

Power. To what extent is power widely or narrowly held? E.g., how many members of the community are involved in amending the constitution, or enacting other prescriptions; or in the function of intelligence, recommendation, invocation, application, appraisal, termination? (The involvement may be direct, as in referenda, or indirect, as in representation.) To what extent are the processes of adjustment coercive or persuasive? E.g., how intense is the expectation of violence? Of peaceful agreement?

Wealth. To what extent is the economy focused upon savings and investments? Upon rising levels of consumption? Upon shorter hours of work? E.g., what tax and other fiscal measures make for forced saving or discourage saving and investment? Is there compulsory labor? Are there minimum income guarantees?

Respect. What is the commitment to caste or to mobile class forms of society? E.g., does status depend upon position of family at birth? Or upon any other characteristic besides individual merit? To what extent is minimum respect accorded to everyone on the basis of mere membership in the human race? E.g., prohibition of humiliating penalties; protection of privacy; protection of freedom of agreement against official and private limitation. To what extent are individual differences protected when they depend upon government? E.g., protection of reputation.

Well-Being. To what extent is continued increase of numbers encouraged even at the expense of immediate improvement of the values available to individuals? E.g., are birth restrictions promoted or opposed? What are the policies regarding care of the old? In what degree is the living population sought to be protected from mental and physical deprivation, *e.g.,* accident, disease and defect prevention; prevention of private and public violence? In what degree is the health, comfort or safety of the population restored after deprivations have occurred? E.g., arrangements for care and cure.

Skill. To what degree is the body politic committed to optimum opportunity for the discovery and cultivation of socially acceptable skills on the part of everyone? E.g., is there universal and equal access to educational facilities? Does the access continue to whatever level the individual is capable (and motivated) to make use of? In what measure does the body politic provide optimum opportunity for the exercise of accepted skills? E.g., are there employment guarantees or suitable levels? Are new skills recognized and assisted readily? E.g., prohibitions upon skill monopolies.

Enlightenment. To what extent does the community protect the gathering, transmission and dissemination of information, *e.g.*, guarantee freedom of press, of research, of research reporting? In what degree does the community provide positive aid, *e.g.*, encourage the use of competent sources (though not permitting monopoly)?

Rectitude. To what degree does the body politic protect freedom of worship and of religious propaganda? To what extent is positive assistance given to foster freedom of worship and religious propaganda, *e.g.*, aid to doctrinal schools?

Affection. What is the protection given the family and other institutions of congeniality? *E.g.*, what are the barriers against disruption? What affirmative aid is given, *e.g.*, freedom in the choice of partner; in group formation; financial and other modes of help?

Next we turn to the description of trends. Our concern is for trends throughout the world community with special reference to all the bodies politic, however incomplete their level of political organization. The term "trend" is used to designate the present distribution of goals sought, the degree of their contemporary realization, and the extent to which this realization has become greater or less through time.

It is perhaps obvious that we are not to be satisfied with taking note of the fact that the ideal of human dignity is verbally accepted. We therefore propose to go beyond the dominant beliefs, assumptions and loyalties (the myth) of any given society and look into its operational technique. It is therefore ultimately necessary to conduct the studies that reveal the true state of affairs throughout the entire social process. Then we can sum up the state of public order according to the degree of effective sharing and the basic institutions that receive protection.

Each value-institution pattern has a specialized system of myth and of operational technique. The myth falls into three parts: doctrine, formula, folklore. Political doctrines, for instance, include the prevailing philosophies of politics and law. Economic doctrines include theoretical justifications of capitalism or socialism. Respect doctrines either justify social class discrimination or the opposite. And every other value has its doctrinal myth.

The political formula takes in all the constitutional, statutory and other authoritative prescriptions of the legal order that relate to the decision process. It is possible to find corresponding rules for the other values, such as wealth. Some of these rules receive legal backing; others are not supported by the community as a whole, but depend solely upon the support of a component group.

The political myth also includes popular lore about the heroes and villains of yesterday and today, and the notable events of history (and the future); similarly, for wealth, enlightenment, and the other values.

The operational technique exhibits the extent to which the perspectives constituting a myth are adhered to, or deviated from.

The foregoing categories provide a broad reference frame within which more detailed consideration can be given to the patterns of authority and control, and particularly the patterns of international law, characteristic of each legal system. We shall devote a separate section to the outlining of such questions.

Turning to the third intellectual task, the analysis of conditioning factors, it is necessary to make an inventory of the categories of factors to be investigated by the scholarly community. . . . We shall go no farther than to indicate the five sets of conditioning (interacting) factors that must eventually receive attention. First, we mention *culture*, which is the term that characterizes the most distinctive patterns of value distribution and institutional practice to be found in the world community. Second, *class*. This word covers the position of individuals or groups in terms of the control of values. One may be upper, middle or lower (elite, mid-elite, or rank and file) in control over each value. Third, *interest*. The word is used to refer to groups less inclusive than a class or unbound by class. Specific occupational skills, for example, may cut across lines of class. Fourth, *personality*. The term designates the basic value orientations, practices and mechanisms characteristic of an individual. Fifth, *crisis* level. This expression, referring to conflict situations of extreme intensity, applies to each of the foregoing categories, but can be separated for convenience. In addition to those factors which pertain directly to values and institutions, place must be found for the impact of the entire resource environment, and of basic genetic capabilities, upon mankind. The fourth task, that of projection of future developments that are likely to affect international law, requires a disciplined consideration of past trends conjointly with the available stock of scientific knowledge. . . .

The ever-present question in everyone's mind is whether we can invent or recognize policy alternatives that are likely to move us most rapidly, and at least social cost, toward a more perfect realization of a universal international law of human dignity. . . .

We turn to a more specific consideration of the existing state of affairs.

COMPARING INTERNATIONAL SYSTEMS OF PUBLIC ORDER

The questions with which we are concerned are those pertinent to the ultimate appraisal of the success or failure of any system of public order as instruments of the overarching goal of human dignity. We are chiefly interested in international systems, and particularly in the external impact of each system. Specific interpretations of many universalistic terms and propositions differ greatly on particular problems. Hence it is especially important to examine the diverse systems of public order whose several commitments affect the flow of events in the world arena.

The following questions about any particular system of public order, to be asked here of any grouping of states, are directed to the identification of its fundamental categories and techniques and to the appraisal of both its inner operations and external interactions in terms of impact upon the values of human dignity. With respect to each specific inquiry, we ask a double question: What is the proclaimed, explicit myth or implied assumption about myth? How in fact is the proclaimed or assumed myth interpreted and applied in particular instances of social interaction? We are concerned both for what values are expressed in the basic conceptual structure of the system about important problems and for how these concepts are applied in practice to affect the sharing of values and the degree of achievement of the basic goal values.

Relevant questions might be directed toward every aspect of social interaction, including any or all of the traditional problems of international law. For convenience we group questions about the conceptions and ap‑ plications of any particular system of public order under the following three main headings: (1) Conceptions of Law (including perspectives of authority and techniques of effective control, as well as myth and practice about the interrelations of authority and control); (2) Features of Power Processes Protected by Law; and (3) Features of Basic Value Processes Protected by Law. It may be emphasized again that the questions we ask are intended to be suggestive only and not exhaustive.

(1) Conceptions of Law

The important questions here relate to both perspectives of authority and techniques in effective control. Most generally the questions are: What processes, structures and functions of authority are established or recom‑ mended? What processes, structures and functions of effective control are established or recommended? And what interrelations between authority and effective control are established, assumed, or demanded.[4]

Concerning authority, more specifically, important questions relate to perspectives about both decision-makers and criteria for decision-making.

First, in regard to decision-makers: Who are regarded as authoritative decision-makers and by what processes are they established and identified as authoritative? What is the degree of community participation in such processes of establishment and identification? Are decision-makers in the various authority functions distinguished from parties to the interactions regulated? Do they include both national and international officials? Do they include representatives of non-governmental groups or parties? Who, with what qualifications, are selected by whom and how? What constitutive, legislative, executive, judicial, and administrative structures of authority are established or recommended? How, in sum, must such structures be appraised in terms of such fundamental *continua* as democracy-despotism, centralization- decentralization, concentration-deconcentration, pluralization-monopoliza‑ tion, and regimentation-individuation?

Second, in reference to criteria for decision: By what distinctive criteria— in terms both of the scope, range, and domain of values affected and of procedures by which decision outcomes are to be brought about—does the system of public order under inquiry recommend that decisions be taken? How are perspectives of authority grounded in terms of fundamental justifications of decision? Are ultimate references to trans-empirical or empirical events? If trans-empirical, are the references religious or meta-physical? If metaphysical, idealistic or materialist? If ultimate reference is empirical, is it to events within or without the social process? If transcendent of the social process, how characterized? If within the social process, is it by unclarified demand for "precedent," "logic," "validity" or other alleged rectitude norms or by systematic reference to expectations about social process values? If reference is to social process values, is demand made for caste or human dignity values? If the system declares an overriding goal of human dignity, what particular values and institutional practices are included in the conception of such goal? What degrees in the sharing of particular values are specified as required by human dignity? With what degree of universalism or inclusiveness are criteria of authority, whatever their ultimate reference, asserted and demanded? For what "community" is "common interest" proclaimed?

Important questions about criteria for procedures relate both to the structures of authority established or recommended for each policy function indicated above—prescription, intelligence, recommending, invoking, apply-ing, appraising, terminating—and to the impact of the modalities by which each function is performed upon human dignity values. For each function the two most general questions are: What structures of authority (constitutive, legislative, executive, judicial, administrative) are specialized to the perfor-mance of this function? How does the performance, which is in fact established or recommended, impact upon all demanded values? Impres-sionistic indication of the type of more specific, relevant question with respect to each function may be indicated *seriatim:*

Prescription. What is the relative reliance, in the performance of this function, upon specialized organizations or tribunals, upon explicit agreement by participants in an arena, and upon unilateral decision by contending participants in the name of "customary law"? What principles and procedures are afforded for expediting the achievement of consensus and the making of agreements? To what "sources" of policy (prior uniformities in behavior and subjectivities of "rightness," general principles of mature systems, considerations of equity and fairness, opinions of the learned, and so on) are unilateral decision-makers authorized to turn in shaping and justifying decision? Does the system purport to accept the notion of "customary law" but reject the inherited general principles of mature societies? To what degree is there community participation in, and acceptance of, all procedures?

Intelligence. How effective and economic are specialized structures in bringing to the attention of decision-makers the information required for rational decision? How widely is available information shared in the com-munity?

Recommending. How many different types of participants are permitted to engage in this function? How open is participation in advocacy of policies or decisions? Are opposition groups permitted or encouraged? Are the mass media of communication accessible to all?

Invoking. What is the degree in equality of access by all types of participants to the invoking machinery of the community? What participants are admitted to what arenas for invoking what prescriptions?

Applying. Is arrangement made or recommended for the impartial, third-party application of community prescriptions? Are appropriate procedures, and dispositions of effective power, afforded for prompt enforcement? Are procedures for enforcement compatible with human dignity?

Appraising. How effective are the structures afforded for appraising the economy and legality of decision? How open is the sharing of results of appraisals? May private groups make appraisals of the legality of government?

Terminating. How efficient is provision for the termination of obsolete prescription? Do the procedures afforded give effective expression to the demands of the people affected? What is the relative reliance upon termination by consensus of the parties affected and upon unilateral decision by one party? Is an appropriate balance sought and achieved between stability in expectations and necessary change, with minimum costs in terms of all values?

Concerning effective control, more specifically, the important general questions are two: What processes, structures and functions, of effective control are brought to bear in support of, and in turn receive reciprocal protection from authority? And, in contrast, what processes of effective power escape the control of authority? The first of these questions will be developed in some detail below. The second requires only brief illustration. The thrust of the inquiry is whether all participants in power processes and all instruments of policy are effectively made subject to processes of authority.[5] In what degree do political parties, pressure groups, and other private associations achieve a privileged position above the law or are subordinated to the legal process? In what degree are the varying instruments of policy—diplomatic, ideological, economic, military—subjected to, or freed from the regime of law?

(2) *Features of Power Processes Protected by Law*

The first questions here relate to the allocation of competence, protected by processes of authority, between particular states and larger groupings, or the general community of states.[6] What inclusive competence is protected in the general community or larger groupings of states? What exclusive competence is protected in particular states? How economic is the balance achieved for the production and sharing of the values of human dignity for all mankind? Is it the balance which is best calculated to maintain minimal security, in the sense of freedom from intense coercion or threats of such coercion and freedom to promote the greatest production and widest sharing of other values? In what degree does the inclusive competence protected both secure democratic access by peoples to participation in decision-making which affects them and achieve an assumption of responsibility adequate to maintain application of inclusive policies in arenas both internal and external to particular states? In what degree does the exclusive competence protected secure states from arbitrary external intervention and promote freedom for initiative, experiment, and diversity in effective adaptation of policies to all the peculiarities of the most local contexts? Are technical concepts proffered by the particular system under inquiry—such as "international concern," and equivalents, for protecting inclusive competence, and "sovereignty" and equivalents (including "domestic jurisdiction," "independence," "equality," and "non-intervention") for the protection of exclusive competence—designed and interpreted in fact to promote a rational, productive balance between competences? Is "sovereignty," for example, subordinated to, or regarded as a part of, international law or is it conceived as a "discretionary power which overrides the law"?[7] Is "international concern" interpreted in practice to protect inclusive decision which is genuinely inclusive or used as a cloak to conceal arbitrary exclusive decision?

For the more detailed posing of these and other relevant questions, brief reference may be made *seriatim* to each of the important elements or phases in a power process: participants, arenas, bases of power, strategies, outcomes, and effects.

Participants

Which of the effective participants in the world power process are accepted as full participants in processes of authority—that is, given access to authority structures and functions for the protection of their interests and subordinated to authority for insuring their responsibility to community policies? Which effective participants are admitted, or subjected, in lesser degree to what authority structures and functions? By what criteria are different types of participants accepted or rejected in varying degree? What territorially organized communities are accepted as authorized participants and in what degree? What provision is made for regional groupings of territorial communities? Is the ultimate goal a monolithic "single state" or a pluralism of balanced regions? What role is accorded international governmental organizations? Are they conceded an independent role or regarded as mere diplomatic appendages of states? What role is accorded non-governmental groups? Are differences made between political parties and other private associations? Are individual human beings a recognized category of participants in processes of authority or are they regarded as mere objects of authority?

Arenas

Are the various particular arenas provided for the performance of authority functions adequate to promote the resolution of controversies by persuasive, rather than coercive, means and to reduce to a minimum the number of decisions not taken in accordance with authority?

Are special criteria, other than those stipulated for the identification of generally authorized participants, imposed to regulate admission to particular arenas? When a new territorially organized community emerges, by changes in effective control and authoritative arrangements, from an older community, do authoritative prescriptions make a distinction between emergence by consent and by violence? Between indigenous internal change and change stimulated by external intervention by peoples from other communities? Between change in the name of a totalitarian world order and in genuine demand for indigenous freedom? Do relevant prescriptions achieve an economic balance between maintaining security in the larger community and promoting genuine self-direction in the lesser communities?

Are principles and procedures about membership, representation, and credentials stipulated for international government organizations compatible with easy access by all interested participants or do they create controversy and continuous world tension?

Is provision made for the reciprocal recognition and protection by governmental participants of the private associations they variously charter and foster for the greater production of specific values, such as wealth and enlightenment? How open is the access of individual human beings to governmental arenas, political parties, pressure groups, and private associations?

Are decisions about recognition, membership, representation, and credentials established as inclusive or exclusive?

BASES OF POWER

A. *Resources*

By what criteria may exclusive claims to resources such as land masses, internal waters, and airspace be established? Is peaceful use and succession protected against violent seizure?

By what criteria is a balance achieved between exclusive and inclusive claims to sharable and strategic resources, such as the oceans, international rivers, international waterways, Polar regions and outer space?[8] Does the balance achieved promote the most productive and conserving use for the benefit of all?

B. *People*

By what criteria are varying degrees of control over people as bases of power honored and protected? What discriminations are permitted between "nationals" and "aliens"? By what criteria may a territorial community impose its nationality upon or withdraw its nationality from an individual for varying purposes? What are the limits upon naturalization and denaturalization? What selective admissions, exclusions, and corrective measures, with respect to both physical access to territory and all value processes, is a territorial community permitted to impose for power purposes upon its nationals and upon aliens? Do relevant prescriptions protect the utmost individual voluntarism in affiliation and activity that is compatible with a reasonable community security?

C. *Institutions*

How adequately are participants protected in their freedom of decision, as to both internal and external arrangements, from external dictation? Are principles of non-intervention fashioned to catch the more subtle modalities of coercion or only the cruder, physical forms? Are protected freedoms appropriately balanced by imposition of responsibility for the maintenance of internal institutions adequate to the performance of community responsibility? Is "self-determination" invoked to secure and protect a genuine self-direction of people or merely as a slogan to promote destruction of existing communities?

Is the equality between states which is protected a real equality in sharing of power and responsibility or is it a pseudo-equality which defers by verbal legerdemain to the security considerations of the greater powers? Is it tacitly expected that discriminations will be made which are not explicitly provided?

Strategies

With respect to each instrument of policy—diplomatic, ideological, economic, and military—what are the prescriptions about who can employ the instrument, with respect to whom, for what objectives, under what conditions, by what methods, and with what intensities in effects?

How adequate are prescriptions for promoting the persuasive, non-coercive use of instruments of policy?[9] Are adequate immunities and facilities afforded to diplomats and others to facilitate negotiation? Does the "peaceful settlement" demanded by a system express a real willingness to compromise and to seek an integrated solution in community of interest or is it a mere tactic in the poising of an opponent for ultimate destruction? Are provisions about the formation, application, interpretation, and termination of agreements rationally designed to protect the reasonable, mutual expectations of parties? When the "validity" of agreements is found, not in the mutual expectations of parties, but in alleged *objective* conditions, by what criteria is it decided which conditions create validity and which do not?

Do prescriptions contain a clear prohibition of the use of instruments of policy in modalities so coercive that they threaten a target participant's continuing bases of power and independence in decision? Does the prohibition upon too intense coercion extend to all instruments of policy, singly or in combination, or only to the military instruments? Is the use of force limited to the conservation, rather than to the expansion of values? Do prescriptions in the law of war about permissible combatants, areas of operations, objectives of attack, instruments and means of attack, and degrees of destruction, achieve a reasonable balance between humanitarianism and military necessity? Do the prohibitions of coercion and violence impose a community-wide responsibility or are "neutrals" tolerated?[10]

Outcome and Effects

By what criteria—territoriality, nationality, passive personality, protective universality, et cetera—are states accorded exclusive competence to prescribe and apply law for particular events or value changes? By what criteria— "acts of state," "immunities," et cetera—is it expected that a state which has acquired effective control over persons or resources will defer in decision to the law prescribed by another state? What varying degrees of competence are accorded states with respect to events within their own territory, in the territory of other states and in areas open to many or all? Do relevant prescriptions both permit states substantially affected in their community value processes by particular events to assert competence over such events and, when two or more states are so affected, promote compromise by requiring claimants to take into account the degree of involvement of the values of others in the same or comparable events? Do the prescriptions as a whole establish an appropriate stability in the expectations of participants that controversies will be handled in agreed ways without the disruptions of arbitrary assertion of power? Do they achieve an appropriate balance between subordinating non-governmental participants—individuals and private associations—to inclusive community authority and freeing such participants from parochial and arbitrary restraint for creative initiative in ordered exploitation of the world's resources, sharable and non-sharable?

Do prescriptions about aggregate changes—state and governmental succession—achieve a necessary balance between continuity in the application of general community policy and freedom for local communities to direct internal changes as they deem their unique conditions to require?

(3) *Features of Basic Value Processes Protected by Law*

Ideally our inquiry here should extend to detailed examination of all the remaining community value processes—such as with respect to wealth, enlightenment, respect, well-being, skill, rectitude, and affection or congenial personal relations—in a manner comparable to that employed above with respect to power processes. . . . For brief indication of the general method of inquiry we make reference only to a few important questions with respect to certain important values. We begin with "security," in its *maximum* sense of the sum of position, potential and expectancy with respect to all values, and then proceed to other values.

Security

By "security" we here refer to demands for the maintenance of a public order which affords full opportunity to preserve and increase all values by peaceful procedures, free from more than a minimum level of coercion or threats of such coercion. In terms of the general analysis of power the questions grouped under the rubric of security emphasize not so much the sharing as the mode by which the social process is carried on. Obviously the fundamental goal of human dignity commits us to the minimum use of coercion compatible with the most advantageous net position for all value outcomes.

For inquiry into any particular system, some of the more general questions may be indicated as follows: What policies are recommended as appropriate for the international community in regard to coercion? What objectives are asserted as permissible, and what impermissible, for employment of coercion? What operational meaning is given to proclaimed policies in terms of policies sought in fact? How are proclaimed and actual policies translated into specific conceptions of permissible and impermissible coercion? What, on the one hand, are the recommended conceptions of "aggression," "breaches of the peace," "threats to the peace," and "intervention," and, on the other, of "self-defense," "collective self-defense" and "police action"? Are these concepts given an operational meaning which in fact authorizes, and promotes, the defense of independence and territorial integrity? Are all instruments of coercion, including the techniques of externally instigated *coup d'etat*, brought within their compass? What factors in the context of the world arena are recommended to decision-makers for consideration in the making of specific interpretations in concrete instance? What structures of community authority are approved and recommended for application and enforcement of community policies? What recommendations are made about the procedures by which decisions are to be taken? What specific sanctions are approved and recommended for securing conformity to community policies? Is there willingness to place adequate effective power at the disposal of community organization or agency . . . ?

Wealth—Economic Growth and Trade

The demand of the lower income groups and nations around the globe to live a better life in the material sense has confronted the world community with most acute problems. Important questions about any projected system of world public order are: Does this order protect an economy which seeks an appropriate division of labor and the development and exploitation of resources on a world (or universal) scale or some lesser scale? By what policies, persuasive and coercive, are resources allocated? Do these policies embrace the most productive sharing of sharable resources? Are appropriate institutions provided for planning and development functions? What balance is achieved between the public and the private control of resources, or between central and decentralized control? Does this balance promote or retard the democratic functioning of other value processes? Are wealth considerations subordinated to power considerations? How adequate is the protection and regulation of private claims to resources, and of the wealth activities of private associations across state lines? Are appropriate institutions provided for the most productive international exchange? What accommodation is afforded between free markets and state trading?

Respect—The Articulation and Implementation of Human Rights

The criterion of human dignity is most obviously applicable in relations including the degree of effective freedom of choice given to individuals in society. To respect anyone is to protect his choosing function so long as its exercise does not seriously imperil the corresponding freedom of others. For inquiry into how diverse systems of public order have distinctive approaches to all that affects human rights, we suggest questions as: Does this system begin with a presumption in favor of private choice? In favor of privacy? Does it provide equality of access to value processes upon grounds of merit or foster discriminations based upon caste, race, alienage, color, sex and so on? Does it prohibit or permit value deprivations incompatible with common humanity? Does it provide positive assistance to individuals on the basis of common humanity in overcoming handicaps? For what territorial community does the system demand human rights . . . ?

Enlightenment and Top Skills

It is generally recognized by observers of the world scene that barriers to the gathering, transmission and dissemination of current information of events around the globe help to sustain the local monopolies of intelligence that stand in the path of peace and order. Further, the enormous significance of scientific and technological know-how has emphasized the importance of prompt enlightenment as to fundamental discoveries about nature or society.

The relevant questions for spotlighting divergence in approach are as above: What positive facilities, governmental and private, are afforded for promoting inquiry, communication, education and training? How open is access to all processes? Are discriminations made on grounds other than merit? Is freedom of expression, assembly, and association encouraged? Does the system promote the sharing of information, scientific knowledge, and cultural exchange across state lines? What content and modes of implementation are proposed for international prescription? What limits are imposed upon the use of the ideological instrument for purposes of coercion?

Well-Being

The importance of maintaining optimum standards of safety, health, and comfort is as axiomatic as the interdependence of all peoples with respect to such standards. Relevant questions relate both to the facilities provided—including all degrees of governmental involvement—for medical care, prevention of disease, healthful housing, appropriate food and clothing, sanitation, working conditions, leisure and recreation, et cetera, and for the area of community concern and effective prescription and application of policy.

Rectitude

The reference here is to the consensus in conceptions of right and wrong sufficient to support all other institutional patterns of the world community toward which we aim. A society of human dignity implies a high degree of unity as to goal values and to the non-coercive practices by which goals are clarified and put into effect. More specifically, what is involved is a high degree of effective application in public and private of the formal standards of responsibility which are essential to attain and maintain the desired society.

Immediate questions relate to varying conceptions of individual and collective responsibility in national and international systems of criminal law and to accommodations between diverse systems, by extradition, protection of political offenders, rights of asylum, and so on. More long-term questions relate to potentialities for adjusting national criminal laws and procedures to more comprehensive unities, for adapting local systems of ethics (with or without religious and metaphysical derivation) to more comprehensive unities, and for adapting prevailing moral sentiments for larger unities. Recurrent inquiry seeks the degree of freedom of choice in beliefs about right and wrong and the adequacy of facilities for the enjoyment of rectitude beliefs.

Affection (Including Loyalties)

Goals here include the development of a sense of belonging to the whole community of mankind and concern for the common good (positive identification), the spread of congenial personal relationships in all groups regardless of cultural or class characteristics, and the development of nondestructive human personalities capable of entering into friendly contact with others. Relevant questions relate to authoritative formulae and procedures affecting the comprehensiveness of loyalties and memberships and the congeniality of personal relations. Of especial concern are any potentialities for adapting local doctrinal systems and sentiments to larger loyalties and for adjusting national and international prescriptions for facilitating more comprehensive memberships. The humanitarianism in family law and the degree to which this humanitarianism is projected across state lines are of obvious pertinence.

What the Scholar Does in Gathering and Processing Data

There remain for brief consideration some of the technical problems that relate to the operations by which scholars gather and process the data required to identify and appraise systems of public order. We shall briefly characterize the strategy by which the facts of any given community context can be obtained. Broadly conceived, the most promising strategy of inquiry moves from the well known to the less known, in this case implying that a beginning is made by employing the operations familiar to all legal scholars, then proceeding to the phases of the situation for which the social and behavioral sciences provide the sharpest instruments. Legal scholars in international law must take direct responsibility for the plan as a whole, and for the execution of those parts that require the traditional training of lawyers. It is also essential that the legal scholar work in close association with specialists from related fields whose contributions are called for. Briefly:

Operation 1. Establish the provisional identity of a public order system within a community context by means of an inventory of explicit legal formulae.

The inventory can be made by examining constitutional charters, statutes and doctrines purportedly applied by decision-makers in specific controversies.

What value patterns and basic institutional practices are given *explicit* protection or aid in fulfillment? What value-institution patterns receive *implicit* support (that is, what does the scholar infer from the formal material, even though the language is somewhat ambiguous)?

By extending research through past time, changes of trend in the public order system, as tentatively understood, can be described.

Operation 2. Add accuracy and detail to the inventory obtained by means of *Operation 1* by describing the frequency with which each prescription found in the legal formulae is invoked or purportedly applied in controversies.

In the formal decision process authoritative prescriptions are mentioned with varying degrees of frequency by the parties who seek to justify their claims, and by decision makers who are performing functions of invocation or application. . . .

The data gathered by *Operation 2* makes it possible to relate the language of authority more directly to the facts of control. As a matter of definition it will often be clarifying for the scholar to specify the minimum level of frequency of invocation and purported application that he requires before accepting a particular pattern of authority and control as "law." The information assembled by *Operation 2* makes it feasible to classify specific authoritative statements, not only as law but as obsolete or obsolescent or emergent law. By extending research historically the trends in the role of each statement can be revealed.

Operation 3. Analyze all other sources for the purpose of making a fuller identification of the systems of public order provisionally revealed by the preceding operations. Describe the legal process in the context of the decision process as a whole, and of the social process within the entire community context.

Most of the scholarly effort at this phase is devoted to obtaining data by methods that are not conventional to traditionally trained legal scholars. Hence reliance is put upon the finding of specialists upon the value-institution processes of wealth, respect, well-being, and so on. . . . To some extent the procedures of data gathering in *Operation 3* will be the interview or participant observation. Insofar as materials must be gathered which are residues of the historical process the basic methods are those familiar to historians. . . .

All the facts assembled in each operation above will of course be contributory to the five intellectual tasks to be performed by scholars in the fields of international law. The data will interact with the clarification of values, the characterization of trend, the analysis of conditioning factors, the projection of future developments, and the invention and appraisal of alternative policies for the optimum realization of the clarified values of human dignity.

The Contemporary Challenge to Scholars

For some decades scholars of international law have been preoccupied with the task of establishing that the subject of their professional concern was in fact law and could not be dismissed as a miscellany of maxims principally useful for the admonishing of decision-makers to act ethically. The implicit assumption appears to have been that unless the universality of international law is established, there is no international law whatsoever; and further, that the most effective means of moving the world toward a universal body of law is to assert its contemporary reality in fact.

It is high time that the community of scholars abandon a conception of their role in history whose principal effect is to condemn them to inaccuracy and futility. The inaccuracy consists in the assertion of universality in fact, and relative futility is demonstrated by the contemporary division of the globe into diverse systems of public order whose leaders use the appeal to universality as a pawn and a screen in the tactics of world power.

The challenge to scholars is to resume their proper function, which is to assist all who will listen to distinguish clearly between the current facts of the global context and estimates of future developments—and between estimates of policy alternatives that will merely move the world closer to some universal system of law and public order, however unfree, and alternatives that will in fact foster the common objective so frequently proclaimed by the authorized spokesmen of existing nation states, namely, the goal of realizing human dignity in theory and fact.

More specifically the challenge to scholars of international law is twofold: (1) to develop a jurisprudence, a comprehensive theory and appropriate methods of inquiry, which will assist the peoples of the world to distinguish public orders based on human dignity and public orders based either on a law which denies human dignity or a denial of law itself for the simple supremacy of naked force; and (2) to invent and recommend the authority structures and functions (principles and procedures) necessary to a world public order that harmonizes with the growing aspirations of the overwhelming numbers of the peoples of the globe and is in accord with the proclaimed values of human dignity enunciated by the moral leaders of mankind.

In this perilous epoch of threatened catastrophe legal scholars have an opportunity of unparalleled urgency to assist in performing at least two indispensable functions: the function of providing intelligence and of making recommendations to all who have the will and capability of decision.

As old orders crumble and dissolve under the ever-accelerating impact of scientific, technological and other changes, the future becomes increasingly plastic in our hands, holding out the possibility of moulding a world order nearer to the aspirations of human dignity, or of losing out to the most ruthless and comprehensive tyranny that man has ever known.

The impact of scholarly research and analysis can be to disclose to as many as possible of the effective leaders, and constituencies of leaders, throughout the globe the compatibility between their aspirations and the policies that expedite peaceful co-operation on behalf of a public order of human dignity. . . .

NOTES

1. Criteria have not been elaborated for even preliminary identification of existing international systems, which vary in territorial spread from two-Power arrangements upward toward demanded or asserted universality. Suggestions are variously made in the literature of possibly useful classifications of systems in such terms as Western European (and North Atlantic), American (North, South), Soviet (European, Asian), British Commonwealth, Islamic, Hindu, Burmese, Southeastern Asian, and so on.

An excellent introduction to the problem may be found, with abundant references, in Jenks, The Common Law of Mankind, Ch. 2: "The Universality of International Law" (1958). Other representative recent writings include Northrop, "Contemporary Jurisprudence and International Law," 61 Yale L.J. 623 (1952); Aaron and Reynolds, "Peaceful Coexistence and Peaceful Cooperation," 4 Political Studies 281 (October, 1956); Snyder and Bracht, "Co-existence and International Law," 7 Int. and Comp. Law Q. 54 (1958); Fifield, "The Five Principles of Peaceful Coexistence," 52 A.J.I.L. 504 (1958); Triska, "A Model for Study of Soviet Foreign Policy," 52 Am. Pol. Sci. Rev. 64 (1958); Berlia, "International Law and Russo-American Coexistence," 79 Journal du Droit International 307 (1952); Kunz, "Pluralism of Legal and Value Systems and International Law," 49 A.J.I.L. 370 (1955); Wilk, "International Law and Global Ideological Conflict: Reflections on the Universality of International Law," 45 *ibid.* 648 (1951); Schwarzenberger, "The Impact of the East-West Rift on International Law," 36 Grotius Society Transactions 229 (1950); Hazard, Law and Social Change in the U.S.S.R., Ch. 11 (1953); Kulski, "The Soviet Interpretation of International Law," 49 A.J.I.L. 518 (1955); Schlesinger, Soviet Legal Theory, Ch. 10 (2d ed., 1951); Taracouzio, The Soviet Union and International Law (1935); Kelsen, The Communist Theory of Law (1955).

2. The common assumption is thus stated in Sauer, "Universal Principles in International Law," 42 Grotius Society Transactions 181 (1957): "It goes without saying that the notion of present-day international law implies universality because this law means a law for all nations of the world." Dr. Sauer notes a certain shrinkage, however, and observes "that the present condition of universal international law is a sad one." *Ibid.* 184.

The "universality" asserted or demanded, too often in attempted self-fulfilling description, by different writers and spokesmen exhibits of course many varying nuances in reference. Sometimes reference is made to the range of participants alleged to be subject to authoritative prescription and it is insisted that a single international law governs Western and non-Western, Christian and non-Christian, or Communist and non-Communist, states alike. On other occasions the emphasis in reference is upon alleged uniformity in application of prescriptions—that is, that the same results are achieved in the same or comparable contexts when the only difference lies in the identity of the parties to the controversy. Still again "universality" may merely express a demand that all states accept and implement the same set of policies relating to their external interactions. On rare occasions, the reference is explicitly and candidly to mere words, accompanied by demands that future interpretations of the words be made to conform to the requirements of a projected world order. *Cf.* Dickinson, Law and Peace 122 (1951).

3. For background and development of social process analysis with special reference to law and politics see, among other studies, Lasswell and McDougal, "Legal Education and Public Policy: Professional Training in the Public Interest," 52 Yale L. J. 203 (1943); Lasswell and Kaplan, Power and Society (1950).

4. We recognize of course that authority and control may overlap and it is indeed precisely this overlap that we recommend as the most useful reference of the world "law." The asking of separate questions about authority and control may, we hope, promote realism in inquiry about their interrelations.

5. *Cf.* Lipson, "The New Face of Socialist Legality," 7 Problems of Communism (No. 4, July–Aug. 1958) 22, 29:

"What the reformers have not touched and will not touch is the political basis that necessarily prevents 'socialist legality,' Soviet-style, from meeting the standards of legality upheld by other countries. There will be no sure legal guarantees that the *troikas* and purges will not recur, that the cult of (some other) personality will not again become the religion of the state, and that terror will not lay waste another generation of Soviet citizens; indeed, there can be none as long as the party, and the elements of Soviet society striving for supremacy through or against the party, remain unwilling to grant effective autonomy to the legal system, keeping it above the political struggle as a safeguard of general order and liberty."

6. It is convenient to use the traditional words, "general community of states," without imputation of universality, to refer to the largest grouping seeking common values.

7. Jenks, note 1 above at 120.

8. These questions are developed in more detail in McDougal and Burke, "Crisis in the Law of the Sea: Community Perspectives Versus National Egoism," 67 Yale L. J. 539 (1958); McDougal and Lipson, "Perspectives for a Law of Outer Space," 52 A.J.I.L. 407 (1958).

9. The distinction between persuasion and coercion may be clarified in terms of the number and cost of alternatives open to a participant. By persuasion we refer to interactions which leave open a number of alternatives with expectations of high gain and low cost. By coercion we refer to interactions which leave open few alternatives, with expectations of little or no gain and high costs.

We assume that the participants consciously pursue a range of realizable alternatives in representative situations in the social process. This assumption is necessary to indicate that people who have been trained to demand and expect few alternatives are not free.

10. More detailed inquiry is outlined in McDougal and Feliciano, "International Coercion and World Public Order: The General Principles of the Law of War," 67 Yale L. J. 771 (1958).

11. The Nature of International Law: Toward a Second Concept of Law

Gidon Gottlieb

I

Law in international relations is unlike law in our domestic system. This has led to doubts about the "legal" quality of international law. These emanate, it will be argued, not from the nature of international law but rather from analyses in terms of only one concept of law. Far from being a "problem" area it will be shown that international law is a paradigm for legal ordering in a decentralized power system.

Consideration of the nature of international law imports assumptions about the concept of law.[1] These assumptions currently rest on a number of dominant legal theories. The problem with theories about the concept of law and about the nature of legal systems is their foundation in the political context of nation states. They all refer primarily to *legal* systems operating in the *political* systems of such states.[2] That is, to the legal order of societies in which the means of coercion are supposedly monopolized by the state. These are systems in which, to borrow Professor Falk's phrase, there is a vertical or hierarchical relationship between unequal centers of power. This is in contrast to systems in which there is a horizontal or nonhierarchical order between equal centers of power:[3] power, that is, in the sense of a capacity to gain one's ends *over the opposition* of others rather than a generalized capacity to attain goals.[4] Vertical and horizontal relationships are a function of actual power relationships—not of formal social arrangements.

Dominant legal theories all relate to the legal order of vertical systems. None investigates the legal order that is characteristic of horizontal systems. Statements about the nature of law and about the existence of legal systems in the writings of Austin, Kelsen, and Hart implicitly accept the pyramidal model of state power.[5] It is by no means evident that they can be successfully transplanted to the alien grounds of international relations.

A productive analysis of the nature of international law requires an overhaul of the conceptual framework in terms of which it is conducted. The first task is to investigate the features of the concept of law that are peculiar to horizontal political orders. Second, to determine whether it is possible to have more than one concept of law in the same way that we have more than one system of geometry. It may thus be possible to develop an alternative to the state-system analogy—or, to mix an old metaphor, something like a non-Euclidian concept of law. Third, to find out whether it is possible to demarcate meaningful boundaries between a concept of law peculiar to horizontal systems and the neighbor concept of politics.

The need to outline an additional concept of law rests on the necessary connection between the structure of a legal order and underlying patterns of power relationships. The distortions caused by reliance on the pyramidal model of state power, in the analysis of "primitive" legal systems at one extreme and on international law at the other, rest upon the unproven proposition that there is only one ideal model for legal systems.[6] Mere *characteristics* of the domestic model are transformed into *prerequisites* for international order. The acceptance of either vertical model as a decisive test of the existence of legal order generates irrelevant cynicism as to the stabilizing claims of international law. . . ."[7]

CONCEPTUAL DISTORTIONS CAUSED BY
VERTICAL CONCEPTS OF LAW

Under the impact of hierarchical concepts of law it is conventional academic wisdom to accept a number of propositions:

- international law is not as fully law as the law of the domestic legal order;
- what gives all law a peculiar legal quality is the establishment of coercive acts as sanctions;
- international law is only at the beginning of a development which national law has already completed. It is a primitive legal order;
- the prophecies of what courts will do are what is meant by the law;
- the structure which has resulted from the combination of primary rules of obligation with the secondary rules of recognition, change, and adjudication is the heart of a legal system;
- when law is violated, it is necessary either to vindicate rights or to punish offenders to preserve the legal system;
- in the absence of applicable norms, decision makers enjoy full discretion;
- fidelity to law requires deference to constituted authority;
- there is a clear line dividing the law that is from the law that ought to be;
- the existence of law is not a matter of degree;
- the power of a sovereign is incapable of legal limitation;
- there is a clear line between the study of law and the study of behavior and other social phenomena;
- a fully developed legal system relies on separate agencies for changing and making laws, for determining infractions of the law, for enforcing the law, and for settling disputes.

Every one of these statements requires qualification when we speak about law in a horizontal power system. Every one of them is predicated upon a hierarchical power structure alien to the international environment. . . .

Investigations of the concept of law should reflect variations in permanent features of power structures. Differences between such power systems are clearly reflected in normative systems.

Despite the manifestly horizontal character of the decentralized power structure of international society, a number of vertical relationships do coexist and alternate with horizontal ones. Decentralized relationships of a horizontal character may become vertical in time of armed conflict, only to reacquire their previous horizontality immediately thereafter. They display, in other words, a considerable degree of elasticity. . . . Except during combat, the limited effectiveness of armed coercion in international and in domestic conflicts is well established. During combat, military victories can be defined in objective "kill ratio" or destruction terms, and coercion then prevails. At other times, however, the will to resist superior power is productive of horizontal relationships which do not reflect coercive capabilities. Horizontal and vertical relationships may thus alternate between the same system units on a time continuum reflecting the alternance of armed conflicts and other forms of coercion. Such modifications may depend also on the character of the issues involved. . . .

The relevance of a second concept of law for horizontal systems should not be limited to international law. It is likely to have a bearing on areas of domestic constitutional law, civil rights, and labor law as well—on all legal fields dealing with power groups and political organizations rather than with individuals' rights and interests. With the spread of horizontal power relationships in characteristically vertical systems, realistic strategies taking this phenomenon into account must be designed for securing compliance with the law. Student disruptions on campuses have thus led some university administrations to adopt a delicate balance between policies of conciliation and enforcement. Changes in attitude to legal ordering domestically may also find expression in expectations about international law. International phenomena may be more understandable in the light of domestic developments pointing to difficulties with law enforcement against determined power groups.

THE USES OF LAW IN HORIZONTAL SYSTEMS

At the present time the rare international disputes that reach settlement are not generally resolved by judicial organs. In the settlement of disputes the International Court of Justice now performs distinctly secondary functions. This is not due to faulty draftsmanship of Chapter VI of the Charter, or of the Statute of the Court, or to a failure on the part of the Framers at San Francisco. Rather, this fact reflects the true position of courts in horizontal system disputes in times of stress.[8] Under United States constitutional law, for example, judicial restraint in the decision of "political questions" or of issues that would present compliance problems is a familiar phenomenon.[9] The political question doctrine has enabled the Supreme Court to avoid deciding cases that would involve serious conflicts with other branches of the government or interfere in the conduct of foreign relations. Disputes between powerful units, between branches of the government, those involving sensitive Federal-State relationships, civil rights issues, and strong labor, racial, or other groups are characteristic of horizontal system disputes. Like international disputes they stand in contrast to vertical system conflicts in which law enforcement presents few problems.

In horizontal disputes, accommodation rather than adjudication is the object generally sought. The goal is conflict settlement, not the vindication of rights. . . . Thus in horizontal system disputes, in which power is not centralized, courts must steer a careful course between the Scylla of ineffective judicial activism and the open defiance of judgments and the Charybdis of exaggerated judicial restraint allowing the erosion of constitutionally binding instruments. But even in matters that do not lend themselves to adjudication, those pertaining to horizontal and to permanent relationships, law may still be invoked and has an important role to play. This has some far-reaching consequences.

States invoke legal norms in nonjudicial contexts when making claims and concessions, in negotiations, in the justification of political moves, in arbitration and mediation, and in other attempts to settle disputes peaceably outside courts of law.[10] Legal norms are also invoked in international organizations, in debates and caucuses, in drafting and legitimizing resolutions, in rallying support for them and getting them adopted. Indeed, law is much used in diplomacy, in drawing attention to particular features of conflicts, in defining issues, in characterizing situations, in building up authoritative practices, in conferring and withdrawing legitimacy, and ultimately in shaping policy options.[11] Such non-judicial uses of law are equally prominent in domestic legal systems, even though they are largely neglected in academic writings and legal education which focus primarily on judicial decisions and on rule formulations.

When dealing with bodies of law that do not lend themselves readily to adjudication—that is, with non-judicial uses of law—clear identification of rules and principles as "legal" is not always appropriate. In the process of making claims and counterclaims, of advancing demands and allowing concessions, much can sometimes be gained by allowing ambiguity about the legal quality of the rules and principles invoked. For it is generally harder to retreat from asserted legal rights than from hoped-for political advantages. . . .

THE CREATION AND ALTERATION OF INTERNATIONAL OBLIGATIONS

Authoritative guidance such as "community policies" and "general principles" would not always be characterized as "law" under operative rules of recognition. Yet in the *South-West Africa* case Judge Jessup maintained that accumulations of expressions of condemnation of apartheid were of decisive practical and juridical value in determining the meaning that was to be given to the mandate provisions dealing with the well-being of the inhabitants of the Territory of South-West Africa. Judges Fitzmaurice and Spender, on the other hand, said "[This] is a court of law and can take account of moral principles only insofar as these are given a sufficient expression in legal form. . . ."

This issue takes on a different complexion where nonjudicial uses of law are involved. While Judge Fitzmaurice would only apply the law of the Court as determined in the rules of recognition in Article 38 of the Statute, the political organs of the United Nations are prepared to claim a much broader and indeterminate set of principles and instruments as being authoritative and "legally" compelling. In the absence of formal legislative procedures, a wide range of unstructured practices are used to accomplish quasi-legislative ends. No secondary rule of recognition can be used to identify the variety of laws and the proliferation of law-making techniques. These techniques share some common features:

- they are based on consensus rather than on consent;
- they erode the status of formal sources of law such as treaties and enhance the importance of informal sources like declarations;
- they favor informal and rapid normative change;
- they involve fairly general principles and standards rather than precise contractual obligations, and therefore leave states with considerable discretion in the interpretation of obligations; . . . [See Gottlieb's essay in Chapter 4—EDS.]

Reliance on legal rules and principles in diplomatic practice is not in general designed with litigation in mind. It therefore matters relatively little whether a particular state accepts or rejects principles invoked against it when these have been recognized as authoritative by the vast majority of states. In such a climate, the shift from consent to consensus is an easy one. It is further accentuated by growing international cooperative activities in which exclusion from participation is an effective sanction. . . .[12]

The trend from consent to consensus is not likely, however, to hasten the settlement of conflicts in which diplomatically isolated states are determined to hold on to their vital interests in the face of adverse world opinion. On the contrary, it is possible that such consensus might well harden the positions of all and delay the elaboration of acceptable common grounds for settlement. A similar situation seems to have developed in the wake of General Assembly Resolution 2145 (XX) terminating South Africa's mandate in South-West Africa and establishing, in Resolution 2248 (S-V), the Council for Namibia (South-West Africa) to take over the administration of the Territory. These decisions, as well as subsequent Security Council resolutions, have made diplomatic accommodation less likely than ever. The prospects for accommodation have not been enhanced by the 1971 Advisory Opinion of the International Court of Justice on the question of Namibia.

The impact of consensus declarations of a legal character on the settlement of disputes remains to be assessed. Judging from the experience of recent years, consensus declarations and resolutions of a legal character can easily be adopted in situations involving a pariah state such as South Africa and its policy of apartheid. Almost any law-making resolution designed further to isolate South Africa is likely to secure majority support. But it is also destined to be ignored by that country. . . .

EFFECTIVENESS OF OBLIGATIONS

. . . Factors making for the effectiveness of legal norms in international relations are not easily identifiable. Foreign policy pronouncements have a distinctive binding force that tends to tie the hands of even the greatest powers. This is true of proclamations, declarations, statements, joint resolutions, treaties, agreements, and other instruments used in foreign relations. But the use of documents, policy statements, treaties, and other international instruments has certain side-effects unrelated to the purposes they are designed to serve. There are consequences inherent in the very use of texts and other policy pronouncements that bear no relation to their contents and functions. These are side-effects analogous to the unchartered repercussions of the use of certain medical drugs. The effectiveness of these pronouncements does *not* depend upon whether they are intended to be legally binding. . . .

The fact that texts, declarations, and other policy pronouncements have a coercive, obligatory force generated independently of their legal quality, enforceability, or acceptance has been largely ignored. . . .

[There exists a] peculiar gravitational pull of authoritative policy pronouncements, authoritative texts, speeches, agreements, and the like. Deviation from them is difficult and states are frequently trapped in webs of past commitments. This gravitational pull, this entrapment, is generated by a variety of factors closely related to the nature of the international system and to the very functions of policy guidance:

Stability. States and bureaucracies generally face demands for consistent and stable policies both domestically and from allies. Verbal formulations serve as signposts and standards for such policies. Even unilateral declarations and unilateral formulations of a nonlegal character, i.e. the guarantee of the freedom of Berlin, acquire an inertial weight of their own. Attempts to abandon or to erode these commitments may lead to strong political reactions from those with a vested interest in the status quo, and stimulate other demands for more far-reaching policy changes.

Legitimacy. Administrations require authority for the conduct of their policies. Such authority is generally derived from authoritative texts, precedents, and past practices. Deviations from past practices and past statements frequently raise questions about the authority or legality of such departures. Reasons must then be given to account for changes. Deference to guidelines, to rules, to institutionally defined goals, and to standard practices are features of all organizations particularly at the bureaucratic level.[13] Changes require leadership, persuasion, authority, and determination. Inertia is not mere laziness; it is the natural temperament of organizations.

Propaganda. Some policies and statements evoke emotional responses both at home and abroad. "Contain Communism," or "Punish the Aggressor" are not mere guidelines for treaty making. They are powerful propaganda symbols. They crystallize and fossilize attitudes and expectations. The staying force of such symbols is independent of the will of their creators. Policy symbols rapidly develop an immunity to change and destruction. They easily become live fossils, so to speak. They are not easily forgotten or destroyed— but generate the emotion and support required to assure their survival.

Deterrence. Much foreign policy is designed to set the boundaries of permissible actions for other powers. Containment, deterrence, collective security, and collective self-defense are all policies which require putting adversaries on notice of actions we would take to meet hostile moves. A key goal of such instruments is to prevent miscalculations by adversaries about our intentions. The sanctity of commitments, on the altar of which former Secretary of State Dean Rusk has performed public rites, is assured by the jealous God of miscalculation.

These four factors are not exhaustive, common ends, reciprocity, retaliation, the pressure of allies—all these are other factors accounting for difficulties in abruptly terminating obligations, abandoning commitments, changing policies, and suspending agreements, which even the most powerful states must consider. These factors would suggest that some policies are more "sticking" than others, harder to abandon. This again does not depend on their "legal" quality or status. For example, the so-called rules of the game governing spheres of influence between the United States and the Soviet Union, which are based on tacit understandings, on unilateral actions and acquiescence, are among the most effectively enforced rules of any system. . . .

There are thus inherent features involved in the very use of guidelines in foreign relations. They cannot be willed away and disregarded. Some of these rest on systemic considerations. All guidance devices play roles that we would not expect of a system that is backed neither by the "power of the sword" nor by that of "the purse." These factors account, however, for the weight of all "commitments" rather than for those of a specifically "legal" character. They point to yet a further link between the political and the legal orders of the international system, confirming difficulties about a meaningful demarcation between the two. . . .[14]

THE PROBLEM OF DEMARCATION
BETWEEN INTERNATIONAL LAW AND POLITICS

This bleak account of political uses of international law could at first sight appear to reinforce arguments for discounting their significance. For if the uses of international law in the political organs of the U.N. are as partisan and unprincipled as is sometimes maintained, what is then the difference between law and politics—or, in other words, what is the point of talking about international law at all when referring to such highly politicized behavior? Is international law then not precisely that positive morality which Austin argued is not law properly so called?

The purists would restrict our concept of law to adjudication contexts, although these are of secondary significance only in the existing horizontal system. To do this, however, would be to exclude from our concept of international law much that states and international organizations do regard as international law. The alternative is to use the concept of law to include also political uses of international law. We are then led, however, to consider as legal some practices that are not easily distinguishable from political maneuvers.[15]

The demarcation between international law and politics can best be understood in terms of the functions of the demarcation itself. In a well-known essay Brierly wrote that the best evidence for the existence of international law is that every state recognizes that it does exist and is under an obligation to serve it. Significantly, when states violate international law—and this is not an infrequent occurrence—they do not deny its binding force. They characteristically attempt to excuse and explain away their conduct without challenging the validity or the existence of the international legal order.[16] This professed acceptance of law by the community of states cannot be dismissed by rule-skeptics or "realists" focusing on actual state behavior—for, in the very process of disregarding international law, such skeptics would lose sight of the ways in which states act upon policy options open to them and take into account considerations of a legal nature. . . .[17]

The argument that there is no meaningful use for international law except in the context of adjudication simply fails to meet the practical needs of states in the conduct of their foreign relations. It also fails to reflect the practice of legal officers in foreign ministries and in international organizations in their day-to-day activities.

Adjudication cannot in any meaningful sense be the touchstone of the international legal system so long as its horizontal authority structure subsists. Some other criterion is required to sort the legal from the political. But all available models have failed—neither Hart's emphasis on primary and secondary rules, nor the Austin-Kelsen concern with sanctions can account for international law. We are thus left with two questions that must be kept separate for they invite different kinds of response:

- How can one demarcate between legal and other obligations in the international system?
- What does it mean to say that an international legal system exists?[18]

The first question about demarcation invites the articulation of criteria for dealing with the practical problems of sorting obligations. The second question about the existence of an international legal system does not involve the application of criteria of demarcation. It is a meta-system question—a question *about* the international legal system, not about problems arising in its operation.

The relationship between these two questions is a matter of some delicacy. The problem of demarcation between juridical and other obligations points to the *need* for rules of recognition such as those set out in Article 38 of the Statute of the International Court of Justice. State practice discloses no other widely accepted principle of recognition. Strict adherence to Article 38[19] would, however, rule out the legal status of much that states accept as legally obligatory—the alternative is to accept the indeterminacy of obligations.

This indeterminacy of obligations raises difficulties about the existence of the international legal system as such. For, if rules of recognition are indeterminate and uncertain, we can either conclude with Hart that we are confronted with something other than a fully realized legal system, or we must argue that Hart's thesis about the combination of primary and secondary rules does not apply to *legal* ordering in horizontal systems however "advanced" they may be.[20] The rejection of Hart's thesis, so far as world order is concerned, would be more persuasive if it were possible to outline a competing idea of legal system. Such an idea would not then be based on a combination between primary rules of obligation and secondary rules of recognition. It should account at least for legal ordering in the international system.

TWO CONCEPTS OF LAW: THE AUTHORITY MODEL AND THE ACCEPTANCE MODEL

. . . I should like to advance the following proposal to account for the existence of a legal system in horizontal power relationships. This is a proposal for an "acceptance model" contrasting with the dominant "hier-archical-enforcement" model. It builds upon systemic distinctions expressed in different types of power relationships. It takes as a point of departure the peculiar features of institutional arrangements in the international society in which power is widely diffused. In such a horizontal system, it is correct to assert that a legal order exists when:

1. international actors (for example, states) accept sets of fairly specific rules, principles, and policies as binding—in the sense that they recognize they are not at liberty to disregard them—and as proper standards for assessing the legality of their own actions;
2. international actors make demands, claims, complaints, and proposals to each other on the basis of such binding rules, principles, and policies and seek to settle their differences by reference to them;
3. international actors attempt to secure compliance with such rules, principles, and policies and there is a measure of congruence between state action and accepted law;
4. there are organizations established under such rules, principles, and policies and acting pursuant to them;
5. there is a measure of consensus between international actors about the content of the rules, principles, and policies accepted as binding, and about criteria for identifying them;
6. these rules, principles, and policies regulate significant aspects of the relationships between international actors and are designed to limit their unfettered discretion in decision-making;
7. international actors are committed to accept the guidance of these binding rules, principles, and policies in good faith and to apply them evenhandedly in all situations.[21]

Such a legal order involves then a *process of authoritative decision-making* leading to unavoidable principled choices between competing goals and policies.[22] It requires a measure of congruence between state action and accepted law. This congruence is a central feature of *the existence of any legal system.*[23] Accordingly, the earnestness with which major powers act upon international law considerations in good faith, and the intensity of their commitment to its principles and objectives, are good measures of the existence of such a system. Deviant practices, invoking one set of standards for oneself and another for adversaries, stretching concepts to legitimize national policies of questionable legality, all these tend to undermine the existence of the international legal order. The health of a legal system is thus subject to fluctuations, declining at times of crisis and tension when legal scruples may be ignored to accommodate pressing political interests.

These seven ingredients can be used as a model concept of law in all horizontal systems. Every one of these ingredients is a goal or target for the fullest realization of the legal nature of the system. At the end of the spectrum farthest from law lie the politics of coercion, in which the strongest but not necessarily the most authoritative influences govern. This formulation evidently contemplates a continuum between law, power, and politics separated by a threshold of considerable indeterminacy. . . .

For in a decentralized power system, indices for the identification of rules, principles, and policies as binding are evolved and applied in a decentralized manner. States and organs of international organizations make their own determinations about the legal status of instruments and doctrines. Such a system can retain its unity only so long as some measure of consensus is achieved. Horizontality, it must be noticed, is not a feature of the concept of law but of systems in which it operates. The legal model for horizontal systems merely *reflects* systemic requirements. Actual power relationships are generally situated somewhere on the continuum between vertical and horizontal extremes.

Evidently the unity and coherence of such a system is open to erosion as consensus breaks down not only about the content and application of primary rules of obligation but also about secondary rules of recognition. The unity and universality of the international legal order remains vulnerable and the line between law and non-law undemarcated. This is in contrast to positivist concepts which provide for clear demarcation resting on accepted rules of recognition.

The erosion of such a system can also occur through a failure of congruence between state action and accepted law. States do not admit to flagrant violations of international law. They invoke a variety of diplomatic explanations, rhetorical justifications, and doctrinal innovations in support of their actions. For example, the Brezhnev Doctrine designed by the Soviet Union to legitimize the Warsaw Pact intervention in Czechoslovakia, was shortly afterward reflected in the revised Soviet draft definition of aggression submitted to the Special Committee on the Question of Defining Aggression. . . .

The question remains—why do we insist on referring to the system of international rules, principles, and policies as a legal order when political uses and abuses of law are so common, when its "internal morality" is so constantly imperiled?[24] This is a recurring question of considerable importance. . . .

The reasons for insisting on a demarcation between international law and politics are perhaps plainest if we were to assert that no international legal system now exists. Such a proposition would clarify what is at stake and would entail a number of conclusions of palpable falsity:

- that every state is at liberty to disregard rules and policies as its interests may dictate and that there is no duty to abide by them or to obey them;
- that there are no legal grounds for impeaching the legitimacy of constituted authorities and the legitimacy of their policies; .
- that since there is no international legal system there is no occasion to respond to violations of the law, to affirm standards, and to maintain claims. In the absence of law all a state can do is to use its power to uphold its interests;
- that in the absence of obligations, and of rules and policies of a binding and constraining character, it is useless to negotiate agreements and to draft international instruments;
- that the establishment of an international legal order would require legal arrangements radically different from those currently in effect.

These considerations do not as yet account for all the qualitative differences between political and legal guidance systems. One crucial aspect of these differences lies in the extent to which decision-makers are limited in their discretion. . . .

The reasoning appropriate to decisions in terms of policies differs from reasoning required by rules. When policies only are available to direct decisions, their executants are free to determine when and what to do provided their decisions lead to the required goal. Policies contemplate the delegation of a considerable degree of authority to their executants and presuppose a correspondingly significant area of indeterminacy in measures to be adopted. For example, the principle contained in Article 2 paragraph 4 of the Charter—that all Members shall refrain in their international relations from the threat or use of force against the territorial integrity or political independence of any state, or in any other manner inconsistent with the Purposes of the United Nations—functions as a policy directive. It is of such generality that it cannot meaningfully guide the decisions of States.

Legal as distinct from political guidance requires that there be a "marked degree" of firmness of guidance, limiting discretion not only with respect to the goals to be achieved but also as to the means to be adopted. Under policy guidance the pursuit of posited ends may take a variety of forms and the means are left to the discretion of executants. Rule guidance, on the other hand, typically requires the performance of specific acts in predetermined circumstances for stated ends. Rules guidance looks not only to the acceptance and pursuit of policy goals, but also to compliance with certain procedures and requirements in promoting them. Arguments that rules are always competing pairs of opposites can be overdone. Similar arguments can be made that policy goals are so vague as to amount to functioning legal fictions. The fact remains that rules no less than policies can be designed to guide, to limit discretion, and to circumscribe unfettered authority. Only in this fashion can we account for the hard bargaining and time-consuming drafting involved in the production of international instruments. Rules and policies operate through the instrumentality of language and of text. Initially at least, they call for deference to verbal guidance rather than to the expectations of their authors.[25] A legal system as distinct from a political system relies on specificity in language about what is required, when, and to what end. This is by way of contrast to systems in which one would only postulate abstract goals, in which general principles, broad standards, and loose precepts permit decision-makers to do pretty much as they please. In such systems, general and frequently conflicting aims provide the only signposts to permitted or required behavior. Here again there looms a vast undemarcated terrain between the legal and the political—but the more specific the guidance in a system becomes, the more specific the norms, the policy goals and their application, the more "legal" this system becomes. On the other hand, a system which requires merely obedience to very specific orders, directives, and commands without regard to policy considerations would not necessarily present a true picture even of a vertical legal system. It should be more accurately characterized as a bureaucratic structure resembling the military, severing consideration of policies from the application of rules and standing orders. . . .

CHARACTERISTICS OF LEGAL SYSTEMS—A RECAPITULATION

Common elements in the two model legal systems suggest that there are some essential qualities for legal ordering that are not shared by other forms of ordering. They possess salient features of their own.

Perhaps the first and most prominent element is the acceptance of guidance. Legal decisions involve primarily guided reasoning—reasoning that relies whenever possible on the authoritative guidance of texts and of enunciated policies formulated in binding fashion. Such reasoning requires *deference* to the preferences of authoritative decision-makers rather than reliance on one's own preferences. In clear contrast, political reasoning looks to no authority to defer to but is designed to promote the claims, needs, and expectations of relevant constituencies. Guided legal reasoning, guided decision-making, accordingly requires "good reasons" for departing from established practices.

A second and closely related feature of legal ordering is the commitment to abide by governing rules and principles and authoritatively enunciated policies. That commitment and the resulting congruence between decision-making at all levels and declared law express the guided nature of legal reasoning. To accept legal guidance in good faith necessarily involves congruence between official action and accepted law. Good faith compliance and deference to rules, principles, and their objectives are essential ingredients in legal ordering. In these circumstances unauthorized modifications and departures from practice are impermissible. The acceptance of legal guidance signifies the acceptance of rules and binding policies that one cannot unilaterally alter at will. In political systems, by way of contrast, policies and objectives can be modified and abandoned without impropriety.

Third, good faith deference to authoritative texts and policies calls for their evenhanded and consistent application. Evenhandedness and consistency in application are no mere moral virtues. They express the essence of legality. Unequal applications of the law or inconsistent decisions that are not based upon "good reasons" are essentially arbitrary. But nonlegal decisions, political decisions for example, those that are concerned neither with justice nor with principle but primarily with the attainment of posited ends, these need be neither evenhanded nor consistent.

A fourth requirement of legal ordering can be discerned in procedures for choosing between competing rules, principles, and binding policies. Legal choices for which no authoritative guidance is available must be made on a principled basis transcending the requirements of each case. In such choices consistency, evenhandedness, and principle express the essentially legal character of the choices involved. Choices expressing merely the preferences of the decision-maker are devoid of this feature. They are political.

A fifth characteristic of legal ordering lies in yet another aspect of authoritative guidance—in a limitation of discretion. The crucial point is the fairly simple one that all acceptance of guidance involves a limitation of discretion. Free decision, as we have observed, involves a choice unbounded by any prior authority. The continuum from discretion to authority spans the full breadth of the division between legal and political reasoning.

A sixth characteristic of legal ordering can be found in the procedures adopted in adjudication. Impartial and informed decisions can be made only when affected parties have an opportunity to present proofs and arguments for a decision in their favor. Procedure is here inseparably related to the very concept of legal ordering.

Then, in addition, reference should be made to the seven ingredients of the acceptance model outlined above. They are, however, peculiar to legal systems operating in societies in which power is widely diffused. But the emphasis on the authoritative quality of the guidance is fundamental. The seven ingredients are a shorthand statement of the specifically juridical character of decision-making in horizontal systems.

In the repeated references placed in this essay upon the distinction between the legal and political systems, no concept of political system was either proposed or attempted. Instead, the strategy of the argument has been to outline what is involved in the existence of a legal system and to proceed by exclusion. The emphasis was placed on models of legal ordering and to contrast the different modes involved in juridical and "other" forms of ordering. *The emphasis in this contrast lies not in institutions but on modes of decision-making and on procedures of reasoning.* The contrast between juridical and political processes does not depend upon the existence of particular institutional settings. Both horizontal and vertical institutional structures and political arrangements can accommodate juridical processes. . . .

NOTES

The author is indebted to Oscar Schachter, Executive Director of UNITAR, and to Abraham Edel, Professor of Philosophy, City University of New York, for their stimulating and perceptive comments.

1. These are considered in a significant body of recent literature—Richard A. Falk, "New Approaches to the Study of International Law," in Morton Kaplan, ed., *New Approaches to International Relations* (New York 1968); Richard A. Falk, "The Adequacy of Contemporary Theories of International Law—Gaps in Legal Thinking," 50 *Virginia Law Review*, 231 (March 1964); Myres McDougal, Harold Lasswell, William Reisman, "Theories About International Law: Prologue to a Configurative Jurisprudence," 8 *Virginia Journal of International Law*, 188 (April 1968); Wolfgang Friedmann, *The Changing Structure of International Law* (New York 1964); Gregory Tunkin, *Droit International Publique, Problèmes Theoriques* (Paris 1965); Charles de Visscher, *Theory and Reality in Public International Law* (rev. ed., Princeton 1968); Karl W. Deutsch and Stanley Hoffmann, *The Relevance of International Law* (Cambridge, Mass. 1968); Cornelius F. Murphy Jr., "Some Reflections Upon Theories of International Law," 70 *Columbia Law Review*, 447 (March 1970); Hans Kelsen, *Principles of International Law*, R. Tucker, ed. (New York 1966); Gregory Tunkin, "International Organizations and Law," *Soviet Law and Government* IV No. 4 (1966), 3; Oscar Schachter, "Towards a Theory of International Obligation," 8 *Virginia Journal of International Law*, 300 (April 1968); Oscar Schachter, "Law and the Process of Decision in The Political Organs of the United Nations," 109 (1963) 2 *Recueil Des Cours*, 171; Michael Barkun, *Law Without Sanctions* (New Haven 1968); Morton Kaplan and Nicholas de B. Katzenbach, *The Political Foundations of International Law* (New York 1961); H. L. A. Hart, *The Concept of Law* (Oxford 1961), Chap. X; Stanley Hoffmann, "International Systems and International Law," in Klaus Knorr and Sidney Verba, eds., *The International System* (Princeton, N.J. 1960).

2. Austin, Kelsen and Hart devote considerable attention to international law. See John Austin, *The Province of Jurisprudence Determined*, Hart ed. (New York 1954); Kelsen (fn. 1) and also Hans Kelsen, *General Theory of Law and State* (Cambridge, Mass. 1949); Hart (fn. 1).

3. See Richard A. Falk, "International Jurisdiction: Horizontal and Vertical Conceptions of Legal Order," 32 *Temple Law Quarterly*, 295 (Spring 1959). See also Inis L. Claude, *Power and International Relations* (New York 1962), Chaps. VII and VIII.

4. The concept of power is usefully analyzed in Talcott Parsons, *Structure and Process in Modern Societies* (Glencoe, Ill. 1960), 182; Harold Lasswell and Abraham Kaplan, *Power and Society* (New Haven 1950). See also Talcott Parsons, "On the Concept of Political Power," *Proceedings of the American Philosophical Society* CIII, No. 3 (June 1963). See also B. de Jouvenel, *On Power* (New York 1949); Guglielmo Ferreró, *The Principles of Power* (New York 1942); Adolf A. Berle, *Power* (New York 1969).

5. In Kelsen's opinion a coercive legal order is an essential feature of law. See Kelsen (fn. 1), 3–177. See also Hart (fn. 1), Chap. X; John Austin, *Lectures on Jurisprudence*, R. Campbell, ed. (New York 1875).

6. See Barkun's well-argued thesis, Barkun (n. 1); see also Fried, "How Efficient is International Law?" in Deutsch and Hoffman (n. 1).

7. Falk (n. 3), 297.

8. See Lon L. Fuller, "Adjudication and the Rule of Law," 54 *Proceedings of the American Society of International Law*, 1 (1960), and see also his "Collective Bargaining and the Arbitrator," *Wisconsin Law Review* (January 1963), 3. See also Milton Katz, *The Relevance of International Adjudication* (Cambridge, Mass. 1968).

9. On the "political question" doctrine in U.S. Constitutional Law see Alexander Bickel, *The Least Dangerous Branch* (Indianapolis and New York 1962); Herbert Wechsler, *Principles, Politics and Fundamental Law* (Cambridge, Mass. 1961); Fritz W. Scharpf, "Judicial Review and the Political Question—A Functional Analysis," 75 *Yale Law Journal*, 517 (March 1966). This doctrine should not be confused with the concept of political disputes under international law. On this second subject, see Rosalyn Higgins, "Policy Considerations and the International Judicial Process," 17 *International and Comparative Law Quarterly*, 58 (Jan. 1968).

10. For interesting comments on the uses of international law outside law courts see Dean Rusk, "Parliamentary Diplomacy—Debate v. Negotiation," *World Affairs Interpreter*, XXVI (Summer 1955); Philip Jessup, "Parliamentary Diplomacy: An Examination of the Legal Quality of the Rules of Procedure of Organs of the United Nations," 89 (1956) *Recueil Des Cours*, I, 185; Hardy Dillard, "Some Aspects of Law and Diplomacy," 91 (1957) *Recueil Des Cours*, I, 449; Percy E. Corbett, *Law in Diplomacy* (Princeton 1959); Louis Henkin, *How Nations Behave* (New York 1968); Arthur Lall, *Modern International Negotiations* (New York 1966), Chap. 26.

11. On the uses of international law by organs other than judicial organs see the works cited in Note 10, and see also Rosalyn Higgins, *The Development of International Law Through the Political Organs of the United Nations* (Oxford 1963); Richard A. Falk, *The Status of Law in International Society* (Princeton 1969); Roger Fisher, "Bringing Law to Bear on Governments," 74 *Harvard Law Review*, 1130 (April 1961); Rosalyn Higgins, "The Place of International Law in the Settlement of Disputes by the Security Council," 64 *American Journal of International Law*, 1 (Jan. 1970); Myres McDougal, "International Law, Power and Policy," 82 (1953) *Recueil Des Cours*, II, 137; Schachter (n. 1); Oscar Schachter, "Dag Hammarskjold and the Relationship of Law to Politics," 56 *American Journal of International Law*, 1 (Jan. 1962), and "The Development of International Law Through the Legal Opinions of the United Nations," 25 *British Yearbook of International Law*, 91 (1948); A. J. P. Tammes, "Decisions of International Organs as a Source of International Law," 94 (1958) *Recueil Des Cours* II, 264; Leo Gross, "States as Organs of International Law and the Problem of Auto-Interpretation," in George A. Lipsky, ed., *Law and Politics in World Community* (Berkeley 1953).

12. See Richard A. Falk, "On the Quasi-Legislative Competence of The General Assembly," 60 *American Journal of International Law*, 782 (Oct. 1966); see also Judge Tanaka's dissent in the *South West Africa Cases* [1966] *ICJ Reports* 248, 292–94. See further Falk (n. 8), 55 (n. 21), Chap. 5; on the sanction of non-participation see Friedmann (n. 1), 88ff.

13. Fisher (n. 18).

14. See United States Senate 90th Congress 1st Session, Hearings before the Committee on Foreign Relations, Senate Resolution 151; U.S. Committments to Foreign Powers (1967), 70.

15. See Stanley Hoffmann, *The State of War* (New York 1965), 130ff.; de Visscher (n. 1), 106ff.; Higgins, *The Development of International Law Through the Political Organs of the United Nations* (n. 18), 1–10; Falk, in Deutsch and Hoffmann (n. 1), 144ff.; J. Fried, in Deutsch and Hoffmann (n. 1), 116ff.; Gerald G. Fitzmaurice, "Judicial Innovation," in *Cambridge Essays in International Law in Honour of Lord McNair* (London and New York 1965).

16. J. L. Brierly, *The Basis of Obligation in International Law* (Oxford 1958), Chap. 1.

17. See Fisher (n. 18); Henkin (n. 17); see also the work of the Panel of the American Society of International Law on Decision-Making in War-Peace Crises.

18. There is a vast literature on this subject. See, in particular, Hart (n. 1), Chap. X; Glanville Williams, "International Law and the Controversy Concerning the Word 'Law,'" 22 *British Yearbook of International Law*, 146 (1945); Herbert Morris, "Verbal Disputes and the Legal Philosophy of John Austin," 7 *U.C.L.A. Law Review*, 27 (Jan. 1960). The first question is generally treated under the heading of "sources" of international law, see Clive Perry, *The Sources and Evidences of International Law* (New York 1965); see also notes 10 and 11; the second question is one about "legal systems"; in addition to the works cited in notes 1 and 2 above, see also Hermann Kantorowicz, *The Definition of Law*, A. H. Campbell, ed. (Cambridge 1958); Julius Stone, *Legal System and Lawyers' Reasonings* (Stanford 1964).

19. "The Court, whose function is to decide in accordance with international law such disputes as are submitted to it, shall apply:

(a) international conventions, whether general or particular, establishing rules expressly recognized by the contesting states;

(b) international custom, as evidence of a general practice accepted as law;

(c) the general principles of law recognized by civilized nations;

(d) subject to the provisions of Article 59, judicial decision and the teachings of the most highly qualified publicists of the various nations, as subsidiary means for the determination of rules of law.

2. This provision shall not prejudice the power of the Court to decide a case ex aeque et bono, if the parties agree thereto."

20. See Hart (n. 1), 91ff. and Chap. X.

21. The reference to "international actors" is not merely a reference to States. It is a reference to all groups and entities with the *capability* to affect international relations. It is a de facto sociological concept—not a juridical construct. The state system happens at this time in history to be the most effective power system in international relations.

There is nothing in this model of law to preclude either reciprocal or common interest arrangements. Horizontal systemic relationships are not confined to barter-like reciprocal associations. Indeed, common enterprises feature prominently in them. Horizontality refers to the distribution of power—power in the sense of a capability to gain one's ends over the opposition of other centers of power. A horizontal distribution of power does not then preclude the agreed subordination of narrow vested interests to a higher vision of the common good. Nor does it rule out the possibility that another authority or power structure might be established for conflict control or for other objectives.

A nonauthoritarian model of law for horizontal systems does not require the attribution of any special status to sovereignty or nonintervention principles. These principles are merely reflections of the interests and claims of states as the most powerful international actors. These principles do not *logically* form a component of our model.

22. For a fuller discussion, see Gidon Gottlieb, *The Logic of Choice* (New York 1968), Chaps. VIII, X and XI; see also Rosalyn Higgins, *Conflict of Interests; International Law in a Divided World* (Chester Springs, Pa. 1965).

23. Lon L. Fuller, *The Morality of Law*, rev. ed. (New Haven 1969), 39ff., 81ff.

24. See Fuller's (n. 42) discussion of the concept of the "internal morality of law."

25. See Gidon Gottlieb, "The Conceptual World of the Yale School of International Law," *World Politics* XXI (October 1968), 108-32, and David Weisstub, "Conceptual Foundations of the Interpretation of Agreements," *World Politics* XXII (January 1970), 225-69; see further Gidon Gottlieb, "The Interpretation of Treaties by Tribunals," and Myres McDougal, "Comments," in *Proceedings of the American Society of International Law* (1969), 122-34.

CHAPTER 4

Lawmaking in International Society

One of the fundamental issues for international legal analysis is to give a clear account of how law can come into being in a society that lacks a government. Jurists can expound at length on the "sources" of international law. The classical sources include international treaties, custom, general principles of law, and the opinions of respected international law experts. These sources are laid out in Article 38 of the Statute of the International Court of Justice (World Court), where, additionally, the decisions of the Court itself are claimed as a subsidiary source.

This section of the book does not attempt an exhaustive treatment of international lawmaking. It seeks to highlight the emergence of new sources, which are the result of the acts of international institutions, especially the resolutions of the General Assembly and the pronouncements of more specialized international agencies. The technical complexity of international life, together with the increased number and diversity of states, engenders pressure to create law rapidly and on a global scale. At the same time, however, notions of sovereignty retain a firm hold. The Soviet Union, its allies, and the recently independent countries of the Third World are especially reluctant to acknowledge legal obligations for which they have not given their consent, especially in the express form of an international treaty.

To the extent that law is effectively created by community procedures based on voting majorities rather than by the meeting of each and every sovereign will, there seems to be a new ingredient introduced into international law. In actuality, it involves restoring an old ingredient, as international law originated in a natural law environment in which the binding content of rules and principles was based on their immutability. This new tendency toward community lawmaking is one indication of a latent disposition and practical necessity to move beyond the state system. The significance of these developments should neither be neglected nor exaggerated. The status of a rule or principle as "law" does not address the separate issue of whether governments feel a "sense of obligation" in relation to normative standards that they reject or have not accorded some indication of approval or, at least, acceptance. It seems clear that most governments do not feel bound under such circumstances, and since patterns of compliance are so dependent on self-enforcement it is doubtful whether the rule or principle will be respected. As a result, "disrespect" weakens the status of law as such, and is thus, in fundamental ways, a setback for international law.

Gidon Gottlieb's contribution in Chapter 4 examines lawmaking themes directly in the specific context of the contemporary world order. He shows us the complexity of the process as well as the variety of instruments actors use to structure their participation in international life. Gottlieb divides international agreements into two basic categories: instruments emerging from "diplomatic modes" of arriving at decisions and those deriving from such formal arrangements. The latter can be classified as treaties, executive agreements, or (legally) nonbinding agreements. Gottlieb tries to give us an understanding of the bewildering array of devices that actors now use to stabilize behavior by agreements and rules. Increasingly, a focus solely on treaties—duly ratified written instruments between states—would overlook the actual scope of relevant authoritative pronouncements regulating interactions.

Thus, for instance, the consensus procedures utilized by the Law of the Sea Conference undoubtedly enhanced the stature of the "informal" texts long before the principles enunciated in these negotiations became formal law through the ratification of a multilateral convention. Similarly, nontreaty agreements that constitute the Camp David accords or the Vietnam Peace Agreements create not only international but also domestic consequences whose importance cannot properly be assessed by relying upon an all-or-nothing dichotomy between formally valid treaty/executive agreements and informal agreements that do not attain treaty status. The blurring of what were once much more clear-cut distinctions is to a certain extent the result of the increasing intensity of interdependencies and of the sheer volume of transactions that make up modern transnational politics. While, formerly, the instruments of "contracts" (treaties) were generally sufficient to stabilize expectations for single "one-shot" transactions, increasing interdependencies make it more and more necessary to develop general modes of agreed coexistence in which too technical a focus on specific rights, legal stipulations, and third-party interests cannot cope with the range and diversity of interaction that requires mutually agreed-upon action. Law, often seen as a "community-building" device, clearly shows its limitations in this respect. It is perhaps better adapted to regulate clearly separable transactions than to structure a more intimate modus vivendi in which, through a continuous process of give and take, mutual bonds are gradually established.

Friedrich Kratochwil's essay follows this line of thought by investigating the role of domestic institutions, in particular domestic courts, in shaping the international legal order. He argues that although domestic courts wear "two hats" in that they are agencies of the international legal system as well as national institutions, most of the time they do not satisfactorily discharge their role in the international legal process. They either defer too much to executive action, or give rather uncritical preference to domestic law in transnational legal disputes. Even when discretion and comity are invoked to justify judicial abstention, the principles as well as the "choice of law" rules applied to a particular "case and controversy" seldom address the system-wide needs of creating an acceptable "regime" for all participants. Thus, while various "balancing acts" might take the conflicting interests of two domestic legal systems into account, the absence of a global frame of reference leaves courts with the sole injunction to act "reasonably," without raising the question of how these discretionary powers relate to the international constitutive process of law creation. Similar tensions between the imperatives of the international legal order and domestic considerations can be observed in cases in which individuals challenge the actions of national institutions by invoking international legal norms such as human rights or the Nuremberg principles.

Kratochwil's analysis takes the form of a discussion of American legal practices as shown in the pertinent case law. His treatment of American courts leads him to consider such constitutional issues as foreign policymaking powers in a federal state, and the locus and limitations of a system of government characterized by separation of powers and checks and balances. In sum, the basic theoretical problem addressed by Kratochwil is how constitutionalism, which is concerned with legitimacy and limited govern-ment, can relate to a more global world order perspective of international legal thought, and whether and how opportunities for a Grotian evolution can be created.

Nicholas Onuf, in the third selection, deals with the problem of codification and progressive development of international law in a historical as well as systematic fashion, arguing that the current enchantment with codification through the drafting of comprehensive "codes" is based on a fundamental misunderstanding not only of the international but also of the domestic legal order. Thus the proliferation of conferences and other lawmaking devices outside the International Law Commission charged with codification is paralleled in the domestic order by the growth of "administrative law." In the burgeoning domestic setting, the rise of regulation by bureaucratic means involves the substitution of individual problem-solving devices for general rules. Thus, a confusing situation emerges. Rulings in a myriad of specific cases proliferate, leading often to incompatible "solutions." These inconsistent rulings can erode the authoritative character of law. In such circumstances, the use of legal rhetoric and the employment of "lawyers" disguise a fundamental change. Internationally, the "growth of law" exhibits similar features. This is perhaps most obvious in relation to the impressive evolution of "European Community" law, wherein rulings by administrative directive have become the most common ordering device. The same process is also observable in transactions governed by "transnational law" and in the international interactions in which lawyer-bureaucrats use their respective foreign ministries, and their recourse to United Nations machinery, to give a certain structure to their undertakings. Given this setting, the law-creating process "codified" by draft conventions represents only the tip of the iceberg. In actuality, law develops more intensively and more usefully as a result of various ad hoc and unsystematic occasions. It grows largely in response to administrative needs of behavioral complexity rather than by reference to formal texts drafted in isolation. In this context, the role of General Assembly resolutions in the evolutionary process of international law must be mentioned. Although "legislative competence" was withheld from the General Assembly by the UN Charter, it is generally accepted that the Assembly can pass resolutions that are "declaratory" of international law. To this extent, if strictly construed, the General Assembly serves as an agency in the articulation of a customary rule, rather than as a "world parliament" passing laws. If stringent requirements of unanimity are upheld in assessing whether a customary rule of international law exists, as well as rules requiring subsequent observance of the articulated rule in state practice, then the General Assembly is merely a modern way of codifying "custom."

A more interesting question is raised by resolutions that claim that the legitimization (or delegitimization) of particular norms derives not from their origins in custom, but rather from the authority of the General Assembly as the most representative organ of the world community. Although one need not fully share the enthusiasm of some Third World jurists for the lawmaking authority of the General Assembly, the conservative position seems to err on the other side, given that there is no doubt that several General Assembly resolutions have been given weight even by such sovereignty-oriented legal institutions as the World Court and arbitration tribunals. Besides, other opinion-forming groups may invoke such "law" to add weight to their claims (as in the case of General Assembly resolutions condemning reliance on nuclear weapons, which are relied upon by peace groups in their efforts to persuade).

The carefully drafted arbitration award in the Texaco-Libyan dispute, for instance, includes some reasoning that bears on the lawmaking status of resolutions. The arbitration enunciates a nearly "Calhounian" position by arguing that the authoritative character of a resolution depends on the *quality* of the consensus that underlies its adoption. Thus, a resolution passed by a majority that comprises members of all relevant power groupings within the UN will be accepted as binding. This conclusion can, of course, be interpreted as weakening the notion of "sovereign equality" that is written into the Charter of the United Nations. It represents a genuine shift in the direction of the "consensus position" (compared to the "consent position") in addition to confirming the increasing relevance of community expectations in the formation process of international law. As such, it constitutes a Grotian seedling that gives some energy and direction to the dynamics of global reform.

The last selection in Chapter 4 is an article by Daniel Partan on the role of the International Court of Justice. Partan introduces us to the reality of the World Court, a reality that amounts to no more than a gesture of judicial centralism in international society. Global reformers at one time had put great stock in the World Court, initially established as part of the peace arrangements at the end of World War I. It was supposed that a genuine judicial alternative to armed conflict would shift the scale of decisionmaking within governments in the direction of the peaceful settlement of disputes. In particular, given the growing complexity of international life, it was supposed that having disputes adjudicated before a tribunal composed of jurists would be a real contribution to the possibility of orderly and fair regulation. And yet the Court has not grown stronger with time. In fact, its role is generally now seen to be marginal at best and, at worst, to be actually on the decline. Why? There have been many efforts at explanation, but the main ones hinge on the reluctance of states to part with their control over a settlement process in their relations with another state and on the failure of international law to give equal weight to disparate ideologies and cultural outlooks. At the same time, however, there is no alternative to judicial settlement in some settings: The law that is created cannot be authoritatively and peacefully applied without organs of judicial interpretation. The Court, for all its shortcomings, is one expression of the Grotian promise of community institutions growing up over time alongside states.

QUESTIONS FOR DISCUSSION AND REFLECTION: CHAPTER 4

1. In what ways does lawmaking in the international arena differ from lawmaking in domestic societies? Evaluate in this respect the role of political institutions and customary norms in both settings.

2. Do you believe that the codification process outlined by Onuf can be a significant factor in developing the international legal order? What factors operate for and against a "progressive" development through codification procedures?

3. Does Partan's article lead you to believe that the International Court of Justice can play an active role in the development of international law? Is it important that ICJ decisions do not enjoy a formal status as precedents? Should national courts be allowed to request advisory opinions from the ICJ on international law questions? What changes, both domestic and international, would be necessary to make this proposal a realistic possibility?

SELECTED BIBLIOGRAPHY: CHAPTER 4

Anthony D'Amato, *The Concept of Custom in International Law* (Ithaca, N.Y.: Cornell University Press, 1971).

Richard Bilder, *Managing Risks of International Agreement* (Madison, Wis.: University of Wisconsin Press, 1961).

Tashlim Elias, *The Modern Law of Treaties* (Dobbs Ferry, N.Y.: Oceana, 1974).

Richard Falk, *The Role of Domestic Courts in the International Legal Order* (Syracuse, N.Y.: Syracuse University Press, 1964).

Leo Gross, ed., *The Future of the International Court of Justice* (Dobbs Ferry, N.Y.: Oceana, 1976).

Louis Henkin, *Foreign Affairs and the Constitution* (New York: Norton, 1972).

Nicholas Onuf, ed., *Law Making in the Global Community* (Durham, N.C.: Carolina Academic Press, 1982).

I. M. Sinclair, *The Vienna Convention on the Law of Treaties* (Dobbs Ferry, N.Y.: Oceana, 1973).

12. Global Bargaining: The Legal and Diplomatic Framework

Gidon Gottlieb

The emergence of a new world order shaped more by bargains, compromises, and necessity than by grand architectural designs is underway. Deep structural changes are taking place. They follow the decline of the big power blocs and the rise of states organized in global political parties; changes include the emergence of a distinct multilateral mode of diplomacy that involves a shift from parliamentary diplomacy to a novel form of diplomacy based on equality between groups of states which I shall refer to as *parity diplomacy*. Changes are reflected also in the growing importance of non-voting procedures in international negotiating arenas and in the variety of instruments designed to accommodate all types of bargains. These instruments are often characterized by a shift from formal, legally binding accords to other forms of commitment, and in the United States such shifts affect the respective roles of the President and of the Congress in the domestic management of interdependence. Informal agreements are evidently harder for Congress to control or even to monitor. Cumulatively these changes constitute new structures for the contemporary world order. Legal theory, as well as economic and political conventions, must be brought up to date and reflect the rapidly evolving practice of states, as well as the new structural framework in which the great economic issues of interdependence must be resolved. These are the main themes of this essay.

DIPLOMATIC MODES AND PROCEDURES OF DECISION IN INTERNATIONAL ARENAS

The headlong flight of developed countries from negotiations in arenas dominated by coalitions of Communist States and Less Developed Countries (LDCs) continues. Since the first meeting of the United Nations Conference on Trade and Development (UNCTAD) in 1964, these coalitions of states have acquired official status. States are formally classified in a number of groups that reflect fairly fixed party alignments in the world economic arenas.[1] These formal groupings function in the economic arena as global

TABLE 12.1
Some Principal Diplomatic Modes

The Parliamentary mode: characteristic of representative conferences and assemblies: the U.N. General Assembly.

The Traditional mode: characteristic of bilateral negotiations: U.S.-Japanese trade negotiations.

The Parity mode: characteristic of conflicting interest groups: North-South conference.

The Managerial mode: characteristic of functional agencies or corporations with agreed objectives: World Bank.

The Conference mode: characteristic of situations in which the parties must act in concert to reach agreement: Vietnam Peace conference.

Third party modes: mediation, conciliation, good offices: U.S. role in Egyptian-Israeli disengagement agreement.

---

bargaining units. They tend to keep their cohesion in political forums as well.

The emergence of economic interest groupings of states has encouraged the shift toward conciliation and away from the majority voting characteristic of the principal United Nations organs.[2] This trend is noticeable in UNCTAD and in the Economic and Social Council (ECOSOC). It has also had an impact in the Law of the Sea Conference where complicated coalitions of states have sprung up along lines reflecting additional special interests such as those of landlocked states.

Powers that are not ready to forego military parity cannot be expected to accept less than parity in negotiations. Yet positions secured by military might can be eroded at the conference table. The significance of issues on the international negotiating agenda is confirmed by the emergence of a new mode of multilateral diplomacy: I refer to it as the principle of *parity*. It reflects the organization of states into global political parties and alignments which do not follow the big power bloc politics of the first years of the U.N. Parity requires that agreement be reached between the main parties or groups of states on the basis of the equality of the groups of states rather than on the basis of the equality of individual states. It requires the consent of the groups before any decision can be taken or agreement reached. It arises from the organization of states into caucuses or alignments. Parity is a principle applicable in negotiations between groups of states and between powers. It is anchored neither in ideological claims of equality nor in the theory of representation. It emanates from the realities of power relationships and from the need to manage the problems of interdependence and of world order. The principle of parity is well suited to a pluralistic international community with few shared ideological premises. It connotes no particular theory of political obligation or consent but rests entirely on actual patterns of relationships and common concerns.

The principle of parity, which is reflected also in collective bargaining, was applied in the Paris North-South negotiations at the Conference on International Economic Cooperation (CIEC).[3]

The principle of parity has recently been tied also to the notion of consensus. This notion was the subject of significant analysis in the arbitral award in the dispute between Texaco and Libya. The sole arbitrator, French Professor Dupuy, stated that resolutions of the United Nations which reflect the state of customary law on a given subject and which are supported by a consensus of a majority of states belonging to various representative groups, could—if other conditions were met—acquire a binding force. The arbitrator underscored the importance of representative groups in the process of the development of international law.[4] This is a notion likely to create problems for isolated states not associated with any particular group or alliance. It stands in contrast to earlier official views of the Department of State.

The parity principle avoids the pitfalls of parliamentary diplomacy in a world order dominated less by single states than by organized state groupings. The parity principle can gradually displace the principle of majority rule in international conferences, which until recently was itself regarded as a novelty. Earlier this century the progression from unanimity to majority rule had marked the emergence of international assemblies as corporate entities capable of taking action as such. This was in contrast to nineteenth-century practice, under which conferences were mere assemblies of states or a medium for negotiating a treaty:

In the historical development it was necessary that the great political organs of the League should adhere to the traditional system so that the corporate personality of the Council and the Assembly soon came to be accepted. It was soon customary to refer to the decisions of the Council or of the Assembly as such and not as the concurrent decisions of the members composing those organs. Yet the complete abandonment of the unanimity rule in the drafting of the United Nations Charter was revolutionary.[5]

Thirty years after the San Francisco Conference on the United Nations, we thus note the further progression from majority to parity.

The range of modes of agreement-making has been broadened. Each mode is endowed with particular attributes that cannot be modified at will. The main diplomatic modes[6] are:

1. The *traditional diplomatic mode* is practiced by states on a bilateral basis and involves consultation, discussion, and negotiation.
2. *Conference diplomacy* is adopted in international meetings in which negotiators meet collectively and are bound only by actions to which they consent. Such conferences cannot take action as an entity, but are only an arena for negotiating agreements.
3. *Parliamentary diplomacy* is practiced in international organs endowed with a corporate character of their own and authorized to act as such by a majority vote.
4. *Parity diplomacy* is a new emerging mode adopted in international arenas in negotiations between groups of states.

5. *Third-party modes* are characteristic procedures adopted for the settlement of international conflicts, such as good offices, conciliation, mediation, arbitration, and judicial settlement and involve varying degrees of authority exercised by third parties.
6. The *managerial mode* is adopted in agencies responsible for performing services requiring managerial decisions.
7. *Informal modes* are unstructured, informal processes adopted without the use of formal instruments or arenas.

The attributes characteristic of each diplomatic mode permeate and sometimes dominate the process of agreement-making. The choice of mode can on occasion determine the outcome of the negotiating effort itself. Significant attributes of each diplomatic mode include: (1) the procedure of decision-making (i.e., voting, consensus); (2) the character of participation (i.e., universal, regional, bilateral, etc.); (3) the basis of representation (i.e., equality, quotas, special rights); (4) the functions of agreements (i.e., operational, goal-setting, or rule-making); and (5) the range of domestic participants (i.e., the executive or legislative branches, private interest groups, and other constituencies).

Attributes cannot be transplanted at will from one diplomatic mode to another. In parliamentary diplomacy it is thus hard to legitimize unequal voting powers. But these modes can be combined and used simultaneously or in sequence. A conference may thus be called to adopt and sign instruments negotiated in the traditional diplomatic mode. This was done for the Japanese Peace Treaties. President Truman had requested the then New York attorney, John Foster Dulles, to negotiate a peace treaty with Japan. The treaty was eventually submitted to an international conference for acceptance.[7]

The weakness of the majority principle is deepened by the declining authority of two other principles which sustain majority rule: equality and representation.[8] The admission of mini-states to world organizations has accentuated the tensions between the formal equality of states and the extreme inequalities in population, resources, and capacity for independent action. Formally the votes of these states count as heavily as those of the big powers in any tabulation of votes cast, but their political weight is evidently far from equal. Increasingly the equality of states is regarded mainly as a jural principle governing legal rights and duties rather than as a guide for the management of global interdependence and decision-making. The principle of the equality of states is vulnerable to claims about the need for planetary reapportionment. The vitality of the equality principle as a basis for majority rule in international arenas is fading as reapportionment remains beyond reach.[9]

The moral weight of an international organization varies with the character of its main actors. Police states carry no greater moral authority collectively than they do in isolation. The problem is well illustrated by the efforts some Communist states made in 1978 in the United Nations Education, Scientific and Cultural Organization (UNESCO) to legitimize press censorship. The increasing number of authoritarian states in the international community has modified the corporate character of international assemblies. Some of these are now analogous to a consortium of tyrannies. The non-aligned group thus had no difficulty in throwing its full support in 1975 behind the Cambodian government of Pol Pot which was then already engaged in the extermination of vast segments of its population. The legitimacy of majority decisions in international organizations is sapped by the repressive and brutal character of many of its constituents.[10] Most cannot in any sense of the word be regarded as representative governments. They meet neither classical nor revolutionary standards of legitimacy.[11] They are not legitimate by reference to their origin, and most are not legitimate under their own principles of constitutionality and law. Many are indeed simply lawless, even in terms of the aspirations which they purport to reflect.[12] Doubts about the domestic legitimacy of authoritarian rulers do not, however, impeach their international standing to participate in the emerging world order and to bargain and negotiate with states that enjoy governments of unimpeachable legitimacy. These ideological doubts never-theless undermine the relevance of the principles of majority rule and equality where rulers indifferent to majority rule and equality in their own societies are involved.

Rulers in power, in effective control of territory and people and able to affect global interdependence patterns, cannot be, and on the whole are not, left out of the diplomatic process. But increasingly gross and consistent patterns of violations of human rights are eroding their international legitimacy in the sense that aid to their regimes becomes controversial and assistance to their domestic adversaries elicits support. The developing and as yet unexplored connection between legitimacy and gross violations of human rights is casting a clouded light on the standing of institutions dominated by regimes which flagrantly abuse their populations.

Universality and equality of representation are appropriate principles for deliberative or legislative organs. But their relevance should not everywhere be taken for granted. In institutional architecture, function shapes the design of an institution, its membership, its procedures, and the decision-making process. Difficulties emerge with attempts to rely, for example, on a quasi-legislative organ for collective bargaining purposes. A broad view of insti-tutional design is required to harmonize decision-making processes and outcomes.

The diplomatic record confirms that effective negotiations can be con-ducted, even in the General Assembly, between influential states that can deliver a decision.[13] It does not follow that the General Assembly and ECOSOC can be converted from majority decisions to consensus procedures. Attempts to deny LDCs and Communist states the benefits of their two-thirds majority may well be futile. Efforts to use the same organs for deliberation, for rule setting, and for collective bargaining were nevertheless attempted. An interesting effort to mix the deliberative and bargaining functions of ECOSOC and the General Assembly with built-in mediation and consensus procedures was made in the 1975 Report of a Group of Experts on "A New United Nations Structure for Global Economic Cooperation."[14]

The collective bargaining process, or "consultative procedure" as it was referred to in the report, was designed to promote agreement on major policy issues "where agreement might otherwise be unobtainable." The report suggested:

With this end in view, the procedures would normally be initiated at an early stage in the discussions of a given subject and before the stage of the passing of resolutions, but the procedures could also be initiated at the end of a process of debate or even after a decision where this seemed to be appropriate. It would be for the Economic and Social Council, if the recommendations in this section were accepted, to work out these consultative arrangements in appropriate rules of procedure which would specify, among other things, the kind of subject on which consultative procedures could take place.[15]

The report drew inspiration from the experience of the UNCTAD in employing the conciliation procedures contemplated in Resolution 1995 (XIX) December 30, 1964, of the General Assembly and from the work of Mr. Jeremy Morse, Chairman of the Committee of Twenty on the Reform of the International Monetary System.[16]

The Report of the Group of Experts did not, however, adopt the UNCTAD conciliation procedure, which postpones for a fixed period voting on resolutions on which no agreement has been reached. Such a procedure would presumably be too considerable a limitation on the majority's voting rights to be contemplated at this stage of United Nations development. The majority's rights are confirmed in Article 9 of the 1969 Vienna Convention on the Law of Treaties, which provides, with regard to voting at international conferences, that "The adoption of the text of a treaty at an international conference takes place by the vote of two-thirds of the States present and voting, unless by the same majority they shall decide to apply a different rule."[17] Although the Report of the Group of Experts on "A New United Nations Structure for Global Economic Cooperation" did not refer to voting procedures at United Nations conferences, it was an attempt to limit the effects of bloc voting in the United Nations.

Neither the recommendations of the Group of Experts nor the procedures adopted at the Conference on the Law of the Sea can modify the basic political attitude of states, and little can be done by way of rules when a majority wishes to avail itself of its voting power or when a significant minority refuses to accept the will of the majority.[18] Consensus procedures designed to get important states to agree on substantive proposals are vulnerable to criticism of the kind made by the Representative of China at that Conference:

A super-Power, under the smokescreen of practicing "consensus," asserted that the rules of a new Law of the Sea would have international observance only if they were supported by all countries and that the holding of the Conference on the Law of the Sea should also depend on the aforementioned conditions. The intent of these remarks was all too obvious: that is, as long as the super-Power alone does not agree, the Conference cannot be held and the new Law of the Sea cannot be established. Is this not typical hegemonism? As is well known to all, it is necessary now to formulate a new Law of the Sea, precisely because the old Law of the Sea protects the interests of the imperialist Powers, while subjecting the numerous small and medium-sized countries to plunder and humiliation. If the new Law of the Sea would be the same as the old, what is the need for the drafting of a new Law of the Sea? Would not the six year work of the Sea-Bed Committee be in vain? The representative of a developing country had put it rightly: that is, an attempt at the "establishment of the veto" at the Conference by big Powers, which consider that their economic interests and political ambitions must prevail over the fate of the rest of the nations of the world. Obviously, if those views of that super-Power were accepted, it would be impossible to work out a fair and reasonable new Law of the Sea. In our opinion, consultations are desirable; but there certainly should be some method of voting in formulating a new Law of the Sea. The Chinese delegation firmly opposes the attempt by a certain super-Power to impose on the Conference the so-called principle of "consensus" which is tantamount to a veto.[19]

In conferences in which all United Nations member states participate, some states will seek an operational outcome that is effective, binding rules of conduct actually followed by states, for which consensus is the best guarantee. Other states will be satisfied instead to modify standards of legitimacy by a full utilization of voting majorities over the objection of dissident states, however important and influential, without being unduly preoccupied with the implementation of texts adopted.

United Nations parliamentary diplomacy cannot escape these tensions. Consensus rules operate only when major states or groups of states are politically disposed to let them work. They fail when a majority is determined to use its voting power to adopt an instrument, or when a minority will be reluctant to continue a process of negotiations under the threat of a reversion to naked voting power. Thus, in economic matters, the Group of Seventy-Seven may find it difficult not to press for the political advantage that voting power assures in the United Nations system, while the less numerous developed states may yet prefer a process of bargaining in a forum far removed from the unsettling influence of a well-organized and hostile voting majority, timidly avoiding confrontation in the U.N. itself.

The introduction of collective bargaining procedures in United Nations parliamentary diplomacy by using the device of representative committees, consultative groups, or small negotiating groups, operating on the basis of unanimity, is an attempt to strike a balance between the principle of unanimity on the one hand and the participation of only those states that are principally interested in the subject matter on the other. This balance is open to the same tensions that affect consensus rules and can work only when major states or controlling groups of states are politically disposed to accept it.

The recommendations of the Group of Experts attempted to strike this delicate balance. Under the proposals of the Group of Experts during the two-year period in which the negotiating groups would operate, "the General Assembly and ECOSOC would be free to consider subjects under discussion in the group and to vote resolutions thereon, but in deciding whether to vote a particular resolution, the General Assembly and ECOSOC would take into account the progress of the negotiations."[20] At its 31st Session, the General Assembly had received proposals to utilize its functions and powers both as the highest policy-making body in the United Nations system and as a negotiating forum. These proposals were intended to strengthen the role of the Assembly in monetary, trade, and financial fields. As part of the restructuring effort, the Assembly also had proposals to transform UNCTAD into an effective institution for deliberation, negotiation, and review in the field of trade and international economic cooperation, "maintaining its close relationship with the General Assembly." UNCTAD was to be a "generator of new ideas and policy approaches," while its "negotiating function" would also be strengthened. UNCTAD, it has been proposed, would exercise an overview of "negotiations being conducted elsewhere," thus subjecting them to the domination of the Group of 77. The terms of reference of the Committee which considered proposals for restructuring the United Nations system in the economic and social sections were set out in Resolution 3362 (S-VII), September 16, 1975. The Seventh Special Session of the Assembly instructed the Committee to take into account also the report of the Group of Experts on the Structure of the United Nations system. But it appears that the Committee favors leaving the existing Assembly majority with the power to initiate its new ideas and policy approaches as well as subject all negotiations of an economic character to the overview of the self-same dominant majority. Predictably, the Assembly followed a different course and adopted resolution 32/197, December 20, 1977, "Restructuring of the Economic and Social Sector of the United Nations System." The proposals of the Group of Experts were not followed.[21]

Collective bargaining arenas and technical two-group or three-group negotiating forums removed from parliamentary diplomacy are multiplying. An incentive is needed if the U.N. is to adopt new consensus procedures. If need be, interdependence and crisis management can be conducted in arenas outside the United Nations: The Paris Conference on Vietnam, the Geneva Conference on the Middle East, and the CIEC are major negotiating efforts insulated to a large extent from majority decisions.

The choice between arenas involves a choice among modes of decision. Voting, the method of collective bargaining, or the hybrid method of consensus procedures, representative committees, and negotiating groups must be seen as alternatives. But other important models also exist. The method of informal meeting and gentlemen's agreements adopted by the Heads of the Central Banks of the industrialized nations in their frequent meetings in Basel, Switzerland, under the auspices of the Bank for International Settlements has shown its value in a period of great monetary and financial turmoil. A French observer wrote that

[D]iversification (or informality) is the second characteristic trait of the international monetary system. International monetary cooperation which has developed so fast in recent years between Central banks and the concentration of national economic policies rests only on informal bases known as arrangements or gentlemen's agreements. Those in charge of national monetary policy have taken care to establish a vast network of consultation and cooperation removed from any juridical link and from any formal basis. For bankers in particular, the very idea of formality is synonymous with ineffectiveness. Moreover, national governments, while concerting their domestic policies or while taking specific unilateral measures which went beyond what they were required to do by the positive juridical norms of the international monetary system, have not wished to crystalize those practices into international obligations. This is how, for example, states have followed the practice of keeping part of their official reserves in the national currencies of third countries, in large measure United States dollars, pound sterlings and to a smaller extent, French francs. Similarly, it had been the traditional policy of the United States until 15 August 1971 to convert on demand gold for dollars held by foreign monetary authorities. In these two cases, and they are not the only ones, these were simple practices which have greatly facilitated the work of the international monetary system; the states concerned did not have the feeling that their action, that their policies in these fields, flow from international obligations assumed by treaties or from international custom. This coexistence of legal factors and factual factors in the midst of the international monetary system makes delicate the determination of its true nature and its classification under the traditional typology.[22]

In the economic field, weighted voting plays an important role. The International Monetary Fund is a model for management by such voting procedures. It is significant, as another observer comments, that

[t]he experience of the Fund demonstrates that even in an international organization in which the principle of the weighted voting power of members prevails, it may be necessary to provide that certain decisions are to be taken on the basis of equal voting power or by unanimity, the practical effect of which is equal voting power. The number of decisions, including action by members to amend the articles, for which weighted voting power has been eliminated in the Fund is modest. Originally, the decisions were limited to those for which the need for special safeguards was almost beyond controversy. . . . Obviously, members with sizable proportions of the total voting power are likely to resist any suggestions for extending the scope of equal voting power or the requirement of unanimity.[23]

The World Bank is also a significant model for management by weighted voting. Just how far this weighted voting can go is illustrated by the method used for drafting international treaties. The Executive Directors of the World Bank formulated treaties which they submitted to member states under which three international organizations in the Bank's structure were created. Again, it is worth noticing that

[t]here was no express provision in the Charter of the Bank empowering the Directors to engage in this activity and there was no opportunity for individual governments (with the exception of those—five in number—who appoint their own Directors) to participate directly in the task of formulating these agreements. Moreover,

the Executive Directors vote in accordance with the weighted-voting formula laid down in the Bank Charter. Under this formula voting strength is closely related to participation in the Bank's capital and the Executive Directors cast a number of votes to which the governments electing or appointing them are entitled. This means that one-third of the Directors can control decisions of the Board by their vote.[24]

An increasingly important model of decision-making is decision by consensus in organs in which decisions can be taken by a vote. Many General Assembly decisions are now adopted by consensus. This mode of decision also has currency in the Security Council where the adoption of "a consensus" of the members of the Council is expressed in a statement made by the President of the Council. During the discussion of the invitation extended to the Palestine Liberation Organization (PLO) to participate in the Council's proceedings, an interesting development took place. The President of the Council reported the "understanding of the majority of the Security Council," not of the Council as a whole, that during discussions on the question of Palestine, the PLO would be invited to participate in the proceedings of the Council.[25] A procedural precedent had earlier been set by Western states during a debate on the Laotian question. It paved the way for agreed statements by a majority of the Council in caucus using the Presidency of the Council to overwhelm the veto. The dangers of such a procedure are apparent:

What we may very well have to come to judge and are seeing here today is the commencement of an effort to subvert the open and public proceedings of the Security Council and replace them by the rule of an extra-legal, semi-secret apparat, which is inaccessible to the membership of the United Nations and inaccessible to the process of inquiry. There is a term for this: the term is totalitarianism.[26]

The form of decision is intimately tied to the type of arena used. The four principles of the sovereign equality of states, of universality, of representative rule, and of majority rule transposed to international organizations have spawned the pattern of majority voting now in common use. The bloc party coalitions of the General Assembly are replicated in many other organizations and agencies.[27] Having captured control of the legitimacy machine, the coalition of Arab, Socialist states and LDCs continues to press the ideological and diplomatic advantages which the United States and its Western allies had enjoyed in the early days of the organization.

As a result, Assembly resolutions such as the Charter of the Economic Rights and Duties of States have been resisted as mere "ideology" by the West. These instruments nevertheless have a tendency to legitimate claims of the 119 members of the non-aligned groups once negotiations begin, although resolutions adopted by consensus cannot acquire legal force in the face of opposition by a major group.[28] The intimate connection between majority votes and the principles of equality, universality, and representation informs the design of other arenas and forums such as the CIEC, in which accommodation and give-and-take are encouraged. In summary, decisions in international organizations are generally taken under one of the following procedures:

1. Unanimity, requiring the concurring votes of member states
2. Consensus, when proposals are adopted without a vote
3. Vote by a majority (simple or two-thirds)
6. Vote by a majority subject to the veto or other special rights of particular states or groups of states
7. Decision by consensus of a majority (the majority must be large enough to be able to obstruct procedural challenges to rulings by the Chair)

THE MANY FORMS OF AGREEMENT

The complexity of global bargaining and its diplomatic modes is compounded by the importance of informal instruments of legal interest that are negotiated in multilateral forums and in traditional channels. The new diplomacy, multilateral as well as bilateral, is characterized by the design of many agreements in forms other than those which constitutional experts in the United States have been accustomed to. These formal changes affect the division of responsibility between the President and Congress. They impact on domestic constitutional arrangements for the management of interdependence. Global and regional bargains are struck in instruments of all shapes and forms. The elusive character of many of these instruments reflects the wish of states to structure not only the substance of obligations, but also their weight, legal effect, and domestic processes. States are intent to structure their freedom to retain, modify or terminate agreements. In a regime of global interdependence, some states find it difficult to end and reduce commitments. The demands of mutually deeply impacting and sustained relationships between the powers give rise to inertial forces that stabilize the agreements which consecrate and define these relationships. This inertial force can make it truly difficult to modify or end them. Less formal instruments give states greater leeway. Informal agreements can be terminated or revised or suspended with greater ease—and this can then be done, in the United States at least, without requiring formal Congressional support.

The international law concept of international agreement must not be confused with domestic constitutional classifications. Internationally binding commitments can be made in writing or orally, with a minimum of formality. Constitutional and statutory requirements regarding treaties and executive agreements contribute to confusion about the international and domestic effects of instruments under domestic law on the one hand and international law on the other.

It is not surprising that the formality or legal character of international agreements and arrangements can itself become the object of negotiations. This should be illustrated.

Some instruments are intended to have an ambiguous juridical status. Thus, the Final Act of the Conference on Security and Cooperation in

Europe signed in Helsinki on August 1, 1975 is neither a treaty nor an executive agreement. A U.S. negotiator commented that

[f]rom the very earliest discussions in Geneva, it became clear that virtually all delegations desired documents that were morally compelling but not legally binding. As the negotiations progressed, however, and as various delegations gained enthusiasm for texts which were to their liking, certain texts took on some of the tone of legally binding instruments. This trend was a cause of concern to the U.S. delegation, which considered that the intent of the participants should be clearly reflected in the language of the documents. Given the predisposition of Congress to question the right of the President to conclude important international agreements without Congressional consent, any ambiguity as to the legal nature of the texts could become the source of unnecessary dispute with the Congress.[29]

Even though the Declaration as such was clearly not intended to be legally binding, it remained possible, on account of the language used, for the "Document on Confidence-Building Measures and Certain Aspects of Security and Disarmament," which is part of the Final Act, to be regarded as binding. Some doubts were dispelled by tabling interpretive statements in the course of the negotiations. Despite the lack of intent to create legal obligations, the United States, the Soviet Union, France, and the United Kingdom faced the problem of how best to protect their existing special rights in Germany under the German Instrument of Surrender at the end of World War II. An express disclaimer of modification of Four Power Rights in Germany was thus included by the three Western powers in the text of their acceptance of the invitation to the second stage of the Conference and in a statement in the opening week in Geneva. The Powers eventually felt, despite the non-binding character of the Final Act, that some form of disclaimer should be included in the Final Act itself.[30]

To have regarded the Final Act as legally binding would have had a number of significant consequences. The Department of State was concerned that "euphoria over this event might lead to increased pressure for withdrawal of U.S. forces from Europe and for other forms of unilateral disarmament." It played down the Conference as an exercise which "was primarily of interest to the allies of the United States and which, in any case, had not produced documents of a legally binding character." The United States was also reluctant to concede that the Conference had finalized the status quo in Europe and recognized the frontiers in Europe, confirming Soviet hegemony in Eastern Europe and in the Baltic States. According to the same participants, it was the view of "all" the Western negotiators that the Declaration does not depart materially from previous international arrangements on frontiers and "does nothing to recognize existing frontiers in Europe."[31] To this end, Western representatives sought to avoid legal obligations of any kind and treated the question of frontiers merely as a facet of the principle of the non-use of force which had been developed in the United Nations Declaration on Principles of Friendly Relations and Cooperation among States.[32] Recognition of the existing frontiers was also

TABLE 12.2
Sets of Necessary Choices Regarding the Character of International Agreements

Process	Legal . . . Mixed (i.e., UNGA Declaratory Resolutions) . . . Political
Participation	Universal . . . Plurilateral, Bilateral . . . Unilateral Treaties . . .
Formality	Executive Agreements, letters, speeches, toasts . . . Understandings
Actors	States . . . Non-recognized States, Non-recognized movements . . . Corporations, Individuals
Institutions	Inter-governmental . . . Mixed IGO/NGO . . . Non-governmental
Stability	Ratification by referendum . . . Commitment of all branches of the government (majority and opposition) . . . Commitment of Executive Branch only . . . Personal commitment of officials
Decision Technique	Unanimity . . . Agreement of Parties, Consensus . . . Majority voting, coalitions, veto
Inputs	State Civil Service . . . Advisory boards, private participation in delegations . . . Private interests
Time Frame	Permanent . . . Temporary
Negotiating Forum	Universal Organization . . . Plurilateral Conference . . . Bilateral Conference, Collective Bargaining Setting . . . Unilateral Proclamation
Representation	Formal equality . . . Weighted participation . . . Special rights . . . Parity of groups
Modification	New agreement or amendment . . . agreed interpretation and development . . . unilateral interpretation and development . . . new practice without reference to old agreement
Termination	Agree termination . . . claim that arrangement is no longer in force . . . unilateral denunciation
Dispute Settlement	Judicial, compulsory or ad hoc . . . Third party binding arbitration . . . Third-party recommendation . . . Third party good offices . . . Bilateral negotiations
Publicity	Public negotiations and arrangements . . . secret negotiations and published agreements . . . secret negotiations and secret agreements
Linkage	Linkage to character of relations . . . Linkage to other non-related issues . . . Linkage to related issues . . . no linkage
Bases of Effectiveness	Agreement . . . Relationship between the parties . . . Expectations of allies or of adversaries . . . common ends . . . reciprocity . . . legitimacy . . . consensus of big powers . . . sanctions
Dissenting and Third Parties	Imposed acceptance . . . negotiated acceptance . . . license action against . . . exclude . . . ignore
Procedure	Formal rules with public debate . . . Formal meetings behind closed doors . . . informal negotiations behind closed doors . . . private talks
Consent	Submission to imposed arrangement . . . deference to recommended arrangement . . . acquiescence to arrangement . . . Tacit agreement . . . Express agreement

resisted because of the interest of the Federal Republic of Germany in a possible reunification with the German Democratic Republic and because of concern by States in the European Economic Community that no language be used in the Final Act that might inhibit an eventual political union of the Community.

The formal character of diplomatic auspices is also often the object of negotiations. For example, the decision to hold the Middle East Geneva Peace Conference under the "auspices" of the United Nations but not under its authority reflected the participants' agreement on the avoidance of Security Council voting majorities and procedures and on limiting the terms of reference of the Conference to resolutions 242 and 338 of the Security Council. It made the conference independent of the major United Nations organs, structured the agenda and, most importantly, postponed the question of the participation of the PLO to a later stage. On the other hand, the Security Council decision to invite the PLO to participate in the debate of the question of Palestine expressed the agreement of the Council's majority, with the ambiguous acquiescence of the United States, to recognize the authority of the PLO to speak on behalf of the Arab people of Palestine.[33]

At times when agreement on a difficult point is beyond reach, efforts may be made to substitute informal unilateral undertakings for agreed provisions in the hope that the desire for progress in negotiations will lead the other side to respect expectations expressed in a unilateral understanding. For instance, at the 1973 Moscow Summit meeting between President Nixon and General Secretary Brezhnev an effort was made to reach agreement on the important definition of "heavy missile" in the SALT negotiations. No one on the U.S. side, which pressed for an agreed definition of heavy missiles (in which the Soviet Union has the advantage), suggested that the negotiations with the Soviets be broken off if the definition was not agreed upon. Instead, in instructions from the White House, the United States delegation was directed to put into the record the following statement:

The U.S. delegation regrets that the Soviet delegation has not been willing to agree on a common definition of a heavy missile. Under these circumstances, the U.S. delegation believes it necessary to state the following. The U.S. would consider any ICBM having a volume significantly greater than that of the largest light ICBM now operational on either side to be a heavy ICBM. The U.S. proceeds on the premise that the Soviet side will give due account to this consideration.[34]

The head of the Soviet delegation made it clear that no understanding had been reached on this point.[35] The Secretary of Defense later stated that the Soviet Union could not be bound by a unilateral understanding on the part of the United States. The device did not work. But it did inject confusion about the question whether the Russians had violated the letter or the spirit of the 1972 SALT agreement to limit strategic arms.

The adoption of conference texts or resolutions in parliamentary arenas is pregnant with legitimizing powers even when these texts lack binding power. They are invoked in disputes and in situations in which the legitimacy of a policy is at issue. Quite apart from the question of their binding effect, assembly resolutions tend to have a self-enabling, self-licensing, or self-authorizing power for states supporting them. Formal limitations on the competence of representative parliamentary organs are *not* an effective restraint in the face of a willful majority.

Emphasis on binding texts has been a costly bias of legal investigation. Preoccupation with binding texts, obligatory resolutions, and enforceable decisions, which are at the core of conventional legal inquiry, has led to the neglect of the authorizing, licensing, recognizing and constitutive properties of resolutions that do not aspire to obligatory status. Concern with binding force and enforcement in the decentralized international system is a relic of legal habits developed in the hierarchical milieu of the state system. The conventional legalistic approach to pay little heed to non-binding texts has encouraged those who would vote for, or permit a consensus on, resolutions inimical to the West on the ground that these texts are only recommendations devoid of obligatory force. It is the licensing, authorizing, recognizing, and constitutive powers of the recommendations of the General Assembly of the United Nations which largely account for its political potency.[36]

Coherent majorities expressed in voting blocs seek to enhance the authority of the arena in which they prevail. The policy of the United States in the General Assembly of the United Nations at the time of the Korean War is a good illustration. In pressing for the "Uniting of Peace" resolution, the United States asserted for the General Assembly powers for the maintenance of international peace and security which at the San Francisco Conference had been reserved to the Security Council. The theory was that when the Security Council fails to exercise its primary responsibility for the maintenance of international peace and security owing to the use of the veto power by one of the Permanent Members, then the Assembly may act to discharge the responsibilities of the organization.[37]

A point may be reached at which multilateral negotiations become simply too involved. The mammouth United Nations Conference on the Law of the Sea has generated intense analysis of the characteristics of the parliamentary mode of negotiations. Policy-makers and analysts have been overwhelmed by the complexities of the negotiating process. Here the magnitude of the task can be numerically expressed. At the 1973 Caracas meeting of the Conference, approximately 1,450 persons were officially accredited by states. Other accredited persons, journalists, and observers numbered about 5,000. In negotiations involving 140 states, with an agenda of 100 issues, or articles, a participant was required to know something about 14,000 "decision cells." But even this was an oversimplification, for "14,000 decision cells presumes unified states without internal dissonance in decision."[38]

Particular useful materials on the formality and legal effect of international engagements can be found in the Senate Hearings on an Early Warning System in Sinai.[39] In seeking the Senate's approval for the American proposal to send technicians to Sinai, the Secretary of State distinguished between several types of documents submitted to Congress. He referred to documents which include assurances, undertakings, and commitments which are considered to be legally binding upon the United States and which were initialed or signed by the United States and one of the parties. He warned that not all the provisions of documents which also contain legally binding commitments are considered to be legally binding. Some are and some are not so binding; some provisions reflect assurances by the United States of political intentions:

These are often statements typical of diplomatic exchange; in some instances they are merely formal reaffirmations of existing American policy. Other provisions refer to contingencies which may never arise and are related—sometimes explicitly—to present circumstances subject to rapid change. The documents submitted to Congress contain all assurances and undertakings which are binding on the United States. That means the Administration will make no contrary claim in the future, nor will it accept any contrary claim by any other government.

The Secretary of State pointed out that

[t]he fact that many provisions are not by any standard international commitments does not mean of course that the United States is morally or politically free to act as if they did not exist. On the contrary, they are important statements of diplomatic policy and engage the good faith of the United States so long as the circumstances that give rise to them continue. But they are not binding commitments of the United States.[40]

He submitted to the Committee extracts from documents in the negotiating record which the Administration believes are legally binding assurances, undertakings, or commitments. These include certain provisions which, although not regarded by the Administration as binding, might be so regarded by others. The Committee was also supplied with documents which are explicitly described *as a part* of the Agreement between Egypt and Israel, without the United States being a party to that instrument.

By inference, other kinds of documents might also be in existence: minutes, notes and other documents in the negotiating record which contain assurances, undertakings, and commitments of a non-binding character only.

The statement of the Secretary of State highlights the delicate distinction between types of assurances, undertakings, commitments, and political intentions of the United States. They suggest several categories of material:

1. Legally binding provisions in an agreement which are recognized to be binding in the sense that the United States recognizes it is not free to disregard them and which are governed by the rules of international law regarding legal agreements
2. Provisions which one party to an agreement may regard to be legally binding but which another party may not

3. Assurances, undertakings, commitments, and statements of political intentions which declare or reaffirm existing American policy and which
   are not intended to be legally binding
4. Assurances, undertakings, commitments, and statements of political intentions which refer to contingencies which may never arise and which
   are related to present circumstances subject to rapid change
5. Undertakings or assurances which are conditional on existing or prior
   legislative authority and approval

Statements and provisions of documents which are not legally binding
engage states politically and morally, in the sense that they are not free to
act as if they did not exist. They engage their good faith so long as the
circumstances that gave rise to them continue.

The distinction between legally binding provisions and those not intended
to bind requires clarification. When a provision is regarded as legally binding,
the parties agree that they:

1. Will make no contrary claims in the future
2. Will accept no contrary claim in the future
3. Cannot fail to honor the binding provisions without being in breach of
   a legal obligation which entails international responsibility
4. Recognize that the provisions agreed upon are subject to the rules of
   international law governing international agreements
5. Consider that all appropriate constitutional requirements regarding existing or prior authorization have been met
6. Affirm that claims, rights, and obligations under relevant treaties and
   other agreements and arrangements under international law are affected
   and modified by the new agreement to the extent required

Provisions and instruments are not binding without the intent to give
them a legal character. Treaties and executive agreements are legally binding
instruments by virtue of their formal character. However, other memoranda
of agreement which may not be binding instruments can contain legally
binding provisions. The requirement of publicity attached to the Senate
consent power involves the Congress in the process of agreement, reducing
the possibility that it may not wish to honor the commitments of the
Administration. In the case of the Sinai Agreements, the Administration
made it clear that the Congress was only invited to approve the American
proposal regarding the limited U.S. role in the Early Warning System in
the Sinai. Dr. Kissinger emphasized that a vote in favor of that proposal
would not commit the Congress to a position on any one of the elaborate
U.S. commitments to Israel made as part of the package deal. Congress
was not asked to approve the undertakings and assurances to the parties,
the relationships with the countries in the area, any given level of budget
support, or policies and programs in the Middle East. The Secretary of
State stressed the distinction between legal obligations of the United States

and the commitments of Congress. What then does a provision which is not a legal commitment involve? Such provisions indicate the agreement of the parties that they:

1. Cannot fail to honor a provision that is not legally binding without being in breach of their moral or political obligations which engage their good faith, provided the circumstances which gave rise to them have not changed
2. Recognize that their rights and obligations under relevant treaties and other agreements and arrangements are not affected, modified, or waived
3. Agree that no new jural acts (such as recognition) can be inferred in the absence of an intent to the contrary

As a result, the legal binding force of particular documents or provisions may become a matter of great delicacy. For example, the Legal Adviser of the Department of State submitted to Congress on a classified basis a memorandum with his assessment of the legal character of all the documents given to the Congress in connection with the Sinai agreements. His judgment about which commitment is legally binding was itself classified, although the documents analyzed were made public.

The Legal Adviser to the Department of State, Monroe Leigh, gave an opinion that the two memoranda of agreement between the United States and Israel, reached in connection with the disengagement agreement, are properly described under U.S. Constitutional practice as "executive agreements." These are the agreements which in the opinion of the Secretary of State also contain provisions which are not considered legally binding. Nevertheless, in the Legal Adviser's opinion, the memoranda of agreement when executed become international agreements. The identification of the provisions not intended to be binding remains classified.[41]

The Legal Adviser did not discuss in his opinion the character of the other legal commitments that were included in the negotiating record.[42] The question arises whether binding commitments found in extracts from negotiating records and other informal materials are included in the constitutional category of internationally legally binding commitments.

When provisions of agreements are publicly declared and when Congress expresses its support for them, for example, in a Joint Resolution, then many of the political distinctions between legal and non-legal undertakings are removed. But a difference that remains regards the duration and termination of undertakings. The case of the Mutual Defense Treaty with the Republic of China is in point. Let us assume that, in lieu of the commitment to the defense of the Republic of China, the President had instead proclaimed a "Defense of China Doctrine" which would have been approved in a Joint Resolution of Congress. Such an American commitment, not in legal form, would in effect have been modified by the Shanghai Communique issued at the end of President Nixon's visit to the People's Republic of China. There would have been no requirement to bring such a commitment formally to an end, assuming the Administration had so wished. On the other hand, abrogation of the Mutual Defense Treaty required formal denunciation, a difficult matter for an Administration facing political constituencies with an interest in the status quo. The role of Congress in terminating treaties is itself unclear. The Shanghai Communique is one of the key diplomatic instruments negotiated in recent years, outlining as it does the character of relations between the People's Republic of China and the United States pending full recognition, and the political commitment of the United States to the People's Republic of China in the event of an armed attack. But this instrument was not endowed with legally binding force, and merely outlined the positions, intentions, and policies of the parties. It did not suggest that the parties intended to enter into a legal relationship capable of modifying existing legal commitments. Only formal recognition could accomplish this.

The subtleties of international negotiations have engendered forms of agreement which Congress finds difficult to control. The Case Act which requires communication to the Congress and publication of international executive agreements has in a sense strengthened the hand of the President in his relations with the Congress, a result not intended by the authors of that enactment. The Act has in effect created a new category of agreements, those that are transmitted to the Congress and on which the Congress takes no position. Where the President would not previously have communicated an executive agreement on a delicate matter to the Congress, he is now bound by law to do so. But as a result, the Congress can no longer claim it was not informed of the President's commitments, and this knowledge implicates it to a greater extent than ignorance would have done. It can no longer pretend ignorance. For example, President Nixon's unpublished assurances to President Thieu with regard to U.S. military assistance in case of Communist violations of the Vietnam-Paris Peace Agreements engaged the good faith of the United States less than if it had been communicated to the Congress at the time. It would then have been necessary for the Congress to take a position on the whole Vietnam agreements package, including the President's assurances.[43] Failure to disavow such assurances would have come closer to acquiescence.

The function and character of an agreement between parties not involved with each other beyond that particular transaction are fundamentally different from those of an agreement which forms part of a complex pattern of interdependence and mutual dealings. In a casual relationship it is natural for the parties to look first and foremost to the performance and enforcement of their accord, which is the raison d'être for their having a relationship. In a complex relationship the parties look to the maintenance of their relationship by honoring their commitments or by further negotiations about the performance and modification of their accords. In such relationships agreements are rarely enforced. They are primarily the basis for future negotiations to modify them. Enforcement is an effective guarantee in a casual relationship. In a fixed relationship the effectiveness of accords rests in the character of the relationship itself.

International negotiations proceed on the basis of agreed rules, principles, and policies that outline the perimeter of what can be claimed. It is difficult for states locked in negotiations—just when good faith is so important—to repudiate principles and rules to which they have subscribed or to which the community of nations defers. International law furnishes an ample store of agreed principles to structure negotiations and their product. The skillful management of principles already agreed upon gives no mean advantage to the negotiator.

Wherever we turn in the design of agreements and of modes of agreements, a recurring feature stands out: the options and the modes are few and the choice between them inescapable. Failure to choose is nothing more than passive acquiescence in the status quo or in a dominant trend. In the international arena, as in social choices generally, the range of possibilities is restricted. Invention consists in the departure from pure formal models and the generation of mixed modes which strive for delicate balances. The narrow range of options is a significant characteristic of social arrangements limited by natural necessity to a range of choices which cannot be meaningfully widened. The practice of agreement-making remains distinct from that of a rule-guided decision. It belongs to a separate logical field. Other objectives are sought, other mental operations are involved. The area of negotiations is a basic skill of lawyering.

In a global society, increasingly vulnerable to domestic and foreign enemies because of the fragility of its technology and its exposed lifelines, a movement toward negotiations and away from the enforcement of accords was to be expected. The confrontations and violence that enforcement imports have become too costly.

The demands of world order politics are in fact no longer ignored.[44] Without prejudice to the question whether world order can be deliberately created, another preliminary question has been considered: What are the diplomatic modes and structures for a world order built on bargaining and accords? The U.S. is now confronted with the necessity of bargaining with others rather than laying the groundwork for the new order by itself. Esoteric new structures for bargaining, the emergence of parity diplomacy, the creation of new arenas for negotiations, and the wise use of a rich variety of forms of agreement, binding and non-binding, are all elements of the world order now taking shape. Flexibility in voting procedures and a greater variety of forms of instruments is required for managing interdependence and moving to the next world order. They are all part of the transition to the world of the 80's.

We have every reason to think that this world order can be neither easily comprehended nor easily made manageable. It does not fit into any of the blueprints for a new order. The ever-widening circle of arenas, both domestic and international, and the variety of procedures for addressing a complex agenda of interconnected issues that deeply influence national economic policies defy anything but expert analysis. They threaten to exclude significant segments of the law and economics community from involvement in the domestic and international dimensions of global interdependence— a development much to be feared in the absence of a commitment by this community to make this field its own.

NOTES

1. See U.N. General Assembly resolution 1995 (XIX), December 30, 1964, and Annex. See, for example, the classification adopted in the Reports of UNCTAD IV on International Financial Cooperation for Development, TD/188/Sub. 1 (1976) Nairobi. Thus the developed countries are formally identified by reference to their membership in Group D of UNCTAD, in the Development Assistance Committee of the OECD, in the Group of Developing Countries, in the Conference on International Economic Cooperation and in the Group of 10 which meets at various levels both in the International Monetary Fund and in the OECD. Less Developed Countries or LDCs are formally identified by their membership in the Group of 77 and participation in its ministerial meetings. For the purposes of development assistance this group is divided into three segments: OPEC members, Less Developed Countries and Least Developed Countries. They are also identified by their membership in Group A and C of UNCTAD and in the Group of Developing Countries of the Conference on International Economic Cooperation. Socialist countries of the Soviet bloc belong to COMECON and to Group D of UNCTAD.

2. Bloc voting and caucuses in international organizations are not a new feature of the world political order. For example, the West European and Afro-Asian groups at the United Nations have been caucusing regularly during meetings of the General Assembly. But the drafting and development of comprehensive proposals in advance of U.N. meetings were less common. The Group of 77 and the nonaligned now come to the General Assembly with an agreed comprehensive program regarding a large number of agenda items. See, for example, the documents agreed at the Colombo Summit of Non-Aligned Countries in 1976 and circulated to the General Assembly, A/31/197 (1976). See also the Manila Declaration and Program of Action of the Ministerial Meetings of the Group of 77, TD/195 (1976). Generally, on the phenomenon of coalitions in international organizations, see Thomas Hovet, Jr., *Bloc Politics in the United Nations* (Cambridge, Mass.: Harvard University Press, 1960), and his "Political Parties in the United Nations," paper delivered at the 1962 Meeting of the American Political Science Association.

On the principle of majority rule, see Cromwell A. Riches, *Majority Rule in International Organizations* (Baltimore: Johns Hopkins Press, 1940); Wellington Koo, *Voting Procedure in International Political Organizations* (New York: Columbia University Press, 1947); Julius Stone, "The Rule of Unanimity: The Practice of the Council and Assembly of the League of Nations," *British Year Book of International Law*, Vol. 14 (1933), pp. 18–42; F. A. Vallat, "Voting in the General Assembly of the United Nations," *British Year Book of International Law*, Vol. 31 (1956), pp. 273–298; Frederick Sherwood Dunn, *The Practice and Procedure of International Conferences* (Baltimore: Johns Hopkins Press, 1929); John G. Heinberg, "History of the Majority Principle," *American Political Science Review*, Vol. 20, No. 1 (February 1926), pp. 52–68, and "Theories of Majority Rule," *American Political Science Review*, Vol. 26, No. 3 (June 1932), pp. 452–469, provide useful reviews of theoretical claims in support of the principle.

3. See the Final Communique of the Conference on International Economic Cooperation, *Department of State Bulletin*, Vol. 74, No. 1907 (12 January 1976), pp.

48–49. See also the Final Declaration of the Second Preparatory Meeting, *Department of State Bulletin*, Vol. 73, 1898 (10 November 1975), pp. 668–669. In some cases, a modification of established instruments of parliamentary organs can be attempted. For example, Rule 59 of the Rule of Procedure of the Economic and Social Council regarding "request for a vote" could be amended to make allowance for the parity mode of negotiation. As it now stands, Rule 59 provides, "[a] proposal or motion before the Council for decision shall be voted upon if any member so requests. Where no member requests a vote, the Council may adopt proposals or motions without a vote." (U.N. Doc. E/5715). This rule could be amended to provide for postponement of votes at the request of a group of states.

4. *Texaco v. Libya*, International Legal Materials, Vol. 17, No. 1 (January 1978), pp. 1–37.

5. Philip C. Jessup, "Parliamentary Diplomacy," Academie de Droit International, *Recueil des cours*, Vol. 89 (1956/I), p. 248.

6. The literature on diplomatic modes is considerable. A good beginning is Jessup (n. 5), pp. 181–320. See also Dunn (n. 2). For a recent survey see *Journal of International Affairs*, Vol. 29, No. 1 (Spring 1975), full issue. See also Harold G. Nicolson, *Diplomacy* (New York: Oxford University Press, 3rd ed., 1969), and his *Evolution of the Diplomatic Method* (London: Constable and Co., 1954); Charles K. Webster, *The Congress of Vienna* (London: G. Bell and Sons, 1945); Nicholson, *The Congress of Vienna* (New York: Harcourt Brace, 1946); Norman Llewellyn Hill, *The Public International Conference* (Stanford: Stanford University Press, 1929).

7. See Jessup (n. 5), and U.S. Department of State Record of the Japanese Peace Conference, Publication 4392 (1951).

8. There is ample literature on these two principles. For example, see the useful work of Hanna Pitkin, *The Concept of Representation* (Berkeley: University of California Press, 1967), and its excellent bibliography. See Edwin DeWitt Dickinson, *The Equality of States in International Law* (Cambridge, Mass.: Harvard University Press, 1920), and bibliography. Adolf Lande, "Revindication of the Principle of Legal Equality, 1871–1914," *Political Science Quarterly*, Vol. 62, No. 2, 3 (June, September 1947), pp. 258–286, 398–417. See also the Declaration on the Principles of International Law Regarding Friendly Relations and Cooperation Among States, U.N. General Assembly resolution 2625 (XXV), October 24, 1970. For a recent study, see Robert A. Klein, *Sovereign Equality Among States* (Toronto: University of Toronto Press, 1974). Different theories were advanced at different times in support of the principle of majority rule. It was only during the lifetime of Locke that the "social compact" theory and principles of "equality" were woven into the majority principle. See Heinberg, "Theories of Majority Rule" (n. 2).

9. The formal emergence of negotiating groups is taking place at the expense of the less influential states. On the theory of apportionment, see Alfred DeGrazia, "General Theory of Apportionment," *Law and Contemporary Problems*, Vol. 17, No. 2 (Spring 1952), pp. 256–267.

10. See, for example, Amnesty International, *Report on Torture* (New York: Farrar, Strauss and Giroux, 1975). See further, Freedom House, *Freedom at Issue*, No. 39 (January–February 1977).

11. See Guglielmo Ferrero, *The Principles of Power* (New York: G. P. Putnam's Sons, 1942).

12. On the concept of the lawless state, see Gidon Gottlieb, "Is Law Dead?" in Eugene V. Rostow, ed., *Is Law Dead?* (New York: Simon and Schuster, 1971). See also the contrasting treatment of the question in Morton Halperin and others, *The Lawless State* (New York: Penguin Books, 1976). The liberal critique of official

lawlessness in the United States remains for the time restricted to a discussion of internal domestic politics. It has not led to parallel studies of the lawlessness of foreign regimes other than those which receive U.S. economic and military assistance. See Irving Kristol, "Mortality, Liberalism and Foreign Policy," *The Wall Street Journal*, 19 November 1976. The critique of foreign lawlessness is so far primarily limited to the consideration of human rights violations, such as torture, to treatment of political prisoners, and the right to immigrate.

See Maurice Duverger, *Droit constitutionel et institutions politiques* (Paris: Presses Universtaires, 4th ed., 1955), for a classical treatment of the concept of legitimacy. See also V.I. Lenin, *The State and Revolution* (New York: International Publishers, 1932). Duverger cites Vychinsky's statement that "laws are made to protect the state from the individual and not the individual from the state," p. 49. For a further treatment of Soviet doctrines, see Hans Kelsen, *The Communist Theory of Law* (New York: Praeger, 1955). Charles Maurras, *Enquête sur la monarchi* (Paris: Hachette, 1928), pp. CVII–CVIII, cited in Ferrero (n. 11), p. 132.

In the past, regimes that sought their legitimacy in the popular character of the revolution that brought them to power often looked for confirmation in a plebiscite establishing the support of the nation. Marxist theory, however, has advanced a new doctrine of legitimacy. It does not claim legitimacy in terms of the ancient order of elective and representative government. Marxist doctrine seeks legitimacy by turning to the future rather than to the past. The dictatorship of the proletariat is the strategy to be followed as long as Marxist legitimacy itself is not solidly implanted. Marxist regimes have been joined by a multitude of other repressive governments in the effort to derive legitimacy from policies for a better future, in the accomplishment of the "public good." In many new states, the legitimacy derived from the overthrow of alien colonial rule is receding into the mist of history. As the original leaders fade from the scene, new vivifying sources of popular acceptance and support are needed—and hard to find—as economic and social conditions worsen. Nearly half a century ago, the French right wing intellectual, Charles Maurras, wrote: "Legitimate government, good government, is that which does what it has to do, which does it well, which succeeds in achieving the public good. Its legitimacy is confirmed by its utility. It is considered useful when its means of action, by their vigor and by their structure, appear to be appropriate in proportion to its aim. Just power is born so that it will provide men with what they need when they are gathered into a community; its existence is determined by the conditions that create it. It exists when this necessary good exists. The absence of this good reveals the absence of the power, that it has been abolished or diverted, or distorted. The harm that the power does is a sign and a confession of its evil nature or of its bad structure, and is proof of its inability to do that for which it was created. . . . But there is a stage at which discussion ceases. This is the criterion before which there can be no doubt. It is called public welfare. A government that does not insure it is a government whose incapacity removes it from power. A government that insures the protection of society and the state acquires an incontestable claim to permanence. It is only a claim, but one that counts. This majesty that surrounds the welfare of the nation and the country is sufficient to create a discipline. This discipline existed at the origin of both transitory government and lasting governments" (Ferrero trans., as cited).

Even the Maurras totalitarian theory of legitimacy sets standards that are too high for many contemporary tyrannical rulers in the international community. Illegitimate governments are not representative—the illegitimacy of regimes vitiates political claims based upon representation. Their illegitimacy weakens their political claims for participation in majority rule.

Freely chosen governments are becoming an anomaly, and a large number of states are afflicted by authoritarian rulers with tenuous domestic legitimacy. According to Freedom House surveys, only 19.6% of the world population is living under free regimes. Only 42 of 159 sovereign countries are classified as free.

Regimes callously indifferent to the majority principle in their own societies have weak claims to participation in majority decision-making internationally. Questions properly raised about the representativeness of the white-racist-minority regimes in Rhodesia and South Africa can be equally raised about scores of military and one-party systems. Ideological doubts about the relevance of majority rule reinforce claims for accommodation of differences between organized groups of states by give-and-take rather than by voting.

13. See Arthur Lall, "Some Thoughts on the UN General Assembly as a Forum for Mediation and Negotiation," *Journal of International Affairs*, Vol. 29, No. 1 (Spring 1975), pp. 63–67. See more generally his *Modern International Negotiations* (New York: Columbia University Press, 1966); K. Venkata Raman, *Dispute Settlement Through the United Nations* (Dobbs Ferry, N.Y.: Oceana, 1977).

14. U.N. Doc. E/AC.62/9.

15. Ibid., p. 30.

16. Resolution No. 27-10, in International Monetary Fund, *Annual Report of Executive Directors* (Washington, 1972), pp. 92–93; see also Joseph Gold, "Weighted Voting Power: Some Limits and Some Problems," *American Journal of International Law*, Vol. 68, No. 4 (October 1974), pp. 687, 702.

17. On the history of this provision, see Shabtai Rosenne, *The Law of Treaties* (Dobbs Ferry, N. Y.: Oceana, 1970).

18. Rule 37 of the Rules of Procedure of the Third Conference on the Law of the Sea provides an elaborate procedure for determining whether all efforts at reaching general agreement have been exhausted. It is worth describing in detail:

(i) Automatic deferment of a vote: When a matter of substance comes up for voting, the President shall defer the question of taking a vote on such matter for a period not exceeding ten calendar days, "if requested by at least 15 representatives." This can be done only once, and the period of deferment could be less than ten days, depending on the circumstances.

(ii) President's right to defer: Even when not requested by a group of representatives, the President "may" make a similar deferment for up to ten days, but again only once with respect to a particular matter.

(iii) Deferment by the Conference itself. The Conference may, at any time, decide to defer the question of taking a vote on any matter of substance, "for a specified period of time." Such decision shall be made by a majority of representatives present and voting. It can be done either upon proposal by the President "or upon motion by any representative." Such a motion can be made "any number of times" and the final decision will be up to the Conference.

(iv) Special negotiating effort during the period of deferment: In order to ensure that the period of deferment is used for intensive negotiations, the President "shall make every effort" to facilitate the achievement of a general agreement, "having regard to the overall progress made on all matters of substance which are closely related." Negotiations should thus be directed not merely to the solution of a particular problem but should, whenever possible, contemplate the conclusion of a package deal, solving simultaneously a number of problems. The conduct of such negotiations is to be primarily in the hands of the President, the role of the General Committee, stressed in some earlier proposals, having been relegated to assisting the President "as appropriate."

(v) Determination that no agreement can be reached: On the basis of a report by the President, to be made before the end of the period of deferment, the Conference may decide, by the double majority specified in Rule 39(1) for matters of substance, that all efforts at reaching a general agreement have been exhausted and that the matters of substance be put to the vote. Should, however, the Conference prove unable to make such a determination because of a lack of sufficient majority under Rule 39(1), the matter can be resubmitted to the Conference after five calendar days for another vote, on the motion of the President or of any representative. This requirement of five days' delay does not apply during the last two weeks of the session.

(vi) Proper notice for each vote on any matter of substance: To avoid surprise votes and to provide a last chance for compromise, the rules require that no vote shall be taken on any matter of substance less than two working days after an announcement that the Conference is to proceed to vote on the matter has been made, and only after this announcement has been published in the Journal of the Conference. In addition, the Convention as a whole shall not be put to the vote less than four working days after the adoption of its last article.

Louis B. Sohn, "Voting Procedures in United Nations Conferences for the Codification of International Law," *American Journal of International Law*, Vol. 69, No. 2 (April 1975), pp. 310, 349; U.N. Doc. A/Conf.62/30/Rev.; Daniel Vignes, "Will the Third Conference on the Law of the Sea Work According to the Consensus Rule?" 69 *American Journal of International Law*, Vol. 69, No. 1 (January 1975), pp. 119–129; John R. Stevenson and Bernard H. Oxman, "The Third United Nations Conference on the Law of the Sea: The 1974 Caracas Session," *American Journal of International Law*, Vol. 69, No. 1 (January 1975), pp. 1–30.

19. Cited in Sohn (n. 18), p. 336; U.N. Doc. A/C.1/PV.1932, pp. 22–23.

20. U.N. Doc. E/AC.62/9, p. 1; U.N. Doc. A/AC.179/L.10/Rev. 1, p. 7.

21. U.N. General Assembly resolution 32/197, adopted without vote on December 20, 1977.

22. Dominique Carreau, *Le système monétaire international* (Paris: A. Colin, 1972) pp. 31–32.

23. See Gold (n. 16), p. 707; see also Joseph Gold, *Voting and Decisions in the International, Monetary Fund* (Washington: International, Monetary Fund, 1972).

24. A. Broches, "Development of International Law by the International Bank for Reconstruction and Development," *Proceedings of the American Society of International Law at its Fifty-Ninth Annual Meeting* (1965), p. 34, quoted in Gold (n. 16), p. 706.

25. U.N. Doc. S/PV.1870, pp. 51–52.

26. Leo Gross, "Voting in the Security Council and the PLO," *American Journal of International Law*, Vol. 70, No. 3 (July 1976), pp. 470–491.

27. See in general Hovet (n. 2); see also Gold (n. 23), pp. 93ff.

28. On decision by consensus see Giuseppe Sperduti, "Consensus in International Law," *Italian Yearbook of International Law*, Vol. 2 (1976), pp. 33–38.

29. Harold S. Russell, "The Helsinki Declaration: Brobdignag or Lilliput?" *American Journal of International Law*, Vol. 70, No. 2 (April 1976), pp. 242–272. For the text of the Final Act, see *International Legal Materials*, Vol. 14, No. 5 (September 1975), pp. 1292–1325.

30. The language adopted is as follows: "The participating states, paying due regard to the principles above and, in particular, to the first sentence of the tenth principle, 'fulfillment in good faith of obligations under international law,' note that

the present Declaration does not affect their rights and obligations, nor the corresponding treaties and other agreements and arrangements."

31. See Russell (n. 29).

32. U.N. General Assembly resolution 2625 (XXV), October 24, 1970.

33. See Gross (n. 26).

34. United States Arms Control and Disarmament Agency, *Arms Control and Disarmament Agreements* (Washington, 1980 ed.), p. 157.

35. See the account of Gerard C. Smith, Chief of the U.S. Delegation at the SALT Talks from 1962–1972, in the *New York Times*, January 16, 1976; see also his account, "SALT after Vladivostock," *Journal of International Affairs*, Vol. 29, No. 1 (Spring 1975), pp. 7–18.

36. See Gidon Gottlieb, "The Nature of International Law: Toward a Second Concept of Law," in Cyril E. Black and Richard A. Falk, eds., *The Future of the International Legal Order, Vol. IV, Trends and Patterns* (Princeton: Princeton University Press, 1972), pp. 331–383.

37. General Assembly resolution 377 (V), November 3, 1950. This episode is discussed in Julius Stone, *Legal Controls of International Conflicts* (New York: Holt Rinehart, 1954), pp. 266–284.

38. The Law of the Sea Conference has generated considerable academic and professional interest. In the vast literature, a good starting point is Robert L. Friedheim, *Parliamentary Diplomacy—A Survey*, Institute of Naval Studies, Center for Naval Analyses, 76-0046 (1976); see also his "The 'Satisfied' and 'Dissatisfied' States Negotiate International Law: A Case Study," *World Politics*, Vol. 18, No. 1 (October 1965), pp. 20–41.

39. U.S. Senate, Committee on Foreign Relations, 94th Congress. 1st Session, Hearings on Early Warning System in Sinai.

40. The testimony of Dr. Kissinger is also printed in *Department of State Bulletin*, Vol. 73, No. 1896 (27 October 1975), pp. 609–613.

41. See U.S. Senate, Committee on the Judiciary, Subcommittee on the Separation of Powers, 94th Congress, 1st Session, Hearings on Congressional Oversight of Executive Agreements—1975. For Mr. Leigh's opinions and letters and the conflicting opinions of the Senate Office of Legal Counsel, see ibid., pp. 365–415. Problems of interpretation may also arise under the Vienna Convention on the Law of Treaties when provisions not included in instruments known domestically as either executive agreements or as treaties may constitute nevertheless international agreements under the Convention.

42. See, for example, interpretations of the concept of international agreement by the Department of State in *Foreign Affairs Manual*, Vol. 11, reprinted in U.S. Senate Hearings, ibid., pp. 279–301. Compare with the text of the Case Act, Public Law 882, September 23, 1950, *Statutes at Large*, Vol. 64, Part 1, p. 980. See also Department of Defense Instruction No. 5530.2 in the selfsame Senate hearings, pp. 97–98. See further Mr. Leigh's letter discussing the definition of an international agreement, ibid., pp. 237–239, citing the Restatement on Foreign Law. See also the text of a letter by Kenneth Rush, Acting Secretary of State, ibid., pp. 187–188.

43. Ibid., pp. 322–326, for the text of the Nixon letters to Thieu.

44. See, for example, the "third century" series of articles by distinguished writers in the review *Foreign Policy*. As Stanley Hoffman observes in "No Choice, No Illusions," *Foreign Policy*, No. 25 (Winter 1976–1977), p. 97, "world order politics is obviously in." For a review of some of the literature on the new order, see Geoffrey Barraclough's articulate if opinionated "Waiting for the New Order," *New York Review of Books*, Vol. 25, No. 16 (26 October 1978), pp. 45–53.

13. The Role of Domestic Courts as Agencies of the International Legal Order

Friedrich Kratochwil

Often used is the imagery of international law as a "primitive" system. Such imagery has been useful in preserving the *legal* nature of prescriptions in the international arena by characterizing them as something other than norms of mere convenience or morality. At the same time, it has been able to account for the indubitable weaknesses of these norms as well as to answer the question of how some of these weaknesses could be remedied— specifically, by suggesting analogies taken from the development of the domestic legal order. Thus "centralization"[1] of sanctioning mechanisms and their further development through codification[2] appear to be the answers to the decentralized and still largely customary "self-help" system of international law.

Implicit in such suggestions, referred to in this article as "domestic analogies," is a theory of law that interprets the force of prescriptions in terms of constraints. It assumes that actors follow rules largely out of fear of threatened sanctions. These inferences, which utilize the metaphor of international law as a primitive system, are open to question and in need of substantial modifications.[3]

Let us begin with the idea of law as a constraining force, and with its logical corollary, law as a sanctioning system of norms.[4] The implicit image here is taken from criminal law. Through the threat of negative consequences "the law" intervenes in the decisionmaking process of a utility-maximizing actor and thus makes him behave in a certain manner. Aside from the question of whether this implicit theory about the functioning of norms as "causes" of decision is appropriate even within the narrow confines of criminal law,[5] viewing all law through the lenses of criminal law leads to serious distortions. This contingency becomes obvious when one remembers that prescriptions (rules and norms) are of different types and are utilized in various contexts. Thus actors in the domestic as well as in the international arena are not merely constrained by norms, but norms enable them to act, to pursue their goals, to communicate with each other, to share meanings, to criticize claims, and to justify actions.[6] Indeed, the blueprint image of a society in which social—and hence legal norms—program individuals in their actions is rightly criticized in sociology.[7] The inappropriateness of viewing law merely as a sanctioning or constraining system has also been noted in the jurisprudential literature.[8]

It is the task of this chapter to clarify the concept of a primitive legal system. As we examine the role played by national institutions as "deputized agents" of the international legal order, some unique features become apparent.

In particular, we are concerned in this investigation with the role of domestic courts in clarifying and applying international legal norms and with the various complications that arise out of the "dedoublement fonctionelle."[9] It is precisely because national courts become "gatekeepers" between the domestic and the international legal order that they reinforce the state system. Courts frequently resort to a national security rationale or invoke some type of political-questions doctrine in order to shelter national conduct from judicial assessment. At the same time, courts are also *arenas*; as such, they create opportunities—within the narrow limits of particular controversies—to question the policies and actions by which national decisionmakers protect and reproduce the state system.

The question of whether these opportunities are utilized *in fact* can be answered only through a detailed study of court practices. The question of whether such opportunities *ought* to be used and for what ends is largely a problem of justification, in which context democratic theory and a world order orientation provide some valuable insights. The term *democratic theory* refers to the normative argument concerning the legitimate exercise of public power within a system of limited government. In this system individual rights are constitutionally guaranteed, and both public and private persons are given the opportunity to have their claims authoritatively decided by independent courts. As for the world order perspective, enough has been said within the present volume that no further explication appears to be necessary.

From these initial remarks, the plan of the present chapter can be derived. The following section examines critically the role of the U.S. courts, particularly the Supreme Court (hereafter occasionally referred to as "the Court") as "gatekeepers" in a federal system. In the section after that, their role is discussed in a different context, specifically through an examination of the judicial strategies that attempt to deal with the complexities of increasing interdependence. Such interdependence makes the domestic arena more vulnerable, or at least more sensitive, to events taking place beyond the (national) jurisdictional boundaries.[10] The natural reflex, then, is the reestablishment of control through the often questionable extension of jurisdiction. The fourth section focuses on the domestic courts as arenas in which state action can sometimes, at least indirectly, be challenged by international legal norms. The evolving human rights law is of particular importance in this context. Finally, a short summary of the main arguments of this chapter concludes the investigation.

THE AMERICAN COURTS AND THE INTERNATIONAL LEGAL ORDER: THE CONSTITUTIONAL DIMENSION

The "law of nations" is specifically mentioned in the Constitution only in connection with the power of Congress to punish individuals for certain crimes under that law.[11] But it is through the definition of the judicial power in Article II, section 2 and through the development of judicial review that domestic courts have become involved in international legal problems. Thus federal courts have jurisdiction in suits of foreign ambassadors, ministers, and consuls and in suits of states against aliens.[12] This jurisdiction not only creates access to the courts for (recognized) foreign governments, but, through the Foreign Sovereign Immunities Act of 1976,[13] it also provides remedies against foreign states for torts arising out of their nonpublic actions.

Even so, the participation of the courts in applying and clarifying international legal principles is incidental to the usual court business in deciding cases between parties, reviewing administrative decisions, and administering civil and criminal justice. A treaty between the United States and another country may be relevant in order to decide a probate case or the tax liabilities of a company. Courts must also apply international customary norms in a variety of circumstances, as the famous *Paquete Habana*[14] case demonstrates. In quoting *Hilton v. Guyot*,[15] the Supreme Court held that

International law is part of our law and must be ascertained by the courts of justice of appropriate jurisdiction as often as questions of right depending upon it are duly presented for their determination. For this purpose where there is no treaty and no controlling executive or legislative act or judicial decision, resort must be had to the customs and usages of civilized nations and as evidence of these to the work of jurists and commentators.[16]

Historically, it was the scope of the treaty power of the federal government and the meaning of the supremacy clause in the Constitution that occasioned the most famous decisions.

Four interrelated issues had to be decided in this context. First, there was the question of state rights (10th Amendment) versus the powers of the federal government in foreign relations. Second, the "foreign relations" powers of the president had to be clarified, as the Constitution was silent on this problem. A third issue thus became relevant—that is, the question of the review of governmental acts in international affairs when they violate either an international legal norm or a constitutionally guaranteed right. Finally, the issue of the extraterritorial validity of foreign as well as U.S. legislation turns courts not only into arenas but, increasingly, into "actors" as well, in areas in which nation states appear to show a heightened sensitivity. It might be useful, therefore, to quickly review some of the major holdings of U.S. courts in these four issue areas and to critically evaluate some of the emerging patterns.

The *locus classicus* for the definition of the *treaty power* of the federal government as against alleged reserved state rights protected by the 10th Amendment is *Missouri v. Holland*.[17] Justice Holmes argued that Congress had the authority to implement treaty provisions through legislation, even if without such a treaty the legislation would have been held invalid. This effectively disposed of the old argument found in Jefferson's manual that treaties could not regulate matters that were reserved to the states.[18] Efforts to "overrule" *Missouri v. Holland* during the period of 1952–1957 by means of a constitutional amendment (the Bricker amendment) failed.

After it had been established that the treaty power of the federal government may "defeat" state rights limitations, the question of the scope and the locus of these international relations powers arose. Both questions were systematically dealt with in the famous *Curtiss Wright* decision (1936)[19] involving the violation of an arms embargo proclaimed by the president on the basis of a joint resolution of Congress. The defendant claimed that this was an improper delegation of power. Holding that such a delegation was proper because foreign relations powers were involved, Justice Sutherland elaborated the origins and location of these powers in the following way:

As a result of the separation from Great Britain by the Colonies, the power of external sovereignty passed from the Crown not to the Colonies *severally*, but to Colonies in their collective and corporate capacity as the United States of America. . . . The Union existed before the Constitution. . . . It results that the investment of the federal government with the powers of external sovereignty did not depend upon the affirmative grants of the Constitution. The powers to declare and wage war, to conclude peace, to make treaties, to maintain diplomatic relations with other sovereignties, if they had never been mentioned in the Constitution, would have vested in the federal government as necessary concomitants of nationality.[20]

Although one might take issue with Sutherland's historical understandings, and although his delegation theory is largely "obiter," this theory nevertheless echoes the reasoning of *U.S. v. Arjona* (1887).[21] In this case the Supreme Court gave the legislative mandate of Congress a much wider scope than the explicitly enumerated delegated powers. "A right secured by the law of nations to a nation, or its people, is one the United States as the representatives of this nation are bound to protect."[22]

The *Curtiss Wright* case went further by lodging these powers predominantly in the office of the president. The presidency is described as "the very delicate, plenary and exclusive power . . . as the sole organ of the Federal government in the field of international relations."[23] This trend is further reinforced in the *U.S. v. Belmont*[24] case, in which the Supreme Court held executive agreements made by the president to be on the same legal footing as treaties requiring Senate approval. Furthermore, the Court established that the substantive determinations entrusted to the "political departments of the Federal Government" are "not open to judicial inquiry."[25]

In the *Belmont* case, such nonreviewable issues concern quite narrowly the question of recognition of the Soviet government and the concomitant acceptance of the extraterritorial effect of Soviet nationalization laws. The *U.S. v. Pink*[26] decision clearly shows some further implications. The issue there was whether the funds of a nationalized Russian company, assigned through the Litvinov agreement to the United States, could be claimed by the federal government in violation of the rights of foreign creditors, which had been vested by virtue of New York decrees. The lower court held that this claim deprived the investors of their property in violation of the due process clause of the 5th Amendment, which extends its protection to aliens as well as to citizens. The Supreme Court overruled, stating: "If the

President had the power to determine the policy which was to govern the recognition, then the 5th Amendment does not stand in the way of giving full force and effect to the Litvinov assignment. . . . Objections to the underlying policy as well as objections to recognition are to be addressed to the political department and not to the Courts."[27]

This leads us to a more fundamental issue with respect to constitutional, as well as international, legal implications—that is, the political-questions doctrine. Since one may doubt whether a clearly defined political-questions doctrine exists,[28] it might be best to discuss this issue within a wider framework. The limitation of judicial power as well as the various "avoidance techniques" that courts have used to sidestep sensitive foreign policy issues become relevant concerns.

The basic tenet of the political-questions doctrine is that no court will sit in judgment concerning an act committed by the Constitution to one of the other branches of government. This raises the issue of remedies in cases in which official acts violate, for example, international legal norms: "Where fairly possible, the courts will interpret actions of the President or of Congress to render them consistent with international obligations, but both President and Congress can exercise their respective constitutional powers regardless of treaty obligations and the courts will give effect to acts within their powers even if they violate treaty obligations and other international law."[29] Hence Henkin argues that the attempts to enjoin Executive Action in Vietnam on the grounds that it violated United States obligations under the UN Charter were "misconceived."[30] This position is certainly based on an accurate assessment of the existing legal order; the case law, although sometimes confusing, supports Henkin's argument. A different issue is raised, however, when such a "statist" perspective on law is questioned.

Let us remember that the "logic" of extraordinary grants of power to the presidency in the *Curtiss Wright* case was justified in terms of international law, especially international custom. But as custom erodes—or is eroded by the deliberate violation of the law, which is beyond the recognition of the court—the weak restraints upon executive power provided by international norms increasingly fail. In a perceptive article, Edward Gordon characterized the situation in the following way:

[A]t the point in history when executive decisions are coming to have no less an impact on private lives than public legislation and judicial pronouncements traditionally do, the checks on governmental excess which usually flow from the principle of the separation of powers are being seriously eroded in the name of that principle. Moreover, because any issue, otherwise justiciable, which touches foreign relations is apt to be dismissed by some courts as nonjusticiable political questions on that ground alone, the availability of a judicial remedy is becoming an uncertain thing in a wide range of disputes whose resolutions may have an impact on this country's foreign relations. Insofar as these results do obtain, the government may be said to have become the beneficiary of constitutional limitations placed on the people.[31]

The last sentence may somewhat overstate the case, but the fears described are not entirely unfounded. Thus national security claims might further enhance executive power without scrutiny. Although the Supreme Court in *Haig* v. *Agee*[32] held that the president's foreign relations powers "must be exercised in subordination to the applicable provisions of the Constitution," it also added that "no governmental interest is more compelling than the security of the nation" and that "measures to protect the secrecy of our Government's foreign intelligence operation plainly serve these interests."[33] This otherwise persuasive argument indicates an approach to constitutional choice in the weighing and consideration of conflicting constitutional principles that is no longer "couched in terms of democratic values and the public interest but in terms of a potentially antagonistic and more limited standard termed governmental interest. . . ."[34]

In this context of fundamental democratic values versus governmental interests, it is quite strange that the interests of investors are considerably better protected than those of the "citizen." For example, U.S. legislation concerning "corrupt practices" is based on and justified by the investor's "need to know" whether a corporation's revenues are "sound" and not the result of bribery (financial materiality). While this protection is only mildly controversial, a second aspect of "materiality" underlying the Foreign Corrupt Practices Act is not necessarily related to the financial performance: It concerns the "quality and integrity of management."[35] At the same time there is a very low opinion of the citizen's "right to know" what his or her government is doing in foreign affairs, even if such conduct includes acts deemed illegal under domestic as well as international law. The right to know is recognized neither by legislation nor by the commonly accepted interpretation of the 1st Amendment.

The issue of the right to information was part of the litigation in *U.S.* v. *Richardson*.[36] In this case, a citizen alleged a violation of his rights by the governmental secrecy surrounding the financing of intelligence operations. Chief Justice Burger's majority opinion held that a federal taxpayer did not have standing since he failed the tests enunciated in *Flast* v. *Cohen*.[37] First, the respondent could not prove that the appropriated funds were spent in violation of a specific constitutional limitation upon the taxing and spending power. Rather, the issue was the *use* of the taxing power. Second, the court argued that there was no logical nexus between the status of a U.S. taxpayer and Congress's failure to make public CIA expenditures. Richardson's claim that he was deprived of important information that would have allowed him to make a reasoned choice in the elections and, hence, to evaluate governmental performance was held to be a "generalized grievance" rather than a specific injury prescribed by *Frothingham*[38] and *Flast*. Only Justice Brennan, dissenting, accepted these claims as sufficient to confer standing, although he added cautiously that these claims may ultimately fail on the merits. This argument raises the more principled question of whether and how secrecy can be justified in foreign relations.

Obviously it is naive to assume that international relations can be conducted under continuous and full public scrutiny. The disastrous consequences of the "open covenants openly arrived at" are well known and need no further criticism. Similarly, the ability of the United States to conduct foreign policy effectively, or even to establish a limited amount of trust among actors with conflicting interests, might crucially depend upon the quality of U.S. intelligence. In other words, the United States must be able unobtrusively to monitor the behavior of other states.

This *functional* need for secrecy, invoked for the purpose of drawing inferences from untampered data, is, however, totally different from many contexts in which implausible secrecy claims are made. Take, for example, the "secret" bombing of Cambodia. Obviously neither a functional secrecy was involved here (since the actors on the receiving line must have been aware of what was being done to them), nor does it take the "world" long to catch on. Secrecy is invoked by the decisionmaker against his *own* society and as a protection against criticism.[39] It seems perfectly sensible to argue that there ought to be ways in which such abuses of executive privilege can be avoided. Furthermore, legal principles will clearly be of decisive importance in such a review, whether it is executed by the courts or by another political branch of government. Whether the courts can, and ought to, play the "neutral arbiter" is, of course, a different question, one that cannot be answered without a closer look at the issue of judicial review and its place within the larger constitutional framework.

But what, then, is the proper place for judicial intervention? It is often forgotten that one of the first and decisive limitations of judicial review was that developed by Justice Marshall in conjunction with foreign relations issues. During the revolution in France, the problem of U.S. neutrality arose. Accordingly, Secretary of State Jefferson addressed the following letter to Chief Justice Jay and the Supreme Court:

Gentlemen:

The war which has taken place among the powers of Europe produces frequent transactions within our ports and limits, on which questions arise of considerable difficulty, and of greater importance to the peace of the United States. These questions depend for their solution on the construction of our treaties, on the laws of nature and nations, and on the law of the land, and are often presented under circumstances which do not give a cognizance of them to the tribunals of the country. Yet, their decision is so little analogous to the ordinary functions of the Executive, as to occasion much embarrassment and difficulty to them. The President therefore would be much relieved if he found himself free to refer questions of this description to the opinions of the judges of the Supreme Court of the United States, whose knowledge of the subject would secure us against errors dangerous to the peace of the United States, and their authority insure the respect of all parties [sic]. He has therefore asked the attendance of such of the judges as could be collected in time for the occasion . . . to present, for their advice, the abstract questions which have already occurred, or may still occur.[40]

This request touched upon a wide variety of legal issues, ranging from the interpretations of treaties between the United States and France to the rights and duties of neutrals, and to questions concerning the powers of the federal government. In other words, the letter presented a virtual compendium of interesting legal questions in which any jurist could have taken delight. Nevertheless, Marshall and his brethren declined the opportunity to decide these questions precisely because of the abstract and hypothetical nature of the request. In a letter to the president (August 8, 1793), the justices presented their reasons in the following fashion: "We exceedingly regret every event that may cause embarrassment to your administration, but we derive consolation from the reflection that your judgement will discern what is right, and that your usual prudence, decision, and firmness will surmount every obstacle to the preservation of the rights, peace, and dignity of the United States."[41]

As Marshall later wrote, the justices considered themselves merely as constituting a legal tribunal for the decision of controversies brought before them in legal form. "Thus . . . these gentlemen deemed it improper to enter the field of politics by declaring their opinion on questions not growing out of the case before them."[42]

The same ideas became central in the argument in *Marbury* v. *Madison*.[43] As a leading scholar put it: "They constitute not so much limitations of the power of judicial reviews as necessary supports for Marshall's argument in establishing it."[44] In other words, no "advisory" opinions were given. When there is no adversary situation, the parties involved cannot show a particular interest that is impacted by the court's decision aside from the more general influence any policy decision might have. Whenever the latter circumstances prevail, the courts will hold that the party desiring an adjudicative resolution on a controversy lacks "standing." Courts thus routinely dismiss cases involving injunctions against governmental actions when such requests are based solely on the alleged violations of the rights of a U.S. taxpayer.[45] Although some scholars have maintained that the test enunciated in *Flast* v. *Cohen* allowed for "standing" to taxpayers protesting the illegality of the U.S. involvement in Vietnam, later case law did not follow that lead.[46]

Another more problematic avoidance technique of the Supreme Court is the "ripeness" principle. This applies when a case and controversy are given and the interests of the plaintiff are held to be demonstrably and specifically affected, but the Court decides to postpone adjudication until the fuller impact of the statute or executive measure can be assessed.

An interesting case, *Goldwater* v. *Carter*,[47] utilizes most of the avoidance techniques available to the courts. Here the president abrogated, without the authorization or concurrent vote of the Senate, the defense treaty with Taiwan. In vacating the judgment of the Court of Appeals, Justice Rehnquist, writing for a plurality of justices, maintained that the issue was nonjusticiable in the absence of a clear constitutional proviso as to the Senate's participation in cases of abrogation of treaties. Thus "the instant case . . . must surely be controlled by political standards."[48] Sharply critical of this position, Justice Brennan focused on the important distinction between invoking "political standards" from the narrower doctrine of "political questions." Noting that the meaning of the political-questions doctrine—as expounded by Brennan in *Baker* v. *Carr*[49]—restrains the courts from reviewing essentially discretionary foreign policy judgments of a coordinate branch of government, Brennan maintained that the doctrine does not apply to questions concerning whether a "particular branch has been constitutionally designated as the repository of political decision making power." This antecedent question has to be "resolved as a matter of constitutional law, not political discretion; accordingly it falls within the competence of the courts."[50] In this sense, then, the abrogation of the defense treaty fell within presidential authority since it was incidental to the president's well-established power to grant and withdraw recognition from foreign governments.

Justice Powell also wanted to have these issues decided within the narrower limits of a constitutional doctrine. Although he did not find an unquestionable commitment of a power to terminate treaties to the president, the suit had to be dismissed nevertheless, because of its lack of "ripeness."[51] This dismissal, however, would not in more appropriate circumstances prevent the court from deciding "what the law is," even if two branches of government had arrived at different constitutional interpretations. By implication, Powell's decision meant that the argument of embarrassing one of the branches of government through judicial action—which had been a point in the original political-questions doctrine in *Baker* v. *Carr*—should not be determinative for the disposition of such a case.[52]

The most controversial avoidance technique, however, is the denial of *certiorari*, which appears to be governed by very few, if any, well-articulated standards. It became an important issue, for example, during the Vietnam War, when draft resisters invoked the illegality of the U.S. commitment in their defense.[53] Although it could be argued that congressional action was tantamount to the constitutional requirement of "declaring war," and although the issue probably raised a nonjusticiable political question, the Supreme Court took the "easy way out" by a flat denial of *certiorari*. This might be considered a "prudential stance" against judicial activism, since activism in controversial cases can be destructive of the effectiveness of judicial review. It is doubtful, however, that such an interpretation is correct, as it misunderstands the historical context in which judicial review takes place and, more important, mistakes the criteria that ought to govern judicial discretion.

Therefore, let us consider in greater detail the argument for judicial restraint. In the words of one of the most articulate advocates of judicial self-restraint, Felix Frankfurter, a prudential course of action is required because the Court's effectiveness depends crucially on two things: first, upon its ability to separate a legal issue from the larger societal tensions; and second, upon the moral authority it can marshall by acting in a "nonpolitical" fashion. The first limitation requires a strict "case and controversy view." It explains Frankfurter's insistence that constitutional questions should not be dealt with abstractly "in terms of barren legal questions," as such dealings would lead to "sterile conclusions unrelated to actualities."[54] The second limitation is justified by the following words: "The Court's authority—possessed of neither the purse nor the sword—ultimately rests on sustained public confidence in its moral sanction. Such feeling must be nourished by the Court's complete detachment, in fact and in appearance, from political entanglements and by abstention from injecting itself into the clash of political forces in political settlements."[55]

In preserving this moral authority, the Court cannot act in a manner that violates the fundamental values of a society. It must decide controversies in light of the applicable principles and fundamental values, given that its own persuasive powers depend upon the continuous creation of a universe of meaning within which societal tensions can be mediated. Therefore, "governmental interests" do not have, a priori, an exclusive, privileged status, nor can courts avoid settling the issues involved. In an opinion concerning a university teacher forced by the state to disclose his political affiliation, but who claimed that this requirement infringed upon his freedom to teach and learn, Frankfurter spoke of a *duty* of the courts to decide the controversy:

To be sure, this is a conclusion based on a judicial judgment in balancing two contending principles—the right of a citizen to political privacy, as protected by the Fourteenth Amendment, and the right of the State to self-protection. And striking the balance implies the exercise of judgment. This is the inescapable judicial task in giving substantive content, legally enforced, to the Due Process clause, and it is a task ultimately committed to this court. It must not be an exercise of whim or will. It must be an overriding judgment founded on something much deeper and more justifiable than personal preference.[56]

In this connection, even advocates of judicial self-restraint have never argued for an inability to decide such cases as soon as a "security rationale" was invoked. In light of this argument, Justice Douglas's dissent from the courts' denial of *certiorari* in *Mora v. McNamara*[57] attains its full importance. Referring to the points raised by the petitioner concerning the legality of the Vietnam War, Douglas concludes that

[t]hese are large and deeply troubling questions. Whether the court would ultimately reach them depends, of course, upon the resolution of serious preliminary issues of justiciability. We cannot make these problems go away simply by refusing to hear the case of three obscure Army privates. I intimate not even tentative views upon any of these matters, but I think the court should squarely face them by granting certiorari and setting this case for oral argument.[58]

Douglas is careful to point out that such an acceptance of jurisdiction involves neither the role of becoming "a committee of oversight or supervision"[59] nor even an implicit validation of the claims of the petitioner. On the other hand, he correctly rejects the idea that a significant difference is created by the fact that this case and controversy arise out of the actions taken by the president as commander-in-chief and as a coordinate "political branch of the federal government." Following his brief review of *Ex parte*

Milligan, in which a presidential act under the commander-in-chief power was struck down, Douglas drew the following conclusion:

> The fact that the political branches are responsible for the threat to petitioners' liberty is not decisive. As Mr. Justice Holmes said in *Nixon v. Herndon,* 273 U.S. 536, 540:

> "The objection that the subject matter of the suit is political is little more than a play upon words. Of course the petition concerns political action but it alleges and seeks to recover for private damage. That private damage may be caused by such political action and may be recovered for in a suit at law hardly has been doubted for over two hundred years, since Ashby v. White, 2 Ld. Raym. 938, 3 id. 320, and has been recognized by this Court."

> These petitioners should be told whether their case is beyond judicial cognizance. If it is not, we should then reach the merits of their claims, on which I intimate no views whatsoever.[60]

The arguments in this section against an automatic deference to the executive branch in foreign relations and against a too uncritical use of avoidance techniques are largely based on constitutional considerations, such as the separation of powers and the political-questions doctrine. It is the task of the next section to show that automatic deference is also, for prudential reasons, dangerous and disruptive of the international order. Strangely enough, such a course of action not only leads to a weakening of the international legal order but is likely, as well, to result in a judicial activism of another kind. Such activism is bound to create serious embarrassment for the executive in foreign relations and a good deal of tension— in other words, exactly the problems that deference and abstention were supposed to overcome.

COURTS AS GATEKEEPERS: THE ISSUE OF EXTRATERRITORIAL APPLICATION OF U.S. LAW

The tendency of courts to view as political any question touching on a foreign relations issue is considered by this author to be problematic, as courts meet neither their domestic nor their international obligations in such cases. Justice White's fears expressed in his dissent to *Sabbatino*[61] were not without foundation, as recent U.S. court practice shows.

Consider, for example, the decision in the case of *Occidental of Um al Qayayn v. a Certain Cargo*[62] of the Fifth Circuit, which dealt with claims arising out of oil concession agreements. The interpretation of the agreement in turn hinged upon a dispute over the delimitation of the continental shelf between Iran and an Arab sheikdom. The court in question refused to decide these issues, calling them "political" for the following startling reasons: "In their external relations, sovereigns are bound by no law. . . . A prerequisite of law is recognized superior authority whether delegated from below or imposed from above. . . . Because no law exists binding these sovereigns and allocating rights and liabilities, no method exists to judicially resolve their disagreements."[63] Equipped with such conceptual blinders, the court could easily dispose of the legal issue concerning the delimitation of the continental shelf.

[A]lthough some standards have been developed, these standards depend in part on the existence of agreement among sovereigns. Because ownership of the continental shelf is derivative of the ownership of the unsubmerged land, the extent and ownership of the [second island's] shelf is necessarily in dispute. No manageable law exists to resolve disputed continental shelf ownership, however. The nexus between the absence of manageable standards and the political question [doctrine] is evident. Resolution of the disputed shelf can only occur by the political action of the sovereigns themselves.[64]

As such, it is surprising to hear that in light of the Convention of the Continental Shelf, the ICJ judgment on the North Sea continental shelf delimitation, and the then ongoing UNCLOS III discussions, a judge could assert that no manageable law exists. True, an application of the existing legal norm might be difficult to bring about, and the applicable law might be susceptible to conflicting interpretations, but these are common problems for practitioners of law. Nobody could possibly accept the inconveniences created by an ambiguous situation in the domestic arena as justifying a judge's refusal to discharge his duty in deciding cases. The destructive influence of a blanket invocation of political questions becomes obvious. If the doctrine is taken to its logical conclusion, courts could refuse to apply international legal norms in general.

A strong case can be made for the proposition that the latent motivation for treating international law . . . as a political question is the belief that the application of international law places a judge in conflicting roles: that is, a conflict may be seen to exist between a judge's role as a public servant of a national legal system which is predominantly self-contained, on the one hand, and as an officer (at least symbolically) of a legal system whose culture is inherently global, on the other. The feeling of conflict may be especially acute when it is the United States government whose actions are challenged as violative of international community standards, or when a challenge to some other government's actions requires a ruling which may also draw into question some analogous conduct or course of action by the United States government.[65]

The uneasiness of the courts in "wearing two hats" (i.e., as institutions of the domestic as well as the international order) is also seen in cases involving transnational interactions. Technically, transnational cases raise issues of "private international law," given that courts must decide which (national) legal prescription is applicable to a particular case and controversy.[66] As public international law permits concurrent jurisdiction (e.g., over nationals abroad) and also, according to the "protective principle," the exercise of jurisdictional power whenever conduct abroad has foreseeable and direct effects on the domestic order, courts must utilize "conflict-of-law rules."

The principle of international "comity" is likewise often invoked in order to reach a decision as to which of the (conflicting) national norms shall be the governing one. Thus, in contrast to conventional legal rules dealing with the definition of the validity of certain practices (such as "promising" or "contracting") as well as that of the respective parties' rights, conflict-of-law rules address largely *policy issues* concerning the way in which the various domestic legal systems interact within the international legal order. In this context, comity is viewed by courts as a discretionary principle. Its case-by-case application is based largely on "political considerations" as well as on reciprocity.[67] Such flexibility and indeterminacy is all the more important given that many transnational litigations touch upon regulatory issues. Hence transnational regulatory cases always involve a decision regarding the rights of *governments*, rather than a simple determination of private rights familiar from the normal conflict-of-law cases. A further discussion of these points appears to be in order.

Let us begin with the classical antitrust case, *United States* v. *Aluminum Co. of America*,[68] which ended the reign of Justice Holmes's dictum in *American Banana*, "All legislation is *prima facie* territorial."[69] The new theory developed by Judge Learned Hand concerned the applicability of the Sherman Act to contracts made abroad among foreigners in setting exports quotas and thus restricting trade. Judge Hand held that "any state may impose liabilities, even upon persons not within its allegiance, for conduct outside its borders that has consequences within its borders which the state reprehends."[70] The important test that courts were supposed to utilize in deciding the jurisdictional question was whether the conduct had "intended and actual" or "substantial and foreseeable"[71] effects within the territory of the state claiming jurisdiction. It does not require much perspicacity to realize that in a period of growing interdependence, "intended, substantial," and even "foreseeable effects" are nearly always present. Thus serious conflicts arising out of the vast overlap of jurisdictional claims can result.

Meanwhile, several important trading countries such as Germany, Canada, Holland, and Austria have legislated or taken administrative action to forbid compliance with the U.S. requirement on the part of their nationals.[72] The British "Protection of Trading Interest Act," passed in 1980, spells out in clearer detail the legal implications. It requires U.K. nationals who carry on trade in a foreign country to notify the secretary of state concerning any requirements or prohibitions threatened or imposed on them. It also authorizes the secretary of state to prohibit compliance with such foreign orders. Clause 2 stipulates that a person required to produce to a court or authority of another country any commercial document "not within the territorial jurisdiction of that country" may be enjoined from doing so if the foreign "requirement infringes the jurisdiction of the United Kingdom or is otherwise prejudicial to the sovereignty of the United Kingdom." Clause 5 provides that judgment of foreign courts in civil suits awarding "multiple damages shall not be enforceable in the United Kingdom."[73]

Obviously required in this connection is an international agreement that regulates these matters, in place of the unilateral extension of jurisdiction by domestic courts. However, even the existence of an international treaty[74] may only alleviate the potential for serious tensions, though it may not do away with them altogether. Accordingly, information can be requested from a foreign firm in civil or antitrust proceedings under American rules of evidence, including details that other countries would not consider to be directly related to the issues under litigation.[75] Germany, for example, attached reservations to Article 23 of the Hague Convention in order to prevent U.S. courts from forcing certain disclosures.[76]

This problem has become an issue not only in civil law countries, whose philosophy concerning the proper role of the judge in a proceeding differs from that of the United States; it is an issue in Great Britain and Canada as well. Four points are of particular importance in this context. First, civil law systems rely primarily on the judge for procedural acts, whereas the common law system makes the parties themselves responsible for obtaining evidence and notifying the opponent of the steps taken. Second, civil law systems view the trial as comprising all the elements of the litigation; hence pretrial proceedings (depositions, etc.) are part of the judge's responsibility. German law, for example, does not provide for a "duty" to supply documents to the opponent or to third parties. Third, §383, section 5 of the German Code of Civil Procedure (ZPO) allows for the refusal of documents based on the protected privilege of keeping "business secrets." This latter provision is directly in conflict with Rule 37 of the American Federal Rules of Civil Procedure, by which even a foreign witness can be charged with contempt of court if he or she refuses requests of this kind.

This leads us to a fourth important point—the use of grand juries and the possibility of the United States to utilize civil proceedings in, for example, antitrust matters. From a civil law system's point of view, treble damages have a punitive character. The same is true in product liability cases in which U.S. law allows for damages beyond the assessment of civil liabilities. Most other legal systems, including other common law systems, draw the lines differently.

Some of these issues surfaced in the antitrust case against the German firm C. F. Boehringer, leading to the *U.S. v. First National City Bank* case.[77] The First National City Bank refused to comply with a Grand Jury subpoena *duces tecum* to produce documents in possession of its foreign branch in Germany, arguing that the German bank secrecy law would make it liable for damages resulting from the disclosure of the subpoenaed documents. The court of first instance therefore adjudged the bank and its vice-president responsible for the refusal to be in civil contempt. The Court of Appeals affirmed this judgment, holding that although the bank might be liable for civil damages, the hardships for City Bank, if suffered at all, were not sufficient to excuse its refusal. In doing so, the court proposed a balancing test concerning the respective interests of Germany and the United States in extending its jurisdictional reach. Given that this test was clearly not only "troublesome" (as the court itself admitted) but quite indeterminate on this level of abstraction, several recent appeals decisions have simply done away with the last restraint. In *Arthur Andersen and Co. v. Finesilver*[78] and *Ohio v. Andersen and Co.,*[79] the Tenth Circuit, for all intents and purposes, held that local law always has to take precedence over foreign law. Hence foreign stipulations protecting the disclosure of information can be taken into account only at the point at which penalties are assessed.

In a similar fashion, traditional restraints observed by U.S. courts in not forcing the production of evidence if such a disclosure violates the criminal laws of the *situs* were set aside in *U.S. v. Vetco Inc.*[80] Here the Ninth Circuit Court found U.S. fiscal interests to prevail over Swiss criminal law prohibiting the production of evidence. Such an extension of U.S. jurisdiction obviously touches on sensitive issues of public policy, such as the protection of information, antitrust matters, general economic policy, consumer protection, and so on. Thus the conjunction of the willingness of U.S. courts to extend jurisdiction, along with the relatively low court costs in the United States, the lack of a requirement to indemnify the other party for its legal expenses in case of an unfavorable judgment, treble damage, and exorbitant jury awards have led to a new speciality in "lawyering," known as forum shopping. As Professor Stiefel once remarked, "the United States has become a relatively risk-free forum of high nuisance value for the stated reasons."[81] Even in proceedings among foreigners abroad, U.S. courts are utilized for forcing disclosures. Recently attempts were made by European litigants to gain evidence from a Frankfurt bank by means of a New York court.[82] Although there was not the slightest indication of an effect on the United States, since the transactions occurred only between Geneva and Israel, the U.S. forum was utilized because the Frankfurt Bank had a subsidiary in New York.

Some of the European fears appear somewhat exaggerated, given that counter examples can also be found. Courts have often invoked comity[83] as a decision principle, or have argued that a balancing of the conflicting national interests could be achieved more properly through international negotiation. Nevertheless, fundamental differences in judicial philosophies and rules of procedures are bound to engender difficulties, particularly when the issue of sovereignty is thereby raised. As Lord Wilberforce stated so eloquently in the *Westinghouse Uranium* case,[84] while dismissing the U.S. requests for evidence as "fishing expeditions":

My Lords, I think that there is no doubt that in deciding whether to give effect to letters rogatory, the courts are entitled to have regard to any possible prejudices to the sovereignty of the United Kingdom. . . . Equally, that in a matter affecting the sovereignty of the United Kingdom, the courts are entitled to take account of the declared policy of Her Majesty's Government, is in my opinion beyond doubt. . . . If public interest enters into this matter on one side, so it must be taken account of on the other and as the views of the Executive in the United States of America impel the making of the order, so must the views of the Executive in the United Kingdom be considered when it is a question of implementing the order here. It is axiomatic that in anti-trust matters the policy of one state may be to defend what it is the policy of another state to attack.[85]

Similar difficulties concerning the role of courts and their impact on policy surfaced when activists tried to use the National Environmental Policy Act (NEPA) as a vehicle to force foreign policy changes through the courts. It appears that the problematic result of these attempts was the strengthening of executive discretion. Claiming extraterritorial validity for NEPA, the Sierra Club in *Sierra Club* v. *Adams*[86] tried to enjoin the federal government from carrying out the construction of the Pan-American highway wholly within the territorial limits of Colombia and Panama. After the district court had held that a voluntary environmental impact statement was deficient, the Sierra Club also challenged the revised Final Environmental Impact Statement (EIS) as insufficient, "in that it did not discuss adequately the possibility of the project contributing to the spread of hoof and mouth disease and because of inadequate treatment of the impact of the project upon the lives of the Cuna and Choci Indians. Also challenged as inadequate was the discussion of alternative routes."[87]

It mattered little to the activists that the environmental impact was totally local, and that the routing of the highways obviously involved the cooperation and consent of foreign governments. Two years later, the court of appeals for the District of Columbia remanded the case, holding that the environmental impact statement had been satisfactory while expressly refusing to decide the extraterritorial applicability of NEPA for U.S. projects producing only local effect. The court stated somewhat incongruously: "[I]n view of the conclusions that we reached in this case, we need only assume, without deciding, that NEPA is fully applicable to construction in Panama."[88]

When the National Resource Defense Council wanted to force the same issue by bringing suit against the Export Import (Ex-Im) Bank, alleging that an environmental impact statement was required for all Ex-Im–financed projects, the suit was finally dismissed after a "compromise" had been worked out. The result was Executive Order 12,114 of January 4, 1979, in which U.S. agencies were directed to consider the effects of their actions on the environment even if they occurred outside the United States.[89] But the trade-off may have been of questionable benefit since the executive order maintained that the purpose of the order was to "further environmental objectives consistent with the foreign policy and national security policy of the United States."[90]

The order explicitly exempts from scrutiny presidential actions, intelligence activities, arms transfers, export licensing permits, and emergency disaster relief. It also notes that "nothing in this order shall be construed to create a cause of action." The order furthers the purpose of NEPA, but it is based on *independent authority.* Thus, far from establishing independent review procedures, activism and the use of courts have basically led to a reaffirmation and grant of power of the executive, a pattern already familiar from other issue areas. In addition, the national security rationale had now been explicitly included in the executive order.

There is still, however, another more principled reason why the present state of affairs remains unsatisfactory, even if it is characterized by comity and discretion rather than by an unreflective attitude on the part of the courts. Even when courts exercise discretion and wrestle with the balancing problem, most often they do not properly take care of their duty within the constitutive process of the international legal order. Interest adjustments are therefore ad hoc at best in the absence of a clearer identification of the system's needs that goes beyond the particular weighing of the concrete interests in a particular case. As Harold Meier has pointed out, the traditional balancing as well as the comity argument, based on the distinction between authority (jurisdiction) and restraint,

frees the court from weighing its decision in the light of its impact on the international law formation process and insulates it from the need to evaluate the impact of the assertion of jurisdiction on the development of reciprocal expectations about the legitimacy of the exercise of power in similar situations by other potential regulators in the international community. . . . Since courts . . . are always operating under legislative language that on its face suggests that the statute is applicable to the foreign events . . . there is some anomaly in a court's finding that a regulation may be applied without violating international jurisdictional standards but that the congressional command will not be followed if the court determines that as a matter of policy the regulation is inappropriately applied. . . . Furthermore, this judicial approach suggests that Congress should regard itself as being free of international legal constraints when drafting legislation, as long as it can identify an appropriate effect upon U.S. commerce within the context of objective territoriality.[91]

Again, it becomes obvious that even when acting "prudentially," courts are often quite oblivious to their proper duties and role within the international legal order.

COURTS AS ARENAS: THE ISSUE OF "RIGHTS" UNDER INTERNATIONAL LAW

The last few cases discussed above reveal how courts often become arenas for cases in which national policies having impacts abroad are challenged on the grounds of alleged violations of congressional legislative intent. Different issues—and from a world order perspective, more important ones—are raised when citizens claim to have vested rights under either treaty or international customary law and when they allege a violation of these rights by national decisions.

This leads us back to the constitutional issue of the legal effects of treaties, particularly in connection with the developing international "human rights law." Can individuals utilize human rights provisos in making valid claims in domestic courts? Two possibilities exist. First, treaties might directly vest individuals with rights. Second, treaties might be "declaratory" of international *custom* and thus become "the law of the land."

Conventional wisdom has it that a direct invocation of international legal norms usually fails because these norms are often embodied in treaties that are not "self-executing."[92] But such an easy answer raises problems: (1) It does not address the issue of the "declaratory" (i.e., customary) nature of many human rights instruments. (2) The doctrinal issues of self-executing versus non-self-executing treaties, though never quite clear to begin with, have become even less so through certain recent decisions introducing the notion of "not wholly self-executing" treaties. (3) Courts sometimes granted a quasi-authoritative status to international accords and documents without holding that they were directly governing the case under consideration. Accordingly, a more detailed analysis seems in order.

Let us begin with the issue of self-executing versus non-self-executing treaties as it relates to the human rights provisions of the UN Charter. Although the problem of whether a treaty is self-executing or not is obviously a different and wider one than the issue of whether a treaty vests rights in an individual, often the latter question can be decided only by answering the former. This was the issue in the case of *Fujii v. California*,[93] which concerned the racially discriminatory Alien Land Law of California. Holding for the Plaintiff, who had challenged the Land Law on the basis of the antidiscrimination articles of the UN Charter—which, as a treaty, had become the law of the land—the lower court found the California Law invalid. It violated both the purpose and the intent, as well as the plain language, of Articles 55 and 56 of the Charter.[94] The holding, which caused a national furor and gave impetus to attempts to pass the Bricker Amendment, was reversed by the California Supreme Court. This court also struck down the Alien Land Law as discriminatory, but it did so on the basis of the equal-protection clause of the Constitution, in noting that the UN Charter was not self-executing. One reason for the lack of self-executing character in Article 56 was stated by Judge Gibson: "The fundamental provisions in the Charter pledging cooperation in promoting observance of fundamental freedoms lack the mandatory quality and definiteness which would indicate an intent to create justiciable rights in private persons immediately upon ratification."[95] To that extent, the holding was in conformity with the classical doctrine developed in *Foster and Elam v. Neilson*[96] and *U.S. v. Percheman*.[97]

The Foster decision deals with the validity of titles based on land grants made by the Spanish king before the cession of the Louisiana territories to the United States in the Treaty of 1819. Article 8 of this treaty provided that "all grants of lands made . . . by his Catholic Majesty . . . in said territories . . . shall be ratified and confirmed to the persons in possession of the lands to the same extent that the grants would be valid if the territories had remained under the dominion of his Catholic Majesty."[98] Justice Marshall read into this clause a separation-of-powers argument that necessitated a "ratification" through explicit legislation by Congress. Relying on legislation by Congress that was inconsistent with an intention to preserve the land grants, Marshall held against the appellants, who had sued for the recovery of a tract of land under the Spanish land grant. The operative passage dealing with the conferral of rights and its dependence upon the self- or non-self-executing character of the treaty reads as follows:

Our constitution declares a treaty to be the law of the land. It is consequently to be regarded in courts of justice as equivalent to an act of the legislature, whenever it operates of itself without the aid of any legislative provision. But when the terms of the stipulation import a contract, when either of the parties engages to perform a particular act, the treaty addresses itself to the political, not the judicial department; and the legislature must execute the contract before it can become a rule for the court.[99]

Four years later, the same court, hearing a case involving the same treaty, came to a different conclusion after the Spanish text suggested that the term *ratified and confirmed* in Article 8 could be construed in a self-executing fashion. Marshall admitted that this could mean that ratification and confirmation were intended by the force of the "same instrument."[100] He added that, given the clearer Spanish text, such a construction was "proper, if not unavoidable."[101]

The *Head Money* case,[102] decided in 1884, confirmed the possibility that treaties might directly vest individuals with rights without further legislative action.[103] But two difficulties arise given the conflicting precedents in Foster, Perchman, and Head Money. First, a clearer criterion is needed by which we can decide whether a treaty is self-executing or not. Second, given such a criterion, under what circumstances can individuals be said to have vested rights directly under international agreements?

The first issue is taken up in the case of *Aerovias Interamericanas de Panama v. Board of County Commissioners of Dade County, Florida*,[104] which dealt with discriminatory user charges leveled against foreign air carriers in violation of Article 15 of the Chicago Convention on International Civil Aviation. The court admitted that, in spite of some guidelines, non-self-executing treaty analysis was in a state of confusion. "Whether a given treaty is 'self-executing' or requires special implementing legislation in order to give force and effect to its provisions, through the aid of the Courts, presents primarily a domestic question of construction for the courts, but it is difficult to extract any clear principle for judicial guidance from the cases discussing the subject."[105] Under such circumstances it is not difficult to see the problem involved in vesting individuals directly with rights—for example, through the UN Charter or declaratory human rights instruments. The U.S. case law seems to suggest that "most treaties do not vest the individual with sufficient legal character to enable him to invoke international law in domestic courts and that such executory international law can only be invoked by sovereign nations."[106] The "statism" inherent in the approaches of most courts is readily apparent in the holdings of *Pauling v. McElroy*.[107] In this case, the plaintiffs sued in order to enjoin the United States from nuclear tests on their native islands, alleging that such tests violated the UN Charter and general international law. The court rejected such reasons by stating as follows:

The provisions of the Charter of the United Nations, the Trusteeship agreement for the Trust Territory of the Pacific Islands and the international law principle of freedom of the seas relied on by the plaintiffs are non-self-executing and do not vest any of the plaintiffs with individual legal rights which they may assert in court. The claimed violations of such international obligations and principles may be asserted only by diplomatic negotiations between the sovereignties concerned.[108]

At first, the evidence appears to be quite clear concerning the conferral of rights to individuals by means of international convenants.[109] However, such an assessment leaves out some important and complicating elements in the ongoing debate about the nature of the self-executing and non-self-executing features of the Charter and in other documents declaratory of international legal principles. First, there is the mandate of Article 6 of the constitution to apply "treaties as the law of the land and to vest individuals with rights whenever the treaty permits."[110] Second, in a variety of circumstances, U.S. courts have used various human rights instruments as quasi-authoritative sources backing the judicial decision[111] without declaring the UN Charter or various human rights pronouncements to be self-executing. Noting the "well-established principle that customary international law is part of the law of the United States," a Connecticut court held that overcrowded prison conditions violated the prisoners' rights to due process as the UN Minimum Standard Rules for the Treatment of Prisoners was not met.[112] These standards were held to be "significant as expressions of the obligations to the international community of the member states of the United Nations . . . and as part of the body of international law (including customary international law) concerning human rights which has been built upon the foundation of the United Nations Charter."[113] Although the court was careful to point out that this did not necessarily mean that UN rules were therefore directly applicable to the case, it was nevertheless "an authoritative international statement of basic norms of human dignity," and the standards embodied in this statement "were relevant to the cancns of decency and fairness which express the notion of justice in the Due Process clause."[114]

Although these passages do not necessarily prove that an individual is vested directly with rights under an international legal instrument, they do suggest that such instruments have been used by courts to fulfill a *constitutional mandate* (e.g., the due process clause). Thus they are far from lacking direct legal relevance. A further step in the direction of vesting the individual directly with rights under international law was made in two landmark cases that, although not binding upon all courts as they are only decisions of an appeals court, nevertheless provided some important indications for the development of a human rights law. This development might soon lead to a sidestepping, if not eventually an overruling, of *Pauling*, and to the abolition of the problematic self-executing/non-self-executing distinction.

A case discussed earlier in this chapter, *U.S. v. Toscanino*,[115] dealt with the complaint of an Italian citizen who had been identified by U.S. authorities as a drug dealer doing business with U.S. distributors out of Uruguay. Toscanino had been kidnapped in Montevideo by the Uruguayan police, with the full knowledge and active help of U.S. officials. He was brought against his will to Brazil and later to the United States, where he was convicted. On appeal from his conviction, which the defendant claimed to be void because the presence within the territorial jurisdiction of the court had been illegally obtained, the Second Circuit Court sided with the plaintiff and remanded the case. Quoting the UN Charter and the charter of the OAS (both non-self-executing agreements), the court took them as evidence of binding principles of international law. Thus the U.S. government's duty under international law—to refrain from kidnapping a criminal defendant from within the territory of another nation, especially while the possibility of extradition existed—violated the rights of the defendant whose international law claims were thereupon remanded for a hearing in the district court.

The second, even more significant case was the tort claim brought by Dolly and Joel Filartiga against Americo N. Peña-Irala[116] in a New York district court. Peña-Irala, the former inspector general of police in Asuncion (Paraguay), was accused by Mr. Filartiga (father) and Ms. Filartiga (sister) of having kidnapped a 17-year-old boy (brother) and of having tortured him to death in retaliation for the political activities of Mr. Joel Filartiga (the father) against the Stroessner regime. Through a variety of circumstances, both plaintiffs and defendant were in the United States at the time the tort claim was brought against Mr. Peña-Irala. The basis for the suit was Section 1350 of the Alien Tort Statute,[117] which provides that "the district courts shall have original jurisdiction of any civil action by an alien for tort only, committed in violation of the law of nations or a treaty of the United States."

The district court dismissed the claim for lack of jurisdiction, arguing that the "law of nations" used in Section 1350 excluded the treatment of a state's own citizens. Thus, the central question in deciding the jurisdictional issue before the Second Circuit Court of Appeals turned upon the interpretation of the term *violation of the law of nations*. In this context, several subsidiary issues had to be decided. First, there was the question of which standards should govern the establishment of a violation. The court stated that a rule of international law must command the general assent of civilized nations in order to exclude idiosyncratic interpretations. Second, the judge held that courts are bound to interpret international law in terms of its evolving standards and not as an ahistorical set of disembodied prescriptions.[118] Third, in evaluating Articles 55 and 56 of the UN Charter ("although [the provisos of these articles are] not wholly self-executing"),[119] the court argued that in this age a state's treatment of its own citizens is a matter of "international concern."[120] Hence the UN Charter as well as the Universal Declaration of Human Rights constitute authoritative evidence as to the binding principles of international law.[121] Fourth, and as a consequence of the reasons stated, the Universal Declaration no longer "fits into the dichotomy between binding treaty against non-binding pronouncement, but is rather an authoritative statement of the international community."[122] Fifth, although there might be no universal agreement as to the precise extent of the human rights and fundamental freedoms guaranteed by the Charter, there is unanimous agreement that "these guarantees include, at the bare minimum, the right to be free from torture."[123]

The implications of these decisions could be of great importance for the future definition and development of the role of domestic courts as agencies of the international legal order. It would make the wearing of the "international hat" by domestic institutions an accepted and important part of their function. It could also provide some innovative solutions to the often artificial and confused statist analysis, in terms of self-executing and non-self-executing treaties, by sidestepping the pitfalls of the conventional categorization. Finally, it could provide a new impetus to the development of international law in the domestic context.

This development, however, will not proceed unimpeded, as the recent Tel-Oren[124] decision shows. The plaintiffs in this appellate case, survivors and relatives of the victims of a PLO terrorist attack in Israel, sued for damages under the alien tort statute, to be paid from the assets of the PLO (or from assets held by others for the PLO) in the United States. The district court had dismissed the action on the basis of lack of subject matter jurisdiction and the applicable statute of limitations. The Court of Appeals took jurisdiction but held that international law did not provide individuals with a "cause of action," i.e., did not directly vest individuals with rights that could serve as a basis of the plaintiffs' tort claim.

Much of Judge Bork's[125] controversial opinion turned on the argument that international law does not designate individuals as a class of possible litigants by vesting them directly with rights, since among others, human rights treaties are not self-executing. Given Judge Bork's sweeping statements, no individual could invoke international customary norms in a U.S. court.

However, although the judges all agreed on the dismissal of the suit, they agreed on little else. Thus, one can hope that this decision will be less of a stumbling block for the development of a human rights law than it at first appears,[126] particularly in view of the other cases discussed above.

CONCLUSION

This chapter has attempted to meet several objectives. Starting with an observation of the institutional weaknesses of the international legal order, it investigated the role of domestic institutions—particularly that of domestic courts—that "double up" as agencies of the international legal system. In this connection, the metaphor of the courts as "gatekeepers" and "arenas" was used. On the one hand, courts reinforce and reproduce the state system; on the other hand, they provide opportunities for challenging state action in violation of international legal norms.

The analysis proceeded with a "case study" of American legal practices, thus permitting a closer investigation of the issues concerning the federal foreign relations powers and, in particular, the definition and limits of presidential power. This led to the second task: a critical evaluation of these practices in terms of the criteria derived from democratic theory and world order concerns. In this context, the need for, and the limits of, judicial review even in the area of foreign relations, as well as the evolving international human rights law, had to be examined. While the discussion of the former issue area was largely informed by constitutional principles and considerations of legitimacy in a democratic polity, the examination of the latter evaluated court practices by applying a world order perspective. Thus strategies of transformation could indirectly be assessed.

Given the complexities of these matters, the suggestions necessarily have to be tentative. Implicit in the argument was a counsel of caution concerning both strategies, either that of delegating too much discretion to the executive or that of extending jurisdictional claims. It also concerned a type of judicial activism well founded in the function of courts as agencies of the international legal order. This, in turn, led to a further discussion of the nature of a jurisprudence based on comity in transnational litigations. In this context, the constitutive role of the courts for the international legal process was emphasized.

Due to the complexities created by the current growth of interdependence between nations, an urgent need exists for greater cooperation and regulation. The main question is whether this regulation will occur largely through unilateral executive action, which is virtually unchecked, through judicial activism, or through abstention. Even if one favors executive action over the piecemeal accretion associated with case law in the courts, the important issue remains whether and how the broad delegation of new powers to the executive shall be governed by identifiable principles, as well as how the executive's conduct shall be subject to some type of review, whether legislative, judicial, and/or "public."

The problem thus posed clearly raises a whole host of puzzling questions regarding the merits or demerits of various strategies. But before deciding the issue, one needs a frame of reference within which these metalegal questions can be systematically discussed. For example, the problem of delegating broad authorities to the executive makes it necessary to inquire further into the problem of the "constituency" to which a given actor is supposed to be accountable. Thus, quite aside from the enormous practical problems of attaining meaningful change in an orderly fashion in an anarchical system (precisely because short-run considerations often conflict with those in the long run and because regime creation and maintenance pose the well-known public goods dilemmas), the absence of a coherent frame of reference for debating these issues is debilitating. Such a frame has to be sensitive to the limitations imposed by political constraints upon activism, judicial and otherwise, but must not exhaust itself in the reaffirmation of the existing situation.

In the state system it was the task of legal thought to reflect critically upon norms and practices and to inquire into the conditions of international order. Whether a world order perspective will be of similar service remains to be seen. Even so, the world order perspective promises to provide an interesting and rewarding starting point for such a discourse.

NOTES

1. See, for example, Hans Kelsen (Robert Tucker, ed.), *Principles of International Law* (New York: Holt, Rinehart & Winston, 1968), who derives the primitive character of international law from the lack of central enforcement mechanisms.

2. See Nicholas Onuf's contribution in this volume, which traces the "codification" debate.

3. See Friedrich Kratochwil, "Thrasymmachos Revisited: On the Relevance of Norms and the Study of Law for International Relations," *Journal of International Affairs* 37 (Winter 1984), pp. 343–356.

4. See Kelsen's argument that law is distinguished from other norms by "sanctions" and that sanctions are a "threatened evil," in Kelsen, *Principles of International Law*, p. 4.

5. See, for example, the attempts by Fritjof Haft to develop a concept of criminal law based on the "dialogue" between the law breaker and "the law," in which the pragmatic aspects (i.e., the acceptance of guilt or exculpatory reasons) figure prominently and provide the necessary conditions for holding a criminal "responsible." Thus the focus shifts from the "punishment" set down by the norms to the process by which these norms are applied to a "case"; the reestablishment of a common universe of meaning is the precondition for the legitimacy of the punishment and also the necessary condition for the "resocialization" of the individual. See Fritjof Haft, *Der Schulddialog* (Frieburg: Alber, 1978).

6. See Friedrich Kratochwil, "The Force of Prescriptions," *International Organization* 38 (Fall 1984), pp. 685–708, and "Following Rules" (forthcoming).

7. See, for example, Judith Blake and Kingsley Davis, "Norms, Values and Sanctions," in Robert Harris, ed. *Handbook of Modern Sociology* (Chicago: Rand McNally, 1964).

8. See, for example, the sophisticated account of rule-guided action in David Miers and William Twining, *How to Do Things with Rules* (London: Weidenfeld and Nicholson, 1976). Louis Henkin makes a similar point in *How Nations Behave*, 2nd ed. (New York: Columbia University Press, 1980), passim; see also Friedrich Kratochwil, "Is International Law 'Proper' Law?" *Archiv fuer Rechts und Sozialphilosophie* 69 (1983) pp. 13–46.

9. Georges Scelle, *Droit International Public* (Paris: Donat Mott Christien, 1948).

10. For a fundamental discussion of interdependence and the resulting "sensitivities" and "vulnerabilities," see Robert Keohane and Joseph Nye, *Power and Interdependence* (Boston: Little, Brown, 1977), Ch. 1.

11. Article I, section 10.

12. Article III, section 2 reads in part: "The judicial power shall extend to all cases, in Laws and Equity, arising under this Constitution, the Laws of the United States, and Treaties made, or which shall be made under their authority; or all cases affecting Ambassadors, other public Ministers, and Consuls; . . . to controversies . . . between a state or the citizens thereof, and Foreign States, citizens or subjects. In all cases affecting Ambassadors, other public Ministers and Consuls, the supreme court shall have original jurisdiction. In all the other cases before mentioned, the supreme court shall have appellate jurisdiction, both as to law and fact, with such exceptions, and under such regulations as the Congress shall make."

13. U.S.C. §1330, 1332(a), 1391(f), 1441(d), 1602–1611 (1976).

14. *Paquete Habana*, 175 US 677 (1900).

15. *Hilton v. Guyot* 159 US 113 (1895).

16. Excerpt from the *Paquete Habana* case, reprinted in Louis Henkin et al., *International Law, Cases and Materials* (Minneapolis: West, 1980), p. 40.

17. 252 US 416 (1920).

18. For an extensive discussion of the constitutional issues involved, see Louis Henkin, *Foreign Affairs and the Constitution* (New York: Norton, 1975), Ch. 5.

19. US 299 US 304 (1936).

20. *Curtiss Wright*, as quoted in William Bishop, *International Law, Cases and Materials* (Boston: Little, Brown, 1962), at p. 89.

21. *U.S.* v. *Arjona* 12 US 479 (1887).

22. *Ibid.*, at 487.

23. *U.S.* v. *Curtiss Wright* 299 US 304, at 320.

24. *U.S.* v. *Belmont* 301 US 324.

25. This is the summary of *U.S.* v. *Belmont* given by the Supreme Court in *U.S.* v. *Pink*; see also *Oetjen* v. *Central Leather* 246 US 297 (1918).

26. *U.S.* v. *Pink* 315 US 203.

27. *U.S.* v. *Pink*, as reprinted in Bishop, *International Law*, p. 324.

28. The *locus classicus* for the definition of the political questions doctrine is *Baker* v. *Carr* 369 US 186 (1962).

29. Henkin, *Foreign Affairs*, p. 171.

30. *Ibid.*, p. 32.

31. Edward Gordon, "American Courts, International Law and 'Political Questions' Which Touch Foreign Relations," *International Lawyer* 14 (1980), pp. 297–329.

32. *Haig* v. *Agee* 453 US 280 (1981).

33. *Ibid.*, at 307.

34. Jordan Paust, "Is the President Bound by the Supreme Law of the Land? Foreign Affairs and National Security Reexamined," *Hastings Constitutional Law Quarterly* 9, no. 4 (Summer 1982), pp. 119–162.

35. Robert Gareis, "The Corrupt Practices Act," *International Lawyer* 14 (1980) pp. 377–382, at 378.

36. *U.S.* v. *Richardson* 416 US 166 (1974).

37. *Flast* v. *Cohen* 392 US 93 (1968).

38. *Frothingham* v. *Mellon* 262 US 447 (1923).

39. I owe this thought to Richard Falk.

40. As quoted in Alexander Bickel, *The Least Dangerous Branch* (Indianapolis: Bobbs-Merrill, 1962), pp. 113–114.

41. *Ibid.*, at 114.

42. *Ibid.*

43. *Marbury* v. *Madison*, vols. 1–5 U.S. (1 Cranch) 137 (1803).

44. Bickel, *The Least Dangerous Branch*, p. 115.

45. See, for example, *Frothingham* v. *Mellon*, which challenged the power of Congress to enact the Maternity Act based on the claim that the interests of Mrs. Frothingham as a U.S. taxpayer were thereby affected. See also *Doremus* v. *Board of Education* 342 US 429 (1952).

46. One could, however, make a case that citizens have standing under the tests enunciated in *Flast* v. *Gardner* (Cohen), which modified the Frothingham rule. For a further discussion of this point, see Lawrence Velvel, "The War in Vietnam: Unconstitutional, Justiciable and Jurisdictionally Attackable," in Richard Falk, ed., *The Vietnam War and International Law*, vol. 2 (Princeton, N.J.: Princeton University Press, 1969), pp. 651–710.

47. *Goldwater* v. *Carter* 444 US 996 (1979).

48. *Ibid.*, at 1003.

49. *Baker* v. *Carr* 369 US 186 (1962).

50. *Goldwater* v. *Carter* at 1007, citing *Powell* v. *McCormack* 395 US 486 (1969), at 519–521 (1969).

51. Ibid., at 997.

52. Ibid., at 1001.

53. See, for example, *Mitchell* v. *United States* 386 US 972.

54. Felix Frankfurter, "Advisory Opinions," in *Encyclopedia of the Social Sciences*, Vol. 1, p. 478, as quoted in Bickel, *The Least Dangerous Branch*, p. 115.

55. Felix Frankfurter dissenting in *Baker* v. *Carr* 369 US 186 (1962), at 267.

56. *Sweezy* v. *New Hampshire* 354 US 234 (1957), at 266–267.

57. *Mora* v. *McNamara* 389 US 934 (1967).

58. *Mora* v. *McNamara*, as reprinted in Falk, *The Vietnam War*, pp. 830–834, at 831.

59. Ibid., p. 833.

60. Ibid., p. 834.

61. *Banco Nacional de Cuba* v. *Sabbatino* 376 US 398 (1964), Justice White dissenting: "I am dismayed that the Court has, with one broad stroke, declared the ascertainment and application of international law beyond the competence of the courts of the United States in a large and important category of cases" (at 439).

62. 577 F. 2d 1196 (Fifth Circuit, 1978).

63. Ibid., pp. 1204–1205.

64. Ibid., p. 1205.

65. See Gordon, "American Courts, International Law and 'Political Questions,'" at 311.

66. For a fundamental discussion of the issues involved see Andreas Lowenfeld, "Public Law in the International Arena: Conflict of Laws, International Law and Some Suggestions for Their Interaction," in *Recueil des Cours*, vol. 2 (Netherlands: Sijthoff and Noordhoff, 1980).

67. See Harold Maier, "The Bases and Range of Federal Common Law in Private International Matters," *Vanderbilt Journal of Transnational Law* 5 (1979), pp. 133 ff.

68. 148 F. 2d 416 (Second Circuit, 1945).

69. 213 US 347 (1909), at 356.

70. 148 F. 2d, at 443.

71. Ibid., at 443–444.

72. See V. Rock Grundman, "The New Imperialism: The Extraterritorial Application of U.S Law," *International Lawyer* 14 (1980), pp. 257–266, at p. 257.

73. Edward Gordon, "Extraterritorial Application of United States Economic Laws: Great Britain Draws the Line," *International Lawyer* 14 (1980), pp. 151–166, at pp. 161–162.

74. The "Hague Convention on the Taking of Evidence Abroad in Civil or Commercial Matters" has been open for signature since March 18, 1970. For a treatment of the types of foreign requests made under this convention to U.S. authorities, see Edward Weiner, "In Search of International Evidence," *Notre Dame Law Review* 58, no. 1 (October 1982), pp. 60–83.

75. On the differences in approaches of obtaining evidence, see United States Department of Justice, *Civil Division Practice Manual*, Vol. 1, International Judicial Assistance, pp. 22–23; see also Robert Augustine, "Obtaining International Judicial Assistance under the Federal Rules and the Hague Convention on the Taking of Evidence Abroad in Civil and Commercial Matters," *Georgia Journal of International and Comparative Law* 10, no. 1 (1980), pp. 101–163. On the difficulties that arise

for U.S. courts out of foreign nondisclosure laws, see Department of Justice, "Foreign Non-disclosure Laws and Domestic Discovery Orders," *Yale Law Journal* (1979), pp. 61–88.

76. On the difficulties that arise in German American discovery proceedings, see Ernst Stiefel, "Discovery Probleme and Erfahrungen im Deutsch-Amerikanischen Rechtshilfeverkehr," *Recht der Internationalen Wirtschaft* 25, Heft 8 (1979), pp. 509–520. For a critical review of recent American practice, see Hans Wiggo von Huelsen, "Gebrauch und Missbrauch U.S. amerikanischer pre-trial discovery und die internationale Rechtshilfe," *Recht der Internationalen Wirtschaft* 28, Heft 4 (1982), pp. 225–235.

77. 369 F. 2d 897 (Second Circuit, 1968).

78. 546 F. 2d 388 (Tenth Circuit, 1976).

79. 570 F. 2d 1370 (Tenth Circuit, 1978).

80. 644 F. 2d 1324 (Ninth Circuit, 1981) as amended October 22, 1981, *certiorari* denied 50 U.S.L.W. 3465.

81. Stiefel, "Discovery Probleme," pp. 517–519.

82. Ibid., p. 518.

83. For a general discussion and a review of cases that exhibit these different tendencies, see Harold Maier, "Extraterritorial Jurisdiction at a Crossroads: An Intersection Between Public and Private International Law," *American Journal of International Law* 76 (April 1982), pp. 280–320.

84. United Kingdom: House of Lords Decision in Westinghouse Electric Corporation, Uranium Contract Litigation; Execution of Letters Rogatory, *International Legal Materials* (1978), pp. 38–76.

85. Lord Wilberforce, quoting from RCA v. Rowland Corp., *Westinghouse Uranium case*, *International Legal Materials*, (1978), p. 43.

86. Sierra Club v. Adams 578 F. 2d 389 (D.C. Circuit, 1978).

87. Grundman, "The New Imperialism," p. 264.

88. 578 F. 2d 389 (D.C. Circuit, 1978), at 391, note 14.

89. Executive Order No. 1211444, Federal Regulations, 1957 (1979).

90. Ibid. For an assessment of this executive order and the issue of the extraterritorial reach of NEPA, see John Pierce, "Exports and Environmental Responsibility," *Cornell International Law Journal* 12 (Summer 1979), pp. 247–268.

91. See Maier, "Extraterritorial Jurisdiction," p. 299; in this context see also the new formulation in the Restatement of Foreign Relations Law of the United States (revised), Tentative Draft No. 2 (1981), which eliminates the distinction between authority on the one hand and abstention on the other by circumscribing the jurisdiction of courts much more narrowly, making it dependent on a whole host of factors rather than on simple factual contacts. For a summary of the draft, see *American Journal of International Law* 75 (1981), pp. 987ff.

92. For an important although somewhat dated discussion, see Alona Evans, "Self-executing Treaties in the United States of America," *British Yearbook of International Law*, vol. 30 (1953), pp. 178–205.

93. Supreme Court of California, 242 P. 2d 617 (1952).

94. 217 P. 2d, at 486.

95. 242 P. 2d, at 621–622.

96. 27 US (2 Pet.) 253.

97. 32 US (7 Pet.) 51.

98. *Foster and Elam v. Neilson*, 27 US (2 Pet.) 253, at 276.

99. As quoted in Henkin et al., *International Law*, p. 158.

100. *U.S. v. Percheman*, 32 US (7 Pet.) 51, at 88–89.

101. Ibid.

102. 112 US 580 (1884).

103. Justice Miller is quoted in *Head Money* as saying, "A treaty, then, is a law of the land, as an Act of Congress is, whenever its provisions prescribe a rule by which the rights of the private citizen or subject may be determined. And when such rights are of a nature to be enforced in a court of justice, that court resorts to the treaty for a rule of decision for the case before it as it would to a statute" (112 US 580 [1884], at 598).

104. 197 F. Supp. 230 (S.D. Fla. 1961), rev'd on other grounds sub nom. *Board of County Commissioners of Dade County, Florida v. Aerolineas Peruanas, S.A.*, 307 F. 2d 802 (Fifth Circuit, 1962).

105. 197 F. Supp., at 245.

106. Jeffrey H. Louden, "The Domestic Application of International Human Rights Law: Evolving the Species," *Hastings International and Comparative Law Review* 5, no. 1 (1982), pp. 161–209, at 197.

107. 164 F. Supp. 390 (D.C. Circuit, 1958).

108. Ibid., at 393.

109. In *Diggs v. Richardson*, 555 F. 2d 848 (D.C. Circuit, 1976), which challenged the U.S abrogation of a Security Council embargo against South Africa, the D.C. Circuit Court decided that resolutions of the UN organs are directed to the political branches and did not confer rights upon individual citizens to challenge the government's policy even if it was in violation of international norms.

110. Louden, "The Domestic Application," pp. 197–198.

111. See, for example, the concurring opinions of Justices Black, Douglas, and Murphy in *Oyama v. California*, 332 US 633 (1947).

112. *Lareau v. Manson*, 507 F. Supp. 1177 (D. Conn., 1980).

113. Ibid., at 1188, note 9.

114. Ibid.

115. 500 F. 2d 267 (Second Circuit, 1974).

116. *Filartiga v. Peña-Irala*, 630 F. 2d 876, at 882, note 9.

117. 728 U.S.C. 1350 (Judiciary Act of 1789).

118. *Filartiga v. Peña-Irala*, at 881.

119. See ibid., quoting *Hitai v. Immigration and Naturalization Service*, 343 F. 2d 466 (Second Circuit, 1965), at 468.

120. *Filartiga v. Peña-Irala*, at 881.

121. Ibid., at 882, quoting *U.S. v. Toscanino*.

122. Ibid., at 883, quoting Egon Schwelb.

123. Ibid., at 882.

124. *Tel-Oren v. Libyan Arab Republic*, 726 F. 2d 774 (D.C. Circuit, 1984).

125. There were three concurring opinions in this case.

126. See the extensive discussion between Anthony D'Amato and Alfred Rubin, entitled "What Does Tel-Oren Tell Lawyers?" *American Journal of International Law* 79 (January 1985), pp. 92–114.

14. International Codification: Interpreting the Last Half-Century

Nicholas Greenwood Onuf

The idea of codification of international law became, with arbitration and free trade, an inseparable part of the liberal peace movement of the nineteenth century. International codification gained practical significance with the emergence during that time of international institutions and entered the realm of public sponsorship with the Hague Peace Conference of 1899 and 1907.[1]

In its time, the League of Nations assumed responsibility for international codification. A Committee of Experts on the Progressive Codification of International Law began work in 1925 by identifying, in consultation with member states, bodies of customary law sufficiently ripe for consolidation in code form. Three topics were settled on—nationality, territorial waters, and state responsibility—preparations undertaken, and the assistance of states solicited, all for the purpose of convening an international conference. The Hague Codification Conference of 1930 drew representatives from forty-eight states, nine of them, including the United States, not members of the League. The conference was universally judged a failure, mitigated, perhaps, by modest concurrence on some aspects of nationality but marked by severe cleavage on the principle of state responsibility for injury to aliens and their property and unanticipated disagreement on the actual limit of territorial seas.

In 1931 the League of Nations adopted procedures for future efforts to transform international law.[2] The new procedures thoroughly integrated governments into the process of selecting and preparing topics while relying on committees of experts to advance draft conventions that states could judge as potential permanent obligations.

The Charter of the United Nations further refined the League's procedures by providing for the General Assembly to encourage "the progressive development of international law and its codification," in Article 13(1)(a). During its second session the General Assembly created a subsidiary body called the International Law Commission (ILC) to assist in this duty.[3] Unimpeded by the great changes and controversies affecting its parent, the General Assembly, and many of its specialized siblings in the UN family, the ILC has an enviable series of accomplishments to its credit. After some early distractions, it prepared detailed drafts that were to become the 1958 Geneva Conventions on the Law of the Sea, the 1961 Vienna Convention on Diplomatic Relations, the 1963 Vienna Convention on Consular Relations, and the 1969 Vienna Convention on the Law of Treaties.[4] Remarkably, half a century has seen the international codification movement come from a condition of virtual self-destruction to one in which success seems almost to have been inevitable.

The codification movement need not be viewed as coherent in content and compelling in consequence, as most writers assume it to be. More plausibly, several intellectual traditions competed for primacy throughout the movement's checkered history. There follows in this essay a brief characterization of three such traditions—continental, British, and American (not to be confused with a tradition often styled as "American" by its Latin American members)—which have dominated the codification movement since 1930. We then consider the appearance of these positions in deliberations of the "Committee of Seventeen"[5] as preferred strategies for meeting the requirements of Article 13(1)(a). The drafting of the ILC Statute is indeed the codification movement in microcosm.

Explication of the Statute's major provisions also serves as a platform from which to observe the subsequent trajectory of the ILC. Simply stated, these two intellectual traditions, with their Procrustean tendencies, canceled each other out in the Committee of Seventeen, allowing the remaining, pragmatically inclined tradition identified with American writers to shape the Statute's contents. What results we will find to be procedurally permissive and organizationally pliable enough to allow the ILC to take advantage of opportunities long heralded but never tapped by the codification movement in its previous incarnations. At the same time, the Statute prefigures a significant change in the character of international codification made possible by the fact that the ILC's place is secure and its work admired. This development is integrally related to the widely observed phenomenon of global bureaucratization but is nevertheless unanticipated in the intellectual traditions guiding the codification movement and, even today, remains virtually unrecognized (see the concluding section of this essay).

Some terminological clarifications are in order before we proceed with the interpretation just outlined. International codification, in its most general meaning, relates to a collection of activities—retrieving and writing down existing law in an orderly fashion and, where necessary, reconciling inconsistencies and filling gaps, all for the purpose of reducing that law to a simpler, more accessible form. Consistent with this general meaning, codification can also involve a more radical reduction of many laws to a few underlying principles applicable to a variety of situations previously regulated individually, or the revision of existing rules, for the purpose of rationalizing the law.[6]

The second, more restricted meaning of codification differentiates it from development, the latter corresponding to those activities other than restatement encompassed by the term *codification* in its larger meaning. If codification is merely restatement, then it need not require official sanction or assistance, and final disposition has no effect at all on the legal status of restated rules.

A restatement, however, may supplant the melange of rules it restates if procedures exist for it to do so. This is typically the case in the history of municipal codification, in which a drafting of the restatement is undertaken by instruction of appropriate public officials with the expectation that the results will take a legislated form and thus acquire extrinsic authority. Some early proponents of international codification even saw privately initiated restatements as a means of prompting the emergence of a global legislative technique, despite the fact that municipal experience with codification is closely associated with a strengthening executive.[7] In the absence of global legislative machinery, the technique for supplanting existing law with restated law lies with opening multilateral conventions for ratification.

Codification can therefore mean (1) restatement, (2) restatement become law, or (3) restatement combined with innovative elements not intended to become law or prevented from becoming law. For our purposes, given that codification is a term of general import, we call restatement alone "reductive law exposition" and restatement become law "reductive law creation." Deliberately introduced innovations in the law, when they stand alone, stand apart from codification by any conception.

It should be evident that the terminology adopted here is not consistent with the UN Charter and ILC Statute. The phrase "the progressive development of international law and its codification" is synonymous with codification in its more general meaning.

We would be mistaken to attach great significance to the wording of the Charter, to which the Statute's definitions are necessarily tied. The drafting history of Article 13(1)(a) strongly suggests that the language found there is an artifact of diplomatic interaction and not the result of careful drafting.[8] The working nomenclature in draft materials before the Dumbarton Oaks meetings (1944) and during the San Francisco Conference (1945) referred to development and revision of international law. The alternative formula, progressive development and codification, was chosen in the end to sound somewhat less radical in spirit. The emphasis throughout had been on upgrading the law rather than on merely digesting it.

Legal scholarship often contrasts, perhaps unduly, Anglo-American and continental schools of law.[9] Their stance toward codification—namely, hostility and attachment respectively—presumably marks their differences.[10] We should not be misled by the fact that the first great advocate of codification was an Englishman, Jerry Bentham, and that the first great critic of the idea on the grounds of law's organic character was a German, Friedrich Karl von Savigny. It is specifically the organic relation of the common-law system of justice to the growth of law that is widely believed to prevent codification in any other sense than reductive exposition unless lawmaking techniques are greatly altered. The choice is to substitute legislation for the common law or to let the latter develop as it will. Enduring support for codification in continental legal thought derives from its long-standing positivist tendencies, which reached their ascendancy in the half-century prior to the world wars. This predilection is strengthened by the recognition that codification on Napoleon's grand scale contributed to political modernization in a number of countries.

If the peculiar character of the "genius" of common law inhibits its codification, that inhibition is far greater for British than for American lawyers. The United States has had a long and varied experience with municipal codification, enabled by the federal principle and consequent multiplicity of jurisdictions within which to codify. But Britain has had no such experience. Nor is there an Anglo-American view of the nature of international law.[11] American scholarship, which has a heritage of pragmatism and legal realism, tends to place considerations of process and context over the content of rules.

The British—far more so than writers from the United States—perceive international law, so much of it customary in origin, as analogous to common law. The absence of effective legislative procedures makes international law, if anything, more resistant even than common law to conscious development. Furthermore, success, if it is possible, brings with it the danger of freezing the law in place. By finding little that is analogous between municipal and international contexts and legal processes, the American view accepts in its own limited terms the opportunities to improve international law uniquely presented by its notorious substantive and institutional underdevelopment. The League's ill-fated experience with conscious law development reinforced already well-established Anglo-American differences. While Americans believed in remedying organizational deficiencies manifest in that experience, for the British long-suspected conceptual flaws in the whole idea of international codification stood confirmed.

For their part, continental writers brought to the international codification movement before 1930 a mood of optimism and a simple conception of method. They generally felt that international law could be consciously developed in a relatively simple two-step sequence—officially sanctioned, expert preparation of a rationalized law followed by its adoption in multilateral form by international conference. Obviously these writers were impressed (and deceived) by the successes in just these terms registered by the Hague Conferences of 1899 and 1907 and the attendant illusion shared by writers in all schools that multilateral conventions were analogous to legislation. The product of such legislation would be a great code promulgated in regular segments without the passage of exceptional periods of time. For continental writers, the main problem was to determine which areas of international law were best suited for treatment and to order them in a long-term program of work.[12]

Even more than in Europe, the tradition of a great code embodying overarching principles of a reconstituted law animated Latin American proponents of the codification movement.[13] Regional differences aside, Latin American, American, and continental ideas bore more in common with each other than did any of them with the British position. Latin Americans were perhaps most concerned with developing principles, continentals with laying out bodies of positive law, and Americans with organizing all such activities. Of them all, the Americans were least interested in doctrinal considerations; but, for all that, they were no closer to their common law brethren, to whom we now turn.

Among the early and more lucid expositions of the British position is P. J. [Noel-]Baker's much-cited article, which begins by differentiating between codification and legislation "in accordance with the best British opinion."[14] Specifically, differences in meaning pointed to differences in purpose and technique.

The purpose of codification is of course to improve not the substance but the form of the law, to make its rules easier to understand and apply, not to alter the rules themselves. It is to improve the form of the law by getting rid of apparent ambiguities or conflicts, by bringing customary law and statutory law together into one coherent and consistent whole, and thus to clarify the obligations of the subjects of the law without adding to or diminishing those obligations.

The method of codification is likewise quite different from that of legislation in that it is necessarily a work for professional lawyers alone. It can only be carried through by the intensive study by commissions of lawyers of existing rules, statutes, custom, practice, decisions of courts, etc. On the basis of such studies the lawyers reduce their conclusions to writing for the acceptance of the law-making authority in substitution for existing law.[15]

Finally, Baker found a difference in the results of codification and legislation. The results of codification were negligible because "an adequate legal basis of existing rules" upon which to build a code simply did not exist.[16] Legislation was more promising because it did not rely on existing rules.[17]

In 1946 Sir Cecil Hurst read before the Grotius Society a paper that reexamined the British view, especially with regard to techniques and results. Hurst's primary argument concerned the effect of convention-making conferences on attempts at codification.

The two processes, that of scientific determination of the law and that of achieving the adoption for rendering the law so defined and determined binding on States, get mixed up together. No matter how well the preparatory work for the conference in the way of scientific investigation and determination of existing law is done, the moment the Government Delegates assemble and decide to conclude a Convention to render the rules so defined binding on States, their efforts are directed to laying down the law as it ought to be and not as it is. This is precisely what happened at the Codification Conference of 1930.[18]

By means of a strict construction of the codification/legislation dichotomy regarding technique, Hurst's immensely influential paper refocused the British view on results. In the Baker interpretation, the nature of international law made codification impractical. In Hurst's interpretation, however, *corruption of technique* had confounded previous attempts at codification. International codification was nonetheless practical so long as the results of a scientific determination of law stood as such. Hence Hurst recommended the creation of national study groups working in coordination with "some central scientific organisation" to deal solely with codification.[19]

Hurst's reinterpretation of the feasibility of codification made an immediate impact on British thinking. The so-called McNair Report to the 1947 Conference of the International Law Association followed the traditional

British view with respect to meanings, purposes, and techniques and explicitly seconded Hurst's proposed program.[20]

Perhaps the most notable articulation of the American position is that of Elihu Root. Root established the need for international codification, which he understood as conscious law development, by pointing out the differences between international and municipal law.

It is curious that codification should be especially necessary in a system of law which is based on custom more exclusively even than municipal law; but that is necessarily so in the case of the law of nations, because there are no legislatures to make the law and there are no judicial decisions to establish by precedent what the law is.[21]

In this context, not only was the necessity of codification clearly established, but its function was indicated as well.

To codify international law is primarily to set in motion and promote the law-making process itself in the community of nations in which institutional forms appropriate for the carrying on of such a process have become so vague, indistinct, uncertain, and irregular that they could hardly be said to exist at all.[22]

If the point of codification was to set lawmaking in motion, then the British distinction between codification and legislation was patently irrelevant.

For Root, reduction and innovation were inextricable elements in a greater process, that of guiding the development of international law. This is the point on which British and American views were diametrically opposed. Because the British did not wish to see the law consciously shaped as law, they maintained a sharp distinction between reduction by exposition and innovation by law-creation, thereby severely limiting the possibility of direct influence by either of these isolated processes on the development of the law. Because an American like Root did wish to see the development of the law consciously shaped, he cast attention on law-creation, combining reductive and innovative elements in such proportion as best satisfied this ambition.

Root recognized that the "codifier's task" was an undertaking too abstract in nature to be of immediate value to governments.[23] Consequently, this work could not be left in the hands of governments, which had neither the time nor the interest to pursue it properly. Instead, preparations for the conscious development of international law had to come from other sources, where interest was deep and sustained. At the same time, approval of governments was essential if such efforts were to mean anything. After private initiative had resulted in the necessary preparations, governments could signify their approval by assenting to international conventions embodying draft texts. Other American writers spelled these themes out in greater detail.[24]

To assist the General Assembly in acting on Article 13(1)(a), the Secretariat in 1947 prepared a policy memorandum on "Methods for Encouraging the

Progressive Development of International Law and Its Eventual Codification."[25] This report, which was adopted by the Committee of Seventeen
as one of its bases of discussion, followed Hurst's argument for codification
by means of restatement. Whereas the convention method was described
as having "many drawbacks when it is considered as a method for securing
general agreement on general rules and principles of international law,"
restatements were "a useful step in promoting international agreement with
regard to the formulation of certain rules of international law which may
lead to their eventual codification in an international convention. . . . If
such restatements, possessing no governmental authority, were to be drawn
up by a committee of jurists functioning under the imprimatur of the
United Nations, they might serve as a useful guide to statesmen and judges."[26]
The striking resemblance of this argument to that of Hurst is no accident.
The chief of the Secretariat division responsible for it, Yuen-li Liang, was
an acknowledged advocate of Hurst's position.[27]

The Committee of Seventeen was exposed to the British view from a
more direct source. The British member of the committee, James L. Brierly,
commanded a position of influence as rapporteur. Brierly took a leading
role in the committee's deliberations, hewing close to the British position
as modified by Hurst, which he summarized in the following terms:

(a) Codification is a scientific and not a political task. (b) The method for drawing
up international conventions, as employed by the League of Nations, is appropriate
for international legislation but not for codification. (c) A small committee of personal
experts would be required. (d) The result of the work of these experts would be
binding on no one, neither on the governments of Members of the United Nations
nor on any tribunal. The authority of the work done by this small committee of
experts would be based solely on its intrinsic merits. (e) This, however, would not
exclude the possibility of giving at a later date a higher authority to the work . . . ,
but it would be preferable to leave this question open for the time being.[28]

Brierly and the British view were challenged point by point by the Soviet
representative, Vladimir M. Koretsky. Soviet doctrine was an unrestrained
version of the historic continental approach, which followed from Soviet
insistence, especially at that time, on treaties as the only valid source of
international obligations. Koretsky attacked the idea of a small body of
experts.

The task of progressive development of international law and its codification is
entrusted by Article 13(a) [sic] of the Charter to the General Assembly itself. If
this task should be entrusted to a Committee of Experts, this would seem to be
imitative of the old custom of isolating those who have to determine the will of
the people. In my opinion there is no need for an Olympic oracle endowed with
greater powers than governments themselves.[29]

Finally, on the question of results, Koretsky argued that "rules resulting
from the work of codification must . . . become generally obligating rules,

but this can only be achieved by the method of concluding multilateral conventions."[30]

Because their positions were consistent, thorough, and irreconcilable, Brierly and Koretsky were the focus of much debate in the Committee of Seventeen. Nevertheless, a compromise was reached and eventually embodied in the ILC Statute. The question of meanings was settled in favor of the British view. Contrary to Soviet preferences, however, a separate commission of experts was created, but it was twice the size preferred by the British; it was obliged to consult governments, and, most important, the question of the independence of its members was left in abeyance. This hybrid of techniques implied nothing certain about the form of results. Provision was made for both possibilities—scientific restatement and multilateral convention-making—with the choice to reside with the Commission itself. In short, the standoff between British and Soviet doctrine enabled a pragmatic solution, which was indeed a part of the American tradition of pragmatism.

The American view offered no middle ground on the question of meanings. Consequently, the Charter formulation sustaining the British view was adopted, but at the price of irrelevance to the Commission's activities. While it is true that the ILC Statute designates separate procedures for codification and progressive development, the substantive differences between them disappear on inspection and in the Commission's subsequent practice. It was the American view that prevailed in matters of technique. As representative of the United States, Philip C. Jessup proposed to the Committee of Seventeen that a commission of experts should provisionally be established for three years. Its members should be "persons of outstanding competence in the field of international law," to be selected either by governments or through a procedure similar to that by which judges are elected to the International Court of Justice.[31]

Although Jessup felt that codification and progressive development deserved separate procedures for their realization, these dual procedures, envisaged by stages, would be substantially interchangeable. In both instances the Commission would initiate work, enlist cooperation from other expert groups and prepare a draft text to be submitted to governments for comments and then revised for transmittal "to the General Assembly for action thereon either by resolution of the General Assembly; by the adoption of a convention to be submitted to governments for ratification; or by simple authorization of publication of the report."[32] The Commission could thus draw on a modest repertory of techniques.

The dual procedures for the progressive development of international law and its codification, finally presented in Articles 16 through 23 of the ILC Statute, share an American pedigree but broader parentage in the procedure for conscious law development adopted by the League in 1931.[33] All three procedures utilize an autonomous body of legal experts who must remain closely informed on the views of states on the topics under consideration. In the case of the League procedure, once a state initiates and the Assembly approves an activity, a committee of experts "will make necessary enquiries." In the case of progressive development in the UN design, once activity has been initiated on a topic, a questionnaire soliciting relevant information from states is circulated for the ILC. Finally, in the case of codification, once activity has been initiated, states are requested to provide the Commission with relevant information. In every instance that the expert body completes a draft on the basis of information so received, the process of securing the comments of states is repeated, although in the League procedure, approval of the Assembly comes first. All three procedures then provide for revision of the preliminary draft on the basis of these comments and for the submission of the final draft to the Assembly or General Assembly.

The need to reconcile scholarly detachment with governmental participation in conscious law development dictates a particular sequence of activities, which are twice stated in the ILC Statute for reason of formal completeness. There are, however, two major differences in the Commission's procedures for progressive development and codification, and they occur at the beginning and end of these procedures. In the instance of progressive development, initiation of work lies with the General Assembly or with states or other agencies upon approval of the General Assembly. Although their interests are directly affected by what topics *are* selected, states are infrequently motivated to do the selecting. A role for the General Assembly follows almost inevitably. In the instance of codification, legal criteria for selecting topics acquire proportionately greater weight. As a consequence, initiation of the reductive procedure is a function of the ILC, with priorities to be determined by the General Assembly.

The differences in the two procedures are a good deal clearer at the point of initiation than at their termination. These differences also point to the question of the proper form for the results of conscious law development. With respect to work undertaken in the name of progressive development, the ILC is instructed to transmit its final draft to the General Assembly with a recommendation on the final disposition of the text. Nothing is stipulated about the nature of these recommendations. With respect to the final draft of codificatory texts, however, Article 23 outlines the four kinds of accompanying recommendations that the ILC may make to the General Assembly:

- To take no action, the report having already been published;
- To take note of or adopt the report by resolution;
- To recommend the draft to members with a view to the conclusion of a convention;
- To convoke a conference to conclude a convention.

Two of these possibilities definitely provide for the reduction of law by exposition (restatements), and two provide for reductive law creation (conventions).

The ILC is generally referred to as an independent body of legal experts. Article 2 of the Statute supports this view by providing that members "shall be persons of recognized competence in international law." Article 8 also presents confirming evidence: "At the election the electors shall bear in mind that the persons to be elected to the Commission should individually possess the qualifications required and that in the Commission as a whole representation of the main forms of civilization and of the principal legal systems of the world should be assured." Observe that while the Statute is amply concerned with the expertise of the Commission's members, there is no explicit reference to independent status. It must be inferred. For example, Briggs stated that "the requirement of Article 8 that representation of the main forms of civilization and of the principal legal systems of the world shall be assured in the Commission as a whole is a clear indication of the General Assembly's decision that members of the International Law Commission, like the judges of the International Court of Justice, shall not be regarded as representatives of States."[34] In like manner, Rosenne remarked that "as in the case of members of the Court, and by the combined effects of Articles 2, 8, and 9 of the Statute, the members of the Commission sit in their individual capacity, and not as representatives of their government."[35]

But the actual procedure for selecting members of the Commission was designed to evade meaningful commitment in the Statute on the question of their independence. Article 3 prescribes that "members of the Commission shall be elected by the General Assembly from the list of candidates nominated by the Governments of State Members of the United Nations." Other articles go on to outline the conditions under which nominations are made. According to Rosenne, the ILC's election procedure is a debased version of the procedure for electing judges to the ICJ. As such, it "represents the abandonment of objective scientific criteria as the primary consideration in the choice of individual members of the Commission and the application of more pronounced political criteria—the General Assembly being itself an exclusively political body."[36] In short, the ILC procedure does not ensure the independence of the Commission's members in the same manner as it is ensured for the Court's judges. Undoubtedly the best hope for independence in either instance is the integrity of competent personnel, on the assumption that independence and competence are correlative qualities of mind. No instrument can guarantee such qualities.

If early sessions established a climate of independence in the Commission, the professional affiliation of members has shifted over three decades. Members with scholarly careers and no concurrent governmental duties have markedly declined in number. New states, as they become better represented in the ILC, send proportionally fewer scholars, if only because they have fewer to draw on.[37] But this explains only part of the decline. The United States, for example, has access to an abundance of scholarly resources. Yet its last two members have also been government officials during their terms of service—increasingly the norm for the Commission. This condition, fully expressing the possibilities contained in the Statute, could be held up as an ideal and not the contradiction in terms (government official versus independent scholar) that it appears to be. Members see themselves as independent and uninstructed because, practically speaking, no one else from their own governments is competent to issue instructions. In fact, many members are the self-same officials who would write instructions if there were any.

Members who work in governments are a significant asset to the Commission in its own eyes. They are likely to serve their governments in the General Assembly's Sixth Committee, which passes on the Commission's work, and in the international conferences called to render ILC drafts in a form suitable for ratification. Given their investment in the Commission's work, it is reasonable to expect that members will take considerable pains to see that all goes well. Clearly, ILC members are part of a tight community of foreign ministry legal personnel who dominate the intricate world of lawmaking. An organizational, or what we have called the American, approach to international codification works as well as it does precisely because this community administers it at every stage. Indeed, the Statute contributes to the community's informal organization and functioning. The consequent blurring of formal role designations is not to be confused with the well-known phenomenon of politicization in the UN system. The presence of governmental personnel does not automatically mean an intrusion of politics in presumably technical activities. Arguably, it lessens the chance that the Commission will be seen as politically irresponsible and an easy target for politicization in the rawest sense.

Long before the ILC was born, at a time when "international legislation" was an organizing metaphor, Max Weber observed that codification (referring, of course, to municipal experience) marks the bureaucratic rationalization of legal orders. As foreign ministries bureaucratize, their need for a rationalized and professionally administered body of law increases at least proportionally, if not exponentially. The conscious development of international law by lawyer-bureaucrats follows upon the earlier phase of scholars and statesmen occupying distinct roles in a less mature legal order.[38] International codification is paradoxically ever more technical, as it is removed from the domain of those whose political disinterest is presumably guaranteed by their private status. The paradox disappears with recognition that conscious law development is becoming a closed system of activity that governments alone can foster and which alone need to have undertaken. Politics and private concerns are equally irrelevant.

Any progress, at whatever stage of formality, contributes to and draws from the bureaucratic milieu of which the ILC's members partake. Law develops dynamically in relation to what the Commission does, not by reference to conclusive texts ultimately acceptable to states as formal obligations. To borrow a metaphor, the Commission is a medium of development in which its deliberations as much as its determinations are the message.

Seen in this light, recent discussions about the Commission's inadequacies seem misplaced.[39] Concern for the fact that the ILC takes so long in its work mistakenly assumes that only the products of such labors matter.

Concern that states choose not to ratify such products when they duly reach final form also mistakes the relation of medium to message.[40] The consequences of unremitting participation by government officials in extended, detailed discussions of successive drafts compel gradual ingestion of their contents. Belief that the drafting process could be expedited and the ratification problem solved if the Commission undertook restatements not only exhumes the distinction between codification and progressive development but misapprehends the value of their respective textual forms as well.[41] Restatements are cheapened by the very fact that they are easier to draft, because governments do not anticipate their adoption as formal instruments. Potential draft conventions, even if they fail to get beyond the drafting stage, require governments to participate in their formulation with complete attention to the diverse implications of possible adoption. Suggestions that the Commission meet for longer sessions or become a full-time body appear to make sense from a bureaucratic point of view but actually overlook the role of ILC members in a larger network of lawyer-bureaucrats populating foreign ministries and the UN. These roles would have to be shorn in order to boost the rate at which work is produced.

The fact that criticisms of the ILC are easy to refute may obscure a deeper problem, one that is perhaps more conspicuous in the constitutional order of a modern state like the United States. Described as pluralism and defended as the free play of interest groups, the political process as it has evolved in the United States permits legislative enactment of only the vaguest guidelines for public policy. Pluralism depends on bureaucracy for its administration.[42] The rise of bureaucratic regulation is indeed a progressive substitution of individual rulings covering specific situations for rules that are general in form but specific enough in content to cover those same situations. While legislative enactments may purport to direct the behavior of subjects of the legal order, they are actually working instructions to bureaucrats. Rulings proliferate into an unruly mass, undercutting the comparability and accountability presumably guaranteed by the rule of law. In effect, administrative order, enabled by permissive legislation, replaces legal order. The presence of lawyers and the persistence of legal forms mask the real character of the change.

The international legal order lacks the constitutional and legislative paraphernalia of advanced pluralist orders, but it nevertheless displays the same tendency for rules of general or generalizing import to fall before rule-like formulae concocted to suit bureaucratic need and circumstance. The latter seem less like rules when we find that their origin, subject, and consequence merge. They are nothing more than factual summaries of deals struck and problems solved, codified for future reference. Here codification has a minimalist meaning, more akin to the place of articulation in converting customary practices into law than to the conscious development of law. If law is forthcoming, it must be seen as a by-product of administrative routinization and then only insofar as this kind of activity acquires predictive value. The ILC appears to be identifying rules as law when indeed it is ruling on fact summaries. These activities can be reconciled if factual conditions and relations hold still long enough for rulings to cumulate as rules. If instead the Commission finds facts constantly changing and cannot fix them in place for long, then its ceaseless quest for law serves the ordering of administrative practices at the expense, but also in the name, of legal order.

The Commission's bureaucratically defined activities stand at the core of contemporary international codification. Other activities, being peripheral and episodic, also fit into the codification movement's complex evolution. More than a decade of arduous discussions under UN auspices produced in 1982 a multilateral convention on the Law of the Sea. Why this cycle of preparation and conference negotiation was conducted outside of existing codificatory machinery casts light on the ILC's drift toward bureaucratic rationalism. Politically sensitive ocean issues not settled at the codificatory conferences in 1930, 1958, and 1960 were thereafter compounded and intensified. The return of the Commission to these issues would have condemned it to unending travails, insurmountable obstacles, and certain politicization. That same fate was happily avoided when the UN also devised an alternative ad hoc mechanism to prepare what were to become the Principles of Friendly Relations and Cooperation Among States. As an articulation and reorientation of principles found mostly in Chapter I of the UN Charter, work on this subject revived the long-standing Latin American dream, taken up by the international community's newer and less privileged members everywhere, of restructuring the international legal order. A necessary preliminary to the current push for a new international economic order and preeminently a matter of high politics, the conscious (re)development of principles proceeded in political arenas unhampered by considerations of the ILC's special history and place. Other such reversions to the codification movement's earlier preoccupations are bound to crop up occasionally. They are important in fostering a larger public awareness that there should be more to law than can be discerned in the successively more detailed drafts of industrious and obscure lawyer-bureaucrats, however useful administratively these never-finished codes might prove to be.

NOTES

Parts of this essay, in substantially abbreviated form, are drawn from my doctoral dissertation, "The Conscious Development of International Law," Johns Hopkins University (1967). I am grateful for this belated opportunity to acknowledge publicly dissertation support from the Woodrow Wilson National Fellowship Foundation. I also wish to thank Larman C. Wilson and Fritz Kratochwil for their critical assistance.

1. On the history of the international codification movement, see "Historical Survey of the Development of International Law and Its Codification by International Conferences," UN Doc. A/Ac.10/5, reprinted in 41 *American Journal of International Law* 29 (Supp., 1947), and Dhokalia, *The Codification of Public International Law* 3–133 (1970).

2. Reprinted as Appendix 11 in "Historical Survey," at 110.

3. Resolution 174 (II), 21 November 1947; ILC Statute annexed thereto. The ILC consists of 25 members (initially 15, later 21, and the current number since 1961), each from a different state but not formally representing those states. Members are elected for five-year terms, with seats carefully distributed among representatives from the world's regions and legal cultures. The Commission meets for ten weeks each spring in Geneva, and its work is debated each fall by the General Assembly's Sixth (Legal) Committee. For detailed treatments of the ILC's Statute, working methods and institutional relations, see Briggs, *The International Law Commission* (1965); Dhokalia at 147–350; Ramcharan, *The International Law Commission* (1977).

4. Conveniently assembled, along with the ILC's Statute, in the UN Office of Public Information, *The Work of the International Law Commission*, Annexes (rev. ed., 1972).

5. Officially known as the Committee on the Progressive Development of International Law and Its Codification.

6. See also Thirlway, *International Customary Law and Codification* 12–13 (1972), on definitions and distinctions.

7. Weber, *On Law in Economy and Society* 256–283 (1954).

8. Rosenne, "The International Law Commission 1949–1959," *British Yearbook of International Law* 109–110 (1960).

9. Lauterpacht, "The So-Called Anglo-American and Continental Schools of Thought in International Law," 12 *British Yearbook of International Law* 31 (1931).

10. See, illustratively, Pound, *Jurisprudence* 673–677, 705–738 (1959).

11. Higgins, "Diverging Anglo-American Attitudes to International Law Introductory Statement," 2 *Georgia Journal of International and Comparative Law* (Supp. 2, 1972).

12. The classic exposition of the continental position, still a monument to scholarship, is De Visscher, "La codification du droit international," 6 *Recherches des cours* 329–452 (1, 1925).

13. Over a period of decades the prolific Chilean jurist, Alejandro Alvarez, consistently placed an architectural emphasis on principles. See, for example, *La codification du droit international* (1912); *Le droit international nouveau dans ses rapports avec la vie actuelle des peuples* (1959).

14. Baker, "The Codification of International Law," 5 *British Yearbook of International Law* 41 (1924). The British position can be traced back much earlier—for example, to British proposals leading to the program of the 1908–1909 London Naval Conference. See "Historical Survey," at 44.

15. Baker, at 43–44.

16. *Id.* 52.

17. Baker was never clear on whether he conceived of codification as reductive law exposition or creation. While the work of codification was to be converted into conventions, this was evidently different from the "quasi-legislative process of general conventions" because no *new* obligations were involved. *Id.* 64.

18. Hurst, "A Plea for the Codification of International Law along New Lines," 32 *Tr. Grotius Society* 147 (1946).

19. *Id.* 153.

20. "Report of the Committee on the Development and Formulation of International Law," A. D. McNair, Rapporteur, *International Law Association Report of Forty-Second Conference Prague 1947* at 83. Membership of this committee was dominated by Britons, including Brierly, Lauterpacht, Colombos, and McNair.

21. Root, "Should International Law Be Codified? And If So, Should It Be Done Through Governmental Agencies or Private Scientific Societies?" 9 *Proceedings of the American Society of International Law* 163 (1915).

22. Root, "The Function of Private Codification of International Law," 5 *American Journal of International Law* 579 (1911). See also Root, "The Codification of International Law," 19 *American Journal of International Law* 681 (1925).

23. Root, "The Function of Private Codification," at 581.

24. For example, James W. Garner, claiming to speak for "most Americans who favor codification," called for a piecemeal approach, thereby introducing the question of ripeness. His emphasis, though, was on a "practical mode of procedure" by which to develop selected topics. He observed that "intelligent codification requires a large amount of careful preliminary work which should be done by a select and relatively small number of jurists and technical experts. This preparatory work cannot be safely left to unwieldy conferences composed mainly of diplomats and statesmen." Garner noted "much sentiment in favor of the view that drafting experts should not be appointees or representatives of particular governments," but he appeared to view the matter pragmatically. See Garner, "Some Observations on the Codification of International Law," 19 *American Journal of International Law* 330-331 (1925).

25. UN Doc. A/AC. 10/7, reprinted in 41 *American Journal of International Law* 111 (1947).

26. *Id.* 115-116.

27. Liang, "The Progressive Development of International Law and Its Codification under the United Nations," 41 *Proc. Am. Soc. Int'l L.* 44-45 (1947).

28. UN Doc. A/AC.10/SR.2, at 5. Since UN speeches are rendered into third-person past tense in summary records, it is here rendered back into the first-person present tense in order to duplicate its original form. The next three quotations have also been changed. It must be remembered, however, that these speeches are not perfect verbatim records.

29. UN Doc. A/AC.10/SR.4, at 6-7.

30. UN Doc. A/AC.10/32, at 2. See also UN Doc. A/AC.10/SR.4. add. 1, at 3.

31. UN Doc. A/AC.10/14, at 1.

32. *Id.* 3.

33. The League's procedure, in turn, shows much in common with the standardized procedure for preparing general conventions (also adopted by the League in 1931) and with the International Labor Organization's 1926 guidelines for preparing conventions. Both sets of generalized procedures sought to establish a sequence of roles and responsibilities for states and international institutions involved in convention-making. Both are reprinted in "Historical Survey" at 97-98, 100-101.

34. See Briggs, at 63; see also *id.* 31-32.

35. See Rosenne, at 123. Article 9 provides for the General Assembly's election of ILC members.

36. See Rosenne, at 122. See also Dhokalia, at 172-173.

37. Lee, "The International Law Commission Reexamined," 59 *American Journal of International Law* 549 (1965).

38. See also Onuf, "Global Law-Making and Legal Thought," in Onuf, ed., *Law-Making in the Global Community* (1982).

39. See especially *id.* 64-85, 202-210, which also presents the views expressed in the ILC's debates over its program of work.

40. Also expressed by De Visscher, "Stages in the Codification of International Law," in Friedmann, Henkin, and Lissitzyn, eds., *Transnational Law in a Changing Society* 18 (1972).

41. The Commission itself rejected this possibility. See UN Doc. A/9010, para. 169 in 2 *Yearbook of the International Law Commission* 1973, at 260.

42. The argument here follows Lowi, *The End of Liberalism* 92–126 (2nd ed., 1979).

15. Increasing the Effectiveness of the International Court

Daniel G. Partan

It is now more than ten years since the International Court delivered what has appeared to some critics as the Court's most "political" and least worthy judgment. On July 18, 1966, by the narrowest of majorities, the Court dismissed Ethiopia's and Liberia's challenge to the racial policies imposed by South Africa under its League of Nations Mandate in South West Africa.[1] In the decade following its dismissal of the *South West Africa, Second Phase* cases, the effectiveness and the future of the Court have been widely debated, with many political and scholarly prescriptions for enhancing the effectiveness of the Court.[2] The General Assembly has extensively reviewed the "role" of the Court and has received numerous proposals for change, including many calling for amendment of the United Nations Charter and of the Statute of the Court.[3] Governments have sought, sometimes quietly and sometimes publicly, to increase the use and stature of the Court.[4] Scholars and scholarly associations have been active throughout, putting forward both general and specific proposals for restructuring the Court and for renewing its role in world affairs.[5] Thus there has been no lack of proposals, some spurious and some sound, arising from political and intellectual attention focused on the Court.

This introduction will review recent developments and will attempt to frame the major issues that must be faced in redesigning and in carrying forward the role of the Court. The concern here is to draw attention to fundamental issues, not to explore particular proposals. There is no expectation that the issues surrounding the Court will have early, or easy, solutions; the hope is, rather, that their articulation will lead to greater clarity and to more forthright consideration of the most difficult issues in the political debate that must precede meaningful change in the role and stature of the Court.

PARAMETERS OF THE COURT'S EFFECTIVENESS

The effectiveness of the International Court, like that of any international institution, must be examined in terms of the purpose and functions of the Court. At the risk of over-simplification, three functions of the International Court might be distinguished. First, the Court functions as a vehicle for the peaceful settlement of international disputes. Second, in articulating international law and applying that law to disputes brought before it, the Court exerts a major influence on the progressive development of international law. Third, in carrying out its dispute settlement and law development roles, the Court must balance claims for legal change against claims for the enforcement of established rights under traditional international law. Within broad limits, and subject to many intense differences of views as to their proper exercise, the three functions just stated would probably enjoy wide acceptance as a framework within which to define the Court's role and measure its effectiveness. The discussion that follows begins with the peaceful settlement function, but combines consideration of the law development function with consideration of the Court's role in balancing tradition and change.

THE PEACEFUL SETTLEMENT OF INTERNATIONAL DISPUTES

The framers of the United Nations Charter, and before them the framers of the League Covenant, viewed the International Court as having its principal role in the peaceful settlement of international disputes.[6] It is this role, from which in a sense the others flow, that the Court has suffered most in the decade following the *South West Africa, Second Phase* decision. United Nations Charter article 33, paragraph 1 includes judicial settlement as one of the means that "shall" be used "first of all" by the parties seeking settlement of dangerous disputes.[7] Article 36, paragraph 3 goes further in directing the Security Council to take into account that "legal disputes should as a general rule be referred by the parties to the International Court of Justice."[8] Article 92 makes the Court "the principal judicial organ of the United Nations,"[9] and article 94, paragraph 1 obligates each United Nations member to comply with decisions of the Court in any case to which it is a party.[10]

The most commonly used measure of "effectiveness" in the Court's peaceful settlement function has been frequency of successful use. By this measure, or even by the more objective test of simple frequency of use, the Court does not appear to be functioning effectively. In the ten years following the *South West Africa, Second Phase* decision, only five controversies have been brought to the Court by states,[11] and in three of the five the respondent governments declined to appear, having decided for themselves that the Court lacked jurisdiction.[12] Of the three controversies in which the respondent government declined to appear, one was decided by the Court, one was dismissed by the Court, and one was withdrawn by the applicant.[13] Thus there have been at most two cases in which it might be said that adjudication before the International Court contributed to peaceful settlement.[14]

Another possible measure of the Court's effectiveness in peaceful settlement might take into account the impact on the parties of potential resort to the Court in controversies not actually brought to the Court.

The presence of an option to litigate may affect the behavior of parties to an international dispute, but no study has been made of this postulated "subjective" peaceful settlement role of the Court, to establish in what cases parties have been more ready to reach a settlement than they would have been had the Court not been available.[15] It would be helpful for scholars and government representatives to address these issues as they review the experience of their countries with international adjudication.

Both measures of the Court's peaceful settlement effectiveness, the objective and the subjective measures, raise to a degree the threshold issue of acceptance of the Court's compulsory jurisdiction. In recent years, cases have been begun by application invoking the Court's jurisdiction under a pre-existing international agreement,[16] although states are also free to submit their disputes by special agreement.[17] If, as postulated above, it can be shown that the availability of an option to litigate facilitates dispute settlement, the willingness of states to accept the Court's jurisdiction may be taken as an independent index of the effectiveness of the court.[18] Considering present limitations on analysis and understanding of government dispute settlement behavior, the simple objective test of frequency of submission is likely for the present not to be the most useful measure of the Court's effectiveness. By this objective measure, success has not been great. It remains to ask why the Court has been so seldom used, and how its use might be increased. This question lies at the center of traditional analysis of the Court's failure. In recent General Assembly discussions,[19] government representatives voiced two general reasons for reluctance to rely more often on the Court: instead of adjudication, they favor broader, less concrete mechanisms as alternatives for dispute settlement; and they reject the existing or traditional international law that they feel the Court will apply in favor of a new law more responsive to the interests and needs of the newer countries.

Alternatives to adjudication have tended to be understated in discussions of the United Nations Sixth Committee, the Legal Committee, about the role of the Court. Delegates often speak generally of the need for negotiation, or of the wide range of freedom of choice available to states under the United Nations Charter.[20] More to the point, the Indonesian delegate has observed that "legal" and "political" disputes are often difficult to differentiate, so that acceptance of the Court's compulsory jurisdiction deprives states of control over the ultimate settlement of matters affecting their vital interests.[21] He saw in these two factors the central explanation of why states are more prone to utilize non-adjudicatory dispute settlement procedures.[22] References to a division between "legal" and "political" disputes tend to be a short-hand expression of the view that certain disputes are too important to be left to judges, at least in the present state of international law and international relations. As put by the British delegate, the reluctance of states to use the Court may have been due in part to lack of imagination or to timidity, but mostly it was "due to an excessive preoccupation with a narrow notion of national sovereignty."[23] Whatever the explanation, the fact is that states are seldom willing to submit disputes to adjudication.

This being so, the delegate of Romania suggested that, rather than review the role of the Court in isolation, the General Assembly would be better advised to consider all means of peaceful settlement together.[24] In this way the interrelationships between negotiation and judicial settlement, for example, might be clarified, and each procedure would be strengthened. Though not acted upon by the Assembly, the Romanian suggestion has indirectly become the approach taken by the General Assembly. The Assembly's formal review of the "role" of the Court has concluded, but its consideration of peaceful settlement procedures, including adjudication, continues as part of the Assembly's study of the Charter of the United Nations and of the strengthening of the role of the organization.[25] The reservations expressed by the Indonesian delegate about allowing the Court to adjudicate "political" issues may be rooted in a suspicion of the law that will be applied by the Court. A representative of India, among others, has noted that the new states are seeking to establish "a new international economic and political order based on equity and justice," and that the Court should "ensure that the law respond[s] to the requirements of international life."[26] The diversity that now characterizes the international community is often contrasted to the League period, when the system was composed of a much smaller number of countries that all espoused traditional international law. According to representatives of various countries, the new system, bringing together societies having different forms of civilization, different legal systems, and different levels of economic development, calls for a new law developed with full participation by all states, not just by the older European and American countries.[27]

The argument thus stated closes a circle around the Court. The Court cannot be used to its capacity for peaceful settlement until its law is adequate to the needs of new states and of the international community. The court's law, however, is in large measure developed through cases brought to it for peaceful settlement. Without cases, the Court cannot generate new law, and without new law, the Court will not be given the cases that it needs to develop the new law.

Can the circle be broken? Insofar as peaceful settlement is concerned, the answer seems to be probably not. When governments perceive that their needs, and the needs of the international community, are not well served by traditional international law, they are not likely to turn to a court, any court, that by its nature is expected to be more responsive to tradition than to change.[28] Fortunately for the International Court, its position does not altogether fit the dilemma just described for two reasons. First, the International Court need not always be a staunch supporter of tradition in the face of change. Second, the Court is not entirely dependent upon peaceful settlement as the source of its judicial custom; alternative sources exist and others can be developed that might provide the Court with the vehicle it needs to become an agent for change in international law. These matters are addressed in the sections that follow.

THE COURT AS ARBITER OF CHANGE

Some of the commentary quoted earlier challenged the Court to adapt itself and the law to the changing needs of the international community. For each such comment one might well find another admonishing the Court to respect established rights, thus providing the "anchor to windward" needed to protect justifiable expectations and to give stability to the law. All governments, of course, are interested both in stability and in change. The most dedicated proponents of the new international economic order, such as the sponsors of the effort to define "international economic development law,"[29] nevertheless rely on established law in most aspects of their relations with other governments. They call for redefinition of rights and duties only in contexts where it will reflect the changing interests of governments and the perceived needs of the international system. What is necessary is a better way of determining when situations have arisen that call for, or indicate, changes in substantive international law. If governments entrusted this role to it, the International Court could function as one such arbiter of change. In the past, the Court has been regarded as having a role in the progressive development of international law as well as in the peaceful settlement of disputes.[30]

Much of the business brought to the Court in the last decade has carried the Court well out towards the cutting edge of change, but it has often resisted the current. In the *North Sea Continental Shelf* cases,[31] although the Court did much to move forward the customary law of the continental shelf, it took rather a traditional view of the source and development of customary international law. Holding that the equidistance method of continental shelf delimitation had not become a part of customary law through state practice, the Court declared that the acts relied upon must not only amount to a settled practice, but that "they must also be such, or be carried out in such a way, as to be evidence of a belief that this practice is rendered obligatory by the existence of a rule of law requiring it."[32] In the *Fisheries Jurisdiction* cases,[33] the Court took modest steps towards validating preferential fishing rights of coastal states, but upheld the established "traditional fishing rights" of foreign flag distant-water fishermen at a time when state practice was moving rapidly towards the reservation to coastal states of as much of the "optimum yield" as their nationals are able to catch.[34] Referring to contemporaneous discussion of fisheries at the Third United Nations Conference on the Law of the Sea, the Court saw the conference proposals and preparatory documents as "manifestations of the views and opinions of individual States and as vehicles of their aspirations, rather than as expressing principles of existing law."[35] In the *Nuclear Tests* cases,[36] the Court turned aside an opportunity when it dismissed the cases as moot because the controversy no longer existed.[37] The Court's decision did develop new law regarding the legal effect of unilateral acts,[38] but avoided the issue of whether states, and their people, have a right under customary international law to be free from radioactive fall-out from atmospheric nuclear weapons tests. Taken together, the three cases illustrate important dimensions of the Court's potential role as an arbiter of legal change. First, the cases show what many would see as healthy judicial conservatism on the central issue of customary law development, sometimes called "proof of custom." The Court, in the *North Sea Continental Shelf* cases, adhered closely to traditional *opinio juris* requirements, and in the *Fisheries Jurisdiction* cases approached with extreme caution the contribution to customary international law of positions taken by governments at international meetings. In the *Nuclear Tests* cases, the Court broke new ground on the issue of unilateral declarations, but did so in the context of declining to reach a highly sensitive issue that would have drawn the Court into fundamental aspects of customary law development. The three cases thus make modest contributions in the field, but leave existing or traditional international law largely undisturbed.

Second, almost as a corollary of the first observation, the customary law development issues decided and left undecided in the three cases show the relatively primitive level reached by the international legal process. There has been in modern times little agreement either as to the continued validity of traditional approaches to customary law development or as to the effect on customary law of the work done and the decisions taken in modern international organizations.[39] These are central issues to which the Court must eventually turn and through which the Court will have an opportunity to shape its role as arbiter of legal change in the modern world.

The Court has missed its most recent opportunities to restructure its approach to customary law development, and there is no assurance that it will soon have another. When it does, there is also no assurance that the Court will take up the challenge and articulate a customary law development framework within which change can be balanced against tradition. Without such a framework there is little reason to expect governments to be willing to use the Court in the peaceful settlement of disputes. The circle is likely to remain closed, though now its dimensions can be stated more accurately: having no adequate theory to accommodate change in customary international law, the Court will be ignored in disputes turning on customary international law, which will, in turn, deprive the Court of opportunities to develop theories adequate to accommodate change in customary international law.

THE ROLE OF GOVERNMENTS

Although the Court may have the formal capacity to redefine the concept of customary international law, its determinations will only be significant if such changes are broadly acceptable to governments. Such changes in theory would have to be put into practice by governments in their ordinary dealings with other governments. In addition, governments could, by their control over the Court's jurisdiction, forestall a trend not to their liking. Sixth Committee discussion, although rarely reaching the detail that would be required for a restructuring of customary law,[40] in one respect moved beyond generalities to reach a basic issue of customary law development. During the concluding debate on the role of the Court, the Mexican delegate suggested referring in the Assembly's resolution to the need to amend article 38 of the Court's Statute to include resolutions and declarations of international organizations among the subsidiary means to be used by the Court for the determination of rules of law.[41] The Mexican delegate gave as his intention the rejuvenation of article 38, by asking the Court to take into account the declarations and resolutions of the General Assembly which he said were "unquestionably a reflection of the most recent developments in contemporary international law."[42] Several delegates opposed any tampering with article 38. The Soviet delegate stated flatly that resolutions and declarations were not sources of international law.[43] The British delegate stated that Assembly resolutions "might reflect or be evidence of developments in international law," but that "that was not the same as saying that General Assembly resolutions could themselves develop international law."[44] As a result, the redrafted Assembly resolution, adopted by consensus, said only that "the development of international law may be reflected, *inter alia*, by declarations and resolutions of the General Assembly, which may to that extent be taken into consideration by the International Court of Justice."[45]

Guidance from governments has thus been both conflicting and superficial. In view of the inadequate development of a theory of change in customary international law, probably nothing more substantial could have been expected. Yet governments should recognize that change in the law development process is urgently needed to bring the Court and its law back into the mainstream of dispute settlement. Given the cases, and aided by the reflections of scholars, the Court is fully capable of working out a theory of change and applying it to shape both customary law and its own role as arbiter of legal change. What is required from governments is basic political support for a theory of change in customary law and some guidance as to the general direction that should be taken.

Without undertaking to restructure the theory of customary law, debate and action in the Sixth Committee, for example, could have a positive effect. The Sixth Committee could hold an annual review of the work of the Court and the state of customary law in which governments could comment generally on the contributions of the Court and seek to develop a consensus on the need for change in the customary law process.

NEW CASES FOR THE COURT

If, without an adequate theory of change in customary law, prospects for a flow of "peaceful settlement" cases are not good, other kinds of cases might serve as an alternative vehicle for developing the necessary theory of change in customary law. Two chief possibilities come to mind: expansion of the Court's advisory jurisdiction; and opening the Court's jurisdiction to new classes of litigants.[46] These possibilities cannot be explored thoroughly here; they will be addressed solely from the standpoint of the need to generate for the Court cases through which the Court might fashion a theory of custom and establish for itself an effective role in the development of customary international law.

Expansion of the Court's advisory jurisdiction has most prominently taken the form of a proposal to permit international organizations, in addition to "organs of the United Nations and specialized agencies," to request advisory opinions "on legal questions arising within the scope of their activities."[47] A second major proposal would permit states to request advisory opinions on legal questions arising in disputes with other states or with international organizations.[48] In both cases, the change could be effected either by amendment of the Charter, or possibly through the establishment of a standing General Assembly committee empowered to request advisory opinions on application by states or by international organizations.[49]

Requests by international organizations for advisory opinions would normally center on the functions and powers of the organizations concerned and thus might seldom raise broader issues of customary international law. Such issues would not be ruled out, however.[50] The same is true of requests by states for advisory opinions. It has been suggested, however, that allowing states to obtain advisory opinions would diminish the prestige of the Court since states might then have recourse to the Court without undertaking to be bound by the results.[51] No such result has followed from the present advisory practice, and to the extent that the non-binding character of an advisory opinion would lead states to make greater use of the Court, the resulting increase in cases would serve the ends here discussed. In the case both of states and of international organizations, there is no basis for considering an advisory opinion as any less effective than a judgment in developing customary international law.

The extension of the Court's jurisdiction to new classes of litigants may be seen in the same light. If, for example, municipal courts were empowered to refer international law questions to the International Court for "preliminary decision" of international law issues,[52] the Court's opinion would be as effective for customary law development as it would be in any other case brought to the Court. There is, in addition, no basis for considering that the law-development effect of the Court's opinions would be diminished if the expansion of litigants were to be accomplished through the existing advisory opinion procedure rather than through amendments to the United Nations Charter and the Statute of the Court.

Three categories of new litigants might come before the Court either through the present advisory jurisdiction or under a wholly new head of jurisdiction. International organizations might simply be offered use of the Court's advisory jurisdiction. They might also be given access to the Court's "contentious" jurisdiction in cases brought by or against states or by or against other international organizations.[53] Article 34, paragraph I of the Statute of the Court presently limits the Court's "contentious" jurisdiction to states, but nothing in the present analysis would bar amendment of that article to permit international organizations as well as states to be parties in cases before the Court.[54] Access to the International Court for two other classes of new litigants would raise somewhat more complex problems, most of which would not be relevant here. Municipal courts might be authorized to seek "preliminary decision" of international law questions arising in their practice; and litigants in municipal court cases might be authorized to seek International Court review of international law questions decided by the municipal court of last resort.[55] In both cases, International Court review could be provided either through requests for advisory opinions or through a wholly new head of jurisdiction added by amendment to the Statute of the Court. The resulting increase in business for the Court would multiply the occasions on which the Court might have an opportunity to review basic issues in the development of customary international law, as well as increasing the opportunities for applicants to participate in the development of customary international law.

RENEWING THE ROLE OF THE INTERNATIONAL COURT

The decade of serious study that has followed from the International Court's *South West Africa, Second Phase* decision has not solved the "crisis of the Court," but may have brought about a better understanding of the Court's role and potential in international affairs. If, as postulated here, that role requires from the Court active involvement in the development of international law, the foremost task facing the Court is the fashioning of a framework within which the Court can balance the need for change in the law against the need for protection of rights enjoyed under traditional international law. The fashioning of such a framework, termed here a theory of customary law development, will be immensely complex and will require both affirmation by governments and close study by scholars. Only the most hesitant of beginnings has been made at the level of official thinking, but even that beginning is cause for hope. Having broached the subject, and perceiving dimly what may be required, perhaps governments, prodded by scholars, will explore the issues and help the Court to develop theory accommodating change and tradition in customary international law.

NOTES

1. Judgment on South West Africa, Second Phase, [1966] I.C.J. 6. Four years earlier the Court had sustained its jurisdiction, Judgment on South West Africa Cases, Preliminary Objections, [1962] I.C.J. 319, but in 1966, after extensive hearings on the merits, the Court dismissed the two cases, holding that the applicants had not established "any legal right or interest" in the subject matter of the dispute. [1966] I.C.J. at 51. Critics could see no justifiable distinction between the "jurisdiction" that the Court found present in 1962 and the "legal right or interest" found absent in 1966; and the 1966 dismissal was most often explained in political terms, as a product of the change in composition of the Court between 1962 and 1966, and of a change in the climate of the times. The two cases are the subject of a rich literature. R. FALK, THE STATUS OF LAW IN INTERNATIONAL SOCIETY 378 (1970);

M. KATZ, THE RELEVANCE OF INTERNATIONAL ADJUDICATION 69 (1968); J. STONE, OF LAW AND NATIONS 331 (1974); and articles and commentary cited by these authors.

2. The reader is referred to the following recent major works on the International Court of Justice: R. ANAND, STUDIES IN INTERNATIONAL AJUDICATION (1969); 1 & 2 THE FUTURE OF THE INTERNATIONAL COURT OF JUSTICE (L. Gross ed. 1976); C. JENKS, THE PROSPECTS OF INTERNATIONAL ADJUDICATION (1964); JUDICIAL SETTLEMENT OF INTERNATIONAL DISPUTES: AN INTERNATIONAL SYMPOSIUM (Max Planck Institute 1974); 1 & 2 S. ROSENNE, THE LAW AND PRACTICE OF THE INTERNATIONAL COURT (1965).

3. The General Assembly's Sixth Committee Review of the Role of the International Court of Justice began in 1970 and was concluded in 1974. 25 U.N. GAOR, Sixth Committee (1210th–18th, 1224th–26th, 1229th mtgs.) 189–237, 263–75, 285–91, U.N. Docs. A/C.6/SR. 1210–18, 1224–26, 1229 (1970); 26 U.N. GAOR, Sixth Committee (1277th–84th, 1293d–95th mtgs.) 173–221, 269–85, U.N. Docs. A/C.6/SR. 1277–84, 1293–95 (1971); 29 U.N. GAOR, Sixth Committee (1465th–1470th, 1486th, 1490th, 1492d mtgs.) 15–41, 133–35, 160, 166–70, U.N. Docs. A/C.6/SR. 1465–70, 1486, 1490, 1492 (1974). The Assembly's resolution, adopted at the close of the debate in 1974, makes no mention of amendments to the United Nations Charter or to the Statute of the Court. G.A. Res. 3232, 29 U.N. GAOR, Supp. (No. 31) 141, U.N. Doc. A/9631 (1974). The Assembly's 1974 resolution was limited to the following six recommendations: (1) that states study the possibility of accepting the Court's compulsory jurisdiction under article 36 of its Statute; (2) that states consider inserting in their treaties clauses providing for the submission of disputes over treaty interpretation or application to the Court; (3) that states keep under review the possibility of identifying cases in which use can be made of the Court; (4) that states consider using chambers established under articles 26 and 29 of the Statute of the Court; (5) that United Nations organs and specialized agencies consider submission of requests for advisory opinions to the Court; and (6) that recourse to judicial settlement of legal disputes, particularly referral to the International Court of Justice, should not be considered an unfriendly act between States.

4. For example, in 1970, United States Secretary of State Rogers said that the United States had asked Canada to submit to the Court the "differences arising from Canada's intention to establish pollution and exclusive fishing zones more than 12 miles from her coast," and that the United States was "presently exploring the possibility of submitting several other disputes to the Court." Address by William P. Rogers (Apr. 25, 1970), *reprinted in* 64 PROC. AM. SOC'Y INT'L. L. 285, 287 (1970). No submissions have followed from this announcement. See the 1976 study, U.S. DEP'T OF STATE, OFFICE OF THE LEGAL ADVISER, WIDENING ACCESS TO THE INTERNATIONAL COURT OF JUSTICE (1976) [hereinafter cited as WIDENING ACCESS], discussed at notes 45–54 *infra.*

5. *E.g.,* 1955 REPORT OF THE AMERICAN BRANCH OF THE INTERNATIONAL LAW ASSOCIATION, COMMITTEE ON THE CHARTER OF THE UNITED NATIONS 70–75 [hereinafter cited as 1955 U.N. CHARTER COMMITTEE REPORT]; 1972 REPORT OF THE AMERICAN BRANCH OF THE INTERNATIONAL LAW ASSOCIATION, COMMITTEE ON THE CHARTER OF THE UNITED NATIONS 142–69 [hereinafter cited as 1972 U.N. CHARTER COMMITTEE REPORT]; and the works cited at note 2 *supra.*

6. The consideration of the Court at San Francisco in 1945, and the role of the Court in the legal order of the United Nations, are briefly reviewed by Steinberger in JUDICIAL SETTLEMENT OF INTERNATIONAL DISPUTES, *supra* note 2, at 191.

7. Article 33, paragraph 1 refers to "any dispute, the continuation of which is likely to endanger the maintenance of international peace and security." The peaceful

settlement means listed are "negotiation, enquiry, mediation, conciliation, arbitration, judicial settlement, [and] resort to regional agencies or arrangements." U.N. CHARTER art. 33, para. 1.

8. U.N. CHARTER art. 36, para. 3. Article 36 deals generally with the role of the Security Council in bringing about the peaceful settlement of disputes likely to endanger international peace and security.

9. U.N. CHARTER art. 92.

10. U.N. CHARTER art. 94, para. 1. Paragraph 2 provides for "recourse to the Security Council" should any party fail "to perform the obligations incumbent upon it under a judgment rendered by the Court." U.N. CHARTER art. 94, para. 2.

11. The following are the five controversies: (1) the *North Sea Continental Shelf* cases, brought by separate special agreements between Denmark and the Federal Republic of Germany and between the Netherlands and the Federal Republic of Germany in 1967 and decided in 1969, Judgment on North Sea Continental Shelf, [1969] I.C.J. 3; (2) India's application against Pakistan concerning an *Appeal Relating to the Jurisdiction of the ICAO Council*, brought in 1971 and decided in 1972, Judgment on Appeal Relating to the Jurisdiction of the ICAO Council, [1972] I.C.J. 46; (3) the *Fisheries Jurisdiction* cases, brought by the United Kingdom and the Federal Republic of Germany against Iceland in 1972 and decided in 1974, Judgment on Fisheries Jurisdiction (United Kingdom v. Iceland), Merits, [1974] I.C.J. 3; Judgment on Fisheries Jurisdiction (Federal Republic of Germany v. Iceland), Merits, [1974] I.C.J. 175; (4) Pakistan's application against India concerning the *Trial of Pakistani Prisoners of War*, brought in May, 1973 and withdrawn in December of the same year, Order on Trial of Pakistani Prisoners of War, Interim Protection, [1973] I.C.J. 328; and (5) the *Nuclear Tests* cases, brought by Australia and New Zealand against France in 1973 and dismissed by the Court in 1974, Judgment on Nuclear Tests (Australia v. France), [1974] I.C.J. 253; Judgment on Nuclear Tests (New Zealand v. France), [1974] I.C.J. 457. A sixth case, the *Aegean Sea Continental Shelf* case, brought by Greece against Turkey in August, 1976, is at this writing the only case pending before the Court, Order on Aegean Sea Continental Shelf, Interim Protection, [1976] I.C.J. 3. For a discussion of the jurisdictional issues in this case, see Robol, *Limits of Consent—The* Aegean Sea Continental Shelf *Case*, 18 HARV. INT'L. L.J. 649 (1977).

Three requests for advisory opinions were submitted to the Court in the same period: (1) the *Namibia* case, submitted by the Security Council in 1970 and decided in 1971, Advisory Opinion on Legal Consequences for States of the Continued Presence of South Africa in Namibia (South West Africa) Notwithstanding Security Council Resolution 276 (1970), [1971] I.C.J. 16; (2) the *Application for Review of Judgment No. 158*, submitted by the General Assembly Committee on Applications for Review of Administrative Tribunal Judgments in 1972 and decided in 1973, Advisory Opinion on Application for Review of Judgment No. 158 of the United Nations Administrative Tribunal, [1973] I.C.J. 166; and (3) the *Western Sahara* case, submitted by the General Assembly in 1974 and decided in 1975, Advisory Opinion on Western Sahara, [1975] I.C.J. 12.

12. In the *Fisheries Jurisdiction* cases, Iceland informed the Court by letter that Iceland considered that the Court had no basis to exercise jurisdiction in the two cases under its Statute, and that, "considering that the vital interests of the people of Iceland were involved, [Iceland] was not willing to confer jurisdiction on the Court, and would not appoint an Agent." Order on Fisheries Jurisdiction (United Kingdom v. Iceland), Interim Protection, [1972] I.C.J. 12, 14; Order on Fisheries Jurisdiction (Federal Republic of Germany v. Iceland), Interim Protection, [1972]

I.C.J. 30, 32. In the *Nuclear Tests* cases, France informed the Court by letter that "it considered that the Court was manifestly not competent in the case, and that it could not accept the Court's jurisdiction. . . ." France declined to appoint an Agent and asked the Court to remove the cases from its list. [1974] I.C.J. 253, 255; [1974] I.C.J. 457, 458. In the case concerning the *Trial of Pakistani Prisoners of War*, India informed the Court by letter that India "declined to consent to the jurisdiction of the Court" and that without such consent the Court could not proceed since "there was no legal basis whatever for the jurisdiction of the Court in the case." [1973] I.C.J. 328, 329.

13. The Court decided the *Fisheries Jurisdiction* cases, [1974] I.C.J. 3; [1974] I.C.J. 175; and dismissed the *Nuclear Tests* cases [1974] I.C.J. 253; [1974] I.C.J. 457. In December 1973, noting that negotiations were being held with India, Pakistan requested discontinuance of the proceedings in the case concerning *Trial of Pakistani Prisoners of War*. [1973] I.C.J. 347, 348. India never appeared in the proceedings. *See* note 12 *supra*.

14. The *North Sea Continental Shelf* cases, submitted by special agreement in 1967, were decided in 1969 after full participation by the parties. [1969] I.C.J. 3. The *Appeal Relating to the Jurisdiction of the ICAO Council*, submitted by India in 1971, was decided in 1972 after full participation by Pakistan. [1972] I.C.J. 46. The *North Sea Continental Shelf* is the Court's outstanding success. Discussions held between the parties on the basis of the Court's 1969 judgment led to treaties signed in 1971 delimiting the continental shelf between the parties and fully settling the dispute. [1970-1971] I.C.J.Y.B. 117-26.

15. Mr. Rosenstock, speaking for the United States in the Sixth Committee, noted, without giving examples, that the existence of the Court not only afforded a solution when disputes could not be settled by negotiation, but also encouraged out-of-court settlement. 29 U.N. GAOR, Sixth Committee (1467th mtg.) 21-22, U.N. Doc. A/C.6/SR. 1467 (1974). Regarding Pakistan's withdrawal, *see* note 13 *supra*.

16. Of the six controversies listed at note 10 *supra*, only one, the *North Sea Continental Shelf* controversy, was submitted by special agreement. Jurisdiction in the other five was asserted under pre-existing agreements between the parties. *See* note 11 *supra*. Countries may make a general submission to the jurisdiction of the Court under the so-called "optional clause." I.C.J. STATUTE art. 36, para. 2. As of July 31, 1976, a total of 45 states had accepted the Court's jurisdiction under this provision. *Declarations Recognizing as Compulsory the Jurisdiction of the Court* [1975-1976] I.C.J.Y.B. 51. Countries may also submit to the Court's jurisdiction in advance of a particular dispute through treaties with other countries. The Court's Yearbooks contain a chronological list of treaty provisions vesting jurisdiction in the Court. *E.g., Chronological List of Other Instruments Governing the Jurisdiction of the Court* [1975-1976] I.C.J.Y.B. 82.

17. I.C.J. STATUTE art. 36, para. 1.

18. Conversely, of course, to the extent that states have not accepted the jurisdiction of the Court, there can be no pressure to settle from the threat of litigation.

19. *See* note 3 *supra*.

20. *E.g.*, statements by representatives of the German Democratic Republic, 29 U.N. GAOR, Sixth Committee (1470th mtg.) 38, U.N. Doc. A/C.6/SR. 1470 (1974); the Soviet Union, *id.* at 36-37; India, 29 U.N. GAOR, Sixth Committee (1467th mtg.) 18, U.N. Doc. A/C.6/SR. 1467 (1974). The delegate of the Federal Republic of Germany said that, notwithstanding his country's recent use of the Court, "direct means of bringing about agreement between parties to a dispute, namely negotiation

and compromise, remained the normal and ideal way of settling disputes." 29 U.N. GAOR, Sixth Committee (1470th mtg.) 39, U.N. Doc. A/C.6/SR. 1470 (1974).

21. 29 U.N. GAOR, Sixth Committee (1470th mtg.) 38–39, U.N. Doc. A/C.6/SR. 1470 (1974).

22. *Id.* A similar statement was made by the representative of India, 29 U.N. GAOR, Sixth Committee (1467th mtg.) 18–19, U.N. Doc. A/C.6/SR. 1467 (1974).

23. 29 U.N. GAOR, Sixth Committee (1468th mtg.) 29, U.N. Doc. A/C.6/SR. 1468 (1974).

24. *Id.* at 26–27.

25. The General Assembly has established a Special Committee on the Charter of the United Nations and on the Strengthening of the Role of the Organization, which, among other subjects, has considered the "means, methods and procedures for the peaceful settlement of international disputes," including the role of the International Court. G.A. Res. 3499, 30 U.N. GAOR, Supp. (No. 34) 52, U.N. Doc. A/10034 (1975). *See* U.N. SECRETARY-GENERAL, ANALYTICAL STUDY § II.B, at 53–63, U.N. Doc. A/AC.182/L. 2 (1976).

26. 29 U.N. GAOR, Sixth Committee (1467th mtg.) 18, U.N. Doc. A/C.6/SR. 1467 (1974). *See* statements by the representatives of Yugoslavia, *id.* at 23, and of Iraq, *id.* at 19.

27. *See* statements by the representatives of Italy, *id.* at 19–20; and Mexico, 29 U.N. GAOR, Sixth Committee (1470th mtg.) 38, U.N. Doc. A/C.6/SR. 1470 (1974).

28. A good example is the Canadian revision of its acceptance of the compulsory jurisdiction of the Court to exclude disputes concerning the actions taken by Canada to protect against the pollution of arctic waters. *Declarations Recognizing as Compulsory the Jurisdiction of the Court* [1970–1971] I.C.J.Y.B. 43, 48–49. Canadian Prime Minister Trudeau said at the time that Canada could not litigate vital issues in an area where the law was either inadequate or non-existent. Press Conference of Canadian Prime Minister Pierre Trudeau (Apr. 8, 1970), *reprinted in* 9 INT'L LEGAL MATS. 600–04 (1970). A Canadian note explained that the new reservation to Canada's acceptance of the Court's compulsory jurisdiction "does not in any way reflect lack of confidence in the court, but takes into account the limitations within which the court must operate and the deficiencies of the law which it must interpret and apply." Summary of Note from Canada to the United States (Apr. 16, 1970), *reprinted in* 9 INT'L LEGAL MATS. 607, 612 (1970).

29. For example, a working paper by the Philippines contained a Draft Convention on the Principles and Norms of International Economic Development Law, U.N. Doc. A/C.6/31/L. 7 (1976).

30. Law development was acknowledged to be a judicial function by the General Assembly in urging in 1947 that the Court be "utilized to the greatest practical extent in the progressive development of international law." G.A. Res. 171, U.N. Doc. A/519, at 103 (1947). *See* Steinberger, *supra* note 6.

31. [1969] I.C.J. 3.

32. *Id.* at 44. The Court thus carried forward the Permanent Court's *Lotus* case approach to custom, casting on the proponent of a restrictive rule the burden of showing the states following a concordant practice have "so acted because they felt legally compelled [to do so] . . . by reason of a rule of customary law." *Id.* at 44–45. The Court quoted from the Permanent Court's Lotus Case opinion the passage in which the Permanent Court said that the fact that states had abstained from instituting criminal proceedings in collision cases was not enough to show that they acted under compulsion of law. The Permanent Court said that "only if such abstention were based on their being conscious of having a duty to abstain would

it be possible to speak of an international custom." The S.S. Lotus, [1927] P.C.I.J., ser. A, No. 10, at 28.

33. [1974] I.C.J. 3; [1974] I.C.J. 175. The quotations that follow are taken from the Court's opinion in the United Kingdom case, [1974] I.C.J. 3.

34. [1974] I.C.J. 3, 31. The Court characterized Iceland's 50-mile exclusive fishery zone as an infringement of high seas freedom of fishing, and stated that coastal state preferential rights "are limited according to the extent of its special dependence on the fisheries and by its obligation to take account of the rights of other States and the needs of conservation." *Id.* at 31–32.

35. *Id.* at 24–25.

36. [1974] I.C.J. 253; [1974] I.C.J. 457.

37. This occurred after France indicated, in statements made outside of the Court, that it did not intend to continue its atmospheric test program. [1974] I.C.J. at 263–67. *See* Note, *The Nuclear Test Cases: Judicial Silence v. Atomic Blasts*, 16 HARV. INT'L L.J. 614, 621–27 (1975).

38. Franck, *Word Made Law: The Decision of the ICJ in the Nuclear Test Cases*, 69 AM. J. INT'L L. 612 (1975).

39. Jenks has an excellent chapter on "Proof of Custom in International Adjudication." C. JENKS, *supra* note 2, at 225–65; *see* J. CASTANEDA, LEGAL EFFECTS OF UNITED NATIONS RESOLUTIONS (1969); A. D'AMATO, THE CONCEPT OF CUSTOM IN INTERNATIONAL LAW (1971).

40. Most contributions took the form either of general references to the need for greater clarity or certainty in the law, or of exhortations that the Court "resolutely apply the new legal concepts," sometimes coupled with general calls upon the Court to take an active role in the progressive development of customary law. The Yugoslavian delegate is quoted. 29 U.N. GAOR, Sixth Committee (1467th mtg.) 23, U.N. Doc. A/C.6/SR. 1467 (1974).

41. 29 U.N. GAOR, Sixth Committee (1470th mtg.) 38, U.N. Doc. A/C.6/SR. 1470 (1974). I.C.J. STATUTE art. 38, para. 1 directs the Court to apply, *inter alia,* "international custom, as evidence of a general practice accepted as law," and "judicial decisions and the teachings of the most highly qualified publicists . . . as subsidiary means for the determination of rules of law."

42. 29 U.N. GAOR, Sixth Committee (1486th mtg.) 133, U.N. Doc. A/C.6/SR. 1486 (1974). The Mexican delegate explained that as the principal judicial organ of the United Nations, the Court should "play a fundamental part in the codification and progressive development of international law." 29 U.N. GAOR, Sixth Committee (1470th mtg.) 38, U.N. Doc. A/C.6/SR. 1470 (1974).

43. 29 U.N. GAOR, Sixth Committee (1492d mtg.) 166, U.N. Doc. A/C.6/SR. 1492 (1974).

44. *Id.* at 167.

45. G.A. Res. 3232, 30 U.N. GAOR Supp. (No. 31) 141, U.N. Doc. A/9631 (1974). The resolution is summarized at note 3 *supra.* The 1974 Assembly resolution has had no noticeable impact upon the willingness of governments to submit their disputes to the International Court.

46. *See* 1955 U.N. CHARTER COMMITTEE REPORT, *supra* note 5; 1972 U.N. CHARTER COMMITTEE REPORT, *supra* note 5; WIDENING ACCESS, *supra* note 4.

47. U.N. CHARTER art. 96, para. 2. Article 96 reads in full: (1) The General Assembly or the Security Council may request the International Court of Justice to give an advisory opinion on any legal question. (2) Other organs of the United Nations and specialized agencies, which may at any time be so authorized by the General Assembly, may also request advisory opinions of the Court on legal questions

arising within the scope of their activities. U.N. CHARTER art 96. International organizations other than the United Nations specialized agencies may not now be authorized to request advisory opinions. *See* WIDENING ACCESS, *supra* note 4, at 4, 29–31.

48. "Steps that might be taken by the General Assembly to enhance the effectiveness of the International Court of Justice," 1972 U.N. CHARTER COMMITTEE REPORT, *supra* note 5, at 142, 153–54, 158–60.

49. *Id.* at 153–54, 156–60.

50. In *Western Sahara*, the Court was asked by the Assembly for an advisory opinion on the legal status of the territory at the time of its colonization by Spain, a question which the Court saw as arising from the functions of the Assembly concerning the decolonization of the territory. [1975] I.C.J. at 26–27. The Court distinguished the question asked by the Assembly from the underlying issue in dispute between Morocco and Spain, but observed that: "The legitimate interest of the General Assembly in obtaining an opinion from the Court in respect of its own future action cannot be affected or prejudiced by the fact that Morocco made a proposal, not accepted by Spain, to submit for adjudication by the Court a dispute raising issues related to those contained in the [General Assembly's] request." *Id.* at 27. This statement takes a large step towards resolving the question of the propriety of rendering advisory opinions on legal questions involved in disputes between states when the states in question have not both asked the Court to hear the case. The *Western Sahara* example shows that offering access to advisory opinions to a broader class of international organizations holds promise for an increase in the number of such requests and thus for more frequent presentation to the Court of opportunities to develop customary law.

51. 1972 U.N. CHARTER COMMITTEE REPORT, *supra* note 5, at 158–59.

52. For a discussion of this possibility, see *id.* at 161–62; WIDENING ACCESS, *supra* note 4, at 1–3, 38–43.

53. *See* 1972 U.N. CHARTER COMMITTEE REPORT, *supra* note 5, at 153–54.

54. The Department of State proposes Charter amendment to permit international organizations to seek advisory opinions and to permit litigants in municipal court cases to achieve indirect International Court review through the "preliminary decision" procedure. WIDENING ACCESS, *supra* note 4.

55. *Id.* at 1–4, 43–56.

CHAPTER 5

Resolving Conflict

Although the essence of law is generally understood to be the application of a preestablished rule or norm to a controversy by an impartial third party, Gottlieb and McDougal and Lasswell have argued in earlier selections that this is far too narrow a view of the way international law, or for that matter *any* law, actually works. The adjudicatory function remains rather undeveloped in international law, being definitely subordinate to coercive and persuasive diplomacy in the settling of disputes. This set of circumstances does not by itself denigrate the role that law plays in shaping alternatives, justifying actions, or communicating intentions in the course of international relations. The first selection in Chapter 5, by Thomas Franck, helps illuminate these various roles by building a frame of reference around three types of law: "first-party" law, the command and/or imposition of a particular will upon a recalcitrant party; "second-party" law, the direct mediation of interacting wills through bargaining and compromise; and "third-party" law, the enunciation of standards and rules designed to resolve controversies in an objective manner and set precedents for the future by a disinterested third party.

These three analytical models provide a useful framework within which to consider positions raised in the subsequent selections by Ibrahim Shihata, Dean Acheson, and Abram Chayes. While it may be true that the purest case of first-party law is the imposition of one's will on the opponent, there do exist certain important distinctions pertaining to type and degree of coercion within the universe of first-party law that need further elaboration. After all, no sensible person would contend that the case of A hitting B over the head is of the same order as a situation in which A is trying to justify imposing his or her will by adducing standards and reasons that are shared by A and B. Although it is true that the weakness of first-party law is often the lack of clarity concerning the principle or rule that has been established (as opposed to deciding who won), the presence of shared norms nevertheless plays an important role in setting boundaries to the outcome of a particular dispute, including the provision of a sense of the content of "appropriate" behavior of the target state conforming to the "winner's" wishes and expectations. In effect, avenues for the resolution of the conflict are suggested. If A can make it intelligible to B that despite the painful experience of coercion associated with the suggested alternatives (in addition to his or her preferences and a shared image of "reasonableness" and fairness), then first-party law need not lead to confusion or disruption of social relationships. Nevertheless, such an outcome depends upon the (re)establishment of a common universe of meaning, which, indeed, is most likely to occur if second-party law (negotiation) plays some part in the process, giving each antagonist a greater opportunity to shape the outcome than would occur if the situation were characterized by unilateral commands. Furthermore, since even two-party law will often resort at least implicitly to precedents, philosophical principles, folk wisdoms, and other sources of guidance that would favor one or the other party depending upon the invoked standard and its interpretation, some pressure arises to rely upon third-party adjudication. This is particularly the case if both parties can agree (that is, agree on how to resolve their disagreement) that the issues shall be settled in accordance with objectively interpreted standards rather than through the mobilization of competing resources of persuasion. Whatever the logic of the analytical situation, in international practice, sovereign states have proved consistently unwilling to take the decisive step that leads from second-party to third-party law. And, in fact, only rarely in matters of vital importance have states been induced to move from first-party to second-party law. The study of international conflict, as matters now stand, involves an inquiry into different types of first-party law situations.

Shihata's essay, which attempts to justify the Arab oil embargo, covers both points mentioned earlier. Shihata attempts to demonstrate that the controversial action undertaken (namely, the imposition of an embargo on oil) is in conformity with legal prescriptions and that the imposed OPEC policy is consistent with such general norms of international law as that of "proportionality." Furthermore, the author relies on the exemption of Japan from the embargo to demonstrate the care taken to minimize damage to "innocent" states. Although this was clearly an unfriendly act and quite arguably violated the letter (Principle 3) and spirit of the *Declaration on Principles of International Law Concerning Friendly Relations and Cooperation Among States* as well as Article 34 of the 1974 *Charter of the Economic Rights and Duties of States*, it is rather unrealistic to assume that in an arena characterized by bargaining and self-help, recourse by states to hurtful retaliatory measures can be avoided by means of general legal standards ("soft law"). Coercive techniques are especially attractive to states when there exists an opportunity to settle old scores. The most that can be achieved from a world order perspective associated with present political arrangements is some assurance that the measures adopted are not excessive, are clearly circumscribed, are taken in response to an alleged injury after other less harmful methods of redress have failed, and are promptly diminished or revoked when other parties disclose a willingness to reach an accommodation with the party seeking redress. Furthermore, while it is natural to focus on oil as a salient instance of "economic coercion," it should be clear that given the differences in economic strength between developing and developed countries, the problem of economic coercion is relevant in many other settings. The proper emphasis should be directed to the whole gamut of unequal economic relationships between states at different stages of development and with differing histories relative to trade and investment. It would be legalism of the worst kind to insist selectively upon the execution of "contracts" that incorporate structural inequalities. Such a regressive emphasis would institutionalize coercion instead of addressing the wider necessity of stabilizing all relationships in accordance with the basic requirements of justice. Such an objective of equity is not, we believe, a starry-eyed vision endorsed by world order enthusiasts in the "North," nor is it merely the cheap rhetoric of "southern" politicos. Rather, a willingness to reconsider the normative basis of international economic relationships is at the center of an ongoing global bargaining process. A sensitive legal analysis can play an important role in providing parties with some ideas on how to alter legal expectations without altogether destroying stability.

The next two selections touch on the Cuban Missile Crisis of 1962, the encounter of superpowers that observers agree brought the world to the brink of World War III. Given the success of U.S. diplomacy in getting the Soviet Union to remove "offensive" weaponry from Cuba, the context has been interpreted from many angles, including that of international law. We offer the views of two lawyers, each of whom had practical experience at top levels of government. Their differences may, in part, reflect their different roles in the crisis: Acheson, a former secretary of state, was a member of the so-called Executive Committee of distinguished Americans set up to advise President Kennedy, whereas Chayes acted during the crisis as legal adviser to the secretary of state.

Acheson's analysis derides the claims of law altogether in crisis diplomacy, and to some extent even scorns the modest claims of guiding and confining choice of means. Such a "realist" view of world politics as largely a play of power is widely held, especially among nonlawyers.

Abram Chayes's investigation of the legal aspects of the Cuban Missile Crisis is an example of first-party law in the context of vital national security policy. In delineating the role of law in crisis decisionmaking, Chayes reacts sharply to the popular notion that law is an influence only when it "determines" whether the grand policy is legal or not. Since the relevance of legal norms is not self-evident and several outcomes are compatible with the various legal principles invoked, the role of law depicted by Chayes in terms of communicating claims, seeking a limited degree of redress, justifying and confining the actions, rallying support, and limiting the stakes to avoid a more serious encounter is far subtler than the imagery of "the law" as the bottom line of assessment of controversial state policy. Nonetheless, one must still face Acheson's challenge. Is Chayes indulging in wishful thinking, public relations, and word play? Each author in his own way is correct to a certain degree.

In their contribution Robert Johansen and Saul Mendlovitz raise the question of implementing legally binding decisions or norms by means of a standing supranational police force. There is an understandable tendency to dismiss such proposals out of hand, pointing to the unrealistic underlying expectation that sovereign states, especially large ones, that have broken international law can be coerced, or would even agree to the establishment of coercive machinery. However, we should realize, to begin with, that "law enforcement" involves much more than the execution of final judgments involved in putting a "criminal" behind bars. Police also monitor the safety of vehicles to achieve greater compliance with relevant standards, and it is unclear as to why such monitoring duties as, say, those levied against polluters on the high seas would not presently benefit most, if not all, members of the international community, or why there should be intense resistance to the creation of such a mechanism. Police often keep violence under control not by arresting people but by separating the contending parties, as when cordons of officers are established during demonstrations and counterdemonstrations. Comparable tasks have been entrusted to UN peacekeeping forces from time to time on an ad hoc basis. Johansen and Mendlovitz's essay surveys types of peacekeeping roles ranging from humanitarian interventions to monitoring activities; it also makes the case for the general usefulness and desirability of a world constabulary as an institutionalized presence, thus moving the UN beyond its current reliance on generating ad hoc forces and arrangements under the sway of an emergency. The underlying world order concern involves such questions as whether the norms of the global arena will continue to be primarily enforced (and/or manipulated) by the strongest actors, often for selfish reasons, or whether some type of accountability to the global community as a whole can be facilitated by the creation of an impartial constabulary. Such a proposal tests the Grotian waters, so to speak. At the moment, the political will on the part of states and international institutions is very weak with respect to supranational innovations of this sort. The failure to adopt, or even to consider, such a proposal confirms the nonadaptive image of statism, whereas significant levels of support might create new faith in the adaptive resilience of statism or could even be seen as evidence that the transition to an altered world order system is significantly under way. As we have stressed throughout this collection, the Grotian moment is full of ambiguities and shifts of mood and apparent direction.

As we approach the mid-1980s, considerable anxiety continues to mount over the collapse (relating to peace, to financial stability, and to trading and alliance relations) of the current framework of order. The political leaders are doing their best, though a not very impressive best, to plug up the gaps in the dikes. There is little receptivity to more idealistic or bold innovations, and in this respect the energy for global legal reform remains latent rather than active.

QUESTIONS FOR DISCUSSION AND REFLECTION: CHAPTER 5

1. It is frequently alleged that force is the ultimate arbiter in international politics. In this section, several authors argue that even when states act

unilaterally, rules of international law can play an important role. Explain what is meant by such theorizing. Is it persuasive?

2. Given explicit prohibitions against the use and threat of force, to what extent should economic or other forms of nonmilitary coercion be considered illegal? What considerations would be relevant here?

3. How effective can "second-party" law be in the absence of a compulsory procedure to clarify the terms of agreement between the parties to a dispute? Is there another way in which this problem can be attacked?

4. The conventional conception of policing is that of using force against the "law-breaker." Johansen and Mendlovitz present a more complex framework for enforcement. How useful do you find this framework, given the present functioning of the state system? Does it suggest an alternative worth pursuing?

SELECTED BIBLIOGRAPHY: CHAPTER 5

R. P. Anand, *International Courts and Contemporary Conflicts* (New York: Asian Publication House, 1974).

Ian Brownlie, *International Law and the Use of Force by States* (Oxford: Clarendon Press, 1963).

M. S. Daoudi and M. S. Dajani, *Economic Sanctions* (London: Routledge & Kegan Paul, 1984).

Richard Falk, *Legal Order in a Violent World* (Princeton, N.J.: Princeton University Press, 1968).

Benjamin Ferencz, *Enforcing International Law*, 2 vols. (London, N.Y.: Oceana, 1983).

Thomas Franck and Edward Weisband, *World Politics* (New York: Oxford University Press, 1971).

Myres S. McDougal and Florentino P. Feliciano, *Law and Minimum World Public Order* (New Haven, Conn.: Yale University Press, 1961).

W. M. Reisman, "The Enforcement of International Judgements," *American Journal of International Law* 63 (1969).

16. The Structure of Impartiality

Thomas Franck

. . . In essence, there are three systems of problem-solving known to the law. They may operate independently, or successively, or they may be integrated in a single process.

The first system is distinguished by its *power* syndrome, and it operates where the community permits (or cannot prevent) the imposition, by force, of the will of one party on another. . . .

In relations between states, unfortunately, the unilateral use of power remains a much more common source of law. Military conquest, annexation, imposed treaties, economic boycott, "police actions," these have all been more-or-less tolerated by the international community as legitimate ways of making law. Such recognition is, of course, little more than a realistic acceptance by that community of the consequence of its weakness and lack of cohesion, and the equally indisputable phenomenon of *force* creating *order*, and of the will behind force justifying itself by reference to certain standards by which it is exercised and thus made "lawful."

In the United States we have examples of the use of power being *permitted* by law—the father is allowed to spank his child, and a man may hit back at an assailant or snatch back his stolen property—but force is not a *source* of law, as it is, still, in the more primitive international community. Primitiveness is, indeed, the style of one-party law-making. Aside from the fact that law made by unilateral exercise of power as often endangers as protects the peace, and that it invariably produces a law favoring the rich and powerful at the expense of the poor and weak, there is another even more serious defect in the power syndrome as a law-making device. It is that law made in this way frequently fails to produce substantive content.

The dispute, in 1962, between the United States, Russia, and Cuba over the placing of nuclear missiles in the Caribbean helps to illustrate this proposition. According to the United States, Russia's action in putting missiles on Cuban soil was an international wrong because it was done in secrecy and deceit, because it forcefully upset the world balance of power, and because it violated the integrity of the Western Hemisphere as declared in the Monroe Doctrine. Russia, on the other hand, contended that the United States could not have it both ways: either all overseas bases are wrongful, aggressive threats to the peace—in which case the United States should dismantle its bases in Western Europe, Turkey, the Philippines, Formosa, etc.—or else all bases are legal, in which case Russia was perfectly within its rights in setting up shop in Cuba.

By its "peaceful blockade," as we know, the United States persuaded Russia to withdraw its missiles from the Caribbean. Such an exercise in the use of unilateral force, accompanied by an extensive polemic, exchanges of notes, debates in the UN, and formal negotiations ought, presumably, to have had some law-making effect. But what law did it yield? Since Russia and the United States never agreed on what the dispute was about, there could not, of course, be agreement as to what the successful use of force actually decided. Those who side with the American view, for example, can assert that the emerging rule is that the Monroe Doctrine remains in effect and all foreign bases in the Western Hemisphere constitute aggression against the collective hemisphere. Those who side with the Russians can allege that the emerging rule is that all overseas nuclear missile bases are hostile, aggressive, illegal, and should therefore be dismantled; that America's continued refusal to apply this rule reciprocally to itself proves Washington's disdain for international law and equity. Still others, more cynically, see the entire polemic as nothing but propaganda window dressing, sound and fury signifying nothing, an exercise in *pure power*. The meaning of this term we will shortly examine. For the present, however, it is sufficient to note that when a problem is resolved by recourse to *power*, to one-party law-making, the solution one party imposes on another does not yield a clear-cut rule of law, when as often happens in a *power*-oriented solution, the various members of the international community and the parties, in particular, retain their different views of *what the issues were*, and therefore will continue to disagree as to *what was decided*. The world will only know *who won*, but not what *principle* the victory established, for they will not have a definitive statement of the issues on which it was decided. For the long-range prospects of peace it is less important to know who won than what principle was established. This is a hypothesis many will not share, but it marks the dividing line between an orderly community and the jungle. A system of decision-making which does not yield an agreed principle is like a rifle without a sight: lacking not in effect but in *predictable* effect. Without these principles of decision, there can be no prediction and thus, perhaps, no future.

Neither two-party law-making, employing the *compromise* syndrome, nor third-party law-making, employing the *impartiality* syndrome, suffers from this important defect. A court of law, for example, will attempt to have the parties agree as to the facts and issues on which the case is to be decided. But failing that, the court will itself decide which facts and what issues are relevant to its decision. In this way the judicial settlement of a dispute generally yields not only a *decision* but a *rule of law.*

The two-party system is marked by a *compromise* syndrome. This operates in disputes where the law sanctions the reconciliation of contending claims in a mutually acceptable agreement devised by the parties themselves. The parties, so to speak, write their own law. Our ordinary everyday business contracts are laws made by compromise, as are the wage agreements negotiated by conciliation boards. Most international agreements, treaties and their genus, are laws made by mutual accommodation and consent.

The system of compromise may simply involve two-party negotiation, or it may call for complex mechanical devices as well as reference to other systems of decision-making. Take, for example, the ingenious scheme for the consensual division of eighty-seven art treasures left "equally" to the Metropolitan Museum and the National Gallery by the will of the late Mrs. Timken of the ball-bearing fortune.

How can two museums, both steeped in the aesthetic prejudice we call "taste," agree to divide a collection of masterpieces "equally"? Had the two beneficiaries litigated the "equality" of every painting in relation to every other painting, the entire collection would probably have ended up being owned by the lawyers. A compromise was inevitable, and a particularly ingenious one was worked out. The directors of the two museums first grouped the items into a series of artistic categories, then divided each category into two sections of roughly equivalent value. Thereafter the directors wrote out, simultaneously, their first choice in each group. Each time both showed a preference for the same section of a particular category, a coin was flipped and the winner had first choice. The process was entirely successful in avoiding litigation.[1] (It should be observed, however, that this procedure yielded not a principle of law but a principle of procedure.)

The *compromise* syndrome manifests two-party law. The parties to the dispute themselves may make law to suit their own needs by a process of negotiation. This is in contrast to the *power* syndrome, which manifests one-party law, and in which the stronger makes the law both for himself and for the weaker party.

Two-party law, unlike one-party law, continues to occupy an important role in the development of even sophisticated legal systems—especially in the continuing and ever-growing use of the adaptable idea of contract. It can also be located closer to the soul of our complex modern national societies, for it is readily apparent that *all* law can only operate within a general framework of applied consensus or compromise. Only when a community produces an expressed or implied agreement as to *how* its law is to be made, as it did with considerable ingenuity in the special circumstances of the Timken case, or with historic genius in the "contract" that is the United States Constitution, can the members of that community begin to distinguish the sheep of legal order from the goats of personal and political expediency. And only when a community has an agreed measure for making that distinction can it be said to have reached its socio-political *take-off* point. This fundamental community consensus, which Professor H.L.A. Hart of Oxford calls a "rule of recognition," generally originates in a confluence of popular opinion or will, although it may also be the product of revolutionary charisma. It is frequently a complex pattern woven of multiple strands of two-party law—although it may also, of course, be imposed unilaterally by a dictator or a revolutionary class, thereby becoming a manifestation of one-party law-making. Without either an imposed or agreed basic norm or group of such norms, however, and in the absence of a new socially conditioned breed of men who act invariably and voluntarily according to harmonious social principles that are natural to them, law would remain in a state of opinion where each man, and therefore *no man*, is king.

Professors Charles Manning and Lon L. Fuller have demonstrated by reference to *games* that communities of children and adults tend to develop imaginatively within their community those agreed guidelines necessary to allow their chosen activity to proceed. Underlying these guidelines of the game is a remarkably seldom-challenged common assumption or set of assumptions which may be unenunciated, but of which the "rules of the game" are symptomatic. . . .[2]

One of the agreed "rules of the game," in particular, merits further attention, for it is basic to the third category of decision-making, which operates by using the *impartiality* syndrome, as well as to law-making that uses the *power* and *compromise* syndromes. If this rule is ignored, neither the *power* nor the *impartiality* syndrome can yield what is generally acceptable to the community as law. This agreed rule of the game is thus obviously one of great importance. It may be described as the rule of philosophical consistency, linear reasoning, or logical deduction. . . .

Plato's dialogues are its fountainhead, and its impact on the West has never diminished in 2,300 years, despite repeated efforts by the early Christian dogmatists to turn it upside down by substitution of the illogical paradox (life through death, joy through suffering, wisdom through simpleness, and even conception through virginity), or the effort of Hegel and Marx to substitute "thesis-antithesis-synthesis" as a way of thinking. Philosophical consistency is the triumph of the intellect, of "pure" reason, and it provides the bridge between arbitrary, selfish, and isolated decision-making and promotes the emergence of a set of knowable and predictable rules for the exercise (and restraint) of authority: In other words, it facilitates *law*. It is not the sole component of good law for which there must also be mercy, feeling-perception, and an awareness of public policy, but it is the indispensable prerequisite to the existence of a legal system.

Suppose the caveman, Ug, has begun his autumnal hunt by killing a dinosaur. Having left his lethal flint-ax in its heart, he continues on his hunt, intending later to return with his family to gather the carcass. Two days afterward, his neighbor, Og, stumbles across the dead animal. With the aid of his wife and ten children and the expenditure of two days work, Og succeeds in dragging the cadaver to his cave. Once Ug has returned from his hunt, he traces the missing carcass to Og's cave and demands its return.

Depending upon the degree of sophistication Ug and Og have achieved, this story can have various climaxes:

1. Ug and Og could simply clout each other with the jawbones of asses in that familiarly primitive manner of problem-solving and decision-making first attributed to Abel and Cain or Romulus and Remus. Such a contest involves no thought for either past or future conduct. The parties are concerned neither with laying down principles for solving future disputes nor with applying to a present dispute the lessons of comparable disputes in the past. They are concerned only with one immediate—and no doubt to them vital—question: Who gets the dinosaur? This, then, is the use of *pure* power to reach a decision, and it yields no law, unless some future disputants, by benevolent induction, read a reasonable principle into Ug and Og's seemingly mindless contest of strength and apply it to solve their own predicament. It is just conceivable that the battle between Ug and Og might in this way gradually come to be accepted as a law stating that dinosaurs killed and left behind on autumnal hunts may be taken by any person strong enough to defend his title. That such a rule of law sanctioning and regulating a contest of pure or mindless power is not entirely fanciful will be seen by recalling the extensive role of trial by combat and its refinement, the duel, in medieval European and also Oriental systems. The role of the law in associating itself with a contest of pure power in order to impart to it a trace of its grace and order is like that of the Church in blessing dictators, senselessly warring armies, and the shrines of pagan cults.

2. On the other hand, Ug might reason: "This dinosaur is mine because I killed it and impressed on it my mark of conquest. To allow you, Og, to take this carcass from me merely because I left it to continue my hunt would be to admit a principle that would make the whole business of organized autumnal hunts impossible." In reply Og might contend that the abandonment of carcasses during a hunt is a socially undesirable, wasteful practice, that it leaves them exposed to the ravages of other beasts, that oft-times carcasses go unclaimed for weeks while they rot in the sun, that moreover, by dragging the carcass home, Og did far more than Ug of the actual work necessary to reduce it to a commodity capable of ownership and use. After that, Ug and Og, if they are deadlocked, may still rely on asses jawbones to club each other to a violent verdict. *But in this case, the outcome would yield a solution based on power as a law-making device.* The difference is a simple one. Suppose Ug is the winner. Suppose that, the following autumn, the same events recur but with the roles reversed. It would be difficult for Ug now to contend that a newly killed dinosaur, temporarily abandoned during a hunt, becomes the property of a finder who drags it home. His sense of honor and consistency would probably shame him into obeying the "law" he made by force of arms only a year earlier. If it does not, Og's neighbors, outraged by Ug's shameless inconsistency, would probably rally to his aid. Ug and Og would have discovered that not only judges and lawyers but the public as a whole, even in primitive societies, have an extraordinary, seemingly innate preference for action that is consistent, and at a more sophisticated state, can be *seen* and *expressed* to be consistent with what has gone before. This preference, which appears as a universal social instinct, is an essential ingredient in the emergence of a rule of law, and it means little more than that men do not simply do whatever they feel like doing, or whatever they think they can get away with, but only that which they can "justify." Power relationships, as we have noticed, often fail to yield such neutral principles, but sometimes, fortunately, they do—either because the contest of power took place between champions of two explicit principles, or because historical forces conspire to pretend that it did.

3. Ug and Og might not fight at all. Instead, they might haggle in the presence of flowing jugs of clover wine. They might, in a soggy euphoria of good fellowship, together set out to kill another dinosaur so the needs of each might be satisfied. Or they might, to the same end, pillage the larder of Hugh, the arch enemy of Ug, taking from it sufficient booty that the needs of both are sated. Or they and their kinfolk might tug and pull at the carcass until it came apart near the middle, whereupon they might simply resign themselves each to their portion and stalk away. Or Og might take one of Ug's ugly daughters as wife, whereupon the grateful father of the bride might bestow the dinosaur upon the groom as dowry. *All of these solutions represent the triumph of pure compromise.* As between Ug and Og they may be *ad hoc* "political" solutions, but they yield no, or very little, law unless others, later, choose to adopt this purely "one-shot" procedure as a model or principle applicable to themselves in a similar dispute, or

again, unless historical forces conspire to "find" a logical principle where, in fact, there had been none.

4. Ug and Og might themselves decide to emulate prior conduct. They might sit down to their clover wine and remember that a similar incident once arose between two fellow villagers, T'Bo and Hun, who could reveal that the earlier quarrel had been happily resolved by an agreement of the parties to divide the carcass: the bulk of it going to the hunter, but the prime hindquarter fittingly being bestowed upon the one who provided the transportation. This would be a solution by reference to the law-making compromise syndrome. Rational principles are here set out, applied, and reapplied to obtain solutions, which, as to both form and substance, are philosophically consistent with each other and generate a tendency toward logical progression and analogy in problem-solving.

Let us now look again at the Cuban missile crisis of 1962.

The difference between *power* and *compromise* as a description of action arising out of pure *will*, and as law-making syndromes generating law through the development of enunciated, logical principles capable of being deductively extrapolated was dramatically illustrated at that time by the important debate that took place within the United States Government over how to explain to the world America's unprecedented action in imposing a peacetime quarantine on Cuba. Some government lawyers argued that these actions—this exercise in power—should be formulated in terms of legal principles. It was suggested, for example, that the United States should have taken the position that the prohibition in the United Nations Charter against use of force against another state except in the event of an armed attack had become obsolete in an age of missile-delivered nuclear weapons; that no nation could be expected to wait until *after* an armed attack before striking back; and that existing law should be reinterpreted to permit the use of force against anticipated, and not merely *actual* aggression.[3] Had this advice been accepted as the official American position, and had the Russians and Cubans joined issue on this basis, the success of the power gambit might have *made law* and thus effected a *de facto* amendment of the United Nations Charter. The State Department, however, shied away from committing itself to a rule that might be taken to authorize any state to respond with force to any alleged *threat* of aggression (and what war has ever been launched without some such allegation?). Moreover, the International Court has already spoken on the matter since the advent of the Atomic Era. In rejecting the British argument that a violation of Albanian sovereignty by Royal Navy minesweepers was a use of force justified as "a new and special application of the theory of intervention," the necessity of which was the failure of international organization to provide a speedy, effective remedy, the majority of judges firmly held the traditional line, saying: "The Court can only regard the alleged right of intervention as the manifestation of a policy of force, such as has, in the past, given rise to most serious abuses and such as cannot, whatever be the present defect in international organization, find a place in international law."[4]

Then, too, some efforts were made to base the Cuban blockade on other principles, such as a conveniently abridged version of the Monroe Doctrine, omitting the doctrine's "other side of the coin," which precludes America from all intervention in Europe. None of these doctrinal approaches carried the day within the United States Government, which followed, instead, the lead of those advisers who urged the position that America owed the world no philosophical explanation other than the self-evident enunciation of national *will*, particularly the will to survive and be omnipotent.

Such *ad hoc* use of power need not be cynical. Indeed, it may proceed from an ethical as well as from a cruder motive—but its reasons will be special to the parties and the occasion, rather than generally applicable and capable of reasoned development by comparison and analogy. Neither the victim nor the victimizer will acknowledge that he has established a pattern for general behavior advancing the good order of society. An unemployed, starving beggar may steal an apple or a loaf of bread to stay alive. He may even vigorously defend his moral right to take by stealth from a society that deprives him of the means of honest gain. But he is unlikely to believe, unless he be mad or an anarchist, that the law condones theft or even that the law *ought* to permit every person who feels himself underprivileged just to take whatever he can carry away.

The International Court has itself recognized this essential difference between *pure* power or compromise on the one hand, and law-making conduct on the other. Speaking in the *Lotus litigation* between France and Turkey. . . . [As] the Court said:

> Even if the rarity of the judicial decisions to be found among the reported cases were sufficient to prove in point of fact the circumstance alleged by the Agent for the French Government, it would merely *show that States had often, in practice, abstained from instituting criminal proceedings, and not that they recognized themselves as being obliged to do so; for only if such abstention were based on being conscious of having a duty to abstain would it be possible to speak of an international custom. The alleged fact does not allow one to infer that States have been conscious of having such a duty* [author's italics].[5]

The element, then, that must be added to the mere event of conduct in order to constitute *law-making* conduct is an expressed or impliable *consciousness of the action being not mere expression of will, but rather of defined obligation*, whether the sense of obligation be induced by consciousness of moral duty, preference for consistency, for a system of practical reasoning, respect for reciprocal benefits, or fear of a coercive power.

Common law, which forms the basis of Anglo-American jurisprudence, was weaned on the consistent application of patterns of applied practical power and compromise by the parties to disputes. The very term "common" reflects the origin of the law in the consciously and repeatedly applied and widely extrapolated customs of the people, the customs that commonly or consistently prevailed among the people in their relations with each other, and that found their content in a balance of popular convenience and consistency. This common agreement to resolve disputes, whether by one-, two-, or three-party methods, in accordance with the principled application of practical reasoned consistency is history's social response to the challenge of chaos.

Ug and Og's problem, for example, continued until a few years ago to be reflected in the whaling industry. Whaling, like some other technologies, has recently become more efficiently lethal. Previously, however, a harpooned whale might continue the fight for a very long time, eventually breaking from, or even towing away, his would-be captors. At what point could such an animal be captured by someone else?

This issue first came before the courts of England in 1788, at the York Assizes. An action was launched by one captain against another, in "trover for a whale, which had been struck first by an harpooner of the Plaintiff's ship, and afterwards by an harpooner of the Defendant's." The counsel on both sides, and all the parties concerned, agreed the law to be, both by the custom of Greenland, and as settled by former determinations at Guildhall, London, as follows:

> While the harpoon remains in the fish, and the line continues attached to it, and also continues in the power and management of the striker, the whale is a fast fish: and though during that time struck by a harpooner of another ship, and though she afterwards breaks from the first harpoon, but continues fast to the second, the second harpoon is called a friendly harpoon, and the fish is the property of the first striker, and of him alone. But if the first harpoon or line breaks, or the line attached to the harpoon is not in the power of the striker, the fish is a loose fish, and will become the property of any person who strikes and obtains it.[6]

With the parties agreed—*compromised*—to the extent of accepting both the binding force of prior solutions and also as to the practical principle emerging from these prior solutions, the work of the court was to apply this past practice taken from the experience of previous disputes to the present one. The word "compromise" is here used in the special legal sense. A *compromis* is, technically, an agreement between the parties to a dispute delimiting the area of concepts within which they or a court may search for a solution to their dispute. Thus a Belgian and a Frenchman may agree that the law of France shall govern their relations. In a large sense all persons engaged in a whaling industry at a particular time and place agree, implicitly, to be governed by its necessary norms—international treaty, long-standing custom, and tradition. Some of these norms are compulsory and thus *legal*, others etiquette that is merely convenient. But beneath all efforts to maintain orderly relationships through law lies a *compromis*, an agreement between the parties that they shall argue their cause, and that the cause shall be decided within a certain circumference of admissible kinds of argument, and not outside it. Thus the use of evidence of past practice is everywhere in the common-law world within—even at the very center of— that circle, while, as Graham Hughes has said, the fact that one of the disputants is ugly, is usually clearly outside the agreed circle.

Most disputes are not quite so easily resolved as our example, the whaling case. While there is usually agreement that prior solutions should be consistently applied, the calculations that go into the extrapolation of one or several precedents to new facts are usually more complex and far less self-evident in human than in mathematical calculations. It is for this reason that an agreement—a compromise—to apply precedent, essential as it is to an organized society, is often not enough *by itself* to resolve a dispute. There are still likely to be disagreements as to *which* of several possible precedents, several arguments all within the agreed circle, is to be applied, and even if there is only one applicable line of precedent, whether differences in circumstances that distinguish the earlier disputes from the present one do not justify modifications in the precedent. Such disputes generally cannot be settled by an agreement between the parties themselves, but require the help of an impartial third party.

This brings us to the third category of law-making. Some years after the *York Assizes* case, in 1808, the House of Lords was asked to consider a whaling case seemingly "similar" to the one raised at the 1788 Assizes. One Luce, captain of the whaler *William Fenning*, harpooned a whale near Greenland. While still fighting it, he hit another whale. Being unequipped to fight on two fronts, he tied the second harpoon-line to a buoy or "droug." By the time the first whale was secured, the second had dragged line and buoy far out to sea. According to the House of Lords:

. . . the wound produced the usual effect of this weapon, it retarded the progress of the fish, by causing it to struggle with the harpoon for a considerable time . . . and the droug floating on the water marked its course, so that it was with the more certainty pursued by Anthony, the master of the "Caerwent," who, in consequence of a signal made to him by Luce, followed the fish, and killed it. He extracted from it the oil and other valuable matter, but rendered no part of it to the Plaintiffs. Numerous witnesses deposed, that a custom had universally prevailed in these seas, from the origin of the fishery, until within a few years past, that the party who first struck the fish with the droug should receive one half of it from the party who killed it. But it appeared by the testimony of the Defendant's witnesses, that for a few years past, since 1792, many captains of the ships employed among the Gallipagos islands, among others, one American, had usually agreed that the striking a fish with a droug should not entitle the striker to a share. In the year 1805, Anthony, with five or six English captains, of whom Luce was not one, had, upon their arrival at the fishing stations, acceded to these terms. The Defendant's counsel contended that the Plaintiff must be nonsuited, because, according to his own claim, he was tenant in common with the Defendant; but on account of the testimony of one witness, who stated that the person who first struck the fish was entitled to the whole, rendering half to the party who killed it, the Chief Justice left the case to the jury, who found that by the custom the Plaintiff was entitled to half the fish, and gave him in damages the value of a moiety.[7]

So must courts choose between contending principles and a multitude of fact-data, similar but not identical to that found in earlier cases, to determine the relevant integers to be taken into account in calculating a logical deduction.[8] Such a process of logical calculus requires an impartial mind.

Having reached the third law-making syndrome, and before going on to a further examination of it, let us briefly recapitulate.

In the international, as in the national community, *power* and *compromise*, the one- and two-party law-making syndromes, may simply be *used*, or they may be *used to make laws*. Hitler's bombing of undefended "open" cities was a use of power bereft of legal intent, and, of course, yielding no law. The Anglo-French invasion of Suez and the Indian invasion of Goa, on the other hand, constituted uses of force in support of strongly urged legal principles, and the outcome in each case has had law-making significance. Not only substantive but also procedural practice, whether derived by power or by compromise, is capable of making law, if it proceeds with an enunciated concept capable of being applied to other than this one instance, and if it works. When in 1961 the Cameroons and Nigeria differed over the disposition of the British Cameroons, they evolved a compromise (*compromis*) reminiscent of the complex solution to the Timken dispute. The area was deliberately divided into two ethnic units in order that each unit might be polled separately in a self-determination plebiscite under UN supervision. The result was a relatively amicable division of the territory in accordance with a principle of ethnic self-determination. This compromise, however imperfect in its execution,[9] must be contrasted with the ethnic dismemberment of Czechoslovakia arranged in Munich in 1938. One yielded procedural law capable of more general application. The other yielded nothing but a dumb event, history without mind or voice to speak to the future, except in animal sounds of triumph and pain. One proceeded along a line of argument within the general agreed circle; the other, being far outside the ambit of principled argument acceptable to reasonable men, was unintelligible, menacing gibberish to the civilized international lawyer.

We have noted how fundamental is the use of agreement or compromise in the conscious development of law; but also that it is an insufficient ingredient in a sophisticated system of problem-solving because the calculations involved in the application of pre-existent principles to new events involves dilemmas of choice not presented by purely mathematical calculations. Let us illustrate this further. A man drives into an intersection while the traffic light is green. An oncoming car ignores the light. Thinking himself the victim of a bluff, or in blind fury, our man fails to yield, insists on his right of way, and collides with the other car. Later it is learned that the driver of the car proceeding against the light had lost control of its braking system. Who is at fault? "Not I," says our man, "I had the green light." "Not I," says the other. "Through no fault of mine, I couldn't stop. The other driver saw me coming and had the last clear chance to avert the accident." Who is right? As it happens, both drivers have some precedent on their side, since some courts apply a simple test of "fault," while others follow the "last clear chance" doctrine to attach responsibility to the man—be he at "fault" or not—who had the last opportunity to prevent the accident. Then too, a fragment of principled reasoning can often be spun out to put a patch of respectability on the exercise of what would otherwise be pure power. If the parties to this dispute are not always able to settle it alone, then an impartial third party is needed if there is to be a settlement without violence. . . .

Suffice it here to point out that the third party is needed, and that his chief qualification is not that he is an expert, or particularly wise—although both may be desirable—but only that he is genuinely a *third* party and not one of the *interested* parties.

Whatever the efficacy of *power* and *compromise* syndromes in the development of national and international law, and it must not be minimized, one- and two-party law-making cannot suffice to guarantee a community against chaos. In the modern state, third-party law has assumed this ultimate law-making function. We return, therefore, to consideration of this third system of law-making. It is identifiable and can be distinguished from the other two systems by its impartiality syndrome—that is, submission to the binding determination of a neutral third party, be he judge in a court of law, arbitrator, administrative civil servant, mutual friend of the disputants, or tax official passing on the validity of exemptions.

Examples of the impartiality syndrome should also include such mechanical devices as that which formed a part of the Timken compromise—that is, the flipping of a coin. The two men flipping a coin are referring their dispute to the mechanical impartiality of fate. They do so because it is one sure, simple way to get a speedy decision, and because they have determined that any decision is better than none. The decision's the thing. Unlike other appeals to the third-party judgment of God, this reference to impartial nondeistic fate is not expected to yield "justice" or "truth" but only a decision—albeit one arrived at with perfect impartiality.

To begin to understand the concept of impartiality . . . requires an initial appreciation of the historical and religious ethos that surrounds it.

The search for a quality of human impartiality comparable to that of God or fate has conditioned the progress of societies toward third-party law-making. In Western, as distinguished from Oriental, religions God is judge and eschatology is concerned with judgment. . . .

As a society we are dedicated to judgment. Moreover, man in his grace relates ontologically and epistemologically to the world, the universe, and to God through a process of impartial, rational, philosophically consistent decisions, which are facilitated by the divinely given power of right-reason. In this way man also "judges" God and all his works. Impartiality thus is a fundamental and religiously related virtue, however secular its manifestation. . . . And the religious origins of impartiality continue to be relevant to the role of courts to this very day. In 1966 Justice Kenneth Keating of New York noted, apparently with satisfaction, that a survey had shown a majority of New Yorkers believe that judges perform their functions under divine guidance. (A trial lawyer commented that "Keating must have meant that Christ only knows what they're doing"!) . . .

So highly was judicial impartiality prized in Roman courts that it was required then, as it is in most legal systems today, that the judges' fairness not only be, *but appear to the litigants to be*, unimputable. The *Codex* of Justinian[10] provides: "Although a judge has been appointed by imperial power, yet because it is our pleasure that all litigation should proceed without suspicion let it be permitted to him who thinks the judge under suspicion to recuse him before issue is joined, so that the cause go to another."[11]

The equally universal concern that judges be protected against biasing pressures is underlined by the Declaration of Independence, in which the American settlers charged that the British king "has made judges dependent on his Will alone, for the tenure of their offices, and the amount and payment of their salaries."

An appreciation of the deep historic-religious roots of the idea of impartiality is essential to an understanding of the future of law in the international community. So basic to our thinking about courts and other decision-makers is this historical and religious ethos that no breakthrough in the direction of peaceful third-party law-making can be expected in the international community until the problem of the impartiality of decision-makers is satisfactorily resolved. In a world divided by politics, economics, race, and geography this is no small challenge. Nevertheless, it comes to this: *Whether the struggle to create a climate of human impartiality succeeds will determine the scope, if any, given by society to a system of third-party law-making.* That there is a direct relationship between the impartiality of third-party impartial decision-makers and the extent to which the community utilizes the third-party decision-making process would appear to be axiomatic. . . .

Put conversely, it is assumed that no administrative or judicial decision-making system, except in a dictatorship, can expect to be widely accepted and routinely resorted to until it has established its essential credential of impartiality.

It has already been said that third-party law-making is not a substitute for, but a supplement to, one- and two-party methods of settling disputes. To place the purpose of this study into perspective, this point might well be sharpened further, now that the three methods of law-making have been introduced. It is not at all intended, by the focusing on third-party law-making, to diminish the importance of, in particular, the two-party system for which there continues to be ample scope. Indeed, paradoxically, the growing intervention of the state in private economic and social relations has, by increasing the real equality of the individual, and therefore his capacity to bargain effectively, placed him in a better position to participate equally with other individuals in private or two-party law-making. The same is true of the growing power-equality among states. . . .

Since the chips are more widely distributed than ever before, so the poker game of direct negotiation has more players than before, and they tend to stay in the game longer. The parties to a dispute must always be given every opportunity to "work things out for themselves" before an outsider is justified in imposing a solution. A good example of this necessary forbearance comes from the traditional jurisprudence of Kenya's Kikuyu tribe. According to Jomo Kenyatta:

The proper procedure adopted in recovering a debt was that a man brewed sugar-cane beer and took it to his debtor. He took with him also one of the elders of his village. The beer was presented to the debtor as a reminder and as a sign of friendship and of the wish to settle the matter peacefully. In this way the debtor might be moved by the friendly approach and perhaps make full settlement of the debt or promise to pay it in installments. If the debt was not paid, another beer was prepared and presented to the debtor, and this time two elders accompanied the creditor. If this failed to bring any successful arrangement towards settlement of the debt, a third visit was made, taking the beer as before, and three elders as witnesses. Now the creditor had full right to take the matter before the kiama because he had tried his best to persuade his debtor to settle the matter mutually out of court and had failed.[12]

Even when the parties to a dispute fail to settle it through negotiation and compromise, it is not always socially essential to interject the third-party method. Rather, it is only when a protracted, unresolved social discord begins to affect not only the disputants, but the peace and good order of the entire community, that the community, as an interested but strictly impartial third party has the right to arrogate to itself the task of settlement. Otherwise the right to disagree, or even to quarrel vigorously, is a part of freedom. A city must tolerate a strike of margarine workers, so long as there is sufficient butter and olive oil to meet its minimal needs. But a strike of electrical or transport workers during a cold winter should certainly bring a rapid but impartial intervention to preserve the essential well-being of the community.

As our national economy becomes more complex and interrelated, the impact of a breakdown in the working of any part is more widely diffused and more strongly felt throughout the entire national community. This in no way militates against continuing the practice of primary recourse to two-party bargaining, even when the road to compromise is rutted by bad faith. It does, however, suggest the need for keeping third-party machinery in constant repair and readiness, and for making constant improvements.

So too, in the international community. No one would wish to apply third-party procedures in every situation of discord. Sovereign states, like free men, should enjoy the right to interact freely, to bargain singly or collectively in pursuit of their national aspirations. Where the search for a legal solution through *compromise* fails to bring the desired result, and this failure endangers the security of the community as a whole, however, there must be an alternative to protect us from the effects of escalating chaos. . . .

There has, of course, long been *ad hoc* third-party decision-making in international relations. It appears to have been used in disputes between ancient Greek city states, Roman provinces, and thirteenth-century Swiss cantons, to have risen and fallen with the medieval papacy, and to have revived in modern times with the Jay Treaty of 1794 and the Alabama Awards of 1872.[13] As long ago as 117 B.C., it has been discovered, two Romans, sons of Quintus Minucius Rufus, were sent to investigate and decide a territorial controversy between the cities of Genoa and Vituria, which they did by fixing and demarcating the boundary and by decreeing a settlement, which is engraved on a bronze tablet discovered near Genoa 450 years ago.[14]

Modern third-party dispute settlement, however, is dated from the Jay Treaty between the United States and England, which was signed in 1794 to settle a number of issues left over from the preceding war of independence. . . .

It is only in the last century, however, that an effort has been made to create *permanent* machinery for the resolution of international disputes by impartial third parties. The stirrings in this direction could be detected in the British-French Treaty of Arbitration of 1903 and the Hague Convention for the Pacific Settlement of International Disputes of 1899,[15] which set up the Permanent Court of International Arbitration.[16] It has been said that the Permanent Court of Arbitration is not permanent, is not a court, and does not engage in arbitration. In any event its relatively long, somnolent life has been disturbed by fewer than two dozen actual calls to service. A very much larger step forward was taken by the creation, in 1921, of the Permanent Court of International Justice, which has since become the International Court of Justice, but even it currently handles an average of fewer than three cases a year.[17] It is surprising that so many of the most intellectually voracious international minds are still willing to be put out to pasture where the grazing is so thin.

While there has been a less-than-phenomenal growth in the direction of permanent worldwide judicial tribunals, more important growth has occurred in the system of problem-solving by special tribunal created for a specific dispute, a particular cause, or a geographic region. Such *ad hoc* arbitral provisions are increasingly commonplace, particularly in defense and commercial treaties. Claims commissions are an historic part of American relations with some states, particularly the United Kingdom and Mexico, although they seem now to have gone out of fashion, to be replaced by national claims tribunals. At Nuremberg a special court sat to try persons accused of "new" international crimes, such as genocide and the waging of aggressive war. Within the developing European communities, a multinational court has jurisdiction over such varied subjects as cartelization and steel quotas and within the Council of Europe a court has jurisdiction in respect of human rights. A new Protocol of the Organization of African Unity provides for an arbitral tribunal to which disputes between African states may be submitted.[18]

Despite this considerable and fairly consistent development in the direction of more, and more frequently used, impartial tribunals, there is no universal theoretical agreement among states that there can even be such a thing as truly impartial third-party decision-making. Such development of the third-party method as is taking place appears to be mainly between friendly states which are unlikely to engage in quarrels endangering international peace. There has been little comparable development between more hostile states.

There are, however, complex reasons for this failure, which bring us straight back to our consideration of our subject of impartiality. Communism, at least in its earlier phases, regarded courts as little more than instruments of power. According to orthodox Russian communist doctrine, the Russian court "is an agency of the Soviet Socialist State. The court may not serve any other cause but the cause of building up a socialist society, may not carry on any other policy but the policy of the Communist Party and the Soviet Government, may not carry out any will but the will of the Soviet people."[19]

. . . The Russian attitude must not, however, be made the scapegoat for the dilemma. In the United States, too, it is not infrequently alleged by reputable observers that some parts of its, or its states', judiciary are much more "political" than most of us comfortably believe. Two important American legal researchers have noted:

> When we observe the judiciary in action, we quickly become aware of how acutely "political" it may be. Not only judges, but sheriffs, prosecutors, and coroners are usually elected officials. In Louisiana, where judges have been indicted for income tax evasion and listed on the board of directors of oil and gas companies, we may infer that their ceremonial insulation from the public has not prevented their getting in on the "big barbecue" that is by now customary in Louisiana politics.[20]

In appraising Russian attitudes toward the third-party system it behooves us to mix our heady brew of *J'accuse* with a dash of sobering *mea culpa*. . . .

It is nearer the mark to say that both American and Soviet attitudes, and the formulation of those attitudes by leaders, have suffered from a lack of precision in their analysis of the institutional manifestations of the *power, compromise*, or *impartiality* syndromes. It has not been widely understood that elements of each syndrome may enter into a single, complex law-making institution. Western observers, applying rigid Montesquieuian standards of divided powers, have sometimes been misled to mistakenly pessimistic conclusions about Russian attitudes toward third-party decision-making. One must begin with the realization that Russia has, indeed, been shy of international courts, but that courts are not the sole machinery for third-party law-making, just as third-party law-making is not the sole system applied by judges, who may also have recourse to two-party (compromise) law-making.

To illustrate: In 1946 Russia's Andrei Vyshinsky argued before the incipient world legislature, the General Assembly of the United Nations, that a question of interpreting the scope of the United Nations Charter, although admittedly a question of law, should not be referred to the International Court of Justice. The proponents of such a suggestion, he said, "having been defeated on the political, the moral-political plane . . . [are] trying to transfer the dispute, the whole question, to the juridical plane . . . anticipating, not without reason, that if the matter is referred to a court, even the International Court . . . it may easily be submerged, as legal soil is very marshy. But I personally do not want the whole matter to be submerged. . . . The Soviet delegation considers that justice must indeed be secured and that it should be secured by an international court; but this international court is here, it is yourselves, it is all of us. . . ."

The issue was the right of the General Assembly to pass resolutions concerning the treatment of Negroes in South Africa in the light of Article 2(7) of the Charter, prohibiting "intervention" in matters essentially within the domestic jurisdiction of any state. Mr. Vyshinsky's likening of the UN's legislative body to its judicial one cannot simply be dismissed as Leninist cynicism. The Soviet diplomat and jurist was here not so much declaring that courts must frequently be guided by political considerations *as the necessary converse*: that legislatures may sometimes act with a degree of objectivity, like a court. When can one expect legislators to behave impartially? One may, of course, doubt the qualities of neutrality the Soviet delegation brought to this particular dispute. But the question raised by Vyshinsky is far more important than any particular instance in which it was raised. . . .

To determine when legislatures can and should act *impartially* requires some further analysis of the nature of legislative decision-making (an analysis which, because we had posited a world without supergovernment, we have so far avoided). In the United Nations, and particularly its Security Council and General Assembly, however, one finds the embryo of a political superlegislature. For the present its *coercive* powers are and probably will remain negligible, particularly insofar as Russia and the United States are concerned. But not its power to make important decisions. What, then, is the nature of the legislative process in terms of the three decision-making syndromes?

Legislatures do, of course, differ significantly from courts in the decision-making tools which they generally employ. In legislating, they lay out the broad, long-term direction of the law, whereas courts, applying this blueprint, build the actual path from one solved dispute to the next. The broad general direction is embodied in legislation that is the product of a political process, usually utilizing the tools of *power* and *compromise*, while the application of general legislation to specific persons and disputes is the prerogative of courts usually acting *impartially*. But it is also possible, and it not infrequently occurs, that courts, in deciding a specific case, must make a decision, the importance of which is so broad and general as to be "legislative." This is particularly true if courts are acting in a dispute for which no prior blueprint has been drawn. Much of the United States Constitution, although a legislative blueprint of sorts, is only sketched in, using deliberately faint and fuzzy demarcations like "due process." Consequently, courts giving specific meaning to the Constitution are placed in the role of a legislature. The desegregation decisions in the United States and the decisions on the right to strike in Britain are among classic contemporary examples of courts having to act in a legislative or blueprint-drafting capacity. When courts legislate, they ought to be sensitive to *power*, to the prevailing political standards and mores of the community, and to the need for *compromise* and agreement between the various interests and factions of that community. They must, in such cases, act at least in part as a legislature. When they fail to do so, they meet, and deserve, the fate of the Supreme Court of the United States in the period 1933–1937, when it irresponsibly chose to block the broad social policies of the Roosevelt New Deal and to substitute, instead, its own political preferences.

Conversely, there are occasions when a legislature is not generating broad and general, but narrow and specific, law. This kind of legislation is exemplified by laws "for the relief of" a particular person—to grant residence or citizenship or exemption from a more general law to one or several persons. In Canada the federal parliament even enacts "relief" laws granting divorces to residents of the two provinces that do not have divorce laws. These specific acts are generally passed on the recommendation of a respected member of the legislative body who indicates to his colleagues how impartial justice and fairness will be advanced by enactment of this "judicial" legislation. In the United States, Congress can try citizens for contempt and obstruction of the legislative process and can imprison them until the end of the legislative session. The British parliament has similar powers. Members of the legislature are in these circumstances expected to vote on the matter impartially, without reference to their political affiliation. . . .

Even when an issue before a legislative body like Congress or the General Assembly is intensely political, a substantial and perhaps controlling number of representatives may have no political interest in, or commitment to, either side and are thus free to bring to the decision-making process an attitude of impartiality. "Neutralism," "nonalignment," or bipartisanship are terms preferred by the jargon of international and domestic politics. But, whatever the name, a third-party status of impartiality is not reserved to judges, any more than political responsiveness is solely the prerogative of the legislature.

NOTES

1. National Gallery of Art, News Release, May 8, 1960; *The New York Times*, May 9, 1960; New York *Mirror*, May 15, 1960; Metropolitan Museum of Art, News Release, May 15, 1960.

2. C.A.W. Manning, *The Nature of International Society* (New York, John Wiley & Sons, Inc., 1962).

3. *Cf.* remarks of Professor Myres McDougal, *Proceedings of the American Society of International Law*, April, 1963, p. 163–65.

4. *Corfu Channel Case*, 1949 I.C.J. 4 at 35.

5. P.C.I.J., Series A, No. 10, p. 31.

6. *Littledale v. Scaith*, I Taunt. 243n.

7. *Fennings v. Grenville* (1808); I Taunt. 241.

8. For similar process also concerning whole salvage see *Ghen v. Rich*, 8 Fed. 159 (1881).

9. The Cameroons took Britain to the International Court of Justice to protest the way the agreement was carried out.

10. 3.1.16

11. See Scott, *The Civil Law: A Translation of Enactments of Justinian*, Vol. XII.

12. Jomo Kenyatta, *Facing Mount Kenya* (London, Secker and Warburg, 1959), p. 218-19.

13. See J. H. Ralston, *International Arbitration from Athens to Locarno* (Stanford University, Calif., Stanford University Press, 1929), pp. 153-298. For a review of the history of arbitration see Julius Stone, *Legal Controls of International Conflict* (New York, Rinehart & Co., 1954), Chap. 4, and authorities cited therein. For a full discussion of the arbitrations under the Jay Treaty, see J. B. Moore, *Digest of International Arbitrations* (Washington, D.C., Govt. Printing Office, Modern Series, 1898), Vol. I, pp. 299-349. For treaty text see W. M. Malloy, *Treaties, Conventions, International Acts, Protocols and Agreements* (Washington, D.C., Govt. Printing Office, 1910), Vol. I, p. 590.

14. Johnson, Coleman, Norton, and Bourne, *Ancient Roman Statutes* (1961), pp. 46, 47.

15. Revised in 1907.

16. Agreement between Great Britain and France providing for the settlement by arbitration of certain classes of questions which may arise between the two governments, Oct. 14, 1903, *Hertslet's Commercial Treaties*, Vol. XXIII, p. 492. First Hague Peace Conference, Convention for the Pacific Settlement of International Disputes, Malloy, *supra*, Vol. II, p. 2016; and Second Hague Peace Conference, Convention of Pacific Settlement of Disputes, *ibid.*, p. 2220.

17. The Statute of the Court, which entered into force on August 20, 1921, may be found in M. O. Hudson, *International Legislation* (1931), Vol. I, No. 37a, p. 530, as amended (1942-45), Vol. IX, No. 654, p. 510.

18. Draft Protocol of Mediation, Conciliation and Arbitration, Cairo, 26 April 1964.

19. Quoted in Gsovski and Grzybowski, *Government, Law and Courts in the Soviet Union and Eastern Europe* (1957), v. 1, p. 521.

20. Jacob and Vines, "The Judiciary in American State Politics," *Judicial Decision Making*, Schubert, ed. (New York, Glencoe Press, 1963), p. 246.

17. Destination Embargo of Arab Oil: Its Legality Under International Law

Ibrahim F. I. Shihata

MEASURES APPLIED BY OIL EXPORTING ARAB STATES

The use of Arab oil as an instrument of pressure for the revival of dormant efforts to restore peace in the Middle East was already a popular demand in many Arab countries before the outbreak of Arab-Israeli hostilities in October 1973. The political argument was simple. Production of oil beyond certain limits did not make economic sense for many Arab countries. Their depleting crude was increasingly converted into depreciating dollars and pounds yielding in fact a lower economic return than that achieved by simply keeping it in the ground. Worse still, this conversion was taking place in countries with few alternative resources and with a rather limited absorption capacity for the generated funds. Unchecked production was thus an economic sacrifice that could only be interpreted as a political favor to the consuming countries. Instead of responding positively to such a favor, the United States and most of its Western allies continued to ignore the vital interests of the Arab states. In particular, they either acquiesced in or actually encouraged the continuation of Israel's territorial expansion at the expense of its neighboring Arab states,[1] and of its refusal to implement the United Nations resolutions on the rights of the Arab Palestinian people. . . .[2]

The weight of this simple argument carried its way after repeated warnings by Arab statesmen had proved futile. Shortly before the outbreak of hostilities in October 1973, officials of Saudi Arabia, the largest Arab oil producer, were revealing plans to check the increase of their crude oil production if the United States did not take a more impartial position in the Middle East conflict.[3] With the outbreak of hostilities the argument unsurprisingly gained full momentum.[4] Less than 24 hours after the fighting started on October 6, the Executive Committee of the Palestine Liberation Organization called for an immediate halt of the pumping of all Arab oil.[5] The Iraqi Government responded on the same day by nationalizing the interests of two U.S. companies, Exxon and Mobil, in the Basrah Petroleum Company.[6] Amidst the warnings issued in various Arab oil producing countries, Kuwait took the initiative, on October 9, of calling for an emergency meeting of Arab Oil Ministers to discuss "the role of oil in the light of current developments."

Held in Kuwait on 17 October and attended by 10 Arab countries,[7] the meeting issued a communiqué[8] indicating that oil production would be reduced by not less than 5 percent of the September 1973 level of output in each Arab oil exporting country, with a similar reduction to be applied each successive month, until such time as total evacuation of Israeli forces from all Arab territory occupied during the June 1967 war is completed and the legitimate rights of the Palestinian people are restored. . . .[9]

The communiqué and resolution defined their objective in no unclear terms,[10] combining escalating cutbacks in production with selective discrimination between friendly and unfriendly states. The "legitimacy" of such an objective was particularly emphasized, along with the concern of the participants for the economic welfare of the industrial world. Production of crude oil in the ten countries attending the meeting averaged in September 1973 around 19.5 million barrels/day. A 5–10 percent cut meant a reduction of 1 and 2 million, or roughly from 3 to 6 percent of the volume of oil exports then moving in world trade. . . .[11]

The embargo of Arab oil to the United States, already recommended at the October 17 meeting, was imposed unilaterally by Abu Dhabi on

October 18, by Libya on October 19, by Saudi Arabia and Algeria on October 20, by Kuwait and Qatar on October 21 and by Oman on October 25.[12] On October 19, it should be noted, the U.S. involvement in the military conflict then going on between Arab and Israeli forces reached such a magnitude that President Nixon requested that Congress appropriate $2,200 million in the current financial year for military assistance to Israel.

On October 21 Iraq, which had not concurred in the cutback decision of October 17, announced the nationalization of the 60 percent Dutch holding in Shell's 23.75 percent interest in the Basra Petroleum Company as a "punitive measure against the Netherlands for its hostile stand towards the Arab Nation."[13] Two days later, Kuwait, which had already adopted an immediate 10 percent cut in production on October 21, embargoed oil shipments to the Netherlands for "its hostile attitude towards Arab rights and its pro-Israeli bias."[14] Oil exports to that country were also curtailed by Abu Dhabi on October 23, by Qatar on October 24, by Oman on October 25, by Libya on October 30 and its curtailment was confirmed by Saudi Arabia on November 2.[15] With the beginning of November, oil production had already been cut back by at least 25 percent in Kuwait, 10 percent in Saudi Arabia, Algeria, and Qatar and by at least 5 percent in Libya, Bahrain, Dubai, and Oman.[16] Before the embargo went into effect, total U.S. imports of Arab oil averaged, according to reliable estimates, around 1.8–1.9 million b/d, equivalent to 28 percent of aggregate U.S. oil imports and 10 percent of its total consumption.[17] Dutch imports of Arab oil reached, on the other hand, 1.47 million b/d or 71 percent of its overall oil imports.[18]

After the cessation of military operations, Arab Oil Ministers held their second meeting on November 4–5 in an attempt to enhance the use of oil for accelerating the process of reaching a peaceful settlement of the Arab-Israeli conflict. They decided on escalation in the initial percentage reduction to 25 percent below the September 1973 level, including the volumes deducted as a result of the embargo. . . . As for future cutbacks, it was decided that a further reduction amounting to 5 percent of the November output should follow in December "provided that such reduction shall not affect the share that any friendly state was importing from any Arab exporting country during the first nine months of 1973."[19]

The trend towards escalation was soon to be reversed, however, partly in view of the less biased attitudes which gradually developed in Western Europe and Japan, and partly because of the relative success of the efforts for reaching a peaceful settlement in the area. On November 18, nine Arab Oil Ministers convening in Vienna decided not to implement the 5 percent reduction for the month of December with respect to European countries (meaning the nine EEC members with the exception of the Netherlands) "in appreciation of the political stand taken by the Common Market countries in their communiqué of 19 November, 1973 regarding the Middle East crisis."[20] The Sixth Summit Arab Conference held in Algiers from November 26 to 28 further exempted Japan and the Philippines from the effects of the 5 percent cutback scheduled for December. It also qualified the progressive monthly reduction formula by adopting a ceiling for reductions in production "to the extent that reduction in income should not exceed one quarter on the basis of the 1972 income level of each producing country."[21] Consuming countries were also to be classified in three categories: friendly, neutral, or "supporting the enemy." The classification was to be applied and reviewed by a committee of the Ministers of Foreign Affairs and Oil of the Arab oil producing states. Any neutral country reclassified as friendly would receive the same quantities of oil as it imported in 1972. . . .

Subsequent to the Sixth Arab Summit Conference, Arab Oil Ministers convened in Kuwait and expressed a greater measure of flexibility. In their communiqué of December 8 they agreed to lift the oil embargo against the United States with the beginning of the implementation of a schedule of withdrawal of Israeli forces from Arab territories occupied since 1967. Furthermore, they decided that once a withdrawal schedule was reached, a schedule for the gradual return of oil production to its September 1973 level would be drawn up to go with the implementation of the stages of withdrawal. Supply of oil to "African countries and friendly Islamic States" was also to continue uninterrupted "to the extent that they have valid contracts even if it means an increase in production."

. . . Emphasizing that the use of oil by Arab states was an instrument of flexible persuasion meant only to ensure respect for the rules of international order in the Middle East, Arab Oil Ministers took further steps in their meeting in Kuwait on December 24–25 for the relaxation of oil production cutbacks. The 25 percent cutback was eased down to 15 percent of the September 1973 level of production with effect from January 1, 1974, while the extra 5 percent originally scheduled for January was dispensed with altogether. Japan, which had already issued two Foreign Ministry statements endorsing UN Security Council resolutions on the Middle East conflict, was allowed a "special treatment which would not subject it to the full extent of the across-the-board cutback measures." This was explicitly justified not only by "the change in Japan's policy towards the Arab cause," but also by "the deteriorating economic situation in Japan." It was also decided to resume oil supply to Belgium via Rotterdam (up to the level of September 1973 imports) and to supply "certain friendly countries," presumably France, Britain, and Spain, with all their actual oil requirements even in excess of that level.[22] The embargo imposed against the Netherlands remained intact, however, despite the earlier declaration of the Dutch Government spokesman on December 4 to the effect that his government "considers that the Israeli presence in occupied territories is illegal."[23]

. . . This gesture was later followed by the much argued decision of Arab Oil Ministers, taken in Vienna on March 18, 1974, to lift the embargo of Arab oil to the United States, to treat both Italy and West Germany as "friendly countries," and to increase oil production in each Arab country to the extent needed to enable it to carry out that decision.[24]

As a result of the above decisions, countries importing Arab oil are, at the time of writing (May, 1974), classified as follows:[25]

1. The "friendly states" which are allowed to import all their actual requirements of Arab oil;
2. the "neutral states," including the United States, which are allowed to import the equivalent of their average imports of Arab oil during the first nine months of 1973 or during the month of September 1973, whichever is greater; and
3. "the embargoed States," the Netherlands, South Africa, Portugal, and Rhodesia, whose supplies of Arab oil are cut off completely (although in the case of the Netherlands, supplies are allowed for purposes of refining and re-exportation to nonembargoed countries).

Measures applied by Arab oil producing countries have thus included nationalization of foreign assets (in Iraq), reduction of oil production, discrimination in oil exports, and embargo of oil shipments to certain countries. The arguments for and against the validity of discriminatory and politically motivated nationalizations are well known.[26] The imposition of limitations on the production of primary commodities is, on the other hand, obviously within the exclusive domestic jurisdiction of sovereign states. Such limitations have, at any rate, been imposed in the past by two Arab states[27] as a conservation measure in respect of oil production, without invoking any international legal controversy. The discussion in this article will therefore concentrate on the legality of the embargo of Arab oil shipments to certain foreign states and the politically motivated discrimination in the export of Arab oil. Since these measures are intrinsically tied to the Middle East conflict, a discussion of certain legal aspects of that conflict seems inescapable in this respect.

ILLEGALITY OF ARMED ISRAELI PRESENCE ON EGYPTIAN AND SYRIAN TERRITORIES

The legal complexities of the Arab-Israeli conflict are many.[28] Although their details do not fall within the scope of this article, one issue has to be clearly established as a basis for the reasoning that follows: Israel has no legal right under contemporary international law to the occupation and, a fortiori, to the annexation of the territories of Egypt and Syria which it has occupied by force since June 1967. . . .[29]

Egypt and Syria, as the states vested with sovereignty but illegally deprived of actual control over territories occupied by Israel, were thus entitled to seek redress for the protection of their territorial integrity. Under the UN system they were probably under the obligation to resort first to peaceful methods. This they have done in vain for more than six years. . . .

Whether these two states and the other Arab states bound with them by regional arrangements including mutual defense pacts[30] were entitled to use against third states such economic measures as those explained in detail in the previous section of this paper is a different question, however. The fact that such measures were taken on the whole as a complementary step in the legitimate struggle of Arab states to regain control of occupied Arab territories and to reach a final peaceful settlement of the Middle East conflict is of great relevance. It remains to be proved, however, that the use of such measures by the Arab states applying them did not constitute a violation of general principles of customary international law or a breach of specific treaty commitments.

LEGALITY OF ARAB OIL MEASURES UNDER CUSTOMARY INTERNATIONAL LAW

In applying the standards of customary international law to the measures adopted by Arab oil exporting countries the following points should be taken into consideration:

1. The measures in question were initiated at a time when many of the states applying them were in an actual situation of war—Egypt and Syria as the major belligerents against Israel, with Iraq, Kuwait, and to a lesser extent, Algeria and Saudi Arabia as cobelligerents with them. This war situation was prompted, as shown above, by Israel's insistence on the forcible occupation of Egyptian and Syrian territories and the attempt by Egypt and Syria to regain control over their occupied territories after exhaustion of peaceful means to achieve that result.

2. The use of the measures was clearly tied, as shown above, to the achievement of the twofold objective of "withdrawal of Israeli forces from occupied Arab territories and restoration of the legitimate rights of the Palestinian people." They were aimed, in other words, at the establishment of two of the basic requirements of a lasting peace in the Middle East.

3. The measures were also in complete conformity with the economic interests of the states applying them. As explained earlier, these measures meant, in fact, the termination by Arab oil exporting states of the practice of doing favors for countries whose foreign policy made them unworthy, in Arab eyes, of receiving such favors. Yet in taking these measures Arab states showed consideration for the welfare of the countries particularly affected, such as Japan, and modified their position towards them accordingly.

4. The measures were taken, on the whole, pursuant to resolutions of the Oil Ministers of the states members of the Organization of Arab Petroleum Exporting Countries (OAPEC). . . .

Identification of the standards of customary international law according to which the legality of the measures in question are to be tested requires a detailed scrutiny of state practice in the matter of the political uses of export controls. These standards will further be clarified by reference to the practice of those international organizations which have considered such uses, either by authorizing them in individual cases or by issuing general statements on the extent of their legitimacy.

State Practice in Peacetime Conditions

U.S. Practice. Special export controls over individual commodities have been long imposed by U.S. legislation for economic and strategic reasons.[31] General U.S. export controls may be said to have begun, however, in 1940, as measures of national defense and economic warfare.[32] Such controls continued to apply after the termination of World War II, resulting in fact in the embargo on shipments of a great number of articles to a wide range of countries. Around the turn of the year 1947, the U.S. Administration began to revive some war regulations and to use them for control of exports to the Soviet bloc. By 1948 most exports to the Soviet Union and Eastern Europe were thus placed under control "in the interest of security."[33] This practice was further formalized in 1949 by the adoption of the Export Control Act which bluntly stated it to be U.S. policy to use export controls, *inter alia*, "to further the foreign policy of the United States."[34] According to that Act, the President of the United States was authorized to "prohibit or curtail the exportation from the United States, its territories and possessions of any articles, materials, or supplies . . . except under such rules and regulations as he shall prescribe."[35] Pursuant to the Act, such rules and regulations were to provide for the denial of any request for authority to export U.S. commodities "to any nation or combination of nations threatening the national security of the United States if the President shall determine that such exports make a significant contribution to the military or economic potential of such nation or nations which could prove detrimental to the national security and welfare of the United States." The Export Regulations actually issued under that Act had a wide extraterritorial effect.[36] They contained a detailed licensing system which required "validated licenses" for certain goods and "general licenses" for others and discriminated between different countries of destination.[37] A sophisticated system of discrimination developed accordingly, culminating in the classification of foreign destinations (excepting Canada) into eight groups, each with a different export control treatment.[38] A complete embargo of U.S. exports to the People's Republic of China, Hong Kong, and Macao was imposed on December 3, 1950, and continued in operation for over twenty years, while a similar embargo imposed on exports to Cuba on October 19, 1960, remains, with a few exceptions, in effect at the present time.[39]

Even when the Export Control Act of 1949 was finally replaced by the Export Administration Act of 1969 (in effect since January 1, 1970),[40] the latter Act, described as "the first significant trade liberalization measure passed by Congress since the end of World War II,"[41] maintained the President's power to prohibit the export of materials under such rules and regulations as he may prescribe. This extensive power was again based on the declared policy to preserve "the national security" and to "further significantly the foreign policy of the United States and to fulfill its international responsibilities." As a result, many of the regulations adopted under the 1949 Act, including the grouping of countries of destination, remain in full force.[42]

This discriminatory trade control system is further reinforced by the Mutual Defense Assistance Act of 1951, commonly called the Battle Act.[43] In this Act the policy of the United States is stated to include an embargo on the shipment of a host of strategic supplies, *including petroleum,* to "nations threatening United States security, including the USSR and all countries under its domination." Such a legislatively sanctioned embargo is unabashedly stated to be imposed in order to "(1) increase the material strength of the United States and of the cooperating nations; (2) impede the ability of nations threatening the security of the United States to conduct military operations, and (3) to assist the people of the nations under the domination of foreign aggressors to reestablish their freedom." A classified list of items embargoed under the provisions of Title I of the Act was thus established and remains, after many amendments, in force to this date. Further steps were also adopted under the Act to strengthen and adjust the control of the export of other commodities which called for a lesser degree of control than outright embargo.[44]

Practice of Other States, Including the Netherlands. 1. Multilateral measures—Internationalization of the U.S. discriminatory practice: Since the beginning of the implementation of its export control system, the U.S. Government has attempted to increase its effectiveness by securing similar action by other countries. It has succeeded in achieving this objective by two means. First, the United States put economic pressure on the countries which received assistance from it by relating, in the Cannon Amendment,[45] the Kem Amendment[46] and the Battle Act,[47] American foreign aid to export control action by the recipient countries against the Sino-Soviet bloc.[48] Secondly, it negotiated with other Western countries, first on a bilateral basis, then multilaterally, the establishment of strategic export controls on the pattern of the U.S. system. Early in 1949 the United Kingdom and France formulated an Anglo-French list of strategic items which was similar to the U.S. lists prepared earlier for the same purpose. Later in November of that year a Consultative Group was founded in Paris by the United Kingdom, France, Italy, the Netherlands, Belgium, Luxembourg, and the United States which was joined on later dates by Norway, Denmark, Canada, the Federal Republic of Germany, Portugal, Greece, Turkey, and Japan. Members of the Group formulated three lists of controlled goods covering items for embargo, for quantitative control, and for exchange of information and surveillance. . . .[49]

It should be particularly recalled that the countries which were intended to be adversely affected by such multilateral measures in many cases maintained normal diplomatic relations with the states applying those measures. The countries affected have not helped directly or indirectly in maintaining forcible occupation of American or Western European territories. Nor have they been involved in any manner in depriving the peoples of the United States or of the other cooperating Western nations of their right to self-determination. Some of the affected countries were accused, however, at the time of the Korean War (December 17, 1950), of providing military assistance to regimes with which U.S. forces were involved in armed hostilities. Only North Korea and North Vietnam could be said to have been engaged in armed conflict with the United States during part of the period in which shipment of all American and West European strategic goods to these two countries was officially embargoed.

2. Domestic legislation: The imposition of export control regulations and discrimination in their application to different countries of destination by no means constitute isolated instances in state practice. Although such regulations are often meant to serve economic purposes, they have been widely used as instruments of foreign policy to secure political advantages for the states applying them, such as the denial to unfriendly countries of badly needed strategic goods. Thus, the European countries cooperating with the United States in the implementation of the multilateral program met with no difficulty in finding a basis in their own domestic legal systems for such a practice. A report submitted to the U.S. Congress in 1962 on export controls in six European countries, including the Netherlands, found that each of the six countries "maintains substantially the same controls on strategic exports to countries of the Sino-Soviet bloc" as those imposed by the United States.[50] It further confirmed that "controls over exports of goods on the international embargo list . . . are carried out through their own laws and regulations."[51]

. . . The politically inspired export control of strategic goods may even be traced in such countries as Sweden and Switzerland.[52] It is, of course, a general practice in the Soviet Union[53] and, one may safely assume, in other Socialist countries where the government exercises a monopoly over foreign trade. A list of the "Laws and Regulations relating to Control of Import and Export Trade in Member Countries" of the Asian-African Legal Consultative Committee also confirms that such restrictive practices have found their way into the legal systems of developing countries.[54] In short, as Adler-Karlsson concluded in his exhaustive study of the subject, "the embargo policy has been world-wide."[55]

State Practice in Time of War

The right of a belligerent state to resort to measures of economic warfare against its adversary and to apply economic sanctions against third states which violate their obligations of neutrality in this regard is so manifest that elaborate treatment is unnecessary. It should be pointed out, however, that neutral states (such as the United States and the Netherlands supposedly were during the Arab-Israeli hostilities of October 1973) are under the obligation of acting towards belligerents in accordance with their attitude of impartiality. This means, in particular, abstention from "the supply in any manner, directly or indirectly, by a neutral Power to a belligerent Power, of warships, ammunition or war material of any kind whatever."[56] It means also that a neutral power should not allow a belligerent to transport war materials or supplies over its territory.[57] As the Dutch Government itself admitted in the course of World War I, a neutral state is bound to prevent the transit of materials likely to strengthen a belligerent when such materials are connected with military operations.[58] A breach of such obligations of neutrality entitles affected belligerents to take retaliatory action in the nature of reprisals[59] (including maritime embargo in the technical sense). It enables them, a fortiori, to resort to retorsion against the delinquent neutral by taking unfriendly or unfair acts in its regard (such as the imposition of an embargo on shipment of strategic goods destined to its ports). Such measures of reprisal or retorsion[60] are not merely punitive retaliatory acts, but must also be considered as instruments for discouraging the offending nonbelligerent from committing further violations of international law with regard to the injured party.

Under the controversial concept of differential or qualified neutrality in its modern sense, a neutral power might be able to discriminate against the belligerent whose recourse to war is unlawful.[61] Such a concept cannot therefore be cited in defense of a neutral state which supplies or helps in supplying war materials to a belligerent in order to enable it to maintain forcible control over territories of other states. This should be particularly so when the military operations during which the supply of such war materials takes place are restricted to the area of the illegally occupied territories, as was the case in the Arab-Israeli hostilities of 1973.

The practice of states, especially that of the United States, in the course of World War II reveals the extent of the use of economic warfare measures, not only among belligerents but also by or against neutrals. The oil policy adopted by the major powers during that war is particularly significant. "It was the general aim of British policy to create an oil famine in Europe."[62] In accordance with that policy, Great Britain requested the United States, early in 1940, and the latter agreed, to complete arrangements to ensure that no U.S. flag tankers would carry oil from the Americas to such "adjacent neutrals" in Europe as Spain and Portugal.[63] The U.S. Government went further by proposing to cut off all supplies of oil to foreign countries including Japan.[64] A presidential order issued on July 25, 1940, extended the application of the Defense Act so that licences would be required for the export of petroleum and its products, and of scrap.[65] Six days later, the U.S. President ordered that export of aviation petrol should be restricted to the countries of the Western Hemisphere.[66] Meanwhile the Soviet and Japanese Ambassadors in Washington were informed that "it was the policy of the U.S. Government to give Great Britain every help short of war and that they intended to give licences for all British oil requirements."[67] As a result of such measures, Japan, which at the time was not at war with either the United States or Britain, and which was believed to be "very short of aviation oil," was deprived of American oil imports on which it was dependent for about two-thirds of its total import requirements.[68] Furthermore, on September 26, 1940, the United States, while still a "neutral" power, declared an embargo on the export of iron and steel scrap as from October 16, 1940 "except to countries of the Western Hemisphere and to Great Britain."[69]

The relevance of the above practice is clear. As explained earlier, Arab oil exporting countries were either cobelligerents against Israel in the hostilities of October 1973 or were merely "nonbelligerents." Along with Egypt and Syria, Iraq, Kuwait, and to a lesser degree, Algeria and Saudi Arabia participated in the war. They were thus definitely entitled to take retaliatory measures against such neutral powers as the United States, which supplied Israel, in the course of operations, with massive quantities of war materials, some of which are reported to have been delivered directly in Arab occupied territories. Sanctions were also justified against such states as the Netherlands and Portugal, which allowed the use of their territory for the transit of some of these war materials to Israel. Other Arab oil exporting countries were following the example of the United States in 1940 by curtailing the exportation of their oil to unfriendly countries. A great many countries have taken similar steps even in peacetime conditions. . . .

LEGALITY OF ARAB OIL MEASURES UNDER PERTINENT RESOLUTIONS OF INTERNATIONAL ORGANIZATIONS

UN Declarations

The UN General Assembly's Declaration of the Principles of International Law concerning Friendly Relations and Co-operation among States, which is generally treated as declaratory of contemporary international law, includes the following statement:

No State may use or encourage the use of economic, political or any other type of measures to coerce another State in order to obtain from it the subordination of the exercise of its sovereign rights and to secure from it advantages of any kind.[70]

The seemingly general language of such a statement which has figured in earlier UN declarations of a more political nature[71] certainly represents a progressive development, not a mere codification of the international practice described above. It should be read in the light of the following considerations:

1. The statement cannot be read in isolation from other parts of the Declaration. That instrument includes, in particular, the following principle:

The territory of a State shall not be the object of military occupation resulting from the use of force in contravention of the provisions of the Charter. The territory of a State shall not be the object of acquisition by another State resulting from the threat or use of force. No territorial acquisition resulting from the threat or use of force shall be recognized as legal.[72]

The Declaration also states that subjection of peoples to alien domination is contrary to the Charter and that the peoples deprived by forcible action of their right to self-determination "are entitled to seek and to receive support in accordance with the purposes and principles of the Charter." When the principles embodied in the latter statements are violated in regard to a certain state, one may reasonably assume from the reading of the entire text of the Declaration that such a state will not be deprived of the right to resort to economic measures of self-defense or of reprisal[73] against the states responsible, directly or indirectly, for that violation.

2. Prohibition of the use of economic measures to coerce another state in order to secure advantages from it cannot be absolute in any case. "[A] certain degree of coercion is inevitable in States' day-to-day interactions for values. Fundamental community policy does not seek to reach and prohibit this coercion. . . ."[74] It will be necessary, therefore, to characterize unlawful economic measures by their objective, not merely by their effect,[75] and to limit this characterization to measures involving the subordinating of sovereign rights of other states, and not merely seeking some advantage from them.

3. The statement under consideration may not, at any rate, be interpreted as imposing an obligation on states to make economic sacrifices for the benefit of other states without receiving a proper consideration therefor. If a state chooses to do favors for other countries at the expense of its long-term economic interests, it is for that state to decide what advantage it should receive in return, as long as the required consideration is permissible under international law. The legitimacy of the action of such a state becomes all the more evident when the consideration required by it is simply the cooperation of the recipients in ensuring respect of international law in regard to itself or to other states.[76]

4. Finally, the language of the above-quoted statement assumes normal peacetime conditions. It cannot apply in an actual war situation where belligerent states are ordinarily entitled, in accordance with the rules of the law of war, to use their economic power to coerce their adversaries and even to inflict damage on third parties violating their obligations of neutrality towards them.

The statement of the Friendly Relations Declaration should also be read in conjunction with other general UN declarations, especially the General Assembly's resolutions on state sovereignty over natural resources. In 1960, the Assembly upheld "the sovereign right of every State to dispose of its wealth and its natural resources."[77] Such a sovereign right to the free disposition of natural resources is confirmed by subsequent resolutions of the Assembly and of UNCTAD's Trade and Development Board.[78] It includes in particular the freedom of each state to develop rules and conditions which it considers "necessary or desirable with regard to the *authorization, restriction or prohibition*" of such activities as exploration, development, and disposition of natural resources.[79] More recently, the UN General Assembly deplored actions aimed at coercing states engaged in the exercise of their "sovereign rights over their natural resources" as violations of the Charter and of the Friendly Relations Declaration. . . .[80]

Action Authorized or Requested
by International Organizations

Economic coercion, including the embargo on shipments of strategic materials to countries in need of them, has also been stipulated by international organizations as an appropriate method for securing collective policy objectives of a noneconomic character. Sanctions of this type have by no means been confined to measures applied by the Security Council under Article 41 of the UN Charter or authorized by it for adoption by regional agencies, pursuant to Article 53(1) of the Charter.

The Security Council is certainly qualified, under these provisions, to employ coercive economic measures and to call upon states to apply them, as it has done in fact with regard to Rhodesia (general embargo on trade including specifically the supply of oil and oil products)[81] and to South Africa (embargo on the supply of arms and ammunition).[82] Similar actions have also been authorized by the UN General Assembly. Early in 1951, the Assembly recommended that every state impose "an embargo on the shipment to areas under the control of the Central People's Government of the People's Republic of China and of the North Korean authorities" of many strategic materials including petroleum. . . .[83] Coercive economic measures were also authorized by the O.A.S. with regard to the Dominican Republic in 1961 and to Cuba in 1962 and 1964.[84] The O.A.U. has similarly assumed competence to authorize and request the adoption of such measures against such states as South Africa,[85] Portugal,[86] Rhodesia,[87] and, indeed, Israel. . . .[88]

With the exception of the 1951 UN General Assembly resolution on China and North Korea, these measures were authorized in peacetime. The measures recommended in the latter resolution were to be taken, on the other hand, by "every State" including nonbelligerents and thus were not meant to be a mere exercise of the rights of belligerents under the law of war.

Such precedents may well be cited in support of the Arab oil measures as a supplementary basis for their lawfulness. On the one hand, they further prove the prevailing trend in international practice, whereby the application of coercive measures is clearly differentiated from the use of armed force, which is subject to a much more restrictive set of rules. . . .

LEGALITY OF ARAB OIL MEASURES UNDER TREATY LAW

Multilateral Conventions

Of all existing multilateral trade conventions, the General Agreement on Tariffs and Trade (GATT)[89] seems to be the only one that has some bearing on our discussion. Other multilateral trade conventions either do not regulate quantitative export controls, or do not include any of the Arab oil exporting countries among their parties. As for the GATT, Egypt and Kuwait are contracting parties to it while Algeria, Bahrain, and Qatar have accepted its *de facto* application to them.[90] These countries have participated, as shown above,[91] in the oil cutback and embargo resolutions.

Article 11 of the GATT contains a general prohibition, subject to exceptions irrelevant to our discussion, on quantitative restrictions imposed on imports or exports "through quotas, import or export licences or other measures." Prohibition or restriction of imports and exports are also to be administered, pursuant to Article 13(1), without discrimination against "all third countries." Furthermore, Article 1, which is entitled "General Most-Favoured-Nation Treatment," provides for the automatic extension to like products imported from or exported to other parties, of any advantage granted by a party in respect of, *inter alia*, "all rules and formalities in connection with importation or exportation."

Such provisions, if read in isolation from other parts of the Agreement, may give the erroneous impression that contracting Arab states are under a general and absolute prohibition in the employment of discriminatory export controls against other contracting parties such as the United States and the Netherlands. The GATT, much like any other treaty, must, however, be read in its entirety.[92] Pursuant to other provisions of the GATT, the above-quoted general principles are subject to two types of exceptions. The "general exceptions" provided for in Article 20 include in particular the right of each party to take measures "relating to the conservation of exhaustible natural resources." Such measures must be made effective "in conjunction with restrictions on domestic production or consumption," and "should not apply in a manner which would constitute a means of arbitrary or unjustified discrimination between countries where the same conditions prevail or a disguised restriction on international trade. . . ." These conditions obviously obtain in the case of production cutbacks employed for the purpose of conserving a depleting resource such as oil. More importantly, the "security exceptions" contained in Article 21 allow each contracting party to take "any action which *it considers* necessary for the protection of its essential security interests," if such an action is taken "in time of war or other emergency in international relations." It is significant to note that in the latter provision the Agreement maintains the freedom of each party to estimate the necessity of the action it takes in such exceptional circumstances. Even if necessity is to be judged by objective criteria, one may easily recognize its relevance in a wartime situation when the vital interests of the state are at stake. Discretion of the state in such matters is, indeed, a question of public policy,[93] which may restrict the application of the most-favored-nation clause even in the absence of explicit provisions.[94]

It is true that Article 22(1) of the GATT requires each contracting party to accord "sympathetic consideration" to, and to afford "adequate opportunity for consultation" with other parties. However, such an obligation is incumbent upon a contracting party only after it receives "such representations as may be made by another contracting party with respect to any matter affecting the operation of this Agreement." Consultation cannot therefore be a precondition for taking measures, but is merely a procedure devised in the

GATT to secure satisfaction to the injured party in cases of alleged violations.[95] None of the contracting parties affected by the Arab oil measures have submitted representations under Article 22 of the GATT; nor have they resorted to the nullification or impairment procedure provided for in Article 23 of that Agreement. . . .

Bilateral Treaties

The relevant bilateral trade agreements concluded between Arab oil exporting countries and countries affected by the Arab oil embargo seem to be limited to three agreements[96] concluded between the United States and Saudi Arabia, Iraq, and Oman, respectively, before any of these latter countries was significantly involved in the export of oil. None of these agreements, it is submitted, presented a legal barrier to the implementation of the Arab oil measures vis-à-vis the United States. Although all agreements include a most-favored-nation clause, the special wording used in each agreement warrants its independent examination.

The U.S.-Saudi Arabia Agreement of 1933[97] confined the application of the most-favored-nation clause included in its Article 3 to treatment "[i]n respect of import, export and other *duties* and *charges* affecting commerce and navigation, as well as in respect of *transit, warehousing* and *other facilities.*" Such a wording obviously excludes quantitative restrictions on exports from the scope of the clause. The same article mentions also "any . . . regulation affecting commerce or navigation," but this is only in stating that *concessions* with respect to them will be immediately reciprocated. Even if the oil measures applied by Saudi Arabia were to be characterized as involving "concessions,"[98] a presumption in favor of an exception on grounds of national security interests can well be derived from a treaty of this type.[99] A similar presumption may also be established "in favor of the overriding character of exemptions on grounds of international public policy."[100] As explained earlier in this article, the Saudi oil embargo was applied in an attempt to secure an objective of the highest international order: the restoration to the lawful sovereigns of illegally occupied territories and the restoration of the rights of peoples deprived of self-determination.

The U.S.-Iraq Agreement of 1938[101] explicitly provides, in Article 2, that "in all that concerns matters of prohibition or restrictions on importations and exportations each of the two countries will accord, whenever they may have recourse to the said prohibitions or restrictions, to the commerce of the other country, treatment equally favourable to that which is accorded to any other country. . . ." Article 4 is equally explicit, however, in permitting exceptions relating to "the adoption or enforcement of measures relating to neutrality or to rights and obligations arising under the Covenant of the League of Nations." Such a codification of the "international public policy exception" could obviously be invoked by Iraq against the United States, which deviated from its obligations of neutrality in the course of the Arab-Israeli hostilities in which Iraqi forces were involved. It should be noted, however, that Iraq did not concur in the cutback and embargo resolutions of the Arab Oil Ministers, and that exportation of its oil through the East Mediterranean terminals was halted due to Israeli military action.[102]

Finally, the trade agreement concluded in 1958 between the United States and the "Sultanate of Muscat and Oman and Dependencies"[103] prohibits, in Article 8, the imposition by either party of restrictions on the exportation of any product to the territories of the other party "unless the exportation of the like product to all third countries is similarly restricted or prohibited." Such a provision, which admittedly would preclude Oman under normal conditions from implementing discriminatory embargo measures on oil shipments to the United States, is restricted, however, by the text of Article 11(d) of the same Agreement. According to this latter article the agreement does not preclude the application of measures "necessary to fulfil the obligations of a Party for the maintenance or restoration of international peace and security, or necessary to protect its essential security interests." The internal security interests of that country would certainly have been further impaired had it deviated from the collective Arab stand adopted during the war crisis. It is unofficially reported, at any rate, that Oman, which is not an OAPEC member, has not participated in the meetings of Arab Oil Ministers, and was the last Arab country to declare an embargo on oil shipments to the United States, was quite lenient in applying that measure, and was the first to lift it.

It may be worth repeating in this respect that the United States has felt free in normal peacetime to impose a quota system for the import of oil, which discriminated in favor of oil imported from certain countries other than Saudi Arabia, Iraq, and Oman. The preferential treatment given under that system to certain countries, such as Canada, could hardly conform to the standards provided for in the above-mentioned agreements. It is not surprising, therefore, that the U.S. Government has not officially characterized the measures adopted by these Arab countries with respect to the export of their oil in a crisis situation as constituting a breach of treaty commitments on their part.

CONCLUSION

In the light of the above analysis, the destination embargo of Arab oil may now be viewed in its right perspective. Far from being a "weapon for blackmailing the West" or a "threat to international peace," it has been employed as an instrument for the respect and promotion of the rule of law in an area of international relations where such a rule has long been forsaken for the rule of superior military force. In their use of that instrument, Arab oil exporting countries were in fact following the steps of a great number of other states which have used their export regulations to further their foreign policies. Only the objective of the Arab states seems to have been more legitimate. The Arab states took that measure not to weaken unfriendly countries but merely to discourage third countries from violating their obligations of neutrality toward them and from continuing their encouragement of, or their acquiescence in, an illegal situation. The Arab states have considered it their moral responsibility to keep the industrialized nations fueled with Arab exhaustible oil, in spite of their awareness that such a policy may not serve their best selfish economic interests. They were not to be expected, however, to do favors indefinitely for states which had refused to cooperate with them in putting an end to the illegal occupation and annexation of Arab territories and to the continuing denial of the right of the Palestinian people to self-determination.

The oil measures taken by the Arab states were the result of the exercise of their "sovereign right" to dispose of their natural resources in the manner which best suits their legitimate interests. . . .

NOTES

Ibrahim F. I. Shihata is a legal advisor for the Kuwait Fund for Arab Economic Development. The opinions expressed in this essay are those of the writer and do not necessarily represent the views of the Kuwait Fund.

1. The "Jewish State" suggested in the Partition Plan of Palestine (adopted by the UN General Assembly by Resolution 181(II) Nov. 29, 1947, GAOR, 2nd Sess., Resolutions, 31–50, UN Doc. A/519) was to cover an area of about 5,655 sq. miles, compared to about 907 sq. m. owned by Jewish settlers and agencies at the time and to about 10,249 sq. m. which formed the total area of Palestine under British Mandate. Territories of Palestine controlled by Israel after the 1949 Armistice Agreements covered, however, 8,017 sq. m., while territories of Arab States occupied by Israel in June 1967 covered 26,476 sq. m., including 23,622 sq. m. in Egypt, 2,270 sq. m. in Jordan (other than the Arab city of Jerusalem) and 444 sq. m. in Syria. See THE MIDDLE EAST AND NORTH AFRICA 398 (19th ed., 1972).

2. For a comprehensive list of these resolutions, see UNITED NATIONS RESOLUTIONS ON PALESTINE 1947–1972, at 176–79, 195–98 (Institute for Palestine Studies, Beirut & Center for Documentation and Studies, Abu Dhabi, 1973). These resolutions have affirmed, in particular, the right of the Palestinians to return to their homes, to compensation for those who opt not to return, to respect for their immovable properties in Palestine, for their human rights, self-determination, and the legitimacy of their struggle for it.

3. See, e.g., statements of Saudi Arabia's Oil Minister Sheikh Zaki Yamani, Washington Post, April 17, 1973, at 1, confirmed by King Faisal, id., July 6, 1973, at 1 and Newsweek, Sept. 10, 1973. In the latter magazine's interview, King Faisal explicitly explained that "cooperation requires action on both sides: not sacrifices on one side and negative, if not hostile attitudes on the other side."

4. Ironically, however, the first cutback in Arab oil production was a direct result of Israeli military action. Two of the four East Mediterranean terminals—Banias and Tartus in Syria—were targets of Israeli air and sea raids which damaged considerably their loading facilities. A third terminal—Sidon in Lebanon—remained open but was not visited by tankers. As a result, throughput from Saudi Arabia and Iraq had to be reduced to a trickle before the cutback decisions on the Arab side were actually issued. See 17 MIDDLE EAST ECONOMIC SURVEY (MEES), No. 1, Oct. 26, 1973, at 2. Israel also suspended operations at the Ashkelon terminal as of Oct. 6, 1973, thus halting a potential 500,000 b/d of exports. See Middle East Oil Emergency, 40 PETROLEUM PRESS SERVICE, No. 11, at 407, 408 (Nov. 1973).

5. 16 MEES, No. 51, Oct. 12, 1973, at 4.

6. Law No. 70, Oct. 7, 1973. English translation in *id.*, at i–iii.

7. Saudi Arabia, Kuwait, Iraq, Libya, Algeria, Egypt, Syria, Abu Dhabi, Bahrain, and Qatar.

8. 16 MEES, No. 52, Oct. 19, 1973, at iii–iv. The communiqué was signed by all participants excepting the Oil Minister of Iraq.

9. Coinciding with this step, a Ministerial Committee representing the six Gulf member states of OPEC (five Arab countries plus Iran) decided on October 16, 1973, to abandon negotiations with oil companies on the price of crude and announced new posting prices adding about 70 percent to the posting for Arabian light crude. *Id.*, at (i). This measure was already under consideration before the flare-up of Arab-Israeli hostilities and was particularly espoused by Iran, a non-Arab country. The establishment of its legality is therefore beyond the scope of this paper.

10. *See also* the communiqué of Arab Ministers dated March 18, 1974, where this objective is reiterated as quoted in note 30 *infra*. Other wild objectives propagated by the Western press and quoted in Paust and Blaustein, *The Arab Oil Weapon— A Threat to International Peace*, 68 AJIL 427ff. (1974), never figured in the original cutback decision or in subsequent official Arab joint statements.

11. Estimates in 17 MEES, No. 4, Nov. 16, 1973, at 3–4.

12. For the attitude of each Arab country *see* 17 MEES, No. 1, Oct. 26, 1973, at 3–7.

13. Law No. 90, Oct. 21, 1973. For English translation of the text, *see id.*, at 12. The reasons stated by the Iraqi News Agency for this action include the use of Dutch territory as "a bridgehead for assistance sent to the enemy," the supply by the Netherlands to Israel of crude oil from its imported stock, the continuous flights of KLM to "transport mercenaries and assistance to the enemy," the initial opposition of the Netherlands to the issue of an unbiased communiqué by EEC members, the declaration of the Dutch Foreign Minister to Arab Ambassadors of his country's support for Israel, the personal participation of the Dutch Minister of Defense in a demonstration staged in the Dutch capital to express support for Israel during the war, and the participation of various Dutch establishments and companies in collecting contributions for the Israeli war effort. *Id.*, at 13.

14. *Id.*, at 5.

15. *See id.*, at 6–7 and 17 *id.*, No. 2, Nov. 2, 1973, at 3–4. It was later explained however that the embargo did not cover oil shipped to Rotterdam for the purposes of refining and reexportation to nonembargoed countries.

16. *Ibid.*

17. *Id.*, 16, No. 52, Oct. 19, 1973, at 4, and 17 *id.*, No. 22, March 18, 1974, at 13.

18. *Id.*, No. 2, Nov. 2, 1973, at 1.

19. *Id.*, SUPP. Nov. 6, 1973, at 4.

20. *Id.*, No. 5, Nov. 23, 1973, at 5. Iraq did not attend the meeting.

21. Considering that oil prices (excluding dollar depreciation adjustments) have risen by 70 percent since 1972, this ceiling meant that oil producing Arab states could in fact reduce output to some 45 percent of the 1972 level before reaching the minimum 75 percent of 1972 revenue level. 17 MEES, No. 6, Nov. 30, 1973, at 1.

22. *Id.*, No. 11, Jan. 4, 1974, at 1.

23. *Id.*, No. 7, Dec. 7, 1973, at 13.

24. *Id.*, No. 22, March 22, 1974, at 1, 6. The Ministers' communiqué reiterated the "basic objective" of the Arab oil measures which is "to draw world attention

to the Arab question in order to create an atmosphere conducive to the implementation of UN Security Council Resolution 242 calling for total withdrawal from the occupied Arab territories and the restoration of the legitimate rights of the Palestinian people" and referred to "the new direction" in American official policy toward the Arab-Israeli conflict. The communiqué provided, however, that the decision would be subject to review on June 1, 1974. Algeria expressed the view that the lifting of the embargo was "provisional in nature and limited to the period expiring 1 June 1974." Syria and Libya dissented to the decision altogether. *See* a translation of the text of the communiqué in *Ibid.*

25. *Compare* a quadripartite classification in 17 *id.*, No. 11, Jan. 4, 1974, at 1.

26. *See, e.g.*, 8 WHITEMAN, DIGEST OF INTERNATIONAL LAW 376–82 (1967); 3 HACKWORTH, DIGEST OF INTERNATIONAL LAW 555, 645 (1943); FATOUROS, GOVERNMENT GUARANTEES TO FOREIGN INVESTORS 249–51 (1962); S. FRIEDMAN, EXPROPRIATION IN INTERNATIONAL LAW 189–93 (1953); Charpentier, *De la non-discrimination dans les investissements,* 9 ANNUAIRE FRANÇAIS DE DROIT INTERNATIONAL 35–63 (1963).

27. Kuwait limited the annual production of its crude oil to 3 million b/d as from 1972 (15 MEES, No. 25, April 14, 1972, at 12), while Libya introduced several successive cutbacks on the production of oil companies operating in its territory beginning in 1968 (12 *id.*, No. 4, Nov. 22, 1968), and continuing in 1970 (13 *id.*, No. 33, June 12, 1970) and in 1972 (15 *id.*, No. 19, March 3, 1972).

28. For enumeration of such legal issues, *see* QUINCY WRIGHT, THE MIDDLE EAST: PROSPECTS FOR PEACE (1969); Quincy Wright, *Legal Aspects of the Middle East Situation,* 33 L. & CONTEMP. PROB. 24 (1968). *And see* a comprehensive, but partisan, discussion of these issues, in MARTIN, LE CONFLIT ISRAELO-ARABE (1973).

29. Occupied Jordanian territory and the Gaza Strip are excluded from discussion only because of their irrelevance to the topic of this article.

30. All Arab states are members of the Joint Arab Defense Council, an organ of the Arab League. For an English translation of some relevant inter-Arab joint military pacts, *see* 2 KHALIL, THE ARAB STATES AND THE ARAB LEAGUE. A DOCUMENTARY RECORD. INTERNATIONAL AFFAIRS 101–05, 242–45, 250–53 (1962).

31. *See, e.g.*, The United States Shipping Act of 1916, as amended, 46 U.S.C. §808, 835, 46 C.F.R. §221.5 *et seq.* (sale and transfer to foreign registry of vessels owned by U.S. citizens); the Act of October 6, 1917, 12 U.S.C. §95a, 95b; 31 C.F.R. §54.1 *et seq.* and the Gold Reserve Act of 1934, 31 U.S.C. §440 (export of gold); the Natural Gas Act of 1938, 15 U.S.C. §717b; 18 C.F.R. §153.1 *et seq.* (export of natural gas); the Tobacco Seed and Plant Exportation Act of 1940; 7 U.S.C. §576 (export of tobacco seed and live tobacco plants); the Agricultural Trade Development and Assistance Act of 1954, 7 U.S.C. §1691 *et seq.*; 68 Stat. 454 (export of subsidized U.S. agricultural commodities to the Sino-Soviet bloc); the Atomic Energy Act of 1954, 42 U.S.C. §2011 (export of atomic materials, facilities), etc.

32. *See* Act of July 2, 1940, 54 Stat. 712, 714 (1940), as amended, 50 U.S.C. App. §701 (expired). For a historical account *see* Comment, *Export Controls,* 58 YALE L.J. 1325 (1951).

33. THE STRATEGIC TRADE CONTROL SYSTEM 1948–1956, Dept. of State, Ninth Report to Congress (1957) on Operations under the Mutual Defense Assistance Control Act of 1951, at 4–5 (excerpt republished in METZGER, LAW OF INTERNATIONAL TRADE. DOCUMENTS AND READINGS 1047, 1051 [1966]).

34. The Export Control Act of 1949, Section 2, 19 U.S.C. §2021 (1949) as extended and amended by Public Law 89-63, 89th Cong.

35. *Id.*, Sec. 3 (a).

36. *See* Silverstone, *The Export Control Act of 1949: Extraterritorial Enforcement,* 108 U.P.L.R. 337–43 (1959).

37. *See* SURREY AND SHAW (eds.), A LAWYER'S GUIDE TO INTERNATIONAL BUSINESS TRANSACTIONS 56–85 (1963).

38. For these groups, *see* EXPORT CONTROL, 99th Rep., 1st Quarter 1972, by the Secretary of Commerce to the President, the Senate and the House of Representatives, 2–3. *And see* a description of an earlier classification in Metzger, *Federal Regulation and Prohibition of Trade with Iron-Curtain Countries,* 29 LAW & CONTEM. PROB. 1000, 1001 (1964).

39. For a critical detailed account of these measures, *see* ADLER-KARLSSON, WESTERN ECONOMIC WARFARE 1947–1967—A CASE STUDY IN FOREIGN ECONOMIC POLICY, particularly at 201, 210 (Stockholm Economic Studies, New Series IX, 1968).

40. 50 U.S.C. App. §§2401 *et seq.* as extended by Senate Joint Resolution 218, April 29, 1972, Public Law 92-284, 92nd Congress.

41. Statement of Senator Mondale of Minnesota as quoted in Berman, *The Export Administration Act of 1969: Analysis and Appraisal,* 3 AMER. REV. OF EAST-WEST TRADE 19 (Jan., 1970).

42. *See* EXPORT CONTROL, *supra* note 38, at 1.

43. 22 U.S.C. S1611 *et seq.*; 65 Stat. 644 (1951), as amended by 75 Stat. 424, approved Sept. 4, 1961.

44. *See* THE STRATEGIC TRADE CONTROL SYSTEM 1948–1956, *supra* note 33, at 11–14.

45. Sec. 1304 of Public Law 843, effective Sept. 27, 1950.

46. Sec. 1302 of Public Law 45, effective June 2, 1951.

47. Sec. 103(b), 104 and 105, 202 and 203 of the Mutual Defense Assistance Control Act of 1951, *supra* note 42.

48. For the effect on the 61 countries then receiving military, economic, or financial assistance from the United States, *see* METZGER, *supra* note 92, at 1066.

49. *See id.,* at 1064.

50. *See* REPORT ON EXPORT CONTROLS IN THE U.K., FRANCE, ITALY, FEDERAL REPUBLIC OF GERMANY, BELGIUM AND THE NETHERLANDS, submitted by Senator Thomas J. Dodd and Senator Kenneth B. Keating to the Sub-Comm. to Investigate the Administration of the Internal Security Act and other Internal Security Laws of the Senate Comm. on the Judiciary. 87th Cong. 2nd Sess., April 4, 1962 at 12.

51. *Ibid.* Reference in the Report is made in particular to Law of June 30, 1931, modified by Law of July 10, 1934, and Decree of January 17, 1955, in *Belgium;* Decree of November 30, 1944 in *France;* Foreign Trade Circular No. 89154 in *Germany;* and Tabella Esport dated July 22, 1957, amended on August 13, 1960, in *Italy.* No mention is made in the Report, however, of the *U.K.'s* Import, Export and Customs Powers (Defence) Act 1939 or, quite obviously, of the Export of Goods (Control) order 1967 which was issued pursuant to the 1939 Act after the date of the Report. For text *see* S.I. 1967 No. 675 reprinted in SCHMITTHOFF, THE EXPORT TRADE 429–33 (5th ed., 1969). The Dutch Laws of 1935 and 1962, referred to *infra,* are also not mentioned in the Report.

52. *See* ADLER-KARLSSON, *supra* note 39, at 75–77.

53. *See, e.g.,* ALLEN, SOVIET ECONOMIC WARFARE (1960).

54. [Asian-African Legal Consultative Committee], ECONOMIC LAWS SERIES No. 1: LAWS AND REGULATIONS RELATING TO CONTROL OF IMPORT AND EXPORT TRADE IN MEMBER COUNTRIES, DECEMBER 1965.

55. ADLER-KARLSSON, *supra* note 39, at 3.

56. Art. 6 of Hague Convention XIII(1907) Respecting the Rights and Duties of Neutral Powers in Naval War. 36 Stat. 2415; TS 545; 1 BEVANS 723. *See also* Art. 44 of the "Rules of Aerial Warfare, 1923," drafted by a Commission of Jurists at The Hague, Dec. 1922–Feb. 1923, reproduced in GREENSPAN, THE LAW OF LAND WARFARE 650 (1959). For the general character of the international custom codified in these provisions, *see* 2 OPPENHEIM, INTERNATIONAL LAW 686 (H. Lauterpacht ed., 7th ed., 1952); Greenspan, *supra*, at 548.

57. *See* Art. 2 of Hague Convention V(1907) concerning the Rights and Duties of Neutral Powers and Persons in Case of War on Land. 36 Stat. 2310; TS 540; 1 BEVANS 654. *And see* 2 OPPENHEIM *supra* note 56, at 690.

58. *See* the argument presented by the Netherlands in answer to Great Britain's protest over the transit of metals from occupied Belgium to Germany and of sand and gravel from Germany to Belgium during World War I, as reported in 2, OPPENHEIM, *supra* note 56, at 690–91.

59. *Accord*, Greenspan, *supra* note 56, at 584.

60. For a clear distinction between the two terms, as used in the above context, *see* 2 OPPENHEIM, *supra* note 56, at 136.

61. *See, e.g., id.*, at 651.

62. J. MEDLICOTT, THE ECONOMIC BLOCKADE 474 (1952).

63. *Id.*, at 476, Furthermore, Medlicott reports that, with a minor exception, "the British and American oil policies were vitually identical" even before the U.S. entered the war. *Id.*, at 481.

64. *Id.*, at 477.

65. *Id.*, at 478.

66. *Id.*, at 479.

67. *Ibid.*

68. *Id.*, at 480.

69. *Id.*, at 485.

70. UN G.A. Res. 2625(XXV), Oct. 24, 1970, GAOR, 25th Sess., SUPP. No. 28 at 122–24 (A/8028).

71. *See, e.g.*, Declaration on the Inadmissibility of Intervention in Domestic Affairs of States and the Protection of their Independence and Sovereignty, UN G.A. Res. 2131, Feb. 21, 1965, GAOR, 20th Sess., SUPP. No. 14 at 12 (A/6220), described by the U.S. representative to the General Assembly as "a political Declaration with a vital political message, not as a declaration or elaboration of the law governing non-intervention." *Id.*, 1st Committee. 143rd Meeting, A/C.1/PV.1422, at 12.

72. *Supra* note 29.

73. *Cf.*, Bowett, *Economic Coercion and Reprisals by States*, 13 VA. J. INT'L L. 1, 7–9 (1972). Mr. Bowett further maintains that "there has been no agreement within the United Nations that economic reprisals are illegal under the Charter. Indeed, given the rather low level of compliance accorded by States to the prohibition of armed reprisals (footnote omitted), *it would seem excessively optimistic to argue that economic reprisals are illegal per se*" (emphasis added).

74. MCDOUGAL AND FELICIANO, LAW AND MINIMUM WORLD PUBLIC ORDER 197 (1961).

75. *Accord*, Bowett, *supra* note 73, at 5.

76. In the light of the above, one may differentiate between the U.S. practice under the Battle Act, where U.S. assistance is tied to the recipient's adoption of economic sanctions against third states which are not necessarily guilty of a breach of international law, and the Arab oil measures, which practically made the unlimited

supply of oil dependent on the expression of friendly attitudes towards the Arabs' claim for the restoration of the *status juris* in the Middle East.

77. UN G.A. Res. 1515(XV), GAOR, 15th Sess., Dec. 15, 1960.

78. *See*, UNCTAD: Resolution on Permanent Sovereignty over Natural Resources, Oct. 19, 1972, UN Doc. TD/B/421 of Nov. 5, 1972 (335th meeting), where reference is made to all earlier UN General Assembly resolutions on this matter.

79. *See, e.g.*, UN G.A. Res. 1803(XVII), GAOR, 17th Sess., Dec. 14, 1962 (emphasis added). For a study of this and earlier UN resolutions in their application to Arab Oil, *see*, MUGHRABY, PERMANENT SOVEREIGNTY OVER OIL RESOURCES (1966).

80. UN G.A. Res. 3016(XXVII), GAOR, 27th Sess., Dec. 18, 1972; Res. 3171 (XXVIII), GAOR, 28th Sess., Dec. 17, 1973. It is surprising therefore to see these two resolutions, which are obviously meant to strengthen the right of states over *their* natural resources against coercion from consuming countries, cited against Arab states, in Paust and Blaustein, *supra* note 10, at 420-21.

81. *See* S/Res/217 (1965), Nov. 20, 1965; S/Res/221 (1966), April 9, 1966; S/Res/ 232 (1966), Dec. 16, 1966; S/Res/253 (1968), May 29, 1968; S/Res/277 (1970), March 18, 1970; S/Res/314 (1972), Feb. 28, 1972; S/Res/318 (1972), July 28, 1972; S/Res/ 320 (1972), Sept. 29, 1972.

82. *See* S/Res/181 (1963), Aug. 7, 1963; S/Res/182 (1963), Dec. 4, 1963; S/Res/ 191 (1964), June 18, 1964; S/Res/282 (1970), July 23, 1970; S/Res/311 (1972), Feb. 9, 1972.

83. UN G.A. Res. 500(V), May 18, 1951, GAOR, 5th Sess., SUPP., No. 20A, A/ 1775/Add.1 (1951), at 2.

84. *See* a discussion of these measures and of the question of the competence of a regional organization such as the O.A.S. to authorize them in the absence of a prior authorization from the Security Council in Claude, *The OAS, The UN and the United States*, 347 INT. CONCILIATION 1 (March 1964); Halderman, *Regional Enforcement Measures and the United Nations*, 52 GEORGIA L.J. 89 (1963).

85. *See, e.g.*, OAU Doc. CIAS/Plen.2/Rev.2, May 25, 1963 in RESOLUTIONS ADOPTED BY THE CONFERENCE OF HEADS OF STATES AND GOVERNMENTS OF IN-DEPENDENT AFRICAN COUNTRIES 1963-1972 at 3, 5; AHG/Res. 5(1), 6(1), July 21, 1964, *id.*, 20, 21; AHG/Res/34(11), Oct. 25, 1965, *id.*, 49. Res. 6(1) of 1964 appealed to all oil producing countries to impose an embargo on shipment to South Africa of oil and oil products. *See also* the following resolutions of OAU Council of Ministers: CM/Res. 6(1), 11 August 1963, 1 RESOLUTIONS, RECOMMENDATIONS AND STATEMENTS ADOPTED BY THE ORDINARY AND EXTRAORDINARY SESSIONS OF THE COUNCIL OF MINISTERS 1963-1967 at 5 (May 1973); CM/Res. 31(III), July 17, 1964, *id.*, 29; CM/Res. 48(IV), March 9, 1965, *id.*, 50, CM/Res. 66(V), Oct. 21, 1965, *id.*, 74; CM/Res. 68(VII), Nov. 4, 1966, *id.*, 102; CM/Res. 102(IX), Sept. 10, 1967, *id.*, 122; CM/Res/138(X), Feb. 24, 1968, 2 *id.*, 1968-1973 at 7, CM/Res. 242/Rev. 1(XVII), June 19, 1971, *id.*, 141; CM/Res. 269(XIX), June 12, 1972, *id.*, 183.

86. *See, e.g.*, OAU Doc. CIAS/Plen. 2/Rev. 2 *supra* note 85; AHG/Res. 9(1), July 24, 1964, *id.*, 26; AHG/Res. 35(11), Oct. 25, 1965, *id.*, 52. *And see* CM/Res. 6(1), *supra* note 85; CM/Res. 83(VII), Nov. 4, 1966, *id.*, 99; CM/Res. 137(X), Feb. 24, 1968, 2 *id.*, 5; CM/Res. 268(XIX), June 12, 1972, *id.*, 178; CM/Res. 272(XIX), June 12, 1972, *id.*, 193.

87. *See* OAU Doc. CM/Res. 62(V), Oct. 21, 1965, *id.* 70, ECM/Res. 13(VI), Dec. 5, 1965, *id.* 86; CM/Res. 78(VII), Nov. 4, 1966, *id.* 94; CM/Res. 102(IX), Sept. 10, 1967, *id.* 116; CM/Res/10(IX), Sept. 10, 1967, *id.* 133; CM/Res/207(XIV), March 6, 1970, 2 *id.* 86; CM/Res. 269(XVIII), Feb. 19, 1972, *id.* 164; CM/Res. 267(XIX), June 12, 1972, *id.* 175.

88. *See* OAU Doc., ECM/Res. 21(VIII), Nov. 21, 1973.

89. Signed at Geneva on Oct. 30, 1947, TIAS 1700; 55-61 UNTS.

90. *See* TREATIES IN FORCE. A list of Treaties and Other International Agreements of the United States in Force on January 1, 1974, at 330 (Dept. of State Pub. 8755).

91. *See supra* note 7.

92. *See* H. Lauterpacht, *Restrictive Interpretation and the Principle of Effectiveness in the Interpretation of Treaties*, 26 BYIL 76 (1949). *And see* for possible exceptions, not warranted in the above context, McNair, *The Law of Treaties*, 213-17 (1961), at 474-84.

93. *See* T. FLORY, LE G.A.T.T.—DROIT INTERNATIONAL ET COMMERCE MONDIAL 83 (1968), where the security exceptions in GATT's Article 21 are also described as constituting matters within the "domestic jurisdiction" of each party.

94. *See* a discussion of this point in relation to bilateral trade agreements, *infra* pp. 623-25.

95. *Cf.*, DAM, THE GATT, LAW AND INTERNATIONAL ECONOMIC ORGANIZATION 221 (1970).

96. The above statement is based on information obtained from some of the Foreign Offices of the Arab states involved, supported by the results of a review of the League of Nations Treaty Series, the United Nations Treaty Series, and the U.S. TREATIES IN FORCE referred to in note 90, *supra*.

97. Provisional Agreement in regard to Diplomatic and Consular Representation, Judicial Protection, Commerce and Navigation, signed at London on Nov. 7, 1933, 48 Stat. 1826 (1933); 11 BEVANS 5456; 142 LNTS 329. The Agreement does not extend, pursuant to Article (4) thereof, to the treatment which the United States accords to the commerce of Cuba and the Panama Canal Zone.

98. As is implied in the testimony of Professor R. N. Gardner to the Subcommittee on International Economics of the Joint Economic Committee of the United States Congress, December 13, 1973, and in his statement quoted in "Saudi Oil Embargo Termed Breach of '33 Treaty with U.S.," N.Y. Times, Dec. 19, 1973, at 12, col. 4.

99. *Accord*, Schwarzenberger, *The Most-Favoured-Nation Standard in British State Practice*, 22 BYIL 96, 110, 111 (1945).

100. *Id.*, at 111, 120.

101. Treaty of Commerce and Navigation, signed at Baghdad, Dec. 3, 1938, 54 Stat. 1790 (1940); TS960; 9 BEVANS 7; 203 LNTS 107. According to the treaty, extension of advantages given by the United States does not include advantages accorded to Cuba, the Panama Canal Zone, border traffic zones, and states in Customs Unions (Art. 1).

102. *See supra* note 4.

103. Treaty of Amity, Economic Relations and Consular Rights (with Protocol) signed at Salalah on Dec. 20, 1958, 11 UST 1835; TIAS No. 4530; 380 UNTS 181. Each party reserved the right to accord special advantages to "adjacent countries" or by virtue of a customs union (Art VIII (4)). Application of the treaty does not extend to Cuba, the Philippines, trusteeship territories in the Pacific, and the Panama Canal Zone.

18. Statement Before the American Society of International Law on the Cuban Missile Crisis

Dean Acheson

To talk of the legal aspects of the Cuban incident reminds me of the story of the women discussing the Quiz Program scandals. One said that she felt the scandals presented serious moral issues. The other answered, "And I always say that moral issues are more important than real issues." Mr. Chayes has cited legal principles to justify the actions taken by our Government in October of 1962, observing in passing that "law was not wholly irrelevant."

Today, in the analyses presented, several legal theories to justify the Cuban quarantine have appeared. Professor Hart has been quoted to the effect that a legal system is all-pervasive, and that an all-pervasive system will necessarily provide an answer for all problems which arise within it. Others found justification within treaties or agreements; still others within the realm of "generally accepted" ideas. What can one expect to find? Clearly, a simple answer that the action was lawful or unlawful will not be found.

In my estimation, however, the quarantine is not a legal issue or an issue of international law as these terms should be understood. Much of what is called international law is a body of ethical distillation, and one must take care not to confuse this distillation with law. We should not rationalize general legal policy restricting sovereignty from international documents composed for specific purposes.

Further, the law through its long history has been respectful of power, especially that power which is close to the sanctions of law. This point is exemplified in the history of English law during the era of Richard II. The Court of the King's Bench was asked to pass on the validity of the Duke of York's claim to the English Crown. The Court refused to consider the question, since it "concerned the king's own estate & regalie." The Court indeed assumed a respectful attitude toward power.

There are indications in our country today which suggest that some segments of our sovereign people resist judicial entry into the inner sanctuary of power. In the field of labor-management relations, where law had once entered boldly, it has withdrawn before power. The same court that was willing to apply a yet-to-be announced doctrine of law to apportionment of legislative representatives has left the issue of featherbedding, where no rules were applicable, to power. Again in the steel price controversy, law has left the arbitrament to other principles.

I must conclude that the propriety of the Cuban quarantine is not a legal issue. The power, position and prestige of the United States had been challenged by another state; and law simply does not deal with such questions of ultimate power—power that comes close to the sources of sovereignty. I cannot believe that there are principles of law that say we must accept destruction of our way of life. One would be surprised if practical men, trained in legal history and thought, had devised and brought to a state of general acceptance a principle condemnatory of an action so essential to the continuation of pre-eminent power as that taken by the United States last October. Such a principle would be as harmful to the development of restraining procedures as it would be futile. No law can destroy the state creating the law. The survival of states is not a matter of law.

However, in the action taken in the Cuban quarantine, one can see the influence of accepted legal principles. These principles are procedural devices designed to reduce the severity of a possible clash. Those devices cause wise delay before drastic action, create a "cooling off" period, permit the consideration of others' views. The importance of the Organization of American States was also procedural, and emphasized the desirability of collective action, thus creating a common denominator of action. Some of these desirable consequences are familiar to us in the domestic industrial area.

In October the United States was faced with grave problems of policy and procedure in relation to its own and outside interests. The action taken was the right action. "Right" means more than legally justifiable, or even successful. The United States resolved very grave issues of policy in a way consonant with ethical restraint.

The most perplexing aspect of the decision was the difficulty of comparing, of weighing, competing considerations. How could one weigh the desirability of less drastic action at the outset against the undesirability of losing sight of the missiles, or having them used against us, which might be avoided by more drastic action from the onset, such as destroying the weapons? The President had no scales in which to test these weights, no policy litmus paper. Wisdom for the decision was not to be found in law, but in judgment. Principles, certainly legal principles, do not decide concrete cases.

19. The Cuban Missile Crisis

Abram Chayes

The legal issues were formally presented at some length by lawyers from the State and Justice Departments and debated at a full session of the Executive Committee on the morning of Friday 19 October.[1] At that time, although there appeared to be a growing consensus for blockade-type action, the decision was by no means clear, and in fact the consensus began to come apart at this very Friday session.[2] The Executive Committee's request for a review of the legal situation was stimulated by a remark on Thursday night by Ambassador Llewellyn Thompson, who had just returned from his tour as Ambassador to the Soviet Union to replace Charles E. Bohlen as Special Assistant to the Secretary of State for Soviet Affairs. Thompson said that the Russians had a penchant for legalities and would be impressed by a good legal case. Lawyers at Justice and State were alerted on Thursday, after Thompson's comments,[3] and on Friday morning, after the ritual intelligence briefing that opened Executive Committee meetings, they made their presentations.[4]

Secretary Rusk called first on Mr. Meeker, but the Attorney General intervened and asked that his Deputy, Mr. Katzenbach, should speak first. Mr. Katzenbach expressed his view that a declaration of war was unnecessary and that United States military action could be justified in international law on the principle of self-defence.

Mr. Meeker followed. He agreed with the judgment that a declaration of war would not improve the United States' position. His analysis was based on the premise that a 'defensive quarantine' of Cuba would amount to a use of force, which had to be considered in relation to the general prohibition against the use of force in Article 2(4) of the U.N. Charter. Meeker pointed out that there were several recognized exceptions to this prohibition. One of these was self-defence in case of armed attack, but Meeker did not think the situation in Cuba constituted an armed attack on any country. A second exception noted was action by the U.N. under Chapter VII of the Charter, but it was obvious that the Security Council would be immobilized, and Meeker thought it was problematical whether the United States could obtain a recommendation from the General Assembly.

A third possibility was presented by the provisions for regional arrangements in Chapter VIII of the U.N. Charter. Meeker emphasized the importance of Article 52, providing that regional arrangements could deal with 'such matters relating to the maintenance of peace and security as are appropriate for regional action.' He concluded that, if the O.A.S. acting under the Rio Treaty approved, a case could be made for the use of force. He pointed to the provisions of Articles 6 and 8 of the Treaty, under which, he argued, the organization could take measures, including a recommendation for the use of force, to meet a situation that endangers the peace of the hemisphere. He referred to Mr. Martin, Assistant Secretary for Latin America, for a judgment about the possibility of getting the necessary two-thirds vote in the O.A.S.

Meeker then addressed the possible argument that O.A.S. action of this kind would amount to 'enforcement action' requiring Security Council authorization under Article 53 of the Charter. He thought there was a reasonably good argument to the contrary. He was not sure that the United States could persuade a majority of the Council to its view, but noted that the veto made it possible to prevent adverse Council action.

Later in the discussion, Mr. Acheson commented that so far as questions of international law might be involved, he agreed with Mr. Katzenbach's position that self-defence was an entirely sufficient justification. He added that if there were to be imported a qualification or requirement of approval by the O.A.S., as apparently suggested by Mr. Meeker, he could not go along with that. Finally, as the meeting recessed for two subgroups to work out detailed scenarios of the alternatives then under consideration, blockade and air strike, the legal aspect was sounded once again. Robert Kennedy, in parting, said that he thought there was ample legal basis for a blockade. Meeker said he was in agreement provided the O.A.S. approved under the Rio Treaty. The Attorney General countered that the O.A.S. action was political, not legal. The issue was left in that state. This comment of Robert Kennedy's at the time contrasts with his retrospective evaluation in *Thirteen Days*. There he said, 'It was the vote of the Organization of American States that gave a legal basis for the quarantine. . . . It . . . changed our position from that of an outlaw acting in violation of international law into a country acting in accordance with twenty allies legally protecting their position.'[5]

. . . A study of the role of law in the Cuban missile crisis inevitably seems to exaggerate that role. The meetings of the Executive Committee were not dominated by debates on fine points of law. Nor would one have wished that they should be.

The factual record is irrefutable, however, that the men responsible for decision did not ignore legal considerations. On the contrary, they made a considerable effort to integrate legal factors into their deliberations. The President and his advisers were properly concerned with the possibilities— for good or ill—in the situation they faced and in the courses open to them. Law and legal institutions played a part in defining and shaping those possibilities.

This much can be said with some confidence about the role of law in the Cuban missile crisis. It remains to restate, though in necessarily tentative form, some more general conclusions that have emerged about the operation of law in crisis decision-making.

Understanding is obscured by two transparent but pervasive misconceptions—one about the nature of law and one about the character of the decision-process. Both are expressions of what I have called the anthropomorphic fallacy. In both law is cast as the superego setting outer limits to permissible action.

But decision-making is *not* a wholly integrated and rational activity. It embodies large elements of misperception, faulty evaluation, miscalculation, failure of communication. These are not occasional or sporadic lapses in an essentially rational exercise. They are massive and they are endemic. Most important, decision-making is a *corporate* process in which individual participants react to different constellations of personal, bureaucratic, and political motives and constraints. All this must be taken into account in any serious effort to understand or explain how the process works.

And law is *not* a set of fixed, self-defining categories of permissible and prohibited conduct. This conception is invalid even as to domestic law, but it is especially so as to international law because of the diffuse modes of establishing and clarifying rules. Its assumptions about the relation of law to decision are reminiscent of Justice Robert's idea of constitutional adjudication. 'The Court,' he said, 'has only one duty—to lay the article of the Constitution which is invoked beside the statute which is challenged and to see whether the latter squares with the former.'[6] Supreme Court Justices and their critics have long since abandoned this mechanistic approach. But there are many who still consider that legal advice or criticism in the international field consists in laying the norm invoked beside the challenged decision and seeing whether the latter squares with the former.

International law, in its normative sense, must be seen as indeterminate with respect to much of the array of concrete choices open in a particular situation. Often the rules have no authoritative formulation in words. Even when they do, the terms are open to a broad range of interpretation and emphasis. They do not dictate conduct so much as orient deliberation, order priorities, guide within broad limits. Moreover, institutional structures that are the product of law can be as important as rules, and more so in organizing and channelling decision.

These more complex concepts of law and decision-making can lead to a richer appreciation of the complicated interplay between the two. Four salient points emerge from this study:

First, law is not self-activating. On the whole, it does not project itself into the deliberations on its own motion. Someone must call the lawyers in. The Cuban missile crisis seems to authenticate a traditional stereotype: in the course of an orderly canvass of considerations relevant to decision, and after the major alternatives had been clarified, government lawyers were asked to present, to the inner circle of decision-makers, a formal exposition of the legal situation and the legal constraints. But our study suggests that this is not the whole story. The impact of the legal presentation will depend on how much time is available for careful and considered development and how early and how insistently it is put before the responsible operating officers. This in turn depends on factors that condition *all* lawyer-client relations, public and private. How do the legal offices fit into the particular bureaucratic structures involved? What are the personal relations between the lawyer and his immediate client? We saw that there were differences in both dimensions as between Defense and State. How does the legal officer view his role? Like the Attorney General, as an active participant in the policy-making process? Or does he wait for questions to be put to him, and then answer only what he is asked? What is his skill in using his professional leverage?

Second, if legal precepts are not exogenous data, dividing the universe of choices into the permissible and impermissible, if legal analysis is always indeterminate, then at best legal reasoning and analysis will impact on alternatives in terms of more or less, not yes or no. Law cannot determine decision, and it is an essential point of this study that we should not expect it to. It takes its place as one of a complex of factors for sorting out available choices.

In return for shedding its oracular pretensions, legal analysis gains a continuous relevance at every point along the spectrum of potential decision. If it cannot divide the universe into mutually exclusive blacks and whites, it can help in differentiating the infinite shades of grey that are the grist of the decision-process. The corporate character of decision-making ensures that these differentiating considerations will be pressed home by the participants whose policy positions they favour. The persuasive force of such arguments and their final influence will depend on infinitely complex moral, psychological, and interpersonal processes of group decision-making. Quantification, as we have said, must always elude us. But the position that the ultimate impact is *de minimis* cannot be maintained.

Third, the significance of legal justification for decision-making is greater and more complex than is customarily supposed. Legal justification is part of the over-all defence of a public decision. It is easy to deprecate the significance of this process. Casual observation is enough to show that public justification is not always based on the 'real' reasons for decision, and may even falsify them. But it is wrong to conclude on this basis that the decision and its announced rationale are essentially independent and self-contained phenomena.

In fact, the requirement of justification suffuses the basic process of choice. There is continuous feedback between the knowledge that the government will be called upon to justify its action and the kind of action that can be chosen. The linkage tends to induce a tolerable congruence between the actual corporate decision-process, with its interplay of personal, bureaucratic, and political factors, and the idealized picture of rational choice on the basis of objectively coherent criteria. We may grant a considerable latitude for evasion and manipulation. But to ignore the requirement of justification too long or to violate its canons too egregiously creates, in a democracy, what we have come to call a 'credibility gap.' The ultimate consequence is to erode the capacity of the government to govern.

Some of the characteristics of law give it special importance for public justification. Because of the scope and variety of the audiences addressed, that process must proceed in terms of more or less universal and generalized criteria. It cannot rely heavily on the detailed factual knowledge, elaborate shared assumptions, personal relations, professional expertise that may be persuasive in internal bargaining over policy. For these reasons, ideological elements, for example, tend to bulk large in public defence and justification of policy. Legal principles also are regarded as quasi-universal or at least generally accepted. They are thus well adapted to the needs of public justification. On the other hand, because of the very prominence of legal standards as criteria for public accounting, failure to justify on these grounds or an inadequate legal defence may compromise the justification exercise over-all. Law thus becomes a prominent element in the justification process.

Comparative justifiability—which is another way of saying the comparative ease of generating political support or acquiescence—is necessarily an important factor differentiating among available alternatives in the intra-governmental process of choice. The perhaps disproportionate significance of law for public justification feeds back on this internal process to enhance the weight of legal considerations there.

Fourth, decision must take account of the international organizational setting against which action is projected. Since the organizational setting is in the strict sense a product of international law, this amounts to identifying a major and continuing legal influence on decision. International institutions, moreover, are a focused and intensified arena of public justification. They are peculiarly sensitive to the legal elements of the position, because the organizations themselves are dominated by legalistic modes of procedure. Most important of all, the international organizations are themselves actors, with some power to create legal relations and alter the legal setting. From a narrowly national point of view, this means that action must be planned with an eye to controlling or neutralizing these actors. From the broader perspective of international law, these not wholly controllable international actors, responsive to legal argumentation and acting by law-created processes, are of increasing importance in the effort to channel national action.

NOTES

1. Abel, *The Missile Crisis* at 72, states that the legal issues were reviewed by Acheson and Ball before the president himself on Thursday, but none of the other accounts corroborate this.

2. Kennedy, *Thirteen Days,* 44–6 (1969); Hilsman, *To Move a Nation,* 204–6 (1967); Sorenson, *Kennedy,* 692 (1965); Abel at 86–9; Allison, *Essence of Decision: Explaining the Cuban Missile Crisis,* 206–8 (1971). Dean Acheson and the Joint Chiefs of Staff, with some support from McGeorge Bundy, were primarily responsible for driving a wedge in the consensus which had presumably been reached on Thursday night.

3. For Thompson's remarks, see Abel at 87; Sorensen at 706. For the start of the legal work, see Abel at 82; Sorensen at 691–2. Meeker states that he was asked on Thursday afternoon to prepare '. . . a paper on legal characterization of the situation and on what the U.S. could do about it.' Letter from Leonard Meeker to Abram Chayes, 21 Apr. 1971. On Friday morning before the ExCom meeting Meeker discussed his paper with Ball, Johnson, and Martin. At that meeting, Meeker suggested, for historical and psychological reasons, the use of the term 'defensive quarantine' instead of 'blockade.' Ibid. The label 'quarantine' was thus born here, although others have made claims to its paternity. It harked back to President Roosevelt's call for a 'quarantine of the aggressors' before the Second World War. See Abel at 73. But it had the further advantage of not implying a characterization of the situation as a 'war,' the only circumstance in which, according to traditional U.S. doctrine, a blockade could be instituted. See [1903] Foreign Relations of the United States 417–41, 452–79, 601–13, 788–805; Dept. of Navy, Office of Chief of Naval Operations, *Law of Naval Warfare* §§631–2 (1955). Avoidance of the harsher term thus contributed to the effort to communicate restraint as well as firmness, to the Soviets. See Sorensen at 694. On Sunday Secretary Rusk voiced a concern that use of the word might be regarded as a semantic 'gimmick' but after I reviewed the foregoing considerations with him, he withdrew his reservation.

4. The following account is based on a number of conversations with participants during or shortly after the crisis. I have also drawn heavily on a memorandum prepared by Mr. Meeker at my request a day or two after the meeting from his notes taken at the meeting. The State Department has declined to permit the full text of the memorandum to be published at this time, but in addition to the copy in my possession, Mr. Meeker has deposited a copy in the Kennedy Library where it will presumably become available in due course. The Meeker memorandum is entirely consistent with the published accounts of the 19 October meeting, see, e.g., Abel at 87–8, but is more detailed on the legal issues.

5. Kennedy at 121.

6. *United States* v. *Butler*, 297 U.S. I, 62 (1936).

20. The Role of Enforcement of Just Law in the Establishment of a New International Order: A Proposal for a Transnational Police Force

Robert C. Johansen and Saul H. Mendlovitz

INTRODUCTION

The central problem of international relations is the willingness of the governments to threaten or use violence to settle disputes. This willingness is unlikely to diminish until nonmilitary means for defending and advancing group interests become more reliable and common. To achieve this requires strengthening nonmilitary norms governing decision-makers' behavior. The strength of such norms depends on internal moral checks, of which there are few in international conduct, and external punishments and rewards. The most familiar and effective external incentive for influencing behavior in all human societies is the enforcement of law or quasi-legal norms. It follows, therefore, that nurturing the development and enforcement of international legal norms—this most maligned subject (often with good reason) among academic analysts and practitioners of international relations—is potentially the most fundamentally transforming element of foreign policy.

Many diplomats, scholars, and social activists remain pessimistic about efforts gradually to replace militarily-backed national self-help with enforcement[1] of international law by officers acting on behalf of a wider world community. At the same time, some useful experience with incipient enforcement mechanisms occurs, for example, with international peace-keeping forces, which have occasionally functioned with success,[2] and with the monitoring activities of the International Atomic Energy Agency.

Although skepticism is justifiable about enlarging the functions of a peacekeeping or law-implementing UN force, excessive pessimism diverts attention from exploring how such a force could help rectify functional inadequacies in the global political system. . . . This essay seeks to avoid both the irrelevant legalism symbolized by treaties such as the Kellogg-Briand pact to outlaw war, and the do-nothing "realism" of those who reject the need to offer specific policies aimed at fundamentally altering the practices of international relations. Our purpose is to examine the need for means to supplement national self-help in law enforcement, to explore their possible nature, to explain the contribution of a transnational enforcement agency to the creation of a more just world polity, and to discuss the transition process for creating such an agency. The process of change that we are examining is more political than legal. If successful, this process domesticates international politics and transnationalizes national politics. By reinforcing norms through more effective enforcement of them, the goal is to increase the governability of world society, as well as to increase the governing ability of global organizations.

To consider how to increase security in the 1980's is a much broader task than to consider how to prevent war. . . . The basic structure and functioning of the present international system bears re-examination, because that system cannot adequately prevent collective violence, promote economic equity, assure worldwide justice and human rights, and secure the environment. To put it bluntly, the present system of international relations has built into it a significant probability of irretrievable disaster for the human race. Yet the impediments to realizing preferred values are political rather than technological or material. They can be changed.

Thus one of the most urgent imperatives is to develop a strategy for moving toward a preferred system of world order in which norms defining the human interest[3] become guides to policymaking. The most critical norms are well known and rhetorically embraced, if not practiced. By increasing the human capacity to enforce specific norms aimed at realizing preferred world order values of peace, economic well-being, social justice, and environmental balance, we can increase the seriousness with which decision-makers will take these values.

With these considerations in mind, the time has come to reconsider the utility of a standing transnational constabulary or police force that can transcend narrowly defined national interests and respond more effectively to the global human interests. . . .

THE NEED FOR A TRANSNATIONAL POLICE FORCE

General Considerations

While a transnational police force would not usher in a golden age, it could, to a significant degree, help meet the need for enhancing the obligatory quality of international norms in each of the four value areas noted above. Nowhere is this need more apparent than in the field of war prevention where a subtle but profound growth of the acceptability of violence is under way.[4]

The Carter and Reagan administrations' overt decision to develop further nuclear capabilities for fighting war with "limited nuclear strikes" will lead to an enormous increase in destructive capability and an erosion of the fragile existing code of conduct against the use of nuclear weapons. The arms race also has been exacerbated by the Soviet willingness to use military force in Afghanistan and the U.S. decision to establish rapid deployment forces. In addition, the past two years have witnessed armed conflict among several socialist societies in Asia and a series of declared and undeclared wars on the African continent. The trend toward violence is further illustrated by the vast increase over the past five years in the sale of arms by the industrialized societies (with roughly 70 percent sold by NATO countries and 27 percent by members of the Warsaw Treaty Organization) and the substantial growth in the number of arms producers.[5]

Although it is true that revolutionaries often use arms in the course of social reform, in the long run it is likely that the sale of sophisticated armaments will aid the repressive, *status quo* forces of the world as much as, if not more than, the bearers of a more just social order. To be sure, dispossessed people in every continent are rightly questioning the legitimacy of past political orders that have not met their needs. As authority erodes, the potential for violence often increases. On the one hand, dissatisfied groups often genuinely feel they have no alternative to using overt violence to combat structural violence to which they have been subjected. On the other hand, repressive governmental tendencies flourish to combat what a dominant group of people see as a threat to their established order. The growth of civil strife provides fertile ground for authoritarian "solutions," whether growing from the right or left, whether from the holders or seekers of political authority. Recurring repression raises the limits for what is acceptable violence and lowers the expectations for what can be done to curtail it.

A transnational police force for these situations as well as others that have occurred in the past could have contributed greatly to alleviating human suffering. For example, the killing and injuring of many innocent people could doubtless have been prevented in the Lebanese civil war in 1976 if a highly trained transnational force could have established a humanitarian corridor in Beirut from which all belligerency was excluded. Similar actions could also have been useful during the Nigerian civil war (1967–70); the conflict, which involved West Pakistan, East Pakistan, and India, leading to the creation of Bangladesh (1971); the chronic violence in Northern Ireland; and the migration of thousands of Kampucheans and their subsequent habitation in areas along the border with Thailand, while under constant threat to their lives (1979–80).

Moreover, a halt to nuclear proliferation and substantial progress in arms reductions cannot be achieved without International Atomic Energy Agency (IAEA) inspection that eventually includes all military as well as civilian nuclear plants and compulsory compliance to universal rules by all states. This can hardly be guaranteed without global enforcement officers.

A transnational police force could also help realize other preferred values of justice, economic well-being, and ecological balance. For example, in the effort to eliminate racist or colonial governments, a UN force to intervene on behalf of racial equality in Namibia or South Africa would be preferable to national intervention. Moreover, in desperate situations, even a human- itarian mission such as food distribution often requires security forces to prevent hoarding by some and inaccessibility by others. Acting on their own behalf, national elites often use grain as a political or military tool against their opponents, as has been alleged by all parties in the Vietnamese- Kampuchean conflict. Among recipients, ethnic quarrels often break out during efforts to alleviate food shortages. Up to now such activities have not required transnational monitoring because assistance has been largely bilateral. But politically divisive uses of world food reserves would be better resisted by multilateral administrative bodies. Transnational inspection and enforcement could provide the monitoring to make major steps toward equity more possible.

Finally, to protect the oceans from ecological decay, tankers flying flags of convenience and multinational consortia of corporations mining deep sea nodules, for example, eventually must be monitored by persons who represent authoritative international decisions.

Advancing toward a preferred world requires moving away from unde- pendable norms, unilaterally interpreted, and enforced only through national self-help. Whether people live in peasant villages or urban skyscrapers, the achievement of a substantially more just life for this planet's people requires movement toward the enforcement of preferred norms on individuals, including heads of governments. The consequences of such a development would produce no permanent state of justice, nor even unmixed social benefits. Nonetheless, the functional and ecological unity of life on Earth means either that some rules will be globally enforced or that human suffering will multiply. The risks of a rationally designed alternative world order, however problematic, are more acceptable than the emerging order shaped by diplomatic drift, official timidity, and reluctance to contemplate fundamental change.

Creating a transnational police force and generating political and moral support for it will nourish the taproot of system change. Such a force would provide an opportunity to begin living a part of the future in the present. When a global police force eventually will be able to monitor national military conduct and enforce laws—whether to guard against clandestine movements of military forces across a border, direct armed attack, racial discrimination, or deployment of weapons of mass destruction— the transformation of human civilization may be comparable in its far- reaching significance to the social metamorphosis that attended the shift from hunting to farming 10,000 years ago.

Even though such a complete transformation obviously is not imminent, focusing on its importance enhances one's understanding of challenges that now press upon us. What proposed innovations could become focal points around which to mobilize support to enhance the reliability of just, global norms? Critical problems, planetary in scope, are now evident in relating population humanely and equitably to the use of food, energy, and non-renewable resources; in handling disposal of persistent, toxic substances; and in decreasing acts of human brutality and collective violence. This essay will focus only on the last of these areas of concern, but the utility of the global enforcement function is present in the other areas as well.

Demand for Four Types of Enforcement

Within the limited scope of this essay, the world's population needs transnational enforcement in four different areas. In the first, enforcement can serve (1) to prevent border clashes from breaking into full-scale war, and (2) to discourage third parties from supplying military equipment to the initial belligerents or from participating in competing military coalitions. This most familiar kind of enforcement activity, which will be labeled here Type A enforcement, has in the past been performed by various UN *ad hoc* peacekeeping forces and observation groups. Along the Lebanese-Syrian border in 1958, for example, UN personnel performed unarmed observation where infiltration of arms was suspected, while along the Israeli-Egyptian border from 1956 to 1957, the UN forces carried arms to prevent violations of the armistice lines.

In recent years the likelihood of border incidents turning into open violence has increased. Examples with ominous portents include: Ethiopia-Somalia, Iran-Iraq, China–Soviet Union, Soviet Union–Afghanistan–Pakistan, North Korea–South Korea, Vietnam-Kampuchea, China-Vietnam, Greece-Turkey, Angola–South Africa, Morocco-Algeria, Lebanon-Syria, and Israel and its neighbors.

Humanitarian intervention represents a second category of activity (Type B), the purpose of which is to use transnational enforcement as an opportunity to aid innocent victims caught in the crossfire of war. This type includes providing sanctuary for non-combatants who seek shelter during civil war, and attempting to quell internal conflicts that have genocidal tendencies.

The growth of political repression and brutalization in the treatment of some ethnic minorities, the poor, and political dissidents suggests that the need for Type B action will be quite high within the next decade. Class conflicts, tribal diversity within many African states, and linguistic-cultural diversity in India, Ireland, Lebanon, Iran, Ethiopia, Sudan, and elsewhere illustrate the potential for future civil strife that might involve heavy human costs and foreign participation.

A third need is to restrain officials who resist internal implementation of norms enjoying nearly universal support in the world community (Type C enforcement). Evidence of chronic brutality, torture, or structural violence might be the basis for this kind of enforcement. It could involve sending a force to Namibia to neutralize officials trying to implement apartheid. Systematic torturing of political prisoners can also be considered a crime against humanity and in violation of the Nuremburg precedent. A global enforcement agency eventually could be empowered to gather authoritative evidence of any alleged violations of that precedent to deter local officials from further violations. Enforcement of the Nuremburg principle could be considered in contexts such as the period after the Chilean military junta seized power from Salvador Allende's administration in 1973. Type C action might well emphasize the positive side of law enforcement, the "do's" as well as the "don'ts" in upholding international law.

In the longer run, transnational monitoring and enforcement will also be necessary to implement arms reductions (Type D).[6] Impartially gathered information about all nations' military deployments and transnational patrol of disputed borders are probably prerequisites to reversing the arms buildup.

A readily available transnational police force could enhance many nations' security, especially along disputed or tense borders. Such a force could also raise expectations for nonviolent conflict resolution so that arms, even though present, would become increasingly superfluous for conflict resolution. Eventually, universal prohibitions of some weapons and armed forces could be enforced by police acting on behalf of all countries.

As Table 20.1 indicates, a wide range of activities, with substantial impact on the international system, are possible even with the kind of police enforcement that is feasible to carry out in the present and immediate future.

National Enforcement, International Ad Hoc Peacekeeping Force, or Permanent Transnational Police Force?

National Enforcement. In any of the four areas, national enforcement carries the obvious and crucial drawback of encouraging either counter national intervention or else "one-sided" enforcement. The latter places the weaker side under duress and promotes partisan conflict resolution without recourse to any community procedure for the weaker side to air its grievances against the enforcing agent. National enforcement neither satisfies elemental requirements for just procedures nor stimulates systemic change.

There are some cases in which the need for third party enforcement is so obvious that, in the absence of transnational police, national enforcement action fulfills a similar—although not equivalent—function. The use of national military forces usually lacks the effectiveness and impartiality that a transnational force should possess. Examples of national action include the Syrian army's occupation of Lebanon to enforce a truce on warring Lebanese factions. In addition, Tanzanian military forces ousted an almost universally criticized Ugandan dictatorship in 1979. Tanzania received almost no protest over its action against President Idi Amin because he had become an embarrassment to most African governments and Tanzania seemed free of imperial ambitions. Vietnamese efforts to replace the widely criticized Pol Pot government of Cambodia have not met with similar approval, perhaps because of ambiguity about Vietnamese political designs on their weaker neighbor. These national efforts, which are rationalized as attempts to enforce

TABLE 20.1

World order value	Goal of enforcement	Concrete objective	Real or hypothetical illustrative activity	
			With host consent	Without host consent
Peace	Type A: to restrain violence across international borders	1. to prevent border incidents from becoming international war	UNEF in 1956	armed patrol of Israeli–Egyptian border in 1967 even after host consent was withdrawn*
		2. to avert intervention by third-party, national forces	UNOGIL in 1958	armed patrol of Angolan–South African border in 1976*
Peace, human rights	Type B: to conduct humanitarian intervention	1. to provide sanctuary for non-combatants during civil war	ONUC 1960–64	Lebanon 1976*
		2. to curtail civil strife with genocidal tendencies	ONUC	Bangladesh 1971*; Thai–Kampuchean border 1978–80*; Lebanon 1976–80*
Peace, human rights, ecological balance	Type C: to restrain officials who resist the domestic application of global norms	1. to decrease structural violence in domestic arenas	N.A.	restrain officials implementing apartheid*
		2. to protect victims of political repression or torture	N.A.	prevent torture of political prisoners in Chile in 1974;* restrain Ugandan President Idi Amin's treatment of political opponents and prisoners*
Peace	Type D: to limit national capability for committing collective violence	1. to monitor arms control agreements	the SALT I treaty; Nuclear Non-Proliferation treaty; Treaty of Tlatelolco*	monitor all borders where infiltration of armed forces is suspected;* monitor missile test firings through an international satellite observation agency;* confiscate equipment or fissionable materials in violation of disarming process*
		2. to enforce arms reduction agreements by: (a) preventing unilateral escalation of the arms race (b) discouraging preemptive war or foreign intervention by one state aimed at stopping a rival from continuing a suspected violation of a process of arms reduction		

*Hypothetical examples
N.A. = not applicable

global peacekeeping norms, further illustrate the need for a transnational force.

Ad Hoc Forces. International peacekeeping forces of an *ad hoc* nature obviously can and have carried out some Type A and B enforcement action. Small or non-aligned nations no doubt will continue to perform a valuable function in providing special training in riot control, peace observation, and border patrol for contingents they earmark for UN duty, to be available when requested. Indeed, for additional countries to provide the necessary training, personnel, and equipment for UN peacekeeping forces would be a genuine service to world peace.

Yet there are ways in which *ad hoc* forces are inadequate for even Type A enforcement. When the second United Nations Emergency Force (UNEF II) was created in 1973, for example, the Security Council required *immediate* placement of the forces in the field. Only because the Secretary-General could transfer some troops from the United Nations Force in Cyprus (UNFICYP) could a force be on the scene within twenty-four hours. Such a procedure could not be depended upon in the future, as there are seldom surplus UN forces available for immediate relocation.

Transnational Police Force. It is even more important for Type B than for Type A action that the peacekeeping forces be seen as agents of the global community rather than as bearers of an alien nationality, simply deputized into international service. Here the force is likely to have substantial involvement with the indigenous population of the host nation. Particularly if the force remains in place without enjoying the continued consent of the host, merely wearing blue arm bands over foreign national uniforms would be a handicap.

A host nation that later terminates its consent for allowing an *ad hoc* UN force to remain in its territory may use bilateral diplomatic channels to persuade the donor states to withdraw their earmarked contingents from the UN force, rendering the latter's continuing operation impossible. Such a chain of events occurred when Egypt requested that UNEF leave Egyptian soil in 1967. Israel had never consented to UN forces being on its territory, and while the Secretary-General groped for a solution, the Indian and Yugoslavian governments informed the UN that their forces could not remain in UN service without Egyptian consent. U Thant withdrew the force. The result was war. This experience with *ad hoc* forces provided two lessons: first, the UN force may need to remain in place without host consent; second, *individuals* directly recruited into a permanent force would be potentially far more reliable than an *ad hoc* group dependent on contributed battalions from member states.

Guidelines for UNEF II suggest that once in place the force cannot be withdrawn without Security Council consent, but whether the force could be relied upon to remain, given the possibility of withdrawal action similar to the Indian-Yugoslavian precedent, is far from certain. In short, although some Type A and B enforcement can be carried out by *ad hoc* forces, such enforcement is severely limited, especially when consent of the host is not present or the force is needed quickly. In addition, for political and psychological reasons, as well as more narrowly military considerations, a permanent, directly recruited police force could handle this type of enforcement more reliably and effectively.

Creative Diplomacy. The purpose of UN peacekeeping to this point has been not only to prevent or decrease violence between two antagonists, such as Israel and Eygpt, but also to isolate the conflict from intervention by outside powers, such as the United States and the Soviet Union. The late Dag Hammarskjold used the term "preventive diplomacy" to describe the use of an international force to prevent national intervention and counter-intervention in conflicts where the major powers preferred a UN peacekeeping role to intervention by a powerful rival. These forces carried out a primarily prophylactic role. In contrast, Type C and D activities might more aply be termed "creative diplomacy." In particular, they have a positive aim to create new attitudes, procedures, and structures in order to implement justice and arms reduction, rather than pour water on hot spots. To be sure, Type C and D actions also perform a prophylactic function insofar as they avert future violence, say, between antagonistic ethnic groups within a country (Type C), or discourage aggressive war because of internationally enforced arms reductions (Type D).

Creative diplomacy upholds the positive law; preventive diplomacy puts out brushfire wars. Creative diplomacy seeks to create conditions conducive to justice and peace, and in that regard it may take sides in order to arrest a violator of community-established norms; preventive diplomacy seeks to restore the *status quo ante* or simply to stop the fighting, and in that regard it is no-fault enforcement, paying heed primarily to only one norm—the prohibition against use of armed force across national boundaries. Creative diplomacy recognizes the need to take action against structural violence; preventive diplomacy is concerned only with overt violence.

The need for a permanent police force is even more evident in Type C enforcement than in Type A or B. Type C action can be most successful when it is absolutely clear that the enforcing agents are acting not for a foreign nationality but instead for the world community. The more the police carry the prestige of the world community with them and the less they carry a vestige of an opposing national interest, the greater will be the likelihood for their success. A small force can often have a dramatic impact upon local authorities if it clearly represents a higher, more embracive, rather than merely an equal and opposing authority. This impact was witnessed in the United States when President Eisenhower sent the national guard to integrate the public schools in Little Rock, Arkansas, and again when Attorney-General Robert Kennedy sent a Federal marshal to ask the Governor of Alabama to stand aside and let a young black woman enroll in the state university. Similarly, the mere presence of unarmed UN observers seemed to interrupt the infiltration of arms across the Lebanese border during the UNOGIL operation. The power of moral principle also expresses itself when its agent is a private actor, as Mohandas Gandhi demonstrated with *satyagraha* against the British. No officer of the world community can, of course, miraculously overturn existing injustices. Many attempts would no doubt fail, at least at first. The U.S. and Indian examples are not fully analogous because they occurred in centralized legal systems. The point is that officials who represent a wider community and act upon prevailing ideas of what is right often wield an authority far in excess of their mere physical strength.

For Type D enforcement a permanent, transnational force seems essential. Arms issues are so sensitive and the arms reduction process likely to be so fraught with obstacles and fears that only inspection and dependable enforcement by genuinely transnational agencies could implement this goal. Indeed, one of the strongest arguments for establishing a police force now is that the process of disarmament in the more distant future will be enhanced by a transnational enforcement agency whose experience and reliability are widely known. Procedures could be well established before the more delicate phases of arms reductions would begin. Transnational enforcement is so vital to this long-range process that it is sensible to begin using transnational monitors for *verification* (even without enforcement) of existing arms control agreements. A permanent police force could have been charged with the responsibility for developing means to inspect the SALT I agreement between the United States and Soviet Union and the Treaty of Tlatelolco for a nuclear free zone in Latin America. It could also be asked to monitor a new, equitable non-proliferation regime[7] and the existing ban on atmospheric testing of nuclear weapons.

Finally, the most important argument for creating a permanent, trans-national, individually recruited, constabulary force is that in modest yet significant ways, it would encourage a humane transition toward a preferred system of world order. This point will be explored in greater detail following a description of the force itself.

THE NATURE OF A PROPOSED TRANSNATIONAL FORCE

Concrete discussions of international organizations that do not yet exist usually convey an atmosphere of unreality because of understandable skepticism about governments' willingness to create such organizations. Yet a brief sketch of a global police force is necessary to suggest here the direction that concerned officials and pressure groups may want to move governments.[8] As the negotiations for the law of the sea make clear, it is occasionally true that what seemed irrelevant theorizing and impractical advocacy a decade ago, now has been written into the text of a treaty—compulsory judicial settlement of all disputes arising out of the exploitation of the sea's hard minerals.

Size

An initial force of 5,000 persons would provide sufficient personnel to carry out most small missions and provide the immediate forces needed to respond to sudden crises. If additional forces are needed in emergency situations before the police force can be adequately enlarged, the original group could serve as the nucleus and officer core for earmarked contingents contributed by various UN members.

Recruitment and Training

The members of the police force should be directly recruited by the UN from among individuals who volunteer. Wide geographic and linguistic representation are essential. No more than 5 percent of any battalion should come from a single national society. . . .

Location

The force could be located in perhaps three or more base camps, so that at least one part of it could be moved quickly to a troublespot anywhere in the world. Such geographic separation would also enable the force to prepare better for action in different climatic, cultural, linguistic, and social contexts. . . .

Financing

Providing appropriate salaries and fringe benefits, modern equipment, careful training, efficient transportation, and necessary logistical support would be expensive.[9] To establish bases and possibly create an international satellite monitoring agency would raise the cost, as would the use of the force in the field. Nonetheless, the amount required would be less than one percent of present world military expenditures.

Perhaps financing could be obtained through conventional UN budgetary procedures and allotments. A new formula might also be considered. When total costs for the force are determined, they could merely be divided among all the members of the UN on a scale proportional to each national government's portion of total global military expenditures. Each country's quota could be figured over the preceding five-year period to avoid wide fluctuations. This idea has the merit of also encouraging decreases in military expenditures because the "tax" for the transnational force would be directly linked to a national government's expenditures on its own forces. . . .

In addition to this financing procedure, an endowment fund could be established to pay for unanticipated costs when the peace force would go into action. Private individuals and organizations could be allowed to contribute to such a fund. . . .

Control

The proposed procedures for controlling the permanent police force are rooted in but move beyond UN experience with *ad hoc* forces. Of course, nothing in the proposals here would take away any existing UN authority to engage in enforcement action. The Security Council may, under Chapter VII, legally require members to take coercive action against a threat to or breach of the peace. In addition, the Security Council may request less

TABLE 20.2

Purpose	Host Consent	Decision Required
1. Unarmed on–site observation	Yes	request of UN Secretary–General alone
2. Unarmed satellite surveillance	No	2/3 GA vote
3. Type A armed patrol or observation	Yes	2/3 GA vote
4. Type A armed patrol or observation	No	2/3 GA vote, including at least 3/5 of the permanent Members of SC
5. Type B humanitarian intervention	Yes	2/3 GA vote, including at least 3/5 of the Permanent Members of SC
6. Type B humanitarian intervention	No	4/5 GA vote, including at least 4/5 of the Permanent Members of SC
7. Type C enforcement	No	4/5 GA vote, including at least 4/5 of the permanent Members of SC
8. Type D enforcement	No	4/5 GA vote, including at least 4/5 of the Permanent Members of SC

GA = General Assembly
SC = Security Council

than obligatory enforcement, by merely asking members to volunteer their forces, as was the case for Operations des Nations Unies au Congo (ONUC). Finally, the General Assembly, under the Uniting for Peace Resolution, may recommend that peacekeeping forces be sent into action in cases where the Security Council is unable to discharge its primary responsibility for . . . peacekeeping due to disagreement among the permanent members. All of these possibilities for enforcement would remain, and the standing police force could easily be put at the disposal of either the Council or Assembly under these time-honored procedures.

In addition, the police force should be allowed to go into action under the somewhat more flexible guidelines indicated in Table 20.2.

A simple idea underlies these suggestions: the more consensus among nations, the more coercive the enforcement may be.[10] The main proposed departure from existing procedure is to allow enforcement action, without host consent, in the absence of unanimity among the permanent members of the Council.[11]

An alternative approach would be to place responsibility for use of the transnational police in the hands of a semi-autonomous, carefully selected body of respected persons, able to commit the force to action and to preside over its command in the field. The group could be selected and guided by policy lines laid down by the Security Council. It is doubtful that the Council would be willing to create such a body at the present time, but it could provide a procedural change in which the permanent members might unanimously agree to delegate some of their authority to an agency they create. The latter could then act without being subject to the veto principle. Its least controversial actions could be taken by majority vote; the most controversial ones should doubtless require unanimity. . . .

Operations

As the preceding description reveals, the proposed force operates more as police than as an army. Wherever possible, violators of law would be treated as individual persons rather than as states, in order to make enforcement more feasible and to avoid a direct attack on the prestige of an entire national society. The transnational force normally would not seek to conquer or hold territory, nor to overwhelm an entire population. No image of an enemy should guide their actions. Only in establishing humanitarian corridors might territory be held, and then it would be of limited size and for a short duration.

Unlike armies, the police would aim to uphold the law, rather than implement the political objectives of a belligerent. Thus the skills and weapons of policemen are required. . . .

THE IMPACT OF A TRANSNATIONAL POLICE FORCE

On the Operations of Enforcement Agencies

A standing police force has several advantages over the *ad hoc* forces that are currently used by the United Nations. A transnational police force can respond to a crisis more quickly because it is always ready to go into action. It can function more effectively because it has an integrated force and command structure. It is more reliable because its members are loyal to the UN rather than to national seats of authority. It would have a helpful tradition of common experience and impartiality that *ad hoc* forces cannot achieve to a similar degree. It could more easily continue operating in the field without host consent. In addition to performing the preventive diplomacy functions associated with past *ad hoc* forces, the proposed police force in some instances could also carry out humanitarian intervention and safeguard the right of self-determination. An impartial use of police during civil strife in Santo Domingo in 1965, for example, could have established a humanitarian corridor for protection of noncombatants, thus removing the justification professed by U.S. officials in sending U.S. marines. Ostensibly sent to protect U.S. civilians in the Dominican Republic, marines in fact were used to influence a local political outcome.

An expanded role for a transnational force raises the question of whether the new enforcement would be fair. The impact of a police force would admittedly not be equal upon all societies. Those with border conflicts might receive the services of the police in a way that those without them would not. Racist regimes would feel more threatened than groups pressing for racial equality. Even more troublesome, the great military powers would seem immune to some kinds of enforcement. However, because the transnational force is designed to function as police rather than as soldiers, different levels of military power among states would not produce the differential in enforcement that would attend the deployment of a transnational conventional military force. The police could not function against a determined, aggressive army, whether fielded by a great or a medium power. In the limited areas in which the police force would operate, it would be more likely to help protect those victimized by regionally or globally dominant states which abuse their power. . . . Such a force could help establish a principle that great powers have no justification for sending their military forces into any nonaligned country, even if seemingly invited, as claimed by the United States and Soviet Union respectively, in Vietnam and Afghanistan.

At worst the transnational force would be inactive in its early years, and therefore would not affect the events that would have occurred in its absence. At best it would help protect the militarily weak against the militarily strong in areas outside the latter's vital interests. No less important, the presence of transnational police would also enable the world community to narrow the scope of the "vital interests" that officials of great powers traditionally used to justify military intervention. . . .

On Attitudes and Behavior

The creation of a universal force would offer a new focal point for developing transnational legitimacy and attract new patterns of human loyalty. As the members of the police force transcend their strict national identities, the legitimizing process will proceed. This in turn would lead to changed behavior in national societies. Diplomats arranging peace settlements would start depending more on the availability of the global police, as has already occurred to some extent with *ad hoc* forces in the Middle East. What would have been the effect of transnational police in Vietnam between 1954–65, in place of the International Control Commission? Might elections have been held as prescribed in the Geneva Accords of 1954?

The existence of a transnational police force would have a profound impact on peoples' consciousness. The type of change this force could promote is similar in its fundamental consequences to the historical attitudinal shift which occurred when people stopped asking "Who should be the king?" and instead began asking "Should we have a king?" A transnational police force will encourage more people to begin asking, "What should be the function of military power in international affairs?" "Should we have national military forces?" Students of attitudinal change report that patterns of loyalty are transferred when new agencies start delivering services one needs or wants. Some day youth may feel that to be a transnational police officer is a calling at least as noble as to become a pilot in a national air force. . . .

THE TRANSITION PROCESS

A strategy for establishing a transnational police force should consider issues of general constituency mobilization, UN enforcement operations, control procedures, and the relevant norms of enforcement. It is useful for analytic purposes to consider the roles of three different sets of people and organizations.

The first group consists of national policymakers, their domestic supporters, and the nation-state system as a whole. The second group includes the United Nations, inter-governmental organizations associated with it, and regional international organizations. The third group is made up of common people acting as individuals and through private organizations. Each group can be viewed as a system or subsystem operating within the overall context of world politics.[12]

The strategy most likely to be effective is for people in the third system to take initiatives to create institutions of the second system to increase the obligatory quality of norms applicable to the first system. The reason that progress has been slow is that the third system has difficulty influencing the second system except by acting through the first system. The latters' dominant members (the great powers) seldom support measures for positive transformation of the international system. Moreover, the third system also is often not enthusiastic about nurturing authority and power in the second system. Progress may now be somewhat more likely because people recognize the first system can no longer provide security, regulate the world economy, protect the environment, insure a dependable supply of resources, or guard against national denials of human rights. In the 1980's there will be more pressures against first system inertia than ever before.

A transnational enforcement agency can be established only if it enjoys at least limited support among all three systems. The strategy proposed here is to increase the leverage of people in the third system by using institutions within the second system to encourage powerful actors in the first system to give greater weight in decision-making to *long-range* self-interest. . . .

UN Enforcement Operations

Selected examples from past UN experience illustrate some progressive development in the effort to provide international—as distinct from national or transnational—enforcement.

- 1947: Establishment of a UN peace observation team in the Balkans (UNSCOB).
- 1949: Establishment of a UN force for cease-fire supervision in Indonesia.
- 1956: Establishment of a UN force for cease-fire supervision and interposition between the belligerents, with the force remaining in place only for the duration of host consent (UNEF).
- 1960: Establishment of a UN force for enforcement of internal law and order, as well as interposition between antagonists in civil war (ONUC).
- 1973: Establishment of a UN force for cease-fire supervision and interposition functions, with the force remaining in place until the Security Council agrees to its withdrawal (UNEF II).

The following sketch of hypothetical developments illustrates how an effectively functioning police force could develop:

1. The Security Council might approve the principle that the presence of *any* UN force cannot be terminated without Security Council consent, as is apparently now true in the single case of UNEF II. The Council might also endorse the principle that a decision to withdraw a UN force once in place should not be subject to a veto, thus establishing a precedent for some vetoless voting procedures. This could be done by agreeing in advance that such a vote would be considered a procedural matter, requiring a simple majority, or that certain actions could be taken by a two-thirds Council vote including, say, three-fifths of the permanent Members. If such a procedure could be agreed upon, it later could be extended to the decision to place the police in the field. This more flexible voting procedure would be helpful but not at first required, as Table 20.2 indicates.
2. Sympathetic governments could carry out intense diplomatic and educational activity to gain official support for the proposed police force. These political initiatives doubtless will come from the smaller powers who have been most supportive of UN *ad hoc* peacekeeping forces.
3. After several years of successful educational and diplomatic efforts, recruitment and training of the force could begin.
4. Some personnel in UNFICYP and UNEF could be gradually replaced with members of the new police force.
5. The Security Council or General Assembly could begin to establish guidelines for Type B enforcement without host consent.
6. A humanitarian corridor might be maintained with the consent of the host state, during a civil war (Type B enforcement).
7. Guidelines could next be established for Type C enforcement, perhaps later to be carried out in Namibia, if independence from South Africa had not already been achieved.
8. After about five years of successful operation, the Council might approve the police taking custody of the Holy Places in Jerusalem, making at least portions of the city immune to control by the police or military forces of any national government.
9. Type C enforcement might be considered to prevent architects of apartheid from impeding the movement toward majority government in South Africa.
10. A humanitarian corridor might next be established during a civil war, even in the absence of consent from the host state.
11. Later on, the UN might request police officers to enforce arms control agreements voluntarily ratified, but from which no state may withdraw without Security Council approval. Still later the transnational force might help implement arms reduction agreements on one or several states which have not adhered to an arms agreement that all other states of the world have ratified.

The police also could enforce restrictions on the transfer of conventional arms. In the more distant future, the police force would enforce a multilaterally negotiated, universally applicable, compulsory procedure for dismantling national armed forces.

Authoritative Control Procedures

A crude picture of the desirable changes in control has already been outlined in Table 20.2. At first, very little enforcement would occur without nearly unanimous consent. Later, as the police force gained experience and political support, its functions could move from Type A and B action to Type C and D.

Norms

The content of a new code of conduct for nations, which can enhance the prospects for peace and justice, is inspired by the values of people in what we have called the third system, and, to a much lesser extent, of the ideals underlying the second system. The old principles of international law, of course, are derived from the traditional preferences of the dominant actors of the first system. The basis for synthesis is to emphasize the convergence, in the long run, between what is ethically desirable and what is politically prudent, between the global human interest and the long-range interest of national societies.

Any effort at enforcement, even in domestic contexts, encounters frequent disputes about which legal norms should be enforced and how they should be interpreted. Third party interpretation and application of rules is almost always preferable to one party's—the stronger party's—enforcement of norms on the other party to a dispute. The latter condition, of course, illustrates both the central problem of international relations today and the virtue of a transnational enforcement agency. Such an agency discourages parties to a dispute from judging their own case by providing third party observation and regulation of deviant behavior.

At the beginning, the police could uphold only those laws enjoying nearly universal support in a relatively uncontroversial context. As new rules eventually are developed to avert nuclear proliferation, to prevent reckless disposal of radioactive wastes or oil tanker ballast, to establish compulsory taxing authority to increase economic equity, to curtail covert intelligence operations, to restrict the transfer of conventional arms, and to enforce a universal disarming process, the role of global police officers will increase. Their utility will be more obvious, and their previous experience will make the world community more willing to rely on global enforcement to apprehend those persons violating the new code of conduct that must eventually be practiced to protect the world's ecosystem and people from the instruments of violence and exploitation. . . .

CONCLUSION

Despite the lack of enthusiasm for the idea by many governments in the past, the creation of a modest transnational police force could become feasible in the near future if medium and small powers initiated a campaign toward that end. Certainly the inadequacies of enforcement through national self-help or *ad hoc* international forces will become increasingly clear and damaging to the interests of many states, including the superpowers, in the future.

The use of a world police force presents many difficulties, but even occasional uses of it in the 1980s will help create a more humane 1990s. A police force can provide rewards and punishments to increase—to a modest yet promising degree—compliance with international laws aimed at enhancing justice and peace. It can help reduce the use of military power and dampen the fires upon which arms buildups feed. Perhaps more important, a global police force can increase justice by strengthening the weak and discouraging the strong from yielding to the temptation to intervene outside their territories and to ignore callously the norms of justice and fair play.

Global norms will increasingly affect our lives whether we like them or not, whether we plan for their impact or not. For example, pollution of the atmosphere or oceans by one state eventually affects all. Inflation in any large national economy damages the economic health of an entire region and, possibly, of the world economy. The use of nuclear weapons by one or two combatants increases radiation for people everywhere. Simply the manufacture of nuclear bombs, because of environmental side effects, affects even future generations. The question is not whether global norms will have growing impact on our lives, but whether the future practices of nations will be based on preferred values instead of ugly outgrowths of the most powerful and selfish political and economic forces of our day. The question is: Will the norms of an emerging global civilization be defined and enforced by what the strongest governments and corporations and the most ruthless and desperate political factions can get away with, or will the code of conduct be implemented by officers acting on the basis of community-established procedures developed in pursuit of the global human interest?

At a time when there are so few initiatives that seem both feasible and likely to promote the transformation of a functionally deficient international system, a carefully established transnational police force looks like an attractive political goal for which to strive.

NOTES

1. In this essay we follow conventional usage of the term "enforcement." It means carefully prescribed action by public officers to prevent illegal behavior and uphold law. This use departs from the technical use of enforcement in Chapter VII of the UN Charter. There the term is reserved for a Security Council decision that legally binds members to take sanctions against a designated state.

2. The utility of several different *ad hoc* peacekeeping forces is beyond dispute. It is fairly clear, for example, that the partial withdrawal of Israeli troops from the banks of the Suez Canal in 1973 was made possible because UN peacekeeping forces were available.

3. The concept of the human interest is elaborated in Robert C. Johansen, *The National Interest and the Human Interest: An Analysis of U.S. Foreign Policy* (Princeton: Princeton University Press, 1980), pp. 19–34, 391–93.

4. This trend and violence-prone structures of dominance are described in Yoshikazu Sakamoto and Richard A. Falk, "World Demilitarized: A Basic Human Need," *Alternatives* VI, 1, pp. 1–10.

5. See, for example, Stockholm International Peace Research Institute, *Armaments or Disarmaments? The Crucial Choice* (Stockholm: SIPRI, 1979), p. 9.

6. For a comprehensive discussion of the need for an alternative security system to reverse the arms buildup and enhance human security, see Robert C. Johansen, *Toward a Dependable Peace: A Proposal for An Appropriate Security System* (New York: World Policy Institute, 1978).

7. The present Non-Proliferation Treaty is inequitable in seeking to place responsibility for the most serious nuclear dangers on those states who do not have weapons rather than those who possess them. It seeks to prevent horizontal proliferation of weapons to additional countries without halting vertical proliferation of weapons in continuously growing stockpiles of nuclear weapon countries. For elaboration of these arguments see *Denuclearization for a Just World: The Failure of Non-Proliferation,* Declaration prepared by a group of concerned scholars at the Lisbon Conference of the World Order Models Project, 13–20 July 1980, *Alternatives* VI, 1980. See also Robert C. Johansen, "The Proliferation of Nuclear Weapons and the Non-Proliferation Treaty," Position Paper for the World Order Models Project, Lisbon Conference, 1980, mimeographed (20 pages); and "Non-Progress in Non-Proliferation," *Sojourners*, September 1980, pp. 3–5.

8. Persons interested in more detailed discussions of the possible nature of transnational forces should see Lincoln Bloomfield, *International Military Forces* (New York: Little, Brown, 1964); Derek Bowett, *United Nations Forces* (New York: Praeger, 1964); Grenville Clark and Louis Sohn, *World Peace Through World Law* (Cambridge, MA: Harvard University Press, 1962); William R. Frye, *A United Nations Peace Force* (New York: Oceana Publications, 1957); Arthur Waskow, *Quis Custodiet? Controlling the Police in a Disarmed World* (Washington, D.C.: Peace Research Institute, 1963); Arthur I. Waskow, *Toward a Peacemakers' Academy* (The Hague: Dr. W. Junk Publishers, 1967).

9. In 1957, William R. Frye (n. 8) estimated that the annual operating cost of a 7,000-person force would be $25 million when it was not in action.

10. Arthur I. Waskow discusses this principle in *Toward A Peacemakers Academy* (n. 8) and in *Quis Custodiet?* (n. 8).

11. These proposals do not discuss the possibility that the category of permanent members may at some point include Japan, India, Brazil, Nigeria or others. Such changes would not affect the suggestions made here for control.

12. This analytic framework is taken from Richard Falk, "Normative Initiatives and Demilitarization: A Third System Perspective," *Alternatives: A Journal of World Policy*, vol. 6, no. 2, 1980, pp. 339–356.

CHAPTER 6

Regulating Force

The abiding content of the Grotian quest is the effective regulation of violence among states. In effect, overcoming war as the ultimate arbiter of disputes and conflicts is the goal that lies beyond all other goals. As matters now stand, aggression is illegal, but a peace treaty that validates the acquisition of the fruits of aggression might be legal. Leaders of an aggressor state that loses are potential war criminals, whereas an aggressor who wins is able to use international law to validate his conquests and, perhaps, punish the losers as "war criminals." The meaning of "aggression" is partly determined by the outcome, as the winner often largely controls the normative debate— especially if the winner is a dominant state. Such a humiliating accommodation to reality is a virtual necessity, given the continuity of interactions that go on after the violence ends and given the possible long-term shift in effective control over territory, people, and resources that may be brought about by war. At the same time, such practicality emphasizes the limited capabilities of international law either to protect the most minimal rights of a sovereign state or to offer weak states any protection if they fail to align or gain protection from a strong state.

There is another basic issue of connection raised here between the development of international law and the character of the overall world order system dominated by sovereign states of unequal size and resource endowments such that each possesses independent military capabilities. That is, international law cannot hope to erode this feature of international life without wider changes in the global political structure, including ideologies of "parts" rather than of "wholes." Moreover, an inquiry into war prevention should not in any sense denigrate other world order concerns. The pursuit of fairness and justice takes precedence over "peace" for many social forces active in the world, especially in societies where the issue of survival is waged by the majority of the people on a daily basis. The establishment and maintenance of "peace" through centralized coercion is not necessarily beneficial. We know from domestic experience that "peace" may coexist for long periods with tyranny and grave injustice. Thus concern for regulating violence needs to be coordinated with the pursuit of other goals, if for no other reason than to win widespread support for its concerns in the world as now constituted.

If one of the main tasks of any legal order is the preservation of the "minimum conditions of social coexistence"—to use Hedley Bull's phrase—then respect for some limitations upon the free resort to violence by actors with conflicting interests can serve as a decisive yardstick for the presence of an operative order. This need not necessarily involve shifting a "monopoly of force" to supranational institutions, the sort of centralization the famous German social theorist, Max Weber, considered crucial for the existence of the domestic order of a state. At a minimum, the existence of international order requires the acceptance of some norms regulating the employment of force by the main "subjects" of international law (i.e., sovereign states).

Lineage systems in ancient societies generally provide at least some demarcation of the group or persons against whom "reprisals" could be directed; letters of marque were issued later by high officials authorizing specific individuals to redress specific wrongs suffered, and, alternatively, independent third parties can be "deputized" to use force on behalf of the public order.

A weakened version of this third type of ordering was implicit in the foundation of the UN security system in which the effective power of the four veto powers, later five "policemen," was supposed to work cooperatively on behalf of the world community to maintain peace. Unanimity among the Great Powers was either "naively" assumed (i.e., as if no conflict would emerge) or "realistically" posited (i.e., as a condition for effective action). In fact, the outlook and record suggest the presence of both naive confidence and realistic caution in the minds of the chief architects of the United Nations system.

A further complication that existed right from the beginning of the United Nations in 1945 was the tension between the universalist aspirations of the envisaged security system and the "regionalist" tendencies that found expression in the Chapter 8 provisions of the UN Charter allowing for "*collective* self-defense." A contradiction existed between Churchill's predilections for stability by way of "spheres of influence" in which a hegemonial power was supposed to preserve the peace in a clearly delineated region through its preponderance of power, and Roosevelt's "universalism" in which global principles of order provided the basis of joint action organized and carried out within the United Nations framework. This contradiction was highlighted by Latin American efforts to insert a "hemispheric organization" directly into the UN framework as an exception to its general competence. The approach of regionalism was intended, among other things, to secure at least a minimum of influence for the many small but powerless states that could use their voting strength in this setting to constrain U.S. supremacy somewhat.

A third difficulty with the United Nations approach arose out of the general tension between the primary responsibility of the Security Council for the maintenance of peace and the "inherent right" of self-defense retained by member states. While this tension does not necessarily imply an irreconcilable contradiction, the lack of any effective fact-finding machinery and the undefined scope of the range of factors to be taken into account by the Security Council in assessing the validity of claims of self-defense led, in practice, to a restriction on the use of force that was so flexible as to be without ascertainable content and, hence, was virtually discounted, except as a propaganda tool. This flexibility invited political considerations to be given primacy, thereby further eroding the legal content of the process. The procedural approach, according to some specialists, was made even more problematic by the Charter's disposition to consider as the aggressor the side that first crossed a border with armed force. For a more adequate conception of aggression, other factors must be examined, including such provocations as threats, terrorist harassment, a consistent refusal to redress wrongs suffered previously, or a refusal to go ahead with negotiations. A more useful conception of "aggression" would take the whole context of violence into account.

The "failure" of the UN security system is thus not fundamentally a consequence of malice or evil ideological cleavages, although malign motivations and adverse circumstances have, on occasion, certainly been strong contributing factors. Rather, this failure is a consequence of the problematic assumptions underlying the security system projected by the Charter. In a central respect, the Charter promised more than it could deliver from the outset. Furthermore, the organization was from the start so paralyzed by ideological conflict as to make only the most modest intrusion on the anarchic self-help systems of separate and unequal sovereign states.

The first selection in Chapter 6, by Thomas Franck, explores in a systematic fashion the reasons for the "failure" of Article 2(4) of the UN Charter. Aside from the factors already discussed, Franck believes that the nuclearization of world politics and the related tendency of war to occur in the "safe" channels of competitive intervention in foreign civil strife constitute a type of "internal" conflict that is not viewed as falling directly within the Charter's competence. Regional and subregional patterns of growing hegemony staked out by the superpowers (i.e., Churchill's vision over Roosevelt's) has made the UN security system virtually inoperative as a real conflict-controlling force. This basic tendency is only partially balanced by the rather dim hope that a more enlightened idea of the national interest will take sufficient hold on the political imagination. Such a wider understanding might also produce a climate of support for a larger role for UN peacekeeping missions in the future.

Responding to Franck's arresting question as to who "killed" Article 2(4), Louis Henkin in the second selection offers us a diagnosis that is far less pessimistic. For Henkin, Article 2(4) has successfully deterred wars and considerably discouraged states from making claims of "anticipatory self-defense" and relying upon other legalistic stratagems that political leaders might be tempted to avow, contending that there is no genuine choice in the absence of a general presumption against initiating uses of force. In addition, Henkin feels that the "regional loophole" is less dangerous than it appears. In fact, no regional authorization contrary to the purposes of the UN Charter can claim a legal effect upon a dissenting state even if it should be backed up by a majority of states in the region. To a certain extent this positive assessment depends upon a particular reading of various interventions (Guatemala [1954], Hungary [1956], Lebanon [1958], Czechoslovakia [1968]) and thus depends on a rather subjective judgment. Nevertheless, the controversy is not quite as pointless as the proverbial dispute between the optimist and pessimist over whether the glass should be considered half full or half empty. Henkin's analysis draws our attention to the legalist conviction that there exists utility for norms even if they are frequently transgressed. Arguing for the continued validity of the Charter prohibition against nondefensive force, Henkin suggests that a first line of justification usually involves some type of assertion that if things are bad now when the norms are still on the books, they would become even worse if such prohibitions were removed. This line of reasoning establishes, though not in an empirically verifiable form, the still quite plausible claim that such norms continue to possess important "deterrent value." Sometimes, skeptics about the role of law argue that legal rules engendering only partial compliance should be eliminated on account of their unreliability, while holding inconsistently that deterrence must be maintained despite its failings. A second type of justification involves various demonstrations that compliance and noncompliance with norms involve a much more complex process than an "all or nothing" view of law suggests, a problem discussed in Chayes's article (Chapter 5).

The next three selections in Chapter 6 elaborate on various dimensions of this central concern. Derek Bowett's piece on reprisals emphasizes the apparent contradiction between an absolute injunction against unauthorized resort to force and its frequent occurrence, which, in turn, leads to a variety of efforts at legal justification. In articulating standards of "reasonableness" for assessing reprisals, Bowett tries to generalize recent state practices and to show the rudimentary review of controversial instances by the Security Council. He also demonstrates that important and legally relevant distinctions can be made even after the breach of the general injunction against force— that is, once force has been used in a situation other than after a prior armed attack (the literal Charter requirement as spelled out in Article 51).

Georges Abi-Saab's essay can be seen as an attempt to show the legality of resort to force under the special circumstances of "wars of liberation." The legal case for liberation movements is thereby construed as resulting not from the *rejection* or the inapplicability of the traditional norms prohibiting nondefensive force, but rather from a delineated *exception* that confers rights as well as duties upon liberation movements. Abi-Saab's position is naturally based on implicit and explicit assumptions that remain controversial. The entire contention that such "movements" are bearers of rights and duties of international law and enjoy a limited status as subjects remains problematic and has not been accepted by some governments, including that of the United States. Nevertheless, recent developments in the codification of the humanitarian law of war definitely confirm the drift of Abi-Saab's argument.

Abi-Saab draws some support for his interpretation by invoking the lawmaking capacity of the General Assembly. Moreover, his position raises more general questions relating to the proper interpretation of the UN Charter, namely, whether the articles dealing with the maintenance of peace and security take precedence over the other purposes of the United Nations or whether considerations of freedom and well-being—and, ultimately, self-determination—enjoy an equal standing. In the latter case, a construction of Article 2(4) in this wider context of Charter rules and principles would be necessary. While some states, such as France and the Soviet Union, definitely favor a historical interpretation of the Charter—thus giving primacy to Article 2(4) over the other purposes delineated in Article 2—this restrictive interpretation has not been generally accepted by most member states. We encounter here, in part, that fundamental conflict between views of international law that elevate the prohibition of force to ascendancy and those views, especially prevalent in the Third World, that bring other concerns to bear with equivalent seriousness.

The last two articles by Terry Nardin and Richard Falk, respectively, concern the issues of compliance, noncompliance, and the validity of norms in the context of the law of war, as distinguished from the earlier discussion dealing with recourse to war.

Nardin examines critiques of the laws of war that contend that the degree of subservience of rules to military technology and strategy has the perverse effect of contributing more to the institutionalization of violence than to its abatement or prevention. Furthermore, according to such critiques, the standards enunciated in the laws of war often appear to be incoherent, as, for instance, when the use of a particular bullet is forbidden but far more cruel weapons such as napalm or antipersonnel mines remain legal. The laws of war could also be criticized as cynical, detailing elaborate protection for prisoners of war while condoning the wholesale destruction of the civilian population by aerial bombardment of urban centers.

These are important objections to the laws of war, and Nardin responds by drawing a crucial distinction between laws and morals. Compared with applicable moral imperatives, the laws of war do, indeed, represent a disturbingly problematic incorporation of moral standards. Nevertheless, Nardin argues that the observation of these imperfect and limited standards is morally, as well as legally, preferable to their abandonment or to a total absence of rules. A crucial element of this argument is the demonstration that the legal standards set forth do have a definite substance and cannot be arbitrarily interpreted by the parties in combat. This latter quality depends also on the clarification of the relevance of claims of "military necessity," which is sometimes advanced as a blanket justification for noncompliance with or suspension of particular norms. A related problem concerns the validity of norms that are alleged to have lost their binding quality through repeated nonobservance or due to changes in the technologies of warfare.

Nardin distinguishes between a narrower and a wider conception of "military necessity" and painstakingly shows that only the narrower version can claim legal relevance. Although the wider version would rule out gratuitous violence that is not connected to any military objective, the invocation of "necessity" for noncompliance with norms due to the incon-venience of compliance or the heightened risk of military failure cannot be allowed as a legal argument without causing a total breakdown of the distinction between legal and illegal activities. A claim of "military necessity" cannot absolve parties in warfare from responsibility for activities prohibited by the laws of war, even if the observance of such norms can be reasonably understood as impairing military effectiveness.

Similarly, *mutual* noncompliance with the rules of warfare does not, as such, invalidate the prescriptions established by this rudimentary legal order—for instance, rules against indiscriminate tactics and weapons. Nonobservance on both sides might give rise to a valid defense if one side seeks to impose punishment for those illegal acts that it has itself also consistently performed.

The question of whether a traditional rule has lost its legal force through widespread noncompliance is a complicated one. Nardin's analysis effectively depicts the main dimensions of the problem. First of all, as in the general case of establishing rules of customary international law, patterns of actual behavior or practice are not by themselves conclusive. Consistent and even universal practices do not technically establish the existence of a legal norm unless the behavior can be shown to be performed out of a sense of obligation. The reverse problem arises in the case of deviations from previously valid norms, in which the noncomplying behavior can be construed as a *violation* rather than as establishing the invalidity or nonexistence of the norm. For example, it would obviously be foolish to infer from the fact that on a given day a majority of drivers were drunk that the injunction against drunken driving has fallen by the wayside, even if on that day no effort at strenuous enforcement was made. Similarly, no one would claim that widespread homicide or rape casts doubt upon the prescriptions contained in the legal order against such behavior, even if the number of actual sanctions dramatically decreases due to the inability of the police and prosecutors to handle an upsurge of crime. At most, such a circumstance calls into question the quality of enforcement mechanisms, but certainly not the validity of the norms themselves.

Of course, it is quite true that certain kinds of prohibitions on behavior ("blue laws") do lose their force when large-scale and repeated noncompliance occurs and is even tacitly tolerated. The difference between these two types of situations should be obvious. Noncompliance with rules protecting the very fabric of society are not invalidated when they are violated, no matter how frequently, whereas rules of societal preference (e.g., those prohibiting drinking on Sundays or on the street) whose violation does no appreciable harm are invalidated by recurrent noncompliance. In addition, efforts to reinforce unpopular rules of this latter sort drain scarce police resources away from more urgent enforcement tasks. The circumstances under which a rule loses its legal force relates to a variety of factors: social goals, perceived effectiveness of a particular means in securing wider social purposes, competing values that strict enforcement would entail, and enforcement costs. The appraisal of all these interacting considerations may often be a complex process, but it is obviously a quite different matter than the claim that the "is" of noncompliance by itself necessarily deprives a rule of its legal "oughtness."

The need for a clear articulation of standards and considerations to be taken into account is all the more important when we deal with the assessment of the (il)legality of a practice for which no specific rules have been formulated. Although there is, in the absence of a clear prohibition, a *prima facie* presumption of legality, the legitimacy of such a presumption can easily be defeated when evidence exists that the action or practice is analogous to clearly prohibited actions or is encompassed by more general prohibitions (e.g., contra cruel or indiscriminate weaponry).

These lines of argument are implicit in Falk's essay dealing with the legal status of nuclear weapons. The worldwide peace movement is preoccupied with the menace of nuclear war and has increasingly moved in the direction of investigating normative (moral, legal, cultural) objections to the present reliance on nuclear weaponry as well as on the arms race generated by this reliance and the prospect that through time more and more countries will acquire nuclear weapons. A milestone along this path was the issuance in 1983 of a Pastoral Letter by the Catholic bishops of the United States. The normative analysis of the Pastoral Letter, drawing heavily on just-war reasoning and traditions, helps create a basic tension between the moral/legal consensus of society on the use of military power and the bureaucratic consensus that guides governments and strategists. This tension also underlies Falk's analysis of the international law of war as applied to nuclear weapons and strategic doctrine, a tension that in a legal context generates questions similar to those raised at Nuremberg about the personal responsibility of leaders and citizens for a course of policy that threatens human annihilation in a manner at odds with the law of war and peace.

Falk also discusses the difficult circumstance of moving toward a "legal" position on nuclear weapons policy, given the possession of such weapons by rival sovereign states in a world system marked by distrust and by the absence of assured means of verified compliance with obligations undertaken. As with the bishops' Pastoral Letter, Falk stresses the unavoidable transition period in which nuclear weapons are retained in a deterrent role though minimized as much as possible by reliance on non-nuclear means of defense. This "legal" indulgence of nuclear weapons is coupled with an insistence on maximum efforts to achieve disarmament and to develop wider "peace plans" (a complement to the various forms of detailed contingency planning associated with readiness for war). What is required, then, is a readiness for peace in various settings, a virtually new policy perspective for the national security planners who act on behalf of the sovereign state. Law and lawyers have a definite role in this peace-planning process.

Note that international law is strained to the breaking point in this transitional period. The law-of-war precepts mandate total renunciation of nuclear weapons, but should this be taken strictly (a political impossibility), it would make the world vulnerable to various forms of nuclear blackmail. Therefore, the threat to use nuclear weapons in retaliation is allowed despite the properties of the weapons that would almost certainly make any actual use of them "illegal." There is a definite element of incoherence here—the threat is legitimated, but carrying it out, almost regardless of the nature of provocation, is not. If law were taken sufficiently seriously as a restraint on governmental discretion, then the credibility of the threat would be eroded, if not destroyed. Falk's legal regime attempts to minimize the role of nuclear weapons while acknowledging these fundamental difficulties with the enterprise of law itself. If the technical means are developed to verify compliance and detect noncompliance, then the ground for total prohibition becomes firmer.

As a short perusal of relevant materials shows, the indiscriminate character and hideous side-effects of nuclear weapons make their use clearly illegal by all traditional standards, even in the absence of explicit treaty prohibitions. Whether the possession of weapons of mass destruction is itself illegal and their "use" a deterrent is a central aspect of the inquiry. It is perhaps one of the saddest paradoxes of our times that we have entrusted the preservation of the minimum conditions of social coexistence in the international arena to weapons that are capable of ending not only any semblance of the "good" life but all of life in general. Here, more than elsewhere, the need for a transformed world order that overcomes the egoism of a state-centered system is evident. Obviously, effective transitional strategies are needed to provide reliable bases of social coexistence for groups without an exchange of dangerous threats of total destruction. The role of law (as distinct from politics and morality) in this context is limited; it can only hope to be persuasive and clarifying, offering guidance for those prepared to listen and adhere. To this extent its main contribution is to strengthen the resolve of societal and elite constituencies determined to question and resist the banality of pure destruction. Note that the conclusion of illegality does not tell law-observant leaders what is to be done now. It would be prudent to implement the prohibition against weapons of mass destruction by stages, perhaps commencing with a pledge or exchange of pledges of "no first use," and then moving on to initiate a disarming process that is coupled with the evolution of new ideas about upholding security (e.g., unarmed resistance, defensive weaponry, unblocked satellite and other technical means of verification, and the like).

Because of space limitations, no readings dealing with terrorism have been included, even though the spread of random violence for political ends has become a major world order problem for which international law has made some facilitative responses—specifically, by easing the task of finding and prosecuting those charged with terrorist acts. We now discuss a few of the international law issues raised by the rise of terrorism as a form of political behavior.

In this context it is important not to exaggerate the scope of the problem of terrorism, especially when compared to the systematic terror wielded by "legitimate" governments or official leaders ranging from Stalin to Pol Pot and from Hitler to Amin, or to overlook the cold efficiency of Latin American "death squads." Since some of these problems will be discussed in the context of human rights guarantees, we turn our attention here to the more spectacular terrorist acts committed by "private" persons, albeit for obvious political and "public" purposes. Terrorism, as normally understood, does not encompass threats to wage nuclear war against cities and other centers of civilian activity; yet this latter activity, officially planned by leading governments, shares on a grand scale all the elements that lead us to affix the word "terror" to other frightening forms of political violence.

The reasons for which acts of terrorism have become so salient and create insecurity and anxiety out of proportion to their actual magnitude is that their occurrence represents a frontal challenge to the idea of an international order based on a monopoly of force by agencies of the state. Beyond this concern is the awareness that everyone is a potential victim. There is no way to protect oneself by claiming "innocence." The randomness of this type of violence differs significantly from the politically motivated violence of earlier periods. Often absent is any logical connection between the victims of terrorism and those conditions against which terrorists act. The destruction of government property and, perhaps, even the physical harm done to the functionaries of an allegedly oppressive regime could be considered justifiable expressions of oppositional politics. It is worth noting that traditional extradition treaties generally exclude alleged perpetrators of "political crimes," although the question of whether political crimes cover violent acts is a controversial one. Indeed, it is the total lack of respect for the notion of "innocence" that makes some of these contemporary events so frightening and shocking. In one instance, Puerto Rican pilgrims to Jerusalem were indiscriminately gunned down in Israel by a Japanese commando allegedly fighting on behalf of Palestinian national rights.

The arguments concerning "solutions" to problems posed by terrorism fall basically into two (not necessarily mutually exclusive) categories: One argues for an attack on the "causes" of terrorism, and the other advocates a better means of transnational enforcement and new international agreements outlawing terrorism.

As might be expected, neither approach without the other promises much success. "Curing" the causes of terrorism is hardly possible, as many of the grievances of terrorists are rather vague and do not command much approval outside a tiny conspiratorial circle, generally reinforced by a larger, but still small, number of sympathizers. For instance, the blind hatred of the Bader Meinhof gang for the "system" represented no genuine social force in West Germany. On the other hand, merely outlawing terrorism is by itself a less than promising solution. The lack of cooperation between various states is one of the reasons for the success of terrorism, a circumstance that cannot be altered significantly by adding another legal document that carries little weight in specific situations. It is precisely because terrorist acts are committed for political purposes that there exists a reluctance on the part of sympathetic governments to treat such political offenders as common criminals. Beyond the general condemnation of random terror we must realize that acts of political violence, which for some observers represent examples of terrorism, are for others instances of heroic struggle. Proposals for stricter penalties for terrorists are also limited in their effectiveness for two reasons. First, it is, in any event, less the severity of the penalty than the certainty of punishment that deters those who act out of extreme political commitment; second, deterrence presupposes rationality and prudence on the part of those to be deterred, and thus will not work as effectively to inhibit those who are desperate or pathological, as is generally the case with terrorists.

The most effective way to prevent terrorist acts is to frustrate terrorist plans through intelligence and surveillance. Such a measure effectively robs terrorists of two of their most powerful weapons: the choice of target and the element of surprise. Surveillance can be largely accomplished by domestic means in the absence of any international arrangements, although elaborate networks of transnational cooperation exist among intelligence services, and situations in which international cooperation is needed and helpful certainly do occur. It is not clear that elaborate additional international arrangements are needed; informal, voluntary cooperation is both sufficient and likely to represent the maximum that can be achieved, even if formal procedures are established. At the same time there are high costs associated with mounting antiterrorist campaigns. Surveillance, even if diligently carried out, poses a danger of abuse for any free society. Experience has validated concern about this danger, given that intelligence operations rarely stay confined to prescribed areas. Worse still, antidemocratic elements often raise the banner of antiterrorism as a pretext for gaining public support for repressive policies and practices.

An entirely different approach to the phenomenon of terrorism proposes the granting of certain rights to terrorist groups in exchange for their adherence to the traditional norms of restraint governing political offenses. Thus one could grant political-offender status to terrorists as long as their behavior respects innocence in its selection of targets. Recently, treaties have been ratified that provide for cooperative procedures of transnational enforcement against hijackers or kidnappers. In general, the practice of granting asylum or political-offender status in extradition proceedings could also be governed by a common framework of law.

Although this idea of granting certain rights in return for the acceptance of duties sounds reasonable and fair, its viability is questionable. After all, it is doubtful whether most terrorists will be interested in obeying rules or entering into a tacit bargain with the official institutions they are out to destroy. Clearly, many modern terrorist groups believe that one of their sources of strength arises precisely from the qualities of randomness and irrationality associated with political violence. Such terrorism frightens far beyond its magnitude precisely because no one is exempt, all claims of "innocence" are implicitly rejected, and the security of all, including those at the very pinnacle of privilege, is undermined. Only through such "irrational" behavior can terrorists expect to exact significant concessions despite their intrinsic weaknesses in such areas as numbers of adherents, general support, firepower, and funds. Thus terrorism, like nuclear war, becomes one of the distinctive threats to the present international order and, in all likelihood, to the evolution of a safer, saner, and more just world order. It is these extremes of tightly organized military command centers and anarchically constituted political behavior that erode the claims of both legitimacy and competence associated with the sovereign state. The Grotian moment is here, to put the issue negatively, partly because the state cannot plausibly or acceptably safeguard its people against either form of violence, and international law, as we know it, can do little more than certify this impotence. In fact, the risk of a breakdown of order, whether through nuclear war or large-scale terrorism, is itself a continuing threat that interferes with the possibilities of peace and general well-being. Chapter 6 largely explores the Grotian potential for legal reform, but the readings are also acutely relevant to the underlying contention that the world order system that came into being with the sovereign state is in a condition of sufficient decay to enable those with conceptions of an alternative to gain a hearing.

QUESTIONS FOR DISCUSSION AND REFLECTION: CHAPTER 6

1. It has been argued that a law that is consistently violated loses its force, at least to some extent. Allowing for the distinction between "blue laws" and fundamental norms safeguarding social existence, how would you assess the significance of the Franck/Henkin exchange concerning the current vitality and usefulness of Article 2(4) of the UN Charter?

2. In civil society, well-founded arguments of self-defense are adequate defenses against criminal charges resulting from the resort to violence. Are you persuaded by Abi-Saab's argument that wars of liberation are justified despite their apparent encroachment upon the prohibition on force contained in Article 2(4) of the UN Charter? Since self-defense is already partially exempt from the prohibition in Article 51, what is the additional legal rationale for uses of force?

3. Given the increasing destructiveness of military technology, both conventional and nuclear, is Nardin convincing in his refusal to make military necessity the ultimate arbiter? How would you argue for military necessity, and what significance should such an argument be given?

4. Recently, there have been several attempts by various professional groups, such as the Physicians for Social Responsibility and the Lawyers' Committee on Nuclear Policy, to raise fundamental questions about nuclear weapons. Even more dramatic, the U.S. Catholic bishops' Pastoral Letter (1983) challenged the moral foundations of relying on nuclear weapons in virtually any context, even for defensive purposes. It is interesting to note,

in this context, that Grotius found it appropriate to use the writings of theologians, philosophers, poets, and historians as sources for his account of the law in his great treatise "On the Law of War and Peace." Is Falk's analysis of the illegality of nuclear weapons persuasive? How is it buttressed? What role can such legal pronouncements and voicings of moral concern play in reshaping official policy?

SELECTED BIBLIOGRAPHY: CHAPTER 6

Geoffrey Best, *Humanity in Warfare* (New York: Columbia University Press, 1980).
James E. Bond, *The Rules of Riot: Internal Conflict and the Law of War* (Princeton, N.J.: Princeton University Press, 1974).
Michael Bothe et al. (eds.), *New Rules for Victims of Armed Conflicts: Commentary on the Two 1977 Protocols Additional to the 1949 Geneva Conventions of 1949* (The Hague: Martinus Nijhoff, 1982).
Philip Jessup, *The Price of International Justice* (New York: Columbia University Press, 1971).
Julius Stone, *Legal Controls of International Conflict* (London: Stevens, 1954).
Telford Taylor, *Nuremberg and Vietnam: An American Tragedy* (New York: Bantam, 1971).
Grant Wardlaw, *Political Terrorism* (New York: Cambridge University Press, 1983).

21. Who Killed Article 2(4)?
OR:
Changing Norms Governing the Use of Force by States

Thomas Franck

Twenty-five years ago, the Allied nations gathered at San Francisco in the warming glow of victory and signed a solemn treaty giving effect to their determination "to save succeeding generations from the scourge of war . . ." and "to ensure, by the acceptance of principles and the institution of methods, that armed force shall not be used, save in the common interest. . . ."[1] Specifically, they undertook in Article 2(4) to "refrain in their international relations from the threat or use of force against the territorial integrity or political independence of any state . . ." They also committed themselves to "settle their international disputes by peaceful means. . . ."[2]

The practice of these states has so severely shattered the mutual confidence which would have been the *sine qua non* of an operative rule of law embodying the precepts of Article 2(4) that, as with Ozymandias, only the words remain. Perhaps the nations, given the changed realities of the postwar quarter-century, could not realistically have been expected to live with

Article 2(4). But its demise does raise a serious question for the nations: Having violated it, ignored it, run roughshod over it, and explained it away, can they live without it?

FACTORS UNDERMINING ARTICLE 2(4)

The United Nations Charter today bears little more resemblance to the modern world than does a Magellan map. The real world is not necessarily nicer, but it is quite different. Chapter VII of the United Nations Charter, for example, makes extensive provision for collective action by the Organization "to maintain or restore international peace and security" when a threat to the peace or an act of aggression occurs. "Such action may include demonstrations, blockade and other operations by air, sea, or land forces of Members of the United Nations." In order to facilitate such collective enforcement actions, Chapter VII provides for a U.N. Military Staff Committee to command the international police forces. It also obligates Member States to "hold immediately available national air-force contingents for combined international enforcement action."

Unfortunately these ambitious projects were founded on an invalid premise: that the Security Council would be able to discharge its responsibility as the United Nations' principal organ for world peacekeeping. Under Chapter VII it is the Council which must decide whether, in any particular instance, a threat to the peace exists, or whether aggression has been committed and, if so, by whom, and, finally, what, if any, collective steps by the world organization would best remedy the situation. The Security Council, however, in all but procedural matters, can only act with the assent of nine members, including the affirmative vote or at least the benevolent abstention of each of the Big Five. Almost from the moment the San Francisco Charter was signed, this essential prerequisite for U.N. collective enforcement action— the unanimity of the great Powers—was seen to be an illusion. Consequently, with the exception of the U.N. action in defense of South Korea, it has never been possible to invoke these collective enforcement provisions. Even in that one instance, U.N. military action could not have occurred but for a fortuitous absence of the Soviet Union from the Security Council. As for the U.N. role in the Congo, it never technically became an enforcement action, since the enemies against which the action was directed were hunger, chaos, tribalism and freebootery, and not a transgressing state. Even at the beginning, when the Security Council authorized a U.N. presence to facilitate the withdrawal of Belgian paratroopers, no actual use of force for that purpose was contemplated. The initial purpose of stationing the U.N. contingent in the Congo was only to relieve the Belgian troops of their reason—or, as some saw it, their excuse—for remaining there, and to assist the Congolese authorities to maintain order.[3]

This paucity of actions under Chapter VII does not, unfortunately, denote a peaceful world community. In the twenty-five years since the San Francisco Conference, there have been some one hundred separate outbreaks of hostility between states. The fact that on only one of these occasions has the United Nations been able to mount a collective enforcement action—and that more by a fluke than by dint of organizational responsiveness—indicates why, for security, nations have increasingly fallen back on their own resources and on military and regional alliances. And the Charter provided them with the necessary loopholes. As Chapter VII was seen to rust, increasing use began to be made of Articles 51, 52, and 53, which set out the rights of states themselves, under certain exceptional circumstances, to resort to various kinds of force outside the United Nations framework, until today, through practice, the exceptions have overwhelmed the rule and transformed the system.

Article 51 of the U.N. Charter permits the use of armed force by a state responding in self-defense to an armed attack. This right to respond can be exercised either individually by the state attacked or collectively by a group of states going to its rescue. At first glance, such an exception would appear to be both inevitable and modest. . . .

Insofar as the facts about the initiation of a dispute have not been satisfactorily ascertainable, the operation of Article 51 is effectively and dangerously unlimited. The temptation remains what it was before Article 2(4) was conceived: to attack first and lie about it afterwards.

The outright lie about who attacked first is not, however, the only or, probably, the principal problem. The most significant factor in complicating the "simple" right of self-defense accorded by Article 51, rather, has been the changing nature of warfare itself. The great wars of the past, up to the time of the San Francisco Conference, were generally initiated by organized incursions of large military formations of one state onto the territory of another, incursions usually preceded by mobilization and massing of troops and underscored by formal declarations of war. Because it was so familiar to them, it was to aggression of this kind that the drafters of Article 51 addressed themselves. Modern warfare, however, has inconveniently by-passed these Queensberry-like practices. It tends, instead, to proceed along two radically different lines, one too small and the other too large to be encompassed effectively by Article 51. These two categories are, first, wars of agitation, infiltration and subversion carried on by proxy through national liberation movements; and, second, nuclear wars involving the instantaneous use, in a first strike, of weapons of near-paralyzing destructiveness.

THE EFFECT OF SMALL-SCALE WARFARE
ON ARTICLE 2(4)

Small-scale warfare takes the form of rural and urban hit-and-run operations by small bands of fighters, sometimes not in uniform and often lightly armed. . . . Insofar as one state merely encourages guerrilla movements within another, an "armed attack," at least in the conventional sense, cannot be said to have taken place. The more subtle and indirect the encouragement, the more tenuous becomes the analogy to an "armed attack." Article 51 does not, however, on its face, recognize the existence of these newer modes of aggression, or attempt to deal with the new problems of characterization which they create for international law.

The deficiency became clear early in the United Nations' history. When, in February, 1948, the Beneš-Masaryk Government of Czechoslovakia appeared about to avail itself of Western economic assistance under the Marshall Plan, it was suddenly overthrown by the internal Communist minority. . . .[4] [S]ince the Charter speaks only of a right to defend against an armed attack, the international community is left to ponder what principles govern the right to retort in instances of lesser trespass.

No doubt a line of continuity runs from invasions by tanks and divisions through training, arming, sheltering and infiltrating neighboring insurgents, all the way down to hostile radio propaganda calling for revolution in a foreign country. However, these acts, while generically related, are also significantly dissimilar, and the law, if there is to be one, cannot simply disregard the differences. Yet there is a strong temptation, in practice, to treat them all as analogous. This is illustrated by our own conduct during the Lebanon crisis of 1958, which is a particularly good illustration of two dilemmas inherent in Article 2(4): that of deciding the factual question of who attacked whom, and that of defining the level of foreign intervention which should suffice to permit counter-intervention by way of collective self-defense.

This particular Middle East crisis flared up in two stages, the first being the civil war which sought to overthrow the pro-Western regime of President Chamoun, whose constitutional status was in dispute. The second stage was the annihilation of the pro-Western monarchy of Iraq, which led to the prophylactic dispatch of U.S. troops to Lebanon and British forces to the Kingdom of Jordan. . . .

Significantly, Lebanon did not at [first] claim that these facts were sufficient to constitute an armed attack within the meaning of Article 51. It brought charges against the U.A.R. before the U.N. Security Council under Article 35 of the Charter, alleging only a "situation" likely to give rise to a breach of the peace and asking the Council to devise "appropriate . . . methods of adjustment" under Article 36(1). Responding on June 11, 1958, at the instance of the Swedish representative, the Council succeeded in establishing "an observation group to proceed to Lebanon so as to ensure that there is no illegal infiltration of personnel or supply of arms or other *matériel* across the Lebanese borders. . . ."[5] The United States supported this resolution, together with all other members of the Security Council except the Soviet Union, which abstained.

The U.N. group went into position and was able to report within a month that their "[p]ermanent stations have been moving progressively closer to the frontiers on all sides"[6] and that with "the increase in the Observer force and the addition of enlisted personnel, together with supporting equipment . . . direct and constant patrolling of the actual frontier will be possible."[7] The Group indicated confidence in its ability to keep the border situation under control: "We have not had anything from the Lebanese Government which would lead us to say there is massive infiltration."[8]

At precisely the same time as this report, however, the governments of Lebanon and the United States were acting on the opposite perceptions. U.S. troops were pouring onto the shores of Tripoli. Two principles justifying the marine landings were advanced, both of them relating to collective self-defense, the rationale of Article 51. The troops had been "asked . . . to preserve Lebanon's integrity and independence" by the Chamoun Government, and they had also intervened in order to "afford security to the several thousand Americans who reside in that country."[9] In addition, Ambassador Lodge noted that the "territorial integrity of Lebanon is increasingly threatened by insurrection stimulated and assisted from outside" since "the overthrow in an exceptionally brutal and revolting manner of the legally established Government of Iraq." This, the United States proclaimed, represents "a *ruthlessness of aggressive purposes* which tiny Lebanon cannot combat without support from friendly nations."[10]

The all-important shift had now taken place from the earlier allegation of a low-yield "intervention" of the kind warranting the dispatch of neutral observers to police the borders, to an "aggressive purpose" justifying the intervention of a super-Power with force by way of collective self-defense. . . . The inherent right of individual and collective self-defense in Article 51 had thus been formally invoked in a non-conventional situation where no foreign army had moved across a border in an "armed attack."

. . . The Lebanese crisis illustrates two problems inherent in applying Article 51. The first is procedural: How is the fact of an armed attack to be established? The Charter provides no answer, and, in its absence, Article 2(4) can be virtually nullified by self-serving allegations. The second problem is substantive: how to define "armed attack" in a way relevant to the modern conditions of indirect, limited warfare without broadening it to the point at which disproportionate armed force can be used under the guise of self-defense against imagined or slight provocation.

Obviously, a rule of law which permits a state to use force whenever it thinks it has been attacked is not much of a rule. If the use of force is to be permitted in self-defense by way of exception to the general prohibition of Article 2(4), there must be some machinery for determining whether that exception applies in particular instances. Although the Charter provides no mandatory machinery to determine when and at whose instigation an armed attack has occurred, some *ad hoc* machinery has been tried. As in Lebanon, so in Viet-Nam an international group had been constituted to police the critical borders against infiltrators.[11] But after the Saigon regime began to lose the ground war, it and United States policy-makers came to the conclusion, albeit one not wholly endorsed by their own principal information-gatherers,[12] that the operations in the South were less a civil war than a covert attack by North Viet-Nam. . . .

As with the Soviet invasion of Hungary in 1956, so in this case the decision to come to the aid of a friendly government under attack may have been permissible joint self-defense by allies within the meaning of Article 51, or it may have been aggression, the use of force in violation of Article 2(4). Which it was depends upon whether the supported regime really constituted the effective government, or was merely a fiction being propped up primarily for the purpose of legitimizing "help" from outside. In the absence of some universally credible fact-determination procedures, the effort to establish whether a use of force is illegal under Article 2(4) or legal under Article 51 is stymied by contradictory allegations of fact by the parties to the dispute and their allies. . . .

Both at present and even in the past, a number of attempts have been made to draft rules taking into account these world-wide phenomena of indirect and vicarious aggression which have recently become endemic but which were not unknown in the past. The Inter-American Convention Concerning the Duties and Rights of States in the Event of Civil Strife of 1928 obliges the parties to

use all means at their disposal to prevent the inhabitants of their territory, nationals or aliens, from participating in, gathering elements, crossing the boundary or sailing from their territory for the purpose of starting or promoting civil strife.[13]

The convention likewise forbids all traffic in arms and obliges the parties to disarm rebels who cross into their territory. In the same cause, the U.N. General Assembly on December 21, 1965, passed a Declaration on Inadmissibility of Intervention[14] which groups together "direct intervention, subversion and all forms of indirect aggression" as equally violating the U.N. Charter. . . . But, of course, this resolution is not binding and it has not notably inhibited Member States' conduct.

Efforts to arrive at a formula that could be incorporated into a new treaty have also been fruitless. Several draft texts submitted to the Special Committee on Principles of International Law Concerning Friendly Relations and Co-operation Among States[15] contain prohibitions against such acts of a state as "organizing or encouraging the organization of irregular or volunteer forces or armed bands within its territory or any other territory for incursions into the territory of another State . . ."[16] as well as against "instigating" civil strife.[17] One definition of force, proposed by neutral states members of this committee, includes

all forms of pressure, including those of a political and economic character, which have the effect of threatening the territorial integrity or political independence of any State.[18]

But none of these efforts has produced agreement as to whether the abetting of civil strife or the exertion of overweaning political and economic pressure should be analogized to an "armed attack" for the purpose of giving rise to a right of self-defense utilizing military force. Indeed, so muddied are these waters that the neutralist definition of the right of self-defense includes the right of insurgents, or states aiding insurgency, to attack with military force "in the exercise of their right to self-determination" in wars of national liberation. Such use of force, in the opinion of the neutralist draft proposal, constitutes "self-defense against colonial domination. . . ."[19]

THE EFFECT OF POTENTIAL NUCLEAR WARFARE ON ARTICLE 2(4)

If the growing fashion for mini-wars or quasi-wars has made the rules devised at San Francisco hard to apply, so, too, has the development of a capacity for warfare far more rapid and devastating than hitherto. Taken literally, Articles 2(4) and 51 together seem to require a state to await an actual nuclear strike against its territory before taking forceful counter-measures. . . .

In construing the language of a treaty one ought not to assume that the drafters intended a patent absurdity.[20] But in correcting for a possible absurdity, it is also possible to over-correct. According to Professor Myres McDougal, Article 51 cannot be taken to read that a military response in self-defense is permitted if, and only if, an armed attack has actually occurred. It would be against reason and nature, particularly in the age of jets, rockets and nuclear weapons, to interpret Article 51 so literally as to preclude a victim from using force in self-defense until it has actually been attacked. From this he goes on to argue that the Article 51 rule should be interpreted to mean that a state may use military force when it "regards itself as intolerably threatened by the activities of another."[21]

. . . The problem is, however, that while a rule which permits a state to use force against another only after it has been attacked may not be satisfactory in the nuclear age, one which permits a pre-emptive strike whenever a nation regards itself as "intolerably threatened" is so subjective as to be no rule at all. Moreover, the McDougal reinterpretation of Article 51 permits a pre-emptive strike not only in cases of apprehended nuclear attack, but against any threatening "activities," including conventional military ones that do not raise the same threat of catastrophic destruction.

Tested against the perceptions of the reasonable man, most of the instances when states perceived themselves about to be attacked or in imminent danger are simply not credible. Perhaps only in the case of Israel's invasion of the Arab states in 1967 does it seem at all convincing, on the facts, that the use of force was truly pre-emptive in a strict sense, i.e. undertaken in reasonable anticipation of an imminent large-scale armed attack of which there was substantiated evidence. . . .

REGIONAL ENFORCEMENT AND ARTICLE 2(4)

Ambiguities and complexities thus lurk behind the misleadingly simple rule in Article 2(4) prohibiting the use of force in international relations and in the carefully delimited exceptions to that rule. Changing circumstances of international relations, of the way nations perceive their self-interest, of strategy and tactics, have combined to take advantage of these latent ambiguities, enlarging the exceptions to the point of virtually repealing the rule itself.

A particularly significant part in this development has been played by regional organizations. Articles 52 and 53 of the Charter have been interpreted to legitimate the use of force by regional organizations in their collective self-interest, and, specifically, the role and primacy of regional organizations in settling disputes between their members. . . .

Intended to supplement the U.N. peacekeeping system, the regional organizations have too often instead become instruments of violence, eroding the Article 2(4) injunction. How this came about must be understood in the context of the historic negotiations leading to the insertion into the Charter of Articles 51, 52 and 53.

The Charter itself represents a compromise between universal and regional international systems: that is, between structured relations among states taking place in one loose, all-encompassing organization and, on the other hand, the norms applied in and between a number of tightly knit, relatively homogeneous groupings based frequently on contiguity, history and shared self-interest. . . .

Formally, the San Francisco compromise between regionalism and universalism is perfectly straightforward. A regional organization may act by means short of force to preserve the peace without having to await an outbreak of armed hostility (*Article 52*), but it may engage in enforcement action only after obtaining a fiat from the Security Council (*Article 53*). An individual state or group of states may use force defensively prior to Security Council approval, but only to respond to an armed attack (*Article 51*). However, between 1945 and 1969, the three articles have melded to produce an increasingly frequently asserted right of regional organizations to take the law into their own hands, to act militarily without Security Council approval even in the absence of an actual armed attack, and to exclude the United Nations from jurisdiction over disputes in which one member of a regional organization is being forcibly purged of ideological non-conformity by the rest. . . .

In the event of a dispute between two members of the same regional organization, who should have primary jurisdiction to bring about a peaceful settlement? Beneath the apparent issue, however, was a more subtle and profound one: To which international organization should the states of a geographic area be constrained to look for the regulation and legitimation of their conduct: the regional or the universal? Again at San Francisco the globalists were compelled to make concessions. The Dumbarton Oaks draft of Chapter VIII, Section C, paragraph 1, was amended at San Francisco by inserting what became Article 52 of the Charter. This provides that members of regional agencies "should make every effort to achieve peaceful settlement of local disputes through such agencies or arrangements before referring them to the Security Council." But even this confusingly non-obligatory prescription was made more ambiguous yet by the additional caveat that it "in no way impairs the application of Articles 34 and 35" of the Charter. These two provisions, in turn, state that the "Security Council may investigate any dispute . . ." and that any "Member of the United Nations may bring any dispute . . . to the attention of the Security Council or of the General Assembly."

Regionalism's potential as a legal loophole for avoiding the duty of Article 2(4) grew as more regional groupings came to see themselves as eligible. . . . [After] all, there emerged from San Francisco no generally accepted definition of a regional organization. There cannot, therefore, be any definitive enumeration of the regional organizations which are today entitled to those exemptions from Article 2(4) that were written into the Charter at San Francisco or which have since been grafted onto it by the practice of states. The discussions at the San Francisco Conference do, of course, clearly support the proposition that the regional groupings then in being regarded themselves, *ipso facto*, as beneficiaries of the new provisions in Article 51 which authorize their use of force in collective self-defense without prior United Nations approval. But does it follow, conversely, that any organization set up primarily to take advantage of the right to act in collective self-defense under Article 51, thereby also qualifies *ipso facto* as a regional organization entitled to maintain "peace and security" among its members under Articles 52 and 53?

. . . The question is, however, of legal importance. The Charter's provisions for regional action in the field of pacific settlement—a field rapidly and alarmingly expanding in scope and practice—do not, at least on their face, apply to organizations for collective self-defense established under Article 51, but solely to regional organizations established under Article 52. When, therefore, a defense organization like the Warsaw Pact brings "peaceful" pressure to bear on one of its members or "settles" a regional dispute under Articles 52 and 53, is it entitled to assert, in the absence of any armed attack from outside, as was done in the case of the "peaceful settlements" in Hungary and Czechoslovakia,[22] that it is acting under the Charter as a regional organization?

. . . In view of the fact that regional organizations are accorded such extensive powers in derogation of Article 2(4), and have garnered much greater powers in practice, it is important to have a clear view of which groupings of states are entitled to regard themselves as regional organizations. Many Americans tend to think that their grouping, the Organization of American States [O.A.S.], is the sole beneficiary. If the inter-American system is to be regarded as setting a minimum standard for recognition as a regional organization, it is argued, no other multilateral treaty organization meets that standard. No other single grouping is as broadly extensive in its coverage of military *and* non-military matters. . . .

Obligations to use force in the common cause are not, however, the sole standard by which a regional system can be measured and its legitimacy determined. Economic integration and the development of common judicial and administrative organs are perhaps even more important. In these other respects, the inter-American system is not pre-eminent. The Treaties of both the European Economic Communities and COMECON impose a substantially higher level of economic cohesion than does that other basis of the inter-American system, the Bogotá Treaty. . . .

A comparison of the various regional arrangements would therefore seem to indicate that in enforcement and collective defense the inter-American system may be somewhat ahead, at least in legal principle, if not in practice, of the level of integration so far achieved in Western Europe and Eastern Europe. On the other hand, both Eastern and Western Europe are far ahead of the inter-American system in economic and related integration. Thus, the inter-American, Western European and Eastern European systems are different in their distribution of strengths and weaknesses, but there is no basis for recognizing one as a "regional organization" while withholding legitimation from the others.

The Organization of African Unity [O.A.U.], the Arab League and several other regional groupings do fall substantially behind the standards set by the Americas and Western and Eastern Europe in the degree of their integration. . . . The test [of a regional organization], if it is to admit to regional status the O.A.S. on the one hand and the Arab League and O.A.U. on the other, cannot be much more exacting than this: A regional organization is any grouping of states in some defined geographic context with historic, ethnic, or socio-political ties, which habitually acts in concert through permanent institutions to foster unity in a wide range of common concerns.

In practice this unity has frequently been established by the use or threat of military force. Both the Soviet Union and the United States have done much to transform their respective regional organizations into instruments facilitating the threat or use of violence in advancing their regional interests. Under the guise of Articles 51, 52 and 53, both super-Powers have succeeded in establishing norms of conduct within their regional organizations which have effectively undermined Article 2(4). These norms have most recently been set out for the "Socialist Commonwealth" in the Brezhnev Doctrine and its corollaries:

1. A dispute within the Socialist "family" or "commonwealth" of Eastern Europe must be resolved within that grouping and not by or in the United Nations.[23]

2. A member of the family of Socialist states must limit its sovereignty to conform to the requirements of the grouping.[24]

3. The family of Socialist states may use force, even military force, by way of collective self-defense against any attempt to divert a member of the Socialist Commonwealth from orthodox conformity.[25]

These are the principles on which the 1968 invasion of Czechoslovakia was justified by the nations of the Eastern European bloc, but the concepts are not new. Rather, they are the restatements by the Soviets of a law of super-Power regional paramountcy which the United States itself did much to formulate through the O.A.S. It is the United States which first insisted that a dispute within a regional grouping should be settled by that grouping to the exclusion of the United Nations. In June, 1954, during what *The New York Times* has described as the "CIA-engineered revolution against the Communist-oriented President of Guatemala," we said at the United Nations that

if the United Nations Security Council does not respect the right of the Organization of American States to achieve a pacific settlement of the dispute between Guatemala and its neighbors . . . the result will be a catastrophe of such dimensions as will gravely impair the future effectiveness both of the United Nations itself and of regional organizations such as the Organization of American States.[26]

. . . It is also the United States which advanced the idea that a state's sovereignty is subject to the overriding right of a region to demand conformity to regional standards. In pushing for a condemnation of the leftist Guzman regime at the Tenth Inter-American Conference in March, 1954, the self-proclaimed aim of the Department of State was to achieve regional "solidarity" and to have "a clear-cut and unmistakable policy determination against the intervention of international communism in the hemisphere. . . ."[27] What was here condemned was not intervention by foreign troops but of a "foreign" ideology. It was against this that the United States pushed the regional organization to commit itself to "take effective measures, individually and collectively. . . ."[28] In announcing the U.S. naval and air "quarantine" during the missile crisis, President Kennedy justified this limitation on a state's sovereignty by pointing out that Cuba was "in an area well known to have a special and historical relationship to the United States and the nations of the Western Hemisphere."[29]

It was during the Dominican crisis that the United States openly asserted the right of a regional grouping to use force to secure conformity—in "self-defense" against the "attack" of an alien ideology and foreign "inspiration."

. . . The United States and the Soviet Union have, in short, both asserted the right to establish regions of super-Power paramountcy to which Article 2(4) of the U.N. Charter does not apply. . . . All this is a long way from the solemn obligation of Article 2(4). Perhaps the world of Article 2(4) never did and never could exist. But the world that has taken its place cannot long exist, either. . . .

THE WAY AHEAD

The prohibition against the use of force in relations between states has been eroded beyond recognition, principally by three factors: (1) the rise of wars of "national liberation"; (2) the rising threat of wars of total destruction; (3) the increasing authoritarianism of regional systems dominated by a super-Power. These three factors may, however, be traced back to a single circumstance: the lack of congruence between the international legal norm of Article 2(4) and the perceived national interest of states, especially the super-Powers. . . .

The failure of the U.N. Charter's normative system is tantamount to the inability of any rule, such as that set out in Article 2(4), in itself to have much control over the behavior of states. National self-interest, particularly the national self-interest of the super-Powers, has usually won out over treaty obligations. This is particularly characteristic of this age of pragmatic power politics. It is as if international law, always something of a cultural myth, had been demythologized. It seems this is not an age when men act by principles simply because that is what gentlemen ought to do. But living by power alone, even in a world of relatively balanced regional spheres of predominance that mutually acknowledge each other's power parity, is a nerve-wracking and costly business. To do it, much must be surrendered by the citizen: individual freedom, a large part of his national budget, and the chance to live in that comparative tranquillity which comes of being liked by others and liking oneself. There are, increasingly, signs that the citizen will not indefinitely pay the price demanded by the conventional national interest, and that his rejection of the traditional values, the realities of old-fashioned, power-oriented *realpolitik* may not be confined merely to one age group of one nation but may turn into a universal, skeptical reassessment of the classical definition of national interest. From such a reassessment could emerge a new set of criteria by which to determine the goals of foreign policy, a *realpolitik* which, for example, measures the national interest in terms of the ecological quality of territory already possessed rather than in new lands to be acquired; or which measures security in terms of the mental health, low level of tension and centeredness of one's own population rather than in control exercised over others. . . .

What killed Article 2(4) was the wide disparity between the norms it sought to establish and the practical goals the nations are pursuing in defense of their national interest. So long as there are nations—which is likely to be for a very long time—their pursuit of the national interest will continue; and where that interest habitually runs counter to a stated international legal norm, it is the latter which will bend and break. The other world that could arise from the ruins of Article 2(4) is one in which the redefined national interest is no longer calculated in integers amenable to military manipulation and in which, consequently, the national interest is perceived to be congruent with a renunciation of the use of military force in inter-state relations.

NOTES

1. U.N. Charter, Preamble.
2. U.N. Charter, Art. 2(3).
3. Security Council Res. 143, U.N. Security Council, 15th Year, Official Records, Resolutions and Decisions at 5, U.N. Doc. S/4387 (1960).
4. "On last Dec. 12, the Soviet Government newspaper *Izvestia* had warned that Czechoslovakia must not be a 'bridge' between west and east. . . . The Russians want to prepare themselves and to take this initiative in Europe before the Marshall Plan can get started." The *New York Times*, Sec. IV, Feb. 29, 1948, p. 1. "The

announcement of the Truman doctrine and the Marshall Plan gave a fresh impulse to the Czechoslovak reactionaries. They decided to pass to the offensive. Through their agents in government and parliament they tried to sabotage the program of the National Front government. . . . This was crude work. The real character of the Marshall Plan is already pretty widely known in Europe." V. Medov, "The February Events in Czechoslovakia," *New Times*, No. 10, March 3, 1948, at pp. 4–5. "Upon orders from Wall Street and the city, the Czechoslovak reactionaries from the National Socialist Party, the Slovak Democratic Party, and others, attempted with all their might to sabotage and to disrupt the social and economic reforms in the country." *Izvestia*, Oct. 28, 1948, found in 4 *Soviet Press Translations* 15 at 17 (1949). *Cf.* B. Polevoy, "The Defeat of Reaction in Czechoslovakia," *Pravda*, March 16, 1948, found in 3 *Soviet Press Translations* 243 (1948), and E. Zhukov, "Marshall's Chicago Address," *Pravda*, Nov. 23, 1947, in 3 *Soviet Press Translations* 39 (1948).

5. U.N. Security Council, 13th Year, *Official Records*, 825th meeting 17; Security Council Res. 128, *ibid.*, Resolutions and Decisions at 5; U.N. Doc. S/4023 (1958).

6. Second Interim Report of the U.N. Observation Group in Lebanon, U.N. Security Council, 13th Year, *Official Records*, Supp. for July, August and September, 1958, 34 at 36–37, U.N. Doc. S/4052 (1958).

7. *Ibid.* at 37.

8. U.N. Press Release LEB/15 of July 7, 1958.

9. U.N. Security Council, 13th Year, *Official Records*, 827th meeting 6 (1958).

10. *Ibid.* 8. Italics added.

11. Agreement on the Cessation of Hostilities in Viet-Nam, July 20, 1954, Geneva Conference Doc. IC/42/Rev. 2; 60 A.J.I.L. 629 (1966); reprinted in *Report on Indochina: Report of Senator Mike Mansfield on a Study Mission to Vietnam, Cambodia, Laos, Oct. 15, 1954*, Senate Foreign Relations Committee, print, 83rd Cong., 2d Sess., pp. 16–26; and 1 *Amer. For. Pol.* 1950–1955 at 750 (1957); "Final Declaration of the Geneva Conference on the Problem of Restoring Peace in Indo-China, July 21, 1954," Geneva Conference Doc. IC/43/Rev. 2; 60 A.J.I.L. 643 (1966); reprinted in Mansfield, above, at pp. 26–27; and *Amer. For. Pol.* 1950–1955, above, at p. 785; Statement by the Under Secretary of State at the Concluding Plenary Session of the Geneva Conference, July 21, 1954, *Amer. For. Pol.* 1950–1955, above, at p. 787; 31 *Dept. of State Bulletin* 162 (1954); 60 A.J.I.L. 645 (1966).

12. Roger Hilsman, *To Move a Nation* 527–528 (Garden City, N.Y., Doubleday & Co., Inc., 1967).

13. Convention Concerning the Duties and Rights of States in the Event of Civil Strife, adopted by the Sixth International Conference of American States and signed at Habana, Feb. 20, 1928. 134 L. N. *Treaty Series* 47, No. 3082 (1932); 22 A.J.I.L. Supp. 159 (1928).

14. "Declaration on the Inadmissibility of Intervention in the Domestic Affairs of States and the Protection of their Independence and Sovereignty." General Assembly Res. 2131, U.N. Doc. A/6014 at 11 (1965); 60 A.J.I.L. 662 (1966).

15. *Cf.* Draft Report of the 1968 Special Committee, U.N. Doc. A/AC.125/L.64/Add. 1 (1968).

16. *Ibid.*, 2.

17. *Ibid.* 3.

18. *Ibid.* 5.

19. *Ibid.*, U.N. Doc. A/AC.125/L.64/Add 2 at 12–13.

20. "Nothing is better settled, as a canon of interpretation in all systems of law, than that a clause must be so interpreted as to give it a meaning rather than so as to deprive it of meaning." Cayuga Indians Claims case, 20 A.F. (1926) at p. 587;

A.D. 1925–6, No. 271. See McNair, *The Law of Treaties* 383–385 (Oxford, Clarendon Press, 1961).

21. 1963 Proceedings, American Society of International Law 164.

22. Ambassador Sobolev (U.S.S.R.), U.N. Security Council, 11th Year, *Official Records*, 754th meeting 10 (1956); also Mr. A. Gromyko, addressing the U.N. General Assembly, U.N. Doc. A/PV.1679, p. 26 at 30–31, Oct. 3, 1968.

23. "The events taking place in Czechoslovakia are a matter for the Czechoslovak people and the States of the socialist community, linked together as they are by common responsibilities, and are a matter for them alone . . . they consider the matter as lying outside the purview of the Security Council." Mr. Malik, U.S.S.R., addressing the Security Council, U.N. Doc. S/PV.1441, Aug. 21, 1968, pp. 48–50.

24. Czechoslovakia "is responsible not only to its own people, but also to all the socialist countries. . . ." It cannot follow a sovereign policy "opposed to the interests of the world of socialism" because the "weakening of any of the links of the world system of socialism directly affects all the socialist countries which cannot look indifferently upon this." *Pravda*, reprinted in the translation of the Soviet Press Agency, the *New York Times*, Sept. 27, 1968, p. 3.

25. When "a danger arises to socialism itself in a particular country . . ." an "encroachment on the foundations of socialism, on the principles of Marxism-Leninism," when "anti-socialist and revisionist elements . . . under the guise of 'democratization' . . . befog the minds of the masses, stealthily hatching a counter-revolutionary coup" and they are "not duly rebuffed inside the country," then the family of states may act to restore normality and to defeat the forces of "world imperialism." *Pravda*, reprinted in *ibid*. "The countries of the socialist commonwealth have . . . their own socialist principles of mutual relations based on fraternal assistance, solidarity and internationalism." Foreign Minister A. Gromyko, addressing the U.N. General Assembly, U.N. Doc. A/PC.1679, Oct. 3, 1968, p. 26 at 30–31. "This [socialist] commonwealth constitutes an inseparable entity cemented by unbreakable ties such as history has never known. . . . The Soviet Union and other socialist countries have on many occasions warned those who are tempted to roll back the socialist commonwealth, to snatch at least one link from it, that we will neither tolerate nor allow that to happen." *Ibid*.

26. Ambassador Lodge (U.S.A.). U.N. Security Council, 9th Year, *Official Records*, 676th meeting 28–29 (1954).

27. Bowdler, "Report on the Tenth Inter-American Conference," 30 *Dept. of State Bulletin* 634 (1954).

28. *Ibid*.

29. "The Soviet Threat to the Americas," 47 *Dept. of State Bulletin* 715, 716 (1962).

22. The Reports of the Death of Article 2(4) Are Greatly Exaggerated

Louis Henkin

Dr. Thomas Franck, pathologist for the ills of the international body politic, has pronounced the death of the heart of the United Nations Charter, and proceeded to tell us who killed it.[1] In my view, the death certificate is premature and the indictment for legicide must be redrawn to charge lesser though aggravated degrees of assault. Article 2(4) lives and, while its condition is grave indeed, its maladies are not necessarily terminal. There is yet time to prescribe, transplant, salvage, to keep alive at all cost the principal norm of international law in our time.[2]

It is difficult to quarrel with Dr. Franck's diagnosis of the ills of the Charter, congenital, hereditary, acquired, and induced: the mistaken original assumption of Big-Power unanimity; the changing character of war; the loopholes for "self-defense" and "regional" action; the lack of impartial means to find and characterize facts; the disposition of nations to take law into their own hands and distort and mangle it to their own purpose. Distracted and distraught by these ills, one can indeed fall into the conclusion that Article 2(4) is virtually dead, but that, I believe, would mistake the lives and the ways of the law.

My principal difference with Dr. Franck's diagnosis is that it judges the vitality of the law by looking only at its failures. The purpose of Article 2(4) was to establish a norm of national behavior and to help deter violation of it. Despite common misimpressions, Article 2(4) has indeed been a norm of behavior and has deterred violations. In inter-state as in individual penology, deterrence often cannot be measured or even proved, but students of politics agree that traditional war between nations has become less frequent and less likely. The sense that war is not done has taken hold, and nations more readily find that their interests do not in fact require the use of force after all. Expectations of international violence no longer underlie every political calculation of every nation, and war plans lie buried deep in national files. Even where force is used, the fact that it is unlawful cannot be left out of account and limits the scope, the weapons, the duration, the purposes for which force is used. Of the "some one hundred separate outbreaks of hostilities" to which Dr. Franck refers, less than fingers-full became "war" or successful conquest, and hundreds of other instances of conflict of interest and tension have not produced even an international shot: cold war has remained cold, threats to the peace have remained threats, issues have remained only issues, for peaceful settlement or non-settlement (as in Cyprus, Kashmir, Berlin).

Many will refuse credit to Article 2(4), attributing the lack of traditional war to other factors—to nuclear weapons and the changing character of war, to greater territorial stability, to other changes in national interests reducing national temptation to use force. If it were so, Article 2(4) would not be the less a norm: law often reflects dispositions to behavior as much as it shapes them. Like others, Dr. Franck concludes that, by the time the Charter came, "new forms of attack were making obsolete all prior notions of war and peace strategy." If it were so, one might yet conclude that that development reflected and supported Article 2(4) and made it viable. In fact, nothing, alas, has rendered war obsolete—between India and Pakistan, India and China, Turkey and Greece, Honduras and El Salvador, Egypt and Israel. The occasions and the causes of war remain. What has become obsolete is the notion that nations are as free to indulge it as ever, and the death of that notion is accepted in the Charter.

The supposed transforming impact of nuclear weapons is also misconceived. For a time the United States had a virtual monopoly and its nuclear weapons might have induced rather than deterred aggressive tendencies. For many years now, the United States and the U.S.S.R. have had an effective duopoly: nuclear war between them is indeed happily unlikely, but many believe that, in their balance of terror, nuclear weapons cannot in fact be used and are effectively neutralized. The overwhelming military superiority of either super-Power over any other nation might encourage rather than deter war, and each has been amply tempted. The nuclear weapons of the super-Powers surely do not deter war by lesser Powers—as in the Middle East.

The fissures of the Charter are worrisome but they, too, are not as wide in international life as they loom in academic imagination. Pre-emptive war as "anticipatory self-defense" has been hypothesized by many professors but asserted by few governments: President Kennedy may have talked about "offensive weapons" in the Cuban missile crisis but he did not claim to be acting in self-defense under Article 51. A few nations have falsely claimed self-defense against actual attack, but there are effective limits to unwarranted claims, in what nations dare assert and what others will believe: no one accepted that North Korea acted in self-defense in 1950, and she was not induced to attack by the expectation that she would be believed. India violated the Charter at Goa but few accepted her rationalizations, and neither act nor justification significantly modified the norm. (Viet-Nam is a very different story, of course, and the applicable law depends on the characterization of the war or wars there in progress; unhappily, as Dr. Franck stresses, that characterization has not been impartially made.) Troops were sent to Lebanon or Jordan upon invitation, not against the political independence and territorial integrity of the host country; if Article 51 was at all relevant, it was invoked, not to justify the use of force contrary to Article (2)4, but only to support collective, defensive deployments by *bona fide* invitation, as in NATO. If some governments have theorized that abiding colonialism is a legitimate target for armed attack from outside, there are few such targets left; and, in fact, few have claimed the right of unilateral force against colonialism, only of collective U.N. action (which has its own justifications and limitations). "Self-defense against colonial domination" invoked by those suffering that domination is rhetoric, not international law, and the law of the Charter, surely, does not forbid a people to liberate itself from colonial yoke.

The regional loophole, too, is not as wide as might seem, dangerous but not fatal. There have been few instances of groups claiming the right to do together what the Charter forbids them singly, and little reason to expect that it will happen frequently in future. Some will say that to suggest that the United States and the Soviet Union have "both asserted the right to establish regions of super-Power paramountcy to which Article 2(4) of the

U.N. Charter does not apply" is to overlook differences of degree (if not of kind) on which all law—and all politics—depend. But even if one equates the O.A.S. with the Warsaw Pact, the Dominican Republic (or Cuba) with Czechoslovakia, surely donning the mantle of regionalism does not dispose of Article 2(4). Short of voluntary, recognized federation eliminating constituent identities and rendering all that goes on [as] "internal," "regional organizations," to whatever degree integrated or dominated, acquire no license for all actions by all means for all purposes. Whatever a regional grouping can do in *bona fide* collective security against armed attack, whatever pressures short of military force it can impose on members that disturb regional peace or relations, no regional organization may collectively use force or take any other action not "consistent with the Purposes and Principles of the United Nations." (Article 52(1)). Whether or not the Warsaw Pact has as good a claim as the O.A.S. to be a regional organization, in 1968 in Czechoslovakia its members abetted the Soviet Union in an indisputable violation of the Charter. Nothing in Articles 52-53 remotely affords the Brezhnev Doctrine a scintilla of legitimacy, and its own proponents have not seriously pursued that construction. There is reason to hope that the Soviet Union will not lightly repeat Czechoslovakia (especially if the victim fights back), with or without a "regional" umbrella. And while I have no legal brief for U.S. actions in regard to Cuba, Guatemala, or the Dominican Republic, neither the United States nor the Organization of American States has claimed the right to invade Cuba or the Dominican Republic, and few believe that the O.A.S. or even the United States alone would use force against the political independence or territorial integrity of any country in the Hemisphere, even in the event of sharp local deviation, if it was not in fact abetted from the outside. (Compare Chile, 1970.)

As Dr. Franck tells us, however, war has not been eliminated but has been channeled into more or less blatant intervention in internal wars and affairs, often by more than one Power, often by major Powers. In various internal wars one group or side, and sometimes both (or all), have sought outside support. Old nations and new nations have seen their interest in inviting, responding to, or tolerating such intervention. The irregular triangle of big Powers—United States, Russia, China—has made competition in intervention a dominant political determinant. International society has no principle for choosing sides in internal wars and has not seen the same interest in excluding external intervention.

Assuming—as many do—that Article 2(4) intended to forbid these interventions, clearly it has not prevented, deterred, or terminated a number of them although, again, one cannot say confidently that it has not deterred many others. To me, if Article 2(4) signaled the effective end of conventional war though not of intervention, even, indeed, if it induced this alternative form of organized violence, it would signify a substantial advance in international order: the temptation to military intervention in internal affairs is largely an affliction of the few big Powers and even for them military intervention to promote or maintain internal wars is not always and everywhere possible; intervention by invitation on one side is not so great an aggression against sovereignty and independence; internal wars are generally limited in area and in scope of military operation and therefore less terrible in their destructiveness.

It makes other real differences: The United States cannot itself invade Cuba; it can connive with Cuban exiles at the Bay of Pigs, but it must do so without providing air cover. The United States could obtain a plausible invitation from someone in the Dominican Republic but not in Cuba. It can send Marines to the Dominican Republic, but only for limited times and purposes, and the political consequences make the next time less likely. If it finds justification in ratification by the Organization of American States, it can do so only for acts which will in fact receive that ratification, and subject to its conditions. It can do less, or nothing, in Chile or Peru. For its part, the Soviet Union, unable to arrange, even to fabricate, an invitation by Czechoslovakia, has to invade, not intervene, and bear even within its family the full onus of blatant violation. The occasional small-Power intervention is also limited and hampered: Syria can send masked tanks, but not its air force, to help Palestine guerrillas against Jordan.

Dr. Franck's dramatic title makes its point, and his cry of alarm is warranted and necessary. But one must not allow it to be seized by the "super-realists" to prove that the effort to control international violence by law has again failed and the Chapter is now as irrelevant as the Kellogg-Briand Pact. For me, if Article 2(4) were indeed dead, I should have to conclude that it rules—not mocks—us from the grave.[3] In fact, despite common misimpressions (from which it suffers in common with other international law) Article 2(4) lives and can live. No government, no responsible official of government, has been prepared or has wished to pronounce it dead. Article 2(4) was written by practical men who knew all about national interest. They believed the norms they legislated to be in their nations' interest, and nothing that has happened in the past twenty-five years suggests that it is not. There is reason to pray and strive for the change in individual and national perceptions which Dr. Franck invokes, but the need is not to condemn Article 2(4) to death and to pray for its resurrection in the end of days when men and nations will not learn war any more. The need is for citizens, policy-makers, national societies, transnational and international bodies to be reminded that this law is indeed in the national interest of all nations; that a decision to initiate force always involves a preference for one national interest over another; that in the cost-accounting of national interest a decision to go to war grossly depreciates the tangible cost to the citizen—in life, in welfare, in aspiration—and usually prefers the immediate and short-sighted to the longer, deeper national interest.

NOTES

1. "Who Killed Article 2(4)? Or Changing Norms Governing the Use of Force By States," 64 *American Journal of International Law*, 809 (1970). [For abbreviated version, see Ch. 21 of this volume.]

2. With some of what I say here I deal at length in *How Nations Behave: Law and Foreign Policy* (1968), especially in Chaps. X and XI.

3. Compare 64 *American Journal of International Law*, at 809 (1970).

23. Reprisals Involving Recourse to Armed Force

Derek Bowett

Few propositions about international law have enjoyed more support than the proposition that, under the Charter of the United Nations, the use of force by way of reprisals is illegal. Although, indeed, the words "reprisals" and "retaliation" are not to be found in the Charter, this proposition was generally regarded by writers[1] and by the Security Council as the logical and necessary consequence of the prohibition of force in Article 2(4), the injunction to settle disputes peacefully in Article 2(3) and the limiting of permissible force by states to self-defense. The U.N. Declaration on Principles of International Law concerning Friendly Relations and Co-operation among States, adopted by General Assembly Resolution 2625 (XXV) on October 24, 1970, contains the following categorical statement: "States have a duty to refrain from acts of reprisal involving the use of force."

In recent years, and principally though not exclusively in the Middle East, this norm of international law has acquired its own "credibility gap" by reason of the divergence between the norm and the actual practice of states. So much is this so that Professor Falk, in a recent article entitled "The Beirut Raid and the International Law of Retaliation,"[2] has suggested a framework for claims to use force in retaliation against prior terroristic acts, thereby conceding the impossibility or unreality of any blanket, unqualified proscription of reprisals involving force.

It cannot be doubted that a total outlawry of armed reprisals, such as the drafters of the Charter intended, presupposed a degree of community cohesiveness and, with it, a capacity for collective action to suppress any resort to unlawful force which has simply not been achieved. Not surprisingly, as states have grown increasingly disillusioned about the capacity of the Security Council to afford them protection against what they would regard as illegal and highly injurious conduct directed against them, they have resorted to self-help in the form of reprisals and have acquired the confidence that, in so doing, they will not incur anything more than a formal censure from the Security Council. The law on reprisals is, because of its divorce from actual practice, rapidly degenerating to a stage where its normative character is in question.

To arrest this process of degeneration may require effective sanctioning by the Security Council of reprisals or, alternatively, a policy of restraint by states which will involve the renunciation of armed reprisals: academic studies are not likely to play any major role in this. However, there is room for a study which is an attempt at clarification of the nature of reprisals, as distinct from permissible self-defense; at an examination of state practice and Security Council practice which will elucidate those features of a claim to use reprisals which will either avoid or minimize condemnation by the Council; and at suggested procedures or assistance by the organs of the international community which might arrest the process of degeneration.

THE DISTINCTION BETWEEN REPRISALS AND SELF-DEFENSE

Clearly, if self-defense is a permissible use of force and reprisals are not, the distinction between the two is vital. To some, the distinction is elementary and obvious. The Soviet representative in the Security Council, Mr. Morozov, in the course of the debate on the Gulf of Tonkin incidents in August, 1964, said:

> The difference between the right of self-defense and the right of retaliation is quite obvious to any first year student at any law school or any institution of legal studies.
>   In fact, contemporary international law categorically denies and rejects a right of retaliation. The recognition of the right of self-defense in Article 51 of the United Nations Charter *ipso iure* precludes the right of retaliation. . . .[3]

The very fact that Mr. Morozov did not explain the "obvious" distinction is sufficient to alert the first-year law student—and even maturer brethren—to the possibility of latent difficulty.

Reprisals and self-defense are forms of the same generic remedy, self-help. They have, in common, the preconditions that:

1. The target state must be guilty of a prior international delinquency against the claimant state.
2. An attempt by the claimant state to obtain redress or protection by other means must be known to have been made, and failed, or to be inappropriate or impossible in the circumstances.[4]
3. The claimant's use of force must be limited to the necessities of the case and proportionate to the wrong done by the target state.

The difference between the two forms of self-help lies essentially in their aim or purpose. Self-defense is permissible for the purpose of protecting the security of the state and the essential rights—in particular the rights of territorial integrity and political independence—upon which that security depends. In contrast, reprisals are punitive in character: they seek to impose reparation for the harm done, or to compel a satisfactory settlement of the dispute created by the initial illegal act, or to compel the delinquent state to abide by the law in the future. But, coming after the event and when the harm has already been inflicted, reprisals cannot be characterized as a means of protection. This distinction would fit neatly into the general theory that punishment is a matter for society as a whole, whereas self-defense must still be permitted to the individual member, as an interim measure of protection and subject to a subsequent evaluation of the correctness of the individual's judgment as to the necessity for self-defense by the organized community of states.

This seemingly simple distinction abounds with difficulties. Not only is the motive or purpose of a state notoriously difficult to elucidate but, even more important, the dividing line between protection and retribution becomes more and more obscure as one moves away from the particular incident and examines the whole context in which the two or more acts of violence have occurred. Indeed, within the whole context of a continuing state of antagonism between states, with recurring acts of violence, an act of reprisal may be regarded as being at the same time both a form of punishment and the best form of protection for the future, since it may act as a deterrent against future acts of violence by the other party. To take what is now perhaps the classic case, let us suppose that guerrilla activity from State A, directed against State B, eventually leads to a military action within State A's territory by which State B hopes to destroy the guerrilla bases from which the previous attacks have come and to discourage further attacks. Clearly, this military action cannot strictly be regarded as self-defense in the context of the previous guerrilla activities: they are past; whatever damage has occurred as a result cannot now be prevented and no new military action by State B can really be regarded as a defense against attacks in the past. But if one broadens the context and looks at the whole situation between these two states, cannot it be said that the destruction of the guerrilla bases represents a proper, proportionate means of defense— for the security of the state *is* involved—against future and (given the whole context of past activities) certain attacks? The reply that this constitutes an argument of "anticipatory" self-defense which is no longer permitted under the Charter, since Article 51 requires an actual "armed attack,"[5] is scarcely adequate. It was never the intention of the Charter to prohibit anticipatory self-defense and the traditional right certainly existed in relation to an "imminent" attack.[6] Moreover, the rejection of an anticipatory right is, in this day and age, totally unrealistic and inconsistent with general state practice.[7]

In fact, the records of the Security Council are replete with cases where states have invoked self-defense in this broader sense but where the majority of the Council have rejected this classification and regarded their action as unlawful reprisals. These cases are worth the study, for they illustrate the importance of this question: Is the legality of the action to be determined solely by reference to the prior illegal act which brought it about or by reference to the whole context of the relationship between the two states?

. . . In the discussion of Israel's complaint of Egyptian restrictions on the passage of ships through the Suez Canal in 1951, the representative of Israel, Mr. Eban, countered the Egyptian plea of self-defense by the argument that self-defense presupposed two conditions: first, an armed attack and, second, the absence of assumption of responsibility by the Security Council.[8] No attempt was made by Egypt to justify the action as a reprisal, possibly because the argument was deemed to be bad in law, and the Security Council condemned the Egyptian action on the basis that the permanent character of the Armistice Agreements precluded any claim to belligerent rights or to a right of search and seizure of vessels in self-defense.[9]

After the Qibya raid in 1953, Israel was perforce obliged to shift away from this restrictive view of self-defense and, for the first time, argued that its action was justified in the whole context of repeated theft, pillaging, border raids, sabotage and injury to Israeli property and life.[10] This argument of an "accumulation of events" became a recurring theme in Israeli statements long before the June, 1967, hostilities: it figured in Security Council debates over the Gaza incidents in February and September, 1955, the Lake Tiberias incident of December, 1955, the Sharafi and Qalqilya incidents of September and October, 1956, the Suez invasions of October, 1956, the Lake Tiberias incident of March, 1962, and the Samu incident of November, 1966. . . .

However this may be, the Security Council has never accepted this widening of the context in which it will assess responsibility. On occasion after occasion . . . , the Security Council formally condemned Israel for illegal reprisals and rejected this form of plea of self-defense. It cannot be said that the Security Council, or even its individual members, have ever been particularly specific in their reasons for characterizing the Israeli actions as reprisals rather than self-defense. Certainly, occasional references to the "punitive" character of the actions are to be found.[11] More frequently emphasis is laid upon their disproportionate character,[12] although strictly this is scarcely relevant if reprisals are illegal in any event, whether proportionate or disproportionate. In some cases the view is expressed that prior incidents directed against Israel are not sufficient "provocation" to justify the reprisal,[13] although here again this is strictly irrelevant if the principle is that *all* reprisals are illegal.[14] There is also to be found an occasional stress on the "premeditated" character of the reprisal,[15] as opposed to the spontaneous reaction of self-defense, possibly a more relevant criterion, although even here one can envisage carefully pre-planned reactions in self-defense which would not cease to be self-defense merely because military prudence had suggested detailed planning for various possible contingencies. Were this not so, the whole basis of military planning such as one finds in N.A.T.O. and other military pacts would be suspect. However, the general conclusion which emerges from a reading of these debates is that the Council will not look to the whole context of the action so as to derive from that and accept the plea of self-defense in the face of continuing and repeated threats which, unless countered, will recur. . . .

In the Security Council discussion of the Gulf of Tonkin incident,[16] though no formal resolution was adopted condemning or deploring the United States action, the Soviet[17] and Czechoslovak[18] representatives rejected the U.S. plea of self-defense, as did the communication from the Democratic

Republic of Viet-Nam.[19] What is of interest is the fact that the United States relied on a series of past incidents, involving attacks on U.S. vessels, and frankly avowed the aim of securing its naval units against "further aggression."[20]

. . . The Security Council's policy of making an assessment on the basis of the action taken and its *immediate* cause, or, to put it in different terms, of isolating the incident in question from the general context of the relations between the parties, has certain advantages. In the first place, since it is a restrictive view of self-defense, it necessarily limits the situations of permissible force; and, if our premise is that the less permissible force the better, this may be regarded as an advantage. Its other advantage is that it permits the Council to make a relatively easy judgment on the limited facts before it. . . .

The disadvantages of this policy are that it may arouse a feeling of unfairness in the state condemned by the Council, and this has certainly been so with Israel, which has repeatedly protested against the Council's refusal to look at the whole context of a situation. It may also place the state claiming self-defense in a very difficult position strategically. Especially in the face of continuing guerrilla harassment, it is notoriously difficult to maintain an adequate defensive system which relies upon meeting attacks incident by incident. This is so whether one confines the defense to one's own territory or, under a doctrine of "hot pursuit,"[21] extends the defense to the territory affording bases to the guerrillas. Even more important, a series of small-scale defensive measures will not have the same deterrent capacity as a large-scale strike and may even be more costly to the defending state. . . .

RECENT PRACTICE ON REPRISALS

Recent practice, particularly in the context of the Arab-Israeli confrontation, suggests that not only have states like Israel, the United States and the United Kingdom not abandoned their wider view of self-defense—based upon the "accumulation of events" theory—despite the Security Council's rejection of the theory, but, even more striking, Israel has relied less and less on a self-defense argument[22] and has taken action which is openly admitted to be a reprisal. The Beirut raid of December 28, 1968, is the obvious example of an action not really defended on the basis of self-defense at all. . . . This shift in argument from self-defense to reprisals may in part be due to the realization that the self-defense argument is unlikely to be accepted in any event. It may in larger part be due to a growing feeling that not only do reprisals offer a more effective means of checking military and strategic gains by the other party but also that they will meet with no more than a formal condemnation by the Council, and that effective sanctions under Chapter VII are not to be feared. Obviously, if this trend continues, we shall achieve a position in which, while reprisals remain illegal *de jure*, they become accepted *de facto*. Indeed, it may be that the more relevant distinction today is not between self-defense and reprisals but between reprisals which are likely to be condemned and those which, because they satisfy some concept of "reasonableness," are not. . . .

After the Nahhalin incident of March 28, 1954, neither the Mixed Armistice Commission nor the Council condemned Israel. Perhaps the most striking feature about the incident is the equation—or proportionality—of the damage: the guerrilla attack from Jordan on an Israeli bus in the Negev killed eleven, the Israeli attack on the Jordanian village killed 9 and wounded 14.[23] A somewhat similar incident, the Karameh incident of March, 1968, brought unanimous condemnation of Israel. But there, after an Israeli bus struck a mine in the Negev, killing two adults and injuring several school children, the Israeli reprisal took the form of a large-scale attack on Karameh with tanks, helicopters and aircraft in support, followed by claims to have killed 150 "terrorists." The debate in the Council emphasized the disproportionate character of the reprisal.[24] Indeed, time and time again (Qibya, 1952; Lake Tiberias, 1955 and 1962; Jordanian complaint of November 13, 1966; Samu Incident, 1966; Es-Salt Raids, 1968 and 1969, Beirut Raid, 1968) condemnations of Israel have followed when the Council has stressed the disproportionate nature of the reprisal.

One suspects that a somewhat similar adherence to the test of proportionality lies concealed in the reasoning that no useful purpose is served by the Council striking a balance-sheet of responsibility. . . . Thus, one arrives at a tentative conclusion that, given a situation in which both sides engage in violence or in breaches of a cease-fire, and given that the Council will not accept the "accumulation of events theory" but will look to the immediate cause and effect, a proportionate reprisal will not incur condemnation. There are exceptions to this "rule." The Israeli invasion of Gaza and Sinai in October, 1956, the British action in the Yemen in 1964 and the Portuguese attacks on Zambia in July, 1969, and on Senegal in 1969, prompted Security Council reactions which are difficult to reconcile with it. The first involved a disproportionate Israeli reaction which was not condemned, largely because of the Anglo-French involvement, which seemed far more blameworthy to the majority of Council members and which could not be condemned because of the power of veto. The latter two instances probably invoked a good deal of the anti-colonialist sentiment which operated against Britain's position in Southern Arabia and the Portuguese position in Africa and therefore brought a condemnation for actions which were probably not strikingly disproportionate.[25]

If a proportionate response is likely to avoid condemnation, it is of equal interest to ascertain what features of a reprisal action, other than disproportionality, are likely to incur condemnation.

There is a good deal of evidence to suggest that reprisals against civilian populations are more likely to be condemned than reprisals against armed forces. . . . It may also be surmised that the Council will be readier to condemn a reprisal against human life than a reprisal against property. Israeli air attacks on the Jordan River development scheme in Syria in July, 1966,[26] and in Jordan on August 10, 1969,[27] have gone uncensored. However, the Beirut Airport raid of December, 1968, in which Israel took special precautions to avoid any loss of life, was nevertheless condemned[28] so that it must certainly not be assumed that reprisals against property will inevitably fall within the area of condoned reprisals. The "balance" between life and property is probably more a part of the general notion of proportionality.

The Beirut raid also illustrates the Security Council's tendency to reject any notion of "collective guilt" which might justify a reprisal against an Arab state irrespective of the origin of the injury which is the immediate cause of the reprisal action. In the Beirut case, Israel failed to adduce any convincing evidence that Lebanon was responsible for the attack on the El Al Boeing 707 at Athens airport by the two Arabs who apparently belonged to the Popular Front for the Liberation of Palestine and who had flown to Athens from Beirut, but who had otherwise no obvious connection with Lebanon.[29] The general allegation by Israel that Lebanon was "assisting and abetting acts of warfare, violence, and terror by irregular forces and organizations"[30] was not accepted as establishing Lebanese responsibility for this incident.[31] Clearly, even under traditional law, the target of any reprisal had to be shown to have committed a prior delict so that, without proof of delictual conduct *by Lebanon*, the Council was disinclined to accept Israel's plea of justification, quite apart from the issue of proportionality. It is possible that the condemnation of Israeli action in the Samu incident in November, 1966,[32] was due not only to its disproportionate character but also to the fact that Israel attacked Jordan rather than Syria, which had been the country alleged by Israel to be responsible for the increase of terrorist activities only a month previously.[33]

. . . The whole notion of responsibility which was central to the Security Council's concern over the Beirut raid (and which is fundamental to accepted notions of state responsibility) would argue against any reprisals policy which allows the selection of targets irrespective of the origin of the particular cause of the reprisal. . . .

A further factor which apparently affects the Security Council's conception of "reasonableness" is the timing of the reprisal action in relation to efforts at peaceful settlement, the argument being that conduct which jeopardizes the chances of a peaceful settlement is the more reprehensible. It is obvious enough that conciliation efforts will be hampered by a spate of reprisals between the parties and this has figured in various discussions within the Council, condemning reprisals.[34] However, while this may be true as a short-term view, it appears to be part of the current Israeli thinking that, in the longer term, the prospects of a peaceful settlement are enhanced by a policy which forces the other party to realize that it has nothing to gain by continued attacks. This thinking certainly runs counter to that of the Security Council, where the theme "violence breeds violence" is a recurring one.[35] Which is the more correct, at least in the Middle East situation, time alone will tell. However, some two years after the June, 1967, conflict, the evidence suggested that Israeli thinking was a less correct assessment of the situation (or of Arab mentality) than the Security Council's. . . .

The degenerating effect of reprisals is possibly the strongest argument against them. Had the Israeli reprisal policy in the Middle East succeeded in the sense that it discouraged recourse to violence against Israel in breach of the cease-fire, whether by states through their regular armed forces or by guerrilla organizations, it would have been difficult for the Security Council to condemn it. Indeed, whatever the *prima facie* illegality of reprisals, the fact that they actively assisted in maintaining the cease-fire would have been enormously persuasive. However, in the event that reprisals produce an escalation of tension and violence, a situation diametrically opposite to the policy objectives of the Security Council, the basic antipathy of the Council towards reprisals is understandable.

THE SPECIAL PROBLEM OF REPRISALS
AGAINST GUERRILLA ACTIVITY

. . . Even a policy of reprisal which might seek to avoid condemnation because of its "reasonableness" encounters the initial difficulty of demonstrating the illegality of the activities against which it is directed. This is amply illustrated by the Arab-Israeli situation. Apart from using emotive terms such as "terrorists," Israel has sought to have the guerrilla activities condemned as illegal and has done so on a variety of grounds. Initially the main ground was violation of the Armistice Agreements and, clearly, the transgression of the Armistice Demarcation Lines (ADL) or other violations of the truce were breaches of these agreements.[36]

. . . The situation since the June, 1967, war has changed in the sense that Israel (but not the Security Council) has now rejected the validity of all the 1948 Armistice Agreements. The case for arguing the illegality of the guerrilla attacks has shifted to the general principle of non-intervention[37] and the Security Council's cease-fire resolutions. . . . In various forms, certain members of the Council have expressed their concern over the continued military occupation of Arab lands[38] and it seems clear that they are not only reluctant to share Israel's characterization of the "terrorist" activities as illegal but also reject any plea by Israel of justified reprisals against these activities. It may thus emerge that Security Council condonation is more likely in respect of reprisals taken to protect territory by the state which is the accepted sovereign over that territory. This view is strengthened by the 1964 condemnation of the British action in the Yemen and the 1969 and 1970 condemnations of Portuguese action against Zambia and Senegal. The sentiment emerging in the Council was that guerrilla activities designed to oust a colonialist Power were not illegal since the colonialist Power's title to the territory or control over it was itself illegal.

However, in relation to Israel, the distinction between the territories occupied in June, 1967, and the territories previously held by Israel is not one on which the Arab guerrilla movements place any great emphasis: both territories are, in their view, "illegally" occupied. This is clearly not the view of the Security Council, and one can reasonably expect a far more sympathetic reaction to reprisals taken in "defense" of Israel proper. Contrariwise, one can expect a more sympathetic reaction to guerrilla activities aimed at challenging the Israeli hold on the newly occupied territories (and confined to bases, police and army posts, etc., rather than civilian targets in those territories) than to guerrilla activities aimed at Israel proper.[39]

The question of the illegality of guerrilla activities (and, correspondingly, the reasonableness of reprisals against them) is inevitably linked to that of the responsibility of the state on whose territory these activities are organized. As we have seen, the Security Council initially had no doubts about the general principle of the responsibility of the territorial state. However, international law has not developed any notion of absolute liability in the field and the basic assumption has been that the territorial state assumed responsibility because it had the power to prevent these activities. This assumption must now be called in question. It is probably unrealistic in relation to Jordan and Lebanon,[40] and partly so in relation to Syria and Egypt. The lack of realism about this assumption depends in part on factors such as the size of the territory and the limited military capacity of a state when compared with the magnitude of the guerrilla activities, and in larger part on purely political factors. . . .

In these circumstances, the aim of "teaching a lesson" to these governments may be misplaced. Reprisals are not likely to affect the toleration shown by a government to guerrilla activities when a show of intolerance would bring the downfall of the government. For these reasons, within a context like the Middle East situation, it would seem that a test of "reasonableness" would require a differentiation between the targets of a reprisal action. Hence, a reprisal aimed at the guerrillas, destroying their camps or bases, might be regarded as reasonable, whereas a reprisal aimed at the government or at state installations, such as airports, dams, irrigation systems, ports, etc., is far less likely to avoid condemnation.

A further indication of "reasonableness" would be the extent to which the state taking reprisals had exhausted all practical measures for the defense of its territory *within its own territory*. The bias against military action which transgresses a frontier or cease-fire line is marked and, in general terms, right. It is common form for reprisals to involve such transgression and, inevitably, the question is posed: "Why could not the state have defended itself against these guerrilla activities by measures of defense adopted on its own territory?"[41] It may be noted that the 10-Power, non-aligned proposal on the definition of aggression combines a concession that a state is entitled to take "all reasonable and adequate steps" against "subversive and/or terrorist" acts with the restriction that these may not take place on another state's territory.[42]

It may well be that some of the lack of sympathy for the Israeli policy stems from the belief that, in her reprisals policy, Israel has chosen the easy way and has not yet tried possible measures of defense against infiltration within her own territory (or that now militarily occupied by Israel). Or, alternatively, if Israel has exhausted all reasonable and possible measures of defense, she has failed to demonstrate this to bodies like the Security Council so as to convince them of the necessity for reprisal actions within Arab territories.

THE RELEVANCE OF SECURITY COUNCIL ATTITUDES ON REPRISALS

Is the Council Ineffective?

Any view on the Council's effectiveness is conditioned by the expectations with which one begins. If the expectation was that the Council would itself take action safeguarding Israel from all attack, then the Council has certainly been ineffective; but the expectation is unrealistic. . . .

The more germane question is whether the Security Council pronouncements are effective in the sense of influencing the "decision-makers." Israel would appear to have adopted the view that it will not now be infuenced by these pronouncements. This is probably not completely the case in practice, for no state lightly incurs the burden of defending itself in more than one international forum, in the press and before world opinion if this can be avoided. And it appears clear that world opinion *is* affected. . . .

Thus, it seems likely that, simply as pronouncements, the Security Council resolutions have little real effect other than as one additional factor in the many which tend to shape world opinion. This can scarcely be accepted as adequate to maintain respect for these pronouncements and, demonstrably, it has not been adequate to check the growing practice of reprisals in the Middle East.

There remains the possibility that the Council might seek to achieve effectiveness by resort to its own punitive measures under Chapter VII. One of the least impressive aspects of Security Council action has been the frequency with which it has, in condemning reprisals, conveyed a threat of sterner action[43]—presumably meaning the use of its preventive or enforcement powers under Chapter VII—but yet never seriously considered the possibility of enforcing respect for its authority. The threat has lost all conviction and is now apparently without any deterrent effect whatever. Of course, the difficulty is that, while the Council can produce sufficient unanimity to condemn a reprisal action, a proposal to take sanctions against either the Arab or the Israeli side would be far more difficult for the Permanent Members to support. However, if we reject military sanctions as patently impossible, there yet remains a variety of measures available to the Council.

Practice in relation to South Africa, Portugal and Rhodesia (none of them a more serious threat to world peace than the Middle East situation) has shown a range of "sanctions" extending from calls for the cessation of arms supplies and the suspension of economic aid to full economic sanctions. It would seem likely that the parties to the Middle East conflict are more susceptible to these sanctions than South Africa, Portugal and, possibly, even Rhodesia, so that arguments about the proved ineffectiveness of such sanctions are not necessarily convincing.[44] Sanctions in the form of an embargo or calculated restraint on arms supplies to the area ought to be perfectly possible. . . .

INSTITUTIONAL DEVICES FOR FACT-FINDING

The retention of a system of "community review" of any reprisal action is fundamental to any policy of restraint and, normally,[45] the Security Council will be the organ of review. Such review is, of course, essential if sanctions are in contemplation and, even apart from this, the possibility of review constitutes an important psychological deterrent to those contemplating reprisals. However, no system of review can operate satisfactorily without facilities for independent fact-finding: it is rarely satisfactory to rely entirely on the evidence adduced by the parties. Moreover, in situations where mutual distrust arises from the holding of different views about the facts, the production of evidence independently of both parties may help to allay that mistrust. . . .

The desirability of accurate reporting of the facts seems so obvious as to need no stress.[46] In practice, however, even the fairly sophisticated machinery of UNTSO has proved inadequate. Experience would suggest that specific improvements to any fact-finding machinery likely to be concerned with reprisals would be the following:

1. The terms of reference of the fact-finding bodies should stem from the Security Council (or other review organ) and not be dependent upon the agreements of the parties.[47]
2. Decisions on the interpretation and application of those terms of reference to specific cases should rest with the review organ and *not* the parties.[48]
3. The fact-finding process should ideally be a continuing one, i.e., involving a continuing scrutiny of the compliance with any armistice, truce or cease-fire or inviolability of a border and *not* limited to investigating a complaint after the event.[49]
4. Observers should have power of investigation of witnesses, though without power of compelling evidence to be given.[50]
5. The observers should be accorded freedom of movement on *both* sides of any frontier, ADL or cease-fire line.[51]

It may well be that one party will either refuse to accord these optimum conditions for fact-finding or, having initially accorded them, frustrate them in practice; such conduct will inevitably, and rightly, affect the review organ's judgment on questions of responsibility for reprisals and, if this be regarded as "bias" or judgment contrary to the facts, the aggrieved party will have no one but itself to blame. Thus, obstruction of optimum fact-finding will create a presumption against the reasonableness of a party's case.

The purely fact-finding or observer function may not, of course, be sufficient in situations when frequent violations of frontiers or cease-fire lines are occurring; and it is this situation which is most likely to give rise to reprisal action. In this situation, while fact-finding remains essential, there are basically two devices which can help: first, the "interposition" force (like UNEF) with power to prevent infiltrations;[52] second, the establishment of a buffer zone or "no man's land" which may reduce the risk of infiltration and facilitate its detection. Obstruction of these expedients by a party could also provide a presumption against the reasonableness of its case on reprisals.

It may also be the case that, with frequent but small-scale violations or even small-scale reprisals, the Security Council is not an appropriate review organ and a local, lower-powered forum is desirable. This, essentially, was the idea behind the Mixed Armistice Commissions established pursuant to the four Arab-Israeli Armistice Agreements.[53]

Indeed, the Middle East experience rather suggests that the various forms of machinery for observation, fact-finding, limited deterrence and even intermediate review of responsibility operate adequately only in a situation where both parties have an overriding interest in maintaining local peace. They all, therefore, have a vital role to play in reducing the risks of reprisals.

But, at the stage where one or both parties decide that their interest lies in an aggravation of the situation, either by initiating activities likely to cause reprisals or by taking reprisals, none of these devices will operate effectively unless they are backed by the authority of the Security Council and a determination by that body to bring real pressure to bear. Thus, in the final analysis, any approach to the problem of restraining resort to reprisals must involve three elements: (1) the serious consideration of guides to moderation by decision-makers (e.g., the Falk "framework") so as to contain reprisals within limits of reasonableness; (2) the establishment of appropriate and effective machinery for fact-finding and intermediate review by impartial agencies, with authority derived from competent international organs rather than the parties; (3) the application of constraint, in the form of sanctions, by the competent organs of final review such as the Security Council or, exceptionally, an appropriate regional body, designed to ensure compliance with authoritative censure of any policy of reprisals or illegal activities likely to give rise to reprisals.

NOTES

This essay was commissioned by the American Society of International Law as the working paper of its study Panel on Reprisals and Retaliation in International Law. The author revised his paper to take account of the Panel's discussion as well as important developments since the original version was written. Because of its significance, the article was referred to the *American Journal of International Law* (*A.J.I.L.*) in its revised Panel form and is being run without attempting to update it further.

The paper focuses on the experience in the Middle East, both because of its richness and importance, and because of the extensive consideration given to that experience by the Security Council and other international organs.—ED.

1. The literature on this point, though not very penetrating on account of the assumed authority of the proposition, is very extensive; the following is no more than a sample: Goodrich and Hambro, Charter of the United Nations 95–96, 102 (London: Stevens and Sons, 1949); Brownlie, International Law and the Use of Force by States, Ch. XI (Oxford University Press, 1963); Higgins, The Development of International Law through the Political Organs of the United Nations 202–205, 217–218 (Oxford University Press, 1963). Both Brownlie and Higgins cite additional authorities: Waldock, 81 Hague Academy, Recueil des Cours 475–494 (1952, II); Sørensen, 101 *ibid.* 219 (1960, III); Skubiszewski, in Sørensen, Manual of Public International Law 754–755 (New York: St. Martin's Press, 1968). The authors maintaining a contrary view, i.e., accepting a continuing, permissible role for armed reprisals, are Colbert, Retaliation in International Law 203 (New York: King's Crown Press, 1948); and Stone, Aggression and World Order 43, 94–98 (1958).

2. 63 A.J.I.L. 415–443 (1969). For a critical reply to this article see Blum, "The Beirut Raid and the International Double Standard: A Reply to Professor Richard A. Falk," 64 *ibid.* 73–105 (1970).

3. U.N. Security Council, Official Records, 19th Year, 1141st Meeting, pars. 82–83.

4. This condition is usually based on the Naulilaa arbitration (Germany-Portugal, July 31, 1928, 2 Int. Arb. Awards 1013), but the arbitrators give no authority for this and, indeed, in the earlier textbooks (and some later) there is little mention of this condition as a specific requirement: see Holland, Lectures on International Law 236–238 (1933); Westlake, International Law: Part II, 8–11 (1913); 2 Hyde, International Law 1660–1667 (1945). The emphasis was more upon the *necessity* for the act of reprisal in the sense that it had to have a lawful motive. As we shall see later in this article, there is little evidence that the Security Council today regards this condition as an essential prerequisite of reprisals, although it would scarcely pronounce on the issue since it is committed to the proposition that *all* reprisals involving the use of force are illegal.

5. This is the thesis ably argued by Brownlie, *op cit.*, Ch. XIII. It has many adherents, of all "persuasions," but it has also been a thesis consistently adopted by the Communist bloc.

6. The author has developed this reasoning elsewhere: see Bowett, Self-Defense in International Law 187–193 (Manchester University Press, 1958). This reasoning also has many adherents.

7. Pakistan justified the entry of her troops into Kashmir in 1948 on this basis before the Security Council, an argument opposed only by India. Israel's invasion of Sinai in October, 1956, and June, 1967, rested on the same argument. The O.A.S. has used the same argument in relation to the blockade of Cuba during the 1962 missile crisis. Several states have expressed the same argument in the Sixth Committee in connection with the definition of aggression and the U.N. itself invoked the principle of anticipatory self-defense to justify action by O.N.U.C. in Katanga in December, 1961, and December, 1963. Following the invasion of Czechoslovakia by the U.S.S.R. in 1968, it is permissible to assume that the U.S.S.R. now shares this view, for there certainly existed no "armed attack."

8. *Ibid.*, Official Records, 6th Year, 551st Meeting, p. 10.

9. Res. S/2322, *ibid.*, 558th Meeting.

10. *Ibid.*, 8th Year, 637th Meeting, pp. 15–38, statement by Mr. Eban. Note that, in this incident, Israel did not concede that the attack on Qibya was by Israeli regular armed forces but maintained that it was by border villagers, driven beyond endurance by Arab guerrilla attacks.

11. For example, China, *ibid.*, 24th Year, S/PV. 1470, p. 27 (Es-Salt, 1969); U.K., *ibid.*, 19th Year, 1109th Meeting, p. 4 (Yemen, 1964).

12. For example, China, *ibid.*, 19th Year, 1166th Meeting, p. 6 (Kibbutz Dan, 1964); France, *ibid.*, 21st Year, 1321st Meeting, S/PV. 1321, p. 2 (Samu, 1966); New Zealand, *ibid.*, S/PV. 1322, p. 7; Netherlands, *ibid.*, S/PV. 1323. p. 6; U.S.A., *ibid.*, 23rd Year, S/PV. 1402, pp. 3–5 (Karameh, 1968); U.S.A., *ibid.*, 23rd Year, S/PV. 1460, pp. 28–30 (Beirut airport, 1968).

13. See the U.K. view, *ibid.*, 10th Year, 710th Meeting, p. 5, and U.S.A., p. 12 (Lake Tiberias, 1955); France, *ibid.*, 23rd Year, S/PV. 1402, p. 22 (Karameh, 1968).

14. For example, U.S.A., *ibid.*, 10th Year, 695th Meeting, p. 9 (Gaza, 1955); U.K., *ibid.*, 10th Year, 710th Meeting, par. 36 (Lake Tiberias, 1955); Australia, *ibid.*, 712th Meeting, par. 11; U.S.A., *ibid.*, 17th Year, 999th Meeting, pars. 100–101 (Lake Tiberias, 1962).

15. For example, China, *ibid.*, 17th Year, 1003rd Meeting, p. 3 (Lake Tiberias, 1962); U.K., *ibid.*, 1003rd Meeting, p. 7; Pakistan, *ibid.*, 23rd Year, S/PV. 1402, pp. 18–20 (Karameh, 1968). And see Security Council Res. 262 (1965), 265 (1969), 280 (1970).

16. *Ibid.*, 19th Year, 1140th and 1141st Meetings, Aug. 5–7, 1964.

17. *Ibid.*, 1140th Meeting, p. 9, and 1141st Meeting, p. 15.

18. *Ibid.*, 1141st Meeting, p. 4.

19. Letter from U.S.S.R. to Secretary General, transmitting the views of the D.R.V., U.N. Doc. S/5888, *ibid.*, Supp. for July, August and September, 1964, p. 170.

20. *Ibid.*, 1140th Meeting, p. 7. And note that the U.K. fully supported the U.S. argument of self-defense: 1141st Meeting, p. 12.

21. For Israeli reliance on this doctrine, see Le Monde, April 20, 1968, and New York Times, Aug. 7, 1968.

22. Although, interestingly enough, in relation to the Israeli incursions into Lebanese territory in May and September of 1970, Israel reverted to the specific claim of self-defense, this was not accepted by the Security Council (S/Res/280 and S/Res/285 (1970)).

23. *Ibid.*, 9th Year, 665th to 671st Meetings; there was no vote on the Lebanese draft resolution condemning Israel for "aggression" (U.N. Doc. S/3209) and no discussion of reprisals.

24. *Ibid.*, 23rd Year, Docs. S/PV. 1401–1407, March 21–24, 1968.

25. U.N. Docs. S/5649, adopted April 9, 1964, and S/Res/268/1969, adopted July 28, 1969; both Britain and Portugal retaliated against repeated armed incursions.

26. 21st Year, 1288th to 1295th Meetings; draft resolution S/7437 condemning Israel was not adopted.

27. The attack on the Ghor Canal is reported in the Times Newspaper, Aug. 11, 1969; the Israeli Army is reported to have claimed this to be a reprisal for guerrilla attacks emanating from Jordanian territory.

28. Security Council Res. 262 (1968), adopted unanimously on Dec. 31, 1968. And note that, prior to its air strike against the Yemen in 1964, the British first dropped warning messages to minimize loss of life: the British action was nevertheless condemned.

29. For a full discussion of this incident see Falk, *loc. cit.* 415–420. A parallel is to be found in the Soviet argument in the Security Council after the Pleiku reprisal in February, 1965: ". . . who gave the U.S. the right to retaliate for the actions of the guerrillas in South Vietnam by bombing the territory of a third country—the Democratic Republic of Vietnam?" (U.N. Doc. S/6178, 20th Year, Supp. for January, February and March, 1965, p. 48).

The validity of the argument of course depends upon the proof of responsibility, and Schick, "Some Reflections on the Legal Controversies Concerning America's Involvement in Vietnam," 17 Int. and Comp. Law Q. 953 at 981 (1968), says: "No evidence has been produced by the American Government that these attacks were committed by North Vietnamese regulars, or with the knowledge and the approval of the Government of North Vietnam."

30. U.N. Doc. S/8946, letter dated Dec. 29, 1968, from Israel to the President of the Security Council.

31. The U.S. delegate stated: "Nothing that we have heard has convinced us that the Government of the Lebanon is responsible for the occurrence in Athens . . ." (U.N. Doc. S/PV. 1460, pp. 28–30).

32. Res. 228 (1966).

33. See the Financial Times, Nov. 14, 1966. Prime Minister Eshkol's speech in the Knesset on Oct. 17, accusing Syria, is summarized in Keesing's Contemporary Archives, 21817A, Jan. 14–21, 1967.

34. See, after the Es-Salt raid of March, 1969, Spain (U.N. Doc. S/PV. 1469, p. 27), and after the earlier Es-Salt raid of August, 1968, Denmark (U.N. Doc. S/PV. 1436, p. 52).

35. Lord Caradon (U.K.) after the Karameh incident of March, 1966, stated: "Violence solves nothing. Violence does not prevent violence. Violence breeds more violence" (U.N. Doc. S/PV. 1403, p. 3). To the same effect, at an earlier stage, see the Netherlands representative (U.N. Doc. S/PV. 1323, pp. 6–7).

36. Especially Arts. III(2) and (3) and IV(3). As early as the debate on the Qibya incident, Mr. Eban (Israel) emphasized the relevance of the agreements to this kind of activity and referred to Art. IV(3) as "the crux of the agreement. Without it Israel's coastal plain becomes an inferno of chaos and lawlessness" (8th Year, 637th Meeting, p. 17).

37. See statement by Ambassador Comay (Israel), U.N. Doc. S/PV. 1323, Nov. 18, 1966 (although, at that stage, the argument was used as one supplementary to, and not in substitution for, the argument based on the Armistice Agreements). He there cited General Assembly Res. 2131(XX): "No State shall organize, assist, foment, finance, incite or tolerate subversive, terrorist or armed activities directed towards the violent overthrow of . . . another State."

38. France has stated: "Nor can we agree that it is possible to speak of necessary measures for the security of the territory and population under the jurisdiction of Israel, because we cannot recognize jurisdiction established by occupation" (U.N. Doc. S/PV. 1402, p. 22). See also Pakistan (U.N. Docs. S/PV. 1435, p. 36 and S/PV. 1468, p. 21); Senegal (U.N. Doc. S/PV. 1436, pp. 63–65); Zambia (U.N. Doc. S/PV. 1469, p. 51).

39. However, it cannot be said that the Security Council has reacted with great energy to Israel's complaint of guerrilla attacks and hijacking of Israel's aircraft. Possibly the matter is not regarded as one with which the Council can deal easily and certainly the Secretary General seems to have assumed ICAO was the more competent: see Eban-U Thant exchange of letters, Feb. 20 and 26, 1969 (U.N. Monthly Chronicle, March, 1969, pp. 12–14).

40. For details of clashes between Lebanese forces and Syrian-backed guerrillas within the Lebanon in April and May, 1969, see Keesing's Contemporary Archives, 1969, 23520. King Hussein had rejected the suggestion that he is under any duty to halt guerrilla activities and had justified those activities (New York Times, March 24, 1968). In the debate on the Es-Salt raid of March 26, the Israeli representative, Mr. Tekoah, alleged complete complicity between the Jordan Government and the guerrilla organizations, citing an agreement between them of Nov. 16, 1968. In 1970 in the debates on the Israeli incursions into the Lebanon in May and September, Mr. Tekoah alleged that similar agreements had been made between the Lebanese Government and guerrilla organizations. This position in Jordan had changed quite radically by the summer of 1970. On July 19, 1970, the Jordanian Government announced that, at the culmination of a series of clashes between its forces and guerrilla forces, it had destroyed the Palestinian guerrilla organization on Jordanian territory and all its bases. The Times Newspaper, July 20, 1970.

41. This is not a question to which lawyers can give persuasive answers. However, there would be advantage in a strategic study of the effectiveness against guerrilla activities emanating from abroad of measures of self-defense confined to the target state's own territory. Possibly, variations in circumstances (terrain, size of respective forces, length of frontier, etc.) are such as to permit no generalizations. But obviously a comprehensive study which demonstrated that self-defense, narrowly construed, is in general ineffective against guerrilla activities would strengthen the case for reprisals considerably. Apparently Israel had seriously considered sealing off the 50-mile cease-fire line with Jordan by a defensive barrier, a technique once regarded as impractical (James Feron in the Herald Tribune, Dec. 20, 1967).

42. U.N. Doc. A/AC. 134/L. 16 of March 24, 1969.

43. U.N. Doc. S/7498, adopted on Nov. 25, 1966, envisaged "more effective steps as envisaged in the Charter to ensure against the repetition of such acts." S/Res. 270 (1969), following the August, 1969, air attack on South Lebanon, referred specifically to the possibility of "further and more effective steps as envisaged in the Charter to ensure against repetition of such acts." Also S/Res. 268 (1969), condemning Portugal for the attack on the Zambian village of Lote, threatened "to consider further measures" if Portugal continued raids on Zambia. Successive threats of sanctions, never implemented, can do little to enhance the reputation of the Security Council and were best not uttered at all.

44. Apparently the threat by the U.S. to cease economic aid to Israel was the means whereby the Israeli project for diverting the River Jordan in 1953 was stopped. Burns, Between Arab and Israel 11 (New York: Obolensky, 1963).

45. One cannot exclude the possibility that organs of regional arrangements will afford other organs of review in situations arising between members. The El Salvador–Honduras conflict of July, 1969, the "football war," would provide a possible situation of this kind and, in fact, O.A.S. mediation was accepted.

46. For the view that fact-finding cannot be objective and is not necessary to prevent recurrence (and that the allocation of blame is undesirable), see Franck and Gold, "The Limits of Perceptual Objectivity in International Peace Observation," in The Middle-East Crisis: Test of International Law, 33 Law and Contemporary Problems 183-193 (1965). This argument appears to rely on the neuro-chemistry of visual perception and, as there stated, is totally unconvincing to this author. No lawyer would claim complete accuracy for any technique of adducing evidence. Indeed, legal systems involve rules of evidence and techniques of proof and cross-examination which assume unreliability of witnesses, etc., but which equally assume that, by these rules and techniques, it is possible to weigh evidence and arrive at

a *reasonably* accurate version of the facts. This author does not accept that neurochemistry has demonstrated the falsity of that assumption and even less that the conclusion that it is unproductive to assess blame is justified in situations like the Middle East.

47. For detailed argument on this point, demonstrating how, with terms of reference dependent solely on the agreement of the parties, it becomes possible for the parties to frustrate the supervision machinery, see Wainhouse, International Peace Observation (Baltimore: The Johns Hopkins Press, 1966), 268–269, 272. This is not to suggest that, as a peacekeeping organ, an observer mission may not need the consent of the host state. The contention advanced above is that, once consent is given and agreement secured to terms of reference, these terms of reference should be contained in a Security Council resolution, and be interpreted by the Security Council.

48. Many disputes of this character arose out of the Arab-Israeli Armistice Agreements. For a useful summary of the dispute over the Israeli project to drain Lake Huleh, which also involved a dispute on the competence of the MAC, see Higgins, United Nations Peacekeeping 1946–1967: Documents and Commentary 86–99 (London: Oxford University Press, 1969).

49. This was the case with the Arab-Israeli MAC's: see Wainhouse, *op. cit.*, 272.

50. Thus, observers should be accorded the right to question civilians, army officers, government officials, etc. Refusal to testify or to allow such testimony to be taken would be made a matter for report to the review organ which would be free to draw its own conclusions. This extensive power of investigation would also suggest that military officers, such as the UNTSO observers, might usefully be supplemented by civilian international officials with police or legal training.

51. By a note of Oct. 5, 1956, Israel informed the Chief-of-Staff of UNTSO that observers had no permission to investigate incidents occurring within Israel: see Burns, *op. cit.*, 172. Obviously, this restriction is crippling if it is to be applied to guerrilla activities. For Security Council insistence on full freedom of movement, see Res. S/3575 and S/3605.

52. For UNEF's limited power to apprehend infiltrators in a zone 500 meters from the ADL (and only on the Egyptian side) and, after interrogation, to hand them over to local police, see UNEF: Summary Study of the Experience derived from the establishment and operation of the Force, Report of the Secretary General, U.N. Doc. A/3943, Oct. 9, 1958.

53. See *ibid.*, p. 4.

24. Wars of National Liberation and the Laws of War

Georges Abi-Saab

Wars of national liberation constitute a category of conflicts which, though not previously unknown, has gained great importance since the Second World War. These are "conflicts which arise from the struggles of peoples under colonial and foreign rule for liberation and self-determination."[1]

The frequency and increasing importance of these struggles in contemporary international relations brought to the fore the numerous and complex problems to which they give rise, especially in the legal field. Among the most important are those concerning the status of wars of national liberation in international law and the extent to which they are governed by the existing laws of war.

THE STATUS OF WARS OF NATIONAL LIBERATION
IN CONTEMPORARY INTERNATIONAL LAW

The status of wars of national liberation in contemporary international law depends on their legal qualification as international conflicts or as conflicts not of an international character.

The Traditional Approach

The traditional legal view of wars of national liberation is that they constitute a category of internal wars and as such are not subject to international legal regulation. This is because such conflicts fall within the domestic jurisdiction of the "established government" and are therefore exclusively governed by its municipal law;[2] any dealings by third States with the "rebels" constitute an intervention in its domestic affairs.

But this legally radical separation of wars of national liberation from the international level is of a relatively recent origin. One has only to remember the active role played by France in the American war of independence, the acquisition and affirmation by the Latin American republics of their independence behind the double shield of the Monroe doctrine and the British fleet, and—last but not least—the proclamation of Greek independence by Great Britain, Russia and France after the destruction of the Ottoman-Egyptian fleet by the British in the battle of Navarino.[3]

However, a changing international context and the rise of the positivist doctrines of the State both in municipal and in international law, led, by the end of the 19th century, to the crystallization of the traditional approach described above.

Even according to the traditional approach, the restrictive attitude to internal conflicts can be radically changed, by resorting to the institution of "recognition of belligerency." If such a recognition emanates from the established government, it entails the application of the international *jus in bello* to its relations with the rebels; if it emanates from third parties, it enables them to apply the rules of neutrality even-handedly *vis-à-vis* both belligerents. But because the recognition of belligerency is purely discretionary for the established government (and, *a fortiori*, for third parties), it has been of very rare occurrence. Moreover, in the few instances in which it took place, it intervened at an advanced stage of the conflict and usually after the rebels had secured control over a sizeable part of the territory, i.e., when the war in its material aspect became similar to an interstate war.[4] For it is only then that reciprocity could come into play and the institution of recognition of belligerency would offer some advantage to the established governments.[5]

This was the state of the law when the Geneva Conventions of 1949 were elaborated. At the same time, as a result of the atrocities of the Second World War and the surge of the movement for the international protection of human rights, there was a strong feeling that a minimum of humanitarian legal regulation should apply in all armed conflicts, regardless of their internal or interstate character.

Thus the *Draft Conventions for the Protection of War Victims,* prepared by the International Committee of the Red Cross (ICRC) and submitted to the XVII International Red Cross Conference at Stockholm, contained a fourth paragraph of common article 2, which read:

> In all cases of armed conflict which are not of an international character, especially cases of civil war, colonial conflicts, or wars of religion, which may occur in the territory of one or more of the High Contracting Parties, the implementing of the principles of the present Convention shall be obligatory on each of the adversaries. The application of the Convention in these circumstances shall in no way depend on the legal status of the Parties to the conflict and shall have no effect on that status.[6]

Two important points stand out in this draft: the classification of colonial conflicts as conflicts not of an international character and, in spite of this classification, the integral application of the Conventions to them.

In fact, the latter point was at the basis of the heavy resistance the draft article met in the Geneva Diplomatic Conference, leading to: (1) the elimination of the examples (including colonial conflicts) for fear of narrowly construing the category of "conflicts not of an international character" by limiting it to these examples; (2) the application to these conflicts not of the totality but only of those principles of the Conventions enumerated in common article 3. This limitation avoids such dangers from the point of view of the established government as the appointment by the rebels of a protecting power,[7] which would in fact if not in law confer on them an international status.

It is precisely to avert this objection that common article 3, paragraph 4, expressly provides (as did draft article 2, paragraph 4 before it) that "the application of the preceding provisions shall not affect the legal status of the Parties to the conflict." In spite of this disclaimer, however, common article 3 does confer a certain objective legal status on "rebels" in conflicts not of an international character.[8] This status is more limited in its legal effects than the one deriving from a "recognition of belligerency," as it does not entail the application of the *jus in bello* as a whole (but only those principles enumerated in common article 3). On the other hand, it is an objective status emanating from the Conventions themselves and thus transcending the discretionary and relative character of the "recognition of belligerency." Its effect is to have a minimum legal standard apply, independently of the will of the established government, as soon as violence attains a certain threshold which has been described by a Commission of Experts convened by the ICRC in the following terms: "The existence of an armed conflict is undeniable, in the sense of article 3, if hostile action against a lawful government assumes a collective character and a minimum of organization."[9]

That was the situation in relation to wars of national liberation at the time of the adoption of the Geneva Conventions in 1949. Has it changed since then? To some it has not:

> The same element of fiction [that non recognition of the other belligerent prevents the conflict from becoming international], but in the opposite sense, seems to be present in the theory according to which "wars of national liberation" against colonial governments are international wars because a people struggling for its liberation should be considered as a subject of international law. Whatever the basic argument may be (the right of self-determination, self-defence, etc.), the factual elements are those which characterize internal conflict. If there is a conflict, it is precisely because the lawful government intends to exercise its sovereignty over the territories in question, a sovereignty which international organization is not able to deny to this government. As long as the insurgents have not succeeded in creating a stable territorial basis, there is no *de facto* entity to which international law could attribute all the rights and duties derived from the laws of war.[10]

Thus, according to this view, as long as there is no territorial control, the conflict by the very nature of its material element cannot be more than a "conflict not of an international character." But this point of view seems unsatisfactory, as it does not take into consideration either the special characteristics or the recent developments both in the "factual elements" and in the law pertaining to wars of national liberation.

Its basic argument can be reduced to one of effectiveness, namely, that the acquisition of legal status is a function of a certain degree of effectiveness in the form of territorial control. This view, echoing the classical doctrine of recognition of belligerency, is based on the assumptions of conventional warfare; it disregards the special nature of guerrilla warfare which characterizes wars of national liberation. In consequence, it conceives effectiveness in very restrictive terms. For effectiveness is not merely formal territorial control; it can also be based on the control and allegiance of populations. Moreover, even territorial control can no longer be measured by a cut and dried rod. Recent experiences have abundantly shown that territorial control over the same area can shift or rotate (e.g., the government controls by day, the rebels by night). In such fluid situations, effectiveness, if rigidly conceived, cannot serve as a criterion for determining the legal status of either party, because of its relative and ever changing character.

A more flexible interpretation would assess the effectiveness of liberation movements not in isolation but in relation to that of the colonial government; it would take into consideration not only the elements which they succeed in controlling, but also those which they succeed in excluding from the control of the colonial government. Such an interpretation would logically lead to the conclusion that, though not exercising complete or continuous control over part of the territory, liberation movements, by undermining the territorial control of the colonial government as well as by their control of the population and their command of its allegiance, muster a degree of effectiveness sufficient for them to be objectively considered as a belligerent community on the international level.[11]

Developments have equally taken place in the law pertaining to wars of national liberation. Unlike the situation under classical international law—which emanated from and exclusively regulated interstate relations—legal status can at present derive from collective legitimization as a result of practice and consensus within the framework of international organizations.[12] Such a status has been conferred on wars of national liberation on the basis of the principle of self-determination.

The Impact of Self-determination

A full examination of the principle of self-determination is obviously beyond the scope of this essay.[13] It is examined here only to the extent necessary for the determination of the legal status of armed conflicts generated as a result of denial of self-determination.

Self-determination as a Legal Principle. Without going into the history of the principle of self-determination, it is sufficient here to recall that it is mentioned in articles 1 and 55 of the Charter of the United Nations. The legal status of this principle has been the subject of a long controversy within the Organization. To certain member States, especially the colonial and ex-colonial ones and their allies, this principle represented a mere standard of achievement towards which member States should strive as an ideal, but not as a matter of legal obligation. To others, especially African, Asian and Latin American as well as East European States, it was a legal principle imposing an obligation on the colonial Powers and establishing a right for all peoples to the exercise of self-determination.

United Nations organs, especially the General Assembly, have confirmed the latter interpretation in many resolutions, dealing with the subject either in general or in relation to a specific situation. This trend culminated in General Assembly Resolution 1514 (XV) of 1960 containing the *Declaration on the Granting of Independence to Colonial Countries and Peoples.* Self-determination was also recognized as a human right in article 1 of the *International Covenant on Civil and Political Rights* and of the *International Covenant on Economic, Social and Cultural Rights* adopted by the General Assembly in 1966 (though not yet in force).

The most significant achievement in this respect, however, is the *Declaration on Principles of International Law Concerning Friendly Relations and Cooperation among States in Accordance with the Charter of the United Nations,* which was adopted by General Assembly Resolution 2625 (XXV) during the 25th session in 1970.

This Declaration was painstakingly elaborated over seven years by a Special Committee representing the whole spectrum of opinion within the

United Nations, including all the major powers (with the exception of the People's Republic of China which was not yet represented in the U.N.). The Committee worked on the basis of consensus, which means that the draft it finally produced was accepted by all those who were represented in it.[14] Moreover, the Declaration itself was adopted in the General Assembly by acclamation, i.e., unanimously, without a dissenting vote. Thus for the first time the Western Powers as a whole recognized self-determination as a legal right and its denial as a violation of the Charter.[15] This consensus was reached not on a vague general formula, but on a detailed interpretation, expliciting the different legal implications of the principle.

It can thus be said that even if self-determination was not universally accepted as a legal principle in 1945, or even in 1960, the practice which has taken place in interstate relations since the adoption of the Charter, leading to the emergence of some sixty new States, as well as the consistent and cumulative practice of the organs of the United Nations, have led in 1970 to the universal recognition of the legal and binding nature of the principle of self-determination.[16]

The Right of Self-determination and the Law of Armed Conflicts. As long as wars of national liberation were considered as internal wars, they fell within the exclusive jurisdiction of the colonial government and outside international jurisdiction. In consequence, both resort to force by the liberation movements and armed repression by the colonial government were considered as internal use of force, and as such not subject to the provisions of article 2, paragraph 4, of the Charter. The recognition of self-determination as an international legal principle radically alters this situation. It entails several important legal consequences particularly affecting the law of armed conflicts in both its facets of *jus ad bellum* and *jus in bello*:

1. As concerns the legal status of questions of self-determination—i.e., colonial situations and conflicts—these can no more be considered as domestic questions. They are international questions over which the jurisdiction of the United Nations can be exercised. This has been the practice of the Organization from the beginning and has been acquiesced to even by the colonial Powers. For, if we admit that the matter is regulated by a principle of international law, it is by definition a matter excluded from the domestic jurisdiction of the States concerned.[17]

Moreover, it logically follows from the above that, in the words of the Declaration, "The territory of a colony or other Non-Self-Governing Territory has, under the Charter, a status separate and distinct from the territory of the State administering it; and such separate and distinct status under the Charter shall exist until the people of the colony or Non-Self-Governing Territory have exercised their right of self-determination. . . ."

2. As concerns the legality of the use of force in the context of self-determination, the Declaration states: "Every State has the duty to refrain from any forcible action which deprives peoples . . . of their right to self-determination and freedom and independence. In their actions against, and

resistance to, such forcible action in pursuit of the exercise of their right to self-determination, such peoples are entitled to seek and receive support in accordance with the purposes and principles of the Charter."

This paragraph resolves several intricate and controversial problems posed by cases of violent self-determination.

(a) It clearly states that the "forcible action" or use of force which is prohibited is that emanating from the colonial governments in denial of self-determination.
(b) Conversely, armed resistance to forcible denial of self-determination—by imposing or maintaining by force colonial or alien domination—is legitimate according to the Declaration. In other words, liberation movements have a *jus ad bellum* under the Charter.[18]
(c) The right of these movements to seek and receive support and assistance necessarily implies that they have a *locus standi* in international law and relations, and this regardless of territorial control, in the traditional sense.
(d) This right also necessarily implies that third States can treat with liberation movements, assist and even recognize them without this being considered a premature recognition or constituting an intervention in the domestic affairs of the colonial government.[19]

3. As concerns the *jus in bello*—i.e., the law governing relations between belligerents and between them and third parties—the most important consequence of the recognition of self-determination as a legal right (a consequence which inexonerably derives also from all the others mentioned above) is to confer an international character on armed conflicts arising from the struggle to achieve this right and against its forcible denial.[20] As such, they are subject to the international *jus in bello* in its entirety.

Thus the evolution of the law culminating in the recognition of self-determination as a legally binding principle, has led, as far as wars of national liberation are concerned, to a situation similar to that advocated at the turn of the century by the adepts of the theory of obligatory recognition of belligerency.[21] As the international status of these wars derives directly from international law, it produces its effects vis-à-vis the colonial government and third parties without any need for recognition by either.

It is worth mentioning in this respect that even before the adoption of the 1970 Declaration, the Security Council and the General Assembly, in relation to several conflicts of this type, called upon the colonial government to apply the Geneva Conventions, thus implicitly characterizing them as international conflicts and, as such, subject to the international *jus in bello* in its entirety.[22] Moreover, in some of these cases, they went even further by recommending (or ordering) sanctions against the colonial government and the provision of aid to liberation movements.

This means not only that these conflicts are international, but also that the position of the colonial government, i.e., the forcible denial of self-determination, constitutes a violation of the Charter which justifies circumscribing the neutrality of the other member States, without engaging their international responsibility vis-à-vis that government.[23]

THE APPLICATION OF THE HUMANITARIAN LAW OF WAR TO WARS OF NATIONAL LIBERATION

The general conclusion that wars of national liberation are international conflicts and consequently that the *jus in bello* is applicable to them in its entirety leaves open the question of the legal basis on which such an application can be founded.

The application of the rules of what has come to be known as the "law of the Hague"—essentially regulating the conduct of hostilities—to wars of national liberation presents little difficulty. With the exception of the Geneva Protocol of 1925 for the Prohibition of the Use in War of Asphyxiating, Poisonous or other Gases and of Bacteriological Methods of Warfare, these rules are basically those included in the Hague Convention No. IV, of 1907, concerning the Laws and Customs of War on Land, and more particularly in the Regulations appended to it. There is a very wide consensus of opinion that the rules contained in this Convention have passed into customary law.[24] In consequence, they apply on that basis to all international conflicts, regardless of the accession of the belligerents to the Convention.

The situation as regards the "law of Geneva"—essentially regulating the treatment of war victims and embodied in the four Geneva Conventions of 1949—is, however, different. For, though in good part these Conventions reiterate, elaborate on, or replace some of the former rules, they go much beyond them and treat other important questions as well. It would be difficult to contend that, as in the case of the Hague Regulations, they are merely declaratory of customary international law. As a result, they can be integrally applied to a conflict only *qua* conventions, which in turn presupposes that the parties to the conflict are also parties to these conventions. In other words, the application of the Geneva Conventions to wars of national liberation poses the problem of the accession of the liberation movements to these Conventions.

Two possibilities are open to non-parties for that purpose in the Geneva Conventions. The first is full accession by virtue of common article 60/59/139/155, which stipulates: "From the date of its coming into force, it shall be open *to any Power* in whose name the present Convention has not been signed, to accede to this Convention."[25]

The other possibility is the *ad hoc* acceptance of the Conventions for the purposes of a given conflict, by virtue of common article 2, paragraph 3: "Although one of the Powers in conflict may not be a party to the present Convention, the Powers who are parties thereto shall remain bound by it in their mutual relations. They shall furthermore be bound by the Convention in relation to the said Power, if the latter accepts and applies the provisions thereof."

The main difficulty facing the liberation movements in resorting to either of these two methods is that accession or acceptance has to emanate from a "Power," a term which is traditionally understood in diplomatic practice and instruments to mean a "State." On that basis, the capacity of liberation movements to become parties to the Conventions, even on a temporary basis, may be put into question.

This argument is not, however, as decisive as it may sound. First, though the term "Power" usually denotes a State in diplomatic language, it has occasionally been used in a wider sense to include some other entities not having this character.[26]

Second, this wider interpretation is the most compatible with the humanitarian object and purpose of the Conventions which, to be fully realized, commend universal application, i.e., application to all types of international conflicts.[27]

Third, there is general agreement that in case of recognition of belligerency, the whole *jus in bello*, including the Geneva Conventions, applies to the conflict. But the recognition of belligerency, even when it emanates from the established government, does not transform the belligerent community into a State.[28] In other words, if the Geneva Conventions are to apply at all, they have to apply to it as a belligerent community and not as a State.

If the Geneva Conventions were open exclusively to States, the consent of the established government or of third States in the form of recognition of belligerency would not be able to change this situation. However, since in practice recognition of belligerency does entail the application of the Conventions, possible obstacles to the accession of liberation movements to these instruments have to be attributed not to their intrinsic legal nature— as long as the international status of these movements is conceded—but to the objection of certain parties, especially the colonial governments and their allies.

It is worth recalling in this context that in 1960 the Gouvernement Provisoire de la République Algérienne (GPRA) notified its accession to the Geneva Conventions to the depository, the Swiss government. In this capacity, the latter took note of the accession and circulated it to the other parties to the Conventions, in accordance with common article 59/58/138/156. But as a party to the Conventions, it made a "reservation" to this accession based on its non-recognition of the GPRA. Moreover, as was to be expected, France, the colonial Power, objected to this accession.[29]

What is the legal effect of such reservations and objections? Can they prevent the acceding entity from joining the conventional community?

The Conventions are silent on that subject. They contain no clauses concerning their application or non-application between objecting parties.[30] Nor can the problem be solved by reference to the general rules concerning reservations to multilateral conventions.[31] However, both the legal nature and the inference of certain specific stipulations of the Geneva Conventions provide sufficient indication as to their position on the subject.

The Geneva Conventions being humanitarian, law-making treaties *par excellence*, their object and purpose commend the widest possible application.

This drive towards universality is reflected in two further characteristics of the Conventions:

1. They are open multilateral Conventions. Indeed, accession to them is not submitted to any conditions of substance or procedure except for a written notification to the depository (common article 59/58/138/156).
2. Though there is no general provision as to the application of the Conventions to conflicts between parties who do not recognize each other, there are certain specific stipulations which almost amount to one. These are articles 13/13/4A, which define the military and assimilated personnel protected by the first three Conventions. They include, in their paragraph 3: "Members of regular armed forces who profess allegiance to a Government or an authority not recognized by the Detaining Power."

This stipulation is based on the precedent of the Free French Forces under General de Gaulle during the Second World War, which raised the problem of non-recognition of Government and not of the entity represented by that Government. But there is nothing in the stipulation itself which would limit its application to cases of non-recognition of governments. Thus, in the conflict between Israel and the Arab States, the latter recognized the applicability of the Conventions, in spite of their non-recognition of Israel as a State.

Indeed, the words used—"a Government or an authority not recognized by the Detaining Power"—are so wide as not to be limited to States. Taken in their ordinary and natural meaning, they can easily cover such authorities as liberation movements.

The ICRC *Commentary* lays down two conditions for the application of this stipulation:

It is not expressly stated that this Government or authority must, as a minimum requirement, be recognized by third States, but this condition is consistent with the spirit of the provision. . . .

It is also necessary that this authority, which is not recognized by the adversary, should either consider itself as representing one of the High Contracting Parties, or declare that it accepts the obligations stipulated in the Convention and wishes to apply them.[32]

Once it is conceded that the legal status of liberation movements derives directly from international law, the first condition set by the *Commentary*, i.e., recognition by third States, becomes superfluous. In practice, however, liberation movements are usually recognized by a number of Third World and Socialist States, and sometimes even collectively by the General Assembly,[33] a measure which consolidates their international status and facilitates their accession to the Conventions.

It can thus be concluded that the Geneva Conventions are open to belligerent entities with an international status. This status can emanate either from a recognition of belligerency or from international law itself as is the case of liberation movements.[34]

But to bring about the full application of the Conventions, it remains necessary for liberation movements to express their consent to be bound by them.

Of the two procedures open for that purpose in the Conventions, the one provided for in common article 2, paragraph 3, may be practically more expedient for liberation movements. According to this stipulation, in case of an armed conflict between a party and a non-party to the Conventions, the party will be bound by the Conventions in its relations with the non-party if the latter "accepts" and "applies" their provisions. This procedure can thus be effectuated by a unilateral declaration of acceptance by the liberation movement and does not depend, to produce its effects, on the acceptance of the other belligerent, i.e., the colonial government, or for that matter, of any other party to the Conventions.[35] This procedure is less formal than full accession and its effects are limited to the ongoing war. As such, it is less susceptible to arouse opposition.[36]

If such a declaration is made—and all liberation movements should make it, as a matter not only of principle but also of interest—the Conventions become applicable to the conflict, regardless of the opposition of the colonial government.[37]

If the colonial government persists in its refusal to apply the Conventions, this would constitute a characterized violation and would put into motion the collective guarantee of common article 1. According to this article, the parties not only "undertake to respect" but also "to ensure respect" for the Conventions. The import of the latter undertaking, according to the ICRC *Commentary* is that "in the event of a Power failing to fulfill its obligations, each of the other Contracting Parties (neutral, allied or enemy) should endeavour to bring it back to an attitude of respect for the Convention."[38] In other words, they should do everything in their power to bring about compliance by the recalcitrant party.

This can be a very strong source of pressure on colonial governments, especially if followed as a concerted policy by the members of the United Nations, including the Big Powers. It is worth recalling in this context that Resolution XXIII of the International Conference of Human Rights, held in Teheran in 1968, explicitly draws the attention to this obligation of the parties to the Geneva Conventions, in its 9th preambular paragraph: "Noting that States parties to the Red Cross Geneva Conventions sometimes fail to appreciate their responsibility to take steps to ensure the respect of these humanitarian rules in all circumstances by other States, even if they are not themselves directly involved in an armed conflict."

THE PROTECTION OF COMBATANTS AND CIVILIAN POPULATIONS IN WARS OF NATIONAL LIBERATION

A fundamental practical question underlying but transcending the legal controversy concerning the application of the Geneva Conventions to wars of national liberation is whether these conventions are adapted to the conditions of such wars. The uncertainty of the answer explains the hesitancy of liberation movements to declare their willingness to abide by the Conventions.[39]

The Geneva Conventions were moulded on the basis of the assumptions of conventional warfare in which regular armies—composed of military personnel clearly distinguishable from civilian populations—confront each other along an equally distinguishable front line. In wars of national liberation, in view of the disparity in strength—especially in firepower, mastery of the air and technological know-how in general—between colonial armies and freedom fighters, the latter have to resort to unconventional or guerrilla warfare. This is a revolutionary method, a "poor man's war" based on mobility, surprise and camouflage. It does not involve a clearly defined front line, and the distinction between combatants and civilian populations is much more blurred and consequently much more difficult to operate than in conventional warfare.

It may therefore be legitimately asked whether the criteria for the application of the Conventions are operative in such wars, and consequently whether the Conventions provide effective protection to war victims, be they combatants or civilians.

The Protection of Combatants

Given the fluidity between combatants and civilians in wars of national liberation, the first and most important question which comes to mind is: Who can be considered as "privileged" combatant in such wars, in the sense of enjoying the rights and protection attached to this category in the Geneva Conventions?

The definition of combatants is provided in the first two articles of the Hague Regulations, Article 13/13/4 A common to the first three Geneva Conventions, reproduces the definition with some modifications and additions. Paragraph 1, 2, 3, and 6 of this article enumerate the categories of fighters who enjoy the status of privileged combatants:[40]

1) Members of the armed forces of a Party to the conflict as well as members of militias or volunteer corps forming part of such armed forces.

2) Members of other militias and members of other voluntary corps, including those of organized resistance movements, belonging to a Party to the conflict and operating in or outside their own territory, even if this territory is occupied, provided that such militias or volunteer corps, including such organized resistance movements, fulfill the following conditions:

(a) that of being commanded by a person responsible for his subordinates;
(b) that of having a fixed distinctive sign recognizable at a distance;
(c) that of carrying arms openly;
(d) that of conducting their operations in accordance with the laws and customs of war.

3) Members of regular armed forces who profess allegiance to a government or an authority not recognized by the Detaining Power. . . .

6) Inhabitants of a non-occupied territory who, on the approach of the enemy, spontaneously take up arms to resist the invading forces, without having had time to form themselves into regular armed units, provided they carry arms openly and respect the laws and customs of war.

At the Hague, and before it at Brussels (in relation to the unratified Brussels Declaration), the debate was between the "militarist" camp, composed of the delegates of the Big Powers favouring the limitation of the status of combatants exclusively to regular army forces, and the "patriotic" camp, composed of the delegates of small States professing the extension of this status to irregular combatants resisting invasion and occupation. The compromise included in article 2 of the Hague Regulations was the recognition of the "levée en masse" (now paragraph 6 above) but only in emergencies and before the territory is effectively occupied. In these circumstances, only two conditions have to be fulfilled in order for the persons involved to acquire the status of privileged combatants: that they carry arms openly and that they respect the laws and customs of war.[41]

The recognition of militia and volunteer corps fulfilling the four conditions of article 1 of the Hague Regulations (reproduced in paragraph 2 of article 13/13/4 A common to the first three Geneva Conventions) as privileged combatants was on the assumption that they function as auxiliaries of the regular forces and not in detachment from them. The innovation of the Geneva Conventions in 1949 was, in the light of the experiences of the Second World War, to extend the same status to resistance movements in occupied territories provided they fulfill the same conditions.[42]

To what extent do freedom fighters in wars of national liberation fulfill the conditions of paragraph 2? This paragraph lays down five conditions:

1. That the movement to which the combatants are attached belong to one of the parties in the armed conflict.

This condition did not figure in article 1 of the Hague Regulations. For as was mentioned above, that article conceived of the militia and volunteer corps covered by it as auxiliaries to the regular armies, a situation which makes the condition superfluous. But if the link with regular armies is loosened, the condition becomes pertinent to exclude "private wars," i.e., wars for private ends and banditism, from the picture.

In the course of the debates in the Geneva Diplomatic Conference, it was clearly pointed out that the link with the party to the conflict should be assessed as a question of fact and not according to formal criteria, such as belonging to the armed forces of that party or even holding its nationality. "It may find expression merely by tacit agreement, if the operations are such as to indicate clearly for which side the resistance organization is fighting."[43]

In wars of national liberation, the party in question is the liberation movement itself, which derives its status directly from international law, as was demonstrated above. The non-recognition of the movement by the colonial government does not affect this situation. Indeed, paragraph 3 of the same article specifically provides for its application to armed forces belonging to a government or an authority not recognized by the other belligerent.[44]

2. That the movement reflects a certain degree of organization, including a certain structure of command, i.e., "being commanded by a person responsible for his subordinates."

Though full details about the identity of military leaders and the structure of command of the liberation movements may not be revealed for security purposes, this condition does not pose serious difficulties. Any movement with a minimum of efficiency needs to have such an organization without which a state of armed conflict is difficult to come into being.

3. That members of the movement have a fixed distinctive sign recognizable at a distance.

4. That they carry arms openly.

These two conditions present the greatest difficulties to freedom fighters who rarely fight in combat formation. They aim at guaranteeing the open character of wars and distinguishing combatants from civilians. The second purpose is of course necessary for the protection of civilians against indiscriminate attacks from the enemy. But "open war" is being abandoned even by regular armies and is not compatible with the nature of guerrilla warfare, unless by open war is meant loyal war, which is another way of describing the respect of the laws and customs of war.

5. That the movement conduct its operations in accordance with the laws and customs of war.

The rationale behind this condition is that if members of such movements want to be treated as privileged combatants, they have to follow the same rules as regular soldiers in conducting their activities. This condition poses some practical difficulties to liberation movements, especially as regards the taking and the treatment of prisoners. But these difficulties are not unsurmountable.[45]

These are the conditions of paragraph 2 of article 13/13/4A common to the first three Conventions. They are not particularly adapted to the new conditions of warfare especially in guerrilla and liberation wars. Indeed there is a general consensus that in the century that has elapsed since these conditions were first formulated in Brussels, the radical changes which have occurred in military technology and in political and strategic conditions and ideas have rendered these conditions obsolete.

But the consensus on this sociological observation about the disparity between the law and the social reality it is called upon to regulate does not extend to the legal consequences to be drawn from it. In the efforts which are under way within the framework of the ICRC, the UN and other bodies to reexamine and update the law of armed conflicts, a wide spectrum of opinion has been expressed on the subject.[46]

Without pretending to examine all these opinions or to analyse them in depth, they can be schematically classified in the following categories:

1. The widest agreement obtains that at a minimum these conditions should be interpreted very liberally with a view to bridging as much as

possible the gap between them and the evolving reality they are supposed to regulate.

(a) Thus it is recognized that most if not all of these conditions attach to the movement as a whole and not to each single combatant.[47] In other words, the compliance which is constitutive of the status is that emanating from the movement and not from its members taken individually.

The language of paragraph 2 is quite clear on that point. It defines the protected persons as being "members of . . . militias and . . . of other volunteer corps, including those of organized resistance movements . . . provided that such militias . . . fulfill the following conditions. . . ." In other words, the status is attributed to the members, while the conditions are attributed to the movement as such.

This is evident as regards the first two conditions—i.e., belonging to a party to the conflict and reflecting a certain degree of organization—which can logically be attributed only to the movement as such. It is equally clear as concerns the fifth condition—i.e., respect of laws and customs of war— for individual members of regular armed forces if they infringe their obligations under the laws of war do not lose their privileged status but can be tried for these violations. It would be an illogical and unjust discrimination to consider that the same violation by an individual freedom fighter would deprive him from the status of privileged combatant, as long as the movement to which he belongs professes respect for the laws and customs of war.[48]

The same reasoning applies to the remaining two conditions—i.e., the fixed distinctive sign and the open carrying of arms. However, acceptance of the same conclusion is more controversial in their case.

(b) Even if one considers that these two conditions (3 and 4) have to be fulfilled by each combatant individually, and especially in this case, they have to be interpreted with great flexibility.

For example, according to a widely held opinion, they are deemed to be fulfilled if the combatant wears a fixed visible sign and openly carries arms throughout each single operation,[49] but not necessarily in between operations.

(c) Finally, it is also largely admitted that these conditions are not all of equal importance.[50] In consequence, the legal sanction of non-compliance with each of them should vary accordingly. Thus, if the major ones, namely 1, 2 and 5, are respected by the movement as a whole, non-compliance with conditions 3 and 4 by individual combatants should not entail their loss of privileged status.

2. Still widely spread, but to a lesser extent, is the opinion that certain conditions have become obsolescent; they are not complied with in practice[51] and consequently are no more required by contemporary international law. There is no consensus, however, on the conditions which are thus discarded and consequently on those which remain valid.

In one opinion, conditions 3 and 4—i.e., the fixed visible sign and the open carrying of arms—should be replaced by one more flexible general condition of waging loyal or "open war."[52] Thus formulated, this condition, it is submitted, is nothing more than another way of requiring the respect of the laws and customs of war, and does not constitute an autonomous requirement.

According to another opinion the conditions of the "levée en masse," i.e., the open carrying of arms and the respect of the laws of war, are a sufficient minimum.

A third opinion, more consistent with practice and the general trend, considers that a minimum structure of organization and command together with the respect of the laws and customs of war are the only two necessary conditions.[53]

Finally, from still another point of view, the only requirement is that of a minimum organization and command structure. The obligation to comply with the laws and customs of war is, to this school of thought, a consequence of the status of privileged combatants, leading to trial for individual violations, but it is not a constitutive condition of this status.

3. It is also agreed that even if the conditions of paragraph 2 were not satisfied, guerrilla and freedom fighters would not be completely deprived of all protection.[54]

Indeed, in the 17th, 18th and up to the middle of the 19th century, neither in practice nor in scholarly writings was there a distinction between regular and irregular forces, provided the latter's war be a *bellum publicum* (not for private ends) and that they be authorized by their sovereign—an authorization which could be presumed. It was only under the influence of the ideology of the Holy Alliance that the restrictive approach as to "privileged combatants" emerged. However, in both the Brussels and the Hague Conferences, this approach met with strong resistance from small States, who vehemently defended the people's right to resist foreign invasion and occupation.[55] They finally accepted articles 1 and 2 of the Hague Regulations, on condition that they be expressly linked to the preambular paragraph which came to be known as the "Martens Clause" and which reads:

Until a more complete code of the laws of war can be drawn up, the High Contracting Parties deem it expedient to declare that, in cases not covered by the rules adopted by them, the inhabitants and the belligerents remain under the protection and governance of the principles of the law of nations, derived from the usages established among civilized peoples, from the laws of humanity, and from the dictates of the public conscience.

The effect of this clause is to safeguard the continued validity of pre-existing customary law, which, as has been described above, is more liberal as to the status of irregular combatants.

As to the "dictates of the public conscience," they cannot be better reflected than in the numerous resolutions of the General Assembly which affirm and reiterate that freedom fighters "should be treated, in case of their arrest, as prisoners of war in accordance with the principles of the

Hague Convention of 1907 and the Geneva Conventions of 1949,"[56] and this without subjecting them to any conditions.

4. On the rather different and more speculative policy level, there is a tendency to consider that the approach most conducive to ensure a humane treatment of captured freedom fighters consists not so much of insisting on their being granted a prisoner of war status, which faces many legal obstacles, but of requesting for them prisoner of war treatment, i.e., treating them according to the standard of the Third Convention, in spite of the fact that they are not legally recognized as privileged combatants. This policy, it is argued, is more acceptable because it puts the emphasis not on the controversial question of legal status, but on the respect of human rights which flatters the wisdom of the Detaining Power and facilitates the prospects of future reconciliation.[57] However, this approach does not afford freedom fighters adequate protection, because to accord such treatment would be a matter of discretion on the part of the Detaining Power, and not a legal obligation. Moreover, though it may lead to a better treatment of freedom fighters in detention, it would not provide them with legal immunity against execution.

A legally better policy approach, which leads to the same result while avoiding the above-mentioned loopholes, would be to clearly disassociate not the *status* from the *treatment* of prisoners of war, but rather the status of *combatants* from that of *prisoners of war*.

Though the latter is the most important legal consequence of the former, they are not identical nor is it necessary that their scope be coextensive. This is because their *ratio legis* is radically different: the status of combatant has military as well as political implications to the extent that it may reflect on the international status of the adversary, while the status of prisoner of war is basically a human right question. Thus not only is it logically and legally feasible, but also desirable, on policy grounds, to widen the latter as much as possible without necessarily widening the former.

Moreover, this approach goes very much in the same direction as the efforts of the UN in the field of "respect of human rights in armed conflicts."

Protection of Civilian Populations

In wars of national liberation, more than in any other type of war, the civilian populations are exposed to the gravest dangers.

Guerrilla tactics being based on invisibility and mobility, the freedom fighters have to hide among the masses and depend on their passive support by not being denounced by them, and on the active support of the most politically conscious and active segment of the population in the form of food, shelter and information as well as new recruits. This support is by definition forthcoming in a community taking up arms to achieve its right of self-determination in the face of its forcible denial.

As a result, one of the most effective ways of reducing both the mobility and the invisibility of freedom fighters is to cut them off from their mass base. Another is to treat every civilian as a potential or a hidden freedom fighter to avoid taking any chances. In both cases, the implications are ominous for the civilian populations. If the colonial government decides to follow the second method, this means that it will resort to mass arrests, the taking of hostages, torture to obtain information, internment, expulsions and even executions and mass reprisals against hostages or in the form of destruction of houses and villages.

If the colonial government decides to use the first method—not trying to get at the freedom fighters among the masses but rather to cut them off from the masses—it usually resorts to forcible transfers of civilian populations from areas suspected of harbouring freedom fighters and their regroupment in camps euphemistically called regroupment centers, fortified hamlets or new villages, but which are in fact a kind of concentration camp. At the same time, the areas thus evacuated are declared "free-fire zones" by the colonial government, which does not hesitate to employ blind weapons both anti-personnel, anti-material and anti-environment in its systematic attacks against them. These weapons are of course indiscriminate in their effect and attain all persons, civilians and combatants alike, who may happen to be in the attacked zones. Moreover, they destroy not only men, equipment and installations, but also the very possibility of life and economic activity in such zones.

In the face of such practices, which unfortunately are current, what protection do existing legal instruments provide to alleviate the plight of civilian populations?

The main legal instrument in this field, namely the Fourth Geneva Convention, suffers from two basic defects. The first is that it covers civilian populations only when they fall in the power of the enemy. Yet the greatest dangers to which civilian populations can be exposed arise from attacks by the colonial government on areas not under its control. This situation is left to the Law of the Hague. But the Law of the Hague, regulating the conduct of hostilities, dates from 1907 (with the exception of the Geneva Protocol of 1925) and is thoroughly out of date in the face of both modern weapons and revolutionary strategy. For example, it does not specifically take into consideration aerial warfare and bombardment.[58] In consequence, even if it is faithfully observed, it still leaves much to be desired.[59]

Nevertheless, the Law of the Hague at least prohibits the use of indis-criminate weapons as well as weapons of mass destruction. This is not only because of the "unnecessary suffering" they cause both to combatants and civilian populations, but also, and mainly, because of their "blind" character, which makes it impossible in using them to distinguish between military and non-military objectives. This also applies to the indiscriminate use of any weapons and to the practice of the so-called "free-fire zones" where all men, objects and even nature are considered as permissible targets.

The second defect of the Fourth Geneva Convention relates to its structure: it uses two basic legal connecting factors, nationality and occupied territory, which are formally inoperative in the context of wars of national liberation. This situation calls for a reexamination of the Convention with a view to determining the articles which are readily applicable and the modifications necessary for the application of the others to such wars.[60]

The difficulty disappears, however, if one interprets the forcible denial of self-determination in terms of military occupation; in other words, if one considers that the presence of the colonial government in the territory in question constitutes an *occupatio bellica* and consequently that all its inhabitants are protected persons under the Fourth Convention.

This interpretation can be defended on the basis of the 1970 Declaration, which expressly states that such a territory (and consequently its inhabitants) has a separate international status from that of the colonial government;[61] it would also logically follow if one considers that the *jus ad bellum* of the liberation movement is based on self-defence.[62]

Otherwise, modifications of or additions to the Fourth Geneva Convention would require new legal instruments, concerning which several proposals have been advanced.[63]

It would be too much to expect from the colonial governments that they accept a new convention or an amendment of the present one to suit the situation of liberation wars. But it would be an important advance all the same to obtain compliance with those articles which are readily applicable to them, as well as with the Law of the Hague, especially as concerns the limits on the use of weapons.

CONCLUSION

In this essay we have tried to demonstrate that wars of national liberation are international conflicts and as such are subject to the international law of war or *jus in bello* in its entirety.

This law is usually divided, for convenience, into the Law of the Hague and the Law of Geneva. The former is principally embodied in the Hague Regulations of 1907 but is generally considered as having passed into custom; the latter is embodied into the four Geneva Conventions for the Protection of War Victims of 1949.

The Law of the Hague, though outdated in many respects, is readily applicable to wars of national liberation, at least as a constraint on the weapons used and the way they can be used.

The Geneva Conventions, on the other hand, though more recent and more detailed, are structured on the basis of different factual situations than the ones arising from wars of national liberation.

However, on the basis of their language, which is broad enough, and the practice which has evolved both within as well as outside their framework, they can be interpreted to cover at least several important aspects of these wars. Moreover, through these means, they are capable of further development in the same direction.

A prime example of this type of interpretation, in the light of the evolving background of general international law,[64] is that of paragraph 2 of article 13/13/4A common to the first three Conventions. This interpretation considers the liberation movement itself as a party to the conflict and requires only that conditions a and d (a certain degree of organization and the respect of the laws and customs of war) be fulfilled by the movement for the freedom fighters belonging to it to acquire the status of privileged combatants. According to another such interpretation, a territory where a war of national liberation is taking place is regarded as an occupied territory and consequently its inhabitants as protected persons under the Fourth Convention.

Development or adjustment through interpretation does not call for new legal instruments. If new instruments can be adopted, however, it would be all to the better; for they would be drafted from the beginning with the specific conditions of wars of national liberation in view. In both cases, the resistance of the colonial Powers and their allies is to be expected.

However this may be, a legal regulation adapted to wars of national liberation is urgently needed.

Those who take up arms to recover their freedom and identity will continue to do so whether they are legally protected or not.

The question which is thus squarely put to the international community is not whether we can do away with wars of national liberation by denying them the benefits of an adequate legal regulation. It is rather whether the humanitarian law of war can afford to ignore wars of national liberation.

ADDENDUM: "WARS OF NATIONAL LIBERATION AND THE LAWS OF WAR" TEN YEARS AFTER

In 1972, when "Wars of National Liberation and the Laws of War" was published, the subject, to the extent that it was perceived at all, was both very vague and highly controversial; moreover, although since 1968 General Assembly resolutions started to demand the application of the Third Geneva Convention on prisoners of war to captured freedom fighters in wars of national liberation, the legal basis and argumentation for such a demand were neither clear nor even explicitly addressed.

The status of liberation movements in international organizations and *a fortiori* in humanitarian law, and more particularly in the Geneva Conventions, was quite tenuous and far from being settled.

The 1972 essay endeavoured to grapple frontally with the legal issues raised by wars of national liberation, to formulate them in terms of relevant and answerable legal questions, and to articulate the legal *rationale* of the prescribed progressive solutions within the context of the then-existing law.

The scope and pace of the evolution of the law in the few years that followed have been truly remarkable, and prove that if a need comes to be strongly felt within the international community, this community can rapidly produce an adequate legal response.

In December 1973, the General Assembly provided for the first time, in its resolution 3103 (XXVIII) on the "Basic Principles of the Legal Status of the Combatants Struggling Against Colonial and Alien Domination and

Racist Regimes," a clear legal classification of wars of national liberation, by declaring, in the third operative paragraph, that

The armed conflicts involving the struggle of peoples against colonial and alien dominations and racist regimes *are to be regarded as international armed conflicts* in the sense of the 1949 Geneva Conventions, and the legal status envisaged to apply to the combatants in the 1949 Geneva Conventions and other international instruments is to apply to the persons engaged in armed struggle against colonial and alien domination and racist regimes. (emphasis added)

In the course of 1974, the status of liberation movements within universal international organizations and the international conferences held under their auspices was greatly clarified to the advantage and satisfaction of those movements.

Also occurring in 1974, in Geneva, was the Diplomatic Conference on the Reaffirmation and Development of Humanitarian Law applicable in armed conflicts; its mandate was to update and supplement the Geneva Conventions of 1949. Its first session of 1974 was almost completely devoted to the controversy over wars of national liberation. The International Committee of the Red Cross (ICRC) all but ignored the issue in the two draft Protocols (additional to the Geneva Conventions), which were to serve as bases of discussions for the conference. But no sooner had the conference started than the controversy broke out; and in spite of great resistance from several quarters, a large coalition of Third World and socialist countries and a few progressive Western states managed to agree on a compromise text of an amendment (along the lines described in the first part of the preceding essay) and to get it adopted. This text constitutes paragraph 4 of article 1 of the First Protocol (on international armed conflicts) adopted in 1977. It reads as follows:

The situations referred to in the preceding paragraph [*i.e.*, situations of international armed conflict] include armed conflicts in which peoples are fighting against colonial domination and alien occupation and against racist regimes in the exercise of their right of self-determination, as enshrined in the Charter of the United Nations and the Declaraction on Principles of International Law Concerning Friendly Relations and Co-operation Among States in Accordance with the Charter of the United Nations.

Similarly, another amendment (along the lines proposed in the second part of the essay, following the model of common article 2, paragraph 3 of the conventions) was put forward and adopted. It constitutes article 96, paragraph 3 of the first Protocol, which provides:

The authority representing a people engaged against a High Contracting Party in an armed conflict of the type referred to in Article 1, paragraph 4, may undertake to apply the Conventions and this Protocol in relation to that conflict by means of a unilateral declaration addressed to the depositary. Such declaration shall, upon its receipt by the depositary, have in relation to that conflict the following effects:

(a) the Conventions and this Protocol are brought into force for the said authority as a Party to the conflict with immediate effect;

(b) the said authority assumes the same rights and obligations as those which have been assumed by a High Contracting Party to the Conventions and this Protocol; and

(c) the Conventions and this Protocol are equally binding upon all Parties to the conflict.

Finally, as far as the substantive protection of combatants and civilians is concerned, as was mentioned in the essay, most of the problems encountered in this respect in wars of national liberation stem from the unadaptability of the Geneva Conventions to the conditions of guerrilla warfare, which is the only realistic method of combat open to liberation movements, at least in the early stages of the struggle. Protocol I has gone some way toward meeting these difficulties and adapting the rules to guerrilla conditions. Most important in this respect is article 44, which introduces some flexibility in the constitutive conditions of prisoner-of-war status, as well as several articles in Part IV of the Protocol on the protection of civilian populations (e.g., 48, 51–58, 75).

The significance of this legislative exercise cannot be overestimated. For even if Protocol I is not adhered to as a separate legal instrument by the handful of governments facing a war of national liberation, its provisions assert themselves as the proper interpretation of the Geneva Conventions on the controversial questions that arose in the course of the application of these conventions to contemporary armed conflicts, including wars of national liberation—an interpretation that is endorsed by the overwhelming majority of the parties to these conventions.*

NOTES

For a detailed account of the controversy in the Diplomatic Conference and interpretation of the relevant provisions of the Protocol on the subject of law and armed conflict, see Abi-Saab, "Wars of National Liberation in the Geneva Conventions and Protocols," 165 *Recueil des Cours*, Hague Academy of International Law (1979, IV), pp. 353–446. The author served as consultant to the Division of Human Rights, United Nations Secretariat, in the course of the preparation of the first two reports of the Secretary-General on "Respect of Human Rights in Armed Conflicts." The article and its addendum, however, exclusively reflect his personal views.

1. This definition figures in numerous General Assembly Resolutions. The quotation in the text is from G. A. Res. 2592 (XXIV) (1969). In some Resolutions, a slightly different language is used: "colonial and alien domination" is substituted for "colonial and foreign rule," e.g., G. A. Res. 2674 (XXV) (1970); G. A. Res. 2787 (XXVI) (1971). The foreign or alien domination, differentiated in these Resolutions from traditional colonial rule, is that of colonies of settlement, which—though they may sever their legal bonds with their countries of origin—impose and maintain a separate and privileged status vis-à-vis the native peoples they subjugate or displace. Throughout this essay, the terms "colonial government" or "colonial power" are used *lato sensu* to cover both these types of rule.

2. For a succinct exposition of this approach see the standard work on "conflicts not of an international character," J. Siotis, *Le droit de la guerre et les conflits armés d'un caractère non international*, Paris, L.G.D.J., 1958; p. 105.

3. This collective "recognition" (which was *constitutive* in more senses than one) is particularly significant. It is reminiscent of the Concert of Europe and a prolongation of its system according to which decisions—even concerning internal questions— were taken in concert by the major Powers, sometimes with, sometimes without the participation of the parties directly concerned, on the basis of what was conceived as the common interest, namely, the preservation of European equilibrium. Though the community was limited and the motives mixed, this system foreshadows the technique of collective legitimization within the United Nations. On this last point see Inis Claude Jr., "Collective Legitimization as a Political Function of the United Nations," *International Organization*, vol. 20, 1966; p. 367.

4. Territorial control was not a condition precedent of recognition of belligerency by the established government, but it was in case of recognition of belligerency by third parties, according to article 8 of the Resolution of the Institute of International Law, adopted in 1900 in Neuchâtel, *I.D.I., Annuaire 1900*, p. 229. This recognition usually took the form of a declaration of neutrality and intervened after the conflict had extended to the high seas and threatened to interfere with the maritime commerce of the third party in question, a fact which explains its rare occurrence in practice. Besides, recognition of belligerency by a third party was not binding on the established government. On the institution of recognition of belligerency in general, see J. Siotis, *op. cit., supra* note 2, p. 108.

5. We leave aside the intermediate situation of recognition of insurgency whose effects vary from case to case, according to the intention of the recognizing party. For this institution, see *ibid.* pp. 117–128; Castren, "Recognition of Insurgency," *Indian Journal of International Law*, vol. 5, 1965; p. 443.

6. Pictet (ed.), *Commentary of the Geneva Conventions of 1949*, III, Geneva, ICRC, 1960, p. 31 (herein after cited *Commentary, III*). The Stockholm Conference adopted this draft paragraph as it stood for Conventions I and II. But in the case of Conventions III and IV, it subjected their application to the provision that the adverse party should also comply with them.

7. *Ibid.* pp. 32–34.

8. Cf. Ch. Zorgbib, "Pour une réaffirmation du droit humanitaire des conflits armés," *Journal de droit international*, vol. 97, 1970; p. 658.

9. ICRC, *Reaffirmation and Development of the Laws and Customs Applicable in Armed Conflicts*, Report submitted to the XXIst International Conference of the Red Cross, Istambul, 1969; p. 99.

10. D. Bindschedler-Robert, "A Reconsideration of the Law of Armed Conflicts" in Carnegie Endowment for International Peace, *The Law of Armed Conflicts* (Report of the Conference on Contemporary Problems of the Law of Armed Conflicts), New York, 1969; p. 52. Certain participants in the Conference of Government Experts on the Reaffirmation and Development of International Humanitarian Law Applicable in Armed Conflicts (Geneva, 24 May–12 June 1971) shared the same point of view. See ICRC, *Report on the Work of the Conference*, Geneva, 1971; pp. 52–56 (paras. 312–356). It should be noted, however, that "[m]ost of the experts who spoke on the subject considered that wars of liberation were international armed conflicts." *Ibid.* p. 54 (para. 321).

11. For a very interesting development of this line of reasoning, see A. Belkherroubi, *La naissance et la reconnaissance de la République algérienne*, Bruxelles, Bruylant, 1972; p. 85.

12. See *supra*, note 3.

13. On self-determination in general, see H. Kamel, *Le principe du droit des peuples à disposer d'eux-mêmes en droit international public positif*, Le Caire, Société d'économie politique, de statistique et de législation, 1961; A. Shukri, *The Concept of Self-Determination in the United Nations*, Damascus, Dar El Fikr, 1965; H. S. Johnson, *Self-Determination within the Community of Nations*, Leyden, Sijthoff, 1967.

14. For a description of the methods of work of the Special Committee and the results achieved during its first two sessions, see P. H. Huben, "Principles of International Law Concerning Friendly Relations and Cooperation Among States," *American Journal of International Law*, vol. 61, 1967; p. 703.

15. In all previous Resolutions on self-determination, including Res. 1514 (XV) (1960), the major Western Powers, especially the USA, the U. K. and France, either voted against or abstained. This was the major argument directed against the legally binding character of the principle, i.e., that a major segment of the international community did not consider it to be so.

16. It is worth recalling in this respect the dictum on intertemporal law enunciated by the ICJ in its most recent advisory opinion: "The Court must take into consideration the changes which have occurred in the supervening [period], and its interpretation cannot remain unaffected by the subsequent development of law, through the Charter of the United Nations and by way of customary law. Moreover, an international instrument has to be interpreted and applied within the framework of the entire legal system prevailing at the time of interpretation." See *Legal Consequences for States of the Continued Presence of South Africa in Namibia (South West Africa) notwithstanding Security Council Resolution 276 (1970).* I.C.J. Rep. 1971, p. 31.

17. On this basis, the great majority of the writers who treated this subject, including many Western writers, reached the conclusion, long before the 1970 Declaration, that a right to self-determination exists in positive international law. See, for example, R. Higgins, *The Development of International Law Through the Political Organs of the United Nations*, London, O.U.P., 1963, p. 90; I. Brownlie, *Principles of Public International Law*, London, O.U.P., 1963, p. 482; R. Pinto, "Les règles du droit international concernant la guerre civile," Académie de droit international, *Recueil des Cours*, vol. 114, 1965 I, p. 494.

18. The acceptance by Western Powers of this interpretation contrasts sharply with their earlier outright rejection of the Soviet thesis that wars of national liberation, on the basis of article 1, paragraph 2 (self-determination), constitute a legitimate case of use of force under the Charter and an exception to the general prohibition of article 2, paragraph 4. For a recent restatement of the Soviet thesis, see I. Blishchenko and M. Solutsvena, "The Struggle Against Portuguese Colonialism in the Light of International Law," *International Affairs* (Moscow), August 1971, p. 60. For a Western critique of this thesis, see G. Ginsburg, "Wars of National Liberation and the Modern Law of Nations: The Soviet Thesis," *Law and Contemporary Problems*, vol. 29, 1964; p. 910.

This acceptance also contrasts with their great indignation against the Afro-Asian theory—advanced for the first time by India during the Goa incident—that colonialism is permanent aggression which can be legitimately repelled at any time on the basis of self-defence. See for an example of the legalistic refutation of this theory C.J.R. Dugard, "The OAU and Colonialism: An Inquiry into the Plea of Self-Defence as a Justification for the Use of Force for the Eradication of Colonialism," *International and Comparative Law Quarterly*, vol. 16, 1967; p. 157.

It is worth recalling that on several occasions, before the adoption of the 1970 Declaration, different organs of the U.N. affirmed the legitimacy of such struggles.

See, for example, in relation to Rhodesia, G. A. Res. 2151 (XXI) (1966) and S. C. Res. 253 (29 May 1968).

Moreover, the General Assembly reiterated the principle in several resolutions, after the Declaration. E.g., Res. 2649 (XXV) (1970): "The General Assembly . . . 1—*Affirms* the legitimacy of the struggle of peoples under colonial and alien domination recognized as being entitled to the right of self-determination to restore to themselves that right *by any means at their disposal*"; Res. 2787 (XXVI) (1971): "The General Assembly . . . 1—*Confirms* the *legality* of the people's struggle for self-determination and liberation from colonial and foreign domination and alien subjugation, notably in Southern Africa and in particular that of the peoples of Zimbabwe, Namibia, Angola, Mozambique and Guinea (Bissau), as well as the Palestinian people, by all available means consistent with the Charter of the United Nations; 2—*Affirms* man's basic human right to fight for the self-determination of his people under colonial and foreign domination" (emphasis added).

It is to be noted that neither the Declaration nor the other Resolutions explicitly base the *jus ad bellum* of the liberation movements on self-defence. This question, far from being a mere theoretical one of legal classification, has extremely important practical consequences, which are discussed *infra*, note 19.

19. In this respect, the Declaration gave formal sanction to a pre-existing practice. See G. M. Abi-Saab, "The Newly Independent States and the Rules of International Law: An Outline," *Howard Law Review*, vol. 8, 1962; p. 111.

After the adoption of the Declaration, the General Assembly reiterated the same principle more explicitly and forcefully: "The General Assembly . . . 3—*Calls upon* all States dedicated to the ideas of freedom and peace to give all their political, moral and material assistance to peoples struggling for liberation, self-determination and independence against colonial and alien domination." Res. 2787 (XXVI) (1971).

A very pertinent and timely question, in view of recent events in the Indian subcontinent, is whether the assistance provided by third parties to liberation movements can take the form of direct military intervention against the colonial or alien government. The answer to this question depends on the legal basis of the *jus ad bellum* of the liberation movements. If it is self-defence, then such an intervention would be legally permissible on the basis of collective self-defence, as specifically provided for in article 51 of the Charter. If it is merely an extension of article 1, paragraph 2 (self-determination), it would be logically inadmissible to extend to third parties this exception to article 2, paragraph 4, of the Charter. As has been mentioned above (*supra*, note 18), the U.N. organs have not pronounced themselves as to the proper legal basis of the *jus ad bellum* of liberation movements.

20. H. Meyrowitz, "La guérilla et le droit international," *Revue belge de droit international*, vol. 7, 1971; p. 64, appositely describes these conflicts as international but not interstate "internationaux, mais non interétatiques."

21. See Siotis, *op. cit.* at 128.

22. For an enumeration of these Resolutions see Secretary-General, Second Report on *Respect of Human Rights in Armed Conflicts*, U.N. Doc. A/8052, paras. 195–203. See also G. A. Res. 2621 (XXV) and 2674 (XXV) adopted in the same session as the 1970 Declaration.

23. Cf. Abi-Saab, *loc. cit.* at 111; Pinto, *loc. cit.* at 494 goes even further: "Dans ces conditions il apparaît que toute assistance au gouvernement légal, au cours d'une guerre civile, menée pour l'indépendance d'un territoire colonial, serait illicite au regard du droit international public. Par contre l'assistance accordée aux insurgés est légale." He thus maintains that aiding the colonial government is prohibited in general, i.e., even where no sanctions are ordered or recommended by U.N. organs.

Certain recent General Assembly Resolutions tend to support this interpretation. See for example, G. A. Res. 2507 (XXIV) (1969); G. A. Res. 2508 (XXIV) (1969); G. A. Res. 2787 (XXVI) (1971). See also *supra*, note 19.

24. See especially the dictum of the Nuremberg International Tribunal: "The rules of land warfare expressed in the Convention undoubtedly represented an advance over the existing international law at the time of their adoption . . . but by 1939 these rules laid down in the Convention were regarded as being declaratory of the laws and customs of war." United Nations War Crimes Commission, *Law Reports of Trials of War Criminals*, vol. 15, 1949, p. 12.

25. Emphasis added.

26. See *Dictionnaire de la terminologie du droit international*, Paris, Sirey, 1960; p. 492 (Puissance).

27. In fact, common article 3, paragraph 3, encourages the integral or partial application of the Convention—beyond the minimum stipulated in the first two paragraphs of the same article—*to conflicts not of an international character*, by means of special agreements between the parties.

28. The effects of recognition of belligerency on the status of the recognized belligerent community is succinctly described by Charles Rousseau, *Droit international public*, Paris, Sirey, 1953; p. 300 (para. 363) as follows: "La reconnaissance de belligérant a des *effets limités et temporaires*, et c'est là une différence profonde avec la reconnaissance d'Etat. Elle vise à reconnaître aux forces insurgées—au moins aux fins de la lutte dan laquelle elles sont engagées et uniquement pour la durée de cette lutte—les droits nécessaires à cette lutte, avec toutes leurs conséquences. Le parti ainsi reconnu sera traité comme un Etat, mais seulement pour ce qui est des opérations de guerre."

29. See M. Bedjaoui, *La révolution algérienne et le droit*, Bruxelles, Association Internationale des Juristes Démocrates, 1961, p. 186, and the documents reproduced, pp. 191-201.

30. An example of these clauses can be found in article 35 of the General Agreement on Tariffs and Trade which provides for the "non-application of the Agreement between" any pair of Contracting Parties in case "either of the Contracting Parties at the time either becomes a contracting party, does not consent to such application."

31. This is because these rules apply to reservations made by a party at the time it gives its final consent to be bound by the treaty and not to reservations emanating from parties already bound by the treaty. The latter cannot be considered as reservations in the technical sense of the term.

32. Pictet (ed.), *Commentary, III*, p. 63.

33. See for example G. A. Res. 2787 (XXVI) (1971) quoted *supra*, note 18.

34. *A fortiori*, there is no legal obstacle to accession to the Geneva Conventions by international organizations whose functions may require the deployment of armed forces.

35. If all the parties object, they obviously can bloc the accession of the liberation movement. They would have in effect departed from the Conventions by limiting their open character; by the same token they would have reduced their effectiveness in realizing their object and purpose.

36. It takes care of a possible objection based on the argument that as long as the fate of the liberation war is not decided, the international status of the liberation movement has to be assimilated to that emanating from a recognition of belligerency. This status exists only to the extent necessary for the prosecution of the ongoing

war and for its duration. (See *supra*, note 28). The effects of full accession transcend these limitations.

37. Indeed, according to the ICRC *Commentary, III*, p. 26, it suffices that the belligerent which is not a party to the Conventions observe them in its conduct of the war for the Conventions to become applicable to the conflict: "The two conditions for the non-Contracting Power are that it should *accept* and *apply* the provisions of the Conventions. In the absence of any further indication, there is no reason to assume that 'acceptance' necessarily implies an explicit declaration." But a declaration has the merit of clarifying the situation.

38. *Ibid.* p. 18.

39. See, for example, on the attitude of the National Liberation Front in Vietnam, "The International Committee and the Vietnam Conflict," *International Review of the Red Cross*, vol. 6, 1966; p. 399 at 400. "The National Liberation Front ('Vietcong') informed the ICRC in October 1965 that, since it did not participate in the Geneva Conventions, it was not bound by them and that *these Conventions contained provisions which corresponded neither with its action nor with the organization of its armed forces.* It declared nevertheless that it was observing a humane and charitable policy towards the prisoners who fell into its hands" (emphasis added).

40. Paragraphs 4 and 5 of this article enumerate certain categories of persons who, though not being part of the armed forces of the belligerents, are assimilated to combatants for the purposes of the Conventions.

41. See I. P. Trainin, "Questions of Guerrilla Warfare in the Law of War," *American Journal of International Law*, vol. 40, 1946; p. 534; R. Bierzanek, "Le statut juridique des partisans et des mouvements de résistance armée: évolution historique et aspects actuels," in *Mélanges Andrassy*, La Haye, Nijhoff, 1968; p. 54.

42. Pictet (ed.), *Commentary, III*, p. 56.

43. *Ibid.* p. 57.

44. Cf. Secretary-General, Second Report on *"Respect of Human Rights in Armed Conflicts,"* UN Doc. A/8052 (1970), para. 214, 230 and 231; M. Veuthey, "Règles et principes de droit international humanitaire applicables dans la guérilla," *Revue belge de droit international*, vol. 7, 1971; p. 505 at 511.

45. ICRC, *Reaffirmation and Development of the Laws and Customs Applicable in Armed Conflicts*, Report submitted to the XXIst International Conference of the Red Cross, Istanbul, 1969; p. 119.

46. See the works of the ICRC, especially *ibid; Preliminary Report on the Consultation of Experts Concerning Non-International Conflict and Guerrilla Warfare*, Geneva, 1970; *Report on the Work of the Conference of Government Experts on the Reaffirmation and Development of International Humanitarian Law Applicable in Armed Conflicts*, Geneva 1971. See also the three reports by the UN Secretary-General on *Respect of Human Rights in Armed Conflicts*, UN Doc. A/7720 (1969); A/8052 (1970); A/8370 (1971). See also Carnegie Endowment for International Peace, *op. cit. supra* note 10; Veuthey, *loc. cit. supra* note 44.

47. Bindschedler-Robert, *loc. cit. supra* note 10, at 40.

48. *Ibid.* p. 41.

49. *Manuel Militaire Suisse*, para. 42; World Veterans Federation Advisory Group, quoted in ICRC, *op. cit. supra* note 45, at 070; Bindschedler-Robert, *loc. cit. supra* note 10, at 44.

50. *Ibid.*

51. Since the Second World War Detaining Powers in general have not insisted on these conditions for the purposes of granting prisoner of war status. See M.

Veuthey, "La guérilla: le problème du traitement des prisonniers," in volume 3 of the *Annals of International Studies* (1972).

52. G.I.A.D. Draper, *The Legal Classification of Belligerent Individuals*, Report submitted to the Conference on Humanitarian Law and Armed Conflicts, Brussels, 1970; p. 21.

53. Bierzanek, *loc. cit. supra* note 41, at 76.

54. There is no reason why the status of freedom fighters should only be examined in the light of paragraph 2 of article 13/13/4A. In certain cases—when the war of national liberation reaches a level in which they are organized in regular forces— it may be more appropriate to apply to them paragraph 1 or 3. The requirements of these paragraphs are, however, more demanding.

55. This historical development is aptly described by Bierzanek, *loc. cit. supra* note 41.

56. G. A. Res 2674 (XXV) (1970); see also G. A. Res. 2621 (XXV) (1970).

57. ICRC, *The Protection of Victims of Conflicts not of an International Character*, Report submitted to the XXIst International Conference of the Red Cross, Istambul, 1969; p. 9.

58. Except for the *Declaration Prohibiting the Discharge of Projectiles and Explosives from Balloons*, adopted in 1907 by the Second Hague Peace Conference!

59. Unfortunately, even this inadequate legal regulation is largely disregarded in wars of national liberation. Indeed, in certain cases, though the colonial and allied governments accept to apply the Law of Geneva, they refuse to abide by the Law of the Hague. See T. Farer, "The Humanitarian Law of War in Civil Strife: Toward a Definition of International Armed Conflict," *Revue belge de droit international*, vol. 7, 1971; p. 20 at 46.

60. For such an essay, see H. Meyrowitz, "Le droit de la guerre dans le conflit du Vietnam," *Annuaire français de droit international*, vol. 13, 1967; p. 179; M. Veuthey, *loc. cit. supra* note 44, at 521.

61. See *supra* p. 100.

62. See *supra* note 18.

63. For a survey of these proposals, see J. Mirimanoff-Chilikine, "Protection de la population civile contre les dangers résultant des opérations militaires," *Revue belge de droit international*, vol. 7, 1971; p. 619.

64. Concerning this principle of interpretation, which has been adopted by the Vienna Convention on the Law of Treaties (article 31, paragraph 3c), see *supra* note 16.

25. The Laws of War and Moral Judgment

Terry Nardin

Reflection on the laws of war seldom fails to produce misgivings. On the one hand, it seems clear that practices as ugly as those of warfare must be regulated, if only to secure society against the emergence of unchecked brutality. Yet when the rules that have been devised toward this end are examined, doubt is cast upon even this cheerless justification by the extent of the violence and destruction with which they are compatible. The laws of war seem to condone the use of force in pursuit of indefensible policies, as well as to allow a degree of suffering by those affected by war that is often disproportionate to the apparent advantages to be had from fighting. Even the few restraints the laws do require are frequently ignored. The result is scepticism concerning every aspect of the laws of war: their effectiveness, their legal validity (and thus their very existence as rules of law) and their defensibility in terms of the requirements of morality from which they appear so often to deviate. Such scepticism is only strengthened by reflection on the vagaries of criminal enforcement and punishment, which at times are not only ineffective, but also introduce their own special injustices. It is a scepticism well expressed in the observation that if international law is at the vanishing point of law, then the laws of war are at the vanishing point of international law.[1] The excesses of present-day warfare have given particular impetus to one aspect of this attitude toward the laws of war, that based upon doubts concerning their moral adequacy.

MORALITY AND THE LAWS OF WAR

Such doubts begin with an examination of the laws of war from the standpoint of some conception of what rules of war ought to be, morally speaking. The laws of war as they exist are judged against this standard and, not surprisingly, found deficient. According to this view our attitude toward them cannot be divorced from the question of the degree to which the laws of war, as an institution, are capable of distinguishing between morally defensible and morally indefensible uses of military force. Acceptable laws of war must promote, not undermine, the moral standards that govern such judgments. It is this basic conception of the proper function of the laws of war that stands behind many of the principled objections to the legal regulation of warfare and that must be taken into account by anyone who wishes to defend the laws of war, not piecemeal against particular criticisms that might in fact be satisfied by partial reforms of existing rules, but against profound doubts concerning the possibility and legitimacy of the institution itself.

In order to determine how vulnerable the laws of war are to this moral challenge, one needs to have in mind a clear conception of its target. The phrase 'laws of war' refers to an intricate collection of legal rules and practices involving elements of both international and national law. Sometimes applied as international law by domestic as well as international tribunals, the laws of war also exist as rules constituting a part of the 'articles of war' or military codes of national states. These codes incorporate the international laws of war, as interpreted by each state, into domestic law, to be applied in military proceedings involving members of a state's own armed forces and, occasionally, members of the armed forces of an enemy. It is this particular feature, the application in war crimes trials of rules regulating conduct in war, that has attracted the most attention and encouraged a conception of the laws of war as a system of criminal prohibition and punishment. The laws of war, in this view, are to be understood as an analogue of ordinary systems of criminal law, that is, as a system of prohibitions backed by threats of punishment for non-compliance. Many particular objections derive their plausibility from this picture of the laws of war. The situation is further complicated, moreover, by the fact that *defences* of the laws of war also often presuppose this conception of them. This is shown by the central place given to war crimes trials in many sympathetic discussions of the laws of war and by the fact that the laws of war are only infrequently mentioned in public debate except in connection with war crimes.

Although I shall argue that this understanding of the laws of war is misconceived, its strengths should not be overlooked. The laws of war do seem to display more of the features of criminal law than, say, of the law of tort or contract. Like crimes, violations of the international laws of war are offences against (international) society and not only against the injured party. Insofar as the law provides the offended state with the means to combat the offence, it is in the form of an authorization to punish captured enemies as war criminals if their acts constitute war crimes under the international laws of war, or to conduct reprisals against the offending state. The purpose, in either case, is to enforce the laws of war and not to exact compensation; the laws of war with few exceptions provide for punishments, not reparations. The contractual aspect of the laws of war is also minimal, because the obligations they impose rest upon a firm substructure of custom. Thus the provisions of international treaties are often taken as declaratory of customary international law and, therefore, as binding even in circumstances in which particular treaties do not apply. Furthermore, the conception of the laws of war as criminal law is even more plausible applied to the versions of its rules contained in national military codes, which typically provide for the criminal prosecution and punishment of offences by individual members of the armed forces whose behaviour is regulated by them and lastly, because of the often atrocious nature of the acts prohibited by the laws of war, the propensity to regard them as crimes—that is, as acts generally injurious to mankind that international law should seek to prevent and to punish—is very great.

However plausible this view may appear at first, it obscures some important distinctions. It attributes to the international laws of war certain features that are more properly characteristic of military law, and takes as defining the essential purpose of the former the criminal law features of the latter. It does this in part by presuming that the international laws of war should restrain the acts of states just as criminal law restrains the acts of individuals. This, however, is the wrong way to conceive the functions of the laws of war; it emphasizes a task that the system, in its international version, is ill-equipped to perform. A better view is one that makes a firm distinction between the international laws of war and municipal systems of military justice and which recognizes that, even though the rules and principles of the international and the various military systems may overlap, they promote different purposes in the regulation of warfare. Military law does seek to regulate the conduct of individuals in much the same way as civilian criminal law and can reasonably rely upon criminal prohibition and punishment, among other means, to implement the law, but the international laws of war, despite the Nuremberg experience which many would like to take as a precedent, do not themselves provide for the international prosecution of war criminals. This is left to the individual states. What the international laws of war are best regarded as seeking to do is to establish authoritative common standards of military conduct. These are standards that national leaders are to take as guiding their decisions with respect to the use of military force in armed conflicts and which are to be reflected and supported by national systems of military law. Thus, instead of providing directly for the punishment of war criminals by international tribunals, the laws of war identify certain acts as war crimes and leave the prosecution of offenders to the belligerents. To this end, many of the rules on enforcement in the Geneva Conventions and in the Draft Additional Protocols to them that are presently being negotiated concern the obligation of governments to co-operate in providing mutual assistance in the apprehension, extradition and prosecution of persons charged with violating the laws of war. In addition, the Conventions and Protocols specify other, non-judicial, modes of implementation, including the requirement that parties instruct members of their armed forces in the provisions of the Conventions and provide legal officers to advise military commanders on their proper application. Criminal prosecution and punishment of offenders in international tribunals is thus only one among a number of possible means for promoting the standards represented by the laws of war. Indeed, to judge the laws of war entirely in terms of the effectiveness of their criminal enforcement in any tribunal is to mistake the means for the end.

There is another reason why we should hesitate to speak of the laws of war as if they constituted a criminal code and this is that they perform a much wider range of functions. The laws of war do concern themselves with matters that are central to any system of criminal law. They define forms of conduct to be avoided as offences against the law, identify the various categories and degrees of offence, provide for their punishment and lay down various justifying and excusing conditions according to which charges of criminal wrongdoing and responsibility may be defeated or mitigated, but the laws of war also perform functions that cannot be fitted into this model of criminal law. For example, they create and define various legal positions (such as belligerent, neutral, combatant and prisoner of war) and confer various rights and obligations on each. They establish certain recognized ways for identifying protected persons, structures and areas by specifying the insignia and signals to be used by units engaged in medical care, civil defence and humanitarian relief. They not only limit, but also facilitate, the war-related activities of states by conferring on them (and on other recognized belligerents) legal rights with respect to a wide range of matters in combat, in the administration of occupied areas and in the maintenance and employment of prisoners of war; and by empowering them to take measures, including reprisals, domestic legislation and criminal prosecution, to secure those rights. The laws of war also empower certain states and international organizations, most notably the International Committee of the Red Cross, to oversee the application of the Geneva Conventions, provide humanitarian relief for the victims of armed conflicts, visit prisoner of war camps and promote the further development of the laws of war. Finally, they increasingly seek to confer rights on individuals affected by warfare and to make it possible, through linking such protection with the international law of human rights, to provide individuals with some recourse, however rudimentary and inadequate, against the violence of military operations.[2] To focus exclusively on the criminal law aspects of the laws of war is to neglect these other features of the system and thus to present a distorted picture that encourages inaccurate and inappropriate expectations with respect to its purposes and functions.

THE WASSERSTROM THESIS

As a source of standards for judgment and action in armed conflicts, the international laws of war may still be deficient. They may be largely ignored and hence fail utterly in the promotion of behaviour that according to those standards ought to be encouraged. Alternatively, they might actively promote the wrong behaviour, because the standards they represent are morally deficient. The latter view is articulately argued by Richard A. Wasserstrom in his essay *The Laws of War*.[3] Wasserstrom takes as the object of his criticism a 'conception' of the laws of war, being careful to avoid the factual claim that the laws of war actually display the features of this conception, but nevertheless suggesting that they come close to doing so. This conception is one that reflects what might be called the 'criminal law interpretation' because in it the laws of war appear as a set of prohibitions backed by penal sanctions (although this last feature receives no particular emphasis). It is also a conception that gives much weight to military considerations where they clash with those that are procedural or humanitarian; this, in fact, is the principal reason Wasserstrom finds it objectionable. His criticism is thus taken up, in a way that will be explained shortly, with what I shall label the 'military interpretation' of the laws of war. What is puzzling in Wasserstrom's argument is that it seems both to criticize and to presuppose the military and the criminal law interpretations of the laws of war. There is no necessary connection between the two interpretations; they simply happen to be related, as a matter of contingent fact, in Wasserstrom's discussion. Perhaps this can be explained by the fact that he leans very heavily on an account of the laws of war by Telford Taylor, a former general and Nuremberg prosecutor, which itself presupposes both the military and criminal law interpretations.[4] Although Wasserstrom is critical of this account, his discussion reflects the same conception of the laws of war. The two differ only in that Taylor accepts and Wasserstrom rejects the practical and moral adequacy of this conception.

In order to forestall misunderstanding, I would like to make it clear that by the 'military interpretation' I mean a conception of the laws of war that gives much more weight to considerations of military expediency than one like that which the International Committee of the Red Cross seeks to promote, which might for the purposes of contrast be labelled 'humanitarian.' Both are marked, however, by considerable deference to the presumed realities of armed conflict; what differentiates them is that the military interpretation is most concerned to forbid only acts of violence that do not confer a military advantage and that in fact may additionally represent a threat to military discipline—such as rape, murder and pillage by an invading or occupying army, or the cruel mistreatment of prisoners of war. While both interpretations grant considerable weight to military consider-ations—even the humanitarian view, after all, begins with an acceptance of warfare as a regrettably unpreventable activity to be regulated by rules that are basically compatible with the military interests of belligerents—they differ in the degree to which such considerations should be allowed to override humanitarian concerns. One of the chief expressions of this difference is to be found in the way in which particular rules of war, which are much the same on both interpretations, are qualified by the principle of military necessity; another lies in the degree of willingness to construe violations as undermining the legal validity of particular rules. To say that Wasserstrom's account reflects the military interpretation is thus to say that it employs certain criteria for specifying what is permitted by the laws of war, according to which more violence is allowed than would be lawful under rules specified according to less permissive criteria; it is not to attribute to him the view, which is in fact just the opposite of that which he defends, that such criteria are morally defensible.

Wasserstrom's basic concerns are these: If the laws of war are judged according to acceptable moral standards, how do they fare? Should there be laws of war, and if so, what—morally speaking—should they be? There are, he suggests, two distinct ways in which the existing laws of war might be defended morally. One would be to try to justify them in terms of the putatively desirable consequences that follow from their acceptance. The other is to argue that the laws ought to be accepted because they "reflect, embody and give effect to fundamental moral distinctions and considerations."[5] Wasserstrom finds versions and applications of each of these views in Taylor's book and is concerned to refute both. Taylor had argued on behalf of the laws of war that, though often violated, they were often enough observed so that many lives were saved in consequence.[6] He had also urged their value in limiting the brutalizing effects of war on its participants by teaching the distinction between necessary and unnecessary killing, arguing that it is of the greatest importance after a war's conclusion as well as during it that soldiers be not permitted to think that unnecessary killing is allowable.[7]

Wasserstrom is unpersuaded by the first argument and repelled by the second; and it is his reaction to the second that is crucial. Far from teaching a necessary moral lesson, the laws of war seem to him to reflect moral standards that are both incoherent and depraved. For example, they prohibit the use of poisons, but allow the use of equally horrible means such as napalm and anti-personnel weapons; they require American prisoners of war to be fed their accustomed diet, but permit the wholesale destruction of centres of civilian population. There is also a consequentialist objection, for not only do the laws of war permit immoral behaviour, they encourage it. They function legally in such a way as to conform themselves to developments in military technology and strategy, so that far from restraining the violence of warfare, they simply institutionalize and promote it. Therefore, the laws of war perform no moral function; the only morally acceptable code of war would be one that forced practice to conform to moral standards and not, as do the laws of war, adjusted moral standards to current practice, no matter how inhumane.

Wasserstrom, then, agrees with Taylor that the laws of war teach a moral lesson, but he thinks it is a bad lesson and this result, together with its further consequences—that is, both the promotion of morally objectionable standards and the encouragement of violence that follows from it—are in turn sufficient to leave Wasserstrom unpersuaded by Taylor's first argument, that the laws of war are worth having because they are sometimes observed and thus save lives. For even if this is so, it is a gain that according to Wasserstrom is likely to be cancelled out by the lives that are lost as a result of violence encouraged by the laws of war. This is scarcely a proof, because it depends upon a series of factual claims and counterfactual hypotheses that [are not being defended adequately—nor is it possible to defend them adequately;] it seems to be advanced here rather as speculation and as a warning that to engage in war according to the laws of war would, under present circumstances, "increase still further our tolerance for and acceptance of the horror, the slaughter and the brutality that is the essence of Twentieth Century war."[8] Where Taylor worried about the corrosive effects of neglecting the laws of war, Wasserstrom is concerned with the corrosive effects of their observance. So instead of "embracing" the laws of war and "concentrating our energies and our respect upon [their] enforcement," we should try to articulate and promote a more morally coherent and ambitious conception of the laws of war, one that requires changes in the practice of war rather than accommodates law to existing practice.

THE WASSERSTROM THESIS: A CRITIQUE

This is a powerful argument, but I think it is a mistaken one. Wasserstrom does very effectively expose some of the inconsistencies and gaps in the laws of war, and one can understand and even share his repugnance for the institution that displays them. Nevertheless, his argument depends upon an account of the laws of war that is fundamentally misleading and thus supports criticism of them that is unwarranted. What is wrong with it can be summed up under two heads. First, the argument attributes to the laws of war defects that the system does not in fact possess, or at least possess to the extent that the criticism supposes. It does this by interpreting the laws of war in such a way that they appear compatible with the kinds of morally substandard conduct which it condemns them for permitting. I wish to argue that a stricter interpretation of the laws of war is the correct one and that if one adopts it the laws of war do not look nearly as bad as the kind of attack voiced by Wasserstrom would lead one to think.

The second difficulty is to be found in the assumption expressed by Wasserstrom, and shared by many others, that the function of the laws of war is to secure, in an immediate way, the application of moral standards to the conduct of war. This is a simplistic way to view the contribution of law to the regulation of warfare. Furthermore, it supports a withdrawal from the idea of publicly accepted standards of conduct in war to a realm of private moral judgment, an attitude that is itself morally questionable. Judged according to more reasonable expectations, the laws of war, imperfect as they are, constitute an institution we should be most hesitant about abandoning or weakening.

On the matter of legal interpretation, Wasserstrom is himself seriously misled in his reliance upon Taylor's understanding of the laws of war. His claim that the legal capacity of the laws of war to restrain violence is vitiated by the principle of military necessity is based upon an unusually broad conception of that principle adopted from Taylor, whose views on this question Wasserstrom takes as authoritative. This conception of military necessity treats it as a general overriding condition that legalizes acts of war otherwise prohibited if they can be shown to confer certain kinds of military advantage. Such acts, for example, killing prisoners of war in circumstances in which maintaining them would threaten the survival of a military unit or the success of its mission,[9] or direct bombardment of civilian populations where the disruption and demoralization that results can hasten the defeat of an adversary by undermining military production and political support for continued resistance,[10] are on this interpretation of military necessity not violations of the laws of war and hence excluded from the category of war crimes. According to this interpretation, the principle of military necessity really rules out only purposeless brutality. This broad view of military necessity may be contrasted with another interpretation, according to which the appeal to necessity is allowable only where explicitly provided for by the conventional laws of war; where this is not the case, the conventional prohibitions must be regarded as absolute. This latter account still leaves much latitude in the application of the laws of war, because as customary law the latter have been construed to allow for considerable deference to the requirements of military operations and its codification in written instruments like the Hague and Geneva Conventions was undertaken with similar considerations in mind. On this narrow view, then, the principle of military necessity retains its place as one of the basic principles upon which the laws of war are based, but it cannot be considered one that has priority over all other rules and principles that constitute the laws of war, according to which the latter can always be overridden. There are some 'necessary' measures—however 'necessary' might be interpreted—that are not permitted by the laws of war.

Although the proper interpretation of military necessity in international law has for many years been a contested issue, the weight of argument supports the narrow interpretation. First, the balance of legal opinion, especially after 1900 and increasingly down to the present, clearly favours it, but more important, for this fact alone could not be decisive, is the consideration that the broad interpretation must be incorrect because it is incompatible with the international conventions that constitute the primary source of the laws of war. It is true that, even on the broadest interpretation of military necessity, there would still be room for rules prohibiting gratuitous cruelty and violence unrelated to any military purpose, but it has in addition clearly been the intention of states, as expressed in these conventions (as well as in the military manuals based upon them), not only to impose restraints on such unnecessary and even inexpedient outrages, but also to impose certain definite, if limited, restraints on the conduct of military operations even where particular acts or policies might confer a momentary advantage upon one side or another, including those that might be construed as necessary for the success of military operations and for the survival of the military units engaged in carrying them out. These restraints include many that have traditionally had a place in the customs of war and have been repeatedly reaffirmed without qualification by successive treaties down to and including the present Draft Protocols. Among the prohibited acts of war that might at times prove to be militarily advantageous or necessary are acts of unusual treachery such as feigning cease-fires and surrenders in order to take advantage of an adversary's compliance; acts of violence against disabled or captive enemy combatants and especially the refusal of quarter; and the imposition of collective penalties by an occupying force. To these traditional prohibitions have been added rules expressly forbidding misuse of the Red Cross emblem and similar protective insignia, torture or mutilation of prisoners of war, taking of hostages and many less serious abuses. Under Article 3 and Draft Protocol II of the Geneva Conventions, these rules apply to civil as well as international conflicts.

The Hague and Geneva Conventions nowhere provide that the rules prohibiting such acts may be suspended on the grounds of military necessity. The evidence that these conventions support the narrow interpretation is both negative and positive. The negative evidence is that the conventions do, on occasion, specifically provide that particular prohibitions may be overridden in exceptional circumstances that can be held to constitute a condition of military necessity; for example, Article 23g of the regulations appended to the Fourth Hague Convention of 1907 prohibits the destruction or seizure of enemy property "unless such destruction or seizure be imperatively demanded by the necessities of war." The clear implication of such explicit references to military necessity is that it cannot be invoked to qualify the prohibitions laid down by other articles in which necessity is not mentioned, and which must, therefore, be regarded as absolute so far as exceptions suggested by military requirements are concerned.

The positive evidence is to be found in assertions to the effect that prohibited acts of the sort mentioned above "are and shall remain prohibited at any time and in any place whatsoever" (Geneva Conventions, Article 3) and that those party to the conventions must respect their provisions "in all circumstances" (Article 1). Similar language occurs throughout each of the four Geneva Conventions of 1949. At least with respect to some acts of war, then, military necessity provides no grounds for overriding the rules that forbid their commission and the laws of war cannot, therefore, be interpreted as conferring on military commanders the discretion to decide whether such rules are or are not in such cases legally binding. It is, furthermore, this narrow interpretation of military necessity that is most often reflected in military codes, judicial opinions and legal commentary. It is an interpretation that corresponds to an obvious need for some restriction on the principle of military necessity if the laws of war are to have any point as rules designed to regulate the use of violence for political purposes and not simply to repress aberrant criminality unrelated to policy.

The arguments that Taylor advances on behalf of the broad interpretation of military necessity are surprisingly weak. He argues that the determination of which acts of war are militarily necessary is "a matter of infinite circumstantial variation."[11] This may be so when the meaning of 'necessary' is to be taken from ordinary usage rather than from legal definition, but the point is irrelevant where acts that are prohibited without qualification by the laws of war are involved. Taylor also argues, in connection with denial of quarter in circumstances under which to take prisoners would endanger the success of the mission or the safety of a unit, that "no military or other court has been called upon . . . to declare such killings a war crime,"[12] but because such acts (in the special circumstances in which military success or safety are truly threatened) occur rarely and no doubt are even more rarely presented for trial, the absence of a judicial ruling does not strengthen the argument in favour of a broad interpretation of military necessity.[13] Even weaker is the argument that Taylor bases on a selective reading of successive United States Army field manuals. He cites a passage from the 1956 version, which states: "The prohibitory effect of the law of war is not minimized by 'military necessity' which has been defined as that principle which justifies those measures not forbidden by international law which are indispensable for securing the complete sub-mission of the enemy as soon as possible." Taylor thinks this is ambiguous and moves on to his claim that necessity is a matter of infinite circumstantial variation and to his prisoner of war example, but it is worth pausing to notice two facts about the statement. Firstly, it implies that military necessity may only be invoked in connection with acts "indispensable for securing the complete submission of the enemy," which seems to imply military victory and does not necessarily include the successful completion of particular missions or the protection of the safety of particular units. Secondly, and far less ambiguously, military necessity cannot be invoked to justify measures forbidden by international law. On the broad interpretation of military necessity, this statement would be rendered circular and meaningless. It is, in fact, a clear expression of the narrow interpretation, similar to those that have appeared in successive American manuals from their beginnings in the Lieber rules of 1863. Taylor oddly ignores both the Lieber and the 1956 definitions of military necessity, which reflect the narrow view and relies instead upon a sentence from the manual of 1917 which says: "A belligerent is justified in applying any amount and any kind of force which is necessary for the purpose of war; that is, the complete submission of the enemy at the earliest possible moment with the least expenditure of men and money." Apart from the fact that this statement again ties the appeal to necessity with military victory, its substance is qualified in the next paragraph (which Taylor fails to cite) as justifying only measures "not forbidden by the modern laws and customs of war."[14] All the editions in fact contain this same limitation on the appeal to military necessity. If these manuals support anything at all, it is not the broad interpretation of military necessity.

Taylor's arguments, therefore, do not undermine the case for the narrow interpretation of the principle of military necessity, according to which the laws of war do not cease to be binding whenever considerations of military necessity, much less of mere military advantage, seem to require the commission of prohibited acts. In his reliance on Taylor's interpretation of military necessity, Wasserstrom is thus led to attribute to the laws of war a moral defect that they do not in fact possess. He is also misled by Taylor on another question of importance, the effect of mutual violation of particular rules of warfare on the legal validity of those rules. Taylor's position is that where both sides have violated a rule, it ceases to be a binding rule of law. His main argument in favour of this conclusion is that the Germans were not prosecuted at Nuremberg for violations of the laws of war, such as the sinking of merchant ships by submarines without warning and without provision for the safety of the former's passengers, that were also practiced by the allies, but this failure to convict can be explained on other grounds than that the Nuremberg Tribunal believed that the relevant rules were no longer legally valid; in fact, the Tribunal appears to have upheld the law in the case of submarine attacks while declining to press the charge in view of comparable violations by the allies.[15] The principle that applies here, *tu quoque*, is that a state that has violated a particular rule may not prosecute an enemy for similar violations.[16] Although there exists controversy about whether *tu quoque* expresses a valid procedural principle, it must not be confused with the quite different assertion that mutual violations invalidate the rules of warfare.

These controversies are exacerbated by the difficulty of ascertaining valid rules of law within the system with which we are concerned. The problem arises because of the thinness and unreliability of other rules, explicitly framed and widely accepted and applied within a framework of established procedures, according to which judgments concerning the validity of substantive rules of war can be authoritatively made. To varying degrees this is a defect of all international law. The problem of uncertainty is most acute with respect to customary law, for it is impossible to identify precisely either the point at which a practice (which may itself represent a departure from existing customary or conventional rules) has become customary and thus gives rise to a new rule, or the point at which an existing rule ceases to be binding because it no longer corresponds to state practice. It is one of the functions of treaties to alleviate such uncertainty, but where the result is a disorderly combination of customary and conventional rules, as is the case with the laws of war, the resulting complexity may sometimes make up for whatever uncertainty is removed by the addition of conventional law to a body of existing custom. What is clear, however, is that the law of war conventions contain no provisions to the effect that particular rules cease to be valid rules of law if violated either by one party or by many; on the contrary, the conventions explicitly define acts that constitute violations, provide for their repression and seek to limit the freedom of signatories to withdraw from the obligations imposed by the conventions. Thus the Fourth Hague Convention of 1907 identifies certain acts as especially forbidden, requires parties to the Convention to issue military regulations in conformity with its provisions and imposes a period of delay before withdrawal from the Convention can take effect. The four 1949 Geneva Conventions each define "grave breaches," prohibit any party from absolving itself or another party from liability for their commission, require the parties to co-operate in their enforcement through national legislation and judicial proceedings, prohibit denunciation of the Conventions by parties engaged in armed conflicts and provide that denunciation and withdrawal by some parties does not affect the obligations of others. There is little here to support and much to counteract any easy connection between violation and invalidity.

Given the uncertainty of the rules, it is hard to show conclusively the error of those who are quick to jump from violations of the laws of war to the conclusion that the latter no longer constitute valid law, but it is even harder to support the claim, not merely that the law is uncertain, but that particular rules have clearly and certainly lost their validity as laws of war. If the rule is a customary one, it must be established that the practice prohibited by it has become so common as to constitute a new custom according to which legal rights and obligations must now be judged. If violations of conventional rules are involved, one must be able to show that such violations invalidate the convention, by pointing either to express provisions to that effect or to accepted principles of treaty interpretation such as those codified in the Vienna Convention on the Law of Treaties. What these principles appear to permit, at most, is withdrawal from a treaty according to specified procedures by one party if other parties violate it; the mere fact of violation cannot itself cancel the treaty. In the absence of any such legal basis for the claim, Taylor errs in concluding that rules that have been violated in a particular conflict can no longer be regarded as constituting a part of the laws of war.[17] As in the case of military necessity, what is being reflected here is the military interpretation of the laws of war, according to which controversies of legal interpretation are regularly resolved in favour of military licence and against military restraint.

There is one respect in which Wasserstrom takes the military interpretation even further than Taylor. He claims that even a less permissive conception than that reflected in Taylor's account would still be morally deficient because it ignores the distinction between combatants and non-combatants. This is thought to follow from the fact that certain forms of warfare, especially strategic bombing and the use of nuclear weapons, are not well-regulated. It is true that there are no treaties presently in force that deal explicitly with these and other novel forms of warfare and, therefore, that the law governing them must be extrapolated—with all the uncertainties that entails—from existing rules which refer specifically to other forms of warfare, or from very general principles, but it does not follow from the fact that a particular mode of warfare is poorly regulated that the laws of war ignore the distinction between combatants and non-combatants. On the contrary, that distinction is quite fundamental to existing customary and conventional law. It is only on an extreme military interpretation of the laws of war, according to which the civilian population might itself constitute a legitimate military objective that may be directly attacked if to do so is thought to contribute to military victory, that this distinction breaks down. Here, as elsewhere, Wasserstrom is too willing to accept, as evidence of law, practices—such as the bombing of German and Japanese cities in World War II—that can just as plausibly be presented as war crimes. It is interesting, for example, how many people remain unaware that in bombing Germany, the British government deliberately chose to attack civilian objectives. Despite what the British public and the flyers in Bomber Command were regularly told, a major purpose of the bombing offensive for much of the war was to destroy the main commercial and residential areas of Germany's principal cities.[18] The rationale of these raids was that Germany might be brought to the point of capitulation by killing, "dehousing" and demoralizing its urban population. Few have appealed to the laws of war to justify *this* policy, which does ignore the distinction between combatants and non-combatants by making civilians the direct object of attack; what is legally defended is rather the myth that any harm to civilians in the strategic bombing was an incidental and unavoidable concomitant of attacks on military objectives, narrowly defined.[19]

CONCLUSIONS

According to Wasserstrom, the significance of objections of the sort that he advances is that they must lead us to conclude that the laws are morally deficient, with respect both to the intrinsic morality reflected by the rules and to the consequences that follow from their acceptance, but even had the argument for this conclusion been less defective, one would have to question its assumptions concerning the functions of the laws of war. The suggestion that a debilitating deficiency of the laws of war is that they embody and give effect to an incoherent and substandard morality reflects the assumption that their function is to secure the immediate application of moral rules to the conduct of war. In this view, not only must the particular rules of a legal system individually correspond to those of morality, but the system as a whole must, in addition, display features like 'coherence' and 'completeness' that are supposed to characterize any adequate morality. This view implies an odd notion of the relationship between law and morality. It is one thing to make a legal system, or some part of it, the object of moral judgment, but quite another to expect it to reflect fully the concerns of morality with respect to a particular area of social and political existence. No doubt the temptation is very great to regard the laws of war as a moral institution that ought to mirror our moral judgments about war or else suffer our rejection. It is an attitude prompted by the reasonable consideration that where so much destruction and suffering is the result of a regulated practice, there must be morally compelling reasons for consenting to rules that permit the usual objections to violence to be overridden. For these reasons, the impulse to subject the law to moral scrutiny cannot be faulted. The mistake arises when, instead of inquiring into the moral merits of a legal system, we begin to think of the law as something that could be directly appealed to in making moral judgments (as Taylor does) or else (as Wasserstrom urges) one that is morally pernicious because it teaches the wrong distinctions.

What is wrong with this propensity to *use* the laws of war as if they could provide a morally adequate basis for judging conduct in war, as well as to *criticize* the laws of war for failing to provide defensible moral standards for making such judgments, is simply that the laws of war are not a moral code, but a legal one. There are differences in function and purpose between moral and legal rules that both Taylor and Wasserstrom, in their different ways, neglect. As a result of these differences, legal rules possess many features that would be inconvenient and unacceptable as morality. For example, law often involves distinctions and principles that are morally trivial, but which are required in the regulation of complex human activities. The law may even prescribe morally dubious action in situations in which the need for having some rule is more important that the precise content, within limits, of the rule adopted, or where a particular moral concern, in being translated into law, must be altered to accommodate the requirements of its practical application within an existing legal system. Thus in addition to the independent moral acceptability of particular rules, one must consider their compatibility with existing law and legal procedures and the practicability of their application in the circumstances which they are intended to regulate. Given the many ways in which legal rules differ in form and content from moral rules, require different action and serve different aims, it is pointless to fault the former for these differences apart from a very general inquiry into the purposes and functions of a particular branch of law. To put it differently, the general justifying aim of the institution as a whole cannot be neglected in the attempt to arrive at sound judgments concerning its moral adequacy or the adequacy of its constituent parts.

In the case of the laws of war, this general justification is to be found in the ways in which they serve to sustain standards according to which judgments of violence can be made that are relatively clear and consensual. To present the laws of war in this light is to emphasize their public character, in contrast to other principles which despite their claims to greater moral adequacy must, in view of their limited recognition, be regarded as private. As international law, the laws of war represent a compromise between divergent interests and principles and can be cited as standards to which almost all nations have given their qualified consent. In spite of both their moral deficiencies and the persistence of disagreements concerning their proper interpretation, the laws of war possess the incontestible advantage of nearly general recognition as an existing, valid system of rules for the regulation of armed conflict. To understand the laws of war in this way is not, of course, to free them from moral criticism. Certainly the system badly needs reform. It is also possible to imagine laws of warfare that depart so far from the standards of morality as to lead us to conclude that the advantages of having them were of little worth compared with the evil of consenting to really depraved standards. If this is the moral critic's fear, I have tried to show that it is an exaggerated one made plausible only by a far too permissive interpretation of what the laws of war allow and an unreasonably elevated expectation concerning the functions they should perform. A more serious problem is that the manner in which the laws of war as public standards are privately interpreted and applied at times goes a long way toward wiping out whatever gains might be thought to follow from the fact of publicity. The remedy for this, however, is to clarify and tighten up those standards and especially to fix the meaning of the concepts used to express them and in this way to limit the discretion of individual belligerents to interpret the rules as they wish.

Meanwhile, however deficient in effective authority and certainty they may be, the laws of war are more adequate with respect to these qualities than any morally superior set of non-legal principles could be. This is one reason why many advocates of reforming the laws of war are reluctant to support the negotiation of a new comprehensive code to be adopted in place of the existing patchwork of heterogenous, obsolescent and undeniably inadequate customary and conventional rules and prefer instead to merely add further to the existing body of accepted law. They recognize the dangers of losing, in the attempt to improve them, the common standards we already have.

NOTES

The author wishes to thank the Baldy Program in Law and Social Policy at the State University of New York at Buffalo for supporting the research upon which this paper is based.

1. H. Lauterpacht, 'The Problem of the Revision of the Law of War,' *British Yearbook of International Law*, xxix (1952), p. 382.

2. The view that the laws of war can be regarded as protecting human rights in armed conflicts is one that has received particular emphasis in resolutions of the U.N. General Assembly, and is defended by G. I. A. D. Draper, 'The Relationship Between the Human Rights Regime and the Law of Armed Conflicts,' *Israel Yearbook on Human Rights*, i (1971), pp. 191–207.

3. *The Monist*, lvi (1972), pp. 1–19.

4. Telford Taylor, *Nuremberg and Vietnam: An American Tragedy* (Chicago, 1970). Wasserstrom's views were initially presented in the form of a review of this book that appeared in *The New York Review of Books* (3 June 1971), pp. 8–13. All references to Wasserstrom are to the later version of his essay (see p. 125, n. 1, *supra*).

5. Wasserstrom, *op. cit.* p. 1.

6. Taylor, *op. cit.* p. 40.

7. *Ibid.* p. 41.

8. Wasserstrom, *op. cit.* p. 19.

9. Taylor, *op. cit.* p. 36; Wasserstrom, *op. cit.* p. 4.

10. Taylor, *op. cit.* pp. 142–3; Wasserstrom, *op. cit.* pp. 6–7.

11. Taylor, *op. cit.* p. 35.

12. *Ibid.* p. 36.

13. Taylor's use of this and other examples is examined by Marshall Cohen, 'Morality and the Laws of War,' in Virginia Held, Sidney Morgenbesser and Thomas Nagel (eds.), *Philosophy, Morality, and International Affairs* (New York, 1974), pp. 71–88.

14. *The Rules of Land Warfare* (Washington, D.C., 1917), p. 14.

15. Cohen, *op. cit.* p. 79. Cohen also notes that if Taylor's view that mutual violations invalidate a rule or principle is correct, then from the fact that both sides in the Second World War committed acts that exceeded the requirements of military necessity one might conclude that the latter principle has itself ceased to form a valid part of the laws of war. Taylor does not, however, press his view of the relationship between efficacy and validity to this conclusion.

16. Frits Kalshoven, *Belligerent Reprisals* (Leyden, 1971), p. 364.

17. Wasserstrom is more cautious, arguing only that it would count against the moral defensibility of the laws of war "if part of the idea of a war crime is, as some of the literature surely suggests it is, that an offense ceases to be an offense once the practice becomes uniform." *Op. cit.* p. 13, emphasis added.

18. These facts are amply documented in the official history of the bombing offensive by Sir Charles Webster and Noble Frankland, *The Strategic Air Offensive Against Germany, 1939–1945*, 4 vols. (London, 1961).

19. Taylor, *op. cit.* p. 143, helps to perpetuate this myth when he writes that in bombing German cities the Allies were "attacking a functioning part of the German war machine with a weapon that could not discriminate among those in the target area." The same misconception is reflected in the claim of Joseph Bishop, *Justice Under Fire* (New York, 1974) at p. 267, that "the massive bombings of Hamburg and Frankfort, though they necessarily inflicted enormous suffering on civilians, were not in my opinion, war crimes, for the RAF had no other way to knock out such legitimate targets as arms factories, submarine pens, and transportation networks."

26. Toward a Legal Regime for Nuclear Weapons

Richard Falk

THE ULTIMATE INTERNATIONAL LAW CHALLENGE

Nuclear weapons have inevitably placed a normative strain on political leaders.[1] This strain was "managed" during the first three decades after 1945 in various ways: by periodic calls for disarmament, by a general Western policy that emphasized defense against aggression, and by a diplomacy that from the 1960s onwards sought arms control arrangements to abate the arms race and maintain public confidence in the stability of the overall nuclear situation. More recently, the rising costs and dangers of a quickening arms race have given rise to widespread public anxiety, in North America, Western Europe, and Japan, about the relationship of nuclear weapons to the security of states and to the viability of a global political order constituted, principally but not exclusively, by sovereign states.[2]

This anxiety has taken several forms, but includes important normative dimensions, that is, moral/legal objections to the role currently assigned to nuclear weapons in the strategic thought and actions of the superpowers. Part of this concern has centered on the combined unwillingness and inability of the superpowers to stabilize the arms race in terms of either resource outlays or risks. Another part of this concern has centered on the provocative deployment of specific weapons systems, such as Pershing II and SS-20s in Europe, which appear to invite first strikes or preemptive attacks in periods of acute crisis. This concern has generated as well a wider questioning as to whether any reliance on nuclear weaponry can ever appropriately serve the ends of state power. Implicit in such questioning is the encroachment upon the sovereign rights of non-nuclear states and junior alliance partners, whose destiny seems entrapped in the dynamics of the rivalry between the United States and the Soviet Union; the old possibility of neutral states opting out of belligerency seems to have become meaningless in a world in which even outer space is understood as a dimension of belligerency, and in which the fallout and the global ecological and economic disruption that would be caused by any major nuclear exchange would certainly ignore national boundaries.

These gathering concerns about the prevailing official thinking on nuclear weapons were most powerfully articulated by Jonathan Schell in his *The Fate of the Earth*.[3] Schell emphasizes threats to human survival contained in the nuclear standoff, as well as the disproportion between tactics and technology, as nuclear destruction far outweighs the state interests supposedly being served by such weapons. This disproportion has been highlighted during the presidency of Ronald Reagan by loose talk about limited nuclear wars, first-strike weaponry, and prevailing or winning in a protracted nuclear war. In fairness to the Reagan administration, their loose talk, in each instance, builds upon earlier entrenched official thinking and war plans about the role nuclear weapons play in relation to the foreign policy of the United States. There also exists a growing public realization that the scale and quality of the Soviet missile buildup in the 1970s went well beyond reasonable defensive requirements. This buildup has raised doubts about Soviet motivations, leading analysts to question Moscow's reasons for building and deploying so many missiles, especially in relation to Europe, including the frequent replacement of missile systems. Perhaps in partial explanation of that buildup, it should be noted that earlier Soviet strategic inferiority produced a diplomatic humiliation for them at the time of the Cuban Missile Crisis (1962), and this undoubtedly gave rise to an attitude of "never again" in the Kremlin, which enabled weapons builders to enlarge their claims on Soviet resources. Furthermore, the Soviet Union has no "friends," and arguably is surrounded by "enemies," including its East European "satellites" and an antagonistic China with enormous manpower resources and its own growing arsenal of nuclear weapons.[4] Each superpower justifies its own continuous search for more and better weapons by its perception and representation of the other, including profound uncertainties about the other's ultimate and proximate intentions.

In early 1983, normative concerns about nuclear weapons are evident in a variety of forms. There is, first of all, a continuing major Western European grassroots effort to prevent the deployment by NATO of 572 Pershing II and cruise missiles. Ronald Reagan's somewhat bizarre espousal of an array of 21st-century advanced defensive weapons, suitably dubbed "Reagan's star wars strategy," which could supposedly provide societies with secure protection against nuclear attack while superseding reliance on deterrence, is acknowledged for the first time at a leadership level to rest on morally dubious threats to devastate foreign societies.[5] The final adoption of the much-discussed pastoral letter of the American Catholic bishops, which places the teaching of the Catholic Church on war as applied to nuclear weaponry in direct opposition to many of the principal tenets of prevailing doctrines of nuclear weapons strategy that have been accepted by NATO and the United States since 1945, is also reflective of a rising consciousness on these issues.[6]

Until this broader political and normative public ferment emerged, international lawyers had been comparatively quiet on these momentous issues. Over the years since 1945 there have been, to be sure, a few scholarly discussions pro and con about the legality of nuclear weaponry, but somehow until the 1980s, the debate never was treated in international law circles as very significant.[7] This neglect has several explanations. The legal issues were clouded from the beginning by the original "popular" and, in this sense, legally "non-controversial" use of atomic bombs "to save lives" and bring peace in the closing days of World War II, generally regarded by the victorious powers as a "just" war.[8] It also seemed futile to mount a legal case against weapons so obviously useful and powerful, because of the prevailing realities and track record of geopolitics. Specifically, the inability of the West to develop sufficient non-nuclear means to defend Europe and other vital interests on the Asian mainland, in light of a perceived threat resting upon an overall Soviet superiority in conventional forces, and reinforced by the logistical advantages of Soviet dominance of the Asian land mass, made it seem self-denying for Western powers to question the legal status of nuclear weapons. Furthermore, aside from a brief movement in England a couple of decades ago, there was no political pressure mounted by way of a grassroots normative attack. Defending the legality of nuclear weapons is such a thankless task that it undoubtedly seemed to most international lawyers upholding official policies to be more desirable to maintain a discreet silence on the subject, as long as this was politically possible. All of these elements contributed to the repression of "the legal question." Nevertheless, it is instructive to realize that legal doubts about the status of nuclear weapons have been objectively "present" ever since the Hiroshima explosion. The importance of posing the legal question of nuclear weapons now in 1983 should be understood not only as a response to a new and more aggravated stage in the nuclear arms race, but also as a belated attempt to consider serious legal issues that, but for the historical circumstances surrounding the original uses, would have been addressed as soon as the first atomic bomb was used as a weapon of war.

If Germany or Japan had developed and used atomic bombs in World War II against the inhabited cities of the victors, the war crimes trials held in Nuremberg or Tokyo would certainly have investigated, and in all probability condemned, the use of this weapon, and would have punished the officials responsible as war criminals, even had due mitigating account been taken of Allied strategic bombing of Axis cities.[9] The magnitudes of the blasts and the fallout from those original fission bombs would, in my judgment, have led impartial international law experts to regard the atomic attacks on the Japanese cities as having been perpetrated by illegal weapons, or at least as having involved an illegal tactic of war, despite the plausibility of arguments from military necessity and the prior disregard by strategic bombing patterns of the traditional limits of the laws of war. Indeed, the only court that ever investigated the legal arguments surrounding the American attacks on Hiroshima and Nagasaki came clearly and persuasively to the conclusion that they violated international law as it existed in 1945.[10] Nevertheless, despite several relatively obscure legal condemnations over the years, which took place in a variety of international settings, the questioning of nuclear weapons has been totally ignored until recently by political leaders and military planners in the nuclear powers, as well as by their publics.

At this time, the international law dimension of the nuclear age is at last becoming prominent, at least in professional and policy-planning circles. A great deal of scholarly work is appearing on all aspects of the topic. International law, as a general rule, is responsive to fluctuations in the political environment, and the last few years have firmly established a climate in which inquiry into the legal status of nuclear weaponry appears "natural," if not unavoidable.

In fact, some of this legal questioning is coming from strange sources. There exists a hawkish school of nuclear strategists, which has for years wanted to shape nuclear weapons policy around traditional moral/legal notions of "defense" and "military targets," thereby hoping to overcome normative inhibitions against an aggressive foreign policy and also hoping to reconcile normative considerations with a reliance on nuclear weapons. Proponents of this approach emphasize the "immorality" of city-busting weaponry that poses the threat of indiscriminate devastation of the urban centers of an enemy society, and the "immorality" of apocalyptic thinking that takes no steps to maximize chances of survival should a nuclear war occur. These "normative" critics of mutual terror do not consider abandoning our reliance on nuclear weaponry, but rather argue on behalf of strategic postures that rest upon a provocative mix of civil defense programs (shelters), defensive technologies, and accurate weaponry that can concentrate its destructive effect on the enemy's military capabilities, including its command structure.[11] The normative paradox here is evident: this type of reconciliation of nuclear weapons doctrine and weaponry with the prevailing conceptions of the law of war and international morality tends toward speeding up the arms race, encouraging the design and deployment of first-strike weapons systems, and making the adoption of attitudes and doctrines that favor nuclear war-fighting options more attractive. In effect, taking international law and morality seriously in *this* manner definitely erodes the crucial firebreak in war planning that separates conventional and nuclear weaponry, thereby making the outbreak of nuclear war far more likely.

Such a perspective has been recently introduced into international law discourse by the recent widely noted RAND study, "The International Law of Armed Conflict: Implications for the Concept of Armed Destruction."[12] The RAND report has proved irresistible to those international lawyers who are opposed to the legality of nuclear weapons—almost too good to be true. It seems to establish the central point that even a think-tank closely aligned with the Pentagon is driven to the conclusion that the principal existing doctrine governing the use of nuclear weapons rests upon a flagrant defiance of international law. In the words of the RAND study, "Destruction of societies, destruction as an end in itself, would appear to be directly opposed to the most fundamental principles of international law governing armed conflict."[13] More pointedly: "The concept of Assured Destruction and its derivatives (e.g., economic recovery targeting) appear to be directly opposed to international law and, hence, contrary to both domestic and DOD directives governing individual actions affecting the acquisition, procurement, and use of weapons."[14] The RAND authors disclose their purpose as being "to help close the chasm that now yawns between international law and U.S. strategic nuclear policies."[15] Indeed, these are extraordinary conclusions, considering their source. In effect, the RAND authors acknowledge an underlying illegality governing United States policy and practice since Hiroshima, a policy and practice characteristic of the United States, of NATO, and of Soviet national security.

But it should be noted that this analysis of international law is confined to a legal condemnation of the doctrine of Mutual Assured Destruction, and has not been applied to the weapons themselves. The RAND study proposes that "actual (as opposed to declaratory) U.S. targeting, strike plans, and military forces should be designed only for attacks against military targets and war-supporting activities (i.e., they should be as discriminate as reasonably possible, consistent with their military purposes). What constitutes war-supporting activities is subject to interpretation; but a safe interpretation under the law would not include civilians or civilian industry unless or until they are converted to military activities that could have a direct effect upon the conflict then being waged (i.e., economic recovery targeting would seem a dubious concept under the international law of armed conflict)."[16] The authors spell out the implications for military research and development as leading to an emphasis on "discriminate, military [sic] effective weapons."[17] The RAND study never genuinely clarifies the extent to which the operational impact of allowing nuclear weapons to be used against military targets is consistent with the fundamental objectives and principles of the law of war. Surely the cumulative effect of nuclear megatonnage and the wide scope of lethal effects creates "problems" for any general validation of nuclear weapons under international law.

The RAND study establishes some important common grounds for inquiry. It affirms the relevance of international law to strategic planning, and it even insists that policymakers and government international lawyers "closely examine" the consistency of "strategic planning concepts . . . with the law of armed conflict."[18] Beyond this, it alerts "defense intellectuals outside the government, in universities and corporations, to appreciate the essentials, if not the details, of the international law as it applies to strategic planning" and urges them to conform their behavior accordingly and on the basis of their opportunity "to be more independent" than those playing official roles. Such a mandate relies expressly on United States Department of Defense official policy, outlined in DOD Instruction 5500.15, which includes the following language: "All action of the Department of Defense with respect to the acquisition and procurement of weapons, and their intended use in armed conflict, shall be consistent with the obligations assumed by the United States Government under all applicable treaties, with customary international law, and, in particular, with the laws of war."[19] In fact, of course, the United States Government position has rested mainly on facile and unpersuasive application of *Lotus* reasoning, namely, that states are permitted to do anything not expressly prohibited by rules resting on consent, and that in the absence of an express treaty prohibition, joined by the United States, nuclear weapons may be legally employed.[20] It seems ludicrous to extend the reasoning of the *Lotus* case of 1927, developed to assess a very narrow question of jurisprudential competence in a criminal negligence controversy arising out of a collision on the high seas, to the drastically different circumstances surrounding the consideration of the legal status of nuclear weapons. For one thing, on a jurisprudential level, the issue of whether or not a given activity is prohibited by pre-existing rules is partly a matter of how *general* is the level of appraisal chosen. For instance, while nuclear weapons are not the explicit subject of any agreement binding nuclear weapons states, the main instruments of the preexisting laws of land warfare prohibit *all* methods of warfare having the characteristics associated with contemplated uses of nuclear weapons. The *Lotus* view of the legal status of new weapons and methods of warfare also flies in the face of the "Martens Clause," inserted in the Preamble to the IVth Hague Convention of 1907, concerning the Laws and Customs of War on Land, and itself generally regarded as a binding element of customary international law. The Martens Clause requires governments to assess "cases not covered by the rules adopted by them" by reference to "the general principles of the law of nations, derived from the usages established among civilized peoples, from the laws of humanity, and from the dictates of public conscience."[21] On such a basis, the overwhelming normative consensus now operative in international society would *legally* condemn all contemplated roles for nuclear weapons, except "possession" as a hedge against nuclear blackmail; not even a retaliatory use of nuclear weapons could be easily reconciled with most interpretations of the laws of war, given the properties of the weaponry and the difficulty of reconciling any actual use with such principles as "necessity," "proportionality," "discrimination," and "humanity."[22]

Even the official American strategic doctrine and war plans, despite the apparent embrace of Mutual Assured Destruction (MAD), seems, on its face, to reject the always emphasized military targeting, and hence has been relatively consistent with the position argued in the RAND study. The service manual formulations with regard to legal status validate nuclear weapons only "against enemy combatants and other military objectives." To the extent that existing doctrines and plans rest on a conception of deterrence based on threats to civilian non-combatants and non-military objectives, these would be illegal under even this narrowest definition of the applicability of international law. However, given such guidelines, the atomic attacks against Hiroshima and Nagasaki should clearly have been repudiated. Furthermore, current counterforce targeting, while superficially repudiating city-busting options, and therefore formally consistent with restricting the role of nuclear weapons to military objectives, is in fact deeply misleading in this crucial respect. Because of the magnitude and properties of nuclear weapons (involving many times the destructiveness of the atomic bombs of World War II), and because of their contemplated use in and around cities (there are, for instance, sixty-two military objectives targeted within the city limits of Moscow!), the cumulative blast and fallout effects from multiple nuclear explosions, the number of targets regarded as "military," and the clustering of military targets near population centers, even an official policy that limits the use of nuclear weapons by reference to the military character of the target is not different in effect from an overtly indiscriminate targeting policy. Furthermore, the World War II experience with the unrestricted bombardment of cities and with unrestricted submarine warfare suggests that a self-limiting framework of policies and tactics confining deliberate destruction to the enemy's military targets gives way in wartime to considerations of battlefield effectiveness, understood to include strikes against cities to weaken the resolve of the enemy society. Either the restriction implicit in counterforce strategy is meaningless, because "military target" is given such a loose definition that it includes everything pertaining to a war effort, even civilian morale, or the confining effect of a restricted definition is overlooked under pressure, as was the case with the atomic attacks in World War II, whose rationale rested on their overall role in helping to end the war successfully. No serious attempt has ever been made to determine whether the contemplated uses of the atomic bomb might be in violation of the law of war despite the justification provided. Without a more focused inquiry on what is permitted and prohibited by law, the general public conception that *some* uses of nuclear weapons are legal has the primary effect of providing a rationalization or loophole for virtually *any* use of such weapons.

This affirmation of the applicability and stature of international law is a challenge to prevailing statist attitudes both within and without government.[23] Let the existing situation be clearly stated. The use of atomic bombs against Hiroshima and Nagasaki was never evaluated in relation to this international law framework by planners and leaders, nor has the subsequent diplomacy of the nuclear age, which has included some twenty documented threats to use nuclear weapons, been in any way sensitive to such legal criteria.[24] In the voluminous literature devoted to the Cuban Missile Crisis, only international lawyers have regarded the international law dimension of the crisis as important, except that it was considered in the detailed planning which was associated with the active carrying out of the strategic decision.[25]

A climate now exists in which to argue the case for the relevance of international law to nuclear issues. This case can be reinforced by action on the part of those who are politically and morally committed to minimizing the role of nuclear weapons. For reasons of state policy, the Soviet Union seems prepared to lend its official support to most efforts to delegitimize nuclear weapons.[26]

There remain, however, several serious preliminary difficulties involved in the application of international law to nuclear weapons. First of all, nuclear weaponry is possessed by state rivals in a world characterized by acute and mutual distrust; nuclear disarmament, beyond certain fairly high thresholds, continues to be viewed as unrealistic, because it would create unacceptable political temptations and vulnerabilities. As a consequence of this practical constraint, rival states are likely to retain offsetting nuclear weapons capabilities for the indefinite future, and to insist on at least a posture of minimum deterrence, that is, their possession and a threat, implied at least, to retaliate with nuclear weapons against nuclear attack. Even this form of the minimization of the role of nuclear weapons is likely to sustain some type of nuclear arms race, as each side will want to be confident that its nuclear weapons capability and its overall capability for response does not become vulnerable to surprise attack as a result of secret machinations by its rival.[27]

Secondly, as the underlying technology needed to produce nuclear warheads becomes more familiar and refined, the possibility of additional political actors, including dissident armed groups, or even criminal gangs, acquiring nuclear weapons will grow greater. In relation to these prospects of nuclear proliferation, the existing nuclear weapons states are unlikely to give up their hedge against nuclear blackmail by altogether renouncing both nuclear possession and use options. In any event, as long as the technological base persists for producing nuclear weapons, their production and reintroduction into defense arsenals can never be reliably ruled out.

Thirdly, and perhaps most disturbingly, as long as nuclear weapons remain under the control of governments, and as long as armed conflict persists in international relations, there exists a grave danger that any available weapon or tactic, regardless of its normative status, would be introduced into battle, if it was perceived by the leaders involved to be centrally decisive. Throughout the history of modern warfare, going at least as far back as the futile effort to banish the crossbow, weapons that are effective on the battlefield or in relation to defeating an enemy society have been used without consideration of legal (or moral, or cultural) restrictions.[28] Nuclear weapons, whatever else they might be, are regarded as effective, at least in their threat role as guardians of political survival. Indeed, it would be easy to contrive rationalizations that "illegal" *threats* to use nuclear weapons against cities and civilians "save lives," safeguard the prospects of "human survival," and make indispensable peacekeeping contributions by way of the prevention of war. Post-1918 efforts to prohibit the use of poison gas weaponry do not provide much reassurance to the contrary. It is true that the legal prohibition may have operated as a marginal factor in discouraging the use of such weapons and in building moral/legal inhibitions against their use in wartime by world leaders. Nevertheless, the evidence suggests overwhelmingly that the non-use of these weapons in major conflicts that have taken place since World War I is related more importantly to doubts about their "effectiveness" under battlefield conditions, and to the existence of alternative methods of carrying out belligerent missions. In essence, the argument I am making rests on the central proposition that because of the way states wage war—the unconditionality of the means they use whenever issues of victory and defeat arise—it is unlikely in the extreme that international law constraints on nuclear weapons by themselves will hold up in times of severe international crisis. Because a large number of these weapons will be retained, under the best of foreseeable circumstances, these weapons will be likely to be used to the extent that it seems to leaders that the outcome of a war is at stake. Countries such as Israel, France, and Great Britain presumably possess nuclear weapons as a warning to their enemies not to push them too far, and there is every reason to suppose that rather than accept military defeat, these countries would use such weapons, regardless of their legal status. To put the matter differently, international law cannot hope to regulate the pursuit of decisive military state interests, and nuclear weapons are manifestly weapons of military decisiveness.

Fourthly, and more obscurely, the indirect reliance on nuclear weaponry to assist in achieving a variety of foreign policy goals is deeply embedded in bureaucratic thinking, at least in the United States and the NATO countries, about upholding "national security" at "acceptable" costs. To relinquish such a reliance will require very determined political leadership in the two superpowers, especially in the West, where first-use nuclear options remain conscious premises of existing foreign policy.[29] Nuclear weapons apologists, including those who reaffirm the explicit relevance of international law to such decision making, argue for "defensive" roles for these weapons (against "aggression") and "military" uses (against silos, bases, and command centers). These lines of argument are consistent with an *abstract* application of the traditional international law of war to nuclear weapons and tactics in the spirit of the Martens Clause. The strategic implications of such an application are to encourage the development and deployment of neutron bombs, ABM and "high frontier" weaponry, civil defense preparations, increasing the accuracy of weapons, and provocative political plans and strategies. The net effect of such strategies is to overcome inhibitions on the first use of nuclear weapons in a conflict situation, because the inhibitions of terror associated with MAD are weakened.[30] In effect, the nuclear/non-nuclear firebreak is eroded, if not cast aside. The ironic result seems to be that taking international law seriously, given the accompanying implausibility of getting rid of nuclear weapons or of transforming international relations in a more pacific direction, may actually clear the path for nuclear war-fighting doctrines, policies, and capabilities.[31] This is the main operative effect of the RAND study, especially in light of the policy directions of those who are presently urging an accelerated arms race and the development and deployment of destabilizing weapons systems.[32]

The complexity of the fifth obstacle to the application of international law to these weapons is as follows: some minimalist variant of MAD provides, arguably, the best hope of avoiding any future use of nuclear weapons and of slowing down the arms race, and yet MAD is presently most flagrantly in violation of international law, as this law has been generally understood.[33] Furthermore, MAD can provide potential adversaries with reassurances that nuclear weapons are being held only against the remote contingency of the necessity of retaliation against prior nuclear attack. The essence of deterrence is to make the potential nuclear attacker anticipate with as much certainty as possible the devastation of his own country. If deterrence is made more compatible with the RAND reading of international law, then all or some of the following effects could come about: deterrence would in fact be hypocritical in its application (that is, because of the nature of the attacking weapons and of the locations and variety of military targets, counterforce limitations will not in fact save either cities or the civilian population from nuclear devastation); MAD would be less effective as a deterrent (that is, the attacker might regard the prospect of retaliation against those of his military targets that are separated geographically from places of civilian habitation as an acceptable and even rational risk to be counted as part of the cost of a nuclear surprise attack and victory); finally, deterrence would prove less and less reassuring to a rival, in a period of acute crisis (that is, if the other side might reasonably attack, then pressure to stage a pre-emptive first strike necessarily grows).

There may be no fully satisfactory way to entirely circumvent this fifth obstacle. However, I think there is a line of analysis that more validly uses the international law heritage to minimize the role of nuclear weapons in diplomacy. The jurisprudential "concession" that will enable this reformulation is a variant of Catholic "just war" moral reasoning, which allows the choice of a lesser evil under certain circumstances of belligerency.

It should be evident by now that serious reflection on the relevance of international law to the status of nuclear weapons will be unavoidably controversial at this stage, and also that it is, to some extent, both inconclusive and tragic. One is not proceeding on the basis of a clean slate. Thousands of nuclear weapons exist, many thousands more are in the planning and development stages, and it is almost inconceivable that the expenditure of so many billions of dollars and the resulting accumulation of towering structures of bureaucratic influence can be easily overcome. At the same time, the overall normative dimension provides firm grounds upon which to premise a critique of existing nuclear weapons policy and practice. Definite improvements can be made in present policies and in public expectations governing the use of nuclear weapons without waiting for the darkness of catastrophe or the lightness of utopia to come upon us. Such improvements might increase the prospects for a peaceful transition over time to a denuclearized world.

TOWARD AN INTERNATIONAL LAW REGIME FOR THE NUCLEAR AGE

The quest for a legal regime rooted in the dynamics of the states system of world order is adversely conditioned by the continuing predominant Machiavellian tradition of political leadership.[34] That is, war as an option of national policy cannot be ruled out by legal fiat, and the legalist efforts of this century to do so by way of renouncing "aggressive war" options largely constitutes a fraud on the public's consciousness and moral concerns. Since the governments of sovereign states are the highest decision makers, especially if the political institutions of the United Nations are either inoperative or are discounted as partisan, self-serving interpretations of the legal status of controversial uses of force are made. These circumstances are the rule, not the exception. That is, politically congenial uses of force are routinely characterized as "defensive," whereas politically hostile uses of force are condemned as "aggressive." To some extent this incoherence flows from polemical uses of the law to serve the interests of state power, but to some extent, it also genuinely reflects a "misperception" that follows from the diversity of perspectives associated with different access to information, ideology, culture, and worldview.

This pervasive subjectivity in international politics makes it exceedingly dangerous to tie any restraint on methods of warfare to a characterization of the context as "defensive."[35] The extension of the aggression/defense framework to the dimension of nuclear weapons policy is seriously flawed on both conceptual and policy grounds: on conceptual grounds, it regressively merges *jus ad bello* analysis with a determination of relative *jus in bello* rights (i.e., allowing the self-styled defending state to use nuclear weapons proportionately and with discrimination);[36] on policy grounds, it weakens the inhibition on the recourse to nuclear weapons, and also dilutes incentives to plan non-nuclear defense strategies.

In articulating the contours of an international law regime responsive to the nuclear age, three goals of policy seem paramount:

1. Avoiding nuclear war;
2. Minimizing crisis instability;[37]
3. Reducing the arms race.

These three overriding objectives are phrased to take account of the international political setting. Also, they are complementary, but they are not necessarily consistent with one another in all applications. For instance, promoting objective 2, crisis stability, may in certain circumstances require increased defense outlays to maintain an assured invulnerability of retaliatory capabilities to a surprise attack and, hence, represents a setback for objective 3.

Each of these objectives requires extensive interpretation to be made operational, and interpretation is necessarily susceptible to a variety of good faith outcomes. One interpreter might argue that the way to avoid nuclear war is to achieve decisive superiority over the other side, because it alone threatens the international status quo. Another equally sincere interpreter might contend that only by renouncing all political violence in international affairs is it possible to avoid nuclear war, because participation in any armed conflict contains unacceptable risks of escalation. In effect, this latter position moves in the direction of conceiving that the realization of objective 1 depends upon the construction of an overall global peace system. Assuming that these difficulties with the operationalization of these objectives are acknowledged, the drawing up of a framework for a legal regime helps to organize and focus inquiry; it cannot hope to resolve all policy differences, except to the extent that it is perceived as a value-oriented appeal to a community of scholars and policy makers.

In order to evolve a useful legal framework, account must also be taken of two features of the international political world: (1) a tendency to risk virtually any level of self-destruction in warfare in order to avoid military defeat; and (2) a general willingness by states to use military power to secure positions of privilege, power, and wealth in human affairs. There is no way to establish a realistic legal regime that is not sensitive to these geopolitical features of international life, as well as to the three previously depicted specific objectives associated directly with nuclear weapons. That is, given the existence of nuclear weaponry, it is difficult to imagine a major state that possesses such weapons reconciling itself to defeat in a conventional war affecting its perceived core interests. The adoption of nuclear weapons prohibitions, in certain forms, could possibly make the outbreak of major warfare more probable in international life, thereby entailing high human costs and even quite unintentionally creating an increased net risk that nuclear weapons would in fact come to be used.

Furthermore, in contouring a legal regime for nuclear weapons, the starting point must be the basic principles constituting the customary international laws of war. These principles, emphasizing discriminate and proportionate warfare, seem impossible to reconcile with a nuclear weapons regime that is responsive to our overall guidelines for nuclear weapons. That is, the possession of a small number of invulnerable, inaccurate missiles (second-strike weapons) seems at present the best calculated way to minimize the danger of nuclear war, encourage crisis stability, and minimize nuclear arms race incentives. With reasonably credible conventional defensive capabilities, and the formulation of foreign policy goals in restrained terms, the dangers associated with nuclear weapons would be significantly reduced— but there is a major catch. This type of minimization of initial threat rests on the claim of last resort to engage finally in indiscriminate destruction, at least in a post-attack situation where its execution would be vindictive in the extreme. However, if nuclear weapons are reduced in number, while at the same time they are made accurate enough to strike at military targets, then it is difficult to maintain either crisis or arms race stability, because the nuclear weapons retained by both sides could be used for offensive as well as defensive purposes. If restraining notions were seriously implemented, they might not deter high-risk war and foreign policy initiatives, because a probability of military targets being destroyed could still be coupled with a projected favorable outcome of a war. Leaders with intense ambitions or great desperation might conceivably be persuaded to gamble on the unwillingness of an attacked enemy to strike back pointlessly with nuclear weapons, or the attacker might even be prepared to absorb some nuclear retaliation in exchange for a prospect of political victory. Because scenario reasoning (projecting hypothetical future situations) is far-fetched, the uncertainties of political behavior in the nuclear age have been allowed to discourage value-oriented breakthroughs on matters of security.

A legal regime responsive to this background must build upon several interrelated aspects of the existing situation: (1) the possession and retention of some nuclear weapons for use in extreme situations; (2) the mutual distrust of adversary states, and a corresponding lack of sufficient confidence in international institutions that disallows any transfer of control over nuclear weapons beyond the level of the sovereign state; and (3) self-determination of occasions warranting recourse to the right of self-defense.

Against this background, a beneficial international law regime for nuclear weapons would have to rest on the following considerations:

1. public support for the idea that *any* actual use of nuclear weapons would violate the international law of war and constitute a crime against humanity;
2. public support for the rule that a first use of nuclear weapons, even in a defensive mode in response to or in reasonable anticipation of a prior non-nuclear armed attack, would violate international law and constitute a crime against humanity;
3. following from point 2, the fact that weapons systems (even at the research and development stage), war plans, strategic doctrines, and diplomatic threats that have first-strike characteristics are *per se* illegal, and that those political leaders, engineers, scientists, and defense workers knowingly associated with such "first-strike" roles are engaged in a continuing criminal enterprise;
4. a definite consensus that second or retaliatory uses of nuclear weapons against cities and primarily civilian targets violate international law and constitute a crime against humanity;[38]
5. a clear obligation, recognized by all nuclear weapons states and by other states as well, to pursue arms control in the direction of minimizing the role of nuclear weapons in conflict behavior through negotiations in good faith; this obligation is a provision, Article VI, of the widely ratified Non-Proliferation Treaty, and is embodied in general terms as well in the Charter of the United Nations and in a variety of formal resolutions adopted over the years by the General Assembly;
6. a definite mandate directed toward citizens to take whatever steps are available to them to achieve a law-oriented foreign policy for their own country, including, as both conscience and good sense dictate, non-violent acts of civil disobedience and efforts to persuade members of all branches of government to overcome the gap that separates the normative consensus of the public as to the illegality of the use of nuclear weapons from prevailing official policies.[39]

These legal conclusions, taken in conjunction with the background of present political circumstances and the general objectives of a stable world order, underscore the importance of reinforcing the firebreak separating conventional and nuclear weapons. Only by minimizing reliance on nuclear weapons can the destabilizing geopolitical interactions surrounding their possible use be reduced. In this regard, a formal no-first-use pledge, coupled with comprehensive plans for non-nuclear defense of vital interests, would be the best overall indication that the normative implications of nuclear weaponry are being taken seriously by policy makers.

The most direct consequence of taking the normative dimension seriously (and law and morality are mutually reinforcing with respect to nuclear weapons), would be to make it "illegal" and "immoral" for a country to seek *any* advantage or positive role for nuclear weapons in relation to national security. From the moral and legal perspective, it is "illegal" to rest national security plans, doctrines, or weapons deployments on first-use options or threats, and it is "immoral" for a country to undertake security commitments without developing adequate non-nuclear capabilities. This development of non-nuclear capabilities assumes great importance because no country will accept defeat if that defeat seriously encroaches upon its political independence and territorial integrity. In such a case it is likely, regardless of the legal status of nuclear weapons, that such weapons would be used because of overwhelming pressure if it was thought that their use would alter the outcome of the war, and, therefore, rules of prohibitions need to be reinforced by making the prohibited activity as unnecessary as possible.

Furthermore, there already exist "legal" instruments to moderate the arms race and to convey reassurances to other countries that foreign policy and national security planning are based on an unconditional renunciation of nuclear weapons as legitimate instruments of war. Measures of arms control, such as a mutually verifiable freeze, including a comprehensive test ban treaty, seem essential embodiments of this approach.

Finally, so long as nuclear weapons are possessed by states, it is important that their possessor act so as not to make these weapons vulnerable to a surprise attack, a theft, or a terrorist attack. Making sure that a nuclear retaliatory capability is reasonably secure against enemy attack further helps to prevent international situations arising in which the risks of nuclear war are increased.

Within the framework of the present structure of international relations, law and morality cannot do more than to minimize the dangers of nuclear war and the use of nuclear weapons, assuming that strategic conflict is kept within manageable limits. However, if geopolitical rivalry produces a world war, then there is little reason to be hopeful that nuclear weapons will not be introduced into it, either to win an ongoing war more easily or to avoid losing it. In the end, over time, assurances against the "illegal" use of nuclear weapons will depend on drastic global reform.[40] A legal regime could never purport to supply unconditional protection. It can only help to establish a series of conditions that would make it less likely that international actors will depart from underlying moral and legal guidelines. In this case, the destructive, even ultimate, consequences of a violation make the task of a legal regime for nuclear weapons unique. Its success will depend on the internalized values, beliefs, and interests of political leaders, military bureaucracies, and the public. Constructing such a legal regime will depend on popular pressure, aided by supportive religious groups and changing cultural perspectives. The survival imperatives of our situation suggest the importance of insisting that our own leaders strive to adhere as closely as possible to international law guidelines in foreign policy, especially with respect to strategic doctrine and planning. The need for such a framework could perhaps be usefully formulated as leading toward a popular demand for a Magna Carta for the Nuclear Age. This call is part of a wider conviction on my part that the citizens of democratic societies have a selfish interest in ensuring that their leaders and institutions adhere to a constraining regime of law, as fully in foreign policy spheres as in domestic domains of public policy.[41] Even such a dramatic resetting of the constitutional order as I have been suggesting here can only hope to achieve, at best, a transitional arrangement, a holding operation. The terrible consequences of the potential use of nuclear weapons place enormous burdens upon our preventive efforts, but even beyond these efforts, building a permanent nuclear peace will depend upon the construction of "a warless world."

CONCLUSION

A haunting question hovers over the foregoing analysis: Is it possible to reconcile *any* reliance on nuclear weapons simultaneously with minimum security functions and with applicable normative traditions, particularly those contained in the international law of war? The legal regime proposed above confines absolutely the role of nuclear weapons to retaliatory uses and, even with respect to such retaliations, offers only a very reluctant, tentative, and ambiguous endorsement. The possession of the weapons for purposes of threatening retaliation seems an unavoidable transitional adjustment, but the normative strain emerges as soon as the character of the threat is specified. If retaliation is restricted in advance to a few *isolated* military targets, then the security function of deterrence is undermined—whereas if it is not so restricted, then it seems to be exaggeratedly vindicative and indiscriminate in a manner that is most manifestly at odds with the law of war.

The bishops' pastoral letter is only "a centimeter of ambiguity" away from an unconditional rejection of nuclear weapons. As the final text emerged, it did leave some political space for a continuing reliance on a much narrowed conception of deterrence, at least for now. In effect, a certain degree of normative incoherence must be accepted in both legal and just war settings, in deference to the realities of our present reliance on nuclear weapons, but with the strong proviso that such deference is a temporary expedient that can be justified even on this qualified basis only if a far stronger effort is made by governments to achieve arms control and nuclear disarmament.[42] If this disarmament effort fails to materialize within this decade, then the burden of persuasion would seem to shift in support of the unconditional prohibition of the threat, use, and possession of nuclear weapons, almost regardless of national security claims. The interim position adopted here, in effect, provides governments with a final opportunity to get their normative house in order, by adapting their security policies to an emergent normative consensus that appears to preclude *any* reliance on nuclear weapons.

NOTES

1. "Normative" is used throughout this article to encompass legal, moral, cultural, and biological standards, which help draw boundaries between what is morally permissible and appropriate and what is morally impermissible and inappropriate at different levels of societal organization. The focus of this article is upon the interplay between legal norms and the nation-state, in relation to external uses of military power and, more particularly, to reliance on nuclear weapons. In the context of the law of war, there has always been a strong relationship of coherence among these various sources of normative authority. There has also always been a tension between the power orientation of the modern state and the acceptance of normative guidelines in relation to issues of war and peace. This tension has been made more serious in recent decades as a consequence of the steady application of technological innovation to warfare, in a way that makes adherence to the normative guidelines strike political leaders as unrealistic. In a sense, this "unrealistic" demand for a modification of such policy prerogatives lies at the core of the current renewed normative inquiry into the status and role of nuclear weapons.

2. This anxiety also reflects the erosion of the position of the United Nations as a source of normative authority, constituted to counterbalance and eventually modify the power-centered, fragmented behavior of independent sovereign states and such alliances of these states that aggregate like-minded and partisan political attitudes. The combined effect of the growing dominance of the state over internal political, economic, and cultural spheres of action and belief, and its autonomy (or sovereignty) in relation to supranational frameworks, especially in matters of national security, fosters an impression that such states, especially the superpowers, operate in a normative vacuum. For these depressing dual aspects of the international situation, see Richard Falk, "Nuclear Weapons and the End of Democracy," *Praxis International* 2, No. 1, April 1982, pp. 1-11; and Falk, "The Decline of International Order: Normative Regression and Geopolitical Maelstrom," *Year Book of World Affairs 1982*, pp. 10-24 (1982).

3. Jonathan Schell, *The Fate of the Earth* (1982).

4. One justification that has been advanced for the Soviet buildup in the European theater is to discourage any Western impulse to intervene in Eastern Europe in the event of future challenges directed at Soviet hegemony.

5. For the Reagan text, see *N.Y. Times*, March 24, 1983, p. A20. The normative aspiration to substitute secure defensive capabilities for current threats to devastate whole societies with weapons of mass destruction is certainly admirable, but there is little reason to suppose that it can ever be made to work with sufficient reliability. Even Reagan talks of this high-frontier scenario as a goal for the 21st century. We are left with the need for a normative framework that can guide our national security policies at the present time and lead us toward a safer future. To the extent that high-frontier thinking is an alternative to peace/disarmament thinking, it represents one more misguided effort to overcome normative problems by proposing another technological fix. For opposing assessments of the feasibility of such developments, see Edward Teller, "Reagan's Courage," and Richard Garwin, "Reagan's Riskiness," *N.Y. Times*, March 30, 1983, p. A31.

6. For a partial text of the pastoral letter, see *N.Y. Times*, May 5, 1983, p. B16; for earlier assessments from a Catholic perspective, see Walter Stein, ed., *Nuclear Weapons and Christian Conscience* (1961); for skeptical assessment, see Bvan Voorst, "The Churches and Nuclear Deterrence," 61 *Foreign Affairs* 827 (1983).

7. Earlier works on the subject include Georg Schwarzenberger, *The Legality of Nuclear Weapons* (1958); N. Singh, *Nuclear Weapons and International Law* (1959); and I. Brownlie, "Some Legal Aspects of the Use of Nuclear Weapons," 14 *International and Comparative Law Quarterly* 437 (1965).

8. A useful depiction of the official thinking surrounding the decision to use the atomic bomb against Japan has been made by the influential Secretary of War at the time. See H. Stimson, "The Decision to Use the Atomic Bomb," 194 *Harpers* 97 (1947).

9. Of course, the "criminal" character of the bombing itself was never considered because of "the victors' justice" limitation on the war crimes proceedings; in other words, to have been condemned, the atomic attacks would have had to have been carried out *only* by the losing side. Victor's justice was not extended in an extreme form to punish the losers for war methods *also* used by the victors; for an excellent discussion of this issue, see R. Minear, *Victors' Justice: The Tokyo War Crimes Trial* (1971); for a more sympathetic construction, see T. Taylor, *Nuremberg and Vietnam: An American Tragedy* (1970).

10. The Shimoda case was decided by the District Court of Tokyo on Dec. 7, 1963. For text, see *Japan Annual of International Law*, pp. 212–252 (1964); for comment and interpretation, see Richard Falk, "Shimoda Case: A Legal Appraisal of the Atomic Attacks on Hiroshima and Nagasaki," 59 *American Journal of International Law*, 759 (1965).

11. A clear and influential instance of this perspective is F. Iklé, "Can Nuclear Deterrence Last Out the Century?" 51 *Foreign Affairs* 267 (1973); see also C. Gray, *Strategic Studies and Public Policy: The American Experience* (1982), and K. Payne, "The BMD Debate: Ten Years After" (Hudson Institute, 1980).

12. Carl H. Builder and Morlie H. Graubard, January 1982, R-2804-FF.

13. *Ibid.*, p. vii.

14. *Ibid.*, p. ix.

15. *Ibid.*, p. xiii.

16. *Ibid.*, p. 48.

17. *Ibid.*, p. 51. Builder's extremely assertive strategic views confirm this interpretation; see Builder, "Why Not First Strike Counterforce Capabilities," *Strategic Review* (Spring 1979), 35.

18. *Ibid.*, p. 57.

19. Air Force Pamphlet AFP, Oct. 16, 1974, pp. 110–31, 6–11; the RAND study also relies on the language of Article 36 of the 1977 Geneva Protocol on the Geneva Conventions, which puts parties to the agreement "under an obligation to determine whether" the employment of a new weapon or method of warfare would "in some or all circumstances" violate international law. The study does not note that the United States representative in the treaty negotiations explicitly ruled out the applicability of the protocol to nuclear weapons. For discussion of the United States Government view on the non-applicability of the Geneva Protocol to nuclear weaponry, see R. Erickson, "Protocol I: A Merging of the Hague and Geneva Law of Armed Conflict," 19 *Virginia Journal of International Law* 557, at 560 (1979).

20. Article 613, U.S. Naval Instructions; also Law of Land Warfare, FM27-10, Department of the Army, 1956, p. 18; for text of *Lotus* case, see "The Case of the S.S. 'Lotus' (France v. Turkey)," Permanent Court of International Justice (1927), P.C.I.J. series A, no. 10.

21. For reasoning on the relevance of Martens Clause to this issue, see Falk, L. Meyrowitz, and J. Sanderson, "Nuclear Weapons and International Law," Princeton

University, Center of International Studies, Occasional Paper No. 10, World Order Studies Program, especially pp. 21–33 (1981).

22. For formulations of these principles, see General Introduction to *Israel in Lebanon* (the Report of the International Commission to enquire into reported violations of International Law by Israel during its invasion of Lebanon), pp. xix–xx (1983).

23. See articles cited *supra*, note 2, and Richard Falk, "Some Thoughts on the Decline of International Law and Future Prospects," 9 *Hofstra Law Rev.* 399 (1981).

24. These uses are carefully documented in an exceptionally important article: D. Ball, "U.S. Strategic Forces: How Would They Be Used?" 7 *International Security* 31, at 41–44 (1982–83).

25. For a legal maximalist interpretation of the relevance of international law to nuclear weapons that manages to avoid being a legalist polemic, see A. Chayes, *The Cuban Missile Crisis* (1974).

26. The Soviet position on the nuclear arms race in general has been well described by the Soviet dissenters Roy and Zhores Medvedev, "A Nuclear Samizdat on America's Arms Race," *The Nation*, January 16, 1982. Soviet adoption of an unconditional no-first-use of nuclear weapons pledge is contained in former Communist Party Chairman, L. Brezhnev's "Special Message" of June 15, 1982, to the Second Special Session on Disarmament. The pledge has been reaffirmed by the current Soviet leader Yuri Andropov.

27. The case for nuclear deterrence along present lines is ably developed by Michael Mandlebaum, "International Stability and Nuclear Order: The First Nuclear Regime," in D. Gompert et al., *Nuclear Weapons and World Politics* (1977).

28. Modern war has grown into an unconditional contest of wills, in which every means and tactic of destruction will be used by political leaders with "a clear conscience." The ideological grounding for this secular absolutism is most clearly formulated in the writings of Machiavelli and Clausewitz. For an analysis of this relation, see W. Gallie, *Philosophers of Peace and War*, pp. 37–65 (1978) and R. Lifton and R. Falk, *Indefensible Weapons*, pp. 239–243 (1982). Despite the normative doubts now being raised about nuclear weapons, there has, as yet, been no serious challenge directed at these unrestricted war-making prerogatives of states, and without a "Magna Carta for the nuclear age," the legal doubts being currently raised about the status of nuclear weapons, even if they come to be embodied in some authorative form, will be cast aside in time of emergency. These doubts may nevertheless be functional, to the extent that they prompt policies and weapons deployments that operate *as if* these weapons were illegitimate; in effect, the legal challenge may contribute to the replacement of "early use" scenarios, and this by itself would greatly reduce the risks and anxieties associated with the existence of nuclear weapons.

29. For an indication of the extent of reliance on the first-use option, see K. Payne, "Deterrence, Arms Control, and U.S. Strategic Doctrine," 29 *Orbis* 747 (1981). In opposition to such reliance lies the main importance of No-First-Use Proposals and Pledges. A main consequence of renouncing first-use policy options is the refashioning of foreign policy in two directions: reducing the overall nuclear undertaking (that is, precluding any credible defense for certain kinds of attacks on foreign societies) or upholding an earlier commitment by reliance on the sufficiency of non-nuclear military capabilities. To what extent, for instance, are current NATO force requirements for the non-nuclear defense of Western Europe being exaggerated by way of a myth of conventional inferiority? How real, in any event, is the threat of a Soviet armed attack upon Western Europe? Even if denuclearization is the exclusive goal, tactical choices are not self-evident, because a process of dealignment

within NATO could produce the opposite results by restoring first-use options by way of a West German decision to develop its own nuclear strike force. For recent discussion of these issues, see McGeorge Bundy, George F. Kennan, Robert McNamara, and Gerard Smith, "Nuclear Weapons and the Atlantic Alliance," 60 *Foreign Affairs* 753 (1982); for a skeptical response see Karl Kaiser et al., "Nuclear Weapons and the Preservation of Peace," 60 *Foreign Affairs* 1157 (1982).

30. The full implications of the main alternative strategic positions are discussed in S. Keeny and W. Panofsky, "MAD Versus NUTS," 60 *Foreign Affairs* 288 (1981–82).

31. At some level of jurisprudential reflection, this "ironic effect" of international law analysis suggests a defect or bias in the RAND rendering of the law of war vis-à-vis nuclear weaponry. One way out, of course, is to condemn the weaponry *per se*, because of its attributes, rather than to focus analysis, as has been traditional prior to nuclear weapons, on the probable contexts of their use, that is, on the targets—in legalist terminology, to consider nuclear weapons illegal *per se*. Another way out would be to formulate a new kind of analysis based on an interpretation of the hierarchy of objectives pursued by the international law of war in the nuclear age, placing the avoidance of any use of nuclear weapons at the pinnacle of the hierarchy.

32. Indeed, overt doctrine since 1974 has emphasized military targeting, under such rubrics as "flexible response" and "counterforce." See M. Leitenberg, "Presidential Directive (P.D.) 59: United States Nuclear Weapons Targeting Policy," 18 *Journal of Peace Research* 311 (1981); Beres, "Tilting Toward Thanatos: America's 'Countervailing' Nuclear Strategy," 34 *World Politics* 31 (1981); L. R. Beres, *Mimicking Sisyphus: America's Countervailing Nuclear Strategy* (1983).

33. The illegality of nuclear weapons is a firm conclusion of the RAND study cited in Note 12; this assessment is reinforced by the analysis in the bishops' pastoral letter, cited in Note 6.

34. See R. C. Tucker, *On Political Leadership*, especially 114–157 (1981); see also Lifton, and Falk cited in Note 28, 239–243.

35. Note that under post-1928 international law, only defensive uses of force in international affairs are "legal." It is also the case that the international law of war is impartial as between the permissible tactics relied upon by "aggressor" and "defender." In effect, the law of peace (*jus ad bello*) renounces "aggressive" uses of force, while the law of war (*jus in bello*) accepts a shared framework of restraining rules, principles, and agreements.

36. This is the consequence of Eugene V. Rostow's and John Norton Moore's analyses of these issues. For Rostow's view, see 1982 *Proc. Amer. Soc. Int'l. Law* (forthcoming), and Moore's views in the *Brooklyn Law Journal*, scheduled to be published in 1983.

37. That is, minimizing the temptation in a period of heightened international tensions to have recourse to war or to nuclear weapons, either because it looks as if an advantage could be seized or a dangerous vulnerability neutralized; mutuality as between nuclear rivals is better assurance of stability than is military superiority, especially forms of superiority that might be nullified or reduced by a surprise attack.

38. There exists a definite normative tension between the legal framework most likely to minimize the risks of the use of nuclear weapons and the legal framework guiding acceptable uses of political violence. The latter framework is most consistent with a *total* prohibition against nuclear weapons and, secondarily, with a prohibition on any use of them directed at non-military targets. The minimizing framework, in contrast, reserves the option for the most legally unacceptable use as the best

practical means to avoid any use and, as well, to eliminate arms race pressures and crisis instabilities. This "tension" expresses the impossibility of "living with" nuclear weapons, and highlights the current tragic reality associated with no longer being able to live without them.

39. These legal conclusions, in relation to the background of the general political circumstances obtaining in the world and in relation to general objectives of a stable world order, underscores the importance of reinforcing the firebreak separating conventional and nuclear weaponry. Only by minimizing reliance on nuclear weapons can the destabilizing geopolitical interactions surrounding their possible use be reduced. In this regard, a formal no-first-use pledge coupled with comprehensive plans for non-nuclear defense of vital interests would be the best overall indication that the normative implications of nuclear weaponry are being taken seriously by policy makers.

40. For some perspectives on this issue, see R. Johansen, "Toward an Alternative Security System," World Policy Paper No. 24, World Policy Institute, 1983, and Richard Falk, *A Study of Future Worlds* (1975).

41. Of course, citizens of non-democratic societies share a similar selfish interest, but, realistically, their prior goal, on the nature of a precondition, is to secure for themselves democratic rights. In this regard the struggle for the democratization of the relations between state and society in the Soviet Union is intimately related to the struggle for the avoidance of nuclear war, yet at the same time, it is partly separable from the preliminary effort needed to construct a legal regime pertaining to nuclear weaponry. This separability arises from the fortunate circumstance that Soviet *state* interests also appear to support the minimizing of the role of nuclear weapons and, in this critical regard, do not depend on responsiveness to democratic pressures.

42. For instance, Bishop Maurice J. Dingman is quoted as saying, "We said this country can keep deterrence only if it works vigorously for arms control. If that isn't achieved, I believe we'll take a far stronger stand." N.Y. *Times*, May 8, 1983, §4, p. E5.

CHAPTER 7

Tensions Between the Individual and the State

In a fundamental sense, modern international law has been organized around the primacy of the territorial sovereign state. As a result, individuals have been subject to the unconditional rule of governments that possess the power and authority of the state. There is no effective set of international institutions capable of upholding some minimal set of decencies for all peoples, nor do governments voluntarily abide by these decencies in relation to their own citizenry, although obviously some records are far better than others.

At the same time, subsisting at the margins of the doctrine of state sovereignty has been a concept of natural law, an idea of inherent limits that restricts the discretion of all political actors, including governments, by reference to universal standards. The international protection of human rights creates an intrusion upon the domain of territorial sovereignty and, for this reason, tends to be rhetorical in impact. To the extent that states give their consent to human rights treaties there exists a formal compatibility between upholding the rights of states and upholding those of individuals, but to the extent that no supranational will or enforcement mechanisms exist, the position of the individual remains precarious in relation to the state.

In considering the Grotian prospect, a new system of world order would undoubtedly give far greater status to the individual and to groups as participants in international life. Any process of transforming statism will accentuate the shared interests of people everywhere in the realization of certain values, including the satisfaction of basic needs, the avoidance of war, the maintenance of environmental quality, and the avoidance of repression. Such values cannot be realized unless there are ways of regulating state behavior, or unless the domestic social order induces appropriate behavior. One expression of this quest for a new world order is to shift the emphasis of law from an instrument for the pursuit of mainly state interests to a means for the protection and fulfillment of the rights (and duties) of the individual in relation to political communities of all sizes, ranging from the neighborhood to the world. The imagery of world citizenship is intended to arouse loyalties based on human identity, and thereby to extend notions of citizenship flowing out of relations with a particular state.

The first selection in Chapter 7, by Rosalyn Higgins, examines the status of the individual within the familiar framework of traditional international law. Higgins reviews whether international law in various specific respects is exhibiting a trend toward greater status for the individual. Higgins displays sensitivity to the conceptual problems of reconciling status for individuals with conventional ideas about state sovereignty.

The tension between the requirements of the state system and individual political aspirations becomes clearest in cases where offenders cross the boundary. There are procedures for the extradition of common criminals who are fugitives from justice. Usually extradition depends on treaties, but such treaties often exempt individuals charged with *political offenses*. At the same time, a foreign country may serve as a base for hostile exile operations designed to overthrow a government. Sometimes these activities are encouraged by the territorial government, as has happened in recent decades in the United States in relation to anti-Castro exiles and, more recently, with the anti-Sandinista exiles.

Richard Falk's essay on the current efforts to keep the Nuremberg conception alive bears on the central theme of Chapter Seven. The Nuremberg conception refers to the trials of Nazi leaders after World War II held before a specially constituted international tribunal established by the victorious governments. The tribunal applied international law standards to individuals who acted on behalf of the German state. It held them criminally responsible and did not allow them to excuse their behavior on grounds that they had acted in their official capacity, that they merely followed superior orders, or that they acted for the sake of their nation.

There was, of course, an element of hypocrisy built into the Nuremberg conception. It was, in part, a matter of victors' justice. The apparent crimes of the winning side were never investigated or prosecuted. At the same time, it was a beginning in the direction of holding individuals accountable for the misdeeds of governments in relation to breaking the peace, as well as with regard to the conduct of war. The Nuremberg Judgment held that "planning, preparation, initiation, or waging a war of aggression" was a crime against peace, the most serious of all international crimes. Recently, the argument has been advanced in "civil disobedience" cases involving antinuclear activists that the construction and deployment of first-strike weapons is itself a violation of this central Nuremberg injunction.

In the decades since Nuremberg no serious attempt has been made to establish a permanent mechanism to deal with crimes of states. Numerous aggressive wars have occurred in the meantime, and there have been many violations of the laws of war. Falk argues that this failure to apply Nuremberg by way of governmental initiatives creates an opportunity and responsibility for individuals to establish their own mechanisms of inquiry and appraisal. To some extent, such developments have been occurring, as when under the aegis of the great British philosopher, Bertrand Russell, a panel of internationalists was established in the mid-1960s to gather evidence and pass judgment on charges that the United States government was guilty of war crimes in Vietnam. The idea of using the Nuremberg conception as a framework within which to assess crimes and criminals of states is one further indication that the state system is being placed under fundamental pressure at a grassroots level. Emerging social forces are using "law" as a means to challenge the claims of the state to be beyond appraisal or restraint, and are creating their own informal institutions as a protest against the failure of the formal ones to take "law" seriously—in this instance, the international law of war and peace.

The focus shifts in the selection by Stephen P. Marks from the issue of holding individuals accountable for official wrong-doing to that of protecting the human rights of the citizenry against abuses of state power. Marks traces the evolution of human rights with respect to the category of rights covered in successive generations—first, freedom from gross abuses of state power; second, social expectations that basic needs for subsistence will be provided by the government; and, third, the upholding of basic planetary concerns. This third generation of human rights, recently emergent, posits by its nature a series of revolutionary claims that, if satisfied, would largely subvert the legitimacy and centrality of the state. These third-generation rights are transnational, relating to peace, ecological balance, and free communication. There is no way in which governments can deal with such concerns without working toward the creation of a new world order.

The final selection in Chapter 7 is a statement by the famous Chilean jurist, Alejandro Alvarez, who here celebrates the emergence of a cosmopolitan orientation toward the rights and duties of both individuals and larger political entities. Judge Alvarez's vision may strike readers as somewhat rhapsodic in light of the chaotic and harsh conditions that exist these days in so many parts of the world. And yet he clearly anticipates the contours and spirit of a new and emergent global consciousness that is necessary for the defense of humanity as well as crucial for further human growth. It is the growth and spread of global consciousness that will determine the pace and shape of the Grotian prospect.

All in all, the state is under simultaneous pressure from above and below. This double reality can be observed in the interplay between individual claims and global consciousness. Each depends on the other for validation. Each threatens the ordering primacy of the territorial sovereign state.

QUESTIONS FOR DISCUSSION AND REFLECTION: CHAPTER 7

1. Classical international law has been defined as "the body of rules binding upon states." Higgins criticizes this conception of absolute statism even for classical international law. How would you assess the current status of individual rights and obligations under international law? Do you find the prospects for improving the protection of individual rights to be favorable at this time?

2. The traditional justification for sovereign immunity rests not solely on the inherent dignity of the state, but also on the practical requirements of nonintervention in the domestic affairs of states. Do the arguments made in the Letellier litigation provide reasons for modifying this deference to a foreign state? If so, how? Is it feasible to have sensitive state-to-state issues resolved in the domestic courts of one of the parties? Are such courts likely to be impartial?

3. Given the frequency of war within and between states, how can anyone seriously argue that human solidarity exists or is at least emergent? How are we to assess Marks's assertion that a third stage of human rights based on such solidarity is taking shape in international law?

4. Justice Alvarez argues the functional case for such solidarity. This visionary position is probably more applicable today than it was thirty-five years ago. Yet why do such claims with regard to international law and its future development seem more remote from realization that ever?

SELECTED BIBLIOGRAPHY: CHAPTER 7

Richard Falk, *Human Rights and State Sovereignty* (New York: Holmes & Meier, 1982).
Richard Falk et al., *Crimes of War* (New York: Vintage, 1971).
Benjamin Ferencz, *An International Criminal Court*, 2 vols. (London and New York: Oceana, 1982).
Thomas Franck, ed., *Human Rights and Third World Perspectives*, 3 vols. (New York: Oceana, 1982).
Louis Henkin, *The International Bill of Rights* (New York: Columbia University Press, 1981).
Richard Lillich, *Humanitarian Intervention and the United Nations* (Charlottesville: University of Virginia Press, 1983).
———, *International Law of State Responsibility for Injustice to Aliens* (Charlottesville: University of Virginia Press, 1983).
A. Robertson, *Human Rights in Europe* (Manchester, England: Manchester University Press, 1972).
Alan Rosenbaum, ed., *The Philosophy of Human Rights, International Perspectives* (Westport, Conn.: Greenwood, 1980).

27. Conceptual Thinking About the Individual in International Law

Rosalyn Higgins

I have thought it appropriate, in a lecture that bears the name of Henry Sidgwick, to choose a theme that focuses on individual rights and on questions of reform and change, with which he was, of course, so much associated.

I shall hope to analyze conceptually, in a manner somewhat different from that usually employed, the status of the individual in the international legal system and to say something of the balance that international law seeks to secure between his interests and those of the state.

What is the place of the individual under international law today and in what ways is this place changing?

Lawyers traditionally think in terms of the notion of "legal personality," or of being a "subject of law." To be a legal person, or a subject of a legal system, is to have rights and duties under that system. To the extent that international law has been regarded as a system of law applicable between states, it has not been easy to see where the individual fits in. To be sure, he is indirectly affected—sometimes quite substantially—by the norms that prescribe what his national state may or may not do. The reference to his "national" state and the scope of the requirement of "nationality" for certain international transactions carries its own overtones.[1] When a state delimits its territorial boundaries, grants nationality under its own rules, asserts territorial jurisdiction and extended jurisdiction over its nationals, then individuals are manifestly affected. That is, of course, quite different from being a subject of the system that authorizes the state so to act. Does the individual have no rights and duties of his own under international law? Is his role in the international legal system merely passively to be affected by the actions of his state and the compatibility of those actions with international law?

The student learning international law for the first time is often simply told that international law is primarily an inter-state law;[2] that the individual may benefit indirectly, however, from treaties made specifically for his advantage; and that in a few isolated areas international law is beginning to acknowledge that he has certain direct rights and duties. Traditionally, the laws of war and in particular the Nuremberg Principles are singled out when mention is made of his duties; and human rights and minimum standards of treatment of aliens are mentioned in the context of benefits to the individual under international law. Undoubtedly the student will be taught the substantive law in each of these areas and will bear away with him the received wisdom that they constitute exceptions to the general rule that international law applies to nations.

But is that all? It is hardly satisfactory as a statement of principle and conceptually it makes little sense. Is there inherent in international law the requirement that it is primarily an inter-state system? Are the topics of the laws of war, treatment of aliens and human rights properly to be regarded as *exceptions* to a different general pattern? Why should these areas be singled out as exceptions which bring rights to and place duties on individuals? What is there in the nature of international law that circumscribes the place of the individual thus?

In the first part of my lecture I shall address myself to these questions; in the second part my focus will be on the delicate balance between the individual and the state and recent developments in international law that affect that balance.

THE INDIVIDUAL AND INTERNATIONAL LAW

To a certain extent, international law has been defined in contradistinction to domestic law. National law, it can be readily agreed, is the law valid in a state, binding on individuals who are subject to that state's jurisdiction. According to the classical definition, international law is the law that is binding upon states; and in recent years it has come to be regarded as the law binding on states and those international organizations which have international personality.[3] The place of individuals in this system of international law has traditionally been identified by reference to whether they are properly to be regarded as subjects of international law. Plutarch and later Francisco de Vitoria in 1532 both wrote in terms that effectively acknowledged that nonstate entities had internationally recognized legal rights. De Vitoria, of course, was speaking of the Indian Kingdoms of America. A century later Grotius, in his *De Jure belli ac pacis* of 1625 was refining the idea. Verzijl has suggested that the first scholar to use the technical term "subject of international law"—albeit to describe the status of a state—was Liebniz in the preface to his *Codex Juris gentium Diplomaticis*, 1693.

The placing of these sovereign political entities within the international legal system thus inexorably led to such examination of the place of individuals within that system being conducted in terms of the same criteria: The search was on to see if individuals could possibly be, along with states, "subjects of international law."

Certain authors have contended vigorously that only states are the subjects of international law.[4] Many of the leading jurists of the positivist school in international law have taken this position, asserting that individuals are the *objects* of international law, but not *subjects* of that legal system. The argument, reduced to its crudest elements, runs as follows: Under a legal system there exists only objects and subjects. In international law "subjects" is the term used to describe those elements bearing, without the need for municipal intervention, rights and responsibilities. Under the existing rules of international law there is no evidence that individuals are permitted to be the bearers of duties and responsibilities. They must, therefore, be *objects*: that is to say, they are like "boundaries" or "rivers" or "territory" or any of the other chapter headings found in the traditional textbooks.

Some of the positivists think that this is the nature of things; yet others,[5] like Professor Georg Schwarzenberger, think that the individual could in principle be a subject of international law, but no existing rule of international law renders him a subject of rights and duties. This is in keeping with Professor Schwarzenberger's insistence on a rigid distinction between the law as it is and the law as we would like it to be. These views—and the reasoning on which they are based—carry with them so many assumptions that, in disagreeing with them, it is hard to know where to begin. The most basic assumption, of course, is that international law—indeed, any legal system—is a set of rules. Yet McDougal and his colleagues have shown that law can be seen rather as a *process*: a particularized form of decision-making process, distinguished from mere political decision-making by the significance of reference to the accumulated trends of past decisions, the emphasis on the authority of the persons making the decision and the *a priori* identification of the purposes of the decision as those that will benefit the community as a whole.[6] Not only is international law not necessarily "rules" (or at least, not only "rules"), but these rules are not fixed indefinitely and thus [are not] wholly unresponsive to the needs of the system. Finally and importantly, the positivist definition assumes that some specific rule is required "permitting" the individual to be a subject of international law.

It has been suggested by one learned author (Carl Aage Nørgaard)[7] that the weakness of the positivist view on the place of individuals is that it fails to distinguish between the possession of rights and duties and the procedural capacity to sue or be sued on them. Nørgaard contends that co-terminosity is not a prerequisite to acknowledgement as a subject of international law: He points to the dictum of the permanent Court of International Justice in 1933[8] that "it is scarcely necessary to point out that the capacity to possess civil rights does not necessarily imply the capacity to exercise those rights oneself." Access to the International Court, as to the Permanent Court before it, is barred to the individual; but he may assert his claim through his national government. Nørgaard, and Alf Ross with him,[9] rest on that distinction. Although he does not directly deal with the point, he does not apparently find it relevant that the individual will be able to assert his claim *only if* his Government so chooses. One may observe, drawing upon a topical example in the field of English industrial law, that Lord Denning thought in the Gouriet case that a right which depended for its enforcement upon the consent of another party was close to being no legal right at all.[10]

Professor Nørgaard, for all his opposition to the view of individuals as mere objects of international law and the distinction that he draws between rights and the procedural capacity to enforce them, assumes that there is something fixed and immutable in the non-access of individuals to the International Court. Yet there is nothing *in the nature of international law* which so dictates. Power, to be sure, rests still to a substantial degree with sovereign states; and it is within their power for the moment to block the access of the individual to certain international tribunals and to continue to assert the old rule of nationality of claims, but the very notion of international law is not predicated on this assumption and the international legal system survives conceptually even were this to change. And it is part of the thesis of this lecture that these assumptions about access to international tribunals and force are in fact changing rapidly, with significant consequences in the delicate balance between the state and the individual.

To assert that international law is, in certain exceptional cases, applicable to individuals, is not conceptually helpful either. It is a statement that does nothing to identify *a priori* such exceptions or to explain those that exist; and it assumes that the place of the individual under international law is necessarily exceptional.

All of this—no matter which side of the line one is on and whether one insists that the individual is a mere object under international law or a subject because of having, in certain limited cases, rights and duties—is based upon the assumption that the correct starting point is an examination of the individual as a subject of international law.

But I believe there is, however, room for another view: that it is not particularly helpful, either intellectually or operationally, to rely on the subject-object dichotomy that runs through so much of the writings.[11] I find it more helpful—and closer to perceived reality—to return to the view of international law as a particular decision-making process. Within that process (which is a dynamic and not a static one) there are a variety of participants, making claims across state lines, with the object of maximizing various values. The values will relate, among other things, to power, wealth, prestige and notions of vindication and justice. The participants will promote their claims by a variety of techniques, ranging from force to diplomacy and public persuasion. And a variety of decision-makers, be they Foreign Office Legal Advisers, or international arbitration tribunals, or Courts, will pronounce authoritatively upon these claims.

Now, in this model, there are no "subjects" and "objects," but only participants. Individuals are participants, along with governments, international institutions (such as the UN, or the IMF, or the ILO) and private groups.[12] In the way our world is organized, it is States which are mostly interested in, for example, sea-space, or boundaries or treaties; it is thus States which advance claims and counter-claims about these. Individuals' interests lie in other directions: in protection from the physical excesses of others, in their personal treatment abroad, in the protection abroad of their property interests, in fairness and predictability in their international business transactions and in securing some external support for the establishment of a tolerable balance between their rights and duties within their national state. Thus, the topics of minimum standard of treatment of aliens, requirements as to the conduct of hostilities and human rights, are not simply exceptions conceded by historical chance within a system of rules that operates as between states. Rather, they are simply part and parcel of the fabric of international law, representing the claims that are naturally made by individual participants in contradistinction to state-participants.

Because states are such influential participants in the international system, they have until now been able to block the access of individuals to certain arenas, including notably the International Court, but over the last twenty years there have been mounting pressures for full access by individuals to international forums and some inroads are being made. Thus—though it is still hedged about with qualifications and reservations—individuals who have claims to make about an identified set of human rights in the Council of Europe Countries may pursue those claims initially in the European Commission of Human Rights and perhaps ultimately in the Strasbourg Court on Human Rights.[13] One sees the beginnings of a parallel system, incorporating the European Convention on Human Rights by reference, in the practice of the Court of the European Communities. Comparable attempts to open up access to arenas for the pursuit of individual claims are being made—though for the moment at a more rudimentary level—in the Inter-American system and the UN system itself.[14]

This access is of course sought not only to Courts, but to other relevant bodies as well. Thus the right of individuals to petition, for example, the UN Commission on Human Rights[15] and the Trusteeship Council,[16] have been of historical and legal importance. It is because I see this right of petition as an important *technique for the promotion of claims* that I cannot join with Professor Eustathiades[17] in seeing the significance of the distinction (factually correct, no doubt, and of which he makes much) between petitions in respect of which the individual has the status of a party, e.g., petitions to the UN from inhabitants of a Trusteeship Territory and petitions which are essentially informational, as under the Mandates system. This type of distinction may have its relevance in a framework where the central issue is the individual as a subject of international law; but not in the sort of model that we have postulated above.

There is, of course, a close relationship between the notion of nationality of claims and the unavailability of particular tribunals to the individual. The fact that Articles 35 and 65 of the Statute of the International Court allow only states and international organs to obtain, respectively, judgements and advisory opinions does not mean that the Court has no interest in, for example, the expropriation of property or human rights. Rather it is that there is the assumption that the state will bring the action on behalf of its national. In an interdependant world, however, Governments will often wish to give priority to not disturbing their good relations with the other state concerned; and the individual has no means of compelling his Government to take up his claim. Indeed, he is often in a Catch 22 situation: If the other state is an ally, his own Government may not wish to offend a trusted friend; if the other state is a traditional enemy, his Government may not wish to lose the chance of détente and of improved relations. The nationality of claims rule can thus militate unjustly so far as the individual is concerned and there are powerful arguments for giving him access—through a revision of its Statute—to the International Court or perhaps to a special Chamber of that Court. Thus in the Barcelona traction case,[18] a company incorporated in Canada had its assets seized in Spain in a manner that arguably was contrary to international law. The Canadian Government had its own good reasons—which had nothing to do with the merits of the case—for not wishing to take up cudgels on behalf of the shareholders. It so happened that a majority of the shareholders were of Belgian nationality and the Belgian Government was persuaded to litigate on their behalf. The Court found, however, that it had no legal standing to do so—it was not possible to go behind the corporate veil of Canadian nationality; and if Canada chose not to act, the individuals were left without remedy.

The European Commission on Human Rights is an interesting example of an institution that has learned to deal with claimants of varying status:

It has to examine both applications from individuals against member Governments who have accepted the provisions of Article 25 of the Convention and the inter-state complaints under Article 24. The European Court of Human Rights, which until now has heard only cases of individual complaint against Governments, now has adjudicated (as it has always been authorized to do) the inter-state complaint that Ireland has made against the United Kingdom.[19] Other than the need for an efficient screening service, there seems to be no necessary reason why an international court— be it restricted geographically or to a certain subject matter, or be it universal both as to parties and subject matter—cannot deal with parties of varying status. The screening function is clearly an important one and in the system of the European Convention on Human Rights it is performed by the Commission, which declares claims in principle admissible or inadmissible. Its yardstick, of course, is the Convention itself. Were individuals ever given access to the International Court of Justice at The Hague, something comparable would be needed to sift misconceived or frivolous claims. No doubt an institution to carry out this task could be devised; but as *its* yardstick would be the whole of international law (because the Court is not restricted to interpreting the UN Charter) rather than the very specific articles of a treaty, its problems would be substantial.

My final comment, in the context of my observations on access by individuals to arenas, is to note that it is not only international courts where international claims are adjudicated upon and where international law is pronounced upon.[20] National courts are from time called upon to respond to international law claims advanced by individuals. The individual may be a foreigner or a national; the action may concern the Government of the country of the forum or a foreign Government. Thus a domestic court can find itself [21] interpreting both its own national laws and international obligations undertaken in a treaty, in response to a request by an individual for release from preventive custody and a claim by a foreign government for the extradition of that individual. Or an individual may claim before a domestic court title to property situated within the forum; and the court will have to look to international law in order to pronounce on those issues. It may, for example, have to look to the validity of acts of expropriation or requisition of foreign property by another Government and international law makes especially significant the requirements of territoriality, non-discrimination and compensation. There is a substantial jurisprudence in this area, especially in the United States in relation to Cuban State Acts. The retreat from this historic function marked by the Supreme Court's decision in the Sabbatino case[22] seems to have been an aberration rather than a watershed.

Here, very often, the problem is not so much the access of the individual to the court—this will usually present no problems if he is a resident of the forum—but his ability to get the other, foreign party before the court. Where the other party is a foreign state or government, it may well plead sovereign immunity. The domestic court, at the very meeting place between international law and domestic law, must decide if the foreign sovereign is indeed immune from process. Those individuals and companies who enter into commercial transactions with foreign state trading companies thus seek the protection of the law in securing commercial certainty. The English courts are engaged in a significant overhauling of the law in this area. The traditional English rule that a foreign sovereign has absolute immunity in our courts is becoming more responsive both to the need to protect the individual trader and to the fact that international law does not itself require such absolute immunity. In *The Philippine Admiral*[23] the Privy Council found that where a state-owned vessel operated purely commercially, the state could not claim immunity *in rem* in respect of the commercial transaction. Lord Cross specifically said, however, that he did not envisage that the rule would be changed so far as immunity *in personam* was concerned—that would continue. Lord Denning, however, in the recent case of *Trendex—Nigerian Central Bank*,[24] found that "an immensely gloomy prospect." Reversing the decision at first instance of Mr. Justice Donaldson, Lord Denning and his colleagues in the Court of Appeal found that, the Central Bank having acted commercially and not for a state purpose, it could not as an arm of the Government claim immunity *in personam* the respect of a failure to meet commercial letters of credit. The significance of this important decision is multifold: In particular, if English as well as United States Courts are now prepared to look at the *nature of the transaction engaged in* and not at the *status* of the foreign state trading company, the individual will be greatly protected in that his international commercial transactions will be subject to the process of law.

What is as yet uncertain is whether, if the transaction in question was a purely commercial one but the breach of it was for a state reason, the foreign state may still claim immunity. This issue has just been before the English Courts which have found that the descent into the market-place by the foreign government does not prevent it from claiming immunity in these circumstances.[25] The case is to go to the Court of Appeal.

THE INDIVIDUAL, THE STATE, AND INTERNATIONAL LAW

I turn now from questions relating to access to the courts by the individual[26] to questions relating to his substantive rights. The individual, as we have seen, can make claims about any area of international law that affects his interests, provided he can get before an appropriate tribunal. Are there, in his relationship with the state—his own, or any other state which affects his interests—any specific rights which international law will recognize? There now exists a network of international instruments which identify human rights. A couple of generations ago human rights were thought of in terms of basic rights of liberty and survival. The existence of the General Assembly of the United Nations has given a tremendous impetus to the extending of these core rights. If the West has been preoccupied, in the retreat around the world from the Westminster model, to preserve the basic political and civil rights long known to it—habeas corpus, the right to vote, jury trial, etc.—the developing world has been concerned to extend the notion of human rights into the hitherto uncharted waters of economic and social progress. For this reason and because also it was appreciated that the ability of states fully to grant economic, social and cultural rights will depend in part on their state of development, there are two separate UN Covenants on human rights. One is the Convenant on Economic, Social and Cultural Rights and the other the Covenant on Civil and Political Rights.[27] As with all international instruments of general scope, the starting point for the Covenant was the Universal Declaration of Human Rights of 1948.[28] This Declaration of the General Assembly, though not a treaty, has not been without legal effect. Many of its clauses have come to be recognized as declaratory of general international law and moreover certain states expressly accepted the Declaration. There have been many instances, in various jurisdictions, where domestic courts have relied on the terms of the Declaration.[29] The intention of the Covenants was to provide a firm treaty basis to build on the experience of the European experiment in human rights and to incorporate those views of the intervening twenty years which sought to translate aspirations into human rights. Above all, the opportunity was to be taken to provide machinery for scrutiny and enforcement wherever possible.

The Covenant on Economic, Social and Cultural Rights thus confirms that self determination is a legal right (albeit very inadequately defined) and not a mere political slogan.[30] There is emphasized in Part I on group rights—self determination, the right of a people freely to dispose of its natural resources, the unlawfulness of depriving a people of its means of subsistence. These are the understandable legacy of the end of colonialism. The Covenant contains a general non-discrimination clause and specific mention of equal rights of men and women.[31] Among the specific rights guaranteed are those relating to a fair wage and decent working conditions[32] and the right to form and join unions.[33] The clause on unions is silent on the question of the closed shop and gives some quarter to Eastern European practice in qualifying the right to strike with the ambiguous phrase "provided that it is exercised in conformity with the laws of the country."[34] Family rights are protected and the right to education is guaranteed. The Covenant provides also for the individual to take part in cultural life.

As for the Covenant on Civil and Political Rights, there is a prohibition against the arbitrary deprivation of life[35] and an absolute prohibition against torture, cruel, inhuman or degrading treatment or punishment.[36] Slavery and forced labour are forbidden,[37] as are arbitrary arrest and detention.[38] Equality of persons before the courts is guaranteed[39] and retrospective panel legislation—retrospective both as to the offence and the punishment[40]—is prohibited. Everyone shall have the right to freedom of thought, conscience and religion.[41] Freedom of speech, of assembly and of association[42] are all provided for.

The mere enunciation of rights does not, of course, of itself much alter the position of the individual under international law, but there is now a legal yardstick against which the behaviour of States may be judged and a point of reference for the individual in the assertion of his claims. More tangibly, the Covenants have built into them certain control mechanisms. The Covenant on Economic, Social and Cultural Rights relies on a complex reporting system, in which the Economic and Social Council and the Commission on Human Rights play their part. The Covenant on Civil and Political Rights is more ambitious. The enforcement measures have teeth, though whether they shall bite is optional. In addition to transmitting reports, Article 41 provides that a state party may declare its recognition of the competence of a new Human Rights Committee to receive and consider complaints from another state party. This is the mechanism for inter-state complaints about human rights. There is, further, a separate Optional Protocol whereby the Committee may receive complaints from individuals concerning violations by state parties to the Covenant.

Both Covenants and the Protocol have entered into effect. The United Kingdom has ratified both Covenants and made the necessary declarations for the state to state system under Article 41 of the Civil and Political Covenant to come into effect. It has not, however, become party to the Optional Protocol. The United States is not yet a party.

To a considerable extent the Covenants build on the European experience where the Convention on Human Rights—which covers a limited number of rights agreed by like-minded democratic States to be basic—itself provides optional procedures for individual petition and ultimate recourse to the Court. The United Kingdom, after a somewhat late start, accepted the provisions whereby individuals could bring complaints against it before the European Commission on Human Rights. It is for the moment prepared to do this only on a regional basis and not on the more universal basis of the UN Covenant. Both the European Commission and the Court have put flesh on the bare bones of the legal rights guaranteed by the Convention. In the European context, at least, case law has now made tolerably clear what is meant by, for example, unreasonably long pre-trial detention.[43] The limits of the scope of the concept of freedom of choice in education— whether it relates to the language in which training takes place, or compulsory sex education—are being shaped by the cases.[44]

All this, it may be thought, represents a substantial improvement in the status of the individual under international law. And so it does. Indeed— as must be the case with every living institution—the law sometimes develops, frequently to the benefit of the individual, in unexpected ways. Let me give two examples. After the passing of the 1968 Immigration Act certain East African Asians sought entry to the United Kingdom. They were British passport holders, they were severely harassed by the anti-Asian policies of General Amin and they had members of their families resident in Britain. They were refused admission, on the basis that their passports now afforded them no automatic right of entry and they would have to take their place in the immigration queue—a process that might well take many years. They took their case to the European Commission on Human Rights. The United

Kingdom claimed, successfully, that the Convention did not guarantee to everyone, including passport holders, a right of entry or residence. The Commission, however, went beyond finding the legislation discriminatory within the meaning of Article 14 of the Convention; it said that discrimination based on race could by itself amount to degrading treatment of the person, which is prohibited under Article 3. Thus a government, operating in an area which it believes substantively to be beyond the reach of the Convention, can find itself caught up via the more generalized provisions relating to the *standard* of treatment of individuals that the Convention requires.[45]

A second example of the same principle: Extradition, expulsion and asylum do not feature as such in the European Convention. An applicant brought a case against the Federal Republic of Germany, which was contemplating expelling him to Algeria (his own country) or to France (which also had some claim over him). The Commission found that, notwithstanding the absence of provisions requiring restraint in matters of extradition and expulsion, to expel him to Algeria would, given the treatment he could have expected there, be an inhuman punishment under Article 3. Germany was thus restrained from exercising this option, though, like the United Kingdom on matters of freedom of entry, it thought the Convention did not cover these substantive aspects of the law.

The Commission drew the line in an interesting—and intellectually unsatisfactory—place; responding to the applicant's plea that if he was extradited to France, France would in fact send him on to Algeria, the Commission found that this was too remote to bring Article 3 into operation.[46]

It is perhaps not generally appreciated how fragile is the right of freedom of movement for the ordinary individual. The rights of entry, sojourn and exit are indivisible: The denial of one makes the assertion of the others a chimera. As early as 1948 the Universal Declaration of Human Rights had provided in Article 13(1) that "everyone has the right to freedom of movement and residence within the borders of each State." Article 13(2) went on to refer to "the right of everyone to leave any country, including his own and to return to his country." And of course these standards in turn are interwoven with and rely for their efficacy upon the prohibition against arbitrary arrest, detention or exile; the right to seek asylum; the right to a nationality and protection against the arbitrary deprivation of nationality. Important too are the provisions on personal liberty, the right to a fair trial and equality before the law.

The right of freedom to move within a country and freedom to leave a country is confirmed in Article 12 of the UN Covenant on Civil and Political Rights. And Article 5 of the 1967 International Convention on the elimination of all forms of racial discrimination specifically forbids discrimination, whether as to race, colour, national or ethnic origin, in the enjoyment of the right to leave any country, including one's own and to return to one's country.[47]

Yet the Soviet Union—a party to all these instruments—does not allow free exit from its shores. And one knows also that the United Kingdom's immigration legislation *is* geared to distinctions between races. The freedom of movement clause of the Covenant is merely one of several clauses that has an *ordre public* caveat: "The above mentioned rights shall not be subject to any restrictions except those which are provided by law, are necessary to protect national security, public order (*ordre public*), public health or morals or the rights and freedoms of others."[48]

. . . The Soviet Union has consistently cited national security reasons for refusals to grant exit visas; and at least until she becomes a party to the Optional Protocol and that Protocol enters into effect, there is no method of effectively testing reliance on that qualification.

As for the right of entry under international law, it is still less than certain that international law guarantees a right of a passport holder to enter at will his country of nationality. The UN Covenant on Civil and Political Rights circumspectly provides that no one shall be *arbitrarily deprived* of the right to enter his own country.[49] Is a queuing system, publicly based on the need to promote good race relations, an "arbitrary deprivation"? The International Convention against Racial Discrimination talks of the right to *return* to one's country,[50] but what if, like the average East African Asian passport holder, one has never been to Britain before? The European Convention on Human Rights does not guarantee this right; one of its additional protocols does.[51] And, to make its legal stance watertight, in ratifying the UN Covenant the UK has entered a reservation covering its position on this issue.[52]

When one looks at the vast battery of rights now guaranteed to the individual under these various international instruments, one must recall that although the pressures of international opinion may now make it hard for a state simply to decide not to become a party, or, if a party does not accept the right of individual petition or the jurisdiction of a court, there is still a further hurdle that the individual has to surmount. In both the UN Covenants and in the European Convention, several clauses are subject to an *ordre public* clawback. Moreover, Article 15 of the European Convention and Article 4 of the UN Political and Civil Covenant both allow for notified derogations in more general terms from the obligations contained therein, in conditions of national emergency. (Some rights, however, are so basic that no derogation is permitted—the prohibition against torture being an example.) In the European model, both these "clawback clauses" and the derogation in times of national emergency are subject to the scrutiny of the Commission. The European Commission on Human Rights has, over a wide range of cases, made clear what the acceptable limits are; and although it has been prepared to allow governments a "margin of appreciation" to use the technical term, it has not hesitated to find the necessary criteria unfulfilled, or the measures excessive or inappropriate.[53] It remains to be seen how the machinery of the UN Covenants will operate in this scrutineer function.

So far I have spoken of the developing rights of the individual under international law, but what of his responsibilities? It has long been accepted that under special treaty arrangements individuals may have duties as well as advantages. The UN servant, for example, has certain duties as well as rights before the UN administrative tribunal. UN sanctions—though these may need enabling legislation in certain countries—bind individuals as well as governments. The law of the European Communities reaches out, in its burdens as well as its benefits, to individuals in certain areas, but these are all special regimes. What of the individual in general international law? It is by now fairly clear that international law has something to say about the use of force by individuals. The Geneva Conventions of 1949[54] (partially revised by the new Humanitarian Law Convention) place upon the individual, through their attempt to protect the non-combatant, certain restraints. And whatever diverse views about its lawfulness are held, the Nuremberg Trials marked something of a watershed. The Nuremberg Trials[55] made clear, and the UN General Assembly has formally affirmed, that the individual—and not only the state—is under international law subject to duties concerning the waging of wars of aggression, crimes against humanity and war crimes. The uncertainties of the extra-territorial reach of a state's jurisdiction (I have in mind the Eichman case) or of so-called "victors' justice" (and here I think of the 1977 trials of the mercenaries in Angola) must not obscure the fact that there is still a solid core prohibition upon certain types of behaviour in warfare; and, as the *My Lai* trials in the United States graphically and properly showed, the defence of "superior orders" is no longer enough.

It is the perimeters of this norm that are now being marked out in the Anglo-Irish case before the European Court of Human Rights. The Commission found that five interrogation techniques used on IRA prisoners together constitute "torture."[56] The United Kingdom publicly accepted this finding and gave an undertaking that the techniques will not be reintroduced. . . .

International lawyers have become acutely aware over the last decade that the changing patterns of warfare—with civil wars replacing inter-state wars as the normal pattern of major violence—have made the traditional norms unrealistic, but at the same time there has been the parallel phenomenon of individual violence—often urban, often indiscriminate—against the state, with individual citizens usually those most hurt. It seems to me that when one tries to draw a balance sheet in this relationship between the state and the individual, the question of international terrorism must be put onto the scales. For if, as I have suggested, the progress made by individuals in the pursuit of their rights under international law is to some extent tempered by the rights of states to derogate from their obligations, then in the matter of terrorism the scales are heavily tipped against the state.

It is perhaps useful to begin by looking at the question of hijacking or air sabotage. International law—in the form of a tryptych of conventions—has sought to bring the individual offender to book. The first of these treaties is the Tokyo Convention on Offences and certain other acts

Committed on Board Aircraft.[57] The Convention applies to unlawful acts done by a person on board the aircraft, but its reach does not include acts or offences by those, such as the saboteur who has planted a bomb, who remain on the ground. It gives to the state of registration of the aircraft authority to apply its laws to the events occurring on board in flight, no matter where this may be. Contracting states in which the aircraft landed were also obliged to bring actions against the person concerned; however, the Convention did not define hijacking and in the majority of states hijacking itself is not a crime. Prosecutions would thus have to be instituted for other offences, perhaps of a less serious character, committed in the course of hijacking. Most importantly, the Tokyo Convention specifically stated that nothing in it created an obligation to grant extradition.

The Hague Convention[58] did define the offence of unlawful seizure of aircraft and it was provided that each contracting state would undertake to make the offence punishable by severe penalties. The gaps of the Tokyo Convention were further plugged by placing an obligation upon the state in whose territory the offender is found, without exception and whether or not the offence was committed in that territory, either to prosecute him or to extradite him. An essential loophole remained, however: The majority of states were unwilling to agree that prosecution or extradition should occur where the offence was for a political purpose.

The Montreal Convention for the Suppression of Unlawful Acts against the Safety of Civil Aviation[59] provides for universal jurisdiction in respect of violence, destruction or damage and the placing of a device on board an aircraft. Significantly, the Convention failed to include a proposal that the acts enumerated as prohibited should not be considered as political crimes for the purpose of extradition.

It will thus be seen that when questions of defining the offence, making them offences under national law, extending jurisdiction beyond the territory, have all been satisfactorily dealt with—then all roads lead to the question of extradition and this has, of course, become apparent equally in regard to land-based terrorism.

In 1973 Secretary General Waldheim placed the issue of terrorism on the agenda of the United Nations, and the United States, in particular, was active in the drafting of a convention. Faced with the feeling among third world states that such a convention could be used to clamp down on one of the most successful methods of waging wars of national liberation, the United States sought only a convention of modest scope—one that would protect diplomats from kidnapping and nationals of neutral states from terror. Thus the convention would *not* have dealt with Irish bombs in London, or Arab bombs in an Israeli supermarket; but the taking of hostages in, for example, Germany, would have been covered.

There was not a sufficient measure of consensus to achieve even these modest aims and instead the Assembly adopted a resolution calling for the study of the *causes* of terrorism as well as for proposals for its elimination in a manner compatible with self-determination. The sharply differing perspectives on this issue are illustrated by the statements made by the United States and Somalia. Secretary of State Rogers said:

We all recognize that issues such as self-determination must continue to be addressed seriously by the international community. But political passion, however deeply held, cannot be a justification for criminal violence against innocent persons.[60]

By contrast, Ambassador Farah observed:

The General Assembly must view this question of terrorism with a sense of historical perspective. While the world organization has a duty to use the peace-keeping machinery at its disposal to deal with all forms of violence, including international terrorism, it must be realised that this phenomenon is not new. It has only been brought closer home because a world which has accepted violence and terror as the natural lot of the poor, the weak and the oppressed, is shocked to see those evils applied to the rich and the successful.

Global agreement thus appears beyond our grasp. It may perhaps be—though I myself doubt it—that it will be easier to make progress on a regional basis. There does, after all, exist the Inter-American Convention on the Kidnapping of Diplomats[61] which specifically states that:

kidnapping, murder and other assaults against the life or personal integrity of those persons to whom the state has the duty to give special protection according to international law, as well as extortion in connection with those crimes, shall be considered common crimes of international significance *regardless of motive.*

They are, in other words, extraditable.

One should not, of course, underestimate the genuine difficulty that faces a democratic state in eroding the long-held principle that persons will not be extradited for political offences. This principle was for decades the mark of a liberal and civilized society. In England, it took us some twenty years to accept the proposition that it was appropriate to make an exception to the principle in the case of genocide. The Genocide Act, giving domestic effect to the 1948 Genocide Convention[62] which *did* make the offence extraditable, with the plea that the crime was political being of no avail, was passed only in 1969. And the narrow point has been taken in English case law that crimes by anarchists *are* extraditable, as anarchy is definitionally the negation of politics. This is hardly a satisfactory basis, intellectually or practically, for dealing with the heart of the problem. Rather, it is surely necessary for states to move towards an attempt to identify across the board certain acts which are so intolerable both to the reasonable security requirements of the state and the protection of innocent persons that a political purpose in committing them will not forbid extradition.

The new European Convention on the Suppression of Terrorism[63]—the text of which was approved in November 1976 by the Committee of Ministers—makes this attempt. Article 1 lists offences—including offences within the scope of the Hague and Montreal Conventions, against diplomats, regarding the taking of hostages and using bombs including letter bombs— which are *not* to be considered political. Article 2 allows a measure of latitude to the requested state in treating certain *other* offences as "political" or not. The Convention is not yet open for signature, but the British Government has announced in Parliament its firm commitment to ratify it.[64]

If, in the balance between the ordinary citizen and the state, the scales still are tipped in favour of the state, where the terrorist is concerned the advantages run his way. Not only have the provisions of international law and domestic law concerning extradition run his way, but the realities of contemporary life make it unlikely, in my view, that the passage of the European Convention will much change the situation. Even had that Convention already been in effect, the Abu Dhaud affair has shown that, so long as nations fear the continued ability of fellow terrorists to strike at will in their cities, ways will continue to be found to make the extradition proceedings non-applicable[65]—though the Convention will certainly make it harder and the relationship between governments and courts is clearly not the same throughout Europe. What the Convention does not do—and what the tool of law can never do—is to compel governments to *seek* the extradition of an alleged offender in the present climate, and save for Israel and perhaps the United Kingdom[66] (so far as Irish, but not Arab offenders are concerned) requests for extradition are unlikely to be made.

While it has been convenient to approach matters this way, this image of a balance sheet is to a certain extent artificial: I can, in concluding, do no better than to quote the words of Sidgwick's good friend, John Stuart Mill: "The worth of a State, in the long run, is the worth of the individuals composing it."

NOTES

This article represents a revised and edited version of the text of the Sidgwick Memorial Lecture given at Newnham College, Cambridge, in March 1977. A similar version of part of this text is to be found in a special issue of the *New York Law Review* (1978) to honour Myres McDougal.

1. See the outstanding analysis by M. McDougal, H. Lasswell and L. Chen, 'Nationality and Human Rights: The Protection of the Individual in External Arenas,' *Yale Law Journal*, 83 (1974), pp. 900–998.

2. See the classic definition in H. Kelsen, *Principles of International Law* (London, 1966, 2nd edition), p. 3: "International Law or the Law of Nations is the name of a body of rules which—according to the usual definition—regulates the conduct of the States in their intercourse with one another."

3. See Lauterpacht-Oppenheim, *International Law*, i (London, 1955, 8th edition), pp. 636–42.

4. D. Anzilotti, *Cours de Droit International* (Paris, 1929), p. 134; T. Gihl, *Folkratt under Fred* (Stockholm, 1956); M. Siotto-Pintor, *Receuil des Cours* 41 (1932–33), p. 356.

5. For example, G. Schwarzenberger, *A Manual of International Law* (London, 1967, 5th edition), p. 52; *International Law as Applied by International Courts and Tribunals*, i (London, 1957, 3rd edition), pp. 140–55.

6. M. McDougal, "Law as a Process of Decision: A Policy-Oriented Approach to Legal Study," *Natural Law Forum*, I (1956), p. 53; and "The Comparative Study of Law for Policy Purposes: Value Clarification as an Instrument of Democratic World Order," *American Journal of Comparative Law* (1952), p. 24.

7. C. Nørgaard, *The Position of the Individual in International Law* (Copenhagen, 1962).

8. Series A/B. No. 61, p. 231.

9. Alf Ross, *A Textbook on International Law* (London, 1947).

10. Gouriet v. Union of Post Office Workers [1977] 2 *Weekly Law Reports*, p. 696. This point was not approved by the House of Lords, which reversed the Court of Appeal's decision favouring Mr. Gouriet.

11. A very important contribution to this understanding is made by D. P. O'Connell. He notes that in the subject-object debate, "The real answer . . . goes to the heart of legal philosophy." He continues in telling fashion, "Is it true to say that the end of the legal action is a philosophical one in which the lawyer can pretend to be disinterested? Does it suffice to admit that the individual's good is the ultimate end of the law but refuse the individual any capacity in the realisation of that good? Is the good in fact attained through treating the individual as an instrumentality of law and not as an actor? Philosophy and practice demonstrate that the answer to all these questions must be in the negative. The individual as the end of community is a *member* of the community, and a member has status: He is not an object. It is not a sufficient answer to assert that the state is the medium between international law and its own nationals, for the law has often fractured this link when it failed in its purpose." *International Law*, i (London, 1965), p. 116.

12. For fuller elaboration of the variety of participants in the international legal system, see M. McDougal, H. Lasswell and M. Reisman, 'The World Constitutive Process of Authoritative Decisions,' *Journal of Legal Education*, 19 (1967), p. 253, and M. McDougal, 'Some Basic Theoretical Concepts About International Law: A Policy-oriented Enquiry,' *Journal of Conflict Resolution*, 4 (1960), p. 337.

13. See Articles 25 and 46 of the European Convention for the Protection of Human Rights and Fundamental Freedoms: L. Sohn and T. Buergenthal, *Basic Documents on International Protection of Human Rights* (New York, 1973).

14. Articles 40, 48 and 53, Regulations of the Inter-American Commission on Human Rights; Optional Protocol to the International Covenant on Civil and Political Rights: Sohn and Buergenthal, *op. cit.* pp. 199–209 and 62–65 respectively.

15. See A. Cassesse, 'The Admissibility of Communications to the United Nations on Human Rights Violations,' *Revue des Droits de l'Homme*, 5 (1972), pp. 375–97; J. P. Humphrey, 'The Right of Petition in the United Nations,' *Revue des Droit l'Homme*, 4 (1971), pp. 463–75.

16. Article 87(b), United Nations Charter.

17. C. Eustathiades, *Receuil des Cours*, 84 (1953–55), p. 553 ff.

18. Barcelona Traction, Light and Power Company Company Case, *ICJ Reports* 1970, p. 18.

19. No. 5310/71, *Yearbook European Convention Human Rights* (1972), pp. 78–254 and judgement of 18 Jan. 1978.

20. See R. Falk, *The Role of Domestic Courts in the International Legal Order* (Syracuse, 1964).

21. As did the French Courts in the recent Abu Daoud affair.

22. Banco Nacional de Cuba v. Sabbatino, 376 U.S. (1964). For opposing comments, R. Falk, 'The Complexity of Sabbatino,' *American Journal of International Law,* 58 (1964), p. 925; F. Mann, 'The Legal Consequences of Sabbatino,' *Virginia Law Review,* 51 (1965), p. 604; 'International Law: Congressional Abrogation of the Act of State Doctrine,' *Columbia Law Review,* 65 (1965), pp. 530–537; M. McDougal, 'Jurisprudence in a Free Society,' *Georgia Law Review,* 1 (1966), p. 1.

23. [1976] 2 *Weekly Law Reports,* p. 214.

24. [1977] 2 *Weekly Law Reports,* p. 356.

25. 1 *Congreso del partido* [1977] 1 *Lloyds Law Reports,* p. 536.

26. For some earlier writing in this area, see E. Borchard, 'The Access of Individuals to International Courts,' *American Journal of International Law,* 24 (1930), p. 364; F. Dunn, 'The International Rights of Individuals,' *Proceedings of the American Society of International Law,* (1941), pp. 14–21; E. Hambro, 'Individuals Before International Tribunals,' *Proceedings of the American Society of International Law* (1941), pp. 22–30.

27. GA Resolution 2200 (XXI) 16 Dec. 1966.

28. GA Resolution 217A (III) 10 Dec. 1948.

29. See L. Sohn and T. Buergenthal, *op. cit.* pp. 518–522; E. Schwelb, *Human Rights and the International Community: The Roots and Growth of the Universal Declaration on Human Rights, 1948–1963* (Chicago, 1964).

30. Article 1.

31. Article 3.

32. Article 7.

33. Article 8.

34. Article 8 (I) (d).

35. Article 6.

36. Article 7.

37. Article 8.

38. Article 9.

39. Article 14.

40. Article 15.

41. Article 18.

42. Articles 20 and 21.

43. Article 5 (3) of the European Convention. See, e.g., the Ringeisen Case, 4465/70, *Yearbook,* 14, p. 476; the Wernhoff Case (European Court of Human Rights, Series A, 1968, pp. 21–24); the Neumeister Case (*ibid,* Series A, 1968, p. 4). See further D. Harris, 'Recent Cases on Pre-trial Detention and Delay in Criminal Proceedings,' *British Yearbook of International Law,* xliv (1971), p. 87; and F. Jacobs, *The European Convention on Human Rights* (Oxford, 1973), pp. 63–75.

44. See Belgian Linguistics Case (merits) (European Court H.R. Series A (1968)); and the Case of Kjeldsen, Madsen and Pederson, Judgement of 7 December 1976.

45. East African Cases: 4403/70, 36 *Receuil* 92.

46. See 3745/68 *Yearbook* 11, 494.

47. Existing international treaty commitments are incorporated by reference into Principle VII of the Helsinki Final Act. The Final Act also includes specified arrangements for the free movement of individuals for the purpose of reunification of families: Cmnd. 6198. See also Y. Dinstein, 'Freedom of Emigration and Soviet Jewry,' *Israel Yearbook of Human Rights,* 4 (1974), p. 226; R. Higgins, 'Human Rights of Soviet Jews to Leave,' *ibid.* p. 275; R. Higgins, 'The Right in International Law of an Individual to Enter, Stay in and Leave a Country,' *International Affairs* (1973),

p. 341; L. Chen, 'Expulsion and Expatriation in International Law,' *Proceedings of the American Society of International Law* (1973), pp. 122–132.

48. Article 12(3).

49. Article 12(4).

50. General Asembly resolution 2106A (XX), Article 5(d).

51. Protocol No. 4, Article 3, The United Kingdom is not a party to this Protocol.

52. UN Doc CN, 193, 1976, treaties –6 (29 June 1976).

53. For a full survey and analysis see the forthcoming article by this author, 'Derogations in Human Rights Treaties,' *British Yearbook of International Law*, xlviii (1976–77).

54. 75 *United Nations Treaty Series*, p. 287 ff.

55. *International Military Tribunal*, 1.

56. No. 5310/71, *Yearbook European Convention Human Rights* (1972), *op. cit.*, pp. 78–254.

57. (1969) UK Treaty Series No. 126, Cmnd. 4230.

58. (1971) UK Treaty Series Misc. No. 5, Cmnd. 4577.

59. *International Legal Materials*, 10, p. 1151. See also the excellent survey by C. Thomas and Kirby, *International and Comparative Law Quarterly*, 22 (1973), p. 163.

60. Press release US/UN 104 (72).

61. 9 *International Legal Materials*, 1177.

62. *UN Yearbook* (1948–9), p. 959.

63. Cmnd. 6176.

64. Enabling legislation was before the House of Commons in February 1978.

65. Recent events in Western Europe and especially in the Federal Republic of Germany, occurring after this lecture was given, may perhaps make it necessary to suspend for future proof the opinion here given.

66. The author would now, for the same reason, add the Federal Republic of Germany to this list so far at least as Baader-Meinhof activities are concerned.

28. Keeping Nuremberg Alive

Richard Falk

The decision to prosecute German and Japanese leaders as war criminals after World War II, although flawed as a legal proceeding, represents an important step forward. It creates a precedent for the idea that leaders of governments and their subordinate officials are responsible for their acts and can be brought to account before an international tribunal. It affirms the reality of crimes against humanity and crimes against peace, as well as the more familiar crimes arising from violations of the laws of war.

The Nuremberg Judgment was also a promise to generalize the occasion of prosecution so as to make it an ingredient of international order. Justice Robert Jackson, the Chief American Prosecutor at Nuremberg, made his famous pledge in the courtroom: "If certain acts and violation of treaties are crimes, they are crimes whether the United States does them or whether

Germany does them. We are not prepared to lay down a rule of criminal conduct against others which we would not be willing to have invoked against us." We know, of course, that what Justice Jackson denied has occurred. After World War II the Allied Powers carried out the sentences passed at Nuremberg (and elsewhere) without subsequently exhibiting the willingness to abide by the commitment embodied in Jackson's statement. To be sure, the legal principles on which the Nuremberg Judgment rested were endorsed by unanimous vote at the first session of the United Nations General Assembly, and some years later these principles were set forth in authoritative form by the International Law Commission, a body of international law experts functioning within the UN system.[1] The Nuremberg Principles provide authoritative legal criteria to assess official behavior and, consequently, are embodied in modern international law.

It is painfully obvious, however, that no willingness has been shown to carry forward the Nuremberg idea as a practical check on sovereign discretion. Jean-Paul Sartre has suggested: "It would have been enough if the organ created to judge the Nazis had remained in existence after having carried out that specific task, or if the organization of the United Nations had drawn all the consequences from what had just been done and had, by a vote in its General Assembly, consolidated the body's existence as a permanent tribunal empowered to take cognizance of and to judge all charges of war crimes, even if the accused should happen to be the government of those countries which through the agencies of their judges delivered the Nuremberg verdicts. *In this way, the implicit universality of the original intention would have been made clear and explicit*" (emphasis added).

Sartre, in his role as President of the Bertrand Russell War Crimes Proceedings, concludes that the organized international community has failed to fulfill this crucial promise to the peoples of the world at a historical time when state power is being used for criminal purposes, especially its interference in the liberation struggles of Third World peoples. As Sartre suggests, perhaps overstating the institutional issue and understating the ideological issue: "There is a cruel lack of that institution—which appeared, asserted its permanence and universality, defined irreversibly certain rights and obligations, only to disappear, leaving a void which must be filled and which nobody is filling."[2] The Russell Tribunal, a distinguished jury of conscience, was assembled on an *ad hoc* basis to fill part of the institutional void created by the special circumstances of American military aggression against the peoples of Vietnam. In truth, even if the Nuremberg idea had been embodied in a permanent institutional framework as Sartre urged, I doubt very much whether it would have been capable, for political reasons, of dealing directly with the central issues of oppression and abuse that result from the imperial structure of international society. It hardly needs to be explained that international institutions established and financed by sovereign governments reflect the balance of political forces operative in international society at a given time. The imperial sector, although greatly diminished in significance since 1945, is still able to prevent most adverse initiatives by international institutions, especially if the initiatives move beyond the rhetorical level of censure. Also, the spread of neo-colonial influence has led to the emergence of elites in many Third World states who are not at all disposed to subject governmental policy to any system of international moral or legal constraint. For this reason, the assessment of state conduct will depend on innovative para-legal political forms such as took temporary shape in the original Russell Tribunal.

As expected, mainstream media attacked the legitimacy of the Russell initiative, ignored its presentation of evidence (fully vindicated by subsequent inquiries from many sources), and scorned its conclusions. The principal criticism of Russell's initiative was contained in a letter by Charles De Gaulle, then President of France, denying Sartre's request to allow the tribunal to meet on French territory: "I have no need to tell you that justice of any sort, in principle as in execution, emanates from the State. Without impugning the motives which have inspired Lord Russell and his friends, I must recognize the fact that they have no power whatsoever, nor are they the holders of any international mandate, and that therefore they are unable to carry out any legal action."[3] De Gaulle's conception of justice tied to state power was in direct opposition to the vision embraced by the Russell Tribunal. As Sartre said at the outset of the proceedings: "The Russell Tribunal considers . . . that its legitimacy derives equally from its total powerlessness and from its universality."[4] Sartre is using "powerlessness" in an ironic sense, as he believes that ultimate power resides in the people and that the findings of the Tribunal can help guide mass opinion to right action. Again, addressing his fellow members of the Tribunal, Sartre states: "We, the jury, at the end of the session, will have to pronounce on these charges: are they well-founded or not? But the judges are everywhere: they are the peoples of the world, and in particular the American people. It is for them we are working."[5] The exposures of the criminality of the Vietnam enterprise encouraged the mobilization of the peoples of the world, including the American people, and this did contribute, in a small way, to the victory of the Vietnamese people against the American military juggernaut.

Nevertheless, a deeper conviction was desired by those who shaped the Russell initiative. As Bertrand Russell declared in a message to the Tribunal: "I hope this Tribunal will remain in existence, so that it may meet when necessary in the future in order to expose and condemn the future war crimes which will be committed inevitably until the peoples of the world follow the example of Vietnam."[6] Sartre also expressed the same sentiment, ". . . the Russell Tribunal will have no other concern as in its conclusions, than to bring about a general recognition of the need for an international institution for which it has neither the means nor the ambition to be a substitute"; "Yes, if the masses ratify our judgment, then it will become truth, and we, at the very moment [in] which we efface ourselves before those masses who make themselves the guardians and the mighty support for that truth, we will know that we have been legitimized and that the people, by showing us its agreement, is revealing a deeper need: The need for a real 'War Crimes Tribunal' to be brought into being as a permanent body—that is to say, the need that it should be possible to denounce and punish such crimes wherever and whenever they may be committed."[7]

The Russell Tribunal, as with Nuremberg, struck a commitment to the future though one, in my judgment, overly expressed in institution-building terms; it may also be wondered whether "commission of inquiry" or "peoples' hearing" is not more appropriate terminology to identify the quality of the proceedings than the more governmentally coercive image projected by use of the term "tribunal." Quite possibly, such naming is not essential, provided the sense of the undertaking can be adequately conveyed to larger and larger segments of the public. This commitment to keep the Russell process in being, however, failed. Such a failure has had serious consequences. International society at least requires a regular procedure of inquiry and exposure so long as the reality of international crimes persists. More than a decade has passed since the Russell Tribunal was established in 1967, and the spread of imperial and fascist crimes is rampant throughout the Third World. The need to expose the truth about these crimes is greater than ever, especially as their commission is so widespread and disguised by a virtual official conspiracy of silence. In Latin America, in Asia, and in Africa, vicious crimes are committed daily against the peoples of these countries. In the North the stockpiling, deployment, development, and threat of nuclear weapons of mass destruction are crimes against humanity of grave character. In addition, severe abuses of indigenous minorities are being neglected by organized international society. These circumstances demand that something must be done outside the formal structures of conventional diplomacy. . . .

As observed, those associated with the original Russell Tribunal emphasized the institutional deficiencies that resulted from the failure to create a permanent International War Crimes Tribunal without indicating any concern about deficiencies in international law. Such an emphasis was partly a reflection of the fact that the rules and standards of post-Nuremberg international law were adequate to enable a tribunal to assess the activities in question. Such is not the case, however, when one extends the scope of concern to embrace the full range of imperialist activities, which include the role of multinational corporations and international financial institutions. In this wider setting of inquiry a new corpus of legal principles is also needed to allow a procedure of inquiry to function in an authoritative principled fashion.

The Algiers Declaration also supplements the work of the United Nations in the human rights field, and constitutes a parallel document to the Universal Declaration of Human Rights (1948). In contrast to the United Nations instruments, the authors of the Algiers Declaration are relatively uninhibited by geopolitical rivalries or by the need to produce agreements that are generally acceptable to principal governmental members. The UN's need to please governments virtually nullifies progressive tendencies in the human rights area because a large cluster of governments are the principal violators.

Unlike the mainstream tradition of human rights law and activity, the Algiers Declaration also emphasizes the structural core of oppression. In its Preamble it notes that ". . . this is . . . a time" during which "new forms of imperialism evolve to oppress and exploit the peoples of the world . . . using vicious methods, with the complicity of governments. . . . Through direct or indirect intervention, through multinational enterprises, through manipulation of corrupt local politicians, with the assistance of military regimes based on police repression, torture and physical extermination of opponents, through a set of practices that has become known as neo-colonialism, imperialism extends its stranglehold over many peoples." The Preamble also endorses the rights of peoples "under subjection, to fight for their liberation and to benefit from other peoples' assistance in their struggle." Specific rights, beginning with the rights of a people to existence and self-determination, are then set forth in the operative provisions of Algiers Declaration. As with any instrument issued after debate, the consensus reflects some compromises in phrasing and emphasis. I would have preferred more emphasis placed on the rights of individuals (as distinct from peoples), and a more direct endorsement of the political rights of dissent, assembly, and opposition than can be found in the Algiers Declaration. Despite these reservations, I regard the Algiers Declaration as a major progressive juridical step which manifests a serious determination to put the rights of people on a solid legal base and reasserts the legitimacy of non-governmental initiatives in the area of human rights and criminal responsibility. Furthermore, by comparison with UN human rights instruments, the Algiers Declaration is a superior statement of political analysis, connecting the roots of imperialist oppression with its manifestations in an array of abuses. It helps fill the normative and ideological gaps that exist alongside the more obvious institutional void.

It is appropriate to ask the skeptical juridical question: On what basis can a group of individuals gathered together at a meeting give any legal status to a document that purports to set forth the rights of people? No conventional source of law supports such a law-making procedure. Even standards of behavior established by the General Assembly of the United Nations are not generally regarded as binding. The status of such resolutions is controversial, and there is a trend toward treating the General Assembly as the agency of the international community and, hence, possessing a law-making capacity. How, then, shall we regard the Algiers Declaration? Does it purport to be law? On behalf of what community does it speak? Who appointed Lelio Basso and his associates to rest their claims of authority to speak on behalf of "the peoples" of the world?

These are difficult perennial issues for both the international jurist and the international moralist. Naturally, to the extent that law and morality in world affairs are a reflection of the state system, the Algiers Declaration will be dismissed with scorn. Governments did not participate in the norm-shaping process, either directly or indirectly. The fundamental claim of the Algiers Declaration, in contrast, is that the peoples of the world possess the ultimate law-making authority, and that the validity of governmental law-making capacity rests on a prior delegation of competence by the people. How such a delegation takes place and is expressed is admittedly difficult to specify. Implicit in this view is also the contention that there is an inalienable competence that has not and cannot be delegated. In an earlier period, theories of natural rights were relied upon. Such explanations are still helpful to the extent that they rest upon the conviction that the most fundamental level of moral and legal reality is associated with the will and character of the people.

This affirmation of competence still leaves the question of representation unanswered: Who appointed Bertrand Russell or Lelio Basso? In the world of today, given the pretensions of the absolute state, there is no procedure by which the peoples can gather to express and assert their own demands as to their rights or appoint others to do so on their behalf. At the same time, patterns of exploitation and oppression obviously exist, although much propaganda prevents their clear discernment. The Algiers Declaration is, in the first instance, an argument and appeal, just as was, indeed, the 1776 Declaration of Independence (who appointed Thomas Jefferson and colleagues? By what authority did they represent even American opinion?).

The claim of representation rests ultimately on the popular acceptance of the Algiers Declaration's understanding of exploitation and oppression as a by-product of an imperial world order that needs to be dismantled to allow the peoples of the world to experience lives of dignity and satisfaction. In this sense, the Algiers Declaration is more of a political document than a legal or moral one and, as such, possesses an educational, mobilizing intention. The Basso group, therefore, has no special competence aside from the persuasiveness of its critique and its positive vision. Its legitimacy is inseparable from its potentiality. It deserves a provisional benefit of the doubt partly because its authors and endorsers have no vested economic or bureaucratic interest and have a long, honorable identity associated with progressive politics.

Of course, such a rationale is shaky in some respects, but no more so than other claims of authority at the margins of accepted legitimacy. Whenever a group of individuals assert rights on behalf of a wider community, their formal position appears weak. Surely the same doubts that we have been considering with respect to the Algiers Declaration pertain to such earlier inspirational documents as the Magna Carta and Declaration of Independence, as well as to the Universal Declaration of Human Rights. Surely the capacity of governments to act on behalf of the world as a whole, as in creating the League of Nations and United Nations, is subject to challenge on representational grounds.

At this stage in international history, those who endorse the Algiers Declaration, and the steps taken to give it impact, are expressing their lack of confidence in existing international procedures and their positive conviction that the rights of peoples must be upheld by new kinds of direct action. The validation of this position will depend upon its eventual effects. In the meantime, it advances an appeal to those who understand its arguments to join in the struggle to make its vision of peoples' rights into a reality. Achieving a widening circle of participation in the struggle would be one aspect of validation, and in this regard, it should be noted that the Basso group is not content with declaring intentions and good sentiments. The Algiers Declaration is the premise for a process of political action designed to exert as much influence as possible.

The issue of effectiveness is the central concern. Even the right to meet and discuss can be impaired by governments refusing to allow such activities on their territory. The Russell Tribunal had difficulty finding a government that would tolerate its presence. Furthermore, those who endorse the Algiers Declaration lack any tax base or military establishment, and because of this there is an absence of power in a tangible sense. Nevertheless, power can be gradually acquired with ingenuity and perseverance, and at this early stage, organization and enthusiasm on the part of a few is critical. This has been understood from the outset by the Basso group.

Accordingly, at Algiers in July 1976, the International League for the Rights and Liberation of Peoples was simultaneously brought into existence to give a continuing institutional backing to the substantive concerns of the Algiers Declaration. The most ambitious project of the League is, of course, to launch an International Peoples' Tribunal that will be available to investigate, assess, and report on allegations of violations of the rights of peoples. This Tribunal, operating on a continuing, professional, and objective basis, may have an historic opportunity to expose the basic structure of imperial abuse in a variety of specific contexts. Its mobilizing potential is enormous, although one must anticipate a hostile response from mainstream media and most governments. An International Peoples' Tribunal carries out one dimension of the promise to the future made at Nuremberg. It keeps the Nuremberg idea alive, and it compensates to some extent for the failure of governments and international institutions to uphold the rights of peoples.

Of course, what Bertrand Russell started and Lelio Basso is continuing and extending is not the kind of legacy of Nuremberg that was contemplated in 1945. Hopes were higher, at that time, for a permanent international criminal framework agreed to by principal governments. As already discussed, subsequent international patterns of conflict and domination, as well as the reluctance of governments to submit their activities to external scrutiny, have confined the original Nuremberg impulse to its original World War II setting. In the setting of the late 1970's, with formal decolonialization virtually complete, only a populist continuation of the Nuremberg idea is plausible. The success of an International Peoples' Tribunal will depend upon the support it generates as a means of carrying on the anti-imperial struggle in a variety of contexts. . . .

NOTES

1. General Assembly Resolution 95(1); for text of Nuremberg Principles as formulated by the ILC, see R. A. Falk, G. Kolko, and R. J. Lifton, eds., *Crimes of War*, 1971, pp. 107–108.

2. Sartre's Inaugural Statement, John Duffett, ed., *Against the Crimes of Silence: Proceedings of International War Crimes Tribunal,* 1968, pp. 41, 42.
3. Text of De Gaulle's letter in Duffett, pp. 28–29.
4. Duffett, p. 43.
5. Duffett, p. 45.
6. Duffett, p. 39.
7. Duffett, p. 44.

29. Emerging Human Rights: A New Generation for the 1980s?

Stephen P. Marks

INTRODUCTION

. . . The difficulty of identifying exactly what is meant by "human rights" is particularly acute as regards the emergence of new human rights. While philosophical and transdisciplinary dimensions of human rights may be far removed from actual law practice, repression, oppression, and exploitation deserve the attention of all lawyers and students of the law. . . .

I do not intend to cover the philosophical and transdisciplinary dimensions; instead, I will attempt to outline the process by which certain standards, identified by the organized international community as "human rights," attain international recognition, and to suggest some directions this process seems to be taking in the 1980s. After some general remarks on this process and on the nature of established human rights (civil and political, on the one hand, and economic, social, and cultural, on the other), I will discuss the notion of a new generation of human rights and the various rights proposed for inclusion in this new generation. In this way, I hope to impart a sense of the dynamic aspect of human rights and their place in international relations and international law today and tomorrow.

THE PROCESS OF THE EMERGENCE OF INTERNATIONAL HUMAN RIGHTS

According to the classical definition of the sources of international law, reaffirmed in article 38 of the Statute of the International Court of Justice,[1] the rules of international law are to be found in international treaties, international custom, general principles of law, and, as subsidiary sources, judicial decisions and the teachings of the most qualified publicists. The law-creating process in international law is based on these sources, and the existence of a rule must be proved by reference to them. The first meaning of the notion of the emergence of international human rights is therefore *the establishment of rules of international law concerning human rights according to the law-creating process as defined in international law.*

Now all this sounds very straightforward. Anyone who has studied international law knows, however, how exceedingly complex it is to determine what the exact rules are. In the field of human rights this determination is rendered even more problematical by the temptation to believe that a desirable proposition is a human right and to rely on the slightest evidence, such as a resolution of the General Assembly of the United Nations, to prove it.

One of the most insightful American human rights scholars, Richard Bilder, has written that "[i]n practice a claim is an international human right if the United Nations General Assembly says it is."[2] He did not, of course, mean that literally. The point is that U.N. resolutions occupy a crucial role in the norm-creating process. This process may be schematized as follows: A constant feature of human existence is the existence of *human needs*. To satisfy them, we generally use self-help. When there are social constraints on the satisfaction of certain needs, they may become *claims* made by individuals or groups seeking such satisfaction through the social process. Other needs become recognized as requiring constant satisfaction and correspond to *values* in the society. One of the social institutions characterizing societies, including international society, is legislation, by which certain claims, values, or interests are formally recognized.

International human rights are those human needs that have received formal recognition as rights through the sources of international law. According to Professor Louis Sohn, the availability of the General Assembly has made a new method of international legislation possible, what he calls "the emergence of a new customary rule of international law relating to the establishment of a new law-creating process in the field of human rights."[3]

The problem with the emergence of human rights is that it is often difficult to distinguish between rules *lex lata* and rules *de lega ferenda*, between positive law and law in the making, between "hard" law and "soft" law. As Professor Georges Abi-Saab put it,

In reality, law does not come out of social nothingness, nor does it come into being with a "big bang." In most cases, it is a progressive and imprescriptible growth over a large grey zone separating emerging social values from the well established legal rule; a zone which is very difficult (and sometimes even impossible) to divide *a posteriori* between the two.[4]

At various stages in the history of human rights, doubts have been expressed—and indeed severe opposition voiced—concerning the appropriateness of proclaiming certain values as "human rights." A look backwards to the human rights of earlier generations may make this clearer before we consider the prospects for the 1980s.

THE HUMAN RIGHTS OF EARLIER GENERATIONS

For reasons that are not our subject here, the commonly recognized starting point for the emergence of international human rights as we know them today is the movement for the "rights of man" in eighteenth-century Europe. By tracing the first international standards in this area to the philosophers and revolutionaries of Europe and America, I in no way wish to give the impression that the concept of human rights is exclusively or even essentially Western. All cultures and civilizations in one way or another have defined rights and duties of man in society on the basis of certain elementary notions of equality, justice, dignity, and worth of the individual (or of the group).[5] Due to the privileged position Western Europe and North America occupied throughout the eighteenth, nineteenth, and the first half of the twentieth centuries in the elaboration of international law, the French and American revolutions have left a permanent imprint on human rights.[6]

For our purposes, we may consider this the "first generation" of human rights. Three points are to be retained. First, the demand for the recognition of these rights arose in a "revolutionary" context. Second, the revolutionaries felt the necessity to proclaim the human rights they defended in the form of a solemn declaration. Third, they proclaimed these rights in the name of all (free) men, in the sense that the rights were not limited geographically. These features will reappear in successive generations of human rights.

Human rights, as they emerged during the first generation, were conceived negatively as "freedoms from" rather than as positive "rights to." They required the prohibition of interference by the state in the freedom of the individual to do as he or she pleased. This conception is epitomized by the statement attributed to H. L. Mencken, that "All government is, of course, against liberty."

The rights that belong to this generation are essentially freedom of opinion, conscience, and religion, freedom of expression and of the press, freedom of assembly, freedom of movement, freedom from arbitrary detention or arrest, and freedom from interference in correspondence. To these should be added the right to property, which was fundamental to the interests fought for in the French and American revolutions and to the rise of capitalism.

It would be an oversimplification to say that the so-called first generation of human rights corresponds exclusively to the notion of "negative rights" or "rights of abstention" I have been describing. The right to participate in free elections, the right to a fair trial, and so on cannot be guaranteed without some contribution by the state. Even rights to relief for the poor and to education, precursors of present-day "economic and social rights," were included in the French constitution of 1791.[7]

The social upheavals of the nineteenth century against the exploitation arising from abuses of the rights of the first generation drew inspiration from the philosophical and political positions of socialist and Marxist writings. They led to the emergence of a new generation of human rights of a different nature than the "negative" rights of the first. The freedoms of the first generation had meant for the majority of the working class and peoples of conquered lands the right to be exploited and colonized. They were regarded as "formal" freedoms that neglected the material realities of social conditions. The national constitutions adopted in 1917 after revolutionary struggles against such exploitation in Mexico and Russia, international instruments, particularly the Constitution of the International Labour Organisation of 1919, and international labor standards ushered in the second generation of human rights, a generation of economic, social, and cultural rights, characterized by the intervention rather than the abstention of the state. Indeed, the rights to decent working conditions, to social security, to education, and to health were inconceivable without an active role by the state. . . .

Quincy Wright summarized the distinction between the first two generations very succinctly in 1947, when he wrote:

Individual rights are in the main correlative to negative duties of the State, and social rights are in the main correlative to positive duties of the State. Individual rights require that the State abstain from interference with the free exercise by the individual of his capacities, while the social rights require that the State interfere with many things the individual would like to do. . . .[8]

Once again, the distinguishing criteria should not be pushed too far. Several economic and social rights had, as I have said, already been recognized in certain texts, and many of these rights as currently formulated may be considered individual freedoms, such as the right to join a trade union. The notion of "generation" is only meaningful if it is used to identify a *trend* and not to establish hard and fast categories.

A NEW GENERATION OF HUMAN RIGHTS

In the literature of human rights it has usually been sufficient to distinguish the civil and political rights from the economic, social, and cultural rights in terms of "catalogues" or "categories."[9] Why have I introduced the notion of "generation"? The answer is simply that the former terms are static, whereas the concept of human rights in international law and politics is eminently dynamic—as is law in general, of course. At the time they are proclaimed, human rights are often couched in terms that would make them, according to their authors, valid for all times. Indeed, the feeling that certain propositions have such an immutable character is one of the reasons the expression "human" rights is preferred for them.

Although the natural law tradition is closely linked with the proclamation of human rights,[10] the history of human rights, both national and international, clearly reveals that the formulation and the very existence of rights vary over time. Slavery was compatible with human rights in the eighteenth century, and property was considered an inalienable right. Freedom from slavery subsequently occupied its proper place among internationally recognized human rights, while the right to property was progessively limited to the point of being replaced, in the documents on the establishment of a new international economic order, by the "inalienable right" of a state "to nationalization or transfer of ownership to its nationals."[11]

In fact, much can be learned by relating a proclamation of human rights to the historical context in which it occurs. The present catalogue of human rights contained in the International Bill of Human Rights can be traced back to three different revolutionary movements, two of which I have already mentioned—first, the "bourgeois" revolutions, particularly in France and America, in the last quarter of the eighteenth century; second, the socialist, anti-exploitation revolutions of the first two decades of this century; and third, the anticolonialist revolutions that began immediately after the Second World War and culminated in the independence of many nations around 1960. The third revolutionary movement affected recent international human rights texts by giving a privileged status to self-determination and nondiscrimination. This is particularly true of the Declaration on the Granting of Independence to Colonial Countries and Peoples of 1960, the Proclamation of Teheran of 1968, and the common Article I of both Covenants of 1966. Principle "e" of Resolution 32/130 of 1977 offers a clear statement of the perspective of the anticolonialist revolution:

In approaching human rights questions within the United Nations system, the international community should accord, or continue to accord, priority to the search for solutions to the mass and flagrant violations of human rights of peoples and persons affected by situations such as those resulting from *apartheid*, from all forms of racial discrimination, from colonialism, from foreign domination and occupation, from aggression and threats against national sovereignty, national unity and territorial integrity, as well as from the refusal to recognize the fundamental rights of peoples to self-determination and of every nation to the exercise of full sovereignty of its wealth and natural resources.[12]

The three movements I have just described were revolutionary in that they involved a radical change in the power structure. That certain historical factors at play in the 1980s may also have that effect is a possible explanation for the emergence of certain new human rights. Such new rights are strongly resisted, but let us keep in mind that when rights were proclaimed following other revolutions, their detractors too were numerous and vociferous. Think of Thomas Paine answering Edmund Burke's attack on the French revolution in his brilliant *The Rights of Man* (1791–1792), or the persistent reluctance in the United States to take economic, social, and cultural rights seriously, or the continued defiance of the international community by *apartheid* regimes.

What then are the factors of historical significance which can justify speaking of a "new generation" of human rights? I maintain that there are certain major planetary concerns, which, although they were always present and sometimes acutely felt in the past, have taken on a renewed urgency at a time when the legislative process in the field of human rights is particularly receptive.

By identifying certain rights as belonging to a new generation, I am actually underlining two features that these rights share:

1. they belong neither to the individualistic tradition of the first generation nor to the socialist tradition of the second; and
2. they are at an early phase of the legislative process and show promise of being accepted as international human rights during the 1980s.

The distinguishing characteristics of the new generation of human rights have been expressed by the person who in fact forged the notion of a "third generation of human rights," Karel Vasak. In his inaugural lecture to the Tenth Study Session of the International Institute of Human Rights in July 1979,[13] he said that the new human rights of the third generation

are new in the aspirations they express, are new from the point of view of human rights in that they seek to infuse the human dimension into areas where it has all too often been missing, having been left to the State, or States. . . . [T]hey are new in that they may both be *invoked against* the State and *demanded* of it; but above all (and herein lies their essential characteristic) they can be realized only through the concerted efforts of all the actors on the social scene: the individual, the State, public and private bodies and the international community.

Vasak has further distinguished the three generations of human rights as corresponding successively to each of the elements of the motto of the French revolution: *liberté, égalité, fraternité*. The third generation is the generation of human rights predicated on brotherhood (*fraternité*), in the sense of solidarity. Vasak has, in fact, called these rights "solidarity rights" or "rights of solidarity."

This notion of solidarity is not unique to the third generation of human rights: a minimum of solidarity, in the sense of a sharing of purpose and an agreeing on modes of action among various elements of society, is essential to the realization of the rights of the first and second generations as well. It is, however, the key feature of the rights of the third generation, which are inconceivable without a very broad sharing of objectives and commitment to certain forms of action. It is in the nature of certain planetary concerns, such as peace, development, ecological balance, and communication, that such solidarity is a prerequisite to action commensurate with the needs.

PLANETARY CONCERNS CURRENTLY PROPOSED FOR REDEFINITION AS HUMAN RIGHTS

I think we can safely say that during the last few decades several planetary concerns have been the subject of genuinely interdisciplinary investigation and enlightened debate by representatives of practically all the peoples of the Earth, in a way that has not occurred previously. Sometimes this investigation and this debate concern matters which have already been consecrated in basic human rights texts. The *right to food*, for example, appears in article 25 of the Universal Declaration of Human Rights.[14] The World Food Conference in 1974 proclaimed the Universal Declaration on the Eradication of Hunger and Malnutrition, the first article of which stipulates that [e]very man, woman and child has the inalienable right to be free from hunger and malnutrition in order to develop fully and maintain their physical and mental faculties."[15] In such a case, there is no need to consider that there is a new human right. However, the right to food is a good example of a right that has been internationally recognized for over thirty years but to which very little thought has been given in terms of effective implementation. In fact, this right belongs among the solidarity rights, since concerted efforts involving radical changes among and within nations will be required before the 800 million hungry can notice the difference. The Executive Director of the U.N. World Food Council has said, "A truly major effort to eradicate hunger . . . is a political imperative for building world cooperation and solidarity among all peoples and all nations."[16] So, although the right to food is not normally listed as a right of the new generation, it is one by its nature.

The other rights to be considered have an interesting and, I think, revealing feature in common. In most cases, before there is an attempt to postulate a "right to . . ." there is the development of a "law of . . . ." In other words, a new body of legal norms or a revision of legal thinking on a given problem provides the conceptual framework for identifying first the legal implications of the problem, then the human rights implications, and finally the reformulation of the whole problem in terms of a new human right.

Six areas are currently under consideration: environment, development, peace, the common heritage, communication, and humanitarian assistance.

The case of *environment* is perhaps the most "classical" case of a set of claims which have been given a holistic formulation in terms of human rights. All the features of a right of the new generation are there: elaboration of a specialized body of law, an easily identifiable international legislative process, incorporation of the right as a human right within municipal legal systems, and need for concerted efforts of all social actors.

The growth of "environmental law" at the national and international levels has been well advanced by the establishment of specialized law reviews, environmental law institutes and councils, systematic textbooks on the subject, specialized courses in law schools, and so forth. This body of law is the result of the popular pressure against mismanagement of the environment and in favor of greater ecological conscience, particularly during the 1960s. The existence of such legislation, however, is not of itself a sign that a human right is involved.

At the international level the first formulation in human rights terms was in the Stockholm Declaration, adopted by the U.N. Conference on the Environment in 1972. Principle I of the Declaration reads as follows: "Man has the fundamental right to freedom, equality and adequate conditions of life, in an environment of a quality that permits a life of dignity and well-being, and he bears a solemn responsibility to protect and improve the environment for present and future generations."[17] That text does not state explicitly that there is a human right to a clean and ecologically balanced environment, but it does express the issue in human rights terms. . . .

An interparliamentary conference on the environment held in Bonn in 1971 resolved that mankind has a right to a healthy environment. In 1972 the Consultative Assembly of the Council of Europe adopted a recommendation proposing to study whether or not the right to a decent environment should be raised to the status of a human right. . . . In the meantime the government of the Federal Republic of Germany proposed that the right to a healthy and balanced environment be incorporated into an additional protocol to the European Convention on Human Rights. That a protocol or other instrument has not been adopted does not mean that this right has been rejected. On the contrary, the constitutions of numerous nations and states—for example, Spain, Portugal, Peru, Yugoslavia—have already affirmed it expressly. Other less explicit formulations exist in the constitutions of Illinois, Rhode Island, Poland, and Hungary, and other constitutions—those of Greece, Switzerland, Czechoslovakia, the German Democratic Republic, the Peoples Republic of China, the U.S.S.R., Sri Lanka, and Bulgaria—stipulate that the government shall protect the environment. These examples and the conclusions of numerous scientific or nongovernmental meetings on the subject[18] justify including this right among the new generation of human rights emerging in the 1980s.

Like other solidarity rights, this one has both an individual and a collective dimension. The individual right is the right of any victim or potential victim of an environmentally damaging activity to obtain the cessation of the activity and reparation for the damage suffered. The collective dimension implies the duty of the state to contribute through international cooperation to resolving environmental problems at a global level. As with all solidarity rights, the collective aspect means, in the last analysis, that the state and all other appropriate social actors have the duty to place the human interest before the national or individual interest.

The right to *development* as a human right has been the subject of extensive reflection and proposed formulations for nearly a decade and is well advanced in acquiring the status of an internationally recognized human right. As with environment, there has grown up a branch of international law on development,[19] with institutes, textbooks, specialized courses, and conferences.

The first formulation of this right as a human right, which is a direct precursor of current international references on the subject, was the inaugural lesson given at the International Institute of Human Rights in Strasbourg in 1972 by Kéba M'Baye, first President of the Supreme Court of Senegal, Vice-President of the International Institute of Human Rights, President of the International Commission of Jurists, and member of the Commission on Human Rights of the U.N. . . .

The content of this right has been analyzed not only by M'Baye and the U.N. study, but also by Hector Gros-Espiell, Georges Abi-Saab, Wil Zerwey, and others. Briefly summarized, it is the *individual right* to benefit from a development policy based on the satisfaction of material and nonmaterial human needs and to participate in the development process, and the *collective right* of developing countries (and "peoples" not yet having exercised their right to self-determination) to succeed in establishing a new international economic order, that is, in eliminating the structural obstacles to their development inherent in current international economic relations. The more precise definition of the subjects, objects, beneficiaries, and duty-holders of this right is too complex a matter for our purposes. Suffice it to say that the notion of "solidarity" is more than evident in the realization of this right of the new generation.

The right to *peace* is not difficult to deduce from the U.N. Charter, the Kellogg-Briand Pact, the Declaration on Principles of Friendly Relations, the Final Act of Helsinki, and many other basic documents. Moreover, the existence of a "law of peace," in contrast to the newer "environmental law" and "development law," is part of the classical subdivision of the subject matter of international law. The formulation of a right to peace as a human right, however, is a more recent phenomenon. Philip Alston has recalled several efforts, in several documents in the late 1940s, to incorporate variations of the right of states to peace.[20]

. . . A brief word about the content of the right to peace: it is the right of every individual to contribute to efforts for peace, including refusal to participate in the military effort, and the collective right of every state to benefit from the full respect by other states of the principles of non-use of force, of non-aggression, of peaceful settlement of disputes, of the Geneva Conventions and Additional Protocols and similar standards, as well as from the implementation of policies aimed at general and complete disarmament under effective international control. What I have just said is no more than an illustration of the sort of considerations that should go into the definition of this right. No authorized formulation exists, but I am convinced that this right will be increasingly refined in the coming years.[21]

The right to *benefit from the common heritage of mankind* has also been suggested as a human right of the third generation. In the Declaration of Principles Governing the Sea-Bed of December 17, 1970, the General Assembly proclaimed that the sea-bed beyond the limits of national jurisdiction was part of the common heritage of mankind. The concept has been broadened to other areas such as space, bodies in space, the Antarctic, and even more abstract concepts such as monuments, sites, and cultural traditions and scientific and technical progress.

. . . If conceived of exclusively as a right of states, this right, like the others proclaimed by the Charter on the Economic Rights and Duties of States, not only is endangered by the neocolonialism of the great powers, which Bedjaoui has warned of, but also runs the risk of benefiting only the elites in the developing countries and perpetuating the inequalities within nations, while reducing slightly the inequality between nations. In this respect the idea that certain human rights may be rights of peoples may be a valid one, particularly for the human rights of the new generation. The concept of rights of peoples is a highly controversial matter in international human rights today. Be that as it may, the right to the common heritage of mankind belongs, as Bedjaoui put it, to the "law of solidarity," which is a further reason to place it within the solidarity rights of the new generation of human rights. . . .

The right to *communicate* has also been considered as involving the redefinition, in the contemporary context, of existing human rights. The International Commission for the Study of Communication Problems analyzed the evolution of this notion and included the following in its report:

The concept of the "right to communicate" has yet to receive its final form and its full content. Far from being, as some apparently maintain, an already well-established principle from which logical consequences might, here and now, be drawn, it is still at the stage of being thought through in all its implications and gradually enriched. Once its potential applications have been explored, . . . the international community will have to decide what intrinsic value such a concept possesses. It will be required to recognize—or not—the existence of a possible new human right, one to be added to, not substituted for, those that have already been declared.[22]

Of course, considerable thought has already been given to the content of this new right and its relation to existing rights, such as freedom of opinion and expression, including freedom to seek, receive, and impart information and ideas through any media and regardless of frontiers.[23] One of the authors of a background paper for the Commission for the Study of Communication Problems, Jean d'Arcy, after recalling the existing rights, affirmed that

Today, a new step forward seems possible: recognition of man's right to communicate, deriving from our latest victories over time and space and from our increased awareness of the phenomenon of communication. . . . Today, it is clear to us that it encompasses all these freedoms but adds to them, both for individuals and societies, the concepts of access, participation, two-way information flow—all of which are vital, as we now sense, for the harmonious development of man and mankind.[24]

The language used in proposing this right is clearly that of the new generation of human rights: the realities of the last quarter of this century justify concerted efforts to contend with a challenge of planetary proportions; the international community is providing a legislative process through which the concepts involved can be expressed in terms of human rights; as a human right it is both a synthesis or composite of existing rights and the expression of an original idea; it has both an individual and a collective dimension. Many of these features, as we have seen, are found in the other new human rights of the new generation.

The final right being considered as a new human right is the right to *humanitarian assistance*. The idea that in time of dire need all human groups have a right to assistance from the international community is perhaps the clearest example of a right of "solidarity" in the most traditional sense of that term. In time of natural catastrophe (epidemics, famines, earthquakes, floods, tornadoes, typhoons, cyclones, avalanches, hurricanes, volcanic eruptions, drought, and fire), mass exodus or massive accumulation of refugees or displaced persons, or similar events, the failure to assist the victims often means death on a wide scale. The task is in many cases beyond the capacity of any single donor state or of an institution like the International Committee of the Red Cross or the United Nations Disaster Relief Office.

Faced with particularly enormous problems of this type, certain assemblies or relief organizations have expressed recently the idea that the victims have a right to international efforts of assistance. It is difficult to find, for the moment, more than a moral right. Nevertheless, the right to international humanitarian assistance has several of the features of rights of the new generation: concerted efforts, both an individual and a collective dimension (the individual victim's right to receive his or her share of the assistance sent and the collective right of the group to benefit from that assistance), and so forth.

The right to humanitarian assistance already exists as a legal right in international humanitarian law. The Geneva Conventions of August 12, 1949, provide for the care of the wounded, sick, and shipwrecked, as well as for prisoners of war and civilian populations. These rights are so absolute that the conventions even specify that the beneficiaries of the rights, including the right to be cared for and the right to intellectual and spiritual assistance, cannot renounce those rights.[25] The Additional Protocols to the Geneva Conventions reinforce this right to humanitarian assistance. Article 10 of Protocol I and article 7 of Protocol II, for example, specify that "[a]ll the wounded, sick and shipwrecked, . . . shall be respected and protected. In all circumstances they shall be treated humanely and shall receive, to the fullest extent practicable and with the least possible delay, the medical care and attention required by their condition."[26] The right to humanitarian assistance is further protected by the provisions concerning respect for the protection of civil defense organizations that carry out "humanitarian tasks intended to protect the civilian population. . . ."[27]

The duties relating to humanitarian assistance in the Geneva Conventions and Additional Protocols are, of course, duties incumbent on the states parties. The idea of a right to international humanitarian assistance would go beyond these instruments, while incorporating certain provisions of them. . . .

SOME OBJECTIONS AND A TENTATIVE CONCLUSION

Much hostility has been voiced against the idea of a new generation of human rights. Not only is proliferation of rights considered to be dangerous, but also the use of the term "generation" implies, the detractors say, that the rights belonging to earlier generations are outdated. It is also frequently said that the rights of the new generation are too vague to be justiciable and are no more than slogans, at best useful for advancing laudable goals of the U.N., at worst useful for the propaganda of certain countries.

Indeed, it would weaken the idea of human rights in general if numerous claims or values were indiscriminately proclaimed as human rights. It is also true that the essential normative task in the field of human rights was accomplished during the first three decades after the founding of the U.N., and that the more urgent task now is implementation. Nevertheless, I have tried to stress the dynamic nature of the process by which these rights are recognized and the consequent emergence of new human rights in the 1980s.

As the 1980s begin, the human rights specialist is, to a certain extent, faced with the choice of resisting the rights which, whether he likes it or not, are emerging, or understanding and contributing to the process by which a limited number of new rights will succeed in attaining international recognition because (a) the need for them is sufficiently great and (b) the international community is ready to recognize them as human rights. He should seek to apply rigorous standards to the definition of new rights, and in particular, as Professor Rivero of France has insisted, see that they have a clearly defined object and an identifiable subject and can be reasonably expected to be enforced. Many human rights already recognized for several decades fall short of these standards. The proclamation of these rights nevertheless increased the likelihood that they would be translated into law and practice. As long as emerging rights are not so unrealistic or trivial as to be treated with mockery, their recognition does serve the advancement of the cause of human rights without endangering the rights of earlier generations. . . .

NOTES

The author is a Program Officer at the Ford Foundation, and he wrote this article while at the Division of Human Rights and Peace, UNESCO. B.A., Stanford University; French State Doctorate in Law, Institut des Hautes-Etudes Internationales, Paris. He is responsible for the choice and the presentation of the facts contained in this article and the opinions expressed therein.

1. Statute of the International Court of Justice, *done* June 26, 1945, 59 Stat. 1055, T.S. No. 993.

2. Bilder, *Rethinking International Human Rights: Some Basic Questions*, 2 HUMAN RIGHTS J. 557, 559 (1969).

3. Sohn, *Protection of Human Rights Through International Legislation*, 1 RENÉ CASSIN AMICORUM DISCIPULORUMQUE LIBER 330 (1969).

4. Abi-Saab, *The Legal Formulation of a Right to Development (Subjects and Content)*, in THE RIGHT TO DEVELOPMENT AT THE INTERNATIONAL LEVEL (Dupuy ed. 1980).

5. Among the publications which illustrate the universality of human rights, see UNITED NATIONS EDUCATIONAL, SCIENTIFIC AND CULTURAL ORGANIZATION, BIRTH-RIGHT OF MAN (1969), and HUMAN RIGHTS: COMMENTS AND INTERPRETATIONS (1949).

6. For a discussion of this heritage, *see* L. HENKIN, THE RIGHTS OF MAN TODAY (1978).

7. *See* CONSTITUTION of 1873 arts. 18, 21, 22, 23, 24 (France).

8. Wright, *Relationship Between Different Categories of Human Rights*, in HUMAN RIGHTS: COMMENTS AND INTERPRETATIONS, *supra* note 5, at 147.

9. *See, e.g.*, Szabo, *Remarques sur le développement du catalogue international des droits de l'homme*, 1 RENÉ CASSIN AMICORUM DISCIPULORUMQUE LIBER 347 (1969).

10. *See, e.g.*, Castberg, *Natural Law and Human Rights*, 1 HUMAN RIGHTS J. 14 (1968).

11. Declaration on the Establishment of a New International Economic Order, G.A. Res. 3201, 6 (Special) U.N. GAOR, Supp. (No. 1) 4, U.N. Doc. A/9559 (1974).

12. Alternative Approaches . . . for Improving the Effective Enjoyment of Human Rights and Fundamental Freedoms, G.A. Res. 32/130 (1)(e), 32 U.N. GAOR, Supp. (No. 45) 151, U.N. Doc. A/32/45 (1978).

13. To be published in HUMAN RIGHTS JOURNAL.

14. *See* Universal Declaration of Human Rights, art. 25, G.A. Res. 217A, U.N. Doc. A/810, at 71 (1948).

15. Report of the World Food Conference, Nov. 5–16, 1974, U.N. Doc. No. E/CONF.65/20, at 2 (1975).

16. *Quoted* in BRANDT COMMISSION, NORTH-SOUTH: A PROGRAM FOR SURVIVAL 90. For a more critical analysis of the world food situation, *see* S. GEORGE, HOW THE OTHER HALF DIES: THE REAL REASONS FOR WORLD HUNGER (1976).

17. Report of the United Nations Conference on the Human Environment, June 5–16, 1972, U.N. Doc. A/CONF.48/Rev. 1, at 4 (1973).

18. *See, e.g.*, An Individual Right or an Obligation of the State? International Colloquium on the Right to a Humane Environment (1975).

19. Schachter, *The Evolving International Law of Development*, 15 COLUM. J. TRANSNAT'L L. 1 (1976).

20. Alston, The Right to Peace, UNESCO Doc. SS-80/CONF. 806/7.

21. *See* Bilder, *The Individual and the Right to Peace: The Right to Conscientious Dissent*, 11 BULL. PEACE PROPOSALS 387 (1980).

22. INTERNATIONAL COMMISSION FOR THE STUDY OF COMMUNICATION PROBLEMS, MANY VOICES, ONE WORLD 172 (1980).

23. *See* G.A. Res. 217A, art. 19, U.N. Doc. A/810 (1948).

24. *See* J. D'ARCY, THE RIGHT TO COMMUNICATE (n.d.).

25. *See, e.g.*, Geneva Convention for the Amelioration of the Condition of the Wounded and Sick, ch. 1, art. 7, 6 U.S.T. 3115, T.I.A.S. No. 3362 (1949). Similar provisions appear in article 7 of the second and third Geneva Conventions and in article 8 of the fourth.

26. International Committee of the Red Cross. Protocol Added to the Geneva Convention of Aug. 12, 1949, at 11, 95 (1977).

27. *Id.* at 45–51.

30. Dissenting Opinion

A. Alvarez

II

. . . The questions concerning the Territory of South-West Africa submitted to the Court for opinion have been complicated and even made obscure in the discussions which have taken place for several years between various Governments and in the Councils and Assemblies of the League of Nations and the United Nations. They have been dealt with from various angles: from the angle of private law, when the nature of the mandate, its termination, the nature of the obligations, the lapsing of contracts, etc., were considered, and from the angle of international law, when sovereignty, treaties and their purposes, certain provisions of the League of Nations Covenant and the United Nations Charter were being discussed. This was done on the basis of traditional views in these matters, and by applying the classical method of interpretation of conventions and treaties.

In fact, the question is an entirely new one and comes under the new international law. It is the duty of the Court therefore to consider it, not only in the light of principles laid down in the Covenant or the Charter, but also, as we shall see later, in accordance with the nature, aims and purposes of this law.

III

For this reason, we must first consider briefly the nature of this new international law and the new criterion which must be applied to the questions before the Court.

This law is the result and outcome of the great transformations in the life of nations which have taken place since the first world war, and mostly after the 1939 cataclysm.

The *community* of States, which had hitherto remained *anarchical*, has become in fact an *organized international society*. This transformation is a fact which does not require the consecration of an international agreement. This society consists not only of States, groups and even associations of States, but also of other international entities. It has an existence and a personality distinct from those of its members. It has its own purposes. On the other hand, international relations present various aspects: political, economic, psychological, etc., and to-day possess a dynamic character, complexity and variety which they did not show formerly.

All these transformations have had a great influence on international law: a new international law has emerged. It is new for three reasons: it includes new questions in addition to traditional questions in a new form; it rests on the basic reconstruction of fundamental principles of classical international law, and brings them into harmony with the new conditions of the life of peoples; finally, it is based on the new social régime which has appeared, *the régime of interdependence,* which is taking the place of the individualistic régime which has, up to now, provided the basis of both national and international life. This new régime has given rise to what may be called *social interdependence* which is taking the place of traditional *individualism.* I prefer the expression "social interdependence" to "social solidarity," which has a variety of connotations.

The purposes of the new international law, based on social interdependence, differ from those of classical international law: they are to harmonize the rights of States, to promote co-operation between them and to give ample room to common interests; its purpose is also to favour cultural and social progress. In short, its purpose is to bring about what may be called *international social justice*.

To achieve these purposes this law must lay stress on the notion of *obligation* of States, not only between themselves, but also toward the international community. It must limit absolute international sovereignty of States according to the new requirements of the life of peoples, and must yield to the changing necessities of that life.

Because of these characteristics the new international law is not of an exclusively juridical character. It has also political, economic, social, and psychological characteristics.

It is not a mere abstraction, a doctrinal speculation without any foundation in fact, as some would have it. In reality it takes root in the new conditions and the new requirements of the life of peoples in numerous recent social institutions of several countries, in the international judicial conscience which has been awakened mainly since the upheaval of 1914; in the Covenant of the League of Nations and in particular in the United Nations Charter (preamble, Arts. 1, 2, Chapters IV, V, IX, X, XI, XII, XIII, etc.) and in several resolutions and drafts of the Assemblies of those organizations; and in the declarations of the heads of former allied countries which have subsequently received the support of the people. It also springs from various resolutions of the last Pan-american Conferences, some of which tend to incorporate new great moral, political and social ideas, either in continental international law, or in world international law.

Therefore, the new international law has a more positive basis than classical international law, which rests on principles and rules often derived from speculation and from doctrines and customs, many of which have become obsolete.

This new law is in formation. It is for the International Court of Justice to develop it by its judgments or its advisory opinions, and in laying down valuable precedents. The theories of jurists must also share in the development of this law.

At this point, I want to stress the idea which I have already expressed in previous individual opinions: the Court must not apply international law such as it existed before the upheavals of 1914 and 1939 but must apply the law which actually exists to-day.

Indeed, since that time the international life of peoples and, consequently, the law of nations have consistently undergone profound changes and have assumed new directions and tendencies which must be taken into consideration.

The Court must, therefore, declare what is the new international law which is based upon the present requirements and conditions of the life of peoples: otherwise, it would be applying a law which is obsolete in many respects, and would disregard these requirements and conditions as well as the spirit of the Charter which is the principal source of the new international law.

In so doing, it may be said that the Court *creates* the law; it creates it by modifying classical law; in fact it merely *declares* what is the law to-day. Herein lies the new and important purpose of the Court.

The Court, moreover, already exercised this faculty of creating the law in its Advisory Opinion concerning Reparation for injuries suffered in the service of the United Nations; it declared on that occasion that the United Nations was entitled to present an international claim; until that time only States had been recognized as possessing this right.

The action of the International Court of Justice combined with the action of the Assembly of the United Nations, which has very broad international powers (Article 10 of the Charter), will greatly contribute to the rapid development of the new international law.

IV

To find the solution of the questions put to the Court in the present case, let us now consider, according to the elements of the new international law, what are the characteristics of international obligations and how conventions and rules of international law are to be interpreted.

Because the new international law is based on social interdependence, many cases may be found in which States are under obligations without the beneficiary of the rights relating to these obligations being known. The beneficiary is the international community. For the same reason it is not necessary that all obligations be expressly laid down by a text. Because of the diversity and the complexity of international relations it is not possible to provide for every contingency. Many obligations result from the very nature of institutions or the requirements of social life.

On the other hand, besides *legal* obligations there are also *moral* obligations and obligations of a *political international character* or *duties*. The latter derive from the interdependence of States and the international organization. The duty to co-operate indicated in the United Nations Charter is a typical example of this last category of obligations. The non-performance of such obligations may result in political sanctions applied by the United Nations.

In each case, the Court must decide whether a State has certain obligations or not, and what is their nature.

The conventions and rules of international law are to be interpreted by applying a criterion different from that which hitherto prevailed.

At present, the strict literal sense of the text is sought and to clarify it, recourse is had to *travaux préparatoires*. Use is also made of postulates, axioms and traditional precepts of general law, in particular of Roman law, and even natural law (except in Anglo-Saxon countries where attention is mostly paid to diplomatic precedents), and of postulates, axioms and precepts of classical international law. Not only are the immediate consequences not drawn from these elements, but deductions are made, by pushing logic too far. To this end a whole juridical technique is brought into play, and as a result, solutions are often found which are unreasonable and unacceptable to public opinion.

Important studies have recently been published by publicists of authority on the interpretation of treaties, but they follow the traditional line and, therefore, are open to criticism.

In future, postulates, axioms and general principles of law or of international law, which have hitherto been accepted may be relied upon only after they have been subject to the test of close scrutiny because many of them have become obsolete and may be replaced by others which will provide the basis of the new international law. This work of reconstruction is mainly a matter of doctrine, but it must also be effected by the International Court of Justice whenever the opportunity arises.

Extreme logic, dialectics and exclusively juridical technique must also be banished. Reality, the requirements of the life of nations, the common interest, social justice, must never be forgotten.

An isolated text may seem clear, but it may cease to be so when it is considered in relation to other texts on the same question and with the general spirit of the institution concerned. In the latter case the spirit must take precedence.

It may also happen that a text contains expressions of a clearly defined legal scope, but that, by reason of the nature of the institution, these expressions appear to have been taken in a different sense. This is exactly the case of the questions now before the Court: the words "Mandate" and "Trusteeship" have a different meaning in the Covenant and the Charter than they have in domestic law.

V

Let us now consider the nature of the Mandate conferred upon the Union of South Africa and its consequences on the questions before the Court in the light of the provisions of the Covenant of the League of Nations and of the United Nations Charter, and the spirit of the new international law. In this connexion I shall not dwell upon the declarations of the Union Government or its representatives, these declarations having been examined in the Court's Opinion.

Under Article 22 of the League of Nations Covenant the well-being and development of the inhabitants of colonies and territories which, as a consequence of the war, had ceased to be under the sovereignty of the States which formerly governed them, and were not capable of standing by themselves under the strenuous conditions of the modern world, form a sacred trust of civilization. The article goes on: "the best method of giving practical effect to this principle is that the tutelage of such peoples should be entrusted to advanced nations who, by reason of their resources, their experience or their geographical position, can best undertake this responsibility, and who are willing to accept it." Article 22 also lays down the conditions and guarantees for the performance of that great trust.

The United Nations Charter has not only taken up these ideas, but it has developed them (Chapters XI and XII).

Our starting point must be the existence of the sacred trust of civilization. The ideas and aims contained in this expression and the general principles of the new international law must be our compass in our quest for the answers to the questions put to the Court. We must not resort to a textual interpretation of certain articles of the Covenant or of the Charter, or to minor considerations.

Article 119 of the Versailles Treaty provides that "Germany renounces in favour of the Principal Allied and Associated Powers all her rights and titles over her oversea possessions."

The Mandate over South-West Africa established by the Council of the League on December 17th, 1920, says: "The Principal Allied and Associated Powers agreed that, in accordance with Article 22 of the Covenant of the League of Nations, a Mandate should be conferred upon His Britannic Majesty to be exercised on his behalf by the Government of the Union of South Africa to administer the territory afore mentioned."

The Union thus received not an ordinary mandate, but a *sacred trust of civilization*, which is quite another thing. The act which has been created is not a *fidei-commissum*, a trust or a contract deriving from any other similar national or international institution. The ordinary Mandate is a contract mainly in the interests of the principal, regulated by the rules of civil law, whereas the mission under consideration is an honorific and disinterested charge for the benefit of certain populations. It is an international function regulated by principles which conform to its nature. It is impossible therefore to apply, even by analogy, the national rules applicable to the Mandate or the other institutions which I have mentioned. Nor is it a treaty between the League of Nations and the Union of South Africa. The League of Nations has undertaken no obligation and has acquired very important rights indicated in the Mandate. It has also other political rights which have not been expressly provided for, such as the right to terminate the Mandate.

VIII

Even if it be admitted that South Africa is under no legal obligation to conclude this agreement, it has at any rate the political international obligation or a duty to conclude such an agreement. If it is impossible to reach such an agreement, the United Nations must then take the appropriate measures which it is empowered to take under Article 10 of the Charter.

The Union of South Africa is not competent unilaterally to modify the international status of South-West Africa. This competence belongs to the Union of South Africa acting in concert with the United Nations under Article 79 of the Charter.

(*Signed*) A. Alvarez

Resources and Responsibilities in a World of States

In the previous chapter we considered the breakdown of pure statism based on sovereign prerogatives in several areas of international law. At the same time we acknowledged that, overall, the emphasis in international law remains on constructing agreements among governments.

In Chapter 8 we examine a more or less traditional subject matter. International law, in its modern form, has always given certain protection to private property owned by aliens—that is, to property located abroad. This exception to the notion of territorial sovereignty worked for the general benefit of richer, more powerful states, those states whose nationals, banks, and corporations were most likely to have overseas assets and investment holdings. Of course, the extent of this protection, which in the premodern period (before World War I) included claims of diplomatic protection as well as recourse even to military intervention, has been a continuous source of grievance for and protest by both socialist and Third World governments. Although the intensity and form of the attack has varied, there has been a consistent repudiation of the notion that the "protection" of alien rights by intervention is a positive goal. In opposition to this internationalist idea of protection has been the territorial notion of "permanent sovereignty over natural resources." Although this notion is statist in nature, it has a progressive side to the extent that it protects weak states against strong ones.

At the same time, some postmodern (since World War II) planetary concerns have surfaced (see the selection by Marks in Chapter Seven) to challenge the capacities of international law to protect the commons, that is, those domains that are beyond the jurisdiction and reach of the territorial sovereign states—the oceans, outerspace, the polar regions, and the biosphere. Guarding the commons generates social pressure for a different type of world order than that descended from Westphalian style statism. Dangers of nuclear war are the most dramatic of these more recent concerns, challenging to a degree the very survival prospects of the human species.

There are also environmental dangers associated with fallout, pollution, piercing the ozone shield, and altering the climate of the planet that require planetary guidance, as well as enlightened national and regional approaches, to uphold the public good. The free market created by interacting sovereign states cannot protect the public good when the interests and activities of one state or a group of separate states imperil the well-being of others in serious respects. "Overfishing" is a clear example of a pattern that arises from the retention by each state of the discretion to maximize its own particular gains. Either such a state is imprudent—in failing, for example, to realize that its activities (say, dispersing DDT into the ground or radiation into the atmosphere) imperil the whole—or the state may knowingly be taking such a risk to accomplish some other end, such as attacking an enemy with nuclear weapons.

In addition to managerial problems, issues of values arise. There is some normative support for fulfilling basic human needs, including education and information, as well as for using some of the untapped wealth of the world located in the commons to assist the poor countries. But this normative perspective is currently quite weak. Its expression takes the form of demands made by poor countries against the global system, demands that seek various concessions collectively discussed as the quest for the "new international economic order." A definite element of globalism is similarly contained in such ideas surfacing in the oceans negotiations as the "common heritage of mankind." Moreover, pressures on international law arise from emergent values and ideological perspectives as well as from the managerial impulse to regulate complexity and vulnerability in light of growing interdependence.

These planetary concerns, as they become part of human consciousness, erode claims by the state to exclusive loyalty from citizens, groups, and certain special economic interest groups. Their natural field of identification is with the general public good or, put differently, with the well-being and durability of the whole. This increasingly global setting in relation to practical everyday international life is creating a political climate supportive of the Grotian quest; yet this quest is moving at a rather slow pace, in conjunction with simultaneous trends in the opposite direction.

In Chapter 8, we concentrate on the ways in which international law is dealing with the protection of private property and with competing claims over the benefits to be derived from various categories of resources. So far, as would be expected, international law has not successfully adapted its framework to accommodate these planetary concerns. At the same time, international lawyers have been active in their advocacy of more globalist approaches to resource policy issues, putting forward the case for negotiated agreements on a global scale and for institutional arrangements to ensure effective implementation.

Governments acting on behalf of states are constantly responding to a variety of influences in their efforts to shape coherent state policy. Their situation in the world is diverse in relation to access to resources beyond their frontiers, and to private property and resource development within their territories. Can this diversity be translated into common standards of regional and global scope? Can these standards, if agreed upon, also serve to uphold longer-range interests in conservation and environmental protection?

There are many complex issues of knowledge, value, ideology, and responsibility bound up in the workings of the legal process. Again, diversity of outlook inhibits the formation of an international consensus. And without such a consensus there is a tendency for the state system to be thrown back upon itself. After all, it is not evident whether most governments, when left on their own, can be relied on even to protect the longer-term interests and values of their own peoples.

Moreover, it remains very difficult to fix responsibility in this area. There is some attempt in the property context to achieve standards of accountability across state lines. There is almost no willingness, however, on the part of states with distinctive capabilities—say, with respect to mining deep sea minerals—to share the fruits of its enterprises with less advantaged states. The basic drives are still overwhelmingly statist. Large states dominate international society, especially along the frontiers of innovation. Accordingly, informal hierarchies emerge as a consequence of technological capabilities. The attempt to balance this sort of unilateralism against the claims of a nascent global community has not yet been achieved.

The first selection in Chapter 8 is by Oscar Schachter, who explores the benefits from resource uses in terms of whether they can be shared with communities of beneficiaries to a wider degree than is traditional. Schachter sympathetically puts forward the claims of the poor, the unborn, the community as a whole, nonhuman beings (do trees have rights? do whales?), and the overall natural environment. In domestic society, we are familiar with the use of taxation, regulatory standards, welfare payments, and subsidies to spread the benefits and to hold those who are reaping rewards accountable for the costs (e.g., deteriorated environment, undue depletion of resources, wastes of various kinds). Legal regimes are a flexible mechanism by which these goals could be pursued *if* the political will existed. Schachter, on the basis of great personal experience, investigates these possibilities, perhaps neglecting somewhat too much the constraints created by the prevailing orientation of leading governments.

The second selection, by Eduardo Jiménez de Aréchaga, illustrates one context in which new claimants for resource benefits are seeking to adjust the legal relationship—namely, the requirement that foreign investors be compensated for expropriated alien-owned property. This dynamic is present mainly in the interplay between the advanced industrial countries and the Third World, and it reflects the underlying view that earlier investment arrangements drained off national wealth and deprived the territorial society of the appropriate share of benefits from its resources. The issue is complicated by the fact that many of these Third World countries are also seeking to attract private capital and international financial backing to proceed with development plans. In addition, there are key ideological questions involving the character of private property and the adequacy of contractual and market mechanisms for purposes of resource arrangements. Finally, governing elites in Third World countries are often beholden to investors in a variety of ways, and their members cut in on the profits to such an extent that the government does not really represent the resource claims of its own society.

Aréchaga discusses the pressures on the traditional international law concept that the expropriating state has to pay "prompt, adequate, and effective" compensation. The new "balance" arises not from renouncing the compensation requirement altogether, but rather from a growing insistence that the level of compensation be reduced to the extent that the investor in the past benefited from "unjust enrichment" (by way of either excessive profits or insufficient taxation). Counterpressures from investment interests have questioned the legality of this attack on the old standards of compensation. The international law on the subject stands in a condition of turmoil. Not only is it a matter of disagreement about legal requirements, but it is also a dispute involving the extent of state sovereignty over the territorial resource base. In this setting, a given Third World country invokes sovereignty as a defensive concept, whereas the investor country invokes strict notions of state responsibility for international economic obligations as a positive attribute of a legal environment that encourages mutually beneficial investment flows across boundaries.

The next three selections deal with various aspects of the long process to create a new law of the oceans that both manages these vast resources and use-rights efficiently, and achieves an agreed balance among the claims and interests of the 170 states that will enlist support. The UN Convention on the Law of the Sea was opened for signature on December 10, 1982. Significantly, the United States was among the four states that voted against the treaty, giving as the principal reason its objections to the deep seabed mining provisions. Four Western European states also declined to sign, but the rest of the major states in the world gave their approval. It remains to be seen whether the treaty regime can be effective without the participation of the United States and, alternatively, whether the United States may not find its nonparticipation in the treaty regime a severe source of inconvenience and disadvantage.

The first of these three selections is by Bernard Oxman, who summarizes a new convention that is highly likely to provide the framework for legal relationships even for states that fail to ratify. Whether these nontreaty states can avail themselves of provisions of the treaty that go beyond prior customary international law remains to be seen and is certain to be hotly contested. Even if we take into account the unexpected withdrawal of the United States from the final phases of the negotiations and its rejection of the emergent text, this is still the most ambitious lawmaking enterprise ever undertaken. Oxman's summary creates a good introductory awareness of the range of issues covered and of the general shape of the emergent new law. To have created a final text that is so generally acceptable to the

170 or so states involved is a remarkable achievement. The United States' repudiation mars this sense of achievement, especially here in the United States. Whether the current U.S. position will endure is hard to say. The repudiation came after years of bipartisan participation in the negotiations and seemed to reflect the Reagan administration's highly ideological commitment to market solutions for resource-related issues. In any event, the struggle to provide a legal regime for the increasingly complex array of ocean uses will provide an important test in the years ahead of the problem-solving capacities of the state system.

The next two selections explore more specifically the process that culminated in the UN Convention on the Law of the Seas. The piece by Philip Allott attempts to assess the structural features of the agreed-upon terms. In this connection, the treaty is analyzed in relation to the pre-existing law and in terms of its relevance to various types of activities. In the background is the broad issue of sovereign rights. In one central sense, the treaty is a triumph of internationalism, a multilateral agreement covering a significant body of behavior. In another sense, by accepting the 200-mile Exclusive Economic Zone, the treaty consolidates and validates an extraordinary extension of sovereign rights in relation to what had been previously treated as high seas belonging to all. Of course, the United States under Reagan wants even more deference to sovereign claims, and refuses to accept some community management of deep seabed minerals. Allott's essay helps us appreciate some of the underlying questions of legal theory posed by the rights, duties, and powers created in the treaty.

The following selection, by Per Magnus Wijkman, examines the resource effects of the treaty regime in relation to fisheries, oil and gas, and deep seabed minerals. The article gives some concrete feeling for the economic stakes in these distinct resource contexts. It also clarifies the main contending positions taken during the negotiations in relation to the central distinction between developed and developing states. The author is rather critical of the resource regimes considered, arguing that they are neither efficient in terms of promoting development nor progressive in the sense of providing redistributions to poorer states.

In the final selection in Chapter 8, Jan Schneider investigates the principles and evolving rules for environmental protection in the international arena. Here, too, the question of the adequacy of the regulations can be raised not only from the viewpoint of world order but also from the more restricted perspective of international order. Since ecological systems do not degenerate consistently, they can collapse rather suddenly. Therefore, it is not sensible, for example, to allow the unregulated release of toxic substances into the environment. In these circumstances, environmental protection depends on both prohibitions and adequate and consistent monitoring, as well as on an understanding of the relevant elements of an ecological system sufficient to identify thresholds of danger in due time. Needless to say, these conditions do not prevail. What regulations exist are plainly insufficient or belated, often adopted to prevent, or at least make less likely, future environmental disasters—and usually only after a serious disaster has already occurred. Such a regulatory reflex generally does nothing to reverse the dangerous trends that give rise to the menace. Although it seems utopian, it would serve the general interest simply to reverse the existing permissive presumption and to allow hereafter only those international discharges of substances that have been established as generally "safe" (either degradable or acceptable up to specified maximums). Naturally, such a radical regulatory shift would cause some immediate disruption for the sake of safeguarding our well-being as a species over the long run. At present, environmental quality is being sacrificed to avoid challenging polluting industries and other users in any serious manner. Questions of equity are also present, especially to the extent that many developing countries, already under severe pressure, would be denied some industrial output through the imposition of costly regulations. But the damaging effects associated with more rigorous environmental standards could be offset by subsidies and the transfer of nonpolluting technologies on advantageous terms. The complex interrelationships among welfare, population growth, the arms race, and ecological problems inform a world order perspective and give a high priority to the realization of shared values for all peoples.

The narrower technical and legal problems have to do with the creation and upkeep of a global information and monitoring system, the choice between regional versus universal standards, and the implementation of standards by a variety of public (licensing) and private actors (insurances) and techniques. Furthermore, levels of liability must be imposed by international means for such hazardous activities as transporting oil on the seas in supertankers. Finally, we must raise the issue of whether any injunctive relief is available against environmentally damaging acts of transnational corporations and governments. What protection to the general global interests at stake is provided by national environmental-protection laws? Does access to domestic courts for claims involving transnational pollution extend to foreign nationals? There are many questions of this sort that mix issues of policy with those of law.

Throughout this section we consider problems that are challenging the organizational capacity and normative content of traditional international law. To what extent can the law adapt? To the extent that these managerial and equity challenges are not being met, the old order is experiencing a loss of legitimacy, and new visions, orientations, and demands are becoming visible on the horizon. It is this dimension of the horizon that marks our time as a period of turmoil, danger, and possible transition. Whether this mixture of organizational and normative challenges engenders an effective response will allow future historians of international relations to assess whether or not we did indeed seize the Grotian moment to create something viable and beneficial for the various peoples of the world.

QUESTIONS FOR DISCUSSION AND REFLECTION: CHAPTER 8

1. To what extent does Schachter's discussion of rights and needs help in analyzing the circumstances of misery afflicting at least half a billion

people? Is it possible for the state system to respond compassionately and effectively to these ethical challenges? If so, how? If not, what changes in the structure of the world system would seem necessary, if satisfaction of the minimum needs of all people was made a political requirement of world order?

2. Aréchaga's argument concerning permanent sovereignty over national resources is strongly reinforced by a historical record of past abuses and by an urgent need for capital in the underdeveloped world to facilitate economic growth. Is his argument persuasive? Is economic development thereby helped, and is nationalization for purposes of modernization useful for advancing world order concerns? Does nationalization reinforce the state system instead, or does it merely equalize relations between different parts of the state system?

3. Given Wijkman's critique of the likely distributive outcomes of the Draft Treaty on the Law of the Sea, is the conception of a "common heritage of mankind" still a useful concept for thinking about sharing the world's as yet untapped resources? What is its status in international law? Has it been accepted within the political arena and, specifically, in the LOS negotiations?

4. Thoughtful commentators have used the metaphor of the tragedy of the commons—a situation in which individual persons benefit at the expense of collective resources until those resources degenerate and all members suffer. Does this dynamic describe the resource depletion and pollution problems of the globe? Do Schneider's recommendations for a better antipollution regime deal adequately with this issue?

SELECTED BIBLIOGRAPHY: CHAPTER 8

Manoush Arsanjani, *International Regulation of Internal Resources* (Charlottesville: University of Virginia Press, 1981).

Norbert Horn, ed., *Legal Problems of Codes of Conduct for Multinational Enterprises* (Deventer, Netherlands: Kluwer, 1980).

Dave Kay and Harold Jacobson, eds., *Environmental Protection* (Totowa, N.J.: Allanheld, Osmun, and Co., 1983).

Robert Meagher, *An International Redistribution of Wealth and Power* (New York: Pergamon Press, 1979).

Michael M'Gonigle and Mark Zacher, *Pollution, Politics, and International Law* (Berkeley: University of California Press, 1979).

Oran Young, *Resource Regimes, National Resources, and Social Institutions* (Berkeley: University of California Press, 1982).

31. Sharing the World's Resources

Oscar Schachter

Problems of equitable sharing among nations are not new. They have arisen for centuries in regard to boundary waters, fisheries, and the terms of trade.

But the scale and intensity of such problems are vastly greater today; they permeate the domestic economies and social life of almost all countries, and they have generated a widespread consciousness of inequalities and dependencies that is surely unprecedented. In the 1970s this has been sharply accentuated by imbalances and scarcities which threaten to destroy the social fabric of many areas and which, even in the most prosperous countries, have reversed the long-prevalent idea of continuous material progress.

It is mainly because of these conditions that some international bodies may be said to have become "justice-constituencies," arenas in which claims of equity and distributive justice are asserted and "internationalized."[1] These bodies vary widely. Some are concerned in concrete ways with allocation of goods or prices; others with access to resources; others, more generally, with cooperative arrangements over a range of economic and social matters (as, for example, the European Economic Community or the Andean organization). They are often specialized or regional organs which lay down rules and standards relevant to allocation of resources or carry out operational and managerial functions that affect the distribution of goods and services. More conspicuous are the general international bodies, typified by the General Assembly of the United Nations and its Conference on Trade and Development (UNCTAD), which are almost continuously engaged in considering demands for more equitable treatment and in formulating collective responses of a normative character. These generally take the form of declarations, charters, and resolutions, often couched in terms of rights and obligations. Whether or not they are accepted as international legal rules, they are likely to engender expectations about future patterns of international distribution, and, in some cases, to delegitimize traditional norms which would otherwise be regarded as authoritative. In that way multilateral conferences and international organs influence the development of customary international law even though they are not explicitly engaged in lawmaking efforts.

Although this may seem surprising, there is actually no sharp line separating the normative judgments of many international bodies from the continuous and ubiquitous process of customary law creation that takes place through the interaction of states.[2] An essential element of that process is the common perception of right and obligation on the part of the states concerned; when such shared perceptions emerge and are expressed clearly in international bodies, they are bound to shape the development of legal norms. All in all, there are a variety of international structures in which demands for equitable distribution may be made and given authoritative force by collective decisions. By examining these collective decisions we can discern the emergence of the normative concepts and criteria which bear on the sharing of the world's wealth. My aim . . . is to examine these emergent concepts and criteria and to consider their practical implications for the resolution of international disputes relating to the use and allocation of global resources.

The scope of that last phrase, "the use and allocation of global resources," can best be indicated by noting the kinds of problems with which I shall deal. They fall into two broad categories. The first category is treated . . . under the heading "Sharing the Common Heritage." The situations discussed include such resource areas as ocean space, water basins and rivers, and, to some extent, the atmosphere and the general global environment. These areas give rise to the kind of problems associated with property or territorial rights, and involve such questions as access and transit, allocation of exploitation rights, the sharing of monopoly rents, responsibility for conservation, and liability for extraterritorial harm.

The second broad category, dealt with . . . under the heading "Equity in Distribution," concerns problems of exchange and transfer of goods and services. Four major problems are examined: (1) the pricing and supply of basic raw materials; (2) the sharing of technology; (3) "sovereignty over natural resources"; and (4) world food security. . . . Consideration is given to proposals for more equitable distributive arrangements, as, for example, a "just" price for oil, limits on monopolistic or oligopolistic practices, commodity agreements, regulation of contracts for purchase of technology, control over transnational companies and foreign investment, and international food commitments and reserves. I realize that each of these subjects is in itself a large and complicated field of study on which a treatise can be written. But it is also possible—and I believe highly useful—to indicate briefly the significant new norms and procedures that are emerging in each of these areas and to consider their utility in meeting demands for equity and the other social ends sought by most governments.

Before dealing with these varied problems, however, I shall discuss the broad principles of entitlement which reflect the basic concepts of distributive justice as manifested in international decisions concerning resource allocation. My object is to clarify the value assumptions implicit in governmental positions and to point up the difficulties and dilemmas faced by collective bodies in seeking equity in the sharing of resources. This will be essentially an empirical analysis in the sense that it is based on the evaluative statements and behavior of governments and international organs rather than on theoretical assumptions. However, the record is complex and many-faceted. One must bear in mind that statements about equity and justice, especially those made by governments, often involve ambivalence and equivocation. When they are made in political bodies it is prudent to follow Wittgenstein's admonition, "don't look for the meaning, look for the use." After all, governments are not engaged in elaborating ideal systems but in coping with real grievances and conflicts. Yet we must also be careful not to wash away normative concepts and principles with an excessive dose of "cynical acid." They are part of the social reality: they shape the expectations and demands that give rise to conflict, and they help define the common basis for cooperative arrangements among states which have conflicting interests. That is why an examination of their meaning and use can have practical as well as intellectual significance, and it is especially with their practical significance in mind that I offer the following analysis. Perhaps "analysis" is not quite the right word; if I may borrow a phrase once again from Mr. Justice Holmes, my effort may be "more like painting a picture than doing a sum."

EQUALITY AND NEED

Tocqueville's comments on the passion for equality, made more than a century ago, do not seem strange to observers of contemporary international assemblies. The political demands for more equitable distribution find much of their intellectual and emotive justification in the ideal of equality, and few question the high, and even primary, position of equality among social values. As one moves from the level of the ideal to practical social policy, however, it becomes apparent that equality is in itself too general a concept to support concrete policy choices. Choices must be made among the different kinds of equality: equality of rights, of opportunities, of conditions, and of outcome. And these different kinds of equality may be incompatible in practice; indeed, this is likely to be the case when there are disparities in resources and capabilities. That is why, since the time of Plato, it has been suggested that "equality among unequals" may be inequitable and that differential treatment may be essential for "real equality." We hear this reasoning echoed today in international bodies. However attractive the ideal of equality, governments (like social philosophers and jurists) are compelled to translate this ideal into specific valuational criteria if they are to resolve competing claims. In effect, then, general egalitarianism must become specific egalitarianism if it is to have practical application. That the selection of specific egalitarianism presents difficulties is readily indicated by the familiar conflicting standards for personal economic rewards—equal return for equal work, return based on productivity, or simply equal income (*tout court*), to which we must add equality of opportunity and of access, equality of property rights, and more. Nearly all of these kinds of equality among individuals have analogues in criteria which have been followed or proposed for relations among nations. As I see it, however, two basic criteria have particular importance in contemporary debates and decisions: one is a standard based on need, the other a standard based on legitimate expectation and historic entitlement. A consideration of these broad principles will throw light on the issues and dilemmas involved in applying the ideal of equity to the international division of the world's product.

I began with the idea of entitlement based on need. This may seem, somewhat paradoxically, both obvious and utopian as a basis for international distribution. It has become virtually platitudinous to suggest that everyone is entitled to the necessities of life: food, shelter, health care, education, and the essential infrastructure for social organization. At the same time, it would be considered quixotic to suggest the classical Marxist maxim "to each according to his need" as a criterion of distribution. Even Marx regarded that principle as the distant goal of a classless and abundant society.[3] Yet when construed as a standard of minimal need it loses its utopian quality. Few today question the commitment of most states, capitalist and socialist, to meeting the minimal needs of their citizens. It is true that ideas of what minimal needs are vary with country and situation, but as a broad normative principle need is now so widely accepted in national societies as to be virtually beyond debate.

It is scarcely startling to find that a similar principle has been advanced on the international level. This does not lessen its importance. The fact that it has emerged as a widely accepted standard of international distribution has far-reaching practical implications. What is striking is not so much its espousal by the large majority of poor and handicapped countries but that the governments on the other side, to whom the demands for resources are addressed, have also by and large agreed that need is a legitimate and sufficient ground for preferential distribution. This agreement is evidenced not only by their concurrence in many international resolutions and by their own policy statements, but also, more convincingly, by a continuing series of actions to grant assistance and preferences to those countries in need. Though it may well be true that these actions fall short of meeting the actual requirements of many of the recipient countries, the scale and duration of the responses have been substantial enough to demonstrate the practical acceptance of the principle of need in contemporary international affairs.[4] It is true that the motivation of donor states will often include an element of self-interest (whether or not objectively well-founded), but this does not cancel out the significance of their response. Nor is its significance reduced by recognizing that state behavior reflects sociohistorical determinants, as Marxists and others suggest. Altruism is not necessary for an action to be equitable in its intent or effect.

It might be asked whether need has not always been an accepted standard for humanitarian assistance by nations as by individuals. It has, but there is an important difference between treating need as a matter of charity and linking it to the notion of justice. In the latter case, the satisfaction of needs is perceived as an entitlement, to be embodied in norms and institutions, and the relationship between donor and recipient is seen in terms of mutual rights and responsibilities.[5] On the other hand, when the provision of need is regarded as an act of charity, the relationship between the parties involved tends to be characterized by a sense of inequality, often with expectations of submissive behavior on the part of the recipient. Moreover, when viewed as charity, assistance is considered a matter of grace and is not readily institutionalized; deprivation is often regarded as an act of fate. Thus, the shift from a concept of charity to one of justice has had considerable importance for international actions and institutions, as shown by recent United Nations relief measures for countries severely affected by food deficits and the high price of essential imports. The shift has probably taken place because of the great increase in productivity and the expectations created by the new and potential patterns of distribution. In a world of meager resources, need was generally felt to be a natural calamity; it is only with the promise of global abundance, stimulated by new productive capability, that we find a widespread sense of injustice about the failure to meet needs. Clearly, this sense of injustice is no ephemeral phenomenon, nor is it one that can be attributed to transient political coalitions in international bodies. We must, I think, recognize it as a profound change in the perception of values, one with significant implications for international policy.

By treating need as a standard of equity (and of "real equality"), we reduce considerably the vagueness and indeterminacy of the concept of equitable sharing. Need, after all, can be ascertained in some objective way; there is even a widespread consensus on basic requirements of human beings everywhere. Still, defining needs on an international scale remains a complex, difficult task. It is not enough to distinguish needs from wants, as Aristotle did, though such differentiation remains a valid principle in the management of limited resources. Nor is it enough to calculate, as many have done, the essential needs of individual human beings for nutrition, health, shelter, education, security, and other factors. The more important and complicated issues involve the definition of needs in the light of social processes and their interaction. For example, in determining the food requirements of a country, one can begin with reasonably determinate facts such as nutritional requirements, population estimates, and available food supplies. But then to define needs in a prospective and operational sense, it is essential to consider the interrelation of several factors that determine supply and demand: the changing means of production, the input of capital and technology, the incentives to produce, the system of tenure and redistribution, the market and credit arrangements, prices, export demands, and several other conditioning elements. These factors are dynamic, and through their complex interactions the level of need for the people of a given region is determined. Obviously, then, the criterion of need does not provide simple answers even for a single problem such as food. It does, however, set a standard that can in principle be applied by objective factual inquiry.

Another type of problem faced in determining needs concerns the relation of collective needs to individual needs. Many have questioned the claims of developing countries which themselves have highly inequitable internal distribution of income. Gunnar Myrdal reports a typical question in donor countries: "Why do they not tax their own rich and reform their countries before they come to us with the begging bowl?"[6] Yet, valid as this question may be, it does not embrace the entire problem. When defining national needs, one must take into account the interaction between the needs of national states as collective entities and the needs of individual human beings. Even if one regards individual needs as the ultimate criterion (based on the premise that the state's only raison d'être is the well-being of its people), the requirements of a national state are relevant to certain public needs (for example, independence, security, growth) which are distinct from the distribution of economic benefits among its people. This distinction between national and personal needs does not mean that inequities within individual countries are of no international concern or that the sovereignty of a state precludes inquiry into such inequities by international bodies. But it does indicate that an international concept of need must take account of collective goods as well as of patterns of distribution.

Let me mention still another complex problem encountered when determining needs for purposes of equitable distribution. It concerns the need to allocate resources between present and future generations. The problem is not entirely a new one. Societies have always had to determine how much of their current consumption should be given up for investment and, therefore, for future generations. Economists see this as a problem of the optimum growth rate and mainly as a choice between private and social ends; that is, how much consumption should individuals be required to forego in order to maintain the economy or to meet other social needs, such as national security. When this is carried to great lengths (consider the Soviet Union's build-up of heavy industry and the consequent demands made on Soviet peoples), it is perceived by some as an issue of equity between present and future generations. In a more general way, some philosophers (for example, Herzen and Kant) have referred to the unfairness of earlier generations laboring for the benefit of later ones without reciprocity.[7] But this kind of inequity is accepted as part of the natural condition and only becomes a point of grievance where forced savings involve severe deprivation for contemporaries.

The issue of intergenerational equity has, however, taken a more acute turn because of the threatened environmental danger and resource depletion brought about by present rates of consumption. Even if the doomsday predictions of the "Limits to Growth" school are highly debatable, there is little doubt that the anticipated growth of population and industry will have serious consequences for future generations.[8] Increased awareness of these consequences means that the issue of the proper rate of growth will no longer be left to market forces or individual decisions. Making it a societal decision tends to bring out more sharply the problem of equity between generations and the extent of the sacrifice that should be made for the sake of posterity. In this context the distinction between needs and wants takes on new significance. We see it manifested in those movements which stress the wastefulness of consumption in affluent countries and those which warn of ecological dangers. The issue is further complicated by the apprehension that limiting economic growth in the interest of posterity will interfere with meeting the present needs of the poor. Formulas for selective growth and preferential distribution are responses to this problem which we shall consider later in more detail. At this point, I merely wish to point out the degree to which the issue of equitable sharing now tends toward a more objective standard of need in contrast to the economist's traditional standard of demand based on individual wants.

Although the issue of limited growth is usually discussed in terms of present versus future need, it is also valid to treat the needs of future generations as a part of present needs. After all, societies regard it as necessary to transmit to their descendants the social institutions and material base which they inherited and developed. That universally felt necessity is generally regarded as a justification for the renunciation of some present consumption through social saving and other transfers for the future. Seen in this way, the question of sacrificing for posterity becomes a matter of fulfilling actual needs of the present generation. It takes us from the much-debated but unanswerable question of reciprocity (what has posterity done for me?) to the determinate issue of how the needs of intergenerational transmission as perceived by specific societies should be satisfied in existing circumstances.

Finally, there is the conception of global needs as distinct from national needs and from an aggregation of individual needs. The recent concern with this dimension of needs had been greatly stimulated by three interrelated attitudes: (1) the apprehension over ecological and resource depletion; (2) the awareness of linkages and mutual interactions, summed up by the term "global interdependence"; (3) the interest in systems theory and systems approaches as methodologies for dealing with international problems. The fashionable metaphor of the "spaceship earth" and the concepts of "inter-dependence," "integrative planning," and "total designs" all figure prominently in the discussion of global needs. Under the influence of natural science systems models, some theorists emphasize the requisites for the "global system" to maintain its equilibrium and to adapt itself to internal and external influences.[9] This emphasis often tends toward formalistic taxonomy, especially when human beings and their aspirations are treated as "black-box" units (i.e., their contents are ignored). But my reservations about some systems theories do not mean that I reject the relevance of global needs. I am only dubious about formalistic approaches which rely too heavily on physical and biological models and exclude actual human goals and socio-historical factors. I think it necessary to give concrete meaning to the concept of global needs, and I should like to mention three approaches to that task.

The first approach is to look to the physical and technological areas which transcend national boundaries. The obvious subjects of current concern are the oceans, the atmosphere, the overall climate; in these areas, needs such as the conservation of resources and protection against dangers to human health and to other species are now identified on a global level. Methods of global monitoring, such as "earthwatch" and the "integrated global ocean station system," are being instituted to determine the specific character of those needs. Meeting them would clearly come within a general policy of equitable sharing, even though such a policy served collective requirements rather than preferential distribution.

A somewhat different approach to the definition of global needs derives from the worldwide character of certain patterns of interaction. Perhaps the best-known example of this is the food-population-resource equation, which is an oversimplified way of referring to a series of interrelated problems that have to be dealt with in terms of global quantities and effects. Another example is suggested by the "international development strategy" adopted by the United Nations in an effort to bring into a coherent relationship the many interactive elements that affect development on a worldwide basis. Both of these examples indicate that in order to define global needs, one must go beyond aggregating separate national requirements.[10] The methodology and empirical data now available are still not adequate, however, and much remains to be done if the generalities about interdependence are to be transformed into reasonably specific conclusions that are usable for policy decisions. It also remains to be seen whether or not governments which are almost entirely concerned with their own national requirements will encourage efforts to identify global needs as an independent category.

The third approach to worldwide needs is rather more political and less technocratic than the two others just described. It focuses on the conception of a world economy composed of three sectors: a core of advanced industrial states, a semiperiphery of socialist countries, and a periphery of underdeveloped countries which are mainly sources of raw materials.[11] The features stressed in this conception are the hegemonic role of the core countries and the inferior position of the periphery. When viewed from this third perspective (which has been advanced by some spokesmen from the Third World), the most critical global need is the elimination of the stratification and the relation of dominance and subordination in the world economy. Although explicitly directed against the core states, this approach claims support based on the universal values of equity and justice. Thus, in a way, it brings us around full circle to our quest for the meaning of real equality and equitable sharing of the world's product.

It is evident from our discussion that in seeking to relate equitable sharing to ascertainable needs, we encounter a number of complex problems. Some of them are difficult to solve because of intellectual limitations; we have insufficient knowledge of causal relations and not enough factual data. Others involve what we may describe as political difficulties; they require choices which will mean sacrifices and high costs for some. Later we shall consider some of the institutional structures and arrangements which have been suggested or employed to deal with these problems. However, these various difficulties do not mean that the criterion of need is chimerical as a standard of equitable distribution. As we shall see in more detail, many international decisions affecting the allocation and distribution of resources seek to meet specific needs on a preferential basis. Of course, the world is still very far from accepting the utopian goal of "to each according to his need" even in theory, but it is undeniable that the fulfillment of the needs of the poor and disadvantaged countries has been recognized as a normative principle which is central to the idea of equity and distributive justice. That this principle has been given a measure of practical effect in collective decisions is attributable, I believe, not to a sudden spread of altruism, but to a widely felt necessity on the part of governmental elites to respond to tensions and grievances which threaten the equilibrium and stability of the international order. The implications of this new response for the norms and structures of the international system are only just beginning to be examined.

LEGITIMATE EXPECTATIONS AND
HISTORIC ENTITLEMENT

Although in international bodies equity has been increasingly identified with meeting the needs of the disadvantaged, other notions of fairness and justice are also evidenced in regard to the distribution of resources. The most significant of these has an affinity to the idea of proportionate equality as used by Aristotle: that equality should be proportionate to what is due or deserved.[12] Initially this idea appears to be little more than a tautology— "to each his due"—but it leads us to consider the basis of entitlement and the legitimate expectations which flow from it. In national societies such expectations usually derive from social norms and institutions, and this would seem to be true on the international level also. Principles of legitimacy and control, norms governing trade and exchange, and an extensive array of accepted practice relating to distribution all create the expectations that enable participants to recognize what is due and deserved.

You will note that these expectations are not usually based on any general valuational principle (such as need, or merit, or efficiency), nor are they dependent on a desired pattern of results. They are generated by the processes of acquisition and transfer, whether the results are considered good or bad. We need only remind ourselves that the great bulk of the world's resources has been divided among numerous sovereignties by a historic process, and that our conception of entitlement to those resources is largely determined by the legitimacy accorded that process. When governments insist on their sovereign authority over their own natural resources and their rights to use and dispose of these resources freely (to determine who may exploit and purchase and at what price and conditions), they are basing their position on the legitimacy of their acquisition and on what they deem to be their just due. We can observe this in the disputes of governments with foreign enterprises, in their claims to adjacent ocean space, in their control over exports and access to their markets, and in various other manifestations of territorial jurisdiction. Their ideas of what is just and fair in their international relations are profoundly influenced by their conception of their sovereign rights. Nor is this influence limited to territorial sovereignty. Just entitlement may also include access to and use of natural resources outside of national jurisdiction, as, for example, historic fishery rights or customary transit rights over land or waters. Efforts to reduce or eliminate such acquired rights run counter to concepts of fairness and justice.[13] The same holds true for entitlements arising from international agreements and the norms governing consensual transactions. These not only create expectations as to future behavior; they also condition attitudes about the equities involved. Holmes's "bad man" theory of contract does not quite fit international dealings; when states enter into treaties they are not simply buying an option to perform or pay damages. The commitment is itself a determinant of what is due and therefore of what is equitable, irrespective of the merits of the transaction. Of course there are exceptions, but we need not have a categorical rule to substantiate our conclusion about the general bearing of entitlement on ideas of equity.

In the light of these observations it may seem strange that in current discussions equity and distributive justice are identified almost entirely with the demands of the poor and disadvantaged for a larger share of resources, and that they are rarely used to refer to the kind of entitlements I have described. Perhaps one reason for this situation is that economists tend to employ the term equity (or distributive justice) as virtually a code word for wider income distribution and transfer payments to the poor. But this special meaning overlooks the significance of entitlements in actual disputes between nations in which strong feelings of injustice have been generated. Consider, for example, the dispute between Iceland and the United Kingdom over Iceland's claim to an extended, exclusive fishing zone, which came before the International Court of Justice in 1974; or the more general class of disputes between capital-exporting states and host countries over nationalization and contractual rights pertaining to foreign investment in natural resources; or the claims of lower riparians to a share of clean river water (as in the dispute between Mexico and the United States over the salination of the Colorado River).[14] In these resource disputes, the equities asserted have been based on each side's conception of what was due to it and that, in turn, rested on historic and consensual processes and norms derived from them. Clearly, the idea of equity has a much wider meaning for governments than it does for economists and others who use it to refer to increasing the share of those less well-off. Nor should this be surprising. After all, the world's resources are distributed in accordance with entitlements based on territorial rights, custom, and consensual transactions, and it is only natural that ideas of equity should be significantly determined by that reality.

But how, it may be asked, can this idea be reconciled with the concept of equity as meeting the needs of the poor and disadvantaged? One way, evidenced in international debate, is to link demands based on needs to entitlements derived from accepted principles. For example, the claims of landlocked states and new states for access to and sharing of ocean resources have been advanced not so much on the basis of needs as on the basis that such access is due these states under the principle of the common heritage (the *res communis*) of the oceans. Similarly, in river disputes lower riparian countries assert not only their need for adequate supplies of water but also a customary or treaty right and on the latter basis may demand changes in the pattern of use and appropriation by the upper riparians. Even the broad and generalized demands of poor countries for preferences and grants are often advanced as entitlements owed to them because of past exploitation, oligopolistic restraints, or other allegedly illegitimate practices of the industrialized societies. Such demands illustrate a general tendency to utilize the two conceptions of equity in harness as mutually supportive rather than antagonistic principles of valuation. This is not merely a matter of "dialectics" or rhetoric. It reflects a political judgment that as an international criterion the maxim "to each according to his need" is too impractical and far-reaching in its implications to win acceptance as a general principle; but that when this maxim is conjoined with and limited by a principle of legitimacy, it becomes more acceptable because less threatening to the international order. In short, the Aristotelian principle of distributive justice may be seen as implicit in the normative assumptions of governments and as providing a counterpoint to competing egalitarian conceptions.

The interplay and linkage of the competing conceptions of equity are evidenced in two international principles which have received wide support in recent years. One is the principle of permanent sovereignty over natural resources. The other is the principle of rectification of past injustices. . . . I should like only to indicate briefly how they are related to the two criteria of equity we have been discussing.

"Permanent sovereignty over natural resources" is linked to what I have called historic entitlement. Its normative premise is that territorial jurisdiction resulting from a historic process of acquisition is the paramount basis for rights over natural resources and that, in consequence, it is just and equitable to recognize the ascendancy of that principle in international decisions pertaining to resources. Each sovereignty has its "proportionate equality," however unequal its actual share may be. At the same time, the concept of permanent sovereignty is perceived by the less-developed countries as a defense against alleged exploitation by the more advanced countries and their enterprises. They use it primarily to obtain a greater share for themselves, and it is therefore asserted to justify nationalization and other take-over measures directed against foreign enterprises, to limit profits and their repatriation, to remove foreign restraints on the transfer of technology, to override contractual arrangements on the grounds of public interest and need, and so on. Significantly, "permanent sovereignty" is rarely, if ever, advanced as an entitlement of the affluent countries in their relations with the less-developed countries. Thus, decisions by the richer countries to restrict exports or to impose restraints on access to their markets are not justified by international bodies as proper exercises of "sovereignty over resources" but are regarded often as undesirable and unfair actions against the poorer countries. From one perspective this difference in attitude can be criticized as a double standard of sovereign rights, yet from another it may be seen as an indication of a single standard, namely, the principle of meeting the needs of the disadvantaged. We thus find in the concept of permanent sovereignty over resources a principle which is, so to speak, conservative in its stress on sovereign rights (based on historic acquisition) yet utilized by poor countries as a weapon of change.

In a somewhat analogous way, the idea of rectification of past wrongs has been advanced primarily as a right of disadvantaged countries with, again, the implication of a double standard in its application to developed and developing states. There is, of course, nothing new in the demand of governments and peoples for correction of historic injustices. In a sense that demand is the other side of the coin of historic entitlement. If entitlements are based on the legitimacy of the process of acquisition, they should also be open to attack on grounds of their illegitimacy and injustice; acts of fraud or the illegal use of force would vitiate an entitlement for reasons of equity, if not in law.[15] We find this general notion of rectification reflected also in claims of unjust enrichment, advanced, for example, by governments which claim compensation for inordinate profits said to have been made by foreign concessions under conditions of political or economic domination. Even though such claims have received little support in judicial cases, they have been expressed in political bodies and in declarations of principle adopted in organs of the United Nations. For example, in 1974 the General Assembly declared that states and peoples which have been under "foreign occupation, alien and colonial domination" have the right to restitution and full compensation "for the exploitation and depletion of, and damages to, the natural and all other resources."[16] One cannot but be struck by the breadth of this asserted principle when one thinks of the numerous countries in the developed areas of the world as well as in the Third World which have suffered even in the recent past from alien domination and foreign occupation. Almost certainly the proponents of the UN declaration had the poor countries primarily in mind as its beneficiaries, but the declaration's sweeping language and the grievances felt in many developed countries about foreign domination may presage its political use outside of the Third World. But even if the declaration is limited to the claims of developing countries, its scope is so wide and its meaning so uncertain as to cast doubts on the feasibility of its practical implementation.

These intrinsic difficulties do not mean that the notion of rectification will be ignored. It is too firmly grounded in widely held conceptions of justice to disappear from political and juridical claims. More specifically, it is a consequence of accepting entitlements based on the process of acquisition rather than on end-results, for, as we noted, if there are historic rights, there will inevitably be historic wrongs. One could say that the principle of rectification is the natural and radical offspring of the conservative concept of acquired rights. Just how far this principle will be carried in international affairs and in what specific forms remain to be seen, but it seems likely that it will be utilized as still another conceptual weapon by dissatisfied governments seeking to change existing patterns of distribution.

My observations on the role of entitlements and need have, I hope, clarified my earlier reference to the dialectical interplay of competing notions of equity. I have sought to show how these two opposing criteria of distributive justice have been applied as mutually supportive grounds for new principles of equity asserted in international bodies and indeed how difficult it would be, in a political sense, to apply either one without the other. This analysis, as I have said, is essentially empirical; it is not based on moral theory or philosophical premises but rather on the actual positions taken by governments in their claims and responses regarding the world's resources. These positions are a product of existing tensions and conflicts. They are not ideal constructions, and they naturally manifest ambivalences and indeterminacies. But, as I have tried to show, they also reveal certain basic normative concepts which influence evaluative behavior and which give some determinate meaning and political force to the ideal of distributive justice.

COMPETING GOALS AND COLLECTIVE DECISIONS

Of course, equity is not the only social value sought in international arenas. Even the institutions which frequently receive and respond to demands for distributive justice (such as UNCTAD) are not specialized structures for dealing with such issues. In fact, their terms of reference are explicitly directed toward other objectives—trade, development, coordination of national effort, integration—so that issues of equitable treatment usually arise in the context of a wider range of goals and criteria. Nor are the stated aims of such international bodies the only aims that matter; the participants always pursue other goals. National security, independence, and prestige may be more important to many of them than either equity or economic efficiency. It is also evident that the multiple goals and the efforts to pursue them are frequently in conflict with each other, and the concrete problem is often one of achieving a proper balance or trade-off among competing values.

The idea of trade-offs is especially prominent when issues of equity are in the forefront. In economic matters, this is linked to the widely held belief that greater equality and wider sharing are likely to be antithetical to the goals of efficiency and productivity. Stated in the language of utilitarian economics, "the sum of utilities would be considerably smaller at complete equality (and near-complete equality) than under redistributive programs allowing significantly more incentive for differentials in retained disposable income and utility."[17] Although this proposition and its variants have been subjected to much refined economic analysis (which has produced certain qualifications), it still expresses a major international and national policy-making dilemma that is relevant to both the allocation and the use of resources. We may observe parenthetically that this dilemma holds for the socialist centrally planned economies as well as for market economies, and for the industrialized as well as for the developing countries. As long as resources are scarce, there will be a problem of relating differentials in income distribution to the requirements of production and efficient use of the resource endowment of national states. The problem is also present (although in somewhat different aspects) in most of the principal international issues relating to the distribution and use of resources. It is manifested or implicit in the debates on international transfer payments, commodity pricing and stabilization, the transfer of technology, the control of multinational companies, the management of seabed resources, fishing rights, the system of food reserves, even in debates on outer space. On the whole, it is reasonably clear to those who are concerned that in these matters claims of equity and wider sharing may have negative effects on other values, particularly on economic productivity and, in some situations, on national autonomy. That a trade-off and balance must be sought is an obvious conclusion.

However, this conclusion leads us to the complexities of international decision making. We must remember that a trade-off among competing values is one thing for a single decision maker and quite another for a collective body. The single decision maker (whether it be an individual or a national authority) can determine its own ranking order for the relevant values and, taking that order into account, can seek to maximize its net value position. In doing so it will strike a compromise among the competing goals of efficiency, autonomy, stability, equity, and so on. In a collective body, however, the existence of divergent individual ranking of ends requires, if decisions are to be taken, a "master" ordering of values that necessarily differs from one or more of the individual orderings. (If it did not, the individual orderings would not be divergent, and if unanimity existed, there would be no problem of choice.) In this sense a master ordering implies an imposed decision; no voting arrangement, however democratic, can avoid such an imposition as long as the individual constituent parties maintain their divergent positions. This truth has been demonstrated in elegant abstract postulational analysis by Kenneth Arrow[18] (and refined and argued over by others), but the basic point is obvious enough in international arenas where participant countries are acutely conscious of their autonomy and sovereignty. The problems of achieving a consensus (or, in the older language, ascertaining the general will) have not escaped the diplomats. They are fully aware (though the point is rarely made explicit) that a genuine consensus on the ranking of social ends is almost impossible to attain in a heterogeneous body of nation-states with different interests and social systems.

This difficulty is especially evident when the issues among countries involve claims of equity as against claims of productivity, national autonomy, or stability. That does not mean that the issues are laid aside or that the demands for justice disappear. Solutions are sought on various levels of international activity. These levels fall, broadly speaking, into two categories: one, bargaining; the other, institutional procedures. Bargaining remains the characteristic and, some might say, the natural modality for striking a balance among competing interests and thus, to a certain extent, among conflicting values. This is so whether transactions are conducted in a free market or under regulated conditions. The recent intensification of demands for distributive justice has not only introduced new elements into international bargaining but has also produced greater concern about the conditions of bargaining on the multilateral level. Such concern is manifested in proposals and arrangements for facilitating the bargaining process and rendering it more equitable. An important aspect relates to improving the "transparency" of international economic dealings by providing a much greater flow of reliable information about the factors affecting demand and supply. Proposals range from an ambitious plan for a global intelligence system that would monitor information regarding resources and prices to more limited measures such as increasing the exchange of information on demand and supply factors for specific commodities or reporting on activities of transnational companies. Although these informational proposals may be justified as facilitating bargaining under market conditions, they are far from noncontroversial. Yet, as we shall see, many of the new schemes affecting resource distribution are premised on mechanisms for greater transparency in sensitive economic matters.

Procedural measures for improved bargaining are also directed toward improving the conditions of negotiation and consultation among the parties to the bargaining process. An important and controversial aspect concerns the relation of producers' associations to collective bodies for the consuming and importing countries. The need for appropriate bargaining between these two sides has produced a variety of proposals on the procedures and modalities of such collective negotiation.[19] Stress also has been placed on the need for consultative procedures in cases affecting resource distribution and use. Proposals to require consultation have been warmly debated in international bodies over a wide range of issues including, for example, environmental damage, the use of water resources, earth satellite sensing, oceanographic research, and commodity pricing. Despite the difficulties of and resistance to such requirements, one can discern a trend toward greater acceptability of consultative procedures in regard to national actions affecting the resources of other countries.[20] There is also increased interest in the exclusion of practices which interfere with good faith negotiation and consultation. The most important, as well as the most debated, issue in this respect concerns restrictions on the use of economic coercion. Of special concern is the use of economic coercion to achieve objectives of a political or strategic kind or to interfere with a state's authority over its own domestic affairs.[21] We can also foresee an interest in rules and procedures that would protect the collective responsibility of negotiating groups against actions, such as bilateral deals, which would make collective bargaining impossible. Finally, there is an interest in promoting conditions for the more reliable fulfillment of expectations, particularly in assuring security of supply and markets, in stabilizing price relationships, and in avoiding disruptive behavior. The mere recital of these problems and objectives is sufficient to delineate the kind of procedural law and "rules of the game" that will be needed to produce conditions of fair bargaining and, in that respect, to facilitate rational choices among competing interests and goals.

Although no sharp line can be drawn between bargaining and institutional procedures (since the latter normally reflect negotiations among the parties concerned), the decisions of international bodies often go beyond bargaining in affecting or determining collective choices among conflicting objectives. Such institutional decisions can be seen as taking place on three levels. The first level is that of general principles and aims typically expressed in resolutions adopted by quasi-parliamentary organs of global scope such as the General Assembly and UNCTAD. Two types of such normative resolutions can be distinguished. One is the classic "balanced" resolution which seeks to accommodate all important interests and thus obtain universal support. Balanced resolutions express diverse and competing aims without laying down a hierarchy of values or a criterion of choice between antithetical objectives. The other type of resolution is the more one-sided, equity-oriented resolution which articulates the intensely felt demands of the majority political coalition for a wider distribution of resources. This type of resolution, now more prevalent than the former in United Nations bodies, lacks a genuine worldwide consensus (though sometimes adopted by a technical "consensus" procedure in order to avoid voting) and is regarded by many of the more affluent states as unbalanced.[22] Obviously, resolutions of this second type do not seek to present a paradigm of rational choice but rather to further a specific type of change. By expressing majority demands as principles and obligations (moral, if not legal), they aim both at delegitimizing norms which were previously influential and engendering expectations as to future patterns of more equitable distribution. Whether or not they are likely to have that effect, in the absence of a genuine consensus of all concerned, has been argued about, especially in the rich countries, but it seems hard to deny that there has been a significant shift in attitudes and expectations in line with the principles of these resolutions. Our earlier discussion of the importance now given to meeting basic needs of the less well-off and disadvantaged countries has already made that point. One need not attribute to resolutions of international bodies a decisive role in bringing about that shift in expectations in order to recognize that they have an influential and probably unique role in that respect.

Although resolutions of the kind just discussed have been in the forefront of discussion, they constitute only a small segment of the institutional decisions concerned with the sharing of resources. Many other decisions are made on a more specific plane by the various international organs composed of territorial or functional groupings, as in fisheries and river basin commissions, commodity bodies, producers' associations, Common Market arrangements, and a variety of other multinational economic institutions. On the whole these bodies, with their limited membership and specialized responsibilities, can more readily achieve consensus than can the heterogeneous global organs. Moreover, the criteria they lay down or apply, whether in the form of rules or policy decisions, are generally complied with, whatever their formal legal character.[23] Their decisions do, of course, involve bargaining, but that bargaining is substantially affected by the institutional context in which it occurs. Obvious examples of this are the influence of international secretariats and of political coalitions as well as the aims and limits imposed by the basic constituent agreement.

As might be expected, these specialized organs, in contrast to the more heterogeneous global bodies, do not address themselves to the larger issues of global reform or rectification of past injustices. Yet they almost always have to be mindful of equity in the sharing of benefits among their parties. Otherwise the essentially voluntary arrangements for cooperation would cease to be viable, and they would either collapse or possibly be transformed into more dictatorial or hegemonial structures. Consequently, issues of equitable treatment among the parties, in respect to both losses and gains, are often critical to the functioning of these bodies and of great concern when their constitutional foundations are laid. In many cases, the only acceptable safeguard for states with substantial resources at stake is a firm requirement of unanimity (or "consensus") for decisions of any importance. In a few situations, more complex voting procedures for qualified majority decisions and constitutional provisions to protect minority rights have been adopted.[24] Agreement on substantive criteria for equitable distribution may, in some cases, be a condition precedent for the acceptance of a rule-making or allocating organ, as we have seen in riparian and fishing commissions or in the new International Energy Authority.

There is still a third level of institutional decisions affecting resource allocation: the level of operational or executive action. Included in this composite category are the acts of international financial agencies in transferring capital, the technical assistance and informational activities of many of the United Nations agencies and of various regional bodies, and even the occasional managerial functions of international bodies directly responsible for resource management (as, for example, in buffer stock operations, or in the embryonic seabed authority). Although all such operational activities take place within a framework of governing rules and precepts, the concrete executive decisions still require choices and trade-offs among conflicting ends. A history of policy trends in the World Bank or of the controversies in the United Nations Development Programme reveal the extent to which demands for greater efficiency, for more national autonomy, and for equity (seen in terms of needs and entitlement) have competed with each other in operational decisions and have required a series of accommodations by the international organs.[25] We note this not to assert that the accommodations reached were satisfactory, but to underline the continuing, almost day-to-day, process of collective international bargaining to reach decisions involving competing social ends.

Clearly such collective determinations cannot always conform to the divergent value rankings of the different states concerned, and in that strict sense, they are imposed decisions. The political implications are manifested in the tendencies of governments to limit such operational agencies and to require the specific agreement of host states to any activities on their territory. Questions concerning the distribution of power and authority for collective decisions generally result in conflicting positions taken by major groups, depending on how these groups perceive their chances of exerting influence and avoiding decisions against their interest. This state of affairs is especially evident when new institutions are being established. The same constitutional issues arise time and again. Should the terms of the constituent agreement be drafted tightly, with detailed prescriptions for operations? How should the intergovernmental governing bodies be composed to give appropriate representation or parity to competing blocs? Should their decisions be taken by general agreement, by special majorities (as in weighted voting), or by a simple majority? To what extent should the executive staff be politically representative of governments and how should their discretionary authority be controlled? These and related questions have become perennial issues in international organization; they are especially contentious when the institutions involved are operational and their decisions managerial rather than advisory. It is true that precedents and patterns have been established, but they are continually being challenged as political coalitions develop and new demands arise. The controversy over the regime for the seabed is a good illustration, as we shall see later. What is evident is that the procedures for international decision making cannot be determined by some ideal model. They have to be seen as problems in the distribution of power to be solved through political processes which take account of relative national capabilities and needs as well as the shared interest in cooperation.

This does not mean that there is no room for rules and standards to promote rational and equitable decision making. Just as bargaining among states may be placed on a firmer basis by suitable rules of the game (as I suggested above), so the institutional arrangements concerned with multi-national resource-sharing problems may benefit from similar measures to improve the rationality and fairness of collective decisions. For example, practical steps leading to the greater transparency of world economic activities and to early consultation on the transnational effects of domestic actions would strengthen many of the regulatory and operational institutions. Nor is it unrealistic to seek the acceptance of standards of behavior which would facilitate collective decisions and avoid unilateral or group action disruptive to cooperative arrangements. Some examples of this may be found in some of the specialized regional schemes that relate to trade and resource management. What is needed, one might optimistically suggest, is a kind of "constitutional law" which would prescribe broad principles of reasonable behavior relevant to international cooperation and which would be applicable to all the diverse economic bodies. We are still far from such law but some of the new proposals for sharing resources and wealth point in that direction.

One should not expect that any such emergent constitutional precepts would prescribe a master order of values for all situations. In our pluralistic and heterogeneous world such a master order would be neither sensible nor feasible. What we might reasonably expect and seek to promote is a more sustained effort to identify and clarify the multiple goals shared by most peoples and to relate these goals to specific situations and proposed actions. In that effort, the goal of international equity with which we have been primarily concerned may become more precise and also seen in a wider context than it previously has been. A process of concretization should occur so that diverse situations may be distinguished for purposes of ordering priorities and goals. We can already see this in the special categories emerging for international preferences—the desperately needy Fourth World, the underdeveloped but financially prosperous oil producers, the landlocked countries, the desert areas, the resource-poor industrialized countries, those threatened by environmental damage, and so on. The main components of international equity that we have discussed above—the satisfaction of basic needs, the respect for entitlement and legitimate expectation, the ideal of equality—must be applied to these special categories and to other diverse factual situations in ways appropriate to their particular characteristics. The conceptions of distributive justice provide standards and a sense of direction; they do not prescribe specific solutions.

Moreover, as we saw, in actual situations legitimate demands for equity must be linked to the other major goals of states and peoples. When resources are scarce, their equitable sharing cannot be isolated from the consideration of productive capacity and the means of increasing supply. Nor can the measures for more equitable treatment be pursued without regard to the intense demands for independence and autonomy which may be antithetical to goals of sharing and production. We cannot, in short, escape from the reality of pluralist goals and the necessities of trade-offs and compromise. But the effort to clarify our values—to analyze their complex and ambivalent meanings—and to relate them to specific circumstances can enable us to see the problems in the round, to detect our intellectual and factual deficiencies, and to identify more precisely the sacrifices and the benefits that may result. These become highly practical objectives at a time when governments are groping uncertainly toward new international structures to meet the grievances and anxieties of a troubled world.

NOTES

1. I have borrowed this phrase from Professor Julius Stone, though he has used it to apply to communities rather than to international organs. See Julius Stone, *Social Dimensions of Law and Justice* (Stanford: Stanford University Press, 1966), pp. 117, 796–98.

2. Oscar Schachter, "Toward a Theory of International Obligation," in *The Effectiveness of International Decisions,* ed. Stephen Schwebel (Leyden: Sijthoff; Dobbs Ferry, N.Y.: Oceana, 1971), pp. 9–31. See also Rosalyn Higgins, *The Development of International Law Through the Political Organs of the United Nations* (London, New York: Oxford University Press, 1963); Jorge Castañeda, *Legal Effects of United Nations Resolutions* (New York: Columbia University Press, 1969); A. J. P. Tammes, "Decisions of International Organs as Sources of Law," in 94 *Hague Academy Recueil des Cours* 1958 (Leyden: Sijthoff, 1959), 2:264–364.

3. Karl Marx, *Critique of the Gotha Programme* (New York: International Publishers, 1938), p. 10.

4. See International Commission on Development (Pearson Commission), *Partners in Development* (New York: Praeger, 1969), chapter 7 and tables 15–19; Robert Asher, *Development Assistance in the Seventies* (Washington: Brookings Institution, 1970), pp. 19–38. For discussions of the legal implications, see Michel Virally, "La 2ème Décennie des Nations Unies pour le développement—Essai d'interprétation parajuridique," in *Ann Française de droit int.* (Paris: Centre National de la Recherche Scientifique, 1970), 16:28–33.

5. Pope Paul VI, *Populorum Progressio,* Papal Encyclical of 26 March 1967, paragraphs 23, 49. See also "Charter on the Economic Rights and Duties of States," U.N. General Assembly resolution 3281 (XXIX), 12 Dec. 1974.

6. Gunnar Myrdal, "The World Poverty Problem" in *Britannica Book of the Year, 1971,* p. 34. On unequal income distribution in less-developed countries, see Irma Adelman and Cynthia Taft Morris, *Economic Growth and Social Equity in Developing Countries* (Stanford: Stanford University Press, 1973), a comprehensive and cogent analysis of the failure of "trickle down" in developing countries and of the concentration of benefits at the upper end of the income spectrum.

7. References to these views are found in John Rawls, *A Theory of Justice* (Cambridge: Harvard University Press, 1971), pp. 290–91.

8. Mihajlo Mesarovic and Eduard Pestel, *Mankind at the Turning Point* (New York: E. P. Dutton, 1974); see also Jan Tinbergen, "Assigning World Priorities," in *Environment and Society in Transition,* ed. P. Albertson and M. Barnett (New York: New York Academy of Sciences, 1975), pp. 25–31.

9. Ernst B. Haas, "On Systems and International Regimes," *World Politics* 27, no. 2 (January 1975):147–74.

10. Philippe de Seynes, "Prospects for a Future Whole World," *International Organization* 26 (Winter 1972):1–17.

11. Raul Prebisch and Célso Furtado in Latin America and Samir Amin in Africa have expressed this view. See Samir Amin, *Accumulation on a World Scale* (New York: Monthly Review Press, 1974); Norman Girvan, "Economic Nationalism," *Daedalus* 104 (Fall 1975):146–50. A comprehensive historical study based on a similar conception is to be found in Immanuel Wallerstein, *The Modern World-System: Capitalist Agriculture and the Origins of the European World Economy* (New York: Academic Press, 1974).

12. Aristotle, *Nicomachean Ethics,* Book V, 3.

13. See International Court of Justice, *Reports* (1974), p. 3, Judgment, Fisheries Jurisdiction (United Kingdom v. Iceland); Judge Dillard's separate opinion notes the relevance of the Aristotelean conception of distributive justice, ibid., p. 71. See also International Court of Justice, *Reports* (1969), Judgment, North Sea Continental Shelf Cases, especially the separate opinion of Judge Jessup, pp. 67–84.

14. More detailed reference to these situations will be found in Parts II and III of Oscar Schachter, *Sharing the World's Resources* (New York: Columbia University Press, 1977).

15. A similar conclusion on the rectification of past injustice was reached by Robert Nozick in his *Anarchy, State and Utopia* (New York: Basic Books, 1975), which, from a conservative perspective, places emphasis on the legitimacy and justice of entitlements derived from the historical process that led to them.

16. U.N. General Assembly, "Declaration on the Establishment of a New International Economic Order," paragraph 4f of U.N. General Assembly resolution 3201 (S-VI), 1 May 1974.

17. Edmund S. Phelps, ed., *Economic Justice* (Middlesex, England: Penguin Books, Ltd., 1973), p. 22.

18. Kenneth Arrow, "Values and Collective Decision-Making" in Phelps, ed., *supra* n.17, pp. 117–36.

19. See, for example, the proposals of Secretary of State Henry Kissinger to the U.N. General Assembly, 7th Special Session, U.N. Doc. A/PV.2327, 1 Sept. 1975, pp. 16–65. See also Richard Gardner, "The Hard Road to World Order," *Foreign Affairs* 52 (1974): 566; Thomas O. Enders, "OPEC and the Industrial Countries," *Foreign Affairs* 53 (1975): 625; U.N. Report of Experts, "A New United Nations

Structure for Global Economic Co-operation," U.N. Doc. E/AC.62/9, 28 May 1975, pp. 30–32.

20. See U.N. General Assembly resolution 3129 (XXVIII), 13 Dec. 1973, and report of Executive Director of U.N. Environmental Programme on "Cooperation in the Field of the Environment Concerning Natural Resources Shared by Two or More States," U.N. Doc. UNEP/GC/44, 20 Feb. 1975, pp. 41–45.

21. Economic coercion directed against the sovereign rights and independence of any state has been declared to be in violation of international law by several declarations of the U.N. General Assembly. See article 32 of the "Charter of Economic Rights and Duties of States" (U.N. Gen. Ass. res. 3281 [XXIX]), the "Declaration of Principles of International Law concerning Friendly Relations of States" (U.N. Gen. Ass. res. 2625 [XXV], 24 Oct. 1970) and the "Declaration on the Inadmissibility of Intervention" (U.N. Gen. Ass. res. 2131 [XX], 20 Dec. 1965). For discussions of the legality of economic coercion see D. W. Bowett, "Economic Coercion and Reprisal by States," *Virginia J. Int. Law* 13 (1972): 1; Gardner, *supra* n.19; R. B. Lillich, "Economic Coercion and the International Legal Order," *Int. Affairs* (London) 51 (1975): 358; J. J. Paust and A. P. Blaustein, "The Arab Oil Weapon—A Threat to International Peace," *Am. J. Int. Law* 68 (1974): 410; I. Shihata, "Destination Embargo of Arab Oil: Its Legality under International Law," *Am. J. Int. Law* 68 (1974): 591.

22. See discussions in U.N. General Assembly, 29th session, plenary meetings, December 1974, U.N. Docs. A/PV.2307, A/PV.2308, A/PV.2313, A/PV.2314, A/PV.2316.

23. See papers and proceedings in Schwebel, ed., *supra* n.2.

24. For a general review of diverse voting procedures see Inis Claude, *Swords into Ploughshares*, 4th ed. (New York: Random House, 1971), pp. 118–62. Specific procedures are discussed in F. Y. Chai, *Consultation and Consensus in the Security Council* (New York: UNITAR, 1971); Elizabeth McIntyre, "Weighted Voting in International Organization," *Int. Org.* 8 (1954): 484–97; Oscar Schachter, "Conciliation Procedures in the United Nations Conference on Trade and Development," *Liber Amicorum for Martin Domke* (The Hague: Nijhoff, 1967), pp. 268–74; Louis Sohn, "Voting Procedures in United Nations Conferences for the Codification of International Law," *Am. J. Int. Law* 69 (1975):310–53.

25. Edward S. Mason and Robert E. Asher, *The World Bank since Bretton Woods* (Washington, D.C.: Brookings Institution, 1973); Robert Jackson, *A Study of the Capacity of the UN Development System*, 2 vols. (New York: United Nations, 1969).

32. State Responsibility for the Nationalization of Foreign-owned Property

Eduardo Jiménez de Aréchaga

INTRODUCTION

Contemporary international law recognizes the right of every State to nationalize foreign-owned property, even if a predecessor State or a previous government engaged itself, by treaty or by contract, not to do so. This is a corollary of the principle of permanent sovereignty of a State over all its wealth, natural resources and economic activities, as proclaimed in successive General Assembly resolutions[1] and particularly in Article 2, paragraph 1 of the Charter of Economic Rights and Duties of States.[2] The description of this sovereignty as *permanent* signifies that the territorial State never loses its legal capacity to change the status or the method of exploitation of those resources, regardless of any arrangements that may have been made for their exploitation and administration.

Traditional international law considered any interference by a State with foreign-owned property a violation of acquired rights which were internationally protected, and thus an unlawful act. Today, measures of nationalization or expropriation constitute the exercise of a sovereign right of the State and are consequently entirely lawful. This fundamental change of approach significantly affects the application of the rules of State responsibility, particularly in regard to the existence and scope of the duty to compensate aliens whose property has been nationalized or appropriated.

LEGAL BASIS FOR THE PAYMENT OF COMPENSATION

The Classical Doctrine

Since acts of nationalization and expropriation were considered under traditional international law to be in violation of acquired rights, the traditional doctrine applied the normal principles of State responsibility for unlawful acts to these measures. A secondary duty was imposed upon the nationalizing State to eliminate all the damaging consequences of its unlawful act. This was to be achieved by restitution of the expropriated undertaking, or if restitution were not possible, by the "payment of a sum corresponding to the value which a restitution in kind would bear," plus the award of "damages for loss sustained which would not be covered by restitution in kind or payment in place of it. . . ."[3] On the strength of this judicial pronouncement, the classical doctrine required, in cases of expropriation or nationalization, that indemnity be determined on the basis of the full market value of an undertaking as a "going concern," plus the value of its future earning prospects (*lucrum cessans*), good will and other intangible assets. This claim was synthesized in the formula, still defended by many industrialized States, of "just" or "adequate" compensation. The formula also requires that compensation be "prompt" and "effective." Payment is expected at the time of dispossession or shortly thereafter in a convertible and freely transferable currency.[4]

The very basis of this traditional doctrine, which is predicated on the existence of an unlawful act, is removed once it is realized that the acquired right to private property—in particular, private ownership of the means of industrial production—is no longer protected by contemporary international law. Different economic systems coexist peacefully in the world today. There is a growing trend toward recognition of the right of each State to organize its economic structure as it chooses and to introduce all the economic and social changes which the government of the day deems desirable. As provided in Article 1 of the Charter of Economic Rights and Duties of States, "[e]very State has the sovereign and inalienable right to choose its economic system. . . ."[5]

Once the measures of nationalization are not *per se* unlawful, but, on the contrary, constitute the exercise of a sovereign right, the general rules of State responsibility that govern unlawful acts can no longer be applied. The assertion of the existence of a duty of restitution of a nationalized undertaking would be tantamount to a denial of the right to nationalize. Consequently, the principle proclaimed by the Permanent Court that the amount of compensation should correspond as closely as possible to the economic benefit which the foreign owner would gain from restitution[6] is deprived of relevance.

The Doctrine of Unjust Enrichment

One might contend, therefore, that there is no duty to compensate affected aliens in the event of nationalizations which further a general program of economic and social reform, particularly when no such indemnity is paid to the affected national owners. However, the practice actually followed by States argues against such a contention. That practice—in particular, the experience of widespread nationalizations following World War II—shows that compensation generally has been granted to alien owners, often through the so-called "lump-sum" agreements between the nationalizing State and the States whose subjects were affected by the nationalization measures.[7] However, it is clear from these examples that the legal foundation for the payment of compensation in the event of nationalizations must be sought in principles other than an internationally protected acquired right to property.

The principle which constitutes the legal foundation of the practice actually followed by States is to be found in the doctrine of unjust enrichment. If the nationalizing State were to grant no compensation when nationalizing alien property, it would enrich itself without justification at the expense of a foreign State—a distinct political, economic and social community. Through the exercise of its sovereign right, the nationalizing State would be depriving an alien community of the wealth represented by the investments it has made on foreign soil. The nationalizing State would be taking undue advantage of the fact that economic resources originating in another State had penetrated its territorial domain.

This principle signifies that it is not the elements of the loss suffered by the expropriated individual owner, but rather the enrichment, the beneficial gain which has been obtained by the nationalizing State, which must be taken into account. Any measure which results in a transfer of wealth in favor of the nationalizing State or one of its agencies gives rise to a duty to compensate. For example, the total suppression of a detrimental or inconvenient industrial or commercial activity, for reasons of general policy, is not subject to compensation. In that case, nothing is gained by the nationalizing State, despite the loss suffered by the foreign owner. Similarly, there is no duty to compensate for loss of good will when the abolition of free market conditions of competition nullifies the value of this intangible asset.

However, the municipal law doctrine of unjust enrichment, in all its aspects, cannot be mechanically transplanted into the sphere of international law.[8] What makes the doctrine of unjust enrichment highly relevant to nationalizations is its equitable foundation, which requires the taking into account of all the circumstances of each specific situation and the balancing of the claims of the dispossessed alien with the undue advantages that he may have enjoyed prior to nationalization. Thus, the principle of unjust enrichment would take into account the undue enrichment gained by foreign companies during a period of monopoly or of highly privileged economic position, as, for instance, during a period of colonial domination.

COMPENSATION UNDER THE CHARTER OF ECONOMIC RIGHTS AND DUTIES OF STATES

Charter Provisions and Interpretation

Article 2, paragraph 2(c) of the Charter of Economic Rights and Duties of States provides:

2. Each State has the right:

. . . .

(c) To nationalize, expropriate or transfer ownership of foreign property, in which case appropriate compensation should be paid by the State adopting such measures, taking into account its relevant laws and regulations and all circumstances that the State considers pertinent. In any case where the question of compensation gives rise to a controversy, it shall be settled under the domestic law of the nationalizing State and by its tribunals, unless it is freely and mutually agreed by all States concerned that other peaceful means be sought on the basis of the sovereign equality of States and in accordance with the principle of free choice of means.[9]

The question arises as to which of the various approaches to the question of compensation the above provision corresponds.

It is obvious that the provision does not correspond to the doctrine of "prompt, adequate and effective compensation." In the early stages of the drafting of the Charter, the industrialized States insisted that such were the requirements of existing international law.[10] A vast majority of States categorically rejected the proposal to refer to "prompt, adequate and effective compensation," thus demonstrating that the alleged customary rule lacked the necessary generality and uniformity.[11] It is apparent from the process of elaboration of the Charter that the classical doctrine does not represent the general consensus of States. Consequently, it cannot be considered as a rule of customary law.

The *travaux preparatoires* of the Charter also show that the provision of paragraph 2(c) is not based on a position which denies the existence of any obligation to pay compensation. This position, originally adopted by the working group which drafted the Charter, was abandoned during discussion of the instrument.[12] The text originally presented to the General Assembly stated that compensation was to be paid "provided that all relevant circumstances call for it."[13] This text clearly avoided the imposition of a duty to compensate and left such payment to the discretion of the expropriating State. It was only a few days before the vote that the Group of 77[14] changed its position and proposed to revise the text by inserting a provision imposing the obligation to pay "appropriate compensation."[15] The text as finally adopted not only imposes the duty to pay "appropriate compensation"; it also provides that such compensation shall be determined by "taking into account . . . all circumstances that the State considers pertinent."[16]

The following exemplify factors which should be taken into account: whether the initial investment has been recovered, whether there has been undue enrichment as a result of a colonial situation, whether the profits obtained have been excessive, the contribution of the enterprise to the economic and social development of the country, its respect for labor laws and its reinvestment policies. Failure to pay taxes would not, in and of itself, determine the amount of compensation due, but it would constitute a credit which may be set off by the expropriating State vis-à-vis the expropriated company at the moment of payment. For this reason or similar ones, there may be cases where, in fact, the indemnity is minimal or nonexistent; but this would not signify legally the nonpayment of compensation. It is for these reasons that the Charter employs the term "appropriate" instead of "just" or "adequate" since it conveys better the complex circumstances which may be pertinent in each case.

Thus, it is clear that the basic features of Article 2, paragraph 2(c)—the recognition of an international duty to pay compensation and the determination of the amount due in light of the particular circumstances of each case—are rooted in equitable considerations. They point to the doctrine of unjust enrichment as the legal foundation for the provision. In this regard, it has been said that "[t]he notion of appropriate compensation is flexible enough to allow a decisionmaker, whether domestic or international, to take into account elements of unjust enrichment in the background of the investment in determining what under the circumstances constitutes appropriate compensation."[17]

Criticisms: Relation of the Charter to Customary International Law

However, this interpretation of the Charter provision has been widely criticized, especially by writers from industrialized countries. The main criticism addressed against this provision is "the absence of any references in article 2 to the applicability of international law to the treatment of foreign investment,"[18] which is described as "the utter rejection of international law" in respect of nationalization or expropriation measures.[19] The Charter is thus interpreted as pronouncing for the exclusive jurisdiction of the territorial State: "so conceived, international law itself would place within the hands of the State all available means to circumvent the obligation it provides."[20] Other critics have concluded that the only obligation "is to grant such compensation, if any, as it is subjectively thought to be 'appropriate,' considering only local law and 'circumstances,' to which international law is not necessarily 'pertinent.' "[21]

It must be recognized that Article 2, paragraph 2, the result of compromise between differing views, is so vague and ambiguous as to lend support to such an understanding of the provision. However, a reading of the entire article in relation to other parts of the instrument and basic principles of international law, compels a different interpretation. It is true that Article 2, paragraph 2(c) does not include the provision of General Assembly Resolution 1803 requiring, in cases of nationalization or expropriation, the payment of appropriate compensation "in accordance with rules in force in the State taking such measure in the exercise of its sovereignty and *in accordance with international law.*"[22] The developed countries continuously asserted that customary international law provided for "prompt, adequate and effective compensation."[23] The phrase "in accordance with international law" was eliminated because of Third World countries' "suspicions as to what Western countries expect from international law."[24] However, once it is established that the alleged customary rule of "prompt, adequate and effective" compensation is no longer accepted by the vast majority of the international community,[25] the reference to international law lost the meaning intended by the developed countries.

Article 2 of the Charter also refers to the application by the expropriating State of its laws and regulations and to its appreciation of all pertinent circumstances. It is perfectly legitimate to accept this determination as the one to be made in the first instance since under the local remedies rule national law and local remedies must be applied and exhausted. But the requirement of Article 2, paragraph 2(c) for the payment of an "appropriate compensation" remains.

Thus, if a nationalizing State, in application of its laws and in its appreciation of the circumstances, were to offer compensation which was not considered "appropriate" by the other interested State (and not just by the individual party), the subjective determination by the host State would not be final. The State of nationality of the expropriated owner would become authorized under the existing rules of international law to take up the case of its national and to make a claim on its behalf, based on the host State's noncompliance with the international duty to pay "appropriate compensation." In that case, an international controversy would arise between the two States, as is expressly recognized in Article 2, paragraph 2(c).

The industrialized States proposed that if an international controversy were to arise out of measures of nationalization or expropriation, then, after national laws and remedies were exhausted, the dispute should be submitted to compulsory adjudication or arbitration.[26] Although the Charter of the United Nations provides that legal disputes should "as a general rule be referred by the parties to the International Court of Justice,"[27] a different principle prevails in practice. The 1970 Declaration of Principles of International Law concerning Friendly Relations and Cooperation among States in accordance with the Charter of the United Nations pronounced the principle of a state's "free choice of means."[28] According to the principle of "free choice of means," no sovereign State is bound to accept a particular method of settlement except on the basis of its own consent. Consequently, compulsory adjudication or an obligation to submit to third-party settlement only exists when it is agreed upon by both interested States, either on an ad hoc basis or by means of a preexisting treaty or agreement. This is the case, for example, when States have accepted either the compulsory jurisdiction of the Court in all legal disputes or are parties to the arbitration agreement sponsored by the World Bank.[29] But unless there is such agreement, no rule of general international law compels States to solve their investment disputes by recourse to international judicial settlement or to arbitration. This is, *in fine*, what is established in Article 2, paragraph 2(c).

By recognizing that an international controversy exists in the event of disagreements over a unilaterally determined compensation, and by referring in its final words to the "sovereign equality of States" and to "the principle of free choice of means," Article 2, paragraph 2(c) triggers Article 33 of the United Nations Charter.[30] The unsettled dispute continues to be an international controversy. A basic rule of international law, and a corollary to the principles of sovereign equality of States and the free choice of means, is that an international dispute cannot be settled unilaterally by any one of the parties, not even by its municipal tribunals.

Conclusion

It follows that it is not entirely accurate to say that international law has been "utterly rejected" by the Charter of Economic Rights and Duties of States. Though expelled through the door because of its alleged identification with the doctrine of "prompt, adequate and effective compensation," it has come back through the window in the garb of an equitable principle which takes into account the specific circumstances of each case and is more likely to be of assistance in the settlement of investment disputes through negotiation or, if the parties so agree, through adjudication.

INVESTMENT AGREEMENTS BETWEEN STATES AND PRIVATE PERSONS

Legal Status

The question of the legal status of investment agreements between States and private companies constituted the chief stumbling block in the way of consensus on the terms of Article 2 of the Charter of Economic Rights and Duties of States.[31] In the words of the chairman of the Working Group that drafted the Charter, Ambassador Jorge Castañeda, "Disagreement on that issue was radical."[32]

The industrialized States favored inclusion of an express reference in Article 2 to these agreements, emphasizing the obligation of States to fulfill the agreements in good faith and to respect any dispute settlement procedures contained in the agreements.[33] This position is supported by the following provision of General Assembly Resolution 1803: "[f]oreign investment agreements freely entered into by or between sovereign States shall be observed in good faith; . . ."[34] The text places agreements concluded by a State with private foreign companies on the same footing as inter-State agreements.

While not denying the general duty of all States to fulfill their obligations in good faith, the countries of the Group of 77 would not classify investment agreements between States and private foreign companies as international agreements. Since these agreements were not concluded between States, they were governed by the domestic law of the State concerned. "They did not have international status, because private companies [are] not subjects of international law."[35] Consequently, the developing countries refused to accept the proposal of the industrialized States "because they felt that it would be tantamount to conferring international status on such companies and making the legal bond between the company and the State a bond of international law."[36]

During the discussion of Article 2, reference was made to the Convention on the Settlement of Investment Disputes between States and Nationals of Other States,[37] which provides a binding arbitration procedure for investment disputes.[38] However, any obligation to comply with this method of settlement results from the consent of the States that are parties to the Convention. The opposition of the Group of 77 to the proposal of the industrialized States in this area was based on the fear that its incorporation in the Charter might give the character of general international law to solutions like the one sponsored by the World Bank. Some Latin American States which had accepted without reservations the compulsory jurisdiction of the International Court of Justice viewed this Convention as an expedient devised by capital exporting countries to remedy the lack of judicial guarantees resulting from the reluctance of such countries to accept without crippling reservations[39] the compulsory jurisdiction of the Court in investment disputes. For this reason a dispute as to whether compensation is "appropriate" is to be settled in an arbitration which places the private company and the developing States on the same level of adversary proceedings rather than in litigation between the interested States.

The opposition of the developing countries is justified by the position of the International Court of Justice in the *Anglo-Iranian Oil Co. Case.*[40] There, the Court rejected the view that a concessionary contract between a government and a foreign private corporation could be considered an international treaty.[41] It follows that the cancellation of a concession of this nature before the expiration of its term, as a consequence of a measure of nationalization, cannot be considered a breach of an international treaty.

But this does not mean that an anticipated cancellation would have no legal consequences. The rights represented by a concession or a contract are no more exempt from expropriation than are mines or factories. The agreement and the expectations thereunder represent property interests which are subject to the eminent domain of the territorial State. Since a cancellation would constitute the expropriation of the contractual rights of a foreign company, the cancellation would be subject to the payment of "appropriate compensation" in accordance with Article 2, paragraph 2(c).

An arbitration clause in a concession would not be affected by the cancellation of the contract. The arbitration clause stands on its own and is separable from the contract: otherwise, the purpose of having such a clause in a contract is defeated. Consequently, the contracting State would be bound by the arbitration agreement and would be obligated to pay the compensation which the tribunal finds appropriate. But this is not an obligation resulting from an international treaty; rather, it is derived from the contract itself and is based on general principles of law, particularly the requirement that a State observe all its obligations in good faith.

Stabilization Clauses

What is the situation if the concession or contract contains an express stabilization clause providing, for instance, that the agreement will not be altered during its term without the consent of both parties?

In his very penetrating studies on this subject, Professor Prosper Weil reaches the conclusion that such clauses deprive the host State of the power to terminate a concession without the private party's consent. He bases his conclusion on the ground that a contract which contains a stabilization clause is governed by international law rather than the law of the contracting State.[42]

We do not believe that there is an international law of contracts. But even if there were such a body of law, the principle of a State's permanent sovereignty over its wealth and natural resources[43] would be recognized as a supervening principle of international law. Professor Weil's conclusion conflicts with the fundamental concept and purpose of this principle.

This does not mean that stabilization clauses have no legal effect. An anticipated cancellation in violation of such a contractual stipulation would give rise to a special right to compensation; the amount of the indemnity would have to be much higher than in normal cases because the existence of such a clause is a most pertinent condition which must be taken into account in determining the appropriate compensation. For instance, there would be a duty to compensate for the prospective gains (*lucrum cessans*) to be obtained by the private party during the period that the concession still has to run.

In contracts between States and private parties, stipulations have been inserted subjecting the contract to international law, or the general principles of international law, rather than the municipal law of the host State.[44] These stipulations are designed to function as indirect or disguised stabilization clauses.

In my view, such stipulations, which are often resisted by developing States, do not achieve the desired purpose of stabilization and, in other respects, are unnecessary and even counter-productive. They do not achieve the purpose of real stabilization clauses since international law does not forbid either a nationalization or the resulting cancellation of the contract, provided appropriate compensation is paid.

Furthermore, they are unnecessary because international law is always applicable to the cancellation of a contract or the nationalization of an enterprise without the payment of appropriate compensation. After the exhausting of local remedies, there would be an international responsibility for expropriation of contractual rights, enforced by diplomatic protection, just as in any other case of expropriation which is not accompanied by an appropriate indemnification. It is unnecessary to stipulate that the contract will be governed by international law in order to reach this result. It is not the contract as such, but rather the situation as a whole which is governed by international law, regardless of the parties' stipulations.

Finally, since international law does not possess adequate rules governing contracts of this nature, the stipulations may be counter-productive. Some of these long-term contracts—for example, the oil concessions of the thirties— had to be adjusted to new circumstances when it became evident that the original conditions were too favorable to the companies. This process of readjustment was conducted on the basis of institutions of municipal contractual law such as the doctrine of frustration of contracts or of administrative contracts. Such a process would have been much more difficult if the strict conditions governing the change of circumstances in the field of treaties had been applied. The exclusion of the flexible methods for contractual adjustment which have been elaborated by the various systems of municipal law and their replacement by the rigidity of international law may lead, in practice, to the complete breakdown of the contractual link, a situation which is unfavorable both to the maintenance of the rule of law and to the interests of the private party.

Calvo Clauses

In certain cases, these contracts contain stipulations in which the private party agrees not to call upon his State of nationality in any issues arising out of the contract's "Calvo clause."[45] The industrialized States have often disputed the validity of these clauses as they involve a waiver by the private party of the inalienable right of the State to protect its citizens abroad. However, just as the governmental party is expected to comply with an arbitration or a stabilization clause of a contract, a Calvo clause must be observed on the basis of the principle of good faith. This is confirmed by important arbitral awards which have recognized the validity of the Calvo clause with respect to any matter connected with the contract provided, naturally, that the governmental party has also complied with the agreement.[46] The principle of good faith binds both parties equally. It constitutes "[o]ne of the basic principles governing the creation and performance of legal obligations, whatever their source. . . ."[47]

The critics of the Charter of Economic Rights and Duties of States emphasize the refusal to accept the proposal of the industrialized States to refer expressly to the principle of good faith[48] in the context of contracts between States and private parties.[49] However, the developing countries maintained that this general principle applies to all State obligations.[50] To insert it specifically in connection with the duties enumerated in Article 2 would have created an unbalanced situation regarding other obligations of States which are enumerated in the Charter, such as the duty to avoid the use of coercion[51] and that of nonintervention.[52]

CONCLUSION

In interpreting the rights and duties of States under Article 2, paragraph 2, it is of overriding importance to consider both the equitable balancing nature of the provision and the concept of good faith as applied to international obligations. The absence of an express reference to the principle of good faith in Article 2, paragraph 2 does not mean that the duty to perform contractual obligations in good faith has been excluded from the Charter. Chapter 1, subparagraph (j) of the instrument, which applies to all obligations dealt with therein, including those of Article 2, provides: "Economic as well as political and other relations among States shall be governed, *inter alia*, by the following principles: . . . (j) Fulfilment in good faith of international obligations; . . ."[53] Furthermore, Article 33, paragraph 2 of the Charter of Economic Rights and Duties of States states that "[i]n their interpretation and application, the provisions of the present Charter are interrelated and each provision should be construed in the context of other provisions."[54] Finally, the interpretation advanced here of the relevant provisions of the Charter is confirmed by the remarks of Ambassador Castañeda, the Chairman of the Working Group that drafted the document:

The Charter accepts that international law may act as a factor limiting the freedom of the State when the interests of aliens are affected, even if Article 2 does not say so expressly. From a legal point of view this follows from the provisions contained in other articles of the Charter which must be interpreted and applied jointly with Article 2.[55]

NOTES

The author was president of the International Court of Justice in the Hague, Netherlands, until the February 1979 expiration of his term of office.

1. G.A. Res. 1803, 17 U.N. GAOR, Supp. (No. 17) 17, U.N. Doc. A/5217 (1962); G.A. Res. 2158, 21 U.N. GAOR, Supp. (No. 16) 29, U.N. Doc. A/6316 (1966); G.A.

Res. 2386, 23 U.N. GAOR, Supp. (No. 18) 24, U.N. Doc. A/7218 (1968); G.A. Res. 2692, 25 U.N. GAOR, Supp. (No. 28) 63, U.N. Doc. A/8028 (1970); G.A. Res. 3016, 27 U.N. GAOR, Supp. (No. 30) 48, U.N. Doc. A/8730 (1972); G.A. Res. 3171, 28 U.N. GAOR, Supp. (No. 30) 52, U.N. Doc. A/9030 (1973).

2. G.A. Res. 3281, 29 U.N. GAOR, Supp. (No. 31) 50, U.N. Doc. A/9631 (1974).

3. The Factory at Chorzow Case, [1928] P.C.I.J., ser. A., No. 17, at 47 (claim for indemnity) (merits).

4. The Hickenlooper Amendment understands this doctrine as requiring "speedy compensation for such property in convertible foreign exchange, equivalent to the full value thereof." 22 U.S.C. § 2370(e)(1) (1976).

5. G.A. Res. 3281, 29 U.N. GAOR, Supp. (No. 31) 50, U.N. Doc. A/9631 (1974).

6. See text accompanying note 3 supra.

7. Even socialist States, whose economic policies are based on the national ownership of means of production, have made and accepted inter se claims for compensation resulting from measures of nationalization. See, e.g., Agreement on the Settlement of Outstanding Property Questions, Feb. 11, 1956, Yugoslavia-Czechoslovakia, 397 U.N.T.S. 199.

8. Lord McNair wisely advised that international law does not import private law rules and institutions "lock, stock and barrel" but regards them as "an indication of policy and principles." Advisory Opinion on International Status of South-West Africa, [1950] I.C.J. 128, 148 (separate opinion of Lord McNair).

9. G.A. Res. 3281, 29 U.N. GAOR, Supp. (No. 31) 50, U.N. Doc. A/9631 (1974).

10. 29 U.N. GAOR, C.2 (1638th mtg.) 382, 384, U.N. Doc. A/C.2/SR. 1638 (1974). See also Alternative 4 to Article 2 of the Draft of the Charter of Economic Rights and Duties of States, U.N. Doc. TD/B/AC. 12/4, at 10 (1974).

11. See 29 U.N. GAOR, C.2 (1638th mtg.) 382, 384, U.N. Doc. A/C.2/SR. 1638 (1974).

12. Castañeda, La Charte des Droits et Devoirs Économiques de États, 20 Annuaire Français de Droit International 31, 50–51 (1974) [hereinafter "Castañeda"].

13. Draft Resolution of the Charter of Economic Rights and Duties of States, U.N. Doc. A/C.2/L. 1386, reprinted in Report of the Second Committee, 29 U.N. GAOR, Annexes (Agenda Item 48) 1, at 3, U.N. Doc. A/9946 (1974).

14. The name comes from the "Joint Declaration of the Seventy-Seven Developing Countries Made at the Conclusion of the United Nations Conference on Trade and Development," Proceedings of UNCTAD, Final Act and Report, Annex B, 66, U.N. Doc. E./CONF.46/141, Vol. 1 (1964). Although several developing States have joined this faction since 1964, the original designation for the group has been retained.

15. See U.N. Doc. A/C.2/SR. 1386/Corr. 6, reprinted in Report of the Second Committee, 29 U.N. GAOR, Annexes (Agenda Item 48) 1, at 7, U.N. Doc. A/9946 (1974); Castañeda, supra note 12, at 51.

16. Art. 2, para. 2(c), G.A. Res. 3281, 29 U.N. GAOR, Supp. (No. 31) 50, U.N. Doc. A/9631 (1974).

17. Falk, The New States and International Legal Order, 118 Recueil des Cours: Academie de Droit International [R.A.D.I.] 1, 29 (1966).

18. Statement by the delegate of Canada, 29 U.N. GAOR, C.2 (1649th mtg.) 446, U.N. Doc. A/C.2/SR. 1649 (1974).

19. Feuer, Reflexions sur La Charte des Droits et Devoirs Économiques des États, 79 Revue Generale de Droit International Public 273, 291 (1975) (author's translation).

20. Id.

21. Brower & Tepe, *The Charter of Economic Rights and Duties of States: A Reflection of International Law?* 9 Int'l Law. 295, 305 (1975).

22. G.A. Res. 1803, 17 U.N. GAOR, Supp. (No. 17) 15, U.N. Doc. A/5217 (1962) (emphasis added).

23. *See* 29 U.N. GAOR, C.2 (1638th mtg.) 382, 384, U.N. Doc. A/C.2/SR. 1638 (1974); U.N. Doc. TD/B/AC. 12/4 at 10.

24. De Waart, *Permanent Sovereignty over Natural Resources as a Cornerstone for International Economic Rights and Duties*, 24 Neth. Int'l L. Rev., 304, 313 (1977).

25. *See* text accompanying note 11 *supra*.

26. *See* proposed amendment to Article 2, U.N. Doc. A/C.2/L. 1404, *reprinted in* Report of the Second Committee, 29 U.N. GAOR, Annexes (Agenda Item 48) 1, at 6, U.N. Doc. A/9946 (1974).

27. U.N. Charter art. 36, para 3.

28. G.A. Res. 2625, 25 U.N. GAOR, Supp. (No. 28) 121, 123, U.N. Doc. A/ 8028 (1970).

29. Convention on the Settlement of Investment Disputes, *opened for signature* Mar. 18, 1965, 17 U.S.T. 1270, T.I.A.S. No. 6090, 575 U.N.T.S. 159.

30. Article 33, paragraph 1 of the U.N. Charter provides: "The parties to any dispute, the continuance of which is likely to endanger the maintenance of international peace and security, shall, first of all, seek a solution by negotiation, enquiry, mediation, conciliation, arbitration, judicial settlement, resort to regional agencies or arrangements, or other peaceful means of their own choice."

31. 29 U.N. GAOR, C.2 (1638th mtg.) 382, 383, U.N. Doc. A/C.2/SR. 1638 (1974).

32. *Id.*

33. *See* 29 U.N. GAOR, Annexes (Agenda Item 48) 1, at 3, U.N. Doc. A/9946 (1974).

34. G.A. Res. 1803, 17 U.N. GAOR, Supp. (No. 17) 15, at 16, U.N. Doc. A/ 5217 (1962) (emphasis added).

35. 29 U.N. GAOR, C.2 (1638th mtg.) 382, 383, U.N. Doc. A/C.2/SR. 1638 (1974).

36. *Id.*

37. Convention on the Settlement of Investment Disputes, *opened for signature* Mar. 18, 1965, 17 U.S.T. 1270, T.I.A.S. No. 6090, 575 U.N.T.S. 159.

38. *Id.* Ch. IV; De Waart, *Permanent Sovereignty over Natural Resources as a Cornerstone for International Economic Rights and Duties*, 24 Neth. Int'l L. Rev. 304, 318 (1977).

39. *See, e.g.,* the Connally Amendment imposed by the Senate on the U.S. declaration of acceptance of I.C.J. jurisdiction, S. Res. 196, 79th Cong., 2d Sess., 92 Cong. Rec. 10692 (1946). The amendment limits U.S. acceptance to matters not within the domestic jurisdiction of the United States, and reserves for the United States the authority to decide what matters are "domestic." *Id.*

40. [1952] I.C.J. 93 (jurisdiction).

41. *Id.* at 112.

42. Weil, *Les Clauses de Stabilisation ou d'Intangibilité Insérées dans les Accords de Developpement Economique*, in Melanges Offerts à Charles Rousseau (1974); Weil, *Problèmes Relatifs aux Contrats Passes entre un État et un Particulier*, 128 R.A.D.I. 101 (1969).

43. *See* text accompanying notes 1 & 2 *supra*.

44. *See* Van Hecke, *Les Accords entre un État et une Personne Privée Étrangère*, 57 Annuaire de l'Institute de Droit International 192 (1977).

45. The Calvo clause is incorporated in article 17 of the Peruvian Constitution and states that: "Commercial companies, national or foreign, are subject, without restrictions, to the laws of the Republic. In every state contract with foreigners, or in the concession contracts granted in their favor, it must be expressly stated that they will submit to the laws and Courts of the Republic and renounce all diplomatic claims." Const. art. 17 (Peru).

46. *See* Manual of Public International Law 591-93 (M. Sørensen, ed. 1968).

47. Nuclear Tests Case (New Zealand v. France). [1974] I.C.J. 457, 473.

48. 29 U.N. GAOR, Annexes (Agenda Item 48) 1, at 6, U.N. Doc. A/9946 (1974).

49. *See, e.g.,* White, *A New International Economic Order?* 16 Va. J. Int'l L. 323, 331 (1976).

50. *See* 29 U.N. GAOR, C.2 (1638th mtg.) 382, 383-84, U.N. Doc. A/C.2/SR. 1638 (1974). *See* text accompanying notes 33 & 34 *supra.*

51. Art. 32, G.A. Res. 3281, 29 U.N. GAOR, Supp. (No. 31) 50, U.N. Doc. A/9631 (1974).

52. *Id.* Ch. 1, subpara. (d).

53. *Id.*

54. *Id.*

55. Castañeda, *supra* note 11, at 54 (author's translations).

33. Summary of the Law of the Sea Convention

Bernard H. Oxman

After fifteen years of treaty negotiations, a new United Nations Convention on the Law of the Sea[1] was opened for signature in Jamaica on 10 December 1982. Although President Reagan found that most provisions "are consistent with U.S. interests" and "serve well the interests of all nations," he, along with the governments of Great Britain, Italy, Luxembourg, and West Germany, declined to authorize signature of the convention because of its deep seabed mining provisions. The five other members of the European Common Market, most other Western countries, the Soviet bloc, China, and most African, Asian, and Latin American countries were among the 117 signatories on 10 December. Japan joined them a few weeks later, and more signatures are likely. There is a substantial possibility that more than the necessary 60 signatories will ratify the convention and bring it into force in this decade.

Except perhaps for the provisions on deep seabed mining and the settlement of disputes, the stipulations of the convention are already regarded by some government and private experts as generally authoritative statements of existing customary international law applicable to all states. The president of the conference, however, joined many other delegates in warning that other countries will not necessarily accord Americans their *quids* if the U.S. government stays out and denies others their *quos.*

There are many facets to the current debate regarding the convention, a treaty of some 200 single-spaced pages whose 446 articles describe the basic rights and duties of states in connection with all activities at sea. Broad issues of process, principle, and precedent are invoked with respect to matters as varied as defense, ecology, economics, ethics, oceanography, politics, and (sometimes) law. Many of these issues are enunciated in other contributions to this collection.

It is not my purpose here to rehearse the debate but merely to give a brief summary of its object: the convention. Still, every sentence and omission reflects some professional judgment with which others might reasonably differ.

HISTORY OF NEGOTIATIONS

As its title indicates, the nine-year-long Third UN Conference on the Law of the Sea was not the first effort to lay down the rules of the law of the sea by universal agreement. Efforts to codify the law of the sea began under the League of Nations, culminating in the adoption by the first UN conference of four conventions on the law of the sea in 1958. Although ratified by the United States and many other maritime countries, the 1958 conventions did not fully achieve the objectives of a modern, universally respected body of law. Negotiated before almost half the current community of nations won independence, they were not ratified by a substantial majority of states, failed to resolve certain important issues, and did not deal adequately with certain new problems. The second conference was called in 1960 to try again to fix a maximum limit for the territorial sea. Its failure, coupled with the breakdown of customary restraint in maritime claims, meant that there remained no sufficiently reliable basis for predicting or restraining the increasingly conflicting claims of states to use and control the sea.

The third conference was charged by the UN General Assembly in 1973 with preparing a new comprehensive convention on the law of the sea, by consensus if at all possible. Beginning in 1975, the officers of the conference combined texts and ideas that emerged from informal negotiations and submitted them as an informal negotiating text at the end of a session. Delegations returned to the next session with a clearer idea of what they were prepared to accept. The final text emerged from the eighth iteration in this process. The few substantive amendments pressed to a vote were defeated.

Following the U.S. request for a record vote, on 30 April 1982 the conference adopted the text by a vote of 130 delegations in favor[2] and 4 against,[3] including the United States, with 18 abstentions[4] and 18 unrecorded.[5] Many Western European countries abstained on the vote because they preferred further improvements in the deep seabed mining provisions and were urged by the U.S. to vote no. Eastern European countries abstained because they were miffed by a technical provision in the conference resolution on protection of preconvention mining investments that they felt discriminated in favor of U.S. companies.

THE LEGAL MAP OF THE SEA

The convention applies to the "sea." Oceans, gulfs, bays, and seas are part of the "sea"; lakes and rivers are not. It has long been accepted that the sea may not be claimed in the same manner as land areas. Some parts are allocated to adjacent coastal states, and the rest is open to all.

The convention seeks to accommodate the interests of a state in two ways. First, it gives each state and its nationals freedom to act in pursuit of those interests (e.g., navigation rights and high seas freedoms). Second, the treaty limits the freedom of others to act in a manner adverse to those interests. Thus it imposes a duty on foreign states and their nationals to act in a prescribed manner (e.g., with respect to safety and environmental restrictions), and it gives a state the right to prevent or control activities of foreign states and their nationals (e.g., to maintain territorial sovereignty or coastal state jurisdiction over mining or fishing). Because rules generally apply to all, states must balance their desire to maximize their own freedom of action with their desire to limit the freedom of action of others. Law is one way to achieve this balance.

Internal Waters

Not only lakes and rivers but also harbors and other parts of the sea are so much enclosed by the land that they are, in effect, internal. An example is a small bay. Emergencies aside, use of internal waters (including their seabed and airspace) generally requires coastal state consent. However, because they are more open and useful to navigation, in those internal waters established by a "system of straight baselines" connecting coastal or insular promontories, foreign states enjoy the same passage rights as in the territorial sea. The convention contains a number of technical rules on how to establish baselines delimiting internal waters. These are largely drawn from the 1958 Territorial Sea Convention.

One innovative provision permits a state to investigate and try foreign ships visiting its ports for discharging pollutants in violation of international rules and standards virtually anywhere at sea.

The Territorial Sea

Every coastal state is entitled to exercise sovereignty over a belt of sea adjacent to the coast, including its seabed and airspace. This "territorial sea" is measured seaward from the coast or baselines delimiting internal waters.

One of the reasons for calling the third conference was that the earlier two conferences failed to reach agreement on the maximum permissible breadth of the territorial sea and, accordingly, on the extent of the free high seas. Respect for the old 3-mile limit had eroded. Some territorial sea claims extended as far as 200 miles. The new convention establishes 12 nautical miles as the maximum permissible breadth of the territorial sea.

The sovereignty of the coastal state in the territorial sea is subject to a right of "innocent passage" for foreign ships, but not for aircraft or submerged submarines. The question of what constitutes "innocence," as well as the extent of coastal state regulatory power over ships in passage, remained in dispute following the 1958 conference. While repeating the provisions of the 1958 convention on innocent passage, the new convention adds a list of activities that are not innocent passage, prohibits discrimination based on the flag or destination of a ship, and clarifies the right of the coastal state to establish sealanes and traffic separation schemes and to control pollution.

Straits

Any extension of the geographic area in which a coastal state exercises sovereignty at sea reduces the area in which the freedoms of the sea, including freedom of navigation and overflight, may be exercised. In narrow straits, extension of the territorial sea or the establishment of straight baselines may eliminate any (or any usable) high seas passage through the area. At the same time, states bordering straits may be subject to political pressures to assert control over transit for military, economic, or environmental purposes.

Under the 1958 convention, a coastal state could not suspend innocent passage in straits used for international navigation. The new convention establishes a more liberal right of "transit passage" for aircraft and submerged submarines as well as surface ships in most straits, including Bab-el-Mandeb, Dover, Gibralter, Hormuz, and Malacca. The debate about whether warship passage is "innocent" is rendered irrelevant. There is no right to stop a ship in transit passage, unless a merchant ship's violation of internationally approved regulations threatens major damage to the marine environment of the strait.

Special long-standing treaty regimes for particular straits (such as the Turkish straits), rights under the peace treaty between Egypt and Israel, and the regulation of artificial canals are unaffected by the convention.

Archipelagic Waters

The new convention generally validates the sovereignty claims of some independent island nations (e.g., the Bahamas, Indonesia, and the Philippines) over all waters within their archipelagos, subject to a right of "archipelagic sealanes passage," similar to transit passage, through the archipelago for all ships and aircraft, including submerged submarines. Specific criteria are established for limiting the situations in which archipelagic baselines may be drawn around an island group and how far they may extend.

The Contiguous Zone

The coastal state may take enforcement measures in a contiguous zone adjacent to its territorial sea to prevent or punish infringement of its customs, fiscal, immigration, or sanitary laws in its territory or territorial sea. The new convention extends the 1958 limit of this contiguous zone from 12 to 24 nautical miles from the coast or baseline. It also permits the coastal state to take special measures to protect archeological treasures.

The Continental Shelf

It is now generally accepted that the coastal state has exclusive "sovereign rights" to explore and exploit the natural resources of the seabed and subsoil of the continental shelf adjacent to its coast and seaward of its territorial sea. The questions are where and for what other activities coastal state authorization is needed.

The new convention permits the coastal state to establish the permanent outer limit of its continental shelf at either 200 nautical miles from the coast or baseline, or at the outer edge of the continental margin (the submerged prolongation of the land mass), whichever is further seaward. Its elaborate criteria for locating the edge of the continental margin are designed to allocate virtually all seabed oil and gas to coastal states. Once approved by an international commission of experts, the coastal state's charts showing the location of the outer edge of its continental margin are final and binding on the rest of the world (or at least on the other parties to the convention). This *ex parte* procedure is intended to lower the risk of investment in a manner similar to the common law action to quiet title.

Under the new convention, the coastal state has sovereign rights over the natural resources of the seabed and subsoil of the continental shelf, as well as the exclusive right to authorize and regulate drilling for all purposes and the right to consent to the course for pipelines. The coastal state's newly elaborated rights regarding installations and marine scientific research on the continental shelf are generally the same as its rights concerning the exclusive economic zone discussed in the next section.

The new convention specifies three new duties of the coastal state. The first, applicable to the entire continental shelf, requires every coastal state to establish environmental standards for all activities and installations under its jurisdiction that are no less effective than those contained in international standards. At the same time, the rigid petroleum installation removal regulations of the 1958 convention have been relaxed in response to oil company concerns.

The other new duties are applicable only to that part of the continental shelf that is seaward of 200 nautical miles from the coast. One requires the coastal state to pay a small percentage of the value of mineral production from the area into an international fund to be distributed to parties to the convention, particularly developing countries. Another prohibits the coastal state from withholding consent for marine scientific research outside specific areas under development.

The Exclusive Economic Zone

The provisions on the exclusive economic zone (EEZ) are all new law. Measured by any yardstick—political, military, economic, scientific, environmental, or recreational—the overwhelming proportion of activities and interests in the sea are affected by this new regime.

Under the convention every coastal state has the right to establish an exclusive economic zone seaward of its territorial sea and extending up to 200 nautical miles from its coast or baseline. Seabed areas beyond the territorial sea and within 200 miles of the coast are therefore subject to both the continental shelf and economic zone regimes.

Two separate sets of rights exist in the economic zone: those enjoyed exclusively by the coastal state and those that may be exercised by all states. The division is by activity, not by area or ship.

The rights of the coastal state in the economic zone are:

• Exclusive sovereign rights for the purpose of exploring, exploiting, conserving, and managing the living and nonliving natural resources of both the waters and the seabed and subsoil;

• Exclusive sovereign rights to control other activities for the economic exploitation and exploration of the zone, such as the production of energy from the water, currents, and winds;

• The exclusive right to control the construction and use of all artificial islands and those installations and structures that are used for economic purposes or that may interfere with the coastal state's exercise of its rights in the zone (e.g., an oil rig or offshore tanker depot);

• The right to be informed of and participate in proposed marine scientific research projects, and to withhold consent for a project in a timely manner under specified circumstances;

• The right to control dumping of wastes;

• The right to board, inspect, and, when there is threat of major damage, arrest a merchant ship suspected of discharging pollutants in the zone in violation of internationally approved standards. This right is subject to substantial safeguards to protect shippers, sailors, and consumers. Even if investigation of the ship indicates a violation, it must be released promptly on reasonable bond. If release if not obtained within ten days, an international court may set the bond and order release "without delay." If so authorized, a private party may seek this release order on behalf of the flag state. The convention establishes a time limit for prosecution, requires that the coastal state observe "recognized rights of the accused," prohibits punishments other than monetary fines, and restricts successive trials by different states for the same offense.

The rights of all states in the economic zone are:

• The high seas freedoms of navigation, overflight, and the laying of submarine cables and pipelines;

• Other internationally lawful uses of the sea related to these freedoms, such as those associated with the operation of ships, aircraft, and submarine cables and pipelines. This category may cover a gamut of uses such as recreational swimming, weather monitoring, and various naval operations.

This allocation of rights is accompanied by extensive duties.

Because both the coastal state and other states have independent rights to use the economic zone, each is required to ensure that its rights are exercised with "due regard" to the rights and duties of the other.

Flag states must ensure that their ships observe generally accepted international anti-pollution regulations, and each coastal state must take measures to ensure that activities under its jurisdiction or control do not cause pollution damage to other states.

The coastal state is required to ensure the conservation of living resources in the waters of the economic zone. Except with respect to marine mammals, it must also promote their optimum utilization by determining its harvesting capacity and granting access under reasonable conditions to foreign vessels to fish for the surplus, if any, that remains under its conservation limits. Neighboring states with small enclosed coastlines, or none at all, enjoy some priority of access to this surplus. International protection of whales and other marine mammals is required, as is regional regulation of highly migratory species such as tuna.

If the economic zones or continental shelves of neighboring coastal states overlap, they are to be delimited by agreement between those states on the basis of international law in order to achieve an equitable solution. This general provision should be read against the background of an increasing number of bilateral agreements and international judicial and arbitral decisions on offshore boundary delimitation.

The High Seas

Like the 1958 Convention on the High Seas, the new convention does not contain an exhaustive list of the freedoms of the high seas. Both expressly name the freedoms of navigation, overflight, fishing, and laying of submarine cables and pipelines. The new convention also lists freedom of scientific research and freedom to construct artificial islands and other installations permitted under international law.

Largely copied from the 1958 convention, the new high seas regime has been augmented by stronger safety and environmental obligations of the flag state and special provisions on the suppression of pirate broadcasting and illicit traffic in drugs. Freedom to fish on the high seas is subject to specific conservation and ecological requirements. Free high seas fishing is eliminated for salmon and can be eliminated or restricted for whales and other marine mammals.

Unlike the 1958 convention, the new convention does not contain a definition of the high seas. Rather it says that its articles on the high seas apply to all parts of the sea beyond the economic zone, and that most of those high seas articles also apply within the economic zone to the extent they are not incompatible with the articles on the economic zone. Thus, for example, the law of nationality of ships and the law of piracy continue unchanged in the economic zone.

The International Seabed Area

The "international seabed area" comprises the seabed and subsoil "beyond the limits of national jurisdiction"—that is, in effect, beyond the limits of the economic zone and continental shelf subject to coastal state jurisdiction. This area is declared to be the "common heritage of mankind." Its principal resource of current interest consists of polymetallic nodules lying at or near the surface of the deep ocean beds, particularly in the Pacific and to a lesser degree in the Indian Ocean. The nodules contain nickel, manganese, cobalt, copper, and traces of other metals.

Nonresource uses, including scientific research, are free, and prospecting is almost as free. On the other hand, mining requires a contract from an International Seabed Authority. Parties to the convention are prohibited from recognizing mineral rights asserted outside the convention system.

To obtain a contract conferring the exclusive right to explore and mine a particular area with security of tenure for a fixed term of years, a company must be "sponsored" by a state party. It must propose two mining areas, one to be awarded to the company, the other to be "reserved" by the Seabed Authority for exploration and exploitation by its own commercial mining company, the Enterprise, or by a developing country.

Assuming procedural requirements are met, the Seabed Authority may refuse to issue the contract to a qualified applicant in essentially four circumstances:

• If the applicant has a poor record of compliance under a previous contract;

• If the particular area has been closed to mining because of special environmental problems;

• If a single sponsoring state would thereby acquire more active minesites, particularly in the same general area, than are permissible under fairly broad geographic limits;

• If there is already a contract or application for all or part of the same area.

Before beginning commercial production, a miner must obtain a production authorization. This must be issued so long as the aggregate authorized production from the international seabed area would not exceed a twenty-year interim ceiling. In the absence of an applicable commodity agreement, this restriction limits the total nodule production to an amount that would generate by any given year no more than the cumulative increase in world demand for nickel in the five years before the first commercial production, plus 60 percent of the cumulative projected increase in total world demand for nickel thereafter.

In exchange for mining rights in a contract that may not be modified without its agreement, the mining company assumes three basic obligations:

- It must abide by various performance, safety, environmental, and other technical ground rules;

- It must pay to the Seabed Authority a specified proportion of the value of production or, at its election, a smaller proportion of production coupled with a specified proportion of profits. The Seabed Authority must use the funds to cover its administrative expenses and may then distribute the remainder to developing countries and peoples designated by regulation;

- Until ten years after the Enterprise first begins commercial production, the company must be willing to sell to the Enterprise, on fair and reasonable commercial terms and conditions determined by agreement or commercial arbitration, mining (but not processing) technology being used at the site if equivalent technology is not available on the open market. Alternatively, it would have the same obligation to a developing country planning to exploit the "reserved" site submitted by that company.

The International Seabed Authority

The Authority would have the standard structure of an intergovernmental organization—an Assembly of all states parties, a Council of limited membership, and a Secretariat.

The thirty-six-member Council must include four of the largest consumers and four of the largest (land-based) producers of the types of resources produced from the deep seabed, as well as four of the states whose nationals have made the largest investment in deep seabed mining. The Soviet bloc obtained an express guarantee of three Council seats in exchange for tacitly conceding at least seven, and probably eight or nine, seats to the West, including a guaranteed seat for the largest consumer, which was intended to be the United States should it become a party. Developing countries will hold most of the remaining seats.

The Assembly is referred to as the supreme organ of the Seabed Authority. However, the adoption of legally binding mining rules and regulations, restrictive environmental orders, and proposed amendments to the deep seabed mining provisions of the convention requires a consensus decision of the Council. Other substantive decisions, depending on their importance, require a three-fourths or two-thirds vote in the Council. A Technical Commission is required to recommend Council approval of applications for mining contracts if they satisfy the relevant requirements of the convention and the rules and regulations. That recommendation may be rejected only by consensus, excluding the applicant's sponsoring state.

The Enterprise—an intergovernmental mining company—is the most unusual feature of the Seabed Authority. The initial capitalization target for the Enterprise is the cost of developing one minesite, now estimated at well over $1 billion. Half would be in the form of private loans guaranteed by the states parties and half in the form of interest-free loans from the states parties.

If Jamaica ratifies the convention, it would be the site of the International Seabed Authority.

GENERAL OBLIGATIONS UNDER THE CONVENTION

The convention specifies a number of duties that apply to all or most of the sea. The most developed are the strong new duties to protect and preserve the marine environment. There are also duties to promote marine scientific research and dissemination of scientific knowledge, to protect archeological treasures found at sea, to use the seas for peaceful purposes, to refrain from any threat or use of force contrary to the UN Charter, and to settle disputes peacefully. There is a special chapter guaranteeing land-locked states access to the sea. Abuse of rights is prohibited.

Settlement of Disputes

The convention is the first global treaty of its kind to require, without a right of reservation, that an unresolved dispute between states parties concerning its interpretation or application shall be submitted at the request of either party to arbitration or adjudication for a decision binding on the other party. There are, however, important exceptions to this rule:

- Disputes concerning the rights of the coastal state in the economic zone or the continental shelf may be submitted by another state only in cases of interference with navigation, overflight, the laying of submarine cables and pipelines, and related rights, or in cases of violation of specified international environmental standards;

- Disputes regarding historic bays and maritime boundary delimitation between states with opposite or adjacent coasts, disputes concerning military activities, and disputes that are before the UN Security Council may be excluded by unilateral declaration.

Arbitration is the applicable procedure unless:

- Emergency measures (e.g., vessel release) are necessary before an arbitration panel has been constituted;

- Both the "defendant" and the "plaintiff" have accepted the jurisdiction of the International Court of Justice in The Hague or the new Tribunal on the Law of the Sea, to be established in Hamburg if West Germany ratifies the treaty; or

• The dispute concerns exploration or exploitation of the resources of the international seabed area. In this event, the case may be brought to a chamber of the Tribunal on the Law of the Sea or commercial arbitration, depending on the circumstances. These forums are open both to states parties and to the deep seabed mining companies sponsored by them.

CONFERENCE RESOLUTIONS

A Preparatory Commission of treaty signatories will draft provisional deep seabed mining regulations that will, in effect, interpret, clarify, and apply the convention text with greater precision. Only when they are drafted will one be able to know the exact nature of a miner's rights and obligations under the deep seabed mining system and the mining contracts to be issued. These regulations will automatically enter into force with the convention a year after 60 states have ratified it.

A conference resolution authorizes the Preparatory Commission to register the deep seabed mining companies that made substantial investments before 1983 as pioneer investors, each with the exclusive right to carry out exploration and testing in a registered area of 150,000 square kilometers at the start. Once the convention enters into force, a qualified pioneer investor sponsored by a state party must be granted a mining contract for that half of the original registered area selected by the investor if the Preparatory Commission has certified compliance with the conference resolution.

France, Great Britain, the United States, and West Germany signed an agreement in 1982 to deal with exploration applications for overlapping areas previously filed under their respective deep seabed mining laws. Such an agreement is envisaged by and consistent with the conference resolution on pioneer investment. It also may be regarded as a first step in establishing an international arrangement for deep seabed mining outside or in lieu of the convention.

RESERVATION, AMENDMENT, AND WITHDRAWAL

The convention does not permit reservations, but does permit other declarations and statements. Amendment is possible, but difficult—perhaps a bit less so with respect to deep seabed mining.

The deep seabed mining system as a whole is subject to review fifteen years after commercial production of deep seabed minerals begins. Should the review conference be unable to reach agreement on amendments within five years after it is convened, it may adopt amendments to the mining system by a three-fourths vote. These would enter into force for all parties a year after ratification by three-fourths of the parties, but would not affect mining under contracts already issued.

A party has the right to withdraw from the convention at any time on one year's notice.

NOTES

1. UN Doc. A/Conf. 62/122 (1982).
2. Australia, the Bahamas, Brazil, Canada, China, Colombia, Denmark, Egypt, Finland, France, Greece, Iceland, India, Indonesia, Ireland, Japan, Kuwait, Mexico, New Zealand, Nigeria, Norway, Panama, Peru, Saudi Arabia, Sweden, Switzerland, and all other countries except for those listed in 3, 4, and 5.
3. Israel, Turkey, the United States, and Venezuela. Israel objected to observer status for the PLO. Turkey and Venezuela apparently prefer to resolve offshore boundary disputes with their neighbors before accepting the convention. The United States objected to provisions regarding deep seabed mining.
4. Belgium, Bulgaria, Byelorussian SSR, Czechoslovakia, German Democratic Republic, Federal Republic of Germany, Hungary, Italy, Liberia (initially unrecorded), Luxembourg, Mongolia, Netherlands, Poland, Spain, Thailand, Ukranian SSR, USSR, United Kingdom.
5. Albania, Antigua/Barbuda, Belize, Comoros, Dominica, Ecuador, Equatorial Guinea, Gambia, Holy See, Kiribati, Maldives, Nauru, Solomon Islands, South Africa, Tonga, United Arab Emirates, Vanuatu, Tuvalu.

34. Power Sharing in the Law of the Sea

Philip Allott

The United Nations Convention on the Law of the Sea is a fact. It exists. Whether or not it becomes a fully operational treaty—signed, ratified, in force, widely supported, generally followed—it is and will be the cause of significant effects. Its very existence modifies political, economic, and legal relationships in countless ways whose direction and intensity we can predict only in a most speculative way. What we can say in advance is that the effect of the Convention—its own fate as a treaty and its impact on international relations—will substantially depend on how it is perceived. It is itself the product of mental processes. It will in its turn intrude into the mental processes of those involved in any way in the activities to which it relates. The purpose of the present article is to suggest a particular and unified structure of ideas within which the significance of the Convention may be perceived as a whole—a structure that, when grasped as a whole, facilitates the task of determining the significance of its individual provisions and has implications for our general perception of contemporary international law and society. . . .

The Law of the Sea Convention takes its place in the long history of international relations. It is already a major event in that history. As a self-standing fact, the Convention meets other objects in the field of international relations: the Geneva Conventions of 1958, customary international law, prenormative state practice, the international constitutional structure, the international class struggle, the New International Economic Order, the world balances of power. These great ideological structures, leviathans in the contemporary international sea, must make room for the newcomer, and countless lesser structures (regional, bilateral, local, temporary) must accept its existence. . . .

There is nothing in the Convention that does not have a relationship with these general structural relationships of international society. This is not to say that there are not other contexts of a still more general character, up to and including, as we shall see, the thought-structures known as Justice, Equity, Law, society, the state system—ideas without which such a far-reaching legal structure could not be articulated. They are the *causae sine qua non* of the Convention. But the *causa causans* of the structure of the whole Convention and of particular relationships within the Convention is to be found in the general structures of the same level of generality in the specific field of international relations.

It is these general structures of contemporary international society that have made possible the particular form in which the Convention has emerged as a social fact. These structures have, through a particular configuration of their interaction over a particular period of time, generated a *legislative* act. The Convention is a legislative act, not in the attenuated form represented by the hallowed formula of "lawmaking treaty," but in the fullest and most literal sense. The Convention has the two defining characteristics of legislation: (1) It transforms social policy into legal rules; and (2) that transformation is effected by an autonomous process. . . .

There is a fine piece of continental European legal terminology that is not used in the common law systems but that reflects the same concept to this day. Continental lawyers speak of "the legislator" as the source of law: *le législateur, der Gesetzgeber, il legislatore.* They would say, "the legislator apparently did not provide for such-and-such a situation." In an international consensus situation, the law is not made by one state or two, not by the majority of states, not even by the unanimous assent of all states. It is made by the disembodied hand of the international legislator, his hand pushed this way and that by the pressures of debate, interests, power. The *ratio legis* is to be found in the real-world forces whose ideological interaction is resolved, on this occasion, in the text of the Convention mediated through the decision-making process of the conference. . . .

The genesis and development of legal texts through such a consensus process is exceptionally obscure. It is very difficult to unravel the story of how a text came to acquire its final form, especially, as at UNCLOS, when all substantive discussion was off the record. Instead of the will of a majority opposed to the will of the minority, there is the interaction of many wills within the groups and among the groups, interacting not merely in relation to a draft text and a limited number of proposed amendments but in relation to an infinite number of possible alternative textual formulations, as various as the ingenuity and the patience of the negotiators will allow. . . .

The nature of the consensus process raises special problems in relation to *travaux préparatoires.* In the case of the LOS Convention the problem is exceptionally acute. The Convention is not quite in the happy position of the Treaty Establishing the European Economic Community, for example, which has no effective *travaux* at all and whose interpretation and application has been much assisted by their absence. Nor is it in the familiar position of leading codification treaties, such as the Vienna Convention on the Law of Treaties, where the four-stage *travaux* (ILC rapporteur's reports, ILC debates, ILC draft articles, conference papers and debates) are well known and their relevance well understood.

Instead, in the case of the LOS Convention, there is already and there will increasingly accumulate an amorphous mass of material, including very miscellaneous conference documents, together with contemporaneous and retrospective accounts purporting to describe the evolution of the texts. It should be understood here and now (before misunderstanding develops) that such material cannot be regarded as *travaux préparatoires* in the traditional sense (as used, for example, in Article 32 of the Vienna Convention on the Law of Treaties). With the possible exception of the successive published texts of the Convention, they do not have the objective character of *negotiating facts*, the actual material chain of causation of the resulting instrument, which is the essence of traditional *travaux*. The random and disorderly character of some of them and the partisan character of much of the rest mean that it would be wiser to regard them as a new kind of phenomenon, a physical manifestation of the decision-making process of consensus. . . .

The legislative view of the consensus process as outlined above throws an especially clear light on the position of those states which repudiate the consensus product at whatever stage of its organic existence. Through the metamorphic process of consensus, the produce undergoes constant changes in form and vitality. It develops in response to the pressures that are applied to it. At a particular moment of metamorphosis (say, the final conference vote on a treaty, signature, or ratification), a participant may repudiate the consensus product, may seek to reform it or to destroy it. Whether the product is strong enough to resist such pressures and whether it is able to adapt itself in response to the pressures are contingent questions, not in the sole control of the repudiating party, not capable of being predetermined by legal rules or principles. The will of the repudiating party meets the combined will embodied in the consensus product. In the case of the LOS Convention, it remains to be seen whether the negative attitude of certain states at the latest stages of the process will destroy, cripple, or transform the product or whether the will of the Convention will be strong enough to cause them to change their attitude or to enable it to become a powerful formative source of general international law for all states, including those which do not choose to be contracting parties to it.

Beyond the outermost structural context (the general structures of international relations) and the second structural layer (the Convention as the fruit of a specific legislative process), the third contextual layer is that of the Convention itself as an organized structural whole.

The Convention's main structural feature is its comprehensiveness. It is comprehensive in dealing with the whole nonland area of the world. It is also legally comprehensive. It has a rule for everything. The rule may be a permissive rule. It may be an obligation. It may confer an explicit freedom or leave a residual liberty by not specifying a right or a duty. But a Flying Dutchman wandering the sea areas of the world, carrying his copy of the Convention, would always be able to answer in legal terms the questions: who am I? who is that over there? where am I? what may I do now? what must I do now? The Convention would never fail him.

The first paragraph of the Preamble to the Convention provides: "Desiring to settle *all issues* relating to the law of the sea" (emphasis added).[1] The last paragraph adds a belt to the braces: "Affirming that *matters not regulated* by this Convention continue to be governed by the rules and principles of general international law" (emphasis added).

The way the Convention makes its rules is the way all legislation makes rules: by the process of legal classification. It recognizes persons by classifying them as legal persons. It establishes relationships between legal persons by applying jural relations to them. It specifies the content of the jural relations by classifying places, things, and activities. That is the transforming process of all legislation; there is no other way that social policy can be transformed into legal rules.

On one possible analysis of the Convention, one might say that it recognizes 57 kinds of legal person to answer the questions: who am I? who is that over there? One might similarly say that the Convention recognizes 58 legal sea areas to answer the question: where am I? The legal situation varies intrinsically as the legal persons participating in the situation vary and as the legal sea area in which activity occurs varies.

Needless to say, the Convention makes constant use of the eight fundamental Hohfeldian forms of jural relation.[2] But the Convention, at the textual level, makes use of a very large number of set formulas for establishing relations between legal persons in respect of places, things, and activities to answer the questions: what may I do? what must I do?

It is worth recalling the way such structural mechanisms operate in lawmaking.

There is a classic and apparently unpromising topic in university jurisprudence courses that is introduced by the injunction, "distinguish ownership and possession." The subject turns out to be very enlightening for the student. He gradually sees that ownership and possession are in fact areas situated on a broad *spectrum* of possible relationships between persons and all kinds of things: ownership of many different degrees, possession, constructive possession, custody, control, and so on. Then he comes to see that each of these relationships is itself a *bundle* of rights: right to exclude, right to possess, right to alienate, right to profit, right to manage, right to bequeath, and so on. He then sees that what the law does is to transform social policy into legal rules by an endless process of manipulating and permuting such possible legal elements, switching them on and off, aligning them in this direction or that. From this it finally becomes clear that the prelegislative stage, before the moment when policy becomes law, consists of a complex dialectical struggle among interested parties, all seeking to have the disembodied legislator do various quite specific things:

1. recognize my *group* as fit to be abstracted into a *legal person*, subject or object of a given legal relation;
2. recognize a given *place, thing, or activity* in which my group is interested as fit to be abstracted into the *material legal base* of a legal relation;
3. recognize an *interest* of my group as fit to be abstracted into the *primary legal objective* of a legal relation, consecrated as a right or protected by a duty.

The long saga of the negotiation of the LOS Convention was nothing other than such a prelegislative process. But there are two other fundamental features of the general legislative process that are of particular importance in understanding the nature of the LOS Convention, what may be called the "layering of legal relations" and the "delegation of power."

The layering of legal relations refers to the fact that the legislator may *superimpose* legal relations on each other, so that the same area, the same interest, the same activity may be the focus of any number of overlapping legal relations. There is the familiar example of a chattel, one and the same chattel, which may be subject to the ownership of A, the right to possession of B, the possession of C, the constructive possession of D, the bailee's possession of E, the custody of F, the control of G, and may be subject to overriding powers of any number of power holders up to and including the powers of local, state, and national public authorities. . . .

Of such potential legal relations, one is of outstanding importance in the structure of the LOS Convention: that of *power*. The Convention is a massive structure of powers. We tend to overlook the extent to which treaties confer powers, as opposed to more static forms of right. It seems that treaties are more and more conferring powers, but the LOS Convention is without parallel or precedent in the scale of its delegation of power. Powers obviously give rise to special problems for international law. Powers are a sort of delegated legislative function. The law allows me to choose at some later date to alter someone else's legal position with impunity and to my advantage. Powers may also be regarded as a form of *licensed wrong*. I may do what in other circumstances would be a wrong and the existence of the power confers on me an immunity from the normal legal consequences. But the license is always a limited license. The area of the immunity is legally and strictly circumscribed by what in administrative law is known as the concept of *vires*. Within the area of the power there is an infinite number of possible discretionary choices of action and inaction. Outside that area, action or inaction may be unlawful.

A great problem of modern international law is accordingly how to make sense of the large-scale conferring of powers within a system that does not have a regular court system to enforce *vires* or a body of administrative law to provide the principles used to identify the limits and to confer a *locus standi* on those who may challenge unlawful acts. Nor does the international system have an organized structure of political accountability to check on the application of powers from day to day and to review the discretionary choices made within the limits of powers, the *intra vires* decisions that are not in any case within the jurisdiction of courts, except to the extent that the administrative law deems them to be the misuse of a power (*détournement de pouvoir*).

Both the layering of legal relations and the delegation of powers are *boundary phenomena*. My right may begin where someone else's right ends. The more extensive my power, the more limited someone else's freedom. The boundaries between powers are expressed by power modifiers, what in English administrative law is called the "fettering" of powers. The fixing of these power modifiers is a major part of the process of negotiation and compromise at international conferences. All the participants at UNCLOS spent countless hours with their attention concentrated on a number of subtle distinctions such as:

generally accepted / applicable / relevant;
taking account of / on the basis of;
necessary steps / all necessary steps;
due notice / due publicity;
due regard / reasonable regard;
prevail / supersede;
without discrimination / on a footing of equality;
have the right to / shall be entitled to;
endeavor / make every effort;
in conformity with / in accordance with;
compatible with / not incompatible with;
where appropriate / as appropriate;
subject to / without prejudice to.

. . . The powerishness of the LOS Convention and the luxuriance of its layering of legal relations account for the vast dispute settlement system created in part XV (together with section 5 of part XI). There was a very general feeling that it would be pointless to create a legal structure of such complexity, containing thousands of subtle legal relationships, if there were no secure means of resolving disputes of interpretation and application. The dispute settlement provisions, in all their own subtlety and complexity, should be regarded as a gloss on every substantive provision of the Convention, integrated into the very functioning of every provision. They are a caution and a guarantee attached to each provision,[3] whose benefit, however, is only available to those states which become parties and not to those which seek to profit from what is advantageous to them in the Convention without becoming parties to it.

The place of the dispute settlement provisions in the Convention is one example of the obsessive concern of UNCLOS with the concept of "the package," another fundamental structural feature of the Convention as a whole. The Preamble refers to the concept: "Conscious that the problems of ocean space are closely interrelated and need to be considered as a whole. . . ." Article 309 prohibits reservations, largely on package grounds. The *travaux préparatoires*, such as they are, will be found to contain countless affirmations of the package concept. If the concept does survive and is used by courts and tribunals in applying the Convention, it could have an important effect, especially, oddly enough, if the convention does not enter into force as a treaty and has to be applied as a formative source of customary international law.

It is not possible to list here all the package aspects of the Convention. Among the most important is the all-embracing package that incorporates the subject matter of all four of the Geneva Conventions into a single Convention, with the addition and integration within that one Convention of what is in effect a major pollution convention and a major piece of international economic legislation (the deep seabed regime). The three main parts of the Convention (general law of the sea, deep seabed, pollution and marine scientific research) should also be regarded as subordinate integrated packages.

Beyond these there are some more recherché packages:

- the links between and among the 12-mile territorial sea, the 200-mile exclusive economic zone (EEZ), and transit passage through straits used for international navigation;

- the link between Article 55 (on the legal regime of the EEZ) and Article 86 (virtually a definition of the high seas);

- the link between the delimitation articles (15, 74, and 83) and Article 298 (optional exception for delimitation disputes);

- the links among Article 76 (definition of the continental shelf), Article 134(4) (limits of the international seabed area), and Annex II (Commission on the Limits of the Continental Shelf).

Of course, there are also countless special links within articles and between neighboring articles where compromises were arrived at by balancing one text against another.

The structure of the main legal sea areas is an instructive illustration of the relationship of continuity and discontinuity between the new Convention and the Geneva Conventions. Geneva law was based on five main legal sea areas (internal waters, territorial sea, contiguous zone, continental shelf, high seas). Several more arose in subsequent state practice and established themselves with more or less legal finality. UNCLOS adds a further four main legal sea areas to the Geneva five (archipelagic waters, EEZ, straits used for international navigation, deep seabed).

Superficially, the legal basis of the Geneva five remains the same, epitomized by the key words *sovereignty* (internal and territorial waters), *control, sovereign rights, freedoms*. But important changes have taken place within those structures.

The territorial sea sovereignty is to be exercised "subject to this Convention and to other rules of international law" (Article 2). The other relevant provisions of the Convention are articulated in terms of rights and duties conferred and imposed now on one party to the territorial sea relationship (coastal state), now on the other (other states, foreign ship), as the different holders are permuted from provision to provision. The rights are mainly in the form of powers and freedoms.[4] The right of innocent passage is "subject to this Convention" (Article 17). Passage is defined in a slightly more elaborate way than in Geneva (Article 18). Passage must take place "in conformity with this Convention and with other rules of international law" (Article 19). The coastal state must not hamper innocent passage "except in accordance with this Convention." The coastal state may adopt laws and regulations "in conformity with the provisions of this Convention and other rules of international law" (Article 21).

This network of rather obsessively interconnected rights, each delicately balanced against others, contains at its core two new lengthy specifications that are not found in the Geneva texts:

1. the long list in Article 19 of activities that are to be considered prejudicial to the peace, good order, or security of the coastal state, which thus becomes an important part of the legal content of the relevant rights (powers) and duties of the parties to the territorial sea relationship; and

2. the long list in Article 21 of matters in respect of which the coastal state may adopt laws and regulations, which similarly becomes an important part of the legal content of the rights (powers) and liabilities of the parties to the territorial sea relationship.

These lists are important evidence of a new balance of power in the territorial sea. It would not be difficult to analyze the real-world forces that generated them. But they symbolize and emphasize the true character of the territorial sea as a legal area. The facile formula of "sovereignty"—subject to the right of innocent passage" is not adequate. The complex layering of superimposed legal relations and the intricate interaction of delegated powers mean that the territorial sea is properly regarded as *an area of legal mutuality* and *an area of legal potentiality*. . . .

Superficially, the legal status of the continental shelf (Articles 77 to 81) is also remarkably similar to that created by Geneva: epitomized in the concept of functional sovereign rights. But the appearance is deceptive. The status is transformed by the fact that the superjacent waters, up to a distance of 200 nautical miles, are EEZ, no longer straightforward high seas. In addition, Article 56 gives functional sovereign rights in respect of the seabed and subsoil of the EEZ. Where the EEZ and continental shelf overlap—

up to a distance of 200 nautical miles—the two sets of sovereign rights overlap. Presumably in that area, the EEZ generally trumps the continental shelf, at least for all practical purposes. But there are important differences: the *inherent* nature of the continental shelf rights in what is perceived as a natural prolongation of the land territory (Article 77(3), read with Article 76(1)), and the emphasis on the *exclusivity* of the continental shelf rights (Article 77(2)). For example, these differences might continue to have a bearing on the delimitation of the continental shelf between neighboring states.

The mystery of the relationship between the continental shelf and the EEZ is aggravated by the problematic relationship between the EEZ and the high seas. Where do the high seas begin? Under Geneva, they begin at the outer edge of the territorial sea. The position is not so straightforward under the LOS Convention. . . . It is not quite right to say simply that the EEZ ends at 200 nautical miles and the high seas begin at that point. Article 58 gives all states a certain status in the EEZ: they have the high seas freedoms of Article 87. And Article 58(2) applies the remainder of the high seas articles (Articles 88 to 115) to the EEZ. It also applies to the EEZ "other pertinent rules of international law . . . in so far as they are not incompatible with" the Convention provisions on the EEZ.

In other words, it is not at first sight clear whether the EEZ is essentially the high seas with a special EEZ regime superimposed upon it (the "high seas minus" view) or whether the EEZ is a new sui generis zone of the coastal state in which the high seas freedoms are the equivalent of the right of innocent passage in the territorial sea (the "EEZ minus" view).

A preferable view is that the EEZ should be regarded as a *horizontally shared zone* between the coastal state and other states. This view is supported by the extraordinarily balanced drafting of the fundamental EEZ article (55), entitled "specific legal regime of the EEZ":

The exclusive economic zone is an area beyond and adjacent to the territorial sea, subject to the specific legal régime established in this Part, under which the *rights and jurisdictions* of the coastal State and the *rights and freedoms* of other States are governed by the relevant provisions of this Convention [emphasis added].

The view is supported further by the parallel provisions in Articles 56 and 58(3) under which the coastal state, in exercising its rights and performing its duties in the EEZ, must have *due regard* to the rights and duties of other states (56), and other states, in exercising their rights and performing their duties in the EEZ, must have *due regard* to the rights and duties of the coastal state (58(3)). It is reinforced still further by the remarkable wording of Article 59, a perfect example of the administrative lawism of the Convention:

Basis for the resolution of conflicts regarding the attribution of rights and jurisdiction in the exclusive economic zone: In cases where this Convention does not attribute rights or jurisdiction to the coastal State or to other States within the exclusive economic zone, and a conflict arises between the interests of the coastal State and any other State or States, the conflict should be resolved on the basis of equity and in the light of all the relevant circumstances, taking into account the respective importance of the interests involved to the parties as well as to the international community as a whole.

Whatever may be regarded as the essence of the relationship of the EEZ to the high seas, there is another fundamental difference in the status of the high seas as compared with the Geneva Conventions. The deep seabed area beyond the limits of national jurisdiction (that is, beyond the EEZ and the continental shelf), called in the Convention "the Area," is subject to the special regime created by part XI of the Convention. Part VII (on the high seas) contains a reference to part XI in Article 87(2), which provides that the high seas freedoms shall be exercised "with due regard for the rights under this Convention with respect to activities in the Area." Article 89 also provides that "no State may validly purport to subject any part of the high seas to its sovereignty" (which might or might not apply to the seabed of the high seas). Part XI itself contains a whole array of provisions on the legal status of the Area and its mineral resources. They are "the common heritage of mankind" (136). No state may claim or exercise sovereignty or sovereign rights over any part of them. No state or natural or juridical person may appropriate any part of them (Article 137). All rights in the resources of the Area are vested in mankind as a whole, on whose behalf the International Sea-Bed Authority (ISA) is to act (Article 137(2)). The general conduct and responsibility of states in the Area are controlled by Articles 138 and 139. Activities in the Area are to be carried out for the benefit of mankind as a whole (Article 140). . . .

In short, therefore, it may be said that, under the LOS Convention, the high seas proper are also a *horizontally shared area*. That area is shared between, on the one hand, mankind and all states and the ISA and legal persons with derived rights and, on the other hand, all states as the holders of the general high seas freedoms. It is accordingly, once again, an area of legal mutuality. And the deep seabed, under the LOS Convention, may be regarded as the *ne plus ultra* of legal potentiality. The deep seabed governmental system (legislative, executive, judicial) waits upon its implementation by countless subordinate decisions taken within the framework of the Convention structure, going to the fourth generation of concretization[5] and beyond: Convention, implementing legislation, executive decisions thereunder, application of decisions, resolution of disputes, and enforcement (judicial and otherwise).

It is apparent that one could demonstrate by a similar analysis that the other UNCLOS main legal sea areas (straits used for international navigation, archipelagic waters, contiguous zone) had the same structural character, and the same applies a fortiori to the numerous minor legal sea areas (safety zones, suspension zones, marine scientific research zones, and so on). In all these cases, boundaries between superimposed legal relations are fixed by critical power modifiers that create an area of interaction of powers among interested states; their legal effect is essentially an administrative law effect, depending on postlegislative activity to extrapolate from, and to interpolate into, the texts, and to extend and to intend the texts—through cascades of derived legal action (prescribing, deciding, enforcing).

The *vertical* boundaries between different legal sea areas and between the legal sea areas of different states are of the same intrinsic nature. Their establishment is the subject of a power conferred on the coastal state or states concerned. That power is in each case subject to critical power modifiers.

One vertical sea boundary has taken on a completely new significance as compared with the Geneva regime: the outer edge of the continental shelf. . . .

In Article 76 the international legislator has wrought a work of exceptional complexity. It is of particular interest and relevance in forming any overall view of the legislative significance of the Convention. The Article 76 system consists of two phases. The first is the *identification* of the outer limits of the continental shelf by reference to geographical and, especially, geological concepts. The second is the *establishment* of the outer limits as legally final and binding by the coastal state, in some cases in conjunction with the Commission on the Limits of the Continental Shelf (CLCS).

The identification of the outer limits makes use of five concepts that are technical in origin but that become legal terms of art by reason of the way they are used in Article 76: natural prolongation of land territory (paragraph 1); continental margin (paragraph 2); outer edge of the continental margin (paragraph 4(a)); foot of the continental slope (paragraph 4(b)); and submarine ridges (paragraph 6). The outer limits of the continental shelf are in principle at the edge of the continental margin, as defined, unless that outer edge does not extend as far as 200 nautical miles from the baselines of the territorial sea (in which case the outer limit is at 200 nautical miles); the outer limits are also subject to a general cut-off point (paragraph 5) at 350 nautical miles from the territorial sea baselines or else, except on submarine ridges, 100 nautical miles from the 2,500-meter isobath.

It follows that there are in principle four possible outer limits to the continental shelf: 200 nautical miles, the outer edge of the continental margin, 350 nautical miles, and 100 miles from the 2,500-meter isobath.

Because of the complexity of these provisions, because they involve questions of sophisticated technical judgment, and because of the new interest of all states in the resulting boundaries, it was agreed to set up an administrative law type of procedure to help to settle particular boundaries. The coastal state first *delineates* the outer limits on the basis of the Convention provisions. It then *submits* information on the limits to the CLCS, a permanent international body of 21 experts. The CLCS follows the procedure set out in Annex II to the Convention. By a two-thirds majority the CLCS approves *recommendations* "on matters related to the establishment" of the outer limits and *submits* them to the coastal state. If the coastal state disagrees with the recommendations, it makes a revised or new submission to the Commission. The coastal state then *establishes* the outer limits *on the basis of* the recommendations of the Commission.

The key sentence is in a form that will bring a sparkle to the eye of any administrative lawyer: "The limits of the shelf established by a coastal State on the basis of these recommendations shall be final and binding."

Each of the critical power modifiers in Article 76 was keenly considered, disputed, and negotiated. The outcome is not only a complex structure of technical and legal elements but also a sophisticated balance of powers and responsibilities. In particular, it raises the archetypal problem of administrative law: who has the last word? Is it the coastal state, the CLCS, or some putative third-party settlement instance under part XV of the Convention?

The outer limit of the continental shelf is thus a boundary for whose determination the international community has delegated intricate powers to the coastal state and others. The international community has also, in one respect, made the continental shelf itself into a partially shared area, where the coastal state acts as an agent of the international community or at least as its statutable benefactor. Under Article 82 the coastal state must surrender a percentage of the value of production from the continental shelf sites located more than 200 nautical miles from the baselines. The percentage eventually reaches a ceiling of 7 percent. It is paid to the International Sea-Bed Authority, which is to distribute the revenues equitably by taking into account the interests and needs of the developing countries. The implementation of these provisions depends on a distribution of powers among the coastal state, the ISA and, to the extent that they might be held applicable, the Convention's dispute settlement procedures. . . .

So far as the other vertical boundaries, between neighboring states, are concerned, the Geneva Conventions contain three slightly differently formulated rules for three cases: territorial sea, continental shelf (opposite coasts), and continental shelf (adjacent coasts). But the structure of the three rules was the same: failing agreement, the median or equidistance line, subject to special circumstances. Those were the three classical elements in the light of which many sea boundaries were settled. On the basis of those provisions, states could delimit the sea areas unilaterally using the residual rule; but the provisions provide the conceptual framework for negotiation and settlement, resulting in an agreed settlement containing any appropriate variation of the median or equidistance line and taking account of such special circumstances as the parties wished to treat as relevant. In the case of a dispute that could not be resolved by agreement, third-party settlement procedures could be used and the Convention provisions could be applied (subject to any reservation made under Article 12 of the Continental Shelf Convention) as governing rules of law.

In post-Geneva state practice, three significant developments occurred:

1. Most actual delimitation settlements were accomplished on the basis of a median or equidistance line adjusted to fit the circumstances of the case.[6]

2. The International Court of Justice told us that the Geneva rule, at least so far as the continental shelf was concerned, was a contractual rule and did not adequately reflect the position under customary international law.[7]

3. The internal balance of the Geneva rule itself was adjusted by state practice and judicial decisions and was brought closer to the International Court's view of customary international law by the displacement of the median or equidistance line as the cornerstone of the rule in favor of "equitable principles."[8]

When UNCLOS came to work on the corresponding provisions, these three factors had to be taken into account in deciding how far to reproduce the Geneva texts. But a fourth factor of fundamental significance also dominated the legislative process: the real-world fact that 50 and more of the states participating in the conference had unresolved sea boundary problems with neighboring states. In formulating rules that might apply to or affect their own situation, they had to temper their natural loyalty to the Geneva Conventions and court decisions with a realistic appreciation of where their interests lay. What happened was that more or less half of the specially interested states decided that their interests would be best served by the apparently more "equitable" approach of the judicial decisions (and they became known as the "Equitable Principles Group"). The rest thought that the original spirit of Geneva had been sound, that (respecting also the Aristotelian tradition) equality was the ultimate equity (and they became known as the "Median Line Group").

During session after session, debates and pseudo-debates and stylized indirect negotiation took place between the two groups. The process by which the final texts of Articles 15, 73, 84, and 298(1)(a) were settled is thus an unusually exposed example of a legislative process. In particular, the growing impatience of the rest of the conference and the threat of a third-party intrusion into their relationship made the groups feel ever less assured as masters of their own fate. . . .

The solution adopted for the territorial sea (Article 15) is the Geneva text (Article 12, Territorial Sea Convention) with minor linguistic changes: failing agreement, median or equidistance line, special circumstances. A completely different solution—and one and the same solution—was adopted for the EEZ and continental shelf (Articles 74 and 83).[9] Judged only by the standards of alchemy could it be said to be anything but bizarre.

The delimitation rule in Articles 74 and 83 has a three-part structure containing a *process*, a *principle*, and a *purpose*:

1. *process* = agreement: if agreement is not reached within a reasonable period of time, resort to the dispute settlement procedures of part XV;

2. *principle* = international law, as referred to in Article 38 of the Statute of the International Court of Justice;

3. *purpose* = to achieve an equitable solution.

The *process* sets the procedural *vires* of the powers of the states concerned. But they are subject to an important qualification introduced by Article 298(1)(a)(i). There is a right for a state to exclude sea boundary delimitation disputes from the compulsory third-party settlement procedures of part XV. Thus, the reference in Article 74(2) and Article 83(2) to part XV, although it is in an obligatory form ("shall resort to"), does not itself necessarily amount to an acceptance of compulsory jurisdiction. However, Article 298(1)(a)(i) does go on to require a state that has excluded such disputes to accept submission of the dispute to conciliation under Annex V, section 2, if agreement is not reached "within a reasonable period of time." The compulsory conciliation system is closely modeled on that contained in the Vienna Convention on the Law of Treaties and its annex. This substitute obligation to submit to conciliation is itself subject to an exception for disputes "necessarily involving the concurrent consideration of any unsettled dispute concerning sovereignty or other rights over continental or insular land territory."

If a dispute is submitted to conciliation under Annex V, section 2, the parties must *negotiate on the basis* of the conciliation commission report. If those negotiations do not result in agreement, there is one last possibility at the end of the road: "the parties shall, *by mutual consent*, submit the question to one of the procedures provided for in section 2, *unless the parties otherwise agree*" (Article 298(1)(a)(ii)) (emphasis added). It is a rare sort of obligation ("shall") that depends on the mutual consent of those subject to it and is subject to their not agreeing otherwise. Sense can only be made of such an apparent contradiction if it is analyzed as a duty coupled with a power rather than a duty coupled with a freedom. That is to say, at the moment when the provision becomes applicable, the parties do not have unfettered discretion to do what they will as if there were no provision at all. The provision contains the policy desideratum of the international community speaking through the international legislator. That desideratum is that the unresolved dispute should not be allowed, merely because it has not been resolved by the procedures followed theretofore and especially because it has not been so resolved, to remain indefinitely unresolved or to become a source of extralegal conflict or the subject of self-help.

Following through this long process chain, we find that Articles 74 and 83 do not contain a substantive default provision, applicable in the case of an absence of agreement; nor do they contain a fully constraining third-party settlement system. The overall change from the corresponding Geneva structure is illuminating. The process aspect of the UNCLOS text is concerned, in what may be seen as a more realistic and sophisticated approach, rather with constraining the *behavior* of the states concerned in relation to their unresolved sea boundaries than with predeciding their dispute by edict.

The same may be said of the mysterious *principle* in Articles 74 and 83. At first sight, it is nonsensical to require states to reach agreement *on the basis of international law*, when that obligation is contained within an instrument that is to be the highest and most authoritative possible source of international law. The apparent nonsense is made worse by the reference to Article 38 of the Statute of the International Court of Justice, which, as has long been recognized, is emphatically not an apt list of either the formal or the material sources of international law. . . . The reference to international law and to Article 38 must be given some meaning. It must be taken to be legislation by means of a symbolic formula. It is saying that the process of delimitation must be conducted in the light of the principles that have been evolved by international law and that, for this purpose, international law must be understood in a special extended sense to include not only fully formed international law but also the material found in formative sources of international law (such as prenormative state practice, judicial decisions, general principles of law). The vital point to understand about such a symbolic formula is that it does *not* transform all these heterogeneous materials into international law by the legislative act of the Convention. It is *not* merely legislation by reference. The complete ragbag of such materials does *not* together constitute the "UNCLOS substantive rule" on delimitation. What the Convention does is to set the parameters of the delimitation *process.* Those parameters are finite in number and kind but not wholly specific. They are not wholly specific, but they are exclusive.

So far as the *purpose* of the process is concerned, the third element of the structure of Articles 74 and 83—"in order to achieve an equitable solution"—similar considerations apply. If one did not firmly believe in the ultimate rationality of the general will and the inevitability of the invisible hand, it might at first seem that the use of this expression is a disaster. It cuts across and short-circuits the subtle concept of "equitable principles," which is also imported, as noted above, by the reference to "international law." Both the International Court of Justice in the *North Sea Continental Shelf* cases and the court of arbitration in the *Anglo-French* case took pains to make it clear that their task was not simply to roam freely in search of equity.

[I]t is not a question of applying equity simply as a matter of abstract justice, but of applying a rule of law which itself requires the application of equitable principles, in accordance with the ideas which have always underlain the development of the legal régime of the continental shelf in this field. . . .[10]

This excellent dictum accords closely with the general theme of the present study. We may say that the reference in the UNCLOS text to an "equitable solution"—which is a phrase that has also been used by the International Court—was designed as an avoidance tactic, so that, in the interest of fairness between the two parties most concerned (the Median Line Group and the Equitable Principles Group), references to *both* the shibboleth concepts could be omitted from the final text.

But the underlying intention of the legislator would seem to be the same as that indicated by the International Court in the passage quoted above.

The concepts of "equitable principles" and "equitable solution" are playing in this context a role analogous to that played by "reasonableness" in English law. They are high-level power modifiers whose referent is a subtle amalgam of an attitude or approach (fairness, common sense) and evolved artificial legal principles. Those principles are both abstract and situational. In the case of the continental shelf, they may include the concepts of natural prolongation, general direction of the coast, proportionality, equidistance, other sea boundaries, natural resource distribution—or, in a given case, one or more of such concepts may not be relevant or may only be subsidiarily relevant. . . .

Articles 74 and 83—and countless other provisions in the LOS Convention—are not simply contractual terms; nor do they lay down rules of law in the classical sense. *They delegate decision-making powers.* The current structural development of international law is involving states more and more not only in the mystical composite personage of the international legislator but also in performing the function of the executive branch of their own *self-government.*

In the mainstream of the Western democratic tradition (exemplified in Locke and in Marx), all government aspires to the condition of self-government. Whether the ideal is articulated by reference to a hypothetical pregovernmental state of affairs (Locke and the state of nature) or to a hypothetical postgovernmental state of affairs (Marx and the "administration of things" in the poststate world), that ideal acts as a constant critical force drawing social arrangements into their future, forever competing with the natural forces of anarchy and disintegration. . . .

The development of the international constitutional structure since the 18th century has proceeded on a different basis. International society has seemed to lack, at least since the 18th century and especially since the Russian Revolution of 1917, a single coherent and distinctive ideological structure (ideal or myth) to sustain and condition its social arrangements, and it has seemed to lack the real-world instruments of organized physical force that, in national society, confer de facto legitimacy on social arrangements through their efficiency and inevitability. These notorious disadvantages may be more apparent than real. From the natural law ethos of early modern international law to the rationalistic naturalism of some modern international law theory,[11] there may be more of a coherent underlying ideological structure, however dimly perceived by the participants in international society, than is normally supposed. But what matters for present purposes is that such apparent inadequacies of the international system have led most participants and observers to import the notion of "consent" wholesale into international theory as the all-purpose solvent of theoretical mysteries and as the validating, sustaining, and conditioning force in the development of international social arrangements.

It is important to realize the particular character of the notion of consent as it is used in modern international theory. It has been derived in part as a deduction from the principle of the sovereign equality of states, partly from a loose analogy with the long established municipal law institution of contract, and partly from the timeless anthropological phenomenon of the sanctity of the promise. It is emphatically not "consent" in the sophisticated sense of the mainstream Western democratic tradition (of Locke and Marx). National society, in its scale and its complexity and its repressive intensity, would not have been able to survive and progress if its ideological basis had been nothing more than "consent" in this direct, literal, contractual sense. The LOS Convention causes us, once again, to realize that such a notion of consent is no longer able to contain and sustain the reality of the post-1945 development of international self-government. In the present study we have considered four aspects of the Convention that illustrate the new reality:

1. *consensus* as the generator of autonomous law, created *by* the subjects of the law but also created *for* them;

2. *powers* delegated en masse and leading to a cascade of derived activity (legislative, decision making, enforcing);

3. *administrative law procedures* integrated in the substantive provisions (as dispute settlement mechanisms and other forms of third-party intervention and, although not the subject of the present study, in the form of international organizational structures, especially the International Sea-Bed Authority);

4. and, finally, the puzzle with which we are presently concerned: the delegation of what seems to be a *power/duty to agree* on the basis of certain substantive principles.

The accidents of litigation have led the International Court of Justice on two recent occasions to consider the phenomenon of a fettered power/duty to negotiate. In the *North Sea Continental Shelf* cases and in the *Fisheries Jurisdiction* case the Court's decisions laid down a series of matters that the parties were to take into account in the negotiation they were obliged by international law to undertake. The individual and dissenting opinions of Members of the Court expressed more clearly than the Court itself the theoretical anguish such a decision engenders: the tension between a freedom and a duty, between the judicial function of the Court to declare the law and/or to decide legal disputes and the responsibility of the parties to settle their dispute by peaceful means. The Court itself hovered between two underlying conceptual structures to explain the form of its decisions: the duty to settle such a dispute by negotiation and the "regime" character of the thing the parties had to establish by agreement. But it also came close to a more novel and fruitful idea.

The legal situation therefore is that the Parties are under no obligation to apply either the 1958 Convention, which is not opposable to the Federal Republic, or the equidistance method as a mandatory rule of customary law, which it is not.

But as between States faced with an issue concerning the lateral delimitation of adjacent continental shelves, there are still rules and principles of law to be applied; and in the present case it is not the fact either that rules are lacking, or that the situation is one for the *unfettered appreciation of the Parties* [emphasis added].[12]

It is one of the advances in maritime international law, resulting from the intensification of fishing, that the former *laissez-faire* treatment of the living resources of the sea in the high seas has been replaced by a recognition of a *duty to have regard* to the rights of other States and the needs of conservation for the benefit of all [emphasis added].[13]

The idea that is here struggling to reach the surface of international consciousness is the distinction between a freedom and a power. The story of the development of international society since 1945 is the story of a progression from legal freedoms to legal powers. A freedom implies the absence of legal control. A power implies the absence of unfettered discretion. The development of modern national society was also the development of powers. The way that national society responded to that development was by extending the notion of self-government from legislation to executive action by means of the concepts of constitutionalism, the Rule of Law, government under the law. The constitutional struggles of centuries cul-minated in the late 17th and 18th centuries in the great Rule of Law achievements, which provided the theoretical basis for the spectacular development of the powers of government in the 19th and 20th centuries.[14] The essence of the Rule of Law concept lies in the idea of Law as the actualization of the general interest. Each holder of a power under the law must act as an agent of all society. In subjecting itself to legal powers, society is appointing agents to whom it delegates the function of acting on its behalf. Especially in advanced societies, society governs itself through the law, which is created by and for it and through the decision making that is carried out in its name and as a series of limits on its natural freedoms. Natural freedom is limited by law and powers under the law. Law and powers under the law are limited by their function of serving the interests of society.

A change of perspective is required to see that all such rights (and the countless other comparable rights in the LOS Convention) are in reality *shared powers*, shared between the holder of the power and the community of states, in which regard for the interests of other states and of all states is of the essence. There are no freedoms from the law. There are no freedoms apart from the law. Freedoms are powers conferred by and under the law. The sovereign of modern international society is the same as the sovereign of the modern Western democratic tradition: *systemic authority*, the authority which flows from participation in the system. . . .

NOTES

1. Texts from the Law of the Sea Convention are taken from the Draft Convention, UN Doc. A/CONF.62/L.78, of Aug. 28, 1981.

2. Right, privilege, power, immunity; no-right, duty, disability, liability. *Cf.* Kocourek's revised list: claim, immunity, privilege, power; duty, disability, inability, liability. Hohfeld, *Some Fundamental Legal Conceptions as Applied in Judicial Reasoning*, 23 YALE L.J. 16 (1913); A. KOCOUREK, JURAL RELATIONS (1927). For a review of post-Hohfeldian developments, see Pound, *Fifty Years of Jurisprudence*, 50 HARV. L.R. 557, 571 *ff.* (1937).

3. *See* Adede, *Law of the Sea: The Scope of Third-Party, Compulsory Procedures for the Settlement of Disputes*, 71 AJIL 305 (1977); Adede, *Law of the Sea—The Integration of the System of Settlement of Disputes under the Draft Convention as a Whole*, 72 *id.* at 84 (1978); Rosenne, *Settlement of Fisheries Disputes in the Exclusive Economic Zone*, 73 *id.* at 89 (1979).

4. In the Hohfeldian sense of such terms (*see* note 2 *supra*). For Hohfeld, a privilege (or liberty) is the opposite of a duty and a power is the correlative of a liability. *Cf.* Kocourek: "Since freedom is the base from which and for which legal transactions are entered into, the significance of the idea of jural relationship becomes apparent—a jural relation is a situation of fact upon which one may affect (through the existence and exercise of a power) or may claim to affect (because of the existence of a duty), the freedom of another with legal consequences."

5. In the sense in which Kelsen used the word. Concretization (or individualization) is the process by which "the general norm which, to certain abstractly determined conditions, attaches certain abstractly determined consequences, [is] individualized and concretized in order to come in contact with social life, to be applied in reality." H. KELSEN, GENERAL THEORY OF LAW AND STATE 135 (tr. Wedberg 1945/49).

6. For inter-state sea boundary agreements, see the series published by the U.S. DEP'T OF STATE, OFFICE OF THE GEOGRAPHER, LIMITS IN THE SEAS; N. PAPADAKIS, INTERNATIONAL LAW OF THE SEA: A BIBLIOGRAPHY 116–23 (1980).

7. North Sea Continental Shelf Cases (Federal Republic of Germany/Denmark; Federal Republic of Germany/Netherlands), 1969 ICJ REP. 3 (Judgment of Feb. 20). *See* Friedmann, *The North Sea Continental Shelf Cases—A Critique*, 64 AJIL 229 (1970); Grisel, *Lateral Boundaries and the ICJ Judgment, id.* at 562 (1970); Blecher, *Equitable Delimitation of Continental Shelf*, 73 *id.* at 60 (1979); Rhee, *Equitable Solutions to the Maritime Boundary Dispute Between the United States and Canada in the Gulf of Maine*, 75 *id.* at 590 (1981). For further references, see N. PAPADAKIS, *supra* note 6, at 120–22.

8. THE UNITED KINGDOM AND THE FRENCH REPUBLIC DELIMITATION OF THE CONTINENTAL SHELF DECISION OF 30 JUNE 1977, CMND. 7438 (1978), *reprinted in* 18 ILM 397 (1979). *See* Bowett, *The Arbitration Between the United Kingdom and France concerning the Continental Shelf*, 49 BRIT. Y.B. INT'L L. 1 (1978); McRae, *Delimitation of the Continental Shelf Between the United Kingdom and France*, 15 CAN. Y.B. INT'L L. 173 (1977); Colson, *The United Kingdom-France Continental Shelf Arbitration*, 72 AJIL 95 (1978), and *—Interpretive Decision of March 1978*, 73 *id.* at 112 (1979); Quéneudec, *L'Affaire de la délimitation du plateau continental entre la France et le Royaume-Uni*, 83 REV. GÉNÉRALE DROIT INT'L PUBLIC 53 (1979).

9. The text of Article 74 is as follows (the text of Article 83 being the same with the substitution of references to the continental shelf): "*Delimitation of the exclusive economic zone between States with opposite or adjacent coasts*: (1) The delimitation of the exclusive economic zone between States with opposite or adjacent coasts shall be effected by agreement on the basis of international law, as referred to in Article 38 of the Statute of the International Court of Justice, in order to achieve an equitable solution. (2) If no agreement can be reached within a reasonable period of time, the States concerned shall resort to the procedures provided for in

Part XV. (3) Pending agreement as provided for in paragraph 1, the States concerned, in a spirit of understanding and co-operation, shall make every effort to enter into provisional arrangements of a practical nature and, during this transitional period, not to jeopardize or hamper the reaching of the final agreement. Such arrangements shall be without prejudice to the final delimitation. (4) Where there is an agreement in force between the States concerned, questions relating to the delimitation of the exclusive economic zone shall be determined in accordance with the provisions of that agreement."

10. North Sea Continental Shelf Cases, 1969 ICJ REP. at 47.

11. It would be invidious to mention any particular names among those who have contributed to such an approach to international law beyond acknowledging the leading role of Myres S. McDougal.

12. North Sea Continental Shelf Cases, 1969 ICJ REP. at 46.

13. Fisheries Jurisdiction Case (UK v. Iceland), 1974 ICJ REP. 3, 31 (Judgment of July 25).

14. Especially the (British) Bill of Rights (1689), the great decided case of *Entick v. Carrington* (1765), the (United States) Declaration of Independence (1776) and (federal) Constitution (1789, with the Bill of Rights amendments of 1791), and the (French) Declaration of the Rights of Man and of the Citizen (1789). For Entick v. Carrington, see (1765) 19 State Trials 1029.

35. UNCLOS and the Redistribution of Ocean Wealth

Per Magnus Wijkman

The Third United Nations Conference on the Law of the Sea (UNCLOS III) has marked time in 1981 as a result of the Reagan Administration's decision to review the convention text before proceeding with negotiations on the few but important outstanding issues. Prior to 20 January 1981 virtually all the 320 Articles and eight Annexes of the Draft Convention (Informal Text) produced at the ninth session in 1980 had received the support of all major delegations. Session ten in Spring 1981 was to have converted this draft into a final text for adoption by the Conference delegations in the fall. The United States' decision delays this process by at least one year.

The new administration will attempt to obtain a more satisfactory accommodation of U.S. interests than the Draft Convention provides. However, if improvements for the United States require concessions by other governments, those nations may no longer feel that they gain more from a convention than they would from continuation of the *status quo* or from unilateral actions. This would destroy the consensus on which the convention must build to be effective as international law. To avoid reducing the negotiations to a zero-sum game, with little hope for a successful conclusion, proposed changes in the convention text should result in greater benefits from ocean resources.

All governments should have a common interest in fostering the efficient exploitation of ocean resources since this generates more income for all nations to share. No reliable estimates of global ocean wealth exist but it can safely be assumed to be significant. The oceans could now produce products worth at least 200 billion dollars or 5 percent of world income.[1] The current annual value of fisheries and hydrocarbon production is worth about 160 billion dollars. Deep seabed mining of manganese nodules might contribute an annual value of more than 10 billion dollars if not regulated. These three industries together with shipping represent a current potential value of about 200 billion dollars. Of this, perhaps one-tenth constitutes rents—the competitive advantage that the oceans hold over landbased production of foodstuffs, energy and minerals. The contribution of these industries, and in particular of hydrocarbons, will increase with time and new uses of the oceans will develop. Thus, inefficient use of ocean resources jeopardizes substantial values.

World national product is maximized by allowing the most efficient producers to produce the most valuable products wherever it is cheapest. The ideal regime would not favor landbased production of foodstuffs, energy or minerals over production from the oceans, or *vice versa*. Nor would it favor production in any particular area of the oceans over another area. Finally, it would discriminate between firms on grounds of efficiency rather than nationality. The Draft Convention frequently breaks these rules.

It is not surprising that efficiency has been sacrificed. Without effective mechanisms for redistributing income, each country will attempt to obtain a larger share of the resource for itself, even at the expense of some inefficiency. Since countries are not required to pay for an increase in their share, the UNCLOS III negotiations are characterized by the coastal states' attempts to enclose any ocean space that might have some future value. Exclusive ownership has become more attractive as growing world population and advances in marine technology have increased the value of these resources. Most coastal nations have attempted to appropriate them unilaterally. . . . The big winners are coastal, broad-margin states and landbased producers of nodule ores. Among these are some of the richest countries in the world. The biggest losers are non-coastal, developing countries which are net consumers of nodule ores. Among these are some of the world's poorest countries. This hardly conforms to the declared goal of the Conference to redistribute ocean income to the poorer countries.

This article considers how the regimes proposed for fisheries, offshore hydrocarbons, and the resources of the deep seabed will affect efficiency in production and will redistribute income between nations. The viewpoint is global rather than national, paying particular attention to the distribution of income between developed and developing countries. . . .

THE FISHING REGIME

The world's annual catch of fish was worth about 20 billion dollars at the end of the seventies, constituting about one-half of one percent of world income (Holt, 1978, p. 53) and about 15 percent of world protein consumption. Ninety-nine percent of the catch is harvested within 200 nautical miles of the coast and the remainder are highly migratory species caught on the high seas (Gulland, 1979, p. 36). The Draft Convention awards coastal states the exclusive rights to manage the world's major fishing stocks and priority rights to harvest them by creating an exclusive economic zone (EEZ) extending 200 nautical miles out from a country's coast. In this zone the coastal state is granted "sovereign rights for the purpose of exploring and exploiting, conserving and managing the natural resources, whether living or non-living, of the sea-bed and subsoil and the superadjacent waters and with regard to other activities for economic exploitation and exploration of the zone such as the production of energy from the water, current and winds . . ." (Article 56.1(a)).

Articles 69 and 70 in the Draft Convention allegedly modify the fishing rights of the coastal state. They allow landlocked states and countries with certain geographical characteristics deemed disadvantageous to harvest "an appropriate part of the surplus of the living resources of the exclusive economic zones of coastal states of the same subregion or region" (Article 69.1 and Article 70.1). They also obligate the coastal state to negotiate with developing landlocked and geographically disadvantaged states in the same region or subregion to establish "equitable arrangements" which would allow them to participate in the exploitation of the living resources of the coastal state's EEZ (Article 69.3 and Article 70.4) even when the coastal state has the capacity to harvest the whole allowable catch.

These concessions by the coastal states are, however, more apparent than real. The coastal state alone determines the size of the allowable catch and of its own harvesting capacity. It can determine unilaterally the size of the surplus it is required to share with landlocked states and those with specified geographical characteristics; it can set that surplus at zero, if it so desires. Furthermore, even though the coastal state may be obligated to allow developing landlocked and geographically disadvantaged countries to participate in harvesting the allowable catch in its EEZ, Article 62.4(a) allows the state to charge foreign fishing vessels a fee for this privilege. Thus, in spite of Articles 69 and 70, the coastal states will enjoy (or dissipate) all the rents from the world's major fishing grounds. The next section considers the size of these rents and how they are distributed.

Income Distribution

The rents from fishing grounds have been estimated to be worth between 2 and 4 billion dollars annually, i.e., up to one-fifth of the value of the total catch. This represents the excess of the value of the fish caught over the cost of the capital and labor needed to capture them *when the fishery is efficiently managed*. Rents are an unearned income provided by the bounty of nature and often dissipated by man through inefficient use of fishing vessels and fishermen as well as through overfishing of the stocks.

Cooper (1975, p. 363; 1977, p. 110) has estimated that these rents constituted 2.5 billion dollars annually in the mid-seventies. . . .

Under the traditional regime of open access to fishing grounds these rents are either enjoyed by fishermen or dissipated by them through overcapitalization of the fleet or congestion on the fishing grounds. The Draft Convention would redistribute income from long-distance fishing fleets and other foreign fishermen to those states with long coasts bordering on rich fishing grounds. The richest fishing grounds, like the richest countries, are located in the temperate zones, and three-quarters of the world catch is taken from waters off the developed countries. . . . Thus, developed countries will get roughly 3 billion of the 4 billion dollars of rents generated currently.

Prior to the extension of fishing limits, non-local fishermen enjoyed (or dissipated) about one-quarter of the rents generated off developed countries' coasts. All these fishermen were from other developed countries. Thus, the draft Convention would redistribute about 800m. dollars annually from developed long-distance fishing nations to developed coastal states.[2] About one-third of the catch in developing countries' waters is taken by non-local fishermen, and these are largely from developed countries. Some 400m. dollars, then, will be redistributed annually to developing coastal countries, of which 300m. would come from the fishermen of developed countries. These rough calculations assume that all fishing grounds are of equal productivity. It is probable, however, that the productivity and rents of fishing grounds bordering developed countries are greater than those near developing countries.

Thus a total of at least 1.2 billion dollars annually is to be redistributed to coastal states, and of this the developed countries would enjoy the major part. Developing coastal countries do gain somewhat at the expense of the developed. The major losers are long-distance fishing fleets and those fishermen who historically have fished in waters that now are declared "foreign."

Whether this redistribution of income is fair is a matter of opinion. Coastal countries claim ownership of the fishing stocks by right of proximity. Less fortunately located nations stress that this resource, too, should be part of the common heritage in which they have a share. Undeniably, the proposed treaty fails to compensate those fishing nations that lose historical rights, and favors currently rich coastal countries over poor ones, and coastal states over others. This is a surprising outcome of the negotiations since non-coastal states have a blocking vote.

Efficiency

Coastal states often justify the awarding of property rights to themselves on the grounds that this is necessary to allow them to manage the fishery and prevent stock depletion which otherwise would threaten common property resources. Since many stocks were seriously depleted in the early seventies, this argument was generally accepted. However, coastal state jurisdiction is neither necessary nor sufficient for efficient management. It could be efficient only if the extension of fishing limits brought the fishing stock (and sometimes also its predators as well as the fish it preys upon) entirely within its jurisdiction. In practice, enclosure of the whole ecosystem will occur only occasionally.[3] Many stocks that migrate along the coast remain transboundary resources even after the extension of fishing limits to 200 nautical miles. With some exceptions (Icelandic cod is notable) major fishing stocks will remain common property resources, albeit common to fewer states than before. The crucial question is whether extension of fishing limits will reduce the number of co-owners of fishing stocks sufficiently to create incentives for voluntary cooperation in managing the stocks. If not, coastal state management will be inefficient: partial management is not necessarily better than no management. A supranational management regime must be given coercive powers in the many cases where too many co-owners share the stock for voluntary cooperation to work. Nevertheless, the Law of the Sea Conference has awarded management rights to coastal states without setting up a mechanism to ensure that management will be effective.[4]

In addition to imperfectly managing stocks, the provisions of the treaty will foster inefficient fishing activities because the treaty does not require that entry to fishing grounds be granted on a non-discriminatory basis. On the contrary, it sanctions use by the coastal state of tariffs or quotas on international trade in fishing rights. Such trade restrictions impose economic losses on society.

It would be unwise to underestimate the frequency of protection and its costs. Programs to control harvesting are unpopular with domestic fishermen, who view extended fishing limits as a means to protect fishermen rather than fishing stocks. In many of the 80 countries which already claim 200-mile fishing limits, domestic fishermen have replaced foreign fishermen. Domestic political opposition as well as the inability to cooperate with other governments sharing the stock has led many governments to postpone introduction of effective controls on total catch. Discriminatory access will create inefficiency in the fishing industry and raise costs because it forces part of the world fishing fleet to move to new waters and to convert to new types of fishing.[5] This leads to higher priced fish products, to which consumers react by substituting landbased foods for seafoods. This reduces the ocean's contribution to solving the world's nutritional problems.

THE REGIME FOR OFFSHORE OIL AND GAS

Offshore hydrocarbons may be the most valuable ocean resource. Today 20 percent of oil production, worth about 140 billion dollars, comes from offshore (Driver *et al.*, p. 2), entirely from the continental shelf. Production platforms currently operate at 350 meters water depths, and production and transportation technology to exploit reserves in deeper and more distant waters is developing rapidly (Mason, 1981). Three-eighths of proved reserves lie offshore (Exxon, p. 5), and half of the hydrocarbon reserves that remain to be discovered are estimated to be there (Klemme, 1977). Consequently, 40 percent of world hydrocarbon production may come from offshore sources by the year 2000.

The right to these resources currently is regulated by the Geneva Convention on the Continental Shelf of 1958. According to this a coastal state has the right to exploit the resources of its adjacent continental shelf out to the 200-meter isobath or as far out as the water depth permits exploitation. It therefore follows that this exploitability criterion allows national jurisdiction to move outward as technology improves. . . .

The Draft Convention embodies a definition that awards coastal states complete jurisdiction over seabed resources to at least 200 nautical miles. When a country's continental shelf extends further than 200 nautical miles, it is awarded resource jurisdiction to "the outer edge of the continental margin," but it is also required to share with the international community the revenues obtained from resource exploitation on its margin beyond 200 miles. The Draft Convention provides a complex set of alternative definitions of the outer edge of the continental shelf (Article 76). . . . Prominent "broad-margin" countries . . . are Argentina, Brazil, Sri Lanka, Australia, Canada and United States. In this area the coastal state has resource rights and the International Seabed Authority limited taxation rights. For this reason it is sometimes called a mixed rights zone.

According to Article 82 of the Draft Convention, the Authority would levy a wellhead tax of one percent of the value of production in the fifth year of production with the rate to rise by one percent per year until it reaches seven percent in the twelfth year. The resulting revenues are to be distributed primarily to the developing countries. How large those revenues will be depends only in part on the distribution of offshore hydrocarbon resources.

Assuming that this reserve is recovered to the last drop, that the annual production volume is constant over the lifetime of the well, and that the wellhead tax does not make production unprofitable, this estimate gives a total tax revenue of 315 billion dollars from oil reserves in the mixed-rights zone. Assuming that these reserves are exploited over a period of alternatively 50 or 100 years, the International Seabed Authority would receive an annual revenue of 6.3 or 3.1 billion dollars respectively.[6] This is a significant amount, and although the estimate contains a wide range of uncertainty, it is not based on any extreme assumptions. Large amounts of money appear to be available for distribution to the developing countries through offshore oil production.

Several factors tend to reduce this amount, however. First, developing countries which are net importers of hydrocarbons do not have to pay the wellhead tax. This would exempt potential offshore producers such as

Argentina, Sri Lanka, India and Malagasy. No logical justification for this exemption can be found on grounds of equity.

Second, the tax rate may be high enough to discourage production in the mixed rights zone for the foreseeable future. These deposits are in deep waters far off the coasts and consequently will be the last to be exploited. Thus, wellhead tax revenues available for distribution to the developing countries may materialize only in the distant future, if at all. . . .

THE REGIME FOR THE DEEP SEABED

Manganese nodules, containing, *inter alia*, nickel, copper, cobalt and manganese, were long believed to be the major resource of the deep seabed. The most controversial task of the Conference has been to design an institution to regulate their exploitation "for the benefit of mankind as a whole, . . . and taking into particular consideration the interests and need of the developing countries, . . ." (Article 140). Paradoxically, the regime proposed by the Draft Convention will harm the world community as a whole, by fostering inefficient production, and most developing countries by reducing their real income. Nevertheless, a majority of countries supports this regime because it provides nonpecuniary benefits and establishes a precedent in their struggle for a new international economic order. We shall first briefly characterize this regime.

Negotiations over the deep seabed regime arrayed developing countries in a cohesive group against most developed market economies, and each side offered proposals reflecting its dominant economic and ideological interests. The developing countries, emphasizing the need to plan production centrally and to modify the free market distribution of income, wished to establish an International Seabed Authority with extensive powers to regulate seabed mining. In their view, the Authority should have a monopoly on seabed mining. Production would be assigned to an Enterprise governed by an Assembly in which each country would have one vote. The Enterprise could cooperate with land-based mineral producers and thereby control total production and prices. If the Council decided to charge monopoly prices, it would maximize benefits to producers rather than maximize consumers' welfare and the rents extracted from the oceans.

Developed countries, on the other hand, believing in the allocative efficiency of the market economy and free enterprise, wished to limit the powers of the Authority. In their view, it should only register claims to mine sites and, if claims competed, the Authority should auction the site to the highest bidder. Competitive bidding would ensure that the most efficient firms would mine the seabed and also that the Authority would maximize both the welfare of consumers as a group and ocean rents.

A compromise between these opposite views emerged during the fifth session in the form of the "parallel system," by which national firms, private and public, may mine the seabed alongside the Authority's Enterprise. An applicant for mining rights must prospect and delineate two mine sites:

upon granting mining rights the Authority keeps one of the sites for its Enterprise or assigns it to a developing country. . . .

Acquisition of prime sites alone is not sufficient for successful commercial production by the Enterprise or by developing countries. They must also acquire mining technology, expertise and risk capital; the conditions for this acquisition remain the subject of negotiation. Likewise, only tenuous agreement exists on the principles by which the Authority will award mine sites to applicants and the closely related question of control over the volume of seabed production. Furthermore, the powers of the Authority to tax both national firms and the Enterprise as well as the question of who controls the Authority and thereby ultimately the Enterprise remains to be settled. Dissatisfaction with these issues and a basic ideological objection to the majority opinion led to the Reagan Administration's decision to review the Draft Convention before proceeding with further negotiations.

Thus, even though the principle of the parallel system has been accepted, no consensus exists on the practical details of technology transfer, capital subscription, allocation of mine sites and production control, taxation powers and voting rights. How these issues ultimately are solved will influence the efficiency of mineral production, the international distribution of income and the economic power of primary producers in commodity markets. . . .

The prospect of seabed mining primarily pits landbased producers against consumer nations. However, developing consumer countries have supported the landbased producers in the Group of 77 and this has transformed the issue into a negotiation between the developed and the developing countries. . . . The annual net gain to the world from seabed mining is small, less than 1 billion dollars of 1980 value, but the transfer from producer interests to consumers is significant, about 5 billion. The developed market economies as a group gain more as consumers than they lose as producers, reaping an annual net gain of over 2 billion dollars. The converse is true for the developing market economies which lose on balance one and a half billion dollars per year. Even if all the rents or taxes collected from seabed production were distributed to developing countries, they probably would not benefit on balance from seabed mining.

Long-term projections are necessarily uncertain.[7] Nevertheless this estimate illustrates that seabed mining poses a major distributional problem: significant amounts of income are transferred from landbased producers, some of them poor countries, to consumer nations, most of them rich countries. . . .

Limiting production from the seabed reduces the harm inflicted on landbased producers, but it reduces the benefits enjoyed by consumers by a larger amount. The production controls proposed by the Draft Convention can be estimated to reduce the share of seabed production to about 25 percent of total production in the year 2000, which is about one-third of what it might be with unregulated mining (Levy, 1979). This would prevent the realization of a world gain of about one-half billion dollars per year and also prevent a transfer of about four billion dollars from landbased producers to consumers.

While the landbased producers have an obvious self-interest in preventing competition from seabed production from inflicting losses on their firms and residents, production limitation is an inefficient way to do this. A deadweight loss is imposed on the world economy; it primarily benefits landbased producers in a handful of developed and developing countries alike (Australia, Canada, Chile, Peru, Philippines, South Africa, United States, U.S.S.R., Zaire, and Zambia). The costs are paid for in the form of higher prices by consumers in all countries—poor as well as rich. A more efficient way to compensate landbased producers would be direct payments to them in proportion to the rents and tax revenues they lose and to finance these by contributions from consuming countries. Compensation payments, controversial as a principle, have not been seriously considered at the Conference. . . .

The production limitation system discussed in the preceding section is the primary cause of misallocating resources between seabed and landbased mining. A second cause is the structure of the proposed tax system. . . . The tax rate on net proceeds moves into a higher column when a firm has recovered its investment costs. Furthermore, within each column, the tax rate is progressive, rising with the annual rate of return on capital invested. The strongly progressive nature of this tax structure is designed to transfer "excess profits" in seabed mining from national firms to the International Seabed Authority.

The ambition to regulate the return on investments utilizing a common heritage resource is understandable. Unfortunately, it also affects firms' willingness to assume entrepreneurial risks. Seabed mining is a high-risk industry: existing estimates of the return on seabed mining vary greatly. Some ventures may make large profits while others take large losses. Firms considering investments in seabed mining face this prospect until the technology is commercially tested. A taxation system that allows the International Seabed Authority to share in higher than normal profits without having to share in losses reduces firms' expected after-tax return from investments in seabed mining. Since landbased production is not subject to a similar system of progressive taxation, this would lead to an under-investment in seabed mining relative to landbased production of nodule ores. In effect, national firms are regulated like public utilities to ensure that they do not earn monopoly profits, but lack the legal concession of a monopoly position to guarantee that they can recover their costs.

Preferential treatment for the Enterprise relative to national seabed mining firms is provided by several provisions of the Draft Convention. This distorts competitive conditions and reduces the efficiency of the seabed mining industry as a whole, thereby providing an additional favor for landbased producers. The major subsidies are the following:

1. *Prospecting subsidy.* Receiving mine sites free of charge gives the Enterprise a competitive advantage over national firms which must expend prospecting costs estimated at 16.4m. dollars per site by the MIT study (Nyhart *et al.*, 1978, p. ES3) and at 69.2m. dollars by the Aachen/Frankfurt study (Diederich *et al.*, 1979, p. 10).

2. *Interest rate subsidies*. The Enterprise will receive the risk capital necessary for one seabed mining operation (about 1.5 billion dollars currently) in the form of interest-free loans and loan guarantees in equal parts. Given an interest cost of 16 percent on the first half and an interest savings of four percentage units on the other half, this subsidy would be worth 150m. dollars per year—a significant competitive advantage. The loans and the interest rate guarantees will be supplied by states party to the Law of the Sea Convention in accordance with the scales for national contributions to the United Nations. This cost will burden the developed nations' taxpayers, not their mining firms. Consequently, this funding arrangement will have insignificant distortive effects.

3. *Technology Transfer*. Technology is to be transferred to the Enterprise on "fair and reasonable" commercial terms (Annex II, Article 5.3a). However, commercial terms are impossible to establish for mandatory transactions. Consequently, if this provision is effective it will transfer technology on concessionary terms. If it is ineffective, no transfer will occur that would not have occurred anyway. Using the MIT and the Aachen/Frankfurt studies, one can estimate that private firms will have invested 250m. or 500m. dollars respectively in research and development of seabed mining technology. Part of this amount may be transferred on concessionary terms to the Enterprise. National firms are also obliged to transfer technology to developing countries which have received a mine site from the Enterprise.

4. *Tax breaks*. It was originally proposed that the Enterprise not be subject to any taxation. This would significantly distort competition. Instead, the Draft Convention proposes that the Authority tax the Enterprise in the same manner as it taxes national firms. The Enterprise can negotiate for exemption from taxation by the host state where its facilities are located. If nodule processing is done on land rather than on ocean floating platforms in international waters, the Enterprise could obtain a competitive edge over national firms unable to obtain similar professional treatment (Annex IV, Art. 13.5).

Control of the Authority and thereby the Enterprise remains the most controversial issue of the seabed mining regime. As long as the governing body has some discretionary power, distribution of voting rights between countries is a crucial question. The developing countries originally wanted each country to have the same voting power in the Council. This would put the developed countries in the minority, and consequently they wanted voting power to reflect the degree of involvement by countries in seabed mining and in the consumption of nodule ores. The proposal embodied in the Draft Convention represents a balancing of these contradictory views. It has been rejected by the Reagan administration.

Negotiating the seabed mining regime involves principles which have been bitterly disputed in the North-South Dialogue. Should resources be allocated by markets or by bureaucrats? Is it possible to transfer technology effectively by fiat? What role do profits play for entrepreneurial risk-taking? Can developing countries increase their economic power by instituting international commodity cartels and establishing economic democracy as a global decision-making principle? The value of the deep seabed regime in setting a precedent in these issues has dwarfed more mundane matters such as the efficiency of production and the distribution of seabed income between developed and developing nations. Transformed into a battleground for the new international economic order, the deep seabed may wind up with a regime that makes seabed mining a boondoggle for international bureaucrats rather than a boon for mankind.

CONCLUSION

The designing of a management regime for ocean resources that is both efficient and fair is a difficult task. Nevertheless, the potential economic value of ocean resources suggests that it is well worth the effort. The provisions of the Draft Convention do not ensure that ocean values will be fully realized or fairly distributed. Under the regimes proposed for fisheries, hydrocarbons and seabed mining, the most efficient firms will not necessarily be allowed to exploit the resources and the most economic resources will not necessarily be exploited first. As in domestic politics where considerations of efficiency are often sacrificed to achieve greater equity, the negotiations at UNCLOS III have been constrained by considerations of political feasibility. However, the resource regimes of the Draft Convention allow inefficient use of resources without redistributing income from the world's richer to its poorer countries.

What can be done in this situation? Attempts to renegotiate the treaty risk the unravelling of the package of compromises so tediously put together during eight years of negotiations. . . . Given the large nonpecuniary values that seabed mining represents for many governments and the potentially large redistributions of income caused by mining, a more efficient regime presupposes that the richer consumer countries compensate the landbased producers in addition to allowing seabed rents to go primarily to developing countries. They have been reluctant to do this so far, perhaps because they fear that implementing the principle of compensation would set a precedent for other resources, in particular those which are not common resources. But if the richest countries combine their pursuit of greater efficiency with willingness to compensate those who suffer from more efficient use of the commons and temper it with understanding for the demands by the poorest countries, UNCLOS III may yet produce a generally acceptable comprehensive treaty.

NOTES

1. Pontecorvo and Mesznick (1974) estimated the gross national product of the world oceans to be 60 billion dollars. Their estimate was presented in an appendix without explanatory text and presumably refers to a year early in the 1970s. Shipping and "other surface uses" constitute the largest item—40–50 billion dollars. This is twice the value of shipping services provided in 1974 as estimated in Wijkman (1980,

p. 278 text and n. 14)—22–25 billion dollars. The value of ocean resources increased significantly with the quadrupling of oil prices in 1973. The output of offshore hydrocarbons currently is worth about 140 billion dollars per year and can be expected to increase steadily. Adams (1980, Table 4, p. 31) estimates the value of seabed production in twenty years to be 15.6 billion dollars in current prices, i.e., about 8 billion dollars in 1980 dollars. This value might have been realized in the eighties if seabed mining had not had to await conclusion of UNCLOS III. The value of fisheries is currently about 20 billion dollars, a value which would be larger under effective management schemes. Thus the potential current value of ocean commodities is at least 200 billion dollars. According to Pontecorvo *et al.* (1980, Table 6, p. 1005), the value of output from the U.S. ocean sector was 30.6 billion dollars in 1972 or 2.6 percent of U.S. gross national product. Additional estimates for the U.S. are provided by Nathan (1971).

2. Note that foreign fishermen can still enjoy some of these rents through a direct investment or joint venture with the coastal state. A foreign fishing interest, refused permission to fish in a coastal state's EEZ, can through a direct investment set up a local corporation as the legal owner of its vessels. In this case, the terms of vessel registration determine how the rents are split between the two parties. For instance, if the coastal state can charge foreign-owned fishing corporations a discriminatory flag fee, it can extract some of the resource rents. If, in addition, the coastal state requires that its flag vessels be built in the coastal state and manned by coastal state residents, then its factors of production can capture remaining rents. If, in addition, the coastal state requires that its flag vessels land their catch in its ports, then any transportation or processing advantage that foreign fishing fleets enjoyed is eliminated. On the other hand, foreign fishermen will be able to enjoy the same rents as before, if the coastal state merely supplies a flag of convenience at a nominal fee while real factors of production used in fishing are unchanged. In the case of joint ventures, the division of rents between the coastal state and the foreign fishing interests depends on the terms of the agreement.

3. Traditionally, management plans have been based on managing a single species at a time. The necessity of managing the whole ecosystem has been increasingly recognized. For instance, the Convention on the Conservation of the Living Marine Resources of the Antarctic adopted by the Antarctic Treaty Nations in December 1980 adopts an ecosystem management approach. For a description of the problems involved in managing even relatively simple ecosystems see May *et al.* (1979) and Donaldson and Pontecorvo (1980).

4. A different conclusion is drawn by Eckert (1979), who argues that national enclosure will prove more efficient than the current situation and is also preferable to international management.

5. Note that discriminatory access is not itself sufficient to cause inefficiency. According to the Hecksher-Ohlin theorem restricting international trade in fishing rights will lead to international factor movements, which will result in factor price equalization if transfer costs are zero. Consequently, restrictions on factor movements or positive transport costs together with discriminatory access cause inefficiency. For instance, coastal state requirements that vessels be locally built and manned prevent the sale of the vessel from foreign to local fishing interests in response to discriminatory access. Should such sales occur, efficiency would be unaffected although the distribution of income is obviously affected.

6. 250 b.b. × $30 = $7,500 bill.; $7,500 bill. × 4.2% = $315 bill. This gives $6.3 billion per year if exploited over 50 years. For comparison, the U.S. government received 18.7 billion dollars for auctioning offshore leases during the decade ending in 1978 (Exxon, 1980, p 4).

7. The main uncertainty in the calculation concerns the size of the cost advantage seabed mining has over landbased production. Adams' assumption of 19 seabed mining plants in operation in twenty years is probably a conservative one. In the absence of international regulations, more may be in operation, and the net social gain and the redistribution from developing to developed countries will be correspondingly greater.

REFERENCES

Adams, F. G. (1980). "The Law of the Sea Treaty and the Regulation of Nodule Exploitation," *Journal of Policy Modelling*, Vol. 2, No. 1.

Akesson, R. (1974). "The Law of the Sea Conference," *Journal of World Trade Law*, Vol. 8, No. 3.

Amacher, R. C., and R. J. Sweeney (1976). *The Law of the Sea: U.S. Interests and Alternatives*, American Enterprise Institute, Washington, D.C.

Cooper, R. (1975). "An Economist's View of the Oceans," *Journal of World Trade Law*, Vol. 9, No. 4.

Cooper, R. (1977). "The Oceans as a Source of Revenue," in Bhagwati, J. (ed.) (1977). *The New International Economic Order*, M.I.T. Press.

Crutchfield, J. A. (1979). "Marine Resources: The Economics of U.S. Ocean Policy," *American Economic Review Papers and Proceedings*, Vol. 69, No. 2.

Diederich, F., W. Muller, and W. Schneider (1979). *Analysis of the MIT Study on Deep Ocean Mining—Critical Remarks on Technologies and Cost Estimates.* Mimeo from The Technical University Aachen and the Battelle-Institut e.V. Frankfurt.

Donaldson, J., and G. Pontecorvo (1980). "Economic Rationalization of Fisheries: The Problem of Conflicting National Interests on Georges Bank," *Ocean Development and International Law Journal*, Vol. 8, No. 2.

Driver, E. S., B. P. Collins, and H. Skolnick (1981). "Petroleum from the Oceans: Resources, Exploration Methods and World Energy," Future of Gas and Oil from the Sea Conference, Center for the Study of Marine Policy, University of Delaware, 17–20 June.

Eckert, R. (1979). *The Enclosure of Ocean Resources: Economics and the Law of the Sea*, Hoover Institution Press, Stanford.

Emery, K. O. (1977). "The Potential and Time Frame for the Development of Petroleum in the Deep Ocean," in Meyer, R. F. (ed.), *The Future Supply of Nature-Made Petroleum and Gas*, Pergamon Press.

Emery, K. O. (1979). "Potential for Deep Ocean Petroleum," *Ambio*, Special Report, No. 6.

Exxon (1980). *The Offshore Search for Oil and Gas*, Exxon Background Series, New York, N.Y.

Frezon, S. (1974). *A Survey of Oil and Gas Statistics for Onshore and Offshore Areas of 151 Countries*, U.S. Geological Survey Professional Paper No. 885, Washington, D.C.

Gulland, J. (1979). "Developing Countries and the New Law of the Sea," *Oceanus*, Vol. 22, No. 1.

Hedberg, H. D. (1976). "Ocean Boundaries and Petroleum Resources," *Science*, Vol. 191, No. 4231, pp. 1009–1018.

Hedberg, H. D., J. D. Moody, and R. M. Hedberg (1979). "Petroleum Prospects of the Deep Offshore," *The American Association of Petroleum Geologists Bulletin*, Vol. 63, No. 3, pp. 286–300.

Holt, S. (1978). "Living Resources," in Borgese, E. M., and N. Ginsburg (eds.), *Ocean Yearbook 1*, University of Chicago Press, Chicago and London.

Katz, R. S. (1979). "Financial Arrangements for Seabed Mining Companies: An NIEO Case Study," *Journal of World Trade Law*, Vol. 13, No. 3.

Klemme, H. D. (1977). "One-fifth of Reserves Lie Off-shore," *Oil and Gas Journal*, Vol. 35, No. 75.

Levy, J. P. (1979). "The Evolution of a Resource Policy for the Exploitation of Deep Sea-Bed Minerals," *Ocean Management*, Vol. 5.

Logue, D. E., R. J. Sweeney, and T. D. Willett (1975). "Optimal Leasing Policy for the Development cf Outer Continental Shelf Hydrocarbon Resources," *Land Economics*, Vol. L1, No. 3.

Mason, J. P. (1981). "Deep Water Drilling and Production Systems for the 1980s," Future of Gas and Oil from the Sea Conference, Center for the Study of Marine Policy, University of Delaware, 17–20 June.

May, R. M., J. R. Beddington, C. W. Clark, S. J. Holt, and R. M. Laws (1979). "Management of Multispecies Fisheries," *Science*, Vol. 205, No. 4403.

Nathan Associates, Inc. (1974). *The Economic Value of Ocean Resources to the United States*. A Report prepared for the Committee on Commerce, 93rd Congress, 2nd Session.

National Petroleum Council (1975). *Ocean Petroleum Resources*.

Nyhart, J. D., L. Antrim, A. E. Capstaff, A. D. Kohler, and D. Reshaw. *A Cost Model of Deep Ocean Mining and Associated Regulatory Issues*, MIT Sea Grant Report MITSG 78-4, Index No. 78-304-EMP.

Pontecorvo, G. *et al.* (1980). "Contribution of the Ocean Sector to the United States Economy," *Science*, Vol. 208, pp. 1000–1006.

Pontecorvo, G., and R. Mesznick (1974). "The Wealth of the Oceans and the Law of the Sea: Some Preliminary Observations," *San Diego Law Review*, Vol. 11, No. 3.

Tollison, R. D., and D. Willett. "Institutional Mechanisms for Dealing with International Externalities: A Public Choice Perspective," in Amacher, R. C., and R. J. Sweeney, op. cit.

U.N. Conference on the Law of the Sea. *Draft Convention on the Law of the Sea (Informal Text)*, A/CONF.62/WP.10/Rev.3/Add.1, 28 August 1980.

Wijkman, P. M. (1980). "Effects of Cargo Reservation: A Review of UNCTAD's Code of Conduct for Liner Conferences," *Marine Policy*, Vol. 4, No. 4.

Wijkman, P. M. (1981). "The Distributional Consequences of Deep Seabed Mining" (mimeo).

36. State Responsibility for Environmental Protection and Preservation

Jan Schneider

Given emerging ecological and political ecological interdependencies and in view of the nature of the contemporary international system, it follows that there is a basic obligation upon states to protect and preserve the human environment, and in particular to use the best practicable means available to them to prevent pollution and other destructive impacts on both exclusive and inclusive resources. This basic obligation may seen obvious and self-evident, but the notion represents a radical departure from traditional *laissez-faire* doctrines of state sovereignty in general and in regard to specific inclusive resources such as the seas. Although it is fundamental to the United Nations Declaration on the Human Environment and to many emanations from customary international law, at present there exists no explicit treaty obligation laying down this responsibility in comprehensive terms capable of effective implementation. In fact, the whole international law of state responsibility for environmental protection and preservation and complementary questions of liability and compensation for environmental injury is currently in a state of obscurity and flux, and it is hoped that the present discussion can make some contribution to its . . . progressive development. . . .

BACKGROUND OF STATE ENVIRONMENTAL RESPONSIBILITY

Less than a century ago it was possible for U.S. Attorney General Judson Harmon without embarrassment to assert that '[t]he fundamental principle of international law is the absolute sovereignty of every nation, as against all others, within its own territory' and therefore to conclude that 'the rules, principles, and precedents of international law impose no liability or obligation' which inhibits a state from using the resources within its territory as it chooses without regard to the impact upon others.[1] Fortunately, this ultranationalistic notion was not adhered to at that time, nor has it won sympathy in the subsequent development of international law. Instead of the Harmon doctrine, the international community has clearly adopted the maxim of *sic utere tuo ut alienum non laedas* (use your own property so as not to injure that of another) fundamental to both Roman and common law. As a result, today state responsibility can be regarded as 'a general principle of international law' or as 'a concomitant of substantive rules and of the supposition that acts and omissions may be categorized as illegal by reference to the rules establishing rights and duties.'[2]

'State responsibility' has traditionally been defined in narrow terms of a wrongful act or omission which causes injury to an alien, but the doctrine has not been confined to that context. As even the reporters of the Harvard draft Convention on the International Responsibility of States for Injuries to Aliens have acknowledged, '[t]he responsibility of a State may also be engaged by a violation of any treaty or any rule of customary international law under such circumstances that no injury to an individual is involved.'[3] Since such responsibility may be either original with the state itself or vicarious as a result of unauthorized acts of its agents or nationals, there are a great number of possible permutations and combinations of international claim situations.[4] Problems may also arise in connection with the participation of several states in the same act, and they can be further complicated by questions of the responsibility of one state for the acts of another state or its nationals.[5] This whole polemic has for several years been under discussion in the UN International Law Commission; and it is interesting to note that in a quite recent draft on state responsibility the ILC said that an 'international crime' may result, *inter alia*, from 'a serious breach of an international obligation of essential importance for the safeguarding and preservation of the human environment, such as those prohibiting massive pollution of the atmosphere or of the sea.'[6]

Meanwhile, *state responsibility* has acquired a more expansive meaning, and the term is now commonly employed by international lawyers to encompass a broad range of conditions under which international obligations may be incurred. In the environmental context, there has been explicit acceptance of the principle that states must bear responsibility for the effects of their actions on the environment of other states or the common environment. The international community has also expressed concern for clarifying the circumstances under which violation of a substantive norm entails an obligation to make reparation or to pay compensation for any resultant damage. Principles 21 and 22 of the Stockholm Declaration . . . embody the current community expectations, and it seems worth repeating them fully in juxtaposition here:

Principle 21: States have, in accordance with the Charter of the United Nations and the principles of international law, the sovereign right to exploit their own resources pursuant to their own environmental policies, and the responsibility to ensure that activities within their jurisdiction or control do not cause damage to the environment of other States or of areas beyond the limits of national jurisdiction.

Principle 22: States shall co-operate to develop further the international law regarding liability and compensation for the victims of pollution and other environmental damage caused by activities within the jurisdiction or control of such States to areas beyond their jurisdiction.[7]

Logically understood, this formulation would have to incorporate responsibility for preventing irremediable or noncompensable effects as well as liability for actual damage, responsibility for warning of reasonably foreseeable environmental consequences of otherwise lawful activities, and responsibility for submitting to peaceful and expeditious settlement disputes related to any of these matters. . . .

PREVENTION OF ENVIRONMENTAL DEPRIVATIONS

Within the overall realm of state environmental responsibility, the first objective of international sanctioning or implementing processes is that of the long-term prevention of environmental losses. Prevention embraces a great variety of measures and activities designed, over a varying range of time, significantly to reduce the probability of undesirable environmental effects. The instruments of policy involved encompass the whole range of diplomatic, economic, ideological, and military strategies available for the maintenance of international public order. . . .

National Environmental Policing Systems

To take as an example what should by now be a familiar piece of legislation, the Arctic Waters Pollution Prevention Act is a model attempt by one state to provide comprehensive environmental policing for its designated area of coverage.[8] No one doubts the particularly severe climatic conditions or other special ecological circumstances of Arctic regions, and the political ecology of the Arctic is exceedingly complex, difficult, and inconducive to joint action.[9] Consequently, taking cognizance of its 'responsibility for the welfare of the Eskimo and other inhabitants of the Canadian arctic and the preservation of the peculiar ecological balance that now exists in the water, ice and land areas of the Canadian arctic'[10] (and of peculiar political imbalances as well), the government of Canada has gone ahead on its own with this legislation. The act prohibits and prescribes penalties for the deposit of 'waste' in Arctic waters or on the islands or mainland under conditions that such waste may enter Arctic waters. It provides for civil liability resulting from such deposit on the part of persons engaged in exploring for, developing, or exploiting the natural resources on the land adjacent to the Arctic waters or in the submarine areas below the waters, or by persons carrying on any undertaking on the mainland or the islands of the Canadian Arctic or on Arctic waters, or by owners of ships navigating within Arctic waters and owners of the cargo of any such ship (which liability is absolute and not dependent upon any proof of fault or negligence). In addition to these basic substantive provisions, the act empowers the Governor General in Council to make regulations relating to navigation in shipping safety control zones and to prohibit any ship from entering such zones unless it meets the regulations concerning hull and fuel tank construction, navigation aids, safety equipment, pilotage, icebreaker escort, and so on; he may also order the destruction or removal of ships in distress which are depositing waste in Arctic waters or are likely to do so. The same legislation furthermore makes arrangement for Pollution Prevention Officers who among other things may, with the consent of the Governor General in Council, seize a ship and its cargo anywhere in Arctic waters within the hundred-mile zone of coverage or elsewhere in the territorial sea or the internal or inland waters of Canada when there is suspicion, on reasonable grounds, that the provisions of the act have been contravened by the ship or by the ship or cargo owners. Upon conviction for such an offence, a court can order the forfeiture of both the ship and its cargo. . . .

As was shown by the example of the Arctic waters legislation, a comprehensive set of preventive measures would encompass regulations for the conduct of operations in regard to the use and enjoyment of ecologically interdependent resources on a functional basis, investigatory powers to oversee compliance, subpoena and other powers for the production of witnesses and documents, seizure powers and/or bonding arrangements for ensuring collateral with which to satisfy an adverse judgment, juridical or administrative procedures to evaluate conformity or non-conformity, and civil and/or criminal penalties for inadvertent or wilful violation. The U.S.

Ports and Waterways Safety Act even goes as far in its criminal penalties as a provision for imprisonment of up to five years as an alternative or in addition to fines.[11]

The references so far have been drawn primarily from the area of marine environmental protection, since that is the subject of most immediate international environmental concern at the present time. It goes without saying, however, that states individually and collectively also have an interest in protecting their air, rivers, lakes, and other resources from pollution and other kinds of environmental deprivations and their people from various additional nuisances (for example, noise) as well. It would be futile to attempt to catalogue all sorts of national environmental legislation and its enforcement provisions here (although that task has already in fact been begun by others elsewhere).[12] There are some variations, but the skeletal enforcement patterns are not fundamentally different in kind, and for the moment it should suffice to grasp the rudiments of what is needed.

Sanctions to Enforce International Prevention Prescriptions

The above examples have dealt with preventive measures to enforce national legislation, but the requirements are not dissimilar as regards either the implementation or the enforcement of international law. . . .

As far as intervention by international machinery itself is concerned, a declaratory judgment by the International Court of Justice or some other international tribunal may have the character of a 'sanction' or 'measure of satisfaction.'[13] The declaration in the *Corfu Channel* case of the illegality of the British minesweeping 'Operation Retail' provides a textbook example.[14] There has, however, been some question about the role of declaratory judgments in cases of potential environmental injury, with at least one writer ruling out resort to them as a means of determining reciprocal rights and duties of parties to a dispute involving extraterritorial environmental interference caused by a *per se* lawful activity in the absence or in advance of actual, provable injury.[15] Yet, as others have pointed out, the arbitral tribunal in the *Trail Smelter* case did, nevertheless, hold that 'it is the duty of the Government of the Dominion of Canada to see to it that this conduct [the future operation of the smelter] should be in conformity with the obligation of the Dominion under international law as herein determined;[16] so the question at the very least remains open.

Unfortunately, clarification has not been provided by the recent *Nuclear Tests* decisions, where the International Court of Justice chose not to confront the problem of illegality.[17] It will be remembered that the ICJ held, in effect, that cessation of the atmospheric testing by France, together with French public statements announcing an intention hereafter to test only underground, rendered moot the issue upon which it had been asked to pass judgment by providing the relief the parties wanted. . . .

In any event, in the overwhelming majority of circumstances, responsibility for the enforcement of international environmental law so as to prevent injury will rest with individual states. When states ratify international treaties and agreements, they quite routinely have to pass detailed implementing legislation (although some of them are, of course, self-executing). . . .

[T]he responsibility of states to conform national legislation and enforcement action to agreed international norms is usually regarded as implied under both conventional and customary international law and is rarely . . . explicitly stated. The specific sanctioning regimes often vary considerably in accordance with domestic constitutional criteria, although certain policing measures have been the subject of international accord. An example of the latter category might be provided by the Oslo and London Ocean Dumping Conventions,[18] which stipulate that states should set up 'special permit' systems for certain grey-listed substances taking account of various specified factors. . . .

On the core issue of what is to be prevented, by whom, and to what extent, conventional prevention prescriptions [yield the following list:] the 1954 International Convention for the Prevention of Pollution of the Seas by Oil with its subsequent amendments and a whole host of related legislation; the 1971 Oslo Convention for the Prevention of Marine Pollution by Dumping from Ships and Aircraft and the following 1972 London Convention on the Prevention of Marine Pollution by Dumping of Wastes and Other Matter; the International Convention for the Prevention of Pollution from Ships; the Paris Convention for the Prevention of Marine Pollution from Land-Based Sources; the Outer Space Treaty; the 1964 Treaty Banning Nuclear Weapons Tests in the Atmosphere, in Outer Space and Under Water and the later Non-Proliferation, Seabed Denuclearization and Tlatelolco treaties; the Antarctic Treaty with its prohibitions, and other agreements to prevent environmental degradation, up to and including the new Convention on the Prohibition of Military or Any Other Hostile Use of Environmental Modification Techniques.[19]

Most of these treaties provide for action by the national state of those carrying out the polluting activities in question. But a new and desirable development from the environmental point of view is the provision for coastal state enforcement in the London Dumping Convention and elsewhere and its elaboration at the Law of the Sea Conference.[20] The extent of action provided for is usually the fullest extent necessary to accomplish the specified purposes according to agreed standards and criteria, and the reach of allowable enforcement measures is not usually an issue. In the debate over coastal state enforcement in the deliberations on the law of the sea, however, there has been sharp and highly vocal disagreement over whether or not such jurisdiction should extend to shore-based or in-port investigation and action only, the detention of vessels, stopping and inspecting ships in territorial waters or the economic zone, the power to order them out of coastal zones, the arrest of offending vessels, the institution of proceedings with only monetary or more drastic penalties, and so on. . . .[21]

Environmental Monitoring

Before passing on to the controversial subject of environmental deterrence measures and to the scarcely considered subject of liability and compensation regimes, however, it should be strongly re-emphasized that the acquisition of accurate and broad-based information is critical to the prevention of environmental injury. An adequate international monitoring system is essential if the effectiveness of existing provisions and the necessity for further preventive measures are to be assessed. The need for ongoing and comprehensive monitoring on a global scale was, of course, recognized at the UN Conference on the Human Environment, and the need for monitoring was referred to in at least twenty-three specific recommendations dealing with very diverse areas of concern.[22] Consequently, planning got under way for the establishment of the Global Environmental Monitoring System and an International Referral Service.[23] By mid-1977, the Executive Director of UNEP was able to state as a practical goal the rendering fully operational of both GEMS and IRS by 1982.[24] It is certainly to be hoped that this goal can be met, and that states will continue to update and elaborate their monitoring efforts thereafter. . . .

DETERRENCE OF IMPENDING ENVIRONMENTAL HARM

Supplementary to their overall interest in long-term prevention of environmental deprivations, states must also be concerned with the deterrence of particular threats or challenges that have emerged or are imminently promised. A danger which one state has an obligation to its own citizens and/or the international community to try to deter may have had its origin either in another state or in the use of inclusive resources. Furthermore, the state which must bear primary responsibility for deterring impending challenges need not necessarily be a state which was charged initially with the obligation to prevent the threatened effects nor is that state or its nationals necessarily likely ultimately to be held liable for any damage which may result.

Admittedly the theory or international legal norm of state responsibility is still nebulous and underdeveloped, and rights and duties in this category are especially difficult to define. Perhaps, therefore, understanding of the problem can be facilitated through concrete illustrations of the types of circumstances that may be involved. When an injurious situation has actually emerged, there is an immediate problem of abating or minimizing the damage, but at times it may seem essential or desirable to seek to avert the risk of grave environmental danger through injunctive or other temporary relief rather than waiting for an actual threat to materialize; interstate environmental warning and notification networks are necessary to accomplish this, and some observations follow about progress to date in this regard.

Abatement and Minimization of Damage

Probably the most dramatic illustration of pollution-abatement measures is still provided by the *Torrey Canyon* catastrophe. . . .[25] The oil started spilling out of her raked tanks almost immediately after grounding. . . . Under the circumstances, the British could hardly have been expected to sit back and wait for the rights and responsibilities to be sorted out among all the interested parties, and indeed the British government would have been sorely remiss in its responsibilities if it had failed to act to avert the danger to its own resources (not to mention those of its neighbours and inclusive resources). Consequently, after the Dutch [salvage team] gave up their attempt to refloat the vessel, the Royal Air Force bombed her to ignite the oil remaining within the hulk so that it would burn rather than leak out into the sea. . . .

It ought again to be emphasized that what is being avoided in [such] cases of abatement measures is not merely impending pollution injury to waters and amenities. There is also a very clear and present danger to living resources in the case of oil spills or other casualties. As one expert has observed:

A slick kills as it goes, often doing some of its worst damage far from the scene of the disaster. . . . The damage a slick does as it travels is comprehensive, destroying both the very foundation of sea life, the plankton, and the highest reach of it, the birds in the air. Phytoplankton, the tiny plants responsible for photosynthesis and for the primary production of more than ninety per cent of the living material in the seas, must function in the upper levels of the oceans, where light penetrates. Fish feed on it, and the fish attract birds. Because of this cycle, all these creatures are victims of oil spills; also destroyed are the surface-mating fish eggs and fry.[26]

This excludes mention of the economic and social dependency of coastal populations on fishery resources and of national and global populations on protein resources from the sea, and so on. All this is but another illustration of the original observation here of inescapable ecological interdependencies.

Short-term measures to abate or minimize environmental harm are not, of course, exhausted by the example of oil spills. They may be concerned with activities in the air, on land, at sea, or elsewhere involving any number of possible substances and dangers. An outstanding example of the variety of factors that may be involved is provided by the Palomares incident.[27] When a U.S. B-52 nuclear bomber collided with a jet tanker during a refuelling mission, four hydrogen bombs managed to escape. Two that fell on land ruptured, and their TNT charges exploded, scattering uranium and plutonium particles near the Spanish coastal village of Palomares and thereby causing a most grave and imminent danger to the inhabitants and the ecology of the area. The governments of the United States and Spain immediately undertook a huge effort to free the region from contamination; this even included burying some 1750 tons of mildly radioactive Spanish soil in the United States.[28] A third bomb hit the earth intact, but the fourth somehow managed to get lost. On the assumption that it lay somewhere on the deep and mountainous bottom of the Mediterranean . . . , naval experts began an intense submarine search. . . . At last, after eighty days, the bomb—reported to be a twenty-megaton device with an explosive force equal to twenty million tons of TNT—was retrieved in a highly specialized forty-eight-hour operation by a U.S. Navy salvage crew. . . .

As all these instances illustrate, once the danger has materialized, the general nature and extent of measures that should be taken to abate it are often quite clear. In the above cases it was also easy to see who had the best means of taking them and the greatest responsibility for doing so. The latter factor is, however, not always so readily apparent. Consequently, to avoid undue haggling and critical delay, for some contingencies specific international arrangements have been made as to who is to take what action.

It is, first of all, firmly established by customary international law doctrines of self-help that any state does not have to await actual catastrophe at its borders but has a right to protect itself from impending disasters, even to the extent of employing necessary and proportional force under the circumstances.[29] And in the particular case of oil spills, the International Convention Relating to Intervention on the High Seas in Cases of Oil Pollution Casualties specifically authorizes parties to take such measures as may be necessary

to prevent, mitigate or eliminate grave and imminent danger to their coastline or related interests from pollution or threat of pollution of the sea by oil, following upon a maritime casualty or acts related to such a casualty, which may reasonably be expected to result in major harmful consequences.[30]

But conditions may arise when it is advisable or desirable that action be taken before the danger becomes 'imminent,' before it is evident which particular state is the primary target of the impending harm, or where there is reason to be greatly concerned over grave and imminent danger to shared resources; and some provisions are being made to meet these situations. Canada and the United States, for example, have adopted a Joint U.S.-Canadian Oil and Hazardous Materials Pollution Contingency Plan for the Great Lakes Region, which fixes spheres of responsibility for the U.S. Coast Guard and the Canadian Ministry of Transport and whose purpose is 'to provide for coordinated and integrated response to pollution incidents in the Great Lakes System by responsible federal, state, provincial and local agencies.'[31] With comparable objectives in regard to a more broadly inclusive resource, the governments of Belgium, Denmark, France, West Germany, the Netherlands, Norway, Sweden, and the United Kingdom, in the Bonn Agreement Concerning Pollution of the North Sea by Oil, have carved up that sea by longitude and latitude into zones of state responsibility '[f]or the sole purposes of this Agreement. . . .'[32]

The International Convention for Northwest Atlantic Fisheries might also be cited in this connection, but the panels of states responsible for the subareas delineated therein are only supposed to oversee developments and then make recommendations to the governments collectively involved as to the need for measures to counteract any observed depletion of the stocks.[33] And there are undoubtedly other examples making varying arrangements in accordance with differing degrees of imminence of harm.

In addition, of course, with regard to inclusive resources in general, any state(s) or international organization(s) aware of circumstances endangering the marine or other environments may always present to the state under whose jurisdiction or control the activities concerned are being carried out, through diplomatic channels, a request for the termination or restriction of such activities and the elimination or reduction of the threat. States can take upon themselves the responsibility to back up such demands by many sorts of political, economic, and other pressures.

Injunctive and Other Temporary Relief

At times it seems essential or desirable to avert the very risk of grave danger instead of waiting until an actual threat has materialized. States may seek to accomplish this through varied channels, drawing on political and other pressures for deterrence. When the United States was contemplating 'Cannikin,' its third underground nuclear weapons test on the Aleutian Island of Amchitka, the Canadian Minister for External Affairs lodged a formal protest with the U.S. Department of State, and Japanese officials also expressed concerned opposition.[34] These apprehensions were supplemented by several unofficial demonstrations by Canadian citizens and environmental groups, in addition to those of U.S. environmentalists. The blast was nevertheless carried out. While no surface radiation was detected and the explosion did not cause the earthquakes that had been feared by some, it did produce high-intensity shock waves affecting large areas. In view of the magnitude of the shock waves registered in Japan, the Japanese government then sent a formal protest to the United States.

Another example of reckless or exceedingly risky behaviour, this time in connection with the use of inclusive resources, was project 'West Ford,' which determined international efforts were made to deter.[35] The U.S. government made plans to release twenty kilograms of tiny copper 'hairs' or 'needles' in outer space to form a belt around the earth about fifteen kilometres wide and thirty kilometres deep, the objective being to test its feasibility to reflect communications signals. . . . After the success of this effort, the Soviet Union made its first formal public protest through the United Nations. . . . The point is that in such cases the determining factor or norm for state responsibility has to be the probability of risk rather than the wrongfulness of the conduct in and of itself. . . .

In addition to the kind of direct effort described above, states and other actors often seek to invoke the authority of relevant courts and administrative bodies for temporary injunctive relief in aid of their causes. The hope is to obtain an official stay of the action either pending further investigation of its likely consequences or as an interim measure on the path to a final judgment disallowing it.

In the Amchitka situation, several conservation groups joined forces to seek an injunction against the tests primarily on the basis that the U.S. Atomic Energy Commission's impact statement did not satisfy the requirements of the National Environmental Policy Act. The U.S. District Court for the District of Columbia entered summary judgment for the AEC, but the Court of Appeals for the D.C. Circuit reversed and remanded. . . .[36]

The U.S. Supreme Court, in a most rare occurrence, agreed to hear on Saturday morning a plea against the blast scheduled for that same afternoon. It rejected the last-minute appeal by a vote of four to three[37] a few minutes before the 12:30 deadline, and the five-megaton warhead went off on schedule[38]—with the dissenters still insisting that they 'would grant the injunction so that the case can be heard on the merits.'[39]

Despite this landmark case, injunctions are a fairly routine occurrence in U.S. environmental litigation. The most notable example from the international point of view occurred in connection with the construction of the Trans-Alaska Pipeline. . . .

International tribunals too have been known to grant the equivalent of injunctions in environmental cases, but often with questionable effect. At an early stage of the *Fisheries Jurisdiction* cases, the International Court of Justice issued Orders Concerning Interim Measures of Protection which, among other things, provided that the sides in the two cases should 'each of them ensure that no action of any kind is taken which might aggravate or extend the dispute submitted to the Court' and also 'each of them ensure that no action is taken which might prejudice the rights of the other Party in respect of the carrying out of whatever decision on the merits the Court may render.'[40] The 1972 Orders also held that the Republic of Iceland should refrain from taking any measures to enforce its purported new fisheries regulations against ships registered in the United Kingdom or the Federal Republic of Germany outside the agreed twelve-mile fisheries zone and that that state should further refrain from applying any administrative, judicial, or other measures against such ships, their crews, or other related persons because of their having engaged in fishing activities between twelve and fifty miles off shore; for their part, the United Kingdom and Germany were directed not to take more than 170,000 and 119,000 metric tons of fish respectively from the 'Sea Area of Iceland.'[41]

A year later, having meanwhile decided that it had jurisdiction to entertain the suits[42] and being aware that negotiations had taken place between Iceland and the other states with a view towards reaching interim arrangement pending final settlement of the disputes, the ICJ issued subsequent Orders Concerning Continuance of Interim Measures of Protection. . . .[43] Iceland continued to disregard the injunctions against it, although a few months after the second set of orders, Iceland and Great Britain reached an 'Interim Agreement in the Fisheries Dispute'[44] (but such was not the result of similar discussions with the Federal Republic). Finally, . . . by ten votes to four, the World Court decided against Iceland on the merits but held that all parties in interest were under mutual obligations to negotiate in good faith for the equitable solution of their differences.[45]

A more unencouraging instance of what were effectively international preliminary injunctions in an environmental controversy occurred in the *Nuclear Tests* cases. In the course of the challenges by Australia and New Zealand to French atmospheric weapons tests over the South Pacific, the International Court of Justice again felt called upon to issue Orders

Concerning Interim Measures of Protection. . . . The orders came down on 22 June 1973, and less than one month later, on 21 July, France exploded another device over its Pacific atoll of Mururoa; the French government also went ahead with another series of tests less than a year later. Subsequently, however, . . . various French officials issued unilateral statements of intention to cease atmospheric explosions and pass on to the stage of underground tests after the 1974 blasts. . . . In the light of these declarations, as has been discussed earlier in this chapter, the ICJ chose not to make a declaratory judgment on the legality of atmospheric nuclear testing or to render any other judgment in the case. . . .

Warning and Notification

During the preparatory processes of the Stockholm Conference, Principles 21 and 22 on state responsibility and liability were accompanied by a third principle relating to the duty to provide proper warning to other states, . . . 'draft Principle 20':

Relevant information must be supplied by States on activities or developments within their jurisdiction or under their control whenever they believe, or have reason to believe, that such information is needed to avoid the risk of significant adverse effects on the environment in areas beyond their national jurisdiction.[46]

. . . In Stockholm the recognition of a duty to warn was effectively blocked by the Brazilian delegation. Brazil was at the time undertaking feasibility studies for a giant hydroelectric installation on the Parana River, which eventually flows into Argentina, becoming the La Plata. Argentina feared that such an alteration in the flow of the river might cause floods, droughts, water pollution, and other injury to Argentine environmental interests, and that government therefore called upon its neighbour to enter into consultations before going ahead with the plans. Accordingly, Argentina proposed at the Conference that the principle be strengthened by adding: 'This information must also be supplied at the request of any of the Parties concerned, within appropriate time, and with such data as may be available and as would enable the above-mentioned Parties to inform and judge by themselves of the nature and probable effects of such activities;'[47] Brazil, on the contrary, wanted expressly to limit it: 'No State is obliged to supply information under conditions that, in its founded judgment, may jeopardize its national security, economic development or its national efforts to improve environment.'[48] The Conference finally avoided deciding the question by referring it to the General Assembly the next fall, in the hope that a consensus might have emerged by that time.

In the General Assembly a few months later, Brazil took the lead in coming forth with something of a conciliatory proposal. The substantially weakened resolution, which was co-sponsored by a large number of developing countries and a few developed countries, recognized that co-operation between States in the field of the environment, including co-operation towards the implementation of principles 21 and 22 of the Declaration of the United Nations Conference on the Human Environment, will be effectively achieved if official and public knowledge is provided of the technical data relating to the work to be carried out by States within their national jurisdiction, with a view to avoiding significant harm that may occur in the environment of the adjacent area.[49]

The next year the General Assembly passed a new and stronger resolution on 'Co-operation in the Field of the Environment Concerning Natural Resources Shared by Two or More States.' General Assembly Resolution 3129 (XXVIII) specifically considers that 'it is necessary to ensure effective co-operation between countries through the establishment of adequate international standards for the conservation and harmonious exploitation of natural resources common to two or more States in the context of the normal relations existing between them'; and it considers further that 'co-operation between countries sharing such natural resources and interested in their exploitation must be developed on the basis of a system of information and prior consultation within the framework of the normal relations existing between them.'[50] It therefore requests the Governing Council of the United Nations Environment Programme to report on measures adopted for the implementation of these two paragraphs and solicits UNEP and member states to take them fully into account. . . .

In some cases and with regard to certain problems, states have very recently begun on a multilateral and bilateral basis to try to elaborate upon and implement these responsibilities for information exchange and prior consultation. The 1974 Principles Concerning Transfrontier Pollution of the Organization for Economic Co-operation and Development specify both that countries concerned should exchange 'all relevant scientific information and data on transfrontier pollution' (an advance over merely 'technical data' or plain 'information' in the previous formulations) and also that they should 'promptly warn other potentially affected countries of any substances which may cause any sudden increase in the level of pollution in areas outside the country of origin of pollution' (which may be taken to imply a responsibility to analyse available information and present it in a readily assimilable form).[51] The 1975 Canada-U.S. Agreement on the Exchange of Information on Weather Modification Activities . . . not only tries to elaborate upon what type of information is to be communicated, in what form, and by and to whom, but also commits the responsible agencies in each country to 'consult with a view to developing compatible reporting formats, and to improving procedures for the exchange of information.'[52] In keeping with General Assembly Resolution 3129, the parties additionally 'agree to consult . . . regarding particular weather modification activities of mutual interest,' except in extreme emergencies. . . .'[53]

Finally, at the Law of the Sea Conference, the international community has been doing some work clarifying and expanding upon evaluation and notification requirements. A draft article has been adopted which obligates states having reasonable grounds for expecting that planned activities under their jurisdiction or control may cause substantial pollution of the marine environment both to 'assess the potential effects of these activities' and to 'communicate reports' of them. . . . This draft article on environmental assessment must be interpreted in the light of another draft article on global and regional co-operation, which provides that a state which becomes aware of cases in which the marine environment is in imminent danger of being damaged or has been damaged by pollution 'shall immediately notify other States it deems likely to be affected by such damage, as well as the competent international organizations, global or regional.'[54] Taken together, the combination of responsibilities is not inconsequential.

In short, slowly and tentatively, there is developing a legal norm of environmental warning and notification the violation of which may entail international responsibility on the part of states.

REPARATION OR COMPENSATION FOR ENVIRONMENTAL INJURY

When environmental deprivations have not been prevented or potential hazards have not been effectively deterred, there then arises the problem of reparation of the harm and compensation for the damages that have occurred. It is in connection with this subgoal of legal sanctioning processes that the reference to concern over 'international law regarding liability and compensation for the victims of pollution and other environmental damage' in Principle 22 of the Stockholm Declaration becomes of direct concern here.[55] As has been explained by other writers at length, there are actually three relevant subsidiary aspects to the problem of what is to be done after the fact of injury: 'restoration' of relationships between or among the parties involved, 'rehabilitation' or immediate reparation of the values destroyed, and 'reconstruction' or long-term avoidance of unauthorized manipulation of the basic value relations at issue.[56] Since international environmental law is still in such a relatively primitive stage of development, however, it is not often possible to distinguish between these aspects in considering existing precedents.

The basic question here is the standard of liability to be applied. It may obviously make a great deal of difference in the respective rights and value positions of the parties concerned if the basis of liability is fault or negligence, on the one hand, or there is strict or absolute liability, on the other. And it is highly important to the protection and preservation of the environment that liability follow upon mere demonstration of causality of injury, rather than only upon proof of intention to harm or some other wrongful behaviour. A second fundamental and related question is who is to be held liable. Assuming that liability attaches to the type of conduct involved, it is clear that a state is liable for damage attributable or imputable to it. When damage has been caused by its nationals or some activity under its jurisdiction or control, however, a state may choose in the first instance to provide appropriate recourse directly against the natural or juridical person(s) involved;

but following exhaustion of any such local remedies, the state that is itself injured or is the national state of a damaged party still has the right to present a claim to the responsible state, and the latter state would then be answerable for any compensation found to be due (although it would probably, of course, then seek to extract payment from the particular relevant actor or actors). Under some circumstances, nevertheless, reciprocally or otherwise, states may wish to assume liability in the first instance for certain activities of their nationals. Further complications can arise in connection with both of these questions. For example, designation of liability and assessment of the nature and extent of damages are likely to be much more difficult when injury has been done to inclusive interests rather than exclusive interests. And on the matter of the respository of the liability, situations are not at all unforeseeable where there will be joint liability and perhaps indemnity from one responsible state or other party to another.[57]

International law on many of these issues is, to repeat, not at all clear. Certain consistent and generalizable patterns of reparation and compensation requirements can, nevertheless, be observed in the contemporary development of international environmental law. The next section discusses the standard of strict or absolute liability both as it is emerging under general circumstances and as it has been applied to certain ultrahazardous activities; then, since the possibility and feasibility of insurance underlies so much of the policy consideration in this area, a commentary on the nature and functions of various environmentally related compensation funds follows.

Emergence of Strict Liability for Environmental Injury

'Strict liability' is liability without fault, and it may be said to exist when compensation is due from one actor to another for injuries caused despite compliance with any particular standards of care. A number of variations on the theme of strict liability have evolved in common law jurisdictions (for example, nuisance, ultrahazardous activities, trespass, and borderline doctrines such as *res ipsa loquitur*), but for present purposes a general comprehension of the generic term should suffice. It cannot be said that there are no defences to strict liability since, depending on the degree of strictness involved, it may be subject to the classic exonerations for tortious acts: *force majeure*, acts of God, or interventions of other third parties. Consequently, while some writers use the terms 'strict' and 'absolute' liability interchangeably, others prefer to reserve the latter for conditions under which very few or no exculpations apply; usage here will attempt to follow that general distinction.[58] But all of these are just words, none of which is very precise, and it must be recognized that what goes on in any given case is a balancing of multiple and multidimensional interests rather than merely pinpointing along some non-existent linear theoretical projection.

One professor has maintained that 'the *Trail Smelter*, *Corfu Channel* and *Lac Lanoux* cases clearly point to the emergence of strict liability as a principle of public international law.'[59] Others who have analysed these very few precedents in the field of international environmental law usually tend to agree with him that there is an evolving norm of strict liability for environmental injury modelled on the century-old rule adumbrated in the famous case of *Rylands* v *Fletcher*.[60] In that case, the defendants, who were proprietors of a mill, had built a large reservoir on their own land for their own business purposes. It was perfectly lawful for them to do this, and they employed for the project a competent engineer and competent con-tractors. Unfortunately, however, due to the unknown and unsuspected presence of an old and abandoned mine shaft, water leaked out of the reservoir and flooded the tunnels in the mine operated by the plaintiff on his adjoining property. The plaintiff therefore sued to recover the damages caused by the flooding of his mine, and the English House of Lords found in his favour. The theory of the case was that the mill owners had put their land to a 'nonnatural use' by collecting on it an unusual amount of water and that they were consequently liable for damage caused to someone else's property; as the Lord Chancellor observed, 'that which the Defendants were doing they were doing at their own peril.'[61]

Parallels in the *Trail Smelter*[62] situation are not difficult to find. That controversy, it will be remembered, involved damage occurring in the territory of the United States and alleged to be caused by an agency situated in Canada. The Consolidated Mining and Smelting Co. of Canada Ltd was operating a smelter at Trail, British Columbia, which was one of the largest and best-equipped such plants on the North American continent. Due at least in part to certain characteristics of river and air currents in the valley shared by the two countries, the fumes were claimed to be causing air pollution and damage to crops in the increasingly populated farming areas around Northport, a town in the State of Washington. The arbitral tribunal set up to resolve the matter found that the Dominion of Canada was responsible under international law for the conduct of the mining company in Canadian territory, that the damage south of the border was indeed caused by the operation of the Canadian smelter, and consequently that indemnity was due from Canada to the United States in compensation for the injury. It based its decision on the much-quoted observation that 'no State has the right to use or permit the use of its territory in such a manner as to cause injury by fumes in or to the territory of another or the properties or persons therein. . . .'[63]

An even clearer illustration of the application of strict liability in the context of environmental injury is the *Gut Dam*[64] arbitration between the same two countries. The facts have been summarized in an earlier chapter but bear repeating here in less skeletal form. In 1874 the Canadian Chief Engineer of Public Works proposed to his government that it construct a dam between Adams Island in Canadian territory and Les Galops, in the United States, for the purpose of improving navigation in the St Lawrence River. After many investigations and reports and formal approval by an act of the U.S. Congress, the Canadian government proceeded to construct the dam in 1903; experience soon demonstrated that it was too low to serve the desired ends and, again with explicit U.S. permission, Canada increased the height of the dam a year later. Between 1904 and 1951 several man-made changes affected the flow of water in the Great Lakes–St Lawrence River basin, and, while the dam itself was not altered in any way, the level of the water in the river and nearby Lake Ontario increased. In 1951–2 the level of waters reached unprecedented heights which, in combination with storms and other natural phenomena, resulted in extensive flooding and erosion damage on both the north and south shores of all the lakes. In 1953, the government of Canada removed its dam as part of the construction of the St Lawrence Seaway, but the problem of U.S. claims for damages allegedly resulting from the presence of Gut Dam still festered for some years. The Lake Ontario Claims Tribunal set up to resolve these matters, after initially determining that Canada had an obligation to all citizens of the United States and not just the owner of Les Galops regarding the construction of the dam and that such responsibility was not limited in time to some initial testing period, observed that 'the only issues which remain for its consideration are the questions of whether Gut Dam caused the damage for which claims have been filed and the *quantum* of such damages.'[65] The arbitral tribunal was, in other words, clearly adopting a standard of strict liability, since it was not interested in hearing any arguments for or against fault or negligence in planning and construction or whether Canada knew or ought to have known what injuries might result. Following upon this holding by the Claims Tribunal, the two governments concerned reached a negotiated settlement of a lump-sum payment from Canada to the United States 'in full and final satisfaction of all claims of United States nationals for alleged damage caused by Gut Dam,'[66] which was then approved by the Tribunal. . . .[67]

Turning now to the other two cases cited at the outset of this section, *Corfu Channel*[68] and *Lac Lanoux*,[69] the existence of strict liability is not difficult to maintain. The former case involved a finding by the International Court of Justice that the People's Republic of Albania was liable for the consequences when British warships struck mines in the Albanian waters of the Corfu Channel. More exactly, the conclusion of the Court was 'that Albania is responsible under international law for the explosions which occurred . . . and for the damage and loss of human life which resulted from them, and that there is a duty upon Albania to pay compensation to the United Kingdom.'[70] The liability stemmed directly from the presence of the mines and the failure to warn the approaching vessels, with no proof required of any malevolence, neglect, or other wrongfulness on the part of Albania. By contrast, the *Lac Lanoux* arbitration was a suit by Spain to block before it was undertaken a hydroelectric project by France using the waters of the lake. It was decided that the proposed project would not be in violation of France's obligation under treaties with its neighbour or under general international law, since it was found to represent a reasonable utilization of the water resources that should not prove injurious to Spanish interests. The tribunal nevertheless added that, if the works did in fact cause pollution or other actual damage, 'Spain could then have claimed that her rights had been impaired.'[71]

Besides these few juridical requirements, there have been certain other instances of voluntary compensation for environmental injury by governments or other actors without proof of fault, but their precedential value is questionable and limited. A much-cited example is the *ex gratia* payments by the United States government to the Japanese government as compensation for Japanese nationals who sustained personal and property damage as a result of the nuclear tests in the Marshall Islands in 1954. Although the tests themselves may be considered lawful measures for security, due to a series of miscalculations or for some other reason, a number of Marshallese, Japanese, and Americans were injured by the test of 1 March of that year, and the series as a whole somewhat disrupted activities of the Japanese fishing industry.[72] The United States tendered $2 million to Japan 'for purposes of compensation for the injuries or damages sustained' and 'in full settlement of any and all claims against the United States or its agents, nationals or juridical entities' as a result of the tests, but did so 'without reference to the question of legal liability.'[73] To take a more recent example on the part of a private actor, the Atlantic Richfield Company, which operated the refinery at Ferndale, Washington, that was the site of the 1972 Cherry Point oil spill, paid an initial clean-up bill of $19,000 submitted by the municipality of Surrey for its activities. ARCO later agreed to pay another $11,606.50 to be transmitted by the United States to the Canadian government for its costs incurred in connection with clean-up operations, but would not consent to provide reimbursement for an additional item of $60 designated 'bird loss (30 birds at $2 a bird).' Again this was done, however, 'without admitting any liability in the matter and without prejudice to its rights and legal position.'[74]

Imposition of Absolute Liability for Ultrahazardous Activities

Many systems of municipal law contain rules creating 'absolute' or exceedingly strict liability for failure to control operations which necessarily create a serious or unusual risk of harm to others. Such designations are, to repeat, only words, and it is essential to look at the varied factors and policies behind them. These rules are based, at least in part, upon principles of loss distribution and liability imposed upon the effective (insured or self-insured) defendant. Ian Brownlie reports that it is the general opinion that international law at present lacks such a doctrine, although Wilfred Jenks has proposed that the law be developed on the basis of a Declaration of Legal Principles Governing Ultrahazardous Activities Generally, which would be adopted by the UN General Assembly.[75] But he also acknowledges that caution is required in accepting the statement that existing law lacks such a principle, 'because the operation of the normal principles of state responsibility may create liability for a great variety of dangerous activities on state territory or emanating from it.'[76] And in every event, absolute liability has at least been recognized in several multilateral conventions as regards certain exceptionally risky or hazardous activities. Of particular interest for present purposes is the increasing imposition of absolute liability in respect of nuclear installations and the operation of nuclear ships, damage caused by space objects, and certain types of oil pollution incidents.

Dealing with a relatively new and obviously dangerous enterprise, the drafters of the 1962 Brussels Convention on the Liability of Operators of Nuclear Ships were quite straightforward: 'The operator of a nuclear ship shall be absolutely liable for any nuclear damage upon proof that such damage has been caused by a nuclear incident involving the nuclear fuel of, or radioactive products or waste produced in, such a ship.'[77] The only narrow exculpation allowed is for intentional wrong on the part of the injured party: 'If the operator proves that the nuclear damage resulted wholly or partially from an act or omission done with intent to cause damage by the individual who suffered the damage, the competent courts may exonerate the operator wholly or partially from his liability to such individual.'[78] The operator may have an independent right of recourse against some other party, but this basic liability is certainly strict enough to deserve its appellation of 'absolute'; the extent of the liability in respect of any one nuclear incident was, however, limited to approximately $100 million.[79]

The 1963 Vienna Convention on Civil Liability for Nuclear Damage was equally succinct: 'The liability of the operator [of a nuclear installation] for nuclear damage under this Convention shall be absolute'[80]—although its exculpatory clause is slightly broader, allowing the competent court if its law so provides to relieve the operator wholly or partly if he proves that the nuclear damage resulted 'either from the gross negligence of the person suffering the damage or from an act or omission of such person done with intent to cause damage';[81] the Vienna Convention allows states to set limits of not less than $5 million for any one nuclear incident.[82] The above are but two of four early conventions in the field of nuclear liability,[83] the others being the 1960 Paris Convention on Third Party Liability in the Field of Nuclear Energy[84] and the 1963 Convention Supplementary to this Paris (OECD) Convention.[85] As in the present context we are interested in the strictness of the standard of liability specified, the precise mechanics of these agreements need not be explored here. It is nevertheless worth noting that, in keeping with their primary concern being the risk inherent in the activities themselves involved, these international conventions treat all nuclear operators—whether government agencies or private corporations—on a similar basis. Finally, as concerns maritime carriage of nuclear material, in order to ensure that the operator of a nuclear installation will be exclusively liable for damage caused by a nuclear incident, the Vienna and Paris Conventions have been complemented by a fifth agreement; the 1971 IMCO Convention Relating to Civil Liability in the Field of Maritime Carriage of Nuclear Material exonerates any and all other persons.[86]

Another area for which there has been designation of liability so strict as to verge on being absolute is the exploration and exploitation of outer space. The various expressions of world community expectations in this realm have already been recorded. The essential point to note is that, while the 1967 Outer Space Treaty states only most generally and summarily that a launching state 'shall bear international responsibility' and 'is internationally liable for damage to another State Party to the Treaty or to its natural or juridical persons by such object or its component parts on the Earth, in air space or in outer space, including the moon and other celestial bodies,'[87] there has been some further clarification of the nature of the liability. The 1971 Convention on International Liability for Damage Caused by Space Objects expressly provides that a launching state 'shall be absolutely liable to pay compensation for damage caused by its space object on the surface of the earth or to aircraft in flight.'[88] There may be exoneration from this absolute liability in accordance with the broader standard, that is, if the state responsible for the launch establishes that 'the damage has resulted either wholly or partially from gross negligence or from an act or omission done with intent to cause damage on the part of a claimant State or of natural or juridical persons it represents,' but no exoneration whatsoever is to be granted in cases where the damage has resulted from activities conducted by a launching state 'which are not in conformity with international law including, in particular, the Charter of the United Nations and the Treaty on Principles Governing the Activities of States in the Exploration and Use of Outer Space, including the Moon and Other Celestial Bodies.'[89] By contrast, where two ultrahazardous activities or in this instance space expeditions clash, in other words where one space object causes injury to another or to persons or property on board, then a fault standard is to be reinstated and the launching state 'shall be liable only if the damage is due to its fault or the fault of persons for whom it is responsible.'[90]

Finally, as the potential hazards of oil spills and other catastrophes are increasing exponentially, more and more strict liability may be finding a place in the legislative regime of the law of the sea as well. It has already been mentioned in passing that liability under the Canadian Arctic Waters Pollution Prevention Act 'is absolute and does not depend upon proof of fault or negligence' (with certain relatively minor exceptions).[91] There is, in addition, some indication of movement multilaterally towards such a standard. During the negotiations of the 1969 IMCO International Convention on Civil Liability for Oil Pollution Damage,[92] there was considerable debate as to whether the applicable standard should be fault or strict liability.[93] Even after the *Torrey Canyon* disaster, there was substantial although diminishing support for a fault basis. But after much deliberation, by the time of the Brussels Conference which concluded this IMCO 'Private Law' Convention, the tide of international opinion had clearly shifted to favour a rather strict standard. The resultant liability provision is worth quoting at length, to give an overall idea of how such requirements are put together:

1. Except as provided for in paragraphs 2 and 3 of this Article, the owner of a ship at the time of an incident, or where the incident consists of a series of

occurrences at the time of the first such occurrence, shall be liable for any pollution damage caused by oil which has escaped or been discharged from the ship as a result of the incident.

2. No liability for pollution damage shall attach to the owner if he proves that the damage:

a. resulted from an act of war, hostilities, civil war, insurrection or a natural phenomenon of an exceptional, inevitable and irresistible character, or

b. was wholly caused by an act or omission done with intent to cause damage by a third party, or

c. was wholly caused by the negligence or other wrongful act of any Government or other authority responsible for the maintenance of lights or other navigational aids in the exercise of that function.

3. If the owner proves that the pollution damage resulted wholly or partially either from an act or omission done with intent to cause damage by the person who suffered the damage or from the negligence of that person, the owner may be exonerated wholly or partially from his liability to such person.[94]

This is obviously not 'absolute' liability, being not nearly as strict as the nuclear or space formulations; but, even without the 'wholly' restriction in paragraph 2, it could still be argued to be a bit stricter than most traditionally allowable defences under international maritime law. The trend of development by which it was reached is, of course, also significant. Moreover, whatever its precise categorization, this convention is also notable for being backed up by supplementary arrangements setting up compensation funds for oil pollution damage.

International Environmental Compensation Funds

The Brussels Conference which adopted the International Convention on Civil Liability for Oil Pollution Damage also passed a Resolution on Establishment of an International Compensation Fund for Oil Pollution Damage, which recommended early establishment of such an insurance fund founded on two basic principles:

1. Victims should be fully and adequately compensated under a system based upon the principle of strict liability.
2. The fund should in principle relieve the shipowner of the additional financial burden imposed by the present ['Private Law'] Convention.[95]

Accordingly, at another IMCO Conference in Brussels two years later, a new agreement was concluded towards these ends. Although its preamble states that the 1971 International Convention on the Establishment of an International Fund for Compensation for Oil Pollution Damage[96] is to be 'supplementary to' the earlier provisions, it is only somewhat so. On the one hand, it did raise the amount of compensation available from the then $14 million limit of the IMCO 'Private Law' Convention to about $34 million (now around $17 and $36 million denominated in terms of 'Special Drawing Rights').[97] On the other hand, however, it still did not expand coverage to pollutants other than oil, nor does it encompass damage outside the 'territory including territorial sea' of the parties.[98] As far as procedure is concerned, when the Fund Convention comes into force on 16 October 1978 and its Oil Pollution Fund is created, contributions in respect of each state party are to be paid in by the petroleum industry on the basis of tons of oil received in ports or terminal installations.[99] Actions for compensation or indemnity will be able to be brought against the Fund in the national courts of the state or states in which the pollution damage has been caused or measures have been taken to prevent or minimize damage.[100]

At the time of this writing, the Oil Pollution Liability Convention has only recently come into effect, and the supplementary Fund Convention enters into force by the end of the year. Meanwhile, however, the provisions of the Tanker Owners Voluntary Agreement concerning Liability for Oil Pollution[101] and the Contract Regarding an Interim Supplement to Tanker Liability for Oil Pollution,[102] known as TOVALOP and CRISTAL, have been applicable.[103] TOVALOP, as its name indicates, is a contract among the tanker owners to the effect that, '[i]f a discharge of Oil occurs from a Participating Tanker through the negligence of that Tanker (and regardless of the degree of fault)' and in addition 'if the Oil causes Damage by Pollution to Coast Lines within the jurisdiction of a Government or creates a grave and imminent danger of Damage by Pollution thereto,' then the tanker owner is obliged to remove the oil or to reimburse the government of the coastal state for the removal costs incurred.[104] Maximum liability in any one incident is limited to $100 (later $125) per gross registered ton or $10 million.[105] Although it does offer something by way of reparation, TOVALOP has certain readily apparent disadvantages, such as requiring proof of negligence, running in favour only of governments, and applying only to oil removal costs and not to other measures of deterrence of or compensation for damage.

The other agreement, CRISTAL, is an oil company attempt to supplement the compensation provisions of the 'Private Law' Convention and TOVALOP pending entry into force of the Fund Convention. It is a contract among the companies to create a fund out of which public or private persons can be compensated for pollution damage up to $30 million per incident.[106] The Oil Companies Institute for Marine Pollution Compensation Ltd, a Bermuda entity organized to administer the fund of CRISTAL, is liable only in cases where liability arises under the terms of TOVALOP or the Liability Convention.[107] As this is being written, both TOVALOP and CRISTAL are in the course of revision. Their limits of liability are expected to be increased, and many of the defects discussed here should be eliminated.[108]

The oil companies are not concerned with their liability solely as regards tanker ownership and operation. In view of the growing impetus towards exploration and exploitation of the resources of the continental shelf and the seabed, the same basic group of corporations felt called upon in late 1974 to conclude an Offshore Pollution Liability Agreement (OPOL).[109] In many respects, OPOL functions for offshore oil facilities as the TOVOLOP and CRISTAL fund and insurance schemes do with respect to owners and operators of oil tankers. The new contract is not restricted to negligence and does provide for compensation to private persons. Its main operative paragraph on remedial measures, reimbursement, and compensation for claims states:

If a Discharge of Oil occurs from a Designated Offshore Facility, and if, as a result, any State or States take Remedial Measures and/or any Person sustains Pollution Damage, then the Party hereto who was the Operator of said Designated Offshore Facility at the time of the Discharge of Oil shall reimburse the cost of said Remedial Measures and pay compensation for said Pollution Damage up to an overall maximum of U.S. $16,000,000 per Incident. . . .[110]

In the same clause, exceptions are allowed for damage which resulted from acts of war or other hostilities, was wholly caused by an act or omission done with intent to cause damage by a third party, was wholly caused by the negligence or other wrongful act of any state or other licensing authority, or resulted from an act or omission done with intent to cause damage or from negligence of the claimant—that is, fairly standard strict liability exonerations. The signatories formed under the laws of England the Offshore Pollution Liability Association Ltd for the purpose of administering this contract and certain other functions.[111] Furthermore, there is also now the 1976 Convention on Civil Liability for Oil Pollution Damage Resulting from Exploration and Exploitation of Seabed Mineral Resources, which stands in very much the same relation to OPOL as the 1969 and 1971 Civil Liability and Fund Conventions do to TOVOLOP and CRISTAL; in the seabed mining case, however, the convention is limited in its applicability to the Western European region and differs significantly in several of its terms from OPOL.[112]

The above examples all deal with internationally and transnationally organized environmental compensation funds. Funds created in pursuance of national legislation may also have international significance, of which a noteworthy example is that established under the U.S. Trans-Alaska Pipeline Authorization Act of 1973.[113] After providing for strict liability for activities in connection with the pipeline right of way on the part of the holder,[114] the Act goes on to create a compensation fund to pay for related incidents. The liability provision is as follows:

Notwithstanding the provisions of any other law, if oil that has been transported through the trans-Alaska pipeline is loaded on a vessel at the terminal facilities of the pipeline, the owner and operator of the vessel (jointly and severally) and the Trans-Alaska Pipeline Liability Fund established by this subsection, shall be strictly liable without regard to fault in accordance with the provisions of this subsection for all damages, including clean-up costs, sustained by any person or entity, public or private, including residents of Canada, as a result of discharges of oil from such vessel.[115]

Exoneration is allowed for damages caused by act of war or the negligence of the United States or other governmental agency and for the negligence of the damaged party, and liability is limited under this subsection to $100 million for any one incident.[116] The Fund itself is to be a non-profit corporate entity that may sue and be sued in its own name, with its resources to be maintained at the level of $100 million by imposition of a fee of five cents per barrel by the pipeline operator against the owner of the oil.[117] Aside from the immediate and obvious interests of Canada and Canadian citizens in this piece of U.S. legislation,[118] it is a matter generally worthy of international concern whether or not provision is made sufficiently to take into account possible environmental costs and ways of meeting them in such a large-scale undertaking as this.

A Note on Private Rights of Action
Under National and Local Laws

Since the present focus of inquiry is on 'state responsibility' in particular within the broader context of 'world public order,' there has been little discussion here of private rights of action in domestic arenas. This should by no means be taken to imply that the possibility of private litigation or other action is not of great significance. Sometimes it is found preferable to international solutions. In *Michie v Great Lakes Steel Division, National Steel Corp.*,[119] for example, plaintiffs who are residents of the Windsor area in Canada and regular recipients of effluents from the Detroit industrial complex in the United States, chose to institute private actions against three industrial corporations and seek remedies for their air pollution in U.S. courts under municipal law rather than wait for a long and tedious international claims process as in *Trail Smelter* or *Gut Dam*.[120] And the new Nordic Environmental Protection Convention,[121] of course, envisions such suits happening on a regular and usual basis among citizens and entities of the four countries involved. Furthermore, in some cases private arrangements may be made to provide rapid compensation without the need for juridical intervention of any type, as the U.S. government undertook to do in regard to 597 claims filed in connection with the Palomares incident[122] and as it is reported ARCO did privately by opening up a claims office to handle claims resulting from the Cherry Point oil spill.[123]

Frequently such private litigation under national and local laws will be capable of resolving the controversy satisfactorily and expeditiously. Often, nevertheless, the juridical tangle likely to result without benefit of additional international liability and compensation arrangements boggles the mind. There was, for example, a good deal of private litigation—some of it effectively resolved—in the wake of the *Torrey Canyon* disaster.[124] Yet in most such situations, with all the parties and countries involved with different applicable fault and limitation provisions and other conflicting legal requirements, truly prompt and adequate compensation seems virtually unimaginable without prior general agreement on a standard of strict liability for some state, company, or other international actor involved imposed in accordance with certain set rules and regulations. And it is only through such agreement that the parties in interest can know reliably beforehand the possible consequences of their activities so as to be able to make arrangements for insurance or other cost-spreading devices.

In short, although this is not the place to discuss comparative national substantive legislation or procedural requirements in environmental cases, it must be noted that municipal law, too, can be critically important. It is unrealistic to try to make any sharp distinctions between international and national legal responsibilities, as these involve multiple interacting and interreactive processes of authoritative decision.

NOTES

1. Treaty of Guadelupe-Hidalgo—International Law, 21 *Op. Att'y Gen.* 274, 281, and 283 (1893-7). For some discussion of this matter see Utton, International Environmental Law and Consultation Mechanisms, 12 *Colum. J. Transnat'l L.* 56, 57-9 (1973).

2. I. Brownlie, *Principles of Public International Law* 418-19 (2d ed., 1973).

3. Convention on the International Responsibility of States for Injuries to Aliens 45 (Draft no. 12, with Explanatory Notes, L. Sohn and R. Baxter reporters 1961). See generally C. Amerasinghe, *State Responsibility for Injuries to Aliens* (1967).

4. On this subject of who is responsible for what, see Fatouros, Developing Legal Standards of Liability for Transnational Environmental Injury: Bases of Liability and Standing to Complain, in *International Responsibility for Environmental Injury* (R. Stein, ed., forthcoming). And there are also questions of agency and joint tortfeasors. See Brownlie, supra note 2, at 441-4.

5. See Brownlie, ibid.

6. *Report of the International Law Commission on the Work of Its Twenty-Ninth Session,* U.N. Doc. A/32/283, art. 19(3)(d) (1977). The ILC has been giving attention at this stage of its deliberations to the responsibility of states for international wrongful acts, leaving aside the problem of responsibility for risks. After it completes work on these draft articles, the Commission has been given a mandate by the General Assembly to turn to the topic of international liability for injurious consequences arising out of acts not prohibited by international law (G.A. Res. 3315, 29 U.N. GAOR Supp. 31, at 144, U.N. Doc. A/9631 (1975)).

7. *Report of the United Nations Conference on the Human Environment,* U.N. Doc. A/Conf.48/14, at 7 (1972) (hereinafter *Report*), quoted previously at chapter 3, 21 and 48.

8. R.S.C. 1970 (1st Supp.) c. 2 (1970); for discussion see Jan Schneider, *World Public Order of the Environment* (1979), chapter 3, 27, chapter 4, 81, 85-6. [All subsequent references to "chapter" pertain to Schneider's book.]

9. The basic political ecological problem is as follows. On the one hand, claims of sovereignty on a sector theory have been raised as to certain parts of the Arctic by the Soviet Union. But on the other, the United States, among others, has strongly and consistently opposed the advancement of any such claims or the drawing of baselines by Canada in its neighbouring northern areas. As a result, any determination in an international forum of rules and regulations to apply to the Arctic, which would in effect refer to the Arctic north of Canada overwhelmingly, is not politically viable from the Canadian point of view. See generally D. Pharand, *The Law of the Sea in the Arctic* (1973).

10. Supra note 8, preamble.

11. 33 U.S.C. § 1227.

12. Reference is made to the Environmental Law Information System and the Environmental Law Centre of the International Union for the Conservation of Nature and Natural Resources (IUCN) at chapter 4, 78 and chapter 5, 126.

13. On state responsibility and the role of declaratory judgments see the report by F.V. García-Amador, Special Rapporteur, [1961] 2 Y.B. *Int'l L. Comm'n* 1, 14–16, U.N. Doc. A/CN.4/134 (1961). He explains that sometimes declaratory judgments 'constitute a simple means of giving satisfaction for "moral and political" injury caused to a State, or, in other words, a method of "making reparation" for an act contrary to international law by formally declaring it to be unlawful and thus sanctioning or censuring the conduct imputable to the defendant state'; at other times such a judgment 'constitutes a type of "juridical reparation" for the unlawfulness of an act or omission capable of occasioning actual and effective injury and therefore constitutes a form of reparation *sui generis*'; see *Black's Law Dictionary* 1507 (rev. 4th ed., 1968), at 15–16.

14. The International Court of Justice stated that 'to ensure respect for international law . . . the Court must declare that the action of the British Navy constituted a violation of Albanian sovereignty' and that '[t]his declaration is in accordance with the request made by Albania through her Counsel [for "the declaration of the Court from a legal point of view"] and is in itself appropriate satisfaction' ([1949] I.C.J. 4, 35). See chapter 3, 49.

15. Handl, Territorial Sovereignty and the Problem of Transnational Pollution, 69 *Am. J. Int'l L.* 50, 72–5 (1975). But see the second use of declaratory judgments described in García-Amador's report, supra note 13.

16. (*United States* v *Canada*), 3 U.N.R.I.A.A. 1938, 1963 (1941). For discussion see chapter 3, 48–9; see also García-Amador, supra note 13, at 15.

17. *Nuclear Tests* (*Australia* v *France*) and *Nuclear Tests* (*New Zealand* v *France*), [1974] I.C.J. 253 and 457. For discussion see chapter 3, 41–2, chapter 4, 91–2. See also Goldie, The Nuclear Tests Cases: Restraints on Environmental Harm, 5 *J. Maritime L. & Com.* 491 (1974); Frank, Word Made Law: The Decision of the International Court of Justice in the Nuclear Test Cases, 69 *Am. J. Int'l L.* 612 (1975).

18. Convention for the Prevention of Marine Pollution by Dumping from Ships and Aircraft, *done* 15 February 1972, in 11 *Int'l Legal Materials* at 262 (1972) and Convention on Prevention of Marine Pollution by Dumping of Wastes and Other Matter, *done* 29 December 1972, [1975] 2 U.S.T. 2403, T.I.A.S. no. 8165; see chapter 3, 35–6.

19. For discussion and citations see chapter 3, 32–3, 35–6, 36, 36–7, 37–8, 39, 40, 40–1, 42–3, and 29 respectively. See also Legault, The Freedom of the Seas: A Licence to Pollute? 21 *U. Toronto L. J.* 211, 216 (1971).

20. See chapter 3, 36, chapter 4, 94.

21. For further specification, see the enforcement provisions of the Informal Composite Negotiating Text (ICNT), arts. 214–23, in 8 *Third United Nations Conference on the Law of the Sea: Official Records* 37–9 (1977). See also the safeguards in ICNT arts. 224–34, ibid, at 39–40.

22. See *Report*, supra note 7, at 59.

23. For description see chapter 4, 76–7. See generally Global Environmental Monitoring System, U.N. Doc. UNEP/GC/31/Add.2 (1975); Development and Implementation of the Global Environmental Monitoring System, U.N. Doc. UNEP/GC/

Inf.2 (1977); Progress Report on International Referral System Development, U.N. Doc. UNEP/GC/Inf.7 (1977).

24. *Report of the Governing Council of the United Nations Environment Programme on the Work of Its Fifth Session*, 32 U.N. GAOR Supp. 25, at 9, U.N. Doc. A/32/25 (1977). See also Decision 84(V)(B), ibid, at 122.

25. For presentation of the facts and analysis of the legal issues raised by this disaster, see Brown, The Lessons of the *Torrey Canyon*, 21 *Current Legal Problems* 113 (1968); McGurren, The Externalities of a *Torrey Canyon* Situation: An Impetus for Change in Legislation, 11 *Natural Resources J.* 349 (1971); Utton, Protective Measures and the *Torrey Canyon*, 9 *B.C. Ind. & Com. L. Rev.* 613 (1968); Comment, Post *Torrey Canyon*: Toward a New Solution to the Problem of Traumatic Oil Spill, 2 *Conn. L. Rev.* 632 (1970).

26. Mostert, Profiles: Supertankers, *New Yorker* 45 and 46 (2 parts, 13 and 20 May 1974), the quotation being from part 2, at 75. See also N. Mostert, *Supership* (1974), which expands upon these articles. On cleaning up these spills, see generally Environmental Emergency Branch, Environmental Protection Service, Canada, *Spill Technology Newsletter* (bimonthly).

27. See generally F. Lewis, *One of Our H-Bombs Is Missing* (1967); T. Szulc, *The Bombs of Palomares* (1967).

28. Radioactive Spanish Earth is Buried 10 Feet Deep in South Carolina, *N.Y. Times*, 12 April 1966, at 28, col. 3.

29. See the discussion of self-defence, self-preservation, and security in M. McDougal and F. Feliciano, *Law and Minimum World Public Order* 213–16 et seq. (1961); see also chapter 3, 46–7.

30. *Done* 29 November 1969, [1975] 1 U.S.T. 765, T.I.A.S. no. 8068, discussed at chapter 3, 33–4.

31. The plan itself was adopted on 10 June 1971 and is reprinted in 6 *New Directions in the Law of the Sea* 464 (S. Lay, R. Churchill, and M. Nordquist, eds. 1975). It was described in and its purpose is here cited from the Agreement on Great Lakes Water Quality, 15 April 1972, [1972] 1 U.S.T. 301, T.I.A.S. no. 7312, Annex 8.

32. *Entered into force* 9 August 1969, in 9 *Int'l Legal Materials* 359, art. 6 (1970). For discussion of other aspects of the arrangement see chapter 3, 34–5.

33. *Done* 8 February 1949, [1950] 1 U.S.T. 477, T.I.A.S. no. 2089, 157 U.N.T.S. 157. The workings of ICNAF were described in chapter 3, 57.

34. On the general subject of the international legal implications, see Stein, Cannikin, in *International Responsibility for Environmental Injury*, supra note 4. On the protests see, e.g., Kentworthy, Nixon May Cancel Aleutians A-Test, *N.Y. Times*, 9 September 1971, at 1, col. 4; Szulc, US, Britain Wary on Security Talks, ibid, 2 October 1971, at 1, col. 7; Walz, 12 Sail for Amchitka to Fight Atom Test, ibid, 3 October 1971, at 14, col. 4; Gamble in the Aleutians (edit.), ibid, 4 October 1971, at 38, col. 2; Kentworthy, Nixon Authorizes Atomic Explosion in the Aleutians, ibid, 28 October 1971, at 1, col. 4; Canada Voices Disquiet, ibid, 28 October 1971, at 26, col. 8; Turner, H-Bombs Tested in the Aleutians Despite Protest, ibid, 7 November 1971, at 1, col. 8; Shock Waves Felt in Japan, ibid, 7 November 1971, at 64, col. 6.

35. On the legal issues involved see Weiss, Project West Ford: Needles in Space, in *International Responsibility for Environmental Injury*, supra note 4. On the protests see, e.g., Finney, Needle Antennas Stir Space Furor, *N.Y. Times*, 30 July 1961, at 48, col. 1; Sullivan, Needles Orbiting to Be Tried Again, ibid, 3 February 1962, at 5, col. 1; Finney, New Panel to Screen Space Experiments, ibid, 10 May 1962, at

16, col. 4; Needles Orbited for Radio Relay, ibid, 13 May 1963, at 1, col. 5; U.S. Assures World Scientists Needles Are Harmless, ibid, 18 May 1963, at 9, col. 7; Soviet Again Hits US Needles Test, ibid, 21 May 1963, at 3, col. 1; Brewer, Soviet Is Accused of Space Secrecy, ibid, 7 June 1963, at 10, col. 3; More Needles in Space? (edit.), ibid, 23 September 1963, at 28, col. 2.

36. See *Committee for Nuclear Responsibility v Seaborg,* 463 F. 2d 783 (D.C. Cir. 1971).

37. *Committee for Nuclear Responsibility v Schlesinger,* 404 U.S. 917, 92 S. Ct. 242, 30 L. Ed. 2d 191 (1971).

38. See Turner, H-Bombs Tested in the Aleutians Despite Protest, supra note 34.

39. See Mr Justice Douglas' dissent, 404 U.S. at 917; Justices Brennan and Marshall would also have granted a temporary restraining order pending plaintiff's filing of a petition for certiorari and action by the Court on the petition (404 U.S. at 930).

40. *Fisheries Jurisdiction (United Kingdom v Iceland)* and *Fisheries Jurisdiction (Federal Republic of Germany v Iceland),* Interim Protection, Orders of 17 August 1972, [1972] I.C.J. 12, 17 and 30, 35. For discussion of these cases, see chapter 3, 58–9.

41. Interim Protection Orders, [1972] I.C.J. at 17 and 35.

42. Jurisdiction of Court, Judgments, [1973] I.C.J. 3 and 49.

43. Interim Measures, Orders of 12 July 1973, [1973] I.C.J. 302 and 313.

44. *Done* 13 November 1973, in 12 *Int'l Legal Materials* 1315 (1973). See also Belgium-Iceland: Agreement on Fishing Within Fifty Mile Limit Off Iceland, *done* 7 September 1972, ibid, vol. 11, at 941 (1972); Iceland-Norway: Agreement Concerning Fishing Rights, *done* 10 July 1973, ibid, vol. 12, at 1313 (1973). Compare Belgium-Iceland: Fisheries Agreement on the Extension of the Icelandic Fishery Limits to 200 Miles, 28 November 1975, ibid, vol. 15, at 1 (1976); Federal Republic of Germany–Iceland: Fisheries Agreement on the Extension of the Icelandic Fishery Limits to 200 Miles, 28 November 1975, ibid, at 43; Iceland-Norway: Agreement concerning Norwegian Fishing in Icelandic Waters, 10 March 1975, ibid, at 875; Iceland–United Kingdom: Agreement concerning British Fishing in Icelandic Waters, 1 June 1976, ibid, at 878.

45. Merits, Judgments of 25 July 1974, [1974] I.C.J. 3 and 175.

46. Draft Declaration on the Human Environment, U.N. Doc. A/Conf.48/4, Annex, para. 20, at 4 (1972), previously quoted at chapter 3, 51. For discussion see Sohn, The Stockholm Declaration on the Human Environment, 14 *Harv. Int'l L.J.* 423, 496–502 (1973).

47. Ibid, quoting U.N. Doc. A/Conf.48/CRP.5 (1972).

48. Ibid, quoting U.N. Doc. A/Conf.48/14, at 119 (1972).

49. G.A. Res. 2995, 27 U.N. GAOR Supp. 30, at 42, U.N. Doc. A/8730 (1972).

50. G.A. Res. 3129, 28 U.N. GAOR Supp. 30, at 48, 49, U.N. Doc. A/9030 (1973).

51. OECD Doc. C(74)224 (21 November 1974), reprinted in 14 *Int'l Legal Materials* 242, 246, Titles G and F respectively (1975). Also relevant is Title E on the principle of information exchange and consultation. See also Council Recommendation on Implementing a Regime of Equal Right of Access and Non-Discrimination in relation to Transfrontier Pollution, 17 May 1977, ibid, vol. 16, at 977 (1977). See chapter 3, 51–2.

52. *Done* 26 March 1975, [1975] 1 U.S.T. 540, T.I.A.S. no. 8056, art. 3.

53. Ibid, the quotation being from art. 5 and the emergency exemption found in art. 6.

54. ICNT art. 199, in ibid, at 35. It is worth noting in passing that warning and consultation provisions have already been written into the London Ocean Dumping Convention, supra note 18, art. 5, and into the regional Agreement Concerning Pollution of the North Sea by Oil, supra note 32, art. 6.

55. Supra 143–4.

56. See M. McDougal and F. Feliciano, supra note 29, at 287–96; M. McDougal, H. Lasswell and I. Vlasic, *Law and Public Order in Space* 404–6 *et seq.* (1963).

57. For a good summary treatment of principles and problems of international responsibility of states and international claims, see W. Bishop, *International Law* 742–899 (3d ed., 1962).

58. See generally Goldie, Liability for Damage and the Progressive Development of International Law, 14 *Int'l & Comp. L.Q.* 1189 (1965); W. Jenks, *The Prospects of International Adjudication* 514–46 (1964).

59. Goldie, International Principles of Responsibility for Pollution, 9 *Colum. J. Transnat'l L.* 283, 306 (1970).

60. L.R. 1 H.L. 330 (1868), extracted in H. Shulman and F. James, *Cases and Materials on the Law of Torts* 61 (2d ed 1952).

61. H. Shulman and F. James, supra note 60, at 70. And as Lord Cranworth added: 'If a person brings, or accumulates, on his land anything which, if it should escape, may cause damage to his neighbour, he does so at his peril. If it does escape, and cause damage, he is responsible, however careful he may have been, and whatever precautions he may have taken to prevent the damage' (ibid, at 71). See also Bohlen, The Rule in *Rylands v Fletcher,* 59 *U. Pa. L. Rev.* 298 (1911).

62. (*United States v Canada*), 3 U.N.R.I.A.A. 1911 and 1938 (1938 and 1941), reprinted in 33 *Am. J. Int'l L.* 182 (1939) and ibid, vol. 35, at 684 (1941). See chapter 3, 48–9.

63. Ibid, at 1965; see chapter 3, 48–9.

64. See Canada-United States Settlement of Gut Dam Claims, 22 September 1968, Report of the Agent of the United States before the Lake Ontario Claims Tribunal, in 8 *Int'l Legal Materials* 118 (1969). For discussion see chapter 3, 50.

65. Decision of 12 February 1968, quoted in ibid, at 138, 140.

66. Agreement on Settlement of Claims Relating to Gut Dam, 18 November 1968, [1968] 6 U.S.T. 7863, T.I.A.S. no. 6624.

67. Communication of 27 September 1968, quoted in 8 *Int'l Legal Materials* 140–2.

68. [1949] I.C.J. 4; see chapter 3, 48, 49.

69. (*Spain v France*), 12 U.N.R.I.A.A. 281 (1957), digested in 53 *Am. J. Int'l L.* 156 (1959); see chapter 3, 48, 49–50.

70. [1949] I.C.J. 23.

71. 12 U.N.R.I.A.A. 303; see chapter 3, 50.

72. See McDougal and Schlei, The Hydrogen Bomb Tests in Perspective: Lawful Measures for Security, in M. McDougal and Associates, *Studies in World Public Order* 763 (1960).

73. Agreement on Personal and Property Damage Claims, 4 January 1955, [1955] 1 U.S.T. 1, T.I.A.S. no. 3160.

74. The terms and conditions were specified in a note from the U.S. Department of State to the Canadian government on 13 November 1974. On reimbursement for the clean-ups, see ARCO Pays $19,000 Cleanup Bill and Oil Spill Billing Will Hit $26,000.

75. I. Brownlie, supra note 2, at 463. See also Jenks, Liability for Ultra-Hazardous Activities, 117 *Recueil des Cours* 166 (1966); Kelson, State Responsibility and the Abnormally Dangerous Activity, 13 *Harv. Int'l L.J.* 197 (1972).

76. Brownlie, supra note 75, at 463.

77. 25 May 1962, in 57 *Am. J. Int'l L.* 268, art. 2 (1963). See chapter 3, 33.

78. Brussels Nuclear Ships Liability Convention, supra note 77, art. 2.

79. Ibid, art. 3. The limit was set at 1500 million francs.

80. *Opened for signature* 21 May 1963, in 2 *Int'l Legal Materials* 727, art. 4 (1963).

81. Ibid.

82. Ibid.

83. On this subject see generally Cigoj, International Regulation of Civil Liability for Nuclear Risk, 14 *Int'l & Comp. L.Q.* 809 (1965); Hardy, The Liability of Operators of Nuclear Ships, ibid, vol. 12, at 778 (1963) and his Nuclear Liability: The General Principles of Law and Further Proposals, 36 *Brit. Y.B. Int'l L.* 223 (1960); Konz, The 1962 Brussels Convention on the Liability of Operators of Nuclear Ships, 57 *Am. J. Int'l L.* 100 (1963).

84. *Done* 29 July 1960, in 8 *Europ. Y.B.* 202 (1960).

85. Convention Supplementary to the (OEEC) Paris Convention of 1960, 30 January 1963, in 2 *Int'l Legal Materials* 685 (1963).

86. *Done* 17 December 1971, in ibid, vol. 11, at 277 (1972).

87. Treaty on Principles Governing the Activities of States in the Exploration and Use of Outer Space, Including the Moon and Other Celestial Bodies, *done* 27 January 1967, [1967] 3 U.S.T. 2410, T.I.A.S. no. 6347, 610 U.N.T.S. 205, art. 7. See chapter 3, 39.

88. *Done* 29 March 1972, [1973] 2 U.S.T. 2389, T.I.A.S. no. 7762, art. 2. See chapter 3, 39–40.

89. Liability Convention, supra note 88, art. 4.

90. Ibid, art. 3.

91. Supra note 8, para. 7. See 110 supra.

92. *Done* 29 November 1969, in 9 *Int'l Legal Materials* 45 (1969). See also Protocol to International Convention on Civil Liability for Oil Pollution Damage, *done* 19 November 1976, in 16 *Int'l Legal Materials* 617 (1977); the protocol converts the limit into special drawing rights (SDRs) as defined by the International Monetary Fund as the unit of account. The 'Private Law' Convention was discussed in chapter 3, 34.

93. See Healy, The CMI and IMCO Draft Conventions on Civil Liability for Oil Pollution, 1 *J. Maritime L. & Com.* 93, 93–8 (1960); Goldie, supra note 59, at 314–17. See also Avins, Absolute Liability for Oil Spillage, 38 *Brooklyn L. Rev.* 359 (1970); Bergman, No Fault Liability for Oil Pollution Damage, 5 *J. Maritime L. & Com.* 1 (1973). See generally Dowd, Further Comment on the Civil Liability and Compensation Fund Conventions, ibid, vol. 4, at 525 (1973).

94. Supra note 92, art. 3.

95. In 9 *Int'l Legal Materials* 66, 67 (1970).

96. *Done* 18 December 1971, ibid, vol. 11, at 284 (1972). For analysis of the working arrangements involved, see Hunter, The Proposed International Compensation Fund for Oil Pollution Damage, 4 *J. Maritime L. & Com.* 117 (1972).

97. The limit was set at 450 million francs. On the problem of conversion rates, see Mendelsohn, Value of the Poincaré Gold Franc in Limitation of Liability Conventions, 5 *J. Maritime L. & Com.* 125 (1973). See also Protocol to the International Convention on the Establishment of an International Fund for Compensation for Oil Pollution Damage, *done* 19 November 1976, in 16 *Int'l Legal Materials* 621 (1977), which converts the limit into SDRs, supra note 92, as the unit of account.

98. See 1971 Fund Convention, supra note 96, art. 3; see also chapter 3, 34.

99. Fund Convention, supra note 23, art. 10.

100. Ibid, art. 7, incorporating by reference art. 9 of the Liability Convention, supra note 92.

101. 7 January 1969, in 8 *Int'l Legal Materials* 497 (1969). The owners of over 99 percent of the free world's tanker tonnage are parties (booklet entitled *TOVALOP* 4 (Int'l Tanker Owners Pollution Federation Ltd, reprint 1973)).

102. 14 January 1971, in 10 *Int'l Legal Materials* 137 (1971). The receivers of over 90 percent of the world's cargoes of crude and fuel oil contracted to be parties to the agreement (Becker, A Short Cruise on the Good Ships TOVALOP and CRISTAL, 5 *J. Maritime L. & Com.* 609, 614 (1974)).

103. TOVALOP and CRISTAL became effective on 6 October 1969 and 1 April 1971 respectively. When the former came into operation, at least 50 percent of the tanker tonnage of the world had become parties (*TOVALOP*, supra note 101, at 4). And the latter required that Oil Companies receiving over 50 percent of the world's seaborne crude oil and fuel oil become signatories in order to come into effect (CRISTAL, supra note 102, clause III(A)).

104. Supra note 101, art. 4.

105. Ibid, art. 6.

106. Supra note 102, art. 4.

107. Ibid.

108. The new limits of TOVALOP are to be $147 per gross registered ton or $16.8 million. Revised CRISTAL limits will match the Fund Convention $36 million ceiling. TOVALOP will also in the future include coverage for third-party damage.

109. *Done* 4 September 1974, in 13 *Int'l Legal Materials* 1409 (1974).

110. Ibid, Clause IV.

111. Ibid, Clause II. The Rules of the Association appear in 14 *Int'l Legal Materials* 147 (1975).

112. *Done* 17 December 1976, in 15 *Int'l Legal Materials* 1451 (1977). This convention, which covers both public and private damage (including preventive measures), sets a limit of liability at 22 million SDRs, supra note 127. For discussion of its purposes and operation, see Dubais, The 1976 London Convention on Civil Liability for Oil Pollution Damage from Offshore Installations, 9 *J. Maritime L. & Com.* 61 (1977). For an excellent review of the whole developing law in the area of prevention of pollution from activities concerned with the exploration and exploitation of the continental shelf, see de Mestral, Study of Offshore Mining and Drilling Carried Out within the Limits of National Jurisdiction, U.N. Doc. UNEP/ WG.14/2 (23 February 1978).

113. 43 U.S.C.A. § 1651 (Supp. 1975).

114. Ibid, § 1653(a) and (b).

115. Ibid, § 1653(c)(1).

116. Ibid, § 1653(c)(2) and (3).

117. Ibid, § 1653(c)(5).

118. See also § 1654 of the Act, which authorizes the President of the United States to enter into negotiations with the government of Canada on a whole range of issues concerned with pipelines or other transportation systems for the transport of natural oil and gas, including environmental and energy issues.

119. 495 F.2d 213 (6th Cir. 1974), *cert. denied* 419 U.S. 997, 95 S. Ct. 310, 42 L. Ed. 2d 270 (1974). Thirty-seven residents of Canada brought this suit against the three corporations, claiming that pollutants emitted by the defendants' plants were noxious and represented a nuisance which resulted in damage to their persons and property. For discussion of why this form of action was preferred to the international

claims route, see Ianni, International and Private Actions in Transboundary Pollution, 11 *Can. Y.B. Int'l L.* 258, 266-70 (1973). See also chapter 7, 194. See generally McCaffrey, Transboundary Pollution Injuries: Jurisdictional Considerations in Private Litigation between Canada and the United States, 3 *Cal. Western Int'l L. J.* 191 (1973).

120. See J. Schneider, *World Public Order of the Environment* (1979), 164-6.

121. Convention on the Protection of the Environment, *done* 19 February 1974, in 13 *Int'l Legal Materials* 591 (1974). For discussion see chapter 3, 53, chapter 4, 91.

122. It was announced on 16 January 1967 by U.S. Embassy sources in Madrid that the United States had paid $558,104 to 475 Spaniards who suffered damage when the four bombs fell. U.S. officials said that 597 claims had been filed and that all of them would be paid. A group of residents from Palomares alleged, however, that only 3 percent of the claims had been paid in full, and they asserted that outstanding claims totaled $2.5 million (U.S. Pays Spanish Claims for Damage by Lost Bomb, *N.Y. Times*, 16 January 1967, at 14, col. 3).

123. See ARCO Sets Up Offices for Oil Damage Bills, *Columbian* (New Westminster), 24 June 1972.

124. For discussion of the *Torrey Canyon* litigation see Brown, The Lessons of *Torrey Canyon*, 21 *Current Legal Problems* 113 (1968); and Comment, Post *Torrey Canyon*: Toward a New Solution To the Problem of Traumatic Oil Spill, 2 *Connecticut Law Review* 632 (1970).

CHAPTER 9

International Law and
World Order Transformation

As we suggested in the General Introduction, the prospects for the old international law of the state system appear more dismal than ever. More so now than at any time since the end of World War II, the major governments of the world seem unwilling to take seriously legal restraints on recourse to war. The only inhibitions on major violence are associated with prudence in foreign policy as a consequence of the danger of nuclear war and a continuing effort to mobilize public opinion against hostile aggressor states (for instance, the West complains about the lawlessness of the Soviet invasion of Afghanistan, while the East and Third World condemn Israel for its 1982 invasion of Lebanon and the United States for its interventions in Central America). Yet it has become increasingly evident that law in these crucial settings is little more than a tool of propagandists, and not a widely respected one at that. Increasingly, also, the United Nations looks the other way when its most vital prohibition on recourse to war is grossly violated, an expression of helplessness in the face of warfare, increasingly accepted once again, as it was prior to World War I, almost as a "normal" exercise of discretion in foreign policy.

It can be argued, of course, that international law never succeeded very well in the war/peace context and that the structure of the state system is to a large extent incompatible with such a legal endeavor. Yet, there was at least serious lip-service paid to the outlawry of war in the years following the Kellogg-Briand Pact (1928) and then again in the period following the creation of the United Nations. The Korean War was widely perceived by Western countries at that time (1950–1952) as a test of the new reliance on collective security, taking the form of providing South Korea with adequate protection in the face of aggression. Admittedly, the world community was to some extent being manipulated by cold war pressures and the desire of Washington for a United Nations fig leaf to endow its essentially unilateral defense of South Korea with a more internationalist quality. And yet it seemed credible to claim that the United Nations was to some extent throwing its support behind a new resolve to uphold an international law of peace.

Even more impressive, perhaps, was the international reaction to the Suez Operation of 1956, an initiation of war by England, France, and Israel in the form of an invasion of Egypt. Here, the United States joined with the Soviet Union to support a demand on behalf of Nasser's Egypt (on bad terms at the time with the United States because of its anti-West positions) that the invading armies withdraw. Once again, the basic Charter norm prohibiting aggressive force was seemingly upheld and effectively protected in the face of a dramatic challenge.

In the 1960s and 1970s, there was a loss of confidence in the willingness of the United States government to throw its diplomatic weight behind either the United Nations or the norms prohibiting aggression. The U.S. involvement in Vietnam, deepening throughout the decade of the 1960s, and entailing major extensions of war beyond the boundaries of the initial intervention in South Vietnam, as well as its post-Castro Western Hemisphere diplomacy (especially the intervention in the Dominican Republic in 1965), made it much more difficult for the United States to urge upon the world a law-oriented foreign policy. At the same time, the rise during this period of anti-Western attitudes in the United Nations included attacks on traditional notions of international law, especially in relation to economic rights and duties. A series of Third World expropriations of foreign investments was regarded in Western international law circles as spectacular instances of repudiation of traditional international law. The U.S. government viewed, in particular, the entire call in the mid-1970s for a New International Economic Order (including an insistence on a far more relaxed obligation to compensate foreign investors) as a foray into the domain of lawlessness. This impression was reinforced by many transnational terrorist incidents— hijackings, kidnappings of foreign businessmen and diplomats, and attacks on banks and corporations—that were often staged by groups with political grievances. This trend, and associated U.S. perceptions and responses, culminated in the seizure on November 4, 1979, of the U.S. Embassy and its diplomatic personnel in Tehran by militant factions associated with Khomeini's Iranian Revolution. The incident, stretching out over a period of more than fourteen months, emphasized the degree to which some of the most widely respected rules of international law—in this instance, diplomatic immunity and the sanctity of diplomatic premises—were under severe pressure from new wielders of power.

The 1980s began, then, in a setting dominated by the breakdown of détente, a renewed strategic arms race, a serious global recession, unchecked instances of large-scale aggressive warfare in several regions of the world, a partial breakdown in the Law of the Sea negotiations, and declining support for international economic institutions. It is not surprising that the prospects for international law, except as a technical ordering process for routine transactions, seem currently dismal. Our effort in this book is not to deny these discouraging developments, but rather to consider the decline of international law from a world order perspective. We argue that this decline reflects, in large part, the inability of the global political system as now constituted to cope adequately with mounting demographic, technological, economic, ecological, and cultural pressures. We further suggest that the revival of militarism in world affairs may be associated with a "sunset effect" created by the collapsing state system. As the afternoon sun nears the horizon it assumes even greater brilliance before it disappears. We are not witnessing the intensification of the most anarchic and militarist patterns of statecraft as a rearguard struggle to maintain statist control despite the fragility, interconnectedness, and downward drift of the world situation. In effect, the efforts to promote tolerable levels of order and justice in world affairs by means of a state system have failed, and yet we have not seen the emergence of an alternative system that possesses the requisite social and political support or seems convincing as a real possibility. We live, in essence, at a painful and dangerous time of transition.

In Chapter 9 we seek to provide a framework for analyzing international law in relation to the behavior of states and to reorient the enterprise of international law and lawyers to recognize and meet the challenges and potentialities of transition.

In the first selection, Friedrich Kratochwil examines the jurisprudential roots of international law. Falling as it does at the end of this volume, Kratochwil's essay summarizes and crystallizes earlier inquiries into the nature of international law, given the reality of national sovereignty and the absence of any supranational governing authority. What we mean by law is not a question for which international jurists have provided a standard response. Kratochwil helps us understand that the reality of international law has been conceived over the centuries in three principal forms: as rules, as authoritative decision, and as rhetorical device. These forms assist us in grasping the structural character and limits of order in a world of separate sovereign states.

Kratochwil ends his inquiry with a reasoned argument for understanding international law now in relation to the quest for world order. He conceives of this quest in terms of "a significant reduction of violence and the improvement of the quality of life throughout the globe." In effect, we are left with a challenge—to reorient the role of lawyers toward the work of making law an instrument of value realization with certain specific societal ends in mind. Can this role be discharged by acting through the formal channels of lawmaking and law-applying provided by diplomatic interaction? Can this role be facilitated by international institutions? One challenge is to develop new frameworks for order that do not depend nearly so centrally upon the interplay of governmental and intergovernmenal actors. Kratochwil gives us the fundamental grounding upon which to grasp the essential reality of international law.

The other selection in Chapter 9 is by Richard Falk, who attempts to put these same challenges in a more historical context. Falk refocuses the Grotian theme that underlies the overall inquiry of the book: If we understand how Grotius helped solve the transition crisis of his time, can we gain insight into the transition crisis of our own era? As earlier selections have made clear, Grotius provided a synthesis of legal ideas to facilitate the construction of a framework for law and justice appropriate for the emerging state system of the seventeenth century. Feudalism was the waning system of the Grotian era. It was the particular genius of Grotius to have facilitated the new without repudiating the old; indeed, he built upon it.

It seems evident, as Falk argues, that a globally constituted system of some kind is emerging. Whether its emergence has progressed far enough yet to allow for a Grotian-type synthesis remains uncertain. Surely the emergent globalism has not thus far taken any definitive form that would reduce the jurist's task to the reportorial one of depicting what exists. There is a confusing amalgam of new identities and actors that are generally perceived as making the world situation more complex and confusing than it had been at earlier stages. Falk responds to this setting by suggesting several plausible forms now being assumed by this emergent globalism. He suggests that a value-oriented and decentralized globalism is the most attractive alternative to be chosen from among the array of plausible prospects. Such an altered world order would be at once more localized and more globalized than the authority power patterns associated with states and superpowers.

Several international lawyers can address and respond to the transitional context in several distinct ways. Some of these potential solutions to the transitional crisis are portrayed by Falk as harmful from the viewpoint of world order values. Falk's article ends with an appeal to international lawyers to work for the emergence of a preferred globalism.

Several conclusions follow from Falk's interpretation. (1) International lawyers need to direct more of their energies to the challenge of emergent globalism, as well as to that of mastering the workings of law within the traditional system of sovereign states; (2) international lawyers should distinguish among the main plausible forms of emergent globalism by reference to value consequences; and (3) international lawyers can contribute best to the successful solution of the transition problem by strengthening support for a new framework of authority built around a mixture of territorial and nonterritorial actors and a blend of local, regional, and global identities. The normative underpinnings of such a system are to be founded on the realization of peace, economic well-being, human rights, ecological balance, and humane scale and ideologies of governance.

A special, perhaps dominant, aspect of the Grotian moment as we are experiencing it at this stage of human history has to do with change induced by survival consciousness. The old ways are not merely being superseded; they are threatening the human experience as a totality with catastrophic collapse. The essence of these threats involves the twin dangers of nuclear war and ecological disruption. The shadow cast by the possibility of such a self-administered "last judgment" imparts urgency to any inquiry concerned with the reconstruction of our legal, political, and ethical life to enhance human survival. In addition, the survival context is increasingly becoming an actual dimension of the ordeal of everyday existence for hundreds of millions of poor people, especially nonwhite people in the Third World. A special survival challenge is being directed at the cultural and psychological identity of indigenous nations—for instance, the territories inhabited by American Indians—trapped in modern states and often languishing as an early casualty of modernization schemes.

The law dimension of reconstruction has, as yet, received very little nonutopian attention. Our plea is to distinguish between legalist forms of utopia (usually culturally specific projections onto a global screen) and the role of law, conjoined with political and cultural elements in the great undertaking of social reconstruction—what we mean by the construction of a preferred world order.

QUESTIONS FOR DISCUSSION AND REFLECTION: CHAPTER 9

1. How pervasive is law in human experience? Why is it essential to have principles and procedures by which to guide behavior and resolve disputes?

2. Do you envisage further growth or decline for international law? In what respects? For what reasons?

3. Does there exist at this stage the credible prospect of moving beyond a legal framework predominantly concerned with the interplay of states (each sovereign over territory, resources, people) toward one preoccupied with the interplay of people and peoples and with spatial boundaries playing a much diminished role? What factors might help encourage such a transition? How can international law and lawyers contribute?

4. What should be the connection between the analysis of legal prospects and the depiction of present and future systems of world order? As Falk's essay suggests, there are several variations *within* the state system that could be achieved in coming years. Should international law experts be neutral with respect to the diverse value effects of these alternatives? What is the Grotian imperative of our age?

SELECTED BIBLIOGRAPHY: CHAPTER 9

Percy Corbett, *The Growth of World Law* (Princeton, N.J.: Princeton University Press, 1971).

Philip Jessup, *Transnational Law* (New Haven: Yale University Press, 1956).

————, *A Modern Law of Nations* (New York: Macmillan, 1956).

William Reisman and Burns Weston, eds., *Towards World Order and Human Dignity* (New York: Free Press, 1976).

37. Of Law and Human Action:
A Jurisprudential Plea for a World Order
Perspective in International Legal Studies

Friedrich Kratochwil

THE TASK OF LEGAL THOUGHT

If it is the task of legal thought to reflect critically on the connection between law and social order, then two important themes can be identified within this enterprise.[1] First, there is the general inquiry into the "nature" of law. Second, there is the issue of exactly how legal norms impinge upon human actions, and how stability and change in a society are related to the normative and, in particular, to the legal structure.[2]

Applied to the problem of international law, this *problematique* means that international legal thought has to answer the question of whether international law is "proper" law[3] and to reflect critically upon the problem of how "regimes" arise, are maintained, decay, or develop and thus mediate between conflicting policies and conceptions of the international "game." A conceptual approach to these interrelated problems must be both stringent and sensitive, especially when it attempts to shed light on the paradox by which the growth and importance of law in the area of transnational law exists side by side with the obvious ineffectiveness of legal prescriptions forbidding the resort to violence.

Finally, such an inquiry must enable us to locate the legal enterprise in a wider set of norms and values that have important implications for legal practices. Since legal rules are never "neutral" in their distributive outcomes— as the granting of rights often gives precedence to the protection of certain value positions over others—they are always in need of further justification. These justifications are systematically provided by a "meta-legal" discourse in which particular outcomes and/or arrangements are assessed in terms of broader principles (just deserts, equity, fairness, etc). Furthermore, precisely because legal norms always require application to a particular context, legal decisions often remain problematic—even after a case has been decided. Indeed, much of legal and social change cannot be appreciated if "legalism"— that is, the insistence on the normative validity of past practices—is maintained to the exclusion of other (meta-)legal considerations. It is the purpose of this essay to address these issues in a more extensive fashion and to show that for such purposes a "world order" framework is particularly helpful for international legal studies.

I begin in the next section with a discussion of some current conceptions of law and show their implications for international legal thought. In this context, I want to argue that it is not fruitful to establish the *legal* character of prescriptions either through some systematic property (pedigree à la Kelsen or Hart)[4] or by deriving their "legalness" from some ultimate goal (human dignity).[5] Rather, I see legal norms as particular "rhetorical devices" that derive their character from the role they play in a distinct mode of decisionmaking (i.e., reasoning), which they guide in choice situations. This conceptualization allows us to place legal decisionmaking within the wider field of "practical reason"[6] and at the same time addresses the interaction between legal and meta-legal considerations. The advantage of such an approach is that it makes the definition of "legalness" no longer dependent upon disembodied normative structures[7] or on certain organizational features, such as courts or the command of a sovereign. Rather, the emphasis is on rule guidance in decision situations and on the particular mode of arriving at a decision that will determine the legal character of norms. The last section focuses more explicitly on the meta-legal concerns of the world order perspective by which legal prescriptions can be appraised and transition strategies can be articulated.

LAW AS A RHETORICAL DEVICE

Let us begin with a concept of law that avoids the excesses of Austinian positivism (command of a sovereign), as this theory disposes of the problem of international law simply by definition. We could call law a "set of prescriptions (rules, norms and principles) that impartial judges apply to a case at hand in order to render an authoritative decision."[8] But this preliminary definition becomes problematic if it is not appropriately modified. Hence we must reflect briefly on the meaning of the term "rule of law." When we talk about a government of laws (and not of men), we refer not to the government of judges but, rather, as Kaplan and Katzenbach have put it, to

the larger formal process through which the members of the society pursue and realize values in an orderly way. It scarcely requires argument that law viewed as a body of authoritative rules pervades all the institutions of modern democratic government and is no monopoly of judges. . . . Legislators, administrators and judges are all parts of a related process; all are subject to legal rules, and all invoke legal rules in their performance of their official tasks. They play different roles and the role of each of them is related in important ways to the existence of and the role played by the others.[9]

Several points are worth pondering in this context. First, there is the implicit argument that law is best understood as a conduct-guiding device—as a special case of rules,* that is, rather than as a command. Second, there is the distinction between a narrower and a wider conception of law—in other words, between rule application by impartial third parties and the

---

*The terms *rules* and *norms* are used interchangeably throughout this chapter.

wider context in which rules are used in order to arrive at and justify decisions. This distinction allows us to see more clearly the limitations of judicial activity that can not longer be identified with "the law" in general. Finally, there is the issue concerning the importance of (legal) rules for certain performances; in other words, law is not simply a constraint but often an enabling instrument, as well as a means of communication pertaining to the nature of the game in which one is involved.[10]

It becomes clear even from this very sketchy analysis that the conception of law as a coercive order needs correction.[11] Its effectiveness can no longer be assessed in terms of compliance patterns with prohibitions. Such a process of assessment would be inaccurate, because it mistakes laws for commands and because compliance with prescriptions involves an intensely dynamic procedure rather than merely a passive following of rules. Let us consider these two points in greater detail.

The mistaking of prescriptions for commands has a long ancestry shared by such unlikely companions as positivists, voluntarist philosophers, and theologians.[12] But even in cases in which the obligatory character of prescriptions is derived from an "absolute sovereign"—God—the language distinguishes between a "command" and a "commandment." While commands are always situation-specific, commandments (which show rule-like characteristics) are thought to be applicable to *broad classes of events* and are valid *erga omnes* (including those who issue them, provided the proper circumstances obtain).[13] Even when rules "empower" to issue commands, rule and command can be distinguished,[14] given that empowering rules refer to specific circumstances in which the giving of orders is authorized. But how is it possible to distinguish *legal* rules and principles from other norms of social life (norms of taste, comity, etc.)?

Basically, there are only two ways of approaching this question concerning the "character tag" associated with a particular rule. Either one traces the rule back to its origin (formal criterion), or one tries to define it according to the influence it has upon an actor's decision. Strangely enough, although fundamentalist mullahs and positivists alike prefer the formal test (i.e., "law is what originates from God, the sovereign, or what can be traced back to a valid, or basic, norm"), the "pressure test" of legal obligation is preferred by sociologists and psychologists. Legal norms, then, are distinguishable from other prescriptions by their solemnity or severity.

Both approaches create severe difficulties for the determination of the legal character of a norm, especially in the international arena. Although some norms can conveniently be traced back to a source (e.g., those created by a treaty), others create nearly insoluble puzzles (custom). Obviously, these puzzles are the reason why we justifiably call the international legal order a "primitive" one, as many arguments cannot advance beyond the stage of *ex parte* contentions. However, it would not be very useful to describe as "nonlegal" all of those activities in which legal norms are invoked simply because an authoritative decision or *stare decisis* is absent.[15] States usually *do* make distinctions between their claims based on "rights" and their preferences, even when the latter can be backed by good reasons.

The second attempt by which a demarcation criterion is sought focuses on the psychological pressure generated by legal norms. Unfortunately, this type of yardstick does not fare much better than the first kind, in that it appears to be seriously under- as well as over-inclusive. On the one hand, legal norms are said to be characterized by a certain gravity and seriousness; on the other hand, it is maintained that legal rules are not as compelling as moral prescriptions. Thus it is not quite clear as to which type or degree of "seriousness of pressure" qualifies a rule as legal. In addition, the most severe psychological pressures in the international arena might be generated not by legal norms but by unilateral policy commitments, which qualify neither as moral imperatives nor as legal obligations. Besides, no legal order can make the private feelings of an actor the ultimate test of legal obligation,[16] and, in any event, "feelings" are probably an inappropriate metaphor in cases of corporate actors.

If the "pressure model" is also seriously deficient, then legal rule guidance has to be conceptualized in a different way. It is the relatively firm guidance, "not only in respect to ends but to the means adopted,"[17] associated with contexts of application and (non)admissible exceptions that distinguishes legal rules from other rules and norms. Moral norms, such as "do not lie," are practically context-free and do not provide for specific ranges of application—a fact, in turn, that accounts for the open-ended nature of the moral discourse. The specificity of legal norms, on the other hand, becomes most obvious in the "rules of evidence" that are intrinsic to a legal order. The finding of "what the case is" (truth) in a legal proceeding is subordinate to provisos specifying what counts as a "proof" and what facts are inadmissible, even when they are germane to the case at hand.[18]

The emphasis in this approach to law is no longer placed on certain institutions (such as courts) or on the mental states of the actors; rather, it is directed to the intersubjectively communicable reasoning process, which is structured in a particularly explicit fashion. A legal order can now be said to exist if actors accept certain rules as obligatory by making principled use of them in defining choices, by making demands as well as proposals for the settlement of disputes in terms of them, and by justifying action through the invocation of these rules and principles.

The shift away from "judicial" to "juridical" (i.e., principled) decision-making is a useful starting point for reflection on legal thought. It places legal norm guidance within the realm of "practical reasoning," which is applicable to all actions and actors rather than only to a particular "role"— namely, that of the judge. This point has important implications for the treatment of rules and norms possessing varying degrees of authoritativeness, a situation characteristic of international law. "Precedents" do not exist, nor does the search for applicable rules resemble that of the "treasure hunt" that is familiar from finding the *ratio decidendi* of court decisions.[19] Nevertheless, the decisionmaker or advocate does not operate in a norm-free vacuum; previous decisions, customary norms, contracted obligations, and pronouncements of varying degrees of authoritative quality (e.g., General

Assembly resolutions) will be relevant to one's choice of legal argument or strategy. Typically, the "opponent" will also have a particular reading of the legal landscape, and the skill of advocacy will consist in turning the attention to the features of the case that buttress one's own side in a plausible fashion. Conversely, various avoidance techniques are available to weaken the authoritative quality of the norms and decisions invoked by the other side: Faulty application of legal rules, fundamental incompatibility of the facts at hand, lack of clarity as to the scope of the rule, changed conditions, and inconsistent subsequent practice may all serve to inhibit adherence to the opponent's argument.[20]

Advocates, however, are not only participants in the legal process who seek to persuade others to accept a particular line of reasoning. Beside their primary task of justifying their decision, judges too may try to persuade their colleagues that a particular legal solution to a dispute is to be adopted. Where a judge is espousing a currently unpopular result, he must rely heavily on his power of persuasion, and he may employ a number of rhetorical devices to bolster and protect his case.[21]

In this view, law is a particular form of arriving at a decision. Instead of the workings of "pure law" by means of logical hierarchies (i.e., deductive entailment or inductive generalization), legal reasoning exhibits features that are fundamentally "rhetorical" in character. Precisely because practical choices deal with the selection of a valued position and not with the truth of a particular alternative, the degree of adherence to this position rather than the check against "reality" is at issue. *Plausibility* in the light of all the norms and facts rather than logical elegance alone strengthens such adherence. Yet, naturally, there is always a tendency to disguise these "weaknesses" of practical reasoning. One might follow this strategy by showing as Aristotle's *enthymeme* did, that a particular value judgment could be logically derived from the conjunction of a valued major premise and a factual assertion in the minor premise.[22] But it should be clear that such a deduction is possible only *ex post*, when through a decision the envisaged goal becomes unequivocal (i.e., the trade-off problem has been resolved) or when the valuation of the major premise is beyond debate. Since in real life these conditions are hardly ever met, there is an understandable tendency in legal reasoning to present value choices as instrumental ones. Thus the valued major premise becomes a minor premise in a new syllogism, if we conceive of this premise as being an instrument to attain the "higher" value. Theoretically, this means that all questions internal to such a hierarchy can be treated as logical entailments. Only the *Grundnorm* à la Kelsen, or the overarching goal of human dignity (or of "pleasure" in the utilitarian system), has to be justified by some means other than deduction.

However, if legal reasoning is better conceptualized as a kind of practical reasoning by which adherence to an alternative is established both through the persuasive power of argument and through authoritative decision, how is adherence through persuasion possible in an arena in which adjudication (authoritative decision) is minimal? Furthermore, *who* is to be persuaded?

After all, the advocate in the domestic sphere need not convince his opponent or the public at large, but, rather, must convince the court. Is persuasion illusory in the absence of third-party adjudication? A short discussion will be helpful.

All persuasion presupposes the reliance upon a discourse, a pleader, and an audience. The reliance on a discourse implies not only the rejection of coercion as a means of gaining adherence, but also common meanings, especially widely accepted "commonplaces" (*topoi*), through which persuasion becomes possible.[23] Although these *topoi* play in the persuasive process a role analogous to axioms in formal systems, they are not "true" by definition and can serve as unproblematic starting points only because of their acceptance by the group as well as their inherent ambiguity. Thus the agreement on a commonplace (such as "one must do good and avoid evil") in no way guarantees agreement on a particular application and therefore does not "entail" the conclusions for which they may be utilized. In the context of application, quasi-logical forms such as the conjunction-dissociation of notions (the opposition of appearance and reality, subjectivity and objectivity, etc.) as well as arguments about the structure of reality become important. These rhetorical figures and their place in legal reasoning[24] have been exhaustively investigated by Perelman and Tyteca[25] and need not be reiterated here.

What do these considerations mean for international legal thought and particularly for answering the questions raised above? First of all, they establish law as a special instrument of persuasion, since the most general principles of law (such as "treat like cases alike," "give everybody his due," etc.) are very powerful commonplaces in the context of practical reasoning. They play a residual, but important, role in judicial pronouncements as well as in the more general justificatory (meta-legal) discourse. Second, through the development of a specialized cadre entrusted with the "finding" of the law, new procedures and standards develop that can be invoked in buttressing a particular decision. Thus, although law (when seen from the adjudicative perspective) retains some essential features of ritualized conflict mediated by a judge through appeals to common understandings, it is increasingly becoming a highly specialized activity with its own logic.[26] The persuasiveness of the arguments presented by judges is increasingly addressed to their peers, whereas the ceremony and ritual of the "day in court" establishes general compliance of the public at large.

Now that we have addressed the central role taken by third-party adjudication in making law function, it also becomes clear that there are definite limits to the effectiveness of adjudicative procedures. Empirically, we observe an increase in noncompliance with judicial pronouncements in instances in which organized groups press their claims—that is, when the separation of a particular case and controversy from the larger social context becomes problematic and the uncommitted "audience" becomes smaller and smaller. Law increasingly functions as a justificatory device in a wider bargaining process. If accommodation occurs, it is generally brought about through extralegal means, without reference to preestablished rules and procedures. What is needed in such cases is the reestablishment of a universe of common meanings within which the legal decision process can function.

The role of law in such a process of accommodation (or conflict escalation, for that matter) is as ambiguous as it is interesting. Since rights, equity, fairness, and so on are powerful commonplaces, they do not lose their appeal in determining a debate, even if their exact "technical" range of application is frontally challenged. The phenomenon in which the rejection of "law and order" occurs largely by means of an essentially legal rhetoric is surprising only if one does not keep the "technical" and "common sense" levels of law in mind. The French Revolution made the "rights of man" the pivotal argument, America seceded in order to secure the "rights of citizens" for representation, and the New International Economic Order was advocated in the name of equity as well as that of sovereignty. Thus the idea that conflict is best solved by legal means is valid only if we have the "technical" level of law in mind. Too strong an insistence on "rights," which, as modern language analysis has shown, are parasitic upon a process of claiming[27] and, therefore, probably also upon institutional frameworks, can be as disruptive of peace as unprincipled conduct.

We can now attempt to answer the question raised before: Who is to be persuaded in the international arena? Clearly, it can now be seen that persuasion takes place on two levels: that of common sense and that of technical application (although the latter exhibits, as a distinctive feature, "executive application" rather than judicial application).

The importance of legal arguments in persuading audiences is well known in the domestic as well as the international arenas. No state (pathological cases excepted) will claim that its policies are in violation of established legal prescriptions. Rather, a plea of inapplicability, desuetude, or exception to violated norms will be advanced. However, persuasion also takes place on the technical level—that is, among the practitioners who are part of the policymaking process. Hence international legal norms provide solutions in thousands of routine decisions for situations that would otherwise escalate into open conflict. The fact that international law works mainly through the imperatives of the bureaucratic state (executive norm application) is not new, but it is often forgotten. The esteem for the practitioners who utilize international legal norms in the administration of policy might not be as high as that reserved for "judges," but the importance of their activity cannot be denied.

THE WORLD ORDER PERSPECTIVE

What remains to be shown is the usefulness of a world order perspective for legal thought. Such a demonstration requires that several objectives be met. First, a clearer definition of *world order* is necessary; second, criteria have to be specified that allow us to evaluate and contrast the world order approach with respect to other theoretical efforts in the field of international law. Although the definitional question will be answered with reference to the value grid developed by the World Order Models Project,[28] I propose to use "heuristic fruitfulness" and the capacity for a critical appraisal of legal practices as evaluative criteria.

The term *world order* refers most generally to the systematic "study and appraisal of efforts of creating a more dependable international environment which would lead to a significant reduction of violence and the improvement of the quality of life throughout the globe."[29] This admittedly rather sweeping first cut can then be specified further by stipulating a set of interrelated goal values such as peace, justice, well-being, and ecological stability, all of which serve as organizing concepts for further inquiry.

This leads us to a more principled discussion of the heuristic fruitfulness criterion. The world order approach meets this requirement in two ways. First, it widens the scope of the inquiry from state practice (international law as the "body of rules binding upon states") to the more general world order *problematique*, which includes claims of subnational groups as well as those of individuals (human rights). Legal thinking is thereby not only fundamentally reoriented but significantly widened in scope. This widened scope, in turn, allows for more interesting questions as the number of topics and their interrelations increase. Second, by placing problem areas, such as that of "justice" (which lies at the heart of the legal enterprise),[30] within the wider framework of other human aspirations, such as well-being, peace, and ecological stability, the world order approach informs us more effectively than does the "world peace through world law" perspective or the ecological holism of the Club of Rome about the difficult value choices and trade-offs that characterize international life.

Such a critical reflection is, however, even more principled than the term *trade-off* suggests. Rather than being a mere "optimization problem" between two or more competing values, the context between justice and peace, between well-being and ecological stability, entails difficult conceptual problems. For example, "justice," if seen in its equitable (rather than merely procedural) dimension, will have different implications in an intergenerational context and within a time frame in which only present claimants count. Moreover, the problem of ecological stability has important repercussions for intergenerational justice, as well as for the value of well-being for which it is usually considered a competing value.

Admittedly, such speculations are more common among philosophers than among lawyers, and the world order framework does not seem to have been successful in producing legal inquiries that take these problems as their point of departure. But the relevance of such considerations even for the classical international lawyer cannot be doubted. This is well exemplified in Oscar Schachter's treatise on the equitable sharing of the world's resources.[31] True, world order proponents cannot claim that everyone dealing with such problems is by definition a "world order theorist." Nevertheless, the world order framework and the research program that can be derived from the world order agenda suggest a more disciplined inquiry that raises these issues in a systematic rather than *ad hoc* fashion.

Beyond these more philosophically inclined investigations, the world order perspective challenges us in still another way. Owing to the growing interdependence in international life, there is a continuing need for the adjustment and creation of "regimes." The international monetary order and the comprehensive regulation of all uses of the oceans are good examples. However, given the somewhat disappointing results of UNCLOS III, in which the vision of a "common heritage" came to be superseded by notions of national appropriation, it is clear that legal thought must reflect more than legally established or proposed practices; it must *evaluate* them, as well, in terms of wider relevant principles.

The last remarks bring the importance of our second criterion—appraisal—to the fore. Given that every evaluation presupposes a preferred value position and that "values" are conventionally held to be beyond rational debate, how can we avoid the miring of such an appraisal in idiosyncrasies? Without entering into the perennial debate about the "value freedom" of the social sciences or about the "neutral principles" in law, I maintain that the assertion that values are nothing more than personal, irrational preferences appears rather exaggerated. After all, we do try to persuade each other; we do seek adherence to a valued position, and we can and do distinguish between spurious and reasoned arguments in this respect. Habermas, Schwemmer, and Apel[32] have shown, each in their own way, that discourses about values are possible in other than a purely dictatorial or idiosyncratic fashion. Besides, even the classical position of value freedom did not argue the lack of relevance of values; instead, it has insisted rather emphatically on the explicit communication of one's own value preferences. One of the main virtues of the world order approach in this respect is its *value explicitness*, which allows not only a critical reflection of one's own value position but also the inclusion of those concerns that often go unrecognized in the legal and political process when no proponents with "voice" can be found (e.g., the environment and its wildlife must rely on the surrogate voices of activists).[33] By starting neither with the "actors" and their ascribed rights nor with certain legal practices (such as treaty-making), the silent value premises embodied in conventional rights and legal practices can be illuminated and alternatives can be assessed in terms of their contributions to preferred value positions.

In evaluating the world order perspective and in comparing it with more traditional modes of legal study, one might be tempted to claim too much. The world order agenda seems to promise (or, at least, to strongly suggest) that a general theory of "planetary society" is in the offing. To put it bluntly, no such claims are made here. Furthermore, it is extremely unlikely that such a holistic theory will ever be developed.[34] Besides, world order thinking is still very weakly articulated in both the theoretical as well as the practical sense. It is more a conceptual grid that links together several important areas of concern than a tightly knit theoretical web. To that extent its concerns might be time bound—indeed, detractors are sometimes fond of debunking it by tracing its intellectual roots to the concerns of the liberal intellectual elite of the 1960s—and it is probably quite culture bound.

Against these objections two short responses might suffice. First, nothing is gained by refusing to start somewhere. Thus a "cultural bias" makes for distortion only when it is not properly reflected upon or when partial insights are misrepresented as "general laws," "eternal truths," and so on. Second, the "topical" character of a question neither determines nor detracts from its heuristic fruitfulness, as the time-bound questions of political theorists from Plato to the Founding Fathers have shown.

An important corollary follows from these short remarks. Precisely because the world order perspective is not a stringent theory but, rather, is a set of concerns calling attention to problems that normal "lawyering" and theory have neglected, its ability to create policy prescriptions is limited in several respects. In particular, such "concerns," even if diagnosed correctly and translated into policy imperatives, still face the obstacle of implementation. "It helps very little to jump," John Ruggie has remarked,

from the emergence of a complex of interrelated global problems, no matter how pressing they may be, to prescribed behavior that the international community must undertake or court disaster. For the international community is not an agency that can act in its own behalf for its own good. . . . Thus while problems may cry out for global solutions, effective measures continue to depend on the willingness and ability of public and private actors at other levels of organization in the world system to change their behavior.[35]

This quotation points to the difficulty of connecting the realm of thought and action; there are, however, two more problems that stand in the way of effective transformation of international relations. One is the tendency of holistic theories to result in technocratic nightmares; the other is the somewhat related problem of viewing law as a mere instrument "in the service" of society or the world community. The tyrannic tendencies of technologies and instrumental rationality have been dealt with extensively by Ellul and need not be rehearsed here.[36] What is usually less well appreciated is that similar tyrannical impulses can spring from well-meaning efforts to substitute for the partial insights of the various sciences a holistic understanding of the world. In its most radical form, such ecological holism visualizes politics

as part of a vast natural system, a biosystem. Therefore, all past units of analysis we became accustomed to—territorial units and functional relationships—are subsumed under the biosystemic perspective. All units and all relationships become relevant; and perhaps they can be ordered as well. The criterion of order and relevance is the key concept of both evolution and ecology: survival. . . . While there can be many human or social purposes beyond survival, collective survival must be considered the minimum purpose; all others depend on its realization. Evolution has a purpose in this sense only.[37]

Action, then, is evaluated in terms of its contribution to the survival of the species, toward a more harmonious (or at least a better) "fit" with nature. But since man is not determined by nature but transcends it by transforming it, the question of survival depends upon a prior specification of the *way of life* that the species called man is supposed to choose for its survival.

Given this *problematique*, a framework is needed that allows for the orderly pursuit of conflicting values. In the most general terms, it is the function of *law* to provide such a framework. Although it is only natural to stress the purposive function of law, particularly when taking the "judge's" perspective, law, as we have seen, is more than the application of rules to a given controversy. Its effectiveness in guiding decisions by delineating the space in which choices have to be made and by providing a particular kind of "rhetoric" is particularly important in an arena (namely, that of international relations) in which adjudication is the exception rather than the rule.

On the other hand, the task for *legal thought*, particularly in periods of rapid change, is the critical reflection upon established practice as well as the giving of form and content to new ways of mediating the conflicts intrinsic to man's social existence. Such an enterprise requires not only rigor but also sensitivity to new elements that can serve as the foundation of a new order. The "Grotian moment" for legal analysis, as Richard Falk so aptly termed it, has definitely arrived, and concerted efforts to bring about a new synthesis are therefore sorely needed. It is for this reason that we, the editors of this volume, have chosen—and consider quite necessary— a world order perspective that goes beyond the "technical" horizon of law and thus can aid in the analysis of the challenges facing the legal order in our present and future world.

NOTES

1. On this point, see Nicolas Onuf, "Global Law Making and Legal Thought," in Nicholas Onuf, ed., *Law Making in the Global Community* (Durham, N.C.: Carolina Academic Press, 1982).

2. See Friedrich Kratochwil, "The Force of Prescriptions," *International Organization* 38 (Fall 1984), pp. 685–708.

3. See Friedrich Kratochwil, "Is International Law 'Proper' Law?" *Archives for Philosophy of Law and Social Philosophy* 69 (1983), pp. 13–46.

4. H.L.A. Hart, *The Concept of Law* (Oxford, England: Oxford University Press, 1961).

5. This is Myres McDougal's approach, of course; for a more extensive discussion, see McDougal and Lasswell's contribution in this collection.

6. For an interesting discussion of the formal properties of practical reasoning and its applicability to legal reasoning, see Robert Alexy, *Theorie der juristischen Argumentation* (Frankfurt, Germany: Suhrkamp, 1978).

7. On the idea that law can be comprehended as a normative system, see Hans Kelsen (Robert Tucker, ed.) *Principles of International Law* (New York: Holt, Rinehart & Winston, 1966).

8. Morton Kaplan and Nicholas de Katzenbach, *The Political Foundations of International Law* (New York: Wiley, 1961), p. 4.

9. Ibid.

10. On the notion of law as a communications system, see William Coplin, "International Law and the Assumptions about the State System," *World Politics* 17 (October 1964), pp. 615–635.

11. On the notion that law is a "coercive" normative order, see Kelsen, *Principles of International Law.*

12. For an effective conceptual distinction between laws, morals, and commands, see Thomas Mayberry, "Laws, Moral Laws and God's Commands," *Journal of Value Inquiry* 4, (Winter 1970), pp. 287–292.

13. Hart, *The Concept of Law,* Chs. 2 and 3.

14. For a further discussion of the situation-specific form of commands versus the "standing order" character of rules, see Alf Ross, *Directives and Norms* (London, England: Routledge & Kegan Paul, 1968), pp. 99ff.

15. On the "primitive law" analogy, see Friedrich Kratochwil, "Thrasymmachos Revisited: On the Relevance of Norms and the Study of Law for International Relations," *Journal of International Affairs* 37 (Winter 1984), pp. 343–356.

16. For a fundamental discussion of the problem of political and legal obligation, see Richard Flathman, *Political Obligation* (London: Croom Helm, 1972).

17. Gidon Gottlieb, "The Nature of International Law: Towards a Second Concept of Law," in Cyril Black and Richard Falk, eds., *The Future of the International Legal Order,* vol. 4 (Princeton, N.J.: Princeton University Press, 1972), Ch. 9, p. 370.

18. See, for example, the "exclusionary rule" of evidence.

19. David Miers and William Twining, *How to Do Things with Rules* (London: Weidenfeld & Nicolson, 1976), p. 176.

20. Ibid., pp. 166ff.

21. Ibid. p. 168.

22. On the topical form of Aristotle's reasoning in value matters, see Hugh Petrie, "Practical Reasoning," *Philosophy and Rhetoric* 4 (Winter 1971), pp. 29–41.

23. Aristotle, *Topik,* translated by Eugen Rolfes (Hamburg, Germany: Felix Meiner, 1960).

24. For an elaboration, see Chaim Perelman, *Logique Juridique* (Brussels: Mouton, 1967), passim.

25. Chaim Perelman and Olbrechts Tyteca, *La Nouvelle Rhetorique, Traite de l'Argumentation* (Paris: Presses Universitaires de France, 1958), pp. 15–28, 45–62.

26. In this respect, see Michael Barkun's, *Law Without Sanction* (New Haven, Conn.: Yale University Press, 1968), Ch. 6.

27. On this point, see Joel Feinberg, *Rights, Justice and the Bounds of Liberty* (Princeton, N.J.: Princeton University Press, 1980), especially Chs. 6 and 7.

28. For a summary statement, see Saul Mendlovitz, ed., *On the Creation of a Just World Order: Preferred Worlds for the 1990s* (New York: Free Press, 1975).

29. See Consortium on World Order Studies (Saul Mendlovitz, director), mimeo, p. 1.

30. Although one could argue that there exist a good many different conceptions of justice, of which legal justice is only one possible dimension, it is clear that any evaluation or judgment as to the "justness" of a cause requires a delineation of whose claims should be entertained. Thus, while a procedural definition of justice might be at odds with substantive conceptions, it seems doubtful whether one can speak of justice without taking minimum procedural criteria into account. On the latter point, see Leon Fuller, *The Morality of Law* (New Haven Conn.: Yale University Press, 1964), who sees in such procedural safeguards a "natural law" component, which is obligatory for any legal system.

31. Oscar Schachter, *Sharing the World's Resources* (New York: Columbia University Press, 1977).

32. See Juergen Habermas, *Communication and the Evolution of Society* (Boston: Beacon, 1979); Oswald Schwemmer, *Philosophie der Praxis* (Frankfurt, Germany: Suhrkamp, 1980); Karl Otto Apel, ed., *Sprachpragmatik und Philosophie* (Frankfurt, Germany: Suhrkamp, 1982).

33. This is also true for the poor who generally possess neither the political nor the "market" power with which to register their preferences. Thus the concern with widely shared economic well-being is a much-needed corrective to traditional economic analysis and the economic analysis of law.

34. On this point, see Ernst Haas, "Is There a Hole in the Whole?" *International Organization* 29 (Summer 1975), pp. 327–377.

35. John Ruggie, "On the Problem of the Global Problematique: What Roles for International Organizations?" *Alternatives* 5, no. 4 (1979–1980), pp. 517–550.

36. Jaques Ellul, *The Technological Society* (New York: Knopf, 1964); for an excellent discussion of these problems, see also Langdon Winner, *Autonomous Technology: Technics Out of Control Theme in Political Thought* (Cambridge, Mass.: MIT Press, 1977).

37. Haas, "Is There a Hole in the Whole?" p. 342.

38. A New Paradigm for International Legal Studies: Prospects and Proposals

Richard Falk

A major reorganization of international life is taking place at the present time that will produce drastic modifications of the world order system that has prevailed since the Peace of Westphalia in 1648. This reorganization is being brought about through the efforts of powerful economic, political, and cultural actors on the world stage to cope with the challenge of growing interdependence during a period in which critical resources may be in short supply. Coping can be conceived in relation to immediate issues, such as disrupted energy or food flows, or, more structurally, as the threat of fiscal collapse, the recurrent failure to satisfy basic human and societal needs, and the constant threat of apocalyptic war. This reorganization of international life has two principal features—increased *central guidance* and increased roles for *nonterritorial actors*. There are many uncertainties concerning the nature and orientation of the nonterritorial actors, the pace of various changes, and the type and control of the emergent central guidance mechanisms.

This article supports the proposition that international law and lawyers can play a significant and beneficial role during this period of transition, but only if they become sensitive to the wider process of change under way in international society and, more controversially, if they give self-conscious support to a set of explicit world order goals that structure both the means and the ends of transition. In the course of arguing that a comparison among various historical types of international law is necessary to achieve an understanding of "what is essential and what is accidental in the transformation of law,"[1] Sir Paul Vinogradoff eloquently describes the potential role of the international lawyer:

In this quest for the spirit of the laws we are certainly not animated by fatalistic resignation. As knowledge of the laws of nature does not deprive men of the possibility of turning them to profit, so the logical force of ideas does not condemn societies to go adrift under the sway of currents of opinion. . . . [F]ar-seeing guides, determined leaders, fruitful workers are no less necessary in the outward social movement than are explorers, inventors, well-equipped craftsmen in the material world. The best vessel may be the victim of shipwreck, but it is the pride of free men to oppose danger by farsighted and stubborn efforts.[2]

I believe it is possible for international lawyers to contribute to the work of constructing "the best vessel" to which Vinogradoff refers, but their contribution is by no means assured. Indeed, international law and lawyers tend to serve and identify with prevailing lines of power and wealth; in the current context this tendency accentuates the deficiencies of the old system and encourages the emergence of regressive variants of central guidance.

It is important not to exaggerate the prospects even for enlightened approaches. Even aside from the question of gaining influence, those with an enlightened view may still not accomplish much. As Vinogradoff suggests, even the best vessel may fall victim to shipwreck. The dimensions of our juridical ship mainly reflect the anthropological, social, economic, political, and technological circumstances that together constitute an historical context. If we are to have any realistic prospect at all of reshaping this context, we must accurately appreciate the constraints as well as the options.

An intriguing passage appears in Henry Kissinger's Harvard dissertation:

The success of physical science depends on the selection of the crucial experiment: that of political science in the field of international affairs, on the selection of the "crucial" period. I have chosen for my topic the period between 1812 and 1822, partly, I am frank to say, because its problems seem to me analogous to those of our day.[3]

I agree with Kissinger that insight into the present situation can gainfully be achieved by a careful study of a relevant historical period. However, I believe that Kissinger, along with many others of his generation, has chosen the wrong historical analogy. The reason for choosing the nineteenth century is obvious. It was a time when an international aggressor, Napoleonic France, was successfully neutralized by a coalition of conservative states through a diplomacy that constructed a relatively stable system. In Kissinger's view, the problem of our age, perhaps of any age, is to prevent revolutionary actors from mounting a challenge against the existing order. In our age, this objective has involved confronting first Hitler's Germany, then the Soviet Union, and, most recently, the Third World. Succinctly put, Kissinger's utopia is stability.[4]

Although the nineteenth-century analogy (or, to use a twentieth-century term, the "Munich lesson") is an important one for policymakers to study, far more important is the analogy that can be drawn from the seventeenth-century transition to the modern state system. In effect, the transition analogy can help us to fashion the "major premise" on which to base a viable strategy of global reform. As I see it, the tragedy of our age is that the leaders of many countries, including our own, act as if the minor premise of deterring aggressors were the major premise of establishing a beneficial world order. Such leaders act, moreover, as if the major premise reflected nothing more substantial than wild musings or wishful thinking.

The world order shift now under way seems to be a reversal of the shift completed in the middle of the seventeenth century, by which time Medieval Europe had given way to the modern state system. The seventeenth century completed a long process of historical movement from nonterritorial central guidance toward territorial decentralization, whereas the contemporary transition process seems headed back toward nonterritorial central guidance. In each context we shall consider the transition interval and try to identify some of the prefigurations of the future embedded in changing forms. Intimations of transition can be found in many elements of cultural expression. Indeed, it is often the artists and prophets who are the first to express the handwriting on the wall.

The transition interval is one during which elements of the new system intermingle with elements of the old. It may go on for several centuries. Its boundaries are often the subject of prolonged scholarly dispute. Even its reality may be controversial, at least until perceived in retrospect. Beyond all doubt, developments of political order occur unevenly. There were European territorial states in existence long before Westphalia; for example, England possessed most of the features of a territorial state from the thirteenth century onward. Indeed, as one specialist writes, "[b]y 1300 it was evident that the dominant political form in Western Europe was going to be the sovereign state."[5] But what this historian had discerned was only an incipient tendency, one that subsequently accumulated momentum over a long period of time. The state is the main building block of "the state system," but its existence did not ensure the emergence of a specific pattern of international relations sufficiently valid to associate the origins of the modern state system with the Peace of Westphalia. This generalization is nothing more than a focusing device to bring broad patterns of change into clearer delineation, admittedly at the cost of blurring details.

In this spirit of seeking to grasp world order patterns, and more especially the characteristics of a transition period during which one pattern gives way to another, several main questions help clarify the role of international law and international lawyers. What can we learn from this prior transition process, which culminated in the birth of the state system? What roles were played by international law and lawyers? To what extent is this historical experience transferable to the present transition context? How can international law and international lawyers help ensure the emergence of a new post-state system of world order that is relatively more peaceful and just? To what extent does the participation of international lawyers reflect specific national, ideological, cultural, socioeconomic concerns? Is it possible to formulate a position on the means and ends of transition that could serve as the basis for a transnational or global consensus? Could such a consensus provide the normative grounding for a political movement dedicated to global reform? This article responds to such questions, to some more directly than to others, but with the overall objective of helping to formulate a world order ideology appropriate to human needs and aspirations, given the present historical situation of challenge and opportunity.

The main features of the position here can be set forth in summary form:

1. The state system is being superseded by a series of interlocking social, cultural, economic, political, technological, and ecological tendencies that are likely to eventuate in some form of negative utopia, that is, in a very undesirable and dangerous structure of overall response (or nonresponse) to the problems posed by the deepening crisis in the state system.

2. Although this disquieting outcome seems probable as of now, it is not inevitable. There are also positive paths available, premised upon an affirmation of the wholeness of the planet and the solidarity of the human species that could bring about a rearrangement of power, wealth, and authority more beneficial than anything the world has heretofore known.[6]

3. Initially, the global reform movement necessary to promote such a positive outcome has to take principal shape outside of and mainly in opposition to the centers of presently constituted political and economic power: In many societies it will have to be populist and antigovernmental in character and origins.[7] Governments are not necessarily adversaries, and one objective of a popular movement is to encourage the emergence of political leaders more attuned to the need and opportunity for global reform.

4. The principal initial focus of a movement for positive global reform should involve education-for-action, that is, a demonstration that the felt needs and frustrations of people in a variety of concrete social circumstances around the world arise from the inability of states or the existing multinational actors to find short-range, middle-level, and long-range solutions to the distresses and dangers of our world.[8]

5. The case for global reform should be premised on a basic assessment of structural trends and options. It need not rest altogether on the collision course that apocalyptic reformers are conveniently programming to take effect around the year 2000.[9] We should be somewhat suspicious about the recent show of millennial egoism, the idea that we either change by the year 2000 or everything is lost.[10] There is a temptation to deliver an apocalyptic sermon to the wayward citizenry of Nineveh, but such a message would probably be shaped by the characteristic desire of mortals to witness

the completion of their own reform projects within the compass of their probable lifetimes. My inclination is to adopt the perspective of that retired French general who wanted to plant in his garden some species of trees that he had grown to love during his years as a colonial administrator in an Asian country. When told by his gardener that such trees would not blossom for 70 years, long after his death, the general is supposed to have said, "In that case, don't wait until after lunch to plant them."

The language and sensibility of law tend to be static. New modes of thought, new orientations are needed if law and lawyers are to adopt a dynamic, processive perspective. Such an outlook is obviously essential to the whole idea of a transition process in the course of which the very framework of legal relations would undergo fundamental change. Can we develop an interpretation of that transition process that international lawyers can use to analyze the main developments of international life that call for the application of legal techniques such as negotiation, adjudication, treaty-making, and institution-building? Without such an interpretation, the characteristic problems of the day—whether they be the status of prisoners of war, claims to impose or disrupt an oil embargo, the status of military reprisals, or satellite surveillance—are fed back into an obsolete framework of interstate relations in which the irrelevant cynicism of the Machiavellians jousts with the irrelevant moralism and legalism of outmanned idealists. We do not need judgments of approval and disapproval nearly as much as we need a set of values that can inform a strategy of change. What was "realism" a generation ago when the state system was able to deal adequately with the main problems of the day becomes "crackpot realism" in the current world setting. Regardless of our normative outlook, we require a new framework to comprehend the dynamics of global transformation.

It is hoped that this new framework can perform a social and political, as well as an intellectual role, by helping to mobilize a normative consensus that challenges the prevailing ethical currents of neo-Darwinian sentiment and policy. As matters now stand, the process of transition is dominated by those who believe that the privilege of the few in the face of the misery of the many is either inevitable or actually beneficial, providing a necessary foundation for human excellence and accomplishment. The central feature of the normative challenge that I would propose as a counter rests upon an acceptance of human solidarity and all of its implications, especially a shared responsibility to seek equity and dignity for every person on the planet without regard to matters of national identity, territorial boundary, or ideological affiliation.

I

Since the seventeenth century the territorial state has been the principal organizing unit in global politics, and national governments have been the principal actors. Modern international law arose to give juridical expression to this political reality.[11] It was a political reality that began to take shape in medieval Europe but subsequently assumed global significance, through a combination of Western superiority over other regional systems of organization, and the actual physical colonizing and missionizing processes that managed to extend the sway of this Eurocentric system over most of the rest of the world. That is, there are other regional systems of multistate law, but none whose claims of universal applicability achieved such plausibility as a result of the extension of actual influence beyond the region of its origins.[12]

Since Grotius, if not before, this juridical consensus has provided international lawyers with a generally shared framework.[13] To transform it will require a new perception of a changing political reality and an awareness that the juridical articulation of the perception can influence the balance of choice among historical options as well as condition the moral quality of the prevailing option. Vinogradoff understood that while not all options are historically plausible, neither is there an inevitable historical current that predetermines the world order outcome. Some human pressure on the rudder of history at the right moment may avert collision, or even ensure that the voyage is a pleasant one. International legal studies remain, by and large, oblivious to the system-changing context. As a result, there has been a failure to fashion new juridical formulations that are responsive to political realities moving the world system from one that is a relatively decentralized, if hierarchically arranged, form of statism to an emerging order that is becoming gradually more centralized, although its specific nature and orientation is by no means yet predetermined.

Thomas Kuhn has attracted considerable attention through his depiction of the structure of scientific revolutions. His basic observation, relevant to our purposes, is that natural scientists at any given time work within a paradigm of shared assumptions, traditions, and procedures to solve the characteristic problems confronting their profession. Kuhn describes a paradigm as "universally recognized scientific achievements that for a time provide model problems and solutions to a community of practitioners."[14] Such a paradigm sets boundaries on research and creates a set of intellectual taboos that prevail until challenged by new discoveries, so-called anomalies, that are not explicable within the reigning paradigm and yet appear too significant to ignore or disavow.[15] It is at such a point that a scientific revolution occurs and a new paradigm is crystallized, in order to allow the work of the profession to proceed with maximum efficiency because a large fundamental area of agreement can again be taken for granted.

Kuhn has been critical of facile extrapolations of his ideas about paradigms in the natural sciences to the disciplines of social science. Indeed, he contends that the social sciences operate without a paradigm of shared perspectives, in the sense that he applies the term to the work of physics, astronomy, biology, and chemistry.[16] With respect to international law, however, I think there has been a sufficiently shared and definite view of the world to make it useful to consider that its practitioners have worked within a paradigm. Assuredly, this paradigm has not been as explicit as the one that has normally guided astronomers, but it has nevertheless provided an authoritative framework that has shaped inquiry and established a generally accepted conception of the political terrain upon which international law must operate. By looking back at premodern types of international law, we can discover that the statist paradigm has not always dominated inquiry, that a major juridical revolution in this direction was heavily influenced by the work of Grotius and consolidated by Vattel.[17] The statist paradigm has been used by the profession to discipline deviant practitioners, mainly by labeling them as "utopian," "legalist," or "idealist"—that is, as unworthy of serious attention either because they worked outside the paradigm or because they challenged prevailing patterns of statecraft.[18] (Occasionally, statist deviants have also been disciplined by being called "cynics" if they went too far in denying the role of law in world affairs.)[19] At the present time, in my judgment, we are on the verge of another juridical revolution of the sort Grotius accomplished, but this time the revolution will dethrone the statist paradigm and put in its place a new framework based on some form of central guidance.

There are several characteristics associated with a paradigm shift. First, it is a mutation rather than a series of increments or minor modifications. Second, it embodies a distinct and coherent explanation of the entire agenda of problems relevant for a current generation of practitioners. Third, the shift (as it occurs in law) will parallel comparable shifts in many disparate fields of human experience, such as art, science, and the humanities.[20] The sweeping nature of a paradigm shift (or system-change) needs to be underlined because its reality is so uncongenial to the American temperament. Paradigm changes are especially uncongenial to American lawyers who tend to view constructive social change as necessarily incremental and who distrust overall explanations of complex social and political phenomena.

At the same time, one main reason for urging consideration of a new juridical paradigm is quintessentially American—namely, that the old juridical paradigm no longer "works," that it no longer seems responsive to the main problems on the international agenda. Thus those who persist in carrying on their inquiries within the old paradigm end up with trivial results, either because they work on irrelevant problems or because they work on relevant problems within an inappropriate framework. Of course, so long as the old paradigm works, it is sensible to take it for granted so that we can concentrate our efforts on the frontiers of knowledge.[21] The more we can safely take for granted, the greater proportion of our time and energy we can devote to that which is not yet adequately understood. The problem in a period of transition is that we are no longer justified in taking very much for granted, and we therefore have to establish a new superstructure that "works" for the problems we seek most to solve.

In creating a foundation for this line of interpretation, it is relevant to look back at the premodern paradigm that existed in medieval Europe, and then at that twilight period of transition when the old feudal paradigm was crumbling but the new statist one had not yet definitively crystallized.

Of course one can always find antecedents, whether for scientific or juridical revolutions, that make the choice boundary markers appear somewhat arbitrary. For instance, one leading interpreter of the origins of the modern state concludes that the process by which this new organizational form came into being was completed by the year 1600, or almost fifty years before the Westphalia treaties.[22] But our concern is with the *state system* as distinct from the *medieval system*, rather than with the process by which the elements of the system were formed. Since politics is a consensus-building compromise-oriented realm, there is a strong tendency by actors to keep the paradigm shift implicit, even disavowed, until long after it has been effectively accepted at the level of ordinary consciousness as conventional wisdom. In the history of international law, the writings of jurists, the great lawmaking treaties, and the contending positions (or claims) of antagonists in the most prominent legal disputes of a given period all manifest an ambivalence toward the contending paradigms. Dual loyalty to the past and that which is emerging injects an element of incoherence in these three characteristic settings of international law activity during any period of transition from one world order system to another. Indeed, the existence of such incoherence is, perhaps, one of the strongest indications that a particular historical period is actually undergoing transition.

A further feature of a transition period is an attitudinal shift toward interpretations that challenge the dominant paradigm.[23] While the dominant paradigm is secure, deviant interpretations, other things being equal, can be ignored, or vitually so, as harmless. But as evolving events undermine the older paradigm's claim to deal adequately with the problems within its domain, new claims based on an alternative paradigm begin to be perceived as credible challenges. The guardians of the status quo begin to perceive deviant interpretations as dangerous and hostile, rather than as merely silly. In effect, previously harmless knowledge becomes dangerous knowledge. It is relevant to recall that Grotius's great treatise on war and peace was perceived by Catholic defenders of the old order as undermining of medieval unity and the special role of the pope, and was accordingly placed on the Papal Index in 1626 and not removed until 1899, that is, until long after the collapse of feudalism.[24]

In writing of the emergence of the modern statist paradigm, James Turner Johnson notes, with special reference to the changing status of war, that "were only the Spaniards thinking along these lines, the new order would never have emerged; its genesis and growth derive not only from changed historical circumstances but also from fairly widespread efforts to think out the implications of these changed conditions with the help of natural law considerations."[25] That is, threshold phenomena such as the Grotius treatise and the Peace of Westphalia are reflections of an emergent, widely shared, disparately formulated consensus regarding changed conditions and their juridical consequences. As Professor Johnson points out, not only Grotius and his Spanish antecedents, but a whole tradition of English speculation, perhaps best represented in the writing of Matthew Sutcliffe[26] and William

Ames,[27] was formulating a similar set of juridical interpretations from premises set forth in the great philosophical treatises of Hobbes and Locke.[28] In other words, a juridical revolution will not occur unless there is a convergence of interpretations based on intersecting perspectives drawn from the many interacting directions of thought.[29] By the time the new juridical paradigm exists unambiguously, it has long dominated the actual patterns of practice in political behavior. That is, defense of the old and resistance to the new delays acknowledgment of reality in the final stages of a transition process.

Let me now briefly consider the juridical paradigm shift that accompanied the wider historical transition from the Middle Ages to the modern world. We are concerned here with the profound effects on the substance and methodology of international law that can be attributed to the emergence of a new world order system at the end of the Middle Ages. We are concerned also with the role that jurists and juridical events seem to have had in accelerating and shaping the new paradigm embodied in the dynamics of the state system. The purpose of this discussion is not to achieve a new historical understanding of the origins of modern international law, a much debated and studied question. Rather, the purpose here is to prepare the ground for studying the actual and potential relevance of international law to the current transition from the state system to some form of new ordering arrangement embodying the juridical and managerial logic of central guidance.

The main world order transition of the seventeenth century involved the substitution of a relatively multipolar state system for the former relatively unipolar imperial system bound together by the authority of the pope and the spiritual unity of Christendom.[30] The medieval system was one in which papal central guidance was coordinated with feudal and localist loyalties to family, church, guild, and prince. The claim, as crystallized in 1075, was one of supremacy for the pope, "that his decision ought to be reviewed by no one, and that he alone can review the decisions of everyone; that he ought to be judged by no one."[31] The historian Joseph Strayer prefers the more compact formulation of Innocent III that popes "judged all and could be judged by no one."[32] In contrast, the modern state is characterized by spatial boundaries sustained through time, by a set of specialized administrative institutions, and by the loyalty of its citizenry. The buildup of this statist order depended heavily, in Strayer's words, on "a shift in loyalty from family, local community, or religious organization to the state and the acquisition by the state of a moral authority to back up its institutional structure and its theoretical legal supremacy."[33]

It is the antagonism between these papal and secular sources of moral authority that characterizes the transition period from medieval Europe to the modern state system; and it is the eventual dominance of statist ideology that marks the end of transition and the beginning of the statist era. This antagonism was personified by the struggle between the papacy and Philip IV of France, who reigned over one of the earliest political units to achieve statehood in the modern sense. The controversy was provoked by Philip's efforts to tax the French clergy without prior consent from Rome. The reigning pope, Boniface VIII, considered this an improper attempt to subject the Church to secular control. It led in 1302 to the famous papal bull *Unam Sanctam*, which has been described as an effort "to sum up and define the plenitude of the Papal power over all the Christian community, including France and her king."[34] It expressed the pure ideology of the medieval system in its first self-conscious confrontation with paradigmatic threats from emergent state units. *Unam Sanctam* staked out a claim of a once single ascendant Church: "At the time of the flood there was, indeed, one ark of Noah, prefiguring one Church; it . . . had one steersman and commander, namely Noah, and we read that outside of it all things existing on earth were destroyed."[35] From this unity springs a hierarchy of authority, rather than two equal swords of temporal and spiritual authority: "Spiritual power exceeds any earthly power in dignity and nobility, as spiritual things excel temporal ones. . . . If, therefore, earthly power err, it shall be judged by the higher, competent spiritual power, but if the supreme spiritual power err, it could be judged solely by God, not by man."[36] Thus, the temporal authority of a king is derived ultimately from the same unity as the Church, but its claims are subordinate to those of the pope, who is the supreme spiritual authority on earth.[37]

It is significant that Philip's views prevailed and that he repudiated the papacy. But this seed of statism would take several centuries of growth before its full flowering would occur. The culmination of this long process of changeover to the state system is not to be found until the Peace of Westphalia, regarded as the decisive *juridical event*, and Grotius's treatise *The Rights of War and Peace*, regarded as the decisive *juridical formulation*.[38] In both instances, the transition context is clearly evident from the way in which the forms of the eroding order are drawn upon to embellish, and perhaps disguise, the substance of the new order. Peace treaties had been, heretofore, the decisive juridical events in international history, because the search for an acceptable political framework within which to manage international conflict has been almost exclusively concerned with the problem of war and peace. The system-changing peace treaties, a small subset, have been those which marked major shifts in managerial conceptions, by altering authority patterns, by staking out new roles for actors, or by expressing a new awareness of the destructiveness of warfare and a temporary determination to cooperate to the extent necessary to keep the peace.

Consider the Peace of Westphalia from this perspective. It took almost four years to negotiate, and, when finally concluded in 1648, it formally brought the Thirty Years War to an end. The treaty (actually two distinct texts) carried forward notions of territorial absolutism on matters of religious preference (at least within the Christian regional system) and removed the issue of religious faith from the list of just causes for which a prince might have recourse to war.[39] The Church could no longer stand above the secular fray and serve as an impartial arbiter among Christian foes, nor could it form an alliance with the Holy Roman Emperor. Thus the Peace of Westphalia signaled the shift in the locus of power that accompanied the rise of strong territorially based nation-states, acknowledging the split in Christendom that led to the Reformation, and then to the Counter-Reformation. The Thirty Years War involved a final defeat of the effort by the Hapsburg Dynasty to reestablish the secular and spiritual unity of pre-Reformation Europe. It thereby ensured the decentralization of power and authority that has become one major attribute of the state system. Recall our earlier contention that harmless knowledge turns to dangerous knowledge as the hour of paradigm shift approaches; it is revealing that Pope Innocent X attacked the provisions on religious tolerance, the very core of the Peace of Westphalia, as "null, void, invalid, wicked, unjust, condemned, reprobated, futile, and without strength and effect" in the bull *Zelo domus Dei* of November 20, 1648.[40] The bull even purported to nullify the oaths made to carry out the treaty; significantly, the treaty was carried out in all its parts, and the papal intervention seemed to exert no influence even on the Catholic rulers who had signed the treaties at Munster and Osnabrück. Nussbaum aptly notes: "Just as there is a spiritual nexus between Grotius's work and the Peace of Westphalia, so there is a similar nexus between the papal condemnations of Grotius's work and of this Peace."[41] And so those who are the bearers of a new paradigm for international legal studies can expect similar harsh treatment.

The military outcome of the final phases of the Thirty Years War also reflected the rise of secularized geopolitics, as Catholic Bavaria allied with Lutheran Sweden to oppose the Hapsburgs while the French Catholic monarchy supported the essentially Protestant effort to halt the Counter-Reformation. Thus, a perceived need to check secular ambitions was a significant element of the pre-Westphalia alliance system, notwithstanding the prevailing rhetoric by which the participants insisted on emphasizing the religious stakes of the conflict. Put differently, Catholic France would undoubtedly have preferred to see Catholicism restored throughout Europe, but not at the cost of making the Hapsburg Empire the dominant actor in Europe. Rather than acquiesce in such a disadvantageous geopolitical situation, France was prepared to help the anti-Catholic cause prevail in the Thirty Years War. The principal loser in the Thirty Years War was the loosely confederated German assemblage of kingdoms and principalities.[42] After Westphalia, it was France that emerged as the most powerful actor, mounting expansionist drives in subsequent periods to achieve hegemony over the whole of Europe, first under the aegis of Louis XIV and later under Napoleon. These efforts resulted in two of the most important peace treaties after 1648—the Peace of Utrecht (1713) and the Peace of Paris (1814, 1815), related to the Congress of Vienna. Manifest in these treaties was a second attribute of the state system, the increasingly self-conscious use of alliance relationships to achieve "balance" despite the multipolarity of the world order system, as well as to contain revolutionary actors who seek a large-scale revision in basic geopolitical relationships.

At Westphalia the realization occurred that in some national societies there were domestic religious differences, and that unless these differences were tolerated they would cause civil strife and generate pretexts for intervention by outsiders. Therefore, the treaty protected the religious autonomy of individuals while reinforcing the new peace framework of sovereign states; it thereby also expressed the philosophy of natural rights underlying the contemporary development of an international law of human rights.[43] In the setting of the seventeenth century this right of personal choice, accompanied by an ethics of religious toleration, reflected the growing influence of an individualistic ethos that had many roots, ranging from the rise of capitalism to the whole outlook of enlightenment and individualism associated with the Renaissance, and extending to the Luther-led revolt on behalf of conscience against the arbitrary authority of the Church.[44]

Thus Westphalia embodies one of those "omnipresent complementarities," as Myres McDougal identifies them, in the prevailing international legal order[45]—on the one side, matters of religion are confined to domestic jurisdiction; on the other, abridgments of religious freedom are made matters of international concern. The tension between domestic jurisdiction and human rights is as old as the persecutions of the Huguenots or Puritans and as contemporary as the persecution of Soviet Jewry. The question as to whether deference to state sovereignty should take precedence over efforts to rescue victims of governmental abuse remains necessarily ambiguous and controversial in each context.

Here, then, are the major elements of the modern state system prefigured in the Peace of Westphalia, although rendered somewhat murky in its express textual language by the residual deference to and reliance upon the outmoded feudal system that was being supplanted. This exhibition of transitional intersystemic confusion is especially interesting for our purposes. First of all, the secularization of international politics is disguised by the adoption of a highly religious rhetoric characteristic of a much earlier mood. The use of this rhetoric may have expressed a measure of nostalgia, and it may indicate a perfectly reasonable attempt to use the shared Christianity of the opposing leaders as a normative common ground above their ecclesiastical divisions. Article I of the Treaty of Westphalia (Munster) expresses this tone: "[T]here shall be a Christian and Universal Peace, and a perpetual, true, and sincere amity, between his Imperial Majesty and his most Christian Majesty."[46]

There are also numerous indications of the residual role of feudal arrangements even at the level of intergovernmental compacts. Indeed, the older feudal paradigm provided a ready-made means of implementing the conflict's main geopolitical outcome, the defeat and frustration of the Hapsburg design to extend the sway of the Holy Roman Empire over the numerous Germanic principalities. The Peace of Westphalia conferred autonomous international status on the more than 300 members of the Holy Roman Empire; they were given the legal capacity to enter alliances with foreign governments and to wage war, provided only that the alliances were not directed at the empire or against the terms of the Peace of Westphalia. These subordinate units of empire "were thereby lifted to an international legal status approximating sovereignty though the old term *Landeshoheit* (territorial supremacy) was preserved."[47] Here, too, we note ironically another characteristic feature of the state system in its Eurocentric phase: the primacy of geopolitics, especially the persisting effort by major governments to prevent any one of their number from achieving continental hegemony.

The closing articles of the treaty include some forward-looking provisions involving an innovative effort to establish an agreed framework of restraint vis-à-vis recourse to war. For one thing, the primacy of the peace obligation is affirmed, even in the event that some aspect of the elaborate plan of "Restitution and Reparation" is not put into effect: "[A]ll Parties in this Transaction shall be obliged to defend and protect all and every Article of this Peace against any one, without distinction of Religion."[48] Even more impressive are the seeds of modern notions of peaceful settlement and the provisions of an ambitious implementing procedure: "[A]nd if it happens any point shall be violated, the Offended shall before all things exhort the Offender not to come to any Hostility, submitting the Cause to a friendly Composition, or the ordinary Proceedings of Justice."[49] Finally, the treaty contains a notion of collective security based on helping the victim of abuse, provided that victim has waited three years to allow settlement to come about by peaceful means.

[I]f for the space of three years the Difference cannot be terminated by any of those means, all and every one of those concern'd in this Transaction shall be oblig'd to join the injur'd Party, and assist him with Counsel and Force to repel the Injury, being first advertis'd by the injur'd that gentle Means and Justice prevail'd nothing.[50]

The treaty also seeks to identify the "infringer of the Peace," what in modern parlance we call "the aggressor," as that party who first departs from the peaceful processes of settlement ("the means of ordinary justice").[51]

Embedded in this extraordinary juridical happening at Westphalia is a constitutional effort to lay down ground rules for a new status of war: At this point of transition the peace treaty became a legislative document seeking to prevent reversion to destructive warfare by taking account of the "new realities." My point here is that Grotius (and other jurists of the time) helped to formulate reformist notions on the status of war that were then translated by statesmen into a juridical formula that could be put into treaty form. International law also performed a critical role in providing a normative bridge between the spiritualist preoccupation of the Middle Ages and the statist orientation of the modern era.

Just as critics were unmasking the pious frauds perpetrated under the aegis of Church-centered normative guidance, ideologists of the state system were working out notions of absolute prerogative at the national level— often, as in the case of Bodin, so as to legitimate claims of domestic sovereignty on behalf of national governments that were internally opposed by feudal loyalists.[52] The danger, of course, was that the collapse of Christian unity would produce a normative vacuum in which there were no shared guidelines of restraint. International lawyers provided an intricate set of procedures by which to uphold and maintain these shared guidelines in the new secular context, thereby working against the abiding impulse toward amorality in interstate relations.

This contribution of international law and lawyers is easy to underestimate, especially as public attention tends to fasten on the spectacular struggles of the day in which all forms of constraint give way. But for recurrent and normal interactions among governments, and even for classes of interactions among antagonistic or warring governments, international law has over the centuries provided a normative framework of immense practical value. This framework has been a constant buffer against more absolutist and cynical approaches to state behavior, and has refuted those simplistic assertions that rest the whole of international relations on considerations of relative military power. Thus, the role of the great international jurists in the Westphalian period was to add a beneficial normative element to the historical drift toward a statist option in international life. To be creative, in other words, required both an understanding of this historical drift and an effort to exert an influence upon it.

The perspectives prefigured in Grotius and Westphalia become much more explicit in the Peace of Utrecht (1713) and in the principal treatise of Emmerich de Vattel.[53] The main contractual undertaking at Utrecht was to formalize the frustration of Louis XIV's effort to extend French control to Spain in the War of Spanish Succession (1702–1713). In the treaty this result was expressed in the form of reciprocal renunciations by the French and Spanish kings of each other's thrones.[54] Of even greater significance from our point of view is the more explicit emergence of the statist paradigm. First, territorial states are acknowledged as the prime actors; semiterritorial actors like the Holy Roman Empire or nonterritorial actors like the pope are now virtually deprived of international status. Second, geopolitics is explicitly recognized to be an element of the international legal order. It is the means to sustain the multistate context, resist hegemony, and preserve balance; thus natural law perspectives on the status of war give way to the balance of power perspectives. Third, governments are accepted as sole agents of the interests of their populations and treated as authoritative spokesmen for their well-being; they exercise "that paternal Care which they delight to use towards their own subjects."[55]

The geopolitical nexus of international relations is worthy of closer scrutiny. In several places, the idea that peace depends on geopolitical equilibrium is not only affirmed but virtually elevated to a principle of natural law.[56] In the Spanish king's renunciation of any claims on the French crown we find this phrasing:

[I]t being to be believed, that by this perpetual and neverceasing Hope, the Needle of the Ballance may remain invariable, and all the Powers, wearied with the Toil and Uncertainty of Battles, may be amicably kept in an equal Poise; it not remaining in the Disposal of any of the Partys to alter this federal Equilibrium by way of any

Contract of Renunciation, or Retrocession: since the same Reason which induced its being admitted, demonstrates its Permanency, a fundamental Constitution being formed, which may settle by an unalterable Law the Succession of what is to come.[57]

Notice that solicitude toward subjects is given as a principal reason for preferring peace to a frequent assertion of unresolved dynastic claims, and that the permanent renunciation of such claims is intended to reinforce the equilibrium among the great powers, thereby discouraging renewal of war. International law provides governments with an authoritative instrument by which to solemnize such undertakings and to express the basis of peaceful relations in a definitive form that diminishes any prospect of future miscalculation. In another ancillary way, international law separates private grievances from public wrongs so as to provide remedies of a limited nature that do not threaten resumption of warfare. Thus, in Article XVIII it is agreed that if any subject of the contracting parties acts in a manner incompatible with the peace agreed upon, it shall not disrupt intergovernmental arrangements; "that Subject alone . . . shall suffer the Punishment, which is inflicted by the Rules and Directions of the Law of Nations."[58]

The Peace of Utrecht manifests the full logical coherence of the new paradigm. The Christian bonds are still evident in the choice of terminology, but not in an integral manner. Peace is now sustained by geopolitical equilibrium, which requires two main things: First, secure boundaries for sovereign states and clear lines of dynastic succession; second, the realization that any attempt by a major power to increase its relative position in the system will set in motion a complex of forces that could eventuate in a defensive alliance and warfare.

The juridical consequences of the Westphalia-Utrecht flow of mainline international political developments is carefully and conveniently explicated by Vattel in his *Law of Nations*, initially published in 1758. Unlike Grotius, who combines nostalgia for the earlier medieval approach with aspirations for a future order based on higher morality, Vattel rather fully expresses the prevailing statist consensus. His work reflects rather than reforms or challenges. As a result, it became generally acceptable to decisionmakers at all levels of the political order, and, as might be expected, it is more influential than other intellectually superior juridical statements.[59]

In my view, Vattel's stature was a direct consequence of his capacity to codify the statist paradigm in clear prose; there was no longer intellectual space available for Grotian-scale originality. Vattel was praised for his "common sense" and "realism,"[60] but such praise meant only that he was a faithful repository of conventional wisdom. With the erosion of the Westphalia paradigm in the twentieth century, especially in the period since 1914, there has been a gradual disappearance of the Vattelian consensus on the contents of "common sense," as well as a neo-Grotian upsurge of sorts. Hedley Bull describes "the Grotian conception," an outlook he himself deplores, as "a certain conception of international society, whose imprint may be traced in the Convenant of the League of Nations, the Paris Pact, the United Nations Charter, and the Charter of the International Military

Tribunal at Nuremberg."[61] These agreements, which prefigure neo-Grotian thought, call to mind Grotius's own effort to substitute a community of nations resting on natural law norms for the collapsing Christian community, which had rested uneasily on ecclesiastic authority and religious tradition.

In my terminology, Grotius endeavored to recreate a plausible ideology of central guidance in a situation of increasing institutional disintegration. As long as the historical drift was against this recentralizing endeavor, that is, in the period between Utrecht and World War I, the more statist jurisprudence of Vattel carried the day because it seemed to correspond more closely with configurations of belief, power, and behavior. As twentieth-century students of the statist paradigm began to uncover anomalies, principally in the form of mutually destructive warfare and of multidimensional interdependence, a swing back toward Grotian conceptions could be discerned both in the work of "far-seeing guides"[62] and even in the characteristic juridical reforms of the time.[63] Instead of a purely normative hope, central guidance of a secular sort became a public demand as well as an objective sought after by practical men of affairs.[64]

The time horizons of such a quest encourage misinterpretations, especially by those with little feeling for the rhythm of major historical transformations. There is a tendency either to expect the process to crystallize almost immediately in a world government or, conversely, to dismiss as irrelevant these early gropings toward central guidance because they have no prospect of taking definitive shape in the near future.[65] Confusion is also generated by contradictions among concurrent trends, and unless attempts are made to interpret the overall process, there is some disposition to conclude that everything is canceled out. For instance, for every move toward central guidance it is possible to point to a neutralizing countermove toward sovereign prerogative, whether it be geographic extension of the state system in this postcolonial period or the upsurge of statist approaches to the control of the oceans,[66] until recently a feature virtually common to all societies.

An historical perspective should enable us to accept the fact that a process of paradigm shift may take place over a period as long as several centuries and that the pull and push of forces in the international legal system may be appreciated without losing sight of the *cumulative drift* toward central guidance. What is "realistic" has fortunately become a matter of increasing controversy. Objective conditions have changed in ways that alter the notion of "equilibrium," the status of war, the prospects for peace and tranquility, and the role and capacities of territorial actors. Today, as in the seventeenth century, the time is ripe for preliminary efforts to give juridical shape to a new paradigm of global relations, one that corresponds more closely than statist thinking to the needs, trends, and values of the present state of global politics. The constituent elements of a new paradigm were planted long ago, most emphatically by the experiences of widespread disillusionment with the balance of power, but only recently has it become plausible to conceive of their existence as powerful enough to establish the political basis for a new paradigm. It is this possibility that will be considered in the next section.

In a sense this analysis can be stated as a plea directed to the international legal profession. It is a normative plea that challenges the implicit conservatism of statism and mocks the pseudo-realism of those who, in a period of transition, make the pursuit of stability their primary goal. It is a plea for international lawyers to stop acting as if their most important task were to clarify the rights and duties of the various passengers on the planetary cruiseship Titanic. It is basically a plea to join forces with an infant movement for global reform, but without any illusion that a "quick fix" can be achieved. Indeed, it is a plea to pursue a set of goals that seems hopeless if we consider the array of forces on the other side. It is a plea to participate in history without calculating prospects of success, precisely and principally because of a personal commitment to the future of the human species and the fate of earth.

II

How, then, can we encourage the development of a paradigm for international legal studies that is at once responsive to the historical tendency toward central guidance and supportive of efforts to realize world order values? Given the preceding analysis, a paradigm will not satisfy these criteria unless it is sensitive to the various transitional currents active in international life. It is, first of all, necessary to depict the general direction of the transitional shift already under way, the array of plausible options, the criteria for choice among the options, and an action plan by which to maximize the possibilities through which the *preferred* option could become the *probable* option. On this basis a new paradigm might be part of a wider effort to resist transition pressures likely to produce a world order solution that is undesirable in terms of either the well-being and development of the human species, or the ecological stability of the planet.[67] The ideas presented here are deeply influenced by the new juridical paradigm that has been evolving under the auspices of Myres McDougal and Harold Lasswell and their numerous co-workers.[68] For present purposes, the McDougal enterprise needs to be adapted to the specific challenges posed by a transitional context.

Barrington Moore, Jr., has urged reform-minded individuals to compare the costs and risks of reform with those of passivity and reconciliation. Moore realizes that such a comparison "can never be more than a rough approximation."[69] But only with it, he says, "can we avoid succumbing to the defeatist illusion of impotence within a permanent present or the opposite one of romantic utopianism."[70] Moore regards these two illusions as themselves "sources of human misery" and argues that "the effort to overcome them . . . is indeed the central justification for the role of the detached observer of human affairs."[71] What Moore emphasizes is similar to what Vinogradoff had in mind when he referred to the role of "far-seeing guides" in reshaping the character of international legal studies. It is what seems critical at the present juncture if we are to grapple in earnest with the twin dangers of cynical realism, which overadjusts to the inadequacies of the existing order, and utopian idealism, which is so unmindful of existing constraints on reform that it can be of no practical relevance. Both are static postures that fail to comprehend an historically *constrained* transition process in a manner that might throw light upon the most relevant range of *options.*

It is the notion of historical constraint that brings into focus the analysis of the present world order situation. This notion makes certain assumptions. For instance, it excludes the occurrence of man-made or natural catastrophe; it excludes an invasion from outer space; it excludes discoveries that enable the whole world population to enjoy affluence and abundance despite the persistence of wide disparities. In other words, the perspective adopted here accepts a developmental view of the transition process that is neither beset nor alleviated by a *deus ex machina.* At the same time it rejects the position that human capacities for response must be confined to marginal adjustment. Changes in overall possibilities are better understood as *mutations* rather than *increments.* The whole conception of paradigm change implies an abrupt discontinuity; the work of Jean Gebser in studying the evolution of human consciousness is highly relevant because he so clearly associates modes of thought with particular conceptions of space prevalent at a given time. Gebser shows that the capacity to deal with the pressures of the contemporary world depends upon holistic ways of thinking, and he argues convincingly that such modes are already imminent in consciousness. It is a matter of actualizing the holistic potential, rather than inventing it.[72] The first phase in an explicit transition[73] strategy is to reshape consciousness in a holistic direction that derives inspiration from an ethical position of human solidarity in a context of material scarcity.[74] The understanding of the crisis in world order that is presented here is summarized in Figure 38.1

Before dealing with paradigm redesign, it seems appropriate to raise some fundamental questions of basic approach. It is important to draw the distinction between adopting a new orientation toward global reform (what is called here "paradigm redesign") and the process of actual reform. The design of a new paradigm is possible immediately and it is also a step in the direction of reform, but the dynamics of implementing an altered vision is likely to be the work of the next several generations.

First, there is the age-old issue of freedom and constraint. It is apparent that the flow of historical forces restricts the plausible array of world order options in rather specific ways. The limits of plausibility are set by functional requirements for effective mechanisms of *nonterritorial central guidance.* The possibilities for creative human intervention depend on a prior understanding of the historical context. I am taking a position that denies both historical closure and indefinite openness.

Second, there is the ongoing debate between the allegedly tough-minded and tender-hearted over who occupies the high ground of "reality." The literature of international law and relations poses a false dichotomy between Machiavellian geopolitics and the globaloney of schemes for instant world government. As argued here, the balance of power approach to world order is increasingly incapable of satisfying the needs of principal governments or their most powerful constituencies, whereas a utopian fantasy of world government is unconnected with any plausible transition scenario. It is true, as declared in a recent letter to the *New York Times*, that "no utopian thinking disregarding the realities of the world scene can move us an inch beyond the balance of power. It can only aggravate the calamities of an imperfect world."[75] So conceived, the only rational course of behavior is to learn the ropes on the Machiavellian ship of state; any more drastic strategy is repudiated as "utopian." This falsely posited dichotomy provides the prevailing obsolescent paradigm with a means to discipline deviants or, at least to label them as harmless oddities.[76] In a sense, advocates of instant world government reinforce the statist paradigm by discrediting a movement for drastic reform in general. I think legalists and other utopians encourage a re-embrace of the status quo; people commonly react that if fantasy is the alternative to some purchase on reality, then it's better to give the devil his due and work with reality.

But apologists for each of these positions are placing their bets on horses that have already lost the race. Both Machiavellian geopolitics and utopian legalism are nonviable world order options because they fail to perceive the dominant integrationist thrust of contemporary issues. At the same time, both positions can be usefully associated with an apt appreciation of prospects for global reform. The intelligent appreciation of the dynamics of geopolitics does moderate the potential for conflict during a period of consciousness-raising that is just now seriously getting under way. We may need an interim period of moderate geopolitics as a "minor premise," to avoid a breakdown of the state system prior to the formation of a widely shared understanding of the prospects for nonterritorial central guidance and of the array of plausible options. Furthermore, we require utopian and semi-utopian models of global reform to structure our awareness, provided we appreciate both their failure to provide a transition strategy and their metaphorical provincialism.[77]

It seems important, also, to consider the frequent claim that only a catastrophe could bring about a transformation of the world system.[78] Here, analysis often concedes that central guidance is likely to come, but not until after another world war. Indeed, among self-styled realists we can identify an optimist as one who believes that the war system can be eliminated from human experience by world order reforms put into practice after World War III; a pessimist believes we may have to wait until after World War IV, or longer. But perhaps we are interpreting the global setting without taking a close enough look at some of its distinctive features. It is, of course, significantly chastening to notice, as earlier indicated, that the main world order adjustments of the past have taken place after wars, as aspects of overall peace settlements. But is this sequence of breakdown and response inevitable? Are there reasons to suppose that precatastrophe prospects for world order mutations are improving?

There are now various pressures in addition to the menace of general warfare that are propelling the human species and its leaders toward a new

FIGURE 38.1
A Conceptual Guide to the Study of Global Reform

Analytic Framework

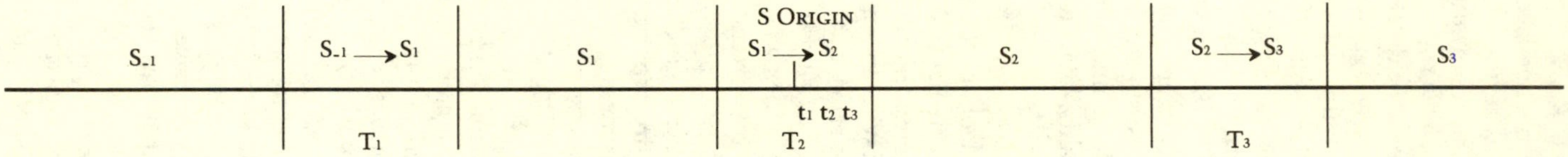

Chronological Framework

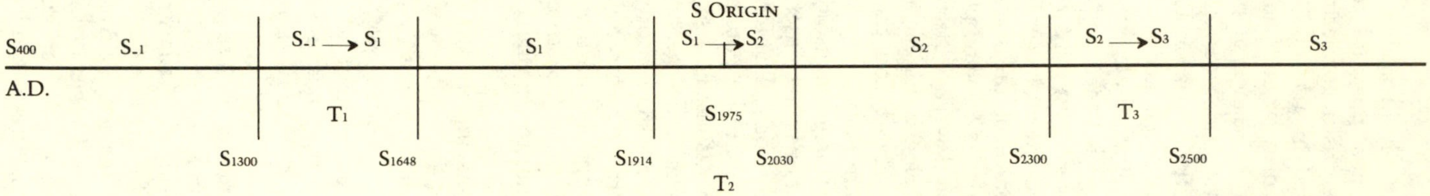

S = System
T = Transition from one
world order system
to another

Detail

$$T_2 \, [S_1 \longrightarrow S_2]$$

S_1	S_0	t_1	t_2	t_3	S_2

T_2

t = transition stage within T

t_1 = consciousness

t_2 = mobilization

t_3 = transformation

Law paradigm for $S_1 \longrightarrow S_2$:

I.   Jurisprudential stage: shift from S_1 to $S_1 \longrightarrow S_2$ framework.

II. Sociological and Epistemological stage: Introduce array of possible central guidance options and alternative redesign options.

III. Axiological stage: select preference model from among plausible array of central guidance and alternative options.

IV. Political stage: Implement transition strategy designed to facilitate $S_1 \longrightarrow S_2$ process in accordance with III in all relevant arenas.

threshold of choice with respect to fundamental issues of social organization for security and well-being. Many major governments in our age believe that general warfare would be both mutually destructive and politically inconclusive—in other words, that the damage would be awesome and there would be no winner who could dictate the terms of peace and reconstruction. Indeed, the main military conflicts since Hiroshima, those fought on center stage in the geopolitical arena, have all been carefully stage-managed to avoid escalation and have been terminated by an acceptance of stalemate rather than by victory and defeat.[79]

The future synapses of transition are not so likely to be postwar rehabilitation, but rather the emergent necessity of governments to strike world order bargains concerning subject matter that is global in scope and nonterritorial in essential character. The prime world order imperative is no longer prudential or redemptive, in the historical sense of liberating world society from what the Preamble of the United Nations Charter calls "the scourge of war." On the contrary, it is ecological, in the broadest sense of interdependence amid scarcity. An overwhelming list of issues makes this perspective inevitable and inescapable: the drive to evolve a sustainable world energy and monetary framework and to establish a mutually beneficial ocean regime; the challenge of space age technologies relating to such crucial matters as the transmission of information, modification of climate and weather, and the identification of earth resources; the prevalence and potency of private armies; the transnationalization of terrorism; the deteriorating world food situation; the mobility of ideas, people, things; and the universality of holistic imagery of the earth—the Apollo vision of the planet in space on which state boundaries are no more natural than the mapmakers' lines of latitude and longitude.

The issue of timing is fundamental and bewildering. A paradigm shift at the intellectual level is both necessary and possible in the years ahead. Such a shift could help to influence the transition process in the direction of preferred world order options. Nevertheless, the duration of the transition process cannot be anticipated with any confidence. It might be as short as a few decades or as long as several centuries.

In sum, I see a buildup of largely peacetime pressures to adopt a central guidance option. It is true that militarism at the state level will be accentuated during this restructuring process and will doubtless distort priorities during the transition period. However, the war system's influence is primarily exerted through shaping the eventual character of central guidance, rather than in discouraging transition altogether. As matters now stand, rampant militarism makes it far likelier that central guidance, should it emerge as a new pattern of world order, will assume a regressive character—that is, a highly centralized and exploitative system of dominance that relies on coercion and deception to maintain control. Can this dismal prospect be changed? Can international law help to alter the present relation of forces now arrayed in support of regressive transition strategies?

III

At this point it seems useful to clarify what is meant by world order options during this period of transition, by considering the prospect of drastic global reform from four perspectives, each of which in my opinion is alert to the possibility in the decades ahead. The perspectives are (1) utopian legalism, (2) the new geopolitics of great powership, (3) the new geoeconomics of the multinational corporate elite, and (4) a global populism based on human solidarity. At this stage the utopian legalist perspective need concern us the least, because it lacks both a credible transition scenario and structural leverage. The next two perspectives are far more relevant to the process and prospects of system change. They serve as examples of the kind of reformist initiatives that are potent because they possess structural leverage, but regressive because they seek to exert it on behalf of values and interests generally incompatible with those put forward as the basis for peace and justice in international relations. The fourth perspective explicitly adopts values that focus on justice and human dignity, and strives to shape an emerging order of nonterritorial central guidance to serve values associated with humanity as a whole, rather than to promote the particular interests of favored religious, ethnic, or geographic segments. This contrast between central guidance *of the whole* and *of the part* is the fundamental ground on which world options are evaluated as positive or negative projects.

Four types of world order options thus deserve serious consideration. One purpose here is to provide a rationale for selecting a preference model that can orient international legal studies within the new paradigmatic circumstance of a system shift from the territorial and hierarchical concentration of power and authority at the state level (emphasizing inequality among states and sovereign rights). For convenience, each type of world order option will be represented by an illustrative case. However, it should be understood that each type of option is itself capable of wide variation with respect to both structure of implementation and normative orientation. Nevertheless, the following four types of options can be usefully selected for study at this stage of inquiry:

Option A: World Government (illustrated by the Clark-Sohn plan)
Option B: Concert of Great Powers (illustrated by Nixon's Geopolitical Management Scheme)
Option C: Concert of Multinational Corporate Elites (illustrated by the Trilateral Commission)
Option D: Global Populism (illustrated by the World Order Models Project)

These four options will be appraised as world order constructs from three additional perspectives: (1) considerations of attainability—whether it is plausible, even if unlikely, to achieve sufficient structural leverage under specified conditions to bring the proposed reforms into being; (2) considerations of desirability—whether the proposed reforms would be likely to operate in a desirable manner as assessed by value priorities; and (3) considerations of durability—whether realization of the reforms would produce a reasonably stable international environment in which there would be no strong likelihood of early collapse. Table 38.1 may aid the reader in the following discussion of these options.

OPTION A

The Clark-Sohn proposals are designed to produce a peaceful and more just world by combining total disarmament with a greatly augmented United Nations.[80] They provide a model of an alternative world system that seeks to realize values of peacefulness and equity. These proposals attempt a balance between the amount of central guidance needed to create confidence in the disarmament process and the amount of protection needed to bar encroachment by the center on the zones of autonomy of national societies. As such, Clark and Sohn have evolved a plausible, carefully conceived, enlightened world order system that is probably best classified as a model of weak or limited world government. In effect, the Clark-Sohn plan expects national governments to implement the scheme voluntarily, entering into a new mutually beneficial constitutional order. The fundamental goal is war prevention; the basic nexus of transformation is a constitutional convention.

Such proposals, as matters now stand, are both unrealistic, since they shed no light on the transition problem, and misleading, since they assume that existing elites will either voluntarily evolve a new world order system that diminishes their relative power, wealth, and prestige or be receptive to such adjustments. To show the promised land across an unbridgeable river is to encourage either quietist despair (because the future is unattainable) or confirm the status quo (because the present setting is the only meaningful one). Either attitude helps power-wielders discourage recourse to more credible strategies of transformation.[81]

These proposals constitute a reasonable solution to current challenges, though not the only statement, or even the best statement, of what the goals of global reform should be. But they drop as dead weights on present social reality.[82] The only "quick fix," one that their proponents usually avoid, would be to tie their advocacy into apocalyptic scenarios of the future; perhaps these proposals are useful instruments to have in the intellectual survival kit should World War III or some other global catastrophe occur that suddenly creates receptivity by elites to structural change.

To be worthy of investigation, a world order option must have a transition strategy that is credible, as well as a reasonably coherent model for dealing with the challenge of interdependence amid scarcity. It is not necessary, and probably would be misleading, to offer a blueprint for a future world order system at this stage of the transition process; "the fallacy of premature specificity" is characteristic of Option A initiatives, which tend to be static and apolitical, depicting the workings of a preferred world system on the basis of naive and ultrarationalistic assumptions about the nature of power and its relationship to benevolent human ends.

TABLE 38.1
A Summary Comparison of Central Guidance Options

	Option A	Option B	Option C	Option D	Option n
Identifying label	Clark-Sohn plan	Nixon's five-power conception	Trilateral Commission perspective	World Order Models Project	Other value-realizing models
Ideological orientation	Utopian legalism	Geopolitics of a great power	Geoeconomics of a transnational corporate elite	Geopolitics of populist humanism	?
Performance criteria (V_1, V_2, V_3, V_4)	V_1+++ V_2+ V_3	V_1+++ V_2	V_1+++	V_1++++ V_2+++ V_3+++ V_4+++	?
Main focus of aspiration	War prevention	Geopolitical stability	Economic growth	Peace, justice and ecological well-being	?
Transition strategy	Persuasion of governing elites and constitutional arrangement	Consensus among dominant governments	Consensus among privileged elites	Populist movement	?

Criteria for global reform:

V_1 = peacefulness
V_2 = economic equity
V_3 = social and political dignity
V_4 = ecological balance

OPTION B

Geopolitical designs of central guidance seek to freeze the geopolitical status quo through the moderation or regulation of political conflict among the most powerful governments.[83] If such moderation is successful, then the prospects of containing Third World discontent can be undertaken with a reduced threat of an overall breakdown or of disrupting existing hierarchies of international relations, especially in political and economic spheres. The design is necessarily hierarchical and exploitative in both conception and societal effects. There is virtually no appreciation of economic misery, ecological decay, political repression, or population pressure as genuine world order issues.[84] In contrast, energy flows, monetary stability, the repression of terrorism, the elimination of drug flows, and the exploitation of ocean resources are high on such a world order agenda. As a consequence, geopoliticians offer us various "law and order" variants of central guidance, whose success is fully compatible with domestic repression and global inequality. Geopolitical managers and architects (i.e., power-wielders and their main advisers in leading governments) do not lose sleep over military repression or even torture instituted by friendly regimes, although they claim great concern about the status of human rights in countries under the rule of a geopolitical rival.[85] Geopolitical orientations to global reform must be taken seriously, since their advocates and supporters control not only the apparatus of state power but also the shaping of public attitudes toward reality and change. The capacity to implement a given geopolitical design seems within the reach of the effective leaders of the two superpowers, especially if their principal allies can be persuaded or induced to go along. Option B, for this reason, is by far the most accessible path to central guidance.

The ethos is neo-Darwinian: In a setting of global scarcity *all* will suffer unless *some* prevail. Therefore, the powerful will, and given the nature of life processes *should*, prevail. In a Darwinian sense their prevalence is adaptive for the species, and is also ethically acceptable because those who tend to shape the future can be considered the most deserving. International legal studies, as one would expect, have generally followed the directions set for it by geopolitical tendencies, and the geopolitical conception of the future is generally, if tacitly, supported by most international lawyers, although without the negative interpretation I have made.[86]

Why is this support ill-conceived? Such central guidance makes likely a continuous cycle of vicious forms of inter-class and inter-regional struggle in the future. The dominant actors will be challenged by immensely powerful social and political forces of discontent that are prepared to suffer greatly to cast off various yokes of hegemony. With expected technological developments it is quite conceivable that a Third World Hitler could emerge and initiate a desperate crusade for global reform that could well include recourse to nuclear blackmail. To forestall such danger, the case for surveillance and repression would seem irresistible. At best (!) we would live in an Orwellian atmosphere, supposedly made secure by a variety of ultrasophisticated technologies of mind control.

There is a second problem. Ecological planning and protection for the planet seem to require longer time horizons and much better planning and coordination than any geopolitical plan provides with respect to the global process of economic development. With inequality structured into the world order system in a setting of rapidly expanding population, especially among the poorest peoples of the world, it will be virtually impossible to put an effective brake on resource use or environmental deterioration. With self-interest as the main engine of economic distribution, there will be no capacity to identify, let alone implement, a concept of planetary interest. Already evident under the pressure of adverse worldwide economic conditions is the decline of what small altruistic element earlier manifested itself in the foreign aid area.

The classic geopolitical design seems self-destructive, violence-prone, and ecologically hazardous. Arguably, a geopolitical management directorate might achieve a few extra years of material prosperity and geopolitical dominance at immense costs in moral and ecological terms, while at the same time incurring grave risks of geopolitical disintegration and ecological collapse. Obviously, in certain phases of international relations geopolitical cooperation is desirable, regardless of what else happens, most notably in calming the strategic arms race and setting some limits on the spread of militarism.

Political leaders are normally reluctant to spell out their endorsement of geopolitical management schemes. For one thing, such schemes seem to undercut existing explanations of foreign policy based on rivalry and implacable hostility. For another, they seem to involve a degree of inter-governmental cooperation that is unprecedented. At times, however, such schemes seem "realistic," especially after breakdowns or near breakdowns of fundamental order. The congress diplomacy of nineteenth-century Europe arose out of a shared realization, for instance, by political leaders of the desirability of more centrally managed systems of geopolitics. In recent times the menace of nuclear war and the fear of economic chaos have made geopolitical management schemes attractive, despite the pervasive endorsement of hostile propaganda about rivals and the associated cold war encounter between the two superpowers and their allies. During the Nixon presidency, a fairly clear embrace of geopolitical management for the sake of global reform took place in the name of establishing "a structure of peace." An era of détente was proclaimed in superpower relations and a vision of geopolitical management under the aegis of five power centers (United States, USSR, China, Japan, Western Europe) set forth. These proposals never became more than a vague vision.[87] More traditional patterns of conflict persisted and the dynamics of militarism made it difficult to examine too seriously shifts in foreign policy orientation that worked to achieve a moderate international political environment. Nevertheless, the Nixon proposals were a clear illustration of a highly pragmatic leader encouraging public consideration of a potentially ambitious geopolitical management scheme.

OPTION C

Option C can be illustrated by the formation in 1973 of the Trilateral Commission, the dream-child of influential banker and private statesman, David Rockefeller. This commission intends "to bring the best brains of the world together to bear on the problems of the future."[88] It is almost exclusively drawn from the ultra-elite ranks of North America, Japan, and Western Europe, and unless "the best brains" are defined as those inhabiting the most affluent bodies, it includes many intelligent individuals, but virtually none of the best brains, among its membership. It does bring together a very impressive array of influentials, almost all of whom possess easy and effective access to the topmost levels of power, wealth, and prestige.[89]

In *Trialogue*, the newsletter of the commission, Rockefeller is reported as believing that "private citizens are often able to act with greater flexibility than governments in the search for new and better forms of international cooperation."[90] What is not explicit but seems to underlie Option C thinking is a fear about the consequence of uncooperative governments that become beholden to domestic ideological or nationalistic constituencies whose interests are defined in narrowly territorial terms and, hence, are increasingly at variance with those of multinational corporations and internationally minded financial institutions with their increasingly nonterritorial spread of interests.

Why is such an initiative worthy of note? First of all, its formation expresses a general recognition by the elites in the most powerful states that there is an emergent global crisis of unprecedented proportions that involves, in particular, the capacity of capitalism to adapt to the future; it deserves comparison with more globalist and academically oriented undertakings such as those sponsored by the Club of Rome.[91] Second, the Trilateral Commission's formation reflects the view that national governments were considered insufficiently capable on their own of working out the adaptations that are necessary to sustain existing elites in power in these three geographical centers of global wealth and technological innovation. Such a nongovernmental initiative can be currently understood as a complement to the managerial geopolitics of Henry Kissinger, which, by its stress on a so-called structure of peace,[92] conceivably imperils the structure of wealth constituted by the capitalist sector of the highly industrialized portion of the world. The Trilateral Commission can be conceived, I think, as a geoeconomic search for a managerial formula that will keep this concentration of wealth intact, given its nonterritorial character, and in light of the multiple challenges to it from Arab oil interests, the Third World, the communist bloc, and economic nationalism in a variety of forms. In a sense, the original vista of the Trilateral Commission can be understood as the ideological perspective representing the transnational outlook of the multinational corporation.

This initiative deserves note, furthermore, because the emphasis on devising transnational solutions and on consensus-building among elites is responsive to the nonterritorial dimensions of the crisis in the state system. The Trilateral Commission is an important initiative because it is constituted in such a way as to possess structural leverage: It has a formidable transition capability through its influence upon the most powerful governing elites and upon media presentation of public policy issues. But its reformist goals are not concerned with globalist solutions based on the interplay of peace and justice considerations. The Chinese sometimes speak of a world divided into predators and prey. Option C represents the initiatives of the predators. Put less ideologically, the Trilateral Commission embodies a strategy of transition that does not emphasize empathy and equity, much less equality, and hence has to rely on patterns of dominance, repression, and violence, administered if possible by territorial governments to provide police protection wherever capitalist interests are locally threatened, but does not tie the definition of interests to any particular territorial domain.

The actual value orientation of the multinational corporate elite as embodied in the Trilateral Commission is difficult to discern, since the commission is reluctant to be very explicit about its overall interpretation of international developments. As matters now stand, it seems complementary to and closely aligned with Option B orientations, but more transnational and less governmental (or static) in perspective orientation. Class affinities are somewhat cross-cultural and transnational, and there is less emphasis upon the distinctive interests of one particular state in the system or of the well-being of its domestic population. The Trilateral Commission also tentatively takes an implicit stand against socialism as a mode of economic organization and as a strategy for carrying humanistic ethics into the real world. The geopolitical management schemes of Option B tend to be agnostic on these questions so long as capitalist modes of organization can be sustained and are enabled to penetrate profitably most other economies. Indeed, domestic political constraints on foreign economic policy should make the welfare of the national population of constituent states much more central to a great power geopolitical solution than to a transnational geoeconomic solution. At the same time, since the formal apparatus of government has been dominated by those who seek to reconcile Options B and C, there is less real tension between the two perspectives than an analysis of the diverse perspectives would lead one to expect.

The main work of the Trilateral Commission has consisted of widely publicized meetings and the dissemination of a series of occasional papers, "Triangle Papers," on broad issues of international policy such as money and energy.[93] These analyses of current issues, stressing items on the international economic agenda, have advocated generally moderate solutions to current problems and have avoided any reliance on neo-Darwinian tactics. Thus despite its socioeconomic class affinities, the Trilateral Commission has, by and large, encouraged a relatively enlightened variant of Option C; it may indeed be partly regarded as an effort to persuade its transnational economic constituency to reject harsher, more selfish strategies for the protection of its various interests.

There is also a genuine globalism present here, well captured by the prominent banker Walter Wriston: "Whether we like it or not, mankind now has a completely integrated, international financial and informational marketplace capable of moving money and ideas to any place on this planet in minutes."[94] To avoid being "irrelevant," the central guidance underpinnings of the contemporary situation must provide the framework for self-interested behavior. As Wriston notes, it has nothing to do with idealism or preference; central guidance embodies the latest technologies harnessed to the spirit of secular (economic and political) expansionism.

George Ball put the positive case for this transnational economic approach to world order in a form that corresponds closely to the central theme of this article: "The multinational corporation not only promises the most efficient use of world resources, but as an institution, it poses the greatest challenge to the power of a nation-state since the temporal position of the Roman Church began to decline in the 15th century."[95] Richard Barnet and Ronald Mueller initiate their book-length inquiry with a related and striking assertion: "[T]he men who run the global corporation are the first in history with the organization, technology, money, and ideology to make a credible try at managing the world as an integrated unit."[96] I do not want to imply that David Rockefeller may be best understood as having aspired to be the new Pope Innocent X, but I do believe that there is a new ideology of geoeconomics that is a secular vision of *Unam Sanctam*. By this I mean only that the transnational ideology of the multinational corporate elite seeks to subordinate territorial politics to nonterritorial economic goals, just as the papacy in *Unam Sanctam* sought to place the spiritual sword of the Church above the secular sword of national kings.

What does this new *Unam Sanctam* offer? It offers efficiency in resource use, maximum economic development, and a dampening of international political conflict. IBM proclaims from a Manhattan skyscraper "world peace through world trade." The corporate boardrooms of the multinational corporation tend to have maps with no political boundaries. In its outlook, and even in its management, the multinational corporation is becoming cosmopolitan; the ideological fervor of the cold war has been replaced by ideological indifference. The world order solution promised by "the cosmocorp" has been described as "the businessman's peace." Or, as a recent article put it: "Alexei Kosygin has a friend at Chase Manhattan . . . and his name is David Rockefeller."[97]

What is wrong? Is it not a viable, indeed the only viable, way of promoting transition to a post-statist system of world order? Unfortunately, most of the criticisms directed at Option B proposals apply here. Option C is a creature of economic inequality and needs a militarist and coercive support structure itself in the face of popular discontent. It is not accidental that International Telephone and Telegraph (ITT) tried to organize illegal interventionary efforts to thwart Allende's ascent to power in Chile, or that multinational corporations find the militarism of regimes in Brazil and even Peru congenial to their interests. Of course, clumsy efforts at business-sponsored intervention are deplored—most of all, I suspect, by the Trilateral Commissioners themselves. They can hardly help but realize that such a fiasco is discrediting, just as counterinsurgency enthusiasts must have been appalled by the Bay of Pigs fiasco. Even ITT has acknowledged its clumsy pursuit of interests by hiring a former State Department official, Samuel de Palma, as its de facto secretary of state, though thinly disguised by a job description that called him adviser to the president for international policy. It's a bit like the CIA cleaning house after the Bay of Pigs: The counterrevolutionary policy is not renounced; only its pursuit by ineffectual and discredited means are abandoned.

To thrive in a Third World setting, the multinational corporation generally prefers a repressive, exploitative governmental structure. If this kind of national economic setting does not exist, then the corporation's well-being may require diplomatic protection, whether it be of the crude sort or of the more sophisticated sort that resulted after Allende was in power. In other words, the multinational corporate solution is viable only in conjunction with the support of powerful governments that possess strong military capabilities. Multinational corporations appear to depend on the state system even as they act as agents of its transformation. Furthermore, the Trilateral Commission perspective has proved as blind to ecological hazard and human misery as that of the geopoliticians. Perhaps to a greater degree even than national governments because of its class character, the Trilateral Commission is likely to be oblivious to the need for humanizing policies even if carried out at a national level.

Therefore, the outlook of the Trilateral Commission seems unacceptable, despite its effort to mobilize a transnational nonterritorial consensus on world order issues. It remains hegemonial in the extreme; as a result, it cannot cope with either the social question (the alleviation of misery), the political question (the elimination of repression), or the ecological question (the defense of the planet and its resources). It is therefore unlikely even to keep its promise to deal with the military question (the avoidance of large-scale warfare), and, indeed, in the late 1970s it increasingly shifted its emphasis to security concerns, especially in lending its prestige and influence to rearmament efforts within the frame of Western alliance politics. Option C, in this instance, has proved subordinate to the mandates of Option B, no doubt reflecting the continuing primacy of statism and geopolitics in the world system, despite the rise of nonterritorially oriented economic actors.

What general principles can we derive from these responses to the crisis in the state system? First, it is impossible to contribute to the process of changing consciousness for a new world order without a credible strategy of transition. Second, a credible strategy of transition is not necessarily to be applauded if it seeks to sustain or solidify existing structures of exploitation and dominance; such initiatives are illustrative of an effective approach but are not conducive to achieving a desirable outcome. It follows from this interpretation that the Clark-Sohn proposals will be ignored, whereas the work of the Trilateral Commission and geopolitical management schemes may achieve practical political relevance.

On this basis, we can proceed to a more positive statement of the problem of the relevance of international law to system change. It is important to proceed on a *transnational basis*, to seek *structural relevance* for a set of *reformist goals* that emphasize peace, the elimination of poverty, the promotion of social and political justice, and the achievement of ecological balance (i.e., both conservation of resources and enhancement of environmental quality). How can international lawyers and international law contribute to such an enterprise? In my view, international law and lawyers can play a positive role in three major respects: first, by discerning trends toward a new system of global order implicit in various lawmaking contexts; second, by evaluating these trends from a transnational perspective that is oriented around the four value positions enumerated above; and, third, by actually using these insights and evaluations in the lawmaking contexts of world policy, of which by far the most important continues to be that of state practice.

OPTION D

The most difficult task is that of specifying "dangerous knowledge" in the special sense of providing a problem-solving paradigm that is a genuine alternative to central guidance Options A, B, and C. Myres McDougal and his numerous colleagues spread around the globe provide a vector for those in search of the grail of dangerous knowledge.[98] McDougal's enterprise, to create a world public order based on the values of human dignity, is a radical vision of normative potential that is, at once, a challenge to Machiavellianism and utopianism. It is universal in scope: The framework of inquiry is nonhierarchical and does not necessarily depend on the persistence of the state system. It is process-oriented in relation to the future; that is, the future can be beneficially shaped by promoting preferred values in all critical arenas, starting now. It is oriented toward the well-being of the species as a whole, and is thus naturally receptive to both an ecological perspective and a futurist concern with ensuring the life-chances of subsequent generations.

Because we are in the historical mainstream, it is thus far unclear as to whether we should regard McDougal (and collaborators) as the immediate precursors of a new world order system, in the way that we view Grotius today, or whether we should take their role to be a more antecedent one comparable to that of, say, Vitoria or Suarez.[99] Such an assessment will have to wait upon the passage of time and events. It is impossible to tell whether some set of elaborate international negotiations in the area of, say, ocean rights and duties, arms policy, or resource regimes will be viewed from the perspective of the future as a decisive normative benchmark, as our Westphalia,[100] or whether the efforts to strike world order bargains among governments in this period will be seen instead as antecedent events in the sense that Augsburg was antecedent to Westphalia.[101] And, of course, we do not yet know whether the McDougal jurisprudence will directly underlie the paradigm that eventually prevails in this emergent era of nonterritorial central guidance. There is even a danger, to which we must admit, that the highly abstract formulations of the McDougal jurisprudence could be stretched by unscrupulous policymakers to indicate geopolitical schemes of the Option B variety. Despite this vulnerability, its humanistic animus is both genuine and directly responsive to the objective realities of the misery that afflicts most of the human race.

The McDougal breakthrough in reformulating on a global level the relevance of law to human affairs is surely "dangerous knowledge." It threatens the prevailing paradigm, and hence draws fire from certain kinds of professionals who continue to believe in the Westphalia paradigm.[102] McDougal himself is an almost ideal purveyor of dangerous knowledge, with his uncanny mix of inconsistent qualities that are essential for discharging such a role. First of all, he has the strength and largeness of personality to build a following that is broader than normal partisan lines. Second, the message is helpfully disguised by the medium; the obscurity and abstractness of formulation actually require someone either to learn the new paradigm as a whole or to ignore the entire effort.[103] And, finally, McDougal's politically conservative views on current issues[104] disguise his real message and permit the subversive reorientation of thinking to gain access to policymaking at high levels without being detected as such.[105] Thus the message has to do with a processive, value-oriented approach to norms that are appraised by reference to global criteria. These criteria are directly at variance with the national interest–oriented, Machiavellian calculus that arises out of the statist paradigm as codified by international lawyers, especially since the mid-eighteenth century, when Vattel's treatise was published.[106] Now, it is true that McDougal's work is transitional, deriving substance from the state system as well as moving beyond it. McDougal is no utopian. On the contrary, his writing always shows a lively sense of realism as well as an understanding of the connection between his appraisals of normative potential and the dominance of states and their rival aspirations.[107]

To deal with the present global situation from a legal perspective, it would be helpful to develop further the McDougal framework in several directions.[108] These developments are implicit in present formulations and applications of the framework, but it is now the time to make them more explicit. The domain of ambiguity must be restricted as we move deeper into the 1980s, because we are confronted, as I have suggested, by a set of relatively discrete competing world order options. The issue of choice and recommendation is becoming paramount. The advocates of Options B and C, the geopolitical minimalists and the geoeconomic maximalists, have ensured power, wealth, prestige, and access to the media. Do advocates of Option D have any offsetting capabilities? I believe they have a superior understanding of the historical situation and an authenticity that is safeguarded by their powerlessness; their line of recommendation appears to have the best insight into the well-being of the human species, and the viability of the planet is also a potential source of political and moral strength. Option D proponents are beginning to become participants in the emerging debate on global reform.[109]

As matters now stand, McDougal's approach to global reform does not relate itself specifically to this context of critical choice. Let me be more specific with reference to several issues:

Values. McDougal's values are not currently specified in relation to any of the outstanding problems of mankind such as poverty, population pressure, violence, and ecological decay. As a result, elitist perspectives can employ his terminology to disguise their indifference to a public order of human dignity. The values informing a new paradigm for international legal studies will have to be placed in direct relation to the agenda of concrete problems facing the human community.

Governments. McDougal tends to associate the representations of non-communist governments with the well-being of the peoples of the world. Such an identification overlooks oppressive patterns of governance that are firmly entrenched in many parts of the world. Even democratic governments treat their own citizens as antagonists when it comes to national security policy, perhaps the most crucial issue of political choice. Therefore, it seems necessary to draw a sharp distinction between the well-being of governments and the well-being of peoples or their countries.[110] This distinction must be drawn vis-à-vis values specified in terms of problems (or social goals).[111]

Central Guidance. McDougal is nowhere explicit about the historical pressures toward nonterritorial global integration and the principal ordering options that can be derived therefrom. It is of critical importance for the new framework to pose these choices and to endorse the image of central guidance that corresponds most closely with the performance criteria set forth. Of course, it should be understood that just as Westphalia did not identify precisely the time at which the state system originated, so any emergent central guidance system will evolve in unexpected directions and goals, embodying the seeds of one or more further paradigms within itself.

Transition Strategy. Because of its noncommittal approach to the policy content of world order values and to the shape of the future world order system, McDougal's orientation never describes any path of transition from the present late phases of the state system to the emergent form of central guidance most likely to realize preferred values.

The World Order Models Project (WOMP) can be understood as a complementary attempt to adapt McDougal orientation toward world order to the specific circumstances of a global reform movement. It was organized in 1967 by Saul Mendlovitz under the auspices of the Institute for World Order (now the World Policy Institute), and consists of eight regional groupings of scholars—the Soviet Union, Africa, India, Japan, Latin America, Western Europe, the United States—and a self-consciously nonterritorial transnational perspective.[112] Following meetings among the directors over the past five years, most of the participating groups in WOMP have produced their own book depicting proposals for global reform by the end of the century.[113] There has been no effort to achieve a consensus, except to agree on a shared normative orientation. The research directors have agreed to regard this orientation as generating a common set of goals for global reform. These goals have been specified as minimization of violence, maximization of social and economic well-being, maximization of social and political justice, and maximization of ecological balance. There is also agreement on the need to make proposals that are desirable and attainable, and to indicate the contours, at least, of a world order solution to the problems of the present system. Despite this shared outlook there is a considerable diversity, and even disagreement, as to the relative weighting of values, preference models, and transition tactics and strategies.[114]

In my contribution to the WOMP series, *A Study of Future Worlds*, I develop a framework (summarized in Figures 38.1 and 38.2) with respect to the realization of a preferred form of central guidance. The change of world order systems comes about as a consequence of a three-stage transition process.[115] To simplify matters, the analysis assumes that the primary concern of the present state (t_1) is consciousness-raising, by which is meant the beginnings of a consensus as to world order challenges and an acceptance of a value orientation implied by Option D. In the $+S_2$ world—that is, a system in which the four value criteria are substantially realized—the patterns of central guidance are organized around four corresponding functional areas. These functional systems are linked with technical organs of coordination and political organs of oversight. The political organs have tripartite representation: peoples, nongovernmental organizations, and governments. The constitutional structure sacrifices efficiency to achieve widely based participation and inhibits abuse of concentrated power. Intermediate types of central guidance—that is, those that involve a net increase in the capacity for global administration but not necessarily a net increase in bureaucratic presence vis-à-vis human existence at most levels of social organization—are treated as the most plausible options. Option D embodies countervailing organizational tendencies: (1) centralization of functional control and planning to enable equitable allocation of scarce resources, and (2) decentralization of political structures combined with localization of loyalty and identity patterns. On the level of bureaucratic presence and loyalty attachments there is envisioned by the end of t_3 an outward mutation in the direction of central guidance and an inward mutation in the direction of localism, subnational autonomy, and participatory relevance.

As an acronym WOMP is, admittedly, not too promising. Nevertheless, this ongoing project is helping to prepare the intellectual terrain and political climate: For the first time a nonaffiliated group of scholars has coordinated on a worldwide basis an inquiry into the prospects for global reform in this century. It is no more than a first step in the consciousness-raising process that must occur, but I believe it is a notable step because it treats the subject matter of global reform as the new essence of practical politics.

Of course, skeptics abound. What difference can such an initiative make in a world ruled by petropolitics and missile postures? There is a Zen saying: "If I raise my little finger I alter the course of the stars." The point is not that the pebble causes a ripple, but that we do not begin to grasp the causal chains that eventuate in specific forms of social change. In these circumstances, it at least makes sense to raise one's little finger, especially when adversaries are raising their hands and stamping their feet. It is also only sensible to be tentative about expectations for the future, and to revise assessments as events unfold. We must constantly improve the map that guides our journey into the future. Much of the literature of global reform has been marred by the prevalence of congealed legalism. Legalism is at variance with the dynamic, process-oriented approach that is required by a context of transition.

CONCLUSION

Although analytic purposes may require us to distinguish as sharply as possible among the principal central guidance options, certain dangers do arise from such artificial separation. The options described here are ideal types; in actuality we are dealing with human beings whose interests, values, roles, and consciousnesses may overlap the boundaries set by the options as depicted. The overall context of concern about the future will lead adherents of one option to react to and learn from adherents of competing options, whether by reading each other's books or by borrowing each other's rhetoric and perspectives. Indeed, Option D, as "the enemy on the left," so to speak, may exert its initial behavioral impact indirectly, via assimilation and co-option by the principal exponents of Options B and C. To illustrate, it seems clear that the importance of Norman Thomas's Socialist party during the mid-1930s should be gauged not by its unimpressive results at the election polls, but by the extent to which its thinking influenced the New Deal programs of the mainstream Democratic party. Similarly, if a populist movement for global reform of any magnitude gets started in key countries such as Japan, France, Germany, India, and the United States, and within the ranks of the Soviet and Chinese Communist parties, then it is likely to reshape the way in which governments and multinationals go about fostering their objectives in the transition interval. Thus Options B and C would most likely be skewed in the direction of D even if D itself is never acknowledged.

The linkages between Options B and C are also of critical importance in the years ahead. One question is whether the proponents of Option C will be able to strike a mutually acceptable bargain with the managerial elite of leading socialist societies, thereby establishing an economic ethos that is global and nonideological in character. Another question is whether the interests of Option C can be safeguarded if they run seriously counter to statist demands, especially if populist pressures intensify in key countries. In essence, this concern involves the degree to which the multinational business elite can pass upon, or at least exercise a veto over, candidates for high governmental office. As the years go by, it will become clearer whether the multinational elites are the servants or the masters of the governmental elites—whether Option C crowds out B, or vice versa. Put differently, will the multinational elite be able to call upon the governmental system to enforce its economic claims and to discourage or shatter overseas political resistance? Or will the governmental system evolve a regulatory approach that superimposes nationalist or populist values upon the profit and productivity ethos of corporate operations?

At present, an alarming convergence of motives is developing between those who adhere to Options B and C. Most governments and virtually all multinationals are threatened by ambiguity and pluralism; their distinct interests prosper through patterns of firm control. So long as a government welcomes business operations according to the profits and productivity rationale, it matters little whether a political ideology drawn from the left or right prevails. Therefore, it is easy for corporate elites increasingly to perceive themselves as apolitical, as well as anational and amoral. It is not surprising that capitalist tycoons return from China filled with enthusiasm, after witnessing order and regimentation on a grand scale. For both global businessmen and managers of government bureaucracies, reliability and predictability are the prime requirements for successful operations; dissension, opposition, and ambiguity are characteristics that can wreck things. Therefore, the populist bias of Option D is antagonistic to the basic drift of Options B and C, at least given the distribution of present value orientations and relation of forces. Such antagonisms could become affinities if the political context were to change in relevant ways—for example, if a world depression or prolonged ecological challenge were to shift the basic political-economic orientation from satisfying the wants of a relative few to meeting the needs of the many. Such a shift is the humanist alternative to a neo-Darwinian response, as we begin to face worldwide shortages of both renewable and nonrenewable resources.

IV

Earlier sections imply an emerging new paradigm of international legal studies. Its contours consist of five elements: (1) a framework of inquiry that is global, explicitly normative, futurist, and systematic; (2) an orientation toward inequity that is shaped by an appreciation of the transitional character of the international system;[116] (3) a recognition that the outcome of transition will be the emergence of a system of nonterritorial central guidance; (4) an understanding that the actual shape of the emergent nonterritorial central guidance system will be conditioned by the interplay of statist, business, and populist social forces; (5) a consensus that the most beneficial of the plausible central guidance options will reflect the priority of populist claims for peace, economic equity, social and political dignity, and ecological balance.

I believe that a jurist who is alert to these five elements will be able to acquire a far more relevant understanding of specific legal controversies than he or she could from the perspective of the older statist paradigm.

For vocational purposes it remains desirable to equip students to operate within the statist paradigm, which remains dominant in most sectors of power, wealth, and prestige. From an educational perspective, however, what is now needed is an approach to international legal studies that is anchored in the statist paradigm, but with one eye cocked on an emergent world order paradigm.

Consider, for instance, the various tides of fervent advocacy among international lawyers generated by the question "Should the United States ratify the Genocide Convention?" It is possible to oppose Senate ratification of the convention because it amounts, as some have phrased it, to "a pious fraud"; the guilty governments are willing to ritualize the condemnation of genocide precisely because they are confident that it will never be enforced against them. At the same time, right-wing agitators are stirred to fury by the prospect of Senate ratification. A group called Liberty Lobby warns that the Genocide Convention is being "pushed by aliens to help destroy our American culture and serve the devious ends of hostile forces carefully planted in our midst!"[117]

On the other side, the proponents of ratification, including Senator Proxmire and a group of Yale Law School faculty members, argue that "[r]ejection of the Convention will diminish United States capacity to influence others to comply with human rights laws and is likely to weaken the international protection of human rights."[118] But is the United States government really committed to the promotion of human rights? If so, why has it trained and supported some of the most repressive police forces in the world? Why has it not responded to the documented accounts of genocide in Burundi?[119] Why does it overlook its own direct responsibility for the torture of political opponents even in societies, such as South Korea or El Salvador, where there is considerable American leverage over official policy?[120]

Oddly enough, all parties to the dispute over ratification have a pretty strong position. It is true that the claims of the Genocide Convention are pious frauds, given the realities of genocide. But it is also true that the claim to hold government officials, including our own, criminally accountable for systematic repression of distinct ethnic groups represents a drastic claim against the state system. This claim is especially drastic given the persistence of widespread hard-core genocidal activity and the pervasiveness of official patterns and practices, including those of leading governments, that strike some foreign and domestic observers as "genocidal."

It is true that failure to ratify would weaken the credibility of U.S. objections to human rights violations elsewhere in world society. However, it is also true that, given the inconsistent U.S. record on human rights issues, ratification would heighten international cynicism about the status of international law. Interpreting this ratification debate in world order terms, we see a tug of war between statism and central guidance, as well as an anticipatory struggle of sorts among contending central guidance options. For instance, those who accept Option D and are firmly entrenched in central guidance thinking would be most likely to find it useful to point an accusing finger at their own government. In that sense they, like the Liberty Lobby, perceive the Genocide Convention as "subversive," but unlike their reactionary colleagues, world order populists welcome such subversion as beneficial.

This point may be clarified by the example of the Nuremberg trials. There are those who speak of "the fallacy of Nuremberg,"[121] by which they mean that because the Nuremberg decisions are incompatible with statism, they will not be respected. However, these spokesmen overlook the second-order effects of the Nuremberg precedent. These second-order effects involve reinforcing a populist and cosmopolitan conscience in matters of war and peace, a conscience made manifest, for instance, in "crimes" of resistance carried out by Americans during the Vietnam War. Daniel Ellsberg is a prime example of a person who was actually influenced by the Nuremberg Obligation to take steps that he perceived at the time to be possibly illegal under domestic law. In other words, he decided to implement his understanding of the Nuremberg Obligation to act in opposition to crimes of war, even when such action was in violation of domestic law.[122]

This form of analysis of international law issues can be generalized. If we are concerned with the relevance of the paradigm shift under way, then there is a variety of subject matter ripe for illuminating analysis. For example, we might explore subject matter in which lines of significant interdependence transcend the boundaries of national jurisdiction, such as the regulation of multinational business or of international terrorism; the assessment of liability for environmental damage, as a result either of spatial diffusion or of territorial and oceanic interaction; the regulation of global monetary policy, of commodity pricing policy, or resource policy. International issues that involve dangerous forms of scarcity, including protection of endangered species of the Great Whale, allocation of rights to fish on the high seas, protection of land, sea, and air against environmental decay, and world population policy (Is it or can it be any longer allowed to be a matter of exclusive sovereign rights to permit a doubling or tripling of population, despite the impacts on neighbors, world resource supplies, and prices, and on the quality of the global environment?) are also appropriate focuses.

World food policy also needs to be studied from this outlook. For example, is it a matter of sovereign prerogative to leave cropland idle or underdeveloped when aggregate world food shortages are producing large-scale famine? Similarly, we might more closely examine matters in which nonterritorial actors are playing increasingly significant roles—for example, the role of multinational corporations, of international financial institutions, of world social and political movements, of humanitarian initiatives like Amnesty International or the International Committee of the Red Cross, of movements for global reform like the Trilateral Commission, the Club of Rome, or the World Order Models Project. Finally, we might look at areas in which legitimacy and loyalty are shifting away from the territorial focus characteristic of the state system.[123]

In my judgment, it is important to appreciate that loyalty and legitimacy are shifting away from the state in two directions simultaneously: toward the center of the globe and toward the local realities of community and sentiment. The role of the individual in war/peace and human rights settings is expanding, as is the role of subnational movements for self-determination. The significance of religious and political movements with cosmopolitan identifications is rapidly increasing.[124] At a minimum, international lawyers should study the transition context and appraise it by reference to the normative criteria associated with various central guidance options. Even more desirable would be an appraisal of legal developments from a WOMP or global populist perspective, an appraisal that would be alert to the desirability of strengthening the prospects for an Option D solution to the world order problems of our era.

We are ineluctably moving toward a new world order system based upon an augmented capacity for central guidance and an increased role for nonterritorial actors. The value predispositions of these actors are not predetermined. Nevertheless, the evidence seems to support a pessimistic view of the capacity of these actors either to sustain minimum conditions of a tolerable world order or to achieve an arrangement that promotes human development and well-being for all the peoples of the world. The drift is toward some new kind of geopolitical and geoeconomic hegemony sustained by a neo-Darwinian ethos and implemented by persuasion where possible, coercion where necessary, and violence wherever indirect forms of coercion fail to produce stability.

International lawyers can take advantage of the fact that choice is still possible in the area of value orientation. They can help create an alternative vision of central guidance that is built around the values of human dignity and oriented toward the possibility of a planetary community joined together by contractual bonds rather than regimented by hegemonical bondage. At this stage in transition, the primary need is to interpret this unprecedented historical opportunity, as well as to expose the multiple jeopardies that also are present and likely to be aggravated if either Option B or C becomes substantially realized over the next several decades without prior shifts in the controlling ethos. International law will be a testing ground for the relative strength of social forces favoring Options B, C, and D; it is up to humanistically inclined international lawyers and others to improve the prospects for Option D.

Can it happen? Can Option D prevail over the forces arrayed against it (or, alternatively, can Option D reshape Options B and C)?

But if you ask me now what prospect it has of being realized, then I would admit: Very slight, if at all. And yet perhaps this may turn out to be the agenda of the next revolution.[125]

It is not a violent seizure of state power that is meant by *revolution*, but an upsurge of energy directed toward reshaping the priorities and perspectives that now dominate the political process. Our educational challenge is to enable the young to emerge as citizens with a global perspective sufficient to be receptive to such possibilities should a favorable climate develop.

NOTES

1. See Paul Vinogradoff, "Historical Types of International Law," *Bibliotheca Visseriana* 1 (1923), p. 8. See also James Brierly, "The Basis of Obligation in International Law," in Hersch Lauterpacht and C.M.H. Waldlock, eds., *The Basis of Obligation in International Law and Other Papers by the Late James Leslie Brierly* 1, 2 (Oxford, England: Clarendon Press, 1958): "There is a subtle interaction between theory and practice in politics, not always easy to trace because the actors themselves may easily be unconscious of their theoretical prepossessions which, nevertheless, powerfully influence their whole attitude towards practical affairs; and at no time has it been so important, as it is today, that we should see the facts of international life as they really are, and not as they come to us reflected in false or outworn theories."

2. Vinogradoff, *supra* note 1.

3. Stephen Graubard, *Kissinger: Portrait of a Mind* (New York: Norton, 1973), p. 10.

4. Henry Kissinger's main academic works dwell on this central theme, which is perhaps most fully and starkly depicted in his principal books on contemporary international relations. See Henry Kissinger, *The Necessity for Choice: Prospects of American Foreign Policy* (New York: Harper & Row, 1961); Kissinger, *Nuclear Weapons and Foreign Policy* (New York: Norton, 1969).

5. Joseph Strayer, *On the Medieval Origins of the Modern State* (Princeton, N.J.: Princeton University Press; 1970), p. 57.

6. In actuality there is a cluster of organizational options following from the adoption and implementation of an orientation toward global reform that is based on a specific set of ecological and ethical premises. See Richard Falk, *A Study of Future Worlds* (New York: Free Press, 1975).

7. Fouad Ajami specifies the contours of such a movement in a stimulating paper, *The Global Populists: Third-World Nations and World-Order Crises* (Princeton, N.J.: Princeton University Center of International Studies, Research Monograph No. 41, May 1974).

8. Rethinking the attachment of people to the state is one essential element in fashioning an adequate strategy of response to world order challenges. In this regard, see John Schaar, "Power and Purity," *American Review* 19 (1974), pp. 162–179; Schaar, "The Case for Patriotism," *American Review* 17 (1973), pp. 59–99.

9. See, for example, Barry Commoner, *The Closing Circle* (New York: Knopf, 1971); Paul Ehrlich, *The Population Bomb*, rev. ed. (Mattituck, N.Y.: American Reprints/Rivercity Press, 1975).

10. See John P. Lewis, "Oil, Other Scarcities and the Poor Countries," *World Politics* 27 (1974), pp. 63–86.

11. There are as many types of international law as there are distinct types of political reality. And, indeed, if states become less predominant in managing global relations, then we would expect a new legal order in which other actors played more significant actual and formal roles.

12. See Bert Röling, *International Law in an Expanded World* (Amsterdam: Djambatan, 1960). For fuller discussion of the legal traditions active in maintaining interstate order in other regions of the world, see Adda Bozeman, *The Future of Law in a Multicultural World* (Princeton, N.J.: Princeton University Press, 1971); F.S.C. Northrup, *The Taming of Nations* (Westport, Conn.: Greenwood Press, 1952).

13. It was Grotius, however, who set forth the normative foundations for a world of separate territorial sovereignties with distinct claims of autonomy, in a major

treatise on the relevance of law to war. See Hugo Grotius, *The Rights of War and Peace* (translated by A. Campbell, 1901). The essence of the modernist element in Grotius was his refusal to recognize a decisionmaker higher than the head of state, or an interpreter of legal obligation other than that head of state. Even though he believed that legal rules have an objective character, he regarded their application as dependent on subjective appreciation by juridically equal state leaders. For an analysis of thinkers who antedate Grotius such as Vitoria, Suarez, and Gentili, see Percy Corbett, *Law and Society in the Relations of States* (New York: Harcourt Brace, 1951), pp. 17–24; Arthur Nussbaum, *A Concise History of the Law of Nations*, rev. ed. (New York: Macmillan, 1954), pp. 79–101.

14. Thomas Kuhn, *The Structure of Scientific Revolutions*, 2d ed. (Chicago: University of Chicago Press, 1970), p. viii. Kuhn defines a paradigm as follows: "A paradigm is what the members of a scientific community share, *and*, conversely, a scientific community consists of men who share a paradigm" (*ibid.*, at 176). He distinguishes between two different senses in which the term "paradigm" is used: "On the one hand, it stands for the entire constellation of beliefs, values, techniques, and so on shared by the members of a given community. On the other, it denotes one sort of element in that constellation, the concrete puzzle-solutions which, employed as models or examples, can replace explicit rules as a basis for the solution of the remaining puzzles of normal science" (ibid., p. 175).

15. Ibid., p. 97. During a period in which a paradigm is securely established, the boundaries of what constitutes knowledge are firm. Claims to discovery or explanation beyond such boundaries are repudiated or ignored, and claimants are regarded as deviants. Indeed, when questions involving the broad issue "what is knowledge?" are posed and taken seriously, then it is a sign that a paradigm is loosening its hold on a given scientific community.

16. Ibid., p. viii.

17. Emmerich de Vattel, *The Law of Nations, or Principles of the Law of Nature, Applied to the Conduct and Affairs of Nations and Sovereigns* (translated by J. Chitty, 1855). Hedley Bull correctly notes that in this century there has been a resurgence of Grotian thinking and a relative decline in the stature of Vattelian thinking. Professor Bull laments this resurgence, as he associates it with an immoderate or revolutionary phase in international relations. See Hedley Bull, "The Grotian Conception of International Society," in Herbert Butterfield and Martin Wight, eds., *Diplomatic Investigations* (London: Allen & Unwin, 1966), pp. 51–73. I interpret this resurgence of Grotian thinking more favorably, as disclosing a growing juridical sentiment for the reform of international relations in the face of mounting evidence of the inability of the statist paradigm (especially in its purer Vattelian form) to meet the main concerns of humankind.

18. See, for example, George Kennan, *American Diplomacy 1900–1950* (Chicago: University of Chicago Press, 1970); Hans Morgenthau, *Dilemmas of Politics* (Chicago: University of Chicago Press, 1958); Hans Morgenthau, *In Defense of the National Interest* (New York: Knopf, 1951). For critical remarks about the influence of lawyers and legal background on the approach of U.S. policymakers to the foreign policy process, see Henry Kissinger, *American Foreign Policy: Three Essays* (New York: Norton, 1969), pp. 29–34. Kissinger notes, *inter alia*, that one consequence of what he calls "the Anglo-Saxon tradition" is that lawyers or legally trained individuals "prefer to deal with actual rather than hypothetical cases; they have little confidence in the possibility of stating a future issue abstractly" (ibid., p. 30).

19. See Louis Henkin's discussion of Dean Acheson's deprecation of the role of international law in geopolitical crises (in that instance, the Cuban Missile Crisis),

in Louis Henkin, *How Nations Behave* (New York: Praeger Publishers, 1968), pp. 265–266. On the general issue of law and its limits, see ibid., p. 251–271.

20. See Jean Gebser, "The Foundations of the Aperspective World," *Main Currents* 29 (1972), pp. 80, 81.

21. Alfred North Whitehead has a concise formulation for this point: "It is legitimate (as a practical counsel in a short life) to abstain from the criticism of scientific foundations so long as the superstructure 'works.' " Alfred North Whitehead, "Principle of Relativity," in Mason Gross and F.S.C. Northrup, eds., *Collected Works of Alfred North Whitehead* (New York: Macmillan, 1953), p. 300.

22. Strayer, *supra* note 5, at 10, dates the process of statist consolidation as between 1100 and 1600. But compare with Edmund Burke's contention that "the generality of people are fifty years, at least, behind in their politics": P. Stanlis, ed., *Edmund Burke: Selected Writings and Speeches* (Ann Arbor: University of Michigan Press, 1963), p. 107.

23. Kuhn, *supra* note 14, at 52–76.

24. Nussbaum, *supra* note 13, at 114, observes that Grotius's treatise was placed on the Index "with the mitigating though practically insignificant proviso 'donec corrigatur' (until amended)."

25. James Turner Johnson, *Ideology, Reason and the Limitation of War* (Princeton, N.J.: Princeton University Press, 1975).

26. M. Sutcliffe, *The Practice, Proceedings and Law of Armes* (1593).

27. W. Ames, *Conscience with the Power and Cases Thereof* (1643).

28. Johnson, *supra* note 25.

29. At the same time, a diversity of interpretations of the juridical situation is evidence that a paradigm shift is under way, and such a diversity, which generates confusion and controversy, is characteristic of a transition period.

30. The political realities of medieval times were complicated and dominated by the character of highly localized power arrangements. In this regard, notions of papal supremacy and spiritual unity were rhetorical more often than behavioral, and should not, in any event, be accepted uncritically.

31. Articles 18 and 19 of "Dictatus Papae Gregorii," translated in E. Lewis, *Medieval Political Ideas* (New York: Knopf, 1954), p. 381.

32. Strayer, *supra* note 5, p. 8 (especially note 2).

33. Ibid., p. 9.

34. S. Ehler and J. Morrall, eds., *Church and State Through the Centuries* (Westminster, Md.: Newman Press, 1954), p. 89.

35. Ibid., p. 90.

36. Ibid., pp. 91–92.

37. The dispute was part of the process that led to the temporary shift of the seat of the papacy to Avignon.

38. Nussbaum, *supra* note 13, pp. 112–114, 115. See also Grotius, *supra* note 13.

39. The principles of religious tolerance had already been anticipated in 1555 in the Peace of Augsburg. But this anticipation was on an intra-German, rather than at an international, level (ibid., p. 116).

40. *Church and State Through the Centuries, supra* note 34, at 196. (The entire text of the bull appears at 193–198.)

41. Ibid., p. 116.

42. "Culturally and economically the war had thrown Germany back more than a century. She had lost one-third of her population according to conservative estimates. To this the Peace added the irretrievable paralysis to the Empire's political might" (Nussbaum, *supra* note 13, p. 116).

43. This concern with the individual or group is an alien element in a purely statist conception of international society. It is like a dormant bacterium that waits for the organism to weaken before it mounts an attack. The natural rights feature is significant because it underscores the inalienable character of fundamental human rights, thereby ensuring their legal status independent of expressions of consent by governments. See note 56 *infra*.

44. This revolt, although triumphant in a politically conservative form, is one of the most significant elements of revolutionary energy present in the Protestant movement as a whole.

45. Myres McDougal, "The Ethics of Applying Systems of Authority: The Balanced Opposites of a Legal System," in Harold D. Lasswell and Harlan Cleveland, eds., *The Ethic of Power* (New York: Conference on Science, Philosophy, and Politics, 1962), pp. 221, 222.

46. *Major Peace Treaties of Modern History* vol. 1 (1967), p. 9 [hereinafter cited as *Major Peace Treaties*]. The entire Westphalia text appears at 7–49.

47. Nussbaum, *supra* note 13, p. 116. Even the language of the treaties is replete with feudal terminology; for instance, in the general amnesty provision, Article VI, we note references to "their Lordships, their fiefs, Underfiefs, Allocations" and to their "Dignities, Immunities, Rights, and Privileges" (*Major Peace Treaties*, vol. 1, *supra* note 46, p. 11). In confirming French royal sovereignty over towns in Alsatia and Sungtau, Article LXXVI refers to "all the Vassals, Subjects, Peoples, Towns, Boroughs, Castles . . ." (ibid., p. 31).

In the Westphalia Treaty there is an acknowledgment not only that national governments are the *main* participants in the new world order system, but also that such governments are not the *only* participants. This view contrasts to that of the late nineteenth and early twentieth centuries, a view that is itself now coming under some pressure. The view that governments of states are the only participants finds its way into some of the most influential earlier definitions of international law. See generally William Bishop, Jr., *International Law*, 2d ed. (Boston: Little, Brown, 1962), pp. 3–6. For a much wider appreciation of the participants in the world order, see Myres McDougal, Harold Lasswell, and Michael Reisman, "The World Constitutive Process of Authoritative Decision," *Journal of Legal Education* 19 (1967), pp. 253, 261–275. The Munster variant of Westphalia included a long list of feudal allies of both principal signatories—the Holy Roman Emperor and the King of France—many of whom achieved great international status even though they could not qualify as states.

48. Article CXXIII, *Major Peace Treaties*, vol. 1, *supra* note 46, p. 46.

49. Article CXXIII, ibid.

50. Article CXXIV, ibid., p. 47.

51. Ibid.

52. Jean Bodin's principal work, K. McRae, ed., *The Six Bookes of a Commonweale* (Cambridge, Mass.: Harvard University Press, 1962), originally appeared in France in 1579. On the evolution and nature of sovereignty in the state system, see Ernest Cassirer, *The Myth of the State* (New Haven: Yale University Press, 1946); Friederich Meinecke, *Machiavellism* (London: Routledge, 1957), translated by D. Scott; R. Sterling, *Ethics in a World of Power: The Political Ideas of Friedrich Meinecke* (Princeton, N.J.: Princeton University Press, 1958).

53. See note 17 *supra*.

54. See *Major Peace Treaties*, vol. 1, *supra* note 46, p. 118, which describes the major aspects of war.

55. Preamble to the Peace of Utrecht (ibid., p. 177): "The Welfare of a People so faithful, is to us a supreme Law, which ought to be preferred to any other Consideration. It is to this Law that We this day sacrifice the Right of a Grandson, who is so dear to us; and by the Price which the general Peace will cost our tender Love, we shall at least have the Comfort of shewing our Subjects, that even at the Expence of our Blood, they will always keep the first place in our Heart" (Renunciation of Spain to the Crown of France, Peace of Utrecht, ibid., p. 184).

56. By "natural law" I mean that jurisprudential tradition which derives the authority of law and its fundamental content from sources of objective authority independent of human will. Among the varieties of natural law are those that rest their claim upon revelation by God, the dictates of reason, or the character of nature itself. What these diverse schools of natural law have in common is the assertion of a criterion of legality that takes precedence over any assertion by a particular person or any interpretation of an historical situation. Natural law is often set off against legal positivism, in which principal stress is placed upon deriving the authority and content of law from the consent of the sovereign or the operations of formal lawmaking procedures. See A. D'Entreves, Natural Law, 2d ed. rev. (London: Hutchinson University Library, 1970).

Note that even at Utrecht the unity of Christendom remains an element in the settlement of conflict; parallel to this, the relationship between the Christian and non-Christian worlds becomes an increasingly critical ethical and legal issue.

57. See Major Peace Treaties, vol. 1, supra note 46, pp. 187–188. The Declaration of Philip, Duke of Orleans, expresses a similar sentiment: "[I]t was necessary to establish a kind of Equality and Equilibrium between the Princes who were in dispute [regarding the prospect of Hapsburg succession to the Spanish Crown]. . . . [T]his house itself, without the Union of the Empire, would become formidable, if it should add a new Power to its ancient Dominions; and consequently this Equilibrium, which is designed to be established for the good of the Princes and States of Europe, would cease. Now it is certain that without this Equilibrium, either the States suffer from the Weight of their own Greatness, or envy engages their Neighbors to make Alliances to attack them, and to reduce them to such a point, that the great Powers may inspire less Fear, and may not aspire to an universal Monarchy." Ibid., pp. 199–200. This statement resolves Spanish succession in an indisputable fashion, confirming the Spanish claimant and renouncing the prospect of the French claimant, Charles of France, who made a comparable statement: "It has been agreed . . . to establish an Equilibrium, and political Boundarys between the Kingdoms, whereof the Interests have been, and are still the sad occasion of a bloody Dispute; and to hold it for a fundamental Maxim, in order to preserve this Peace, that Provision ought to be made, that the Forces of these Kingdoms may not become formidable, nor be able to cause any Jealousy; which it has been thought, cannot be settled more solidly than by hindering them from extending themselves, and by keeping a certain Proportion; to the end that the weaker being united together may defend themselves against the more powerful, and support themselves respectively against their Equals" (ibid., pp. 195–196. The entire text of the Peace of Utrecht appears at 177–239.)

58. Ibid., pp. 187–188.

59. A. Nussbaum, supra note 13, p. 160, notes, "Among the legal learned Vattel has never met with much praise." Jeremy Bentham's famous summary of Vattelian reasoning is somewhat, but not entirely, unfair: "It is not just to do what is unjust." Nevertheless, Vattel's influence was without serious peer. Edwin Dickinson's study of the relative influence of continental international lawyers during the period from 1789 to 1820 is revealing:

	Citations in Pleadings	Court Citations	Court Quotations
Grotius	16	11	2
Pufendorf	9	4	8
Bynkershoek	25	16	2
Vattel	92	38	22

See Edwin Dickinson, "Changing Concepts and the Doctrine of Incorporation," *American Journal of International Law* 26 (1932), pp. 239, 259, n. 132, cited and commented on by Nussbaum, *supra* note 13, p. 162. See also the fuller depiction of Grotian ideas in Hersch Lauterpacht, "The Grotian Tradition in International Law," *British Yearbook of International Law*, Vol. 23 (1946), p. 1.

60. See Nussbaum, *supra* note 13, pp. 161–163.

61. Bull, *supra* note 17, p. 50. Bull refers to Hersch Lauterpacht, *International Law and Human Rights* (New York: Praeger Publishers, 1950), and to C. Wilfred Jenks, *The Common Law of Mankind* (New York: Praeger Publishers, 1958), as further evidence of the revival of Grotian thinking.

62. See, for example, Wolfgang Friedmann, *The Changing Structure of International Law* (New York: Columbia University Press, 1964); Jenks, *supra* note 61; Lauterpacht, *supra* note 61; Lauterpacht, *The Function of Law in the International Community* (Oxford: Clarendon Press, 1933).

63. These include the constitutional documents of international organizations, especially the Covenant of the League of Nations and the Charter of the United Nations; the Nuremberg Judgment and the later formulations of its conclusions in a document called the Nuremberg Principles; and the main developments in the international law of human rights. For the texts of the United Nations Charter and principal human rights developments, see Ian Brownlie, ed., *Basic Documents in International Law* (New York: Oxford University Press, 1972), 2d rev. ed., pp. 1–31, 144–232. For a convenient text of the Nuremberg Judgment and Principles, see Richard Falk, Gabriel Kolko, and Robert Jay Lifton, eds., *Crimes of War* (New York: Vintage, 1971), pp. 88–108.

64. The enthusiasm for central guidance in the period after World War I, and the subsequent disillusionment, is well-documented in Friedmann, *supra* note 62, pp. 275–276.

65. Friedmann provides a characteristic, if restrained, dismissal of central guidance when he concludes that its proponents "ignore the basic social factors of international society" (ibid., p. 276). In the slightly altered context of the basis for a universal system of international law, see the critique of this "make-believe" or "spurious universalism" in Myres McDougal and Harold Lasswell, "The Identification and Appraisal of Diverse Systems of Public Order," *American Journal of International Law* 53 (1959), p. 1.

66. I refer here to the extension of state sovereignty over ocean activity formerly regarded as part of the high seas and thus, by legal right, open to all on an equal basis. Given the need to replace the historic regime of "freedom," it could have been possible to allocate regulatory authority to the world community or regional subcommunities rather than to allocate the bulk of authority over the most valuable activities among coastal states. The efforts under United Nations auspices to evolve a new law of the seas started with an idealistic vision of the oceans as "the common heritage of mankind" and ended with an extension of sovereignty achieved mainly at the expense of an earlier domain of community prerogatives. See L. Alexander,

ed., *The Law of the Sea* (Proceedings of Annual Conferences of the Law of the Sea Institute, 1966–1973).

67. The ethical foundations of such a new paradigm are beginning to be developed. See Garrett Hardin, *Exploring New Ethics for Survival: The Voyage of the Spaceship Beagle* (New York: Viking, 1972); V. Potter, *Bioethics: Bridge to the Future* (Englewood Cliffs, N.J.: Prentice Hall, 1971).

68. For representative formulations of McDougal's approach, see Myres McDougal and Florentino P. Feliciano, *Law and Minimum World Public Order* (New Haven: Yale University Press, 1961); Eisuke Suzuki, "The New Haven School of International Law: An Invitation to a Policy-Oriented Jurisprudence," *Yale Studies in World Public Order*, Vol. 1 (1974), p. 1; Myres McDougal, "Jurisprudence for a Free Society," *Georgia Law Review* 1 (1966), p. 1. For assessment and analysis by a sympathetic scholar, see John Norton Moore, *Law and the Indo-China War* (Princeton, N.J.: Princeton University Press, 1972), pp. 47–76.

69. Barrington Moore, Jr., *Reflections on the Causes of Human Misery and upon Certain Proposals to Eliminate Them* (Boston: Beacon Press, 1972), p. 13.

70. Ibid.

71. Ibid.

72. See Gebser, *supra* note 20; see also Gebser, "The Integral Consciousness," *Main Currents* 30 (1973), pp. 107–108. Gebser's principal work, *Ursprung und Gegenwart* (2 vols., 1966), remains untranslated.

73. In Figure 38.1, "t" (transition) is the historical process of drift from the state system in the direction of some new globalist system of world order, whereas "T" (Transition) is the study of explicit ideas about facilitating the realization of a given program for global reform.

74. Richard Falk, *This Endangered Planet: Prospects and Proposals for Human Survival* (New York: Random House, 1971), pp. 215–245, develops such a position. See also Falk, *supra* note 6, pp. 277–439.

75. Steven Borsody, "Letter to the Editor," *New York Times*, July 28, 1973, p. 22, col. 5; for a full and eloquent defense of balance-of-power thinking, as adapted to an ideological interpretation of global conflict, see Eugene V. Rostow, *Peace in the Balance* (New York: Simon & Schuster, 1972). Even idealistic thinkers lend their authority to the attitudes Borsody expressed. See, for example, Wolfgang Friedmann, *Introduction to World Politics*, 5th ed. (New York: St. Martins Press, 1965).

76. For perceptive critiques of reformist thinking from the perspective of the statist paradigm, see F. H. Hinsley, *Power and the Pursuit of Peace* (Cambridge: Cambridge University Press, 1963); Walter Schiffer, *The Legal Community of Mankind* (Westport, Conn.: Greenwood Press, 1954). For an advocacy of world government as the sole alternative to the anarchy and warfare of the state system, see Arthur Holcombe, *A Strategy of Peace in a Changing World* (Cambridge: Harvard University Press, 1967); Emery Reves, *The Anatomy of Peace* (New York: Harper & Row, 1946).

77. For example, the Clark-Sohn model must be understood as an American fantasy to be perceived, at most, as a particular cultural hypothesis about global reform that must be related to parallel fantasies drawn from the utopias depicted in other world cultures. See Grenville Clark and Louis B. Sohn, *World Peace Through World Law*, 3d ed. (Cambridge: Harvard University Press, 1968). See also D. Plath, ed., *Aware of Utopia* (Urbana, Ill.: University of Illinois Press, 1971); C. Negley and J. Patrick, eds., *The Quest for Utopia* (New York: Schuman, 1952); George Kateb, ed., *Utopia* (New York: Lieber-Atherton, 1971). It is notable that even Aristotle in *The Politics* proposed the study of ideal states as well as real ones. Aristotle, *The Politics*, translated by B. Jowett (New York: Penguin, 1943), pp. 80–107.

78. For a scenario based on postcatastrophe global reform, see McGeorge Bundy, "After the Deluge, the Covenant," *Saturday Review*, August 24, 1974, p. 14. André Webre and Paul Liss, *The Age of Cataclysm* (New York: Putnam, 1974), pp. 153–197, examine the general case for imminent catastrophe as politically regenerative, but base the prospect for a new world order system on their anticipation of natural (rather than man-made) catastrophe.

79. The 1948, 1956, 1967, and 1973 "wars" in the Middle East can be regarded as phases in a continuous war to resolve the status and domain of Israel; the Indo-Pakistan War of 1971 seems an exception to the proposition in the text because it ended in an all-out Indian victory. But it was not a major war in the geopolitical sense, because the nuclear superpowers were not arrayed in a serious way on opposing sides. Moreover, the main stake of the conflict was to encourage a secessionist effort within Pakistan.

80. See Clark and Sohn, *supra* note 77; for a recent perspective on proposals by Sohn, see Clark and Sohn, eds., *Introduction to World Peace Through World Law* (New York: Seabury, 1973).

81. For an overall critique of legalist thinking about drastic global reform of which the Clark-Sohn proposals are an example, see Schiffer, *supra* note 76; see also Schiffer, *A Critical Analysis of the Modern Concept of World Organization* (Westport, Conn.: Greenwood Press, 1954). For specific critical comments on the Clark-Sohn proposals along these lines, see McDougal and Feliciano, *supra* note 68, pp. 369–370, 374.

82. Legalists tend to overestimate reason and rationality in human affairs, as well as the potency of men of good will. As a result, they maintain a naive conception of power that fails to cope with the problem of evil and with irrationality, passion, and vested beliefs. In this regard, the Clark-Sohn proposals, as expectations rather than as statements of preference, seem almost totally apolitical or, what is worse, even antipolitical. Such a posture on politics for putative reformers constitutes a serious flaw. Nietzsche has delivered the message against the voice of reason in its clearest form; among modern writers who stress the ascendancy of evil in social and political realms are Thomas Mann, Harold Pinter, and William Irwin Thompson.

83. There can be projected a wide array of plausible Option B schemes, some more overtly imperial (concentrating managerial authority in two or more centers of state power), others more informal and dispersed (as with regular administration of global economic policy by governments of leading industrial governments).

84. This allegation is not refuted by references to speeches by Kissinger in which a sensitivity to these issues has been expressed. Rhetorical postures do not entail behavioral positions, but may operate as substitutes for them. I believe that the Kissinger conception of world order, to the extent it has been embodied in policy, has not been responsive to the issues mentioned in this text.

85. Specific reinforcement of this charge is made in a careful recent assessment of this aspect of Kissinger's foreign policy: David Binder, "The Pragmatism of Nixon's Foreign Policy," *New York Times*, Jan. 15, 1974, p. 6, col. 3.

86. See, for example, Rostow, *supra* note 75.

87. See, for example, Richard Nixon, "Remarks to Midwestern News Media Executives," Kansas City, Mo. (July 6, 1971), in *Public Papers of the Presidents of the United States, 1971* (Washington, D.C.: Government Printing Office [1972]), at pp. 802–813.

88. D. Rockefeller, quoted in *Prospectus of the Trilateral Commission* (1973). The Trilateral Commission is described in the subtitle of the *Prospectus* as "A Private American-European-Japanese Initiative on Matters of Common Concern." For wide-

ranging critical assessment, see Holly Sklar, ed., *Trilateralism: The Trilateral Commission and Elite Planning for World Management* (Boston: South End Press, 1980).

89. The membership of the Trilateral Commission is listed in the *Prospectus, supra* note 88.

90. *Trialogue*, Vol. 2 (Nov. 1973), p. 5.

91. See, for example, D. Meadows, J. Randers, and W. Behrens, *The Limits to Growth: A Report for the Club of Rome's Project on the Predicament of Mankind* (Washington, D.C.: Potomac Associates, 1972); M. Mesarovic and E. Pestel, *Mankind at the Turning Point* (New York: E. P. Dutton, 1974).

92. For perhaps the most authoritative statement of the character of "the structure of peace," the cornerstone of the Kissinger foreign policy, see Richard Nixon, *Annual Report on Foreign Policy*, H.R. Doc. No. 96, 93d Cong., 1st Sess. (1973), pp. 2–13.

93. The first cluster of Triangle Papers has been collected in a volume of *Trilateral Commission of Task Force Reports: 1–7* (New York: New York University Press, 1977).

94. Quotation taken from Karin Lissakers, "World Loan Responsibility," *New York Times*, July 7, 1982, p. D2.

95. Quoted in House Committee on Foreign Affairs, 93d Cong., 2d Sess., Report of Official Visit to Congress by a Delegation of the European Parliament (Committee Printing, 1973), p. 40.

96. Richard J. Barnet and Ronald Mueller, *Global Reach: The Power of the Multinational Corporation* (New York: Simon & Schuster, 1974), p. 1.

97. Harvey Shapiro, "Alexei Kosygin has a Friend at Chase Manhattan . . . ," *New York Times Magazine* (Feb. 24, 1974), p. 11. It seems useful to add a caveat referring to *the* multinational corporation or *the* multinational corporations, with various interpretations of the world and of their interests, and with varying effects on the societies in which they operate. To illustrate, there is a great difference between the manufacturer of consumer durables (requiring a middle-class market) and the builder of economic infrastructure in the form of bridges, dams, and roads. Nevertheless, despite these crucial diversities, it remains useful and valid to generalize the outlook and impact of the multinational corporation as a globalizing phenomenon of prime significance.

98. This dangerous knowledge is embodied, of course, in the long list of scholarly publications emanating from the New Haven School. For a useful introductory sampling, see McDougal and Lasswell, *supra* note 65; *Yale Studies in World Public Order*, Vol. 1, 1974.

99. The main role of these pre-Grotians was to begin to formulate the basis of a law of nations by distinguishing between *jus naturale* and *jus gentium*, the latter being susceptible to human modification and discernible by custom and consent. For a brief discussion of the contributions of Vitoria and Suarez in relation to the work of Grotius, see Corbett, *supra* note 13, pp. 17–24.

100. It remains unclear whether the 1974–1975 effort to negotiate a new law of the seas will eventuate in a widely ratified and seriously implemented treaty. It appears likely that no major innovation in supranational authority will result, either with respect to administration, revenue-sharing, environmental protection, or dispute settlement, with the possible exception of the regulation of deep sea mining operations. Hence the major effect of this attempt at global reform is likely to be an extension of coastal sovereignty over a 200-mile economic zone. Such a development can be regarded as an accentuation of the state system rather than as a step toward its supersession. See note 66 *supra*.

101. The Peace of Augsburg (1555) foreshadowed the principal terms of the Peace of Westphalia by almost 100 years. At Augsburg each prince was given the right

to determine whether Catholicism or Lutheran Protestantism would prevail within his territory; dissenters were assured a right of emigration. In 1648 the idea of religious toleration was broadened at Westphalia to include non-Lutheran Protestant sects and adherents of the Christian faith at variance with that of the prince; both could choose between emigration and toleration. Perhaps in retrospect the breakup of the oil tanker *Torrey Canyon* in 1967 will be seen as the comparable originating event in the nuclear age.

102. Because of the decorum of the profession, much of this hostility to McDougal's works is expressed indirectly by mocking asides and the like, and is deleted from published texts. One interesting example of criticism that comes from an international lawyer who shares McDougal's conservative views on immediate issues but senses an underlying cleavage is Alwyn Freeman, "Professor McDougal's Law and Minimum World Public Order," *American Journal of International Law* 58 (1964), p. 711. I have written a response explaining my bases for supporting McDougal on a fundamental level: Richard Falk, *The Status of Law in International Society* (Princeton, N.J.: Princeton University Press, 1970), pp. 654–659.

103. Corbett makes an intriguingly similar comment about Grotius's tendency to confuse the law of nature with the law of nations when he conjectures that it was "conceivably a calculated confusion designed to endow his law of nations with the authority of the law of nature." See Corbett, *supra* note 13, pp. 23–24.

104. See McDougal and Lasswell, *supra* note 65, pp. 763–843; McDougal, "Foreword" to Moore, *Law and the Indo-China War* (Princeton, N.J.: Princeton University Press, 1972), pp. vii–xiv; McDougal, "The Soviet-Cuban Quarantine and Self-Defense," *American Journal of International Law* 57 (1963), p. 597.

105. See generally Falk, *supra* note 102, pp. 342–377, 642–659; Falk, *Legal Order in a Violent World* (Princeton, N.J.: Princeton University Press, 1968), pp. 80–96; Henry Kissinger, "The White Revolutionary: Reflections on Bismarck," in D. Rustow, ed., *Philosophers and Kings: Studies in Leadership* (New York: Braziller, 1970), pp. 317–353.

106. All of the principal international law treatises illustrate the predominance of the statist paradigm. See, for example, Charles Cheney Hyde, *International Law Chiefly as Interpreted and Applied by the United States*, 2d rev. ed. (Boston: Little, Brown, 1951); D. P. O'Connell, *International Law*, 2 vols. (Dobbs Ferry, N.Y.: Oceana, 1965); H. Lauterpacht, ed., *International Law: A Treatise* (New York: Longmans, 1948).

107. This point is evident in an influential study of the relevance of domestic public order to the prospects for the growth of world law. See McDougal and Lasswell, *supra* note 65, p. 3.

108. I appreciate the difficulty of implementing such a recommendation. A radical (in the sense of "root" or "fundamental") redefinition of what constitutes knowledge for lawyers underlies the work of the New Haven school. To extend that redefinition in new social and political directions would require a degree of intellectual flexibility not common among intellectual innovators, who tend, perhaps out of necessity, to be purist rather than eclectic in their evolution. Nevertheless, the argument for innovation is advanced in the text in the hope that at least an altered dialogue arising out of a dynamic challenge and response will result.

109. These include even such a mainstream analyst of foreign policy as Zbigniew Brzezinski, "U.S. Foreign Policy: The Search for Focus," *Foreign Affairs* 51 (1973), pp. 708–721.

110. A characteristic of statist-paradigm thinking is to grant national governments a monopoly over representational legitimacy—that is, the competence to represent

the well-being of the citizenry. But *cf.* McDougal, Lasswell, and Lung Chu Chen, "Nationality and Human Rights: The Protection of the Individual in External Arenas," *Yale Law Journal* 83 (1974), p. 900. Where national governments sustain power by repressive as distinct from voluntaristic and contractual means, such a presupposition does violence to any ethical assessment of public well-being. Most preferred models of future central guidance (and clearly Option D) distribute representational legitimacy among several categories of actors.

111. This distinction becomes clearer (and easier to make) if one shares William Irwin Thompson's brilliantly expressed skepticism regarding governmental capacities: "Some of our problems stem from the fact that authority today pretty much comes from those who have power. What we need is a clear distinction between authority and power—as in the days of Christ and Caesar before the papacy. We must realize that there are areas of human culture in the imagination, in religious instincts, in the full dimensions of human culture rather than its mere technocratic husk that are important and that have to be affirmed. If we look upon our Presidents as colorless managers and develop alternative systems for cultural regeneration, then I think we have ways of creating new institutions that aren't weighted down with institutional inertia." See Thompson, "The Mechanists and the Mystics," *Noosphere* 1 (1973), pp. 1–2.

112. See Saul H. Mendlovitz and Thomas Weiss, "Toward Consensus: The World Order Models Project of the Institute for World Order," in *Introduction to World Peace Through World Law, supra* note 80, pp. 74–97.

113. Each book is an independent venture. However, early drafts were commented upon at meetings of the research directors held in the 1970–1973 period, and a common acceptance of the four world order values underlies the work of WOMP. In actuality the manuscripts exhibit a surprising degree of diversity; they treat the transition concept in quite different ways, ranging from superseding the state system to merely reforming it. The series consists of Rajni Kothari, *Footsteps into the Future* (New York: Free Press, 1975); Ali Mazrui, *A World Federation of Cultures* (New York: Free Press, 1975); Saul H. Mendlovitz, ed., *On the Creation of a Just World Order* (New York: Free Press, 1975); Gustavo Lagos and Horacio Godoy, *Revolution of Being: A Latin American View of the Future* (New York: Free Press, 1977); and Johan Galtung, *The True Worlds: A Transnational Perspective* (New York: Free Press, 1980).

114. I have depicted the WOMP/USA conception of central guidance more fully in Falk, *supra* note 6, pp. 224–276. My approach to global reform is developed in this book.

115. See Figure 38.1.

116. Hence, in acting to overcome poverty and economic disparities in the world, priority should be given to those approaches that help create procedures, norms, and institutions of the sort that would facilitate the emergence of Option D as a world order solution. In other words, with any concrete issue of world policy, short-term tactics should reflect long-term preferences for global reform.

117. Quoted in Allen J. Large, "Senate is Due to Vote on a Treaty Soon—One Submitted in 1949," *Wall Street Journal*, Jan. 17, 1974, p. 1, col. 3.

118. Letters to the Editor, *New York Times*, Feb. 7, 1974, p. 36, col. 9.

119. For news accounts, see *New York Times*, May 21, 1972, p. 11, col. 1; June 11, 1972, p. 1, col. 2; and June 17, 1973, p. 1, col. 2; see also R. Morris, M. Bowen, G. Freeman, and K. Miller, *Passing By: The United States and Genocide in Burundi 1972* (Washington, D.C.: Carnegie Endowment, 1973).

120. H. Brown and D. Luce, *Hostages of War: Saigon's Political Prisoners* (Washington, D.C.: Indo China Mobile Education Project, 1973); R. Orman, "The Ultimate

Form of Corruption," in *Crimes of War, supra* note 63, pp. 255–257; "An Interview with Philip Agee: Inside the CIA," *Intercontintental Press,* Feb. 10, 1975, p. 173.

121. The most careful account along these lines is Eugene Davidson's appropriately titled volume, *The Nuremberg Fallacy: Wars and War Crimes Since World War II* (New York: Macmillan, 1973). Davidson's book illustrates the dichotomous view that since world governmental ideas do not work we are thrown back on unrestrained statism. See note 76 supra.

122. On this line of reasoning, see Richard Falk, "Ecocide, Genocide, and the Nuremberg Tradition of Individual Responsibility," in Virginia Held, Sydney Morgenbesser, and Thomas Nagel, eds., *Philosophy, Morality and International Affairs* (New York: Oxford University Press, 1974), pp. 123–137.

123. See generally Schaar, *supra* note 8.

124. It is relevant to note that the Chilean junta under Pinochet in the mid-1970s has, in addition to moving against its political opponents, sent activists in Eastern religious sect movements—such as that of Maharaj Ji—to prison for indefinite periods. A religious movement with ethical goals and a transnational frame of reference dilutes loyalty to the state and often undermines its claims of legitimacy.

125. Hannah Arendt, *Crises of the Republic* (New York: Harcourt Brace, 1972), p. 233.